ENCYCLOPEDIA OF APPLIED ETHICS

VOLUME 2

E–I

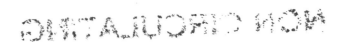

ENCYCLOPEDIA OF APPLIED ETHICS

VOLUME 2
E–I

ACADEMIC PRESS

SAN DIEGO   LONDON   BOSTON   NEW YORK   SYDNEY   TOKYO   TORONTO

Copyright © 1998 by ACADEMIC PRESS

Academic Press
a division of Harcourt Brace & Company
525 B Street, Suite 1900, San Diego, California 92101-4495, USA
http://www.apnet.com

Academic Press Limited
24-28 Oval Road, London NW1 7DX, UK
http://www.hbuk.co.uk/ap/

Library of Congress Card Catalog Number: 97-074395

International Standard Book Number: 0-12-227065-7 (set)
International Standard Book Number: 0-12-227066-5 (v. 1)
International Standard Book Number: 0-12-227067-3 (v. 2)
International Standard Book Number: 0-12-227068-1 (v. 3)
International Standard Book Number: 0-12-227069-X (v. 4)

PRINTED IN THE UNITED STATES OF AMERICA
97 98 99 00 01 02 MM 9 8 7 6 5 4 3 2 1

CONTENTS

CONTENTS OF OTHER VOLUMES

CONTENTS OF VOLUME 3

CONTENTS OF VOLUME 4

CONTENTS BY SUBJECT AREA

LEGAL ETHICS

ETHICS IN EDUCATION

ETHICS AND POLITICS

CONTRIBUTORS

G. JOHN M. ABBARNO
HOMELESSNESS
D'Youville College
Buffalo, New York

FRANCIS J. AGUILAR
CORPORATIONS, ETHICS IN
Harvard University
Cambridge, Massachusetts

WILLIAM AIKEN
CHILDREN'S RIGHTS
Chatham College
Chatham, New York

TIMO AIRAKSINEN
PROFESSIONAL ETHICS
University of Helsinki
Helsinki, Finland

LARRY ALEXANDER
FREEDOM OF SPEECH
University of San Diego
San Diego, California

ANDREW ALEXANDRA
EXECUTIVE COMPENSATION
Charles Sturt University
Bathurst, New South Wales, Australia

GARLAND E. ALLEN
GENETICS AND BEHAVIOR
NATURE VERSUS NURTURE
Washington University
St. Louis, Missouri

JONATHAN ALDRED
WILDLIFE CONSERVATION
Cambridge University
Cambridge, England, UK

DAVID ARCHARD
CHILD ABUSE
University of St. Andrews
Fife, Scotland, UK

MARY BETH ARMSTRONG
CONFIDENTIALITY, GENERAL ISSUES OF
California Polytechnic Institute
San Luis Obispo, California

RICHARD J. ARNESON
EQUALITY AND EGALITARIANISM
University of California, San Diego
San Diego, California

ROBERT L. ARRINGTON
ADVERTISING
Georgia State University
Atlanta, Georgia

RICHARD ASHCROFT
HUMAN RESEARCH SUBJECTS, SELECTION OF
University of Bristol
Bristol, England, UK

SUE ASHFORD
TERRORISM
University of Western Australia and Murdoch
University
Medina, Western Australia

ROBIN ATTFIELD
ENVIRONMENTAL ETHICS, OVERVIEW
University of Wales, Cardiff
Cardiff, Wales, UK

ROBERT D. BAIRD
HINDUISM
School of Religion, University of Iowa
Iowa City, Iowa

DOUGLAS BAKER
LAND USE ISSUES
University of Northern British Columbia
Prince George, British Columbia

NORMAN BARRY
WELFARE POLICIES
University of Buckingham
Buckingham, England, UK

BERNARD BAUMRIN
DIVORCE
    City University of New York
    New York, New York

JOHN D. BECKER
NATIONAL SECURITY ISSUES
WARFARE, STRATEGIES AND TACTICS
    United States Air Force Academy
    Colorado Springs, Colorado

HUGO ADAM BEDAU
CAPITAL PUNISHMENT
CIVIL DISOBEDIENCE
    Tufts University
    Medford, Massachusetts

RON L. P. BERGHMANS
COERCIVE TREATMENT IN PSYCHIATRY
    Institute for Bioethics
    Maastricht, The Netherlands

ROBERT H. BLANK
FETAL RESEARCH
    University of Canterbury
    Canterbury, England, UK

PAULA BODDINGTON
SELF-DECEPTION
    Australian National University
    Canberra, Australia

ANNIE BOOTH
LAND USE ISSUES
    University of Northern British Columbia
    Prince George, British Columbia

STEPHEN ST. C. BOSTOCK
ZOOS AND ZOOLOGICAL PARKS
    Glasgow Zoo and University of Glasgow
    Glasgow, Scotland, UK

ANDREW BRENNAN
GAIA HYPOTHESIS
    The University of Western Australia
    Nedlands, Western Australia

ANDREW BRIEN
JURY CONDUCT
MERCY AND FORGIVENESS
    Australian National University
    Canberra, Australia

ROGER L. BURRITT
ENVIRONMENTAL COMPLIANCE BY INDUSTRY
    Australian National University
    Canberra, Australia

EDMUND F. BYRNE
PRIVACY
    Indiana University
    Indianapolis, Indiana

JOAN C. CALLAHAN
BIRTH-CONTROL ETHICS
    University of Kentucky
    Lexington, Kentucky

EAMONN CALLAN
PLURALISM IN EDUCATION
    University of Alberta
    Edmonton, Alberta

ARTHUR L. CAPLAN
INFORMED CONSENT
    University of Pennsylvania
    Philadelphia, Pennsylvania

ALEXANDER MORGAN CAPRON
DEATH, DEFINITION OF
    University of Southern California
    Los Angeles, California

ALAN CARLING
EXPLOITATION
    University of Bradford
    Bradford, England, UK

STANLEY R. CARPENTER
SUSTAINABILITY
    Georgia Institute of Technology
    Atlanta, Georgia

RUTH CHADWICK
GENETIC SCREENING
ORGAN TRANSPLANTS AND DONORS
    Centre for Professional Ethics
    University of Central Lancashire
    Preston, England, UK

TIMOTHY CHAPPELL
PLATONISM
THEORIES OF ETHICS, OVERVIEW
    University of Manchester
    Manchester, England, UK

VICHAI CHOKEVIVAT
AIDS IN THE DEVELOPING WORLD
    Thai Department of Health and Human Welfare

JOHN CHRISTMAN
PROPERTY RIGHTS
    Virginia Polytechnic Institute and State University
    Blacksburg, Virginia

JOHN P. CLARK
POLITICAL ECOLOGY
    Loyola University
    New Orleans, Louisiana

ANGUS CLARKE
GENETIC COUNSELING
    University of Wales College of Medicine
    Cardiff, Wales, UK

MARGARET COFFEY
BROADCAST JOURNALISM
    Australian Broadcasting Corporation
    Malvern, Australia

DAVID CONWAY
LIBERALISM
    Middlesex University
    London, England, UK

LINDSEY COOMBES
MENTAL HEALTH
Oxford Brookes University
Oxford, England, UK

WILLIAM COONEY
RIGHTS THEORY
Briar Cliff College
Sioux City, Iowa

PRESTON K. COVEY
GUN CONTROL
Center for the Advancement of Applied Ethics
Carnegie Mellon University
Pittsburgh, Pennsylvania

CHRISTOPHER J. COWTON
SOCIALLY RESPONSIBLE INVESTMENT
University of Huddersfield
Queensgate, Huddersfield, England, UK

CHARLES CRITCHER
MEDIA DEPICTION OF ETHNIC MINORITIES
Sheffield Hallam University
Sheffield, England, UK

THOMAS CLOUGH DAFFERN
NATIVE AMERICAN CULTURES
University of London
London, England, UK

TIM DARE
APPLIED ETHICS, CHALLENGES TO
The University of Auckland
Auckland, New Zealand

MICHAEL DAVIS
CONFLICT OF INTEREST
Illinois Institute of Technology
Chicago, Illinois

ANGUS DAWSON
PSYCHOPHARMACOLOGY
University of Liverpool
Liverpool, England, UK

JUDITH WAGNER DECEW
WARFARE, CODES OF
Clark University
West Newton, Massachusetts

C. A. DEFANTI
BRAIN DEATH
United Hospitals of Bergamo
Bergamo, Italy

CARLOS DEL RIO
AIDS IN THE DEVELOPING WORLD
Emory University

PHILIP E. DEVINE
HOMICIDE, CRIMINAL VERSUS JUSTIFIABLE
PUBLISH-OR-PERISH SYNDROME
Providence College
Providence, Rhode Island

BERNARD DICKENS
PATIENTS' RIGHTS
University of Toronto Law School
Toronto, Ontario

SUSAN DIMOCK
CRIME AND SOCIETY
JUVENILE CRIME
York University
North York, Ontario

SUSAN DODDS
SEX EQUALITY
University of Wollongong
Wollongong, Australia

STRACHAN DONNELLEY
HUMAN NATURE, VIEWS OF
The Hastings Center
Briarcliff Manor, New York

JUDE P. DOUGHERTY
THOMISM
Catholic University of America
Washington, DC

NIGEL DOWER
DEVELOPMENT ETHICS
DEVELOPMENT ISSUES, ENVIRONMENTAL
WORLD ETHICS
University of Aberdeen
Aberdeen, Scotland, UK

HEATHER DRAPER
EUTHANASIA
University of Birmingham
Birmingham, England, UK

DENIS DUTTON
PLAGIARISM AND FORGERY
University of Canterbury
Christchurch, New Zealand

SUSAN EASTON
PORNOGRAPHY
Brunel University
Uxbridge, England, UK

ANDREW EDGAR
QUALITY OF LIFE INDICATORS
SPORTS, ETHICS OF
University of Wales
Cardiff, Wales, UK

BENGT ERIK ERIKSSON
PREVENTIVE MEDICINE
University of Linköping
Linköping, Sweden

GAVIN FAIRBAIRN
SUICIDE
North East Wales Institute of Higher Education
Wrexham, Wales, UK

JOHN FENDER
ALTRUISM AND ECONOMICS
University of Birmingham
Birmingham, England, UK

DAVID E. W. FENNER
ARTS, THE
University of North Florida
Jacksonville, Florida

J. CARL FICARROTTA
MORAL RELATIVISM
United States Air Force Academy
Colorado Springs, Colorado

BETH A. FISCHER
SCIENTIFIC PUBLISHING
University of Pittsburgh
Pittsburgh, Pennsylvania

ANTHONY FISHER
CHRISTIAN ETHICS, ROMAN CATHOLIC
Australian Catholic University
Ascot Vale, Australia

CHARLES J. FOMBRUN
REPUTATION MANAGEMENT BY CORPORATIONS
New York University
New York, New York

NORMAN FORD
FETUS
Caroline Chisholm Centre for Health Ethics
East Melbourne, Australia

CLAIRE FOSTER
RESEARCH ETHICS COMMITTEES
King's College
London, England, UK

LESLIE PICKERING FRANCIS
RAPE
University of Utah
Salt Lake City, Utah

LUCY FRITH
REPRODUCTIVE TECHNOLOGIES
University of Liverpool and University of Oxford
England, UK

K. W. M. FULFORD
MENTAL ILLNESS, CONCEPT OF
University of Warwick
Coventry, England, UK

SUSANNE GIBSON
ABORTION
ACTS AND OMISSIONS
University College of St. Martin
Lancaster, England, UK

CHRISTOPHER GILL
GREEK ETHICS, OVERVIEW
University of Exeter
Exeter, England, UK

RAANAN GILLON
BIOETHICS, OVERVIEW
Imperial College
London University
London, England, UK

ANDREW GILMAN
PERSONAL RELATIONSHIPS
Andover Newton Theological School
Stratham, New Hampshire

DONALD A. GRAFT
SPECIESISM
Software Engineer Manager
Pondicherry, India

WILLIAM GREY
PLAYING GOD
University of Queensland
Queensland, Australia

MATTHEW W. HALLGARTH
CONSEQUENTIALISM AND DEONTOLOGY
United States Air Force Academy
Colorado Springs, Colorado

JOCELYN Y. HATTAB
PSYCHIATRIC ETHICS
Eitanim Mental Health Center
Hebrew University
Jerusalem, Israel

HETA HÄYRY
GENETIC ENGINEERING
PATERNALISM
University of Helsinki
Helsinki, Finland

MATTI HÄYRY
GENETIC ENGINEERING
University of Helsinki
Helsinki, Finland

TIM HAYWARD
ANTHROPOCENTRISM
University of Edinburgh
Edinburgh, Scotland, UK

ADAM M. HEDGECOE
GENE THERAPY
GENOME ANALYSIS
Centre for Professional Ethics
University of Central Lancashire
Preston, England, UK

ERIC HEINZE
VICTIMLESS CRIMES
University of London
London, England, UK

SIRKKU HELLSTEN
DISTRIBUTIVE JUSTICE, THEORIES OF
University of Helsinki
Helsinki, Finland

ALAN HOLLAND
ECOLOGICAL BALANCE
  Lancaster University
  Lancaster, England, UK

SØREN HOLM
AUTONOMY
EMBRYOLOGY, ETHICS OF
  University of Copenhagen
  Copenhagen, Denmark

TERRY HOPTON
POLITICAL OBLIGATION
  University of Central Lancashire
  Preston, England, UK

J. STUART HORNER
MEDICAL ETHICS, HISTORY OF
  University of Central Lancashire
  Preston, England, UK

GILLIAN HOWIE
GENDER ROLES
  University of Liverpool
  Liverpool, England, UK

RICHARD HUGMAN
ETHICS AND SOCIAL SERVICES, OVERVIEW
  Curtin University of Technology
  Perth, Australia

GEOFFREY HUNT
WHISTLE-BLOWING
  European Centre for Professional Ethics
  University of London
  London, England, UK

DOUGLAS N. HUSAK
DRUGS: MORAL AND LEGAL ISSUES
  Rutgers University
  New Brunswick, New Jersey

JENNIFER JACKSON
BUSINESS ETHICS, OVERVIEW
  University of Leeds
  Leeds, England, UK

MARJA JÄRVELÄ
ENVIRONMENTAL IMPACT ASSESSMENT
  The University of Jyväskylä
  Jyväskylä, Finland

MARGOT JEFFREYS
AGED PEOPLE, SOCIETAL ATTITUDES TOWARD
  Centre of Medical Law and Ethics
  King's College
  London, England, UK

MARIANNE M. JENNINGS
ELECTION STRATEGIES
  Arizona State University
  Tempe, Arizona

EDWARD JOHNSON
INTELLIGENCE TESTING
MEDIA OWNERSHIP
POLITICAL CORRECTNESS
  University of New Orleans
  New Orleans, Louisiana

JEFFERY L. JOHNSON
NUCLEAR DETERRENCE
  Eastern Oregon State College
  LaGrande, Oregon

PAULINE JOHNSON
SEXISM
  Macquarie University
  Sydney, Australia

TREVOR JONES
POLICE AND RACE RELATIONS
  Policy Studies Institute
  London, England, UK

RABINDRA N. KANUNGO
LEADERSHIP, ETHICS OF
  McGill University
  Montreal, Quebec

HELMUT F. KAPLAN
VEGETARIANISM
  University of Salzburg
  Salzburg, Austria

PAUL KELLY
CONTRACTARIAN ETHICS
  London School of Economics
  London, England, UK

DAMIEN KEOWN
BUDDHISM
  Goldsmiths College, University of London
  London, England, UK

JACINTA KERIN
SEXUAL ORIENTATION
  Monash University
  Toronto, Ontario

EDWARD W. KEYSERLINGK
MEDICAL CODES AND OATHS
  McGill University
  Montreal, Quebec

JUKKA KILPI
MERGERS AND ACQUISITIONS
  University of Helsinki
  Helsinki, Finland and Monash University
  Clayton, Victoria, Australia

DAHLIAN KIRBY
TRANSSEXUALISM
  University of Wales
  Cardiff, Wales, UK

STEPHEN KLAIDMAN
FREEDOM OF THE PRESS IN THE USA
  Georgetown University
  Washington, DC

JAMES W. KNIGHT
BIRTH-CONTROL TECHNOLOGY
  Virginia Polytechnic Institute and State University
  Blacksburg, Virginia

LORETTA M. KOPELMAN
FEMALE CIRCUMCISION AND GENITAL MUTILATION
MEDICAL FUTILITY
  East Carolina University School of Medicine
  Greenville, North Carolina

MARK KUCZEWSKI
CASUISTRY
  Medical College of Wisconsin

PAUL A. KURZMAN
WORKPLACE ETHICS: ISSUES FOR HUMAN SERVICE
  PROFESSIONALS
  Hunter College, City University of New York
  New York, New York

KRISTIINA KUVAJA-PUUMALAINEN
ENVIRONMENTAL IMPACT ASSESSMENT
  Jyvaskyla University
  Jyvaskyla, Finland

WILL KYMLICKA
ETHNOCULTURAL MINORITY GROUPS, STATUS AND TREATMENT OF
  University of Ottawa
  Ottawa, Ontario

OLLI LAGERSPETZ
TRUST
  Abo Academy
  Abo, Finland
  and The University of Wales at Swansea

DAVID LAMB
DEATH, MEDICAL ASPECTS OF
  University of Birmingham
  Birmingham, England, UK

HAROLD Q. LANGENDERFER
ACCOUNTING AND BUSINESS ETHICS
  University of North Carolina
  Chapel Hill, North Carolina

DUNCAN LANGFORD
INTERNET PROTOCOL
  University of Kent
  Canterbury, England, UK

ROBERT LARMER
IMPROPER PAYMENTS AND GIFTS
  University of New Brunswick
  Fredericton, New Brunswick

OLIVER LEAMAN
JUDAISM
  Liverpool John Moores University
  Liverpool, England, UK

GRANT S. LEE
TAOISM
  Colorado State University
  Fort Collins, Colorado

KEEKOK LEE
BIODIVERSITY
  The University of Manchester
  Manchester, England, UK

STEVEN LEE
NUCLEAR TESTING
  Hobart and William Smith Colleges
  Geneva, New York

BURTON M. LEISER
CORPORAL PUNISHMENT
SLAVERY
  Pace University
  Briarcliff Manor, New York

A. CARL LEOPOLD
STEWARDSHIP
  Boyce Thompson Institute for Plant Research
  Cornell University
  Ithaca, New York

HARRY LESSER
AGEISM
  University of Manchester
  Manchester, England, UK

CAROL LEVINE
CUSTODY OF CHILDREN
  The Orphan Project
  New York, New York

MAIRI LEVITT
RELIGION IN SCHOOLS
  University of Central Lancashire
  Preston, England, UK

XIAORONG LI
WOMEN'S RIGHTS
  University of Maryland
  College Park, Maryland

JUDITH LICHTENBERG
OBJECTIVITY IN REPORTING
  University of Maryland
  College Park, Maryland

C. DAVID LISMAN
ETHICS EDUCATION IN SCHOOLS
  Community College of Aurora
  Aurora, Colorado

ANDROS LOIZOU
THEORIES OF JUSTICE: RAWLS
  University of Central Lancashire
  Preston, England, UK

VALERIE C. LORENZ
GAMBLING
Compulsive Gambling Center, Inc.
Baltimore, Maryland

ROBERT B. LOUDEN
VIRTUE ETHICS
Westfalische WIlhelms-Universitat
Munster, Germany

JOHN LYDEN
CHRISTIAN ETHICS, PROTESTANT
Dana College
Omaha, Nebraska

CHRIS MACDONALD
EVOLUTIONARY PERSPECTIVES ON ETHICS
University of British Columbia
Vancouver, British Columbia

CARLOS MAGIS
AIDS IN THE DEVELOPING WORLD
Conasida, Mexico

THOMAS MAGNELL
EPICUREANISM
Drew University
Madison, New Jersey

RUDOLPH J. MARCUS
GOVERNMENT FUNDING OF RESEARCH
Ethics Consultant
Sonoma, California

IAN MARKHAM
RELIGION AND ETHICS
Liverpool Hope University College
Liverpool, England, UK

GARY T. MARX
ELECTRONIC SURVEILLANCE
UNDERCOVER INVESTIGATIONS, ETHICS OF
Center for Advanced Study in the Behavioral
Sciences
Stanford, California

RICHARD O. MASON
GENETIC RESEARCH
INFORMATION MANAGEMENT
Southern Methodist University
Dallas, Texas

TODD MAY
POSTSTRUCTURALISM
Clemson University
Clemson, South Carolina

MARY ANN MCCLURE
INFERTILITY
John Jay College of Criminal Justice
New York, New York

PATRICIA E. MCCREIGHT
ENVIRONMENTAL COMPLIANCE BY INDUSTRY
Australian National University
Canberra, Australia

TONY MCGLEENAN
GENETIC TECHNOLOGY, LEGAL REGULATION OF
The Queen's University of Belfast
Belfast, Northern Ireland, UK

C. B. MEGONE
ARISTOTELIAN ETHICS
University of Leeds
Leeds, England, UK

GREGORY MELLEMA
COLLECTIVE GUILT
Calvin College
Grand Rapids, Michigan

MANUEL MENDONCA
LEADERSHIP, ETHICS OF
McGill University
Montreal, Quebec

MICHAEL A. MENLOWE
SAFETY LAWS
University of Edinburgh
Edinburgh, Scotland, UK

BEN MEPHAM
AGRICULTURAL ETHICS
University of Nottingham
Loughborough, England, UK

SEUMAS MILLER
TABLOID JOURNALISM
Charles Sturt University
Wagga Wagga, Australia

JEAN-NOËL MISSA
PSYCHOSURGERY AND PHYSICAL BRAIN MANIPULATION
Free University of Brussels
Brussels, Belgium

DARRELL MOELLENDORF
IMPERIALISM
University of Witwatersrand
Johannesburg, South Africa

PETER MOIZER
AUDITING PRACTICES
University of Leeds
Leeds, England, UK

DAVID WENDELL MOLLER
DEATH, SOCIETAL ATTITUDES TOWARD
Indiana University
Indianapolis, Indiana

J. DONALD MOON
COMMUNITARIANISM
Wesleyan University
Middletown, Connecticut

EMILIO MORDINI
SUGGESTION, ETHICS OF
   Psychoanalytic Institute for Social Research
   Rome, Italy

JONATHAN D. MORENO
INFORMED CONSENT
   SUNY Health Science Center at Brooklyn
   Brooklyn, New York

MAURIZIO MORI
LIFE, CONCEPT OF
   Center for Research in Politics and Ethics
   Milan, Italy

STEPHEN J. MORSE
INSANITY, LEGAL CONCEPT OF
   University of Pennsylvania Law School
   Philadelphia, Pennsylvania

PETER MUNZ
DARWINISM
   Victoria University of Wellington
   Wellington, New Zealand

TIMOTHY F. MURPHY
AIDS
   University of Illinois College of Medicine
   Chicago, Illinois

CHARLES R. MYERS
MILITARY CODES OF BEHAVIOR
   United States Air Force Academy
   Colorado Springs, Colorado

JAN NARVESON
CONSUMER RIGHTS
EGOISM AND ALTRUISM
STOICISM
   University of Waterloo
   Waterloo, Ontario

DEMETRIO NERI
EUGENICS
   University of Messina
   Messina, Italy

NINA NIKKU
PREVENTIVE MEDICINE
   University of Linköping
   Linköping, Sweden

RICHARD NORMAN
PACIFISM
   University of Kent
   Canterbury, England, UK

DAVID NOVITZ
LITERATURE AND ETHICS
   University of Canterbury, New Zealand
   Christchurch, New Zealand

KATHERINE O'DONOVAN
FEMINIST JURISPRUDENCE
   Queen Mary's Westfield College
   University of London
   London, England, UK

JOHN O'NEILL
TRUTH TELLING AS CONSTITUTIVE OF JOURNALISM
   Lancaster University
   Lancaster, England, UK

GERALD M. OPPENHEIMER
HEALTH CARE FINANCING
   Brooklyn College, City University of New York
   Brooklyn, New York

WILLIAM OUTHWAITE
DISCOURSE ETHICS
   University of Sussex
   Sussex, England, UK

GUILLERMO OWEN
GAME THEORY
   Naval Postgraduate School
   Monterey, California

ROBERT A. PADGUG
HEALTH CARE FINANCING
   Brooklyn College, City University of New York
   Brooklyn, New York

GABRIEL PALMER-FERNÁNDEZ
CIVILIAN POPULATIONS IN WAR, TARGETING OF
   Youngstown State University
   Youngstown, Ohio

MARK PARASCANDOLA
ANIMAL RESEARCH
   Smithsonian Fellow
   Washington, D.C.

JENNETH PARKER
PRECAUTIONARY PRINCIPLE
   Lecturer
   Hastings, England, UK

MICHAEL PARKER
MORAL DEVELOPMENT
   The Open University
   Milton Keynes, England, UK

ELLEN FRANKEL PAUL
AFFIRMATIVE ACTION
SEXUAL HARASSMENT
   Bowling Green State University
   Bowling Green, Ohio

MICHEL PETHERAM
CONFIDENTIALITY OF SOURCES
   The Open University
   Milton Keynes, England, UK

JON PIKE
STRIKES
   Glasgow University
   Glasgow, Scotland, UK

EVELYN PLUHAR
ANIMAL RIGHTS
   The Pennsylvania State University, Fayette Campus
   Uniontown, Pennsylvania

GAYNOR POLLARD
RELIGION IN SCHOOLS
University College Chester
Chester, England, UK

NELSON POTTER
KANTIANISM
University of Nebraska-Lincoln
Lincoln, Nebraska

IGOR PRIMORATZ
PROSTITUTION
Hebrew University
Jerusalem, Israel

JANE PRITCHARD
CODES OF ETHICS
Centre for Professional Ethics
University of Central Lancashire
Preston, England, UK

ROBERT PROSSER
TOURISM
University of Birmingham
Birmingham, England, UK

LAURA M. PURDY
CHILDREN'S RIGHTS
Wells College
Aurora, New York

K. ANNE PYBURN
ARCHAEOLOGICAL ETHICS
Indiana University
Indianapolis, Indiana

MAUREEN RAMSAY
MACHIAVELLIANISM
University of Leeds
Leeds, England, UK

DOUGLAS B. RASMUSSEN
PERFECTIONISM
St. John's University
Jamaica, Queens, New York

KATE RAWLES
BIOCENTRISM
Lancaster University
Lancaster, England, UK

RUPERT READ
COURTROOM PROCEEDINGS, REPORTING OF
University of Manchester
Manchester, England, UK

FREDERIC G. REAMER
SOCIAL WORK
Rhode Island College
Providence, Rhode Island

MICHAEL REISS
BIOTECHNOLOGY
Homerton College, Cambridge
Cambridge, England, UK

TONY RILEY
HOMOSEXUALITY, SOCIETAL ATTITUDES TOWARD
Yale University School of Medicine
New Haven, Connecticut

SIMON ROGERSON
COMPUTER AND INFORMATION ETHICS
De Montfort University
Leicester, England, UK

BERNARD E. ROLLIN
VETERINARY ETHICS
Colorado State University
Fort Collins, Colorado

RICHARD D. RYDER
PAINISM
Tulane University
New Orleans, Louisiana

MARK SAGOFF
ENVIRONMENTAL ECONOMICS
University of Maryland
College Park, Maryland

HANS-MARTIN SASS
ADVANCE DIRECTIVES
Kennedy Institute of Ethics
Georgetown University
Washington, DC

GEOFFREY SCARRE
UTILITARIANISM
University of Durham
Durham, England, UK

UDO SCHÜKLENK
AIDS IN THE DEVELOPING WORLD
HOMOSEXUALITY, SOCIETAL ATTITUDES TOWARD
ORGAN TRANSPLANTS AND DONORS
SEXUAL ORIENTATION
Centre for Professional Ethics
University of Central Lancashire
Preston, England, UK

ADINA SCHWARTZ
PUBLIC DEFENDERS
John Jay College of Criminal Justice
City University of New York
New York, New York

ANNE SELLER
PACIFISM
University of Kent
Canterbury, England, UK

JOHN J. SHEPHERD
ISLAM
University College of St. Martin
Lancaster, England, UK

RUBEN SHER
AIDS TREATMENT AND BIOETHICS IN SOUTH AFRICA
National AIDS Training and Outreach Program
Johannesburg, South Africa

DARREN SHICKLE
PRIVACY VERSUS PUBLIC RIGHT TO KNOW
RESOURCE ALLOCATION
    University of Sheffield
    Sheffield, England, UK

KRISTIN SHRADER-FRECHETTE
HAZARDOUS AND TOXIC SUBSTANCES
NUCLEAR POWER
    University of South Florida
    Tampa, Florida

DEBORAH H. SIEGEL
ADOPTION
    School of Social Work
    Rhode Island College
    Providence, Rhode Island

ANITA SILVERS
DISABILITY RIGHTS
    San Francisco State University
    San Francisco, California

NIKKY-GUNINDER KAUR SINGH
SIKHISM
    Colby College
    Waterville, Maine

ANTHONY J. SKILLEN
RACISM
    University of Kent
    Canterbury, England, UK

JOHN SNAPPER
TRADE SECRETS AND PROPRIETARY INFORMATION
    Illinois Institute of Technology
    Chicago, Illinois

EUGENE SPAFFORD
COMPUTER SECURITY
    Purdue University
    West Lafayette, Indiana

CLIVE L. SPASH
WILDLIFE CONSERVATION
    Cambridge University
    Cambridge, England, UK

PAUL SPICKER
POVERTY
SOCIAL SECURITY
SOCIAL WELFARE: PROVISION AND FINANCE
    University of Dundee
    Dundee, Scotland, UK

R. E. SPIER
SCIENCE AND ENGINEERING ETHICS, OVERVIEW
    University of Surrey
    Guildford, England, UK

DEAN A. STEELE
HONOR CODES
    United States Air Force Academy
    Colorado Springs, Colorado

ELIZA STEELWATER
HUMANISM
    University of Illinois
    Champaign, Illinois

EDWARD STEIN
SEXUAL ORIENTATION
    Yale University
    New Haven, Connecticut

JON STEWART
EXISTENTIALISM
    Søren Kierkegaard Research Center
    University of Copenhagen
    Copenhagen, Denmark

TADEUSZ SZUBKA
FREUDIANISM
    University of Queensland
    Brisbane, Australia

WIN TADD
NURSES' ETHICS
    University of Wales
    Cardiff, Wales, UK

CARL TALBOT
DEEP ECOLOGY
ENVIRONMENTAL JUSTICE
    University of Wales, Cardiff
    Cardiff, Wales, UK

JULIA PO-WAH LAI TAO
CONFUCIANISM
    City University of Hong Kong
    Kowloon, Hong Kong

LAURENCE THOMAS
FRIENDSHIP
    Syracuse University
    Syracuse, New York

JOHN J. TILLEY
HEDONISM
    Indiana University/Purdue University
    Indianapolis, Indiana

G. E. TOMLINSON
GENETIC RESEARCH
    University of Texas
    Dallas, Texas

ROSEMARIE TONG
FEMINIST ETHICS
    Davidson College
    Davidson, North Carolina

MAX TRAVERS
COURTROOM PROCEEDINGS, REPORTING OF
    Buckinghamshire College

JOHN C. TULLOCH
VIOLENCE IN FILMS AND TELEVISION
    Charles Sturt University
    Bathurst, Australia

MARIAN I. TULLOCH
VIOLENCE IN FILMS AND TELEVISION
Charles Sturt University
Bathurst, Australia

RICHARD H. S. TUR
LEGAL ETHICS, OVERVIEW
Oriel College
Oxford, England, UK

ROBERT TWYCROSS
PALLIATIVE CARE
Oxford University and Churchill Hospital
Oxford, England, UK

CAROLE ULANOWSKY
FAMILY, THE
The Open University
Milton Keynes, England, UK

GREGORY UNGAR
ELECTRONIC SURVEILLANCE
University of Colorado
Boulder, Colorado

JORGE M. VALADEZ
INDIGENOUS RIGHTS
Marquette University
Milwaukee, Wisconsin

JOHANNES J. M. VAN DELDEN
DO-NOT-RESUSCITATE DECISIONS
Center for Bioethics and Health Law
Utrecht University
Utrecht, The Netherlands

WIBREN VAN DER BURG
SLIPPERY SLOPE ARGUMENTS
Tilburg University
Tilburg, The Netherlands

PAUL VIMINITZ
NUCLEAR WARFARE
University of Waterloo
Waterloo, Ontario

ANDREW VINCENT
MARX AND ETHICS
University of Wales, Cardiff
Cardiff, Wales, UK

ROBERT WACHBROIT
HEALTH AND DISEASE, CONCEPTS OF
Institute for Philosophy and Public Policy
University of Maryland
College Park, Maryland

NEIL WALKER
POLICE ACCOUNTABILITY
University of Aberdeen
Aberdeen, Scotland, UK

DANIEL WARNER
CITIZENSHIP
Graduate Institute of International Studies
Geneva, Switzerland

DAVID WASSERMAN
DISCRIMINATION, CONCEPT OF
Institute for Philosophy and Public Policy
University of Maryland
College Park, Maryland

JOHN WECKERT
SEXUAL CONTENT IN FILMS AND TELEVISION
Charles Sturt University
Bathurst, New South Wales, Australia

CHARLES WEIJER
RESEARCH METHODS AND POLICIES
Joint Centre for Bioethics
University of Toronto/Mount Sinai Hospital
Toronto, Ontario

D. DON WELCH
SOCIAL ETHICS, OVERVIEW
Vanderbilt University School of Law
Nashville, Tennessee

JOS V. M. WELIE
PLACEBO TREATMENT
Creighton University
Omaha, Nebraska

CELIA WELLS
CORPORATE RESPONSIBILITY
Cardiff Law School
University of Wales
Cardiff, Wales, UK

CAROLINE WHITBECK
RESEARCH ETHICS
Massachusetts Institute of Technology
Cambridge, Massachusetts

MARGARET WHITELEGG
ALTERNATIVE MEDICINE
University of Central Lancashire
Preston, England, UK

URBAN WIESING
MEDICAL ETHICS, USE OF HISTORICAL EVIDENCE IN
University of Münster
Münster, Germany

JOHN R. WILCOX
HIGHER EDUCATION, ETHICS OF
Manhattan College
Riverdale, Bronx, New York

RICHARD R. WILK
ARCHAEOLOGICAL ETHICS
Indiana University
Indianapolis, Indiana

BERNARD WILLIAMS
CENSORSHIP
University of California, Berkeley

CHRISTOPHER WINCH
AUTHORITY IN EDUCATION
Nene College
Northhampton, England, UK

EARL R. WINKLER
APPLIED ETHICS, OVERVIEW
University of British Columbia
Vancouver, British Columbia

CLARK WOLF
THEORIES OF JUSTICE: HUMAN NEEDS
University of Colorado
Boulder, Colorado

PAUL ROOT WOLPE
INFORMED CONSENT
University of Pennsylvania
Philadelphia, Pennsylvania

MICHAEL WREEN
PATENTS
Marquette University
Milwaukee, Wisconsin

MICHAEL J. ZIGMOND
SCIENTIFIC PUBLISHING
University of Pittsburgh
Pittsburgh, Pennsylvania

A GUIDE TO THE ENCYCLOPEDIA

The *Encyclopedia of Applied Ethics* is a complete source of information contained within the covers of a single unified work. It is the first reference book that addresses the relatively new discipline of applied ethics in a comprehensive manner; thus in effect it will provide the first general description of the components and boundaries of this challenging field.

The Encyclopedia consists of four volumes and includes 281 separate full-length articles on the whole range of applied ethics. It includes not only entries on the leading theories and concepts of ethics, but also a vast selection of entries on practical issues ranging from medical, scientific, and environmental ethics to the ethics of social relationships and social services. Each article provides a detailed overview of the selected topic to inform a broad spectrum of readers, from research professionals to students to the interested general public.

In order that you, the reader, will derive maximum benefit from your use of the *Encyclopedia of Applied Ethics,* we have provided this Guide. It explains how the Encyclopedia is organized and how the information within it can be located.

ORGANIZATION

The *Encyclopedia of Applied Ethics* is organized to provide the maximum ease of use for its readers. All of the articles are arranged in a single alphabetical sequence by title. Articles whose titles begin with the letters A to D are in Volume 1, articles with titles from E to I are in Volume 2, and those from J to R are in Volume 3. Volume 4 contains the articles from S to Z and also the Index.

So that they can be easily located, article titles generally begin with the key word or phrase indicating the topic, with any descriptive terms following. For example, "Distributive Justice, Theories of" is the article title

rather than "Theories of Distributive Justice" because the specific phrase *distributive justice* is the key term rather than the more general term *theories*. Similarly "Sports, Ethics of" is the article title rather than "Ethics of Sports" and "Human Nature, Views of" is the title rather than "Views of Human Nature."

TABLE OF CONTENTS

A complete alphabetical table of contents for the *Encyclopedia of Applied Ethics* appears at the front of each volume of the set, beginning on page v of the Introduction. This list includes not only the articles that appear in that particular volume but also those in the other three volumes.

The list of article titles represents topics that have been carefully selected by the Editor-in-Chief, Prof. Ruth Chadwick, Head of the Centre for Professional Ethics, University of Central Lancashire, UK, in collaboration with the members of the Editorial Board.

In addition to the alphabetical table of contents, the Encyclopedia also provides a second table of contents at the front of each volume, one that lists all the articles according to their subject area. The Encyclopedia provides coverage of 12 specific subject areas within the overall field of applied ethics, as indicated below:

- **Theories of Ethics**
- **Ethical Concepts**
- **Medical Ethics**
- **Scientific Ethics**
- **Environmental Ethics**
- **Legal Ethics**
- **Ethics in Education**
- **Ethics and Politics**
- **Business and Economic Ethics**
- **Media Ethics**
- **Ethics and Social Services**
- **Social Ethics**

ARTICLE FORMAT

Articles in the *Encyclopedia of Applied Ethics* are arranged in a single alphabetical list by title. Each new article begins at the top of a right-hand page, so that it may be quickly located. The author's name and affiliation are displayed at the beginning of the article. The article is organized according to a standard format, as follows:

- Title and Author
- Outline
- Glossary
- Defining Statement
- Main Body of the Article
- Cross-References
- Bibliography

OUTLINE

Each article in the Encyclopedia begins with an Outline that indicates the general content of the article. This outline serves two functions. First, it provides a brief preview of the article, so that the reader can get a sense of what is contained there without having to leaf through the pages. Second, it serves to highlight important subtopics that are discussed within the article. For example, the article "Genome Analysis" includes the subtopic "The Human Genome Project."

The Outline is intended as an overview and thus it lists only the major headings of the article. In addition, extensive second-level and third-level headings will be found within the article.

GLOSSARY

The Glossary contains terms that are important to an understanding of the article and that may be unfamiliar to the reader. Each term is defined in the context of the particular article in which it is used. Thus the same term may appear as a Glossary entry in two or more articles, with the details of the definition varying slightly from one article to another. The Encyclopedia includes more than 1,000 glossary entries.

The following example is a glossary entry that appears with the article "Precautionary Principle."

indicator species A particular species whose presence (or absence) is regarded as characteristic of a given environment, and whose ability or failure to thrive there is thus thought to be indicative of the overall ecological status of this environment.

DEFINING STATEMENT

The text of each article in the Encyclopedia begins with a single introductory paragraph that defines the topic under discussion and summarizes the content of the article. For example, the article "Biotechnology" begins with the following statement:

BIOTECHNOLOGY is the application of biology for human ends. It involves using organisms to provide humans with food, clothes, medicines, and other products.

CROSS-REFERENCES

Nearly all of the articles in the Encyclopedia have cross-references to other articles. These cross-references appear at the end of the article, following the conclusion of the text. They indicate related articles that can be consulted for further information on the same topic, or for other information on a related topic. For example, the article "Biotechnology" contains cross-references to the articles "Agricultural Ethics," "Animal Research," "Eugenics," "Genetic Counseling," and "Genetic Engineering."

BIBLIOGRAPHY

The Bibliography appears as the last element in an article. It lists recent secondary sources to aid the reader in locating more detailed or technical information. Review articles and research papers that are important to an understanding of the topic are also listed.

The bibliographies in this Encyclopedia are for the benefit of the reader, to provide references for further reading or research on the given topic. Thus they typically consist of no more than ten to twelve entries. They are not intended to represent a complete listing of all the materials consulted by the author in preparing the article, as would be the case, for example, with a journal article.

INDEX

The Subject Index in Volume 4 contains more than 5000 entries. The entries are listed alphabetically and indicate the volume and page number where information on this topic will be found. Within the entry for a given topic, references to the coverage of the topic also appear alphabetically. The Index serves, along with the alphabetical Table of Contents, as the starting point for information on a subject of interest.

PREFACE

Applied Ethics has come to prominence as a field of study in the last 25 to 30 years, after a period in which the prevailing view among philosophers, at least, was that Philosophy could not usefully be applied to practical problems. The importance of Applied Ethics became obvious first in the medical context, where in the aftermath of World War II and the expanding interest in human rights, developments in technology gave rise to challenging ethical issues such as the use of transplant technology and the allocation of scarce resources such as kidney dialysis. Questions such as the extent to which health care professionals should intervene to extend life became extensively debated. Medical Ethics as a defined area became established, with principles such as autonomy being given central importance. In more recent times contested topics have included assisted reproduction and the advances in and implications of human genome analysis. The latter have led to controversy not only about the options concerning the applications of the technology in medical practice, but also about their wider social uses and even their implications for the meaning of what it is to be human.

Applied Ethics is, however, by no means confined to the medical context and to the social implications of technologies that have been developed for medical purposes or have clear medical applications. Ethical issues arise in any area of life where the interests of individuals or groups conflict, including the interests of different species. In compiling the Encyclopedia we became increasingly aware of the enormity of the task—the list of topics covered could have been expanded indefinitely. We chose to concentrate, however, on areas we regarded as central in contemporary society such as issues concerning the environment, law, politics, the media, science and engineering, education, economics, the family and personal relationships, mental health, social work, policing and punishment, minority rights.

In addition to these areas in which particular issues arise, it is essential for those engaged in Applied Ethics to reflect on what, if anything, is being applied. We therefore included a number of entries on ethical and philosophical approaches, both historical and contemporary, religious and secular. There are different models concerning what is involved in Applied Ethics—for example, whether it is a matter of "applying" a particular theory to a specific ethical dilemma; or whether phenomena, specific developments, particular cases, can affect the development of appropriate theory; whether there is room for a ëbottom-upí rather than a ëtop-downí approach. Some would argue that a central task of Applied Ethics, and one that is prior to the application of theory, is the very identification of the moral dimensions of a situation. Thus we have also included entries on Applied Ethics itself and on challenges to it.

Several disciplines may be involved in Applied Ethics; one branch of Applied Ethics, for example, Bioethics, is commonly explicated in terms of ethical, legal and social issues. In this Encyclopedia by no means all the entries are written by philosophers: some are written by practitioners in the particular field in question; other disciplines represented include law and economics. The Encyclopedia will be a reference work for use by a number of readerships, working in a variety of specialisms; but particularly for students in higher education studying on Applied Ethics courses, for which there is increasing demand. It also has much to offer the general reader interested in the ethical issues arising in contemporary social life.

The number of people who have enabled this enterprise to come to fruition is very large. I should like to thank, first, the members of the Editorial Board and Advisory Council, for participating in the project and for their expert advice on and help with the selection and reviewing of material; the reviewers of the articles, for their time in making the assessments of individual submissions; the University of Central Lancashire, for providing research assistance in the Centre for Professional Ethics—first Jane Pritchard and then Adam Hedgecoe, without whom I cannot imagine how the task would have been completed; and of course Academic Press, especially Scott Bentley and Naomi Henning, for their unfailing support throughout, but also their colleagues in the San Diego office who looked after me extremely well on my visit in 1996. All of my colleagues in the Centre for Professional Ethics have given their support to the project—some by writing entries themselves. Finally, the authors of the articles deserve a very large thank you, for contributing their expertise in their field and for working to very tight deadlines to produce the 281 entries in this Encyclopedia.

RUTH CHADWICK

ECOLOGICAL BALANCE

Alan Holland
Lancaster University

GLOSSARY

climax A condition of vegetation that is the culmination of a process of succession.

community (ecological) A historical association of interacting species.

diversity (ecological) The variety, and capacity to vary, possessed by living organisms and the ecological complexes in which they occur.

diversity-stability hypothesis The hypothesis that the stability of a system tends to increase along with an increase in its diversity.

ecology The study of those interactions of organisms with their environment that determine the characteristics, distribution, and abundance of organisms and systems of organisms.

ecosystem A natural unit or physical system composed of both organic and inorganic components and exhibiting an interdependence of parts and a degree of self-regulation.

ecosystem health The normal occurrence of the eco-logical processes and functions of an ecosystem sustaining a capacity for self-renewal.

food-chain, food-web A sequence of relationships between animal species, or between animal and plant species, ordered or structured by the "*x* eats *y*" relation.

inertia The capacity or propensity to resist disturbance.

integrity (ecological) An unimpaired condition in which the historical range of ecological elements, structures, and processes is maintained.

niche The "occupation" of a species or population, its place or role in the biotic community, and especially its place in the food chain.

pyramid of numbers The pyramidal pattern of abundance of animals according to their place in the food chain/web, with the most abundant at the "bottom" and the least abundant at the "top"; the relation of parasitism reverses the pyramid.

resilience The capacity or propensity to recover from disturbance.

stability The capacity or propensity to persist in a particular state (static) or on a particular path (dynamic), due to inertia or resilience in the case of "static" stability, or due to the operation of predictable processes in the case of "dynamic" stability.

succession (ecological) A directional and law-governed sequence of vegetational states occurring in a given terrain and exhibiting a recurring pattern.

ECOLOGICAL BALANCE is a kind of stability or persistence that is attained through counterposed forces, and may be conceived of as either precarious, in the analogy of a tight-rope walker, or resilient, in the analogy of a well-balanced character (see Figure 1). A structure can be stable or persistent without being balanced—for example, a mesolithic stone circle. Ecological balance involves the relations and interdependencies between living things, and between living things and their (non-living) environments. It may be understood in a functional, structural, or a dynamic sense. Specifically, it may be a feature of ecosystem function, population dynamics, or community structure, and different models of balance—for example, hydraulic, organicist—are appropriate in the different cases. Ecological balance is subject to relativities of both time and space, in the sense that a process or structure that is balanced in relation to a particular period of time or a particular region of space may not be so in relation to some other period or region, and vice versa. The time scales involved may vary from short-term cultural time, through medium-term ecological time, to long-term evolutionary time (or even longer term geological time). The spatial region involved may vary from that of pond to that of the whole planet. The mere fact that matter or energy is conserved in any given system is not sufficient to found the notion of ecological balance, which clearly requires the repetition or persistence of features at an ecologically meaningful level. Among the more obvious apparent signs of balance in terrestrial nature are the daily and seasonal cycles, and the fixity and fittingness (or adaptation) of species. Opinions differ over the degree and kind of balance that characterizes the natural world. One view is that balance is an inherent feature of the natural world. Another view is that it is a contingent feature of the natural world. A third view might be that, like the curate's egg, it is balanced in parts. A fourth, moderately skeptical, view is that it is not a feature of the natural world at all, although it might have been. A fifth, radically skeptical, view would be to question whether it is even meaningful to ascribe balance to the natural world. It is a further epistemological question whether, given the great complexity of the natural world, we could ever get to know which, if any, of these views is true.

I. HISTORICAL CONSPECTUS

A. Pre-Darwinian Conceptions of Balance

1. The Ancient Period

The conception of nature as balanced long precedes modern ecological analysis. Often, this conception has had a "religious" basis—on a broad understanding of that term; thus, many "worldviews" have regarded the natural world as providentially ordered. But the notion that such ordering is the work of a supernatural agency, rather than built into the fabric of things, is arguably the exception rather than the rule. Both Buddhist and Taoist philosophies, for example, like Western Stoicism, feature the idea of nature rightly ordered, not by some external governance but from the inside, and accordingly recommend a life "following nature." Popular religion, however, perhaps answering the needs of common people who "felt the draft" rather more than the privileged, was less convinced. The anarchic world of Homer's gods, for example, provided little reassurance that the world was rightly ordered. The legend of Pandora's box, which, when opened, released a host of evils upon the world, leaving hope as the only solace, gives characteristic expression to this outlook.

Early Western cosmologists construed nature as composed either (i) of a single element, such as water or fire, capable of many transformations; or (ii) of a finite number of different elements, such as earth, air, fire, and water interacting with or being transformed into one another; or (iii) of an infinite number of elements finite in kind, such as atoms and void. The majority, while aware of fluctuating forces and elements—conflagrations in the case of Heraclitus, love and strife in the case of Empedocles—pictured such changes as staying within fixed limits. A notable exception were the atomists, whose almost "modern" outlook is most completely described in the work of the Roman author, Lucretius, *On The Nature of Things* (1st century B.C.). They postulated a real infinity of time and space in which temporary pockets of stability, in the form of clusters of vibrating atoms, occurred at random—literally, on account of a random "swerve"—in the incessant rain of atoms. The current denizens of earth are merely the survivors from trial-and-error processes that the earth "mother," in recent times thought of as

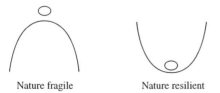

FIGURE 1   Conceptions of ecological balance. After C. S. Holling (1979) Myths of ecological stability, pp. 99–100.

Nature fragile   Nature resilient

failing in her powers, has yielded up. While sharing with Stoicism a belief in the value of attaining an internal psychological balance—ataraxia, or tranquillity—the Epicurean atomists believed this was achieved by understanding rather than by following nature.

As regards living nature, the myth of Epimetheus recounted in Plato's *Protagoras* sets the prevailing tone. The Titan, Epimetheus, charged with distributing to earth's creatures their proper characteristics, gave to each the means of sustenance, and the means to protect themselves against the elements and against each other, "with the view of preventing any race from becoming extinct." The Greek historian Herodotus suggests that practices of cooperation between species, and differential rates of reproduction, have the same effect; while Aristotle contributes the thought that physiological limitations built into a creature's form constrain its ecological impact. What Egerton (*The Quarterly Review of Biology* 48, 1973) has termed "providential ecology" is epitomized in the Stoic picture of a stable and coherent world, held together and suffused by divine intelligence, and possessing the integrity of a living organism, so that, in Cicero's words, "nothing better adapted to endure could be imagined." Although it was a system arranged "for the safety and preservation of all," in which every thing had its place and nothing was superfluous, human convenience was frequently emphasized. Chrysippus, a leading Stoic, notoriously suggested that pigs are given souls in order to keep their meat fresh, and that the role of fleas and mice, respectively, is to encourage cleanliness and tidiness in humans.

2. The Early Modern Period

Belief in providence, hierarchy, and order was readily assimilated into the medieval worldview. But views of the natural world tended to oscillate thereafter between the opposing poles of turmoil and tranquility, often appearing to reflect contemporary social concerns. At the same time, these contrasting views were seldom found in purely unmixed form. In the seventeenth century, darker visions surfaced in the likes of Thomas Hobbes' depiction of the state of nature as "nasty, brutish and short," and John Milton's "dalliance" with Satan in *Paradise Lost*. The belief in a providential ecology, associated with natural theology, and expressed in the metaphor of a great "chain of being," however, experienced a revival in the seventeenth and eighteenth centuries. Richard Pulteney spoke of "that perfect order and just subordination of all the several parts of nature," a point illustrated by William Derham, who remarked how the balance of the animal world was "kept even" by the trade-off between rates of reproduction and life

expectancy. In citing differential longevity as a cause of the balance he was anticipated by Thomas Browne, who added the suggestion that hibernation served to keep fierce animals out of mischief. Gilbert White, meanwhile, found evidence aplenty of cooperative accommodation, noting how dung from the cattle in his local ponds harbored insects that provided food for the fish. (This spirit of collaboration, however, did not extend to noxious insects, concerning which he declared that a compendium of known and likely means of destroying them would be a most "useful and important work.") These harmonious relations, which served to maintain not just species, but also permanent forms of association, were in turn codified by Linnaeus, whose analysis of the natural world suggested that propagation, preservation, and death were the chief factors maintaining the balance. Under this view, apparent exceptions to ecological balance did not go unnoticed, but they were easily explained away: plagues were sent to chastise or test us; apparently extinct species were still to be found in so-far unexplored regions. Only when extinction was taken seriously would these explanations of plagues and pests cease to be acceptable. New sources of tension emerged with the early nineteenth-century debate over the formation of the earth's surface, between catastrophists led by Georges Cuvier, who believed that the present state of the earth's surface could only be explained on the supposition that it had undergone periodic convulsions, and the uniformitarians led by Charles Lyell, who believed that the phenomena could be adequately explained by familiar and more gradual processes. A twist to this debate was that the catastrophist position, rather than the uniformitarian, was thought to be more consonant with religious belief and supernatural agency.

B. Darwin's "Considerable Revolution"

1. The Theory

Against the background warnings of geological instability that had been sounded by Hutton, Cuvier, Humboldt, Lyell, and others, and whether the cause of change was catastrophic or uniform, Engels in his *Dialectics of Nature* was later to comment on the striking anomaly of postulating fixed organic species in a changing inorganic environment. When Darwin offered his theory of natural selection as a credible explanation of species mutation, he modestly claimed to "dimly foresee" how it might involve a "considerable revolution" in natural history (*The Origin of Species* 6th ed., ch. 15). Essentially the theory of natural selection shows how the hereditary characteristics of a population of organisms may change over time due to their differential reproduction arising out of the "struggle for life." Its effect was to replace the conception of the natural world as an enduring, and usually closed, system with a conception of it as an open-ended historical process. A further effect was to render the notion of balance problematic. One view is that the theory of natural selection undermines the notion of ecological balance completely. But another view is that it simply serves to explain it. Ecological theory since Darwin, while adding enormously to our understanding of the constraints and contingencies to which natural phenomena are subject, has so far failed to resolve the issue.

2. The Implications of the Theory

In favor of the view that natural selection undermines the notion of balance is the emphasis in the theory on struggle—the "dreadful but quiet war," as Darwin called it (*Notebooks*, 1838)—with its implication that no particular outcome is assured. Under the hypothesis of natural selection the only constant is change, while responses to change are provisional and makeshift. Stability might be compatible with change if the change exhibits recurring pattern or direction, but natural selection assures us of neither. In favor of the contrary view that natural selection explains balance, it might be observed that the scientific worldview had already assimilated corpuscular, that is, atomic, theory and therefore the idea of wholesale motion at the microscopic level, without this apparently destroying the belief in a well-governed universe. Furthermore, evolutionary change was sufficiently long drawn out to leave the relatively stable world of ordinary experience intact. Even the subsequent idea that the course of evolution has been "punctuated" by periods of rapid change, given that these are externally caused, need not disturb the belief in the overall stability of the system, in light of its demonstrable powers of recovery. Moreover, Darwinian theory does not supplant, but indeed explains, the phenomenon of adaptation, because it yields the idea that, through the mechanism of natural selection, populations of organisms at least have the capacity to track the changes that are constantly occurring around them.

II. THE CONCEPT OF BALANCE IN ECOLOGICAL THEORY

A. Introduction

Whether, as some might have hoped, the new "science" of ecology that Darwin's work ushered in has succeeded

TABLE I

Types of Resilience

Type	Characterization
(i) Elasticity	The speed of recovery to some initial condition, following disturbance
(ii) Amplitude	The extent of the disturbance from which recovery to the initial condition will occur
(iii) Hysteresis	The extent to which the pattern of recovery mirrors the pattern of disturbance
(iv) Malleability	The degree to which the state following recovery simulates the initial state

in placing the question of balance on a sounder, or more testable, footing, still remains unclear. But at least there have been considerable conceptual advances made, and a resulting clarification of the issues. Three types of balance have been distinguished: constancy, or the extent to which some population, community, or system remains unchanged; inertia, or the capacity to resist disturbance; and resilience, or the capacity to respond to disturbance. The two latter notions of balance are "static" inasmuch as they refer to a propensity to retain or revert to some initial state. One thing that can immediately be inferred from this analysis is that the issue of balance may not be an all-or-nothing matter: something that is constant might not be resilient, and so forth. Moreover, the presence of inertia or resilience is clearly relative to the nature of the disturbance involved: resilience in the face of disturbance of kind X—for example, fire following a lightning strike—will not imply resilience in the face of disturbance of kind Y—for example, a flash flood. In his classic account of inertia and resilience, W. E. Westman (*Bioscience* 28, 1978), following G. H. Orians, has distinguished four kinds of resilience; see Table 1.

Ecologists usually discuss the issue of "balance," or near equivalents such as "stability" and "equilibrium," in connection with segments of the natural world identified as "communities" or "ecosystems." It should be noted, however, that some strongly prefer to use a more noncommittal term such as "patch" to refer to these segments, on the grounds that the use of terms such as community and ecosystem are likely to *predispose* one to find structure. In a given community, among the commonly recognized signs of apparently nonaccidental balance or stability are: constancy of its constituent populations, recurring patterns of abundance, correlations between abundance and size of organisms, patterns of feeding relations, and so forth. Two questions arise: whether this apparent stability is real; and what might account for it. It is natural to think that relations between the constituent organisms—"biotic interactions"—will play a large part in determining the structure, composition, and dynamics of a community. One early attempt to explain community structure focused on the feeding relation.

B. Trophic Relations, Trophic Structure

Although Charles Elton notoriously remarked that "the balance of nature does not exist," his work on animal communities was nevertheless seminal in its approach to community structure. Elton held that all animal communities are structured in a particular way and that the crucial factor determining this structure is FOOD (*Animal Ecology*, 1927). He distinguishes four general principles that regulate animal communities, namely food size, the food chain, the niche, and the pyramid of numbers:

(i) Food size. Although there are exceptions, Elton was struck by the fact that there are upper and lower limits to the size of food that any particular animal can eat (he cites the difficulty that a human would find trying to make a meal of bilberries). This is a function of physiological and anatomical features such as bite size and the degree of nourishment afforded by any particular source of food in relation to the effort, size, and talent needed to acquire it.

(ii) Food chain. Facts about what an animal can and cannot eat broadly determine a chain of predator–prey relations. More realistically, the "chain" is in fact a web, because any given species will probably eat and be eaten by a number of different species.

(iii) Niche. Narrowly conceived, an animal's niche is precisely its place in the food chain, as determined by the kind of animal it is (so distinguishing it from Darwin's concept of place that is occupied by individual animals). More broadly, it is the animal's status, role, or "occupation" in the biotic community of which it forms a part, and how it relates to its food and to its enemies.

(iv) Pyramid of numbers. The most abundant animals will be those at the bottom of the food chain who constitute food for the rest, and who themselves consume plants, detritus, and other nonanimal material. In the middle of the pyramid will be animals that both eat and are eaten by other species. The top predator is simply the species which is not numerous enough to constitute a food supply for any other species.

Elton held that these four principles ensure certain "constancies" in the structure of animal communities, which invariably are found to comprise three main classes—of "producers," "consumers," and "decomposers." Also, remarkably similar niches—scavenging, sap-sucking, and so forth—are found in widely differing animal communities both on land and sea.

Although Elton's work continues to attract interest—for example, the intriguing problem of why the number of trophic levels rarely exceeds four or five—much of it has been superseded. Perhaps the chief limitation in Elton's approach concerns his exclusive focus on trophic relations. Many other kinds of biotic interaction, such as competition for resources, interference, mutual support, and converging or competing habitat requirements are now thought to play a crucial role in structuring community relations and therefore, possibly, in explaining community stability. Moreover, the trophic analysis itself has been found to obscure both (i) forms of organization within trophic levels, and (ii) the subtlety of relationships between trophic levels—involving the number, type, and strength of the links. There is growing evidence that both these factors of food-web structure affect the dynamics and stability of the community at large. Finally, the niche concept has proved neither sufficiently fine-grained nor sufficiently well-defined in operational terms. Thus, although the theory suggest that niche overlap should be minimal, such overlap is common when resources are abundant. Moreover, species assigned to different niches on grounds of spatial or temporal separation may nevertheless be in competition if their (common) food source is excessively mobile, or if it is consumed at different times or at different stages in its life cycle.

C. Fluctuating Populations

When Elton denied the reality of the balance of nature he cited, in particular, irregularity in the fluctuations of animal populations both as regards frequency and degree. But this seems to have more bearing on the presence of constancy than of resilience. Indeed, his further point, that variations in the numbers of one species have repercussions on the numbers of others, might be thought to tell as much in favor of balance—or at least of a balancing mechanism—as against it. Whether there is a mechanism regulating animal numbers and if so what it is, is a matter of contention.

Competing accounts can be divided into those that cite an external cause and those that cite an internal one. Possible external controls that are biotic include insect parasitism, disease, and shortage of food; possible abiotic controls include climate and lack of suitable habitat. Among internal controls to have been suggested are genetic (self) regulation—the idea that an increasing number of less viable genotypes accompany rapid increases in population (G. Chitty), and territorial (self) regulation—the idea that among some species there is an instinctive territorial sense that permits a certain number but no more to occupy a given habitat (V. Wynne-Edwards). A question raised about both hypotheses, however, is how far they are compatible with the theory of natural selection. How far such fluctuations are a function of the density of the relevant populations (i.e., how far they are "density dependent" or "density independent") is also an issue. What seems to be true of most, if not all of these hypotheses, is that they are capable of explaining the pattern of fluctuations that are known to have occurred. But the processes that they posit do not carry any guarantee about what the pattern of fluctuation is going to be in the future; they carry no built-in guarantee of balance. Moreover, they do not and cannot guarantee that numbers will not drop below the level at which a species is viable: clearly, they do not ensure against extinction.

One way in which excessive fluctuation might actually, and paradoxically, contribute to constancy has been recently proposed by S. Pimm and J. Lawton. The usual explanation for the limit to the number of trophic levels is that the available community "energy" is not sufficient to support another level. If that were true, Pimm and Lawton argue, one might expect that communities in which primary productivity (i.e., the amount of energy captured by the "producers") was greatest would support more levels—which is not generally true. They suggest instead that top predator populations are simply not stable enough to support a further trophic level.

D. The Ecosystem

In 1935, Arthur Tansley proposed a new concept, the "ecosystem," which provided a unified framework within which to study both plant and animal communities together, their interactions with inorganic nature, and their interrelations with human communities also. Since Clausius formulated the Second Law of Thermodynamics in 1850, it had been understood that in a general trend toward disorder the tendency was for energy to become dispersed. By capturing some of the sun's energy and making it available to animals, plants temporarily reverse this process. Set within Tansley's newly devised concept of the ecosystem, food could be viewed functionally, as partly comprising the means by which both energy and nutrients are transmitted through the biosphere. It was R. Lindeman's landmark paper on "The Trophic-Dynamic Aspects of Ecology" (*Ecology* 23, 1942) that paved the way for this more comprehensive level of analysis. He sets out what is essentially an "economic" analysis of energy transfer, measuring the productivity and efficiency of each trophic level, thus building a picture of what happens to captured solar energy as it moves through the ecosystem. Besides the transfer of energy, the movement through the system of minerals and nutrients such as carbon, oxygen, nitrogen, and sulphur could be studied in the same way. The analysis of systems in terms of energy enables new facets of community structure and ecosystem function to be revealed. For example, there is recent evidence to suggest that both the rate of energy flow and the efficiency with which it is transferred (aspects of the type and strength of trophic links) contribute to stability.

During the middle part of the century, "ecosystem theory" was developed and formalized, notably by the brothers, Howard and Eugene Odum. Nature was conceived as a series of hierarchically ordered ecosystems at various stages of development. Distinguishing features of mature as opposed to immature ecosystems were drawn up, such as greater stability, increased diversity, and minimal loss of minerals and nutrients. These energy, mineral, and nutrient cycles, and the circumstances that facilitate and obstruct their operation, were open to quantitative measurement and became the subject of extensive study. Their existence served to reinforce the conception of nature as systematic and to that extent "balanced." Moreover, the discovery of mineral and nutrient cycles operating on a planetary scale, together with the moderating effects of life on oxygen levels and circumambient temperature, have encouraged some to believe that life has the capacity for self-regulation and self-organization at a higher level. The idea has been given eloquent expression in J. Lovelock's "Gaia" hypothesis, which posits that the planet itself is just such a self-regulating system. The salinity of the sea, and oxygen and temperature levels, are far more constant, it is argued, than they would be if there were no life; and furthermore, this (relative) constancy is essential for the continuation of life. A more cautious reading of the same phenomena, however, would argue that the mineral and nutrient cycles, and the inevitable effect of the existence of life upon oxygen and temperature levels, simply explain how it is "as if" the planet is regulating itself—much in the way that Darwin's theory explains how it is "as if" nature were designed.

E. Ecological Succession

1. The Theory

Communities (ecosystems—or patches) appear to undergo repeatable directional and convergent changes of structure. This is the phenomenon known as "succession." As with evolution, so with succession, it is important to distinguish between the process and the theories advanced to explain the process. The "classic" theory of succession was anticipated by Thoreau and developed by Eugenius Warming, Henry Cowles, and Frederick Clements. It is nearly always advanced as a theory of plant succession, although, as Rory Putman observes, there is no obvious reason why its scope should be limited to plants—given the interdependence of plant and animal populations. In brief, the theory maintains that the character of the vegetation in any terrain is fundamentally determined by climate (and to a lesser extent, by geophysical factors). Following any process that yields a site relatively free of vegetation—whether natural such as fire, volcanic activity, or the retreat of a glacier, or caused by human agency—the site will first be colonized by "pioneering" species. According to Clements's version of the theory, these will affect the site in such a way as to render it suitable for new species, and facilitate their establishment. In some cases the new species will displace the original occupants. The process will continue until a relatively stable or climax state is reached that is most favored by the prevailing climatic conditions. In practice the process may be affected by a variety of contingencies; but these are both anticipated and provided for by the theory. For example, the process may be interrupted, diverted or arrested. If interrupted, the succession is repeated. If diverted or arrested, it will, predictably, settle into a relatively stable form of substitute climax—called in these cases a "proclimax" and a "plagioclimax," respectively. It is by virtue of postulating that plant communities, although changing, are changing according to ascertainable laws, and that deviations are fully explicable, that the theory tends to support the conception of nature as balanced; furthermore, these communities are conceived as tending towards a steady state.

In Clements's hands the theory was overlaid with a metaphysical view which saw plant communities formed in this way as "super organisms." He describes them as similar to organisms in undergoing birth and death and in having the capacities of regeneration and reproduction. Although this metaphysical reading of plant succession is a graphic way of underlining the predictability of the process, it is not essential. The scientific theory of plant succession could survive intact even if the organismic interpretation of it were abandoned.

2. Problems with the "Classic" Theory

To accommodate the growing number of exceptions requiring special explanation, the number of variations on the climax concept began to proliferate implausibly, with Tansley at one point seriously suggesting the concept of a "mowing climax." One of the theory's sternest critics was H. Gleason, a younger contemporary of Clements. Gleason took an individualistic view of plant communities, referring to them as "fortuitous juxtapositions" and as "no more than the mass effect of the action or behaviour of individual plants." He found the attribution of overriding agency to climate implausible and cited existing vegetation, migration, soil, and geography, as equally important factors. In particular he highlighted instances of oscillating succession—between prairie and forest and back again, and between mangrove swamp and open sea, depending in part on whether the shoreline is rising or sinking, so undermining the idea of directional change. Empirical evidence lending support to Gleason includes disparities in the species composition of allegedly similar communities, absence of boundaries between communities, and only fitful evidence of the close-knit dependencies that Clements' theory postulates.

3. New Explanations

Later theorists have tended to accept the reality of the phenomenon, but have offered a number of competing explanations of its occurrence. F. E. Egler suggested that existing vegetation often inhibits rather than facilitates new arrivals, and that the order of arrival affects the composition of the resulting plant community. Others propose that most of the phenomena of succession can be explained in terms of the differential colonizing abilities of the available organisms, together with their growth patterns and survival capacities. Thus, organisms with high dispersal abilities (r-strategists) will tend to predominate in the early stages, while the longer lived, more competitive organisms (k-strategists) gradually gain a foothold, and predominate in the later stages. As these explanations indicate, there is increasing evidence to suggest that succession may be governed more by external than by internal factors.

A more radical proposal is that the phenomena of succession may be the consequence, merely, of random or "stochastic" processes; for directional change and repeatable convergence are a statistical property of "Markov chains"—processes in which what happens next depends entirely on what is happening now, and not at all on what has happened previously. The extent that stochastic events may be responsible for ecological processes raises the general question of how far the apparent signs of ecological stability are signs of stability at all; or whether they are just transient patterns in what are basically nonequilibrium systems. Of course, ecological processes need not be exclusively one or the other. Just as stochastic processes can mimic deterministic ones, so can processes that are "chaotic" (but deterministic) mimic stochastic ones—with apparently random developments in fact reflecting extreme sensitivity to initial conditions, which is the mark of a chaotic system. Methodologies for distinguishing between chaotic, stochastic, and deterministic systems are still undeveloped.

F. The Diversity–Stability Thesis

1. The Thesis

The apparent correlation between stability and diversity has been a particular focus of interest, since it first featured as an assumption in the work of Robert MacArthur—to the effect that the measure of diversity could be used as a way of estimating the balance or stability of a system. Its appeal rests on a combination of empirical and apriori considerations. Among apriori considerations is the belief that a diversity of interaction relations—for example, feeding options—will make for stability in numbers—for example, of both predator and prey. For predators can turn elsewhere if a particular prey becomes scarce, preventing further losses of both the predator and prey species. Further, it would seem that diversity of characteristics within a given population would present that population with more chances of surviving environmental vicissitudes. Empirical observation meanwhile had suggested:

(a) that species rich systems (i.e., systems with large numbers of species) such as tropical rain forests were relatively stable;
(b) that species poor ecosystems were particularly prone to fluctuations in populations; and
(c) that monocultural systems were relatively unstable.

2. Problems with the Thesis

However, both empirical and theoretical considerations have seemed to undermine the thesis. It was noted, for example, that extremely simple systems are also sometimes extremely stable, while extremely diverse systems such as tropical rain forests were proving vulnerable. Correlations appearing to support the thesis could be explained in other ways: in one study where the stability of certain bird populations correlated with their diversity, it was found to correlate also with an east-west and a wet-dry spectrum, and in general with the availability of more suitable habitat (D. Goodman, *The Quarterly Review of Biology* 50, 1975). Moreover, R. M. May showed on theoretical grounds that diverse systems need not be more stable than simple ones.

3. Responses to the Problems

Commenting on May's results, Putman has noted that the type of stability that, according to May's models, is lacking in diverse systems, is constancy rather than resilience, and that some degree of correlation between diversity and resilience might still be affirmed, particularly if the diversity involved is diversity of interaction rather then species richness, for there appears to be no necessary correlation between diversity of interaction and species richness. Further, differences between number and strength of interaction appear to affect inertia, constancy, and resilience in different ways. May himself has gone on to propose that such correlation as is observed in complex natural systems between diversity and stability is to be explained by reference to a common cause—the stability of the natural environment in which they have arisen and by which they are sustained.

This is consonant with a speculation of Bryan Norton's. Noting that the concept of stability assumed by the original diversity–stability thesis, in focusing on recovery to some more or less original state, was therefore "static," Norton has used the work of Ramon Margalef to propose a "dynamic" concept. Dynamic stability refers to the autogenic character of a system—that is, the extent to which the later states of the system are a function of, and therefore predictable in the light of, earlier ones. Persisting species, stable populations, and recovery to some initial state—the marks of static stability—are not required. Dynamic stability, Norton suggests, will be a characteristic not of systems that are internally diverse, but of systems that are themselves formed within a wider context of diversity. This situation will entail intense competitive pressure and therefore result in a system that is highly interconnected internally and likely to be inured to further disturbance. Dynamic stability will tend to correlate with maturity but not necessarily with diversity. Such an analysis will explain how simple systems can be stable, and also how diverse and mature systems can be vulnerable to specifically human pressure, if this should be of a novel kind.

G. Discordant Voices

Recent theorizing in ecology has seen a resurgence of scepticism about the notion of ecological balance, with disturbance increasingly being regarded as the rule rather than the exception. We have seen that conceptions of the natural world that emphasize chaos and complexity and randomness are gaining ground. Weather systems and randomly generated computer graphics are regarded as more appropriate models for natural processes than clockwork mechanisms, organisms, and homeostatic systems. Empirical considerations at best serve only partly to explain this development. It is in part also a matter of the availability of these new models and in part, too, a matter of residual conceptual difficulties over the concept of balance.

A number of factors may be identified as lying behind the new outlook:

(a) The first is a softening of edges, which is an aspect of natural processes to which certain strands of "deep ecology" have been sensitive. Once the relatively sharp boundaries separating individual organisms are left behind, and once Darwin had disproved the constancy of species, the drawing of both spatial and temporal boundaries around natural processes becomes problematic. Units larger than organisms, such as communities and ecosystems, lack clear criteria of identity. Plant "communities," for example, are found to vary considerably across geographical distances along gradients of elevation and moisture, making the separation of one from the other problematic; and their composition is found to vary considerably depending on the order of arrival of their formative species, making the identification of community types problematic.

(b) Lack of clear criteria of identity places the notion of "disturbance" in question, because the latter seems to presuppose a clearly identifiable item undergoing the disturbance.

(c) Lack of clear boundaries places in doubt also the correlative notion of "the surrounding environment," and throws doubt on the validity of the properties that are ascribed to it. There is more than a hint of circularity, for example, in the concept of a "stable environment," which seems partly to gain its sense from the degree of disturbance undergone by that whose environment it is.

(d) If there are functional, evolutionary, or even historical constraints on the changes that characterize natural processes, there has been difficulty in detecting them. For example, neither the mathematically inspired Lotka-Voltera equations describing predator–prey rela-

tions in terms of a "competitive balance," nor the organically inspired succession theory of vegetation, has held up well under empirical study (Goodman, 1975).

(e) Although mere change and variety are not in themselves incompatible with notions of balance, if the change and variety exhibit some constancy or regularity, change in the natural world seems to be inconstant and irregular, and its course to vary greatly, depending on initial conditions. The history of climate change and of vegetational changes as revealed by pollen analysis are both tending to confirm the point.

(f) Natural events traditionally regarded as "disturbances," such as storms, fires, and floods, are increasingly being seen as creative and integral features of natural processes. Accordingly, there are good grounds for viewing such disturbances as endogenous rather than exogenous features of those processes. Yet their occurrence is erratic, and they must be presumed to pass on this feature to the processes of which they are now seen to form a part.

(g) There are increasing pressures to "count in" the effects of human activities. A practical reason is that ecology needs to deal with the real world, and separating out human activity is increasingly difficult in view of its global impact. Moreover, the recognition of the erratic character of much natural disturbance makes humanly caused disturbance seem less out of place.

It is possible, however, to exaggerate the significance of these points. Concerning points (a), (b), and (c), it is not clear that the notion of ecological balance requires there to be sharply defined boundaries in nature. If, as some prefer, we speak of "patches" rather than of communities or ecosystems, these may still be regarded as representative *samples* of natural processes—and the regularities and patterns that are found as therefore illustrative of the way the natural world works. Concerning (d), a number of authors have drawn attention to the apparent operation of morphological and physiological constraints in the history of evolution, citing, for example, the fact that different lineages are often found to pursue strikingly similar behavioral and morphological paths. Concerning (e) and (f), neither inconstancy nor disturbance rules out stability. For example, there are known cases where species richness is greater under moderately severe than under slight disturbance; and cases where irregular disturbance keeps competitive species in balance—by preventing one or the other from wholly gaining the upper hand. Concerning (g), it can be argued that humanly caused disturbance is qualitatively different from anything natural, outside of the great mass extinction events. The inference to be drawn from these various considerations may not so much be that nature is revealed as inconstant, irregular and unstable, as that we still do not know how far any of these features obtains, and more radically, that we still lack clear criteria for deciding what counts as stability or instability in the first place.

III. THE SOCIAL CONSTRUCTION OF NATURE

Challenges to the idea of ecological balance do not only arise from within ecological theory, but also come from outside, and in particular from perspectives such as the sociology of knowledge that emphasizes the extent to which scientific concepts may be culturally determined or shaped. Such a perspective generates apparently oxymoronic talk of the "construction" or "invention" of nature—oxymoronic, because nature is usually conceived as something that is "given." Stronger versions of the perspective will claim that culture determines theory; weaker versions will claim only that cultural factors form an essential ingredient of any comprehensive explanation of why a particular scientific theory or claim is accepted.

Against this framework of thought there would seem to be at least two ways of attempting to preserve some substance to the idea of ecological balance. One is simply to accept the idea of construction and nevertheless insist on the practicality or usefulness of construing nature in this way. But the question is how far the belief that one is actually saying something about nature can survive the admission that this is *merely* a way of construing it. Perhaps a more promising way, therefore, of perserving a degree of objectivity in the idea of ecological balance, while granting the weaker version of the constructivist point some purchase, is to insist that nature lends itself to being construed in one way rather than another, and cannot in fact be construed in any way we please.

Indeed, the scope for invention in our descriptions of the natural world is contained from the start in the inherent elasticity of ecological concepts. It has already been remarked that ecological processes do not manifest sharp edges and clear boundaries: whether a given event counts as a disturbance depends on where boundaries are drawn. Similar considerations apply to "invasion," "indigenous," "population," "colonize," "alien," and a host of other concepts that appear in ecological theory. A moment's reflection reveals that these terms are parasitic upon the way in which certain boundaries are

drawn (as well as being very clearly metaphors with an ideological load); and that a different choice of boundary will entail a different reading of the event. Other sources of elasticity stem from the nature of the tools and instruments used to process ecological data. The point is nicely illustrated in a recent paper by P. Alpert, who describes how the boulders that formed the actual habitat of the mosses that he studied came inevitably to be modeled as spheres during the process of analysis. He shows also how much the results that he produced were a function of the choice of hypotheses that he decided to test and those that he chose to leave alone.

What survives such revelation, however, is the fact that the boulders lent themselves more to analysis in terms of spheres than—say—rectangles, and that the results could at least be justified in the light of the hypotheses chosen. To the extent that nature is "socially constructed," there would appear at least to be a certain construction manual. Hence the "constructivist turn" need not take the ecologist entirely by surprise; many ecologists will take the view that such elasticity in their findings is endemic to their activity. They might well agree that, given the slack between theory and data, it is not unreasonable to suppose that cultural and psychological factors will help to explain why one theory rather than another is chosen, and why a third, perhaps, is not even considered.

IV. HUMANS AND ECOLOGICAL BALANCE

Judgments about the impact of human activity upon ecological balance go a long way to shaping not only current perceptions of our environmental predicament but also the image that human beings have of themselves and of their lives. It raises, for example, the question whether humans are, or are not, to be considered "part" of nature, and how far they can consider themselves to be "at home" in the world: it matters to us to know what kind of world we are thrown into. In fact, humans pose a problem for the thesis of ecological balance inasmuch as the part they increasingly play in relation to the rest of the biosphere is in many ways unprecedented. The single fact, for example, that being only one species they nevertheless appropriate about 40% of the terrestrial biomass, is prima facie difficult to assimilate within that thesis.

There are three responses to this phenomenon that would save the thesis. One response is to treat humans as separate from the rest of nature, and therefore as falling outside the scope of the thesis. But this is a difficult position to maintain in the light of Darwinian theory. At what point exactly in the history of evolution did the separation occur? Another response is to postulate at some future date some answering violence or correction that may or may not spell the end of the human race, but would restore the biosphere to some kind of balanced state. A third response is to place humans firmly within the natural world but construe their apparently uncontrolled growth as a form of disease. Earlier writers had sometimes likened the human race to a plague or pestilence with respect to their effect upon other species. Against the background of a belief in nature as a system in balance, a more favored analogy has been to see humans as a disease of the system—specifically, cancer. Carleton S. Coon, for example, in his *History of Man* refers to mankind as "that terrestrial skin-cancer"; and a contributor to the *Gaia Atlas of Planet Management* refers to humanity as a "supermalignancy." Coon is equally clear about the mechanism by which humans upset this natural balance: it is through the practice of artificial selection and the "thwarting" of the processes of natural selection. Other analysts have not been slow to add to the list of symptoms. Attention has focused most notably on the way in which human activity ruptures the existing food-web relations, and thereby also the energy and nutrient cycles. It has focused also on the loss of biodiversity.

Where humans are not cast as themselves the disease, they are cast as being responsible for disease. Thus Leopold writes of the wounds that only ecologists can detect and calls upon them to practice the science of land health. He saw the conservation schemes that had so far been attempted as merely "local alleviations of biotic pain." This last image at least presents humans in a slightly less negative light. For while they are accused of being responsible for the patient's illness, they are also seen as in principle having the opportunity to effect a cure—in their capacity as "land doctors."

V. ECOLOGICAL BALANCE AND NATURE CONSERVATION

The idea of ecological balance has been of major importance for nature conservation. This is because, to be true to its name, if nature conservation is about maintaining stability of any kind, it must be about sustaining *nature's* stability, or trajectory. If, therefore, the idea of nature's stability or trajectory is placed in doubt, ideas about nature conservation that presuppose such a stability or

TABLE II

Conservation Objectives

Initial state of affairs	Appropriate response	Mode of response
Intact	Conservation	(i) Keep things the same (ii) Keep things going (iii) Let things be
Damaged	Restoration	(i) Undo the damage (ii) Allow "natural" regeneration (iii) Restore to "natural" state
Destroyed	Compensation	(i) Create the same thing elsewhere (ii) Create an equivalent elsewhere (iii) Create a substitute

trajectory must be in question, as must the very idea of nature conservation itself.

Conservation objectives that in one way or another assume some preexisting state of ecological balance can be tabulated (with admitted simplifications) in the way indicated by Table II, depending on whether the site is viewed as relatively intact, "damaged," or virtually destroyed.

Such a schema is not free of internal difficulties. Consider the third mode of response to damage—restoration to some natural state. This might suggest restoration to how things naturally were—which may be impossible to effect in a changing situation; restoration to how things naturally would have been—which may be impossible to predict; or restoration to how they might naturally have been—which makes it unclear what exactly is ruled out.

There may also be some immanent tension between two of the "guiding stars" of conservation thinking that is broadly governed by the assumption of balance, namely, ecological health and ecological integrity—and this despite their both having the imprimatur of Aldo Leopold. For whereas health is a functional concept, integrity contains the idea of being true to origins. Like sustainability, both concepts are still undergoing critical development, but picking up a suggestion of J. Baird Callicott's, we might usefully think of health as being more appropriately predicated of ecosystems, and integrity of communities. Whereas communities are partly defined by reference to the populations and species of which they are composed, ecosystems are functioning entities not requiring the persistence of any particular population or species for the functional role to be maintained. But herein lies the source of tension that at present is manifest in debates about the proper conservation approach to so-called "exotic" or "alien" species. A number of extermination schemes are in operation designed to protect indigenous species against "invasion"—rats and ruddy duck being among the target species. Although this is usually billed as a conflict between conservationists and animal welfare groups, it is at least as much a conflict within conservation thinking itself. For while rats and ruddy duck may well be a threat to integrity, they are not obviously a threat to health, especially if they perform a similar role to that of the species they replace.

It seems likely that any relaxation from the governing model of preexisting balance, although it will not remove sources of conflict, will permit more creative responses to environmental problems. Creative conservation, as it is sometimes called, looks to "future nature" and "new nature" and tends to be skeptical of the human/nonhuman divide. It questions the systems view of nature and associated notions of stability and health, but on the other hand will also tend to be in conflict with approaches that stress the importance of the indigenous and the rare. It will be in tune with the notion of nature as an open-ended historical process and be ready to come to terms with a nature that is unpredictable and wild. It will view nature conservation as less a matter of protecting nature's balance from humanity's destructive power, and more a matter of preserving the destructive wildness of nature from humanly imposed stability and monotony. But if "anything goes" in nature conservation, on the grounds that "anything goes" in nature, skeptics will worry lest it legitimates practices that, as was famously said of politics, merely prosecute the old war against nature, but by other, more diplomatic, means. Accordingly, many conservationists will still argue for the existence of real functional, evolutionary, and historical constraints as being characteristic of natural processes, and therefore factors that nature conservationists must heed. Their fear is that creative conservation, as described, will inevitably lead to homogenization and loss of biodiversity within and among regions.

VI. CONCLUSION

There are recurring patterns that characterize the natural world at the level of individual organisms, both in the conformity to type which grounds the notion of species, and in the pattern of individual development. Because this recurrence is partly constitutive of life, and because life does not and probably cannot occur in isolation, it seems reasonable to suppose that collections or groupings that incorporate living things will also exhibit recurring forms. Thus, life and collections of living things both presuppose and exhibit a degree of relative stability. And just as individual organisms possess various degrees and kinds of recovery capacity, from the healing of wounds to the regeneration of whole limbs, so it also seems reasonable to suppose that collections or groupings of living things will constitutionally possess similar powers of recovery. In short, it may be said that life itself is "a balancing act." But from the fact that, if there is life, it will manifest balance of a certain kind, it does not follow that nature manifests a kind of balance that will ensure the continuation of life in all but the most extreme of circumstances.

The abandoning of providential ecology appears to mean that ecological balance can no longer function as an indispensable explanatory assumption, but itself stands in need of explanation. The issue is whether it can be shown to be an inevitable concomitant of those factors now perceived to determine natural processes, or whether it is nothing but a contingent epiphenomenon of those processes.

The elegant swan looks different viewed from above and below the water line. To a considerable extent current disagreements over the balance of nature may reflect where people choose to stand and where to direct their attention. To a certain extent they may also reflect the room for cultural construction or invention allowed for in the application of ecological concepts. But a deeper question is whether and to what extent physical and biological processes may be reducible one to the other, or whether one must settle for an irreducible plurality in scientific explanations. On a pluralist view, the issue of ecological balance can be seen as an empirical question to be provisionally decided on in the light of prevailing ecological theory. On a reductionist view, the notion of balance might or might not be confirmed. The observed regularities are there; but whether they manifest a real ecological balance depends on how far they are underwritten by the fundamental laws of nature (whatever they may be). For example, one can speculatively imagine a mediating theoretical role here for the concept of the gene. To the extent that the distribution of genes turned out to be some function of the chemical affinities of their material substrate, and to the extent that species distribution turned out to be some function of the distribution of genes, then physico-chemical processes could conceivably turn out to determine ecological regularities. But whether reductionism is true is a hard question to resolve, and for as long as questions of this kind cannot be decisively resolved, whether and in what sense ecological balance is a feature of the natural world is likely to remain unresolved.

Also See the Following Articles

ANTHROPOCENTRISM • BIODIVERSITY • ENVIRONMENTAL JUSTICE • SPECIESISM • WILDLIFE CONSERVATION

Bibliography

Begon, M., Harper, J. L., & Towsend, C. R. (Eds.). (1996). *Ecology* (3rd ed.). Oxford: Blackwell.

Botkin, D. (1990). *Discordant harmonies.* New York: Oxford University Press.

Brennan, A. (1988). *Thinking about nature.* London: Routledge.

Callicott, J. B. (1995). The value of ecosystem health. *Environmental Values* 4, 345–361.

Costanza, R., Norton, B., & Haskell, B. (Eds.). (1992). *Ecosystem health: New goals for environmental management.* Washington, DC: Island Press.

Feidler, P. L., and Jain, S. K. (Eds.). (1992). *Conservation biology: The theory and practice of nature conservation, preservation and management.* London: Chapman and Hall.

Golley, F. B. (1993). *A history of the ecosystem concept in ecology.* London: Yale University Press.

Johnson, K. H. *et al.* (1996). Biodiversity and the productivity and stability of ecosystems. *Trends in Ecology and Evolution* 11, 372–377.

May, R. M. (1986). The search for patterns in the balance of nature: Advances and retreats. *Ecology* 67, 1115–1126.

Norton, B. G. (1987). *Why preserve natural variety?* Princeton: Princeton University Press.

Noss, R. (1996). Sustaining ecological integrity. *Global Bioethics* 11.

Pimm, S. L. (1991). *The balance of nature.* Chicago: University of Chicago Press.

Putman, R. J. (1994). *Community ecology.* London: Chapman & Hall.

Soper, K. (1995). *What is nature?* Oxford: Blackwell.

Westra, L. & Lemons. J. (Eds.). (1995). *Perspectives on ecological integrity.* Dordrecht: Kluwer.

Worster, D. (1994) *Nature's economy* (2nd ed.). Cambridge: Cambridge University Press.

EGOISM AND ALTRUISM

Jan Narveson
University of Waterloo

GLOSSARY

altruism In its broadest sense, the denial of egoism. But many degrees of denial are possible, notably the following three: *partial* altruism—*Some* other people's interests count, and count more than those of others—friends above strangers, say. *impartial* altruism—That the interests of oneself and any others should count *equally*. In between egoism and impartial atruism is *extreme* altruism—The view that other people's interests count and that one's own do *not*.

deep egoism The view that the state of ourselves that we are motivated by is not accessible to the agent but must be reached by special means, such as Freudian psychiatry or neurological investigation.

egoism The theory that all human behavior is (psycho-logical egoism) or ought to be (ethical egoism) motivated *entirely* by self-interest.

ethical egoism The view that the best theory of general action, or life, is to do what is best for oneself, regardless of effects on others, except when those are indirectly necessary for the best result for oneself.

moral egoism The view that the correct rule for groups of people tells each member to do whatever is in his or her interest, regardless of consequences for others in the group.

superficial egoism Egoism identified in ordinary language, with our usual vocabulary concerning what agents "intend" to do, as they see it.

EGOISM is the theory that all human behavior is or ought to be motivated entirely by self-interest. Altruism, in its broadest sense, is the denial of egoism. Many degrees of denial are possible, including partial altruism, in which some other people's interests count, and count more than those of others, impartial altruism, in which the interests of oneself and any others should count equally, and extreme altruism, which is the view that other people's interests count and that one's own do not.

I. PSYCHOLOGICAL VS. ETHICAL EGOISM

The topics of egoism and altruism are subject even more than is usual in philosophy to crucial ambiguities, which must be sorted out before one can say anything helpful.

Egoism, to being with, comes in two species—"psychological" and "ethical." The first is a theory about human motivations: what makes us tick? According to egoism, we are actuated entirely by *self-interest,* even when it appears to be otherwise. Altrium, of course, denies this. But the second is a *normative* theory, a theory about what we *should* do. It says that we *should,* or *ought to,* act only in our own interest. How these are related is perhaps the central question for the subject.

II. SUBSTANTIVE VS. TAUTOLOGICAL PSYCHOLOGICAL EGOISM

The need for still more distinctions arises very soon. Just what is "self-interest," to begin with? Here the ground-breaking work of Joseph Butler paves the way for us. Does self-interest mean (a) interests *in* ourselves, or only (b) interests *of* ourselves? Everything hangs on that one-letter difference!

Interests "in" ourselves are interests that one's own self have certain things, held to be good by the agent, that can be identified and had *independently* of the goods of others. For example, hunger is a desire for food in one's *own* stomach; desires to avoid physical discomfort, for optimal temperature or absence of pain in one's *own* body are further examples. The desire to feel pleasure is the most widely held candidate for the status of fundamental motivator of all action, and pleasure is subjective, *in* the "soul" or psyche of the agent. Interests "in" others, by contrast, would be such desires as love or hatred, where we are essentially directing our actions toward the production of certain states of *other* people. The kind of psychological egoism holding that we are exclusively motivated by the first kind of interests might be called "strict" or "substantive" psychological egoism.

Interests "of" ourselves, on the other hand, simply refer to *whose* interests they are, but not at all to *what* the interests are taken in—what they are aimed at affecting, either in or outside of ourselves. And as Butler pointed out, it is trivial to say that all action is motivated by interests or desires *of* the agent—that is what makes them the agent's actions at all. The so-called "theory" that we always act on motives of *ours* may therefore be called "tautological psychological egoism." By contrast, it seems not at all trivial to say that the *object* of our actions is *only* to produce conditions of ourselves.

Still, the situation is complicated by the fact that we can get pleasure, say, from our perception of the condition of certain other people, or even of all other people. When we do so, are we motivated by the prospect of pleasure from our relations to those people? Views have differed greatly on this. If so, is that to be accounted "egoism," despite the fact that the source of our pleasure in these cases is the pleasures—or perhaps the pains—of others? On the face of it, we need yet another distinction. This would be between theories that deny that we even get pleasure from other-regarding acts, and theories that accept this, but insist that it is only because of the pleasure we get from them that we perform them.

III. SUPERFICIAL VS. DEEP THEORIES

The question whether the nontautological version of psychological egoism may be true becomes very difficult, however, when we distinguish between what we may call "superficial" or, in the terminology of contemporary philosophers of mind, "folk-psychological," and what we may call "deep" theories. At the superficial level, psychological egoism has it that we are all selfish schemers. That is, as Butler pointed out, overwhelmingly implausible. People make huge sacrifices for those they love, including sacrifice of their very lives. Moreover, they sometimes go out of their way to do evils to other people even at the cost of ruining their own lives in the process. At this level, it is surely obvious that we are very interested in at least some others, both positively (as with love) and negatively (as with hatred).

But no one can claim to have refuted the view that there is some variable deep within the soul (or the nervous system) such that all actions really do maximize *it,* regardless of all else in the environment. Except, of course, that other factors in the environment would certainly interact with that variable, whatever it is. The most plausible candidate for what we may be trying to maximize, perhaps, is "net pleasure": the quantity, pleasure minus pain, or more plausibly, of "positive affect" less "negative affect" (or "plus" negative affect if we think of the latter as a minus quantity). Perhaps the man who falls on the grenade to save his comrades reckons that he couldn't live with himself if he didn't do it. Or perhaps, as Kant—not himself a psychological hedonist—supposed, our self-interested motivations are hidden from our own view, so that despite our pretentions to altruism, we are really always acting in our own interest after all. Clearly, appraising such a view is very, very difficult. But if we stick to common-sense distinctions, then psychological egoism must be accounted as simply wrong.

IV. ALTRUISM—PSYCHOLOGICAL QUESTIONS

If psychological egoism has its difficulties, "psychological altruism" is even more problematic. But this requires great care with definitions. Altruism may be understood as concern with others—but how much, and which others? At the opposite extreme from egoism would be the view that we *only* act for the sake of others, and *all* others. To the author's knowledge, no one has ever seriously advocated such a theory. However, David Hume hypothesized that *some* altruism is to be found in every human—a variable but general feeling for all other humans. Taken as a superficial level generalization about people, this is rather plausible, especially if taken as the thesis that *nearly* everyone is *at least slightly* altruistic regarding *nearly* all other humans. But it is, of course, not very precise, and how to describe it more accurately, and account for it, is an interesting question. Interaction with one's mother in infancy, for example, may play a role in the genesis of such dispositions.

V. ETHICAL INCOMPATIBLE WITH PSYCHOLOGICAL EGOISM

Let us now turn to the "ethical" versions of egoism. Here we do well to begin by recognizing that in order for ethical egoism to be meaningful at all, strict psychological egoism, at least in its "superficial" forms, must be false. If Jones is *unable* to seek anyone's well-being but his own, then there is obviously no point in telling him that he *ought* to be seeking someone else's: "Ought," as philosophers put it, implies "can." Even here, to be sure, the distinction of shallow from deep theories is essential, for it is by no means clear that ethics is incompatible with deep self-interest. Possibly, highly altruistic behavior *is* best for oneself, and the "truly" selfish person is the saint or the hero who devotes his life to helping others! Nevertheless, ethical egoism ought to be advocated in a meaningful way, and in order for it to be so, the theorist must explain in what way his proposed message to us is nonredundant. If he is saying "Do what will be best for you!" but this turns out to mean "Do anything whatever!" his message is a nonmessage. But if he is saying "You'll do better by helping those in need," his message is certainly meaningful, and incompatible with "You'll do better if you ignore those in need." Neither of those concrete pieces of advice is entailed by "deep" psychological egoism, nor by any but the shallowest of the "shallow" versions—and those, we

have seen, are surely false anyway. Nor, surely, is it completely obvious which one is true.

VI. ETHICAL VS. MORAL EGOISM

Let us now assume the "plain" or "superficial" level of discussion, which we all understand fairly well, and ask whether ethical egoism is plausible in those terms. But now we must make still another distinction, and again a crucial one—this time with the word ethical. By ethical, do we refer to what we may call the *general theory of how to live?* Or do we mean, much more narrowly, *rules for the group?*

Egoism will look *very* different in these two differently understood contexts. If the question is, "should I aim to live the best life I can?" it is extremely difficult to answer that in the negative. But if our question is, "which rules are we going to insist on people adhering to in our society?" then that is quite another matter, as we will see below. Let us, then, consider the ethical and the moral versions in turn.

VII. EGOISM IS NOT NECESSARILY SELFISH

Egoism as a theory of life may be very different from what the word at first suggests. When we think of egoists, we think, first, of people who are highly self-centered, who tend to ignore others and their needs, even their rights. At the extreme, we think of the sociopath, who will kill, rape, steal, lie, and cheat without compunction in order to achieve certain narrow ends for himself—sexual pleasure, the increment of his monetary income, and so on. But does the sociopath live a *good* life? Would someone setting out to live the happiest, most rewarding life he can choose to become psychopathic if he could? That is extremely implausible. The wisdom of philosophers down through the millennia has been uniform on this point: if you want to be happy yourself, then you need friends, loved ones, associates, and you need to treat all those people with trust and respect, most of them with kindness as well, and some of them with real love. (The true sociopath may not have his choice about it; if he spends most of his time in jail, that may seem to him just a fact of life, like thunderstorms.)

It is difficult to deny that each one of us should try to live the best life we can—the most satisfying, the most rewarding, most fulfilling. Of course this gets us quickly into the very large question of the ultimate values (the "meaning") of life, and what sort of life will best achieve them. For example, as already noted, it is quite possible that a life of "self-sacrifice" is nevertheless the most fulfilling or rewarding. Perhaps it is even the most pleasant, although it seems to strain the idea to think so. But perhaps there are other values more important than pleasure? This has frequently, and plausibly, been advocated by many philosophers.

This last discussion shows the difficulty of generally *opposing* egoism and altruism at this level. Should we literally sacrifice our own *overall* happiness or well-being for others? Which others? And especially, of course, *why?* To suggest that one should do such a thing—if it is even meaningful—seems to be to suggest that those other persons are somehow superior to you. But why should we believe any such thing? On the other hand, someone may be very close to you—children, spouse, close friends. You may find the very idea of living without them intolerable, and reject without a moment's hesitation the very idea of neglecting important needs of theirs. If you are like that, are you really "sacrificing your happiness" if you lay down your life or fortune for the loved one? Or is it that your happiness is totally bound up with the loved one's? The difficulty of demonstrating genuine incompatibilities between unselfish lives and personally fulfilling lives is sufficiently clear from this discussion.

VIII. EGOISM AND MORALITY

At this point, let us turn to the other subject, of what we will call "morality": what should be the rules governing the general behavior of "the group"? One question this raises is, which group? We will dodge the question of cultural relativism by saying that it is the group "in question," recognizing the possibility that it is, in the end, the group consisting of literally everybody, as the classical moralists assumed.

What matters, though, is that we are now addressing the question, not simply what to do in life generally, but what to do *in relation to our fellows:* how do we carry on our dealings with them, our *inter*actions? Morality, so construed, is public: people react to each other, and they are to enforce as well as comply with the rules. It is when we address this question that egoism, in any sense of that word in which it is meaningful, becomes enormously implausible. For if we think of the egoist as the one who pursues *only* his own interest, *regardless* of others, so that our image is of psychopathic behavior, then to recommend that as the rule for a group seems completely absurd. Egoism, again speaking at the "superficial" level, must address the question of conflicts of interest. If A's interests are satisfied only if B's are frustrated, then a "rule" addressed to the two of them, telling them both to ignore the other and "go for it," is silly. If both try to follow it, at least one will fail. In fact, most likely both of them will, especially if we take into account any aspects of their values that extend beyond the narrow one that was the subject of conflict: if the two come to blows, say, probably both will suffer injuries that they would prefer not to have inflicted on them. A rule for a group, if it is to be even remotely plausible, will have to do better than that. When there are conflicts, it is going to have to tell us who is in the "right," who is in the "wrong"—who gets to go ahead, and who has to back down.

Trying to incorporate real egoism, of the first kind identified at the outset, into the very heart of moral rules themselves, is an invitation to conceptual disaster. That Jones ought to do X, and Smith ought to do Y, even when X entails not-Y, is rightly regarded as a nonsense rule. Two boxers in the ring ought both, of course, to *try* to win; but to say that both ought *to win* is nonsense, because by definition that is impossible. A morality for all cannot look like directions to the cheering section for one of the fighters, but rather, like the rule book for boxing, which tells *both* contestants that they have only so many minutes between breaks, that they may not hit below the belt, and so forth. Morality in our second and narrower sense of the term, consists of the rules for large, "natural" groups—that is, groups of people who happen, for whatever reason, to come in contact with each other, rather than groups that come together intentionally for specific purposes. Such rules must, in the first place, be such that everyone can comply with them. And second, they are going to have to be impartial rather than loaded in favor of one person or set of persons as against another. If they are not impartial, then the rule, we may say, is not really a rule *for* the group: it is a rule that may benefit some, but only at the expense of others—in which case, why should those others accept it? For both reasons, egoism is a nonsense "theory" of morality, however plausible it may be as a fundamental ethical view of life or of rational decision-making. What is especially striking is that *egoists* in the group will not accept an "egoistic morality." Self-interest on the part of each, it seems clear, will motivate them to accept an impartial morality. The alternative is no morality at all—but Hobbes (*Leviathan*, Ch. 13) supplies a gruesome depiction of what the latter option would be like. Again, it seems vastly implausible that a rational egoist would want to do without anything resembling a social morality. (Game-theoretic investigation of these matters has been intensively pursued in recent decades—see the Bibliography.)

IX. ALTRUISM AND MORALITY

This brings us to our last question. If we are persuaded that moral rules cannot be egoistic, can they, then, be *altruistic?* Should the rules for groups tell everyone to love everyone else, as fully as if everyone were your dear child or spouse? The answer to this is surely in the negative, as Nietzsche pointed out. (*Morgenröte,* sec. 147) One or at most a very few lovers or loved ones is all any of us can handle. Truly to love someone, we must elevate that person well above the crowd, pay *more* attention to her than to others—not merely an equal amount—and so on. In any case, there is a "budgetary" problem. You cannot love someone and devote *no* time and attention to him; but there are 5 billion people in this world! Altruism construed as the general love of humankind, therefore, simply cannot be speaking of love in its full normal sense; a doctrine of general altruism must retreat very far from that. Indeed, it is clear that in this respect, general altruism has the same formal problem as general egoism: both are shipwrecked as soon as we see the inevitable asymmetries and partialities necessarily involved in full-blooded love, whether of oneself or anyone else.

X. DUTIES AND VIRTUES

How far, then, do we "retreat"? Here a fair variety of answers has been given—and here we need to make one last distinction: between two departments or "branches" of morals. One branch is stern, and associated with duties and with justice, rules that are to be reinforced by such heavy-duty procedures as punishments. The other is associated with commendations and praise, warm sentiments, criticism but not punishment for nonperformance, and so forth. Following Kant, we may call these respectively the theories of justice and of virtue; or, in a slightly different vein, justice and charity. One is the morality of the "stick," the other the morality of the "carrot." Now, our question may be put thus: is altruism to be regarded as figuring prominently in, or perhaps even the basis of, either of these, of both, or of neither?

Again it seems clear that we must deny altruism any significant role in the first. If you and I are enemies, it is pretty pointless to tell us to love each other, but not at all pointless to tell us to draw some lines and then stay on *our* side of them. We are to refrain from killing, stealing from, lying to, cheating, maiming, or otherwise damaging each other, even if we "hate each other's guts." We shall all do better if we simply rule out such actions. This is "negative" morality, the morality of "thou shalt not!" and it applies between absolutely everyone and absolutely everyone else, be they friends, enemies, or strangers—the sole but important qualification being that those who themselves are guilty of transgressing one of those restrictions make themselves eligible for punishment.

It is plainly absurd to point to love as the basis of such rules. Rather, it is, more generally, our full range of interests, rather than the restricted set that consists in positive affection for others. These general interests, considered in relation to how things are and how other people are, undergird these vital rules of social life. On the other hand, when it comes to helping those in need, showing kindness to people, being thoughtful, useful, supportive, and so on—in short, of being, in the words of Hume, "agreeable and useful to others," it is plausible to ascribe this, at least to some extent, to sentiment, some degree of altruism. Our general interests are still not lost sight of, for in being nice to others, we inspire them to be nice to us, and so even considerations of self-interest fairly narrowly construed will teach us the value of these other-regarding virtues. Thus we admire and praise people who go well beyond the "minimum" in these respects: we put the Mother Theresas, the heroic life-savers, those who go the extra mile and then some, on pedestals, and rightly so. As Hume conjectures, it seems implausible to *confine* those tendencies to self-interest in any narrow sense of that word. Thus we find room for both altruistic sentiments and egoistic interests in the foundations of morals, when we view the latter as more than just a set of duties.

XI. CONCLUSION

Egoism and altruism are fascinating but complicated matters, because the terms are used in varying though related senses. Are people "ultimately" egoistic? If so, it is in a sense that is compatible with what is usually thought of as altruism: love and kindness, self-sacrifice, charity, and other phenomena familiar to all. Is the ultimate theory of the good life egoistic? Not if that means excluding affection and interaction, certainly. But if it means trying to live the best lives we can, however that is to be done, it seems very plausible and perhaps inescapable. Is *morality,* construed as social rules for the group, egoistic? Here we get a resounding negative. It can make no sense to tell a set of people that they are all to do what it is impossible for them all to do; but egoism involves pursuing one's own interest even at the expense of others. So a concern with self-interest tells us to accept rules limiting self-interest—especially, to refrain from murder and other serious harms to others. On the other hand, the recognition of kindness and charity as virtues is stimulated by both self-interest and warm human sentiment of the kind that we readily identify as "altruistic."

Also See the Following Articles

ALTRUISM AND ECONOMICS • KANTIANISM • PERSONAL RELATIONSHIPS

Bibliography

Baier, K. E. M. (1958). *The moral point of view.* Ithaca, NY: Cornell University Press.
Butler, J. *Sermons in the rolls chapel.* (Esp. Sermons xi and xiii.)
Danielson, P. (1992). *Artificial morality.* New York: Routledge.
Gauthier, D. (1986). *Morals by agreement.* New York: Oxford University Press.
Hume, D. *An inquiry concerning the principles of morals.* (Esp. Sections V, VI, and Appendix II.)
Medlin, B. (1957). Ultimate Principles and Ethical Egoism. *Australasian Journal of Philosophy.* More widely accessible in S. M. Cahn & J. G. Haber (1995). *20th century ethical theory,* pp. 316–321. Englewood-Cliffs, NJ: Prentice-Hall.
Nagel, T. (1970). *The possibility of altruism.* Oxford: Clarendon Press.
Parfit, D. (1986). *Reasons and persons.* Oxford and New York: Oxford University Press.

ELECTION STRATEGIES

Marianne M. Jennings
Arizona State University

political speech Ads and any other forms of communication regarding candidates or ballot initiatives.

Senate Election Ethics Act A set of voluntary guidelines passed by the U.S. Senate on campaign spending limits, PACs, independent expenditures and soft money.

GLOSSARY

commercial speech Ads and any other forms of communication regarding products, services, or business.

Federal Election Campaign Act (FECA) A federal law governing maximum levels of campaign contributions with requirements of public reporting of campaign donations and expenditures.

Federal Election Commission (FEC) A federal agency charged with enforcing FECA and location for filing of required campaign financial information.

First Amendment A provision in the U.S. Constitution that guarantees an individual the right to speak without censorship of content (with only limited exceptions).

political action committee (PAC) A formally created group of citizens, trade associations, businesses, or employees organized for the purpose of raising funds or making campaign expenditures to or on behalf of candidates or ballot propositions.

ELECTION STRATEGIES are the methods and techniques used by candidates to gain the support of the electorate. These strategies can involve either an effort to influence voters to favor a candidate or to influence them against an opposing candidate. Election strategies raise important ethical questions concerning issues such as campaign funding, political advertising, and the limits of negative campaigning.

I. INTRODUCTION

When George Washington ran for a seat in the Virginia House of Burgesses in 1767, he gave away approximately 160 gallons of liquor in order to win the support of the 391 voters in his district. Since that time, the strategies used to gain the support of voters have grown in variation and expense. For example, in 1860, both candidates for the office of U.S. President spent $150,000. Ronald Reagan and Jimmy Carter spent $58 million in the 1980 presidential election. Bob Dole and

TABLE I

Election Strategies

Fund-raising and contributions: Limitations, disclosures and uses
Polling: Consultants and nature of polls
Opposition research: Privacy vs. character vs. voter information
Advertisements: Truth vs. negativity
Platforms and promises: Misrepresentation vs. emotion

Bill Clinton spent a total of $250 million in 1996. The average cost for an incumbent in the U.S. House to win reelection in 1994 was $389,000. Liquor or money may be parts of effective strategies designed to gain votes. However, there are both legal and ethical issues in the strategies candidates use to seek the votes of the electorate.

There are five different election strategies commonly used by candidates in order to win votes. Those strategies are summarized in Table I and include: fund-raising and contributions; polling; opposition research; advertisements and platforms coupled with promises.

II. FUND-RAISING AND CONTRIBUTIONS

A. The Problem of Quid Pro Quo

Since 1867 (see Table II), the United States has struggled legislatively with the conflict of interest issues that

exist when funds are raised by or donated to candidates for public office.

The ethical issues that surround fund-raising and contributions arise because of concerns about degrees of influence as well as the appearance of impropriety. The notion that an individual, group, or business can "purchase" power in government operations is one that creates a conflict between the public servant's fiduciary duty and the concept of representative government and being in a possible position of payment in exchange for favorable government action toward the donor. There is an abundance of money available to candidates from corporate, union, and trade organizations. These groups form political action committees to raise and disburse funds to candidates in order to assist those candidates in their election campaigns. The problem of perception of a quid pro quo relationship or favorable legislation in exchange for donation is one exacerbated by the legislative successes of the richest PACs. Tables III and IV provide the lists (as of 1996) of the richest corporate and noncorporate PACs, respectively, in federal election campaigns.

However, the reality of elections is that dissemination of information about candidates to voters is both necessary and expensive. The value of the free exchange of information has been a cornerstone of democracy in the United States. Justice Holmes of the U.S. Supreme Court wrote in his dissenting opinion in *Abrams v. United States* that it is the dissemination of information to the electorate that is critical for voter autonomy and noted, "truth is the only ground upon which their wishes can be carried out."

TABLE II

Federal Regulations on Campaign Fund-Raising and Expenditures

Statute	Date	Purpose
Naval Appropriations Act	1867	Illegal to solicit campaign contributions from government workers in U.S. Navy yards.
Civil Service Reform Act	1883	Federal employees prohibited from soliciting or accepting political contributions from other federal employees.
Tillman Act	1907	Corporations prohibited from making contributions to election campaigns.
Federal Corrupt Practices Act (FCPA)	1925	Mandated campaign contributions and expenditures disclosures.
Hatch Act	1939	Limits on individual campaign donations.
War Labor Disputes Act	1943	Labor organizations prohibited from making contributions in federal elections.
Federal Election Campaign Act	1971	Repealed FCPA 1) Required detailed disclosures on spending; 2) Limits of $1,000 per candidate and $25,000 preelection donations for anyone; 3) PAC maximum limitations of $5,000 per candidate donation.
Presidential/Election Campaign Fund Act	1971	Permitted taxpayers to contribute funds to presidential campaigns.

TABLE III

Top 20 Corporate PACS (1996 Elections)
(Funds raised and available)

1. American Telephone & Telegraph Company Political Action Committee (AT&T PAC)
2. United Parcel Service of America Inc. Political Action Committee (UPSPAC)
3. Black America's Political Action Committee
4. Federal Express Corporation Political Action Committee "FEPAC"
5. Lockheed Martin Employees Political Action Committee
6. Banc One PAC
7. Team Ameritech Political Action Committee
8. Union Pacific Fund for Effective Government
9. Philip Morris Companies Inc. Political Action Committee (AKA PHIL-PAC)
10. BellSouth Telecommunications Inc. Employees Federal Political Action Committee
11. RJR Political Action Committee RJR Nabisco Inc. (RJR PAC)
12. UST Executives Administrators and Managers Political Action Committee (AKA USTEAM PAC)
13. General Electric Company Political Action Committee
14. MBNA Corporation Federal Political Committee
15. Compass Bancshares Inc. Political Action Committee (Compass BANCPAC)
16. Tenneco Inc. Employees Good Government Fund (AKA Tenneco Employees Good Government Fund)
17. Civic Involvement Program/General Motors Corporation
18. Ford Motor Company Civic Action Fund
19. WMX Technologies Inc. Employees' Better Government Fund ("WMX PAC")
20. Employees of Northrop Grumman Corporation Political Action Committee (ENGPAC)

B. Government Regulation

It is through regulation of funds that many of the ethical issues surrounding campaign contributions and fundraising have been resolved. To avoid excessive influence, federal law places maximum limits on contributions one individual can make to any one candidate. To provide full public information about the nature and sources of fund-raising and remove the secretive nature of donations, federal law also requires that candidates file disclosure statements with full disclosure of the names of donors, the amount of their donations, and the nature and amount of expenditures made with those funds. While these federal laws are applicable only to campaigns for federal office, most states and local governments also have similar limitations on contributions and disclosure requirements for state and local elections.

C. Gray Area One: Personal Expenses and Campaign Funds

Within these extensive state and federal election regulatory systems, however, there are certain gray areas. For example, the proper use of funds raised for a candidate's election has been a subject of great debate. In 1967, after having been in public office for 20 years, Senator Thomas Dodd was censured by a U.S. Senate vote of 92–5 for his use of campaign funds to make improvements on his Connecticut home, pay household bills and country club dues, and finance a trip for him and his wife to the Caribbean. Then Senator Dodd stated on the floor of the Senate,

This ... strikes at my heart because it has the connotation of treachery, deceit, dishonesty—the connotation that I fooled people—which I did not do. If you want to mark me as a thief, do it today. Do it before the sun goes down, and let me skulk away, ashamed to face you tomorrow.

TABLE IV

Top 20 Noncorporate PACs (1996 Elections)
(Funds raised and available)

1. Emily's List
2. Campaign America
3. National Committee for an Effective Congress
4. Americans for Free International Trade Political Action Committee Inc.
5. National Conservative Club (FKA) National Congressional Club
6. Voters for Choice/Friends of Family Planning
7. Time Future Inc. (FKA Bill Bradley for U S Senate)
8. National PAC
9. Majority Leader's Fund
10. Hollywood Women's Political Committee
11. Ernst & Young Political Action Committee
12. New Republican Majority Fund
13. Arthur Andersen PAC (FKA) Arthur Andersen/Andersen Consulting PAC
14. Effective Government Committee
15. GOPAC Incorporated
16. Monday Morning Political Action Committee
17. Deloitte and Touche LLP Federal Political Action Committee
18. Council for a Livable World
19. Coopers & Lybrand PAC
20. American AIDS Political Action Committee

Senator Dodd lost his next election and retired from public life. Today, however, the notion of the "proper" use of campaign funds has changed dramatically. Alan Keyes, a candidate for president in the 1996 election, is paid $8,500 per month from his campaign treasury. Most members of Congress have two residences (one in their home districts and one in the Washington, D.C., area) and they maintain one of those residences at campaign treasury expense. Car purchases or leases for candidates are considered routine campaign expenditures.

D. Gray Area Two: Consulting Firms and Spouse Employment

Other candidates use campaign treasury funds in the more creative fashion of paying them to media consulting firms owned by them and operated by their spouses or other members of their families. In many cases, the media consulting firms are operated from their homes. These consulting firm payments are disclosed in public records only as payments for services to consulting firms when the funds are actually being used as a means of paying a spouse and supplementing a candidates' income.

While both the Senate and the House have ethics rules that prohibit personal use of campaign funds, the line for what constitutes personal versus campaign use is difficult to draw and the rules of both bodies are no longer enforced. As these rules are written, they permit uses of campaign funds for "officially connected" purposes. However, some legislators see the use of campaign funds for the personal expenses of public office as a means of saving taxpayers' money. Rather than fund expenses through their offices, they use campaign funds to allow donor funds to pay them. The only legislators to be punished in the last 15 years at the federal level for misuse of campaign funds were those who used funds for escorts for donors, for investments in the commodities markets, or to pay off personal debts.

Some members of the House of Representatives have argued for a strict rule that prohibits the use of campaign funds for anything that personally benefits the candidate rather than offering a sole and exclusive benefit to the campaign. However, other members respond that the need for elected officials to continue an ongoing campaign even while in office justifies the recoupment of living expenses from campaign funds. While the Federal Election Commission (FEC) is responsible for the oversight of expenditures, it has been reluctant to

become involved in the review of these expenditures and their debatable benefits to a campaign.

For candidates, the ethical high road is to have disclosure of all uses of campaign funds and to put in place the necessary internal controls so that the funds do not become simply a personal account for the candidate. Those who donate funds to the campaign should be aware of the potential uses of the funds so that there are no misunderstandings between donor and candidate about the purpose of funds solicited or given.

E. Gray Area Three: Soft Money

Yet another gray area in campaign funding is what is referred to as "soft money." Soft money is money available for use on behalf of a candidate, although not directly under the candidate's control. A political party can raise unlimited funds with unlimited amounts given by individual donors. That party, in theory an autonomous entity, is then free to expend or donate funds as it sees fit in order to advance its ideals. However, federal law does not permit the parties candidates themselves to control the flow nor use of the funds. Nor can any candidates be part of the decision-making process for expenditures of "soft money." Former Senator Robert Packwood wrote in his diaries of a meeting he had in 1992 in his office with Senator Phil Gramm in which Packwood alleged that Gramm promised to use $100,000 in soft money to help Packwood. Packwood wrote, "What was said in that room would be enough to convict us all of something."

F. Gray Area Four: Independent Expenditures

Another aspect of campaign financing that is fraught with ethical issues is the right of independent organizations to expend funds on behalf of any candidates. However, the expenditures of these independent organizations on behalf of individual candidates are often made in consultation with the campaign managers of these candidates. It is the element of independence that is at the heart of the statutory exemptions for independent organizations on spending and fund-raising. In *Buckley vs. Valeo,* the U.S. Supreme Court ruled that the First Amendment mandates that those who are not affiliated with a particular candidate be permitted to speak at any time and expend any amount of money in so doing. The absence of direct candidate involvement is the distinction that permits these expenditures and exempts them from limitation and regulation. Candidate control of fund-raising and spending by independent organizations is a violation of the spirit of the First Amendment. Nonetheless, the relationship between independent organizations and candidates continues to be an area of concern because of the potential for close contact with candidates. At one point, the U.S. Senate proposed ethics rules to prohibit contact between a candidate running for office (and any of the candidate's staff or consultants) and any independent organizations engaged in campaigning for the candidate or issues particularly associated with the candidate. The Senate Ethics Act continues to be a subject of debate as the members of the Senate grapple with the First Amendment protections of independent organizations and the need for their arms length relationships with candidates.

In all areas of campaign finance, the keys to avoiding ethical breaches are disclosure of sources and uses of funds, arm's-length transactions in fund disbursements and in relationships with other independent organizations, and clear guidelines on proper and improper campaign expenditures.

III. POLLING

The purposes of polling may be to discover voters' feelings on particular issues, certain candidates, or reactions to advertisements. A poll may also be conducted in a way to determine how demographics affect voters' reactions to issues, positions, and candidates. Polls are necessary and enormously useful devices in structuring and executing a campaign. It was in the 1996 presidential election that the term "push polling" evolved. The strategy of push polling is to commission a political consultant who will conduct a poll that produces the result desired by the candidate. That result could be obtained honestly, but is guaranteed to be obtained using certain constructs that might not be part of a valid statistical sample. For example, a polling consultant could release the results of a poll of a random selection of residents of a city. Or a polling consultant could release the results of a poll of a random selection of residents who voted in the last election. In other words, the results of a poll can be manipulated according to the "n" group chosen by the consultant as the data base.

Once the favorable results for a candidate are released, the voters may be influenced by the results with the poll then serving the purpose of pushing voters in a certain direction. The results of a poll may also cause those who favor the opposing candidate to resign themselves to a loss and have a resulting effect on the turnout on election day. The poll results from one narrowly defined group can often control the issue focus of a campaign. In the 1996 presidential election, the polls on the highly publicized "soccer moms" revealed that single women with children were more likely to vote for President Clinton because of his campaign proposals on college funding, hospital stays for delivery, and day-care policies and facilities.

The critical ethical issues in any polls commissioned or released by candidates are disclosure of who conducted the poll (for possible bias), the nature of the group polled, the phrasing of the questions, and the margin for error in the poll. While that information is generally always provided by media organizations conducting a poll, similar disclosures are not made in polls commissioned by candidates. Whether candidates have such an obligation presents an ethical dilemma that many would say raises a discovery responsibility on the part of the opposition rather than an affirmative duty of disclosure on the part of the candidate conducting the poll.

IV. OPPOSITION RESEARCH

The novel, *Primary Colors,* by Joe Klein ("Anonymous") highlights a character known as "Libby" who has the responsibility of collecting information on her candidate's opponent in order to have ammunition against that opponent. Her damaging information harms the opponent but is also used to silence detractors. Her skill is searching long and hard for background and history on opponents and detractors. Her background work is simply research put to effective political use. One political consultant has observed that "elections are won in the library."

Opposition research consists of gathering information about a political opponent on everything from a voting record to whether there are tax liens on his or her property. Some candidates have been embarrassed by the revelation that they failed to vote in the last general election. Within the political consultant field, a new group of researchers has emerged. These consultants are the experts in researching public records for revelations that are embarrassing to a candidate's opponents. An estimate for the 1996 federal elections puts the total expenditures on opposition research at between $25 and $30 million.

For some, private-eye sleuthing such as that conducted as opposition research is offensive. For others, these research consultants are simply performing a function that used to be done by the media: providing the voters with information about the background, lifestyle, character, and record of candidates for public office.

The ethical issues that arise in this sophisticated snooping include whether it is appropriate to go beyond public records. For example, a question often asked among opposition researchers is whether it is ethical to search through an opponent's trash looking for potentially damaging information because of the privacy implications associated with such a search. Other experts worry that the level of opposition research turns political campaigns into nothing more than a game of "Trivial Pursuit," in which the candidates try to outdo each other with disclosures that may have little to do with the issues of the campaign or the concerns of the voters. The information may, however, have some impact on those issues. In the 1992 California U.S. Senate race, Republican Bruce Herschensohn accused incumbent senator Barbara Boxer of "lacking" religious values. Opposition research in the form of following Herschensohn revealed that he had been to nude bars. Herschensohn confirmed that revelation as true and lost the election. The ethical issue that remains in many minds was whether the election should turn on such a revelation.

Personal versus public information has emerged as the definitive line for opposition research. Voting records, litigation, liens, and compliance with campaign finance laws are all issues of relevance in terms of a candidate's character. When information such as this is not disclosed, voters make their judgments without evidence that may be relevant. A candidate in a California legislative race uncovered, through opposition research, a significant number of mortgage defaults by his opponent. He declined to use the information against his opponent. He lost the election. The mortgage-defaulting candidate has been ranked as a very poor legislator. Voters were deprived of this relevant information obtained through opposition research.

V. ADVERTISEMENTS

A. The Nature of Political Ads

Political ads (as summarized in Table V) run from those that simply describe the candidate to those that associate a voter hot-button issue with the opposition. Other ads use information on the candidate's record or personal life to provide voters with a negative image. Still other ads tie a societal harm to an opponent or focus

TABLE V

Political Advertisements

Touting personal record
Touting personal characteristics
Revealing/describing opponent's record
Revealing/describing opponent's character
Societal harm—cause and effect
Single issue hot-buttons

on a hot-button issue that reflects negatively on the opposition.

In the 1988 presidential election, George Bush ran an ad that described the conduct of Willie Horton, an African American who raped and murdered a woman while he was on furlough from a Massachusetts prison. Mr. Bush's opponent, Michael Dukakis, was the governor of Massachusetts at the time Mr. Horton was furloughed and committed the crimes. The ad was a classic example of a single issue that hit voters' hot button. Concerns about crime, parole, and recidivism were all social issues of great concern to voters. The Horton ad became a turning point in the election and is often cited by political scientists and consultants as an example of the power of political advertising.

In the 1996 presidential elections, President Clinton's ads on Speaker Newt Gingrich and presidential candidate Bob Dole and their roles in the reduction of Social Security and Medicare had the effect of frightening many senior citizens into voting for Mr. Clinton. Mr. Dole's ads, which included a clip of Mr. Clinton telling an MTV audience that he might inhale if given another chance at smoking marijuana, were used in conjunction with statistics on drug use being up among teenagers. The ad was one used to try to have voters associate Mr. Clinton's personal views as the cause of the drug use increase.

B. Regulation of Political Ads

These ads represent the most dramatic forms of political advertising. Whether the ads are true or false or fair or deceptive is not the issue. The Supreme Court has carved out a clear niche for political advertisements. While commercial speech, or ads for products are subject to government regulation for accuracy and fairness, political speech, or speech on behalf of issues or candidates, enjoys an immunity from such regulation. As noted earlier, the desire to have a fully informed electorate fuels the protection candidates enjoy in making their cases through television, radio, and print ads. Any form of content regulation of election ads would fall under a constitutionally mandated and highly suspect category of regulation. To date, states have not enjoyed much success in passing constitutional content regulation on political advertisements. Some states have passed statutes requiring all candidates to participate in public forums in order to give voters more information than that offered in carefully constructed political ads. Other states have required that pamphlets with position statements from candidates be distributed to voters to supplement the slanted candidate-constructed political ads. With respect to ballot initiatives and propositions, many states have disclosure requirements on the sources of financing for such ads. For example, an organization opposing a smoking ban initiative would be required to disclose that one of its sources of funding was a tobacco company.

The fairness of political advertising, the issues of mudslinging and the rough-and-tumble nature of politics have been with us since the days when Alexander Hamilton engaged in a duel to protect his political reputation. In 1850, Mississippi Senator Henry Foote pulled a pistol on Missouri Senator Thomas H. Benton during a debate on slavery. However, recent campaigns have caused political scientists, such as Kathleen Hall Jamieson to remark, "never before in a presidential campaign have televised ads sponsored by a major party candidate lied so blatantly as in the campaign of 1988." Alexander Kroll, the chairman of Young & Rubicam noted, "Political advertising is so wretched that most of it wouldn't be approved by our own self-governing boards."

C. Self-Regulation of Political Ads

Based on the concerns about the truth and political ads, proposals have been advanced for forms of self-regulation of these forms of political speech. For example, during her 1994 campaign for governor of California, Kathleen Brown asked all candidates for office to sign a notarized document that read, "We pledge to be honest." Thomas Jefferson's response to pledges and claims of honesty was, "The more he spoke of his honesty, the faster we counted our spoons." Paul Alvarez, chairman of Ketchum Communications, proposed that political ads be held to the same standards as are other ads: no lies and no disparagement. Mr. Alvarez has proposed a committee to work on a code of ethics for political advertisements that would offer to consultants and candidates the opportunity to establish standards

for political ads that would not violate the U.S. Constitution because of their voluntary nature.

Others maintain that the function of political ads is to place information for the public to evaluate and consider. Just as not all products are purchased by all people because they are skeptical about the claims, not all candidates win voter approval simply because an ad offers certain claims about him or her or the opposition. H. L. Mencken once wrote that the role of every philosopher is to establish that every other philosopher is an ass. Mencken also noted that they all accomplished their goal. There are those who maintain that political ads are reviewed by voters with the idea that there is an agenda at work, and that voters are capable of scrutiny and discernment.

Difficulties also arise in controlling forms of ads. While candidates may pledge to conduct an "issues" campaign, many do view the character and personal life of a candidate as an issue. Negative information about one's opponent record is negative, but it is also relevant information for voters. One distinction that has emerged in the debate over the control of political ads is that the line on content should be drawn on truth and falsehood. In other words, it is not the negative aspect of the ad that creates the ethical issue, it is whether the information that gives rise to the negative perception is true or false. If an incumbent has been absent on 50% of all votes taken in the last legislative session, that information is negative, but it is not unethical to advance that information in the form of an ad if in fact the 50% figure is accurate.

VI. PLATFORMS AND PROMISES

In recent years, no campaign platform promise has been more recalled or had greater significance than George Bush's 1988 campaign promise of "Read my lips. No new taxes." During his administration, Mr. Bush did raise taxes and those words were used by Mr. Clinton in the 1992 campaign to demonstrate a contrast between his character and that of Mr. Bush in the sense of keeping promises. It was a campaign promise not kept, and Mr. Bush's credibility suffered in his reelection campaign.

With election platforms and promises, there is perhaps a prevailing Albert Carr philosophy of "so long as we all understand we're lying to each other, it's okay." There is a certain acceptance in election strategy that the rhetoric of a candidate is different and does not carry accountability. Therefore, many promises are made during campaigns that simply cannot be fulfilled.

In the 1992 presidential primaries, Democratic candidate Bruce Babbitt became a household name when he stood in a debate and said that he was standing up for new taxes because they were inevitable. His honesty was the demise of his candidacy. Some have compared campaign promises to romance—the words must later be discounted. However, the Bush experience taught campaign strategists that clear and unequivocal promises carry expectations with voters.

Also See the Following Articles

ADVERTISING • FREEDOM OF SPEECH

Bibliography

Alexander, H. (1984). *Financing Politics: Money, Elections, and Political Reform* (3rd. ed.). Washington, DC: CQ Press.

Carr, A. (1968). Is Business Bluffing Ethical? *Harvard Business Review.*

Colford, Steven W. (1994, December 8). Coming clean on political ads. *Advertising Age.*

Corn, D. (1995, October 9). Money Talks. *The Nation,* p. 373.

Faber, R. J. *et al.* (1993). Negative political advertising and voting intent: The role of involvement and alternative information sources. *Journal of Advertising,* **22**(4): 67–76.

Hazlett, T. W. (1994, June). And that's the truth. *Reason,* p. 66.

Impoco, J. (1996, October 21). The fine art of digging dirt. *U.S. News & World Report,* 44–45.

Moran, T. J. (1992). Political Debate without Suppressing Free Speech. *Indiana Law Journal,* **67**, p. 663.

Note, Constitutional Law. (1986). Campaign finance reform and the first amendment—All the free speech money can buy. *Oklahoma Law Review,* **39**, p. 729.

O'Neil, R. M. (1992). Regulating speech to cleanse political campaigns. *Capital U. L. Rev.,* **21**, p. 575.

Overby, P. (1992, September). Charge it to my campaign. *Common Cause,* p. 23.

Shipper, F., & Jennings, M. M. (1989). *Business Strategy for Political Arena.* Westport, CT: Quorum Books: Greenwood Press.

Sittig, R. F. (1995, January). Campaign reform: Interest groups, parties and candidates. *Annals,* p. 537.

Teinowitz, I. (1996, July 8). The politics of vice. *Advertising Age,* p. 1.

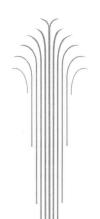

ELECTRONIC SURVEILLANCE

Gary T. Marx and Gregory Ungar
University of Colorado at Boulder

GLOSSARY

minimization A principle of personal data collection in which only the amount of information essential to the goal is gathered

new surveillance A term for a family of technologies for extracting personal information, such as computers, video cameras, and electronic location monitoring devices, in which data can often be gathered, combined, and analyzed inexpensively without a person's consent or knowledge

personal borders The boundaries (whether physical, spacial, relational, or symbolic) that separate the individual from others

privacy An expectation that an individual can control his or her personal information

SURVEILLANCE of individuals has changed markedly with recent developments in electronic, biochemical, and data base forms of personal information collection and analysis. Computer data bases, video cameras, drug testing, and work monitoring are routine. They are or will be joined by new means that may become equally prevalent: DNA screening and monitoring for insurance and employment; electronic location and other forms of monitoring via computer chips that are worn or even implanted under the skin; Internet monitoring that keeps a record of what one has viewed on a computer and for how long; "intelligent" highway systems that record where a vehicle is and its speed; "smart cards" that contain extensive personal information (e.g., passport, banking, credit, medical, and arrest records, driver's license); satellite photography; the linking of video and facial recognition technology that permits scanning faces to find subjects of interest; and "smart homes" in which data flows (whether electricity, communications, or energy) into, or out of, the home are part of the same monitored system.

I. THE NEW SURVEILLANCE

These technologies constitute the "new surveillance". The new surveillance has a number of characteristics that separate it from traditional forms. It can

1. transcend boundaries of time, distance, darkness, and physical boundaries such as walls and skin that traditionally protected privacy;
2. permit the inexpensive and immediate sharing, merging, and it can
3. permit combining discrete types of information such as voice, computer data, facsimile, electronic mail, and video;
4. permit simulating realities and altering data;

5. involve remote access;
6. often be done invisibly;
7. often be done without the subject's knowledge or consent;
8. permit more intensive information collection, probing more deeply;
9. permit more extensive information collection, covering broader areas.

The boundaries that have defined and given integrity to social systems, groups, and the self are increasingly permeable. The power of governmental and private organizations to compel disclosure (whether based on law, circumstance, or technology) and to aggregate, analyze, and distribute personal information is growing rapidly.

We are becoming a transparent society of record such that documentation of our past history, current identity, location, and physiological and psychological states and behavior is increasingly possible. With predictive profiles there are even claims to be able to know individual futures. Information collection often occurs invisibly, automatically, and remotely—being built into routine activities. Awareness and genuine consent on the part of the subject may be lacking.

The amount of personal information collected is increasing. New technologies have the potential to reveal the unseen, unknown, forgotten, or withheld. Like the discovery of the atom or the unconscious, they bring to the surface bits of reality that were previously hidden, or did not contain informational clues. In a sense people are turned inside out.

To be alive and a social being is to automatically give off signals of constant information—whether in the form of heat, pressure, motion, brain waves, perspiration, cells, sound, olifacteurs, waste matter, or garbage, as well as more familiar forms such as communication and visible behavior. These remnants are given by contemporary surveillance technologies. Through a value-added, mosaic process, machines (often with only a little help from their friends) may find significance in surfacing and combining heretofore meaningless data.

The ratio of what individuals know about themselves (or are capable of knowing) versus what outsiders and experts can know about them has shifted away from the individual. Data in diverse forms from widely separated geographical areas, organizations, and time periods can be easily merged and analyzed. In relatively unrestrained fashion new (and old) organizations are capturing, combining, and selling this information, or putting it to novel internal uses.

To a degree these technologies are controlled by laws, organizational policies, etiquette, and counter-technologies that seek to protect personal information. Such efforts imply ethical assumptions that are often unstated. In this article we suggest an ethical framework for thinking about personal surveillance.

II. ETHICS

It might appear that an ethics for surveillance is an oxymoron. Is surveillance with its connotation of spying and suspicion incompatible with ethics? This article suggests that an ethics of, or for, surveillance is not only possible, but necessary. Yet given the gravity and complexity of the issues and the risks, we suggest this gingerly and tentatively. There are extremes of surveillance and good and bad uses. Reasoned discussion can enhance the former and minimize the latter.

Surveillance, broadly defined as attentiveness to one's external environment, is a fundamental part of complex living organisms. Societal attitudes in democracies are profoundly ambivalent about it because it can offer protection via the eye of a benevolent God, leader, or parent or domination by a Leviathan. We cannot live without it, but neither should we live with its excesses. It can be linked (although not necessarily always reduced) to issues of power and authority.

This chapter suggests an ethics for those who carry out the surveillance or data collection. It assumes that under appropriate conditions they may have a *right* to do this, but they also have a *duty* to do it responsibly. Reciprocally, those subject to legitimate surveillance may have duties as well (e.g., not to distort the findings), even as they also have rights not to be subjected to some forms of surveillance. Given the tilted (if not outrightly downhill) nature of the playing field, in which powerful interests and organizations are practically unopposed in emphasizing their rights to gather personal information rather than their duties, and offensively take the behavioral initiative, our emphasis is on creating an ethics that applies to them rather than to their subjects. Yet it is also well to note that given the multiple roles we play, we all rotate between being "surveillors" and the surveilled, if hardly equally.

Our discussion is based on conventional domestic settings in a democratic society for those with full adult citizenship rights. In situations of extreme crisis, such as war, when dealing with very different countries or cultures, children, the ill, the incompetent, or those juridically denied certain rights such as prisoners, a different discussion is needed and the lines in some ways will be drawn differently. That, however, does not negate the value of the principles to be discussed here as ideals that should apply more broadly, other factors being equal.

One form of ethical theory or principle is sweeping, categorical, and absolutist. It declares certain behaviors as either prohibited or required. Biblical commandments are an example. The Bible, for example, does not say "in considering whether to kill the following factors should be considered."

In contrast, the form of ethics treated here considers right and wrong in relative, context-specific terms. In doing so it recognizes the contingent nature of many ethical assessments—that principles may conflict and be subject to different understandings and weighing, that the facts on which an assessment is to be made may be unclear, in dispute, or subject to different interpretations, and that complex situations likely involve multiple dimensions, each subject to ethical analysis.

The relational perspective would say "a situation becomes more or less morally acceptable to the extent that the following conditions are present," or "situations in which these elements are present are morally preferable to situations where they are lacking." Such a perspective requires one to compare a given means to alternatives and to the consequences of taking no action.

In evaluating any behavior we might begin with the law and with whether or not a behavior does what it claims to. While there is much to debate regarding what the law ought to be or how it is to be interpreted and whether or not a tactic works, one does not need to be an ethical theorist to know that the application of a technology should be legal and it should make sense. We take that for granted. But just because an extractive technology is legal and valid does not necessarily make it morally acceptable. Ethical criteria also need to be considered. Of course these can be related—laws can be grounded in morality or be immoral and to use an invalid technique can be unfair and wasteful, but they are empirically and, for some purposes, analytically distinct.

Many positive uses are not in dispute—video cameras and sensors for monitoring the flow of anonymous traffic or a data base containing the names of doctors and lawyers with suspended licenses. Other cases represent obvious abuses—surreptitious video or audio taping among friends or selling of confidential information by medical or criminal justice personnel. Of much greater interest theoretically and for public policy are the cases in which there is disagreement—listening in to a cell or cordless telephone communication that is equivalent to a radio broadcast; drug testing in noncritical contexts such as the employees of retail stores, the selling of consumer lists, or going through a person's trash.

Here we operate inductively. Rather than starting with an ethical framework and applying it to behavior, we start with behavior and examine the beliefs and feelings it engenders. What arguments underlie beliefs about whether personal surveillance is justified or not? Of course, ideas from the major deductive ethical systems such as Kant's emphasis on consistency and dignity or utilitarianism are reflected in commonly held attitudes, although not in an integrated and consistent manner.

Let us begin the analysis by making a distinction between (1) *the means* (instrument) of data collection, 2) *the context and conditions* under which the data are gathered, and 3) *the uses/goals* to which the data are put. There is a temporal sequence here as we start with the means and then move to collection and use.

A given means such as video can be used for a variety of goals and a given goal such as drug testing can be done in a variety of ways. Means and goals apart, the conditions under which these appear also show enormous variation. The ethical status can vary from cases in which the means, the context, and the use are all abhorrent to those in which they are all acceptable or even desirable, to varying combinations. Ethical analysis needs to consider all three factors. Beyond different value priorities and interpretations, disagreements in evaluation often involve persons emphasizing one rather than another of these elements.

A. The Means

Are there some means of personal information collection that are simply immoral? Torture is the obvious case. For many observers the polygraph with its tight-fitting bodily attachments, manipulation, and questionable validity; a drug test requiring a person to urinate in front of another; and harming or threatening friends or relatives of a suspect in order to obtain information, are also generally unethical. Similarly, most persons recoil at the thought of certain coercive bodily intrusions such as pumping the stomach of a suspect believed to have swallowed evidence or removing a bullet from the body for ballistics matching (practices that the courts have generally also prohibited).

For many moral theorists and much of society, lying, deception, and manipulation are a cluster of means that in and of themselves are ethically questionable. These come together in the case of undercover tactics. Such means (unlike many other surveillance means) always present a moral dilemma. This is not to suggest that under certain conditions and for certain ends they may not on balance be appropriate. But no matter how compelling the latter, this does not alter the fact that in our culture neither lying and trickery nor physical force and coercion are morally preferred techniques.

We have identified a folk or common sense morality that underlies judgments made about the collection of personal information. A popular expression claims "if it doesn't look right, that's ethics." And when the means do not look right, the act of collecting personal data is likely to involve saying "yes" to one or more of the following questions:

1. Does the act of collecting the data (apart from its use) involve unwarranted physical or psychological harm?
2. Does the technique cross a personal boundary without permission (whether involving coercion or deception, or a body, relational, or spatial border)?
3. Does the technique violate trust and assumptions that are made about how personal information will be treated such as no secret recordings?
4. Does the technique produce invalid results?

To the extent that one or more of these concerns are present the means as such raise ethical concerns.

Of course, the generality of these concepts offers ample room to ask when they apply. With cleverness or sophistry one can make them problematic. Is harm to be measured by objective or subjective accounts? What about culture or individual differences in definitions of harm, trust, and the drawing of personal boundaries? However, our argument in the first instance is empirical and even intuitive, like Supreme Court Justice Stevens's definition of pornography ("I can't define it, but I know it when I see it"). Within American culture certain data collection means simply feel wrong. Whether this sense extends empirically (or ought to extend morally) to other Western or industrial societies, or more broadly to all societies (if one accepts the idea that there are universal human rights that all persons should be entitled to) is an important question, but beyond our concern here.

In spite of the fact that some data collection or surveillance means are inherently undesirable, most contemporary disputes do not involve the means as such; rather, they involve the context and the end. Ethical disagreements and problems are more likely to be found in the conditions around the data collection and/or in the use of the data.

B. The Data Collection Context

With respect to the context, we ask how the technique is applied and we ask about its social setting. Even if we have a means that is morally acceptable, that is not sufficient justification. We also need to attend to the context of its application and then to its use.

A distinction here can be made between (1) the actual collection of the information, and (2) the broader conditions surrounding this. In the first case we are again concerned with the presence of harm, unwarranted border crossings, trust, and validity. At the most general level these represent respect for the dignity of the person. In this case we assume that it is possible to collect the information in an ethically acceptable fashion. We draw attention to the discretion surveillors have to behave *within* or *beyond* ethical bounds in their use of a means that *is* capable of being ethically applied.

1. Data Collection

With respect to harm during the process of information collection, tactics such as interviews, psychological tests, drug tests, and searches can be done to minimize or maximize discomfort.

Validity here refers to whether the tactic is applied correctly and measures what it claims to measure. Situations in which invalid readings result (whether out of malevolence, incompetence, good faith errors, faulty machines, or unaccounted-for confounding factors) are obviously unfair and wasteful (not to mention the liability issues involved in wrongful application and use). There must be a means to verify results, and those in charge must have enough confidence in the system that they would willingly submit to it themselves when appropriate. It must not be assumed that fallible humans can design and operate infallible machines (or given the complexity, that machines are infallible).

Lack of validity may apply to an individual case, as with the switching of a positive for a negative drug test or factors that can confound a drug test, such as that the subject ate poppy seeds prior to giving a urine sample. Or problems of validity can apply to a broad group as when a large number of false readings result because of faulty lab procedures. A pattern of systematic errors is particularly troubling given what amounts to the institutionalization of unfairness.

Borders have legitimate and illegitimate crossing points and interstitial and gray areas. Being invited in the front door is very different from breaking it down or sneaking in the back door. Information collected in a public setting such as a street or park is different from that taken in a private setting. Regardless of the setting, information available to the unaided senses has a different moral status than that which can only be assessed with sense-enhancing technologies.

Personal border crossings and trust are related to (and even defined by) whether (1) individuals are *aware* that personal information is being collected and, if so (2) whether they agree to the collection and subsequent uses of the data. These are difficult concepts because no one can be fully aware of all the possible consequences of the act of data collection, nor of subsequent uses. In the same way, "consent" is always conditioned by the range of choices and their relative costs and benefits.

While to consent means to be aware, the reverse is not necesarrily true. Whether or not consent is sought is perhaps the most important ethical question with respect to the collection of personal data. Of course, there are social roles granted the right to transcend personal boundaries without consent, such as police and emergency medical personnel. However, in conventional settings the failure to inform, or a coercive lack of choice, is of a different order.

Taking information without consent may also be seen to violate a proprietary right the individual has to control his or her personal information. At one extreme this is reflected in the Fifth Amendment's protection against self-incrimination.

A component of justice is fair warning—providing people with information about the rules, procedures, rewards, and punishments they are subject to. Beyond showing respect for the person, full disclosure can be a means of shaping behavior, as individuals know they will be assessed and they may behave accordingly (e.g., paying bills on time to avoid being data base-labeled as a bad credit risk). Openness about data collection can also help bring accountability to the data collectors because it comes with an address.

We can also ask if consent has the quality of "opting in" or "opting out." In the latter case individuals are told that if they give their permission their individual data will be collected. In the former, individuals are told that their data will automatically be collected *unless* they request that it not be. Those with an interest in gathering the data strongly prefer the latter system of opting out—that is, requiring persons to ask that they *not* be included. To be sure that is better than offering no choice at all. But because many persons will be ignorant of the possibility of opting out or will not want to take the time, not remember, or be unaware of the potential negative consequences, "opting in" is preferable.

There are also degrees—such as full awareness that a tactic may be used, versus knowing that it will be used but not in precise detail where and when (e.g., where a hidden camera is, or whether or not there is a monitor/recorder behind a known camera). A nice example of being informed and consenting are some Internet websites that inform users that "cookies," a program that charts what the individual views, may be activated or blocked as the user chooses.

Even if the data gatherer does not offer a formal choice, it may be possible to, in effect, have this by using a countertechnology to block the collection of personal information. If devices to prevent the unwarranted collection of personal information are widely available but nevertheless are not used, then there is a sense in which persons do choose to release their information. Yet that is not the case if such means are very expensive or are difficult to use.

An element of choice may also be present when privacy becomes commodified such that persons can choose by payment or compensation the level of privacy they desire. Yet it is still important that privacy thresholds be available below which no one falls.

The concept of consent, of course, can be very problematic, given the role of culture in shaping perceptions and the fact that choices always occur within situations that are not fully free, or within the making of the person choosing. For example, the meaning of choice with respect to agreeing to take a drug test is very different in a one-industry town than in a setting where one can find equvialent work settings in which not all employers require such a test.

In flying on a domestic Canadian airline a friend saw the following sign:

> Notice: Security measures are being taken to observe and inspect persons. No passengers are obliged to submit to a search of persons or goods if they choose not to board our aircraft.

Rather than spend days in the car or on the train, the friend had chosen to fly and "agreed" to be searched. Most persons would do the same. But to claim the choise is somehow voluntary as the sign suggests is disingenuous in the extreme. Choice to be meaningful should imply some genuine alternatives and refusal costs that are not wildly exorbitant.

We also need to ask, "consent to what?" Thus, a mass marketing executive reports "the data isn't out there because we stole it from them. Someone gave it away, and it's out there for us to use." In a legal sense that is true. But the element of "giving it away" was not a willful choice in the obvious sense. Rather, the data became available indirectly as a result of taking some other action. At the time, were the individuals to be asked if they agree to have their information used for marketing purposes, it might not be "out there" waiting for specious disclaimers about its nontheft.

We can also ask "who consents?" Thus, when children follow the advice of a television clown and hold their telephone receivers in front of their set and a remote signal sent through the television set activates the phone and sends its number over a toll-free line, they have acted voluntarily. But they did not know that this was to be used for direct mail marketing purposes for candy and even if they did, the "consent" of small children obtained by a clown seems specious.

Given the complexities and competing values, the absence of informed consent is not automatically a sign of unethical behavior, but situations where it is present are clearly morally preferable to those where it is not.

One aspect of harm and crossing into possibly perilous personal borders involves going farther than is required or than has been publicly announced (and perhaps agreed to by the subject). Here we ask, does a principle of *minimization* apply to the collection of personal data?

One should go no farther than is necessary for the task at hand, in spite of temptations and incentives to go beyond. Granted that many of these tactics by their very nature cross personal boundaries and may subject the person to feelings of embarrassment, shame, and powerlessness, we can still ask was this done in a professional manner and only to the extent necessary to obtain the informational end, or does it go beyond that? For example, is wiretapping applied in a categorical way such that all communications are listened to or only those pertaining to the focused goal? If federal minimization rules are followed regarding wiretapping it will be only the latter. A related example is the very precise time and place limits of well-drawn search warrants.

In contrast, many private-sector data gatherers face no such limits. As an "insurance" policy, data collectors often favor gathering more rather than less information, because they can never be sure that sometime in the future they might not need it, or that a new way of using it might not be discovered. Consider large retail chains that may routinely ask (even cash purchasers) for names and telephone numbers, or the extraneous data collection about life-style and demographic characteristics that accompany warranty forms. Much of that information ends up in a massive data base in Denver. Medical samples taken for employment purposes may be analyzed for conditions for which informed consent has not been given.

The potential to go too far is also found with the system operators for many networked computers. For example, some interactive computer games or other services that involve using software at a company's Web page also give the company the opportunity (although certainly not the right), to explore everything in a user's computer. There may be valid reasons for doing this (e.g., to see if a player has stolen or misused files), but there is no justification for looking at other unrelated files. In the same way, providers of telephone and e-mail services may need to monitor communication to be sure their systems are working, but to listen to conversations or read e-mail beyond what is technically required for service reasons is wrong. Yet the temptation can be great.

2. The Social Setting

The second aspect of the conditions of data collection involves the broader social context, rather than the direct application of the tactic as such. We identify 10 procedural conditions. In the absence of these, problems are more likely to occur. The presence of these policies and procedures does not make a tactic ethical, but it does increase the likelihood of ethically acceptable outcomes.

Some procedural conditions:

1. *Public decision-making:* Was the decision to use a tactic arrived at through some public discussion and decision-making process? For example, are the conditions of computer and telephone work monitoring of reservation clerks jointly developed through a management-union or worker's council committee?

2. *Human review:* Is there human review of machine-generated results? Given the acontextual nature of much of the data the technology generates and the possibility of hardware and software failure, this is vital. Generally, individuals as interpreters of human situations are far more sensitive to nuance than are computers, even if they are much more expensive.

3. *Right of inspection:* Are people aware of the findings and how they were created? Being entitled to know the evidence and, as the next condition suggests, to challenge it are fundamental aspects of procedural justice.

4. *Right to challenge and express a grievance:* Are there procedures for challenging the results, or for entering alternative data or interpretations into the record?

5. *Redress and sanctions:* If the individual has been treated unfairly and procedures have been violated, are there appropriate means of redress? Are there means

for discovering violations and penalties to encourage responsible surveillant behavior? In Europe and Canada there are official data commissioners who may actively seek out compliance. But in the United States it is up to individuals to bring forward complaints. But in order for that to happen they must first be aware that there is a problem and that there are standards.

6. *Adequate data stewardship and protection:* Can the security of the data be adequately protected? There must be standards for who has access to the data and audit trails, for whether and when data is to be updated, for how long it is to be kept, and the conditions under which it is to be destroyed.

Finally, three more general questions deal not with a given individual, but with broader social consequences:

7. *Equality-inequality regarding availability and application:* This involves three questions:

    a. Is the means widely available or is it restricted to only the most wealthy, powerful, or technologically sophisticated?

    b. Within a setting, is the tactic broadly applied to all people or only to those less powerful or unable to resist?

    c. If there are means of resisting the provision of personal information (whether technically, economically, or legally) are these equally available, or restricted to the most privileged?

The first question applies particularly to conflict and hierarchical settings and relates to Kant's principle of universalism or consistency, which asks "would it be acceptable if all persons or groups used the tactic?" The democratization of surveillance through low cost and ease of use can introduce a healthy pluralism and balance (as well as reiprocal inhibitions in use for fear of retaliation). On the other hand this may also help create a more defensive and suspicious society with an overall increase in surveillance.

We can also apply a principle of consistency that asks if the tactic is applied to everyone (which is different from asking what if everyone applied it?) Here we ask about equality within a setting—is the tactic (particularly if it is controversial) applied to all, or only to some (usually those lower in status)? For example, are executives drug tested and are their phone and e-mail communications subject to monitoring as with other employees? If there is inequality, is the rationale for differential application clear and justifiable?

Finally, we need to consider (in the absence of being able to just say no) whether there are means available that make it possible for people to maintain greater control over their personal information and, if so, how widely available these are. Some, such as providing a false name and address when the request is irrelevant (as with paying cash for consumer electronics) or free, anonymous e-mail forwarding services, are available to anyone. In other cases privacy may come with a price tag, as with the purchase of a device for shredding records, having an unlisted phone number, or possessing the technical skill to encrypt one's e-mail or telephone communications.

8. *The symbolic meaning of a method:* What does the use of a method communicate more generally? Some practices simply look bad in being deeply violative of a broad principle such as respect for the dignity of the person. Something much broader than the harm to a particular individual seems present here. There is a sense in which a social value is undermined and the community as a whole may be harmed.

9. *The creation of unwanted precedents:* Is it likely to create precedents that will lead to its application in undesirable ways? Even if a new tactic seems otherwise acceptable, it is important to apply a longer range perspective and consider where might it lead. The social security number, which has become a de facto national identification card that Congress clearly did not intend when it was created, is an example.

10. *Negative effects on surveillors and third parties:* Are there negative effects on those beyond the subject? For example, what is the impact on the personality of being a professional watcher or infiltrator? In another example, there is some evidence that police who use radar guns in traffic enforcement have higher rates of testicular cancer. Audio and video tapping may record the behavior of suspects, as well as that of their family and friends. Tactics rarely stand alone, and their possible implications for persons beyond the subject need to be considered.

III. USES OF SURVEILLANCE DATA

Let us move from the tactic itself and the social context in which information is collected to its actual use. The first two may be ethically acceptable even as the uses to which the data are put is ethically unacceptable.

It is easy to identify relatively noncontroversial positive goals such as productivity, health, and crime prevention. It is more difficult to identify questionable goals because by their very nature they are less likely to be publicized (e.g., DNA insurance exclusion examples based on future predictions). These may involve using inappropriate means for strategic gain or profit, an effort to enforce an employer's morality, politics, or opposition to unions onto employees, or illogic or ignorance. The gray area here is large, even if cases at the extremes are clear. For example, is use of a pulmonary lung test to measure whether employees are not smoking (in conformity with a company's nonsmoking policy), a necessary health and cost-saving measure good for both the company and the employee, or is it a wrongful crossing of the boundary between work and nonwork settings?

In considering goals we need to be alert to the possibility that the publicly stated goals may mask other less-desirable goals. Even when that is not the case, moral worth must be sought in the consequences of the use, beyond the good intentions of those applying the technology.

To help in assessing the "use" issue the following questions need to be asked. Other factors being equal, the first response suggests an ethical use and the second an unethical use.

1. *Appropriate vs. inappropriate goals:* Are the goals of the data collection legitimate? Are they publically announced? Consider the following contrasting cases:
    —drug testing bus drivers vs. junior high school students who wish to play in the school band;
    —a doctor asking a female patient about her birth control and abortion history in a clinical setting vs. asking this of *all* female employees (as one large airline did) without indicating why the information was needed.

2. *The goodness of fit between the means and the goal:* Is there a clear link between the information collected and the goal sought? How well a test measures what it claims to—drug and alcohol use, miles driven, or location—can be differentiated from second-order inferences made about goals only indirectly related to the actual results of the measurement. As we move from the direct results of a measure that is immediately meaningful given the goal (e.g., a drug test to determine if a person has abided by the conditions of their parole), to more distant inferences about goals, questions may arise. For example, some research suggests that drug tests may not be associated with the employment performance behaviors they are presumed to predict. In that regard a test for transportation workers that directly measures reflexes is preferable to a more inferential drug test.

3. *Information used for original vs. other unrelated*

purposes: Is the personal information used for the reasons offered for its collection and for which consent may have been given? Does the data stay with the original collector, or does it migrate elsewhere? For example, are the results of medical tests undertaken for diagnostic and treatment purposes sold or otherwise obtained by potential insurers, employers, or pharmaceutical companies? Using data for unrelated purposes may violate shared understandings and can also involve deception, if collectors know from the start how it will be used and do not reveal that.

4. *Failure to share secondary gains from the information:* Is the personal data collected used for profit without permission from, or benefit to, the person who provided it (or at least participated in its generation)? This implies a private property defense of personal information and contrasts with a definition based on universal human or democratic citizenship rights. To sell another person's information without asking them and without letting them share in the gain might even be seen as a kind of theft. The issue of ownership of personal information raises novel copyright issues, whether they involve sale of information about a person's purchases or a clone of their cell structure.

5. *Unfair disadvantage:* Is the information used in such a way as to cause unwarranted harm or disadvantage to its subject? There is, of course, much room for debate over whether these occur and are warranted or unwarranted. Yet some major types can be identified and at the extreme examples are easy to find:

    a. An unfair strategic disadvantage or with respect to a situation in which there is a conflict of interest (for example, a bugged car sales waiting room that permits the seller to learn a customer's concerns and maximum payment).

    b. Unfairly restricting social participation (for example, denying someone an apartment, insurance, or employment based on information that is invalid, irrelevant, discriminatory acontextual, or according to policy, not to be a factor in the decision made (e.g., not hiring someone because their DNA suggests they have a better-than-average chance of developing a serious illness in the future).

    c. The unwarranted publication or release of personal information that causes embarrassment, shame, or otherwise puts a person in a negative light. The emphasis here is on the subjective harm the individual experiences as a result of the release of confidential information, apart from its validity. State laws that protect against the "tort" of privacy invasion apply here. Direct tangible,

TABLE I

Questions to Help Determine the Ethics of Surveillance

A. The Means

1. *Harm:* Does the act of collecting the data (apart from its use) involve unwarranted physical or psychological harm?

2. *Boundaries:* Does the technique cross a personal boundary without permission?

3. *Trust:* Does the technique violate trust and assumptions that are made about how personal information will be treated, such as no secret recordings?

4. *Validity:* Does the technique produce invalid results?

B. The Data Collection Context

5. *Awareness:* Are individuals aware that personal information is being collected?

6. *Consent:* Do individuals consent to the data collection?

7. *Minimization:* Does a principle of minimization apply?

8. *Public decision-making:* Was the decision to use a tactic arrived at through some public discussion and decision-making process?

9. *Human review:* Is there human review of machine-generated results?

10. *Right of inspection:* Are people aware of the findings and how they were created?

11. *Right to challenge and express a grievance:* Are there procedures for challenging the results, or for entering alternative data or interpretations into the record?

12. *Redress and sanctions:* If the individual has been treated unfairly and procedures have been violated, are there appropriate means of redress? Are there means for discovering violations and penalties to encourage responsible surveillant behavior?

13. *Adequate data stewardship and protection:* Can the security of the data be adequately protected?

14. *Equality-inequality regarding availability and application:*
    a. Is the means widely available or restricted to only the most wealthy, powerful, or technologically sophisticated?
    b. Within a setting, is the tactic broadly applied to all people or only to those less powerful or unable to resist?
    c. If there are means of resisting the provision of personal information are these equally available, or restricted to the most privileged?

15. *The symbolic meaning of a method:* What does the use of a method communicate more generally?

16. *The creation of unwanted precedents:* Is it likely to create precedents that will lead to its application in undesirable ways?

17. *Negative effects on surveillors and third parties:* Are there negative effects on those beyond the subject?

C. Uses

18. *Appropriate vs. inappropriate goals:* Are the goals of the data collection legitimate? Are they publically announced?

19. *The goodness of fit between the means and the goal:* Is there a clear link between the information collected and the goal sought?

20. *Information used for original vs. other unrelated purposes:* Is the personal information used for the reasons offered for its collection and for which consent may have been given, and does the data stay with the original collector, or does it migrate elsewhere?

21. *Failure to share secondary gains from the information:* Is the personal data collected used for profit without permission from, or benefit to, the person who provided it?

22. *Unfair disadvantage:* Is the information used in such a way as to cause unwarranted harm or disadvantage to its subject?

material harm can more easily be determined than subjective harm involving embarrassment, shame, stigma, humiliation, and the uncomfortable feeling of being invaded by the prying eyes of others, whether known or unknown.

d. A feeling of betrayal of confidence. The failure to use information only as promised or to maintain confidentiality and security as promised applies here. This can involve friends telling something they should not, violations of professional confidentiality, or a phone company revealing unlisted numbers through a new service such as caller-ID.

e. Intrusions into solitude. An important element of privacy is the right to be left alone in a busy world. The indiscriminate traffic in personal information may result in unwanted mass marketing intrusions via telephone, mail, e-mail, or face-to-face solicitations.

Given the variety of tactics for extracting personal information and the conditions under which they are applied, an ethics of surveillance must be very general, and categorical imperatives mandating prohibition, or use, are difficult to defend. It is unrealistic to expect a general principle to apply equally in all contexts and across all technologies. But we can talk in relative terms and contrast tactics, situations, and uses as being more or less ethically acceptable depending on the play of the factors discussed.

The questions asked about the means, data collection context, and use offer a guide for assessing surveillance ethics. The more the principles implied in these questions are honored, the more ethical the situation is likely to be, or, conversely, the fewer of these present, the less ethical. We intend this additive approach as a sensitizing perspective and do not suggest that equal moral weight necessarily be given to these factors. But, hopefully, they do touch the major ethical elements. There are no simple equation, or cookbook, answers to the varied and complex situations in which personal data are collected and used. Suggesting an ethics for a particular tactic such as computer data bases or drug testing can be worthwhile in offering focused guidelines, but it is important not to ignore the commonalities and to see the broader social picture. In spite of the above limitations, awareness of the complexity and asking the questions in Table I (which summarize our argument) will likely yield better results than ignoring them.

Also See the Following Articles

COMPUTER AND INFORMATION ETHICS • COMPUTER SECURITY • CONFIDENTIALITY, GENERAL ISSUES OF • INTERNET PROTOCOL • PRIVACY

Bibliography

Foucault, M. (1977). *Discipline and punish: The Birth of the prison.* New York: Vintage.

Gandy, O. (1993). *The panoptic sort.* Boulder, CO: Westview Press.

Johnson, D. (1994). *Computer ethics.* Englewood Cliffs, NJ: Prentice-Hall.

Lyon, D. (1994). *The electronic eye: The Rise of Surveillance Society.* Cambridge: Polity Press.

Marx, G. T. (1994). New telecommunication technologies require new manners. *Telecommunications Policy,* Vol. 18, no. 7.

Marx, G. T. (1986). The iron fist in the velvet glove: Totalitarian potentials within democratic structures. In J. Short (Ed.), *The social fabric.* Beverly Hills: Sage:

Regan, P. (1995). *Legislating privacy technology, social values and public policy.* Chapel Hill: University of North Carolina Press.

Rule, J. (1973). *Private lives, public surveillance.* London: Allen-Lane.

EMBRYOLOGY, ETHICS OF

Søren Holm
University of Copenhagen

GLOSSARY

abortion The termination of a pregnancy. Abortion can be spontaneous or induced.

conceptus, zygote, preembryo, embryo, fetus Developmental stages of the developing human being; see Section I.

embryology The science that studies the development of the embryo, fetus, etc., from just prior to conception to birth.

gamete A reproductive cell; sperm and eggs are gametes.

IVF *In vitro* fertilization, a technique developed to treat infertility. IVF involves the fertilization of ova outside of a woman's body. IVF is one of a range of techniques usually called the "new reproductive technologies" or "assisted reproductive technologies."

EMBRYOLOGY is the science that studies the development of the embryo, fetus, etc., from immediately before conception to birth (or hatching in the case of birds, fish, reptiles, etc.). Although the terms "embryo" and "fetus" denote different stages of the developing being, this is not reflected in the name of the science dealing with all these stages. There is no separate science of "fetology." The science of embryology contains both descriptive and explanatory elements; i.e., it describes the various development stages (their anatomy, physiology, etc.), but it also tries to unravel the mechanisms which control the development.

For the purpose of the present article embryology will be used as synonymous with human embryology.

Embryology is a scientific area where there are still large lacunae in our knowledge, but it is also an area of very rapid development. This means that some of the things we think we know today may very well be superseded by new discoveries in the coming years.

I. A SHORT OUTLINE OF THE DEVELOPMENT OF THE HUMAN EMBRYO

The first step in the process leading from fertilization to birth is fertilization itself; i.e., the process whereby the male and female gametes (i.e., the ovum (egg) and spermatozoon (sperm)) unite to form a new entity. This step in the process is also sometimes referred to as conception.

There is no moment of fertilization; it is a process which is extended in time. When a spermatozoon penetrates the outer membrane (the zona pellucida) around the ovum, the membrane changes configuration and becomes impenetrable to further spermatozoa. The head of the spermatozoon then penetrates the cell membrane of the ovum, and its genetic material is injected into the cytoplasm of the ovum where it forms the male pronucleus.

Over a period of hours the male and female pronuclei fuse and form the nucleus of the newly formed entity called the zygote. When one nucleus has been formed we talk of syngamy. The zygote then begins its first division, the single cell becoming two. Genetic studies have shown that the genetic material from the father is not activated until 24–48 hr after the beginning of the fertilization process, that is, after the occurrence of syngamy and after the first division.

In normal fertilization, after sexual intercourse the fertilization usually takes place in the fallopian tubes (the tubes leading from the ovaries to the uterus (the womb)) and the initial divisions take place while the zygote is transported through the fallopian tubes.

After the first division the zygote continues to divide, forming a 4- and an 8-cell stage. At the 8-cell stage all the cells are still totipotential (or pluripotential); i.e., they can all form a new complete zygote if separated. At this stage the zygote looks like a mulberry and is called a morula. It is possible to induce a human ovum to begin its divisions without having been fertilized by a spermatozoon. This activation can be done with a range of different chemical and electrical stimulations. However, such parthenogentically activated ova never develop further than the 8- to 16-cell stage. True parthenogenesis (virgin birth) is impossible in humans.

As cell divisions continue the mass of cells develops a central cavity and is called a blastula or blastocyst, and later the embryo proper begins to develop as a localized mass of cells (the embryonic disk) protruding into the central cavity. If development goes wrong at this stage it may in some cases lead to the creation of a tumor known as a mola which consists only of the kinds of cells which would have formed the placenta in normal pregnancy.

It is at the stage of the formation of the embryonic disk that monozygotic (identical) twinning can occur by a division of the embryonic cell mass. As far as we know, monozygotic twinning is a random process; i.e., the embryo is not genetically predestined to twin (dizygotic (nonidentical) twins arise when two ova are fertilized by two different spermatozoa).

The reverse process of twinning, where two embryos fuse and form a chimera consisting of two genetically different lines of cells, is also possible.

After the appearance of the embryonic disk the zygote is called a preembryo (preembryo may also be used for the entire period prior to the embryonic stage). At about 11 days gestational age (g.a., gestational age, is counted from fertilization) the embryonic disk begins to develop a central depression (the primitive streak) which marks the position of the future brain and spinal cord. When the primitive streak is fully formed at 13–14 days g.a., twinning is no longer possible and the preembryo is now called an embryo.

The term preembryo was first used in the early 1980s and there has been considerable debate over the use of the term. It has been claimed by opponents of embryo research that it was deliberately invented to make research on embryos seem more palatable by redescribing them as preembryos. The term is, however, now in common usage in embryology.

The process of nidation runs simultaneously with the development of the zygote. At 6–7 days g.a. the embryo starts embedding itself in the lining of the uterine wall, and this process is finished at about 14 days g.a. when the first primitive placenta is also formed.

More than 50% of all fertilized eggs do not develop properly in the early stages or do not nidate properly and are expelled with the mothers next menstural flow.

From 2 to 8 weeks g.a. the embryo develops very rapidly, and at 8 weeks all major organs are formed (although very few are functioning), and the embryo is clearly recognizable as a human embryo.

The first brain waves appear at 8 weeks g.a., but the cerebral cortex, which is presumably the part of the brain supporting consciousness, is only developed around 20 weeks g.a.

From 8 weeks g.a. until birth we talk of a fetus. Given present techniques, a fetus is viable outside its mothers womb from 22 to 24 weeks g.a. Prior to this time the lungs of the fetus are not sufficiently developed to sustain extrauterine life.

The mother is able to feel the movement of the fetus from about 16 to 18 weeks g.a. The time when she first feels fetal movement is called "quickening."

The exact time at which the fetus can feel pain is not known, and there is still disagreement on this point among embryologists.

The period from 24 to 40 weeks g.a. is characterized by growth and final maturation of the organs of the fetus. Birth usually takes place at 40 weeks g.a.

II. EMBRYOLOGY AND IN VITRO FERTILIZATION

In vitro fertilization (IVF) is a technique originally developed as a treatment for infertility. In IVF a number of ova are removed from a woman's ovaries and fertilized outside of her body. When they have developed to the eight-cell stage they are transferred back into her uterus, or the uterus of another woman. A number of variations of the IVF technique have been developed, each with its own acronym. These include GIFT (gamete intrafallopian transfer), ZIFT (zygote intrafallopian transfer), ICSI (intracytoplasmatic sperm injection), and SUZI (subzonal sperm injection). As a group these techniques are usually called the "new reproductive technologies" or the "assisted reproductive technologies."

The development of IVF opened new possibilities for embryological research, and new possibilities for intervention at the embryonic stage of human life. Some of these possibilities are briefly outlined here.

Zygotes can be frozen and stored indefinitely, although 25–50% are lost in the process. Zygotes can be split to form two individuals (cloning), or two or more zygotes can be fused. These two possibilities have not yet been tried in humans. The genetic makeup of the zygote can be determined by preimplantation diagnosis where one cell is removed and the genetic material in this cell amplified through modern gene-amplifying techniques. Genetic engineering can be performed on the zygote.

Ova can be donated from one woman to another, or one woman (a so-called surrogate mother) can bear a child for another couple. Ova from aborted female fetuses can be matured and used in IVF procedures. The normal reproductive span of women can be extended by hormonal treatment and egg donation.

These possibilities can furthermore be combined in various ways and can give rise to quite exotic scenarios. By cloning and embryo freezing a woman could, for instance, give birth to her own identical twin.

It is fairly obvious that some of these possibilities raise ethical questions.

III. WHAT IS THE CONNECTION BETWEEN EMBRYOLOGY AND APPLIED ETHICS?

Embryology is important for applied ethics in three ways: (a) it creates new ethical problems by being the basis of a range of new reproductive techniques, (b) it delivers empirical premises which are part of many of the arguments in biomedical ethics concerning the old problem of abortion and the new problems concerning the reproductive techniques, and (c) the early developments of the fertilized egg have proved a fertile field of examples for developing and testing more general theories of personhood and individuation.

Confusion may be created in the mind of the reader of articles of embryology and ethics if the authors do not make it clear whether they are trying to "solve" the ethical problem at hand or to develop a new ethical theory. The reader looking for answers to real world ethical problems is not always satisfied with philosophical analysis performed purely for the sake of its intrinsic philosophical interest.

A. The Moral Status of the Embryo

The moral status of the human embryo and fetus is not a new subject in philosophy. It has a history going back to Aristotle who wrote about the development of the human fetus and identified three consecutive ensoulments with a vegetative, an animal, and a rational soul. In scholastic philosophy in the middle ages this idea was further developed in connection with discussions of the proper punishment for abortion, and some scholastic philosophers maintained that male fetuses were finally ensouled with a rational soul 40 days after conception whereas female fetuses were similarly ensouled 80 days after conception.

In modern applied philosophy the question of the moral status of the embryo again emerged in the early 1970s in connection with discussions about the morality of abortion, and the question has continued to be prominent in discussions about ethical problems in the new reproductive techniques. Knowledge about embryology has been used extensively in these discussions. The question has often been stated in terms of whether or not embryos are persons, where a person is taken to be an entity with the moral status of a normal adult human being, including rights not to be harmed and not to be killed.

It is possible to discern two basic positions on the moral status of the human embryo: (1) The human embryo has no intrinsic moral status, but its status depends on the value conferred on it by others (e.g., its mother). (2) The human embryo has intrinsic moral status, independent of how others value it. The third possible position, that embryos begin with very little or no moral status and then gradually acquire more and more moral status as they develop, is probably the common sense view. This gradualist view has, however, been rejected by most ethicists as unsustainable. This may in part be because it shares the problem of many gradualist theories—it is often easier to argue for the extreme positions than for the middle ground. The gradualists will be attacked from both sides and will be vulnerable to the claim that their distinctions are arbitrary. Some versions of the argument from potential do support gradualist conclusions (see the last part of Section III.A.2).

1. Embryos Have No Moral Status

The position that embryos have no intrinsic moral status or value can be reached in a number of different ways. The two most common are via (a) a theory of rights, or (b) a preference consequentialist theory. The first approach usually proceeds by arguing that interests are a necessary condition for the ascription of rights, and that an entity has interests only if it is possible for the entity to know that these interests have been harmed. An entity therefore has an interest in not experiencing pain if and only if it can experience pain, and it has an interest in not being killed if and only if it is conscious of its life as a life, and not just as a series of unconnected experiences. In the context of the embryo this leads to the conclusion that it does not have any rights until it develops sentience in the fetal stage, and that it never develops a right not to be killed, because it does presumably not develop a conception of its own life as a life before well after birth.

The second (preference consequentialist) approach proceeds by arguing that what really matters ethically is preference satisfaction, and that the wrongness of doing specific acts can be located in the degree to which they thwart the preferences of the entities concerned. Since embryos and fetuses do not have a preference for going on living (or anything else), it is not wrong to kill them.

One problem for views of this sort is that they necessarily lead to the conclusion that full moral status is not attained until well after birth, since it is highly unlikely that infants have any idea of themselves as existing over time (i.e., of having a life). Infanticide is therefore not intrinsically wrong.

Proponents of the view that embryos have no moral status also usually argue that intrinsic value can come only from intrinsic properties; i.e., if an entity has intrinsic value (value in itself), this value must derive from some intrinsic property of the entity, and not from its relationship to other entities. The main problem with this argument is whether it is possible to provide a compelling account distinguishing intrinsic and extrinsic properties of entities.

2. Embryos Have Moral Status

The claim that embryos do have moral status has been supported by a number of different arguments.

The traditional Christian view, which is presently used primarily by Catholic moral theorists and by some evangelical groups, claims that an embryo has full moral status from the point of conception/fertilization. Similar views are held by some Orthodox Jewish and Islamic scholars. This view can be based on a theory of immediate ensoulment, or by reference to the fact that at fertilization a human being is created with a unique genetic makeup.

The main problems for this view are: (a) that it relies on a theological premise if it makes reference to ensoulment, and such premises are not generally accepted in a secular context; (b) that there is a possibility of twinning until 14 days after fertilization, which would require either two souls in one entity prior to twinning or the infusion of a new soul at the point of twinning; (c) that there is a possibility of chimera formation where two zygotes fuse, and this would seem to lead to an entity with two souls; (d) that the argument referring to the embryo as a human being may be guilty of speciesism (i.e., relying on the mere fact that something is human as an argument for giving it moral status); and (e) that there are other human cells with a unique genetic makeup which we do not accord the same status.

A different argument for the full moral status of the human embryo proceeds by localizing the core wrong in killing adult humans in the fact that we deprive them of "a life like ours"—we deprive them of all the experiences and other things which their life would have contained if we had not killed them.

This is also true of any embryo we might kill, and thereby makes killing embryos wrong. There may be other wrong-making characteristics involved in killing adult human beings (the pain, the fear, etc.) which play no role when we discuss killing embryos. This indicates that it may be more wrong to kill adults than embryos, but it does not show that killing embryos is morally innocuous. The main problem in this argument is that it makes killing wrong in all cases, even in cases where a person might want to be killed. This is not a problem if we are only concerned with embryos or fetuses, but it could be a problem if the account is intended to be a general account of the wrong done in killing human beings.

A third way of arguing for the proposition that an embryo has moral status is through an argument from potentiality. Arguments of this kind acknowledge that embryos do not have present conscious interests or present preferences, but they then proceed to the claim that an entity with a potential for possessing such interests or preferences does have moral status.

Such arguments rely on a clarification of what "potential" really means. Potential cannot be the same as logical possibility, since it is not logically impossible for most things to turn into other things (e.g., it is not *logically* impossible for the egg of a hen to develop into a human fetus). Potential also cannot be mere material possibility, i.e., the possibility that a certain piece of marble could turn into a statue of David in the hands of Michelangelo. It must, in the present context, entail that the entity having the potential also is responsible in some sense for the development leading to the fulfillment of the potential. Finally, the notion of potential must rely on some background notion about a stable environment. If this stable environment requirement is not brought in it would be the case that the potential of an embryo would depend upon whether or not its mother wanted to abort it.

If a coherent notion of potential can be established, there still has to be an argument for the move from "entity X has the potential to be Y" to "entity X now has the moral status which it will have when it becomes Y." It is often mentioned in the criticism of the argument from potential that the fact that someone is a potential president of the USA does not give him or her the same powers and prerogatives as the incumbent of the position. This is obviously correct, but it is equally possible to find examples where someone being a potential incumbent of a position does give special privileges, although these privileges may not be exactly the same as those of the actual incumbent (think of the role of the heir to the throne in monarchies).

Another problem for the potentiality argument is that two gametes also have the potential to become a human being. After all, the gametes have a potential to become a zygote, and the zygote has a potential to become a human being. The proponent of the argument from potential therefore seems committed to a prohibition of contraceptives in order not to frustrate the potential of the gametes. This problem has been dealt with either by arguing that potential is a property of entities such as zygotes and not of assemblies of entities such as sperm and ova, or by arguing that gametes do not possess the same degree of control over the developmental process as does the zygote and the later stages of the human embryo.

B. Replacement Arguments and Personal Identity

A specific class of arguments based on an intriguing observation about personal identity have become a standard feature of discussions about ethics and embryology. These are the so-called replacement arguments which all proceed from the observations that (a) if a woman conceives a child this month, the child will be different from the child she could have conceived next month, because they will come from the union of different gametes and be genetically different, and more generally (b) any change in reproduction which entails a change in the timing or manner of conception leads to the production of different children (children with different identities).

This has implications for many arguments of the type, "It is not good for children to grow up in condition X, Y, or Z, therefore it is wrong to procreate in condition X, Y, and Z because it harms the future children." Proponents of the replacement argument argue that there is an underlying conceptual confusion at play here. We may believe that we are comparing the welfare of the child growing up in adverse conditions with the welfare of the *same* child growing up in better circumstances and deciding which would be better, but this is not true. What we are doing is comparing two *different* children, the child growing up in adverse conditions and *another* child growing up in better circumstances. The life of the child in adverse conditions is the only life this child can have, and what we have to decide is not whether there are better lives, but whether the life of this child is so bad that it would be better not to have it. This is an unlikely proposition in most cases, so the argument that it would be better for the child not to be born than to be born disadvantaged is in most circumstances false.

The argument thus maintains that children born to single mothers, to lesbian mothers, or after IVF using matured eggs from aborted fetuses could only have been born this way, and that it makes no sense to prohibit or discourage such pregnancies for the sake of the children.

The replacement type of argument is just one of a larger class of arguments concerning the connection between the adult human being and the zygote. This class of arguments are concerned with the question of whether or in what way the adult and the zygote can be said to be identical. Common sense seems to indicate that I, the adult, am identical with the zygote from which I developed, but there are arguments against this view.

First of all it can be questioned whether the important thing is biological or personal identity. I may be biologically identical with the zygote without having any kind of personal identity with the zygote. This follows, for instance, if we accept a view of personal identity in which it is exclusively a function of psychological connectedness. Since the zygote has no psychology I cannot be psychologically connected to it.

Secondly the possibility of twinning and chimera

formation makes it questionable whether I am even numerically identical with the zygote from which I developed. If I am a monozygotic twin both my brother and I developed from the same zygote, and it is logically impossible that both he and I can be identical with the same entity, since we are undoubtedly at the present time distinct and numerically nonidentical. It is simply logically impossible for A and B to be nonidentical at the same time that they are both identical to C. This assertion of logical impossibility is, however, only valid in all cases in a nontemporal logic like the usual first-order predicate logic. A full discussion of the possibilities of resolving the logical problem within a suitably enriched temporal logic is, however, beyond the scope of the present article.

Arguments about personal identity and individuation have been important in discussions about time limits on embryo research. Many countries now have a legal regulation stating that destructive embryo research is permitted only prior to 14 days g.a. This similarity in the legal regulations is most likely the result of a direct transfer of the 14-day limit suggested by the British Warnock committee which, with the moral philosopher Mary Warnock in the chair, published a report in 1984 on the ethical issues created by the new reproductive techniques (republished commercially as M. Warnock, Ed., 1985. *A Question of Life: The Warnock Report on Human Fertilization and Embryology*. Basil Blackwell, Oxford). The committee based its recommendation of a 14-day limit on the following argument (reconstructed from the text):

1. Prior to 14 days g.a. the primitive streak is not fully formed and there is a possibility of twinning
2. If there is a possibility of twinning the embryo cannot be an individual
3. Only individuals can have moral status
4. It is not wrong to perform destructive experimentation on entities without moral status

Therefore, the embryo becomes an individual at 14 days g.a. (the time of individuation). Prior to this time it has no moral status, and it is not wrong to perform destructive embryo experimentation.

There must obviously be a hidden premise stating that being an individual is not only necessary but also sufficient for some kind of moral status, otherwise the argument would not justify a limit at 14 days g.a. as the committee proposed, but only be an argument to the effect that no limit lower than 14 days g.a. could be justified. All the nonempirical premises of the argument have been criticized, but as could be expected proponents and opponents of embryo research cannot agree on which premises are wrong, or in what way they are wrong.

C. Is the Moment of Fertilization Important?

The simple answer to the question in the head of this section is "no," since there is no moment of fertilization but a process extended over time from the first penetration of the sperm to the occurrence of syngamy. A proponent of the view that fertilization is important could, however, without losing very much, move to either syngamy or the first activation of paternal genes as the important step marking the creation of a unique human being. What is important for the proponent of the view that fertilization matters is presumably not the exact point in time but the fact that at a specific point in time a genetically unique entity is created which is undeniably human.

There is, however, also a more radical challenge to the view that fertilization is important. A challenge which casts doubts on any specific moment in human life as carrying special significance, be it fertilization, birth, sexual maturity, childbearing, or death. This view would point to the way life is presently conceptualized in biology.

If we look at life not as something bound to specific identifiable individuals or entities, but as a process encompassing the whole species and all its members, we find that sexual reproduction is just one of many subprocesses necessary for the continuation of life, but a subprocess which is neither more nor less important than others. Cooperative food gathering may be equally, or more, necessary for the continuation of life in some societies. The same point can also be illustrated if we look at species which reproduce both sexually and asexually (like the common hydra), where it seems odd from a biological point of view to say that sexual reproduction is more important than asexual reproduction, or that entities (new hydras) created by sexual reproduction are more important than entities (new hydras) created by asexual reproduction.

D. Is Viability or Birth Important?

On most views, both those claiming that a fetus has moral status and those claiming that it does not have moral status, there is no direct change in this status just because the fetus is viable outside its mother's womb or just because it has actually been born. The fetus is the same, it is just its possible or actual relationship to its mother which has changed.

This means that a view not according moral status to the fetus would necessarily entail that there is nothing intrinsically wrong in killing viable fetuses or neonates and infants. There may be social reasons not to allow such killing, but it is not wrong in itself. It has been claimed that this consequence of the main theories depriving the fetus of moral status amounts to a *reductio ad absurdum* of these theories.

The fact that the viable fetus is potentially independent of its mother, and that the neonate is independent of her, does, however, entail a difference in decision making. The strength of any reasons to allow the mother to control her own body, and have the embryo or fetus killed in the process, diminishes considerably in a situation where the question is no longer only a question about bodily integrity, but also a question about decision making for incompetent individuals. The mother may have a right not to have the embryo implanted into her body or a right to have the fetus dispelled from her body, but these rights do not necessarily entail that she has a right to have the embryo or fetus destroyed.

E. Are There Specific Problems in Creating Embryos for Research?

Embryos can be used in research for a number of purposes ranging from basic embryological research to improvements of IVF techniques. It is often claimed that embryo research is necessary for the further development of IVF techniques, and that the information produced about the earliest development of the human being may prove useful in the understanding of aging and of cancer. The embryos used in embryo research can either be so-called "spare" embryos that are surplus to requirements in the context of IVF treatments (e.g., because the treatment is a success and there are stored embryos which the parents do not need anymore), or they can be created specifically for research. There has been some debate about whether it is ethically acceptable to create embryos specifically for research.

The arguments produced to show that it is not acceptable to create embryos, but acceptable to use spare embryos, usually refer to Kant's categorical imperative and its prohibition against using someone merely as a means and not at the same time as an end. It is claimed that embryos created specifically for research are used merely as means to further the researchers project, and that this is wrong. The problem with this argument is that it does not really distinguish between spare and specifically created embryos. All embryos are created as means to somebody else's project (the "progenitors" or the "researchers"), and even if we want to deny this, it seems incontrovertible that even if a spare embryo was created as an end in itself it is transformed into a mere means as soon as it is donated to research. The Kantian argument may, however, be more applicable in the context of custody or inheritance disputes about frozen embryos. In many of these cases it is obvious that the embryos in question are even further reified than they were as part of the IVF procedure.

There is also the further empirical problem that the number of spare embryos is not a natural given. Any number of spare embryos can be produced by manipulating the number of eggs retrieved and the number of eggs fertilized. Since there is usually no clearcut distinction between the people performing IVF treatment and the people performing embryo research, the researcher may, in his guise as physician, ensure that a sufficient number of spare embryos are produced.

Also See the Following Articles

ABORTION • FETAL RESEARCH • FETUS • INFERTILITY • REPRODUCTIVE TECHNOLOGIES

Bibliography

Chadwick, R. (Ed.) (1987). "Ethics, Reproduction and Genetic Control." Croom Helm, London.

Evans, D. (Ed.) (1996). "Conceiving the Embryo—Ethics, Law and Practice in Human Embryology." Nijhoff, The Hague.

Harris, J. (1993). "Wonderwoman and Superman." Oxford Univ. Press, Oxford.

Hursthouse, R. (1987). "Beginning Lives." Basil Blackwell, Oxford.

Kamm, F. M. (1992). "Creation and Abortion: A Study in Moral and Legal Philosophy." Oxford Univ. Press, New York.

Sadler, T. W. (1995). "Longman's Medical Embryology," 7th ed. Williams & Wilkins, New York.

Steinbock, B. (1992). "Life before Birth: The Moral and Legal Status of Embryos and Fetuses." Oxford Univ. Press, New York.

ENVIRONMENTAL COMPLIANCE BY INDUSTRY

Roger L. Burritt and Patricia E. McCreight
The Australian National University

GLOSSARY

code of practice A code that establishes guiding principles of behavior toward the environment that become moral obligations for any organization adopting them.

command and control Regulation by government authority.

compliance A reactive strategy to government environmental legislation.

economic instruments Measures that aim to change behavior by changing prices or creating new markets, altering the costs to users of financial resources and thus providing financial incentives to avoid waste or environmental damage.

enforcement Civil and/or criminal sanctions taken against an organization or an individual in breach of environmental legislation or regulations.

NGOs Nongovernment organizations that are not influenced by government or business.

precautionary principle The principle that if there is

an environmental problem, action to protect the environment must be taken without waiting for scientific evidence about the cause of the problem.

sustainable development Development that meets the needs of the present without compromising the ability of future generations to meet their own needs.

ENVIRONMENTAL COMPLIANCE BY INDUSTRY considers the extent to which organizations act in accordance with standards established by government to protect the environment. The notion of ecologically sustainable development is being employed to encourage organizations to be mindful of the need to consider ecological as well as economic factors when developing organizational activities. There is a range of instruments available to influence the attitudes and behavior of people in industry toward environmental and ecological issues. The range extends through various "command and control" instruments, market-based measures, and self-regulatory devices. Command and control instruments require little in the way of ethical judgment, apart from the decision of an organization whether to comply with mandated behavior given the associated penalty and reward structure. On the other hand, at the latter end of the spectrum ethical issues have a role at two stages—the decision to undertake voluntary regulation, and the decision to comply with the norms of self-regulation once introduced. This article explores available instruments, the motivation to comply with each type of instrument, and incentive structures including the monitoring and reporting of compliance and noncompliance by industry.

I. INDUSTRY, SUSTAINABLE DEVELOPMENT, AND ENVIRONMENTAL COMPLIANCE

"Industry's response to pollution and resource degradation has not been and should not be limited to compliance with regulations. It should accept a broad sense of social responsibility and ensure an awareness of environmental considerations at all levels" (The Bruntland Report, 1987).

Development of industry has made it possible for us to increase the number of human beings the world can support. At the same time, environmental problems have accompanied industrial development. Until the 1980s industrial development and the environment were looked at as separate issues. The concept that has brought them together is ecologically sustainable development (ESD). This concept is attempting to get industry to perceive the environment as an asset—one to be nurtured, one to maintain, one to invest in, one to protect for present and future generations and promote intergenerational equity. Indeed, a commonly quoted definition of sustainable development, as recorded in the Bruntland Report 1987, is "development that meets the needs of the present without compromising the ability of future generations to meet their own needs."

In order to establish whether progress is being made in attempts to achieve ESD processes in industry, there is a need, first, to measure the adverse impact an organization is imposing on the natural environment; second, there is a need to disclose information about the environmental impacts of each organization to its stakeholders; and third, there is a need to assess the extent to which organizations have attempted to achieve the environmental standards set down for them. One set of standards is established through legislation. Compliance with legal standards has received much attention, but many organizations go "beyond compliance" with basis legal requirements. The pertinent ethical question is how far should we expect an organization to feel morally responsible for voluntary self-analysis with regard to the impact of its activities on the well-being of our environment? Against a background of differing legislation, is it justifiable for multinational organizations to undertake the same operations in developed

and developing countries while varying the environmental standards they adopt?

Crucial monitoring, investigating, and reporting of environmental standards achieved by industry has really only begun in earnest in the last decade. It is hampered by cost, by creative disclosure, and by the sheer volume and diversity of industrial activities that have an impact on the environment. These range from issues of biodiversity and air and water pollution to land degradation. Progress tends to have been implemented in an incremental way with emphasis initially being focused on identifying industry sectors that are thought to have a significant impact on the physical environment. These are shown in Table 1.

Three particular concerns relate to industries:

• where the environment is being destroyed through irreversible processes—such as the wholesale destruction of tropical rainforest and the loss of biodiversity;
• where environmental problems are common to a number of different industrial sectors—such as the greenhouse effect or "global warming";
• where sustainable development is a global rather than a local issue—such as transboundary pollution caused by industrial waste fouling the waters of the Rhine.

TABLE 1

Industry Sectors Thought to Have a Significant Impact on the Environment

Industry	Environmental Problems
Agriculture	Land degradation; soil erosion; desertification; salinity and acidification
Energy production and use	Global warming and air pollution caused by use of fossil fuels
Fisheries	Depleting stocks; endangered species
Forest use	Logging of old growth forests; water and air pollution from pulp and paper manufacture; rain forest depletion
Manufacturing	Air, water and land pollution
Mining	Depletion of natural resources; land degradation at mine sites; global warming; water pollution from open cast tailings
Tourism	Destruction of wilderness
Transport	Air pollution; global warming

Solutions are being explored at local, national, and international levels.

II. HOW ARE ENVIRONMENTAL STANDARDS EXACTED ON INDUSTRY?

A. Establishing Environmental Standards for Industry

Environmental standards with which individual organizations may or may not comply can be established in six main ways:

- directly by government through legislation;
- indirectly by government through the introduction of economic and administrative incentives designed to encourage acceptable environmental behavior;
- through pressure from community interest groups;
- through third parties that bring pressure to bear on organizations;
- through voluntary self-regulation by indusry associations; and
- through self-regulation by individual organizations.

1. Environmental Legislation

At federal, state, and local levels of government many thousands of environmental laws have been implemented in recent years. For example, at the federal level in the United States there are more than 11 thousand environmental laws. Sovereign states are also under pressure to ratify international environmental conventions, thereby adding to the volume of legislation.

Environmental legislation has traditionally been the method used by governments to establish standards with which organizations must comply if they are to avoid penalties. Organizations are aware that they are only allowed to exist because governments recognize that they provide something of value to society. Hence, most organizations respond favorably to required behavior mandated by legislation. To encourage compliance, legislation usually specifies penalties for noncompliance. This represents a "command and control" approach to achieving environmental compliance. Penalties may be imposed for any form of behavior toward the environment that is unacceptable to society as reflected in legislation. Unacceptable behavior includes such actions as excessive pollution of the air, destroying the potability of water, and degrading soils with toxic substances. Penalties range in form from simple monetary fines imposed on organizations, or individuals such

as company directors who are responsible for organizational activities, to time spent in jail for company officials who are found guilty of the crime of degrading the environment in a number of specified ways. One problem with using legislation to achieve environmental compliance by industry is that organizations tend to try and achieve the environmental standards laid down, but they do not attempt to improve performance beyond this legally required minimum. Legislation does not encourage an ethical commitment to go beyond legislated standards of behavior. Neither does it promote the ethos of a constant search for improvement in environmental performance.

Finally, complete compliance with legislation is not assured without a moral commitment by the organizations affected. In the absence of a police state it is not possible to attempt to monitor the environmental impacts of all organizational activities at all times. As controls proliferate, the costs to government of monitoring begin to outweight the benefits of protecting the environment. Hence, emphasis tends to be placed on legislation that is designed to ensure compliance by organizations that are easy to target, such as large companies rather than small business, and environmental problems that are easy to focus on, such as point-source pollution of waterways by chemical companies rather than broad runoff water pollution caused by agricultural practices. In summary, while direct environmental regulations may be effective in achieving the goals established, legislated solutions can be inflexible and can impose high administrative costs of compliance on the community.

2. Economic and Administrative Incentives

a. Economic Incentives

One way for government to encourage a moral commitment to consider environmental impacts when organizations make decisions is to provide incentives for good environmental behavior rather than penalties for noncompliance with legislation. There are two main types of incentives to consider: economic and administrative (see Table 2).

Economic instruments are designed to induce rather than direct compliant behavior. Their appeal lies in a shift of responsibility from the regulator to the user, and a focus on the efficient and innovative use of resources to meet environmental quality targets. While legislation is aimed at directly changing the behavior of polluters by fiat, economic instruments aim to make environmentally damaging behavior cost more.

Economic instruments engage only when an organization transacts in a market. In some cases markets have

TABLE 2

Typical Penalties and Incentives Designed
to Protect the Environment

Penalties	Incentives
Economic	*Economic*
Direct user charges	Direct grants and subsidies
Emission and effluent charges	Bounties
Licensing fees	Commissions
Environmental taxes	Environmental tax credits
Tradeable quotas	Tradeable emission rights
Performance bonds and guarantees	Deposit refunds
Proportional noncompliance fees	
Administrative	*Administrative*
Tighter monitoring	Favorable administrative consideration—ease monitoring of compliant organizations
Poor publicity	Prizes and rewards as symbols of good behaviour—ecolabelling, and certificates for the voluntary introduction of environmental management systems
Condemnation	Praise

to be established in order to help solve environmental pollution. Such markets create rights to use environmental resources, or to pollute the environment up to a predetermined limit, and they allow these property rights to be traded. One example is tradeable pollution rights. These rights permit factory emissions into the atmosphere. If an organization owns some of these rights to pollute, but it does not need to pollute up to the maximum permitted because of, say, the introduction of environmentally benign technology, the rights can be sold to another organization that wishes to buy the right to pollute the air. Such an organization might be a new business that is trying to establish itself in a region where the total volume of a particular air pollutant (such as carbon dioxide emissions) has been established and the rights to pollute issued. In practice, the United States is the only country where emissions trading is widely applied, and the aim is to achieve economic efficiency rather than environmental effectiveness. In other words, the aim is to reach a predetermined air quality standard at the least cost to industry, and to promote growth despite restrictions on increasing air pollution.

A number of problems exist with tradeable pollution rights. These include: high administrative costs of establishing and trading in the market; difficulty in establishing the assimilative capacity of the atmosphere for different pollutants; thin trading in pollution rights making quoted prices unrealistic; and the moral problems associated with treating the right to pollute the air as a commodity to be bought and sold for profit when it was previously considered as a common good to be maintained in good condition and to be freely used by all biota.

Opposition to emissions trading suggests that it encourages the view that polluters should decide whether there should be a trade-off between economic development and environmental quality, rather than regulators who represent individuals with inalienable rights to clean air.

Where property rights in markets are already established, market prices can be adjusted to bring about a more desirable outcome than an unfettered market would achieve on its own. Price-based measures are used to achieve optimal levels of environmental damage by internalizing environmental costs in organizations that would otherwise have passed these costs on to third parties by treating environmental resources as a free good.

It is argued that if polluting industries pay for the full cost of the environmental damage they cause, then society is no worse off because the payment can be used to rectify any environmental damage. There are several problems with this argument. First, money obtained from pollution charges is rarely used to correct environmental damage; rather, it is used as general revenue by governments. Even if it was so used it is not clear that the environment could be restored. The case of ozone depletion is illustrative. Certain chemicals released into the atmosphere by industry track into the stratosphere and deplete ozone. Destruction of the ozone layer may threaten the existence of biota. Should industry be allowed to buy pollution rights to release ozone depleting chemicals, such as halons, into the atmosphere? Concern in the world community about the irreversibility of ozone depletion led to the decision that this was not a gas that could be released into the atmosphere at any price. Production and use were banned through international convention, national legislation, and a willingness by industry to find replacement chemicals.

Second, the computation of the environmental costs for which compensation is to be sought is difficult. Environmental accountants are slowly beginning to address this issue. Third, in ethical terms, selling rights to pollute today stands in opposition to the notion of humanity acting as a steward of nature for the benefit of future generations. Likewise, the need for intergenerational equity is one reason why it is argued that future environmental quality should not be determined by those who currently possess the financial resources to buy a current right to pollute. Fourth, the use of economic incentives encourages an anthropocentric rather than an ecocentric approach to resolving environmental problems. Anthropocentric views treat humans as the center focus of analysis, whereas ecocentric views treat human beings as only one part of an ecological system. To an ecocentric, what might be justified from an anthropocentric perspective may have no moral justification. For example, from an anthropocentric view trade in endangered species is to be encouraged using economic incentives to protect and increase numbers of species that will otherwise disappear. From an ecocentric view it is considered unethical to determine the fate of a species based on the amount of profit that can be made from trade. Trade in endangered species is regarded as akin to trade in human slaves.

b. Administrative Incentives

Administrative instruments provide an alternative way of getting organizations to act in a benign way towards the environment. They also rely on the market, but they act to enhance the reputation and the legitimacy of organizations in the view of people operating in the market. Hence, good reputation and increased legitimacy in environmental affairs can command a price premium for an organization, through the moral involvement of shareholders, customers, and employees. A price premium may also be obtained from government as a good environmental performer may have the administrative costs of monitoring by regulators eased. Governments have considerable discretion in the extent to which they enforce the requirements of environmental legislation.

There is a range of administrative incentives available to encourage compliance with government environmental policy. First, as a reward for organizations that are proactive in their consideration of environmental impacts, local and national governments, and international bodies, may reduce the administrative burden of compliance. When an organization has developed a record of good environmental behavior, and has taken effective action to rectify any problems that have come to light, it may be appropriate to demonstrate that a degree of trust exists between the regulator and the regulated. Recognition could be given by reducing the extent and periodicity of monitoring of organizations that have an established record as good performers, or as performers that have gone beyond the legislated standards, or that are industry leaders. This would help reduce their costs of compliance and it would provide

a competitive advantage over organizations that have a record of noncompliance. The problem with this approach is that the system might be open to abuse. Enforcement agencies could be subject to pressure to provide exemptions when they were not merited.

Second, excellence in the presentation and disclosure of information about an organization's environmental performance could be rewarded by the award of a prize and the associated good publicity that would accompany a presentation. For example, in the United Kingdom an annual award is made to the organization publishing the best corporate environmental report. In 1995 the award, made by a professional accounting body, was presented to Thorn EMI. Thorn EMI was praised for presenting a life-cycle assessment of each segment of its business showing the environmental impacts at each stage of the life cycle; for including physical measures of environmental targets and an assessment of the extent to which targets were achieved; for including information about the use of ozone depleting substances; and for reporting separate categories of environmental expenditure during the year. Although there is no clear direct economic benefit to an organization from gaining an award, indirect benefits include improved standing in the community and improved employee motivation, and disclosures reduce the risk that unidentified environmental liabilities might emerge to reduce the wealth of shareholders. Certificates awarded for voluntary implementation of audited internal environmental management systems, and logos for display on environmentally benign products, have similar symbolic effects. Both provide motivation for organizations to internalize the environmental management challenge and to go beyond a strategy of grudging compliance with government legislative requirements.

3. Community Interest Groups

Community interest groups, such as environmental nongovernment organizations (NGOs), play an increasingly important role in bringing pressure on industry to comply with environmental legislation. The reason is that government and industry in many countries respond to public opinion, and public opinion about the environmental record of companies is molded by NGOs. They take direct action to raise awareness about suspected environmental abuses. For example, in 1995 Greenpeace waged a campaign against the Shell Petroleum Company's decision to sink an oil rig in the North Sea. The main impact of Greenpeace was to encourage consumers not to buy Shell's petroleum products, particularly in Europe. The effect was such that eventually Shell was obliged to reverse its decision and it agreed to break the rig up on land. NGOs also attempt to educate the public about poor environmental practices in industry. In the process they bring moral suasion to bear on industry.

4. Third Parties

Banks and insurance companies are also bringing overt pressure on organizations to comply with environmental legislation and to introduce environmental management systems that can identify environmental risks. If property offered as security for a loan has been polluted by toxic waste, the client might go bankrupt. In this case, the bank takes over as mortgagee. In some countries, for example in the United States under the "Superfund" legislation, the bank then could become responsible for the cost of cleaning up the contamination. To avoid this possibility, before they lend money to industry, banks now insist upon an environmental audit of property offered as security by a prospective mortgagee. Similar precautions are taken by banks when they lend to organizations that are involved in takeovers and amalgamations.

Insurance companies provide another example of third-party pressure for improved environmental performance. Before they will issue insurance cover against environmental risks they need to receive evidence that an environmental audit has been undertaken.

5. Codes of Environmental Management Practice and Industry Associations

In the last decade codes of environmental management practice have emerged as a third method of establishing environmental standards and monitoring compliance by organizations. General and industry specific codes dominate. Several countries in the developed world encourage the voluntary adoption of standards set for environmental management by the International Standards Organization (ISO). Best practice environmental management systems are outlined in the ISO14000 series of standards. These were first introduced in Britain as the British Standard BS 7750. Examples of a general code include the International Chamber of Commerce's (ICC) Business Charter for Sustainable Development (see Table 3), and the principles of the Coalition for Environmentally Responsible Economies (CERES), which came into being following the grounding of the Exxon Valdez and the consequent spill of oil in Prince William Sound.

The packaging industry's voluntary Environmental Code of Practice for the post-production impact of new packaging materials provides a case in point (see Table 4). In the Code functions of packaging are identified. These functions include ensuring that products are protected and preserved, waste is minimized, quality, health and safety are assured, retail self-service is promoted, and that stocks are secure prior to sale. But the Code also recognizes that the environmental impact of some new forms of packaging is hard to gauge before their introduction into the marketplace. The bodies responsible for establishing the Code see adherence to it, both literally and in spirit, as applicable to all members of the packing and filling industry. In short, an ethical commitment and a moral responsibility to the new Code, which acts as a supplement to legislation already covering existing packaging materials, is sought from members. Enforcement of the Code resides with an advisory council, which is charged with the task of promoting the Code to industry and developing, assessing, and reviewing implementation measures considered necessary to ensure conformance with the Code by industry. In addition, if a new package does not conform to the code, the council will work with the manufacturer to improve the package on a case-by-case basis.

The chemical industry's Responsible Care Program and its accompanying Code of Practice represent the most sophisticated, advanced, and potentially effective scheme of self-regulation of environmental performance by an industry. Chemical industries in more than 20 countries have established a Responsible Care Program. Anxiety and distrust of the chemical industry, a series of major environmental disasters throughout the world, and the threat of greater government involvement in regulation combined to promote the development of principles that act as statements of intention. These principles can be found in Table 5. Individual organizations evaluate their own performance against these principles, and their reports are collected and used to tell the public how well the industry is doing. Moral suasion, or peer pressure, is used to encourage chemical companies to remain within the program. Lack of compliance with the guidelines can lead to expulsion from the chemical industry association. The importance of the Responsible Care Program is that it is an attempt to introduce industry self-regulation in order to preempt further government regulation.

6. Self-Regulation

Growing concern over environmental problems is leading organizations to consider the acceptance of a moral duty to protect the environment. Government legislation, third-party influences, and codes of practice offering guides to benign environmental action all bring pressure on organizations to go beyond compliance

TABLE 3

International Chamber of Commerce and the Business Charter for Sustainable Development

Principles

1. Corporate priority.
To recognize environmental management as among the highest corporate priorities and as a key determinant to sustainable development; to establish policies, programs, and practices for conducting operations in an environmentally sound manner.

2. Integrated management.
To integrate these policies, programs, and practices fully into each business as an essential element of management in all its functions.

3. Process of improvement.
To continue to improve corporate policies, programs, and environmental performance, taking into account technical developments, scientific understanding, consumer needs, and community expectations, with legal regulations as a starting point; and to apply the same environmental criteria internationally.

4. Employee education.
To educate, train, and motivate employees to conduct their activities in an environmentally responsible manner.

5. Prior assessment.
To assess environmental impacts before starting a new activity or project and before decommissioning a facility or leaving a site.

6. Products and services.
To develop and provide products or services that have no undue environmental impact and are safe in their intended use, that are efficient in their consumption of energy and natural resources, and that can be recycled, reused, or disposed of safely.

7. Customer advice.
To advise, and where relevant educate, customers, distributors and the public in the safe use, transportation, storage, and disposal of products provided; and to apply similar considerations to the provision of services.

8. Facilities and operations.
To develop, design, and operate facilities and to conduct activities that take into consideration the efficient use of energy and materials, the sustainable use of renewable resources, the minimization of adverse environmental impact and waste generation, and the safe and responsible disposal of residual wastes.

9. Research.
To conduct or support research on the environmental impacts of raw materials, products, processes, emissions, and wastes associated with the enterprise and on the means of minimizing such adverse impacts.

10. Precautionary approach.
To modify the manufacture, marketing, or use of products or services, or the conduct of activities, consistent with scientific and technical understanding, to prevent serious or irreversible environmental degradation.

11. Contractors and suppliers.
To promote the adoption of these principles by contractors acting on behalf of the enterprise, encouraging and, where appropriate, requiring improvements in their practices to make them consistent with those of the enterprise; and to encourage the wider adoption of these principles by suppliers.

12. Emergency preparedness.
To develop and maintain, where significant hazards exist, emergency preparedness plans in conjunction with the emergency services, relevant authorities, and the local community, recognizing potential transboundary impacts.

13. Transfer of technology.
To contribute to the transfer of environmentally sound technology and management methods throughout the industrial and public sectors.

14. Contributing to the common effort.
To contribute to the development of public policy and to business, governmental, and intergovernmental programs and educational initiatives that will enhance environmental awareness and protection.

15. Openness to concerns.
To foster openness and dialogue with employees and the public, anticipating and responding to their concerns about the potential hazards and impact of operations, products, wastes, or services, including those of transboundary or global significance.

16. Compliance and reporting.
To measure environmental performance; to conduct regular environmental audits and assessment of compliance with company requirements, legal requirements, and these principles; and periodically to provide appropriate information to the Board of Directors, shareholders, employees, the authorities, and the public.

Source: Willums, J. O., and Goluke, U. (1992). *From ideas to action: Business and sustainable development.* Oslo: International Environmental Bureau of the International Chamber of Commerce.

TABLE 4

Environmental Design Considerations for New Packaging

General principles

7.1 The package should be designed with due regard for its ultimate disposal in order to minimize its impact on the environment.

7.2 The waste management options which should be considered are: reduction, re-use, recycling, disposal.

7.3 It may be useful to include consumer education relating to the package in promotion and marketing materials.

7.4 If the package is to be exported it should be determined whether a special export pack is required to satisfy environmental and other requirements of the export market.

7.5 Consideration as to how the package is to be distributed and whether distribution requires special conditions such as refrigeration should be determined. The impact of the proposed distribution system on the environment and the energy usage of the system should be taken into consideration.

Source: The Packaging and Filling Industry. (1992). *Environmental code of practice for the packaging industry*, pp. 11–12.

with the minimum standards and codes. Ultimately, however, many environmental problems will not be solved without a moral commitment from the individuals who are responsible for organizational activities.

Management philosophies that consider an organization's impact on the environment are being encouraged.

Mention has already been made of the ISO 14000 series, which addresses environmental management systems (EMS). In addition, the present popularity of the philosophy of Total Quality Management (TQM) places emphasis on the need for continuous improvement in processes, products, and services, looks toward the involvement of suppliers and customers in the process of continuous improvement, and reduces the emphasis on inspection-based quality controls.

Adoption of these systems is purely voluntary. Some of the reasons they might be adopted include:

• Organizations adopt environmental management systems in order to control and promote their own activities rather than have them regulated by government;

• Organizations perceive that they can make financial gains by building up an image of being environmentally concerned;

• Voluntary environmental disclosure may lead to improved legitimacy of the organization, especially if reported information puts the organization in a good light;

• The direct costs of collecting and collating environmental information are falling as improvements in information technology facilitate the development of systems to measure and record environmental data; and

TABLE 5

The Responsible Care Program in the Chemical Industry: Statement of Intention

Abiding principles

1. To recognize and respond to community concerns about chemicals and our operations.

2. To operate our plants and facilities in a manner that preserves the environment and protects the health and safety of our employees and the public.

3. To develop and produce chemicals that can be manufactured, transported, used, and disposed of safely.

4. To give health, safety, and environmental considerations priority in our planning for new products and processes.

5. To report information on relevant chemical-related health or environmental hazards promptly to appropriate authorities, employees, customers, and the public, and to recommend protective measures.

6. To give advice to customers on the safe use, transportation, and disposal of chemical products.

7. To increase knowledge by conducting and/or supporting research on the health, safety, and environmental effects of our products, processes, and waste materials.

8. To cooperate with customers, authorities, and affected groups and individuals to resolve problems created by the handling and disposal of chemical substances considered hazardous.

9. To cooperate with government in developing laws and regulations to safeguard the community, the workplace, and the environment; to endeavour to ensure that such laws are based on scientifically supported data and/or expert opinion.

10. To promote these principles and practices by sharing experience and offering assistance to others who produce, handle, use, transport, or dispose of chemicals.

Source: Beder, S. (1993). *The nature of sustainable development*, p. 237. Newham, Australia: Scribe Publications.

TABLE 6

The Advantages and Disadvantages of Legislation and Economic Incentives

Legislation	Economic instruments
Advantages	
• They determine the objectives and means independently of economic factors and market forces.	• They allow each polluter to choose the most effective and efficient way of reducing pollution.
• They are the surest means of preventing irreversible effects or a totally unacceptable level of pollution.	• They provide an incentive to continue reducing pollution in order to reduce costs.
• Their objectives, criteria, and surveillance measures are widely understood.	• They minimize the cost of achieving pollution reductions.
	• They provide finance for other things including restoration of damage.
Disadvantages	
• They may not be the most cost-effective way of ensuring environmental standards are met.	• They depend on trial and error to get the charges for environmental degradation right.
• They do not provide an incentive for polluters to do better than standard.	• Setting up arrangements for supervising and measuring is expensive.
• They are generally difficult to administer, and enforcement of standards depends on the resources available to the regulatory authority.	

Source: House of Representatives Standing Committee on Environment and Conservation (HRSCEC). (1987). *Fiscal measures and the achievement of environmental objectives,* pp. 14–15. Canberra, Australia: AGPS.

• The direct costs of reporting environmental information are falling as experience increases. Experimentation has begun with the disclosure of environmental performance data within annual reports and in separate environmental reports. For example, over a number of years The Body Shop International has produced environmental reports on all aspects of its activities and has published them in *The Green Book*. Thorn EMI, a British company that won a prize for the best environmental report in 1995, includes a summary 4-page environmental report in its annual report and accounts targeted towards investors. The information is gleaned from a separate 36-page environmental report available for the specialist environmentalist.

Some organizations are unlikely to adopt sound environmental management principles voluntarily because:

• Their organization is having financial difficulties, and cannot make the necessary investment in environmentally benign technology;
• Their organization is too small to muster the resources, including specialized skilled personnel.

B. Regulatory Mix

In practice, a combination of these methods is used to achieve the goals of environmental policy. The choice of this combination in any particular country is referred to as the "regulatory mix." For example, when comparing legislation with economic instruments the advantages and disadvantages need to be balanced on a case-by-case basis. An appropriate combination of compliance techniques may sometimes be more effective (see Table 6).

III. PROBLEMS OF MONITORING AND ENFORCEMENT OF STANDARDS

No recognition of compliance by industry can be established unless adequate monitoring, reporting, and inspection takes place. Whatever methods are exacted on industry—legislation, incentives based mechanisms, or self-regulation—monitoring and reporting of environmental performance is crucial. Because it is time-consuming and expensive for governments to monitor each organization directly, and because there has been a change in perceptions about the appropriate scope and means of government intervention in general, indirect and voluntary means have been encouraged in recent years. Successful self-monitoring of the extent of compliance depends upon periodic reports about the environmental performance of each organization. This forms one element of an environmental compliance program.

An environmental compliance program is an organized, systematic approach to ensure that an organization is in compliance with all applicable environmental laws, regulations, and standards. The purpose of a compliance program is to minimize the risk that an organization will have to spend time and resources dealing with environmental problems at some point in the future, or will receive adverse publicity from an environmental disaster caused by the organization. By drawing attention to possible environmental problems it permits managers to act in advance to remove environmental risks to the community, to employees, and to the organization. The concept of ESD gives explicit support to this approach by invoking the proactive "precautionary principle" in environmental management.

An environmental compliance program is necessary when an organization:

- Faces significant environmental risk because of the nature of its industry;
- Has many permits and needs to monitor compliance with the permits where there are administrative benefits to be gained from a good record, or penalties to be incurred in the event of noncompliance;
- Has a poor historical record in relation to its management of environmental matters;
- Has been the subject of previous civil or criminal enforcement actions;
- Has ethical investors who invest only if environmentally responsible behavior can be demonstrated;
- Is anticipating acquisition activity, or the need to undertake insurance against environmental risks.

The main elements of an environmental compliance program include:

- A set of compliance policies that are tailor-made for the organization;
- Compliance audit procedures that are independent of operations, and are designed to identify and correct areas of noncompliance;
- Internal and external reporting systems designed to encourage continuous improvement and innovation in environmental matters;
- A formal identification of who is responsible for organizing a response to environmental emergencies, and who is responsible for provision of "right-to-know" information to the community;
- Education and training for staff responsible for possible environmental mishaps;

- A mechanism for identification, measurement, and disclosure of both positive and negative environmental information;
- Incentive schemes that encourage improved environmental performance; and
- Procedures for classifying environmental expenditures and a mechanism for linking these to responsible individuals or groups.

The key component of an environmental compliance program is a suitable auditing, monitoring, reporting, and tracking system. Demonstration of a successful compliance program can be used as evidence in a defense against any action brought for noncompliance.

One way an organization can demonstrate that it has complied with legislated environmental standards is to publish a Compliance with Standards (CWS) Report, either as part of its annual accounts or in a special environmental report. A CWS Report demonstrates the extent to which an organization has satisfied the various elements of a compliance program.

IV. CONCLUSIONS

As the regulatory mix is gradually extended, ethical issues are growing in significance in the calculus designed to ensure environmental compliance by industry. The global trend in the developed world toward a small public sector means that greater reliance will be placed in the future on voluntary conduct by national and multinational organizations. Voluntary compliance with environmental norms established as a basis for industry performance is likely to continue to be driven by financial incentives as well as by ethical considerations for community welfare.

Also See the Following Articles

ENVIRONMENTAL ECONOMICS • ENVIRONMENTAL IMPACT ASSESSMENT • HAZARDOUS AND TOXIC SUBSTANCES • PRECAUTIONARY PRINCIPLE

Bibliography

Beder, S. (1993). *The nature of sustainable development*. Newham, Australia: Scribe Publications.
Fortune, L. (1994). Environmental Management in Packaging: Responding to the Dream, In D. Shillito (Ed.). *Implementing Environ-*

mental Management: Policy and Techniques. Rugby, UK: Institution of Chemical Engineers.

Gray, R., Owen, D., & Adams, C. (1996). *Accounting and accountability: Changes and challenges in corporate social and environmental reporting.* London and New York: Prentice Hall Europe.

House of Representatives Standing Committee on Environment and Conservation (HRSCEC). (1987). *"Fiscal measures and the achievement of environmental objectives"* Canberra, Australia: AGPS.

Organisation for Economic Co-operation and Development. (1994a). *OECD environmental performance reviews.* United Kingdom and Paris.

Organisation for Economic Co-operation and Development. (1994b). *The distributive effects of economic instruments for environmental policy.* Paris.

Stone, C. D. (1993). *The gnat is older than man: Global environment and human agenda.* Princeton, NJ: Princeton University Press.

Willums, J. O., & Goluke, U. (1992). *From ideas to action: Business and sustainable development.* Oslo, Norway: International Environmental Bureau of The International Chamber of Commerce.

World Commission on Environment and Development. (1987). *Our common future* (The Bruntland Report). Oxford, UK: Oxford University Press.

ENVIRONMENTAL ECONOMICS

Mark Sagoff
University of Maryland

GLOSSARY

contingent valuation methodology (CVM) Surveys and other methods intended to elicit stated preferences from individuals on the basis of which "shadow" or surrogate market prices may be established for goods not priced by markets.

efficiency (allocative efficiency) The allocation of resources to those willing to pay the most for them and, accordingly, those who will benefit most (or benefit others the most) from owning those resources.

existence value The value that an individual attaches to the simple existence of an environmental asset he or she may have no interest in consuming or using.

externality or external cost (or benefit) An uncompensated cost (or benefit) to a person or firm that results from the economic activity—production or consumption—of another. Externalities are prominent forms of "market failure."

free rider A term for an individual who uses a good or service others pay for.

marginal cost or marginal value The addition to total cost (or value) caused by the last incremental unit of production.

market failure The inability of a free market system, because of various structural deficiencies, to allocate resources efficiently.

normative economics Systematic propositions about how economies ought to behave, toward what goals, and on what grounds they should be regulated.

perfect competition A system of exchange in which many firms sell the same products, buyers and sellers are fully informed of the qualities of products and the conditions of trade and property rights in all assets are fully defined and enforced, market entry or exit is easy, and the costs of making transactions are low, among other ideal conditions.

positive economics Predictions, descriptions, and other empirical statements about the performance of economies that in principle may be tested by appeal to facts.

preference A theoretical construct of economic theory covering all the reasons, beliefs, attitudes, habits, character traits, moral principles, desires, and so on that lead people to make choices.

private cost The price an individual pays for the use of a resource.

public goods Goods and services that can be consumed by one individual without diminishing the amount available to others (at least up to a congestion limit) and from which would-be users cannot be excluded.

social cost The cost of an activity to society as a whole, including the cost of "externalities."

transaction cost The cost incurred by willing buyers and sellers in finding each other and agreeing on prices.

welfare (or well-being) That which willingness to pay measures; the generic quantity (sometimes called "utility") people always seek in their economic and other behavior.

ENVIRONMENTAL ECONOMICS has so far enjoyed some successes and has encountered some problems in developing methods to measure the costs and benefits of alternative environmental outcomes. The article begins by explaining that environmental economics is a *normative* as distinct from a *positive* science insofar as it proposes goals (principally *social welfare*) for regulatory policy. The article then introduces the concept of *preference,* which economists use as the building block of social welfare. The ideal of a perfectly competitive market then introduces the thesis that *market failure* causes a divergence between the *private costs* of a transaction (i.e., costs reflected in prices paid by parties to that transaction) and its *social costs* (i.e., those passed on to those not party to the exchange). There follows a brief introduction to the kinds of market failure, such as *externalities, public goods,* and *transaction costs,* thought to justify governmental intervention in or regulation of markets. The article then reviews techniques environmental economists have proposed to help public officials to regulate environmental resources to correct these and other forms of market failure.

The article also identifies problems environmental economics still must resolve. The first of these concerns the extent to which the concept of *welfare* or *well-being,* which economists define in terms of *willingness to pay,* can be related to goods or goals, such as human happiness or contentment, as these concepts are understood by noneconomists. (Critics contend that environmental economists use "welfare" in a technical sense that bears no relation, conceptual or empirical, to what we ordinarily understand by that term.) A second difficulty relates to the possible circularity that arises in the description of preferences. Because preferences are unobservable they are inferred from descriptions of behavior. To describe behavior, however, one must already make

assumptions about the preferences that underlie it. Third, critics question whether economists can assemble information more accurately than markets, however flawed; here the problem of disagreement among experts ("dueling cost-benefit analyses") arises. Finally, in empirical studies, people report that they value environmental goods for ethical, cultural, or spiritual reasons unrelated to their own well-being. It is not clear how these "commitment" values, if unrelated to the individual's welfare, can enter into the social welfare calculus on which environmental economists believe public policy is to be based.

I. EQUITY AND EFFICIENCY

In 1981, President Reagan ordered all federal agencies to refrain from undertaking major regulatory actions "unless the benefits to society from the regulation outweigh the costs." Executive Order 12291, published in the Federal Register on February 10 of that year, sought insofar as possible to replace the cumbersome regulatory contraptions created by statute with scientifically based techniques of policy analysis environmental economists had developed. Environmental economics is the branch of welfare economics that is concerned with helping society to use natural resources in ways that provide the greatest net benefits to society as a whole. Many environmental economists saw Executive Order 12291 as a mandate for the objective evaluation of environmental assets a guide to public policy.

"The basic premises of welfare economics," as Stokey and Zeckhauser observe, "are that the purpose of economic activity is to increase the well-being of the individuals that make up the society, and that each individual is the best judge of how well off he or she is in a given situation." Because each individual is the best judge of his or her own welfare gains or losses, the individual's preferences, measured by his or her *willingness to pay* to satisfy then, indicates the welfare change—gains or losses— the individual expects as a result of a particular environmental decision. Economist A. Myrick Freeman defines "the benefit of an environmental improvement as the sum of the monetary values assigned to these effects by all individuals directly or indirectly affected by that action." Environmental economists Joseph Seneca and Michael Taussig concur, "The *benefit* of any good or service is simply its value to a consumer."

According to the science of welfare economics, as economists Edith Stokey and Richard Zeckhauser explain, "the purpose of public decisions is to promote the welfare of society." They add that "the welfare levels of the individual members of society are the building blocks for the welfare of society." From this perspective, a regulation is rational—it promotes the welfare of society—only it confers on members of society in the aggregate benefits in excess of costs. Because the benefits and costs may well accrue to different individuals, welfare economists recognize two fundamental values in terms of which regulatory policy may be justified. The first is economic *efficiency*, which is to say, the extent to which the benefits of a policy exceed the costs for society as a whole. The second goal is *equity*, that is, the extent to which the distribution of costs and benefits is equitable or fair.

Seneca and Taussig define efficiency as the "maximum consumption of goods and services given the available amount of resources." They characterize equity as "a just distribution of total goods and services among all consumer units." As economist Arthur Okun has written, "To the economist, efficiency implies getting the most out of a given input." He explains: "This concept of efficiency implies that more is better, insofar as the 'more' consists in items people want to buy." Roughly speaking, efficiency in the allocation of resources makes the social pie as big as possible; equity in the distribution of resources fairly divides that pie.

Many economists, such as Okun, propose that economics as a science properly addresses issues of efficiency, while equity concerns may be considered by others, such as politicians and philosophers. Other economists, including Burton Weisbrod, have argued that because preferences over the distribution of wealth seem indistinguishable from other preferences, they might be assimilated into the analysis of overall welfare. Economists could derive social policy scientifically from the preferences of individuals, whether these preferences involve the allocation of resources or the distribution of income. On the other hand, equity concerns may be said to differ from other preferences because they have a public, political, or objective dimension. They reflect what an individual believes is good from the perspective of society as a whole—what is objectively right—not desires about his or her private consumption opportunities. This would seem to be true, however, of many other preferences concerning society, politics, or the environment. Later we shall consider the problem economists encounter in dealing with moral or "commitment" values that express the individual's view of the "good society" rather than of the "good life."

II. THE DIFFERENCE BETWEEN POSITIVE AND NORMATIVE SCIENCE

Environmental economics, as an application of the more general theory of welfare economics, presents itself as a normative discipline. As economists explain, its goal has been "to evaluate the social desirability of alternative allocations of resources" and "to formulate propositions by which we may rank, on the scale of better or worse, alternative economic situations open to society." As a normative discipline, environmental economics distinguishes itself from the "positive" study of the functioning of an economy. "Positive economics is the study of what is," a textbook explains, "normative economics is the study of what ought to be." To describe the way an economy works, offering predictions without evaluations, is the province of positive economics. "However, a study to determine the kind of regulation we ought to adopt for a particular environmental problem is a case of normative economics because it ... involves value judgments."

Normative welfare and therefore environmental economics bases itself on "one fundamental ethical postulate"—that the preferences of individuals are to determine the allocation of resources. "In this framework," economist Alan Randall notes, "preferences are treated as data of the most fundamental kind. Value, in the economic sense, is ultimately derived from individual preferences. ..." Environmental economist A. Myrick Freeman III explains the relation between individual preferences and social value:

> Since the benefits and costs are valued in terms of their effects on individuals' well-being, the terms "economic value" and "welfare change" can be used interchangeably. Society should make changes ... only if the results are worth more in terms of individuals' welfare than what is given up by diverting resources and inputs from other uses.

David Pearce, a prominent British environmental economist, argues that the only values that should count in environmental policy are subjective consumer preferences. He writes: "Economic values are about what people want. Something has economic value—is a benefit—if it satisfies individual preferences." Three economists observe, "Economic value for the society arises from individual preferences which are taken to be exogenously given." Michael Bowes and John Krutilla similarly argue that the goal of environmental policy is to allocate environmental resources "to provide the greatest discounted net present value from the resulting flow of goods and services." To say that environmental economics is a normative science is to note that it prescribes the goal of environmental policy, namely, to give the members of society as much as possible of the things that they believe will improve their welfare, which is to say, the things they want to buy.

III. TWO FRAMEWORKS FOR PUBLIC POLICY

It is important to recognize that the framework of welfare economics is not the only one that has been proposed for justifying environmental policy. James G. March, in his *Primer on Decision-Making* (1994), distinguishes between two conceptions of rational collective choice. He distinguishes between utilitarian or economic (preference-based) and deontological or Kantian (principle-based) decision-making. The *utilitarian* approach, which underlies the science of environmental economics, chooses among given alternatives "by evaluating their consequences in terms of prior preferences." Environmental economists appeal to utilitarian moral theory to justify policies intended to allocate resources to those willing to pay the most for them—and who thus may be supposed to benefit the most (or be able to benefit others) by possessing and using those resources.

James March contrasts utilitarianism with a rule-based or *deontological* approach to policy making. When decision-makers adopt the deontological perspective, according to March, they "pursue a logic of appropriateness, fulfilling identities or roles by recognizing situations and following rules that match appropriate behavior to the situations they encounter." In this context, individuals typically do not ask, "what outcome will most benefit me as an individual?" but, "What do I believe is appropriate for society as a whole, given our shared principles, beliefs, and commitments?" From this perspective, political processes and institutions are supposed to provide the context in which citizens try to convince each other of their views and enact them by majority vote within limits set by political, personal, and civil rights. "The reasoning process," March writes, "is one of establishing identities and matching rules to recognized situations."

What distinguishes these two approaches most fundamentally is the way they regard or interpret disagreement among members of society. The utilitarian understands disagreement as conflict or competition for the use of scarce resources. On this view, resources must be allocated to satisfy "given" wants and desires. The way to resolve conflict, then, is to allocate resources in ways that provides individuals the most of the goods and services they wish to buy.

The opposing approach, which is associated with the eighteenth-century German philosopher Immanuel Kant, analyzes disagreement in terms of the logical opposition of moral or political beliefs. In answering questions such as, "what sort of people are we?" and "what do we stand for as a nation?" individuals express opposing views of the common good rather than reveal their preferences with respect to their personal good. Some citizens may assert that society should maximize welfare, but others may hold, for example, that we are committed as a nation to value nature for its own sake or as a heritage for future generations. From the Kantian perspective, these views about the public interest are not to be assimilated to the self-regarding welfare concerns of individuals. They are to be understood as political assertions about the appropriate goals of public policy.

The two frameworks for decision-making differ, then, in the way they conceive the decision-maker. In the utilitarian perspective, the decision-maker is the individual whose judgments about his or her welfare with respect to consumption opportunities result in sets of preferences over environmental goods, services, and outcomes. The individual functions as the location at which subjective wants or desires are found. The problem of public analysis is therefore to ascertain the preferences of the individuals in the client society and determine the most efficient way to allocate resources to satisfy them. Many economists believe that all rational individuals should agree on this approach, and therefore their hypothetical consent to it may be assumed, because it promises to give them the most of the goods and services for which they are willing to pay.

The opposing deontological approach may accept the precepts of welfare economics as far as the subjective consumption desires of individuals are concerned. The deontologist, however, emphasizes the importance of what people believe or stand for, not just what they desire to consume. In the spirit of the eighteenth-century philosopher J. J. Rousseau, deontological theory regards the individual as a source of judgments, views, or arguments about public policy, that is, as defending conceptions of the common good. In other words, the individual is conceived as a person whose views about public policy are to be weighed on the merits, not as a container of preferences that are to be priced at the margin. Of course, if everyone agreed that the goal of environmental policy is to maximize "welfare," as economists understand that term, there would be little reason for political as distinct from economic decision-making. Because citizens differ in their views and conceptions of public policy, however, they must rely on democratic institutions and processes to sort out disagreements. Democracy is the appropriate political system for those who agree to disagree about the normative and conceptual foundations of public policy.

The deontological view entertains the possibility that citizens will espouse views of the good society and not just preferences concerning their own good. The utilitarian approach, in contrast, regards all such values as subjective preferences directed to personal well-being. Within theoretical framework of welfare economics, only views about policy that are scientifically valid, namely, those of welfare economists, are to be accepted on the merits. This does not mean that environmental economists dismiss the views of others, for example, people who believe that a good society would not trade off the existence of species for economic gain. Rather, these views about public policy are assumed by economists to express a special kind of want or subjective preference—say, an "existence" value—that must be factored into the cost-benefit analysis on which policy is to be based.

Because environmental regulation in our democratic society has not been poetry in motion—regulations can impose great economic costs for modest benefits—environmental economists have welcomed Executive Order 12291 and other administrative attempts to establish the goals of public policy on rational scientific grounds. As one textbook suggests, the move from political to scientific judgment is needed because politicians seek their own good, while economists are dedicated to the good of society as a whole. "It is the politician's job to compromise or seek advantage" while economists and other scientists "produce studies that are ... as objective as possible."

IV. ENVIRONMENTAL ECONOMICS AND MARKET FAILURE

There is a great deal to be said in favor of free markets as instruments for allocating environmental resources. First, we know from experience that free market economies have done a far better job protecting the environment as well as producing wealth than socialist economies, such as the former Soviet Union. Prosperity—for example, full employment, low inflation, low interest rates, and so on—is good for the environment insofar

as it produces wealth needed to control pollution and preserve nature. Few environmentalists, indeed, would endorse centralized planning as an alternative to a free market economy.

Second, free markets encourage individuals to take responsibility for their own choices rather than to seek favors from or lay blame on an all-powerful government. Third and most important, markets function marvelously well in gathering information not available to any public official or agency. The political economist Friedrich Hayek argued that the principal advantage of a market is not the organization of self-interest but the organization of knowledge. Markets thus address "the constitutional limits of man's knowledge and interests, the fact that he *cannot* know more than a tiny part of the whole society."

Political economists in the tradition of Hayek doubt that centralized planners or scientific managers can either master enough information or detach themselves so thoroughly from their own interests and prejudices to allocate resources better than individuals will themselves through voluntary systems of exchange. Hayek notes that the practice of experts to refer to the wants or preferences of individuals

> either as "data" or as "given" (or even by the pleonasm of "given data") often leads economists to assume that this knowledge exists not merely in dispersed form but that the whole of it might be available to some single mind. This conceals the character of competition as a discovery procedure.

Environmental economists, as we have seen, concern themselves primarily with the goal of allocating resources to those who are willing to pay the most for them in order to maximize social welfare. It is important to understand that this goal—*allocative efficiency*—bears little or no relation to the reasons, such as those just listed, that lead many environmentalists to favor a free market system. There is no connection, empirical or conceptual, for example, between allocative (or microeconomic) efficiency and social prosperity. Prosperity, that is, the macroeconomic performance of a society—expressed in measurements of employment, inflation, interest rates, balance of trade, and so on—depends on such things as fiscal and monetary policy, the education and skill levels of citizens, their technological progress and prowess, and so on, far more than on the efficiency of resource utilization for consumption. Some economists believe (following Marx) that efficient markets must drive down prices to costs, eliminating profit and therefore leading to massive unemployment. Others contend, on the contrary, that involuntary unemployment is impossible within efficient markets, because wages will fall sufficiently to clear the labor pool. In fact, nobody knows how to make sense of the macroeconomic effects of allocative efficiency, if there even are such effects. Accordingly, environmental economists, as a rule, make no claims about the relation between microeconomic efficiency, which is their concern, and macroeconomic performance.

Environmental economists, again differing from Hayek and other political economists, put little store by the ability of free markets to gather and utilize information. On the contrary, environmental economics point out that only under certain ideal conditions that rarely if ever hold will decentralized market exchange allocate resources efficiently. Under these ideal conditions, the *private costs* of production and consumption equal the *social costs*. This means that the prices both firms and individuals pay reflect the full costs (including the pollution costs) of producing goods and the full costs (including disposal costs) to society of consuming them. When markets meet these conditions, they are perfectly competitive and will provide exactly the mix of goods and services people most want given the limits imposed by the scarcity of resources.

The conditions that define perfectly competitive or efficient markets, however, may never fully be realized. For markets to function efficiently, property rights in everything anyone wants must be fully defined and enforced. Every would-be party to an exchange must understand its terms and conditions and the qualities of the goods and services for sale. All the costs and benefits associated with a transaction must be captured in the prices paid, so that no uncompensated costs are borne by third parties. Finally, the costs of making transactions cannot be too onerous. In these ideal circumstances, everyone affected by a transaction may be supposed to benefit from it, for otherwise he or she would not have entered into it.

As environmental economists Alan Kneese and Blair Bower wrote in 1972, economic theory "developed on the presumption that virtually everything of value is suitable for private ownership with little or no 'spillover' to other persons, households, and firms when the private property is put to use by its owner." Kneese and Bower added: "Of course, it was realized that sometimes adjustments had to be made for 'market failure,' but these were implicitly, if not explicitly, regarded as minor with respect to the overall allocation." Kneese and Bower, who pioneered the application of welfare economics to environmental policy, wrote that by the 1960s, economists began to recognize that market failures were pervasive and ubiquitous. It had become clear "that the pure private property concept applies satisfactorily to a progressively narrowing range of natural resources and economic activities." Kneese and Bower concluded, "Private property and market exchange have little applicability to their allocation, development, and conservation."

As environmental economists identified more and more ways markets fail with respect to the environment, it became clear to them that the government would have to direct the allocation of environmental resources. Environmental economists therefore developed techniques, some of which we shall discuss presently, to gather the given data concerning individual willingness to pay for environmental goods and services. William Baumol and Wallace Oates, in their popular textbook on environmental policy, for example, argue that with many environmental assets such as clean air, "the process of direct negotiating and agreement will generally be unmanageable." As a result, the government must determine the prices at which these environmental assets may change hands.

In the regulatory agencies, public officials were quick to argue that whatever rules they proposed were needed to "correct" market failures. During the 1960s and 1970s, in academic departments and think tanks, environmentalists joined environmental economists in playing the role of sorcerer's apprentice in the discovery of "external" or third-party "spillover" costs of actions that damaged the environment. Externalities, defined as costs and benefits markets fail to price, flooded the intellectual landscape; they appeared to overwhelm the costs and benefits markets do price, that is, those that are "internalized" or reflected in market prices. And every "spillover" or "unpriced" cost of an action suggested a reason to reallocate resources efficiently, that is, away from actual (as opposed to ideal or hypothetical) market transactions.

During the 1960s and 1970s, environmentalists found the externality argument gave them instant legitimacy within the established legal and scientific culture; therefore they either played down their deontological—that is, ethical and cultural—values, ideals, and commitments or recast them in the language of spillovers, welfare, and willingness-to-pay. Those environmentalists who were motivated by spiritual or moral commitments opposed to a utilitarian ethic found themselves locked in the language of contemporary utility theory. Critics of the "market failure" approach charged, then, that it came primarily "from economists desperately eager to play a more significant role in environmental policy and environmental groups seeking to gain the support of conservatives."

Because market failure stories proved so easy to tell, libertarian economists in the tradition of Hayek have worried that they provide an automatic basis for public officials to second-guess market outcomes. In a book defending the ability of free markets to protect the environment, libertarian economists Terry Anderson and Donald Leal portray the cost-benefit approach of environmental economics as a pathway to collectivism. They write:

> To counter market failures, centralized planning is seen as a way of aggregating information about social costs and social benefits in order to maximize the value of natural resources. Decisions based on this aggregated information are to be made by disinterested resource managers whose goal is to maximize social welfare.

According to Anderson and Leal, environmental economics "stresses the potential for market failure in the natural resource and environmental arena on the grounds that externalities are pervasive." They add: "Economic analysis in general and natural resource economics in particular, have approached resource policy as if there were a 'socially efficient' allocation of resources that will be reached when scientific managers understand the relevant trade-offs and act to achieve an efficient solution." Anderson and Leal argue in the spirit of Hayek that resource managers cannot acquire "the 'correct' information about resource values" in order to find "the socially optimal allocation." Managers often disagree, moreover, especially when hired to defend opposing positions. Opposing sides to a policy are able to present opposing cost-benefit analyses. Anderson and Leal deny, therefore, that cost benefit analysis, which they equate with "scientific management" and "centralized planning," will succeed any better than actual markets, however flawed, in allocating resources.

V. THE MANY FACES OF MARKET FAILURE

"The assertion of market failure," one economist writes, "is probably the most important argument for government intervention." Another agrees: "It is the failure of the market system to allocate and price resource and environmental services correctly that creates the need for economic measures of values to guide policy making." A third states that any governmental intervention to achieve environmental goals

> should be based on the existence of a market failure (an "externality"). An "externality" is a cost that is borne by a person other than the person who caused the cost to arise. ... Absent market failure, environmental degradation is not by itself sufficient to justify governmental action.

Among the kinds of market failure, three are the most prominent. They are *externalities, public goods,* and *transaction costs.* An externality arises, for example, when a cement company casts its dust on its neighbors without obtaining their consent. It will be able to charge less for cement than a company that purchases pollution control equipment or compensates its neighbors. As a result of this uncompensated cost, more cement will be produced relative to clean air than people want. Anderson and Leal summarize:

> Market failure is said to result when any benefits are not captured or costs are not borne by decision makers. The existence of these externalities or third-party effects means that either too little of a good is produced in the case of uncaptured benefits or too much in the case of unborne costs. ... Such under- or over-production is often taken as a sufficient condition for taking political control of resource allocation.

A second form of market failure arises when assets are not privately owned but belong as property to no one or to the public in common. Everyone can benefit from these *public goods* (national defense is an example) whether or not he or she pays for them. Those who own private property—a painting, for example—can charge people to see or use it and can exclude people from having access to it. The consumption of a private good involves rivalry or competition, moreover, because if one person puts the painting in his or her home, another cannot. Public goods, such as highways or sidewalks, if open to one, are open to all. Thus, individuals have an incentive to *free ride,* that is, to use the public resource while letting others pay for it. Once again, one is tempted to reap the benefits oneself while imposing on others the costs of providing or maintaining the resource.

If everyone can access a public environmental good—wild fish stocks, for example, or clean air—people tend to use as much of them as they can while paying nothing for the privilege. As a result, the resource will be overused, for example, as more and more people try to capture it for themselves. The air will get dirtier, the wild stocks of fish become depleted, roads congested, and so on, as the logic of this well-understood "tragedy of the commons" works itself out. To avoid depletion and overpollution, economists recommend that the "commons" be privatized or that a regime be established to impose on those who use the resource a charge reflecting its value to others and to society in general.

Finally, *transaction* or *bargaining costs* (sometimes described in terms of "isolation paradoxes") constitute the most general reason market prices may fail to allocate resources efficiently. Suppose a cement company moves into a neighborhood destroying its amenity by creating fumes, dust, noise, and so on. Each of the neighbors may be willing to pay an amount that, in the aggregate, would be sufficient to bribe the plant owners to locate elsewhere, but the costs of organizing themselves, overcoming free-rider problems, and bargaining with the company may defeat these disorganized or isolated individuals. In general, millions of people may each be willing to pay a small amount that, when added together, would purchase many environmental goods, but no one will incur the costs of contacting everyone, taking up a collection, and bargaining for the good in question.

Many economists believe on theoretical grounds that all forms of market failure can be analyzed in terms of transaction costs. Polluters would pollute only to optimum levels, for example, if their victims could costlessly organize themselves to pay them not to pollute or to demand compensation, depending on the way legal or property rights are initially distributed. Nobel laureate Ronald Coase explained that in the absence of transaction costs people will always negotiate to the same outcome (an agreement that maximizes wealth) no matter how property rights are initially distributed, or even if no such rights exist. George J. Stigler dubbed this result the Coase Theorem, which he formulated as follows: "... under perfect competition, private and social costs will be equal."

In the light of the Coase Theorem, the principal question of environmental economics may be put this way: How would individuals allocate environmental resources in the absence of transaction costs? This is a way of asking how a perfectly competitive market would allocate those resources. Three strategies suggest themselves for answering this question. First, we might try to reform institutional arrangements to minimize transaction costs, for example, by building up the infrastructure of associations and organizations in civil society

capable of negotiating solutions to environmental conflicts. The field of institutional economics takes up this kind of concern. Second, environmental economists are developing complex scientific techniques, such as contingent valuation methodology, which we shall discuss presently, to determine what people would pay in a market if they could organize themselves costlessly to bid for environmental assets, goods, and services. Finally, we might accept the status quo, where people do the best they can to negotiate in markets and may also regulate behavior through the political process.

Because there is no ideal market against which we can test predictions about what individuals would do in the absence of transaction costs, disagreements over the "correct" price of any resource are in principle unresolvable. Economists themselves incur costs, moreover, when they undertake cost-benefit analyses and employ other scientific techniques to determine how much individuals will pay for public goods in hypothetical markets. These costs mount as more and more economists are hired as expert witnesses in litigation over opposing cost-benefit analysis. For example, public officials estimate that they have spent more than $100 million to assess the natural resource damage caused by the *Exxon Valdez* incident, although the costs of determining the value even of a single oil-soaked otter may be unlimited, as long as "deep pockets" exist to support different scientific estimates. Accordingly, a lively debate has arisen whether environmental economists are better positioned than individuals themselves to overcome transaction costs and thus to determine the "true" or "correct" prices of resources.

Economist C. J. Dahlman argues that the fact that markets fail hardly shows "that there is good reason for assuming that somebody else, outside the market, can do it better." Charles Perrings, who is associated with the emerging discipline of ecological economics, observes that the cost-benefit approach rests "on an ideological assumption that the state has privileged knowledge of the ... optimal outcome, and is better equipped, informationally, to achieve it." He asks whether official experts can deal with transaction costs better than individuals. Perrings adds, "The implication is that if neither the state nor any other nonmarket agency can do it better, then there is no difference between private and social cost and no cause for believing an external effect to exist."

VI. AIR POLLUTION: AN EXAMPLE

Pollution control provides a clear example of the opposition between utilitarian and deontological or rule-based conceptions of collective choice. A utilitarian approach regards pollution primarily as an "external" or "social" cost of production and therefore may seek to "internalize" this cost in prices paid for goods and services that pollute. A Kantian perspective, in contrast, regards pollution as a form of coercion, invasion, or trespass to be regulated as a violation of the rights of person and property. From this perspective, pollution constitutes a tort or nuisance—like a punch in the nose. Thus, pollution control protects the rights of individuals against trespass, which is not the same thing as—indeed, it may conflict with—satisfying their consumer desires or preferences.

If society adopted a utilitarian approach, it would bring pollution up or down to "optimal" levels, that is, levels at which the benefits of controlling pollution further do not equal the costs. A Kantian framework, in contrast, minimizes pollution until the cost of further reductions become prohibitive. Both common law and public law in the United States take this deontological approach to pollution. For this reason, as economists Maureen Cropper and Wallace Oates observe, "the cornerstones of environmental policy in the United States," such as the Clean Air and Clean Water Acts, "*explicitly* prohibited the weighing of benefits against costs in the setting of environmental standards."

The Clean Air Act of 1970 required the then new Environmental Protection Agency (EPA) to set standards for a list of "criteria" pollutants to assure that air pollution would not endanger public health or welfare or harm even particularly sensitive individuals. In calling for "an adequate margin of safety," Congress pretended that safe thresholds for air pollutants could be found and that NAAQS could come under these levels. Congress knew at the time that no such levels existed; nevertheless, it set EPA to the task of ratcheting pollution down to safe standards even at considerable cost to society.

To understand this, one might consider the case of *Boomer* vs. *Atlantic Cement Company,* which played in the New York State courts as Congress worked on the Clean Air Act. There, plaintiff Boomer, a farmer, sought to enjoin Atlantic, a major manufacturer, from spewing dust and fumes on his land. New York State is a jurisdiction that usually grants injunctions in nuisance cases. In this instance, however, the trial court awarded Boomer compensatory damages instead, because in order to cease polluting, Atlantic, an immense plant supporting the local economy, would have to cease operations. Thus, the court effectively gave the polluter the power of eminent domain—the power to coerce the plaintiff off his land at a price set not by the plaintiff but by the court.

What the court did was efficient from an economic point of view: it allocated resources according to market-based prices. This approach establishes economically "optimal" levels of pollution—levels at which those who benefit from polluting activities could still benefit even after compensating their victims for whatever damage they suffer. These "optimal" levels, however, can be understood only in terms of a hypothetical market where people will always sell property rights to the highest bidder—not in terms of an actual market where people like Boomer just want to be left alone. By denying Boomer injunctive relief, the court departed from the common law protection of property rights to give the polluter effectively the right of eminent domain to coerce its neighbors off their land at a price set by appraisers and not by the neighbors themselves.

Many commentators believe that in enacting the Clean Air Act, Congress in part reacted against the outcome of *Boomer* to insist that the nation regard pollution not as an external cost of production but as an enjoinable nuisance or tort. The Clean Air Act, in setting air quality standard at "no-risk" levels, treated persons as ends-in-themselves rather than as means in the overall maximization of social wealth. Executive Order 12291 and the cost-benefit criterion it imposed then sought to replace the health and safety based imperatives set by statute with the efficiency goals suggested by welfare economics.

VII. THE VALUE OF BIODIVERSITY: A SECOND EXAMPLE

Congress passed the Endangered Species Act (ESA) in 1972 to prevent or at least greatly to slow the extinction of species in the United States. The Fish and Wildlife Service has since listed about 956 species as endangered in the United States. No market player—for example, food, pharmaceutical, or seed company—has acted to protect habitat in the expectation that one or another of these creatures might prove useful. Are there economic benefits that justify the costs of species preservation?

Everyone knows that biodiversity as a whole or in general is essential to all life (indeed, it *is* all life), but this is irrelevant to economic value, which is always computed at the margin, that is, as a relation between supply and demand. For example, carbon, which is found in all organic compounds, is essential to life. Yet the economic value of carbon is computed "at the margin," for example, as the price of a lump of coal.

One might argue that species by sustaining ecosystems possess economic or instrumental value. This may apply to prevalent species, such as worms, but no endangered species has been shown uniquely to support any ecological or other economic service. What such function, for example, does the American burying beetle, a listed species, perform? What ecosystem service on which we depend would collapse in its absence? As biologist David Ehrenfeld, the former editor of *Conservation Biology,* argues:

> Even a mighty dominant like the American chestnut, extending over half a continent, all but disappeared without bringing the eastern deciduous forest down with it. And if we turn to the invertebrates, the source of nearly all biological diversity, what biologist is willing to find a value—conventional or ecological—for all 600,000-plus species of beetles?

The lack of market demand for all or virtually all endangered species in the United States confronts environmental economists with a dilemma. They could conclude that it is simply irrational for the nation to preserve endangered species. Yet the Endangered Species Act is immensely popular. In surveys, Americans by large majorities agree with the statement that destroying species is wrong because God put them on this earth. Some commentators conclude, "It seems that divine creation is the closest concept American culture provides to express the sacredness of nature." The ESA appears, then, to reflect an obligation that Americans believe the nation ought to respect. This moral rule calls on us to preserve species for their own sake, not for the benefits they provide us.

Rather than declare species protection to be irrational, environmental economists have recognized the need to bring moral, spiritual, and other nonconsumption values into the welfare calculus. They have sought to show, therefore, that extinction is a kind of market failure. Environmental economists generally argue that markets fail to "price" plants and animals correctly because "biodiversity is a public good." From an economic perspective, the authors of the monumental *Global Biodiversity Assessment* declare, "the allocation of biological resources on the basis of market signals is inefficient." They conclude that "governments might intervene to correct the signals to private resource users."

The concept of a "public good" plainly does apply to some animals, such as tigers and whales, that people hunt in the wild. Economists quite properly recommend that private property regimes replace the rule of capture with respect to those organisms, such as salmon or halibut, that people seek to consume. Regulations that limit harvests by restricting access respond to the familiar problem of the commons.

Hunting and gathering wild plants and animals, however, is only an occasional cause of extinction these days. Endangered species are not generally threatened because humans consume or directly use them. The problem is that humans, having no use for these creatures, wish to convert their habitats in economically profitable ways. Not hunting but habitat destruction or loss threatens the vast majority of endangered species.

Endangered species, moreover, like paintings, some of which hang in museums and some in private homes, often are found on property a government or an individual owns. The owners of property control access to these species, just as the owners of private and public galleries control access to art. As of 1993, about 80% of all species listed as endangered in the United States had some or all of their habitat on private land. Plants that grow on a person's land—flowers in one's garden, for example—seem to be examples of private not public goods. Even if species that reside on one's land are endangered, they seem to share the same properties of private goods—for example, rivalry and excludability in consumption—that belong to the ordinary flora and fauna found there.

Environmental economists generally reply that endangered species, even when found on private lands, are public goods because individuals are willing to pay to protect them, but this willingness to pay may be so dispersed that these individuals cannot make it effective by purchasing habitat. As a result, environmental economists have developed methodologies to assess "existence" and other values that express moral, cultural, and religious commitments to goals other than personal welfare or well-being—goals people associate with the good of society rather than their own good. Much current theoretical work in environmental economics concerns the measurement of these "non-use" values. This theoretical research has encouraged economists to bring into the welfare calculus the moral, aesthetic, and cultural commitments of Americans to goals other than welfare.

VIII. EXISTENCE AND OTHER NONUSE VALUES

Over the last 20 years, resource economists have sought to find ways to bring into the social welfare calculus moral, religious, and other principled commitments to goals other than personal consumption. In the 1960s, environmental economists observed that individuals derive satisfaction when they forego material consumption to support policies they believe are intrinsically right. "There are many people who obtain satisfaction from the mere knowledge that part of wilderness North America remains," John Krutilla wrote, "even though they would be appalled by the prospect of being exposed to it."

Building on Krutilla's theoretical insight, economists have developed many concepts—including "existence," "vicarious benefit," "bequest," and "stewardship" values—to capture in welfare terms amounts people are willing to pay for policies for reasons other than their own consumption opportunities. Much of the theoretical research in environmental economics during the past decade has concerned the problem of assigning "shadow" (i.e., hypothetical market) prices to these moral beliefs or ethical principles. Contingent valuation methodology (CVM) uses surveys to elicit individual willingness to pay (WTP) for environmental public goods. This method, which involves direct questioning of respondents, has inspired a large literature responding to many technical problems of measurement that cannot be considered here.

The CV approach appears most applicable to those preferences that reflect self-interested goals, for example, an individual's desire to obtain a "warm glow" or sense of psychic satisfaction in knowing certain species exist. In these instances, a connection holds between the "existence" value of species and the welfare or well-being of individuals. Thus, insofar as economists are concerned about the welfare effects of environmental policies, their surveys should ask how much individuals would pay for the "warm glow," or psychic income, or other personal benefit associated with environmental protection. As a rule, however, these surveys inquire how much people are willing to pay simply to protect species or to secure other nonconsumption goods. As long as people care about environmental goals for reasons besides their own advantage, however, the survey results would have no clear relation to their welfare or well-being.

Empirical research has found that "responses to CV questions concerning environmental preservation are dominated by citizen judgments concerning social goals and responsibilities rather than by consumer preferences." Responses to CV surveys reveal "social or political judgments rather than preferences over consumer bundles." A careful study by two economists concurred that ethical commitments often dominate economic or welfare considerations in responses to CV surveys. "Our results provide an assessment of the frequency and seriousness of these noneconomic considerations: They are frequent and they are significant determinants of WTP responses."

That a person's desires "are all *his* desires," as philosopher Mark Overold has written, "does not seem sufficient for saying that satisfying one or all of them would promote his welfare." On the contrary, the principled beliefs on the basis of which individuals form environmental values may reflect spiritual, religious, moral, political, cultural, and other commitments that bear no clear connection to benefits individuals may expect themselves. Critics have concluded that "existence" and other non-consumption values are unrelated to personal welfare or well being and thus to the welfare goals of environmental economics.

As philosopher Ronald Dworkin has pointed out, most Americans attribute intrinsic value to natural objects such as other species. We "think we should admire and protect them because they are important in themselves, and not because we or others want or enjoy them." Economist Amartya Sen has observed that our commitment to moral values drives a "wedge between personal choice and personal welfare," although "traditional economic theory relies on the identity of the two."

IX. THE RELATION BETWEEN WILLINGNESS TO PAY AND WELL-BEING

If distributive or equity goals are considered separately, environmental economists believe that human welfare or well-being is the only object that has intrinsic value for the purposes of public policy. (Economists such as Burton Weisbrod have pointed out that equity concerns are also preferences for which people are willing to pay and so may be folded into the cost-benefit calculus on the same basis as any other good.) When one considers what mainstream economists mean by "welfare"—the satisfaction of preferences taken as they come bounded by indifference and ranked by willingness to pay—one may ask why it provides a normative basis (indeed, the only normative basis) of environmental policy. The term "welfare," as used by economists, has no connection, either logical or empirical, with concepts such as contentment or happiness. Having a preference (for example, to smoke a cigarette) may give the individual who has it a reason to try to satisfy it. Why has society a reason, however, to satisfy these personal or private desires?

The central normative postulate of environmental economics asserts that preferences should direct allocation. The postulate rests on the assumption that insofar as a person's preferences are satisfied, his or her well-being is increased. The term "satisfy" is used in this context in the mathematical sense in which equations or conditions are "satisfied." The unexamined postulate of welfare economics is that to "satisfy" a preference in this *mathematical* sense is also to satisfy a person in the *psychological* sense of making him or her happier or more content.

Empirical studies show, however, that once people meet their basic needs, they do not become happier or more content as their income increases and therefore they are more able to satisfy their preferences. Social research confirms what common wisdom suggests: Money and with it preference satisfaction do not buy happiness. One review concludes, "Studies of satisfaction and changing economic conditions have found overall no stable relationship at all." Those "who win large sums of money in football pools or lotteries are not found to be on the whole more happy afterwards."

Contentment depends more on the quality of one's desires and on one's ability to overcome them, than on the extent to which they are satisfied. The things that make one happy—friends, family, achievement, health—depend on virtue and luck; they are not for sale. Consumption does not produce contentment. A philosopher explains, "this is virtually inevitable because the faster preferences actually *are* met, the faster they escalate."

A legal theorist correctly notes that the "most important thing to bear in mind about the concept of value [in the welfare economist's sense] is that it is based on what people are willing to pay for something rather than the happiness they would derive from having it." If social welfare is defined as a function of "what people are willing to pay for something" rather than "the happiness they would derive from having it," it is not surprising that a policy that allocates resources to those willing to pay the most will maximize welfare. The goal of maximizing well-being—if "well-being" is merely a function of willingness-to-pay—merely restates but does not justify the goal of allocating resources to those willing to pay the most for them.

Welfare economists, in other words, offer no method for measuring changes in well-being other than willingness-to-pay. Thus, for them, the relation between willingness-to-pay and improvements in well-being is a stipulative or definitional rather than a contingent or testable one. Accordingly, "welfare" is just another name—a proxy or a stand-in—for "efficiency." By allocating resources to satisfy the preferences of those who are willing to pay the most for them, society will, of course, maximize social welfare, because "social welfare" is itself defined in terms of the satisfaction of those preferences.

If one could assume that the individual always prefers what he thinks will increase his or her well-being, then the relation between well-being and preference might be more than a stipulative one. But surveys have shown again and again that people value objects and outcomes for many reasons besides the benefits they offer them. The question then arises if these reasons—for example, a moral obligation to protect individuals from the "trespass" of pollution or to prevent extinction—offer as important grounds for policy as the satisfaction of "given" preferences on the basis of willingness to pay. The ESA, the Clean Air Act, and other environmental statutes apparently base policy on deontological rather than utilitarian grounds—on principles rather than on preferences. For the environmental economist, however, the goals of public must be utilitarian for otherwise they would be irrational. If we take this scientific position, we must base public policy not on the moral principles implicit in public law but on the given data of private preferences. The objective description of these data is at present the principal preoccupation of the science of environmental economics.

X. CAN PREFERENCES BE DETERMINED?

One of the most difficult technical problems confronting environmental economists is that of identifying the preferences that motivate behavior. This problem arises because preferences, being private psychological states, are not directly observable. Indeed, of all the factors that determine action—long-term goals, habits, beliefs, mistakes, impulses, obligations, hopes, fears, and so on—preferences may not figure prominently. Preference may best be understood as a theoretical construct of welfare economics inferred from descriptions of behavior, not as a mental entity otherwise of interest to psychologists.

Economists infer preferences from descriptions of behavior. Behavior, however, does not describe itself; indeed, the bodily actions of an individual can be interpreted in any number of ways. Every object one might choose, moreover, possesses an indefinite number of qualities, any one of which might motivate that choice. Everything we do may be explained in the context of a thousand impinging concerns unique to the person and the situation. It would be hard for the individual to reconstruct the alternatives he or she chose among and thus to describe the exact choice he or she made. Welfare and environmental economists circumvent this problem by stipulating the "opportunity set" and by describing the choice and then inferring a preference from that description. But choices are rarely if ever transparent or obvious, and even the greatest psychoanalysts have despaired at plumbing the soul.

XI. ENVIRONMENTAL ECONOMICS AS APPLIED ETHICS

From the perspective of applied ethics, the problem with the normative policy sciences is that there are so many of them. Libertarians, Marxists, utilitarians, egalitarians, Kantians, and others propose "foundations" for various areas of the law; they disagree not only with each other but also with legal realists, economic determinists, and environmental catastrophists. The deep ecologist who sees the earth as an organism thinks he or she is just as objective—just as scientific—as the economist who speaks in terms of commodities. There may be as many objective and scientific views of any policy question as there are opinions, since nobody believes his or her view is only a subjective preference.

Because so many scientific positions contend for political vindication, as philosopher John Rawls has argued, the conception of justice in a constitutional democracy "should be, so far as possible, independent of controversial philosophical and religious doctrines." Democratic political processes provide the best means we know to work out controversies about the philosophical basis of public policy. Welfare and environmental economics presents one controversial doctrine about the appropriate goals of public policy. The goal of maximizing the satisfaction of preferences taken as

they come and as determined by experts may be an important one. It must be defended, however, against other approaches to environmental policy, for example, deontological views of pollution as an enjoinable tort and extinction as a kind of crime. These alternative views of public policy have carried the day in Congress. They are based on moral and community-regarding judgments at least as worthy of consideration on their merits as are the opinions of environmental economists. Instead, economists too often dismiss these opposing views as weird kinds of nonconsumption consumer preferences that markets have failed to price and for which they must therefore develop techniques of elicitation and measurement.

Also See the Following Articles

BIODIVERSITY • CONSUMER RIGHTS • DEVELOPMENT ETHICS • ENVIRONMENTAL COMPLIANCE BY INDUSTRY • RESOURCE ALLOCATION

Bibliography

Cropper, M. L., & Oates, W. E. (1992). Environmental economics: A survey. *Journal of Economic Literature* **30**, 675–740.

Freeman, A. M. III. (1993). *The measurement of environmental and resource values.* Washington, DC: Resources for the Future.

Hausman, J. A. (Ed.). (1993). *Contingent valuation: A critical assessment.* Amsterdam: North Holland Press.

Kahneman, D. & Varey, C. (1991). Notes on the psychology of utility. In J. Elster and J. Roemer (Eds.), *Interpersonal Comparisons of Well-Being*, pp. 127–163. New York: Cambridge University Press.

March, J. G. (1994). *A primer in decision making.* New York: The Free Press.

Perrings, et al. (1995). Economic values of biodiversity. Pp. 823–914 In Heywood, V. H. (Ed.), *Global Biodiversity Assessment*, pp. 823–914. Cambridge: Cambridge University Press.

Sagoff, M. (1994). Should preferences count? *Land Economics* **70**(2), 127–144.

Tietenberg, T. H. (1994). *Economics and environmental policy.* Brookfield, VT: E. Elgar.

U.S. Environmental Protection Agency. (1991, March). *Economic Incentives: Options for Environmental Protection.* Report of Economic Incentives Task Force, Ch. 1. Washington, DC: EPA Doc. #21P-2001.

ENVIRONMENTAL ETHICS, OVERVIEW

Robin Attfield
University of Wales Cardiff

GLOSSARY

anthropocentrism The theory of normative ethics that locates independent value solely or predominantly in human interests, as opposed to nonhuman interests.

anthropogenic Originating from human beings, or originated by their actions.

biospheric egalitarianism The theory that every living organism in the system of ecosystems of the planet (biosphere) has the same moral significance.

biotic community A community consisting of living organisms, such as the community of all of Earth's creatures.

ecofeminism A branch of feminism that unites ecological and feminist themes.

ecology (a) The science of biological systems and communities. (b) The kind of concern or activism that focuses on interactions between humanity and the natural environment or ecological systems.

ecosystem A localized and generally self-regulating system of interacting living and nonliving organisms, such as a wetland or a forest.

intrinsic value Value that is neither instrumental nor in any other way derivative, and that depends entirely on the nature of its bearer.

metaethics The study of the nature and status of valuational and ethical claims and discourse.

moral significance The degree to which a creature's interests warrant moral consideration or carry moral weight.

moral standing (or considerability) The property of being worthy of moral consideration or respect.

natural environment The environment (partly living, partly nonliving) either of particular human beings or groups or of humanity in general, insofar as it remains significantly unmodified by human activity. Also the ecosystems or the system of ecosystems which environ humanity and other living species, comprising the terrestrial (or planetary) biosphere.

patriarchy The domination of society by the power of males.

Precautionary Principle The principle that action, involving the best available technology, or in other cases prohibitions of action, may justifiably be adopted to avert environmental harm in advance of the availability of scientific evidence confirming that harm.

quantum physics The study of subatomic phenomena (and their discrete charges of energy, or quanta), including the indeterminate behavior of electrons, as discovered by Werner K. Heisenberg.

sentient creature A living organism capable of feeling pleasure or pain, and/or capable of suffering, and/or capable of having emotions.

speciesism Discrimination for or against organisms on the sole basis of their species.

sustainable development Development that meets the needs of the present generation without compromising the ability of future generations to meet their own needs. Or alternatively, desirable socioeconomic change capable of being sustained into the indefinite future without undermining either other desirable socioeconomic processes or natural species and ecosystems.

———————

ENVIRONMENTAL ETHICS consists of the study of normative issues and principles relating to human interactions with the natural environment (and, to some extent, to this environment as modified by previous human activity, e.g., through agriculture and human settlements), and to their context and consequences. It forms a crucial area of applied ethics—crucial for the guidance of individuals, corporations, and governments in determining the principles affecting their policies, lifestyles, and actions across the entire range of environmental issues. It is equally crucial for the appraisal of such actions, lifestyles, and policies.

I. WHAT IS ENVIRONMENTAL ETHICS?

Sometimes the phrase "environmental ethics" is used, contrary to the previous definition, to refer simply to the quality of people's behavior insofar as it relates to the natural environment. However, if this were held to be the central meaning of "environmental ethics," the implication would be that ethics consists of (ethically significant) behavior, that ethical principles are invariably manifested in people's conduct, and perhaps also that no critical study of normative ethics is possible. While the usage just mentioned has to be acknowledged, it is important that there are also other uses of the phrase "environmental ethics" which concern not just such behavior, but also the normative principles applicable to it and their critical study. This critical study is standardly known as "environmental ethics," the subject of this overview.

Environmental ethics is sometimes defined instead as the kind of approach to environmental issues which finds independent value to be located not only in the interests of sentient creatures—creatures which can feel pleasure or pain—but also in natural living creatures (or in their good) in general, or in the natural world in general. While many influential philosophies are committed to this approach, many others are not, and base their justifications on the interests of sentient creatures only. Since the latter kind of approach is the approach of many environmentalists, and undeniably offers both specifications of environmental problems and solutions to them, it is advisable not to adopt a definition of "environmental ethics" which treats this approach (let alone more limited approaches) as lying outside environmental ethics. In this way, the debate about the location of independent value can continue to take place within environmental ethics, and the boundaries of the subject or discipline of environmental ethics avoid being treated as themselves a battleground about values. Also environmental ethics can be allowed to be a neighbor of, e.g., health-care ethics or business ethics, concerned about a different sphere, but not a rival discipline with essentially different values of its own.

While environmental ethics is distinguished by its sphere rather than its values, its sphere has made it much more alert than ethics has traditionally been to the interests both of future generations and of nonhuman creatures. Where the interests of coming centuries used to be neglected in general theories of normative ethics, such neglect has now become unsustainable, and this is at least partly due to several pioneering works in environmental ethics. Meanwhile the anthropocentrism of traditional ethics has widely been modified so that at least sentient interests are taken into account, as a result, not least, of the work of philosophers such as Peter Singer and Tom Regan. Thus environmental ethics tends to stress the interests both of future generations and of nonhumans. Meanwhile anthropocentric philosophers are increasingly aware that they hold a minority position in normative ethics, which stands in need of defense.

II. THE SCOPE OF ENVIRONMENTAL ETHICS

The scope of environmental ethics is as extensive as its sphere: the realm of actions, policies, and lifestyles which impact on the natural environment, together with their contexts and their consequences, and the principles and attitudes which underlie these actions, lifestyles, and policies. The spatial extent of its scope is at least as extensive as the biosphere of planet Earth, if not larger, for space probes and their related debris result from human interactions with nature, and have extended the realm of environmental ethics to distant zones of the solar system. On the other hand, abiotic (nonliving) nature is not usually regarded as a principal concern of environmental ethics, at least not for those theories of value which find no value where there is no life, for in lifeless realms there is nothing which can be harmed or benefited. However, philosophers who locate value either in abiotic nature or in nature in its entirety are consistent in including in environmental ethics human impacts on distant stars and galaxies, however long delayed they may be.

The temporal scope of environmental ethics extends for as long as human action can exercise any kind of impact, and as long as something of value remains on which significant impacts can be made. While this may sound like a purely theoretical point, nuclear energy generation and experimentation is already bringing into being radioactive substances with half-lives of millions of years, with predictable harmful effects on almost any living creature which comes into contact with them. Hence the temporal scope of environmental ethics turns out probably to transcend the future existence of humanity, in that its reasoning concerns the long-delayed impacts of current and of projected policies; only on an anthropocentric theory could nothing of value be affected for good or ill after humanity becomes extinct. This means that normative ethics, which used to be preoccupied with such localized problems as the returning of misdirected postal packages, cannot now avoid comprehending vast tracts of space and time if it is to be seriously applied to current practice.

Environmental ethics also studies the past in order to discover the traditions which often underlie current values, and which often turn out to supply limits to possible change in ethical attitudes or resources for such change. The rediscovery of past ways of life, or the discovery of historical saints or heroes, whether in our own culture or in alien cultures, can facilitate present imitation; the discovery of factors which have suppressed desirable patterns of living can generate powerful movements of present resistance. While environmental ethicists need to beware the invention of fictitious pasts, there remains an important ethical component to environmental history.

Fictional utopias, however, should not be considered irrelevant. Depictions of possible worlds or of possible communities living more harmoniously with nature ("ecotopias") comprise a further part of the scope of environmental ethics. They have to be scrutinized, however, for their consistency, and for adverse side effects which their nonfictional adoption might generate; the work of ethicists is seriously incomplete if such scrutiny is neglected. Yet this very exercise shows how environmental ethics is not confined to the actual past or future; counterfactual judgments, ones relating to thought experiments and to the possible rather than to the facts of history or of science, are frequently indispensable when normative theories need to be appraised.

III. ORIGINS OF MODERN ENVIRONMENTAL ETHICS

The widespread acceptance in the late 19th century of Charles Darwin's theory of evolution by natural selection made possible a recognition of the interdependence of living species, and, relatedly, of the extent of the unintended side effects of human action. The perceived importance of preserving tracts of wild nature led to the setting up of National Parks such as Yellowstone (in Wyoming) and Yosemite (in California).

But proposals for an extension of ethics to cover all the species of the living systems of the Earth first emerged in the 20th century, in Aldo Leopold's *A Sand County Almanac*. In Leopold's Land Ethic, the land is the community of the interdependent species of the planet, plus the other components of their ecosystems. It was Leopold's proposal that "a thing is right when it tends to promote the integrity, stability and beauty of the biotic community. It is wrong when it tends otherwise" (Leopold, 1949. *Almanac*, pp. 224–225. Oxford Univ. Press, New York).

Environmental concern became much more widespread during the 1960s, with increasing alarm being voiced about nuclear fallout, population growth and its impact, and pesticides, as in Rachel Carson's *Silent Spring* (1962). In 1973 the Norwegian philosopher Arne Naess classified ecology movements by their depth in a celebrated article (1973, *Inquiry,* **16**, 95–100), and related issues were presented to a World Congress of Philosophy by the New Zealand philosopher Richard Routley, based at Australian National University, Canberra. The distinctive nature of such a new ethic was investigated in a groundbreaking paper by Holmes Rolston of Colorado State University (1975. *Ethics*, **85**, 93–109). By this time, an environmental philosophy conference had already been convened by William T. Blackstone at Athens, Georgia, and environmental ethics courses were already being taught at Universities, both in Wisconsin and in the University of Wales at Cardiff.

The first major journal in the subject, *Environmental Ethics*, was founded at the University of New Mexico in 1979, with Eugene C. Hargrove as Editor-in-Chief; Rolston serves as Associate Editor. By now there are a number of other journals in the field, such as *Environmental Values* based at the University of Lancaster, and work in this field is increasingly found in mainstream journals of philosophy. But the subject owes much to Hargrove's dedication, resilience, and breadth of editorial vision. Having moved in 1981 to Athens, Georgia, and having weathered a controversy about his own tenure there, Hargrove later moved to the University of North Texas, where the journal continues to be based. Meanwhile in 1990 Rolston, by then the author of the leading monograph in the field (H. Rolston III, 1988. *Environmental Ethics, Duties to and Values in The Natural World.* Temple Univ. Press, Philadelphia) founded the International Society for Environmental Ethics, of which he became President and Newsletter Editor, with Laura Westra (University of Windsor, Ontario) as Secretary. The Society has organized sessions at many conferences all over the world, and has a worldwide array of representatives. Its newsletter continues to carry a remarkable wealth of news and reviews.

Thus the discipline of environmental ethics is by now institutionally entrenched in many parts of the developed world, and is increasingly chosen by philosophy researchers as the subject of their dissertations. Third World scholars too have played an active part in its development. The late Henry Odera Oruka was the founding director of an Ecophilosophy Center at Nairobi, Kenya, and organized in Nairobi in 1991 a World Conference of Philosophy on the themes of environment, development, and their philosophical bearing. (It was Odera who drew my own attention to environmental philosophy in 1975.) A further example is supplied by the International Conference on Development, Ethics and the Environment, organized in Kuala Lumpur, Malaysia, in 1995 by Azizan Baharuddin of the University of Malaya and of the independent Institute for Policy Research. Third World environmental philosophers frequently stress the importance of blending environmentalism with the need for economic and social development to remedy the blights of poverty and injustice. Priorities between these diverse values continue to be debated.

IV. SOME NORMATIVE DEBATES

It will already be clear that not all practitioners of environmental ethics argue from interests independent of human interests. Nevertheless, most environmental ethicists do not confine moral standing to human beings and organizations, thereby distancing themselves from anthropocentrism (in the sense previously defined). Sometimes this is argued on the basis that many nonhuman animals are sentient, and that their interest in not being made to suffer has to be regarded as morally relevant; indeed discrimination on the sole basis of species membership has been labeled "speciesism" and compared to other kinds of discrimination such as sexism and racism. Others appeal beyond sentience to the capacity of all living organisms to develop and flourish in the manner of their own kind, or again claim that rights belong to species, or even to ecosystems.

Anthropocentrists respond that human beings cannot help appropriating resources from the natural world, and thus prioritizing their own interests, and that, as agents, they inevitably operate from within a human-centered perspective. However, these claims are consistent with a nonanthropocentric stance in ethics; an ineradicably human-centered cognitive perspective is compatible with recognizing ethical considerations independent of human interests, whether motivated by identification, by sympathy, or by admiration of nature's otherness. Others claim that the underlying ground for identification with nature is the good of the person whose understanding is thus enlarged and humanized, but this stance has been accused of narcissism, and also seems blind to the independent significance of, e.g., animal suffering.

With greater sophistication, others again call "anthropocentric" those judgments of intrinsic value for which no objectivity is claimed, labeling them in this way simply in virtue of their being made by human beings, and designate the kind of value thus ascribed "weak anthropocentric intrinsic value"; the scope of such value is, they hold, by no means confined to human interests and their objects (E. C. Hargrove, 1992. *Monist*, 75, 183–207). But since this is a different sense of "anthropocentric" from the usual sense, conveying a metaethical rather than a normative classification of value, and rather than support for anthropocentrism in the traditional, unsophisticated sense, clarity is better served by using some other term (such as "anthropogenic") for judgments and theories of this nature, and retaining "anthropocentric" for its traditional role.

Among those who reject anthropocentrism, another debate is between those who regard all individual creatures with moral standing as having equal moral significance and those who recognize differing degrees of moral significance, related usually to differing capacities (such as sentience and intelligence). The egalitarian camp regards belief in degrees of significance as discriminatory and arbitrary; the other camp responds that environmental justice demands that priorities be observed when clashes of interest occur. While the kind of biospheric egalitarianism which makes each organism count equally may be a theoretically consistent position, it suffers from the handicap of making life unlivable in practice.

Another debate arises between (on the one hand) campaigners for animal welfare and (on the other) campaigners for the conservation of species, ecosystems, or wilderness. This debate often corresponds to a radical difference of values, with animal welfarists arguing from the importance of the well-being of individual sentient animals, and conservationists, when not appealing to human interests, sometimes arguing that species or ecosystems have some kind of independent, holistic value. While these camps are allies for many practical purposes (as over preserving the last members of an endangered species and their habitats), they often diverge, as over the culling of deer in Scotland, of seals in Canada, and of elephants in southern Africa.

Debates on this and other issues among environmental ethicists often turn on "intrinsic value" (the kind of value which is neither instrumental nor in any other way derivative, but depends entirely on the nature of its bearer) and on its extension or location. Both animal welfarists and many conservationists reject an anthropocentric view of its location. But while the former locate it in individual well-being, some of the latter locate it in diversity, in wildness, in independence from human impacts, or simply in nature (understood as the realm independent of human agency), and sometimes suggest that pain and suffering are intrinsically neutral (rather than bad), besides being instrumentally good insofar as they contribute to the maintenance of ecosystem stability. However, the value of diversity seems to depend on its (by now controversial) contribution to stability; the criterion of wildness would deprive all domestic animals of intrinsic value; and the independence criterion elides the distinction between abiotic nature and living creatures. And if pain does not count even in general as an independent reason against what causes it, it is difficult to see what else counts. This holds true irrespective of whether the pain is experienced by a human being or by a nonhuman animal.

Yet this is not to suggest that welfarists have nothing to learn from the conservationist camp. Conservationists, for example, can explain the importance of predation to the existence of both predators and prey, and thus why human beings should seldom if ever intervene to prevent it. Predation, parasitism, and such-like apparent evils turn out to carry a positive, albeit derivative, value for the species and the systems involved. Further, if human society is to attain sustainability, and avoid undermining the interests of future generations (whether of human beings or of nonhuman creatures), ways must be found of not undermining the ongoing operation of those natural systems on which human life depends. Unless welfarists grasp the networks of interdependence pervading the natural world, their contribution to environmental ethics is fatally flawed. This, however, need not make their principled objections to factory farming, or to hunting as a sport, any less valid.

A further debate concerns whether environmental philosophy should concern itself with values or with ethics at all. In face of trenchant criticisms from Richard Routley concerning deep ecology, with its belief in the value of nature as a whole, and in the self-realization which this belief makes possible, Warwick Fox claimed in its defense that talk of value on the part of deep ecologists such as Arne Naess and George Sessions should not be taken literally, that advocacy of beliefs about value and ethics was futile, and that the real message of deep ecology concerned the identification of the self with the greater Self of nature. Once self-realization of this kind had been achieved, agents would in any case be motivated to defend nature, and no purpose would be served by ethical talk or talk of values. (W. Fox, 1990. *Toward a Transpersonal Ecology*. Shambala, Boston/London). Responses have mentioned the self-undermining character of identification with nature as a whole, the lack of guidance available once values are discarded, and the need for interpersonal reasons implicit in values if actions are to respond proportionately to current problems. Deep ecology also seems to underplay nature's otherness, an equally important source of environmental concern as identification and empathy.

V. METAETHICAL DEBATES

Besides enriching value theory and normative ethics through its stress on future generations and on nonhuman creatures, environmental ethics has had to examine the status of its own claims, and has thus breathed new life into the discipline of metaethics. Objectivists hold that claims about value, rightness, and obligation admit of truth, and comprise interpersonal reasons for action as opposed to comprising expressions of taste or prescriptions. Objectivists usually also hold that knowledge is sometimes possible in these areas (Rolston,

1988; R. Attfield, 1995. *Value, Obligation, and Metaethics*. Rodopi, Atlanta, GA/Amsterdam). Subjectivists, by contrast, maintain that value is always value for someone or some group, or in some valuational framework, and that ultimately there are no merits by which such valuings or frameworks can be compared. Such views appear to deprive claims about value or about obligation from supplying reasons for action capable of being treated seriously.

Recently the claims have been made that developments in quantum physics have made the distinction between subjects and objects untenable, and that the discourse of value must be understood as relative; the very language of objective value is claimed to belong to an obsolete modernist paradigm (J. B. Callicott, 1989. *In Defense of the Land Ethic*. State Univ. of New York Press, Albany). It has been replied that quantum physics itself presupposes the language of objectivity, and does not require a subjectivist interpretation (Attfield, 1995). Another discipline concerned with value, economics, conventionally treats value as a function of preferences; the relations between economic value and intrinsic value currently form a growth point for environmental ethics. An important distinction which has been made in this connection distinguishes our valuations as consumers (typically functions of our preferences) and our valuations as citizens (usually unrelated to preferences or to willingness to pay) (M. Sagoff, 1982. *Arizona Law Review*, **23**, 1281–1298).

Related debates concern whether any single theory of value or obligation should be accepted, or whether working with a plurality of theories might be preferable to this quest for closure, and also whether the very concept of truth should be relativized to kinds of discourse. Such debates continue to figure in *Environmental Ethics* and in mainstream philosophy journals too, such as *The Monist*.

VI. METAPHYSICAL DEBATES

Other relevant debates concern the nature of the environment and of nature itself. These apparently abstruse questions turn out to have a crucial bearing on practice, as different answers to them prompt different policies. Thus if (as is often held) the environment is always *someone's* environment, then environments are always local, and much depends on the perspectives of the local human inhabitants. Principles concerning the global environment thus depend on some less localized concept of environment and on the existence of a globally shared environment on which local environments depend (see Glossary).

By contrast with the concept of environment, the concept of nature (traditionally contrasted with convention or with culture) might seem to demand an objectivist understanding. Yet the perspectives of different cultures about what is natural are so various that for many theorists nature and the natural are to be regarded as constructions. This view has important implications both for the value of nature (understood as something utterly independent of human agency) and for the project of preserving natural wilderness, and could potentially undermine the very idea of identification with nature. In some ways this debate overlaps that between realism and idealism in the theory of knowledge, but even if realism were finally vindicated, that would not undermine all claims about the constructed character of many ideas of nature. However, since constructivists believe that it is embodied people who construct such ideas, there is a significant inbuilt self-limitation to their claims about natural entities as constructions.

Feminist writers have often compared traditional attitudes to nature and to women, and complained of the oppression of both (C. Merchant, 1982. *The Death of Nature*. Wildwood House, London). Sometimes it is also held that through their roles as lifegivers (childbearing) and nurturers, women are closer to nature than men, and that current problems will remain insoluble unless related feminine qualities (such as caring) are allowed to mold social life and policies. Debates about such ecofeminism and its bearing on the concept of nature continue in journals such as *Environmental Ethics*. The patriarchal nature of much of the inherited discourse about nature is undeniable, and there are important parallels between the past exploitation of women and that of nonhuman creatures. It is unclear, however, whether gender-related qualities as such exist, or whether the claim that there are such qualities may not be a further instance of gender stereotyping. What is more cogent is that alliances can be formed between the different movements against oppression, including, importantly, feminism.

VII. RELIGIONS AND ENVIRONMENTAL ETHICS

Recently, Max Oelschlaeger has argued that the best hope for the environmental movement in the United

States is to enlist the support of the churches (1994. *Caring for Creation.* Yale Univ. Press, New Haven, CT). He cites widespread support for the preservation and conservation of nature as God's world, both among believers and (more surprisingly) among nonbelievers. These findings also generate surprise in view of the controversy concerning the supposed religious origins of the environmental crisis.

Nearly three decades ago, Lynn White, Jr., argued that the roots of our ecological crisis lay in the Jewish and Christian doctrine of creation, or rather in the activist variant of it distinctive of the Western churches, as opposed to the Eastern Orthodox churches. The impact of this doctrine was delayed until post-Renaissance science became allied with technology in the 19th century, but its anthropocentric and despotic tendencies were already present in the early Middle Ages (L. White, Jr., 1967. *Science,* **155,** 1203–1207). Other historians have questioned White's account of medieval history, while theologians and historians of ideas have disputed White's intepretation of the Bible. By now it is agreed that theistic religions often regard humanity as steward of creation, answerable to God for its care, and that this stance has ancient origins. Disagreement concerns the extent to which it was or was not a characteristic view until the current century, and the extent to which those who adhered to it were or were not free of exploitative attitudes themselves (Merchant, 1982).

While Christian attitudes to nature in previous centuries have been too various to fit White's rather simplistic interpretation, the debate about White's theory is often seen as a distraction from the theory and practice of problem solving in the present. In the United States, most of the churches are nowadays strongly environmentalist and strong enough to exercise considerable political influence, and even philosophers and ethicists committed to the independence of ethics from religion may need to take all this into account, if only on pragmatic grounds. (Whether this kind of environmentalism encompasses concern for the environment of the Third World or for the global environment remains to be seen.)

In most European countries, religion is not as influential as it is in North America. But Oelschlaeger's theory still has an international relevance, if suitably adjusted, for there are currently influential voices in Islam (as at the 1995 Kuala Lumpur Conference) representing a stewardship interpretation of the faith as historically central and as ethically mandatory. Nontheistic religions also have their environmental relevance, but it is the activist theistic religions which could transform the prospects for conserving the global environment.

VIII. CAUSES OF ENVIRONMENTAL PROBLEMS

The identity of environmental problems (problems resulting from human interactions with nature) depends on values; for example, nonanthropocentric theories are much more concerned with extinctions of species and habitats than anthropocentric theories. Nevertheless, problems such as pollution, resource depletion, loss of cultivable land, and loss of wilderness are often assigned common causes. For example, the theory that religious attitudes are to blame for these problems has often been put forward, without securing agreement. More material causes have to be considered.

Population growth is often suggested as a principal cause, and many ecologists actually favor reductions of the human population and international sanctions to secure such reductions. Yet environmental problems are more concentrated in areas of intense industrial activity than in areas of population concentration, and average impacts on the environment are often many times greater in the former areas than in the latter. While some problems can be correlated with population growth, this kind of growth in turn is often driven by poverty, and these problems are unlikely to be resolved until poverty itself is tackled. Meanwhile the causes of problems in industrial areas cannot be set down to population growth; for such problems, the proposed causes include affluence and also modern technology, and proposed solutions accordingly sometimes commend an ethic of simpler lifestyles reliant on technology of a simpler and less consumptive kind.

Yet economic forces, rather than individual consumption levels, are likely to drive the polluting processes, and this has led to advocacy of limits to economic growth, and sometimes of abandonment of modern technology. But humanity is unlikely to be fed, let alone global problems to be solved, without the aid of modern technology, and so not all growth should be rejected. Nor would the withdrawal of individuals or regions into self-sufficiency contribute much to the solution of these problems. The problems have to be understood against the background of the current inequitable international economic order, and are unlikely to be solved unless this order is radically restructured. Ethical theories in which all this is neglected are likely to prove transitory.

IX. SUSTAINABILITY

Where environmentalists in the 1970s used to advocate limits to growth, their successors from the late 1980s have instead often been advocates of sustainable development. Sustainable development was the central theme of the Brundtland Report (World Commission for Environment and Development, 1987. *Our Common Future*. Oxford Univ. Press, Oxford), where it was defined as "development that meets the needs of the present without compromising the ability of future generations to meet their own needs." Besides stressing that not all growth should be regarded as beneficial change (or development), the authors of this report stressed that development must be sustainable, and thus inaugurate or fortify economic and social processes capable of being continued indefinitely, without undermining either themselves or the ecosystems on which both nonhuman creatures and human economic systems depend. The United Nations Conference on Environment and Development at Rio de Janeiro (1992) took some promising steps toward converting this notion into reality.

Advocates of sustainable development, however, encounter problems of definition, and also opposition from diverse directions. When they attempt to specify what precisely is to be sustained, one account, which makes this the economic value of natural resources, would allow the elimination of species and wild habitats whenever this would result in (say) enhanced technological options for humanity, while another, which would forbid all such changes, would prevent almost all development in regions (for example) of rainforest, at the cost of failure to satisfy basic human needs. Sustainable development, insofar as it diverges from traditional economics, needs to blend the criteria of satisfying current human needs, allowing equivalent options for satisfying future needs, and preserving the bearers of intrinsic value (nonhuman creatures included).

Radical environmentalists would still criticize the concept and the pursuit of sustainable development for permitting "business as usual," and for being too easily appropriated into the vocabulary of capitalist enterprises. Certainly conventional politicians and representatives of business often pay lip service to "sustainable development," meaning thereby nothing more than sustained economic growth. The radical critics sometimes urge an ethic which would reject development and/ or industrialism altogether, and focus on stabilizing economic processes. Meanwhile other critics object to potential departures from cost effectiveness, and claim that sustainability is not always a virtue. However, both sustainability and development embody values which, as their supporters are aware, should not be discarded lightly. Accordingly, work continues on both the theory and the practice of sustainable development at international, national, and local levels.

X. SOME FRAGMENTARY SOLUTIONS

Ethics is concerned not only with ideal solutions, such as a radical restructuring of the world economy would involve, but also with what should be done while things remain largely as they are, by agents with limited powers and a limited scope for action. Despite their greater powers, governments and corporations are often in this position, rather as individuals are. The approaches which follow are suited to agents and agencies in situations of these kinds.

A. The Precautionary Principle

In view of the danger that environmental impacts will cross critical thresholds or prove irreversible, and in the light of evidence that environmental risks are often underestimated, a principle that has increasingly been accepted by European governments in recent years is that action such as regulation may justifiably be taken to avert environmental harm in advance of the availability of scientific evidence confirming that harm. This principle is sometimes supplemented by the requirement that the best available technology be used; its supporters, however, reject the inclusion of the qualification that this technology should not incorporate excessive costs. This Precautionary Principle is not a basic principle, is all too liable to be given an anthropocentric interpretation or a pro-Western bias, and needs to be applied in conjunction with principles both of sustainability and of justice; yet its adoption involves little more than common prudence, and its earlier implementation could have curtailed acid rain, ozone depletion, and even global warming.

B. Comprehensive Weighing

In this approach to environmental decision making, all the entities liable to be affected by a development or policy are identified, including future people and nonhuman creatures both present and future, and the probability and extent of the impacts are calculated (as far as quantitative calculation is possible) and then aggregated, like interests being treated alike. Factors which cannot be quantified are identified alongside those which can be when overall impacts are reported. This method is one tool among others for decision makers, who are also encouraged to consider giving additional weight to impacts affecting the poor and the vulnerable. In requiring the inclusion of nonhuman interests, this approach diverges from conventional economics; in this connection, human proxies would estimate impacts on the creatures concerned. A further divergence would involve discounting future interests only where special reasons (such as inflation) make this appropriate. This approach is presented in *Values, Conflict and the Environment* (R. Attfield and K. Dell, 1996. 2nd ed. Avebury, Aldershot); its adoption would strengthen the quest for sustainability. The danger that monetary costings would be used too widely could be countered by frequent use of the nonquantitative category of impacts.

C. An Example

Global warming is now recognized to be caused by human activity, through the emission of greenhouse gases such as carbon dioxide and methane, and to be likely to raise the level of the oceans through the melting of polar ice caps to an extent which threatens the continued existence of islands such as the Maldives and of low-lying areas such as much of Bengal, plus all their flora and fauna, human beings included. Even before scientific consensus was reached, applications of both the Precautionary Principle and of comprehensive weighing implied that constraints on carbon emissions were ethically obligatory, despite the interests to the contrary of energy-producing countries and corporations. Developing countries, however, cannot justly be expected to curtail carbon emissions until they are able to satisfy the basic needs of their citizens. Emission quotas must therefore be recognized and observed by the industrialized countries, whether through an agreement or treaty, or (if this cannot be negotiated) through informal policy decisions. Negotiations, originating from the Rio Conference, are due to be concluded in Kyoto in 1997. Ethical arguments, such as those put forward by the Association of Small Island States (AOSIS), have played a significant role in persuading the representatives of both developing and industrial countries of the validity of these principles.

While an agreement on carbon emissions will not make the Earth an ecological paradise, rudimentary steps such as this one are ethically indispensable, and could supply a paradigm for the further measures which the global citizens of the future will need to take.

Bibliography

Attfield, R. (1992). *The Ethics of Environmental Concern,* 2nd ed. Univ. of Georgia Press, Athens, GA.

Attfield, R. (1994). *Environmental Philosophy, Principles and Prospects.* Avebury, Aldershot/Ashgate, Brookfield, VT.

Attfield, R. (1995). *Value, Obligation and Meta-Ethics.* Rodopi, Atlanta, GA/Amsterdam.

Attfield, R., and Dell, K. (Eds.) (1996). *Values, Conflict and the Environment,* 2nd ed. Avebury, Aldershot.

Evernden, N. (1992). *The Social Creation of Nature.* Johns Hopkins Univ. Press, Baltimore/London.

Fox, W. (1990). *Toward a Transpersonal Ecology: Developing New Foundations for Environmentalism.* Shambala, Boston/London.

Hargrove, E. C. (1992). Weak anthropocentric intrinsic value. *Monist,* **75,** 183–207.

Oelschlaeger, M. (1994). *Caring for Creation: An Ecumenical Approach to the Environmental Crisis.* Yale Univ. Press, New Haven, CT.

O'Neill, J. (1993). *Ecology, Policy and Politics.* Routledge, London/New York.

Passmore, J. (1974). *Man's Responsibility for Nature.* Duckworth, London.

Regan, T. (1983). *The Case for Animal Rights.* Routledge and Kegan Paul, London.

Singer, P. (1976). *Animal Liberation, a New Ethic for Our Treatment of Animals.* Jonathan Cape, London.

Thompson, J. (1990). A refutation of environmental ethics. *Environmental Ethics,* **12**(2), 147–160.

ENVIRONMENTAL IMPACT ASSESSMENT

Marja Järvelä and Kristiina Kuvaja-Puumalainen
The University of Jyväskylä

GLOSSARY

ecosocial morality The principle or practice of adjusting values or way of life according to the principle of sustainable development.

environmental impact assessment A tool used in environmental management that examines the environmental consequences of development actions in advance.

nature contract An idea of a symbiotic relationship between humanity and nature to be taken as a parallel of the social contract, or to reform this contract.

policy of small action A policy of making everyday life choices in accordance with ecosocial morality.

social impact assessment A tool used to complement environmental impact assessment by predicting and evaluating the impact of planned actions on social and human aspects of changes in the living environment.

sustainable development Development that meets the needs of the present without compromising the ability of future generations to meet their own needs.

way of life The process of everyday life that is based upon its essential social conditions and people's perspectives.

ENVIRONMENTAL IMPACT ASSESSMENT (EIA) is one of the main tools used in current environmental management to produce sustainable development. Sustainable development has most often been defined in terms of economic development and biological reproduction. In its narrow sense it refers to the balance of economy and environment, but new formulations also emphasize free intellectual activity and development of cultural diversity. The authors of this entry perceive that the wider interpretation of sustainable development includes a moral obligation to transmit a viable living environment to future generations. This moral obligation can be treated as part of the social impact assessment (SIA) related to EIA processes. This involves basically the problem of promoting and integrating a layperson's perspective into the experts' activity in EIA.

The policy of small action by the common citizens and other activities referring to the new norms of ecosocial morality should be considered seriously as social resources for sustainable development and for EIA processes.

I. INTRODUCTION

Environmental impact assessment (EIA) is one of the main tools used in current environmental management to produce sustainable development and to prevent the accumulation of environmental risks. "EIA is a *process*, a systemic process that examines the environmental consequences of development actions, in advance" (J. Glasson, R. Therivel, & A. Chadwick, 1995. *Introduction to environmental impact assessment* (p. 3). *The natural and built environment*, series 1. London: UCL Press). Taking a technical stance, the EIA process can be analyzed by its steps (e.g., identification of key impacts and prediction of impacts on natural environment) in terms of its efficiency in physical and biological risk minimizing. Yet a broader view of EIA refers to the comprehensive idea of sustainable development and even to the capacities of the civil society to act as a social agent in building a sustainable heritage for future generations.

This entry does not describe in detail the process and potentialities the EIA has in technical risk minimizing; neither do we argue that the current EIA processes are "unethical" or valueless. Our aim is merely to propose that the concept of ecosocial morality be considered as an integrative ethical element referring to the social aspect of EIA and to the concept of sustainable development, which is the ultimate aim of EIA processes.

II. ENVIRONMENTAL ETHICS

Sustainable development has most often been defined in terms of economic development and biological reproduction. In its narrow sense it refers to the balance of economy and environment. The concept of sustainable development was used already at the time of the Cocoyoc declaration on environment and development in the early 1970s. The concept gained wide popularity after the Brundtland Commission's 1987 report *Our Common Future* (Oxford: Oxford Univ. Press), in which sustainable development was defined as a tool for economic growth and equity among the world's nations. The United Nations Conference on Environment and Development (UNCED) in Rio de Janeiro in 1992, in turn, gave a new emphasis to this concept. *Agenda 21*, which was formulated during the conference, comprised three operational dimensions: an ecological dimension, a social dimension, and a cultural dimension. Hence, in addition to the Brundtland Commission's definitions of ecological and socially just economic development, the new formulation of the concept also emphasized free intellectual activity and development of cultural diversity.

As the authors of this entry perceive it, the wider interpretation of sustainable development refers to the totality of environmental and social policies and their practical implications. The basic argument we propose is that there is a moral obligation inherent to the concept of sustainable development: we should do at least as well for our successor generations as our predecessors did for us. We refer to the responsibility to transmit the common patrimony to an unspecified number of generation as understood, e.g., by François Ost.

Discussion on environmental ethics has previously led to a dramatic division of anthropocentric and biocentric interpretations (B. Norton, 1987. *Why preserve natural variety?* Princeton, NJ: Princeton Univ. Press). According to the anthropocentric approach, humans are the sole moral and valuable entity, and therefore nature is considered valid only when it is related to our goals and aims. Based on this premise, all values connected to nature are derived from human beings. Biocentric environmental ethics, in turn, argues that nature has internal values in itself which make nature equal to humans. Furthermore, our attitudes toward nature should create a more respectful behavior in relation to nature.

Humans, as individuals and communities, assume values and behavior in everyday life. Ways of life can be understood along anthropocentric and biocentric lines of reasoning. An anthropocentric position is represented by ways of life pursuing the well-being and happiness of human kind as ultimate aims. The biocentric position is represented by ways of life dedicating intrinsic value to nature and to populations of various species, as exemplified in the discourse of Deep Ecology.

III. WAYS OF LIFE AND THE ENVIRONMENT

In a study of self-regulation in modern society, there are at least two levels at which we can meaningfully use the conceptual tools of the social sciences to examine the relationship of changing ways of life to the environment. (The concept of the way of life is considered here as a process of everyday life which is based upon its essential social conditions and people's perspectives. People's perspectives refer here to the subjective goals, aspirations, and visions attached to their activities (see P. Ahponen & M. Järvelä, 1987. In J. P. Roos and A. Sicinski (Eds.), *Ways and styles of life in Finland and Poland* (p. 71). Gower: Avebury).) On the one hand, there is the question of what kind of environment individual people can and will produce for themselves through everyday life choices. On the other hand, it is important to understand how the individual, as an integral part of nature, adapts and adjusts to changes in nature, and what sort of impacts and interactions are caused by human activity on and in different ecosystems.

The first level of recognition refers to the human–environment relationship, which starts with considering how people can interact with their environment without causing serious harm to themselves, to others, or to nature. Promoting sustainable development implies recognition of the ecosocial point of view in all development efforts. Robert Tessier refers to a shift in motivation that is expected to favor the community over individual survival or interest. In analyzing the concept of sustainable development Tessier even refers to collective instead of individual salvation, because he finds structural similarity in the rational action inspired by "sustainable development" and Max Weber's protestant ethic.

As regards the second level, the key thing is to look at the foundations of the ecological self-organization of way of life. Edgar Morin and Anne-Brigitte Kern have said that one relevant measure for a human society is whether it operates like a living machine rather than a built machine. A living machine is capable of self-corrective action, in spite of its functional deficiencies, whereas a built machine needs external intervention in an event of any malfunction. The same principle of ecological self-organization could be thought to apply to people's everyday way of life.

The discussion on environmental ethics has only recently been connected seriously to the discussion on Western ways of life and consumption. In the 1980s the concept of sustainability referred more to the environmental stress and catastrophes resulting from increased population and industrialization in the developing world or from such accidents as Chernobyl. The present discussion focuses more on the effects of daily life of an ordinary Western citizen and refers to the aggregated environmental and social impacts of the consumption culture.

As far as large-scale environmental risks are concerned, a major problem lies in the difficulty of predicting the ecological impacts of human activity. The environmental sociologist faces the additional difficulty of predicting human activity in modern society. We still know fairly little about how and why people move about in their daily labyrinths: we know much more about the restrictions that limit the scope of our choices and about what members of modern society can do and what they leave undone. For many people it is difficult not to take the car out of the garage every morning, even though they are well aware that the catalyzer does not completely eliminate the environmental impacts of driving. On a very general level, then, we can conclude that ways of life are structured by modern economic and social systems that tend to mobilize interests and rational action that are not fully conscious of environmental risks inherent to them. Yet each citizen may, as a moral being, take a critical position on the risks induced by his or her choices, or on the reproductive policies of one's community as regards the environmental and social impact of daily decisions.

IV. THE NATURE CONTRACT

Ervin Laszlo's caricature of modern Man describes him as an accumulation of false beliefs about his chances of controlling nature (1989. *The inner limits of mankind.* London: Oneworld). In his critique Laszlo says that the idea of us being able to externalize the environment derives from the belief that nature is an inexhaustible reserve of raw materials. Laszlo is also sharply critical of urbanization and the urban way of life, drawing attention to the pompous aspects of a consumer society's way of life, which are products *not* of the independent logic of economy, but of human greed, short-sightedness, and oversized desires.

The French philosopher Michel Serres (1990. *Le contrat naturel.* Paris: Bourin) goes even further when describing the unbalanced relation between humans and nature. Serres argues that our relation to the environment is parasitical; we use environmental resources, reaping all the rewards without giving any returns. Modern social structures formulate their own justification: the fundamental misbelief that human rights be accorded "every human being." According to Serres this is the very essence of the parasitical relationship—there exists no justification which includes the whole global system as a value in the final assessment.

Serres argues that in order to establish a new balance in human societies' relation to their environment, the "social contract" should be replaced by the "nature contract," in which the environment is an equal counterpart to humans. In *Le Contrat Naturel*, Serres presents the idea of this symbiotic relationship, which is based on the ecosocial morality of the unique human being.

The policy-making processes of modern societies reproduce elements of the social contract that refer back to the constitutional history of modern nation states. In those contracts nature is not included as an inherent entity of vital interest or of intrinsic value. Traditionally, in modern societies social norms refer to the social contract, where nature remains an external entity to be conquered and exploited. From the sociological point of view, Serres' idea of a symbiotic relationship between man and nature, the nature contract, implies development of new norms by the ecosocial dynamics of the present civil society. This, in turn, addresses the final moral responsibility of the social community to develop the natural contract. This moral call is universal in the sense that each community has a common heritage, including the environment, to be maintained or restored not only for the benefit to us, but also for that to the future generation.

V. ECOSOCIAL MORALITY IN THE COMMUNITY

For the common person, environmental changes appear as global and comprehensive entities that are often difficult to reduce into a chain of causes and effects. If a community is to aim at a critical review of the effects of citizens' everyday life at the community level, it has to evaluate its common heritage of ecological and social ways of life. In addition, the community should be able to project impacts of any major development on the living environment, including the impact of the human–nature relation in that particular community. According to Mary Douglas and Aron Wildavsky, communities actually have a strong tendency to define impacts of change as risks that are morally loaded. However, in self-protective communities risks may become "village secrets" if no procedural evaluative practice is created.

The process of perceiving risk and of taking responsibility of the common heritage by the community is specific to particular cultural forms. Anthony Giddens refers to the culture of modern societies as post-traditional (1994. In U. Beck, A. Giddens, and S. Lash (Eds.), *Reflexive modernization*. Cambridge: Polity). In

post-traditional cultures risks are not defined "domestically," but in the situation where impulses from the outside have a generative function. Giddens compares today's experts to traditional guardians who formulated local wisdom. But expertise, from the angle of the community, is a much more situational role that has to be tested not only in terms of knowledge but also in respect to the moral values it represents. In the final analysis, then, what is important is the trust between expert and layperson which may or may not be confirmed in any process of "environmental impact assessment." Thus, the assessment should include as its consituent element a building up of a common ecosocial morality that generates new patterns of reflexive modernity in societies which seem to have lost much of their traditional capacity for guarding the common heritage.

Even in a post-traditional society, there is a sense of solidarity with future generations. This aspect has been underlined by the discussion of sustainable development, even if it is often neglected in experts' assessments finding shortcuts in practical technologies to deal with environmental problems and "development." Particularly in families, children represent the potential victims of environmental risks. Their children's fate make parents reflect on the threat of environmental risks and consider how long "we (our descendents) can be safe."

VI. GLOBALIZATION AND ECOSOCIAL SOLIDARITY

Many manifestations of environmental risks (such as depletion of ozone layers, the accelerated greenhouse effect, and scarcity of potable water) have led to the conclusion that risks of human impact on nature are not only local but also global by character. Correspondingly, there has been strong agreement that principles of environmental policy should be agreed upon at the level of international politics or even defined by the "global community." The critical point for globalization of environmental risks and the call for sustainability and the nature contract is whether ecosocial solidarity may be raised high enough to result in a new moral comprehension at the world level. According to this comprehension, factors which were considered as "development" in the past may not be considered as such any longer (see also Laszlo, 1989).

In relation to poverty, the controversy between economy and ecology is of vital interest. Particularly, the "developing countries" have had difficulties in finding sustainable options that serve their own interests and that meet with critical Western projections (as manifested, e.g., by "green" movements). Nevertheless, there has appeared a new kind of a solidarity concerning "distant others," not only the members of future generations, but also individuals who live far away. This kind of solidarity has increased simultaneously with the globalization of environmental risks, but has also facilitated the globalization of culture (mass media, exported cultural products, etc.). Nowadays many people are aware that "their day-to-day actions are globally consequential" (Giddens, 1994, 57). Social morality thus acquires a new dimension of global solidarity that may restructure the way of life of the individual or even of the community.

VII. POLICY OF SMALL ACTION

Citizens' response to the challenge of changing their way of life through their own choice is in most cases a policy of small actions. Apart from those who choose a radical alternative of asceticism, citizens show their solidarity toward distant others through small actions that do not reverse their own way of life (such as recycling, rejecting harmful products and packaging, and saving electricity and gas). Yet, no matter how minute the acts may appear even to the actors themselves, they lead to the formulation of a new ecosocial norm in civil society. The formulation of ecosocial norms in the daily patterns of action indicates that the personal assessment of environmental changes may lead to new ecological adaptation—or defense mechanisms—from the bottom up and not only by top-down experts' strategies. For example, in Finland citizens commonly believe that they may affect their own ways of life and, to a certain extent, even introduce to others ecosocial morality. New ecosocial norms are, therefore, increasingly a part of daily discussions in families, workplaces, and schools, as well as of other everyday interactions (M. Järvelä & M. Wilenius, 1996. In *The Finnish Research Programme on Climate Change, final report*. Publications of the Academy of Finland).

The application of the personal nature contract and the policy of small actions creates a new ecosocial moral community which emphasizes frugality as a civil virtue. The interpretations of frugality may vary from conserving a household's electricity to choosing second-hand shopping. The main idea is that everyone is able to make some of these choices and become a member of the new ecosocial community. Some acts are practiced very consciously as symbolic manifestations of an ecosocial orientation. In Finland, two of these widely adopted representations are giving up the use of plastic bags (used by the majority) in daily shopping or using the bicycle when going to work. Based on these symbolic actions, the members of the ecosocial community can recognize each other in the middle of daily routines.

The policy of small actions reflects citizens' orientation to a new possible future in which society has chosen a more ecological direction of development. It is considered more valuable as an act of human solidarity to "do even something" in the face of an unsecure future than just to wait and see what will happen. Even if there is no radical change of the frames or patterns of ways of life, ecosocial norms gradually generate new environmental awareness. Instead of the externalized threat of nature expressed by the agonizing relation, "nature versus me," as many come to realize the globalized risks of living as we have, people will start to think in terms of "I and nature" to prepare more or less consciously a reformed basis to pursue community-level sustainability. Consequently, the policy of small actions and acts of frugality can be seen as elements of a more general ecosocial self-regulation of everyday practices. This social development seems to be crucial for the transition of awareness and action that will bring the issue of environmental reproduction and impact assessment to the community level.

VIII. LEGITIMACY AND POLITICAL EFFICIENCY

There is, however, a basic problem of legitimacy and of political efficiency inherent to citizens' policy of small actions. The everyday norms of ecosocial morality and their strong attachment to the daily policy of small actions keep citizens' world of living (*Lebenswelt*) at a considerable distance from the society's environmental politics, which remains to a great extent an experts' "playground" (Järvelä & Wilenius, 1996). It can also be argued that the members of ecosocial moral communities do not necessarily identify themselves with environmental movements which have become familiar through the media. Frugality and prudence as commonly appreciated virtues of civil society lead to a situation where, for example, Greenpeace's acts—if they are considered to be legal at all—gain only passive support by members of the ecosocial community. Legality is considered not only in social movements' activities, but is also in personal norms. Environmental actions ought to meet the demands of legality. Consequently, ecosocial moral norms do not, in fact, replace traditional social norms referring to the social contract. Rather, the norms deduced from the nature contract, as perceived by laypeople of the post-traditional society, should be added to the "contract basis" that sets norms and values in social policy and in everyday life.

IX. ENVIRONMENTAL IMPACT ASSESSMENT AS RATIONAL ACTION

The formulation of the ecosocial moral community follows a certain reasoning in which the principles for personal action are formulated through an individual implementation of the "nature contract." Personal frugality and a policy of small actions may be based on a generalized moral obligation without any further development of the rational strategy that is usually called for in societal environmental policy and expert discourse. In a highly technological modern society with complex policy-making patterns it is, however, important to ask in what social arena and how the values and goals can be mutually understood by experts and laypeople. How is the civil society mobilized to protect nature or to secure a sustainable living environment?

According to our view the responsbility of sustainable environmental policy cannot simply be transferred to experts or environmental movements from the community level. Civil society should create particular rational models of self-regulation to guarantee a social arena for risk perception, for dealing with values and preferences, and for democratic choice of policy action. This would be an arena where experts and laypeople could meet on an equal basis. Personal impact assessment and ecosocial profiles built and represented in everyday life would, then, serve as social resources to increase the self-regulative capacities of the society.

The personal mode of action commonly follows the model of teleological reasoning which may be composed as follows (M. Järvelä & M. Wilenius, 1993. *Climate change, living environment and ways of life*, working paper 9/1993. Tampere: Research Institute for Social Sciences, Univ. of Tempere): (1) The actor recognizes a factual situation that has to do with a highly appreciated object. (2) Having realized the factual situation, the actor chooses another situation in relation to the appreciated object. The more preferred situation is set as the ultimate goal of action. (3) The actor then pursues this goal by specific means that are considered to be essential for achieving the goal. For example, in the case of the accelerated greenhouse effect, the members of the ecosocial moral community can choose appropriate means in their daily lives to prevent the increase of carbon dioxide emissions and to join in this way a more global strategy of rational action to mitigate environmental risk. This kind of reasoning is structured in the way that usually is recognized as an ideal model of expert discourse, no matter how much the actual mitigation may differ from the ideal model. As an ideal model, it may, however, serve as an analysis of the gap between the expert and the lay perspective on the issue of sustainability of the environment and environmental risk.

As said before, the formulation of the ecosocial community in civil society is usually actualized through a policy of small actions: there is rarely involved any direct structural changes at the level of state policies due to these actions. However, communication between experts, professionals, and laypeople can be considered a desired outcome of the development of ecosocial communities. The personal impact assessment and ecosocial profiles of individual families provide a channel of information which is likely to offer new resources for environmental planning and administration, if this agency of the civil society can be channeled to the societal management processes, such as environmental impact assessments.

X. MODEL OF SOCIAL ACTION

There can be drawn a crude distinction between (1) a strategy of rational political influence and (2) a mythical survival strategy. It is commonly assumed that experts and professionalists are inclined to follow a strategy of rational environmental influence and that laypeople are inclined to resort to a mythical environmental survival strategy. The baseline assumption is that there is an important difference in the strategic approach or in the form of rationality between experts and laypeople (Järvelä & Wilenius, 1993). It is likely that a pure division of social values and action orientation, such as presented by the model of "theoretical teleologies" (see Figure 1), has never been found historically. A more reasonable approach is to argue that there is a large scale of variation around the ideal types. Both experts and laypeople can and do combine elements of both rational and mythical analysis in their strategic approaches. Yet it is more probable that we find the ideal types when analyzing the strategic behavior in different social

Theoretical Teleologies

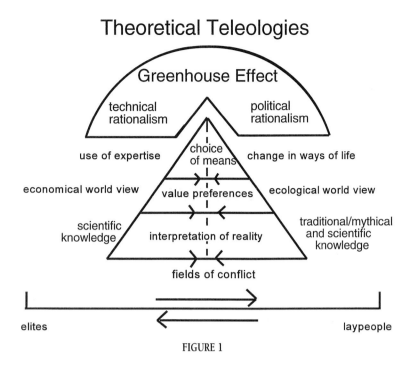

FIGURE 1

fields, as dominating strategies on each side (Järvelä & Wilenius, 1993). To facilitate communication between two relatively distant partners, it is of general interest to develop methods of auditing and participation by civil society such as the environmental impact assessment. There is, however, no technological solution to the problem of social distance between experts and laypeople. This is why environmental impact assessment needs to be completed and reformed by social impact assessment.

tion of the "parties interested" in each EIA process *separately*. From the point of view of sustainable development, however, a good environmental standard may be defined to be a *general interest*. Consequently, it is important to discuss in what framework this general interest can be presented.

From a sociological point of view, EIA has recently been introduced with reference to reflexive modernization, society risk, and communicative planning. It is

XI. ENVIRONMENTAL IMPACT ASSESSMENT

Environmental impact assessment was institutionalized rapidly in the 1980s as an internationally recognized strategy for environmental policy. Since the 1980s EIA procedures have developed into multiple strategies and vary by country (see A. Gilpin, 1995. *Environmental impact assessment* (pp. 16–35). Hong Kong: Cambridge Univ. Press). As a process, EIA may, however, be defined by its phases. According to Glasson *et al.* (1995, 4), the main steps of the EIA process can be defined as in Table I.

Public consultation is a formal part of the EIA, which may be attached to several phases of the process. More important here is that this involves the official recogni-

TABLE I

Step	Tasks
I.	Project screening (is an EIA needed?)
	Scoping (which impacts and issues to consider?)
	Description of the project/development
	Description of the environmental baseline
	Identification of key impacts
II.	Prediction of impacts
	Evaluation and assessment of significance of impacts
	Identification of mitigating measures
III.	Presentation of findings in an environmental impact statement (EIS)
IV.	Review of the EIS
V.	Decision making
VI.	Postdecision monitoring
	Auditing of predictions and of mitigation measures

assumed to develop into a tool of environmental management in order to promote ecological modernization of a society. A critical view of EIA is concerned with the introduction of an effective shift from scientific-data-based impact assessment to a value-based assessment of environmental change. It also calls strongly for the mobilization of the social action resources of the civil society, and, furthermore, it emphasizes developing linkages between laypeople's perceptions and expert knowledge.

XII. SOCIAL IMPACT ASSESSMENT

While *environmental* impact assessment has focused mainly on the physical and biological properties of natural environments, *social* impact assessment (SIA) concentrates on the distinctively human side of particular environments. The very heart of the SIA is to examine the social impact of formulating policies, instituting programs, and building projects. As does the environmental impact assessment, SIA aims to predict and evaluate the impact and outcomes of planned actions. This is, however, approached from the individual, family, or community point of view. SIA methods have been developed since the 1970s in parallel with EIA methods, but often with a distance and distinctiveness from the development of EIA expertise. Today the problem of the (re)integration of EIA and SIA appears to be one of the basic questions not only from a pragmatic policy point of view, but also when considering ethical aspects of the more indirect human impacts related to development acts.

According to its basic idea, SIA uses local citizens' environmental awareness as an input to the societal process of environmental impact assessment. The SIA process should bring forth the shared or controversial values of the community and create a value-based process of mitigation in the interest of the local community. There are several alternatives of practical strategies for the SIA. Auditing may be part of the institutionalized process of EIA, citizens may be involved in the debate concerning EIA in mass media, or a local future workshop can be created. We suggest one more action idea that could be practical as a more permanent participative appraisal for ecosocial communities.

There have been, e.g., in Finland, some recent tentative experiences of integrating social work in local communities with the zoning processes of the cities in a way which we find to be a very interesting example of a new community-level policy of sustainable development. The ecosocial approach to social work pursues in this case an empowerment strategy, trying to match city planning to the ecosocial profiles and projection of the local population. The conventional experts of the EIA process are involved, of course, but there is an additional contribution by the local social workers to mediate between experts and laypeople. In this case social workers are developing capacities as negotiating professionals in ecosocial mitigation. By outlining community values to the experts they help the experts to determine the relevant criteria of a good living environment. On the other hand, the experts' knowledge and technical resources can be translated to the members of the community. The application of this two-way process of advocacy and empowerment calls for an open professionalism where traditions of social closure may be avoided among social workers. The capacities of the reflexive and open professionalism are tested particularly in controversial cases such as in construction of new roads or supermarkets at the next neighborhood of the ecosocial community.

We mention the example of the Finnish social workers as a particular application of SIA mainly because their experiences have further clarified some basic elements of the lay perspective on the immediate living environment. The social workers' activity as SIA agents also increased our understanding of what kind of social mechanisms are applicable to channel laypeople's ethical purposes to the EIA process in order to promote sustainable development. The most crucial qualities or basic values of the urban living environment were brought to the fore through the process of reciprocal participation between citizens and experts. The SIA interpretation by the social workers of the vital value basis refers to the preference for three qualities of an urban environment: (1) good quality or state of the physical and biological environment, (2) social and ecological diversity of the environment, and (3) facility of quotidian life. The ecosocial community is, of course, expected to appreciate highly qualities (1) and (2), whereas the third element is not as easily assumed as part of the quality of a sustainable environment. From the community's point of view, this aspect may, however, be very decisive in everyday life when people choose the particular acts of their ecosocial policy of small actions. Thus, the final outcome of the SIA process should be balanced as an assessment of the man–nature relationship and should include even the feedback the man-to-man relationship has on the former relation.

XIII. CONCLUSION

Environmental problems are inherently social problems. They have been generated mainly by the industrial societies and by consumers' ways of life. Hence, it is consistent that particularly these societies create strategies of social action aiming at mitigation of these problems. Environmental impact assessment has been developed into a legitimate tool for experts to define the impacts of environmental change. In a modern society ecological development is, however, a major social issue in the everyday life of the common people. Daily choices by individuals and communities do have global consequences. This is why environmental impact assessment ought to be reformed and complemented by social impact assessment.

Social impact assessment involves communication not only from expert to expert but also between experts and laypeople. It is ultimately the mission of the civil society to create a culture of self-control in relation to the living environment. In highly individualized societies—and in the world of globalized risk for the environment—the social resources of sustainability can be restored to a great extent to the moral obligations of the solidarity the citizens feel for the "distant other," whether these others are represented by faraway people or by people of future generations. The new ecosocial morality of small steps of environmental protection in everyday life is not to be minimized but to be recognized as an element of a new culture promoting ecosocial morality in civil society. The more communities are empowered by the new ecosocial morality, the stronger the capacities they have in generating political impulses to the process of environmental impact assessment in order to support future prospects for sustainable development.

Also See the Following Articles

ECOLOGICAL BALANCE • ENVIRONMENTAL ETHICS, OVERVIEW • ENVIRONMENTAL JUSTICE • SUSTAINABILITY

Bibliography

Bourdieu, P. (1987). *Choses dites*. Paris: Les Éditions de Minuit.

Douglas, M., & Widavsky, A. (1983). *Risk and culture, an essay on the selection of technological and environmental dangers*. Berkeley: Univ. of California Press.

Finsterbusch, K., Llewellyn, L. G., & Wolf, C. P. (Eds.) (1993). *Social impact assessment*. Beverly Hills, CA: Sage.

Hofbeck, J. (1991). La deep ecology: Essai d'évaluation éthique. In J. A. Prades, J.-G. Vaillancourt, et R. Tessier (Eds.), *Environnement et développement: Questions éthiques et problèmes socio-politiques*. Québec: Éditions Fides.

Morin, E., & Kern, A. (1993). *Terre-Patrie*. Paris: Seuil.

Norton, B. (1987). *Why preserve natural variety?* Princeton: Princeton Univ. Press.

Ollikainen, M. (1992). Kestävä kehitys: Talouden ekologisointi eettisten ja taloustieteellisten periaatteiden nojalla (Sustainable development: Ecological perspective on economy with reference to principles of ethics and economy). Yhteiskunta ja ympäristö, Ympäristöpolitiikan arvo-ongelmia M. Järvelä ja Y. Uurtimo (Eds.), Julkaisuja Yhteiskuntatieteiden tutkimuslaitos, Tampereen yliopisto 2/1992, 101–123.

Redclift, M. (1987). *Sustainable development*. London: Methuen.

Sairinen, R. (1993). Environmental impact assessment in Finland. In A. Haila (Ed.), *Cities for tomorrow—Directions for change*. Espoo: Helsinki Univ. of Technology, Centre for Urban and Regional Studies.

Tessier, R. (1991). L'éthique du développement durable: Quels fondements? Une comparaison avec l'ascétisme séculier chez Weber. In J. A. Prades, J.-G. Vaillancourt, et R. Tessier (Eds.), *Environnement et développement. Questions éthiques et problèmes socio-politiques*. Québec: Éditions Fides.

Wolf, C. P. (1983). Social impact assessment: A methodological overview. In K. Finsterbusch, L. G. Llewellyn, and C. P. Wolf (Eds.), *Social impact assessment*. Beverly Hills, CA: Sage.

ENVIRONMENTAL JUSTICE

Carl Talbot
Cardiff University of Wales

GLOSSARY

ecofeminism A brand of environmentalism that takes its influence from feminism and suggests that the exploitation of women and the exploitation of nature both result from patriarchal oppression, and further, that women, because of their biological and/or social roles, have an innate concern for nature.

job blackmail The tactic employed by industry to secure labor's compliance to its demands by the threat of unemployment or the promise of jobs.

proletarianization The process by which people are dispossessed of the means of production, such as land, so that they must resort to selling their labor.

sustainable use The use of natural resources in a manner that does not deplete their overall stock in such a way as to compromise the opportunities and well-being of present and future generations.

ENVIRONMENTAL JUSTICE challenges the view that environmental matters are external and prior to issues of social justice, arguing instead that social and economic relations of class, race, and gender are central to how environmental issues are identified and how they are fought. The differences in power and opportunity that discrimination on the grounds of race, class, and gender create mean that some sections of the population suffer a disproportionate burden of the detrimental effects of environmental degradation. Environmental justice recognizes the connection between environmental and human well-being and the organization of production in society, whose present relations of exploitation and inequality are directed at the continuation of privilege for some sections of society.

I. REINTERPRETING ENVIRONMENTALISM: A BRIEF HISTORY OF THE ENVIRONMENTAL JUSTICE MOVEMENT

A. The Everyday Environment

The environmental justice movement emerged in the United States in the 1980s as a development of the movement for social justice which sought to challenge racial, sexual, and economic discrimination. The movement strove to politically empower communities so as to include them in decisions that were to affect them, and campaigned to improve home and workplace conditions.

Increasingly the concerns of this community-based movement came to be centered around environmental issues of public health, occupational safety, and, in particular, the siting of polluting industries and technologies and waste disposal facilities. This was especially the case in communities of color which were (and remain) disproportionately exposed to hazards of these sorts. Emerging from these urban, community-based concerns came a movement for which the term "environment" took on a radically new meaning. As Dana Alston, speaking at the first national People of Color Environmental Leadership Summit in 1991, stated,

> The environment, for us, is where we live, where we work, and where we play. The environment affords us the platform to address critical issues of our time: questions of militarism and defense policy; religious freedom; cultural survival; energy-sustainable development; the future of our cities; transportation; housing; land and sovereignty rights; self-determination; employment—and we can go on and on. (quoted in R. Gottlieb, 1993. *Forcing the Spring: The Transformation of the Environmental Movement,* p. 5. Island, Washington, DC)

For this new movement for environmental justice, matters of the environment are not confined to how to best manage or preserve some extra-urban "wilderness"; rather, the environment is part of a broader framework of economic, racial, and social justice. This perspective represents a significant challenge to the way mainstream environmental groups have commonly presented the environmental agenda as primarily occupied with the conservation of pristine wilderness and wildlife. The exclusion of any discussion of urban and industrial concerns in mainstream environmentalism is reflected in the histories of environmentalism, which concern themselves with the romantic champions of wild "Nature," such as the 19th century national parks advocate John Muir and Aldo Leopold, whose "land ethic" has become so revered by much of modern environmentalism, but say nothing of struggles to improve the urban and industrial environments.

By redefining environmentalism, the environmental justice movement has endeavored to rewrite environmental discourse and restructure environmental campaigning to represent the concerns, organizational strategies, and demographics of communities who are confronted by the worst excesses of environmental degradation.

B. Some Historical Landmarks

Because of its community-based approach to organization, the environmental justice movement is defined by the numerous activities of groups and individuals, each of which has its own story of its evolution to tell; nevertheless, a number of significant landmarks stand out in the development of the movement.

Although the issues and campaigns may have been called something other than environmental justice, it is possible to discover a long history of what it encompasses. Friedrick Engels, for example, in his description of the living and working conditions of the working class in mid-19th century England, documents the "environmental racism" suffered by the Irish communities in Manchester (see F. Engels, *The Condition of the Working Class in England*).

Environmental justice advocates in the United States see their campaigning as a continuation and development of a long history of struggles against such "social problems" as dangerous work conditions, poor housing, and poor sanitation, although they have now become framed as "environmental problems."

The demonstrations in Warren County, North Carolina, in 1982 by a community of mostly African-Americans against a proposed PCB landfill site are held by many within the environmental justice movement to mark the birth of the national environmental justice movement. It was during these protests that the term "environmental racism" was coined.

The landmark study of what had become called environmental racism was carried out in 1987 by a civil rights organization, the United Church of Christ Commission for Racial Justice. Entitled *Toxic Wastes and Race in the U.S.* (Public Data Access, New York), the study exposed a link between the location of hazardous waste disposal sites and the racial profile of the neighboring communities. The study concluded that race was the most significant variable with regard to the siting of hazardous waste industries: communities of color had the largest number of hazardous commercial waste operations, with three out of every five black or Hispanic Americans living in communities with at least one toxic waste site. These findings were confirmed in Robert Bullard's book, *Dumping in Dixie,* published in 1990, which documented this form of racism in the southern United States. This particular brand of environmental inequity was found by subsequent studies to operate in the location and through the detrimental impact of other environmentally hazardous industries and practices, such as the manufacture and use of pesticides, and health and safety concerns such as lead poisoning.

In 1990 the environmental justice movement sent a direct challenge to the mainstream U.S. environmental groups, known as the Group of Ten (which includes organizations such as the Audubon Society, the Sierra Club, and the Wilderness Society). In two open letters of protest to the Group of Ten the environmental justice groups, the Gulf Coast Tenants Organization, and the Southwest Organizing Project, criticized the environmental movement for its racism in terms of the racial composition of the staff of the organizations making up the Group of Ten, its agenda, which failed to concern itself with poor and ethnic communities despite evidence to suggest that they were the main victims of pollution, and its "clear lack of accountability" to communities of the Third World. These letters represented a protest against the institutionalization and professionalization of the environmental movement and its agenda, which failed to incorporate concerns of social justice.

The centrality of the link between ethnicity and those communities at greatest risk from environmentally hazardous industries and practices to the redefinition of environmentalism pursued by the environmental justice movement was registered by the first national People of Color Environmental Leadership Summit held in Washington, DC, in October 1991. This meeting represented an opportunity for the numerous environmental justice groups and networks which had developed in the 1980s—many of which, such as the National Toxic Campaign of Boston and the Citizens Clearinghouse for Hazardous Wastes, had been making explicit links between social issues such as poverty and racial discrimination and waste disposal since the 1980s—to collectively define a new kind of environmentalism from a multiracial and social justice perspective. The summit discussed organizational questions of the movement, such as whether campaigning ought to be centralized or remain the domain of regional networks, and whether the central organizational concern of environmental racism would best be served by multiracial groups or ones whose membership exclusively represents the ethnic group concerned. These debates are still current and have formed an important part of the agenda of subsequent regional follow-up meetings (the meeting in New Orleans in 1992 was attended by over 2000 people).

Importantly, delegates to the 1991 summit ratified a statement of the Principles of Environmental Justice (see Appendix) which placed themes of sustainable development, pollution control, health and safety at work, production practices, cultural self-determination and political empowerment, and environmental racism into a single framework, giving this new form of environmental politics a clear identity.

II. RACE AND THE ENVIRONMENT

A. Communities of Color and Environmental Hazards

Benjamin Chavis of the Commission for Racial Justice has defined environmental racism as

> racial discrimination in environmental policy making. It is racial discrimination in the enforcement of regulations and laws. It is racial discrimination in the deliberate targeting of communities of color for toxic waste disposal and the siting of polluting industries. It is racial discrimination in the official sanctioning of the life-threatening presence of poisons and pollutants in communities of color. And, it is racial discrimination in the history of excluding people of color from the mainstream environmental groups, decision making boards, commissions, and regulatory bodies. (B. F. Chavis, 1993. Foreword to *Confronting Environmental Racism: Voices from the Grassroots* (R. Bullard, Ed.), South End, Boston)

Racism has not only shaped the social, economic, and political landscapes of countries such as the United States, it has also played a significant part in the formation of the environmental landscape of countries. Racial discrimination has meant people of color are concentrated in communities that are segregated from white residential areas, and it is these identifiable communities of color that are targeted for a disparate exposure to environmental risks (see J. A. Kushner, 1980. *Apartheid in America*, Associated Faculty, Frederick, MD). Environmental racism is seen by the environmental justice movement as an extension of institutional racism in housing, education, employment, and so on.

Studies conducted by environmental justice advocates, and recently by the U.S. Government's Environmental Protection Agency (in a 1992 two-volume report entitled *Environmental Equity*, EPA Office of Policy, Planning, and Evaluation, Washington, DC), conclude that communities of color are subjected to a disproportionate share of the burden of environmental hazards.

Racism has been, and continues to be, a decisive factor in environmental planning and policy making.

This disproportionate concentration of environmental hazards in communities of color indicates that the siting of polluting waste treatment facilities, and other environmentally dangerous operations, is decided not by considerations of environmental suitability, but by an evaluation of the social power of neighboring communities and the subsequent likelihood of effective organized opposition. Poor communities, particularly those of people of color, with high levels of unemployment, poverty, ill health, poor housing, inadequate educational resources, and poor political representation, are considered the most likely to be able to offer the least resistance to these highly contentious and contested policy decisions. Measures by governments to tighten environmental regulations on industry have had the unconsidered effect of intensifying this burden of environmental racism by increasing the demand for waste treatment facilities.

B. Work, Health Care, and Racism

In work, ethnicity is a factor which generally compounds problems of economic injustice. People of color are concentrated in occupations with high risks to health. Studies, such as those edited by Bunyan Bryant and Paul Mohai (1993. *Race and the Incidence of Environmental Hazards: A Time for Discourse.* Westview, Boulder, CO), show that farmworkers and their children, the vast majority of whom in the United States are people of color, are commonly exposed to poisonous levels of pesticides. This is also true of the workers involved in the production of the pesticides and the communities, again most likely to be people of color, who neighbor these production sites.

Not only are communities of color disproportionately exposed to environmental risks, the effects of this exposure are unlikely to be adequately treated by a health care system which, as studies such as Vicente Navarro's (1991. *Monthly Review* 43(4), 1–13) have shown, is also permeated by racial discrimination and subsequently offers a reduced and impoverished service to people of color.

C. Native American Lands

In the United States the lands of native Americans have suffered from the attention of waste disposal industries, with reservations targeted for landfills and incinerators, although a great many of these planned developments have been frustrated by community opposition.

Less successful has been the defense of these native American communities against "economic blackmail." Ward Churchill and Winona LaDuke have described how the Navajo and Lakota Indian Reservations have been held "economic hostages" by the uranium extraction industry while their health and environment have been decimated by the resultant radioactive waste (1985. *Socialist Review, 81,* 95–119). Poor communities generally are susceptible to "job blackmail," which offers unemployed communities the lure of jobs with the threat that should corporate demands be challenged these employment opportunities will be dissolved. In the case of the Navajo and Lakota peoples the success of this intimidation has resulted in such severe radioactive pollution that the U.S. government is considering designating these, and other affected lands, National Sacrifice Areas. The implementation of this plan would effectively dispossess Indian peoples, who would be forced to leave these areas, of their homelands. As Churchill and LaDuke conclude, such a decision would effectively designate these Indian communities as "National Sacrifice Peoples."

III. WOMEN AND THE ENVIRONMENT

While much of the work done in this effort to redefine environmentalism has been conducted on the issue of environmental racism, environmental injustice is not confined to discrimination on grounds of race. The framework of environmental justice examines the distribution of harmful effects of environmentally destructive practices along class and gender lines as well.

A. Women and Responsibility for Waste

A great many of the slogans of mainstream environmentalism, and their transmission by the media, rest on the assumption that our present environmental insecurity is the result of a culpable universal human endeavor to "dominate" nature. This view has important implications for the ascription of responsibility for environmental degradation. The perceived domination of nature by humanity as a whole implies a universality with informs a discourse of responsbility that blames indiscriminately. The received media expression of this perceived universal responsiblity has allowed the widespread circulation of a mentality which is informed by the self-accusatory assertion, "the enemy is us." As a result a great deal of campaigning by environmental groups, sometimes with the support of governmental agencies, has been directed at the reform of individual behavior; for example, we are given the opportunity to redeem ourselves via "environmentally friendly consumption." This "privatization" of environmental costs has resulted in a disproportionate burden of responsibility being placed on women.

One area of environmental concern where this displacement of responsibility from the wasteful productive practices of industry to the individual is particularly obvious concerns the perceived responsbility for waste. Despite the fact that household rubbish makes up approximately only 10% of the total waste of towns, since their inception in the 1980s, waste reduction and recycling schemes have been concentrated on the household. The high-profile efforts of the state have given rise to a "waste ethic" which informs waste coordination and sorting efforts and environmental information campaigns which are relayed through consumer associations, the media, and governmental bodies. Waste education, which instructs the household to reduce waste at the point of purchase by favoring "environmentally friendly" produced and packaged goods, and at the point of disposal by sorting waste for recycling, is a strategy of displacement in which the household is not only required to absorb the consequences of unhealthy working and living conditions, but is further burdened with the responsibility for environmental recovery and sensible management of valuable natural resources and dangerous waste products. As Irmgard Schultz notes, this state-sponsored "waste ethic" is targeted specifically at women:

> The goal is to create a waste consciousness among women. The method is to burden women with a guilty conscience if they do not correctly sort the rubbish.... The goal of this huge information campaign is to discipline women to collect and separate rubbish, dovetailing both with the teaching of cleanliness to children and with women's overall management of the household. (I. Schultz, 1993. *Capitalism, Nature, Socialism* 4(2), 59)

This tactic of displacing responsibility for waste management onto the household, in which women ultimately bear the greatest responsibility, identifies waste as a problem of individual households whose patterns of consumption and disposal are in need of improvement and reform, and not as a problem of market-governed production principally interested in profitable sales. In this manner the costs of environmental degradation are passed onto the household and thereby privatized. Schultz concludes that this tactic must also be seen as a "moralizing strategy" against women by maintaining that the waste problem is a consequence of women's moral behavior, thereby pressing women to adopt responsibility for waste management.

Schultz believes that women are particularly susceptible to this environmental blackmail because of their established role as domestic caregivers. A guilty conscience about waste can be engendered in women because of an existing "gender-specific" responsibility for health. For the most part it is women who have been allocated responsibility for the health of the household members, and it is out of a concern for the detrimental impact of waste on health that women have engaged with the demands of the "waste ethic" peddled by the state.

This moralizing ethic also facilitates the co-option of unpaid female labor into the production process, thereby aiding the accumulation of capital. To make productive and profitable use of recyclable waste products, it is necessary for the materials to be sorted prior to technological reprocessing, and this sorting of waste is performed in the private household, most often by women. This moralizing strategy therefore not only displaces responsibility for waste reduction and disposal onto the private household, but also co-opts unpaid domestic labor into the production process. In this respect the strategy is a twofold disciplinary mechanism: not only does it morally discipline women by engendering a guilty conscience about the volume and environmental impact of waste, it also represents a form of work discipline requiring the ordered sorting and disposal of recyclable products for the advantage of corporate industry.

B. Women in the Third World

The inequalities that women suffer in the developed world are compounded by economic vulnerability; it is poor women in the developed world, often women of color, who are likely to suffer the consequences of a degraded and polluted environment. In the Third World gender inequality means that women suffer most as a result of the inequalities between rich and poor countries. The inequalities that women suffer in the developed world are intensified for women in the Third World.

The marginalization of women in the policy statements of environmental organizations, and the conservation strategies they evolve, is well illustrated by the inclusion of women, along with indigenous people and the young, in the classification "other groups" in Agenda 21 of the Rio Declaration on Environment and Development issued from the Rio Summit of 1992. Although these three groups together make up the majority of the world's population, with women making up about half of that total, the male dominance of the perspective that sees women as "other" ensures their marginalization in such prominent statements of intent as the Rio Declaration.

Yet it is women in the Third World who are confronted by the worst excesses of unsustainable, environmentally destructive practices. Degraded agricultural land and poor and limited access to food, potable water, health care, and energy supplies—the results of the degradation of the environment and unsustainable, environmentally destructive state and capitalist activities—have their initial and greatest impact on the lives of women and their children. This is borne out by the enormous disparities in infant and maternal rates of ill health, malnutrition, and mortality between the developed world and the Third World.

Women of the Third World have not met these injustices with passivity (despite prevailing stereotypes). Numerous women's groups exist in countries of the Third World to secure the needs of women in both rural and urban regions. These groups have not only engaged in activities which might conform to the often favored view of women as carers, such as the defense of natural habitats and the reclamation of land, but women's groups like the Self-Employed Women's Association, founded in 1972 in Ahmedabad, have involved themselves in trade issues in pursuit of more equitable trade conditions for women. Women have also sought involvement in urban planning—as exemplified by CEFEMINA, a Costa Rican group formed in 1981 to petition for environmentally sensitive housing development—and the provision of literacy programs, like the Chilean group MOMUPO. These groups, which have arisen to combat the environmental, social, and economic injustices that women of the Third World disproportionately suffer, are evidence that the politics of gender must be included in any credible account of an environmentally sustainable world.

C. Women and the Environmental Justice Movement

Since the environmental justice movement's beginnings in the antitoxic campaigns of the early 1980s, women, predominantly women of color, have played a vital role. This membership profile reflects the fact that the majority of community groups that make up the environmental justice movement are located in working class communities in urban and industrial centers. The disproportionate representation of people of color,

women, and the poor in this movement reflects the disproportionate burden of environmental hazards these sections of the population suffer.

In these communities the vital environmental issues are those everyday ones concerned with health and survival, and it has been suggested by some theorists that it is women's biological or social affinity with these concerns that has led to their predominance in the environmental movement generally. While some ecofeminists claim that it is a women's biological role of reproduction that informs an innate appreciation of the unity of all life and encourages them to lead the fight for a clean and healthy environment for their families, others have argued that it is women's gendered social roles as "mother" and "carer" that have determined this involvement.

However, some women campaigners in the environmental justice movement have been cautious of such ecofeminist theorizing, questioning its political usefulness and strategic value; Dana Alston, for example, has stated, "Personally, I like spending my energy trying to change how we are perceived and how we move forward rather than analyzing why we're there in the first place" (quoted in G. Di Chiro, 1992. *Socialist Review* 22(4), 94–130). Whatever the reason, there is no doubt that women do suffer environmental injustices as a result of their gender and that women like Lois Gibbs and Penny Newman of the Citizen's Clearinghouse for Hazardous Waste have made a vital contribution to the environmental justice movement.

IV. CLASS AND THE ENVIRONMENT

A. Labor and the Environmental Movement

The environmental movement has, for the most part, distanced itself from labor-organized opposition to the activities of industry. The loyalties and motives of labor appear to be viewed with a certain cynicism and disdain. Some environmentalists, like the deep ecologist Warwick Fox, have suggested that the working class colludes with corporate interests responsible for environmental destruction, while others, such as Ulrich Beck, have suggested the very notion of class is itself redundant. It seems that from the viewpoint of environmentalism the working class, if it exists at all, is untrustworthy because it is corrupted by the bribes of capital and will seek to defend these interests by siding with industry against an environmentalism which may threaten them.

Similarly labor has opposed environmental protest and activities which it perceives as a threat to continued employment in industries which the environmental movement has identified as environmentally hazardous. The mutual hostility and suspicion of environmentalism and labor finds much of its motivation in the perceived opposition between the interests of labor in securing its continued means of subsistence—employment—and the interests of the environment, which may require the drastic curtailment, and even the cessation, of the activities of many industries (the source of employment). By manipulating the character of this discussion, capital has been able to promote the belief that regulations on industries which seek to defend the environment will lead to losses in employment, thereby contriving the myth of "jobs versus environment," which translates as "labor versus environmentalists" and creates deep divisions between labor and the environmental movement.

B. Labor's Environmental Agenda

Labor's struggle for improved work and living conditions has been a continuous element of class conflict. Demands for a healthy environment, both inside and outside the factory, and challenges to the operating procedures of industrial capital have been a central component of the historical opposition of labor. Capital in turn has sought to resist the internalization of the costs of its destructive practices. These costs are presently borne by society (most severely by the working class and racial minorities, and, with the international mobility of industrial capital, by the poor of the Third World) in the form of pollution, occupational disease, and widespread public ill health. The economic burden of these consequences of capitalist production is met by social institutions, such as health services, where these exist, but otherwise directly by the individual and his or her family and friends.

The unwillingness of industry to take account of the costs of its operations to the environment, communities, and workers is not solely driven by economic considerations; regulations designed to protect the environment, worker, and public health are resisted because they increase worker and public involvement in production and investment decisions of private industry, and represent an interference with the jealously guarded "exploitive rights" of capital. While capital is successful in fending off these challenges to its authority, businesses collect, as Richard Kazis and Richard Grossman describe it, "a subsidy coined in blood, broken bones, broken health, physical pain, mental anguish and the

ultimate trauma of death" (1991. *Fear at Work: Job Blackmail, Labor, and the Environment,* 2nd ed., p. 47. New Society Publications, Philadelphia).

The poor suffer disproportionate exposure to environmental hazards at work (when they are able to get work), whether it be in the production of toxic substances or in their use, and in their communities, which are most likely to be the location of polluting industries. For the working class, health and safety at work, involvement in production decisions, and community conditions are environmental issues. The framework of environmental justice recognizes the essential relationship between these concerns of the working class and environmental problems.

C. Job Blackmail

Efforts to include labor into the environmental justice movement have centered around the issue of job blackmail; employers are able to intimidate workers by threatening to close factories and move to alternative sites elsewhere in the country or abroad, leaving unemployment in their wake. This intimidation is also leveled at communities who are told to conform to corporate requirements if they are to retain existing employment or attract new opportunities.

With increased pressure on industry to clean up its practices, this ultimatum is ever more frequently made to counter public demands for environmental and occupational health and safety protection. By a clever public relations exercise, which focuses on the employment benefits which its present, or proposed, investment promises, business is able to present its own private interests as synonymous with the public's interest: the pursuit of profit dons the benevolent mask of a public service—the creation of employment opportunities. This lure of jobs is reinforced by the threat of unemployment devised to intimidate workers into accepting that their only alternative, if they are to avoid the economic hardship of unemployment, is to support the proposals of employers in spite of their detrimental and exploitative character. This job blackmail represents economic bondage and is used by industry to define the terms of labor's good behavior. Aware of the brutal consequences of its market-governed performance, in both human and environmental terms, business seeks to disarm and deflect challenges to its priorities by pitting jobs against the environment, and subsequently workers against environmentalists.

Job-related benefits reinforce this economic bondage; after workers have sacrificed environmental and health and safety regulations for continued employment, poor health resulting from occupational diseases and possible untimely unemployment or death resulting from occupational accidents become a fearful reality. Insurers, quick to spy the supply-side advantages of worker's concern in the face of such threats, have eagerly offered the "solution" of health and life insurance. By tying such schemes to employment, capital is able to further subjugate labor and police its good behavior. This move seems to go hand-in-hand with government underfunding and privatization of public health care provision.

By manipulating the public's perception of possible alternatives, corporations and their supporters are able to impose the terms of the debate. Speaking of the clash of interests between the northwest American timber industry and environmentalists concerned to preserve the forest habitat of the endangered spotted owl, then President George Bush stated, "We want to save the little furry-feathery guy and all that but I don't want to see 40,000 loggers thrown out of work" (*The Times*, 28 May 1992). Such "definitional sleights-of-hand" allow governmental officials and business to avoid basic considerations of what it is that is being produced and for what purpose, and how, if at all, it should be produced. The contrivance of this false conflict between jobs and the environment provides capital with the opportunity to continue with "business as usual."

In an effort to create a link between employment and the environment, environmental justice groups, such as the National Toxics Campaign, proposed the establishment of a "Superfund for Workers." This concept recognizes the importance of job loss to both labor and environmental groups by calling for financial and training assistance for workers who become unemployed as a result of the termination of environmentally hazardous industries. Similarly environmental justice calls for the restructuring of industry so as to reduce environmentally harmful production and requires the support of labor initiatives, such as that of the Lucas Aerospace Campaign in the 1970s, which sought the opportunity for workers to turn their skills and equipment to the production of environmentally benign, socially useful products (see H. Wainwright and D. Elliot, 1982. *The Lucas Plan*. Allison and Busby, London).

D. Production and the Environment

The framework of environmental justice recognizes that the degradation of the environment is sourced in the procedures of production. It is the organization of production in society, with its relations of exploitation, that is the object of the environmental justice critique.

Current production is organized for the realization of profit and privilege, and pays little heed to the consequences for the health of humanity or the rest of nature. The impact of environmentally hazardous products on wild nature is preceded by their production and their detrimental effects on the health and quality of the lives of workers and their communities during this production. Environmental justice appreciates, therefore, that the terrain of production and the support of labor are fundamental to environmental campaigning.

Thus the link between the interests of labor and the interests of the environment is forged by the realization that environmental issues are questions about the social organization of production; environmental justice dictates that it is not enough to ask, "What is produced?", but also "How do we produce?" and "Who is in control of this production?" Concern about what kind of environment we want to live in presupposes concern about how we labor. The environmental justice movement argues that at present the interests of profit and privilege determine the answers to these questions; it campaigns for justice to determine them.

V. THE THIRD WORLD AND THE ENVIRONMENT

The struggle for environmental justice is an international one reflecting the global character of environmental problems. The Third World has become a dumping ground not only for the wastes of developed countries, but also for products considered too hazardous for the domestic market, including pesticides and medicines. The poorer countries of the world have also received the attention of corporations seeking cheap labor and a way of avoiding costly environmental and health and safety regulations on their operations; the great loss of life at Bhopal is a testament to the enormous dangers Third World peoples face as a result of these cost-cutting exercises.

A. The Trade in Toxic Waste

As restrictive regulations on industrial practices and the disposal of waste have been applied in the industrialized countries, companies have sought out cheaper alternative sites in the Third World, where regulations are nonexistent or ignored. The cost of waste disposal in the United States, for example, may be over 20 times more than that in a country in Africa. As the regulation of toxic waste disposal has tightened and the demand for legitimate domestic sites has outstripped provision, companies have found a cheaper and largely unrestrained alternative abroad in countries of the Third World.

Some of the international trade in waste is carried out legally with Third World waste importation companies and governments eager to earn foreign currency. The Third World Network, who monitors this trade, identifies two "waves" of such waste disposal contracts:

The first, in 1980, involved the U.S. and coincided with the tightening up of laws concerning toxic waste there. The second wave in 1987 and 1988, involving European countries, was probably linked to the 1986 EEC directive and decisions arrived at by the Organization of European Cooperation and Development (OECD) on the transportation of toxic waste. (Third World Network, 1989. *Race Class, 30*(3), 49–50)

There is also a complementary, and widespread, illegal trade in waste often involving the unscrupulous complicity of governments of the developed and underdeveloped worlds.

This "toxic imperialism" represents the globalization of the environmentally racist practice of targeting domestic communities of color for the siting of environmentally hazardous facilities, as uncovered in the United States in such studies as the Commission for Racial Justice and those of Robert Bullard. The institutional nature of this racism was recently made explicit in a leaked memo from Lawrence Summers, chief economist of the World Bank. Part of this memo was published in *The Economist* in February 1992 under the title, "Let Them Eat Pollution." The memo presents an "economic" argument for an increased trade in toxic waste between the developed world and the Third World based on such reasoning as the differential loss of earnings resulting from health-impairing pollution between these two populations, favoring an increased level of pollution in countries with the lowest wages, and the "inefficiently low" levels of pollution in African countries compared with those of the developed world.

B. Conservation and Injustice

There is increasing concern within the environmental justice movement that peoples of the Third World are suffering injustices resulting from the conservation strategies promoted by mainstream environmental groups and governments of the developed world. A good example of this are the "debt-for-nature" ex-

changes initiated by the World Wildlife Fund (now the Worldwide Fund for Nature), and sponsored by the United States government, which enable transnational forces—economic and cultural—to penetrate the political economies of Third World countries and secure control over the conservation programs of these countries, often at the expense, and to the detriment, of indigenous peoples. Since the first debt-for-nature exchange in 1987, when protection for 3.7 million acres of Bolivian tropical forest was negotiated in return for money raised by Conservation International (from public and private financial institutions, governments, and the United Nations) to buy $650,000 of Bolivian debt, such swaps have been arranged, or considered, in a large number of countries, including Brazil, Argentina, Ecuador, Venezuela, Guatemala, Zambia, the Dominican Republic, and Jamaica.

While it does appear that this initiative has extended some protection to an extremely limited and select portion of the biosphere, what is clear is that these new relations between conservationists and the international financial community have seriously undermined the struggles of indigenous peoples for self-determination and control of their homelands. This concern was addressed by the Coordinating Body for Indigenous People's Organizations of the Amazon Basin (COICA), which represents 1.2 million Indian people in Colombia, Peru, Bolivia, Ecuador, and Brazil, in an open letter to the international conservation community in 1990:

We are concerned about debt-for-nature swaps that put your organizations in a position of negotiating with our governments the future of our homelands. We know of specific examples of such swaps which have shown brazen disregard for the rights of the indigenous inhabitants. . . .

We want to make it clear that we never delegated any power of representation to the environmentalist community nor to any individual organization within the community.

We propose joining hands with those members of the world-wide environmentalist community who recognize our historical role as caretakers of the Amazon Basin, support our efforts to reclaim and defend our traditional territories, and accept our organizations as legitimate and equal partners. (quoted in D. Alston and N. Brown, 1993. In *Confronting Environmental Racism: Voices from the Grassroots* (R. Bullard, Ed.), p. 189. South End, Boston)

It seems that the economic vulnerability of these countries, on which this program trades, is likely to lead to financial expediency suppressing matters of social justice.

C. Environmentalism and Development

Environmentalism as pursued by the domestic governments of countries of the Third World is supported to an ever increasing extent by the development assistance of foreign agencies. Such foreign-sponsored environmentalism serves to reinforce dependency relations between poor countries of the Third World and the wealthy developed nations. Not only do environmental conservation and rehabilitation programs cost enormous sums of money, which a debt-burdened Third World cannot afford, but with the increasing "industrialization" of environmentalism, and its monopoly of "expert" technologies of assessment, reconstruction, and management, industrial nations are able to regulate the conservation of the natural resources of the Third World and manage their exploitation. Such a relation of financial and technological dependency means that the economies of the developed countries are able to determine the agenda of the environmental policies of Third World countries so as to control global environmental resources and secure continued, and often improved, access to them. In this manner environmentalism represents another avenue for the insertion of political economies of the Third World into the global corporate system. By reinforcing relations of dependency, environmentalism becomes another example of "dependent development" which enables developed nations to discipline the political economies of countries of the Third World.

D. Conservation Programs and Inequality

The discourse of environmentalism has also been pressed into service by the domestic elites of countries of the Third World to legitimize the reproduction of social inequalities. State-led environmentalism frequently identifies the poor as responsible for environmental degradation: condemnation by vocal elites is leveled against the sexual practices of the poor in their failure to reduce family size and the subsistence practices of the poor, such as the clearance of forest for cultivation and collection of firewood for cooking. In this fashion attention is diverted from the role that corporate interests play in the destruction of the environments of countries of the Third World by their intensive logging, fishing, and agricultural industries, while collaborative domestic elites further enhance their economic wealth.

It is the poor, who suffer the brunt of environmental degradation, who are identified by state environmentalism as to blame. Subsequent elite formulated and foreign-funded responses to the environmental crisis comprehend and objectify the poor only as "passive participants," for example, as paid laborers in reforestation programs. The poor are dispossessed and proletarianized as they are forced out from degraded environments which are no longer sufficiently productive into paid labor, often recruited by elite-led, foreign-funded development programs.

These elite-driven environmental protection programs act as a disciplining mechanism against the poor. These measures may often involve incorporating poor farmers into the "Green Revolution," with the result that food production becomes increasingly dependent on the technologies of chemical pest control, chemical fertilizers, agricultural machinery, and genetically engineered seed varieties, control and distribution of which is monopolized by corporations of the developed world. Moral discipline of the rural poor, directed at their sexual practices, is thereby closely accompanied by the disciplining of their agricultural practices and the creation of a dependency on the technologies of the developed world.

E. Wilderness Designation and "Ecotourism"

Conservation initiatives such as the debt-for-nature swaps are also pursued with the intention of defending the "wilderness" as a leisure opportunity for the wealthier people of the developed world. With a number of tour operators taking an active involvement in conservation programs, the idea is to develop a "low-impact" tourism, or "ecotourism," in countries of the Third World. Ian Munt has disclosed the implicit racism of the primitivistic nostalgia surrounding the romantization of wilderness and native peoples which informs the rhetoric of this tourism, with its frequent employment of colonial imagery and recreation of forms of colonial travel, such as safaris, in a new "ecofriendly" guise as "ecosafaris" (I. Munt, 1994. *Race Class, 36*(1), 49–60).

The designation of wilderness preserves in the Third World is resulting in severe injustices and deprivation. Ashish Kothari, the founding member of the Indian environmental group Kalpvriksh, says of the establishment of the national parks in India,

The approach was essentially one of saving wild-life *from* the people, rather than *with* them. In other words, local communities in wildlife-rich areas were seen to be enemies to the conservation cause, and were either physically displaced or denied access to these areas. While in the short run this approach has led to habitat and species protection in several parts of India, it has also had two detrimental impacts: first severe human rights abuses as peoples' basic survival resources have been denied them; second, the alienation of local people from the very areas which they could have been instrumental in conserving. The approach is therefore not only anti-human, it is also short-sighted from the wildlife conservation point of view. Increasingly, as a sharp backlash, communities are demanding the denotification of national parks and sanctuaries in order to regain their rights over resources. (in an interview with J. M. Alier, 1993. *Capitalism, Nature, Socialism, 4*(3), 111)

The Third World poor, dependent on the lands subject to wilderness designation for their means of survival, cannot afford the luxury of a "museumized nature." Conservation efforts in the Third World which are conducted to the exclusion of the welfare and interests of indigenous communities are unjust insofar as they have led to the dispossession of people of their lands, and subsequently their means of survival. Environmental justice demands equitable access to, and distribution of, the resources of nature, in a manner which is sustainable for present and future generations.

VI. INTERGENERATIONAL AND INTERSPECIES JUSTICE

The demands of justice, at their very least, are met when the basic needs of a person which enable one to live a life that is worthwhile and devoid of such harms as hunger, malnutrition, ill-health, and a polluted environment are satisfied (where this is possible). It is unreasonable, though some have suggested it, to assume that relations of justice and injustice are bounded by the domestic concerns of any particular country or culture, or the limited obligations defined by relations of reciprocal advantage, or some special relationship, such as those of the family. If one person's basic needs are to count, then the demands of moral equality require that those of anyone else count equally, regardless of

their geographical location, or relationship, or lack of it, to any other person.

The pertinent question in considerations of just treatment is, "Do they have needs and interests of moral significance which may be aided or frustrated by our actions?" If this is the requirement for relations of justice to exist, then, as is recognized in "Principles of Environmental Justice" (see Appendix), their sphere of application is not confined to the present population of human beings.

It is widely accepted that our present actions may have serious repercussions for future generations of human beings. It does not take much imagination to recognize that the legacy of a polluted, exhausted, unhealthy environment will significantly frustrate the satisfaction of the interests of future generations and their ability to meet basic needs, such as clean air and water, sufficient energy supplies, and a healthy environment in which to live, and the fact that the identities of future people are currently unknown does not affect this recognition. Justice, therefore, requires that we consider the needs and interests of future generations when evaluating the acceptability of present actions, like those that have a detrimental environmental impact.

The realm of justice does not end with the treatment of humans, although there is considerable debate about what in the natural world is worthy of moral consideration, whether it be sentient animals or all animals, whether plant life ought to be included in the moral community, or whether it is collectives such as species or ecosystems which ought to be the objects of our moral concern. While these debates in environmental ethics and animal welfare ethics are ongoing, it does seem clear that nonhuman species do have basic needs which certain of our actions (particularly those of an environmentally destructive character) can frustrate and to which we therefore owe concerns of justice.

Environmental justice not only mandates that we ensure a healthy environment for present and future generations of human beings, but also for present and future generations of nonhuman life.

VII. APPENDIX: PRINCIPLES OF ENVIRONMENTAL JUSTICE

Preamble
We the people of color, gathered together at this multinational People of Color Environmental Leadership Summit, to begin to build a national and international movement of all peoples of color to fight the

destruction and taking of our lands and communites, do hereby re-establish our spiritual interdependence to the sacredness of our Mother Earth; to respect and celebrate each of our cultures languages and beliefs about the natural world and our roles in healing ourselves; to insure environmental justice; to promote economic alternatives which would contribute to the development of environmentally safe livelihoods; and, to secure our political, economic and cultural liberation that has been denied for over 500 years of colonization and oppression, resulting in the poisoning of our communities and land and the genocide of our peoples, do affirm and adopt these Principles of Environmental Justice:

1. *Environmental justice* affirms the sacredness of Mother Earth, ecological unity and the interdependence of all species, and the right to be free from ecological destruction.

2. *Environmental justice* demands that public policy be based on mutual respect and justice for all peoples, free from any form of discrimination or bias.

3. *Environmental justice* mandates the right to ethical, balanced and responsible uses of land and renewable resources in the interest of a sustainable planet for humans and other living things.

4. *Environmental justice* calls for universal protection from nuclear testing and extraction, production and disposal of toxic/hazardous wastes and poisons that threaten the fundamental right to clean air, land, water, and food.

5. *Environmental justice* affirms the fundamental right to political, economic, cultural and environmental self-determination of all peoples.

6. *Environmental justice* demands the cessation of the production of all toxins, hazardous wastes, and radioactive materials, and that all past and current producers be held strictly accountable to the people for detoxification and the containment at the point of production.

7. *Environmental justice* demands the right to participate as equal partners at every level of decision-making including needs assessment, planning, implementation, enforcement and evaluation.

8. *Environmental justice* affirms the right of all workers to a safe and healthy work environment, without being forced to choose an unsafe livelihood and unemployment. It also affirms the right of those who work at home to be free from environmental hazards.

9. *Environmental justice* protects the right of victims of environmental injustice to receive full compensation and reparations for damages as well as quality health care.

10. *Environmental justice* considers governmental acts of environmental injustice a violation of international law, the Universal Declaration On Human Rights, and the United Nations Convention on Genocide.

11. *Environmental justice* must recognize a special legal and natural relationship of Native Peoples to the U.S. government through treaties, agreements, compacts, and covenants affirming sovereignty and self-determination.

12. *Environmental justice* affirms the need for urban and rural ecological policies to clean up and rebuild our cities and rural areas in balance with nature, honoring the cultural integrity of all our communities, providing fair access for all to the full range of resources.

13. *Environmental justice* calls for the strict enforcement of principles of informed consent, and a halt to the testing of experimental reproductive and medical procedures and vaccinations on people of color.

14. *Environmental justice* opposes the destructive operations of multi-national corporations.

15. *Environmental justice* opposes military occupation, repression and exploitation of lands, people and cultures, and other life forms.

16. *Environmental justice* calls for the education of present and future generations which emphasizes social and environmental issues, based on our experience and an appreciation of our diverse cultural perspectives.

17. *Environmental justice* requires that we, as individuals, make personal and consumer choices to consume as little of Mother Earth's resources and to produce as little waste as possible; and make the conscious decision to challenge and reprioritize our lifestyles to insure the health of the natural world for present and future generations.

Adopted October 7, 1991, national People of Color Environmental Leadership Summit, Washington, DC.

Also See the Following Articles

DEVELOPMENT ETHICS • ECOLOGICAL BALANCE • SUSTAINABILITY

Bibliography

Alston, D. (Ed.) (1991). "We Speak for Ourselves: Social Justice, Race, and the Environment." The Panos Institute, Washington, DC.

Bryant, B., and Mohai, P. (Eds.) (1993). "Race and the Incidence of Environmental Hazards: A Time for Discourse." Westview, Boulder, CO.

Bullard, R. (1990). "Dumping in Dixie: Race, Class and Environmental Quality." Westview, Boulder, CO.

Bullard, R. (Ed.) (1993). "Confronting Environmental Racism: Voices from the Grassroots." South End, Boston.

Churchill, W., and LaDuke, W. (1985). Radioactive colonization and the native Americans. *Socialist Rev.* **81**, 95–119.

Di Chiro, G. (1992). Defining environmental justice: Women's voices and grassroots politics. *Socialist Rev.* **22**(4), 93–130.

Foster, J. B. (1993). Let them eat pollution: Capitalism and the world environment. *Monthly Rev.* **44**(8), 10–20.

Gottlieb, R. (1993). "Forcing the Spring: The Transformation of the Environmental Movement." Island, Washington, DC.

Hofrichter, R. (Ed.) (1993). "Toxic Struggles: The Theory and Practice of Environmental Justice." New Society Publications, Philadelphia.

Kazis, R., and Grossman, R. L. (1991). "Fear at Work: Job Blackmail, Labor and the Environment," 2nd ed. New Society Publications, Philadelphia.

Munt, I. (1994). Eco-tourism or ego-tourism? *Race Class* **36**(1), 49–60.

Navarro, V. (1991). Class and race: Life and death situations. *Monthly Rev.* **43**(4), 1–13.

Shiva, V. (1989). "Staying Alive: Women, Ecology and Development." Zed Books, London.

Third World Network (1989). Toxic waste dumping in the third world. *Race Class* **30**(3), 47–56.

A Note on Sources

An important part of the development of the environmental justice movement has been the establishment of alternative sources of information concerning environmental hazards and problems. Two valuable journals dedicated to making technical information more accessible are *Rachel's Hazardous Waste News,* published by the Environmental Research Foundation, and *Race, Poverty and the Environment,* published by the Earth Island Institute. A directory of people of color environmental justice groups in the United States and Canada is produced by the Environmental Justice Resource Center based at Clark Atlanta University and is entitled *People of Color Environmental Groups Directory.*

Issues of environmental justice in the Third World are reported by the Third World Network in their journal *Third World Resurgence.*

The Internet has become a valuable site for the communication of information for the environmental justice movement. The EcoJustice Network provides on-line news and resources for the environmental justice movement. Its World-Wide Web address is http://www.igc.apc.org/econet/.

EPICUREANISM

Thomas Magnell
Drew University

GLOSSARY

ataraxia Contentment found in an untroubled condition free of fear and pain.

atomism The view that all material things are made up of small, indivisible units of matter.

autarkeia An ideal of self-sufficiency.

empiricism The view that all knowledge of the world requires sensory experience.

ethical hedonism The view that the only things that *we ought to desire,* or *are good for us to desire,* as ends, are pleasures that bring about or tend to bring about happiness.

free will The view that what we do is at least sometimes due to choices we make that in principle we could have made otherwise.

hedonism At the most general, a view, whether psychological or ethical, according to which there is an intimate connection between pleasures that bring about happiness and things desired.

katastematic pleasures Passive, tranquil pleasures, generally of the mind.

kinetic pleasures Dynamic, lively pleasures, generally of the body.

"ought" implies "can" In ethics, the principle that we can only be morally required to do things that are possible for us to do.

psychological hedonism The view that the only things that we *do desire,* or perhaps *can desire,* as ends, are pleasures that bring about, or tend to bring about, happiness.

social contract theory In ethics, a theory that accounts for rights, duties, and perhaps justice, in terms of some sort of civil agreement.

EPICUREANISM, the philosophy of Epicurus and his followers, is perhaps the most commonly misunderstood ancient philosophy. It is not that the doctrines of Epicurus are particularly abstruse or enigmatic. To the contrary, Epicureanism is a clearly set out, straightforward empirical philosophy. It could be characterized as a garden variety empiricism. Nor is it that Epicurus lacked followers to spread and record his views. His school gained considerable popularity while he was alive and remained so for nearly half a millennium. Thus, Epicureanism could be expected to stir controversy—there was plenty of time for that. What is surprising is that it met with mendacious opposition that deliberately encouraged misunderstandings of the philosophy. Epicurus and his followers were maligned and slandered. This proved an effective tactic, relieving others of the burden of careful thought.

Epicureanism was characterized as a pig's philosophy for its unabashed materialism, mechanism, and hedonism. To this day, the gourmet, if not the gourmand, the oenophile, if not the drunkard, all those who indulge in sensual satisfaction without reservation, are called epicures or epicureans. The common idea of Epicureanism is summed up in the epithet: Eat, drink and be merry; for tomorrow ye dieth. But all this is nothing less than slanderous to the teachings of Epicurus. He and his followers would have found the attitude revealed by such injunctions vile and irresponsible. This will become evident when we come to Epicurean ethics.

I. EPICURUS AND LUCRETIUS

A. Epicurus and His Writings

Epicurus was born in 341 or 342 B.C. on the island of Samos, but of Athenian parents. His father, Neocles, had moved to the island around 10 years before Epicurus was born. At about the age of 18, Epicurus left Samos for Athens. This was shortly after the deaths of Alexander the Great and Aristotle at the onset of what is sometimes called the Hellenistic age. After a brief stay, he moved on, first to Colophon to be with his father, and then to Mytilene and Lampsacus to teach. In 306 B.C., when he was in his mid-30s, Epicurus moved to Athens for good. He established a school at his home, teaching, it is said, in his garden. The school flourished and became known, aptly enough, as the garden. Women as well as men were admitted to it as full members from the start. Slaves were also welcome. Epicurus died after a prolonged illness in 270 B.C. at the age of 72. Afterwards, under the terms of his will, his property was transferred to the school.

Epicurus was prolific. Diogenes Laertius goes so far as to say that "Epicurus was the author of very many books, surpassing all men in the number of his works" (*Life of Epicurus,* 26b). Unfortunately, most of his writings have been lost. We have three of his letters: one to Herodotus—not, however, the celebrated historian—largely concerning epistemology and physics; another to Pythocles, mainly on astronomy and meteorology; and the last to Menoeceus, dealing with ethics and theology. We also have a compilation of 40 aphoristic statements of his Principal Doctrines or Cardinal Tenets, the *kuriai doxai,* and a similar collection of aphorisms in a manuscript at the Vatican Library known as the Vatican Sayings. Finally, there is a remarkable collection of Epicurean fragments from the *Casa dei Papiri.* These are scrolls that were unearthed in the middle of the eighteenth century from a house at Herculaneum, which may account for their fragmentary state.

B. Lucretius and *De Rerum Natura*

Despite the loss of most of Epicurus' own writings, we have a reliable and full record of Epicurean philosophy from the magnificent work of the Roman poet Titus Lucretius Carus, *De Rerum Natura.* Lucretius lived between 98 and 55 B.C. It is sometimes said that he died at his own hand, although this is questionable. Lucretius was an ardent Epicurean. He is thought to have written his extended poem with a large but no longer extant work of Epicurus that is referred to as the *Greater Epitome. De Rerum Natura* presents Epicurean doctrines with thoroughness, clarity, and beauty. It is among the greatest of the literary products of Rome and a fitting tribute to Epicurus.

II. EPICUREAN PHYSICS AND EPISTEMOLOGY

A. Mechanistic Atomism

The Epicureans offered a coherent set of views on physics and epistemology that had considerable bearing on their ethics. Their physics developed the materialistic and mechanistic atomism of Leucippus and Democritus. The Epicureans were avowed empiricists, maintaining, as they did, that knowledge of the world is obtained through sense–experience. As Epicurus put it:

> [W]e must use our sensations as the foundations of all our investigations; that is, we must base investigations on the mental apprehensions, upon the purposeful use of the several senses that furnish us with knowledge, and upon our immediate feelings (*Letter to Herodotus,* 38b).

The reference to immediate feelings is important for his ethics. But here, let us turn to three questions that are central to his epistemology: What are sensations? Where do they come from? And how do sensations give rise to knowledge?

Epicurus held that a sensation, or sense–experience, is an image. It is an image of an object, an image that serves to represent the object of our perception (*aisthesis*). I stare at the ceiling. What do I see? Do I see the ceiling? Strictly speaking, on Epicurus' view, I do not. To be sure, the ceiling is the object of my perception. But my sensation or sense–experience is only an image of the ceiling, an image that serves to represent the ceiling. He called such an image an *eidolon,* a word that unfortunately is usually simply transliterated as "idol."

B. Straightforward Empiricism

The idols of sense–experience come from the objects we perceive. As an atomist, Epicurus maintained that everything is made up of atoms—extremely small, uncuttable units of matter—at motion or rest. Apart from atoms, there is only the void of empty space. What then of the idols? They too are made up of atoms. Epicurus argued that the idols are thin films of atoms that "flow from the surfaces of a body in a constant stream" (*Herodotus,* 48). The atoms are "unsurpassed in fineness" and emanate from objects at a "velocity [that] is also unsurpassed" (*Herodotus,* 47b). These assertions that so closely resemble the claims of contemporary science are all the more remarkable for being backed by plausible arguments. The films come from the surfaces of objects, because surfaces are all that are open to our perceptions. They travel in a constant stream, because there are no gaps in our perceptions. The films are thin and the atoms comprising the films are unsurpassed in fineness, because the idols generally represent the surfaces of objects accurately. If the films were thick and the atoms comprising them large, then they would collide with the atoms of the atmosphere and become thoroughly disorganized, scattering and destroying a faithful image. The films travel at a velocity that is unsurpassed, because the atoms of the films are so small that they do not hit the atoms of the atmosphere. The less atoms bounce around, the less they are prevented from traveling unhindered in straight lines. The less hindered they are, the faster they can move. If the atoms of the films are so small that they can, for the most part, travel straight through the atmosphere, it follows that they can move as fast as anything can go, and so at an unsurpassed, although not infinite, velocity.

How do the thin films of atoms, the idols (*eidola*), give rise to knowledge? The beginning of Epicurus' answer is in two parts that tie the past and the future together with the thread of the mind or soul. Repeated experiences of idols in the past make impressions on our minds or souls, and are thus remembered. By bringing together our memories of idols to find their significant similarities, we form anticipations or *prolepseis* of future sense–experience. They act as general concepts or ideas. My memory of former idols of tables enables me to anticipate future tables, but not future cabbages and kings. For that I would need to have memories of cabbage and king idols. Here is how Diogenes Laertius put it in his *Life of Epicurus:*

Our concepts are framed from sensations as we experience and compare them, recognize their similarities, and combine them, not without the assistance of our reason. ... By "concept" they [the Epicureans] mean a mental picture, right opinion, notion, or general idea that has been stored up—in other words, the memory of something external that has often been the subject of sensation, as for example the concept that such and such is a man. As soon as you hear the word "man," the image, man, is at once mentally formed in accordance with the concept, which was originally due to sensation. The basic meaning of each word is clear. If we did not first know the thing for which we are searching, we could not search for it [Cf. Plato's *Meno*] (Diogenes Laertius, *Life of Epicurus,* 32 and 33a).

Little more is needed to complete Epicurus' account of how the idols of sense–experience give rise to knowledge. With general ideas, we can form opinions. I can form the opinion that there is a table before me or that the ceiling is high above my head. If, when I look, I see that there is a table before me, if, that is, I have an idol of a table, then my opinion is true. If I do not have a sense–experience of a table, my opinion is false. My opinion about the height of the ceiling is similarly capable of being verified or falsified. Sense–experience can usually verify or falsify opinions. When it can, sense–experience gives us a criterion of true opinion. If, knowledge is identified with true opinion, as Epicurus was inclined to do, then we have at hand a criterion of knowledge: verification of opinion by the idols of sense–experience. Thus we have one way that idols from the past that enable us to form anticipations or general ideas, and idols from the future that allow us to verify opinions based on the anticipations or general ideas, can give rise to knowledge.

Epicurus recognized that his criterion of verification could not always be applied. Some opinions are not verifiable in practice. Epicurus had no way to verify or falsify the opinion that the moon is made of green cheese. Worse, opinions that take the form of generalizations are not verifiable in principle. "All swans are white" may be false no matter how many swans inspected so far have been found to be white. Of course the discovery of a single swan that is not white can falsify the opinion. But the problem of verifying generalizations remains. Epicurus did not address this problem specifically in the writings of his that we have. But he does suggest that whenever opinions fail to be verified or falsified by the idols of sense–experience, we may accept as true any that do not conflict with the opinions that we have verified. We have here an alternative criterion of true opinion, a test of coherence.

C. Accounting for Error

What are we to say of mistaken opinions, opinions that we take to be true, although they are false, or false, although they are true? One answer that Epicurus gave is that we may, in framing opinions, "be full of bad judgement and confusion" (*Principal Doctrines,* XXII). As we have seen, we frame opinions by forming anticipations (*prolepseis*) that act as general ideas by bringing together and comparing remembered idols from the past. It is not too much to suppose that when our judgment and memory fail us, we are left full of bad judgment and confusion leading us to frame mistaken opinions.

Epicurus suggested another source of mistaken opinions, one that lies external to us. While the idols emanating as thin films of atoms generally represent the surfaces of objects accurately, they are not *always* faithful representations, true to the surfaces of objects. As Epicurus noted:

> For a long time the idols keep their atoms in the same relative position and order that they occupied on the surface of the solid, although sometimes the idols do become confused, and sometimes they combine in the air. This combination takes place quickly since there is no need of filling up their substance within. There are also some other ways in which idols come into being. No one of these statements is contradicted by sensation if we examine the ways in which sensation brings us clear visions of external objects and of the relations between them (*Letter to Herodotus,* 48).

Thus illusions, mirages and, in general, mistaken opinions about objects of perception could be due to factors external to us. A square tower may seem round to us at a distance because the idols leaving the surface become slightly disorganized by the time they reach us. A distant green hill may appear purple to us for the same reason. Idols combining in hot air over certain surfaces may take on the appearance of water and produce a mirage. In all such cases we may be led to frame mistaken opinions.

Epicurus' theory of knowledge is not without problems. The most obvious is that as it stands, it is not strictly speaking a theory of *knowledge* at all. As Plato pointed out, knowledge is more than true opinion. Another is that the deep and difficult problems of epistemology are not seriously taken up: Nothing is said about our knowledge of logical, mathematical, and necessary truth; the introduction of idols conflates science with epistemology; the account of general ideas is too pithy to be of use; the criteria of verification and coherence are not critically examined. As well, the recourse to sight as the model for perception in general is simplistic and potentially misleading.

In reply to criticisms along these lines it should be said that we only have a small portion of the works of Epicurus. Given the systematic nature of what has come down to us in a few short letters, it is not implausible that Epicurus did address at least some of the deeper problems in his long-lost texts. As for the visual model of perception, to this day nearly all philosophers have made heavy use of it, and our language readily allows us to take it for granted, as when we say: "I see that"; "That is clear"; or "I am in the dark on that." At least in passing, Epicurus did do a little to take into account our sense experiences of sounds and smells. In any event, Epicurus provided an early, uncompromising, empirical approach to epistemology and to philosophy in general that is not wrapped up in Aristotelian teleology.

III. EPICUREAN NORMATIVE ETHICS

A. Psychological and Ethical Hedonism

Epicurus was a hedonist. Epicurean ethics is hedonistic, as is Epicurean psychology. The Epicureans were not the first proponents of hedonism, but they were among the first philosophers to try to win intellectual respect for hedonism. If they did not succeed, part of the reason may be that pleasure has always been suspect by certain unhappy thinkers. The terms "hedonist," "hedonistic," and "hedonism" come from the Greek word for pleasure, *hedone.* All hedonists hold that there is an intimate connection between pleasure and the things we desire. Inasmuch as the connection may be normative as well as descriptive, we may distinguish two forms of hedonism, psychological hedonism and ethical hedonism:

> *Psychological hedonism* is the view that the only things that *we do desire,* or perhaps *can desire,* as ends, are pleasures that bring about, or tend to bring about, happiness.

Ethical hedonism is the view that the only things that *we ought to desire,* or *are good for us to desire,* as ends, are pleasures that bring about, or tend to bring about, happiness.

Further distinctions may be drawn among types of hedonism. In particular, we might wish to separate egoistic forms of hedonism from altruistic forms of hedonism. Some hedonists have sought to maintain that all actions spring from motivations of self-gratification, although this seems largely due to a conflation of ourselves as authors of our desires with ourselves as objects of our desires. Our status as the authors of our desires is necessary but immaterial: that I desire what I desire is truistic but mute on motivation. Our standing as objects of our desires is material but not necessary: that what I desire is to satisfy myself is a substantive thesis that is unlikely to be true of all my desires. Even the most narcissistic individuals may have desires that are directed toward others.

When someone advances a hedonistic doctrine that ties pleasure to the ends of human conduct, it is always pertinent to ask whether the doctrine is being put forward as a psychological thesis about the things that we *do* desire or as an ethical thesis about the things that we *ought to* desire. The two do not have to go together. It is possible to be an ethical hedonist without being a psychological hedonist. It is possible to hold that only those things that provide pleasure are good to desire as ends, while yet denying that such things are the only things that are or can be desired as ends. Indeed, an ethical hedonist might call on us to renounce just those sorts of desires—desires that do not, ultimately, bring about pleasure. Is the converse possible? Is it possible to be a psychological hedonist without being an ethical hedonist? On the widely accepted principle that "ought" implies "can" the answer is no, at any rate for a consequentialist. For on that principle, we cannot be called on to desire something other than what we are capable of desiring.

Hedonistically inclined philosophers are commonly both ethical hedonists and psychological hedonists. For Epicurus and the Epicureans this was undoubtedly the case. In his *Letter to Menoeceus,* for instance, Epicurus wrote:

> [P]leasure is the beginning and the end of the blessed life. We recognize pleasure as the first and natural good; starting from pleasure we accept or reject; and we return to this as we judge every good thing, trusting this feeling of pleasure as our guide (Epicurus, *Letter to Menoeceus,* 129a).

This gives expression equally to ethical hedonism and psychological hedonism. But if Epicurus and the Epicureans in general did not draw the distinction between these two forms of hedonism, it was because they were so thoroughly imbued with the psychological hedonistic principle. Still, the distinction is important.

B. *Katastematic* and *Kinetic* Pleasures

Epicurus did not regard all pleasures as being on the same plane. Some pleasures, he held, are more desirable than others. In particular, the pleasures of the mind, he maintained, far outweigh the pleasures of the body. These he distinguished as *katastematic* or passive pleasures on the one hand, and *kinetic* or dynamic pleasures on the other. *Katastematic* pleasures are restful and tranquil in nature. *Kinetic* pleasures are forceful and lively. This is, perhaps, supposed to be more of a distinction in degree than a distinction in kind. It is, in any case, a distinction set in his physics no less than this ethics.

As an atomist, Epicurus maintained that all pleasures, indeed all things that have to do with change, are due to the motion of atoms. In a sense, all pleasures may be said to be *kinetic,* because everything that affects us results from atoms in motion. The mind or soul is supposed to be composed of fine, wispy atoms, in contrast with the body, which is composed of gross, coarse atoms. The mind is a storehouse of idols and anticipations. Little force is needed to set the atoms of the mind into motion. The atoms of our body, and so of our sense organs, require considerable force to be activated. Thus the pleasures due to touch, sight, hearing, smell, and taste, as when we gain sensual delight from food or drink, or for that matter sex, require strong, even violent motions of atoms. The pleasures of our gross senses are all *kinetic.* The pleasures of the mind, in contrast, require very little motion. Violent motion is almost sure to disrupt rather than please. The *katastematic* pleasures of the mind involve only light and gentle movement. And it is the *katastematic* pleasures of the mind that are the most satisfying and long lasting. Here is how Epicurus set out his position in his *Letter to Menoeceus:*

> When we say that pleasure is the end, we do not mean the pleasure of the profligate or that which depends on physical enjoyment [*kinetic* pleasure]—as some think who do not understand our teachings, disagree with them, or give them an evil interpretation—but by pleasure we mean the state wherein the body is free from pain and the

mind from anxiety [*katastematic* pleasure]. Neither continual drinking and dancing, nor sexual love, nor the enjoyment of fish and whatever else the luxurious table offers brings about the pleasant life; rather, it is produced by the reason which is sober, which examines the motive for every choice and rejection, and which drives away all those opinions through which the greatest tumult lays hold of the mind (Epicurus, *Letter to Menoeceus*, 1412b–132b).

It should be evident from this that Epicurus was no Sybarite. If anything, his ideals were more those of the ascetic than the aesthete. Epicurus did not renounce sensual pleasures. But he was inclined to shun them. In a fragment from a letter he went so far as to say:

I am thrilled with pleasure in the body, when I live on bread and water, and I spit upon luxurious pleasures not for their own sake, but because of the inconveniences that follow them (*Letters to Unknown Recipients*, 37).

C. Free Will and the Swerve

We choose how to act. We decide what to do, at least some of the time. We have free will. Or do we? This perennial problem of philosophy has serious ramifications on normative ethics. Free will is arguably a precondition of moral responsibility, and so, of moral agency. If we are not really free to choose courses of action, then it is hard to see how we can be morally culpable for what we do. Again on the principle that "ought" implies "can," if we are to be morally required or forbidden to act in a certain way, we must be able to perform or refrain from the conduct at issue. Without free will, the ability to do anything other than what we end up doing would be illusory and the belief that we may bear moral responsibility as moral agents would be misplaced.

The Epicureans showed a great concern for the problem of free will. Accepting from the outset the mechanistic, atomistic hypothesis of Democritus and Leucippus, they nevertheless rejected the strict determinism of these pre-Socratic atomists. They thought that strict determinism was not compatible with our having free will. To allow for free will, the Epicurians introduced the possibility of occasional, unpredictable swerves in the motion of the atoms. The idea was that the swerve, or *parenklisis*, would break the otherwise inexorable course of events. The apparent freedom of our will was argued to be due to the unpredictable swerves of the fine atoms making up our minds.

Can free will be accounted for in this way? Few philosophers think so. It would make free will a matter of chance, and this does not seem to be correct. But even if the swerve does not serve its stated purpose, it does bear an unmistakable resemblance to the contemporary notion of causal indeterminacy that has entered quantum mechanics through the Copenhagen interpretation of Werner Heisenberg's uncertainty principle. There are differences, of course. But the similarities are nonetheless remarkable. More than one contemporary physicist has tried to solve the problem of free will by appealing to the uncertainty principle, much as the Epicureans argued for freedom of the will by appealing to the swerve.

IV. EPICUREAN ETHICS IN PRACTICE

A. *Ataraxia* and Moderation

Pleasure and pain often come together, or the one may lead to the other. The things that bring us pleasure may also bring us pain, if not in the present, then in the future. This is partly why Epicurus was wary of sensual, *kinetic* pleasures. The pleasure we gain from drinking tonight, we pay for with a hangover tomorrow. The pleasures of the mind, the *katastematic* pleasures, are largely free of concomitant or future pain. They are relatively pure. As a practical matter then, the best way to maximize pleasure may be to seek to minimize pain. This was the view that Epicurus expressly held. Absence of pain sets an upper limit to pleasure. As Epicurus put it:

The removal of all that causes pain marks the boundary of pleasure (*Principal Doctrines*, III).

For Epicurus and the Epicureans, the greatest overall pleasure lay in a state called *ataraxia*—tranquility, serenity, peace of mind. *Ataraxia* is an untroubled condition, a freedom from fears and pains that characterizes contentment. The contentment that comes from simple living and the *katastematic* pleasures is what Epicurus advocates above all else.

Like Aristotle, Epicurus condemned excess as a vice. Moderation in our desires, prudence in our conduct, the *meden agan* in general, is the mark of virtue and wisdom:

Of all this the beginning and the chief good is prudence. For this reason prudence is more precious than philosophy itself. All the other virtues spring from it. It teaches that it is not possible to live pleasantly without at the same time living prudently, nobly, and justly, (nor to live prudently, nobly, and justly) without living pleasantly; for the virtues have grown up in close union with the pleasant life, and the pleasant life cannot be separated from the virtues (*Letter to Menoeceus,* 132b).

Epicurus consistently carried over this ideal of moderation in all things to his predilection for the simple life. It served to mitigate his ascetic inclinations. One of the *Vatican Sayings* is:

There is also a limit in the simple living. He who fails to heed this limit falls into an error as great as that of the man who gives way to extravagance (*Vatican Sayings,* LXIII).

B. Fear or Dread, and Death

Epicurus regarded fear or dread as the greatest source of pain. Fear of what the future may bring, the dread of misfortune, worries in general wreck havoc with our souls. They keep us from being content. *Ataraxia* or peace of mind calls for the removal or dissolution of fears. The refrain "Don't worry! Be happy!" would have pleased Epicurus.

What is our greatest fear? The answer, of course, is death, and also, for those who take seriously the teachings of religion, what may come after death. Strictly speaking, Epicurus was not an atheist. He maintained that there probably were gods, largely for reasons having to do with his epistemology. But he also argued that the gods kept to themselves and had nothing to do with human affairs. The gods have no concerns for us. They do not intervene on our behalf. But neither do they oppose our interests. The gods do nothing to harm us. Epicurus was a near-atheist. This was one reason why Epicureanism was reviled for so long.

Epicurus argued that the atoms that comprise our soul are dissipated upon our death. Thus we do not survive our death. There is no afterlife. But then, if death is not a release to future pleasures, neither is it a passage to future pain. Death is simply an end, and so no cause for anguish. It may be a happy end, if we have had the wisdom to aim for *ataraxia* while we live. If there is no torment to come, what is there to fear? In a word, nothing. In Epicurus' words:

Death is nothing for us; for what has been dissolved has no sensation, and what has no sensation is nothing to us (*Principal Doctrines*, II).

Epicurus himself met death with equanimity. But does religion promote a fear of a life to come which may, for all we know, be even nastier than this one? Can such a fear seriously disrupt our serenity, peace of mind, or contentment? There is probably no character in all of literature with less serenity, peace of mind, and contentment than Hamlet. Consider just a few of the lines from his justly celebrated soliloquy:

To die, to sleep;
To sleep, perchance to dream. Ay, there's the rub;
For in that sleep of death what dreams may come,
When we have shuffled off this mortal coil,
Must give us pause (*Hamlet,* Act III, Scene I).

Epicurus was, perhaps, not far off the mark.

C. Contentment and the Importance of Friendship

Epicureanism placed contentment, basically a passive state brought on by the absence of pain, in place of positive joy or happiness. As a counsel of prudence, satisfaction in mere contentment is not to be despised. Many people would be happier than they are if they were at least content. Contentment is, at any rate, a sensible, minimal goal to seek. But is it enough? Is the conservatism of spirit that it demands truly gratifying? Withdrawal from the hazards of the world and, ultimately, death are ways of freeing oneself from pain. The Epicureans, unlike the Stoics, withdrew from active social and political life. They adopted minimalist lifestyles. By and large, they did not choose to hasten death, even if Lucretius was said to have committed suicide. Epicurus in fact counseled against suicide saying:

He is of very small account who sees many good reasons for ending his life (*Vatican Sayings,* XXXVIII).

But clearly, the goal of contentment has its own costs.

Epicurus' school was organized as a society of friends. The Epicureans placed a high value on friendship. As Epicurus stressed:

Of the things that wisdom prepares for insuring lifelong happiness, by far the greatest is the possession of friends (*Principal Doctrines*, XXVII).

This may seem unexceptionable, but in fact it posed a problem. For the Epicureans, no less than the Stoics, the other highly influential philosophers of the Hellenistic age, set great store in *autarkeia* or self-sufficiency. Friendships create obligations, duties to help friends in need. The bonds of friendship lessen our autonomy insofar as they require us to pay heed to the needs and wishes of our friends. Does this conflict with the ideal of *autarkeia* or self-sufficiency?

Epicurus did not deny that it does conflict, or at any rate that it may do so. Yet friendship is desirable even so. We may gain much pleasure from the friendships we form. But more than this, friends may come to *our* aid when *we* are in need. Friends afford us protection; they increase our safety; they allow us to feel more secure, and so less troubled. Thus friends may promote our serenity and peace of mind. Still, friendship is a risky business and not to be entered into lightly. Two of Epicurus' *Vatican Sayings* sum up all of this:

> Every friendship in itself is to be desired; but the first cause of friendship was a man's needs (*Vatican Sayings,* XXIII).

> Those who are hasty in making friends are not to be approved; nor yet should you commend those who avoid friendship, for risks must be run for its sake (*Vatican Sayings,* XXVIII).

V. EPICUREAN POLITICAL PHILOSOPHY

Epicurus advanced a social contract theory of justice. He took the view that society has its basis in a mutual agreement made by people in order to increase their security. And the concept of justice, he held, can be given application only within the context of such a mutual agreement. Plato presented this sort of view in his discussion of the minimal state in Book II of the *Republic*. But the idea of a social contract played no part in his fully developed theory of obligation or justice. Epicurus adopted the social contract theory as his own. He was among the first philosophers to do so. He anticipated the position set out by Hobbes so closely that the following three brief remarks from the *Principal Doctrines* of Epicurus could well serve as a preface or introduction to *Leviathan*:

> Natural justice is a compact resulting from expediency by which men seek to prevent one man from injuring others and to protect him from being injured by them.

> There is no such thing as justice or injustice among those beasts that cannot make agreements not to injure or be injured. This is also true of those tribes that are unable or unwilling to make agreements not to injure or be injured.

> There is no such thing as justice in the abstract; it is merely a compact between men in their various relations with each other, in whatever circumstances they may be, that they will neither injure nor be injured (*Principal Doctrines,* XXXI, XXXII, and XXXIII) [Cf. Lucretius, *De Rerum Natura,* Ch. V, 1010–1027].

With the resurgence of social contract theories in our own time, Epicurean political philosophy has a decidedly contemporary ring. In any event, what should command attention in a century that has seen so much suffering come about in the name of political ideologies is the emphasis on preventing injury. We might well wish to do more than minimize harm. But as a political objective we should demand nothing less.

Also See the Following Articles

GREEK ETHICS, OVERVIEW • HEDONISM • THEORIES OF ETHICS, OVERVIEW

Bibliography

Annas, J. (1992). *Hellenistic Philosophy of Mind.* Berkeley: University of California Press.
Diogenes Laertius. (1979–1980). *Lives of eminent philosophers* (Hicks, R. D. Trans.). London: W. Heinemann.
Epicurus. (1994). *The Epicurus reader: Selected writings and tetimonia.* (Inwood, B. & Gerson, L. P. Trans.). Indianapolis, IN: Hackett Publishing Co.
Epicurus. (1993). *The essential Epicurus: Letters, principal doctrines, Vatican sayings, and fragments.* (O'Connor, E. Trans.). Buffalo, NY: Prometheus Books.
Epicurus. (1964). *Letters, principal doctrines, and Vatican sayings.* (Geer, R. M. Trans.). Indianapolis, IN: The Bobbs-Merrill Co. Inc.
Lucretius. (1994). *On the nature of the universe* [*De rerum natura*]. (Latham, R. E. trans., Godwin, J. rev.). London: Penguin Books.
Mitsis, P. (1988). *Epicurus' ethical theory.* Ithaca, NY: Cornell University Press.
Osler, M. J. (Ed.). (1991). *Atoms, pneuma, and tranquility: Epicurean and stoic themes in European thought,* Cambridge: Cambridge University Press.
Rist, J. M. (1977). *Epicurus: An introduction.* London: Cambridge University Press.
Santayana, G. (1910, 1953). *Three philosophical poets.* Garden City: Doubleday & Co.

EQUALITY AND EGALITARIANISM

Richard J. Arneson
University of California, San Diego

GLOSSARY

distributive justice The branch of social justice that proposes principles to regulate the processes by which individuals acquire and hold resources.
justice Fair treatment of persons.
social democracy The view that to qualify as democratic, a society, besides being governed by majority will, must provide the education and resources to each member to enable her to be a full participating citizen.

THE IDEA OF EQUALITY comes in various flavors. The ideal holds that all persons should be treated the same. But people are treated differently from each other for many innocent and unproblematic reasons. Different substantive norms of equality single out particular ways in which people should be treated alike or particular aspects of people's condition in which the conditions of all are supposed to be the same. Egalitarian ethics is diverse. Many different moral views, although not all, assert that people should be treated the same in some respect or in some dimension. This article concentrates on ideals of equality that are especially associated with two moments of the intellectual history of Western Europe: the liberal and free market critique of feudal hierarchy, and the socialist critique of the free market economy and capitalist democracy in the nineteenth century along with the communist and social-democratic descendants of this critique in the twentieth century.

I. THE CHRISTIAN BACKGROUND

Christianity, a religion that aspires to acceptance by all humans, contains an ideal of equality. According to Christian doctrine, each human is endowed with an immortal immaterial soul, and each soul is equally precious in the eyes of God. The soul is taken to be the seat of our consciousness and mental life. Because all humans equally possess souls and are equally loved by God, in our dealings with fellow humans we should treat each individual as worthy of equal respect and caring. The Christian doctrine of the equality of souls is not opposed to inequality of fortune and rank among persons as they conduct their earthly affairs but it invites us to adopt a standpoint from which these earthly distinctions will appear unimportant.

Some Christians have found grounds for opposing some forms of unequal treatment in the doctrine of the equality of souls in the eyes of God. It is also possible that in cultures influenced by Christianity some secular advocates of equality have been primed to find egalitarianism congenial by common-sense patterns of belief that are of religious origin.

II. THE CRITIQUE OF FEUDAL AND MONARCHICAL HIERARCHY

On a feudal manor such as existed in Europe during the Middle Ages, serfs were born to the land. They had by custom a claim to stay on it, but also obligations to live where they are born and to labor for the lord of the manor, who enforced compliance with these obligations. Being born to noble or common status fundamentally determined one's place in society. The kings who eventually imposed centralized national order on the patchwork anarchy of feudal obligations claimed the authority to command the obedience of their subjects by divine right, just as a father was thought legitimately to exercise absolute mastery over his family.

In contrast, John Locke's manifesto for individual rights and limited government asserts that individuals are initially in a state of "perfect equality" (1988. *Second Treatise of Government,* Indianapolis: Hackett Publishing; first published 1678). By this he means that no one is naturally in a state of subjection to another. Each is free to live her life as she chooses so long as she does not violate the rights of others. One becomes subject to the will of another person and obligated to obey only by one's voluntary consent. This holds for subjection to government authority as well. Locke famously or infamously attempts to show that the legitimate authority of government derives from the consent of each individual subject.

The equality that Locke upholds is equality of natural rights—moral rights that each person has independently of institutional arrangements. Just in virtue of being an adult human being, one is free to behave as one chooses within certain limits, and other persons are obligated not to interfere. Feudal hierarchy, slavery, the organization of society by castes, and absolute monarchy are all ruled inadmissible because their pretensions conflict with individual natural rights.

In Locke's text, the character of the rights is complex. It may be useful to note the existence of a tradition of Lockean libertarianism, sometimes called "classical liberalism," that upholds a version of Lockean ideas and has continuing intellectual vitality today. For the Lockean, the core natural right is a right of self-ownership. Each person is the rightful moral owner of herself and may dispose of her body as she chooses so long as she does not harm others in certain ways, by force, fraud, theft, or violence, that are deemed violations of others' rights to the undisturbed use of their own bodies. From self-ownership morally legitimate private ownership of objects is derived. Owning myself, I am free to do whatever I choose so long as I do not wrongfully harm others, and this freedom includes the freedom to appropriate parts of the earth as my private property so long as such an appropriation does not wrongfully harm others. The right to trade what one legitimately owns with others on any mutually agreeable terms so long as nonconsenting third parties to the transaction are not wrongfully harmed then follows. In the Lockean liberarian tradition (though not in Locke), one's natural rights are altogether negative in character. They are rights not to be interfered with or harmed by others in certain ways. One's natural rights do not include any positive rights to be helped by others, except that one may freely contract with others in ways that then obligate one to help the others according to the terms of the contract, and one may also do certain acts, such as bringing a child into the world, that then give rise to obligations to aid the child for whose existence one is responsible.

III. DEMOCRATIC EQUALITY

The ideal of democratic citizenship as formulated in the eighteenth-century age of democratic revolution holds that all adult property-owning males in a society should be equal citizens with a right to vote and to stand for office in free elections, the winners of these elections being legislators and government heads. Later this ideal is expanded in two ways: the property qualification is removed and women as well as men are entitled to full citizenship rights.

The democratic ideal of equality under the law prescribes that there should be a single set of laws governing a society that applies equally to all citizens and does not make distinctions of ascriptive status as between aristocrat and commoner, slave and free, or between groups of citizens depending on the ethnicity, tribe, or race of their ancestors. In a later day the ideal is expanded to require equality of status between men and women. All citizens are entitled to equal protection of the laws.

Equality of opportunity is the norm that positions and roles in a market economy and in the bureaucratic institutions that administer democratic government should be open to all on a fair competitive basis. For bureaucratic governmental posts, equality of opportunity requires that any citizen should be free to apply for any post, and that appointments should be made on the basis of qualifications impartially administered and reasonably related to the function of the post. For the market economy, the norm of equality of opportunity means that any citizens should be legally free to buy and sell on mutually agreeable terms. For market employment, the norm of equality of opportunity can be interpreted to imply a constraint on the freedom to buy and sell in order to implement careers open to talents: any citizen should be free to apply for any position of employment in a market firm, and appointment should be made on the basis of relevant qualifications, as in the public sector.

Under democratic equality, with its threefold norm of equal citizenship, equality under the law, and equality of opportunity, superior status and good fortune are to be earned, not ascribed.

IV. THE RADICAL CRITIQUE OF DEMOCRATIC EQUALITY

The origins of an alternative contemporary doctrine of equality lie in the radical critique of democratic equality (sometimes pejoratively labelled "bourgeois" equality). In a nutshell the critique claims that the equality the liberal democrat proclaims is undermined in practice by unearned inequalities of wealth, power, and inheritance. Let us consider wealth. Democratic citizenship gives every adult man and women an equal vote, but the vast inequalities of wealth associated with unregulated market economies render this equality of citizenship illusory. Democratic politics is controlled by the wealthy, and the poor have neither the time nor the financial resources needed to influence the outcomes of political processes. In a similar way, equality under the law is perfectly consistent with the imposition on all citizens of a set of laws that bear very unevenly on rich and poor: the law in its majesty may equally forbid the poor and the rich to sleep under bridges, but only homeless poor people need to sleep under bridges and suffer deprivation from the loss of this freedom. Finally, under a market economy the formal equality of each

person to buy and sell as she chooses is fully compatible with great disparities in people's real opportunity to make deals with others. Even if the norm of careers open to talents is perfectly implemented, so that the more-qualified applicants for posts are always given preference over the less qualified and qualifications for posts are always reasonably related to their purpose, all of this is fully compatible with great and arbitrary inequalities in the opportunities of individuals to acquire talents depending on their parents' wealth and social connections and on the extent of their parents' devotion to their welfare.

The radical critique of democratic equality is that these formal equalities fail to have any tendency to bring about equality of life prospects for individuals. Indeed the implementation of democratic equality does not even guarantee decent life prospects for all members of society.

A. Karl Marx's Views

Karl Marx's "Critique of the Gotha Program" (reprinted in Robert Tucker (Ed), *The Marx-Engels Reader.* New York: W. W. Norton and Co, 1978; written in 1875) contains a classic example of this critique. Writing in the latter half of the nineteenth century, when the development of the capitalist market economy is transforming European societies, Marx imagines social progress leading to the abolition of the capitalist market economy and the evolution of a better, communist form of society. He envisages a lower and a higher phase of communism, the former being still marred by the birth pangs of the transition from capitalism. In this lower phase of communism as pictured by Marx, the economy is still a market economy, but there is no class division between capitalists (owners of business firms) and propertyless workers hired by these capitalists. Instead all are workers laboring for wages, and all wealth created by workers as they labor on society's resources is either returned to them in the form of wages or benefits society as a whole. According to Marx the norm that individuals are entitled to the fruits of their individual exertion is more fully and genuinely fulfilled in lower-phase communism than in capitalist market economies. Only in the former are individuals remunerated in proportion to their labor contribution to the economy. Yet this form of society according to Marx is stigmatized by a bourgeois limitation.

Marx's precise meaning is perhaps unclear, but the general drift of his remarks is plain. To each according to his labor contribution is an inadequate conception of distributive justice and an inadequate ideal of human equality. People differ through no fault or merit of their own in their ability to contribute socially useful labor and in their life circumstances, so equal remuneration for equal contribution is unfair. Marx writes, "This *equal* right is an unequal right for unequal labour. It recognizes no class differences, because everyone is only a worker like everyone else; but it tacitly recognizes unequal individual endowment and thus productive capacity as natural privileges. *It is, therefore, a right of inequality, in its content, like every right.* Right by its very nature can consist only in the application of an equal standard; but unequal individuals (and they would not be different individuals if they were not unequal) are measurable only by an equal standard in so far as they are brought under an equal point of view, are taken from one *definite* side only, for instance, in the present case, are regarded *only as workers* and nothing more is seen in them, everything else being ignored."

In Marx's vision of the future, these defects in the initial, lower phase of classless, communist society would be resolved with further economic and social progress, and "only then can the narrow horizon of bourgeois right be crossed in its entirety and society inscribe on its banner: From each according to his ability, to each according to his needs!"

B. Objections

Egalitarian theories of distributive justice hold that justice requires an economic distribution among persons that makes them equal in their life prospects or conditions of life. A question arises about these last phrases: In exactly what respects are people supposed to be rendered equal? This question is discussed under the subheading, "Equality of What?" Leaving this further specification aside for now, we note that egalitarian theories of distribution have been criticized on various grounds.

One objection is that the pursuit of equality may conflict with other goals that have greater ethical worth. It is claimed that efficiency in the sense of Pareto optimality is such a goal. (A change in a state of affairs is a Pareto improvement on an initial situation just in case the change makes someone better off and no one worse off. A state of affairs is Pareto optimal just in case it is not possible to make a Pareto improvement on it.) Suppose that we start with a situation in which some people are better off than others. Some people have ice cream cones and others lack them. Imagine that we cannot transfer ice cream from the haves to the have-nots. The ice cream will melt before we can get it into the hands of those who now have none. Nonethe-less, we can achieve a state of affairs in which everyone's condition is equal. If we take away the ice cream from those who have it, let us suppose we can end up with a situation in which no one is better off than anyone else, and no one has any ice cream. If justice requires equality above all, and achieving justice has priority over all other ethical goals, then we should welcome equality even when it is achieved by making the better off worse off without making anyone better off. Many people will balk at this. This reaction shows at least that many of us do not give priority to the achievement of equality. Noting that the norm of equality does not demand that people be well off rather than badly off, just that they have the same, a commentator has remarked that equality is as well pleased by graveyards as by vineyards.

The maintenance of equality of distribution might require foregoing schemes that would harness incentives so as to make everyone better off, but some better off than others.

A second objection against distributive equality appeals to the moral principle of self-ownership. Self-ownership asserts that each person is the rightful owner of herself, and is entitled to dispose of herself as she chooses. Imagine a simple village society in which individuals live by the ocean and gain their livelihood by fishing along the shore. The shoreline is large in relation to the village, and is for all practical purposes a non-scarce resource, access to which all villagers are equally entitled. The individual villagers differ in their native talent for fishing. Some catch many fish and live well. Some catch few fish and eke out a marginal existence. An advocate of justice as equality proposes that the villagers share their catch equally. Against this proposal it is objected that to force individuals to share their catch against their will in these circumstances is to fail to respect the principle of self-ownership and to treat the villagers as mutual owners of one another's talents. But each individual owns her own talents andd is entitled to the full fruits of their use, provided she is entitled to the materials on which she deploys her talents, as is the case in this example.

Systems of slavery, in which some persons claim ownership of other persons and force the latter to work for their benefit, blatantly and outrageously violate self-ownership. But forced sharing arrangements that pool people's talents and force the more talented to help the less talented also violate self-ownership, even if in a less outrageous way, and are wrong for the same reason that slavery is wrong.

A third objection against justice as equality is that sometimes unequal outcomes come about because some persons behave responsibly, prudently, and virtuously, while others behave irresponsibly, imprudently, and nonvirtuously. To correct these outcomes of variously meritorious individual conduct by restoring equality is to reward the irresponsible and punish the virtuous. Over time an economic system structured in this way would tend to promote irresponsible conduct and diminish the incidence of responsible and virtuous conduct, and a system of this sort is very likely to be inefficient in the sense of violating Pareto optimality. But even setting aside worries about efficiency, we should condemn proposed moral principles that fail to recommend treating people as they genuinely deserve.

In the "Critique of the Gotha Program" passage on the lower and higher stages of communism quoted above, Marx gives examples of variable life circumstances to indicate the unfairness of the rigid rule "to each according to his labor contribution." One example is that one worker is married while another is not. A second example is that one worker has more children than another. The examples are evidently supposed to illustrate the unfairness of giving people the same pay for the same work, when their life circumstances and needs are so different. (Marx is assuming that if a male worker is married, he is the sole support of his wife and any children they may have.) But some readers will have a response to the examples that differs from what Marx takes for granted. Getting married and having children are not afflictions that fall from the sky. They are the intended or predictable outcomes of individual voluntary choices. One might be inclined to hold the individual, not society as a whole, responsible for such choices and their outcomes, particularly those that are foreseeable.

V. COMMUNISM AND SOCIAL DEMOCRACY

Twentieth-century intellectual life generated two broad types of responses to the objections against egalitarianism just described. The two intellectual traditions were stimulated by opposed reactions to the emergence in Russia after World War I and in Asia and Eastern Europe after World War II of political regimes that identified themselves as Communist and claimed to be inspired by Marxist political idealogy. One tradition is communist, the other social democratic.

Very roughly, the communist position takes human selfishness or limited human altruism to be the fundamental obstacle that stands in the way of constructing a society that would be egalitarian in its distributive practices and would impress the common-sense observer as fair. If individuals were not predominantly disposed to be selfish, to give priority to advancing their own interests and the interests of those near and dear to them, the efficiency objections against egalitarian distributive schemes would lose their force. The communist version of egalitarian political theory supposes that the widespread disposition to selfish conduct can be eliminated or at least reduced to tolerable scale by appropriate socialization and education combined with selfishness-dampening institutions. To guide social progress in this direction, an educational dictatorship of the politically enlightened is needed, and the market economy, thought to be a mechanism that magnifies the human tendency to selfishness, is done away with.

Twentieth-century history has not been kind to the communist egalitarian program. The political regimes that have represented themselves as inspired by this program have been repressive single-party dictatorships. They have been somewhat successful at instituting centralized, state-run, modern industrial economies and efficient at squashing political and cultural freedom and extending a harsh state control over private life. No signs of the hoped-for transformation of human nature showed themselves.

The social democratic position is committed to taking men and women as they are and laws and institutions as they might feasibly be made, in order to organize society so as to achieve egalitarian goals. The goal of transforming human nature is firmly eschewed. Political democracy is viewed not merely as a possible means to securing other justice values, but as valuable for its own sake as a fundamental aspect of egalitarian justice. In the social democratic perspective, the institutions of a market economy are regarded neutrally, as means to egalitarian justice goals. The social democrat is respectful of the market economy's capacity to promote the creation of wealth and to generate efficient outcomes, at least under idealized conditions. Beyond that, the market shows no inherent tendency to bring about outcomes the social democrat can recognize as just. The strategy to be explored is democratic state regulation of the economy to achieve egalitarian goals.

VI. JOHN RAWLS'S VIEWS

John Rawls's theory of justice is a powerful and clear philosophical statement of moral principles expressive of the social democratic tradition. His book, *A Theory of Justice* (1971. Cambridge, MA: Harvard University

Press), clarifies and revises egalitarianism, and has in turn stimulated philosophical exploration of egalitarian themes by other theorists. This section briefly describes Rawls's proposed principles of justice and examines his arguments for them in the light of the objections against egalitarianism already noted.

According to Rawls, the principles of social justice regulate the basic institutions of society, which determine the division of the benefits of social cooperation. Justice trumps other social values: we should give priority to securing justice, whatever the cost to other values such as market efficiency. The doctrine of social justice that Rawls espouses consists of two principles: First, each person has a right to the most extensive basic liberty compatible with a similar liberty for others. Second: social and economic inequalities should be set so they are (a) attached to positions and offices open to all under conditions of fair equality of opportunity and (b) to the greatest benefit of the least advantaged. These principles are in nested order. The First Principle has priority over the Second, and within the Second Principle clause (a) has priority over (b). The former clause is known as fair equality of opportunity; the latter as the difference principle.

The basic liberties of the First Principle include fundamental civil liberties, especially freedom of expression, the right to vote and to stand for office in free elections, equal protection of the laws, and freedom of movement and the freedom to choose one's occupation. These basic liberties are to be the same for all citizens.

Rawls's Second Principle can be regarded as encapsulating the liberal critique of feudalism and the radical critique of a pure private ownership economy. Imagine a fedual or caste society that establishes special privileged positions and assigns these privileged positions on the basis of birth. Those born of noble or high-caste parents are entitled to superior positions. In one way or another the rest of society is forced to pay for the advantages enjoyed by the aristocrats. Rawls takes it for granted that his readers will agree that such a system is unfair. Chance determines whether one is born to superior or inferior position. One's place in society is set by accidents entirely beyond the individual's power to control, and independently of any voluntary choices for which the individual might be deemed responsible. One can then imagine society reformed so that these positions of advantage are open to all who apply for them. Appointment to positions of advantage is determined by relevant qualifications. Society conforms to the norm of careers open to talents. But still whether

one comes to possess these qualifications is strongly influenced by arbitrary luck, which is beyond the individual's power to control. Some parents have wealth, education, and social connections and are motivated to use these advantages to give their children a leg up in competitions for social positions that confer special advantages. Other parents lack these resources or the motivation to use them for their children's benefit.

In theory one can imagine a further reform of society that institutes a more demanding conception of equality of opportunity than careers open to talents. This is Rawls's fair equality of opportunity. This norm is satisfied in a society when the advantages of being born, as it were, on the right side of the tracks are entirely offset by social provision that enables each person a similar opportunity to develop her talents. The institution of a system of free public education in democracies is a small step in this direction. Fair equality of opportunity obtains in a society when any individuals who have identical native talent and the same ambition to succeed will enjoy exactly the same prospects of success in competition for positions of advantage. Being born a man or a woman, of rich or poor, educated or uneducated parents, of one or another race or ethnicity—no such factors are predictive of competitive success unless they happen to correlate with native talent and ambition, which alone determine one's prospects.

This same line of thought can be pressed further. Even in a society in which the fair equality of opportunity principle was completely satisfied, it would remain the case that the system of social cooperation distributes advantages so that individuals are rewarded or punished because of matters that lay entirely beyond their power to control. In the regime of fair equality of opportunity, two individuals with different levels of native talent who have the same ambition and work equally hard to achieve will have unequal prospects of success. In this case no plausible account of deservingness could find the individual with better prospects more deserving of her superior prospects. If we accept the norm that society should eliminate the influence of arbitrary luck or contingency on the determination of an individual's fundamental life prospects as set by the basic institutions of society, further justice reform is needed beyond fair equality. At this point, enter the difference principle.

Further light on the character of Rawls's egalitarianism is shed by considering how his principles of justice fare against the three criticisms of the ideal of equality of life prospects noted above in Section IV.B.

A. Objection: Efficiency Versus Equality

Rawls does not embrace strict equality as a value at all, and substitutes the difference principle norm for it. Like equality, the difference principle is a comparative norm. To determine what it requires with respect to a group of people, one must know the relative standing of these people—who is better off and who is worse off. But unlike equality, the difference principle does not conflict with the fairness requirement that if one can make someone better off without making anyone worse off, one should do it (or move to some other arrangement from which no Pareto improvement can be made). At least, this is so if we amend the difference principle slightly, so it asserts: Institutions and social practices should be set so that, as a first priority, the benefit level of the least advantaged individuals is maximized, as a second priority, the benefit level of the second-worst-off is maximized (without subtracting from the benefits that go to the worst-off), and so on, up to the best-off individuals.

Rawls then is not subject to the objection from efficiency because he does not espouse distributive equality. After all, the difference principle is "egalitarian" only in an attenuated sense. In many circumstances the difference principle prefers a more equal to a less equal pattern of distribution, but only because the former is better for the worse off, not because the difference principle attaches any value to equality for its own sake.

B. Objection: Self-Ownership Versus the Difference Principle

The libertarian norm of self-ownership opposes the difference principle. Suppose that in a society ruled by the difference principle Karen, a virtuoso opera singer, earns 10 million dollars per year, and the redistributive mechanism of the Rawlsian state taxes her earnings to aid the needy. On the assumption that the society implements Rawls's principles, this taxation policy fits into a set of institutions and practices that, taken together, maximize the benefits of the worst off class in society over the long run. The Lockean libertarian sees here a clear violation of self-ownership. It would be acceptable for the government to request that Karen contribute her earnings to a fund to aid the needy, but a violation of her rights to coerce her to contribute.

The Rawlsian egalitarian sees the issue differently. Some accident of fortunate genetic endowment or favorable early socialization has given Karen her extraordinary singing talent. She can take no credit for these background facts; she is simply the winner of these lotteries that all must undergo quite independently of their will. She does not deserve the extraordinary voice that she possesses. Nonetheless, it is hers. It is not as though on a Rawlsian view, society may do anything it likes with the bodies of the talented. The basic liberties protected by Rawls's First Principle include a right of bodily integrity, so if medical researchers discovered that Karen's rare larynx, ground up, could be used to make medicine that could alleviate serious illnesses threatening many of the worst-off citizens, Karen has a right to her own body that denies society the right to expropriate her larynx even for a good cause. The basic liberties protected by Rawlsian justice also include the right to free choice of careers and avocations. If Karen, bored by fame and wealth, renounces her career in opera to pursue life as a mendicant friar, she is within her rights, in a Rawlsian society, to make such a choice. The Rawlsian violation of self-ownership comes at this point: If Karen chooses to engage in a lucrative career, then even if she earns her money by singing for people who voluntarily pay to hear her sing with money that is uncontroversially theirs to spend as they want, these earnings are subject to redistributive taxation.

The Rawlsian egalitarian will say that because Karen does not deserve the native talent that enables her to earn big bucks, it is not unfair to require her to share her income with the less fortunate, so long as this is done in a manner that is consistent with her right to basic liberties and the maintenance of fair equality of opportunity.

C. Objection: Responsibility and Deservingness Versus the Difference Principle

The difference principle says that society should be arranged so as to maximize the sustainable benefit level enjoyed by its least-advantaged members (provided that basic liberties are respected and fair equality of opportunity prevails). This may seem fair if we recall that one's native ability is beyond one's power to control and we imagine all members of society being roughly equally diligent in developing and using their talents. But in fact people are not equally diligent. Other things being equal, the more diligent and ambitious will do better. Like a principle of equality, the difference principle makes it a requirement of justice that society redistribute from better off to badly off individuals. The difference principle holds that we ought to set practices so they redistribute just to the point at which further redistribution would be counterproductive and begin to worsen the condition of the worst off over the long run. Liberals and conservatives would disagree on the difficult empirical issue, where this tipping point lies. But there is also room for moral disagreement here. The difference principle implies that even if (some members of) the least advantaged class are irresponsible and undeserving, nonetheless society should be organized to make their benefit levels as high as possible. The difference principle in these circumstances endorses redistribution from the deserving to the undeserving. This seems unfair.

The Rawlsian has two responses. First, he denies that it is the business of society to reward the deserving and punish the undeserving. In a diverse democracy, people can be expected to disagree about such contentious moral issues, and enforcing any ideal of deservingness would be sectarian. Moreover, the idea of identifying truly responsible and deserving conduct becomes more elusive the more we think about it. The willingess to put forth conscientious effort and thus to be deserving in the ordinary sense comes easily to some people and is far more difficult for others. The disposition to try is a trait that varies with accidents of genetic inheritance and the quality of one's early socialization and education, like any other talent. Also, the more talented one is, the more rewarding will be the experience of trying hard, so other things being equal, the more talented can be expected to be more disposed to put forth efforts toward chosen goals. These points do not show that there is no such thing as being truly deserving, only that it is extraordinarily difficult to distinguish the truly deserving from the undeserving. It would be folly to accept a theory of social justice that assigns a public agency the responsibility of making such determinations, which cannot be made nonarbitrarily in practice.

Rawls's second response to the deservingness objection is more accommodating. His theory of justice presupposes that ordinary members of society are capable of cooperating with others on fair terms and of reflectively choosing their values and a plan of life to achieve their values. In Rawls's scheme each individual is responsible for acting to achieve her plan of life. In the Rawlsian conception there is a division of responsibility between society and the individual. Society is responsible for giving each individual a fair share of access to general-purpose resources, the primary social goods. What the individual does with those resources, as well as the quality of life she gains from them, is her own business, not the responsibility of society.

The second response opens the door on a wider issue. Insofar as we care about distributive equality,

equality in people's life prospects, what exactly should we be caring about?

VII. EQUALITY OF WHAT?

Any standard of distributive equality needs some measure of the advantages and disadvantages that accrue to individuals, so that we can tell whether their conditions are equal or unequal. Many issues are involved in the choice of a measure. A brief survey of possible measures follows.

A. Resources and Opportunities for Resources

Suppose one agrees that social justice should be concerned neither with the quality of people's chosen aims in life nor with the extent to which they achieve their aims. The individual herself must take responsibility for these matters in a free society. It does not follow that justice should be responsible for getting fair shares or equal shares of resources into people's hands. The level of resources that I gain over the course of my life depends to a great extent on voluntary choices that I make. But it also depends on initial circumstances beyond my power to control. Responding to these points, one might hold that the just society should strive to equalize not people's actual resource shares but their opportunities to gain resources by reasonable and lawful conduct. To a first approximation we might say that equality of opportunity for resources obtains among a group of persons when each could gain the same level of resources if she behaved prudently throughout her life that anyone else, behaving with similar prudence, could gain.

B. Achievements and Opportunities for Achievements

Focus on an individual's resource share as the measure of her condition for purposes of distributive justice theory may be fetishistic. After all, people do not ordinarily care about resources or means for their own sakes, but with what a given level of resources enables one to be or do.

Moreover, individuals differ in many ways, and they are able to transform resources into being and doing achievements at varying rates. Consider a simple example. Suppose that income in dollars is the measure of resource shares. Smith and Jones have equal incomes, but Smith is legless, so must spend virtually his entire income on crutches and wheelchairs, whereas Jones has healthy legs, and can spend her income on a wide variety of goods. It is hard to see how equality of condition in any sense that matters obtains between Smith and Jones in this example. Instead of measuring people's condition by their resource levels, we might measure the extent to which their resources enable them to achieve various valued conditions, such as being adequately well nourished, being able to move freely around one's neighborhood, being able to clothe oneself so that one may appear in public without looking shamefully out of place, and so on. We could take the relevant measure to be either the achievements they actually achieve or the opportunities they have to attain various achievements. The latter measure, the opportunity to achieve, could be interpreted as representing the real freedom that the individual enjoys.

C. Well-Being and Opportunities for Well-Being

Many of the things that people are enabled to be or do with a given share of resources are utterly trivial. They are things no one cares about. One's freedom to attain various achievements in a given situation will amount to an infinitely long list of heterogeneous possibilities ranging from the trivial and silly to the weird to the truly important. It would seem that if we want to use some measure of people's opportunities as the aspect of their condition that egalitarian justice bids us to equalize, we need some way of winnowing down the lists of people's possible achievements by eliminating opportunities that do not really matter. To do so would in effect be to arrive at a conception of people's well-being, of what makes their lives go better rather than worse.

One possibility to consider would be preference satisfaction. The proposal would be that the achievement possibilities that count are those that satisfy one's basic preferences, those that one wants satisfied for their own sake, not as a means to any further goal. Egalitarian justice would then be asserting that we ought to equalize people's opportunities to satisfy their basic preferences.

This will not do. Or at least, there are serious difficulties with the proposal. One problem is that some preferences are ill-considered. I come to want things for their own sakes that later, or if I reflected more carefully or with more complete information, I would see are not really part of my good. My single overriding basic preference now might be to love and be loved by

Tom, but my friends and neighbors may be right that this romance would be a disaster for me in terms of things that I ought to care about more but that in my mood of infatuation I could care less about.

One's preferences may be formed in part by one's situation, and crimped or reduced (or badly inflated) by unfortunate and unjust circumstances. The housewife in a patriarchal culture may only want to stand by her man and serve his needs, but satisfying these preferences, some may think, is not achieving a good life. The stunting of one's preferences may be an aspect of the unfairness of one's circumstances. Also, it may be reasonable for an individual to induce in herself limited desires as a way of coping with grim circumstances. Being a poor peasant in a time of famine, I may reasonably try to want only to keep my family alive and not aspire after the impossible. But the extent to which one's resources enable one to satisfy one's preferences will not then in general be a good measure of how well off one is, and equalizing people's opportunities for preference satisfaction may then seem an inadequate conception of egalitarian justice.

A theory of the good life, if we had it, would determine what constitutes well-being, genuinely living well, for each individual. The proposal then to be considered would be that insofar as we think that justice requires equality in some aspect of people's condition, we should be trying to render equal people's opportunities for well-being. Some may think that we do in fact possess enough lore about what is choiceworthy in human life to use our theory of the good life to shape our theory of what justice as equality requires. Others will disagree.

VIII. EQUALITY AMONG WHOM?

So far we have written as though distributive equality is satisfied when in each country, people's condition in that society is sufficiently close to the same. But there does not seem to be any rationale for this limitation. If inequality is bad, the inequality in life prospects between the richest people in the richest countries on the earth and the poorest people in the poorest countries is far greater, and so far worse, than the inequality between most advantaged and least advantaged in affluent, economically advanced societies.

One could regard the norm of distributive equality as applying to households on a global scale rather than individuals. But a focus on individuals seems preferable, because looking only at interhousehold differences masks morally troubling inequalities in opportunities and powers within families between men and women.

In contemporary public discussion unease is expressed at inequality among groups, especially between what are called racial and ethnic groups. This focus is appropriate, given the pervasive tendency for groups defined along these lines to oppress one another. The question arises whether inequality among such groups should be thought to be morally undesirable in its own right, or whether when we speak about the plight of groups our sole underlying concern should be for how individuals fare in comparative terms.

IX. WHAT ENTITLES US TO THE STATUS OF EQUALS?

The discussion to this point has presupposed that some substantive conception of the equality of all human persons is to be incorporated into any adequate morality. The issue then becomes how to pick out the appropriate ideal of human equality. But the presupposition of human equality is open to challenge. In virtue of what traits of human persons are all of them entitled to an equal fundamental moral status?

All human persons are alike in being equally members of the human species. But mere species membership by itself seems an inadequate basis for ascribing a fundamental moral status. We can imagine coming in contact in the future with intelligent beings from outer space, who are clearly persons, but equally clearly not members of the human species. It would be morally arbitrary to restrict the application of moral principles to the boundaries of the human species and to deny that it is wrong, for example, to murder outer space persons just because they are not biologically human.

The claim of human equality is open to challenge from another direction. The egalitarian holds that all human persons share an equal moral status that is not rightly extended to nonhuman animals. All humans are equal and should have equal basic moral rights, we may think, but we do not proceed to assert that all humans, whales, dolphins, monkeys, apes, chimpanzees, zebras, lions, tigers, wolverines, chipmucks, lizards, and scorpions are equal and should have equal basic moral rights. Why not? A tempting response is that membership in the human species confers a moral status equal to that of all other humans and superior to the status of nonhuman animals, but we have already seen that the appeal to species membership by itself does not suffice to establish distinctive moral status. What then is it about humans that renders them equal to all fellow humans and superior to other animals?

The answer may seem to be obvious. Humans have conscious experiences, can experience pleasure and pain, desire some things and are averse to others. A being with these capacities can be benefitted and harmed and so can be an object of moral concern. But many nonhuman animals have these capacities as well, so these capacities do not establish a unique, privileged moral status for humans alone. In broad terms, intelligence or superior cognitive capacity does distinguish typical humans from members of the other species that happen to inhabit this planet. Humans have capacities of rational agency. They can formulate possible courses of action, reflect on their situation to elicit reasons for and against these courses of action, weigh reasons, and decide how to act so as to satisfy goals and constraints that they have chosen or accept as binding. In response to reasoned challenges they can reconsider and revise their choices and values. And they can do all of this over extended periods of time, giving a coherent shape to stretches of their lives. Nonhuman animals either lack these rational agency capacities altogether or have them in attenuated form. Moreover, it is plausible to hold that beings with these rational agency capacities are something special, and entitled to special moral consideration.

With these points in place, we can identify a threshold of rational agency capacities such that of the animals known to us, only humans meet the threshold, and reserve the term "persons" for any and all beings that are beyond this threshold of rational agency. The claim of human equality then gets reformulated as the claim that all persons should be treated according to the same basic moral principles (accorded the same basic moral rights).

To be credible, this account of human equality must confront one large and one small difficulty. The small difficulty is that not all living beings that are members of the humans species can meet the rational agency qualifications for personhood, wherever the threshold is set, if the threshold is set sufficiently high that no nonhuman animals will be able to pass. Human fetuses and developing infants lack developed capacities for rational agency, even if they have the potential to develop these capacities. Even if we confine attention to mature adults, we observe that some are severely cognitively impaired. Some never develop any significant rational agency capacity, and some develop it but lose it at some point in their lives as a result of injury or disease or degeneration. This means that on this threshold account of human equality, not all human beings, but only human persons share the status of fundamental moral equality. If there is a constraint forbidding the murder of human persons, this constraint will not straightforwardly and unequivocally apply to the severely cognitively impaired. Perhaps other grounds sufficient to justify a right to life possessed by severely cognitively impaired humans can be located, but the issue is, so far, open. Those who find this conclusion to be disquieting may be stimulated to produce an alternative account of human equality that accords a fundamental equal moral status to all humans without appealing to mere species membership to justify this way of drawing lines, but it is not clear how such an alternative account would go.

The more important difficulty with this account of human equality is that the setting of a threshold level of rational agency to establish an equal moral status may be inescapably arbitrary. The various capacities that combine to yield rational agency vary by degrees across some large range. If the extent of one's capacity of these various sorts matters enormously up to the threshold level, why don't further differences matter above the threshold? Suppose I am barely at the threshold level of rational agency, and you are far above the threshold level. Why doesn't your possession of superior abilities to identify and assess reasons, deliberate about proposed courses of action, understand the causal structure of the natural world, reason and calculate correctly, make sensible decisions, and implement them render you more morally considerable than me and give you greater rights? The threshold account tries to explain and justify an either–or distinction (either you are a person or not) in terms of factors that vary by degree. It is not clear an account of this type can succeed. It is as though one were attempting to define an aristocratic class by appeal to distinction of physical height, and held that taller is better than shorter and that those above some threshold of height, say six feet, are thereby rendered aristocrats, but distinctions of height matter not at all within the class of aristocrats, who are equally distinguished by virtue of their height even though they are variously tall. To render this analysis coherent one needs to develop a plausible account of why being taller than six feet matters morally but that further differences of height above this level are irrelevant to the determination of fundamental status. The same goes for the threshold rational agency account of human equality.

Also See the Following Articles

CITIZENSHIP • CHRISTIAN ETHICS, ROMAN CATHOLIC • DISTRIBUTIVE JUSTICE • MARX AND ETHICS • RIGHTS THEORY • THEORIES OF JUSTICE: RAWLS

Bibliography

Nozick, R. (1974). *Anarchy, state, and utopia.* New York: Basic Books.
Pojman, L., & Westmoreland, R. (1997). *Equality: Selected readings.* Oxford: Oxford University Press.
Rae, D. (1981). *Equalities.* Cambridge, MA: Harvard University Press.
Sen, A. (1992). *Inequality reexamined.* Cambridge, MA: Harvard University Press.
Walzer, M. (1983). *Spheres of justice: A defense of pluralism and equality.* New York: Basic Books.

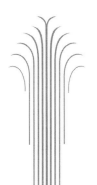

ETHICS AND SOCIAL SERVICES, OVERVIEW

Richard Hugman
Curtin University of Technology

I. Introduction
II. The Ethics of Social Welfare
III. Ethical Codes
IV. Ethics and Difference
V. Conclusion

GLOSSARY

casework The application of social theories and interpersonal skills to aid individuals or families in resolving personal or interpersonal problems (including those associated with structural issues or formal agencies).

ethical code A systematic statement, in summary form, of the standards of conduct required in a given profession.

health Physical and mental well-being, including the absence of disease.

justice Principles of decision making that seek to achieve fair outcomes for all persons; these principles may be applied in areas of social control (criminal justice) or generally (social justice).

probation Sanctioned by a legal process such as a court order, an interpersonal intervention with a person who has been convicted of crime seeking to assist the person in avoiding further criminal behavior.

social services Organized services to assist persons, families, or communities in need; may also be known as community services or human services.

social welfare The set of responses within a given society that are directed toward the alleviation of distress and the promotion of well-being.

welfare mix The balance or pattern of arrangements between different social sectors in the provision of social services.

SOCIAL SERVICES as now understood are a development of the modern era. Although many of the activities which compose social services (for example, nursing) have existed for many centuries, their contemporary *social* organization is a phenomenon of the industrialized world. The growth of social services is most advanced in the more developed countries, while in the poorest countries of the world social services are either highly underdeveloped or are confined to major cities.

Social services may also be known by the terms "human services" (for example, in the USA), "community services" (in Australia), or "health and welfare," which may be considered more generally applicable. This latter term also recognizes more explicitly the inclusion of medical, nursing, and allied health services along with general welfare and "correctional" services (such as probation and prisons). In this discussion the term "social services" is used to encompass all these aspects.

I. INTRODUCTION

A. Comparative Social Policies

1. Political and Economic Factors

Approaches to the provision of social services differ between countries. Nations which share political and economic systems tend to show some similarity with regard to types of social services and their organization, but even so there can be smaller variations which reflect differences in culture and history. Such variations can be understood under comparative social policy through an examination of the differences between countries in their policies for creating and developing social services.

The major distinctions between approaches to social services have political, economic, and organizational dimensions. In the area of politics, the balance between the state and other parts of society is the primary consideration. The issues in this respect are *who* should provide social services and *what* type of services should be available. Economic considerations relate to the amount of resources in a society which are devoted to social service provision. The issue is *how much* social services should be provided. The third aspect, the organization of social services, concerns *how* they should be provided.

2. Resources and Responsibility

The question of who provides social services is most usually addressed to the balance between the state and independent citizens, at least in respect to responsibility for organizing and funding services. In practice, in almost every instance the state has some involvement while independent citizens may also play a part. At opposite ends of the spectrum are those countries in which the state plays a residual role, providing services only for those people who are deemed to be unable to find other assistance, and those in which the state provides all main services and independent citizens are concerned only with marginal or esoteric situations. These different patterns represent varying answers to the question of who should take responsibility for ensuring the well-being of persons in a society. The balance between sectors evident now in most countries is referred to as the "welfare mix."

The amount of social resources devoted to health and welfare varies between countries. Overall, the higher the percentage of gross domestic product (GDP) allotted to social spending, the more extensive the scale of social services in a country. The Scandinavian countries spend over 30% of GDP on social services and have extensive formal provision. However, the amount of GDP spent is not necessarily related to the balance seen in the welfare mix. Although Scandinavian countries represent the most extensive state welfare systems in western capitalism, with high levels of social resources allocated, there are also countries where such connections do not appear to hold. For example, in 1991 the USA spent 13.5% of GDP on health while the United Kingdom spent 6.5%; the USA has a much higher proportion of nonstate health provision than does the United Kingdom, where the state is the main provider of health services. Such patterns are politically determined and reflect social values.

The means by which social services are provided may include formal agencies, including both government departments and independent organizations. Informal local networks and even families may also be providers of social services. Only correctional services (probation, prisons, police) are almost universally the responsibility of the state, whether directly or indirectly. In developed industrial countries such services are likely to be organized and provided by professionals; in developing countries this is increasingly the case. In developing countries medical and health services are likely to be the most professionalized, while social work and community development services may be less so. Here, too, correctional services are the responsibility of the state. The pattern of means by which social services are provided is also part of the welfare mix, in which state agencies, commercial companies, not-for-profit agencies (e.g., charities), and individuals may all play a part. Again, the exact pattern in any country reflects social and political values.

B. Ethical Considerations in Social Policy

1. Ethics and Ideology

Underpinning the pattern of social policy in any given country are moral concerns with what is right for a society in respect to health and welfare. The political, economic and organizational dimensions of social services reflect the moral value which is placed on individual responsibility or collective responsibility for health, well-being, and community cohesion. In most societies there is a balance between the two, with some responsibility ascribed to individuals and some to collective aspects of society (including the state).

V. George and P. Wilding (1976. *Ideology and Social Welfare*. Routledge & Kegan Paul, London) have identified four main value positions:

a. Total individualism/anticollectivism (free market liberalism)

b. "Reluctant" collectivism, emphasis on individual-ism (Keynesianism)

c. Limited individualism, emphasis on collectivism (social democracy)

d. Total collectivism/anti-individualism (Marxism)

Each of these positions, which express social and political ideologies, has implications for ethical responses made toward various forms of "need," including poverty, illness, and crime. Each position is composed of views about the nature of and relationship between freedom and liberty, equality, justice, and responsibility.

2. Ethics and Value Difference

Within any one national society there is unlikely to be total agreement about the balance between individual and collective responsibility for health and welfare because the objectives of social services (children, young people, elderly people, physical or mental disability, deviance and crime, and the family) are issues over which it is possible for there to be different ethical positions within a single society or culture. Actual social policies will reflect particular values—those of the dominant sections of society. Thus political and economic systems in which "liberty" is valued over "equality" have patterns of social services reflecting individualist approaches to responsibility while those in which "equality" is more highly valued than "liberty" will tend toward collective patterns of social service provision.

The moral framework of social services, therefore, is highly contested. Competing ideologies contain different views of what is right and wrong in deciding the who, what, how much, and how of social services. At the same time, proponents of different perspectives claim to be trying to achieve the same overall goal, namely the promotion of human dignity and the best possible life for all.

II. THE ETHICS OF SOCIAL WELFARE

A. Competing Perspectives

1. Liberal Individualism and Social Services

The liberal individualist seeks the greatest freedom possible for the individual person, which must therefore be accompanied by the least possible compulsion from the state. In moral philosophy, the basis of this position can be seen in the work of Kant. Liberal individualism is "deontological," beginning from an absolute view about the nature of human life. Each individual person is seen as distinct, as morally autonomous, and as an end in him- or herself (not a means to an end). The ethical elements of liberal concepts of freedom and liberty are grounded in this moral philosophy.

In the realm of social services, this requires that only those aspects of society which contribute to the achievement of basic freedoms should be the responsibility of the state. Defense, law, and social order are seen as the limits of legitimate state activity, so only these should be funded by compulsory taxation. Some liberals (e.g., J. S. Mill or Friedman) would also allow basic income support to ensure that extreme poverty is alleviated, precisely because this benefits everyone in society. Such a position would require that no reciprocal obligations were attached and that services were only in the form of cash payment. It addresses the distress and not the morality of the poor. Others (e.g., Hayek or Nozick) would posit that distress is the business of the market, not of the state—the business of the state is to ensure that the market remains free to address health and welfare wants.

Liberal individualism, therefore, effectively supports only those social services concerned with the maintenance of social order. This would include the police, the courts, probation, prisons, some social security, and those elements of health and welfare that have "policing functions" (such as social work in child protection, community nursing in mental health, or environmental protection). All other forms of social services are regarded as the responsibility of private individuals, to be provided through free markets or by voluntary effort (charity).

The problems of individualism in social services lie in the extent to which the market can be demonstrated to be capable of responding efficiently or effectively to health and welfare needs. Although there is evidence that in the advanced industrial countries, charitable giving rises with increased incomes, and philanthropy increases with falling taxes, there is also evidence that the level of social services which can be supplied on this basis is less than that which has been supplied by the welfare state, for example, in Scandinavia and Western Europe.

Liberal individualism and a highly developed welfare state are therefore incompatible on ethical grounds. The emphasis within the former on *individual* liberty is valued more highly than the meeting of needs, which are, in any case, seen as "wants" because they are seen as the property of individuals and not as benefits for the maintenance of social order. This ethical position is associated with anticollectivists and to a lesser extent with some "reluctant" collectivists.

2. Utilitarian Collectivism and Social Services

In contrast to liberal individualism, utilitarian collectivism and a highly developed welfare state are compatible. In part derived from other aspects of the work of J. S. Mill, the utilitarian position advocates that the achievement of the "greatest good of the greatest number, at the expense of the least possible number," is the ethical goal of society. Compulsion exercised by the state is therefore a necessary means through which not only social maintenance but also a level of redistribution sufficient to promote the "greatest good of the greatest number" can be achieved. Individuals are seen to derive their moral status from the society of which they are part. The basis of this position in moral philosophy is "teleological," because it justifies means by the ends to which they are put. The coercion of individuals (such as through taxation to pay for social services) is regarded as ethically acceptable in so far as it seeks to achieve the greatest good of the greatest number of people within the society, and at the same time does not cause any undue "pain" (rule utilitarianism). For example, a person's overall level of wealth may be reduced through taxation providing that their *relative* position in the society is not changed and their well-being is not placed at risk. Particular actions can be judged ethically in relation to whether they are the most efficient and effective means of achieving this end (act utilitarianism). For example, it would be acceptable to levy high rates of marginal taxation only in so far as this can be demonstrated to promote the welfare of the greatest number of people.

This approach accepts the state acting to organize and supply not only those social services which maintain the social order, but also those which promote the health and well-being of the large masses of the population. Indeed, without state intervention there is no guarantee that those individuals who possess the greater part of a society's resources will act to distribute them for the benefit of the greatest number. Such a position is based, at least implicitly, on an analysis of social structures which concludes that the spread of resources is neither the result of moral worth nor just good fortune, but reflects a social order which creates and maintains inequality in favor of those in particular groups. Utilitarian collectivism therefore promotes those services which serve the greatest majority of the population.

Within a utilitarian collectivist approach, services such as schools, hospitals and clinics, social centers for people who are disabled, unemployed, or aged, and those aspects of the health and welfare services which are concerned not only with "policing" functions but also with the enhancement of personal well-being may all be funded and organized through the state. The criminal justice system also will be a state responsibility, but this may include some support for access to legal services for those accused of crimes. Highly developed welfare states therefore embody the ethics of utilitarian collectivism.

Critics of collectivism make two charges. The first is that its utilitarian basis makes no allowance for individuality, either in its approach to questions of choice (for a particular type of service) or in its responsibility. Second, collectivism is seen to produce standards of social services which tend toward a low common denominator. As a consequence it may be bad at meeting the needs of very small minorities in situations of limited resources. For example, the costs of minority services might be seen as too great relative to the numbers of those who would have to go without another service in order for it to be funded.

Utilitarian collectivism is therefore highly compatible with a strong welfare state, and inimical to a free market model. Value is placed on *equality* between members of a society and its promotion through social policy. The management of the social system is seen as necessary and beneficial to alleviate inequalities and the needs arising from them, as these are seen as the products of the system. This ethical position is associated, in different ways, with social democrats and Marxists.

B. Contradictions and Compromises

1. Rawls and Social Justice

Two particular attempts to resolve the contradictions between the liberal individualist and the utilitarian collectivist perspectives are worth noting in respect of these issues. The first of these is the work of J. Rawls (1972. *A Theory of Justice.* Oxford Univ. Press, Oxford). Rawls argued that although morality is grounded in the acts of individual persons, nevertheless a just and ethical arrangement of society, especially with regard to welfare (social services), would be one that all reasonable persons would agree to if they did not have prior knowledge of their fortunes in life. There are two key principles in Rawls' theory:

1. Inequalities are just in so far as they benefit the least well off
2. Individuals are not the "owners" of their talents (e.g., knowledge and skills)

The implications of Rawls' approach is that the welfare state is ethical in so far as it is based on taxation of income which derives from skills or knowledge, or indeed from inherited wealth. It also suggests that the just level of coercion (taxation of parts of society to provide benefits to all) is that up to which the least advantaged cease to benefit. There are obviously practical problems in determining quite where such lines might be drawn, as these are questions of value, social and political. For this reason, although Rawls' theory is of analytic use (for example, it could be used to illustrate points of similarity between "reluctant" collectivists and social democrats) and would support limited forms of collective social services provision, it has been little applied in concrete social policy.

2. Bauman and Moral Action

A more recent formulation of the ethical contradictions facing theorists of social welfare is that in Z. Bauman's examination of modernist and postmodernist dimensions to moral philosophy. Bauman (1989. *Modernity and the Holocaust*. Polity, Cambridge) argues that in the modern era (post-Enlightenment), morality, like the rest of the natural and social world, has been treated as if subject to abstract and rational law. There are, for Bauman, two great institutions which modernity has produced, each of which plays a part in the practical application of individualist and collectivist ethics to social services. These are business and bureaucracy, both of which have the effect of removing the human actor from private belief and sentiment while in the public sphere.

Business is based on instrumental rationality. The "good" is achieved through the use of means to the greatest possible effect (of profit, market share, or both). Honesty is the primary virtue, defined in terms of contractual integrity, and the specifics of either the outcome or the people with whom one must deal to achieve business ends are of at best secondary significance. Business has no place for other ethical issues.

Bureaucracy is based on procedural rationality. The "good" is achieved through following correct procedures. The primary virtue is loyalty to legitimate authority and to fellow members. This leads to "floating responsibility" (that is, it becomes separated from persons and attached to positions) coupled with "ethical indif-

ference" ("good" and "bad" are replaced by "correct" and "incorrect").

These institutional forms are of considerable importance because throughout the world, including the former and present communist bloc countries, debates about the organization of social services are couched in terms of the choice between business or bureaucracy. This is not to suggest that all ethical considerations are dispensed with, but that the form moral thinking takes within these institutions also has been framed in modernist terms. "Professional ethics," whether of the nurse, psychologist, or social worker on the one hand, or of the accountant and marketing executive on the other, are codifications which for Bauman can be used to prevent the individual from exercising moral responsibility. Put simply, ethical codes can become sets of contractual or procedural rules which may be followed technically, even mechanically, without demanding of the practitioner that responsibility accompanies action; rather, they may serve to limit such moral autonomy.

The irony of the situation described by Bauman is that professional ethics have often been the driving force of the development of social services. Indeed, the *value* dimension of social services is usually the point of contention from which the urgency of judgments about the who, what, how much, and how is generated. The issue is that the enactment of the responsibilities and powers of social services must be exercised by professionals (and others) who have the capacity to engage with the ethical questions behind such services and not simply by people concerned to maximize resources or carry out functions in a procedurally correct manner.

III. ETHICAL CODES

A. Professions and Ethical Codes

1. Kant and Ethical Codes

All professions have a code of ethics of some kind. Codes of ethics are sets of statements concerning the actions of a member of a profession which will be seen as acceptable by the wider membership of that profession. Such codes are most often composed of detailed declarations of those actions which will produce an outcome that accords with the values of the occupation. In this way, ethical codes can be seen as the connections between means and ends in which the relationship between means and ends is seen as coherent, specific, and having integrity. "Integrity" in this sense means that the means and the ends should be congruent. A well-known example is the demand of medical practitioners that in seeking to promote health they should at least do no harm (from the Hippocratic oath). Almost all social service professions incorporate some notion of "confidentiality" in their ethical codes.

Such an approach owes much to the deontological strand of moral philosophy, which is associated with the work of Kant. That is, the statements that make up an ethical code tend to be abstract rather than concrete, categorical rather than questioning, and absolute rather than conditional. It may be argued that this is necessary, in that such codes must cover all possible actions which might be taken by a member of a profession. It is not possible in advance to anticipate the details of any one situation, and so an ethical code must have a sufficient level of generality to be applicable in all situations.

Arising from the abstract, categorical, and absolute nature of ethical codes can be the criticism that they are, therefore, idealist. In this context idealism refers to the plausibility of such principles in the realm of ideas while at the same time their problematic relationship with the concrete historical world of social action. In other words, they may be "fine in theory" but "difficult in practice." Although being "difficult" to implement does not of itself make ethical codes implausible, if this problem arises, as critics argue, because the codes fail to take account of the social realities in which social services are provided, then either the specific codes are badly constructed or else codes are inappropriate. The former position is adopted by those who would wish to (radically) reform professional ethics, while the latter may be associated with those who would wish to abolish the professions altogether.

Nevertheless, without codes of ethics, it may be countered, how would members of the public know what standards of action they could reasonably expect from the members of a profession? The proponents of such codes stress this point, and emphasize the role played by codes in making professions accountable to those who may not have the level of knowledge to evaluate the technical aspects of their work. The role of ethical codes, from this perspective, is in providing the basis for the openness of social services to those who use these services, as well as to everyone in a society who might contribute to their funding through taxation.

2. Ethics, Professionalism, and Agency

Codes of ethics form an essential component in claims by occupational groups to professionalism. Indeed, it is unlikely that an occupation making such a claim would ignore the extent to which possession of a code of ethics is seen as an essential element of professional standing. The role of the code of ethics in this context is for a profession to provide guarantees of good faith, such that any member in breach of a code will be "struck off" (that is, removed from the profession either temporarily or permanently). An occupation may be granted a high degree of autonomy if it can show the rules by which it will regulate itself. Codes of ethics, and associated procedures, provide just such a means by which self-regulation can occur and through which the actions of a profession are clear to the public.

Where the practices of an entire profession may appear to be incongruent with its stated ethics, however, can lead to the criticism that codes form a "smoke-screen" to disguise the incompatibility of professional interests and the interests of others. It was this observation that led G. B. Shaw to conclude that professions are a "conspiracy against the laity" (1911. *The Doctor's Dilemma*. Constable, London). Such inconsistencies may appear where a profession charges a fee for its services but is committed to helping all without favor (medicine, for example), or if a profession is required to control the actions of some service users while being committed to promoting "self-determination" (social work). Most obviously the employment of social services professions in large agencies, especially state agencies, may create situations where ethical principles are seen to be compromised by organizational requirements. Limits to confidentiality, the restriction on freedom of action imposed by resource constraints, and the management of professionals by those who are not members of the same profession may each serve to obstruct the implementation of ethical codes.

For these reasons, contemporary debates focus on three questions. First, is it possible to practice professionally in agencies at all? The implication may be that professions and managed organizations do not go together. Second, do ethical codes have to be rethought to take account of the predominant (agency) site of practice? In other words, acknowledging limitations to confidentiality or simply being open to a service user about the way an organization functions is honest (and therefore ethical). Third, is it the responsibility of the professional within an agency to always side with the interests of the service user over the organization, even where this may mean resignation (or dismissal) rather than compromising ethical standards? A rather different sense of "agency" is implied here, one which accords with the morally autonomous person (in the sense implied by Bauman).

B. Ethical Codes in Practice

1. Biestek and Beyond

Probably the most influential statement of ethics in social services has been that contained in the work of Biestek (1961. *The Casework Relationship*. George Allen & Unwin, London). Biestek proposed seven principles of casework:

i. Acceptance (of the client as the person she or he is)

ii. Nonjudgmentalism (of the moral worth of the client to receive help)

iii. Individualization (of the client as a person—the avoidance of categorization)

iv. Purposeful expression of emotion (not just for its own sake or for the gratification of the caseworker)

v. Controlled emotional involvement (to protect the integrity of both the client and the caseworker)

vi. Confidentiality (safeguarding all information about the client)

vii. Self-determination (of the client in her or his own decision making)

Each of these principles makes a value statement about the relationship between means and ends in social casework (and by implication, all social services). They are intended to create the basis for an ethical practice in which the interests, needs, and rights of the client are protected by setting constraints on the caseworker's actions, to which the caseworker can give explicit moral consent.

Biestek's principles have been extensively criticized in the last three decades. These criticisms are of two types. The first is that the principles themselves are inadequate in relation to the practical context in which social services are provided. The second is that the moral philosophy at the root of Biestek's thinking is inappropriate in contemporary society.

Where these principles are held to be inadequate practically is a consequence of the problems of "agency" outlined above. Quite simply, Biestek appears to assume both that the caseworker has autonomy at the level of individual practice and that the objectives of their work are freely negotiable with the service user. Not only do most social service contexts not permit the practitioner this much scope, but also some or all of the work undertaken by the caseworker may be in an institution that has aims of social control (in criminal justice, mental health, and so on). Some specific professions, such as social work, may thus seek to balance "control" with

"care," seeing the latter as their primary aim and the former as a means to achieving it (and so be acceptable only at the least possible level), while others, such as the police, may see the former as a primary goal. Whichever the balance, the juxtaposition of "control" and "care" as objectives may render Biestek's principles idealistic, that is, unattainable in practical terms.

The other objection to Biestek's principles is that their deontological assumptions, based on the work of Kant, do not accord with the "postmodern" tendency. That is, the individualist humanism inherent in the absolute values on which Biestek's work is based is in turn based on the Enlightenment view of society and human nature. This approach does not take account of social divisions, for example, nor of the limited resources that most societies consider they have at their disposal for social services. Some critics have proposed the replacement of these ethics with a critical form of utilitarianism. This position is usually identified with "radical" professionals and with a "collectivist" approach to social welfare. In the late 1960s and the 1970s forms of socialism or Marxism provided the basis for this criticism. More recently, the recognition of "social difference" (see Section IV) and its diverse forms (gender, race, culture, disability, sexuality, and age, as well as social class) has become influential as the foundation of a reevaluation of social welfare ethics and of Biestek along with other perspectives. In turn, this has been reflected in the ethical codes, or pronouncements, of social service professions.

2. New Ethical Codes in Social Services

It may be said that the debate between deontological (such as Kantian) and relativist (such as utilitarian) perspectives has led, in the contemporary situation, to something of an impasse. To reject the seven principles of casework as unworkable may need to be done with caution, unless it is to be accepted that all the values embedded in them are likewise to be jettisoned. For example, *absolute* confidentiality may be impossible to guarantee if a service is provided through a managed agency, but this does not of itself render the question of confidentiality irrelevant. In so far as knowledge about the client confers power to the professional, recognition of the responsibility this places on the professional and the institution in practice is shared by individualists and collectivists alike. Underlying all Biestek's principles is the need to set constraints on the use of social power by professionals, which the professionals themselves accept as desirable and so will seek to implement. This ethical concern may have shifted in focus from the *needs* of service users (the basis of Biestek's absolutes) to the *rights* of service users, but the importance of defining what is "good" social services practice, the right relationship between ends and means, remains.

The shift in ethical thinking to respond to the wider developments in social thought (especially the emergence of postmodernism) has impacted some social service professions in the form of revised ethical codes or statements. While for the most part these continue to be constructed as categorical statements, there is also a trend toward the relating of statements to the broad objectives of a profession. In some instances, such as the statement by social work that it seeks to promote "social justice," professions may be seen by the wider society as making "political" statements and so going beyond the remit of professionalism. However, no one would expect the negative instance to apply (that social work should participate in the promotion of "social injustice"). What is at issue is the exact meaning of "social justice" in specific contexts, and the role of social services professions in defining such terms. Ethics and politics are, in this way, inextricably interconnected.

Where categorical statements are redefined in relation to the debates between different moral philosophies, the importance of social diversity, or difference, has become more prominent. References to the ethical dimension of discrimination, for example, are now contained in the ethical codes of nursing, psychology, and social work in many countries. Therefore the next section of this article will examine this important contemporary issue.

IV. ETHICS AND DIFFERENCE

A. Social Difference as an Ethical Issue

1. Social "Difference"

Social "difference" as a concept derives from the structural analysis of society, in which the broad objective relations between social groups are seen to define the social position and life opportunities of members of these groups. For example, the positions of women and men are structured differently, such that to be female or male is to have certain opportunities more or less accessible. Similarly, the racial or ethnic group to which one belongs will structure one's location in society. To be black in a white-dominated society is highly likely to lead to oppression (in the form of disadvantage or discrimination). The same analysis can be applied to other social divisions, e.g., between disabled and able-bodied people, between homosexual and heterosexual people, and between age groups.

The concept of social difference goes beyond acknowledging distinct social divisions to the recognition that society is composed of multiple membership of groups, in which identity comprises many possible elements (a sophistication of "role set" theory). Advantage or disadvantage may accrue in relation to each aspect of identity. For social services, this requires recognition of the way in which advantage and its opposite are differentially distributed by social structures. The interests, needs, and rights with which social services are concerned may be expected to differ between social groups. At the same time, attempts to evaluate and to rethink ethics also will have to deal with social diversity, where the very bases of moral thought will be quite diverse.

2. The Ethics of Difference

Is it possible, therefore, to speak of an encompassing ethical framework for social services, or does the recognition of diversity lead inevitably to a situation of ethical multiplicity? Even within a more traditional understanding, there has been a degree of convergence between the various professional groups, as their ethical standards were all derived from common sources and were couched in the same social and cultural assumptions. In terms of culture, the differences between white cultures and indigenous cultures in Australia or North America, or between white majorities and black minorities in Europe, or between eastern and western countries not only suggest that different ethical positions may be plausible, but also that the very ethic of social welfare itself may be culturally contentious. Similarly, feminist ethics and gay and lesbian ethics make challenging claims on the moral thought of social services professionals.

At one level it may be possible to explore an accommodation between diverse value positions. For example, the notion of "respect for persons," derived from the deontological perspective, may be applied to social divisions. "Respect" as a value is open to empirical examination through a consideration of what actions on the part of the professional would constitute "respect," and which would not (that is, be disrespectful). Assuming that social welfare needs, and the rights with which these are associated, are grounded in social structures, it is feasible that good (that is, ethical) practice could be achieved by the process of accurately grasping the world view of the person or group for whom services are being provided and seeking to respect that reality in the way in which a service is provided.

The problem with this position is twofold. First, it assumes that all social services are of a nature that their provision can be experienced as respectful. Those services that are associated with social control functions clearly are problematic in this respect. Second, the problem may become confined in these circumstances to one of technical competence in communication across social divisions (for example, cultural awareness). While acknowledging that cultural awareness is vital in a multicultural society (indeed, to fail to address this point could be construed as unethical), it is the social structures of differentially distributed advantage that are at issue. These structures are patriarchy, racism, homophobia, disableism, and ageism. Unless social services ethics address these issues also, then they may be seen as unethical because they cannot respond appropriately (and so in the above example could not demonstrate the criterion of "respect").

B. Antioppression and Antidiscrimination

1. A New Ethical Debate

Recognition of the importance of social divisions, and the ethics of difference, has generated a new ethos within the realm of social services. Where previously ethical questions were concerned with the general issues of the means–ends relationship in service provision, the contemporary situation, by highlighting social difference, has become focused on the connections between individual practice and the structural understanding of society. Talk of values now necessarily deals with the links between different groups. For example, in respect of racism judgments about the appropriateness of both *types* of services and the *technical delivery* of services are based on values as much as on knowledge or skills. That is, the social and political values which support the analysis of racism as a key ethical issue provide the foundation for professional and community decision making. Thus, whether a separate service is provided for an ethnic minority group, or work is undertaken to change mainstream services to make them appropriate and accessible for members of ethnic minorities, is a decision which is guided by ethical reasoning as much, if not more, than by technical concerns.

Social services are thus faced with a dilemma that they may become fragmented if they attempt to address the challenges raised by a recognition of social difference. The argument in favor of separate services is that this reflects the reality of society, and that to fail to respond is unethical because it leads to the imposition of the world view of one group over others. Even though this may be an unconscious effect of social power, it is

the exercise of power nevertheless. The argument against separate services is that they exacerbate the structural social divisions which are constructed around difference. Both approaches face the same problem that any minority may find itself marginalized, and neither solution guarantees that this will not happen; both require further conscious effort by policy makers, practitioners, and communities who use the services to ensure that marginalization does not occur.

The underlying question within this and related debates around other social divisions (gender, disability, sexuality, age) is that of *who* makes the judgments about *what* services are to be provided and *how* they are to be provided. The social power exercised by social services professionals brings with it ethical responsibility to make clear the answers to these questions. It has been argued (R. Hugman, 1991. *Power in Caring Professions.* Macmillan, Basingstoke) that the only way in which social welfare professions can grasp this responsibility is by working to form a dialogue with service users in which the "voice" of both may be heard. Determining the appropriateness of ends and means in social services must involve both service users and service providers if the power relations which sustain discrimination and oppression are to be altered. For this reason, the new ethical debates around social difference of necessity involve a concern also with the concrete social structures of services. The "ethical" is indissolubly linked with the "political."

An objection to this view has been made by D. Webb (1991. Puritans and paradigms. *Social Work & Social Sciences Review*, 2(2), 146–59). The focus on social divisions and related questions, it is argued, leads to a position where only one course of action is seen as "correct." This, for Webb, creates a moral straightjacket, because it denies individual people the capacity and the right to exercise moral discretion. This is refuted by L. Dominelli (1991. 'What's in a name?' A comment on 'Puritans and paradigms'. *Social Work & Social Sciences Review*, 2(3), 231–235), who argues that the abstract liberal individualism which underpins Webb's position may suggest ethical liberty (in a deontological framework the only basis for ethics), but because it fails to recognize the unequal distribution of social power it ignores the structured capacity of certain groups to generalize from their own partial vantage point and mistakenly believe that their values are universal. For an ethical community to develop (that is, with certain core values capable of being shared by a profession), the issue of social divisions must, for Dominelli, be central for that group to be adequately located in the wider society.

2. Ethical Code or Ethical Competence?

A structural analysis of the relationship between social services users and providers as the basis for ethics may still be comprehended through a comparative approach to deontological (categorical) and relativist (utilitarian) perspectives. However, each of the positions discussed in the preceding section are moving toward a compromise between the two. Webb's liberalism draws heavily on a Kantian view of moral autonomy as a prerequisite for ethics and on responsibility as a consequence of autonomy. This position would lead to a situation in which the ethical base of social services shifts according to the identity of the practitioner. Dominelli, on the other hand, while drawing on the structural analysis associated with utilitarianism (in which different groups might legitimately be treated differently), leads to a position in which an ethical requirement to respond to social divisions may be codified into professional ethics, such that a common code is shared by the social services community.

There are some senses in which the debate between these positions can be overstated. The former position would not allow for consciously discriminatory or oppressive practice as ethical (which would, for example, fail the test of Kant's maxim of generalizability). In contrast, the latter position cannot dispense with the autonomy, and hence responsibility, that rests with each practitioner to act in ways which are ethically acceptable to the professional community. What is a matter of dispute between the two positions is *what* counts as discriminatory or oppressive and *who* should determine this. The liberalist claims that all members of a society should be the same in this regard; the utilitarian argues that such a view, however unintentionally, privileges the socially advantaged, so the disadvantaged should be consciously privileged in order to rectify this deficit.

A compromise between these two positions is that, although there is marked divergence between them, neither abrogates the individual person (policy maker, practitioner, or service user) from ethical responsibility, nor does either fully remove the practitioner from the professional community in this respect. Professional codes are both possible and necessary, but not as means of restricting the autonomy or responsibility of the individual. Rather, it is necessary for the morally autonomous practitioner to be located within the structures of a professional community. Such a community provides the setting in which ethical debates are enabled to take place. Similarly, professions along with service users and policy makers are located in the wider society, in which such debates are also framed. Indeed, the

extent to which a society is democratic or totalitarian will set the context for the shape of social services, including the ethical dimension. The same techniques (such as counseling or community organization) may be perceived as liberating or repressive according to their context and purpose, as well as how they are implemented. In this way, a stance taken by social services professions in different national contexts may in one place be contributory to the social order while in another may be seen as oppositional to the social order.

A professional code, therefore, to be a means of promoting the ethical basis of social service, must be seen as a framework for judgment by morally active persons and not as a simplistic set of rules. At the same time, such a code must address the nature of society. Indeed, it could be said that this is an ethical requirement.

V. CONCLUSION

Ethical thought and practice lie at the core of social services. In the application of ethical reasoning to this field various contradictions must be faced.

First, these concern the purposes and scope of social welfare. Is it to care or to control? Can it be both? Is social welfare the responsibility of the individual or of the society? Can it be both? The answers to these questions are inherently value laden and so any response will have an ethical core around which political and technical issues are resolved.

Second, as formal social services are a development of the modern era, the predominant debates about ethics have been couched in terms of the dichotomy between liberal absolutism and utilitarian relativism. All positions on ethics in social services, from a modernist perspective, may be understood in relation to the competing claims of these two moral philosophies. It has been argued here that the limits of modernism have begun to require a reappraisal of this bifurcation and a consideration of a new way forward.

Third, the question of ethics can be constructed as that of an appropriate code for practitioners against which they and others might judge their practice, or as the need for each person to be an autonomous moral agent capable of exercising independent judgment. It has been argued here that while the latter is essential for the development of services which do not discriminate or oppress, the scope for moral autonomy is not limitless. The moral practitioner is active in the context of a society and a profession. Codes of ethics therefore serve to provide the explicit framework within which the person may be located and set the terms of thinking, even where thought leads to critical debate.

The consequence is that for *social* services to continue to develop what is required is neither a rigid constraint codified in a set of rules, nor limitless autonomy. Rather, what is necessary is an ethical discourse around social services in which all members of a society may participate. As has been noted in this discussion, the capacity for all to participate must also be addressed consciously. Such a conclusion carries certain social, political, economic, and professional implications. It is not possible to reach a conclusion which accords equal status to all combinations of social life. The form of social services and the ends they accomplish within a society will, ultimately, reflect the values of that society, and it is for this reason that ethics remain the core of social services.

Also See the Following Articles

CODES OF ETHICS • SOCIAL ETHICS, OVERVIEW

Bibliography

Banks, S. (1995). "Ethics and Values in Social Work." Macmillan, Basingstoke, UK.

Barry, N. (1990). "Welfare." Open Univ. Press, Buckingham.

Bauman, Z. (1994). "Alone Again: Ethics after Certainty." Demos, London.

Hugman, R., and Smith, D. (Eds.) (1995). "Ethical Issues in Social Work." Routledge, London.

Kleinig, J., and Zhang, Y. (Eds.) (1993). "Professional Law Enforcement Codes." Greenwood, Westport, CT.

Wearing, M., and Berreen, R. (Eds.) (1994). "Welfare and Social Policy in Australia: The Distribution of Advantage." Harcourt Brace, Sydney.

ETHICS EDUCATION IN SCHOOLS

C. David Lisman
Community College of Aurora

GLOSSARY

character education The view that the grounds for ethical decisions are founded in the virtuous qualities of the individual making the decision. Consequently, the most important task for ethics education is that of attempting to help promote the development of virtuous individuals.

cognitive moral theory The view of moral education advocated by Lawrence Kohlberg that emphasizes the role of moral dilemmas in promoting moral growth through stimulating young people to confront dilemmas and develop their capacity of moral reasoning, and to pass through lower levels of moral thinking represented by basing one's decision on pleasing authorities or one's social group, and to develop higher levels of moral theory epitomized by Utilitarian and Kantian thinking.

ethical dilemmas Case studies embodying conflicting values that we independently accept in which we need to decide which has priority. An example would be a dilemma of euthanasia in which we must wrestle with whether the value of preventing suffering overrides the value of life.

ethics-across-the-curriculum An approach to teaching ethics that integrates ethics case-based discussion into specific academic disciplines, such as English, biology, psychology, and sociology, and that emphasizes the ethical relevance of the specific subject.

ethics of care An approach to ethics maintaining that there are gender-specific differences in approaches to ethics decision-making. It is claimed that females generally adopt a caring orientation and males a principles-based approach.

indoctrination A view of teaching ethics that attempts to influence people to adopt ethics beliefs on the basis of unquestioning authority.

multicultural ethics An approach to ethics maintaining that ethical values are relative to specific ethnic groups, such as Hispanics and African Americans.

philosophical liberalism The view that individuals are the primary reality and that ethics is grounded in some form of social contract.

republican theory The view that individuals can only find true fulfillment through society and that the grounds for ethics is the common good.

service-learning An approach to teaching that integrates community service into the curriculum. Typically, a student engages in community service as a way to research an academic topic.

values clarification An approach to moral education of the young that helps students clarify their values through exercises that confront students with ethical issues. The teacher is generally expected to avoid taking a stand on moral issues and to reassure students that they are entitled to their own opinions.

ETHICS EDUCATION IN SCHOOLS is extremely important at this time in history to counter the widely perceived concern about moral decline. The general purpose of this kind of education is to help students grow in the ability to be moral beings and to make effective moral decisions, especially in light of increased technological development; and to reinforce the democratic process. Ethics education is challenged by conflicts of diversity and unity involving conflicts of liberals and conservatives over how best to morally educate the young and conflicts over the importance of providing ethics education that respects gender and ethnic diversity.

I. BACKGROUND

Beginning in the eighties, we witnessed a resurgence of interest in ethics education and debates about its appropriateness and the method of how ethics should be taught in the schools. This growing interest in ethics education was a response to a number of factors. One was a sense of moral decline in our society, epitomized by the savings and loan and bond market scandals and the Iran-Contra controversy. It was widely feared that our business and government leaders were promoting and practicing an ethos of greed and selfishness, and that something must be done to impede this phenomenon. Hence, many thoughtful individuals, organizations, and foundations began to call for a greater effort to help people recognize the importance of doing the right thing.

Another converging factor contributing to an interest in ethics education was the increase of an array of ethical dilemmas resulting from technological development and increased concern about the environment. Technological development provoked a great deal of controversy in biomedical ethics. Reproductive rights were increasingly controversial as it became possible to provide *in vitro* fertilization and surrogacy. Other controversial areas include genetic research and animal organ transplants to humans. These kinds of technological development have created a sense of urgency regarding the need to provide useful frameworks for ethics analysis and to provide people with the necessary critical tools for developing sound policies regarding

the ethical use of technologies and for being able to make wise personal decisions.

II. ETHICS CONTROVERSIES

Subsequent to this clarion call from many quarters for a renewed effort in providing ethics education, we have seen a certain degree of polarization regarding how ethics should be taught. This controversy has been, of course, much more prominent in the public schools; although there has been a similar set of issues that has affected higher education as well. The underlying motif regarding ethics education for both public schools and higher education resides in a fundamental conflict in our society over finding unity in diversity. Conservatives tilt toward emphasizing the importance of unity. Liberals toward diversity. According to Elshtain (1995), achieving a happy balance between unity and diversity is not easy.

Turning first to public education, in the early eighties a popular theory emerged that attempted to mediate between concern with the right of each person to their own moral opinion and the need to help stimulate moral growth. This was values clarification. This theory advocated that the teacher should refrain from expressing his or her opinion on ethical issues and should create a classroom atmosphere where students were comfortable with expressing their own moral beliefs. The role of the instructor through the use of examples and exercises was to have students "clarify" their values regarding a wide range of issues.

Values clarification was unpopular among both social liberals and conservatives. Liberals attacked the theory for its unwillingness to emphasize that ethics needs to be grounded in moral theory and that students need to come to see that some positions are not as reasonable as others. Conservatives criticized values clarification for promoting ethical relativism by a pedagogy of unwavering moral neutrality.

Following this controversy ethics education moved along several separate tracks in the public schools. Some opposed having any form of values education in the schools, advocating that this was a parental prerogative. Others advocated some form of character education, where the role of the teacher was to be explicit about what was right and what was wrong. Character educators emphasized not only the role of the adult in declaring right from wrong, but in modeling moral values for the young to emulate. The use of stories that had moral themes or lessons was encouraged.

On the other hand, those being influenced by the

work of Lawrence Kohlberg emphasized the importance of helping students move from more infantile and juvenile forms of moral reasoning to a more universalistic ethics and were critical of value clarification and character theories. For Kohlberg, individuals move through a sequence of stages of moral development. Less mature forms of moral reasoning were epitomized by approaches to ethics in which decisions were based on moral authorities or peer influence. Kohlbergian thinking recommended using moral dilemmas embodying conflicts over values that we independently accept but that are in conflict to stimulate moral discussion that hopefully would get students to become more critical and sophisticated in their moral thinking. Kohlberg has been criticized for attributing to a natural process of cognitive development what is in effect a somewhat arbitrary theoretical construction.

Despite these differences about how to best promote moral development among the young in the schools, fairly widespread agreement exists over the fact that any effective approach to promoting moral growth among the young must be done in an age-appropriate way. Young children are not conceptually able to engage in abstract critical thinking about ethical issues. Some of the best practices for instilling moral values in the young include creating a loving home environment that is conducive to the development of trust among children. Also, at times young children simply need to be told that something is right or wrong reinforced by parents and adults who practice what they preach.

Greater controversy has existed over ethics education for older children. And here is where we see what I have called the conflict over unity and diversity appearing. We have seen a schism between social conservatives and liberals over this method. Social conservatives, especially religious fundamentalists, have been suspicious of public schools attempting to provide any form of moral education at all. For extreme conservatives two concerns seem to be paramount. One is the desire to leave all moral education to the prerogative of parents. One school district in Colorado Springs reportedly forbids teachers from mentioning words such as "values." This, of course, is an extreme example but illustrates where this kind of close-mindedness can lead.

The other conservative motive is that of indoctrination, that is to attempt to get students to accept ethical beliefs on the basis of unquestioning authority. Many conservatives are reluctant to educate young people to be independent thinkers. Or at the very least, they wish to delay when independent thinking is permitted. People of this ilk emphasize an authoritarian approach to ethics and emphasize children reading stories that have moral lessons and uphold the Bible as a source of moral edification.

In contrast, social liberals subscribe to the belief that it is imperative that young people develop independence of mind and spirit and that they be equipped with the critical tools necessary to make sound, independent moral decisions. For liberals the value of authority and independence of thought is honored; whereas for conservatives, independence is subservient to the promulgation of authority.

This controversy over how ethics should be taught mirrors a deep split in our society over how to approach the analysis of moral and social issues. Social conservatives tend to locate the moral failings in society in the failures of individual character; whereas liberals locate moral failure as much as anything in the systemic problems of our society. For example, conservatives tend to blame the poor for poverty whereas liberals tend to see poverty as a product of an unjust political economy.

It is important to keep this ongoing societal conflict about ethics education in mind as we think about the need for and the value of ethics education in higher education. Teachers and professors of ethics must not be lulled into the complacent assumption that they always will be allotted a high degree of social tolerance for the standard critical and analytic examinations of the ethical issues of the day. Social conservatives argue that this approach, rather than contributing to the development of a people able to more effectively make informed ethical decisions and better understand the issues of the day, in fact promotes "relativism." This is believed to be the case because it is feared that acknowledging that there often are not unequivocal answers to weighty ethical questions may cause people to arrive at the belief that we simply make up ethics as we go.

Turning to higher education, the unity/diversity polarity is reflected in feminist ethics and multiculturalism. The ethics of care movement, especially in the words of Gilligan (1982) and Noddings (1984), has proclaimed that there are fundamental gender differences in the way men and women think about ethics and make ethical decisions. Some ethics of care advocates have argued that women primarily adopt a "caring" approach to ethics, emphasizing emotions over mind, forswearing attention to moral principles. Men are said to be purveyors of a principled approach to ethics decisions. Some feminists would not go so far as to advocate a strict gender difference in ethics decision-making. But at the same time, they caution that standard ethical discussions exhibit decided male preference for principled-based decision-making.

Similarly, we have seen the emergence of a multicultural approach to ethics. Cortese (1990) has argued that there are unalterable ethnic differences in moral thinking, similar to that attributed to the difference between men and women. It has been argued, for example, that we must be suspicious of principles of justice, because they are a product of Western Anglo culture. One must be cautious of this kind of debunking of the concept of justice, because this concept is evoked in the critique of the dominant culture. Getting rid of the concept of justice would be to get rid of an absolutely essential conceptual arsenal in the desire to seek social vindication for an oppressed ethnic group.

A final unity/diversity conflict in social thought that has important implications for ethics analysis is the current debate between philosophical liberalism and republican theory. Philosophical liberals are epitomized by the thinking of Rawls (1971), an economic liberal, and Nozick (1977), an economic conservative. Philosophical liberals tend to adopt the theory of atomistic individualism, the view that individuals are sufficient unto themselves and are the fundamental producers of value. Advocates of this view, such as Rawls, maintain a social contract theory of ethics or an enlightened self-interest view. We allegedly are moral because we regard it as ultimately in our self-interest to be moral.

In contrast, republican theory, promoted by thinkers such as Sandel (1996) and Taylor (1994), maintains that human beings are fundamentally social and that we can only find individual fulfillment in society. Philosophical liberalism is regarded as contributing to the breakdown of social values by reinforcing egoism and by providing a rationale for the market economy that tends to undermine community.

A postmodernist version of republican theory exists. Barber (1984) argues that we should dispense with the desire to provide a foundation for ethics. According to Barber, the very effort of seeking a foundation results in the production of an ethos of individualism at the expense of our fundamental commitment to working for the good of society. Barber advocates that we adopt a social pragmatic approach to ethical decision-making in which we should be committed to supporting those decisions that work for the good of society. This approach is, of course, very similar to utilitarianism with the exception that Barber grounds ethics in social survival needs whereas utilitarianism grounds ethics in the affective dimension of human nature.

III. VALUE OF ETHICS EDUCATION IN SCHOOLS

It is in the context of great social division over the nature of ethics education, its grounding, and how we should best teach this subject, that we meet our challenge in attempting to provide effective ways to teach ethics and discuss the ethical issues of the day. It is interesting that unlike the sciences, the foundations of ethics itself is as controversial as the applied issues that we deal with. Any college instructor of ethics can attest to the finesse required to mediate between these zones of contestation.

Because of this great disparity of outlooks alongside the urgent moral and social issues of the day, it is more imperative than ever that we work to ensure that ethics is at the heart of education. Teachers and professors of ethics will agree that one of the great values of ethics education in higher education is that we have a forum for promoting thoughtful consideration of ethical issues. In our information age, it seems that our capacity to thoughtfully deal with ethical issues is inversely correlated with the increase in the flow of information. The more information at our disposal, the more difficult it is to make informed decisions. Students at times may be overwhelmed by the barrage of information. Just as significant to promoting thoughtful consideration of ethics is the kind of information and the manner in which this information is conveyed. Much information is simply "newsworthy facts" chosen to be presented with regard to what captures the public's interest. It is not so much the moral relevance of the information that is considered but simply its newsworthiness. Many have commented on the way in which television and now computers have affected the capacity of people to process information. Students are malnourished by a media diet of passive entertainment, causing them to be passive learners, wanting to be entertained.

Being overwhelmed by a sea of information and perhaps not being adequately equipped for critically digesting the necessary facts in the service of moral decision making can lead to a certain indifference and cynicism about ethics. One also is tempted to rationalize a sense of being overwhelmed by this complexity by saying that it makes no difference how hard we work at making thoughtful decisions because of the high degree of unethical conduct that abounds around us. This tendency to escape the burden of moral inquiry feeds into the fact that we have some reason to believe that our society is experiencing a degree of moral erosion, reinforced by corporate capitalist policies that encourage bottom-line approaches at the expense of community and the environment. Additionally, few would doubt that we, as human beings, have a tendency to egoism, to put individual self-interests ahead of others.

Although developing the ability to think more clearly and critically about ethical issues and to make more effective ethical decisions does not necessarily mean that we will improve moral character, engaging in this form of deliberation can accomplish this purpose indirectly. It can do so in at least two ways. In the first place, as we become better equipped with the tools of ethical analysis, we can more comfortably and effectively attack the issues of the day. Instead of being overwhelmed by information, we can begin to sort out the relevant from the irrelevant. Also, as we gain greater clarity over how to apply moral concepts to the issues of the day, we increase our sense that we can exercise some thoughtful influence on social policy and make more informed personal ethical decisions.

Second, many of us who teach ethics have found that providing students with the opportunity to think more clearly about ethical issues in a controlled public form, such as the classroom, indirectly tends to remind students of their fundamental moral responsibilities. In this sense there is a grain of truth in the Socratic view that ignorance is the cause of vice.

One of the important values of ethics education is its contribution to democratic understanding. Advocates of philosophical liberalism and republican theory are emphasizing important aspects of the moral life, the philosophical liberal, the importance of rights, republican theory, the importance of the social good. But regardless of where one falls out on this debate, there is little doubt that being ethical and having the capacity to make informed ethical decisions is at the heart of an effective democracy.

A vital democracy requires that we have a healthy respect for the rights of individuals and that we are committed to working for the good of society. Helping students to arrive at an increased understanding and appreciation of the importance of individual rights in relation to issues, such as abortion, euthanasia, and welfare reform can inhibit tendencies to advocate moral and social policy that minimizes the importance of the individual in favor of the social majority. Similarly, a healthy discussion of the social consequences of some corporate decisions on the environment can help us recognize the need to achieve a balance between our desire to maximize individual rights and aggregate social well-being. Moreover, the very justification of democracy is grounded in ethical theory. Developing a deeper understanding of the relationship of ethics to democratic theory can only have the indirect consequence of reinforcing our commitment to the democratic process.

IV. CURRENT SITUATION OF ETHICS IN THE SCHOOLS

This encyclopedia draws upon writers who represent a variety of ways that ethics is taught in our schools, and it will serve as an excellent resource regardless of one's approach to teaching ethics. There seem to be three approaches that are current. One is the familiar stand-alone ethics courses offered in philosophy departments. This approach has a long history of success in contributing to enlightened ethical understanding and it represents a tried-and-true approach to teaching ethics.

Increasingly, we are seeing ethics courses being offered in specific disciplines, such as nursing and business ethics. Sometimes philosophers teach these discipline-specific courses. One of the challenges that we face for these sorts of courses is to be sure that these are not watered-down courses. If so, students can come out worse for the experience. As indicated above, one of the challenges we confront in ethics education is to equip students with the necessary analytic and critical skills to cope with the profusion of ethically relevant information—here discipline-specific information. If a discipline-specific course merely raises ethical issues but fails to provide students with a critically grounded approach for thinking through these issues, the result may be that students are more cynical than ever about the importance of careful ethical thinking.

Another approach that is gaining currency is the curricular integration of ethics, which is the subject of my book (Lisman, 1996). Many faculty are beginning to see the relevance of including attention to the ethical dimensions of their disciplines as a part of teaching their subject. Why should one do this, it may be asked. I would respond that as educators we have a fundamental social responsibility to help our students understand the social and ethical relevance of their discipline. An effective way this can be done is through presenting discipline appropriate case studies embodying ethical dilemmas containing conflicts between values that we accept independently or case studies that challenge the student to applying a broadly accepted ethical principle to a specific issue relevant to the course material.

While advocating this as a valuable way to teach ethics, if discipline-specific courses run the risk of treating ethics in a shallow way, this approach may do that even more so. I would recommend that if an institution of higher education were considering developing an ethics-across-the-curriculum approach, students should be encouraged to take a basic ethics course in a philosophy department as well. Also, it is important that faculty have some exposure to ethics theory and approaches to teaching ethics. They do not need to be experts in ethical theory, but it is helpful for them as they conduct discipline-specific ethics discussions in their courses.

Having noted the difficulties, the curricular integration of ethics is valuable. It is so because of the fact that our stock and trade of scholarly subjects has an ethical dimension. This is the case whether the subject is business, science, mathematics, or literature. Some sacrifice in ethical depth may be justified if such an approach helps students understand that moral concerns cut across all aspects of our intellectual, professional, personal, and public life.

All of these forms of ethics education should be in our schools. We need traditional philosophy courses for the depth and clarity that is achieved through sustained analysis and reflection. But also people preparing for professional life need to have some in-depth understanding of the ethical dimension of their profession. Finally, the curricular integration of ethics can help students see the ways in which ethics is cross-disciplinary and forms an integrated dimension to life's choices.

V. THE NATURE OF ETHICS EDUCATION

There appears to be fairly common agreement among college and university ethics educators and ethicists regarding how to effectively teach ethics, bearing in mind sharp difference in opinion over the appropriate theoretical approach, whether it be the ethics of caring, character education, multicultural ethics, or a more traditional one of utilitarianism or Kantian ethics. Here are what I see as some of these commonalities.

First, it is generally agreed that teaching ethics is not indoctrination. Indoctrination is prompting people to hold fundamental beliefs in an unquestioning way. But good ethics education is the very opposite. Students are encouraged to examine their most fundamental moral concepts with a view toward attaining a more informed understanding of those concepts or even replacing unquestioned concepts that do not survive critical scrutiny with those that do. Of course,

this is a continual concern for the educator. Students often resist questioning their most basic assumptions. Getting students to confront these unquestioned assumptions or concepts requires some patience and finesse on the part of the instructor. Instructors need to sense when they are pushing a student too hard. If pushed too hard, a student may simply shut down and quit thinking, resenting the effort of the instructor.

As a strategy for dealing with this possible form of student resistance, it may be desirable to treat an initial concept or topic in an ethics course more lightly than one does later topics. In the first place, this enables students to become acquainted with the nature of ethical enquiry in a nonthreatening way. If students are pushed too much in the beginning, they may emotionally opt out of the remainder of the course. Second, the first issue discussed always raises the gamut of theoretical and practical concerns about ethics, such as the justification of fundamental moral norms, relativism, the relationship of religion to ethics, and general ethical skepticism and cynicism. Students need to be reassured that we need not tackle all of these issues at once.

A fundamental principle of effective ethics teaching is liberal neutrality. This is the belief that we should respect the right of each student to make up his or her mind about ethical issues. At times it may be important for the instructor to model what it means to take a thoughtful and committed approach to ethics decision-making by revealing his or her opinion on an issue. However, I recommend keeping this at a minimum. Getting on one's own ethical soap box mainly serves to marginalize those students who do not agree with the instructor. It is far more effective for the instructor to play a mediating and facilitative role in being sure that all relevant sides of ethical issues are presented and discussed.

This perspective could be challenged by a classroom situation in which a student expresses racist beliefs. Of course, this rarely happens. Students usually are smart enough to keep "fighting words" to themselves. Also, as public institutions, we are legally obliged, if not morally as well, to avoid treating members of ethnic groups in a denigrating way. But still one might ask, how should an instructor deal with a student who advocates a racist position?

If I were the instructor in this situation, I would be sure to make my own stance against racism known. I would do this first and foremost to reassure any underrepresented students I might have in my class. I would do it secondly in order to model taking a stand on an issue of consequence. Having done that, I would not simply tell the racist student that he/she is wrong. I would attempt to get the student to explain why he/she espouses such a position. I, of course, would encourage opponents of this position to develop their own position and to challenge the racist position. It is unlikely that the racist student will change his/her mind. But by attempting to get the student to clarify why he/she adopts such a position, the student is challenged to come to terms with the most fundamental beliefs that undergird this viewpoint. At the very least the student will confront the fact that ethics education involves taking a thoughtful and discerning approach to ones' beliefs.

In the vein of respect for liberal neutrality, it is important that the divergence of foundational ethical theories are presented. While an instructor may be an advocate of the ethics of care, it is important that consequentialist, deontological, and virtue theories are discussed. Perhaps the most difficult theories to discuss are theocratic ones, such as the Divine Command theory. Many students ground their ethics in religious faith and find criticisms of theocratic ethics in favor of a more secular approach very threatening.

No perfect solution to this problem exists. While providing some fairly trenchant criticisms of this kind of faith-based approach to ethics, I usually tell students that I appreciate the fact that criticism of this theory falls outside their comfort zone, and that I am only challenging them to stretch a bit and think about some of the difficulties that may be associated with their approach, not necessarily to give it up. I usually end by saying that for the purposes of the course, I am operating from the premise of a secular approach to ethics and hoping to get students to appreciate the possibility that ethics can be founded on non-faith grounds.

I might conclude by mentioning one fairly recent effective pedagogical tool for teaching ethics, and that is service-learning. Service-learning is the incorporation of community service as a tool of educational inquiry. As applied to an ethics course, students are encouraged to put in 10–15 hours of service during an academic semester at an agency, such as a homeless shelter, hospital, senior center, or engage in environmental activities such as trail building or improving a nature sanctuary. As they provide community service, they are expected to investigate an ethics issue, such as poverty, reproductive rights, attitudes about euthanasia, or a variety of issues of environmental ethics, and incorporate their findings into the class through presentations, class discussion, and papers.

Service-learning can be a very effective approach to the study of ethical issues. It helps make ethical issues come alive for the student as they confront issues through community service. Moreover, it provides a way to indirectly overcome resistance to studying ethics, resulting from students being a product of the above-referenced rampant individualism and isolation from community-embedded ethical issues. For example, through working at a homeless shelter, students confront the everyday realities of hunger and homelessness. Many revise their initial beliefs that poor people are the cause of their poverty, as they are startled to discover that hard-working people have fallen into poverty through tragic circumstances.

And perhaps most important, engaging in community service helps students rediscover the value of their connection with other people. They realize that essential to being a well-rounded individual capable of attaining a measure of human happiness is developing those "habits of the heart" in which we care about the well-being of others and having a healthy community. Some research has found that ethics students who do service-learning exhibit a greater degree of ethical development than those who merely study ethics in the traditional ways.

Regardless of the approach one takes to teaching ethics or one's theoretical approach, it is safe to say that this article is grounded in the belief in the importance of equipping students and others with the skills and conceptual ability necessary to being able to attain a sounder understanding of the social issues that confront our society and world and to be able to make more effective personal decisions.

Also See the Following Article

THEORIES OF JUSTICE: RAWLS

Bibliography

Barber, B. (1984). *Strong democracy: Participatory politics for a new age.* Berkeley: University of California Press.

Cortese, A. (1990). *Ethic ethics: The restructuring of moral theory.* Albany: State University of New York Press.

Elshtain, J. (1995). *Democracy on trial.* New York: Basic Books.

Gilligan, C. (1982). *In a different voice: Psychological theory and women's development.* Cambridge, MA: Harvard University Press.

Lisman, C. D. (1996). *The curricular integration of ethics: Theory and practice.* Westport, CT: Praeger.

Noddings, N. (1984). *Caring: A feminine approach to ethics and moral education.* Berkeley: University of California Press.

Nozick, R. (1977). *Anarchy, state, and utopia.* New York: Basic Books.

Sandel, M. (1996). *Democracy's discontent: America in search of a* *public philosophy.* Cambridge, MA: The Belknap Press of Harvard University Press.

Taylor, C. (1994). *The modern identify in Communitarianism: A new public ethics.* (M. Daly, Ed.). Belmont, CA: Wadsworth Publishing Company.

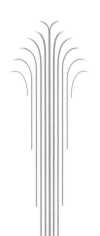

ETHNOCULTURAL MINORITY GROUPS, STATUS AND TREATMENT OF

Will Kymlicka
University of Ottawa

GLOSSARY

ethnocultural group An intergenerational group whose members share one or more of such characteristics as common descent, homeland, history, language, or culture. Although sharing a sense of common identity and belonging, such groups differ dramatically in the degree to which they have separate institutions and are politically mobilized or territorially concentrated.

group rights Technically, those rights that are exercised by, or on behalf of, a group. Used in this way, the term is a synonym for "collective rights," and would include the rights of unions, corporations, governments, or even participants in class-action suits. In many contexts, however, the term is used to refer to rights that are group-specific, i.e., that are accorded to the members of certain groups rather than to all persons regardless of group membership. For example, if Sikhs are exempted from motorcycle helmet laws, this is often called a "group right," even though it is exercised by and for an individual. In this sense, "group rights" (or, more accurately, group-specific rights) are contrasted with universal human rights or common citizenship rights.

immigrant groups Ethnocultural groups which were formed by the migration of individuals or families from one country to another. Their decision to migrate may be more or less voluntary, but if entirely involuntary, or done to avoid persecution, then they are termed refugees. The status of immigrant groups has largely depended on whether they were admitted as part of a deliberate immigration policy, with the right to gain equal citizenship, or whether their entry was illegal, in which case they may be denied legal equality and social acceptance.

indigenous peoples Culturally distinctive groups that are descended from the inhabitants of a territory prior to its invasion by colonizing settlers. They are part of larger settler societies and they generally have profound connections to their land and a continuity of identity with their ancestral past. Often the terms "aboriginal" or "native" are used synonymously with "indigenous."

multiculturalism The view that institutions in pluralistic societies should respect cultural differences. In some countries, this refers primarily to the accommodation of ethnocultural groups, but in other countries it extends beyond this to include religious and lifestyle groups, as well as groups defined by gender, sexual orientation, disability, or even political belief.

national minorities Groups that formed complete and functioning societies in their historic homeland prior to being incorporated into a larger state. The incorporation of such national minorities has typically been involuntary, due to colonization, conquest, or the ceding of territory from one imperial power to another. National minorities therefore include indigenous peoples in New World settler societies, but also include minority cultures in Old World countries.

pluralism The coexistence under common political institutions of groups divided by ethnicity, language, religion, or other cultural criteria that may generate conflicting political demands.

racial groups A set of non-scientific classifications used to identify humans, traditionally based on geographic origin and on visible body features; e.g., hair and facial characteristics. The use of race to categorize people has almost always been done by a dominant group in order to justify a system of dominance and hierarchy. For the members of subordinate races, therefore, race is almost always an imposed identity that does not correspond to their own ethnocultural identity, although a long history of racial oppression can lead to the creation of a common identity among the oppressed.

ETHNOCULTURAL MINORITY GROUPS' demands for greater rights and recognition have surged in the past few decades. This is one component of a wider intellectual and political trend, sometimes referred to as the "politics of difference" or "multiculturalism," which emphasizes the need for sensitivity to pluralism and diversity. However, these general terms can obscure important differences between various kinds of ethnocultural minority groups. Immigrant groups, indigenous peoples, racial groups, and national minorities all differ in their needs and aspirations, and so typically demand different kinds of minority rights (e.g., recognition rights, legal exemptions, affirmative action, representation rights, and self-government rights). All of these demands can be seen as challenging the myth of culturally homogeneous "nation-states," but each raises distinctive ethical issues, and so must be examined on its own terms. While some demands appeal to widely held values of justice and tolerance, other demands appear to threaten basic values of individual liberty, democracy, and solidarity.

I. HISTORICAL BACKGROUND

While most organized political communities throughout recorded history have been multiethnic, Western political theorists have typically operated with an idealized model of the polis in which fellow citizens share a common descent, language, and culture. The culturally homogenous city-states of Ancient Greece have been seen as the paradigmatic model of a political community.

To achieve this ideal of a homogenous polity, governments throughout history have pursued a variety of policies regarding ethnocultural minorities. Some minorities were physically eliminated, either by mass expulsion or by genocide. Other minorities were coercively assimilated, forced to adopt the language, religion, and customs of the majority. In yet other cases, minorities were treated as resident aliens, subjected to physical segregation and economic discrimination, and denied political rights. Such measures were often justified on the grounds that ethnocultural minorities threatened national security or international peace and through ethnocentric denigration of the value of other peoples and cultures.

There were isolated attempts at protecting ethnocultural minorities in the past, but only in this century has the status and treatment of such minorities become a matter of international concern. Under the League of Nations, for example, a number of treaties were signed to protect the rights and collective autonomy of minorities in various European countries. After World War II, many people hoped that "human rights" would resolve minority conflicts. Rather than protecting vulnerable groups directly, through special treaty rights for the members of designated groups, cultural minorities would be protected indirectly, by guaranteeing basic civil and political rights to all individuals regardless of group membership. Where basic individual rights such as freedom of speech, association, and conscience are firmly protected, it was assumed, no further rights needed to be attributed to the members of specific ethnic or national minorities.

Indeed the importance of individual civil and political rights in protecting minorities cannot be underestimated. Freedom of association, religion, speech, mobility, and political organization enable individuals to form and maintain groups and associations, to adapt these groups to changing circumstances, and to promote their views and interests to the wider population. However, it is increasingly recognized that many ethnocultural groups are not satisfied with the common rights of citizenship, and seek greater accommodation of their ethnocultural practices and increased recognition for their ethnocultural identities. This is occurring throughout the world, from the "ethnic revival" in the United States in the 1960s to the rise of minority nationalisms in the former Soviet Union in the 1990s. An increasing number of "group rights" are being demanded, and many of these demands are being accepted.

Yet this trend raises a number of important ethical issues, both theoretical and practical. How are these group rights related to individual rights? What should we do if group rights come into conflict with individual rights? Can a liberal democracy allow minority groups to restrict the individual rights of their members, or should it insist that all groups uphold liberal principles? Can a democracy maintain its stability and solidarity if it allows minorities to maintain and promote their distinctive identities?

After a period of relative neglect, moral and political philosophers are increasingly focusing attention on the ethical aspects of these demands. These are genuinely difficult issues. Ethnocultural relations are often full of complications which defy simple categories or easy answers. To begin with, however, we need to distinguish different kinds of groups, and different kinds of "group rights."

II. FORMS OF ETHNOCULTURAL DIVERSITY

Virtually all countries contain some degree of ethnocultural diversity. They can all be described, therefore, as "multicultural." But the patterns of ethnocultural diversity vary dramatically between countries, and these variations are important in understanding the claims of minority cultures. A complete typology of the different forms of ethnocultural diversity would be an immensely complicated task, but for the purposes of this entry we can start with a very basic distinction between two forms of ethnocultural pluralism—national minorities and immigrant groups—and then examine some more complicated cases.

A. National Minorities

In everyday parlance, we often describe independent countries as "nation-states." But many countries are in fact multinational; they contain more than one nation. By "nation" I mean a historical community more or less institutionally complete, occupying a given territory or

homeland, and sharing a distinct language and culture. A "nation" in this sociological sense is closely related to the idea of a "people" or a "society"—indeed, these concepts are often defined in terms of each other.

If a nation's homeland becomes incorporated into a larger state, then it becomes what are often called "national minorities." The incorporation of national minorities into a larger state has typically been an involuntary process. Some national minorities have been invaded and conquered by another nation; others have been ceded from one imperial power to another; and yet others have had their homeland overrun by colonizing settlers. But some multination state have arisen voluntarily when different cultures agree to form a federation for their mutual benefit.

These national minorities can be found in both "Old World" and "New World" democracies. In North America, for example, they include the American Indians, Puerto Ricans, and Chicanos in the United States, and the Aboriginal peoples and the Québécois in Canada. Some Old World countries are multinational, either because they have forcibly incorporated indigenous populations (e.g., Finland) or because they were formed by the more or less voluntary federation of two or more European cultures (e.g., Belgium and Switzerland). The consequences of incorporation have often been much more catastrophic for indigenous peoples than for other national minorities.

However they were incorporated, national minorities have typically sought to maintain or enhance their political autonomy, either through outright secession or through some form of regional autonomy. And they typically mobilize along nationalist lines, using the language of "nationhood" to describe and justify these demands for self-government. While the ideology of nationalism has typically seen full-fledged independence as the "normal" or "natural" end point, economic or demographic reasons may make this infeasible for some national minorities. Moreover, the historical ideal of a fully sovereign state is increasingly obsolete in today's world of globalized economics and transnational institutions. Hence there is a growing interest in exploring other forms of self-government, such as federalism.

B. Immigrant Groups

A second source of ethnocultural diversity is immigration, that is, the decision of individuals and families to leave their original homeland and emigrate to another society, often leaving their friends and relatives behind. This decision is typically made for economic reasons, although sometimes also for political reasons in order to move to a freer or more democratic country. But it is essential to immediately distinguish two categories of immigrants—those who have the right to become citizens, and those who do not. Much confusion in the academic literature, and the wider public debate, has arisen from conflating these two cases. I will use the term "immigrant group" only for the former case, and will discuss the latter case, which I will call "metics," further on. Immigrants, then, are people who arrive under an immigration policy which gives them the right to become citizens after a relatively short period of time—say, 3–5 years—subject only to minimal conditions (e.g., learning the official language, and knowing something about the country's history and political institutions). This has been the traditional policy governing immigration in the three major "countries of immigration"—namely, the United States, Canada, and Australia.

Until the 1960s, all three of these countries adopted an "Anglo-conformity" model of immigration. That is, immigrants were expected to assimilate to existing cultural norms and, over time, become indistinguishable from native-born citizens in their speech, dress, leisure activities, cuisine, family size, and so on. However, beginning in the 1970s, it was increasingly accepted that this assimilationist model was unrealistic and unjust. All three countries gradually adopted a more tolerant or "multicultural" approach which allows and indeed encourages immigrants to maintain various aspects of their ethnic heritage. Immigrants are free to maintain some of their old customs regarding food, dress, recreation, and religion, and to associate with each other to maintain these practices. This is no longer seen as unpatriotic or "un-American."

Some people worry that this new "multicultural" approach to immigration is encouraging immigrant groups to develop the same attributes and ambitions as national minorities—i.e., to start thinking of themselves as "nations" with the right to govern themselves, and to develop a more or less full set of separate institutions operating in their own language. Others downplay this concern, arguing that multiculturalism is not a rejection of the idea that immigrants should integrate into common institutions which operate in the majority language, but rather a commitment to reform these common institutions so as to better reflect and accommodate the identities of immigrants. I return to this debate about the impact of multiculturalism on the integration of immigrants in Section VI.

In any event, as a result of extensive immigration, combined with the increased toleration of ethnic identities, countries like Australia and the United States have a number of immigrant groups as loosely aggregated subcultures within the larger English-speaking society, and so exhibit what is often called "polyethnicity." So some countries are "multinational" (as a result of colonization, conquest, and confederation), others are "polyethnic" (as a result of immigration), and some, like the United States, are both. Of course, there are many ethnocultural groups which do not follow either the immigrant or the national minority model. I will briefly look at three such groups—isolationist ethnoreligious groups, metics, and African-Americans.

C. Isolationist Ethnoreligious Groups

Whereas most immigrants wish to participate in the larger society, there are some small immigrant groups which voluntarily isolate themselves from the larger society and avoid participating in politics or civil society. This option of voluntary marginalization is only likely to be attractive to religious sects whose theology requires them to avoid all contact with the modern world. This is true, for example, of the Hutterites in Canada, or the Amish in the United States, both of whom came to North America to avoid persecution for their pacifist religious beliefs in Europe. The Hutterites and Amish are unconcerned about their marginalization from the larger society and polity, since they view its "worldly" institutions as corrupt and seek to maintain the same traditional way of life they had in their original homeland. Indeed, they have demanded the right to take their children out of school before the legal age of 16 in order to ensure that they are not exposed to such corrupting influences.

Jeff Spinner calls such groups "partial citizens" because they voluntarily waive both the rights and the responsibilities of democratic citizenship (J. Spinner, 1994. *The Boundaries of Citizenship: Race, Ethnicity and Nationality in the Liberal State.* Johns Hopkins Univ. Press, Baltimore). They waive the right to vote and to hold office (and their right to welfare benefits), but by the same token they also evade their civic responsibility to help tackle the country's problems. Morever, they are often organized internally in illiberal ways. For this reason, many people have thought that the state should intervene in such groups, at least to ensure that children are adequately informed about their opportunities in the outside world. However, in practice, most democratic states do tolerate these groups, so long as they do not harm people inside or outside the group, and so long as members are legally free to leave. This toleration is typically justified either on the grounds of freedom of religion or on the grounds that these groups were given specific promises of toleration when they entered the country—historical promises which were not given to other immigrants.

D. Metics

While isolationist groups like the Amish voluntarily waive their citizenship, there are some migrants who are never given the opportunity to become citizens, either because they entered the country illegally (e.g., North Africans in Italy) or because they entered as students or "guest-workers" but have overstayed their initial visa (e.g., Turks in Germany). When they entered the country, these people were not conceived of as future citizens, or even as long-term residents, and indeed they would not have been allowed to enter in the first place if they were seen as permanent residents and future citizens. However, despite the official rules, they have settled more or less permanently. In principle, and to some extent in practice, many face the threat of deportation if they are detected by the authorities or if they are convicted of a crime. But they nonetheless form sizable communities in certain countries, engage in some form of employment, legal or illegal, and may marry and form a family. Borrowing a term from Ancient Greece, Michael Walzer calls these groups "metics"—that is, long-term residents who are nonetheless excluded from the polis (M. Walzer, 1983. *Spheres of Justice: A Defence of Pluralism and Equality*. Blackwell, Oxford).

Metics raise different challenges from those of immigrant citizens. Metics face enormous obstacles to integration—legal, political, economic, social, and psychological—and so tend to exist in the margins of the larger society. Where such marginalized communities exist, the danger arises of the creation of a permanently disenfranchised, alienated, and racially defined underclass.

E. African-Americans

African-Americans do not fit the voluntary immigrant pattern not only because they were brought to America involuntarily as slaves, but also because they were prevented (rather than encouraged) from integrating into the institutions of the majority culture (e.g., racial segregation and laws against miscegenation and the teaching of literacy). Nor do they fit the national minority pattern, since they do not have a homeland in America or a common historical language. They came from a variety of African cultures, with different languages, and no attempt was made to keep together those with a common ethnic background. On the contrary, people from

the same culture (even from the same family) were typically split up once in America. Moreover, before emancipation, they were legally prohibited from trying to recreate their own cultural structure (e.g., all forms of black association, except churches, were illegal). The situation of African-Americans, therefore, is virtually unique, although the use of "race" to define subordinate groups is certainly more common.

One could also mention other distinctive ethnocultural groups; for example, consider the situation of Roma (gypsies) in Europe, whose homeland is everywhere and nowhere, and the Russian settlers in the Baltics, who saw themselves as members of a Russian majority throughout the Soviet Union, but who now find themselves as a minority within newly independent states. There are many such groups around the world with a distinctive history and set of needs. However, immigrants and national minorities are the most common types of ethnocultural groups found in most liberal democracies. Other groups, by contrast, are typically the result of unique historical processes which only occurred in one or two specific countries.

Moreover, liberal democracies have, over the years, learned a great deal about how to accommodate these two major forms of diversity. Both immigration and minority nationalisms continue to raise many conflicts and challenges for liberal democracies, but there are some well-established norms which help to regulate and manage these conflicts. By contrast, with many of these other groups, there is often much greater uncertainty and disagreement about how the relationship should be conceived.

Indeed, it is interesting to note that even when groups clearly do not fit the immigrant or national minority model, there is nonetheless often great pressure to redefine them so as to fit one of the more familiar patterns. For example, the civil rights movement in the United States was seen by many of its proponents as enabling blacks to follow the immigrant path of integration through a more rigorous enforcement of antidiscrimination laws. Those African-Americans who were skeptical about the possibility of following the immigrant path to integration, however, have pursued the opposite tack of redefining blacks as a "nation" and promoting a form of black nationalism. Much of the recent history of African-American political mobilization can be seen as a struggle between these two competing projects.

Similarly, recent debates over the rights of Russian settlers in the Baltics can be seen as a struggle over whether to redefine them as immigrants (who should have to learn the local language to acquire citizenship) or whether to redefine them as a national minority (who should therefore have extensive language rights and collective autonomy). And many commentators argue that the only long-term solution for metics is to redefine them as immigrants and give them the right to equal citizenship, even though they were not admitted as future citizens.

III. TYPES OF MINORITY RIGHTS

All of these groups are, in different ways, seeking greater rights and recognition. In the case of metics, the primary demand is often simply for citizenship. But with the other groups, the demand is for something more than, or other than, the common rights of citizenship. Groups are seeking distinctive rights, suited to their specific situation as ethnocultural minorities. We can distinguish four types of minority rights which have been adopted to accommodate these ethnocultural differences: (a) self-government rights, (b) recognition rights, (c) special representation rights, and (d) affirmative action. I will say a few words about each.

A. Self-Government Rights

As I noted, national minorities typically view themselves as "peoples" or "nations," and, as such, as having the inherent right of self-determination. They demand certain powers of self-government which they say were not relinquished by their (typically involuntary) federation into the larger state. They want to govern themselves in certain key matters to ensure the full and free development of their cultures and the best interests of their people.

One important mechanism for recognizing claims to self-government by national minorities is federalism. In Canada, for example, the federal division of powers gives Quebec extensive jurisdiction over issues that are crucial to the survival of the French culture, including control over education, language, culture, and immigration. However, for some national minorities, particularly those who are now outnumbered even in their historical homeland, federalism may not provide a feasible mechanism for self-government. In such cases, other ways of devolving power are necessary. For example, self-government for indigenous peoples in many countries has often been tied to systems of "reservations"— i.e., certain lands are legally reserved for the exclusive use and benefit of the indigenous peoples, and the tribal councils which govern each reserve typically seek control over a wide range of issues, from health, education, policing, and criminal justice to resource development.

Other arrangements which have been adopted to accommodate the demand for self-government include confederations, consociations, federacies, protectorates, legislative unions, associated states, and condominiums. Each of these models has its own strengths and weaknesses. But whatever mechanism is adopted, it seems unlikely that the demand for increased self-government will go away. Self-government claims are not seen as a temporary measure. On the contrary, these rights are often described as "inherent," and so permanent.

B. Recognition Rights

Many immigrant groups and religious minorities have demanded various forms of public support and legal recognition of their cultural practices. In some cases, this takes the form of positive assistance—for example, the funding of bilingual education and ethnic studies in public schools, or the public recognition of a minority's religious holidays. In other cases, it takes the form of exemptions from laws that disadvantage them, given their religious practices. For example Jews and Muslims have sought exemption from Sunday closing legislation; Sikhs have sought exemption from motorcycle helmet laws and from the official dress codes of police forces.

Like self-government rights, these rights are not seen as temporary, because the cultural differences they protect are not something we hope to eliminate. But unlike self-government rights, recognition rights usually go hand-in-hand with integration into the larger society. Indeed, recognition rights would not be necessary for ethnocultural groups which govern themselves through their own institutions. Recognition rights are only needed insofar as ethnocultural groups are working within majority institutions, governed by majority laws; the point of recognition rights is precisely to revise these laws and institutions so as to make them more accommodating of ethnocultural identities. As such, they are more likely to be demanded by immigrant groups than national minorities. These measures are intended to help immigrant groups and religious minorities express their cultural particularity and pride without it hampering their success in the economic, educational, and political institutions of the dominant society. Indeed, it could be argued that these rights actually assist in the long-term integration of immigrants, by making them feel more at home in the institutions of the larger society.

The major exception, as I noted earlier, is the demand for exemptions by isolationist ethnoreligious groups, like the Amish. They are not seeking to reform common institutions, but rather seek the right to withdraw entirely from them (e.g., exemption from mandatory schooling legislation, mandatory military service, or mandatory pension schemes).

C. Special Representation Rights

While the traditional concern of national minorities and immigrant groups has been with either self-government or recognition rights, there has been increasing interest by these groups, as well as other nonethnic social groups, in the idea of special representation rights.

Throughout the Western democracies, there is increasing concern that the political process is "unrepresentative" in the sense that it fails to reflect the diversity of the population. Legislatures in most Western countries are dominated by middle-class, able-bodied, white men. A more representative process, it is said, would include members of ethnic and racial minorities, women, the poor, the disabled, etc.

One way to reform the process is to make political parties more inclusive by reducing the barriers which inhibit women, ethnic minorities, or the poor from becoming party candidates or party leaders; another way is to adopt some form of proportional representation, which has historically been associated with greater inclusiveness of candidates. However, there is increasing interest in the idea that a certain number of seats in the legislature should be reserved for the members of disadvantaged or marginalized groups, either explicitly (through a quota scheme), or de facto (through redrawing electoral boundaries to create districts in which the minority forms a local majority).

Group representation rights are often defended as a response to some systemic barrier in the political process which makes it impossible for the group's views and interests to be effectively represented. For example, Iris Young argues that special representation rights should be extended to "oppressed groups" because they are at a disadvantage in the political process, and "the solution lies at least in part in providing institutionalized means for the explicit recognition and representation of oppressed groups" (I. M. Young, 1990. *Justice and the Politics of Difference,* pp. 183–191. Princeton Univ. Press, Princeton).

Insofar as these rights are seen as a response to oppression or systemic disadvantage, they are most plausibly seen as a temporary measure on the way to a society where the need for special representation no longer exists—a form of political "affirmative action." Society should seek to remove the oppression and disadvantage, thereby eliminating the need for these rights.

However, the issue of special representation rights for groups is complicated, because special representation is sometimes defended, not on grounds of oppression, but as a corollary of self-government for national minorities. A minority's right to self-government would be severely weakened if some external body could unilaterally revise or revoke its powers without consulting the minority or securing its consent. Hence it would seem to be a corollary of self-government that the national minority be guaranteed representation on any body which can interpret or modify its powers of self-government (e.g., the Supreme Court). However, this has been a relatively minor part of the recent debate over group representation. Recent work on group representation has focused much more on the claims of African-Americans and women than on the claims of indigenous peoples or other national minorities.

D. Affirmative Action

The issue of representation rights is really just one example of the broader issue of "affirmative action"— i.e., measures taken to increase the representation of particular minorities within educational institutions, public service, or even private sector employment. I will not discuss this at length, since it is examined elsewhere. I will just note that, like representation rights, affirmative action is usually defended on the grounds that it helps overcome a history of unjust barriers to full and equal participation in the larger society. It is, therefore, different from the demand for self-government, which aims to create separate institutions, rather than to promote participation in mainstream institutions.

IV. INDIVIDUAL AND GROUP RIGHTS

These demands for minority rights are often controversial, and many of them are seen (by the majority) as deeply objectionable. To oversimplify, we can divide the objections into two broad categories. One line of criticism is that these minority rights violate basic liberal democratic principles of individual freedom and equality. A second line of criticism is that they will undermine social unity and political stability, leading to the balkanization and possible breakup of the country. I will start with the first line of criticism, and discuss the balkanization objection in Section VI.

Demands for minority rights are often described, by both their defenders and their critics, in the language of "group rights." Defenders, however, typically describe group rights as *supplementing* individual rights, and hence as enriching and extending traditional liberal democratic principles to deal with new challenges, whereas critics tend to assume that group rights involve *restricting* individual rights, and hence as threatening basic democratic values.

The relationship between individual rights and group rights is complicated. Consider two kinds of rights that a group might claim: the first involves the right of a group against its own members; the second involves the right of a group against the larger society. Both kinds of group rights can be seen as protecting the stability of national, ethnic, or religious groups. However, they respond to different sources of instability. The first kind is intended to protect the group from the destabilizing impact of *internal* dissent (e.g., the decision of individual members not to follow traditional practices or customs), whereas the second is intended to protect the group from the impact of *external* pressures (e.g., the economic or political decisions of the larger society). To distinguish these two kinds of group rights, we can call the first "internal restrictions," and the second "external protections."

Of the two, internal restrictions tend to be more controversial. Many groups seek the right to legally restrict the freedom of their own members in the name of group solidarity or cultural purity. Such rights are invoked by theocratic and patriarchal cultures where women are oppressed and religious orthodoxy enforced. This obviously raises the danger of individual oppression.

Of course, all forms of government involve restricting the liberty of citizens (e.g., paying taxes, undertaking jury duty, or military service). Even the most liberal of democracies imposes such restrictions in order to uphold individual rights and democratic institutions. But some groups seek to impose much greater restrictions, not in order to maintain liberal institutions, but rather to protect religious orthodoxy or cultural tradition.

Such internal restrictions are widely opposed in Western democracies. Groups are free to impose certain restrictions as conditions for membership in voluntary associations, but it is widely considered unjust to use *governmental* power, or the distribution of public benefits, to restrict the liberty of members. From a liberal-democratic point of view, whoever exercises political power in a community must respect the civil and political rights of its members.

External protections, by contrast, are often seen as more legitimate. Many groups seek to protect their distinct identity by limiting their vulnerability to the decisions of the larger society. For example, reserving land for the exclusive use of a minority group ensures that it will not be outbid for the land by the greater wealth of outsiders. Guaranteeing representation for a minority on advisory or legislative bodies reduces the chance that the group will be outvoted on decisions that affect the community. Devolving power to local levels enables the group to make certain decisions on its own.

These sorts of external protections do not seem inconsistent with liberal democracy, and may indeed promote justice. They may help put the different groups in a society on a more equal footing by reducing the extent to which minorities are vulnerable to the larger society. Of course, some claims for external protections are unjust. Apartheid in South Africa is perhaps the clearest example, where whites, who constituted less than 20% of the population, demanded 87% of the land mass of the country, monopolized all the political power, and imposed their language on other groups. But in most cases, the minority has no ability or desire to dominate larger groups. The external protections they seek would not deprive other groups of their fair share of economic resources, political power, or language rights. As a rule, minorities simply seek to ensure that the majority cannot use its superior numbers and wealth to deprive the minority of the resources and institutions needed to sustain their community. And that is widely (though by no means unanimously) seen as a legitimate demand.

So whereas internal restrictions are almost inherently in conflict with liberal democratic norms, external protections are not—so long as they promote equality between groups, rather than allow one group to dominate or oppress another. It is important, therefore, to determine whether the claims of ethnocultural groups involve internal restrictions or external protections. This is not always an easy question to answer. Representation rights and affirmative action are primarily matters of external protections. They do not give groups the power to restrict the liberty of their own members. But self-government rights and recognition rights are more ambiguous. They can be used either to secure external protections or to impose internal restrictions.

Some ethnocultural groups are only interested in external protections. They are concerned with ensuring that the larger society does not deprive them of the conditions necessary for their survival, but not with controlling the extent to which their own members engage in untraditional or unorthodox practices. These are the easy cases, at least in principle. There is no reason in principle why liberal democracies cannot accommodate the demands of ethnocultural groups which are themselves liberal. The more difficult case concerns groups which are not liberal—i.e., groups which are concerned with controlling internal dissent and so seek to impose internal restrictions. This issue has arisen both in the context of national minorities and immigrant groups. For example, Pueblo Indians in the United States—who have extensive rights of self-government—discriminate against members who have abandoned the traditional tribal religion in the distribution of housing. They also discriminate against women who have married outside the tribe. (If female members marry outside the tribe, their children are denied membership. But if men marry outside the tribe, the children are members.)

Similarly, some immigrant groups and religious minorities invoke "multiculturalism" as a justification for imposing traditional patriarchal practices on women and children. Some groups may demand the right to stop their children (particularly girls) from receiving a proper education, so as to reduce the chances that the child will leave the community, or the right to continue traditional customs such as clitoridectomy or compulsory arranged marriages.

V. THE NATURE AND LIMITS OF TOLERANCE

How should liberal states respond to these cases in which immigrant and national groups demand the "right" to protect their historical customs by limiting the basic civil liberties of their members? Should minorities be able to reject liberal democratic principles and to organize their society along traditional, nonliberal lines? The mainstream society may find this offensive, but is not this part of what makes the minority culturally distinct? If the members of a minority lose the ability to enforce religious orthodoxy or traditional gender roles, have not they lost part of the raison d'etre for maintaining themselves as a distinct society? Is not the insistence on respect for individual rights a new version of the old ethnocentrism which sets the (liberal) majority culture as the standard to which other cultures must adhere? Indeed, is not it fundamentally *intolerant* to force a national minority or religious sect to reorganize their community according to "our" liberal principles of individual liberty?

These are difficult questions, and have given rise to important conflicts, not only between liberals and nonliberals, but also within liberalism itself. For tolerance is itself a quintessential liberal value, alongside other liberal values like individual freedom and personal autonomy. The problem, of course, is that these values can conflict: promoting individual freedom may entail intolerance toward illiberal groups, while promoting tolerance of illiberal groups may entail accepting restrictions on the freedom of individuals. What should be done in such cases?

If an illiberal minority is seeking to oppress other groups, then most people would agree that intervention is justified in the name of self-defense. But what if the group has no interest in ruling over others or depriving them of their resources, and instead simply wants to be left alone to run its own community in accordance with its traditional nonliberal norms? In such cases, some liberals may think that tolerance should take precedence over autonomy. So long as these minorities do not want to impose their values on others, should not they be allowed to organize their society as they like, even if this involves limiting the liberty of their own members?

A. Two Models of Tolerance

There is a large and growing debate among liberals about whether autonomy or tolerance is the fundamental value within liberal theory. The autonomy-based view is often described as the "Enlightenment," "comprehensive," or "Kantian" conception of liberalism, in contrast to the "Reformation," "political," or "modus vivendi" conception which is gounded on the value of tolerance. Defenders of tolerance argue that there are many ethnocultural groups within the boundaries of liberal states which do not value personal autonomy and which restrict the ability of their members to question and dissent from traditional practices. Basing liberal theory on autonomy threatens to alienate these groups and undermine their allegiance to liberal institutions, whereas a tolerance-based liberalism can provide a more secure and wider basis for the legitimacy of government. On a tolerance-based view, liberals should seek to accommodate illiberal groups, so long as they do not seek any support from the larger society and do not seek to impose their values on others.

Defenders of the tolerance-based view often argue that liberalism emerged out of the idea of religious toleration. Religious tolerance developed in the West when Catholics and Protestants realized that a stable constitutional order could not rest on a shared religious faith; liberals have simply extended the principle of tolerance to other controversial questions about the good life.

There is some truth to this claim that liberalism is an extension of the principle of religious tolerance, but this connection may not support the tolerance-based view, for the sort of religious tolerance which emerged in the West, and which was subsequently generalized, was precisely an autonomy-based conception of tolerance. Religious toleration in the West was based on the idea of *individual freedom of conscience*—tolerance was achieved by giving each individual the right to worship freely, to propagate one's religion, to change one's religion, or indeed to renounce religion altogether. To restrict an individual's exercise of these liberties is now seen as a violation of a fundamental human right.

There are other forms of religious toleration which are not based on individual freedom. They are based on the idea that each religious group should be free to organize its community as it sees fits, including along nonliberal lines. In the "millet system" of the Ottoman Empire, for example, Muslims, Christians, and Jews were all recognized as self-governing units (or "millets") and allowed to impose restrictive religious laws on their own members. This was a group-based form of toleration which did not recognize any principle of individual freedom of conscience.

So when liberals extended the principle of religious tolerance to other areas of life, they were extending an individual freedom-based notion of tolerance. This suggests that a liberal conception of tolerance will probably deny the legitimacy of internal restrictions which limit the right of individuals within the group to revise their conceptions of the good. For example, liberals will oppose attempts by a religious minority to legally prohibit apostasy and proselytization, or to prevent their children learning about other ways of life (as with the Amish).

So the appeal to "tolerance" does not resolve the conflict between liberal values and illiberal minorities. Insofar as liberal tolerance has historically been individual freedom-based, not group-based, it cannot justify internal restrictions that limit individual freedom of conscience.

B. The Limits of Intervention

If internal restrictions are unjust, according to liberal principles, should liberal states coercively intervene in illiberal minority cultures to ensure that individual freedom is respected? Not necessarily. After all, the question of *identifying* a defensible liberal theory of minority rights is separate from that of *imposing* that liberal the-

ory. Internal restrictions may be inconsistent with liberal principles, but it does not yet follow that liberals should impose their views on minorities which do not accept some or all of these liberal principles.

In the case of immigrants who come to a country knowing its laws, the imposing of liberal prinicples is relatively uncontroversial. This can be seen as one of the terms of admission to a liberal polity, and immigrants have no obvious basis for denying that the state has legitimate authority over them. But the situation is more complicated with self-governing national minorities, particularly if (a) they were involuntarily incorporated into the larger state, and (b) they have their own formalized governments, with their own internal mechanisms for dispute resolution. In these circumstances, the legitimate scope for coercive intervention by the state may be more limited.

Recall the case of the Pueblo Indians in the United States, whose tribal council violates the rights of its members by limiting freedom of conscience and by employing sexually discriminatory membership rules. Liberal principles imply that the Pueblo tribal government is acting unjustly, since individuals have certain claims which their government must respect, such as individual freedom of conscience. But if the Pueblo government fails to respect those claims, does the American federal government have the authoritiy to step in and force compliance?

Many liberals have assumed that all governments within a country should be subject to a single Bill of Rights adjudicated and enforced by a single Supreme Court. Hence many American liberals supported legislation to make tribal governments subject to the federal Bill of Rights, even though Indian tribes have historically been exempt from having to comply with the Bill of Rights, and their internal decisions have not been not subject to Supreme Court review.

This legislation was opposed by the Pueblo, for understandable reasons. For one thing, the federal constitution and courts may have no legitimacy in the eyes of an involuntarily incorporated national minority like the Pueblo. After all, the American Supreme Court legitimized the acts of colonization and conquest which dispossessed the Pueblo of their property and political power. Moreover, the Pueblo have never had any representation on the Supreme Court. Why should the Pueblo agree to have their internal decisions reviewed by a body which is, in effect, the courts of their conquerors?

It is important to note that the Pueblo have their own internal constitution and courts which prevent the arbitrary exercise of political power. To be sure, the

Pueblo constitution is not a fully liberal one, but it is a form of constitutional government which provides meaningful checks on political authority and preserves the basic elements of natural justice, and which thereby helps ensure that the tribal government maintains its legitimacy in the eyes of its members.

The nonliberal constitutionalism of the Pueblo is obviously unsatisfactory from the point of view of liberal principles. After all, the Pueblo courts upheld the rules which discriminated against Christians and women. But for the federal courts to overturn the decisions of the Pueblo courts and impose liberal principles is very controversial. To impose liberalism on such an involuntarily incorporated and self-governing group is to denigrate the group's own system of government and courts, even though it has high levels of legitimacy in the eyes of its members, and to impose instead a court system which has no legitimacy, since it has historically justified the dispossession of the Pueblo and has never had a Pueblo member of the Supreme Court.

For these reasons, imposing liberal principles on self-governing national minorities is similar, in important respects, to imposing liberalism on other countries. In both cases, attempts to impose liberal principles by force may backfire, since they are often perceived as a form of aggression or paternalistic colonialism. The experience of postcolonial Africa suggests that liberal institutions are unlikely to be stable when they have arisen as a result of external imposition rather than internal reform. Some commentators believe that liberal institutions can only work if liberal beliefs have been internalized by the members of the self-governing society, be it an independent country or a national minority.

Insofar as it is illegitimate to impose liberalism in these cases, the liberal state and the illiberal national minority will have to come to some sort of modus vivendi. The terms of this modus vivendi may involve exempting the national minority from federal Bills of Rights and judicial review—as indeed the Pueblo Indians are partially exempted. This means that the majority will be unable to prevent the violation of individual rights within the minority community. Liberals in the majority group have to learn to live with this, just as they must live with illiberal laws in other countries.

This is not to say that the federal government cannot provide incentives for liberal reforms within illiberal minority groups, or promote international mechanisms for protecting human rights which are acceptable to minority groups. Moreover, even those who wish to limit intervention in the internal affairs of national minorities are likely to make an exception in the case of gross and systematic violation of human rights, such as slavery, genocide, or mass torture and expulsions (just as these are grounds for intervening in foreign countries).

An intermediary case between that of self-governing national minorities and newly arriving immigrants is that of long-standing ethnic groups or religious sects which have been allowed to maintain certain illiberal institutions for many years, even many generations. This would include the Amish, or the Hasidic Jews in New York. For various reasons, when these immigrant groups arrived, they were given exemptions from the usual requirements regarding integration and were allowed to maintain certain internal restrictions. Many people may now regret these historical exemptions, but they were granted, and it is unclear whether they can now be disregarded. Relying on certain tacit or explicit assurances about their right to maintain separate institutions, these groups have now built and maintained self-contained enclaves that depend on certain internal restrictions. Had those assurances not been given, these groups might well have emigrated to some other country. It is not clear how much weight, morally speaking, should be given to these sorts of historical arguments, but it is arguable that these groups do have a stronger claim to maintain internal restrictions than newly arriving immigrants.

VI. INTEGRATION OR SEPARATISM?

As I noted earlier, minority rights are often opposed, not simply because they may violate liberal democratic principles, but also because they will be a source of disunity and inhibit the development of a sense of shared political identity. They could lead to the dissolution of the country or, less drastically, to a reduced willingness to make the mutual sacrifices and accommodations necessary for a functioning democracy. If groups are encouraged by the very terms of citizenship to turn inward and focus on their "difference" (whether racial, ethnic, religious, sexual, etc), then citizenship cannot perform its vital integrative function. Nothing will bind the various groups in society together and prevent the spread of mutual mistrust or conflict.

This is a serious concern. In evaluating it, however, we need to keep in mind the distinction between the different types of minority rights. Generally speaking, the demand for representation rights, recognition rights, and affirmative action often reflects a desire for *inclusion*. Groups that feel excluded want to be included in the larger society, and the recognition and accommodation of their "difference" is intended to facilitate this.

For example, the right to special representation can be seen as an extension of the familiar democratic idea of guaranteeing special representation for underrepresented regions (e.g., an equal number of Senate seats for all states, whatever their population). This practice is widely seen as promoting both participation and fairness, and hence integration. Proponents of special representation simply extend this logic to nonterritorial minorities, who may equally be in need of representation (e.g., ethnic and racial minorities, women and the disabled).

Similarly, affirmative action is intended to give minorities greater access to, and opportunities in, the mainstream society. There are familiar practical obstacles to such proposals for group representation and affirmative action. Nevertheless, the basic impulse underlying these proposals seems to be integration, not separation.

Many demands for recognition rights can also be seen as evidence that members of immigrant groups want to participate within the mainstream of society. Consider the case of Sikhs who wanted to join the Royal Canadian Mounted Police, but, because of their religious requirement to wear a turban, could not do so unless they were exempted from the usual requirements regarding ceremonial headgear. Such an exemption was opposed by many Canadians as a sign of disrespect for one of Canada's "national symbols." But the fact that these men wanted to be a part of the national police force suggests a desire to participate in and contribute to the larger community. They insisted that the recognition right they were requesting would promote, not discourage, their integration.

The same can be said of other recognition rights, from the recognition of Muslim and Jewish holidays in the school calendar to the inclusion of ethnic history within the school curriculum. Leaving aside the special case of isolationist religious groups, these recognition rights are all intended to increase the likelihood that the members of ethnic groups will choose to participate in mainstream institutions, and that they will feel comfortable doing so.

As I noted earlier, critics worry that "multiculturalism" policies (including the granting of recognition rights) are encouraging immigrants to reject integration and instead to view themselves as separate and self-governing groups, akin to national minorities. Since the adoption of multiculturalism policies for immigrants only occurred 20–25 years ago, it may be too early to assess the merits of this objection. However, it is a striking historical fact that no immigrant group in any of the major immigrant countries

has mobilized along nationalist lines for secession or self-government. Historically, such a quasi-nationalist strategy has been neither desirable nor feasible in the context of immigrant groups, and many commentators argue that it remains an infeasible strategy for groups which have been formed by the decisions of individuals and families to uproot themselves and move to a new land. On this view, immigrants know that integration is the only viable route to success in their new land, and current "multiculturalism" policies make no attempt to change that fact. In public life, immigrants still mix with native-born citizens in common educational, economic, legal, and political institutions, all of which operate in the majority's language. And immigrants to America are still required to learn English to acquire citizenship, and learning English is a mandatory part of children's education. Multiculturalism, then, is not a rejection of the idea that immigrants should integrate institutionally and linguistically into their new society. Rather, it is the view that in return for integrating into common institutions, these institutions should be reformed (through the granting of recognition rights) to accommodate the identity of immigrant groups, in terms of their symbols, holidays, uniforms, rules, and so on.

Self-government rights, however, do raise problems for the integrative function of citizenship. While both representation and recognition rights take the larger political community for granted, and seek greater inclusion in it, demands for self-government reflect a desire to weaken the bonds with the larger community, and indeed question its very nature, authority, and permanence. If democracy is the rule of the people, group self-government raises the question of who "the people" really are. National minorities claim that they are distinct peoples, with inherent rights of self-determination which were not relinquished by their incorporation into a larger country. Self-government rights, therefore, divide the people into separate "peoples," each with its own historic rights, territories, and powers of self-government, and each, therefore, with its own political community.

It seems unlikely that this sort of minority right serves an integrative function. If citizenship is membership in a political community, then self-government rights necessarily give rise to a sort of dual citizenship and to conflicts about which community citizens identify with most deeply. Moreover, there seems to be no natural stopping point to the demands for increasing self-government. It limited autonomy is granted, this may simply fuel the ambitions of nationalist leaders who will be satisfied with nothing short of their own nation-state. Democratic multination states are, it would seem, inherently unstable for this reason.

It might seem tempting, therefore, to ignore the demands of national minorities, avoid any reference to such groups in the constitution, and insist that citizenship is a common identity shared by all individuals, without regard to group membership. This is often described as the American strategy for dealing with ethnocultural pluralism. But with a few exceptions—such as the (mostly outlying) Indian, Eskimo, Puerto Rican, and Native Hawaiian populations—the United States is not a multination state. It has faced the problem of assimilating voluntary immigrants and involuntary slaves, who arrived in America as individuals or families, rather than incorporating historically self-governing communities whose homeland has become part of the larger community. The "ethnicity-blind" strategy was briefly applied to American Indians in the hope that they would integrate like immigrants, but the policy failed miserably and was soon replaced with the recognition of self-government rights. Indeed, there are very few democratic multination states that follow the strict "common citizenship" strategy. This is not surprising, because refusing demands for self-government rights may simply aggravate alienation among these groups and increase the desire for secession.

Of the four kinds of minority rights, therefore, self-government rights pose the greatest threat to social unity and political stability. Both the granting and the withholding of self-government rights may threaten social unity. The recent breakup of Czechoslovakia and Yugoslavia, and the ongoing constitutional crises in Canada and Belgium, suggest that we have not yet found a successful formula for ensuring the stability of multination states.

VII. CONCLUSION

Liberal democracies have a long history of seeking to accommodate ethnocultural differences, and many democracies have enviable records of peaceful coexistence between ethnocultural groups. Yet many groups continue to feel oppressed or excluded, and demands for new or strengthened minority rights show no sign of fading away. There are no magical formulas for resolving these disputes, which often have a long and complicated history. Indeed, perhaps the major lesson to be drawn from this survey is the sheer heterogeneity of group difference and of the mechanisms for accommodating them. The sorts of demands made by national, immigrant, and racial groups differ greatly in their content and their relation to traditional liberal democratic principles of equality, freedom, and democracy.

Also See the Following Articles

CITIZENSHIP • DISCRIMINATION, CONCEPT OF • EQUALITY AND EGALITARIANISM • INDIGENOUS RIGHTS • PLURALISM IN EDUCATION • RACISM • RIGHTS THEORY

Bibliography

Baker, J. (Ed.) (1994). "Group Rights." Univ. of Toronto Press, Toronto.

Galston, W. (1995). Two concepts of liberalism. *Ethics* 105(3), 516–34.

Gurr, T. (1993). "Minorities at Risk: A Global View of Ethnopolitical Conflict." Institute of Peace Press, Washington, DC.

Kymlicka, W. (Ed.) (1995). "The Rights of Minority Cultures." Oxford Univ. Press, Oxford.

Levy, J. (1997). Classifying cultural rights. In "Ethnicity and Group Rights: Nomos 39" (W. Kymlicka and I. Shapiro, Eds.). New York Univ. Press, New York.

McGarry, J. and O'Leary, B. (1994). The political regulation of national and ethnic conflict. *Parliamentary Affairs* 47(1), 94–115.

Phillips, A. (1995). "The Politics of Presence: Democracy and Group Representation." Oxford Univ. Press, Oxford.

Taylor, C. (1992). The politics of recognition. In "Multiculturalism and the 'Politics of Recognition'" (A. Gutmann, Ed.), pp. 25–73. Princeton Univ. Press, Princeton.

EUGENICS

Demetrio Neri
University of Messina

GLOSSARY

DNA (deoxyribonucleic acid) The macromolecule responsible for the expression and transmission of genetic information.

gene The stretch of DNA containing the genetic information necessary to determine a somatic trait.

genetic counseling A form of medical advising for couples who risk giving birth to a child with serious genetic conditions.

genetic engineering A complex of techniques allowing intervention on genetic material through manipulation of DNA.

genetics The science of heredity, which studies the structure and function of genes on how they are transmitted over generations.

genetic screening Research aimed at ascertaining, through the identification of carriers, the diffusion of a genetic disease in a given population.

genome The genetic patrimony of a cell or of an individual.

genotype The genetic endowement of an organism influencing the phenotype.

germ-line cells Reproductive cells from which sperm and ova develop.

heredity The transmission from one generation to the next of factors (genes) that determine the phenotype.

natural selection The process of selection of the fittest individuals to survive in a given environment.

phenotype The physical characteristics of an individual as determined by interaction between genes and environment during development.

pre-embryo The embryo in the first 14 days following conception.

reproductive technologies Techniques that substitute one or more stages of the natural process of reproduction.

somatic cell Every cell of the body, exclusive of the reproductive ones.

EUGENICS can be defined as the application of the principles of genetics and inheritance to the improvement of the human race, in order to secure, by analogy with the selective breedings applied from immemorial time to plants and domestic animals, a desirable combination of physical characteristics and mental traits in the offspring of suitable mated parents. The idea is an old one, but the word is a relative neologism coined in 1883 by the English scientist Francis Galton. The word is derived from Greek roots (*eu* meaning well and *ghenos* meaning birth, descent) that literally mean well born, which can be understood both in the sense of "born in good wealth" and "born from noble descent." This ambivalence of meaning marks the history of eugenics from its very beginning. While the first sense captures a concern every decent person should have toward his or her progeny, the second sense expresses an idea of phenotypical excellence that can easily degenerate (as actually happened at the beginning of the eugenic movement) in elitism and racism.

Currently, the word is emotionally loaded, perhaps irremediably, with negative connotations. The concept of eugenics in the present debate is used mainly to express through one word all that one finds potentially worrying or undesirable in recent developments in genetics and molecular biology and in their application to genetic engineering. These developments and appliations are interpreted in the framework of the ambivalence of scientific progress: on the one hand, there is the hope that biomedical progress can free mankind from illness and suffering while, on the other hand, there is the fear and the anxiety generated from the complete mastering of human life that genetic engineering seems to involve.

I. HISTORICAL ASPECTS

A. Eugenics in Antiquity

1. Plato, the First Eugenicist

Although the word "eugenics" is relatively new, the idea of eugenics is very old. Arguably the first eugenicist was Plato, who in his *Republic* submitted a complete eugenics-minded program of control of human reproduction as an example of the most important basis for founding his ideal state. Plato upheld that the inability of rulers-philosophers to control "scientifically" the "cycle of birth" was one of the most important causes of the corruption of the state. In the fifth book of the *Republic* (458d–460a), he begins by pointing out that selective breedings are commonly used to obtain "more suitable"or "better" domestic animals (Plato referred to hunting dogs and to ornamental birds). He then reaches the conclusion that "the best of either sex should be united with the best as often, and the inferior with the inferior, as seldom as possible; and that they [the rulers] should rear the offspring of the one sort of union, but not of the other, if the flock is to be maintained in first-rate condition." In addition, he suggests that "the proper officers will take the offspring of the good parents to the pen or fold, and there they will deposit them with certain nurses who dwell in separate quarter; but the offspring of the inferior, or of the better when they chance to be deformed, will be put away in some mysterious, unknown place, as they should be."

It is worth noting that, fearing this sort of arrangement for the improvement of race could cause opposition and even rebellion, Plato suggested that such a plan be kept secret and that it should be implemented by appointing "certain festivals at which we will bring together the brides and bridegrooms, and sacrifices will be offered and suitable hymeneal songs composed by our poets." It is curious that after more than 2000 years the idea of favoring the meeting between suitable couples has been planned, as we will see below, in the eugenic proposals of the state of Singapore (1984). In debating these proposals someone suggested that Singapore, like the ancient Greek republic, might decline if its upper-class women could not give birth to talented people.

2. An Old Idea

Plato's eugenic views were not novel in ancient cultures. Elements of eugenics, associated with what we today would label "disgenic worries," were widerspread in many cultures and in prescriptions or prohibitions included in customs and religious practices. The empirical outlook on heredity diffused in ancient cultures included the idea that inborn as well as acquired characteristics were inherited from parents, and that they could be influenced by external practices at conception and during pregnancy. There was a complex of popular beliefs (partially surviving today) about suitable times and rituals to propitiate a "good birth." The general principle was that "like produces like," and some reckoned (as in ancient Egypt in the age of pharaohs) that the best way to preserve the purity and qualities of descent was to marry among close relatives. This is the very first example of a eugenic elitist drift. It is also eugenically wrong, because empirical observation have shown that blood marriages should be avoided because they produce what we label today a "disgenic trend." This was likely the rationale for the canonic prohibition of such marriages in the Christian tradition, even if this concern was not explicitly mentioned until the seventeenth century: marriages of close relatives "weaken the blood." "Blood" was the word used in the past (and it is still used today in common language) to indicate the essence of heredity. As we will see, such a term was used also by Francis Galton and by the biologists of his time who knew no more about the mechanism of hereditary transmission than "like produces like." Galton did not know the work of Gregory Mendel, who in 1865 published a paper describing the results of his experiments on plant hybridization. The old idea of the inheritance of acquired characteristics was not scientifically disproved until the end of the nineteenth century by the German biologist August Weismann, although some scientists still adhered to the old doctrine at least until the 1930s.

B. Eugenics in Modern Times

1. Galton and Darwin

The description above can be termed the prehistory of eugenics. The true history of eugenics begins with the creator of the word, the English mathematician Francis Galton, a cousin of Charles Darwin and the pioneer in the field of statistical treatment of heredity. Galton developed his ideas in two articles published in 1865 (Hereditary Talent and Character, *Macmillan's Magazine.* 157–166; 318–327), followed by several articles and books in which he discussed the results of his statistical research on the distribution over generations of natural abilities that lead to the acquisition of a social "reputation." In 1883 he published *Inquiries into the Human Faculty* in which eugenics is defined as "the study of the agencies under social control that may improve or impair the racial qualities of future generations, either physically or mentally." Profoundly influenced by the Darwinian doctrine that natural selection through the survival of the fittest can improve the adaptive characteristics of a species, Galton thought that the human species too was naturally progressing toward improvement. But he was also convinced that it was necessary to control and accelerate this process because with humans the action of natural selection was somehow thwarted by philanthropic and compassionate concerns allowing the "weak" or "unfit" to survive and reproduce.

The practical goal of the new science of eugenics was to help natural selection by giving "the more suitable races and strains of blood a better chance of prevailing speedily over the less suitable" (*Inquiries,* 24–25). To achieve this Galton considered measures of control and prior restraints on human reproduction. Nevertheless, he realized the practical difficulties of implementing such measures and he ended up envisioning the development of a sort of "secular religion" that would foster voluntary eugenic marriages (Kevles, D. J. (1985). *In the Name of Eugenics: Genetics and the Use of Human Heredity*, p. 12. Berkeley and Los Angeles: University of California Press).

In a passage worthy to be quoted extensively, containing both the rationale for eugenics and the enunciation of the central (moral as well practical) problems involved, Darwin wrote,

With savages, the weak in body or mind are soon eliminated; and those that survive commonly exhibit a vigorous state of health. We civilized men, on the other hand, do our utmost to check the process of elimination; we build asylums for the imbecile, the maimed, and the sick; we institute poor-laws; and our medical men exert their utmost skill to save the life of everyone to the last moment. There is reason to believe that vaccination has preserved thousands, who from a weak constitution would formerly have succumbed to smallpox. Thus the weak member of civilized society propagate their kind. No one who has attended to the breeding of domestic animals will doubt that this must be highly injurious to the race of man. . . . The aid which we fell impelled to give to the helpless is mainly an incidental result of the instinct of sympathy, which was originally acquired as part of the social instinct, but subsequently rendered, in the manner previously indicated, more tender and more widely diffused. Nor could we check our sympathy, even at the urging of hard reason, without deterioration in the noblest part of our nature. . . . We must therefore bear the undoubtedly bad effects of the weak surviving and propagating their kind; but it appears to be at least one check in steady action, namely that the weaker and inferior members of society do not marry so freely as the sound; and this check might be indefinitely increased by the weak in body or mind refraining from marriage, though this is more to be hoped for than expected. (Darwin, C. (1871). *The Descent of Man and Selection in Relation to Sex* pp. 501–502. New York: Random House Library Edition.)

2. The Eugenic Movement

Galton's doctrines gained immediate approval among European and American scientific circles, which were already influenced by Darwin's evolutionary theory by the end of the nineteenth century. In the first years of the twentieth century this complex of ideas became a social movement, which quickly spread to many countries and assumed different forms according to different cultural and social frameworks (see Adams, M. B. (1990). *The Well-born Science: Eugenics in Germany, France, Brazil and Russia.* New York: Oxford University Press). Conservative members of the cultured middle and upper classes adhered to the movement, attracted by the possibility of finding a scientific solution for problem of social "degeneration." But liberal and even socialist intellectuals (such as Havelock Hellis and

George Bernard Shaw) who considered eugenics as an instrument of betterment of the popular masses were also attracted to the movement.

Eugenic societies were created in various part of the civilized world with the dual goal of fostering research on heredity (which received a great boost from the rediscovery of Mendel's theory of the mechanism of hereditary transmission) and of promoting eugenic education and eugenic measures to control the population level.

One of the first effects of the movement was the creation of scientific institutions devoted to research on heredity. Among the most important were the Galton Laboratory for National Eugenic at the University College London, founded in 1905 and directed by Karl Pearson; the Eugenics Record Office at Cold Spring Harbor (Long Island, NY), founded in 1910 and directed by the biologist Charles B. Davenport; the Kaiser Wilhem Institute for Research in Psychiatry founded in Munich in 1918; and the Kaiser Wilhem Institute for Anthropology, Human Heredity and Eugenics, established in 1927 in Berlin and directed by the anthropologist Eugen Fischer, who later played a leading role in the elaboration of the Nazi's racist program.

Although most of the research on heredity in the first decades of the century was pursued in these centers, methodologies were poor and the results were seriously weakened by scientific errors and by class and race prejudices. Most eugenicists favored the idea that each phenotypical trait is the espression of a single gene. This view led to a strong genetic determinism that underestimated cultural and environmental factors in the formation of biological organisms. Moreover, most eugenicists were willing to believe that social phenomena such as poverty, alcoholism, prostitution, and criminality had genetic roots and therefore were inherited: the poor were poor not because they had inadequate education or limited economic opportunities, but because of some genetic defect. In this way social problems became part of genetic research, along with the complex of mental disorders called "feeblemindedness."

3. Elitist and Racist Drift

Although the mainline eugenics movement was not conservative and reactionary, it soon assumed a strong elitist drift. The original idea of improvement of the human species was beneficial and universalist in nature, and it showed traces of the influence of the eighteenth-century ideal of human perfectibility. The Enlightenment nevertheless taught that the perfecting of humankind should be pursued through social reforms and the education of the masses. On the contrary, most

eugenicists thought that humankind could be more effectively improved by applying the science of heredity; and because the improvement of the species implies the selection of individuals, the idea that this goal could be more speedily obtained by selecting the "best" was clearly presented at the First International Congress of Eugenics (London, 1912) as the only way to bring about an elite endowed with the desired somatic and mental characteristics. Such an elitism favored the idea that the purity and superiority of one race (almost always White, aryan, or nordic, and Protestant) over others should be protected from mixing with biologically inferior strains. In 1924 the U.S. government passed the Immigration Restriction Act, which limited the flux from southern and eastern (but not from northern) European countries on the grounds that immigrants from those areas were biologically inferior.

Between 1907 and 1930 many U.S. states passed laws on the compulsory sterilization of habitual criminals, epileptics, idiots, and so on. The American model then appeared in Germany in 1933 when the Nazi regime passed the Eugenic Sterilization Act, which was to prevent people affected by alleged hereditary diseases from propagating their kind. In the beginning the law had no specific anti-Semitic characteristics, but it became soon the first step of a program culminating in the physical elimination of all the "undesirables"or the "useless" (Jews, gypsies, the handicapped, etc.). In 1935, the American genetist Hermann J. Muller denounced eugenics, stating that it had been perverted into a pseudoscientific façade for "advocates of race and class prejudice, defenders of vested interests of church and state, fascists Hitlerites, and reactionaries generally" (Muller H. J. (1935). *Out of Night: A Biologist's View of the Future*, pp. IX–X. New York: Vanguard Press).

4. Eugenics after World War II

After the end of World War II, reports on Nazi crimes gave eugenics and the doctrine itself very negative connotations. Many scientists working in genetics felt the need to eliminate any eugenic shadow from their work. A typical case was that of the English physician, Lionel Penrose, an authority in the field of mental deficiency. At the end of World War II, Penrose was appointed head of the Galton Laboratory and Galton Eugenics Professor: he was so worried about the "stigma of eugenics" that in 1954 he changed the title of the laboratory's annual from *Annals of Eugenics* to *Annals of Human Genetics* and later renamed his chair Galton Professorship of Human Genetics.

Although some eugenic societies discreetly continued their work and new societies with eugenic goals have been created, they carefully avoid the word eugenics: a typical example is the American Society of Human Genetics, established in 1950. A proper eugenics movement no longer exists. Since the end of World War II the history of eugenics has become mainly a history of the scientific and ethical debate about some of the issues that involve eugenics.

In the 1950s and 1960s the main issue was the concern for the "genetic health" of the human species, which according to some scientists, was threatened by a "disgenic trend" associated with the process of improvement (in rich countries, at least) of the conditions of life and medical care. A leading role in denouncing this alleged risk was played by Hermann J. Muller, Nobel laureate in 1946 for his work on X-ray-induced mutagenesis. Muller developed the concept of "genetic load," which is the complex of "harmful genes" present in the gene pool of humankind. He held that each individual carries an average of eight potentially harmful genes and that, under certain conditions, genetic load could reduce the evolutionary fitness of the species (1950. Our load of mutations. *American Journal of Human Genetics*, 2). Nevertheless, although in the 1960s genetic epidemiology and population genetics confirmed Muller's thesis, the risk of a "genetic Apocalypse" was believed to be very unlikely. In any case, Muller's proposals to check disgenic trends appealed to the exercise of responsible human freedom and insisted on the voluntariness of any means suggested to fight genetic deterioration. After the Nazi experience, no one (at least in Western democratic countries) may seriously advocate illiberal or repressive measures to control the biological evolution of the human species.

C. The New Eugenics

1. Creative Eugenics

The locution "new eugenics" was created by biologist Robert L. Sinsheimer in 1969 (April. The prospect of designed genetic change. *Engineering and Science Magazine*), and is now commonly used to indicate the new possibilities that are generally opened by genetic engineering applied for eugenic purposes. Sinsheimer used such a locution to indicate what can be properly called "creative eugenics." It aims not only at the improvement of the present human species by "the conversion of all the unfit to the highest genetic level," but it also aims at the creation of a new human species, endowed with "new qualities yet undreamed." During the 1970s, Sinsheimer's ideas seemed to be confirmed by the dramatic developments opened through the application of DNA-recombinant technologies. These made it possible to "manipulate" the genome of living beings in order to create new forms of life and, moreover, to operate for therapeutical as well as enhancement purposes on the genomic structure of human beings.

Such a biological progress immediately stimulated an already flourishing science-fiction literature, which today is influential in the mass-media. Sometimes popular culture presents future worlds populated by clones or monsters, or by people created only for the purpose of carrying out difficult jobs or so that they can live in inhospitable environments. Of course, these science fiction nightmares have nothing to do with eugenics; it would be meaningless to say that monsters or people like that are "well born" in any sense of the expression. Moreover, the central idea of eugenics had been the amelioration of the present human species, and eugenics might be considered a kind of homage to it. We should ask if the creation of a new (different) human species has to be included within the semantic sphere covered by the concept.

2. The Specter of Eugenics

Since the late 1960s the specter of eugenics has colored the debate on the prospective application of genetic engineering to human beings; the history of eugenics is now the history of this debate. The rejection of eugenics appears almost in every document enacted by official institutions such as, for instance, the European Parliament, or by commissions created in many countries to study this or related issues (such as the new reproductive technologies). For example, in 1980 just after the decision of the U.S. Supreme Court to allow patents on new forms of life, representatives of the three largest religions in the United States, sent a letter to President Jimmy Carter that, while recognizing that the possibility of creating new forms of life could be an exceptional opportunity for the amelioration of human life, expressed fears concering the immense power conferred to scientists by this new possibility: "Control of such life forms by any individual or group poses a potential threat to all of humanity. History has shown us that there will always be those who believe it appropriate to "correct" our mental and social structures by genetic means, so as to fit their vision of humanity. This becomes more dangerous when the basic tools to do so are finally at hand. Those who would play God will be tempted as never before" (The letter is in Appendix A of Capron, A. *et al.* (1982). *Splicing Life. The Social and Ethical Issue of Genetic Engineering with Human Beings*. Washington DC: US Government Printing Office).

3. Old Style Eugenic Efforts

In singular contrast to the science fiction prospects imagined in this section, we can note that the techno-cratic government of Singapore in 1984 proposed a scheme of family planning that has many similarities with Platonic eugenics. Concern for the decrease of the fertility rate of educated women (compared with that of less-educated ones), together with the acceptance of the ideas of Cyril Burt and Arthur Jensen about the inheritance of intelligence (see below), led Singapore's Premier Lee to propose guidelines to reverse this trend, ensuring incentives for less-educated women who undergo voluntary sterilization in order to control the growth of their families and other incentives for edu-cated women who had large families. Among the incen-tives were free "love-boat" cruises to favor (like in Plato's festivals) the meeting of suitable males and spe-cial, higher-level education for their children.

A few years later (from 1988 until 1993) a few prov-inces in the People's Republic of China proposed and sometimes adopted old-style eugenic measures aimed at forbidding the marriage of people with a medical history of "undesirable" traits unless they first accepted sterilization. Apart from the charge of illiberalness, these measures have been criticized as inconsistent and ambiguous (for example, they lumped together genetic diseases, mental illness, hepatitis, and so on as counter-indications to marriage) even from a genuine eugenics point of view (see the editorial, 1994, January). China's misconception of eugenics. *Nature*, 367, 6, p. 1).

II. CONCEPTUAL AND SCIENTIFIC ASPECTS

A. Types, Levels, and Techniques of Eugenics

Before discussing the moral problems associated with the issue of eugenics and in order to focus them ade-quately, it is important to point out some features and distinctions mentioned so far that form what can be called the conceptual structure of eugenics.

To begin with, it is common to distinguish between negative and positive eugenics. Negative eugenics pur-sues good effects by lowering or eliminating unwanted characteristics from a population. Positive eugenics pursues its effects by trying to increase the frequency of desirable traits in a population. This distinction presupposes the rather problematic identification of desirable and undesirable traits; but before discussing

this troubling issue, we mention a more recent distinc-tion drawn between macro- and microeugenics that depends both on the size of the projects and on their final goal.

Macroeugenic projects are expressly aimed at ob-taining changes over several generations and seek the amelioration of the human species as a whole. Such projects emphasize the interests of the species (i.e., of future generations), giving them preeminence over the interests of individuals (and of the present generation). On the other hand, we speak of microeugenic projects in relation to practices that affect small groups and sometimes families. The goal is to benefit individuals, while the potential impact of these practices on the level of species is neither intended nor desired.

Although the proper meaning in which we should use the word eugenics is the first one, the distinction between macro- and micro- (sometimes also called home-made) eugenics stresses an important feature of the current debate. Because it is now very unlikely that a large-scale eugenics project will be launched, many hold that eugenic purposes might pass through other limited and (apparently) innocent programs aimed at preventing genetic maladies by relying on the individual free choice of the parents. From the wish to have "healthy children" to the wish to have children with certain desirable qualities (the dream of the "perfect child") the distance is short and the programs of *in-vitro* fertilization plus the prospective pre-embryo gene surgery promise to make it even shorter. So people became used to the idea of amelioration of the genome and in a more-or-less distant future might be prepared to accept a macroeugenic project.

Finally, until a few decades ago the technique avail-able for eugenic projects involved controversial forms of control of human reproduction: discouraging "unfit" matings and favoring the "fittest" ones, sterilization of the unfit, and so on. Recently they have taken advantage of the advent of genetic counseling and screening, and selective abortion or selective forms of assisted procre-ation. We may define as "indirect or environmental" these techniques, distinguishing them from those that can be called "direct" because they operate directly on the unit of heredity, the genes: these include somatic gene therapy (SGT) and germ-line gene therapy (GLGT). Briefly, SGT is the attempt to introduce a properly functioning gene into the somatic cells, that is, into the cells of the body, with the hope that the added gene will compensate for a malfunctioning one. GLGT requires the insertion of the gene into the repro-ductive cells or into the genome of an early pre-embryo before cell differentiation. In this case there will be a change in the individual and this modification will pass to the progeny.

It is difficult to say if and when these techniques will be practically available: there are many difficult technical problems to be solved, associated with the correct integration of the modified or even new gene in the genome and with the control and regulation of its expression over several generations. These technical problems are even more complicated in the case of polygenic traits, that is, phenotypical complex traits—a favorite target of positive eugenics—whose genetic component is controlled by a cluster of genes interacting in ways that are still unknown.

B. Desirable and Undesirable Traits

As mentioned above, the starting point of any strategy aimed at obtaining eugenic effects is the possibility to individuate wanted and unwanted characteristics. What counts as a "desirable " or an "undesirable" characteristic in human beings varies by time and place and this, of course, raises the problem of who should make the decision (whether the scientists, society as a whole, the parents, etc.). Historically, eugenics dealt with this issue by stressing somatic and behavioral traits possessed by celebrated individuals (for desirable traits) or by individuals from lower social classes (for undesirable traits), and then trying to individuate the hereditary patterns of each trait through family studies. We have seen that these studies were scientifically controversial and that they were often biased by class and race prejudices or, at least, by a questionable anthropology. Developments in biology and a deeper understanding of the biochemical basis of heredity weakened most of the results of this research, but it did not make easier the task of identifying what sorts of desirable or undesirable traits are suitable candidates for eugenic interventions. These are interventions that, by definition, must be beneficial to mankind over generations and statistically significant at the population level. This is particularly true for undesirable traits, which are the target of negative eugenics.

C. Undesirable Traits

Today, such traits mainly coincide with serious hereditary diseases or abnormalities, or with mental disorders that are thought to be genetically determined. Biological research has identified many genes that cause abnormalities or disorders; population genetics, especially its most recent branch, genetic epidemiology, allows us to identify the frequency of these genes and to study their dynamics in a targeted population. Therefore, it seems easy to identify the target of negative eugenic intervention, that is, the so-called "harmful genes." Nevertheless, the concept of harmful gene is scientifically questionable. When we speak of a gene as harmful, we do so because its malfunctioning causes the carrier a harmful or lethal effect. The problem is that we do not know if this gene, in addition to the known harmful effect we want to eliminate, has other positive effects. These might be manifested alone (because of the property called pleiotropy, i.e., the capacity of a gene to influence different traits) or through the interaction with the expression of other genes. On this subject—commenting on the results of the researches carried out by the Centre d'Etude du Polymorphisme Humaine in Paris—a recent editorial in *Nature* (1994, More Fuss about Genetics and Embryo, 367:99–100) warns against defining a gene as harmful because of its known harmful effect and calls for caution in trying to eliminate it. At present we know very little about the mechanisms of genetic expression and we cannot rule out that attempts to "clean up" the genome of the so-called "harmful genes" might have adverse results, including the loss of important adaptive advantages in the human species. More generally, this issue is related to the preservation of genetic diversity, or the presence of different forms of the same gene in mankind's gene pool. Genetic diversity is thought of as a crucial evolutionary resource, because it favors the adaptability of the species to environmental changes. Many think that incautious and massive interventions on the gene pool might cause a reduction of genetic diversity, weakening the adaptive capability of the species. As we are not able to establish the possible future value of what we lose today, we risk depriving future generations of a crucial evolutive resource. Of course, harmful genes do cause suffering and death in affected individuals and therefore we have to decide whether their interests or those of the species should have preeminence. As we will see, this morally puzzles both those who are in favor of eugenics and those who are against it; but now let us focus on some conceptual aspects of negative eugenics.

D. Negative Eugenics

Negative eugenics is often called "preventive," because it is strictly linked to various forms of preventive medicine aimed at avoiding the diffusion of genetic defects. This generates many moral problems, among which perhaps the least important, from a scientific point of view, is the risk, if any, that health preventive policies might turn out to be "old style" eugenics.

At macroeugenic level, the selection of undesirable traits is very slow. As noted, "in terms of human life, allowing 30 years for one generation, it would take 50 generations, i.e., 1500 years, to reduce the frequency of a harmful recessive gene from 0.02 to 0.01, provided every affected individual in every generation is sterilized before reaching reproductive age "(Szebenyi A. L. (1972), Reflection of a biologist. *Theological Studies,* 33:455).

Under less ideal conditions the process of selection would be even slower: for example, if the program is (as it should be today) voluntary; the initial gene frequency is less than 0.02; more than one pair of genes are involved in the production of the disorder; and lastly, if we take into account the fresh mutations that occur at every generation.

Therefore, the eugenic effects that one can expect (or fear) from negative macro-eugenic projects are very modest and so far into the future that it is difficult to imagine how the initial conditions could be maintained through the centuries. Perhaps we have to think (as Galton did) of a new religion, with a priestly caste responsible for such a program.

A microlevel (families or small groups), on the contrary, negative eugenic effects are more evident and can be certified scientifically. Such effects are the outcome of programs of genetic counseling for couples at risk for giving birth to children with genetic defects and of massive programs of genetic screening for common and severe recessive diseases that are being carried out in many parts of the world. For example, the program of genetic screening for Tay-Sachs disease, which is a genetic condition diffused among Jews in the United States and Canada, that has been conducted since the early 1970s, allowed a remarkable reduction (about 90%) in the frequency of the disease. In Sardinia (Italy) a screening program for B-Talassemia healthy carriers gave similar results. In recent years, thanks to the rapid advances in genetics and its technological applications, there has been a dramatic increase in the ability to test for a wide range of genetic conditions as well as for presymptomatic diseases and disease susceptibility. This capability is increasing and it should reach its peak with the Human Genome Project, allowing complete localization of about 50,000 to 100,000 genes.

It is important to note that the decrease in morbidity and mortality due to infective or parasitic diseases corresponds to an increase in morbidity and mortality due to genetic conditions. Given the social costs (economic as well as human) of taking care of such (genetic) patients, it is likely that the attention toward health policies of preventive medicine will increase as well.

E. Desirable Traits and Positive Eugenics

Moving now to positive eugenics (also called "progressive"), we have to remark that this is the most controversial form as far as morality is concerned, but also the most difficult to achieve. In this case the problem is not so much identifying desirable traits as knowing if we have suitable means to improve them. Let us consider the classical case of intelligence, which appears invariably among the desirable traits in the lists prepared by proponents of eugenic projects. As with all phenotypical complex traits, intelligence (not considering the problem of defining and measuring it) is influenced by the interaction between genes and the environment. The debate on how much of individual variation in a population depends on genes and how much depends on environment, has accompanied the development of eugenics from the beginning. This also has to do with potential social implications in the field of educational policies. At the end of the 1960s, the issue again became a very topical question with an article by the psychologist Arthur R. Jensen (1969. How much can we boost IQ and scholastic achievement? *Harvard Educational Review,* 33:1–123). Jensen was referring to the research carried out between 1943 and 1966 by the English psychologist Cyril Burt on identical twins who were separated and grew up in different environments. These studies seemed to confirm the idea of the strong hereditary nature of intelligence, but methodologies used in collecting empirical data were quite inadequate (sometimes even fraudulent; see Rose S., Lewontin R. C., Kamin L. J. (1984). *Not in our genes. Biology, ideology and human nature,* London: Penguin Books). Recently, the controversy reemerged with the publication of Richard J. Herrnstein and Charles Murray's book, *The Bell Curve: Intelligence and Class Structure in American Life* (1994. New York: Free Press). But, despite the impressive quantity of empirical data now available after a century of research, the controversy on the relative importance of the genetic component is still far from being solved scientifically.

Nevertheless, for the sake of our topic, let us set aside the age-old dispute, nature/nurture, and follow Jonathan Glover's suggestion that "we need take no stand on the relative importance or unimportance of genetic factors in the explanation of the present range of individual differences found in people. We need only the minimal assumption that different genes could give us different characteristics" (1984. *What sort of people should there be*, p. 26. Harmondsworth: Penguin Books). The problem of how to improve the genetic component of a desirable characteristic remains. The traditional way of reaching positive eugenic goals, which consists of favoring suitable matings, affects a private domain that, as Plato already envisaged, people wish to protect from external influences. To be effective, a eugenics program in this field should be strongly compulsory and, therefore, it would have a very small chance of being implemented. On the other hand, the likelihood of achieving eugenic effects (i.e., effects on a population level) in this way, on a voluntary basis, is scientifically even lower than in negative eugenics. Under this condition, even the prospective eugenic application of genetic engineering seems no more promising. We should still consider the fact that the desired presence of a trait in the offspring (also of genetically modified individuals) is uncertain because of the unpredictable processes of segregation and recombination that are typical of sexual reproduction. It is not true that intelligent (or idiot) parents necessarily give birth to intelligent (or idiot) children.

To avoid such an unfortunate circumstance, in 1966 the geneticist Joshua Lederberg (Experimental genetics and human evolution. *American Naturalist*, 100:519–526) suggested a new eugenic technique, cloning, which consists of the substitution of the nucleus of a fertilized ovum for the nucleus of a somatic cell of an adult. The new individual will have the identical genetic constitution of the donor and should show the same phenotypical qualities. Nevertheless, apart from the problem of who should decide what sort of people should be cloned, the eugenic effectiveness of cloning is doubtful. It is not always true that individuals with identical genotypes have identical phenotypes. The genes of the organism determine the potential realization of its characteristics. During the development (including embryonic development), this potential capacity is influenced by interaction with other genes and the environment so that an identical environment including an identical intrauterine environment would be necessary to develop a second identical organism. It is difficult to imagine how this could be done.

III. ETHICAL ISSUES

A. Focusing the Moral Problem

As mentioned above, in the current debate the issue of eugenics is raised mainly as an argument to criticize medical practices or technologies that seem to be morally controversial. Labelling them as eugenic means transferring to them the moral repugnance aroused by the association with Nazi crimes and, more generally,

with the authoritarian, illiberal, and discriminatory feature associated with (and perhaps essential to) every macroeugenic project.

If that were the whole story, the issue of eugenics could be still the subject of historical and sociological inquiry or it could enlighten certain aspects regarding the social conditioning of science, but from the moral point of view it alone would not have great interest. It would be enough to demonstrate that today no one believes to be either desirable or possible an "old style," illiberal, and authoritarian eugenic project. Moreover, it is difficult to imagine how such a project could be implemented practically at the present time. In affluent Western societies, endowed with both technologies and resources, there are difficulties concerning the creation of political conditions for such projects. From a conceptual point of view, moreover, eugenic programs can be thought of as being universal in nature and they can be articulated without any exclusivist, class, or race categorization, while their implementation would be respectful of individual rights and liberties.

But not even this is the whole story. Even if it were free of its historically repugnant traits, the concept of eugenics contains the idea of modification of the genetic composition of the human species. The question is whether it is right or wrong (or wise or unwise) to undertake such a modification, given that we are really doing this through several practices. This seems to be the most basic question underlying the issue of eugenics as a whole. Answers vary in relation to the type and the level of interventions, but all of them have to do with our obligations toward future generations. There is wide agreement upon the responsibility toward the genetic composition of future generations, but there are varied opinions about what sort of actions this responsibility includes or excludes.

B. Obligations Toward Future Generations

The moral soundness of eugenics-like policies depends to a large extent on the existence of an obligation to protect and/or to improve the genetic composition of the human species, as part of the obligations that each generation has toward future ones. A classical formulation of this obligation can be found in John Rawls: "In the original position, then, the parties want to insure for their descendents the best genetic endowment (assuming their own to be fixed). The pursuit of reasonable policies in this regard is something that earlier generations owe to later ones, this being a question that arises between generations. Thus over time a society is to take steps at least to preserve the general level of natural abilities and to prevent the diffusion of serious defects" (1971. *A theory of justice*, p. 108. Cambridge, MA: The Belknap Press of Harvard University Press).

Although it is not at all clear, Rawls seems to endorse both negative and positive eugenics, commonly grounded in principle of nonmaleficence and beneficence, respectively. From those principles we can derive different argumentative strategies in favor of eugenics-like programs, according to the weight and the extension assigned to them.

There is extensive agreement upon the obligatory strength of the traditional medical as well as the general moral rule to "do no harm," and perhaps less forcefully, "do not fail to prevent harm." Many authors hold that this rule might be the foundation of an ethics of genetic control with preventive purposes even independently of its negative eugenic effects. More controversial are the implications of the principle of beneficence: as this principle's obligatory force seems to be weaker than in the case of nonmaleficence, many of us maintain that the improvement of the human gene pool is not a moral requirement, although this does not mean that it is morally impermissible. Further difficulties derive from uncertainty about the threshold between prevention and amelioration.

C. Negative Eugenics as Preventive Medicine

Preventive medicine today relies on most of the means from which negative eugenic effects are expected. The application of such means in programs of genetic counseling or genetic screening brings about important results in preventing serious hereditary diseases that may affect certain families or limited and identifiable populations. There is no doubt that the application of genetic diagnostic technologies has an effect on the genetic composition of future generations. Nevertheless, even though these technologies raise specific moral issues—regarding, for example, the morality of abortion, problems of violation of privacy, or of justice in the allocation of resources—the mere fact that they have effects labeled as eugenic should not advise against their use. Many people think that it is unjustified to say that the mere taint of possible eugenic effects might be a reason not to fight against serious diseases that cause suffering, disability, or premature death. This is a form of "inescapable eugenics."

In reference to this, a problem associated with eugenics, the discriminatory effects of such practices, is often raised. The idea is that any identification of genetic conditions to be avoided by preventive means presupposes the concept of "genetic normalcy," so labeling as "abnormal" those whose genome departs from the average. According to this view, individuals born with genetic defects would be exposed to the risk of being considered second-class human beings. This might involve a progressive erosion of benevolent attitudes toward such unlucky individuals, because an increase in our capacity for early identification and prevention of genetic defects could expand social reluctance to invest financial resources in order to deal with avoidable conditions.

Many say that it would be unwise to underestimate such a risk in societies where discrimination still exists. Nevertheless, others observe that this risk—if it exists at all—should lead us to a stronger ban on any form of social discrimination, being in itself insufficient reason for failing to prevent the birth of handicapped people.

Other problems may arise from the potential to prevent some adverse genetic conditions not simply by trying to prevent the birth of these carriers, but by trying to correct such genetic defects through gene therapy. Such a solution is considered less controversial from the moral point of view because it does not involve selective abortion nor does it recommend the assisted procreation for healthy carriers of hereditary defects. Let us begin with a short examination of the main problems of somatic gene therapy.

D. Somatic Gene Therapy and Future Generations

Generally speaking, SGT is the equivalent of standard therapies substituting bodily parts including blood transfusions and transplants. Therefore, moral norms ruling such medical therapies are extended to this case. The equivalence is strengthened by the fact that the introduced modification (which may be corrective, but also ameliorative) affects only the individual subjected to medical treatment and is not passed on to progeny. Nevertheless, it is evident that SGT, like traditional medical therapies for genetic conditions (e.g., diet for a condition known as phenylketonuria), constitutes a manipulation of the genetic composition of future generations: it enables individuals to reproduce and therefore to transmit their genetic defects to offspring. It seems that an intergenerational conflict arises between the obligation, on grounds of benevolence, to cure people as best as we can and the obligation, on grounds of nonmalevolence, to avoid worsening the genetic patrimony. As a rule, the obligation of nonmalevolence is thought of as being stronger than the obligation of benevolence, but in this case the opposite opinion seems to prevail. In any case, there are two ways to avoid the conflict. The first is to pose restrictions on the reproductive activities of persons who have access to SGT or to traditional therapies for genetic conditions, hoping to minimize the disgenic trend. It is difficult to imagine how this could be implemented without turning to odious compulsory means such as precautionary sterilization.

The second way to reconcile the interests of current and future generations is at present only theoretical: the germ-line gene therapy, by which—when and if it becomes available—individuals as well as future generations will be cured. But it is just this form of intervention that generates major problems. Many of us think that there are strong reasons to suppose that use of this technology will not be restricted to purely medical uses. This technology will be applied also to other goals, both in order to justify the enormous cost of its development, and because it would be unreasonable not to use all the new potentialities it makes available.

E. GLGT, Eugenics, and Future Generations

"Once we decide to begin with the process of human genetic engineering, there is really no logical place to stop. If diabetes, sickle-cell anemia, and cancer are to be cured by altering the genetic makeup of an individual, why not proceed to other 'disorders': myopia, color blindness, left-handedness? Indeed, what is to preclude a society from deciding that a certain skin color is a disorder?" Jeremy Rifkin is one of the first and fiercest opponents of genetic engineering, and in this well-known passage he points out the difficulty of drawing a clear-cut line between therapy, amelioration, and eugenics.

On this issue (where and how to draw a line in order to avoid eugenic risks) currently there are several different opinions, which basically go back to three fundamental positions.

The first maintains that it is possible to draw a line between therapeutical and ameliorative/eugenic purposes, pointing to the difference between remedying a recognized genetic defect and aiming at improving a "normal" person: by therapy we try to rid future individuals of illnesses, by improving we decide what sort of people there should be. It is worth noticing that the authors who hold this position are worried by the possibility that negative attitudes associated with eugenics might discredit future developments in biomedical research, generating visceral reactions that lead to the loss of important prospective benefits for mankind.

Such a position resorts to a narrow conception of therapy and, in order to exorcise the ghost of eugenics, it seems to exclude any other use of GLGT, even in the preventive and protective sense. However, if the sole purpose of GLGT must be the strictly therapeutical one, we should ask if it is cost effective to invest financial resources in the development of this technology. After all, if our purpose is only to avoid the diffusion of genetic diseases, we might boost programs of genetic screening followed by abortion. It is true that the availability of GLGT would increase the reproductive options of couples at risk, but the current opinion is that this would be too little to justify the investment.

The second position holds that the line to be drawn in order to avoid any eugenic aim should not necessarily exclude any ameliorative purpose. For example, W. French Anderson considers as ethically acceptable, under very specific conditions, what he defines as "enhancement genetic engineering," that is, the attempt to enhance some known characteristics on grounds of preventive medicine (e.g., an additional growth hormone gene or an additional LDL receptor gene to prevent atherosclerosis). Anderson also suggests identifying as "eugenic genetic engineering" any attempt to alter complex polygenic traits such as personality, intelligence, formations of body organs, and so on. He considers it to be both scientifically implausible and ethically unacceptable to do so.

Finally, holders of the third position—while taking note of the present technically limited malleability of complex traits via genetic engineering—do not exclude the ethical acceptability of ameliorative modification, if possible and safe, of traits of personality (e.g., aggressiveness) as well as of intellectual traits. They observe, for example, that we already try to enhance intellectual performance by offering the best educational opportunities to our children and that there is nothing special in trying to do something similar through genetic engineering. Of course, this possibility gives rise to several social problems that could have a heavy social fallout. For example, we might foresee that the good "ameliorative genetic modifications" will likely be rare and limited so that only the upper classes of rich countries will have access to them. This will increase social inequality and widen the gap between the developed and underdeveloped parts of the world. Nevertheless, some think that this kind of problem will not be radically different from those we already face in our societies: not all of us can have access to the exclusive school Eton, but the worst way to solve the problem would be to close Eton.

Holders of this position certainly refuse eugenics as developed in the first part of this century, but they think that it would be wrong not to use what science offers to pursue the old dream of the improvement of mankind. However, some recognize that the obligation, on grounds of beneficence, to improve the human race via genetic engineering could be overridden by real-world considerations (e.g., the scarcity of resources and the priority of other programs). On the contrary, some hold that our generation has the moral obligation to assign a "high priority" to financial investments for a long-term project of genetic improvement of the human race. Why would it be wrong if we can arrange to do that within the framework of the principles of justice and with respect for individual rights and liberties typical of Western societies, on a voluntary basis and without discrimination toward individuals or social groups? According to many, even in these ideal conditions, it would still be wrong to tamper with the human genome, because this represents an arrogant interference with God's design or, in secular form, with the order of nature.

F. Playing God

The very popular expression "playing God" represents a cluster of ideas that have to do with anxiety and fears generated by the awareness that men are on the way to reaching the core of the great mystery of the construction of life. Once this is obtained, they will be tempted to extend the technological manipulatory power from exterior to the interior nature of man, which should be kept out of our reach. This seems to be an arrogant usurpation of God's power, all the more deplorable because we do not possess God's wisdom and omniscience. According to such a view, the genetic constitution of human beings is supposed to be dependent on a divine project: because God has manifested a special predilection toward our species, it would be in a sense sacrilegious to modify its internal constitution or even to create a new one.

However, some observe that this "hands-off" conception is founded on a traditional and static vision of God's creative design, which is no longer universally agreed upon in Christian theology. The human race, created in the image of God, participates in his creative power: in this sense, man is a created co-creator and this suggests that attempts to improve human genetic constitution could be considered as exercising a power conferred upon us by God himself.

G. Playing Nature

The secular version of the argument against "playing God" begins with the idea that our attempts to introduce modifications that have not been submitted to natural selection into the genetic pool of our species might have unpredictable consequences. Such an attempt seems to be imbued with a benevolent attitude, but on closer inspection, eugenic genetic engineering results in an arrogant and unwise interference with the natural processes that have required millions of years. The outome is the risk of deteriorating genetic conditions that might cause the extinction of our species. Bearing this radical risk in mind, no matter how small its probability, the principle of nonmaleficence obliges us to abstain from tampering with the human genome, or rather with the genome of any living being, and to stop research in this field.

From the moral point of view it is not clear how far this objection can impose abstension in order to protect the interests of future generations. This position seems to assume that such interests lie mainly in the preservation of the genetic status quo, with its ups and downs (that is, with its present genetic load) and no in its improvement. If we hold that any intervention can have unpredictable consequences on the genetic status quo, then we have to ban any form of GLGT, including the therapeutic one. Such a form would be certainly more dangerous than the ameliorative one. In fact, by adding new information to the genome we simply do not know what sort of consequences this might have in the future, because we have not yet solved the highly complicated problems of the correct integration and expression of the new or modified gene. Therapeutical GLGT, on the contrary, operates by eliminating (harmful) genetic information. We know that such interference with genetic diversity is harmful because, as mentioned above, genetic diversity is essential for the future adaptation of the species. But this is not the whole story: abstention from the therapeutical use of GLGT is not enough! As we said earlier, we negatively modify the genetic status quo by means of therapeutic SGT and also by traditional medical therapies for genetic conditions. It is difficult to believe that the interests of future generations can override the medical imperative to cure people of illnesses by any means possible. This is a position that few are prepared to endorse.

IV. CONCLUSION

In the strict sense eugenics is now a marginal question in the ethical discussion concerning the fascinating and worrying pespectives opened by genetic engineering. If in the future human beings have the ability to change their nature, then society will have to face this. We must decide whether or not to allow this practice and the sorts of changes that should be permitted. In the current debate it is clear that no one understands eugenics in the historical meaning of the word. Even those who conjure up the nightmare of eugenics seem to be worried about alleged catastrophic consequences that might result from an unwise use of our capacity to manipulate the human genome. This illustrates the heart of the concern surrounding eugenics.

These worries derive mostly from the "defensive ethics" holding that innocence is the equivalent of abstention when we have to face a new problem presented by technology, where unpredictable consequences are themselves judged to be negative or even catastrophic. However, such an assumption is not always true: many observe that if we cannot foresee all the consequences of our actions, we cannot foresee all the consequences of our inaction either. This is the age-old dilemma of being damned if you do and damned if you don't. This remark by itself does not justify launching programs of eugenic genetic engineering; nevertheless, it weakens a "hands-off" policy and it might justify a cautious "open-door" policy in this controversial field.

Also See the Following Articles

DARWINISM • GENE THERAPY • GENETIC ENGINEERING • GENETIC SCREENING • NATURE VERSUS NURTURE • PLATONISM • PLAYING GOD • PREVENTIVE MEDICINE • SPECIESISM

Bibliography

Adams, M. B. (1990). *The well-born science: Eugenics in Germany, France, Brasil and Russia.* New York: Oxford University Press.

Chadwick, R. F. (Ed.). (1987). *Ehtics, reproduction and genetic control.* London: Routledge.

Duster, T. (1990). *Backdoor to eugenics.* New York: Routledge.

Harris, J. (1993). Is gene therapy a form of eugenics? *Bioethics,* 7:179–187.

Juengst, E. T. (Ed.). (1991). Germ-line gene therapy: Back to basics. *Journal of Medicine and Philosophy, 16.* (Special issue).

Kevles D. J. (1985). *In the name of eugenics: Genetics and the use of human heredity.* Berkeley and Los Angeles: University of California Press.

Kevles, D. J., & Hood L. (1992). *The codes of codes: Scientific and social issues in the human genome project.* Cambridge, MA: Harvard University Press.

Kitcher Ph. (1996). *The lives to come. The genetic revolution and human possibilities,* New York: Simon & Schuster.

Ledley F. D. (1994). Distinguish genetics and eugenics on the basis of fairness. *Journal of Medical Ethics,* 20:157–164.

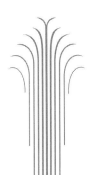

EUTHANASIA

Heather Draper
University of Birmingham

GLOSSARY

advanced directives Documents that state in advance the treatments that people want or do not want if they are incompetent when clinical management is decided. They usually refer to decisions such as not being artifically fed in PVS, or resuscitated or ventilated under certain circumstances.

Cardiopulmonary resuscitation Combined cardiac massage (compressing the heart, which may be achieved by pressing on and off the chest) and artificial ventilation/oxygenation of the lungs (which may be achieved by the "kiss of life" or intubation and mechanical ventilation). Drugs may also be given to maximize the chances of restoring spontaneous heart beat.

Persistent vegetative state (PVS) An extreme form of damage to the upper brain that does not extend to the brain stem. Physicians are generally reluctant to diagnose PVS until a patient has been deeply unconscious for at least 1 year. Where an accurate diagnosis is made, the patient will never regain consciousness; indeed, the upper brain may completely and irreversibly disintegrate. Patients in PVS usually breath without assistance, but they may have to be tube fed, they may exhibit sleep/wake patterns but they are never aware, and they may live for many years—even decades.

EUTHANASIA is sometimes considered a manifestation of autonomy and the control of one's destiny, and at other times it is associated with the failure to provide adequate palliative care for the terminally ill and dying. It brings into focus discussions about the quality and the value of life, and the rightness and wrongness of killing. It is argued that euthanasia is a legitimate barrier against a slippery slope to intrusive medical intervention in dying, and conversely it is argued that to legitimize euthanasia is to begin a slide into the killing of other vulnerable members of society. Some believe that euthanasia is an acceptable expression of the clinical imperative to act always in the interests of patients, and others believe that it is never acceptable for clinicians to take a patient's life. Few debates in health-care ethics result in such polarization of opinion as euthanasia, and few things worry patients more than being left to die in agony or being killed against their wishes by those caring for them.

I. DEFINING EUTHANASIA

Before beginning to discuss the ethical arguments for and against the practice of euthanasia, it is important to understand what euthanasia is. No one disputes the fact that euthanasia is a form of killing; so too are murder, manslaughter, suicide, capital punishment, and war. To state that each is a form of killing warns us to proceed with care, but it need not be decisive in determining the rightness or wrongness of the act. We need, therefore, to address the question of what it is about euthanasia that distinguishes it from, or places it in a separate category to, say, self-killing or murder. We also need to be familiar with different categories of euthanasia—primarily the difference between active and passive euthanasia, and between voluntary and nonvoluntary euthanasia—and we need to be clear about whether these distinctions are merely semantic or of moral relevance.

A. What Is Euthanasia?

Euthanasia is often defined simply as a gentle and easy death. This is not an adequate description for one might die peacefully in one's sleep, thereby having a gentle and easy death. Euthanasia is also the act of bringing about a gentle and easy death, and if it is to be distinguished from self-killing, this bringing about must be done by one person to another. It is, however, not difficult to imagine a premeditated killing that uses gentle and easy means but that is performed solely for material gain. We would want to describe such a killing as a murder and not a euthanasia. Likewise, it is possible to imagine a gentle and easy death that is caused accidentally perhaps due to a genuine miscalculation of a dose of morphine by an inexperienced doctor or a medically unqualified relative. Here, negligence or manslaughter might be more a appropriate description. Set against such examples, it becomes clear that euthanasia is the deliberate causing of death—the intention is to kill—but the motive is of paramount importance. Indeed, the motive forms a crucial part of arguments used to justify euthanasia, because it must be motivated solely by considerations for the best interests of the person on the receiving end.

Euthanasia must be defined as death that results from the intention of one person to kill another person, using the most gentle and easy means possible, that is motivated solely by the best interests of the person who dies (see Table 1). This definition also makes clear that the person giving euthanasia causes the death. To be held morally responsible for something, one has to have

TABLE 1

Components of Euthanasia, All of Which Must Be Present

Agent and subject	Euthanasia is given by one person to another
Intention of the agent	To bring about the death of the subject
Motive of the agent	*Solely* that of the best interests of the subject
Causal proximity	What the agent does or chooses not to do causes the subject's death
Outcome	The subject dies

a hand in causing it to happen, but, as we shall see, simply to be causally responsible for something does not necessarily imply moral responsibility.

Even a momentary thought about euthanasia being in someone's best interests suggests that it is not something that fit and well people might need. Rather, it is associated with a poor quality of life or with imminent death. A distinction is sometimes drawn between mercy killing and euthanasia, where mercy killing is undertaken by a close relative or friend, and euthanasia is performed by a doctor, a nurse, or another person professionally charged with the care of a patient. Most of our discussion concerns the euthanasia of patients by professional carers.

B. Voluntary and Nonvoluntary Distinction

1. The Distinction

The distinction between voluntary and nonvoluntary euthanasia turns on the capacity of the patient to give her consent—her competence to make her own decisions. Voluntary euthanasia occurs when the patient consents and nonvoluntary euthanasia occurs when the patient is incapable of giving her consent.

In order to consent, a patient has to be given all the necessary information, she must be free from coercion, and she must be able to understand the information, its relevance, and its implications for herself. Consent is held to be the clearest expression of a patient's autonomy in the caring relationship so that nothing should be done to a patient without her consent or against her express refusal of consent. The obligation to respect consent is a legally binding one. A patient is wronged when she has the capacity to act autonomously—when she is competent—but is denied the opportunity to do so. Disrespect for consent may involve deliberately withholding information or misinforming the patient—lying to her even—or putting her under pressure to agree to a particular course of action. This might be done perhaps by threatening to withhold other therapies or even basic sympathy, or by failing even to consult her or simply to overrule her decision. In these instances, a therapy is administered involuntarily. In the case of euthanasia this would amount to involuntary euthanasia, which would probably be better described as murder. Voluntary euthanasia occurs, then, when the patient is competent to request it, or to agree to it, having taken account of all the relevant information. The patient must be free to refuse it if she so chooses.

Nonvoluntary euthanasia occurs when the patient is incompetent to make a decision for herself. It is dangerous to give categories of incompetent patients because competence is decision specific. This means that in order to decide upon a therapy, the patient does not need to be competent to make decisions in all departments of life, just the decision currently facing her. However, this accepted, it is clear that neonates, very young children, unconscious patients or patients in PVS (persistent vegetative state), patients in extreme pain, and patients with very severe learning problems will not be competent to decide for themselves whether euthanasia is or is not in their best interests. Making a decision to die requires a high degree of competence.

2. Is the Distinction between Voluntary and Nonvoluntary Euthanasia a Morally Relevant One?

It is argued that voluntary euthanasia enables patients to act upon their autonomous wish to die, based upon their decision that their life is so bad, for various reasons, that death is preferable to living. Permitting voluntary euthanasia, therefore, is seen as part of respecting a patient's autonomy. (This argument is outlined in detail in Section IV). Nonvoluntary euthanasia is performed upon those who are unable to make such a decision; it requires someone other than the patient to determine that death is preferable to life. Yet, when each of us is asked to state what would make life unbearable for us, we will each give roughly different circumstances, and consensus seems impossible. For this reason it is often held that while voluntary euthanasia is acceptable, nonvoluntary euthanasia is not. There are, however, several counterarguments to this view.

First, although the final decision is left to the patient in the case of voluntary euthanasia, in order to convince someone to perform the euthanasia, the patient must also convince him that she has a good reason to suppose that her life is not worth living. This implies that although no consensus would be reached about precisely when life in general would not be worth living, it is possible to reach some agreement on when life might

not be worth it for someone else, that is, to agree with someone that *her* life is not worth living from *her* point of view. This observation blurs the apparently clear moral distinction between voluntary and nonvoluntary euthanasia because both depend upon a second person's assessment of a person's quality of life. The patient's autonomy may be compromised by her inability to persuade a second person (her doctor, perhaps) that her life is not worth living. The second person effectively holds the veto, just as they do in nonvoluntary euthanasia.

Second, accepting voluntary euthanasia and not nonvoluntary euthanasia might also be regarded as extending a benefit to one group of patients that is not available to another group by virtue of their inability to request it. This seems to discriminate against incompetent patients in a way that would not be acceptable when considering other benefits.

Finally, respect for autonomy could be interpreted not in terms of giving patients euthanasia when they want it, but in terms of not giving them euthanasia when they do not want it. It would then be permissible to give euthanasia to an incompetent patient provided that one believes it to be in her interests because to do so would not violate her autonomy. By virtue of being incompetent, she has no autonomy.

3. The Difference between Active and Passive Euthanasia

The difference between active and passive euthanasia is essentially one of the means by which death is achieved. Active euthanasia involves doing something positive that will result in the patient's death: giving a lethal injection, for instance. Passive euthanasia involves not doing something, the absence of which results in the patient's death: not performing surgery, not giving antibiotics, not feeding, for instance.

4. Is the Difference between Active and Passive Euthanasia a Morally Relevant One?

It is sometimes argued that passive euthanasia is permissible whereas active euthanasia is not. The example that is most frequently cited to show how this belief works in practice is that of a baby that is born with Down's Syndrome and an intestinal blockage. Such a blockage is easily remedied; it requires a routine surgical procedure that would be performed without question on a baby who did not also have Down's Syndrome. Without the operation, a baby will die of starvation and dehydration, perhaps over several days. This is sometimes described as nature taking its course, as allowing the baby to die, rather than as the baby being killed.

While there are many occasions where the withdrawal of, or failure to initiate, therapy should not be counted as euthanasia (see Section II), it is now widely accepted that no moral distinction should be drawn between active and passive euthanasia. At least no moral distinction should be drawn that permits passive euthanasia and prohibits active euthanasia, or vice verse. Some writers argue that whenever a decision to start passive euthanasia is made, active euthanasia should be given because by definition euthanasia should be performed using the most gentle and easy means at one's disposal. Others argue that if one is opposed to active euthanasia, one must also resist the temptation to perform passive euthanasia.

James Rachels is now closely associated with the debunking of the distinction between active and passive euthanasia. (J. Rachels, 1986, "Active and Passive Euthanasia" in *Applied Ethics,* edited by P. Singer, OUP, Oxford, pp. 29–35.) He did this by dissecting euthanasia into its component parts and arguing that where the end result, intention, and motive are identical, the means by which the end is achieved is irrelevant (See Table 2). He also argued that the motive of acting in the patient's best interests can only be achieved by administering active euthanasia, because passive euthanasia extends the dying process and involves needless suffering for both the patient and for those who care for and are related to her. It does not, therefore, use the most gentle and easy means possible. Of course, this need not be the case. It might be possible to both allow a patient to die and to administer drugs that would ease the passing. It has been argued that where this is the case, allowing death to be a gradual process rather than an event might be preferred both by the patient and by those caring for her, in whatever capacity this care is given.

Ethical analysis of the varieties of reasons why a life-saving therapy might be omitted is now extremely

sophisticated—as we shall see. Many of the cases historically cited as examples of passive euthanasia have been comfortably accommodated within different models. The force of the argument in favor of passive euthanasia in the remaining cases is based on an understanding of the moral relevance of the distinction between acts and omissions in others circumstances where the distinction has initial intuitive appeal. For instance, if one ignores a drowning man, one is not to be held responsible for his death if one does not jump in and attempt a rescue. One would, however, be responsible for the death if one held him under the water until he drowned. The difference here, however, does not seem to be that one has no obligation to rescue whereas one does have an obligation not to murder. Rather, it turns on motive and intent. If one watched him drowning (confident that one could save him if one chose) as an opportunity to enjoy watching him die or even to film a "snuff movie," one's actions would be reprehensible even if one were not actually a killer. Likewise, one would be guilty of something—manslaughter, even—if one were the lifeguard on duty at the time. Motive is of vital importance here, for if euthanasia is to be justified at all, then its justification will rest in large measure on the motive for the action: namely, that one was acting in the best interests of the patients and that one's motive was therefore wholly benevolent.

II. OMISSIONS THAT ARE CONFUSED WITH PASSIVE EUTHANASIA

We have noted that withdrawal or withholding of therapy—even when this may lead to the death of the patient—is not always passive euthanasia. In passive euthanasia, the omission must be intended to cause the death of the patient and it must be motivated solely by the patient's best interests (because death is deemed preferable to living). Discussions about euthanasia are centered on beliefs about what makes life worth living or on the quality of life. There are other circumstances under which therapy is withheld or withdrawn: when it is futile, when it is likely to produce more harm then benefit, when it is withheld or withdrawn at the request of the patient, and when resources are scarce.

A. Futile Therapy

The term futility is derived from the Latin word *futilis,* which means leaky. This has its origins in Greek mythology, where the daughters of Daneaus were con-

TABLE 2

Rachels' Argument that Active and Passive Euthanasia Are Morally Equivalent

Active		Passive	
Agent and subject	Yes	Agent and subject	Yes
Intention (as Table I)	Yes	Intention (as Table 1)	Yes
Motive (as Table I)	Yes	Motive (as Table 1)	Yes
Causal proximity (as Table I)	Yes	Causal proximity (as Table I)	Yes
Outcome (as Table I)	Yes	Outcome (as Table 1)	Yes

demned to draw water in leaky vessels. A futile exercise is one that is doomed never to achieve its objective. One strong definition of futile therapy is that which cannot achieve even its physiological objective. A weaker definition might be therapy that is almost certain to fail, or that may succeed, but where its success will offer no improvement to the patient's underlying quality of life. Futile therapy is that which "has proved useless in the face of inevitable death" (Lamb, 1995, p. 19).

The strong definition is most straightforward in an ethical sense—although it may be difficult to determine in practice. Moral responsibility requires some causal link between one's actions or omissions and the outcome for which one is deemed responsible. Cause is a necessary though not sufficient prerequisite for moral responsibility. If it makes no difference to the outcome whether an action is performed or omitted, then the outcome is beyond the control of the agent and he cannot be held responsible for it. If a therapy will fail to achieve even its physiological objective, whether it is given, withdrawn, or withheld will make no difference to the outcome. This does not always mean that such a therapy should be withheld, but the reasons for giving it will lie beyond the physiological objective for which it was designed. For instance, once a patient is brain-stem dead, further ventilation is futile. It may, however, be continued in order to preserve body parts for transplantation.

The weaker definition of futile therapy lies more obviously on the border with euthanasia, unless the definition of underlying quality of life is clarified and tightened quite substantially. Operating on the intestinal blockage of a Down's Syndrome baby will not alter the underlying condition of Down's Syndrome. If the withholding or withdrawal of therapy on this weaker definition is to be distinguished from passive euthanasia, this underlying quality of life has to be defined in such a way that it goes beyond a subjective assessment that life is no longer worth living and it moves toward one that death—from a different or related cause—is fairly imminent. This weak definition of futility is often applied in the case of "do not attempt to resuscitate" orders on patients where CPR (cardiopulmonary resuscitation) would achieve its physiological objective of restoring the heart beat of a patient for whom death is imminent. Therapy would also be regarded as futile where death was inevitable—although perhaps not imminent—and where, in addition, the quality of the patient's life is in an irreversible decline. Under these circumstances it would seem futile to treat a patient for anything not directly related to her comfort and that

TABLE 3

Withholding/Withdrawing Futile Therapy

Agent and subject	Yes
Intention (as Table 1)	No, there is no intention that the patient will die (although death is foreseen)
Motive (as Table 1)	Yes
Causal proximity	No, if the therapy is futile then nothing which is given or withheld will alter the outcome
Outcome (as Table 1)	Yes

is not itself life threatening within the anticipated life expectancy for this patient. It does not much matter that a dying patient is addicted to morphine or has operable secondary tumours.

The argument from futility is strongest where the link between what is done, or is not done, and the death of the patient is weakest. Once some link is established, it stands in danger of collapsing into an argument for passive euthanasia. The withholding or withdrawl of futile therapy can be distinguished from passive euthanasia both in terms of the absence of the causal link and also because it does not turn on the judgement that it is in the best interests of the patient to die (see Table 3).

B. Where Therapy Causes More Harm Than Benefit

Lamb (1995, pp. 67–68) cites the case of a Mrs. R who had progressive liver failure, an accumulation of fluid in her peritoneal cavity, severe gastrointestinal bleeding, inflammation of the brain, and kidney failure. She weighed only about 45 kilograms. Her doctors said of her, "When we grab hold of her to turn her the skin comes off down to the middermis. When you move her you can feel her tiny brittle ribs coming in and out of their joints. My God! If we perform CPR on this poor woman we'll literally break her into pieces." CPR in this case is probably a good example of futile therapy in the sense that this woman was going to die soon anyway. However, her case also exemplifies the sense in which a therapy can have benefit in terms of extending life, but where the cost in terms of side effects outweighs the benefit. This is not a comment on the quality of her current existence; rather, it is a matter of looking at just how much worse off she would be if she receives CPR.

What distinguishes this kind of withdrawal or withholding from passive euthanasia is that it addresses not *whether* the patients should die, but *how* they should die. The argument against this kind of analysis is that it still supposes that death is preferable to life in these given circumstances. That is to say, Mrs. R—despite an increased burden of pain and suffering—would remain alive, and being alive is always better than being dead, and to determine otherwise is precisely what euthanasia is about. This is true, but it cuts at a tangent across this distinction that is not focused on the quality of life per se, but rather on what the doctor has a duty to do: namely to decide—on balance—which therapy is most appropriate, taking all things into account.

This difference can be illustrated with reference to two further examples. It is sometimes argued that patients in a PVS cannot benefit from tube feeding because tube feeding will not improve the underlying quality of life and because their current existence is of no benefit to them. It is not futile to feed them because the feeding achieves its physiological objective and death is not imminent. However, what is also clear is that the feeding does not impose a burden upon those in a PVS for precisely the same reasons as they are regarded as gaining no benefit from life—they are unable to experience *anything*. Moreover, it is not clear that the feeding is costly in terms of its side effects, which are no different than those experienced by patients who have recovered from strokes without regaining their swallowing reflex. For patients in a PVS, the decision about whether or not to feed is not being made on the basis of the harm that the feeding will produce, but rather on whether being in a PVS is a life worth having. Contrast this with the case of a child who has already had one unsuccessful multiple organ transplant of heart, lung, liver, stomach, and bowel: is it worth proceeding with another multiple transplantation with little prospect of success with all the attendant pain and discomfort that this will cause? Is it worth proceeding with aggressive surgery and chemotherapy—which may foreshorten life just as it may prolong it a litte— when the alternative is palliation and a period of good quality of life before death? To answer "no" to these questions is not to answer that the *life* is not worth having, but rather that the *therapy* is not worth having.

The difference between these cases and passive euthanasia turns on the doctor's intention at the time, which is not to cause the patient's death but to select the best therapy, under the circumstances, taking the benefits and burdens for the patient into account (see Table 4).

TABLE 4

Where Therapy Causes More Harm Than Benefit

Agent and subject	Yes
Intention (as Table 1)	No, the intention is to select the most appropriate therapy
Motive (as Table 1)	Yes
Causal proximity (as Table 1)	Yes
Outcome (as Table 1)	Yes

C. Where an Autonomous Patient Refuses to Consent to Therapy

The legal and ethical significance of consent has already been discussed. It is illegal and also unethical for a doctor to initiate or continue therapy against the competent wishes of his patient. Clearly, this assumes that the patient is indeed competent, and the fact that it is unethical to proceed does not absolve the doctor of the responsibility for ensuring that the patient is actually competent and understands the implications of her actions, or even from making his own concerns for her well-being clear.

Not all patients who refuse life-saving or prolonging therapy do so because they find life intolerable. The classic example here is that of Jehovah's Witnesses who refuse blood transfusions in the belief that it is against the will of God to proceed with them. Rather than embracing death, such patients may wish to live, and may even be praying for life. Other patients may not find life itself intolerable, but when asked to consider the burdens and benefits of the proposed therapy, they may decide that the therapy will not be tolerable. This does not mean that other patients do not find their life intolerable and refuse or withdraw from therapy in order to die.

The distinction between withholding and withdrawing therapy and passive euthanasia in any of these cases turns on the question of who is responsible for the outcome—the patient's death. Euthanasia is something that one person does to another. When a patient refuses consent to a life-saving procedure, while the doctor has some role in causing the patient's death (because what he does or does not do contributes to the cause of death to a greater or lesser degree, depending on the circumstances) it is not clear that it is he rather than his patient who is morally responsible. It is arguable that because the doctor is unable to act against the competent wishes of his patient, it is she rather than

TABLE 5

Patient Withholds Consent to Life Saving/Prolonging Therapy

Agent and subject	No, the patient is both subject and agent
Doctors intention	To respect the consent of the patient (i.e., not as in Table 1)
Doctor's motive	Yes, as in Table 1
Causal proximity (as in Table 1)	Yes, but the patient is the agent
Outcome (as Table 1)	Yes

TABLE 6

Where Resources Are Scarce

Agent and subject	Yes
Intention (as Table 1)	No, the doctor intends to reallocate resources
Motive (as Table 1)	No, the motive is to maximize resources or target them most effectively
Causal proximity (as Table 1)	Yes
Outcome (as Table 1)	Yes

he who is responsible for the outcome. This conforms with the widely held view that it is part of being autonomous to be responsible for the outcomes of our actions. This does not of course necessarily mean that a patient is to *blame,* any more than it can be said that a doctor who performs passive euthanasia is to blame. Allocating responsibility is only the first stage in passing a judgment about praise- or blameworthiness: further arguments are needed to establish the rightness or wrongness of action or omissions.

The distinction between refusal of consent and passive euthanasia plays on the difference between the intention of the doctor in each case. In the case of passive euthanasia, the doctor intends the patient's death; but when acting on the patient's competent wishes, his intention is to respect her autonomy (Table 5).

D. Where Resources Are Scarce

In the United Kingdom, we have become accustomed to hearing stories about patients who have died because they were unable to gain access—or sufficiently speedy access—to a therapy that would have saved their lives. This has been a particular problem in intensive care, where wards (sometimes called units) are typically small and sized according to estimated need over a year rather than maximum need at particular times of the year or in the event of some major incident. This gives rise to situations where a doctor may not be able to admit to the unit a patient who needs intensive care, or where he may have to consider withdrawing one patient in order to benefit a newcomer. In either case, a potentially life-saving therapy is withdrawn or withheld, which may result in the death of the patient.

This would not be an act of passive euthanasia provided that the decision to withdraw therapy was based solely on the desire to use the resources for another patient, or, in the case of withholding, because there was no resource to give. The doctor certainly does not

intend that the patient will die. If he does not have the resources to save the patient, then he cannot be held responsible, unless he is also responsible for the resource being in short supply. (see Table 6) This is not to say that the withholding of such therapy is therefore acceptable; on the contrary. But whatever condemnation is to be made cannot be made by arguing that euthanasia is wrong. Similarly, to argue that doctors should be able to target resources where they are most effective is not to argue for the permissibility of euthanasia.

A similar confusion occurs when doctors seek to withhold or withdraw therapy because they believe the emotional reserves of the patient's family have been, or soon will be, stretched to breaking point. This argument is based on killing and not on the interests of the patient, but it is based on the interests of the family. Therefore, it cannot be described as euthanasia (which must be performed to serve the patient's best interests) even if it is justified under some utilitarian calculation of harms and benefits.

III. ACTIONS THAT ARE CONFUSED WITH ACTIVE EUTHANASIA

In the previous section, a distinction was made between a variety of cases where therapy was withheld or withdrawn but that were not, it was argued, to be confused with passive euthanasia. Common to each of the examples was that the doctor had a different intention to that given in the definition of euthanasia defended in the first section. The correct identification of intent becomes even more significant in this section, where it will be argued that it is possible for a doctor to perform an action that he may foresee will end the life of the patient, but where his intention is solely the relief of pain. The death is the foreseen side effect of the action and it is not the intended consequence. The distinction being made in this section is based upon the credibility of the doctrine of double effect, which will be outlined and discussed shortly.

It is recognized that when caring for the terminally ill, over time the analgesics required for effective pain relief may begin to foreshorten the patient's life. Indeed, it is not uncommon for a point to be reached when one can be fairly certain that the next injection required to relieve the pain will also kill the patient. Likewise, strategies for relieving a patient of other distressing symptoms, such as breathlessness, may depend upon actually causing the patient to breath more shallowly. As their illness progresses this may mean that the patient is no longer able to breath enough to sustain herself, even when oxygen is supplied. Choices have to be made, therefore, between giving a drug that may kill the patient or allowing her to die in dreadful pain, and between the patient becoming distressed by fighting for every breath or suppressing breathing to the point where she may die as a result.

In cases such as these, it has been argued that even though the doctor causes the patient's death and he knew that he would, he is not morally responsible for the death, because the death is not intended. The resulting death cannot, therefore, be described as euthanasia because it was not intended. What was intended was the relief of pain or distress. This distinction appears irrelevant to those who believe that it is permissible to kill someone in order to prevent them from dying horribly. Such a view might be taken as a defense of euthanasia in such circumstances. The distinction is vital, however, for those who want to argue that it is not permissible to kill, even to bring about some good end. That is, it is vital for those who want to argue that euthanasia is not permissible.

The distinction draws heavily on the deontological view that moral responsibility is based upon what we intend—our policies for action—and not the consequences of our actions, as, for instance, utilitarianism is. This view has been formularized into the doctrine of double effect (DDE). This doctrine addresses circumstances where the known outcome of action would usually give a deontologist pause for thought, because it is so closely related to actions that are prohibited. The DDE is a set of four conditions, *all* of which must be met to ensure that the proposed action conforms with the wider deontological rules governing action. These are:

1. What is intended must be permissible.
2. What is intended must only be the good that is permissible, and not the bad effect.
3. The bad effect must not be the means by which the intended good is achieved.
4. The good that is intended must be in proportion to the bad effect that unavoidably follows from it.

To illustrate how the DDE works, it can be applied to two actions: the one outlined above, involving pain relief, and the other an active euthanasia justified on the grounds that the patient is in such pain that she is better off dead. In the United Kingdom, the latter is exemplified by the killing of Lillian Boyd by Dr. Cox, using potassium chloride. He believed that the only remedy for her pain was death.

It is unlikely that anyone appealing to the DDE will regard active euthanasia as permissible, so active euthanasia fails to satisfy the first condition. It fails the second condition because the death is intended, and it fails the third because the death is intended as the means whereby the pain of the patient is relieved. It may satisfy the fourth condition, for it could be argued that foreshortening a life about to end to prevent terrible pain is a good that is in proportion to the premature death.

The giving of pain relief in a dose necessary to relieve the pain of the patient, but that will also cause her death, passes the test because it satisfies all four conditions. What is intended is permissible. Not only is it permissible to relieve pain but doctors have, under ordinary circumstances, a duty so to do. The death is not also intended—a quick double check is that one would be relieved if, by chance, the patient survived. The death is not the means by which the pain is relieved, but the analgesics are. A quick but not infallible check here might be whether this is a drug that is normally used for the relief of pain. Finally, there is proportionality between the good and bad effects for the same reasons outlined in the case of active euthanasia.

This distinction is echoed in English law. In *R v Cox* (12 British Medical Law Review 38, 1992) it was made clear that it was a criminal offense for a doctor to kill a patient, even in order to prevent further suffering. By contrast, in *R v Adams* (Criminal Law Review 365, 1957), Devlin ruled that:

> If the first purpose of medicine, the restoration of health, can no longer be achieved there is still very much for a doctor to do, and he is entitled to do all that is proper and necessary to relieve pain and suffering, even if the measures he takes may incidentally shorten life.

The emphasis here should be on the *incidentally*. Euthanasia remains illegal in the United Kingdom, but caus-

TABLE 7

Pain Relief that Foreshortens Life

Agent and subject	Yes
Intention (as Table 1)	No, the doctor only intends to relieve pain, not to cause the patient's death
Motive (as Table 1)	Yes
Causal proximity (as Table 1)	Yes
Outcome (as Table 1)	Yes

ing death—even knowingly—is tolerated if it is an unavoidable side effect of otherwise sound clinical judgment.

The DDE is not accepted by all commentators on medical ethics nor by all moral philosophers. John Harris (1986, *The Value of Life,* London: RKP, 1986), for instance, considers that it is a kind of moral alchemy that enables deontologists to perform actions they would otherwise have to avoid. He considers that any event that satisfies the conditions laid down by the DDE could be redescribed, without changing the facts, so that the undesirable side effect becomes the main effect or even the means. Of proportionality, he says that if something is sufficiently good that it outweighs some bad effect, this alone is sufficient to justify action. Jonathan Glover (1977, *Causing Death and Saving Lives,* Middlesex, U.K.: Penguin) adds to these criticisms that it is impossible to divorce the foreseen from the intended.

Criticism of the DDE often comes, not surprisingly, from those who are committed to consequential resolutions to ethical problems. Undoubtedly, its sincere application by those who are not thus committed does enable important ethical distinctions to be drawn.

If the DDE is convincing, actions that involve killing a patient are permissible where all four conditions are satisfied. In which case, the relief of pain that incidentally ends a patient's life can be distinguished from active euthanasia. (see Table 7)

IV. ARGUING FOR THE PERMISSIBILITY OF EUTHANASIA

A. Respect for Autonomy and the Life Not Worth Living

Perhaps the strongest argument in favor of permitting euthanasia concerns only voluntary euthanasia, because it asserts that if there is one thing over which we should be able to exert absolute control, it is our own lives. If an individual decides that death is preferable to the life she currently has, then she should be free to end that life. If she is not in a position to end her life without help, it is not wrong for her to ask others for assistance to do so and it is not, therefore, wrong for them to give that assistance.

This argument rests on two contentious premises: that self-killing is an acceptable or permissible expression of autonomy, and that control over one's life can extend to requesting and receiving help in dying. In respect of the first, two counterclaims have been made: that self-killing is *never* an acceptable expression of autonomy, and that self-killing is not *always* an acceptable expression of autonomy. The first counterclaim may be based on the view that all killing is wrong, even the killing of the self; or it may assert that it is nonsense to use autonomy to defend an action that will, in a stroke, put an end to the capacity for autonomous action. The second counterclaim is that while one's autonomy is to be respected, one can only be free to exercise one's autonomy in ways that will not bring harm to others: control over one's life is not, therefore, absolute. One may kill oneself, then, only when to do so will not cause harm to others. Such an argument may be modified to balance the harm to oneself of continuing to live against the harm to others of one's death. Both of these arguments are well rehearsed with reference to suicide and self-killing.

All arguments in favor of euthanasia must reckon with the view that killing is absolutely wrong. For those without any particular religious belief, the wrongness of killing is located in the fact that it deprives someone of the remainder of her life. Returning to the argument from autonomy, it could, therefore, be argued that if someone does not value or even desire to live out the rest of her life—a judgment that rests entirely with her—she has not been harmed if she does not continue to live, particularly if this is what she wants.

However, in order to make a link between the acceptability of an autonomous decision to end one's life and euthanasia, it must also be shown that one can engage the help of another to die. It is not clear that just because it is permissible for a person to do something she is also entitled to expect help to do it. As James Rachels says, "a man may have the right to sleep with his wife, without having the right to delegate that privilege" (J. Rachels, 1986, *The End of Life,* Oxford: OUP, p. 86). Likewise, granting that it is permissible for a person to end her own life is different from arguing that ending her life is a positive right in respect of which she can demand assistance. Rachels sums up the link between the permissiblity of self-killing and the permissibility of euthanasia: "If it is permissible for a person ... to do, or bring about a certain situation, then it is permissible for that person ... to enlist the freely given aid of someone else in so doing the act or bringing about the situation, provided that this does not violate the rights of any third party" (Rachels, 1986, p. 86). If Rachels is correct, then it is permissible for doctors, acting on the wishes of a competent patient, to give euthanasia.

Moreover, if each of us can imagine a life not worth living—even though this life might vary from person to person—each of us should accept the injustice of imposing such a life on another just because her view of a life not worth living is different to our own. Such a position could be used against intervention in a self-killing, but it is a rather weak argument for committing a reluctant doctor to perform a euthanasia. For his help to be "freely given" he presumably must be in agreement that the life is not worth living. It is difficult to see that a completely fit and healthy person could enlist help in dying simply by appealing to the principle that it is up to each of us to define for ourselves that life is not worth living and for others to respect that judgment. If, on the other hand, our individual assessments vary only on the margins of detail, then it begins to look unfair to impose a life not worth living on someone simply because they are unable to request help in dying. This then shifts the argument from one for voluntary euthanasia to one for nonvoluntary euthanasia, which might be doing more with the argument than those supporting it wanted or imagined.

B. Beneficence, Mercy, and Utilitarianism

Undoubtedly, many people die in circumstances of pain, distress, fear, and misery. The response of those attending them—both as professional carers and family members—is to draw attention to the fact that, in the United Kingdom at least, it is considered an act of great humanity or kindness to kill an animal rather than let it die suffering. "You wouldn't put a dog through this," doctors are told. Indeed, animal euthanasia is common for a variety of reasons, ranging from old age to incontinence, from a diagnosis of terminal illness to the breaking of a leg.

Where there is no other means of reducing suffering, euthanasia may be justified as the only remaining benevolent option. The imperative to act benevolently is considered to be one of the most important ethical principles, along with nonmalevolence, governing medical practice. Doctors, more than most, have the means at their disposal to ensure that a peaceful death is provided for those who will otherwise die horribly. So, it has been argued, doctors may be obliged to give euthanasia rather then watch lamely as a patient dies a protracted and painful death.

Appeals to the principle of beneficence are reinforced by utilitarianism. Utilitarians such as Peter Singer, John Harris, James Rachels, and Jonathan Glover have asserted that the goodness of any action—even that of causing death—must be assessed solely in terms of the consequences that flow from it. Killing a patient may conflict with a previously held taboo, but it is not wrong if it prevents suffering and it achieves a desirable end: a peaceful death.

This argument is used not just in relation to actual physical suffering, but also mental suffering, the frustration of being unable to perform everyday tasks for oneself, and the erosion of dignity as personal and previously private tasks have to be performed by someone else as one reverts to behavior not experienced since infancy. Dying patients may suffer distress from physical symptoms other than pain, such as nausea, the sensation of burning, itching, and so forth.

The argument from beneficence or utilitarianism will be strongest where there is no alternative but death to the misery that one is witnessing, both when the period of suffering is likely to be unremitting and prolonged or when death is fairly imminent. When death is fairly imminent, it can be argued that little of life is lost by this action (which will have considerable gains); and when it is likely that, without access to euthanasia, the patient will suffer for many months (or even years) there is even more suffering to outweigh any value that life might otherwise have.

The argument from beneficence or utilitarianism is equally compelling whether or not it is possible to gain the consent of the suffering patient. It can be used to justify the euthanasia of those who are incompetent to request death for themselves; it is used to support infanticide, for instance. Few, if any, utilitarians would argue that someone should be given euthanasia against their express and competent wishes. This is because beneficence can be expressed equally by respecting autonomy as it can by relieving suffering. Indeed, it is often argued that some suffering of others must be tolerated in order that liberty should flourish. When liberty is granted this order of value, it is unlikely that one can justify overruling it to prevent harm to the very person who seeks to defend her own expression of it.

V. ARGUING AGAINST THE PERMISSIBILITY OF EUTHANASIA

A. Life Is Inherently Valuable, and Giving the Benefit of Doubt

This argument is not the same as one that argues that killing is always wrong. Rather, it provides a limited defense against the move from voluntary to nonvoluntary euthanasia grounded in some understanding of a life that is not worth living.

Without appeals to the *sanctity* of life, that is to say a view about the value of life that is ordained by some deity whose wishes form absolute rules, it is difficult to generate an argument for the wrongness of a killing carried out at the express and competent wish of the person who dies. It is quite a different case when the argument about life not worth living is applied to those who are unable to make or express this judgment for themselves. The argument from the inherent value of life asserts that it is not quality or quantity of life that gives it value, but the fact that life is the vehicle for all experience, both good and bad, that gives it its value. For instance, Thomas Nagal (1979, *Mortal Questions,* Cambridge: Cambridge University Press, p. 2) argues:

There are elements which, if added to one's experience, make life better; there are other elements which if added to one's experience, make life worse. But what remains when these are set aside is not merely neutral: it is emphatically positive. Therefore life is worth living even when the bad elements of experience are plentiful, and the good ones too meagre to outweigh the bad ones on their own. The additional positive element is supplied by experience itself, rather than by any of its contents.

The difference between these two positions has been highlighted by discussions not only of the value of lives spent in enormous suffering, but also of lives spent in PVS or in similar states. Those who want to extend the definition of brain death from the irreversible loss of brain-stem function to the irreversible loss of upper-brain function base their arguments on a difference between biographical life and biological life. They argue that once one is no longer able to experience one's own existence, one is effectively dead. So, for instance, it is argued that the noted PVS victims Karen Anne Quinlan

and Tony Bland died at the time when they lost the capacity for consciousness, and not when they were certified dead as a result of either cardiopulmonary failure or the loss of brain-stem function. Against this it has been argued that the fact they both lay in a prolonged state of unconsciousness before their deaths was part of the tragedy of their lives and not separate to those lives: it was the final chapter of their biographical life.

The argument that we should decide for ourselves when our life is not worth living and that it would be cruel to impose such a life upon someone who does not want it, is an understandable response to some of the religious arguments that appear to suggest that we should accept without question the ills that life throws at us, and face our pain with courage and not with despair. It is not, however, inconsistent to argue that faith in some religious reward or duty of tolerance is compatible with each of us making our own assessment of when life ceases to be worth living. Indeed, recognizing that different things are given different value by different people is precisely part of the argument.

Giving the benefit of doubt to a pro-life position—coupled with renewed efforts to ensure the maximum comfort of those whose lives would otherwise be miserable—is a strong argument against nonvoluntary euthanasia despite being a poor defense against voluntary euthanasia. A contentious premise of the pro-euthanasia argument is that there is some pain and some distress that cannot be relieved. Those working within hospices and specializing in palliative care deny this; they claim that at worst a patient can be kept in a state of unconsciousness. It is sometimes said that a request for euthanasia is a sign that the patient is being inadequately cared for, and that giving euthanasia is the easy escape from providing this care.

Likewise, it is argued that the dignity of patients can be preserved by treating them with dignity whatever their circumstances, and that dignity is not something that patients lose, it is something they are deprived of by careless or callous carers, or by a system of care that is inadequate for their needs.

Similar arguments have been made by disability rights lobbyists. They argue that people are prepared to write off the lives of disabled babies, partly because of a prejudice against difference and partly because this prejudice itself erodes the quality of life of the disabled. Whenever the issue of infanticide is debated publicly, people write to the national press commending their lives as disabled people and urging parliamentarians (and others) to think carefully about what they may be sanctioning. The following is typical:

> Thank God this "abnormal" foetus was conceived in 1947. I was born with spina bifida. My parents were told that I would die within three days (wrong!), wouldn't walk (wrong!) and would be ineducable (wrong!) ...
>
> Years ago we kept the handicapped in institutions, out of sight, out of mind. Now ... we can destroy them before we need to look at them or think about them. But we the handicapped are still here, still playing a part in society. Funnily enough, not only do many of us contribute to society, *we even enjoy being alive* (*The Guardian*, 26 October 1986).

B. The Slippery Slope

The slope, or thin end of the wedge, argument claims that once one form of euthanasia is accepted, other forms will inevitably follow. The argument is commonly applied to voluntary euthanasia from which, it is claimed, nonvoluntary euthanasia and even involuntary euthanasia will follow.

Arguments about slippery slopes take various forms. Some claim that having permitted one form of euthanasia, one may become logically committed to accepting another. An example of this was seen in the argument from autonomy where it was stated that it would be wrong to deny to those unable to consent for themselves the benefits awarded to others by virtue of their being in possession of the faculties that enable them to request these goods. Another claims that one form of euthanasia will incline people toward other forms as they become habituated to the idea. Against this, proponents of euthanasia direct attention to other societies where one form of euthanasia is practiced without leading to other forms (see, for instance, H. Kulse, & P. Singer, 1985, *Should the Baby Live?* Oxford: OUP, 1985, chap. 5). Another potential slope is created because the arguments used to promote euthanasia are indeterminate and can be extended without contradiction to include more and more cases. Concepts such as beneficial killing, life not worth living, poor quality of life, accelerating the process of dying, and so on, may each mean different things to different people.

It is possible to make slippery slope arguments against euthanasia, while simultaneously agreeing that at least some of the arguments for permitting euthanasia are convincing, or even when one agrees that euthanasia is the most appropriate response to a particular case. The strength of the argument lies not in the assertion that euthanasia is never justified or appropriate but that, human nature being what it is, it is potentially dangerous to relax laws and professional codes to permit its use. One weakness of the argument is that those people for whom euthanasia may be justified are sacrificed to save those who may be endangered because euthanasia would not be appropriate. (For a detailed discussion of the slippery slope arguments against euthanasia see D. Lamb, *Down the Slippery Slope* Beckenham, U.K.: Croom Helm, 1988.)

VI. CONCLUSION

When looking at arguments about euthanasia, one has to do more than look at whether or not euthanasia is permissible. One has to have a clear understanding of what euthanasia is—and therefore whether the case in hand is actually a case of euthanasia at all. The category *euthanasia* involves a particular and specific combination of intentions, motives, and outcome (see Section I), and these need to be rigorously applied if confusion and arguing at cross-purposes is to be avoided (see Section II).

The various kinds of arguments offered both in support of the permissibility of euthanasia and against the practice of euthanasia have been reviewed in Sections IV and V. It should be recognized, however, that it is one thing to generate arguments in support of euthanasia and quite another to argue for the legalization of euthanasia. Formulating legislation requires us to focus on other issues, like the protection of the vulnerable (for instance, those who are incompetent) and the possibility that the law may be misused for personal or societal gains. We must also consider the position of doctors, and others, who cannot in conscience perform euthanasia, and the fate of patients in their care attempting to gain access to legal euthanasia. On the other hand, in resisting attempts to legalize euthanasia we must reckon with the suffering of those seeking access to it, and the appropriateness of prosecuting and punishing those who break the law in good faith.

Also See the Following Articles

AUTONOMY • BRAIN DEATH • DEATH, DEFINITION OF • DO-NOT-RESUSCITATE DECISIONS • INFORMED CONSENT • PATIENTS' RIGHTS

Bibliography

Battin, M. (1994). *Least worse death: Essays in bioethics on the end of life*. Oxford: Oxford University Press.

Dworkin, D. (1995). *Life's dominion*. London: HarperCollins.

Keown, J. (Ed.). (1997). *Euthanasia examined: Ethical, legal and clinical perspectives*. Cambridge: Cambridge University Press.

Lamb, D. (1995). *Therapy abatement, autonomy and futility*. Avebury, U.K.: Aldershot.

Singer, P. (1995). *Rethinking life and death*. Oxford: Oxford University Press.

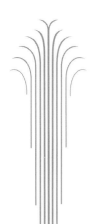

EVOLUTIONARY PERSPECTIVES ON ETHICS

Chris MacDonald
University of British Columbia

GLOSSARY

altruism As used by biologists, any act that increases the inclusive fitness of another organism at some cost in inclusive fitness to the actor.

game theory The study of decision-making in situations in which the results of one's actions depend in part on the actions of others.

inclusive fitness A measure of an organism's reproductive success, including the reproductive success of the individual's close relatives.

naturalistic fallacy The logical error committed when one attempts to claim that because something is natural, it is therefore good.

sociobiology The study of the biological basis of behavior, often based on evolutionary considerations.

EVOLUTIONARY PERSPECTIVES ON ETHICS is a general term used to refer to any of a number of views that claim to derive ethical insight from evolutionary theory. Such views have ranged from those that attempt to draw moral inspiration—moral principles or values—directly from the functioning of evolutionary pro-

cesses, to those that attempt to use evolutionary theory to strengthen the factual bases upon which ethical arguments are based.

I. EVOLUTIONARY THEORY

Evolutionary ethics has its intellectual roots in the work of Charles Darwin (1809–1882), although—contrary to popular belief—Darwin did not "discover" evolution. While an in-depth exploration of evolutionary theory is beyond the scope of this article, some understanding of the details of the theory is necessary in order to appreciate its ethical implications.

A. Evolutionary Thought before Darwin

By the time Charles Darwin was born, just after the turn of the nineteenth century, evolution was a familiar, if still controversial, idea among natural scientists. Most generally, the word "evolution" refers to the idea of one species changing, over a long period of time, into another species or even into several. This idea was (and is) at odds with the traditional (literal) interpretation of the Bible, which held that the animal species extant today are the same ones placed on Earth by God as part of the act of creation. But in the nineteenth century, the growing fossil record was beginning to cast doubt upon the biblical account of things. Yet the idea of evolution was slow in catching on, not least because of the difficulty in explaining just how it was that one species could transform, over time, into another. A few thinkers, however, found the evidence that evolutionary changes had in fact occurred compelling, regardless of whether or not the mechanism by which such changes might have occurred was known.

B. Charles Darwin's Contribution

It was Charles Darwin who finally put his finger on what is widely regarded as the primary mechanism that drives evolution. In 1859, Darwin published his masterpiece, *On the Origin of Species*. In it, he outlined a theory based on three considerations:

1. Left unchecked, populations tend to grow geometrically.
2. Within a species, individuals tend to vary from one another.
3. Individuals tend to pass their particular characteristics on to the offspring.

These three facts, combined with the environment's capacity to support only a limited number of organisms, imply a struggle for survival. In this struggle, some particular characteristics will give some individuals an edge over others. Those individuals that possess advantageous traits are more likely to survive long enough to reproduce. Nature, in a sense, "selects" such individuals for survival—hence the term "natural selection." Individuals "selected" for survival and reproduction will thus have more of an opportunity to pass their traits on to the next generation. Over numerous generations, those successful traits will proliferate within the population, and unsuccessful traits will tend to be eliminated. This means that over time the characteristics of the species will shift in response to the demands of the environment. Given enough time, a whole new species may arise. An important aspect of Darwin's theory is that it illustrated how evolution could proceed without central direction and without goals. In Darwin's account, evolution involves a species changing in response to transient environmental conditions.

C. Modern Theories of Genetics

The one major element missing from Darwin's account of evolution was the specific mechanism by which individual characteristics were passed from one generation to the next—that is, a theory of genetics. Gregor Mendel is credited with having discovered the basics of genetic theory; he published a paper on the subject in 1865. However, Mendel's insights went largely unnoticed un-

til around 1900, and were not given a central place in evolutionary theory until the 1940s. Our modern understanding of genetics tells us that an individual's genes constitute a kind of blueprint. Any individual's particular combination of genes is inherited—with half of the total blueprint being inherited from each parent.

D. Moral Implications

The core implication of evolutionary theory appears to be that human moral norms and moral sentiments are best seen as the result of evolutionary processes, rather than reflecting some eternal, objective moral truth. This reflects the fact that evolution provides an explanation for the development of life on Earth, without reference to supernatural intervention. Darwin provided a workable theory that gave a *naturalistic* account (as opposed to a supernatural, theistic account) of human origins. And while evolutionary theory does not "disprove" the existence of God, it does seem to render God unnecessary as an explanatory hypothesis.

II. INFLUENCE OF DARWIN ON SOCIAL THOUGHT

A. Early Influence on Ethical Thought

1. Charles Darwin

Darwin saw clearly that his account of evolution was ethically significant, in at least one sense: he thought that evolutionary theory could account for the existence of human moral sentiments. Darwin held that the moral sentiments had evolved from the sorts of social instincts possessed by other social animals, but that in humans these sentiments were refined and reinforced by habit. Darwin claimed that the purpose of our moral sentiments is the promotion of "the general good" (i.e., the good of the community) and that this concept provides the standard of morality. For the most part, Darwin put this forward as an *explanatory* hypothesis: he really made no attempt to defend, or justify, the force of the moral sentiments. To the extent that he discussed ethics, Darwin primarily sought to provide a plausible evolutionary account of the origins of human moral sentiments, in order to bring human beings fully within the borders of his theory.

2. Herbert Spencer and Social Darwinism

The most well known nineteenth century moral philosopher to give evolutionary theory a central role was

Herbert Spencer. Unlike Darwin, Spencer saw in evolution a critical perspective from which to reexamine the moral beliefs of the day. Spencer wanted not only to explain the *existence* of our moral sense, but to examine its *validity*.

Spencer's ethics (as outlined most fully in his 1879 *The Data of Ethics* and his 1893 *The Principles of Ethics*) begins with a teleological, or goal-directed (and to that extent, non-Darwinian), view of evolution. That is, he believed that evolution involved an upward trend toward ever greater complexity and perfection. On Spencer's account, an organism is "more evolved" the more it is able to modify its actions to meet its goals. Thus, for example, free-floating protozoa (which take no actions at all) are low on the evolutionary scale, mollusks (which take some simple actions) are higher, and humans (who perform complex actions to achieve their goals) are highest. Spencer thought it clear that the primary goal of every organism was to extend its own life. He held that any optimist— anyone who thought life worth living—must necessarily agree that the extension of life is good. In order for an individual to be skilled at extending its own life, preceding generations must also have been skilled at the preservation of offspring. But in attempting to preserve self and offspring, an organism is often in competiton with others: *effectively* preserving self and offspring involves compromise and cooperation with others. Spencer thus held that the goals of action must be to foster life—in oneself, one's offspring, and one's fellow humans.

Spencer's name has come to be associated, not entirely fairly, with the worldview known as "social Darwinism." Central to the very idea of evolution is the idea of a struggle for existence, in which some emerge as winners and others as losers. Spencer had publicly suggested that governments and institutions ought not to impede the natural course of social evolution (though he argued in favor of *individual* benevolence). These laissez-faire ideas caught on with particular zeal in the United States, where they seemed to fit nicely with existing ideas about capitalism. William Graham Sumner, for example, thought that evolutionary thinking vindicated capitalism and rugged individualism, and the continuing existence of social inequalities. Oil magnate John D. Rockefeller is said to have told his Sunday School class that the growth of large business, at the expense of competitors, is both a law of nature and a law of God. Social Darwinists have generally held that the struggle for existence, in which some succeed and others fail, is (a) positively a good thing, and/or (b) an inevitable fact of life.

3. The "Is/Ought" Distinction and Moore's Naturalistic Fallacy

Attempts to build moral systems on foundations of evolutionary theory (particularly those attempts as simplistic as those of the social Darwinists) immediately ran into philosophical objections associated with what is commonly known as "the fact/value distinction." The initial credit for this distinction goes to David Hume. In *A Treatise of Human Nature* (1739), Hume pointed out that one cannot validly deduce a normative statement (a statement of what "ought" to be done) from a factual statement (a statement about how something "is"). In Darwin's own time, this point was taken up by Henry Sidgwick, the leading moral philosopher of the last quarter of the 19th Century. In *The Methods of Ethics* (1874), Sidgwick claimed that the origin of our moral faculty was irrelevant to the study of ethics. Further, he echoed Hume in suggesting that attempts to derive claims about what *ought to be the case* from claims about what *is the case* are doomed to fail. Simply describing a moral position in no way validates it. And to call a type of behavior "natural" can provide no guidance, since presumably all behavior is natural in some sense. This last point was later taken up by Sidgwick's student, G. E. Moore.

G. E. Moore was one of the preeminent philosophers of the first half of the twentieth century. Few philosophical refutations have seemed more solid than Moore's accusation that Spencer—and anyone else seeking a natural foundation for ethics—committed the naturalistic fallacy. In his famous *Principia Ethica* (1903), Moore dealt what was seen to be a crushing blow to evolutionary perspectives on ethics. Moore held that any attempt to define "good" actions in terms of some natural property (e.g., being "pleasurable," or "altruistic") of those actions thereby committed what he called the "naturalistic fallacy." Actions that are good would, of course, have other properties, but none of those properties would be equivalent with the action's goodness. For any property we can name, if we say that an action has that property, it is still a valid question whether that action is *good*. Moore held that those who attempted to ground ethics in evolution committed the naturalistic fallacy blatantly and on a grand scale. As a specific example, he pointed to Spencer's claim that conduct that is more evolved is better. Although Hume's account of the same worry was perhaps more clear, it is largely because of Moore that many philosophers have thought the naturalistic fallacy insurmountable. The force of Moore's critique can be questioned, however, on the grounds that while it is true that no "ought" statement can be logically *deduced* from an "is" statement, an "is" statement might *lend support to* an "ought" statement, in some nondeductive way.

B. Sociobiology

1. Observed Behavior

By the middle part of the twentieth century, evolutionary theory had become the reigning paradigm in the biological sciences, particularly in those sciences that had to do with the *physical* makeup of various organisms. As well, a number of biologists were turning their attention to the study of the biological basis of *behavior*—including the basis of human behavior—and sought to investigate it in evolutionary terms. This new field, which came to be known as "sociobiology," has as its fundamental—and controversial—assumption that an organism's behavior, like its physiology, is a product of its genes. Sociobiologists observe patterns of behavior, and seek to understand why evolution has favored those forms of behavior over others.

Among the central observations that sociobiologists have sought to explain is the fact that animal relationships show evidence of a good deal of cooperative behavior. This cooperation at first seems odd, given the Darwinian emphasis on competition for survival. If evolution is primarily a matter of competition, why should we find so much evidence of cooperation in nature? Sociobiologists have advanced two explanations—or rather two mechanisms—each of which purports to explain some instances of cooperative behavior among potential rivals.

The first such mechanism is "kin-selection," which works as follows. If two organisms are closely related, they share a significant portion of their genetic codes in common. In other words, relatives share genes, and close relatives share many genes. By promoting the survival and reproductive opportunities of close kin, an organism can increase the likelihood that some of those shared genes will make it into the next generation. Genes that make this sort of cooperative behavior more likely will tend to spread in a population. Clearly, this mechanism only serves to explain instances of cooperation between relatives.

The second mechanism, the one which is thought to explain instances of cooperation between nonrelatives, is known as "reciprocal altruism." Simply put, it makes sense, from the point of view of survival, for one organism to help another if there is sufficient likelihood that the favor will be repaid in the future.

It is important to note, however, that the way in which sociobiologists use terms like "selfish" and "altruistic" is entirely metaphorical. for a sociobiologist, an act is "selfish" if it tends to increase one's long-term reproductive success. Conversely, an act is called "altruistic" by sociobiologists if it tends to increase another's long-term reproductive success, while decreasing one's own long-term reproductive success. In everyday language, "selfishness" and "altruism" rerfer to human motivation. But when sociobiologists use them, they properly refer only to the *consequences* of an organism's actions, and have nothing to do with the organism's *motivation,* if any. However, critics have charged that sociobiologists often tend to confuse the two usages.

Critics have also charged that sociobiologists make the implausible claim that important human behavioral traits are not just *influenced,* but actually *determined,* by our genes. They argue that the meager empirical evidence available with regard to human behavior does not justify the grand claims that sociobiologists are sometimes seen to make. The claim that sociobiology implies "genetic determinism" has been one of the most influential arguments against the field.

Perhaps no writer has been more central to the discussion of evolutionary ethics in the late twentieth century than Harvard biologist E. O. Wilson. Wilson's 1975 book, *Sociobiology: The New Synthesis,* is both famous and infamous, and many modern philosophers take Wilson's work as being representative of the field of sociobiology as a whole. Wilson's book deals, for the most part, with nonhuman behavior, and as such it was generally very well received. In its final chapter, however, Wilson turns his attention to human behavior. There he argues that many morally questionable forms of human behavior—for example, male dominance—are a natural result of our evolutionary history. Whether Wilson intended this or not, his claim that these behaviors are *natural* has been seen as an attempt to defend the status quo. That is, Wilson has been seen as reaching morally conservative (i.e., right-wing) conclusions, based on evolutionary considerations. Wilson elaborates his views on ethics in his 1978 book, *On Human Nature.* There, Wilson claims, among other things, that reciprocal altruism is superior to truly selfless kin-altruism (due to the latter's inability to be effective for large groups). In both books, Wilson establishes himself as one of the most optimistic advocates of evolutionary ethics—that is, as someone willing to derive substantive moral claims from evolutionary theory.

Another prominent sociobiologist, Richard Alexander, is more cautious than Wilson in his pronouncements concerning the relation between biology and ethics. He puts forward what has been called an "engineering" view. Rather than claiming that answers to moral questions are to be found in our biology, Alexander makes the more modest claim that a better understanding of the biological basis of our human moral practices will better prepare us to solve pressing social and political problems. For example, Alexander argues that a proper understanding of our evolutionary past would show the extent to which selfishness is likely to be a key human characteristic that must be overcome in the pursuit of social harmony. Further, Alexander suggests that an understanding of the conflict of interests inherent in the evolutionary struggle points to a conventionalist understanding of moral systems.

2. Evolutionary Game Theory

One important branch of sociobiology is the relatively new field of evolutionary game theory. The most influential proponent of evolutionary game theory has been John Maynard Smith, whose classic 1982 text, *Evolution and the Theory of Games* brought unprecedented rigor to the evolutionary perspective on animal behavior. Game theory itself (a branch of applied mathematics) can be thought of as the study of decision-making in situations in which the results of one's actions depend in part on the actions of others. That is, it is the study of strategic decision-making. As applied to populations of organisms, evolutionary game theory asks questions like "in competitive situations, what strategy—or combination of strategies—will maximize reproductive success for the individual?" It is central, of course, to the Darwinian perspective that the evolutionary process is not subject to conscious control—that is, evolution does not *literally* have "strategies," and most organisms do not *literally* play games. But the working assumption of evolutionary theorists is that evolution can be said (metaphorically) to "design" organisms to "have strategies." This assumption works because the ways in which competing organisms act result in winnings and losses (measured objectively in terms of reproductive success), and thus their interaction can be modeled as a game, regardless of whether or not their behavior is consciously motivated. Because reproductive success provides an unambiguous measure of success in competition, the application of game theory to biology (as opposed to economics) does not require that we attribute preferences (which are hard to measure) to the players of the game.

An interesting recent example of the use of evolutionary game theory in ethics is to be found in Brian Skyrms' 1996 book, *Evolution of the Social Contract,* in which Skyrms uses game theory to show that the familiar egalitarian conception of justice can be accounted for in evolutionary terms. Skyrms shows that in an evolving population engaged in a game of resource division, (given certain plausible initial conditions) the strategy most likely to come to dominate is one that implies approximately equal division of the resource among the participants. Thus Skyrms shows how the structure of interaction, combined with evolutionary processes, can result in a particular shared standard.

3. Evolutionary Psychology

Evolutionary psychology is, in a sense, an intellectual descendant of sociobiology. Evolutionary psychology is simply psychology informed by the fact that the human mind is a product of evolution. It is predicated on the idea that, contrary to the beliefs of behaviorists such as Pavlov and Skinner, the human mind is anything but a "blank slate." Rather than seeing the mind as a general purpose computational device, evolutionary psychologists see it as a collection of special purpose algorithms, or tools, each designed by natural selection to solve a particular problem faced during human evolutionary history. Evolutionary psychologists use theories about the evolutionary pressures under which the human mind developed to generate testable hypotheses about its particular features. Simply put, evolutionary psychologists work under the assumption that the structure of the human mind reflects the demands of our evolutionary past.

Anthropologist Donald Symons has approvingly pointed out a significant difference in approach between sociobiology and evolutionary psychology. According to Symons, evolutionary psychology proceeds upon the assumption that "reproductive success" is too vague a goal for any organism, and too vague a goal for the evolutionary process. In fact, Symons points out, organisms are designed by selection to strive for *specific* goals subsidiary to reproductive success. Symons argues that Darwinism illuminates behavior only to the extent that it illuminates *particular* adaptations—for example, particular mental characteristics. The strength of evolutionary psychology, according to Symons, lies in its focus on such characteristics. In contrast, Symons charges that sociobiologists often attempt to explain all behavior *directly* in terms of the goal of reproductive success.

Why is (or should be) evolutionary psychology of interest for those studying ethics? Clearly, human moral behavior involves a number of particular mental capacities. For example, our moral lives may require us to identify friends, remember promises, and categorize behavior. Emotions such as *sympathy, anger,* and *shame* also figure significantly in our moral lives. Evolutionary psychology holds the possibility of predicting which of those mental capacities will be most well developed, and which ones thus form a reliable basis for moral behavior. Evolutionary psychologists John Tooby and Leda Cosmides have found convincing evidence, for example, for a special human aptitude for detecting cheaters in situations of social exchange. This sort of insight might one day help us decide which of several competing moral norms is the most psychologically plausible, and hence most likely to be adhered to.

III. INFLUENCE OF DARWIN ON MODERN MORAL THEORISTS

A. Proponents of the Darwinian Perspective

Despite the considerable influence of critics such as G. E. Moore, a number of modern moral theorists have claimed to draw insight from evolutionary theory.

Intellectual historian Robert Richards is one of the more aggressive modern proponents of a biologicized ethics. Richards, in his 1987 book, *Darwin and the Emergence of Evolutionary Theories of Mind and Behavior,* argues that human beings are naturally motivated to serve the good of the community. Richards bases his argument on two claims. First, he appeals to our shared moral intuitions, and claims that our intuitions identify morality with altruism. Second, he argues that evolutionary theory shows that humans generally have been constructed (by kin- and group-selection) to hold altruistic behavior in high esteem. In arguing in this manner, Richards explicitly rejects the claim that the derivation of values from facts necessarily involves fallacious reasoning. Richards' argument can be summed up this way: Evolution has constituted human beings in such a way that they are naturally motivated to serve the good of the community, and to call such motives "moral." This shared understanding of what morality *is* serves as a standard by which to judge actions.

Although he is not an advocate of evolutionary ethics per se, utilitarian philosopher Peter Singer was among the first philosophers to take note of, and to take seriously, Wilson's book *Sociobiology.* Singer argues that the evolutionary perspective "debunks" many of our moral beliefs by showing that there are biological explanations for them. Once we see that many of our moral beliefs are remnants of our primitive past, Singer claims, we will be better able to examine critically such beliefs in order to determine whether they meet our modern needs. The only moral belief that can survive this sort of scrutiny, according to Singer, is the belief—really a dictate of reason, on his account—that in making moral decisions we need to take into account the interests of all concerned, that is, utilitarianism. Singer has also pointed out that in a Darwinian world, the differences between humans and other animals are differences of degree, rather than of type. Singer thus claims that Darwinian theory undermines the notion that there is a large—and morally significant—gulf between humans and other animals.

Another utilitarian philosopher, James Rachels, makes a similar argument in using Darwinian theory against what he calls "the human dignity thesis"—the thesis that holds that human beings deserve special consideration as a result of their central place in some divine plan. Rachels claims that while an evolutionary account does not *disprove* the truth of the human dignity thesis, an evolutionary account *does* serve to take away support for that thesis. Rachels claims that once the human dignity thesis is seen to be ungrounded, we are forced to look for a morality that does not treat humans as being of unique or paramount moral significance. Rachels argues that this conclusion has important implications both for views concerning issues such as the abortion of defective fetuses and end-of-life decision-making, as well as for our treatment of nonhuman animals. For example, Rachels claims that if humans can no longer be seen as the center of the moral universe, then there is no justification for the nearly infinite value that some people place on human life as such, and for the negligible value that most people place on the lives of most nonhuman animals.

Among philosophers, Michael Ruse is perhaps the most enthusiastic and prolific advocate of evolutionary ethics today. According to Ruse, the most significant contribution of the evolutionary perspective to ethics is negative: it lies in the evolutionary perspective's ability to debunk the objectivist pretensions of morality. The evolutionary perspective does this, according to Ruse, by providing an explanation of the source of our moral sentiments. Ruse argues our moral sentiments are merely evolution's way of getting us to cooperate. That is, evolution has designed us to have cooperative (i.e., altruistic) tendencies. According to Ruse, morality is a "collective illusion" foisted on us by our genes. Importantly, Ruse points out that it is a *useful* illusion: Ruse echoes the earlier claim by J. L. Mackie (in Mackie's 1977 book, *Ethics: Inventing Right and Wrong*) that morality is more likely to function well if we *believe* it to involve objective truths. Hence Ruse agrees both with the sociobiologists who point out that altruistic behavior must in some sense be selfish, and with moralists who assert that "true" altruism is decidedly *not* self-interested: the roots of our behavior are, and must be, hidden from us.

B. Modern Critics of Evolutionary Ethics

Although most modern moral philosophers have merely ignored evolutionary theory, a number of them have been more actively skeptical of the significance of evolution for moral inquiry.

Thomas Nagel, for instance, maintains that ethics is an autonomous theoretical realm (in some ways like mathematics), to which biology can contribute little if anything. Nagel holds that morality, like mathematics, has its own internal standards of justification and criticism, and argues that knowing the biological roots of our moral beliefs is as unhelpful as knowing the biological roots of our mathematical beliefs would be. Nagel further points out that the very idea of moral progress—the idea that we can *improve upon* existing moral views—suggests that moral views must be critiqued based on standards unique to the moral domain, rather than standards derived from evolutionary theory.

Philosopher of science Philip Kitcher has made strong criticisms of sociobiology, in his 1985 book, *Vaulting Ambition: Sociobiology and the Quest for Human Nature*. In Kitcher's view, the greatest weakness of sociobiology lies in the haste with which its proponents have often sought to reach conclusions, based on inadequate evidence. Human sociobiology is a discipline that promises insights into human nature—insights that could be useful to those tasked with forming social policy. Such being the case, Kitcher argues that the standard of evidence in human sociobiology must be extremely high (and higher than it typically has been), in order to avoid basing social policy on erroneous conclusions.

Yet even harsh critics of attempts to "biologicize" ethics (such as Nagel) admit that evolutionary considerations are important in so far as they illuminate human nature. One proponent of the evolutionary perspective, namely Ruse, has suggested that this is a considerable concession indeed.

IV. CONCLUSION

A. Significance for Applied Ethics

Applied ethics is a young discipline. And evolutionary ethics, though arguably over 130 years old, is underdeveloped. In fact, key theorists disagree over just what the field is about. This makes it hard to say just what

the significance of the one field for the other will be. The answer to this question depends largely upon what the two fields are taken to encompass.

To start with, the significance of evolutionary ethics for applied ethics depends on just what applied ethics is taken to be. If applied ethics seeks simply to apply established ethical theories to particular situations, then it seems that those engaged in applied ethics can leave evolutionary considerations (along with other abstractions) to those who actually build the ethical theories which they seek to apply. On this view, *moral theorists* may need to take evolutionary considerations into account, but applied ethicists need not. But if, instead, applied ethics involves an attempt to arrive at new theoretical insights, then those engaged in applied ethics will need to take into account relevant considerations brought to light by the evolutionary perspective.

Next, just what sorts of conclusions can evolutionary ethics product? As illustrated in this article, the answer to this question varies considerably from one author to the next. In some accounts, evolutionary ethics holds the promise of producing new ethical principles. In other accounts, the evolutionary perspective serves to explain how it is that our moral capacities or particular moral standards evolved. In still other views, the evolutionary perspective provides an explanation of the nature of moral obligation, and the status of moral principles. The first claim is generally greeted with the most skepticism. The second is widely accepted, but its practical implications are unclear.

The third sort of claim is perhaps most significant for those interested in applied ethics. Just what does the evolutionary perspective say about the nature of moral principles? It seems that the evolutionary perspective strongly suggests a pluralist approach that fits in well with the pragmatic moral pluralism that characterizes so much current work in applied ethics. The most commonly cited implication of evolutionary theory is that it provokes skepticism regarding any absolutist moral theory (see Section III A above). In the evolutionary perspective, it seems, morality is a tool that evolved to suit human needs. This seems to imply some version or another of pragmatic moral pluralism: we need a range of moral principles suit a range of human needs. Pluralist approaches—that is, ones that base moral evaluation on a *number* of core moral principles or values—constitute what is arguably the dominant paradigm in the various subdisciplines of applied ethics today. Most current work in bioethics, for example, pays homage to a small cluster of moral principles—"autonomy, beneficence, nonmaleficence, justice," and sometimes "caring"—without providing much in the way of theoretical foundation for the use of that cluster. Similarly, major texts in business ethics point to the importance of justice, utility, and rights, without justifying these in terms of any overarching theory. On one common version of the evolutionary perspective (i.e., the version that is skeptical of universal moral truths), this refusal to commit to any one moral theory makes perfect sense.

B. Prospects for the Future of Evolutionary Ethics

If intellectual history tells us anything, it is that it is foolish to try to predict its course. However, two factors inspire the prediction of a healthy future for evolutionary perspectives on ethics. The first is the fact that for over 100 years, at least some philosophers have suspected that the truth of evolutionary theory could not be irrelevant to the study of ethics. The power of Darwinian thinking is such that the temptation is strong to apply it to the questions—some old and some new— with which ethicists struggle. This temptation becomes a worry, however, when evolution is seen as providing easy answers to questions that have troubled ethicists for centuries.

The second factor is the increasingly multidisciplinary and interdisciplinary nature of ethics research: many of the disciplines with which ethics has recently allied itself find evolutionary perspectives useful. Ethics is no longer done in a vacuum. Where once moral philosophers relied on introspection and personal experience of the world, they are increasingly realizing that accurate information about human beings is central to their project. Moral philosophers are, more than ever, looking outward for the data upon which to build their moral theories. In Darwin's time (and at all times prior),

there were few disciplinary borders. Natural scientists *were* philosophers. Soon after Darwin's death a process of specialization began. The result was academic parochialism and territoriality. Today, disciplinary borders are once more becoming porous. Applied ethicists often work with fellow academics from a wide range of disciplines, including medicine, economics, anthropology, and psychology, to name just a few. Evolutionary perspectives are now being applied in many of these disciplines. To the extent that the evolutionary perspective influences these disciplines, it will also find its way into the ethical theories that are informed by them.

Also See the Following Articles

BIODIVERSITY • DARWINISM • GAME THEORY • SPECIESISM

Bibliography

Barkow, J. H., Cosmides, L., & Tooby, J. (1992). *The adapted mind: Evolutionary psychology and the generation of culture.* New York: Oxford University Press.

Bradie, M. (1994). *The secret chain: Evolution and ethics.* Albany, NY: State University of New York Press.

Dennett, D. C. (1995). *Darwin's dangerous idea: Evolution and the meanings of life.* New York: Simon & Schuster.

Farber, P. L. (1994). *The temptations of evolutionary ethics.* Berkeley, CA: University of California Press.

Nitecki, M. H., & Nitecki, D. V. (1993). *Evolutionary ethics.* New York, NY: SUNY Press.

Rachels, J. (1990). *Created from animals: The moral implications of Darwinism.* Oxford: Oxford University Press.

Ruse, M. (1991). The significance of evolution. In P. Singer (ed.), *A companion to ethics.* Oxford: Basil Blackwell.

Thompson, P. (1995). *Issues in Evolutionary ethics.* New York: SUNY Press.

Wright, R. (1994). *The moral animal: Evolutionary psychology and everyday life.* New York: Vintage Books.

EXECUTIVE COMPENSATION

Andrew Alexandra
Charles Sturt University

I. Causes of Concern
II. Fairness in Pay
III. Is Executive Compensation Determined by the Market?
IV. Reforming Executive Compensation Practice

GLOSSARY

executive For the purposes of this article, an executive is taken to be one of the senior operational personnel in a company, in particular the Chief Executive Officer and those immediately below in the hierarchy, such as the Chief Operating Officer and the Chief Financial Officer.

executive compensation package The sum of benefits offered to executives by firms in return for their labor.

firm In this context, publicly owned commercial organizations. The word "company" is used as a synonym.

incentive package That component of the total executive compensation package whose payment is contingent on a company's performance, such as profit, return on equity, and the like.

stakeholder theory The view that the firm exists to serve the ends of those who have a legitimate stake in its functioning, including stockholders as well as consumers, workers, and so on.

stockholder theory The view that the end of a firm is to make profit, and, correspondingly, that the role of the executive is defined by the duty to increase the wealth of the firm's owners, the stockholders.

EXECUTIVE COMPENSATION is high in both absolute and relative terms. This creates social, moral, and financial concerns. There are two approaches to fairness in pay. The first approach sees pay as reward. Current levels of executive pay cannot be justified in this way. The second approach sees pay as fair if it is the outcome of market forces. However, executive pay is not the result of market forces. Executive compensation packages need to be reformed. Changes should be made to the structure of these packages, the level of remuneration, and the methods for determining packages.

I. CAUSES OF CONCERN

The value of executive compensation packages has been rising for some decades and these packages are now very high in absolute terms—in some cases executives are paid literally hundreds of millions of dollars. They are also very high relative to pay in almost every other area of the workforce. Furthermore, these differences are widening. U.S. figures indicate that in dollar terms the wage of the average worker increased approximately 6-fold between 1960 and 1992, while earnings of chief executive officers of large corporations increased more than 20-fold. For at least part of this period the growth in executive compensation was accompanied (although not matched) by growth in real wages in other parts of the workforce. Now, however, while executive compensation packages continue to skyrocket, wages for much of the rest of the workforce are static or even falling, and work has become increasingly scarce and insecure—often as the direct result of policies devised or implemented by executives who use their success as part of the justification for their own spectacular earnings.

The current levels of executive compensation generate a number of concerns. There are moral concerns about fairness. While most people appear to agree that senior executives are entitled to be paid considerably more than wage-earning employees, the amount that is generally taken to be fair is far below the levels that have become normal in recent years. There are financial concerns that executives are enriching themselves at the expense of their employers or of the wider economy. There are political and social concerns about the rise in social inequity and the accompanying envy and discord.

II. FAIRNESS IN PAY

A. Pay as Reward

Consideration of such political and social concerns involves broad issues of social justice that are beyond the scope of this discussion. Here the focus will be on the moral and financial concerns. There are two broad approaches to the issue of fairness in pay. On the first pay is taken as a kind of reward, allocated according to factors such as the arduousness and danger of the work, or the effort and productivity of the worker. A fair pay regime will be one in which all those workers who are ranked the same according to these criteria receive the same amount.

Attempts have been made to justify high executive remuneration along these lines. Executive work is often demanding in terms of time and intensity; and it is likely to involve high levels of responsibility, with executives making decisions, often in situations of deep uncertainty, that may affect the well-being of many others. No doubt these facts are relevant to the determination of fair rates of pay for executives. It should be noted, however, that there are many aspects of executive work that are intrinsically appealing and rewarding—indeed high levels of responsibility and discretionary control are found attractive by at least some. Furthermore, even if the nature of executive work merits substantial reward for those who undertake it, it seems extremely unlikely

that deserved rewards could be as great as they presently are. Members of other occupations—judges, politicians, vice-chancellors, urban planners, and the like—have jobs of similar levels of responsibility and difficulty, without any general perception that their typically comparatively much lower (though still high in absolute terms) levels of remuneration are unfair. On the other hand, the outraged response to the large increases in remuneration gained by executives of recently privatized utilities in countries such as Australia and Britain may reflect a feeling that because the nature of the work done has changed little or at all, greater rewards are not deserved.

B. Pay Fixed by the Market

Proponents of the second, market-based approach to fairness in pay point out that in certain contexts there is no a priori method of determining what counts as a fair outcome. Rather, an outcome is fair if it is the result of a fair procedure that has been properly followed. So if two people bet on the spin of an unbiased coin, the result should be seen as fair. This is true even though the winner could not be said to be more deserving than the loser in terms of skill or effort. Similarly, when people come together without coercion to trade, the terms on which they agree to trade will count as fair. Labor power is a good to be traded like any other, so its value can only be determined by the price it commands in the market.

On this approach, unlike the first, fairness and equity can come apart. Fairness in pay is compatible with large differences in the amount received for work that is similarly demanding, skilled, and so on. Perhaps unsurprisingly it is some version of this approach that has been most favored by executives themselves and by their apologists. The claim is that current levels of executive pay are fair and justified because they are simply the outcome of the workings of the market in executive labor. Given the capacity of, and incentive for, companies to pay employees as little as possible, the present high level of executive remuneration must reflect the scarcity of effective executives, and the high value of such executives to their employing organizations.

III. IS EXECUTIVE COMPENSATION DETERMINED BY THE MARKET?

Is executive compensation actually determined by the market? Although this is a factual question, it has evaluative implications because, as discussed above, if executive remuneration is set by the market then there is at least a prima facie reason to consider it fair. It is to a consideration of this question that we now turn by examining the level and structure of executive compensation packages, and the means of determining such packages.

A. Levels and Structure of Executive Pay

If there is really a free market in executive labor then it would seem that executive earnings should be comparable to those in other areas where similar skills are in demand. There are really two quite distinct markets for executive skills, and two radically different norms for determining rewards in these areas. Modern corporations are usually highly bureaucratized structures, and much executive work consists of what are essentially high-level bureaucratic tasks. The relevant reference class for determining executive pay then is that of nonexecutive bureaucrats. Although, obviously, executive remuneration is usually considerably higher than that of the rest of the reference class, in other respects executive pay regimes tend to echo the norms applicable in that class. Bureaucratic pay is usually determined by the importance of the office occupied, understood as a function of its rank in the organization and the size of the organization. The same is largely true of executive pay. Conceived of in this way, then, executive compensation seems greater than would be produced simply by the workings of the market.

The bureaucratic role is, however, not the only one undertaken by many executives. To a greater or lesser extent they also play entrepreneurial roles. Rewards for entrepreneurial activities are simply a function of their economic success. Again, it may be claimed that the high levels of executive compensation simply reflect the rewards that would accrue to entrepreneurial executives if they were to use their skills on their own account. High compensation must be paid to entrepreneurial executives to give them an incentive for working for companies rather than on their own account.

The structures of executive compensation packages belie this claim. Typically, executive compensation packages consist of two components. There is a large fixed salary component, worth between 70 and 90% of the total package, and an "incentive package" consisting of payments and opportunities that can be exploited by the executive in the case of certain contingencies. For example, executives may be given stock options, whereby they can purchase stock in their employing company at some future date at current prices.

The structure of executive compensation packages shows that executives are not rewarded as entrepreneurs, because unlike entrepreneurs they are well rewarded irrespective of the financial consequences of their actions and, again unlike entrepreneurs, while they stand to benefit handsomely given good company performance, there is no corresponding penalty if performance is bad. Indeed in some cases, given agreements about "golden handshakes" and the like, it seems that executives can actually benefit from being terminated for poor performance.

B. Methods for Determining Executive Compensation

On the face of it current methods of fixing executive compensation appear fair and impartial, made according to strictly commercial considerations. Almost all large publicly held firms assign the supervision of executive compensation to a special committee of the board of directors. Such committees usually are composed of nonexecutive directors, who often make use of specialized consultants to assist their determinations. However, many of those who are nonexecutive directors of one company are or have been executives of another, and in any case are usually of the same social class and group as those whose compensation they are determining; and outside consultants often have reason to wish to curry favor with executives, who may subsequently be deciding whether to make use of the consultants' services in other areas.

In any case, employers trying to determine appropriate compensation levels to offer executives appear to be faced with a prisoner's dilemma. As a group, it would be rational for them to cut rates, because they would be able to attract executives at the lower rate. However, for each individual employer it is rational to offer compensation at roughly the prevailing level, because they are less likely to attract talented executives if they do not. This appears to be a problem that employers are unable to redress on their own—in fact, it appears to be an instance of market failure.

IV. REFORMING EXECUTIVE COMPENSATION PRACTICE

In either of the approaches to fairness discussed above, current executive compensation practices appear to be unfair. They are not simply morally objectionable, they are also economically inefficient, placing a burden on individual firms and the economy as a whole. They therefore stand in need of reform. What should the content of this reform be, and how should it be implemented?

A. The Executive Role: Stockholder and Stakeholder Theories

Any attempt to answer these questions must take place within the context of an account of the nature and purpose of the firm, and the role of the executive within it. There are two main approaches here. The first, known as "stockholder theory," takes the firm as fundamentally a profit-making concern: the role of the executive is to act in ways which maximize profits. "Stakeholder theory" on the other hand sees the market, like other major social institutions, as existing to serve socially desirable ends. Correspondingly, the firm ought to be seen as not simply a device to maximize owners' wealth, but rather as having a broader function in the production and distribution of goods. This understanding of the social role of the firm allows for a more nuanced approach to both the ends of particular firms and the levels and structure of executive compensation packages. An agricultural firm, for example, may be seen as having such ends as the provision of needed goods, while maintaining the viability of the land that it utilizes and the communities where it is located. Maintaining profitability is presumably a necessary means to the achievement of these ends, but not a final end in itself. Correspondingly, executives should be judged, and rewarded, according to their (joint and individual) contribution to the achievement of company goals, rather than simply according to their contribution to the production of profits.

These theories obviously are likely to diverge at points—some of which are alluded to below—in their approach to executive compensation. However, there will also be a good deal of congruence in their approach, because both see ensuring profitability as defining (partly or wholly) the executive role.

B. Restructuring Executive Compensation Packages

Executive compensation packages need to be restructured. The "incentive package" component is typically rationalized as a way around a problem inherent in the structure of the modern corporation, where ownership (in the hands of stockholders) and control (in the hands of managers) have been split asunder. With this split has come the possibility of fundamental conflicts of interest between owners and managers. On the face of it, the issue of executive pay would appear to be one where such opposition of interests is inevitable: every dollar of executive pay is a dollar that cannot be distributed in dividends or reinvested to promote future profitability. Much of the discussion of executive compensation has attempted to show how this conflict can be, and in many cases has been, overcome. In particular, it is often claimed that the relationship between management and owners should not be seen as a "zero-sum" game, where what one side gains the other necessarily loses. Rather, suitably structured executive compensation packages can induce executives, even if motivated by financial self-interest, to increase the total pool of wealth that is available for distribution to both stockholders and management.

This rationalization seems problematic in a number of ways. First, if monetary rewards are the primary motivating factor for diligent performance, then given the relative importance of the components of the total package, presumably the fear of losing the fixed salary component as a result of being dismissed for inadequate performance should be sufficient motivation. The need for further rewards would seem to indicate that this fear is insufficiently live. Second, it must be doubtful, given the large amounts obtained as fixed salary and the diminishing marginal utility of money, that the incentive package component will really act as a powerful motivating force. (Although what may be true is that executives, like other groups, value pay at least in part as an expression of their comparative worth. Monetary incentives motivate not so much—or at least not exclusively—for financial reasons, as because they give executives a means of improving their status among their fellows. This motivating force would still be felt even if there was an across-the-board cut in the absolute amount of the incentive component.) Third, the link between the performance of the individual executive and the financial performance of the firm on which incentive payments are usually contingent is in many cases at least highly tenuous. As suggested above not all executives have much influence on financial performance. Furthermore, that performance is often the result of forces outside executives' control, such as general economic conditions, currency depreciations, and the like.

Nevertheless there is a legitimate place for payment contingent on outcome for at least some executives. However, such payments need to be made in a way that is sensitive to the realities of the executive role. First, they need to be more directly related to the actual tasks that particular executives undertake. This may mean that the criteria used to determine performance in some cases will be nonfinancial. Second, they must be structured so that incentives are given to executives to act in ways that further the aims of the firm. Notoriously, some executives in the past have responded to poorly conceived compensation packages that rewarded them for increasing short-term profits or stock prices by acting in ways that provided them with substantial benefits, but did great damage to the long term viability of the firm and the interests of the other concerned parties. Incentive packages must be sensitive to the peculiarities of the industry of which they are part. In some industries, for example, innovation is at a premium, and conservative strategies should be discouraged: in others the reverse is true. There are in fact indications that an increasing number of companies are tailoring their executive compensation packages along these lines.

Stakeholders theorists would also insist that in some cases considerations other than increasing the wealth of stockholders should inform the structure of executive incentives. In an increasingly mechanized, technologically, and organizationally complex, and capital-intensive production process the role of management has become more significant and that of the work force comparatively less so, with a corresponding shift of power toward management. Executive compensation packages structured purely to reward wealth production for shareholders encourage management to reduce labor costs by cutting the work force, wages and conditions and so on. In certain situations, they also encourage management to act in ways that are harmful to consumers, for example, by encouraging them to shift investment away from the production of goods where return to equity is comparatively low.

Finally, the percentage of the compensation package constituted by incentive payments should more accurately reflect the mix of bureaucratic and entrepreneurial roles the individual executive actually undertakes. At the moment many executives are paid at rates comparable to those achieved by (successful) entrepreneurs, even though their work is not entrepreneurial; while those whose work is entrepreneurial are paid as if they are successful, even if they are not. The case of Michael Eisner, who became the chief executive officer of the poorly performing Disney Corp. in 1984 is instructive. Eisner actually took a drop in the salary component of his pay on joining Disney, but stood to reap large gains if he could lift the company's performance sufficiently—and not if he did not. Over the next 5 years profits rose more than 500% and the share price rose more than 400%. Eisner made a lot of money, but in the process provided large benefits to stockholders and employees.

C. Reforming Methods for the Determination of Executive Compensation

The creation of executive compensation packages of the kind suggested requires that companies be willing to enunciate clearly their understanding of their mission and long-term strategy, and of the tasks and criteria of payment for executives. They also require a willingness to put in place methods for determining executive remuneration that accurately reflect such understandings. This may, for example, require that in calling on expert advice they deal only with specialized consultants, not with those who are in the market for other sorts of work with the company and so could face a conflict of interest.

D. Cutting Levels of Executive Compensation

While companies presumably have the capacity to make these sorts of changes, given the collective rationality problems alluded to above, they may not be able to bring down the levels of executive compensation on their own. At least in the short term state intervention may be required. It is not, however, a simple matter to determine the form such intervention should take. It has been suggested, for instance, that the state should simply put a ceiling on levels of executive compensation, or raise marginal tax rates to the point where there is no point in executives seeking very high remuneration. But as the example of Michael Eisner indicates, such moves could be undesirable in some cases, because they will deter the genuinely entrepreneurial executive.

Also See the Following Articles

CORPORATIONS, ETHICS OF • MERGERS AND ACQUISITIONS

Bibliography

Ehrenberg, R. E. (Ed.). (February 1990). *Industrial and Labor Relations Review* 43, no. 3 (Special issue).

Foulkes, F. K. (1991). *Executive compensation: A strategic guide for the 1990s.* Boston: Harvard Business School Press.

O'Neill, G. L. (1990). *Corporate remuneration: Strategies for the 1990s.* Melbourne: Longman Cheshire.

Patton, A. (1961). *What is an executive worth?* New York: McGraw-Hill.

Pavlik, E. L., & Belkaoui, A. (Eds.). (1991). *Determinants of executive compensation.* New York: Quorum.

Watts, R. I., & Zimmerman, J. L. (Eds.). (1985). *Journal of Accounting and Economics,* 7.

Wood, A. (1978). *A theory of pay.* Cambridge: Cambridge University Press.

EXISTENTIALISM

Jon Stewart
Søren Kierkegaard Research Centre, University of Copenhagen

GLOSSARY

autonomy In Kant's ethical theory, the ability to legislate a moral law for oneself. The opposite of heteronomy.

facticity According to Heidegger and Sartre, the necessary relation between the individual and the world or between the individual and his past actions. The term refers to unalterable facts of the matter about one's own life, such as one's birth, or about the world at large, such as a war or an earthquake.

heteronomy In Kant's ethical theory, the receiving of a moral law from an external source. The opposite of autonomy or self-legislation.

metaethics The sphere of inquiry that examines the role and status of ethical theories and claims generally instead of proposing or evaluating concrete ethical virtues or rules for conduct.

nihilism (Latin, *nihil*, nothing) Literally, the belief in nothing. In this context: (1) The claim that moral judgments and values are ultimately arbitrary and cannot be justified rationally. (2) The claim that human life itself is devoid of meaning. Often associated with atheism or ethical relativism.

transcendence The term used to refer to the indefinite future realm beyond the individual and his present actions. In the view of both Heidegger and Sartre, we always live in part in the realm of transcendence since our plans and projects, by which we define ourselves, are always projected into the future.

universalization In Kant's philosophy, the test of individual moral maxims by generalizing the principle of the intended action to see if it can be conceived as a universal rule for all rational agents without there resulting a contradiction. For example, the maxim of telling a lie that one will keep a promise that one has no intention of keeping cannot be universalized since if everyone acted in this fashion, then the very practice of making promises would be destroyed.

utilitarianism The school of ethical theory associated with Jeremy Bentham and John Stuart Mill; the view that makes the promotion of the greatest happiness for the greatest number the supreme principle for ethical action.

THE ENGLISH TERM "EXISTENTIALISM" was originally a translation of the German word *"Existenzphilosophie"* or "philosophy of existence," which was intended to refer to the thought of the Danish philosopher and theologian Søren Kierkegaard (1813–1855) and the handful of German philosophers at the turn of the century who were influenced by him. With time the term came to enjoy a wider currency in popular culture and by degrees lost its meaning such that today it has come to be associated with so many different things that it means virtually nothing at all. This fact was lamented by many of the later existentialists, who for precisely this reason rejected the label at least for a time. The radical split that separates the Christian from the atheistic existentialists attests to the broad nature of the term, which covers many different kinds of thinking which are by no means necessarily consistent with one another. Therefore, it is perhaps easier to say which thinkers were important in the philosophical and literary movement referred to as "existentialism" than to try to locate a single doctrine or thesis upon which every exponent of the movement would agree. In its philosophical context, "existentialism" designates the series of thinkers in the post-Hegelian tradition of European philosophy. Kierkegaard is often referred to as the founder of this movement, and the term "existentialism" itself derives from his uses of the words "existence," "the existential," and their cognates, which he contrasts to the abstract or purely theoretical. Other 19th-century thinkers such as the Russian writer Fyodor Dostoevsky (1821–1881) and the German philosopher and philologist Friedrich Nietzsche (1844–1900) are frequently counted as forerunners of the existentialist movement if not as existentialists in their own right. In the 20th century, existentialism has referred to the German school of phenomenology founded by Edmund Husserl (1859–1938) and continued and transformed by Martin Heidegger (1889–1976). The main proponents of religious existentialism in the 20th century are Karl Jaspers (1883–1969) and Gabriel Marcel (1889–1973) who, distinct from the phenomenological wing of the movement, can be seen as continuing in the tradition of Kierkegaard. Existentialism enjoyed its most popular phase in the French school whose leading exponents were Albert Camus (1913–1960), Jean-Paul Sartre (1905–1980), Maurice Merleau-Ponty (1908–1961), and Simone de Beauvoir (1908–1986).

For a number of reasons the issue of ethics in existentialism is somewhat problematic; indeed, many philosophers would dismiss the very notion of an existentialist ethic as an intractable oxymoron. As a school, existentialism is generally averse to both all forms of traditional morality and abstract ethical systems. If one understands by ethics, a systematic set of universal maxims, laws, or principles which are intended to govern action, then existentialism has no ethics since all of the existentialist

thinkers expressly deny the possibility of adequately justifying action based on rational principles or discursive arguments. For this reason, it is hardly surprising that some of the leading theoreticians of the existentialist movement such as Heidegger and Merleau-Ponty, despite their prolific and, indeed, varied writings, never wrote an ethics per se. The primary problem involved in explicating or reconstructing an ethics of existentialism lies in the critical or negative focus of the foremost existentialist thinkers. Since systematic moralities and organized religions are viewed by existentialists as the most pernicious obstacles in the way of an authentic realization of human freedom, the last thing existentialists wish to do is to concoct yet another morality in the traditional sense. For this reason, existentialist thinkers often describe their positions in overwhelmingly negative or privative terms. Existentialists characteristically deny the validity of supposedly overarching, objective, or pre-existing structures that might lend antecedent meaning to human experience. In itself, human experience is radically meaningless, and it acquires meaning and value only through subjectivistic acts of choice and decision. At face value, this would not seem to leave much material with which to work in the construction of a positive ethics.

Moreover, since the existentialists reject traditional forms of ethical theorizing, their comments on ethics have more the look of cultural criticism or philosophical psychology, as in the case of Kierkegaard or Nietzsche. Existentialist discussions of ethics can be considered metaethical in that, instead of offering a positive ethical doctrine, they provide general reflections on the very nature of ethics and the individual's moral situation in the world. Just as the existentialists rejected the *content* of abstract ethical theorizing, so also did they reject its discursive *form*; thus, many of the existentialists' insights on ethics are not found in abstract philosophical treatises but rather in novels, plays, and short stories. The literary works of Dostoevsky, Camus, and Sartre are rich in situations of ethical import and characters caught in illustrative ethical dilemmas. For these reasons, when one examines the issue of ethics in existentialism, one must approach the subject matter somewhat differently than one would when dealing with a discursive or propositional ethical theory such as that of Aristotle, Kant, or Spinoza.

Insofar as one may speak meaningfully of an ethics of existentialism, then this enterprise would comprise two related moments, one negative and one positive: (1) existentialists often speak as if positive value accrues to the project of debunking religious dogmas, objective verities, and preordained orders. Much of the enduring interest in figures like Dostoevsky, Nietzsche, and Kierkegaard is attributable to their antinomian iconoclasm in their ability to expose and discard the saving fictions under which most human beings feebly labor. (2) Having penetrated to the basic meaninglessness of human existence, existentialists believe that a positive moral value accrues to the resolute act of choice, whereby one displays one's attainment of authenticity, which is the closest existentialist thinkers come to a moral ideal. *What* one chooses is not important; *that* one chooses is all that counts. Those who cannot (or will not) choose for themselves the meaning of their existence must wallow in inauthenticity, which is that state wherein one chooses to believe that one has an essence or destiny, which is impervious to choice. Most people, most of the time, live in inauthenticity. The authentic life is reserved only for the existential hero, that quasi-mythical creature who can somehow affirm the meaninglessness of human existence and revel in the freedom afforded him by the "death of God" or the collapse of all stable foundations or points of reference.

Aside from these purely philosophical concerns there are a number of historical factors which explain the rise of the set of ethical concerns that existentialism attempts to address. The existentialist movement is perhaps best seen as a logical outgrowth of a specific zeitgeist characteristic of the 19th and above all the 20th century. Existentialism is often associated with fundamental questions of the finitude of human existence such as death, alienation, suffering, and anxiety. These questions tend not to be particularly pressing in times of stability or affluence. By contrast the rapid changes in human life since the 19th century accompanied by the violent upheavals in our own age have made the need to return to these questions much more urgent. For example, it is no accident that French existentialism was born and flourished in the context of the Second World War and the German occupation of France.

Among the radical changes of the last two centuries must surely be numbered the rapid recession of the Church and organized religion from its once central role in social life. Concurrent with this movement toward secularization there occurred the explosive advancement of the natural sciences. The seemingly miraculous advances in science and the development of technology, which have utterly transformed human life over a relatively short period in human history, have been seen by many as a straightforward proof of the veracity of science. This efficacy simultaneously seems to attest to the falsity of religious belief, which the critical, self-correcting scientific method seems to reduce to mere

superstition characteristic of past ages and unworthy of further consideration.

Existentialism is also characterized by a return to the individual, which can be seen as a natural reaction to the rise of mass culture and the anonymity of modern society. The transfer from traditional forms of communal life to modern mass society has in countless ways relegated the individual to a marginal position. Out of this situation existentialism appears as an attempt to speak for the individual and for his power of free self-determination when everything in his world appears to negate even the very possibility of this. This must suffice as a general characterization of existentialism and the set of ethical issues that it aims to address. We must now turn to the individual thinkers and to the role of existentialism in the tradition of ethical thought generally.

I. KANT'S ETHICAL THEORY

In order to appreciate the orientation of the existentialists toward the field of ethics, it is necessary to say a few words about Kant's theory of autonomy, which can be seen as setting the context for much of the discussion of modern moral thinking. While it would be a mistake to portray Kant himself as an existentialist, his theory of autonomy nevertheless clears the ground for the existentialist theories of choice, responsibility, and ethical action. Many of the existentialists can be seen as adopting Kant's theory of autonomous choice, while rejecting his account of the rational will subject to universalizable moral laws. Indeed, this can in many ways be seen as the formula for existentialist ethics in general.

The central notion for Kant is that of the moral will. According to his view, acts performed on the basis of external commands or authority are devoid of moral value. Human beings, he argues, would not be free if they were subject to a moral law imposed by God or some other external source. On the contrary, the moral agent must give himself the moral law and act out of respect for it. Autonomy involves legislating a moral law for oneself and thus imposing on oneself specific moral obligations. By contrast, heteronomy means being subject to a law which has an external source beyond the acting agent. Kant thus rejects all forms of heteronomy, including both divine command and altruistic motivations, and instead locates moral action in the autonomous agency of the individual. The moral law must be an expression of one's own will, regardless of the will of God, traditional morality, or the wishes of others. One result of this movement of the locus of moral action from an external source to the rational will of the individual is that the moral concepts of good and evil are no longer conceived as independent, self-substituting properties of the world. On the contrary, they arise concurrently with the moral decisions of the individual will.

According to Kant, the rational will is able to determine what actions are morally right by means of a rational procedure. Specifically, the moral agent is obliged to subject proposed maxims for action to the test of universalizability. Kant believes that by means of this test internal contradictions will arise in morally fallacious maxims and that these contradictions will then be self-evident to the moral agent. The proposed action is morally permissible only if it can be willed by all rational agents without contradiction. A proposed action that proves to be self-contradictory must then be discarded. The criterion of the rational will is therefore internal consistency, which is, according to Kant, the necessary and sufficient condition for moral action. The moral action, *qua* consistent and universalizable, is the expression of the rational moral will.

An appreciation of Kant's theory of morality is essential for understanding the background for the existentialists' deliberations on ethics. Kant breaks with classical moral theory by in large part rejecting the conception of a human being with a fixed essence with a determinate content. To be sure, he conceives of humans as essentially rational, but he limits this conception to the notion of a rational will that demands self-consistency. Kant thus prepares the ground for thinkers like Sartre who categorically deny any *a priori* human essence that could serve as the basis of a moral theory. Second, Kant breaks with medieval moral thought in his rejection of heteronomy. For freedom to be meaningful, only the individual moral will itself can form the moral law. Kant discards the notion of God or any external source for moral commands and focuses on the will of the individual. His theory of autonomy thus prepares the way for the existentialists who insist on a form of voluntarism of the individual and deny that a given situation can ever fully determine an individual's action.

With these points of commonality a certain continuity between Kant's moral theory and that of the existentialists can be discerned. However, of equal importance are the ways in which the existentialists depart from Kant's view. Most importantly, they reject his insistence on the ultimate rationality of the will and the ability of the individual to determine the morally correct action by means of a rational procedure. For the existentialists, reason, like a given moral situation, is itself always indeterminate and thus cannot ultimately be used to guide action. A number of given maxims may be internally consistent but yet at odds with one another. Here reason alone cannot adjudicate, and it becomes clear that logical consistency is not a sufficient condition for determining moral action. Thus, to appeal to it as a justification for a given action is inauthentic since it would be no different than appealing to an external fact of the matter which purportedly compelled one to act as one did. The existentialists therefore in essence retain Kant's conception of autonomy while freeing the will from the shackles of a necessary moral law dictated by reason.

II. KIERKEGAARD

The Danish thinker Søren Kierkegaard was profoundly concerned with a number of ethical issues in the life of the individual. He was a deeply religious thinker, and his views on ethics are tightly bound up with his views on Christianity. While there is no single book which one can point to as the definitive statement of Kierkegaard's ethical views, his works *Either/Or* (1843), *Fear and Trembling* (1843), and *Works of Love* (1847) all contain extended analyses of ethical questions. Discussions of Kierkegaard's ethics are complicated by the fact that he wrote under various pseudonyms, which he often used to illustrate opposing views. The result is that one can find varying, often contradictory, statements on ethics throughout his literary corpus. Moreover, Kierkegaard's thinking developed over time, and it is clear from some of his later journal entries that he came to reject at least some of the positions he argued for at any given earlier period. Thus, it would be a mistake to talk about a single Kierkegaard or a single ethical theory in his works. It is far more advisable to attempt to locate individual strands of his ethical thought and to discuss them on their own terms.

One dominant strain of Kierkegaard's understanding of ethics is his rejection of all attempts to ground ethical action in rationality. For Kierkegaard, every attempt to justify a given action must necessarily fail since there is always a gap between the reasons and arguments given for an act and the demands of morality. This gap can only be spanned by a free decision of the individual. Kierkegaard distinguishes between the realm of science, which is characterized by a concern for evidence, justification, and discursive reason, and the realm of religious belief and ethics, which is the sphere of individual choice. For Kierkegaard, scientific fields such as logic and geometry can justify certain conclusions from a given set of assumed premises without any gaps in the reasoning. Other fields such as philology or history, although not wholly deductively valid, can nevertheless reach impressive levels of approximation based on the rigorous employment of basic investigative principles. All of this may be fine and good for these academic disciplines or for "the realm of objectivity," as Kierkegaard calls it in the *Concluding Unscientific Postscript* (1846), but it has nothing to do with ethics or religious faith, which fall within the province of subjectivity. For Kierkegaard, the realm of objectivity is a realm of necessity and logic, whereas the realm of subjectivity is governed by its own laws. Regardless of how much objective knowledge one has or how rigorous a logician one is, the individual will always be confronted by moral choice where discursive knowledge and logic have no relevance and can offer no normative guidance. Kierkegaard argues that if morality were simply a matter of working out a certain equation according to a utility calculus or of subjecting a maxim for action to the Kantian test of universalizability, then choice would be eliminated and humans would not be free. Such procedures in effect produce a result and a plan for action independent of the individual since they are universal, objective procedures which, like a problem in mathematics, can in principle be worked out by any given moral subject. The real choice, which is perniciously hidden by theories of rationality, takes place much earlier when one chooses to allow one's action to be governed by a certain objective procedure of, for example, universalization or an equation of a utility calculus. Thus, when one avails oneself of such methods, a decision has already taken place, and one has tacitly forfeited one's freedom in order to escape into the illusory security of the realm of rational foundations. For Kierkegaard, any theory which purports to ground morality in objective rational standards is simply a sham.

The ultimate indeterminacy of ethical choice can be illustrated by Kierkegaard's early work, *Either/Or*. There Kierkegaard presents two different conceptions of life which he calls "the aesthetic" and "the ethical." The anonymous aesthete resembles in many ways the romantic: he lives whimsically, cultivating his tastes in theater, music, and women, while seeking to satisfy his insatiable desire for pleasure. He criticizes bourgeois institutions and glorifies the spontaneous desire of passion. By contrast, Judge Wilhelm, the representative of the ethical view, argues for the staid life of marriage, family, and order. The two views are presented as mutually exclusive alternatives on an equal footing, and they come to no result or conclusion. The work thus enjoins the reader to make an absolute decision between the

two positions. The title of the book is intended as a criticism of Hegel's doctrine of dialectical mediation which purports to overcome contradictions and raise them to a higher unity. This kind of mediation would seem to destroy both ethical decision and human freedom since in the end there would be no conflicting positions which would call for a choice; thus, for Kierkegaard, ethical life consists in absolute choice between opposing views without compromise or any possible mediation.

Kierkegaard also develops a third category, "the religious," which introduces a new aspect into his ethical thought. The religious is the third and highest category in the sequence, and thus even the ethical is subordinate to it. This is illustrated by his famous analysis of the Abraham and Isaac story, which Kierkegaard analyzes in detail in *Fear and Trembling*. God commands Abraham to sacrifice his son Isaac, a command which, when seen from the ethical point of view, would clearly be unacceptable. But, says Kierkegaard, the religious "suspends" the ethical in the sense that normal human ethical understanding must cede to divine command. But once again when answering the call of the religious as when answering the call of the ethical, one does not have recourse to objective reasons, arguments, or principles. One simply decides and acts. Without the security of rational foundations, we, like Abraham, always experience a "fear and trembling" (Psalms 2:11 and Philippians 2:12) in our moral life as a result of our uncertainty about the correctness of our moral decisions. For Kierkegaard, true religious and ethical life is lived with this fear and trembling and never ultimately comes to a stable place of certainty or rest.

In the religious writings, such as *Works of Love*, which were published under his own name and not under a pseudonym, Kierkegaard advocates a Christian ethics but places the weight on the individual interpretation of the ethical commands enjoined by Christianity. Acting morally for a Christian involves in the first line doing God's will. Our access to God's will is via Christ and the scriptures. Thus, our moral goal as Christians should be to imitate Christ in our actions, but this requires an interpretation based on our reading of the scriptures and of the particular ethical situation in which we find ourselves. Christian injunctions, such as "love thy neighbor," share, for Kierkegaard, the same shortcomings as secular moral commands; namely, they are ultimately indeterminate and require interpretation on the part of the believer if they are to be applicable in individual cases. According to Kierkegaard's Protestantism, the interpretation of scriptures and the response for moral action in the individual case lie wholly with the believer, and there can be no intermediary such as the Church, a priest, or the Pope between the individual and God. If ethical action were simply the mechanical execution of moral principles issued, for example, by some such external authority, then freedom of individual choice would be destroyed. For Kierkegaard, a key ethical concept with respect to the individual interpretation of moral precepts is that of "repetition." The individual must first make a conscious interpretation and inward appropriation of a general Christian principle. Then, in the particular ethical action, the individual repeats or exemplifies the principle. But just as Kierkegaard denies the possibility of any ultimate justification for particular actions, so also he denies the possibility of general criteria for the interpretation of moral laws since this too would destroy freedom. Thus, the interpretation of a particular act within a general framework of Christian ethics is, like faith, something inward and subjective.

At the time of his death in 1855, Kierkegaard was generally unknown outside Denmark, but at the beginning of the 20th century when German and English translations of his works began to appear, he emerged from his obscurity to become one of the most influential thinkers of his age. Although never read by Dostoevsky or Nietzsche, Kierkegaard decisively influenced the work of the later existentialists such as Heidegger, Camus, and Sartre. Today Kierkegaard is generally regarded as the founder of existentialism as a philosophical movement and as the leading exponent of the school's theistic branch. Despite the profoundly religious nature of Kierkegaard's thinking, many of his main ideas were taken up and developed by the atheistic existentialists such as Camus and Sartre, whose work can largely be seen as a secularized version of his views.

III. DOSTOEVSKY

The Russian novelist and essayist Fyodor Dostoevsky has often been regarded as an important forerunner of the existentialist movement. In his works, he treated a number of the themes for which existentialism eventually became popular. Although he was not a philosopher per se, Dostoevsky was far from being simply a *littérateur*. His novels are rife with philosophical themes, and his reflections also touch on fields such as theology, psychology, anthropology, politics, and social criticism. His most relevant works for ethics are *Notes from the Underground* (1864), *Crime and Punishment* (1866), *The Possessed* (1871), and *The Brothers Karamazov* (1880).

Perhaps the central theme in Dostoevsky's work is that of human freedom. Dostoevsky was consistently critical of materialism, determinism, and other contemporary movements, which he saw as the enemies of freedom. Such movements seemed in the eyes of many to be merely the logical outgrowth of the advances in the sciences in the 19th century. At that time fields such as psychology, economics, biology, and chemistry seemed to be able to explain human behavior better than ever before and even to offer the promise of a complete explanation in the future when, for instance, the social sciences became more developed or when more was known about the functions of the human brain. The view that science presents is that humans are simply biological machines determined wholly by nature and that once we understand fully the workings of nature, we will *ipso facto* have understood human beings. The idea of free will then comes to be regarded as an antiquated vestige of the dark ages of superstition which has no place in the mechanistic world of science where every effect has a cause. For Dostoevsky, this view is one that human beings will rebel against for all eternity. He does not offer metaphysical refutations of this view but instead simply claims that its results are intolerable for moral reasons. Humans need to posit the idea of freedom as a sort of regulative ideal, even though it may be empirically unprovable.

Dostoevsky likewise criticized various forms of communism and utopian socialism that were in vogue in his day. The rapid growth of technology during Dostoevsky's time led some theorists to the view that it would be possible in the future to organize human society such that the physical needs of everyone were met. Given the high productivity made possible by modern machinery and mass production, it was thought to be merely a matter of organizing labor and distributing society's resources in an equitable fashion along socialistic lines. The belief was that individuals must merely be educated to recognize their rationally calculated best interest and they would act on it. If this could be done, then a new utopian age could be attained. Dostoevsky argues against this view once again on moral grounds. He contests the claim that humans will be happy and content if their physical needs are met. Humans are more complex than cows and require more than the satisfaction of physical needs. There is a longing in mankind which remains even when all physical needs have been met. Humans are more than simply utility maximizers, and their actions cannot be explained merely as the result of enlightened self-interest. They do not simply lucidly perceive their best interest and then act upon it. Dostoevsky was suspicious of all utilitarian or socialist theories which claimed to know the rational best interest of man. He believed such theories could only lead to a limitation of human freedom. They fail to take into account the vast realm of the irrational in the human soul and therefore can never be a satisfactory explanation of human beings and human existence.

Dostoevsky rejects all rationalistic attempts to understand human nature and to ground morality. In his view, reason is simply a formal ability which is employed, for example, to work out a mathematics problems, but in and of itself it is unable to recognize or distinguish between good and evil. Thus, modern science, which is founded on reason, is ultimately a moral void since it produces new technologies and new information but can offer no moral guidelines with regard to how to use them. The seat of morality for Dostoevsky thus lies not in reason but in a spontaneous inner feeling which he sometimes refers to as conscience. For Dostoevsky, all human beings are in possession of a natural moral impulse which immediately protests against immoral acts; in these cases, it is absurd when the Kantian or the utilitarian seeks the universal rule that applies to the particular case in question in order to demonstrate that the act is wrong. Moral conscience already knows that it is wrong, and reason can only obfuscate this by, for example, trying to rationalize an immoral action by giving discursive arguments and general laws which seek to portray it as morally correct. In this sense, reason is merely sophistry since it cannot of itself distinguish between good and evil or offer moral insight.

For Dostoevsky, the essential freedom at the center of human existence is not a liberating thing as for later writers such as Camus; instead, it is a negative formula, a prescription or invitation for nihilism. Dostoevsky's memorable character Ivan Karamazov says, "If God does not exist, then everything is permitted." The idea is that if we understand ethics to be the result of divine command as either the old law handed down to Moses or the new law uttered by Christ, then ethical principles and values have an absolute sanction in God. Thus, although individuals and particular cultures might have differing ethical ideas, these are *merely* human constructions which do not have absolute validity since only God's divine commands enjoy this absolute, universal status. There is therefore a fundamental ontological difference between divine commands and human ones. Thus, to deny God's existence is to invite ethical nihilism since this denial is tantamount to a denial of absolute ethical values. To say that God does not exist is at the same time to sweep away the ontological grounding of ethics. The only values which would be left would be relative, contingent human ones. In this sense everything is permitted since no one set of human values or no one human moral code could be erected over or preferred to any other. Every ethical command or prohibition would merely be the statement of an individual culture, tradition, or person, which could be called into question by reference to other moral laws from other cultures. Dostoevsky thus understands the question as a kind of either–or proposition: either God exists and there is a transcendent meaning and value, or he does not exist and everything is permitted. Dostoevsky is sensitive to the fact that the modern secular age has made the belief in God problematic, but he is worried by the consequences of a world without God. The choice that he presents is then essentially between Christ, the God-man, or any number of forms of the demonic which try to make man into a god.

To opt for making man into a god raises the specter of the demonic, which Dostoevsky explores under its various guises. One form of the demonic is the radical nihilistic individualism of Kirilov in *The Possessed*. He commits suicide in order to become a god—in order to demonstrate his absolute freedom over religion. Likewise, the nihilism and cynicism of the underground man in *Notes from the Underground* are a form of the demonic. He rejects all customs, conventions, and human soldarity. Perhaps the best-known form of the demonic in Dostoevsky's work is the character of the Grand Inquisitor from *The Brothers Karamazov*. The Grand Inquisitor criticizes Christ for demanding man to be free without the assistance of arguments or proofs and offers instead a life in which man's will is subordinated while his physical desires are met. For the Grand Inquisitor, it is better for man to live out his life in a sedated, bovine illusion than to realize his true freedom which is a burden too heavy for the masses.

Dostoevsky's importance lies in the fact that he articulated the problem of an ethics without God that became a central issue for the atheistic existentialists. Moreover, he provided the model for later existentialist literature: his characters, the underground man, Kirilov, and Ivan Karamazov clearly prefigure later antiheroes in existentialist literature such as Camus' Mersault from *The Stranger* and Sartre's Roquentin from *Nausea*. Although Nietzsche refers to Dostoevsky by name in two of his late works, *Twilight of the Idols* (§45) and *The Antichrist* (§31), he knew only a French translation of *Notes from the Underground*. It is regrettable that he did not know more of Dostoevsky's thought given the striking similarities in some of their views. Dostoevsky is counted along with Kierkegaard as a leading spokesman for theistic existentialism, although his influence has been most profound among the atheistic existentialists.

IV. NIETZSCHE

The German philosopher Friedrich Nietzsche was important in shaping much of the thinking of the later tradition of atheistic existentialism in that he was the first to try to offer a positive solution to the problems posed for ethics and morality by the absence of God or any transcendent power. His attack on Christian morality is in many respects original and unique within this tradition. In contrast to Kierkegaard and Dostoevsky, he did not seek the answers to the basic problems of existence in Christianity but tried a radically new course in many ways at odds with basic Christian views. Virtually all of his books are replete with ethical considerations, but the main works which are usually referred to in this context are *Thus Spoke Zarathustra* (I–II, 1883; III, 1884; IV, 1892), *Beyond Good and Evil* (1886), *On the Genealogy of Morals* (1887), and the posthumous notes that bear the title, *The Will to Power*.

Nietzsche was a classical philologist, and in *On the Genealogy of Morals* he employs his philological training to investigate the origin and evolution of moral terms. There he argues that with the coming of Christianity a number of key ethical concepts took on a new meaning. For the ancient Greeks, words such as *agathos* (good, well-born) were associated with the class of nobles and aristocrats, while the term *kakos* (bad, base) was associated with the common people. In the context of ancient Greek society, as portrayed, for instance, in the Homeric poems, "the good" meant exercising one's strength and abilities on the battlefield or in the political arena, whereas "the bad" meant simply the inability to do so due to a lack of strength, status, or ability. For the ancients, "the good" thus meant correctly fulfilling the duties of one's office as a noble. With the coming of Christianity, these terms shifted in meaning, and there came a radical reevaluation of values. The experience of Roman occupation led the Jews to criticize the Roman virtues, such as strength and the exercise of power, as vices. Thus, what was once the good—strength and power—now came into criticism, and what was once bad was erected into a whole host of new Christian virtues—humility, meekness, self-denial, etc. For Nietzsche, these new "virtues" could only by perceived as something positive by an oppressed people. Although the wretched are deprived of earthly strength, they are, according to the new virtues, the ones truly blessed by God. Christianity thus inverted the meanings of these

moral terms to fit its own purposes. By an unfathomable historical process, even the conquerors, the Romans, came in time to adopt the inverted value system of the conquered. Thus, Christianity created a new morality which modern Europe has inherited.

Nietzsche's criticism of Christian morality is that it is not a positive view that affirms the individual's life and strengths but rather is what he calls a "slave morality" based on a profound sense of *ressentiment* which criticizes and censures the strength of others, which it is itself lacking. This ressentiment is, for Nietzsche, clear in the new meanings of the moral terms. For the Greeks, the opposite of "the good" with its connotation of the exercise of power in the fulfillment of one's duty was simply "the bad" or "the common." Thus, the noble class distinguished itself from the lower classes. But when the Jews and the Christians reinterpreted "the good" to mean "the downtrodden," "the oppressed," and "the miserable," they set as its opposite term not "the bad" but rather "evil." In this way the exercise of strength and power became branded as something morally wicked.

Since the Christian has no power in this world, he consoles himself with the promise of emancipation in another sphere. This conception of morality, for Nietzsche, inverts and distorts mankind's nature, which is a will to express and exercise its own power. Nietzsche often uses the metaphor of an illness to describe the effect of Christianity on modern Europe. Like a cancer, it has deprived modern man of his natural strengths and abilities by making him feel embarrassed and leaving him with a guilty conscience when he does exercise his natural powers. Nietzsche is critical of any number of contemporary movements such as socialism, democracy, and utilitarianism, which he sees as mere outgrowths of Christian morality. These movements merely coordinate the weakness of the masses or "the herd" into a collective strength with which it can effectively oppress the great spirits and enforce a rule of mediocrity in which the weakness and ignorance of the individual become less visible. These movements are, for Nietzsche, pessimistic and life-denying in that they stifle the creative natural impulses of the individual.

Nietzsche never worked out a systematic ethic in response to his moral diagnosis of the age, but he did manage to formulate a number of suggestions which might be regarded as guidelines leading in the direction of an ethic. One of these suggestions is his doctrine of the eternal return. This is essentially a metaphysical doctrine which Nietzsche regards as implying a kind of regulative moral principle. One problem with Christianity, as he sees it, is that it understands life as a linear progression leading teleologically to an eternal existence in heaven. This tends to take value and importance away from mundane life, which is then regarded as a mere trial or warm-up for the real life which only comes later. Nietzsche suggests that we replace this linear conception of time with a cyclical view in line with that often found in Greek thought. If we consider the universe to be like the seasons which come and go and then return again for all eternity, then we are obliged to think of our lives and actions in radically different terms. If the universe is a repeating cycle, then all of our deeds will be repeated for all eternity. Thus, each action is equally important in itself and is not merely of relative importance in relation to some illusory future event. The ethical result that Nietzsche hopes to achieve with this view is that one will try to live one's life such that one can affirm all of one's actions without regret or misgiving. One must conceive of each action as a good in itself and not merely as a means or stepping stone to some future action. One must be able to will each of one's actions to be repeated for an eternity. It should be noted that this principle is normatively neutral and offers no guidance about precisely what is good or bad or worthwhile.

A second, extremely debated and misunderstood doctrine in Nietzsche's positive ethical program is that of the overman or superman (*Übermensch*). This doctrine has often been misread as a forerunner of the Nazi ideology of the superiority of the Germanic race, but Nietzsche, who never hesitated to express disapprobation for his fellow countrymen, was anything but a German nationalist or racist. It has also been disputed whether the notion of the overman is intended as a prediction about the future in a nihilistic age or as a concrete normative proposal for ethics. On a sympathetic interpretation, the overman can be regarded as an ideal or positive model for an ethics without transcendent grounding. In a world after the death of God, the overman is one who has the strength and sobriety to accept life on its own terms without illusions or promises and who has the ability and creativity to posit his own values in place of the traditional Christian moral code. Here once again there is little by way of concrete normative prescription. The overmen and -women could and would presumably all have radically differing conceptions of the good, each based on their own creative individualities. The one normative thing that they would have in common would be their affirmation of life as it is and their expression of this in the exercise of their natural powers.

Nietzsche's view of moral life can be seen as a response to Kant's account of autonomy. While he agrees with Kant in regarding the self-determining will of the individual as the focus of ethical action, he departs radically from the Kantian view in his conception of how the will decides and acts autonomously. For Nietzsche, morality is concerned with ideals or virtues which are posited by the individual. Unlike in Kant's conception, these ideals are not in need of any universal validity or internal consistency; moreover, they need not be conducive to the compatibility of individual wills in the social sphere. The ideals and virtues of the overmen are the expression of their own individual choice and require no further justification either from the inherent nature of the virtue or ideal itself or from the general approbation of others. The only criterion seems to be that the virtues be life-enhancing in the sense that they are conducive to the expression of the will to power. Likewise, the ideals posited by the overmen have a claim on them alone and are not universalized or extended to others.

Despite the fact that he has been badly misunderstood and misappropriated, Nietzsche has exerted a profound influence on 20th century thought in the work of thinkers such as Heidegger, Jaspers, Camus, and Sartre. He can be seen as the founder of the tradition of atheistic existentialism. But even within this tradition, Nietzsche is in many ways unique in his attempt to carve out conceptions of the good and of moral life that depart radically from the traditional Christian model. Even among the later atheistic existentialists such as Camus, for example, there is often an attempt to preserve the actual content of Christian ethics and values while rejecting their metaphysical grounding. In his posthumous notes, Nietzsche prophesied an age of nihilism which Dostoevsky feared would be the result of a godless world, but, instead of retreating back to a Christian position as Dostoevsky did, he attempted to offer positive secular solutions with doctrines such as the eternal return and the overman. Nietzsche thus sets the paradigm of inquiry for the later atheistic existentialists by showing that the problem lies in avoiding the Scylla of rationalistic or transcendent groundings for ethics, which offer the illusory security and certainty of metaphysical comfort, and the Charybdis of nihilism, which seems in many ways to be the logical result of such a denial.

V. HEIDEGGER

The German philosopher Martin Heidegger was a student of Edmund Husserl, and it was under Heidegger's hand that Husserl's phenomenological method took on a new form which proved to be profoundly influential for later thinkers such as Sartre and Merleau-Ponty. Unfortunately, his highly idiosyncratic writing style has for a long time hindered his reception in the anglophone world of philosophy. While Heidegger's work must be mentioned in any account of existentialist thought, it is ostensibly concerned primarily with ontology and not ethics. Although Heidegger never developed an ethical theory, the way in which ethical terms enter into his ontological analyses attests to a deep overriding ethical concern. Clearly the best-known of Heidegger's works is *Being and Time* (1927) in which he gives his highly original account of the existential experience of the human subject, which he refers to as *Dasein*. It is from this quasi-anthropological account that at least a sketch of an ethical theory can be discerned.

Heidegger conceives of Dasein as being always already in a relation to the sphere of objects. Much of *Being and Time* is dedicated to uncovering or disclosing this, for Heidegger, primordial relation to objects by means of an extended phenomenological analysis. Heidegger's critique of much of the scientific and philosophical tradition is that it has forgotten this precognitive sphere by abstracting individual objects out of their original context and thus giving an account of them as monadic and isolated. According to Heidegger, our fundamental relation to objects is that of use. Objects are "ready-to-hand" (*zuhanden*) in that they already exist in a larger schema of use before it is possible for us to abstract them from this schema and analyze them scientifically. Heidegger says that human beings are thrown into the world in that we find ourselves surrounded by objects, practices, and meanings which we did not create. He calls this "facticity," which is intended to refer to the overarching network of meaning and practice which Dasein always already finds itself in. It has been noted that Heidegger has a much more unified or integrated conception of human existence than Sartre, whose Cartesian dualism of *en-soi* and *pour-soi* seems radically to separate the subject from the world and thus to bestow on that subject an absolute and radical freedom. Heidegger avoids this with the very notion of Dasein, which is fundamentally constituted by its being-in-the-world, i.e., by the fact that it is always already surrounded by objects and is bound up in their uses and meanings.

For Heidegger, time is an essential dimension of the constitution of human subjects. Dasein is the kind of being which always projects toward a future. It is the future which contains countless possibilities and in which Dasein will realize its projects. Its orientation in the present is always with respect to this transcendence. However, the projection into the future is compromised by the countless petty distractions of daily life. One falls into routines and habits and busies oneself with the chores of daily existence, and by so doing one forgets the original question of one's being and one's projection into a future. One seeks refuge in the crowd or what Heidegger calls the "they" or "*das Man*" in order to escape from the question of one's own being. In this way Dasein becomes inauthentic. Much of the first part of *Being and Time* is dedicated to outlining these forms of inauthenticity.

In Part Two Heidegger attempts to determine the form of Dasein's possible authentic existence. For Heidegger, the key to authenticity lies in the concept of *Angst*, usually translated as dread or anxiety. Angst is the vague feeling or mood that we experience when contemplating the finitude of our human existence. We see in the future the termination of our life in death. The feeling of Angst is crucial for authenticity since it tears the individual out of the routine of daily habit. Moreover, the Angst in relation to one's own death specifically calls attention back to the individual and does not allow him to seek refuge in the crowd. Thus, what Heidegger calls being-toward-death represents the possibility of an authentic existence.

From *Being and Time* one can discern the vague outlines of an ethics of authenticity. Despite Heidegger's interest in history and his concept of being-with (*Mitsein*), according to which Dasein is always already in relation with other human subjects, his ethics seems to be confined to the individual. Heidegger's conception of authenticity is a call to the individual to keep resolutely before his eye the finitude of his own existence. Like the overman's virtues for Nietzsche, Heidegger's account of authenticity has a reflexive or self-referential character in that it concerns only the particular moral agent and does not make any claim to govern intersubjective human relations. Unlike Nietzsche, who claims that the overmen could have a number of different and even conflicting virtues or moral ideals, with the only overarching criterion being that the virtues be expressions of the will to power, Heidegger seems to limit the possible virtues to one—authenticity. Unfortunately, in his later work Heidegger never developed an ethics or social theory explicitly, and thus we must look to some of the French existentialists, who were inspired by him, to see his ethical views explored in more detail.

VI. CAMUS

The French-Algerian writer Albert Camus was one of the leading figures in the French existentialist movement. Although not a philosopher in the strict sense, he was nevertheless strongly influenced by the Western philosophical tradition. His entire literary career has been characterized not without justice as a struggle with the problem of nihilism. In his novels *The Stranger* (1942) and *The Plague* (1947) as well as in his philosophical essays *The Myth of Sisyphus* (1942) and *The Rebel* (1951) he examines the ethical implications of nihilism and tries to formulate an appropriate response to the challenge of a godless world. It has been noted that Camus' thought cannot be seen as a single theory but rather must be regarded as a movement from a relativistic or even nihilistic position in his early works to a form of secular humanism in his later thought.

Absurdity is, for Camus, the fundamental fact of human existence which poses the moral problem. Human beings have a deep-seated need for order or unity in the universe, an order which would lend our existence a meaning and value. This nostalgia for a world which is hospitable to human beings and their ends is what Nietzsche called "metaphysical comfort." For Camus, the modern age has rendered this conception of the universe implausible. Science tells us that the universe is indifferent to our human goals and that our very existence is merely the result of chance. Likewise, the belief in God has become problematic as has every other form of transcendent value. Thus, we are confronted by a universe essentially devoid of meaning. This, says Camus, we experience as absurdity. The incongruity between our hopes and desires and the ultimate meaninglessness of our existence leave us strangers in the world.

There are several possible responses to the problem of meaninglessness and absurdity. One might opt for the religious solution as Kierkegaard and Dostoevsky did. Camus rejects this solution since it posits a metaphysical comfort and thus ultimately moves beyond the existential condition of absurdity to a position of stability or security. Camus criticizes Kierkegaard for beginning with paradox, absurdity, and despair and ending up with a nonabsurd, meaningful universe via the belief in God. It is not clear, however, that Kierkegaard's solution leads to complacency as Camus charges given that Kierkegaard claims that fear and trembling are permanent features of our moral and religious existence regardless of whether we are Christian or not. Camus likewise rejects metaphysical systems such as Hegelianism or Marxism which in effect create a form of secular religion to answer the problem of meaninglessness and nihilism. These philosophical systems appeal to a metaphysical comfort in the absolute belief in human reason and thus differ from the traditional Christian belief system only in their content. For Camus, such systems must fail in the end since their belief in the power of rationality is ultimately unfounded. Such systems are merely a fragile house of cards that is unable to withstand critical examination. Thus, it is useless to try to employ human reason to supplant God as the source of absolute moral values and meanings.

Another possible response to absurdity and nihilism is, of course, suicide, which Camus likewise rejects. Camus takes up this theme in *The Myth of Sisyphus*, which can be seen as a continuation of the discussion by Dostoevsky in *The Possessed*. The question is whether suicide is the logical result of the realization and full comprehension of the meaninglessness of the world. Can a human being continue to live, knowing that his existence has no grounding or justification? For Camus, suicide cannot be regarded as a viable solution since it represents an admission of the inability to live in a world devoid of meaning. This admission stands in contradiction to the human spirit and is an insult to human pride.

Camus tries to resolve the issue by an appeal to human dignity. The only truly human response for Camus is that of revolt against the universe and the meaninglessness. Only in revolt is the dignity of mankind preserved. Thus, as an allegory for his view he chooses the ancient Greek myth of Sisyphus. As a punishment for his crimes against the gods, Sisyphus is condemned to roll a boulder up a hill for all eternity. His useless labor is a metaphor for meaningless human striving since despite all his efforts in the end the boulder always rolls down to the bottom and he must begin his bitter task again. Camus imagines that Sisyphus continues his task merely out of spite for all eternity even though he knows it is destined to failure. Sisyphus is, for Camus, a model for the integrity of the human spirit which has the courage to carry on in the face of the absurdity.

For Camus, all of the other solutions fail since they attempt to offer a cure for the disease of nihilism. The only correct and authentic response, says Camus, "is not to be cured, but to live with one's ailments." To propose a cure is implicitly to presuppose the old religious belief system and to expect that there should be a transcendent meaning. The goal is to reject not just any such transcendent meaning but also the very hope and expectation of one, and this involves learning to live in a world devoid of such meaning. Not only is this possible, says Camus, but it is also accompanied by a feeling of liberation. The value of life comes not from without, from some transcendent external source, but rather from within the unique concrete situations in which we find ourselves. A given moment or experience is beautiful, unique, and precious precisely in its finitude and transience.

The ethical implications of this view are manifold. Given that there can be no normative ethical system which commands specific action since all such systems and commands ultimately lack a metaphysical grounding, it follows that any discussion about qualitative values is misguided. It is impossible to debate whether something is better or worse, or more or less moral than something else. All such qualitative differences in values must have some kind of necessity or transcendent anchor, which is ultimately impossible. Thus, Camus proposes what he calls an "ethic of quantity." By this he seems to understand the maximizing of the unique individual experiences without the attempt to evaluate them qualitatively and without the hope or illusion of anything more. One might characterize this by saying that Camus puts weight not on living best but rather on living most. In *The Myth of Sisyphus,* he provides examples of character types which embody this ethic. He discusses, for instance, the stage actor who by virtue of the constant repetitions is compelled to recognize the contingency and meaninglessness of his performance. He nevertheless endeavors to give his best effort each time with the awareness that each performance is unique and precious. He accepts that his skill will only be viewed and appreciated by the audience on that given day, and he accepts the ephemeral nature of his fame without hoping for any further redemption. Here the stage actor differs from the film actor who believes in an immortality through the constant playing of the film. This sort of teleology destroys the existential moment and thins out the existential experience of the original performance.

Despite Camus' apparent relativism with respect to qualitative value judgments, later in his literary career he does seem to affirm a secular humanist ethic of solidarity. In the novel *The Plague,* it is Jean Tarrou who expresses Camus' moral ideal. Tarrou realizes that the plague from which the town of Oran suffers is a metaphor for all human suffering and for the incongruity of the universe with our human life and projects. He advocates a doctrine of human solidarity but without any illusions or flights to metaphysical comfort. The task that the novel posits is "to try to be a saint without God." The idea is to affirm ethics and moral values for their own sake without the need for a transcendent

grounding or anchor. Thus, the moral imperative for the later Camus seems to be that we should strive to become secular saints.

Although Camus cannot be regarded as the leading theorist of existentialism, his novels and essays did much to introduce the existentialist movement into the popular culture and to make the themes of existentialism known outside the walls of the university. Moreover, Camus' interest in philosophy was primarily ethical in character. Like Kierkegaard, he was most influenced by those philosophers such as Socrates who insisted on the unity of philosophical thought and life. In this sense Camus can be regarded as making an important contribution to applied ethics.

VII. SARTRE

In the final pages of his philosophical masterpiece *Being and Nothingness* (1943), Sartre tells his readers that he will provide a companion volume to the work which will treat the ethical consequences of the ontological theory sketched there. This book never materialized, although among the notebooks published after his death there are extensive writings on ethics which evidence a clear attempt to fulfill the promise made in *Being and Nothingness.* But one will be disappointed if one hopes to find in these *Notebooks for an Ethics* a systematic statement of his ethical views since the notes, although providing a fuller picture, nevertheless remain rather fragmentary and fall short of a complete account. However, a great deal of other material on ethics from Sartre's hand is still yet to be published, and it is conceivable that a more systematic picture may eventually emerge. Until that time, we must avail ourselves of the published statements of his ethical views.

In the body of *Being and Nothingness* itself, Sartre sketches an elaborate ontological theory, but the focus is not exclusively on ontology since it is clear that he ultimately wants to draw ethical consequences from the ontological basis that he establishes. The central theme in all of Sartre's writings as well as in his ethical views is that of human freedom. Like Kierkegaard, Sartre emphasizes the choice of the individual independent of rational arguments or discursive reason. With his famous slogan, "existence precedes essence," he denies traditional claims that there is some kind of human nature which could determine the individual ahead of time. On the contrary, for Sartre, human beings have no predetermined essence; rather, they simply exist. As a result, it is the responsibility of the individual to create his own essence through his actions. Human beings are essentially defined by their deeds, or, as Sartre puts it, "Man is the sum total of his actions." This, however, implies a mutable essence which changes with one's actions.

For the Sartre of *Being and Nothingness,* the central ethical virtue is to accept this freedom and to lead one's life accordingly by being aware of one's free choices and by taking responsibility for their consequences. But this is by no means an easy task. The ontological fact of radical freedom which Sartre announces is both liberating and terrifying. Sartre says, "Man is condemned to be free," by which he means that the fact of freedom is not something that we can greet with unqualified joy but instead is something which, like a prison sentence, we are condemned to, something we face with uncertainty and anguish. When the individual realizes that the world is essentially a nothingness without human beings and their projects and that only through free acts do individuals create themselves, then this nothingness and the concomitant responsibility become something terrifying since each individual alone must bear the entire burden of responsibility for his own life. However, this freedom is not merely terrifying, for it is also liberating. Sartre's character Orestes in the play *The Flies* (1943) embodies this double-edged sword. He is aware of his freedom, which liberates him to the point that he is capable of anything, even challenging the gods, but it also makes it possible for him to commit terrifying acts such as killing his mother, acts which he must take responsibility for and live with.

Human beings create many mechanisms by means of which they try to deny the fact of freedom to themselves and thus escape from the responsibility of their moral choice. This denial Sartre calls "bad faith." In an insightful psychological analysis, Sartre explains two forms which this denial takes. (1) "Escape to facticity" is the denial of one's freedom by attempting to define oneself as an object with a fixed essence. If one had a pregiven essence, then one would enjoy a metaphysical certainty, and there would no longer be any contingency in one's existence. When one defines one's being, for example, by saying, "I am a doctor," there is often an attempt to portray one's position as a fixed fact about the universe, as if there were no history of choice behind it, as if one were born a doctor and could never have been anything else. One pretends to be a doctor in the same way a chair is a chair, namely as a fixed fact of the matter. But unlike chairs, humans have no fixed essence and are always creating themselves. Likewise, when one tries to justify one's actions by fixed facts about the world, one tries to portray oneself as something fixed and determined by outward circumstances.

If these assertions and self-definitions were true, then one would be relieved of the burden of moral responsibility since things are simply what they are by nature and cannot change. When one says, for example, "I could not come because I was too busy," one tries to portray one's being busy as a fact of the universe independent of one's individual choice or will. One forgets that one has already made certain choices and has already set certain priorities such that doing one thing is more important than doing another. This is in bad faith since what was originally a choice is later portrayed as a fixed fact beyond the individual's control. According to this version of bad faith, one tries to escape one's freedom by becoming a fact or a thing.

(2) "Escape to transcendence" is the other form of bad faith. Here the individual always defers judgment based on past actions and refers to an indefinite future where one's true essence is thought to lie. This represents an absolute and inauthentic denial of certain past actions by means of a retreat into the transcendent realm of the future. Despite, for example, one's history of cowardice and knavery, one is still free to define oneself and to create one's essence in the future. The individual portrays himself, not as a knave, but rather a hero since in the future, he asserts, he will perform heroic acts. For Sartre, this is an attempt to escape from the responsibility and the free choices of one's past by appeal to an indeterminate future. There is no deed so ignominious that one cannot try to ignore it and make it unimportant by pointing into the future. One is one's actions, and to that extent one must own being a coward; but this does not mean that one is condemned to be a coward forever since one is always creating oneself through new actions and thus one might in part erase an ignominious past through heroic actions, but the proof is in the actions themselves not in good intentions and promises about a future. Thus, in this version of bad faith, one escapes freedom by fleeing into the transcendent future.

For Sartre, human beings are caught in the dialectic of facticity and transcendence. He says paradoxically, "Humans are what they are and are what they are not." By this he means that on the one hand we are in a sense a certain set of facts of the matter, i.e., we are the sum total of our past actions, but this is not something static or fixed as a tree or a table is a set of facts. On the contrary, our past is always being reinterpreted by the future and the present as our goals and projects change. Our past is indeterminate since it lends itself to an infinite number of possible interpretations, and in this sense we are what we are not since there is always a part of us which is indeterminate, namely that part with relation to our future. Authenticity lies in being aware of both aspects of this dialectical relation and as a result in taking responsibility for oneself and the world.

Sartre's theory of responsibility is often couched in somewhat radical terms, which has led to a great deal of misunderstanding and criticism of his views. He says, for instance, in reference to his own experience in World War II, that there are no innocent victims in war, but rather that everyone is in a sense responsible for it. By this he clearly does not mean that each and every individual is responsible for the war in the same sense that leaders of nations are responsible for it; rather, he seems to mean that each person is responsible for the interpretation that he gives to the war and thus for the way in which he will live it. One can choose to live the war as a member of the Resistance or as an informant for the enemy, but either way one is free. It is with this freedom that we have chosen what the war will mean to us as individuals and how we will live and experience it.

Sartre's ethics is clearly focused on the individual, and there is at least in his early work no attempt to sketch a theory of social ethics. On the contrary, in *Being and Nothingness* Sartre argues that human relations invariably reduce to either sadism or masochism and that a social ethics based on solidarity or mutual recognition is in principle impossible. He illustrates this in his famous play *No Exit* (1944), in which three characters are condemned to hell, which to their surprise does not consist of the rack or fire and brimstone but, instead, of having to be together with each other indefinitely. Sartre's character Garcin summarizes the situation with the memorable line, "Hell is other people." In his later work, the *Critique of Dialectical Reason* (1960), Sartre attempted a grand synthesis of existentialism and Marxism in which there is a clear attempt to sketch a social ethic along Marxist lines. But in order to do so, he was obliged to revise radically and even reject a number of his earlier views.

Sartre's work has been highly influential in a number of different fields. His personality was the focal point of the French existentialist movement during its most popular period. Along with Merleau-Ponty, he was largely responsible for introducing the work of Husserl and Heidegger into the francophone world. His diverse literary works, which include novels, plays, and essays, make him perhaps the best-known and most read of all the existential thinkers. Although it is clear that he was profoundly interested in questions of ethics, his contributions to the field are limited primarily to moral psychology. It can only be regretted that the companion piece to *Being and Nothingness* dedicated to ethical the-

ory never materialized and that so much of his work remained a preface to ethics rather than an ethical theory in its own right.

VIII. CONCLUSION

In order to understand and appreciate existentialism's contribution to ethical thought, it is useful to place it within the larger tradition of ethics and social theory. In the history of ethics, a distinction is often drawn between theories that concentrate on the cultivation of virtuous character traits in the individual, which are designated "virtue-based ethics," and those that aim to give rules for proper conduct, which are generally referred to as "rule-based ethics." Much of ancient ethical theory is characterized by the former and much of modern by the latter. Ancient theories of ethics such as those of Plato, Aristotle, Stoicism, Epicureanism, and Augustine focus primarily on the moral character of the individual as such. Theories of this sort are characterized by the fact that they concentrate primarily on what virtue amounts to and how to live in accordance with it. Given that rules cannot guide moral action in this view, the goal of a moral life is to cultivate a virtuous character which can make the right decisions in the particular moral situation. In addition, these theories enumerate the various vices and try to explain how to avoid them. Like the virtues, the vices, e.g., gluttony, garrulousness, and incontinence, also focus primarily on the individual. Modern philosophy tends to conceive of the question of moral life differently. In the modern world "after virtue," ethics is considered not to be something which concerns virtue alone but rather universal rules for action. For modern theories such as those of Kant or the utilitarians, the focus is on some universal principle which transcends the individual and which should govern individual conduct and intersubjective relations. These general principles are, for example, the categorical imperative or the greatest happiness for the greatest number. For these theories, the moral life of the individual is conceived as the general correspondence of the individual will with some universal. While there are areas of overlap and the distinction between virtue-based theories and rule-based ones cannot be conceived as absolute, it is nevertheless useful for understanding the various approaches to ethics in the history of Western thought.

The existentialists in some respects revive the ancient tradition in large part in protest against the modern focus on the universal. Like these ancient theories, existentialism is skeptical of the possibility of universal laws giving direction in particular moral situations. No universal rule or system can tell the individual what to do in the particular instance since such rules are always indeterminate and every ethical situation unique. For the existentialists, the individual must decide on his own without recourse to rules. Thus, the existentialists are primarily concerned with the inward, subjective life of the individual. Although the existentialists, with the exception of Nietzsche, do not tend to speak of virtue per se, there is a clear family resemblance between their accounts of the ethical life and traditional virtue-based theories. Seen in this light, the primary, if not the only, virtue for existentialism is authenticity, which amounts, generally speaking, to the acceptance of one's freedom and moral responsibility.

While authenticity can be regarded as the highest virtue among the existentialists, the way in which this is interpreted among the individual thinkers varies. For Kierkegaard, the development of one's inwardness and subjectivity before God distinctly has the look of a virtue. For Dostoevsky, virtue involves listening to the voice of conscience or spontaneous moral sentiment and not allowing oneself to be led astray by the sophistry of reason. For Nietzsche, independence, strength, creativity, and other classical Greek virtues are revived and reinstituted as moral character traits worth striving after in a godless world. Heidegger's conception of virtue is an authentic mode of existence in being-toward-death. For Camus, there is a sense in which maintaining human dignity and avoiding giving way to despair can be regarded as virtues. Virtue, for Sartre, is clearly the acceptance of one's freedom and moral responsibility according to the dialectic of facticity and transcendence.

By the same token, all of the existentialists have some sort of theory which corresponds to the ancients' account of the vices or character flaws, namely, a theory of what constitutes an inauthentic human life. Any attempt to escape from one's freedom via inauthenticity is for the existentialists a moral vice, but once again the way in which inauthenticity is interpreted is different among the various thinkers. For Kierkegaard, inauthenticity is the mark of the absent-minded objective thinker, who forgets his own inwardness and subjectivity in the course of his striving for objective knowledge. For Dostoevsky, it is found in one who allows himself to be subjected to the false rules and conceptions of the good life offered by the various demagogues and ideologues of the modern world. Inauthenticity is a feature of the collective mass or, for Nietzsche, "the herd," where the individual finds comfort for his own weakness, and by so doing loses his individuality and natural strengths. This is of course similar to Heideg-

ger's notion of "the they" or "*das Man*" to which the individual tries to escape. Camus' criticism of those thinkers who seek solace from the absurd by retreating to a position of metaphysical comfort can be seen as a theory of inauthenticity and modern vice. Likewise, for Sartre any attempt to escape from one's freedom is inauthentic and represents a clear sign of a moral character flaw or vice.

While existentialism can be seen as a continuation of ancient virtue-based theories in the sense that it focuses on virtues and vices and in the sense that it rejects universal rules for conduct, it nevertheless departs from the ancient tradition not only in its conception of these virtues and vices but also in its denial of the notion of a natural good or of human nature. For Plato and Aristotle, for example, human beings have a fixed essence. From this objective account of human nature they generate a theory of virtue which indicates how the individual can lead a flourishing, virtuous life given that fixed nature. Likewise, they believe that there are specific natural ends which all humans strive after, and from this objective account of natural ends, such as happiness, they derive an account of how one ought to act to achieve these ends. If we take Sartre's definition that existence precedes essence as existentialism's principle dogma, then existentialism clearly rejects both the notion of a fixed human nature and of natural ends or goods. Human beings are essentially a nothingness until they create themselves through their actions. Likewise, there are no universal *a priori* or fixed goods apart from determinate projects which humans posit for themselves. (It seems that all of the existentialists except Nietzsche would accept this. Contrary to the other existentialists, for Nietzsche, there is a sense of a determinate human nature which has been corrupted by Christianity and Christian ethics.) Existentialism's rejection of natural essences and ends is bound up with the very conception of authenticity which, as we have seen, all of the existentialists espouse in one form or another. In order to be authentic, one must be free and must take responsibility for one's freedom. A fixed human nature or essence would seem to limit one's freedom ahead of time. If there were such an essence, then one would have natural proclivities to do or not to do something, and human freedom would be no greater than the freedom of animals which are determined by nature. One might argue, as indeed the ancient virtue theorists do, that a determinate human nature does not necessarily preclude freedom since one's essence or nature might only determine one's actions partially. But in this view, one could always escape from one's freedom by appeal to one's essence or nature. Any number of failures to live up to the standard of full authenticity could always be minimized with platitudes to the effect that such failures or shortcomings are only human. Thus, for the existentialists, the very possibility of virtue, understood as authenticity, is only made possible by the denial of a fixed human essence and of natural human ends. In this sense, the existentialists, in the rejection of the metaphysical underpinnings of classical virtue-based theories, can be seen as making an original contribution to the discussion while working within the same general tradition of ethical thought. Understood as a theory in line with the classical doctrines of virtue, existentialism can be seen as perhaps the most significant alternative to the formalistic, rule-based theories of ethics which have dominated modern ethical thought.

Also See the Following Articles

KANTIANISM • UTILITARIANISM • VIRTUE ETHICS

Bibliography

Anderson, T. C. (1979). *The Foundation and Structure of Sartrean Ethics.* The Regents Press of Kansas, Lawrence.

Bell, L. A. (1989). *Sartre's Ethics of Authenticity.* Univ. of Alabama Press, Tuscaloosa.

Bernstein, J. (1987). *Nietzsche's Moral Philosophy.* Associated Univ. Presses, London/Toronto.

Detmer, D. (1988). *Freedom as a Value: A Critique of the Ethical Theory of Jean-Paul Sartre.* Open Court, Peru, IL.

East, B. (1984). *Albert Camus, ou l'homme à la recherche d'une morale.* Bellarmin, Montreal.

Hunt, L. (1991). *Nietzsche and the Origin of Virtue.* Routledge, London.

Lauth, R. (1950). *Die Philosophie Dostojewskis.* Piper and Verlag, Munich.

Olafson, F. (1967). *Principles and Persons: An Ethical Interpretation of Existentialism.* The Johns Hopkins Press, Baltimore.

Scott, C. E. (1990). *The Question of Ethics: Nietzsche, Foucault, Heidegger.* Indiana Univ. Press, Bloomington.

Stack, G. J. (1977). *Kierkegaard's Existential Ethics.* Univ. of Alabama Press, Tuscaloosa.

EXPLOITATION

Alan Carling
Bradford University

GLOSSARY

analytical Marxism An academic movement that uses the analytical tools of contemporary philosophy and social science to test, and if possible defend, the work of Karl Marx and his intellectual descendants. Its most prominent exponents are the Oxford philosopher Gerald Cohen, the California economist John Roemer, the Wisconsin sociologist Erik Wright, and the Chicago political scientist Jon Elster.

basic income The provision at regular intervals of an equal and unconditional payment to every adult member of a given society. This proposal has been widely discussed in Europe as a radical alternative to current welfare systems.

cross-class family A household in which, contrary to the usual pattern in most countries, the principal female member of the household has a higher class position from her employment than the principal male member has from his.

exploit (In social science applications) To gain at the expense of another by taking unjust advantage of the social situation in which they are placed.

extort To act deliberately so as to extract a benefit unjustly from another.

general equilibrium theory The modern theory in economics that analyzes the behavior of perfectly competitive markets in terms of simultaneous optimization.

oppress To restrict unjustly the activities or opportunities of another.

self-ownership A doctrine in political philosophy, said to underlie the thought of Robert Nozick, according to which persons are the rightful owners of all their parts, powers, and the full fruits thereof.

TO EXPLOIT SOMETHING is to turn that thing to one's advantage. Thus, a chess player might exploit a particular opening gambit, or a mistake by an opponent; a spider might exploit a favorable environment, or a corporation might exploit a technological advance. In its more specialized usage within the social sciences, the term exploitation is used instead to refer to a certain kind of unequal relationship between individuals or groups. In this usage, one individual (or group) exploits another individual (or group) only if the first individual (or group) gains an advantage at the expense of the second individual (or group).

The importance accorded to the concept of exploitation within the social sciences depends on the extent to which the basic relationships of society are thought to be exploitative. If, as right-wing authors tend to maintain, exploitation is an exceptional feature of major social relationships, then the concept does not have a great deal to offer to the critique of societies; if, on the other hand, as left-wing authors tend to maintain, exploitation is a widespread and inherent feature of major social relationships, then it assumes a central role in the characterization of societies. Thus there is considerable controversy over the applicability of the concept to putative cases of exploitation involving social class, gender, race, ethnicity, and social division.

I. THE CONCEPT OF EXPLOITATION

In its colloquial usage, the term "exploitation" is sometimes used in a morally neutral way: a tennis player who exploits an opponent's weak backhand would not be thought to be doing anything reprehensible. On the other hand, most academic writers maintain that the term carries a moral connotation when used in the description of societies: it is part of the meaning of the term that an exploitative social relationship is also an unjust relationship. The analysis of exploitation therefore resolves itself into a positive question—does one individual (or group) gain an advantage at the expense of another?—and a normative question—is this advantage unjustly gained? A relationship may then be deemed exploitative if and only if affirmative answers are forthcoming to both these questions.

Exploitation is distinct from, yet related to, a number of other concepts that are widely used in similar contexts of social criticism: the concepts of social disadvantage, oppression, tyranny, abuse, and so on. The distinctive feature of exploitation is that the party in the advantageous position (the exploiter) benefits as a result of the deficit imposed on the party in the disadvantageous position (the exploited). This is in contrast to, say, oppression, which can occur when the oppressor merely restricts the freedom or the opportunities of the oppressed without receiving any tangible benefit in return.

Exploitation thus conceived is a variety of unequal exchange, but this is not quite sufficient to identify it as a concept, because both ordinary gifts and cases of extortion (when the highwayman says "your money or your life," and you prefer life) also involve unequal exchange, yet seem to be distinct from exploitation. The differences within this family of concepts might be illustrated as follows: if you are unjustly imprisoned, then you are oppressed; if someone takes advantage of your imprisonment so that you make over your fortune

to them in return for one cigarette, this is exploitation; if a person imprisons you in order that you shall hand over your fortune in exchange for one cigarette, this is extortion; and if you bequeath your fortune to someone with whom you fall in love over a cigarette while in prison, this is a gift.

From such an analysis it follows that the concept of exploitation is especially geared to cases in which a person (or a group) finds herself in a disadvantageous situation, and some other person (or group) makes the disadvantaged person (or group) an offer it may be in the interests of the disadvantaged person to accept, *given* the situation that the person is in. Because the existence of exploitation is thus consistent with the freedom of the exploited group (because indeed it is an *exercise* of the immediate freedoms of the exploited group), exploitation as a social concept assumes significance in societies that are free but unequal. It is therefore particularly apposite in modern liberal democratic societies (which tend to have this character), but its application to them is challenging, because it shows that a society might be unjust despite being free. The concept thus tends to disturb the prevailing self-images of liberal democratic societies.

Although an exploited person will typically consent to the exploitation, *given the situation that they are in,* they would by implication prefer not to be in the original predicament from which exploitation arises. The role of coercion thus tends to lie not in controlling the behavior of exploited individuals or groups directly, but in maintaining the inequalities out of which exploitation grows—maintaining an unequal distribution of private property, for example, or the institutions of a sexist society.

II. THE SCOPE OF THE CONCEPT

The situations of social disadvantage from which exploitation may arise include:

- lack of property (poverty);
- lack of education or earning power;
- lack of talents or abilities;
- lack of power in an organizational setting;
- social discrimination or adverse social expectations;
- political or communal exclusion and oppression.

Although these factors will almost certainly interact in practice to create composite situations of disadvantages, issues of class exploitation arise especially from lack of property and lack of organizational power, issues of gender exploitation from social discrimination and differential expectations; and issues of exploitation by race or ethnicity from processes of social discrimination and communal exclusion.

Some writers have argued that the scope of the concept should be restricted to particular dimensions of benefit and cost, such as those concerning work rather than, say, sexual satisfaction. Other authors have tended to focus on exploitation in relation to specific kinds of social division—class *or* gender *or* race, and so on. A related issue is the possibility of welfare comparison between different instances of exploitation, and between exploitation and other kinds of social injustice: are low wages (as a source of exploitation) worse than, say, religious persecution (as a form of oppression); is racial disadvantage in a particular historical context worse than the exploitation of household labor in the same society? Where as a general issue should the priorities lie among many potential forms and sources of injustice?

We should not expect to find easy consensual answers to such difficult evaluative questions. For what it is worth, this author would argue, first, that it is not generally helpful to restrict the potential scope of application of a concept like exploitation to particular kinds or sources of inequality, and second, that there are dangers in organizing a beauty competition (more accurately: an ugly competition) for different varieties of social injustice. Perhaps social wrongs are incompletely ordered: it does not follow of every pair of social wrongs that one of them is worse than the other. So it may be more important to analyze the specific causes of the different wrongs, and say that each one is in its own way unacceptable.

III. THEORIES OF EXPLOITATION

A. Causal-Explanatory Theories

1. In the Free Market Domain: John Roemer's Core Theory

The idea of exploitation has been much clarified in recent years through the work of the Analytical Marxist school, and especially in the new theories of class exploitation developed by John Roemer. These theories address the first dimension in the analysis of exploitation: the mechanisms by which one group gains an advantage at the expense of another. To understand these developments, it is necessary to know a little of their background in the work of Marx.

Karl Marx had argued that systems of private enterprise capitalism are inherently exploitative because they rest on the "extraction of unpaid labor" from the working proletariat (i.e., those in the society who do not own productive facilities) by the nonworking bourgeoisie (i.e., those capitalists who do own productive facilities). In this view, part of the workers' efforts are rewarded by the wages they are paid, but there is an extra portion of their total efforts that is unpaid (also called "surplus value"). Because (i) it is the existence of the latter "unpaid" portion that enables capitalists to make a profit out of their investment in the production process, and because (ii) the capitalists live off of these profits, there is in effect an unreciprocated transfer of labor from workers to capitalists. This is the basis for saying that a relationship of *class exploitation* exists between the two major classes in a capitalist society, which is moreover inherent in capitalist society, so long as capitalists are making positive profits (and if they are unable to make positive profits, the capitalist society has already broken down).

This theoretical diagnosis was in its turn the foundation for a Marxist political program under which the class division inherent in capitalist society had to be overthrown in order to end the exploitation of the working class.

Quite apart from any of the political problems connected with this program, its theoretical weakness lies in the dependence of the theory of exploitation on a part of Marx's economic theory called "the labor theory of value." The labor theory of value holds that the prices at which goods exchange in a competitive market economy are proportional to the amount of labor required directly and indirectly to produce them. Marx had developed this theory in the light of the most advanced economic ideas available to him in his day—the classical economics of David Ricardo—but, ironically, Marx utilized these ideas just as they were about to be superseded as a result of the neoclassical revolution instigated in the 1870s by William Jevons and Leon Walras.

It is now widely accepted, even by many Marxists, that the labor theory of value in its original form is untenable on logical and theoretical grounds. John Roemer's great achievement—above all in his 1982 work *A General Theory of Exploitation and Class*—has been to reconstruct Marx's theory of class exploitation using contemporary neoclassical economic models, thereby placing Marx's fundamental insight on a firmer scientific foundation. The Marxian critique of capitalism is no longer dependent on the discredited labour theory of value.

Specifically, Roemer assumes:

• a society of self-interested utility maximizers;

who must satisfy their economic requirements by

• working, trading, or employing other people;

in a

• perfectly competitive private ownership market economy;

with

• known productive technology linking economic inputs (materials and labor) to economic outputs (products for consumption or sale).

This is the same theoretical picture as that adopted by what is called *general equilibrium theory* in modern economics. According to these theories the mechanisms of supply and demand operate to clear markets, thereby determining competitive prices for all commodities, and also establishing the relationship between money wages and the general rate of profit in the economy. When all markets are cleared, with no pressures of supply and demand acting to change prices, and all agents are doing as well as they can, given their circumstances (which implies that all economic agents have optimized their behavior) the economy is said to be in an equilibrium.

Roemer's work adds a double twist to these standard models:

(i) An unequal initial distribution of wealth is envisaged. This differentially affects the ability of economic agents to pursue the various economic options open to them.

(ii) A comparison is made between the initial levels of individual wealth and the individual's final position in the economy once an equilibrium outcome has been attained.

What emerges from such a comparison is a remarkable series of *correspondences* between agents:

• initial resources (their wealth);
• their behaviors (whether they are self-employed, employ others, or have to work for others in order to optimize);

and

• their welfare levels (given that the more you have to work, the worse off you are).

TABLE I

Wealth, Class and Exploitation Correspondences in Roemer's Theory of Exploitation*

Wealth level	Economic behavior	Class designation	Welfare designation
Very high	Only an employer	Pure capitalist	Exploiter
High	Employer and self-employed	Small capitalist	Exploiter
Adequate	Only self-employed	Petty bourgeois	Neutral
Low	Self-employed and employee	Semiproletarian	Exploited
Zero	Only an employee	Proletarian	Exploited

*The entry "Employer and Self-employed" means that a person optimizes by both working on their own account, and employing others to work for them; a person described as "Self-employed and Employee" is someone who works on his or her own account, and also works for someone else on the side.

Because economic behavior is closely related to social class (employers are the capitalists, and the employed are the working class), the upshot is shown in Table I, which presents correspondences between wealth, class and welfare.

Looking at the table, you might ask: "What's 'high wealth', and 'low'? It's all very vague, how many dollars are we talking about?" The answer is that the threshold levels of wealth exhibited in Table 1 depend on both the technology available and the needs or aspirations of the individuals in the economy.

Imagine, for example, a person in a purely agricultural economy who has to grow a certain amount of corn in order to survive, requiring a certain minimum amount of land, say 40 acres, which he or she must cultivate for, say, 50 hours each week in order to produce the crop to feed the family. These data establish the benchmarks on the scale of wealth. Anyone who owns just 40 acres of land will have "adequate" wealth, according to these models, enabling them to survive by working 50 hours a week, each on his or her own farm. But people wealthier than that—those who own more than 40 acres—will be able to hire the poorer people—those owning fewer than 40 acres—to work for them, initially using the extra land the wealthier people possess. It is not difficult to see why the wealthier people would prefer this arrangement, because it enables them to get the most from their extra land. But the poorer people will also want to work for wages to make up their subsistence, *given* that they cannot survive wholly on their own resources. This is why a deal can be struck—in effect a wages-for-work bargain—between the richer and the poorer people.

It turns out however that once an equilibrium has been established the employers who do the hiring will always end up working for less than 50 hours in the week themselves (if they are rich enough to be pure capitalists in this example, they won't have to work at all) whereas those they hire will be working for more than 50 hours a week in order to make ends meet. The effect is that the employing classes gain from the employment relationship (they gain the benefit of not having to work as much as 50 hours) while the working classes lose (from the cost of working more than 50 hours). Finally, as we have seen, the person in the middle with "adequate" wealth, who neither employs nor is employed, is in a neutral, intermediate position also from the welfare point of view, judged by the prevailing standard of effort—the 50-hour week. "Adequate" wealth thus acts as a crisp dividing line between the people who gain at the expense of others—the relatively wealthy exploiting classes—and those at whose expense the advantage is gained—the relatively poverty-stricken exploited classes.

Three points about Roemer's theory are especially noteworthy:

• The relationships between wealth, class, and exploitation status emerge endogenously—as logical consequences of a model that does not presuppose them. This is in contrast with many sociological accounts, which tend to assume that the disadvantaged, say, are also the exploited. Roemer's theory shows *why* the disadvantaged tend to become the exploited.

• The theory detects exploitation in the heart of a capitalist private ownership market economy, even under idealized conditions of free trade and perfect competition. This is in sharp contrast with the prevailing orthodoxy of our time, which tends on the contrary to detect exploitation only when markets are working *imperfectly*—when powerful corporate monopolies or trade union organizations are keeping prices or wages artificially above their "natural" competitive levels. In this dominant view, one eliminates exploitation by opening up the society even further to the action of competitive market forces. Roemer's theory shows the opposite: that a more competitive market economy may well be a more exploitative market economy, because it may allow the wealthy even greater freedom to take advantage of their wealth. The institutional culprit in this case is not restraint on trade, but inequality of resources.

• As has been said, Roemer's theory of exploitation no longer depends on Marx's labor theory of value, because prices in the general equilibrium models are determined not by labor content, but by the effects of supply and demand in a given environment of production technologies. Labor time nevertheless retains a role as an index of welfare for individuals, by means of which their exploitation status is assigned: a person's exploitation is measured by the amount of time he or she has to work over and above the work norm mandated by general technological and social conditions (the 50-hour week in the example above). I think it can be argued that this conclusion preserves the critical thrust of Marx's theory, while saving it from dependence on his flawed economics. But whether Roemer's ideas represent a successful rescue attempt on Marx, or another nail in his coffin, they stand by themselves as a powerful modern statement of the causal theory of exploitation in a market economy.

2. Beyond the Free Market Domain

It is not surprising that Roemer's achievement in refurbishing the theory of exploitation applied to the market domain has led to a number of attempts by himself and other authors to generalize the basic ideas across other domains of inquiry.

• Roemer has modeled international trade in cases in which (i) the markets in final commodities are open, but there are no international markets either for labor or capital and (ii) all the international markets are open. In the first case, the restrictions on competition imply that wage and profit-rate differentials may exist between the various "nations" in the idealized world economy; in the second case, international flows of capital and labor migration will act to equalize wage and profit rates. But it transpires that in either case there is a mechanism of unequal exchange analogous to the core examples discussed above: the "advanced" countries with a higher capital/labor ratio, or the wealthier countries that export capital (or, equivalently, import labor) gain at the expense of the less-advanced countries. This amounts to a demonstration of a precise mechanism for *imperialist exploitation,* as this general topic has been discussed in the extensive literature concerning "the development of underdevelopment."

• Feudalism is the name for the system of production prevalent in Europe before the onset of capitalism. It involved workers—serfs—being tied to the land in various ways, and compelled to contribute labor services, or other benefits in kind or in cash, to the feudal lords who controlled the countryside. Roemer has phrased the contrast between feudalism and free market capitalism in terms of a concept of *feudal exploitation:* whereas capitalists exploit the workers' lack of wealth, the feudal lords exploit the serfs' lack of freedom. This is noncompetitive behavior on the part of the lords, because in effect they enjoy a local monopoly over the labor capacity of "their" serfs. (Indeed, the system looks so much like a protection racket that it might be more accurate to use the term "feudal extortion" instead of "feudal exploitation.")

• The model of capitalist exploitation implies that if resources are equalized, exploitation will disappear: if everyone owns just 40 acres, no one is in a position to take economic advantage of anyone else in the population. But would this mean that all sources of class inequality are eliminated in the society? Roemer suggests that differentials in skills, needs and abilities would still exist, and that these could form the basis of new social inequalities, as the skilled or able took advantage of the unskilled and needy. This he calls *skills exploitation,* or sometimes *socialist exploitation;* the latter on the grounds that it is the type of exploitation that might survive in a socialist society that had nevertheless equalized the distribution of alienable wealth.

• The sociologist Erik Wright has taken up Roemer's theory and adapted it to the circumstances of corporate capitalism (and also to the "actually existing socialism" of the Soviet states as it actually existed prior to 1989). The different types of exploitation may be regarded as arising from a series of different assets possessed (or unpossessed) by individuals: private wealth, labor capacity, skill, and so on. Wright suggests that there is another important category of *organization assets* possessed by virtue of occupying an official position in a hierarchical structure, as opposed to the possession of wealth per se. Because this asset can be used as a lever to direct benefits toward the office holder at the expense of a range of different client groups, organization assets can form the basis for systems of *bureaucratic exploitation.* These are certainly to be found within the corporate hierarchies of capitalist business, where their effects are conjoined with the effects of private ownership in the struggles between managers and shareholders over the spoils of enterprise. But they exist (or used to exist) in a less alloyed form among the *Nomenklatura* of the Soviet regime, who only had the workers, and not also the shareholders, to dispute their claims over the net economic product.

• I myself have used Roemer's approach to investigate some questions of gender division and ethnic division.

It can be shown, for example, that mechanisms governing the distribution of labor within households can easily lead to forms of *domestic exploitation* directly analogous with Roemer's core findings. In particular, if there is differential earning power between two domestic partners, economic logic dictates that the higher earner should go out to work, with the lower earner running the home. This is obvious enough. What is less obvious is that the bargaining process within the couple over the domestic division of labor will lead to the lower-earning partner working longer hours overall than the higher earner. The relationship between the two members of the couple is therefore directly analogous in welfare terms to the exploitative relationship discussed above between the wealthy peasant who owns more than 40 acres and works less than 50 hours, and the poor peasant who owns less and works more. (The difference is that the source of exploitation in the domestic case is not lack of land, but lack of earning power.)

Because the domestic labor model was designed to reflect an empirical reality in which women's wage rates are systematically lower than men's, this finding converts into a prediction of *exploitation along gender lines* in the vast majority of (heterosexual) households.

• In relation to *ethnic exploitation,* it can be shown that the theoretical conditions are easily fulfilled by which one segment of a population can sustain a position of advantage that excludes another section from a variety of different possible social benefits. The relevance of this result should be obvious enough to situations of ethnic exclusion, in which one ("majority") community benefits at the expense of another ("minority") community. The system of Apartheid which used to exist in South Africa was a particularly flagrant example (where the Black "minority" group of course constituted the overwhelming majority of the population); but there are all too many other, and some less obvious, cases around the world.

Roemer's ideas have thus proved surprisingly fruitful beyond their original field of development, and have contributed to unifying the causal theory of exploitation in a wide range of applications in sociology, gender, and ethnic studies, and even history.

But there is one important distinction to bear in mind regarding these applications: some of the generalizations rest on the theoretical specifications of a precise causal mechanisms, just like the core theory as it applies to free market societies. This is true, for example, of the analyses of international trade, household labor, and communal division (albeit that the relevant models in the two latter instances are less sophisticated technically than Roemer's originals). But the other generalizations—involving differential skill, bureaucracy, and feudal society—represent insightful applications of general principles to new situations, as opposed to explicit formal models of social process. As such, they do not enjoy quite the same explanatory leverage as the first set of generalizations of Roemer's remarkable core theory.

B. The Normative Dimension

1. For Libertarianism: Nozick's Challenge

It was said above that the term "exploitation" comes freighted with moral significance: any case of exploitation represents an unjust state of affairs. The term has thus been bandied about rather loosely in the previous section, without benefit of the normative discipline to be introduced in this.

In general terms, theories of social justice can investigate the justice of:

• an initial distribution of resources;

or

• the transactions that take place between individuals on the basis of their initial holdings of resources;

or

• the final outcome of such transactions.

Procedural theories of justice focus on the first two loci of justice; *substantive,* or *end-state,* theories focus on the third locus.

The Harvard philosopher Robert Nozick has been the most influential exponent of a procedural approach in recent years. Because his theories tend to deny that the unequal exchanges considered above are unjustly unequal—hence deny that they are exploitative—Nozick's right-wing libertarian ideas represent an important counterpoint to the more left-wing and egalitarian theories of justice to be considered below.

Because Nozick's theory is purely procedural, it allows considerations of justice to impinge only on the ethical standing of the initial distribution of resources—whether or not they were justly acquired—and the nature of the transactions involving the resources—whether or not the transactions were

conducted "above board." It rules out independent reflection, so far as justice is concerned, on any further *consequences* that may flow from the transactions.

His theory holds, in particular, that the outcome of a set of transactions represents a just state of affairs if and only if (a) the resources held by all individuals going into the transactions had been legitimately acquired by their owners ("justice of acquisition") and (b) the transaction procedures themselves are legitimate, leading to justified transfers of resources between prior owners ("justice of transfer"). The theory says in short that I possess something fairly now if and only if I got it fairly from someone else who had it fairly in their turn.

But this immediately prompts the question; how do we know that *they* had it fairly? Nozick's answer can only be: because they got it fairly from yet another person who had it fairly. But how do we know that this third person had it fairly? Because this series of questions can be extended indefinitely, the application of the two principles of justice (justice of acquisition and justice of transfer) evidently draws the Nozickian investigator back into an analysis of the lengthy moral prehistory of any current resource distribution. Nozick's theory would then give a resource—a piece of land, say—a clean bill of moral health if and only if it were justly acquired by some primitive owner, and then passed cleanly from hand to hand down a morally continuous line of ownership culminating in the present day. It therefore becomes important to the application of the theory to give some further content to the justice principles: *how* is a resource legitimately acquired for the very first time, and *what conditions* legitimate its subsequent transfers?

Nozick's answer on the first point is that a person can acquire just title in a previously unowned resource (such as virgin land) if no other person is disadvantaged by the acquisition. This we may call the "Nozickean proviso" regarding primitive acquisition. His answer on the second point is essentially that a transaction—a gift, purchase, sale, bequest, and so on—gets a clean bill of moral health so long as it is not accomplished through either force or fraud.

It is easy to see how this theory might cut the ground from under would-be radical critics of the social order. Let us say, for example (i) that the land, and all the other natural resources of the United States were acquired by their initial private owners in a manner consistent with Nozick's proviso, and (ii) that all subsequent transactions in cash and kind were free of force and fraud. (These are large assumptions, as we will see, but let them stand for the time being.) Then the current highly unequal resource distribution would be justified. And if all current contracts—including labor contracts—were free of force and fraud, then there could be no complaint about their outcome, even if this perpetuated, or exacerbated the existing inequality. The whole of John Roemer's causal theory could in other words be accepted, and it could be agreed that the labor contract gives rise to unequal exchange in the manner stipulated in Roemer's models, and yet it could be claimed that exploitation was not occurring, because the outcome, although unequal, was not unjust.

This finding would also, of course, cut the ground from under any political program designed to rectify the relevant inequalities, because you cannot rectify in the name of justice something that is not unjust. Indeed, the attempt to do so, by, for example, taxing or redistributing property to help the disadvantaged, will itself be unjust (to the current property owners), because it infringes the *cordon sanitaire* that Nozick's argument throws up around unequal property holdings under the assumptions introduced above. This is why critics of a left-wing bent have been so anxious to take on Nozick's theory of social justice.

2. Left-Wing Libertarianism

There are two possible responses from the left to the challenge posed by Nozick's theory: either (a) stick with a procedural conception of justice, and dispute his version of it or (b) abandon the procedural conception in favor of a substantive theory that attends directly to the justice of outcomes ("end states"). The first type of response is covered in this subsection; the second in the subsequent two.

Nozick says that transactions accompanied by force or fraud are unjust transactions. If it could be shown that, say, typical capitalist transactions are accompanied by force—that they are *coerced* transactions—then even Nozick might have to admit that capitalism was an unjust, hence exploitative, system. The difficulty here is that capitalism is conducted in an atmosphere of formal freedom: this is precisely how it differs from feudalism. Workers are not forced to work for particular employers, who can adopt a "take it or leave it" attitude to the wage negotiation. Workers without any other means of support are nevertheless forced (have no other alternative but to) work for *some* employer, because otherwise they face starvation. Although this conclusion is a matter of debate among political philosophers, it might be said that workers without property are coerced into employment, even if no particular employer coerces them into his or her employment.

Accepting this line of argument implies that some parts of most labor contracts are exploitative: specifically, those parts that act to bring the workers up to subsistence level, and therefore up to the point where they are no longer compelled to work by the threat of hunger. This analysis would justify the institution of a welfare state that acted to bring all citizens up to a subsistence level of income. This could be implemented in a variety of ways, but a scheme that has recently attracted much interest in Europe is a proposal to pay *basic income*—that is, an equal and unconditional payment to each adult citizen of a given country. This can be advocated for a number of different reasons, but here a subsistence-level basic income emerges as a useful remedy against wage market exploitation.

Another line of dissent sets out to challenge Nozick's Lockean view of primitive acquisition. It has been pointed out (by G. A. Cohen and Hillel Steiner, among others) that Nozick assumes a situation in which resources are originally unowned. The Nozickean proviso then establishes a ground rule by means of which resources can legitimately pass from a state of nonownership to a state of private ownership by some individual. It is worth noting that this conception is not entirely unmotivated historically. It can be imagined how congenial it would be to the early European colonizers of North America, for example, moving out into what they were pleased to regard as a morally empty landscape. But why assume with the colonizers that resources are initially unowned? Why not assume that the resources start out as owned collectively by the whole population—of the globe, if need be? In that case, it may be that natural resources at least can never be legitimately owned by individuals, because private ownership of, say, land infringes the prior ownership rights of the bulk of the human population.

This would give a deeper connotation to the notion of the *exploitation of a natural resource*. If the resource—say, oil pumped from the ground—deteriorated as a result of any productive use of it by a private interest, this would constitute exploitation in the full sense. It would represent (i) a benefit gained by the producer—an oil corporation, say—at the expense of the population at large, which was (ii) unfairly gained because of the infringement of the population's ownership rights over the resource in its original underground condition.

The philosopher Hillel Steiner has recently developed a theory beginning from the premise of collective ownership of natural resources that harks back to the ideas of the nineteenth-century radical reformer Henry George—a man who advocated a universal land tax. Because Steiner accepts Nozick's libertarian framework, his contribution shows that a left libertarian position is an eminently credible one—Nozick's rejection of end-state theories of justice does not entail right-wing conclusions.

3. Against Libertarianism

John Roemer's theory establishes that unequal exchanges are caused in general by unequal distributions of assets. So inequality of assets is *causally fundamental* to exploitation. But does this mean that inequality of assets is also *normatively fundamental*? If it were, a final allocation would be unjust (and therefore exploitative) if and only if its antecedent asset distribution was independently unjust (because, for example, the assets had been distributed in violation of Nozick's first principle). Roemer himself has adopted this position.

To help see whether this is a plausible doctrine, and to show how the idea of exploitation can be applied in areas beyond the classical Marxist agenda, consider the case of sexual exploitation—that is, the situation in which one party to a sexual encounter gains sexual satisfaction at the expense of another's satisfaction, or perhaps the latter's sense of self. Now the reasons why this occurs may well involve a variety of background inequalities—poverty that drives women who have few other opportunities into a career of prostitution; patriarchy that creates double standards of sexual satisfaction; organizational hierarchy that makes the secretary vulnerable to the attentions of her boss. Among these background inequalities, there may be some that are just and some that are unjust, but it does not seem that the justice or otherwise of the background inequality determines the justice of the sexual exchange itself. To take an entirely hypothetical example, there may be nothing unjust about there being a high-powered position as governor of New York; what might be unjust is the *use* of this position to obtain sexual favors on, let us imagine, unequal terms. And what would make such an exchange unjust is the lack of reciprocity itself: that one person has gained at the expense of another who does not gain likewise for themselves. It is the very inequality of the outcome that makes it unjust.

It is of course dangerous to infer general propositions from intuitions about specific cases: intuitions differ, and one can be misled by contingent features of particular examples. This example nevertheless suggests powerfully to me that asset distributions are not fundamental to exploitation from the normative point of view. While it is an anterior inequality—of economic or social power, or perhaps of physical strength or aggression—which *enables* one person to take advantage of another sexually, what renders the outcome unjust is the in-

equality of the outcome itself, judged against a normative principle applicable to outcomes—in this case a principle of equal satisfaction, or perhaps of equally attempted satisfaction. In that case, Nozick's position is untenable, and it is possible to judge the outcomes of social transactions directly by end-state criteria.

4. For Egalitarianism

The most relevant end-state criteria for assessing exploitation are egalitarian ones: that is, an outcome is regarded as unjust precisely because it is unequal. Moreover, the tables can be turned on the historical entitlement approach to the legitimacy of particular holdings: in some cases we might want to say that an existing unequal distribution is unjust precisely *because of* the unjustly unequal outcomes to which it is likely to lead. Here we have come a long way from Nozick. With his theory, it was difficult to see how any transaction was going to come out as exploitative, no matter how unequal. Now it looks as if it may be difficult to *prevent* every conceivable inequality coming out as an instance of exploitation. At all events, the moral field is now wide open for proposals of injustice.

• Marx's position on the justice issue is the subject of much debate, including the question of whether he took any position at all on the justice issue. (Some critics say he did; some say he did not, and the cleverest critics tend to say that he did, but was not aware that he did when he was doing it.)

Marx certainly seemed to allow some inequalities as justified: he implied that people who work more deserve higher rewards, and that people with what are now called special needs are entitled to special consideration in the allocation of goods. Because both of these suggestions involve compensating individuals for deficits in their welfare (induced by extra work and extra needs, respectively), I think it is plausible to suggest that Marx adhered to a concept of *welfare egalitarianism,* as one strand at least of his rather complex (and no doubt somewhat confused) thinking on the justice issue. The effect, however, would be to make the capitalist labor contract, say, unjust because it chronically violates this principle. The character of the injustice comes out in answer to the rhetorical question: what reason is there that some able-bodied people rather than others should carry the burdens of laboring on behalf of all?

• Strict welfare egalitarianism is too strong a principle for many critics once interpersonal variations are allowed into the equation. If some people are congenitally miserable, do the rest of us have to keep pouring resources into them in the vain hope that it will lift their welfare level fractionally closer to the norm? And what is the scope for individual responsibility in this scenario? If somebody destroys his resources, or fritters away his inheritance, does he still deserve compenstion from the social fund?

Considerations such as these have led some critics to fall back on principles of *equal opportunity* (for welfare or income) rather than equality of welfare per se. These principles imply that everybody has equal chances in the game of life, but they do not guarantee equal results. One might say that they are end-state regarding (because they are geared to the prospective outcomes of interaction), but they are not end-state principles in the strict sense, because they do not act retrospectively on the outcomes that have occurred. They are nevertheless quite radical in their implications, because it may be that very substantial redistributions of existing resources—in money, education, health care, or cultural recognition—would be necessary to bring people up to the starting gates of life on equal terms.

• There has been a considerable, perhaps slightly obsessive, interest in recent political philosophy about returns to talent: do the talented deserve to keep their higher rewards? I have always wondered if the interest has arisen partly from the fact that political philosophers on the whole regard themselves as pretty talented people, so it is both personally agonizing and professionally challenging to try and come up with some reason why such special people should not deserve rather special rewards.

In a maneuver that does for talents what Henry George did for the land mass, the conclusion is now widespread in anglophone philosophy that God's gifts are a species of natural resource, whose fruits belong, if they belong to anyone, to the human collective, and not to the happy individuals whose fleeting vessels they are. This conclusion denies the thesis of *self-ownership*: a thesis that does for a person's entitlement to the rewards from their own talents what Nozick's theory intended to do for the private owners of external resources. And, as in the parallel case of external resources, inequalities arising when talented people make use of their internal, God-given talents at the expense of the less talented will be treated by the dominant academic view as unjust, and hence exploitative.

There are just three examples of the kind of arguments which come into play on the justice issue when

the Nozickian constraints on the scope of the debate are broken through.

IV. EMPIRICAL FINDINGS

A. The Normative Dimension

1. The Relevance of History

The normative domain is distinct from the empirical domain: one cannot infer an ought from an is. But this does not imply that empirical considerations are irrelevant to the evaluation of existing social systems. Far from it, empirical data can in principle establish whether a given system lives up to the standards set by precepts derived independently of the facts.

From what has been said in the previous section, the normative evaluation of any contemporary society will depend *inter alia* upon:

• its history of property acquisition
• its transaction history
• evidence of current inequalities

In one sense, the historical entitlement approach to justice is stacked against the status quo. If present title is invalidated by the existence of a single shady deal that occurred in the transaction chain in, say, the County of Lincolnshire in 1534, it is very unlikely that any current allocation will survive moral scrutiny—and the farther back we look, the less likely is purity to be vindicated. To maintain perspective, we need to be looking only for the legitimacy of the gross events that determine the subsequent shape of whole systems. But even by this laxer standard, it is not obvious that typical current systems have legitimate foundations.

The land of England, to take just one example, was forcibly occupied by a warrior caste after 1066, and this self-appointed aristocracy proved very adroit during the subsequent millennium in ramifying and diversifying its holdings, and absorbing new wealth, in agriculture, in commerce, and, briefly, in industry. And too many of the great cities of England–Liverpool and Bristol, to name but two (not to speak of their great universities) owe their wealth to slaves. What would be the effects on current distributions of unscrambling this whole bloody history? It is very difficult to say, but there is little doubt that they would be considerable: the accumulated London rents of, say, the Dukes of Westminster represent a tidy sum. Or, to take the U.S. example, what about the combined impact of the criminal activities of all the Mafia connections, not to speak of the extermination of the Native Americans or the accumulated dealings of the Rockefellers and the Morgans?

These are sobering reflections. On the one hand, there is an academic debate that makes fine conceptual distinctions, and delicate moral judgments; on the other a reality in which force that keeps its gains acquires a patina of respectability. I doubt that there is any defensible current theory that could defend current property distributions; and there is much truth in the old dictum that if you scratch a state all you will find is a forgetful terrorism.

2. The Relevance of Inequality

End-state egalitarianism makes evidence of inequality directly relevant to the assessment of current exploitation, regardless of transaction history. Such evidence may be used to highlight either

• situations of disadvantage from which exploitation may arise;

or

• the existence of exploitative transactions themselves.

Thus, evidence of unequal current property distributions, or of educational qualifications unequally shared by gender or race, may establish the existence of disadvantaged groups, who become thereby *vulnerable to exploitation,* but do not constitute grounds for inferring current exploitation itself. To show the latter, one usually requires evidence of the consequences of the exploitative acts. Such evidence is actually performing a

dual role: on the one hand, it figures as evidence of the *existence* of the causal process that leads some people to benefit while others suffer (strictly, it is providing evidence of this process by means of providing evidence for the results of the process); on the other hand, it figures as evidence of the *injustice* of the process, where inequalities of the demonstrated kind are regarded as unjust.

Incomes from work are perhaps the most salient index in the case of class exploitation; for sexual abuse it could be evidence of long-term psychological damage; for cases of gender and race exploitation it might be evidence of low self-esteem (being the consequences of exploitative practices conducted by dominant groups). To show the variety of types of evidence that could be relevant to such an assessment, consider the following data presented in Table II on health from Britain in 1991. Although age is obviously the predominant factor in the loss of teeth, class is a powerful compounding influence: as a member of the lowest social group you are roughly *seven times* more likely to have lost your teeth than a member of the highest professional class. Now the interpretative significance of this fact is, like most facts, not immediately transparent. It is presumably not the case that the manual workers' poor teeth are a direct consequence of their work. It is not true that they have no alternative but to be employed chewing for 40 hours a week in the testing plant of a gum factory, which wears down their teeth. Toothlessness is presumably connected to working conditions via low income, or diet, or general life-style. And one can imagine certain sociologists elaborating theories according to which the manual classes are gripped by a culture of dental poverty, leading them to refuse all attempts at preventive medicine, seeking out instead every opportunity for

TABLE II

Percentage of Adults with No Natural Teeth: By Age and Socioeconomic Group, Great Britain 1991

Socioeconomic group	Age							
	16–24	25–34	35–44	45–54	55–64	65–74	75+	All 16+
Professional	0	—	2	2	7	23	32	5
Employers and managers	0	—	2	5	15	33	51	10
Other nonmanual	—	1	2	7	23	42	56	14
Skilled manual	1	1	5	13	33	55	75	20
Semi-skilled manual	0	—	4	18	44	59	77	25
Unskilled manual	0	4	8	26	49	75	81	34
All groups	—	1	3	10	29	49	67	17

Source: General Household Survey.

TABLE III
Mean Annual Individual Incomes by Class Location in Sweden and the United States, 1980*

Owners		Nonowners (Wage laborers)		
	Assets in the means of production			
1. Bourgeoisie	4. Expert manager	7. Semi-cred. man.	10. Uncred. manager	
US: $52,621	US: $28,665	US: $20,701	US: $12,276	+
SW: $28,333	SW: $29,952	SW: $20,820	SW: $15,475	
2. Small employers	5. Expert super-	8. Semi-cred. superv.	11. Uncred. superv.	Organization
US: $24,828	visors	US: $18,023	US: $13,045	>0
SW: $17,237	US: $23,057	SW: $19,711	SW: $15,411	Assets
	SW: $18,859			
3. Petty bourgeoisie	6. Exp. Nonmanager	9. Semi-cred. workers	12. Proletarian	
US: $14,496	US: $15,251	US: $16,034	US: $11,161	−
SW: $13,503	SW: $14,890	SW: $14,879	SW: $11,876	
	+	>0	−	
	Skill Assets			

* United States, $N = 1282$; Sweden, $N = 1049$. Income is gross before tax. Swedish income converted to $ at the 1980 rate.
Source: J. E. Roemer. (1986). *Value, Exploitation and Class* Table I, p. 80. Chur: Harwood (after E. O. Wright, *Classes*).

decay. So the issue of responsibility may rear its head. But if the basic dental data is adduced as one of the unanticipated welfare consequences of a given distribution of occupations, why should it not figure in judgments about social exploitation? Why should the rich grow rich on the teeth of the poor?

B. The Causal–Explanatory Dimension

1. Class Structure

A putative causal theory such as Roemer's theory of exploitation should in principle be susceptible to empirical tests: do its predictions come good in practice? The following data presented in Table III were obtained by Erik Wright from a large-scale comparative research project conducted with this aim in mind.

The main pattern of the findings in Table 3 conforms with the predictions of the theory. There are systematic inequalities of mean income, and the differences in income increase monotonically in the United States and in Sweden with increases in all the assets concerned. Greater wealth, higher skill (as measured by credentials), and higher bureaucratic position invariably translate into higher average income. The magnitudes of the differentials are also surprisingly similar in the two countries, given that Sweden was chosen for comparison with the United States precisely because its strong social democratic political culture (which existed for many years up to the survey date) was felt to place it near the egalitarian end of a value spectrum of major capitalist countries, at the opposite end to the United States.

The only major difference—and it is of course a significant one—is that the average income of Swedish capitalists (and small employers) was considerably lower than that of their U.S. counterparts. One might infer very cautiously that the main shape of class relations is set by the underlying private property systems in each country, but that political considerations—both in terms of state policies and the impact of prevailing cultural norms—can make an important difference to their detailed incidence.

2. The Household Division of Labor

In a survey of data from studies of the distribution of labor in households I found that the predictions of the exploitation theory are once again broadly confirmed. Women with lower earning power generally work longer hours in total than their male partners.

There are, however, two caveats to enter. First, the theory relies solely on the logic of material incentives, and there is good evidence that other considerations affect the allocation of household labor. Specifically, the theory predicts that there will be a role reversal in the small minority of households in which the woman's earning power exceeds that of her male partner: he rather than she will remain at home to manage the house and look after the children. A careful study in the United Kingdom investigated 30 such couples. And it found that role reversal had in fact occurred . . . dear reader, close your eyes and guess . . . in *just one* instance out of 30. In the remaining 29 cases it was sometimes the men who refused to accept the economic logic of their positions; and sometimes it was high-earning "Superwomen" who were deliberately taking on household duties as if to make up for the unconventional nature of their role outside the home.

Thus, while the finding for the majority of "ordinary" couples (wherein wives earn less than their husbands) is consistent with economic exploitation theory, the inconsistent result for these so-called *cross-class families* suggests that the economic theory appears to work in the majority of cases only because material incentives point in the same direction as the socialized gender expectations. For what it is worth, my guess is that the true explanation involves the interaction of economic incentives with cultural expectations, as these evolve over a period of time in the lives of individual families and the wider community. But we do not presently possess good analytical models of the interaction between economic and cultural processes.

3. Two Limitations: Multiple Equilibria and Imperfect Information

The contemporary theory of exploitation has gained a great deal in clarity in rigor from its reformulation in terms of individual rational choice. But there are two features of the architecture of these theories which hamper their empirical assessment.

• First, there is the possibility of *multiple equilibria*, and associated failures both in identifying rational actions and in predicting social outcomes. When the formal specification of a choice situation implies the existence of multiple equilibria, the predictive power of the theory breaks down, because the theory is unable to establish in general *which* of several (or many) possible equilibria is liable to prevail in practice. This problem can be compounded when the paths leading to different equilibria are "balanced on a knife edge," so that very small changes in initial conditions will lead to considerable variations in the outcome. In cases such as these— which occur for example in the analysis of public goods, and the answer to mundane questions like "who does the wash"—it may be clear *that* a particular situation of exploitation exists, but impossible to explain from general theory why *this particular* situation of exploitation exists.

• Second, the theory of general market equilibrium relies on the assumptions both of *perfect competition* and *perfect information*. Perhaps one can phrase the effects of this bluntly: the causal theory of exploitation is at its strongest theoretically where it is at its weakest realistically. The perfect competition assumption is the less troubling of the two assumptions. Many markets approximate the condition of multiple buyers and mul-

tiple sellers. In any case, the achievement of the theory was to show how exploitation could arise even under these circumstances; it is easier conceptually to adapt the theory to monopolistic conditions. Perfect information is, however, a considerable stumbling block, because agents in real economies are always making decisions against a limited knowledge of costs, techniques, and opportunities. For example, the people who replied to Eric Wright's questionnaires were not in this respect the people they were imagined to be in the theory tested by their answers.

It is difficult to know how to cope with the reality of imperfect information. All that can be said is that economists of every stripe are here collected in the same boat. In particular, those who trumpet the superiority of capitalist market organization on the basis of general equilibrium theory have just as slender an empirical warrant for their claims. What Roemer has done is to raise egalitarians to the level of the general difficulty, rather than leave them trapped in the special difficulties of their own created by Marx's labor theory of value.

4. Incentives and Counterfactuals: Roemer vs. Rawls

A final issue involves what is called *the incentive problem*. Roemer's theory implies in its general form that the equilization of some currently unequal resource will (i) make the better off worse off and (ii) make the worse off better off. It is the contrast between these two counterfactual effects that allows one to infer current exploitation. But suppose that these presumed effects of equalization are not empirically valid. The equalization of resources might lead *everyone* to be worse off than before, by killing the goose that lays the golden eggs. Perhaps the talented, say, will sit on their hands and refuse to play ball unless they are able to make a lot of money from their talents.

Exploitation theory has nothing to say about such circumstances, because the distribution of benefits and burdens falls beyond its purview (no one is gaining *at the expense of* anyone else according to the scenario just described). Another famous type of theory, due to John Rawls, does, however, come into play at this point. According to Rawls inequalities are justified so long as they benefit the worst-off members of society. Rewards to talent, for example, might be justified if they were necessary to draw forth efforts from the talented that would benefit everyone (including the worst off). Wherever an egalitarian redistribution would leave the worst off better off, there is unjustified exploitation (according to Roemer); where it would leave them still worse off, there is a justified inequality (according to Rawls).

Although the two approaches to social justice are complementary, in the sense of being geared to the distinct sets of circumstances just outlined, it is a matter of empirical judgment where the boundaries lie in the spheres of application of the two approaches, and therefore in one's impression of the overall justice of particular societies. Will the talented, for example, contribute or not if they are paid the same as everyone else? If you think that the talented, or the rich, are incentive insensitive, you will be a Roemerian, and deduce exploitation as widespread within society; if you think the talented or the rich are incentive sensitive, you will be Rawlsian, and tolerate a good deal of inequality.

V. CONCLUSION

The social sciences have sometimes tried to eschew moral and political concerns by marching under the banner of "value freedom." In my view, this is an irresponsible attitude to take toward the large questions of social change and social inequality. To remain neutral between the winners and the losers in society is to back the winners, begging the questions how and why they came to win. But this does not mean that social scientists enjoy *carte blanche* either as writers or as teachers to promote their personal values in the name of science.

It is very important to distinguish between causal issues and normative issues, and to approach each with the discipline they deserve. Causal proposals stand or fall by the canons of science—theoretical power and empirical validity. The role of reason may be less direct in relation to normative questions, but reasoned reflection still has much work to do in isolating and defining values, tracing out their implications, and specifying their points of contact with the world.

The theory of exploitation well illustrates this rich mixture of empirical and moral concerns. It remains to be developed in many ways—applied to further domains of society, revised to take more account of dynamic social process; of ideology, culture, and uncertainty. But the contemporary theory stands nevertheless as one of the most impressive achievements of recent social science.

Also See the Following Articles

EQUALITY AND EGALITARIANISM • ETHNOCULTURAL MINORITY GROUPS, STATUS AND TREATMENT OF • MARXISM • POVERTY • SOCIAL ETHICS, OVERVIEW • THEORIES OF JUSTICE: RAWL'S

Bibliography

Carling, A. (1991). *Social division.* London: Verso.
Carling, A. (1991). Exploitation, extortion and oppression. In P. Abell (Ed.), *Rational choice theory,* pp. 313–328. Upleadon: Edward Elgar.
Cohen, G. A. (1995). *Self-ownership, freedom and equality.* Cambridge: Cambridge Univesity Press.
Roemer, J. E. (1988). *Free to lose.* London: Radius.
Van Parijs, P. (1995). *Real freedom for all: What (if anything) can justify capitalism?* Oxford: Clarendon Press.
Wright, E. O. (1985). *Classes.* London: Verso.

FAMILY, THE

Carole Ulanowsky
The Open University

GLOSSARY

conjugal Joined together in marriage; relating to the married state; as constituting the functional, familial role in society.

cohabitation The act of living together as husband and wife when not legally married.

contraception The prevention of conception or impregnation by use of contraceptive methods.

divorce A legal dissolution of the marriage relationship.

extended family A unit that includes three or more generations of near relatives, in addition to the nuclear family.

household People dwelling under the same roof; a domestic arrangement composed of family.

infancy The early period of human life.

kin Family, race, genus; a group of persons having a common ancestry; blood relations, consanguity.

marriage The state of being united with a person of the opposite sex as husband and wife; wedlock; a legally recognized personal union with the intention of sexual relations and entailing property rights.

monogamy Marriage with one person at a time; having a single mate.

nuclear family A group consisting of father, mother and children; regarded as the basic social unit.

nurture To nourish, protect, and support; to rear, educate, and morally train.

parent One who begets offspring; progenitor; or, a person standing in loco parentis although not a natural parent.

procreation The act of bringing into existence by process of reproduction.

reproduction The act of forming, creating, or bringing into existence again, the production of new organisms by or from existing one.

THE FAMILY is an institution found in all societies that are committed to their biological and social reproduction. The Latin origin of the word *family* or *familia* implies domestic, or household—a group habitually sharing a common dwelling. This aspect of family can be called a locational criterion; however, it is more usual for definitions of *family* to include important kinship criteria—relationship by blood or marriage. Additionally, notions of family include a functional criterion based on the sharing of activities. One's *kin* will comprise a group of persons descended from a common blood ancestor, but a biological, reproductive focus will define family as a *nuclear* unit—a residential group of parents and their children: a simple biological form with a primary conjugal link. The term nuclear family arises from its definition as the smallest kin unit. Given that family groups, consisting of parents and their offspring—the nuclear form—occur apparently instinctively among many animal species, it is increasingly accepted that this form was perhaps the first unit of *human* culture—a social unit based primarily on the biological facts of procreation. While the Euro-American nuclear form is often assumed to be the global "type" case, there are examples where nuclear families operate a system of roles rather than as concretely defined persons. For example, Malinowski discovered that in some societies the father role might be played by the mother's brother. In their lifetimes, most people will have intimate experience of at least two families—the one they are born into, known as the family of orientation, and the one that they create through parenthood, known as the family of procreation.

In most human societies, the family is the fundamental unit of sexual and social organisation—largely through selected mating on the pattern of monogamy. Situations of polygamy—one man, usually powerful within the group, mating with several women—and, more rarely, polyandry, one woman mating with several men, have been recorded through history and very occasionally in anthropological studies of the present time. By providing structures and guidelines for the regulation of sexual conduct and care, the monogamous family has, over time, *institutionalized* procreation, thus protecting young offspring who require committed care and attention during a lengthy period of infancy.

Families can supply a collective well-being for all their members: for children this means parents meeting adequately a multiplicity of needs. The family, as the first instrument of socialization and education for the young, can contribute to the well-being and stability of the society of which it is a part. Psychological studies suggest that the family from which people originate and the one that they might create have the potential for influencing significantly what individuals are and what they might become from birth to death.

While the nuclear family consisting of a biological child or children in the care of a mother and father committed to a lifelong marital relationship remains pervasive, important sociological changes in the late 20th century are challenging this traditional model. A number of factors have produced these changes, including new perceptions of the role of women and new ways of thinking and acting that have served to deconstruct a range of beliefs and values to which people have been committed over time. So, at the level of the family, alternative personal and procreative life-styles are being

forged. In Western society, therefore, while most households or families are still comprise adults and their children, a number of these now deviate from the standard nuclear type, operating in the traditional mode. These alternative structures include for example, step-families, adopted families and reconstituted families, as well as a significantly increasing number of single-parent families (see below). And the assumption of the central role of parents in the care and upbringing of their children is changing also as outside agencies increasingly are drawn in to fulfill the care, guidance, and educational functions.

I. HISTORICAL PERSPECTIVES

Interest in the *history of the family* as a serious subject for academic research is comparatively recent. Predating this interest, insights into family life of ancient times and through medieval and renaissance periods derived primarily from excavated remains, art, and artifacts, and from legal documents, although such evidence is biased toward the propertied and the literate. Additionally, historical surveys, conducted by individuals researching their own genealogies, have contributed to an understanding of family structures and settings and to a broader understanding of the economic and social conditions of past times.

A. Complex and Simple Structures

Clear evidence of a common pattern of children and their biological parents sharing the same household as single-family occupancy emerges from Europe from as early as the fourteenth century. This has largely discredited the idea of the nuclear structure as a product of nineteenth century industrialisation. (Laslett & Wall, and the Cambridge Group, 1972). However, exceptions can be found, in renaissance France, for example, and beyond, where familial communities of several related family units operated as grand, patriarchal, authoritarian households of a complex nature. Additionally, the large patriarchal families, common over the centuries in China and Japan, persist today in some segments of the Indian subcultures. While most Western households at their core have comprised parents and their offspring with or without extended family members, in many cases servants would have been part of the family unit: around 12% of all households of preindustrial England had servants or live-in workers, subject to the jurisdiction of the head of the household.

B. Patriarchy and Inheritance

In ancient times in the majority of cultures, males held most of the power. In Roman times, the head of the family even had the authority to kill his own sons, and medieval families in some ways were influenced by patriarchal systems practiced throughout the Roman Empire, although Teutonic women had a somewhat higher-than-usual status in the household and could inherit property. Indeed, over the centuries, a woman's rights to have influence in the family home has often depended upon her ownership of goods and property.

Through time, whatever the power relations within families, laws and traditions relating to land distribution, inheritance, and succession have played a significant part in the structure and organization of household groups, particularly among the rich and powerful. For poorer groups, household structure and function was determined in part by food search, by agricultural practices and laws relating to land usage in feudal times and beyond, and later by the requirements of urban living and work practices brought about by industrialization.

There is evidence from literature and other sources of a general belief in the continuance and health of a society as reliant upon the "integrity" of the family, especially at times of change and disruption. The French historian Le Play viewed the "stem" family—inheritance by the eldest son, who after marriage would occupy the family home and inherit it upon the death of his father—as the unit of stability in a changing world and a bastion of traditional values. Thus, a growing weakness in patriarchal authority and the dividing of property between siblings at each succession was seen as diminishing family stability. The good of society, Le Play maintained, relied upon the preservation of the stem family, discernible still, although with questionable effect, in some aristocratic families of present-day England.

C. Family Values in Historical Context

The literature and figurative art of different cultures and nations, while offering useful insights into family settings of particular places and times, can sometimes oversimplify perceptions by offering stylized versions (for example, *The Puritan Family of Seventeenth Century England*) that suggest notions of the family as uniform over a geographical area and over units of time. Be that as it may, following the Reformation, it is clear that under the influence of Luther and the Protestantism of the 17th century and beyond, marriage and the family were greatly valued, and family life was presented as a distinct vocation for those involved. For this reason, family life was structured and supported in such a way as to allow time and effort for everything that fell under its umbrella—the practical and work tasks, as well as its emotional and social dimensions.

Bailyn, in his 1960 study, "Education and the Forming of American Society," noted that in transit across the Atlantic, the family, leaving behind its "extended" elements, was "stripped to its nuclear core": sociologically these early settlers represented the family in its simplest form. Even so, in colonial times, over individuals, in addition to the biological group, might have shared the household. Primarily, these would be servants and apprentices, but also boarders—single unattached people living with the family group. Indeed, these individuals would be encouraged "for the good of themselves" as for the society of which they were a part, to integrate with their local communities. (This is in contrast with current trends in Western society. For example, in the United Kingdom it is predicted that by the end of this century, one in three households will be single occupancy.) If nonfamily members coexisted with the family, then, by implication, nuclear families of earlier times would have been less private and more subject to scrutiny than those of today. This is the case also in other settings where extended family members—grandparents, for example—share the family home.

For more than a century, from the mid-1800s, in the United Kingdom as in most parts of the Western world, attitudes and behavior concerning marriage and the family changed little, and marriage as a social institution guaranteed long-term commitment for children from both parents. Even so, from as early as 1895 in England, wives could obtain separation orders from their husbands for certain unlawful or unacceptable behaviors, although few of them did. Thus, social more and perhaps also social pressures encouraged long-term commitment. In present times, however, more exacting requirements of the couple relationship has meant that many prefer to separate. It has been more than 4 centuries since Thomas Cranmer changed the English liturgy to take account of marriage for the "mutual comfort of the partners," in addition to the procreation of children, but few couples until the later part of the twentieth century have thought it appropriate to end the marriage when this requirement was not fulfilled.

D. Family Size

While families of past times were large by present standards, the average survival rate of children meant that they were not overly large. Toward the end of the nineteenth century there was a positive trend towards restricting family size in most parts of the industrialized world, particularly as children were no longer seen primarily as workers contributing to the family income, but as dependents involved, for the early part of their lives at least, in education. Into the 20th century a variety of contraceptive methods increasingly became available and there is evidence that abortion was not uncommon. Decline in family size through the late-19th and early-20th centuries meant that more emotional effort could be expended on each child, a requirement argued for in a growing body of psychological theory. This commitment to the parenting task also had implications for images of mothers. Carl C. Degler, in his 1980 study of women and the family, observed that during that particular period: "the more children were cherished the more women would be honoured as the parent most directly and 'naturally' concerned with them..."

E. Status, Paid Work, and the Family

With the advent of industrialization, most employment occurred outside the home, and fathers in particular moved with it, into waged activities—deemed to be of higher status than domestic and family work, which was, and still is, unpaid. In an increasingly commercial world, money gave individuals a sense of personal worth, so, into the 20th century, a nonworking woman would increasingly refer to herself as *just* a housewife or *just* a mother.

II. FAMILIES OF PRESENT TIMES

Over the past three decades, traditional assumptions about personal relationships within and around families increasingly have been subject to challenge and debate. Some believe that consensus about what constitutes today's family and how it should be formed and managed is no longer available, but others would argue at least for the formulation of and commitment to child-sensitive structures by adults in their management of family groups. It is the case that overall, as the 20th century has progressed, and more particularly since the 1960s, family structures and systems have become increasingly more complex and fluid. Sexual

proclivities plus flexibility and informality in the establishing and maintenance of relationships through the expression of individual preference that led to this situation, as has the changing aspirations of women. Additionally, economic and structural pressures within the wider society over which individuals have little or no control have demonstrated a potential for disrupting families in no small degree. In particular, unemployment, residential mobility, and homelessness are worthy of note.

It is the case then, that in any single community within Western society, but particularly in urban settings, a range of structures expressing families of significant variety will be in evidence:

Traditional nuclear (biological parents, married or cohabiting)
Reconstituted family (two families together following divorce/separation)
Complex (stepparent with natural parent and his/her children or with a mix of stepchildren and shared children from the relationship)
Widowed parent and children
Divorced/separated lone parent plus her/his children
Gay/lesbian parent (with or without partner, plus children—naturally or artificially conceived)
The "living together/living apart" model (unmarried parents sharing parenthood from two separate residences—sometimes the case with teenage parents)
Single/lone parent (partner deserted or not acknowledged)
Extended/three generation family (more usual in families of Asian or Afro-Caribbean origin)
Commune (of mixed kith and kin)
Household (two or more unrelated adults, with or without children)

Some of these structures challenge the traditional, biological understanding of family by equating it with "household" or "group," so denying its traditional kinship associations. The overall picture is of more fluid and in some cases a less secure and less permanent arrangements for individuals.

Primarily this situation has arisen from choices and changes concerning the couple relationship. For example, more nonmarried couples are rejecting marriage, and about one-third of all children are born out of wedlock. More couples are divorcing, and more than half of all divorces involve children (1995 UK statistics). Almost three-quarters of all divorce petitions are filed by the woman of the partnership. Since about 1970, it

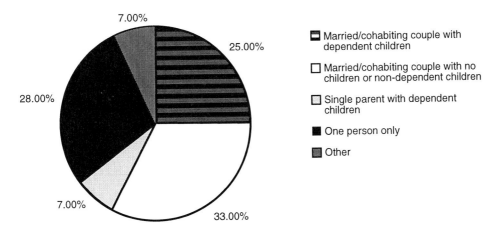

7.00%
25.00%
28.00%
7.00%
33.00%

■ Married/cohabiting couple with dependent children

□ Married/cohabiting couple with no children or non-dependent children

□ Single parent with dependent children

■ One person only

▨ Other

FIGURE 1   Households categorized by the type of family they contain, United Kingdom, 1994 (Office of the Population Census Survey). In the single-parent and married-couple households, other individuals who were family members may also have been present. *Other* includes households containing two or more unrelated adults, two or more families and single parents with nondependent children.

is recorded that throughout the Western world, more marriages have ended in divorce than through the death of the spouse. One outcome of this is an increasing number of single-parent families.

Figure 1 illustrates a situation where almost 30% of all families with dependent children are headed by a single parent.

1. Single-Parent Families

Aside from divorce, single parenthood can arise from other factors, including desertion of a partner, or by never-married individuals choosing "go-it-alone" parenthood. Unmarried teenagers, by opting for motherhood, in some ways challenge norms relating to life stages accepted as partical through time. For example, following the birth of their children, many young women seek opportunities for personal and occupational development through further education, training, and careers—activities traditionally undertaken *prior* to parenthood. Childcare, and the energy required for pursuing dual lifestyles, present particular challenges for individuals, and the kinds of state support required for these to be met is an issue for serious political debate in many Western countries. For example, a 1991 U.K. Department of Social Security report showed that 73% of single mothers depended upon income support for their survival—90% if they happened to be teenagers. Soon after this statistic emerged, the U.K. Child Support Act was passed. Drawing on models developed in Australia and in Wisconsin in the United States, this measure sought to extract maintenance from absent fathers, but in practical terms it has met with only partial suc-

cess, and ideologically it has been fiercely resisted, particularly by the feminist lobby.

Table I presents a situation where almost 50% of families with dependent children are headed by a single parent.

Overall, it is the case that most people make some attempt in their lives to form family groups, but within an increasing variety of structures. And many would defend and promote the rights of people to choose alternative styles even if they require considerable state help to do so.

TABLE I

Family Groups in United States with Children under 18 Years Old

	Number (1000)				
	Total Family Groups	Total Family Households	Subfamilies		
			Total	Related	Unrelated
Totals	37,008	34,016	2,989	2,305	684
Two-parent family groups	25,598	25,055	540	505	34
One-parent family groups	11,410	8,961	2,449	1,800	650
Maintained by mother	9,854	7,647	2,207	1,636	571
Maintained by father	1,556	1,314	242	164	78

Adapted from U.S. Bureau of the Census, *Current Population Reports* No. 72.

2. Influences of Law on Personal Life-Style Choice

The law can influence people in the choices they make in relation to family structure and in their management of personal relationships. For example, the 1987 U.K. Family Law Reform Act removed the legal distinction between *legitimate* and *illegitimate* children by deleting from registration all reference to the marital status of the parents. And U.K. tax/benefit systems also have in some ways favored the single-parent family. Indeed, some would argue in relation to fiscal policies, that the traditional nuclear family currently is in danger of becoming marginalized, lacking funds from central governments and support via pressure groups (sometimes themselves funded by the state) whose agenda seems inclined toward the rights of alternative families (in particular where low income is an issue). A liberalizing of divorce law can likewise be seen to influence the choices people might make and the values they might hold regarding commitment to marriage, although generally speaking, the law will reflect normative trends already prevalent within a society.

3. Marriage

Traditionally, marriage has been linked with particular rights concerning sexuality and procreation; it has been instrumental in ensuring economic and social stability within the family, and it has provided a legal basis for the control and transmission of property. From the 19th century onward, however, in Western industrialized countries, wage-earning opportunities outside the home and the locational requirements of these, plus changing norms and values around sexuality, have released individuals from the strictures of extended family and community with regard to choice of spouse and the management of households. So the modern marriage in Western culture has become is a *conjugal* affair, with partner love and compatibility seen as primarily important and as part of an overall quest for individual self-fulfillment.

With a situation in the United States and increasingly in Western Europe where almost half of all marriages are expected to end in divorce and, as part of a growing fluidity in relational structures, an increasing number of couples are opting to cohabit outside marriage. However, because most cohabitees share property, and often children, if the relationship should break down, the situation may well equate with legal marriage in terms of the emotional, material, and social costs, and also in its impact on children. However, research would indicate a lower level of commitment within cohabiting relationships compared with marriage.

It is the case in present-day Western society that cohabitation has been perceptively legitimized, from "living in sin" to an acceptable domestic and sexual arrangement that in some cases replaces engagement as a prelude to marriage. While logic might suggest that this would provide opportunity for a couple to explore their partnership in helpful ways before full commitment, so leading to a more successful marriage, often the opposite is the case. For unions that began as cohabitation are more than twice as likely to dissolve within the first 10 years, compared with all marriages. A variety of reasons are suggested for this phenomenon.

There is a growing incidence, particularly in the United States, for couples to stake out what they expect of each other prior to marriage. "Prenuptual contracts" mark out expectations of personal behavior within the relationship, and practical outcomes will be detailed in the event the marriage does not work out. It appears that the optimism, confidence, and trust usually expected of those contemplating marriage are missing here, although some interpret a growth in prenuptial contracts as part of a new realism about an increasing gap between what adults aspire to and what they feel they might actually achieve in their intimate relationships.

4. Divorce

Easier and cheaper divorce and the opportunity for legal aid has enabled persons of all socioeconomic groups to opt for divorce where marriage has irretrievably broken down. While, statistically, divorce is more common among those who marry early or who cohabit prior to marriage; among those with lower educational qualifications, lower income, and lower status occupations, divorce in all Western countries and among all groups is rising. The trend toward 'no-fault divorce' began with legislative changes in the early 1970s, for example, in California; by the 1980s, divorce in most Western countries, on purely "relational" grounds, was commonplace. A liberalizing of the law is blamed to some degree for a high rate of divorce, although other pressures play a part. These pressures may be both environmental and economic—for example, the stress of unemployment—but, also in relation to the growing personal aspirations of women and their material independence, ideological.

a. Children's Experience of Divorce

Whatever its cause, the process of relational breakdown and divorce affects all family members. Aside from the separation from a loved parent, in practical ways the parents' divorce can mean many unwelcome changes for children. For example, it may be necessary to have a change of house and move to a different neighborhood and a new school, leaving behind established friends and activities. Some argue that there is still insufficient research to make judgments on how the impact of divorce compares overall with the daily experience of tensions, perhaps violence, between parents who stay together, but it is clear that there are some disturbing aspects concerning the effects of divorce on children.

For the single parent life after divorce may be hard. The likely deterioration in economic circumstances perhaps will need to be offset by more time spent in paid employment. In addition, the custodial parent may be required to be the sole source of both authority and affection for their emotionally traumatized children. Socially, most newly divorced parents (along with single, never-married parents), take up a "single-person" life-style, with its intermix of activity outside the home, often with different partners, resulting in disrupted and incoherent routines for their children. Some perceive a mismatch between the singles life-style and adequate childrearing, which can result in poor levels of satisfaction for both parent and child. In their turn, youngsters of single parents may be expected to take on additional responsibilities in the home, in general having a more "grown-up" and independent status conferred upon them. It is of note that, on average, children of divorced parents are more likely to be sexually active at a younger age than children from intact families, and that these children are more likely, in their turn, to become divorced themselves, for insecurity often begets insecurity.

Should the parent remarry or establish a combined household with a new partner, the children of either or both partners will need to adjust to their new "quasi-kin" relatives, who may present alternative norms and values to their biological family. While this experience may offer richness and variety and a more settled feel to the home, children of divorcees experience a challenging scenario, especially if they resent the parent's intimacy with a new partner.

It is for some or all of these reasons that parents, contemplating separation and divorce, often wait until their children are "old enough to cope," usually in their teens. However, psychological research would indicate that adolescents, above all other age-groups, can experience the crisis of divorce most severely, and disruptive behavior and lower educational attainment may be measurable responses. One recent survey amongst 13–19-year-olds in Britian (1996) revealed that, in addition to secure paid employment, settled family life was the element of existence that they valued the most. However, based on current divorce trends in the United States (and figures would be comparable for some West European countries, in particular the U.K. and Denmark) it is estimated that half of all children born since 1975 will have spent some part of their lives in a single-parent home.

5. Families without Fathers

There is a growing concern about the increasing number of Euro-American families headed by women, meaning an overall loss of the father's role both in terms of general discipline and the care function, and in relation to financial support. Fatherless boys may lack appropriate role models—adult males, in the home interacting in ordinary ways with the rest of the family—as alternatives to distorted media images and the macho ethos of their male social group. An increasing number of social commentators equate this fatherless phenomenon with a rise in social dysfunction and crime—Norman Dennis and A. H. Halsey in England, and Charles Murray in the United States have promulgated theses concerning this connection.

Dennis sees as mistaken the interpretation of growing crime statistics as "moral panic," argued by a growing body of liberal-minded academics, feeling that their attention should be directed more to the realities *behind* the statistics. And he challenges the view that rising crime among young people can be attributed solely to rising proverty and unemployment, observing that in times of comparative affluence and good employment prospects (1965–1975) the rate of crime in the United Kingdom doubled its score over the previous 10 years. Criminal lawyers in the United States who defend minors in the 1990s state that these children lack the moral awareness required for an understanding of right and wrong. In particular, the rising incidence of child-on-child violence, in extreme cases involving murder, is of particular concern.

III. FERTILITY TRENDS AND NEW TECHNOLOGIES

A. Birthrate Trends

In spite of a biblical encouragement to "Go forth and multiply," fertility has, through time been constrained by a variety of health and ethical objectives linked to religious and social mores. In the later 20th century, as with the relationship between sex and marriage, the link between the sexual act and procreation—through extensive use of reliable contraception—has been increasingly weakened. Without artificial methods and other factors inhibiting a woman's fertility cycle, the natural family size for each woman during her 30 to 35 fertile years, could be as high as 15. In Western developed countries, the peak child-bearing age of 25 to 29–biologically, the most favorable period—is declining, due in part to women's career aspirations and the establishment of partnerships later in life. There is a marginally increasing number of births at the onset of the fertility period (in adolescence), particularly in lower socioeconomic groups, and a marked increase at its end—toward menopause, although many of these women may experience problems with fertility.

Currently, around one couple in six experiences problems with fertility. (1994 U.K. statistics) Aside from postponement of the first pregnancy beyond the years of highest fertility, scientists look for environmental causes to explain ever-lower sperm counts in men and to behavioral and other causes for women's infertility. For example, the higher incidence of certain sexually transmitted diseases can impair the reproductive function.

In the United Kingdom as elsewhere in the Western world, there is some concern about a growing imbalance between increased life expectancy and the decreasing birthrate with important economic and social implications. It is estimated that by the year 2000 personal decisions around fertility, including contraception, abortion, and choice to remain childless, will cause the rate will stabilize at 1.9, below the level of 2.1, the figure necessary for long-term replacement of the population. By 2000 it is expected that one woman in five in the United Kingdom will choose not to have children. On average, worldwide, slightly more boys than girls are born, but due to higher mortality rates in males, by adulthood the proportions are practically equal, except where the balance is upset by a cultural preference for male children when parents may ensure the nonsurvival of girls as, for example, in some parts of India and China.

B. Abortion

Although abortion continues to be a controversial and divisive issue, through time, there is clear evidence of a liberalizing of attitudes where legal frameworks increasingly are drawn upon to provide moral frameworks. New medical technologies increase the ethical complexity—for example, in the case of a twin pregnancy, when elective abortion can destroy one fetus in utero, where there is parental preference for a singleton child. This kind of choice appears to reflect a growing consumerism in Western society regarding procreation.

In addition, many view fertility, abortion, and the choices around these as a part of a wider agenda relating to gender, power, and control. Radical feminists in Western developed countries assert that the contents of a woman's body should be hers to do with as she chooses—to abort the fetus, to bring a child into the world, or to decide *how* that child will be cared for, and by whom. Some will opt for parenthood where men play no relational part at all—achieving intimacy and support from other women and becoming pregnant through artificial insemination. For their "sisters" in developing countries, liberal feminists would support the "power of voluntary parenthood" encouraging resistance, for example, to birth control imposed by external agencies. And the growing incidence of genetic screening worldwide will present new choices and new dilemmas that have an impact on the ethics of human identity and human relationships.

C. Biotechnology, Fertility, and the Family

In 1978, with the birth of the first ever test-tube baby, a milestone was reached in reproductive technology. Now, in the late 1990s, women of pensionable age can become mothers, preferences of race and gender for one's progency can be realized, and it is technically possible for a person to be created from the ova of an aborted fetus—a living child from a never-living mother. In addition, the possibility of artificial and surrogate wombs introduces ever more complexity into an already ethically charged landscape around procreation. The problem is to try to establish which changes are likely to increase possibilities for human fulfillment, and which changes are unlikely to do so; critically, to take steps to ensure that "change," whether biological or sociological, does not bequeath too many problems for the future to solve. The ever-increasing possibilities for the treatment of infertility must draw upon scarce resources, thus, serious ethical debate is required as to how these should be apportioned out. Some suggest that subfertile individuals should be screened to check their suitability for parenthood before expensive treatment is made available to them, but others feel this would be difficult to uphold morally when those who conceive naturally are not subject to such screening.

IV. THE IMPACT OF TWENTIETH CENTURY IDEOLOGIES

For an understanding of the kinds of changes concerning the family in the late-20th century, it is important to explore some of the more recent perspectives on relationships that have attempted to influence and explain how the family operates.

Following the Second World War Western society registered in many ways a growth of "opportunities for all" in education and employment. From this, a distinctive youth culture with increased spending power and increasing freedoms emerged in the mid-1960s. At the same time, the contraceptive pill, available to a broad section of the population, effectively released constraints on sexual behavior by allowing sex reliably to be separated from procreation. However, the incidence of divorce was still relatively rare (although due to conditions in law, it was more common in the United States than in Western Europe). Most people got married and stayed married, and few babies were born out of wedlock. Western society was changing, but the family, in its traditional, nuclear form, was intact.

A. Alternative Systems, Alternative Styles

While the 1960s brought new challenges to established ways of thinking and behaving, traditional family systems had in fact been challenged both philosophically and structurally as far back as the ancient Greeks, and, more recently, in post-war Israel through its Kibbutz system of collectivist childcare. Importantly also, 20th-century Marxist regimes, like those of China and the Soviet Union, made efforts to abolish the family in its bourgeois and traditional form. Later, middle-class young people on the American west coast in the 1960s, linked to a pervasive pop culture through the "flower-power" movement, gave expression to values that offered an alternative to those of their families of origin, from which they felt alienated. They searched for a sense of "belonging" through the formation of communes. These communal "families," with their freed-up structures, challenged prescribed notions of commitment as expressed through marriage and family, and all the formal institutions that accompanied these. Connected in some ways with this new thinking were anti-family psycho-dynamic perspectives arising from work of, for example, R. D. Laing, highlighting the negative effects of the family on its individual members, and at the least interpreting the nuclear family as a potential habor of selfishness and reclusive self-interest. A growing awareness of the extent of abuse against women and children within families compounded these negatives.

At the same time, within more conventional structures, the middle-class 1960s "new man" challenged his machismo in a search for more nurturant dimensions. In supportive attendance at the birth of his child and sharing with care responsibilities in partnership with his wife, "new man's" input opened up opportunities for his partner to sustain interests outside of the home, even to work part-time. But, the child, whose upbringing they both shared, remained very much at the center of the parents' concerns. In some ways, connected with a search for males to develop their care and nurturing role, a strand of recent thinking has sought to effect this more 'familial' model of operation in the public arena: the so-called "ethics of care" position (see Ruddick, 1989). However, both women's and men's career-role aspirations into the 1990s are inclined to express the more masculine/antinurturant modes of thinking and operation.

B. Politics, Action, and Feminism

In the later 1960s, at the macro level, politically motivated groups developed strategies of increasing challenge to Western-style capitalism, promoting left-wing and generally more liberal ways of thinking and acting. Students rioted in Paris, and the American anti-Vietnam demonstrations offered "lawbreaker as hero," while "Black Power" activists expressed in action the radicalism of Franz Fanon and Malcolm X. These were clear signs of a growing dissatisfaction with institutional structures registered, for example, in marriage and in the family with their perceived agenda of promoting unequal and ideologically unacceptable lifestyles for people at an individual level.

Intellectuals promoted equal opportunities—not just for different racial groups, but for women also, Indeed, it was the 1960s civil-rights movement that had helped to shape the topics and language of the feminist themes of representation and the sexual division of labor, and, more recently, reproduction. But the feminist equal-rights viewpoint had been argued by writers well before this century. More than 200 years ago Mary Woolstonecraft recognized a mismatch between the rights women had and the duties they were expected to perform. And John Stuart Mill had expressed serious concerns about marriage and how women, by entering into this legally bound structure, would allow additional rights and powers to their husbands, to the detriment of their own situation. In more recent times, the ideas of Simone de Bouviour, Germain Greer, and Shulamith Firestone have renewed the call for women to challenge more radically a structural environment designed for men. In the 1970s and 1980s university gender studies departments grew apace out of a perceived need for new frameworks of thinking to account for women. Feminism became an influential movement with broad impact, especially on what traditionally had been at the center of most women's lives—the home and the family.

The personal is political became the feminist credo, as women increasingly interpreted relations in the home as political structures that formed and constrained how they might act. As with the workplace, home would be seen as an arena of women's subservience to men's needs and men's power—the traditional view of rights and freedoms viewed as a construction of male thinking. A decade before, Shulamith Firestone had argued that women's "natural" feelings and responses would be their undoing, and this perspective became part of a new challenge around the care role of women. Drawing on ideas from deconstruction analysis and from the 'nature/culture' debate presented, for example, by Levi-Strauss, feminists argued that gender role is not, in fact, predetermined, for persons have an built-in variability. Thus, the required altruism for motherhood, previously accepted as a biological inevitability, part and parcel of a time-honored framing of universal concepts and values about gender—the so-called "essentialist" perspective—was called into question by women who were no longer prepared to tolerate what they perceived as its injustices. However, the thinking of feminist intellectuals, in spite of its impact on family and social policy as well as on behavior and attitudes as a personal level, can be out of step with the thinking of many women who are less vociferous in their expression.

C. Postmodernism

The challenge to established ways of thinking around procreation and the care role has been linked in some ways to postmodern thinking—of increasing influence in academia through the 1980s into the 1990s. Postmodernism offered an epistemological skepticism about enlightened modernism and its belief in universally accepted truths to be discovered and imparted for the improvement of people's lives at an individual level. Thus, thinkers such as the French philosopher, Lyotard, identified the demise of the universal truth paradigm reached through scientific rationality that he argued would be replaced by a relativism of different knowledges, arising from "multiple wisdoms." He claimed this perspective would offer a nonhegemonic strategy for breaking down the structures of rationality and power, with the hope of moving toward new and "more meaningful wisdoms." More recently, Richard Rorty has developed these ideas with his view of individuals "making" rather than "finding" truth. It is important to consider the impact that such thinking might have on

ethical debate around the family and on those who engage in it—parents and policymakers, young people, and professionals in care and educational settings, with regard to their roles and responsibilities. For, taken to its limits this argument can present a world devoid of time-honored and unassailable truths, where the only force that counts will be the individual at the center, concerned only with her own subjective interpretations and desires. In interesting ways, in its subjectivism and moral relativism, this position might be seen to mirror the adolescent stage of development.

At the same time, personal behavior and lifestyle is interpreted on the "social model" suggesting individuals as victims of environmental forces with only limited capacity to act on the basis of individual decisions. This is because, as the argument goes, conditions are fixed and ideas and values imbibed, rather than rationally sorted out; thus, people are subjects of powerful forces rather than forces within themselves—a perspective contrasting starkly with the words of John Locke, penned in 1690: "A person is a thinking, intelligent being, that has reason and reflection, and can consider itself as itself, the same thinking thing, in different times and places. ...."

V. ADULTS' VALUES AND CHILDREN'S NEEDS

Notwithstanding changes and new thinking at the macro level of society, it is important to look at children and what universal and continuing needs must be addressed. According to psychological theory, the establishment of a secure identity for children is dependent primarily upon their being linked with significant others—a sense of common stock, a rootedness. This usually begins with their first unit of connection—the biological family. Where in past times the physical well-being of children was frequently hazardous, in current Western society it is their well-being in relation to the emotional, psychological, moral, and spiritual dimensions that are now seen to be at risk.

The provision of adequate conditions for the preservation and flourishing of life and health—food, clothing, shelter, with opportunities for recreation, intellectual stimulus, and social interaction along with affection and the sense of being loved and valued—are commonly accepted as essential for children. Additionally, children need to link into appropriate social norms within their intimate family settings as well as within the wider community of which they are a part. The

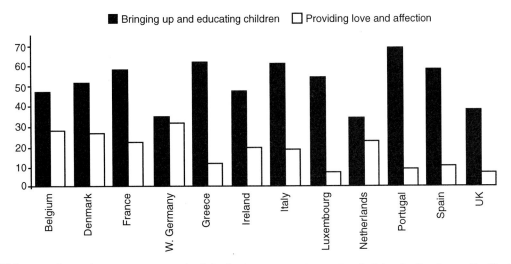

FIGURE 2   Attitudes on the most important role of the family in society. Source: Family Policy Studies Centre, *Families in the European Union* (1994).

critical challenge here is the requirement for inculcation into desirable patterns of moral behavior within a wider context of increasingly undesirable and unethical behavior, where materialism, individualism, and self-indulgence serve to undermine some important and time-honored values regarding human relationships, including the altruism required for committed parenting.

Self-centered, atomized individuals will create a self-centered, atomized society, and parents as the first and most critical role models have the potential to influence their children in the way they think best. Functioning with integrity and altruism, and directing their energies to positive ways both externally and within the home, it is argued that parents can contribute, through example, to their children's moral well-being and ultimately to the future well-being of the society of which they are a part.

Data from a survey of European attitudes, provided in Figure 2, demonstrates that in every country except the United Kingdom bringing up and educating children is seen as the most important role of the family in society. The British, however see providing love and affection as more important.

A. Who Should Care?

The feminist perspective has been considered above, but locked into the debate about equal opportunities for women is the issue of who should take on the care role so that children might also claim *their* equal rights and opportunities. The perceived importance of paren-

tal time and commitment during the human child's attenuated period of helplessness has never been seriously challenged until the last 20 years, when mothers in particular have been required to rationalize the emotional, biological, ideological, economic, and cultural pressures of the parenting role.

The United Kingdom is closer to the United States than to other European countries regarding elements of employment legislation and practice that have a negative impact upon parenting. A good example concerns policies around maternity leave and the lack of opportunity for part-time work and job sharing, which all militate against mothers who wish to respond flexibly to their own and their children's needs.

Overall, parenting is unconditional and imperative (with many of its satisfactions of a future order), but this may not mesh with the values of a present-time search for instant and personal fulfillment. And children's requirements for "unstructured availability" from their parents will be at odds with the limited availability of "quality time"—when children's needs must be slotted into the routines of the working, or otherwise occupied, parent.

B. Work and Care Outside the Home

If the home was traditionally the site for children's early experiences of loving and learning, economic, sociological, and ideological changes over the past two decades have meant that increasingly this has become the task of external agencies. Where in the past extended family members, particularly grandparents, fulfilled the care role if required, today for many, care has been professionalized. For example, more than half of women with preschool children in the United States now work, and the United Kingdom presents similar statistics.

Yet women still appear to bear the burden of household responsibilities, and recent research at the London School of Economics (see Catherine Hakim, 1996) suggests that the majority of women continue to give priority to home and family. Taxation law can work for or against women who stay at home. For example, in Sweden policies are oriented to favor the working mother, whereas the policies in Germany in some ways support the return of the mother to "mothering." Perhaps some systems have not yet achieved an appropriate balance between the interests of society, children's rights, and the rights of parents. We are approaching the first generation of grown-up children of full-time working mothers, so research findings into the effects of this situation on a variety of elements, including child/parent relationships, are just beginning to emerge. But part-time employment, while seen as more advantageous for young children, remains insecure, low-paid, and exploitative for parents and, in its lack of permanence, it can have a destabilizing effect on the family, especially when it represents the only wage coming into the home.

C. Changing Perceptions of Childhood

There is considerable evidence to suggest that factors in current Western society as explored above—divorce and single parenthood, the atomized existences of small family units away from wider kin and community, and the demands of paid employment—are inhibiting parents' ability to meet fully the needs of their children. In recent *nonclinical* studies it was found that two out of five children are not securely attached to the parent figure, and clinical trials present even more grave evidence with regard to malfunctioning parent/child attachment.

In addition, ideological influences around roles and relationships in society serve to deconstruct childhood as they are deconstructing gender. (Indeed, the orientation toward alternative lifestyles and structures threatens to deconstruct the family itself, at least in its traditional nuclear form.) The need for children to be separated from home and parents at earlier ages than traditionally would have been thought desirable requires that they become more independent, because parents' individual freedoms, increasingly highly prized, will be inextricably connected with this require-

ment. Some perceptions of the parental role as compared with their children's moral and social development would seem to suggest that even quite young infants will be deemed to require more to be "listened to" than "guided." In some ways, therefore, children's rights predominate over children's welfare. For example, in a recent survey among parents in the United Kingdom, more than 50% were opposed to teaching their children specific moral values, preferring for them to settle these on their own. Yet parental culpability for children's antisocial and criminal acts is a growing area of litigation as parents increasingly are held more responsible for their children's behavior in both educational and social settings.

VI. THE FAMILY: TOWARD THE THIRD MILLENNIUM

Throughout the 1990s the family has been under the spotlight, and the central question is whether its private troubles are rooted in public issues, or public troubles are rooted in what happens in the private domain of the family. A leveling of personal and social values reflected in the language of relativist morality by professionals has in some ways served to legitimize a general rebellion against structure and authority as expressed through the operation of parents and preparents on the reductive individual choice model of human relationships: the "right" to become pregnant; the "right" to terminate that pregnancy ... Overall, there grows a resentment against any constraints on personal choice, which increasingly are viewed negatively, as measures of social control.

A. Gender: Challenges and Changes

For young men, the erosion of opportunities for self-realization through work and family is experienced keenly in a climate of growing opportunity for women with emphasis on *their* choices, for example in "go-it-alone" parenthood and increasing involvement in paid employment outside the home. Structural changes in work opportunities in postindustrial society, particularly through a decline in manual and factory occupations, restrict opportunities for regular employment for many young men. Without this and the civilizing effects of marriage and parenthood, in the company of other young males they may turn toward macho, aggressive and, at times, the criminal behavior. It would be impossible and certainly undesirable to attempt to turn back the clock on women's hard-won rights, and impractical, too, in an employment setting that in many ways favors women's work. But, clearly, as part of a broader consideration of family policy, it is important that the needs of all are adequately accounted for, and especially those of children—the next generation of parents.

B. Family and Fiscal Policies

Over the past half century, the development of welfare and its growing input into the lives of families has meant that many responsibilities that once were private have devolved to the state. When governments of Western nations are required to provide for an growing burden of need, the call to review policies becomes ever more pressing. The ethical choice between reducing support to single parents and their children, as against providing *more* support to offset the deprivations of their condition with all its present and future implications, is ever present. Increased support might carry an endorsement for single parenthood and it might appear to discriminate against the two parent family; reduction in benefit would penalize children and especially those parents whose condition is not of their choosing. These are weighty issues to be confronted by those in a position to influence and implement policy. Some Western nations, particular, the United Kingdom, operate a tax system that shows no recognition of the financial burden on parents of rearing children.

Perhaps one way forward would be once again to accept the necessary centrality of children by setting out a clear account of their needs and meshing these with a recognized *care charter* expressing *their* fundamental rights, outside the arena of political and factional lobbies. This might be done by drawing upon an appropriate ethical framework, psychological and sociological research, and the wisdom culled from centuries of successful child rearing, but with a realistic awareness of modern conditions. The decision can then be made concerning what children require at different stages of their development, who might best provide for these needs, and how these persons be might best be supported and sustained.

It is clear that to raise the status of children, parents, and the parenting process requires some fundamental changes at policy level. British sociologists Halsey and Young have developed some interesting ideas on these matters, including the implementation of a "parent wage" for those with children under age 5 by way of making parent and home management a real option in economic terms. In addition, these academics recommend taxes with a "children tag," earmarked for the education of parents as well as of children, and for the improvement in the physical environment of both. Proxy votes placed by parents on behalf of their children would ensure that these issues were adequately accounted within government programs, they argue. And they would implement structural changes within employment to ensure that workplace routines mesh more satisfactorily with the needs of children, parents, and home life.

C. Educating for Parenting: Skills and Processes

It appears that natural parenting skills are no longer a "taken as read" resource, although some would refute the idea that they ever were. The idea of parenting skills as requiring to be "learned" has grown in credibility as some parents, operating within personal and economic constraints and locationally separated from extended family, appear to lack the cognitive and functional skills to cope adequately in their role. Research is strong regarding as essential correlation between social and antisocial behavior in children and young people, and the quality of imput and care that parents have provided in their early years.

A growth area in the United Kingdom and elsewhere in the 1970s and early 1980s, *education for parenthood* with teenagers in schools initially was integrated within a broader personal, social, sex, and moral education program. In the 1990s, some countries have remained committed to such programmes. In the United Kingdom, with the establishment of a national curriculum's greater emphasis on academic core subjects in schools and skills for the workplace in vocationally oriented colleges, areas of the curriculum in all institutions, perceived as "nonessential," have become marginalized and underfunded, including education for parenthood.

What would appear to be required of family-life education toward the third millennium (for work both within schools and within community settings in addition to a knowledge curriculum on children and their needs), is a more holistic program of personal and social and ethical education. This would allow opportunity for reflection on the moral dimension of personal life, and the development of the self—for example, to explore the difference between such concepts as hedonism and self-fulfillment, and the likely potential of each for individuals and their families as for the society of which they are a part. In turn, this program should include consideration of the emotional dimension of human experience—an exploration of feelings, and why these matter. In addition, and particularly with regard to the present-day emphasis on the personal choice ethic, it would be beneficial to learn the practice of philosophical reasoning: for learners to practice the logic/rhetoric/dialectic model of explaining their views, while placing these alongside the views of others.

During the late 20th century when postmodern Western culture equates notions of "the good" with "change," and to be "radically enlightened" means to reject what has gone before, it is the case that a natural resource both for parent education and support—the "third" generation—is undervalued. With the advent of smaller families and early retirement, middle-aged and older grandparents and great-grandparents could be part of a holistic education and support process— and as learners, too, both within the community and in their own family settings. While some grandparents gain "new" grandchildren through the remarriage of their children, important kinship links and the richness of integenerational family are often compromised by divorce. An *interfamily* model of support, encompassing three, or even four generations, could have positive spin-offs for individuals within both reconstituted and nuclear families, as well as for the communities of which they are a part.

The photograph below is of retired Yorkshire miner, Henry Chipchase, celebrating 60 years of marriage with his wife Dora, 5 children, 14 grandchildren, and 12 great-grandchildren.

Research across Europe demonstrates that intergenerational contact is very important to family members and arguably to the society of which they are a part. Unstable family systems with broken connections to the family line are demonstrating an undermining of personal and parental fulfillment, in the same way that an unsound parent/child attachment will register seriously negative outcomes. Toward the millennium, a blueprint for the family in a pluralistic age would be inappropriate, but critically, family contexts must provide opportunity for human flourishing as for the development and promotion of critical social values.

Also See the Following Articles

CHILDREN'S RIGHTS • DIVORCE • GENDER ROLES

Bibliography

Almond, B. (Ed.). (1995). *Introducing applied ethics*. Oxford: Blackwell Publishers Ltd. (Especially "The Personal Dimension.").

Berger, B., Carlson, A., & Davies, J. (1993). *The family: Is it just another lifestyle choice?* London: Institute of Economic Affairs.

Gatens, M. (1991). *Feminism and philosophy: Perspectives on difference and equality*. Bloomington, IN: Indiana University Press.

Hakim, C. (1996). *Issues in women's work: Female heterogeneity and the polarism of women's employment*. Atlantic Heights, NJ: Humanities Press International, Inc.

Held, V. (1993). *Feminist morality: Transforming culture, society and politics*. Chicago: University of Chicago Press.

Morgan, P. (1995). *Farewell to the Family*. London: Institute of Economic Affairs.

Nock, S. L. *Sociology and the Family,* 2nd ed. Englewood Cliffs, NJ: Prentice Hall, Inc.

Ulanowsky, C. E. (Ed.) (1995). *The family in the age of biotechnology*. Avebury, U.K.: Ashgate Publishing Company.

Whitfield R. (Ed.). (1987). *Families matter*. Basingstoke, U.K.: Marshall Pickering. (Available through National Family Trust.)

Young, M., & Halsey, A. H. (1995). *Family and community socialism*. London: Institute for Public Policy Research.

FEMALE CIRCUMCISION AND GENITAL MUTILATION

Loretta M. Kopelman
East Carolina University School of Medicine

I. Health Hazards of Female Genital Mutilation
II. Assessing Reasons for Female Genital Mutilation
III. The Debate over Ethical Relativism and Cross-Cultural Moral Authority
IV. Conclusion

GLOSSARY

circumcision: Type 1 Removal of the clitoral hood or prepuce (skin around the clitoris).
circumcision: Type 2, or intermediary Removal of the entire clitoris and most, or all, of the labia minora.
circumcision: Type 3 Also known as Pharaonic circumcision, removal of the clitoris, labia minora, and parts of the labia majora.
descriptive relativism The view that cultures have differences. It takes no stand on whether these differences are good or bad, or right or wrong.
ethical or cultural relativism A moral theory holding that an action is right if it is approved in a person's culture and wrong if it is disapproved; if something has cultural approval, it is right, and if something has cultural disapproval, it is wrong. On this view, something cannot be wrong but approved in a culture, or right but disapproved in it.
infibulation A procedure in which the wound to the vulva from genital cutting is stitched tightly closed, leaving a tiny opening so that the woman can pass urine and menstrual flow.

FEMALE CIRCUMCISION is a widespread and popular practice in north African and southern Arabian regions that involves the removal of some, or all, of the external female genitalia. Eighty million living women have had some form of this mutilation, and it is being performed on an additional 4 or 5 million girls annually. These procedures deny women sexual orgasms and are leading causes of disease, disability, and death in women, girls, and infants in these regions. These surgical rites, usually performed on girls between infancy and puberty, are intended to promote chastity, religion, group identity, cleanliness, health, family values, and marriage. Most of the people practicing this ritual are Muslim, but these rituals are neither required by the Qur'an, nor practiced in the spiritual center of Islam, Saudi Arabia (El Dareer, 1982; Ntiri 1993). These rites predate the introduction of Islam into these regions and are condemned by many Muslims.

Influential international agencies including UNICEF, the International Federation of Gynecology and Obstetrics, and the World Health Organization (WHO) openly condemn and try to stop the practices of female genital mutilation. Many important national groups such as the American Medical Association have also denounced these rituals. Around the world, women's groups protest the practice of female genital cutting, denying it is just a cultural issue and arguing these rites should be treated with the same vigor as other human rights violations (Schroeder, 1994; Toubia, 1994). Pressure from such human right's groups, for example, forced some governments to ban all registered health professionals from performing female circumcision or infibulation and helped women find political asylum in other countries to avoid genital cutting.

Female genital cutting is viewed as child abuse in many parts of the world including the United Kingdom, France, Canada, and the United States (Kluge, 1993; Thompson, 1989; Schroeder, 1994). Despite this, many parents from these cultures find ways to perform these rites in other countries. In the United Kingdom, for example, about 2000 girls undergo the surgery annually (Thompson, 1989). Exact numbers are difficult to collect, however, because these rites are often done in secret, or families return to their countries of origin to have them performed.

People who want to continue these practices resent such criticisms, seeing them as assaults upon their cultural traditions and identity. They receive theoretical support from certain versions of ethical relativism, a moral theory contending that there is no moral authority for the intercultural condemnation of this or other cultural activities, because there is no rational basis for establishing that one set of culturally supported moral values is right and another wrong. Female genital cutting serves as a test case for such versions of ethical relativism because these rites have widespread approval within the cultures where they are practiced, and thus according to this theory they are right. Yet they have widespread disapproval outside them for reasons that seem compelling, but that according to this theory lack any moral authority. Thus, many discussions in ethics about female genital mutilation, such as those of philosophers Susan Sherwin and Loretta Kopelman examine which forms of ethical relativism entail that genital cutting is a justifiable practice in societies where it is approved.

Other moral traditions reject this version of ethical relativism and deny that to say something is morally right means it is popular. These traditions hold that to say something is morally right means that the claim can be defended with reasons showing its merit. Saying that some things are approved in a culture such as invasion, war, slavery, or oppression does not settle whether they are morally right, because something can be wrong even when it is approved by most people in a culture. Moral judgments do not describe what *is* approved but prescribe what *ought* to be approved. If worthy of being called moral or ethical judgments, they must be defensible with reasons that are, among other things, consistent and empirically defensible.

In the first section we examine the harms associated with female genital mutilation and in the second the reasons given for performing these rites. In the third

and last section, we consider the debate about the possibility of genuine moral assessments between cultures over female genital mutilation. The debate will center on the following questions: (1) Do we have any shared, intercultural methods to assess moral judgments including possible inaccuracies and inconsistencies? (2) Can we sharply differentiate and count cultures, or do we live in multiple and intertwined cultures? (3) Do we share any goals? and (4) Does ethical relativism avoid or promote oppression and cultural imperialism?

I. HEALTH HAZARDS OF FEMALE GENITAL MUTILATION

There is good evidence the rites of female genital mutilation cause pain, disease, disabilities, and, occasionally death. Yet these rituals are prevalent in many countries, including Ethiopia, the Sudan, Somalia, Sierra Leone, Kenya, Tanzania, Central African Republic, Chad, Gambia, Liberia, Mali, Senegal, Eritrea, Ivory Coast, Upper Volta, Mauritania, Nigeria, Mozambique, Botswana, Lesotho, and Egypt (Abdalla, 1982; Ntiri, 1993; El Dareer, 1982; Koso-Thomas, 1987). More modified versions of the surgeries are performed in Southern Yemen and Musqat-Oman (Abdalla, 1982). It is also practiced by Muslim groups in the Philippines, Malaysia, Pakistan, Indonesia, Europe, and North America (Kluge, 1993; Thompson, 1989; Abdalla, 1982; Koso-Thomas, 1987).

Of the three forms of female genital mutilation, Type 1 is the least mutilating type and may not, unlike other forms, preclude sexual orgasms for women. Type 1 circumcision, however, is very difficult to perform without removing additional tissue. Dr. Nahid Toubia writes, "In my extensive clinical experience as a physician in Sudan, and after a careful review of the literature, I have not found a single case of female circumcision in which only the skin surrounding the clitoris is removed, without damaging the clitoris itself" (1994, p. 713). The tools commonly used by traditional practitioners, razors and knives, make it even more likely that additional tissue will be taken. In the southern Arabian countries of Southern Yemen and Musqat-Oman, Type 1 circumcision is commonly practiced. In African countries, however, Type 1 circumcision is often not regarded as a genuine circumcision (Koso-Thomas, 1987; Abdalla, 1982). Only about 3% of the women had this type of circumcision in an east African survey conducted by Sudanese physician Asthma El Dareer (1982).

Types 2 and 3, both of which preclude orgasms, are the most popular forms of circumcision. More than three-quarters of the girls in the Sudan, Somalia, Ethiopia, Egypt, and other north African and southern Arabian countries undergo Type 2 or Type 3 circumcision, with many of the others circumcised by Type 1 (El Dareer, 1982; Ntiri, 1993; Koso-Thomas, 1987). One survey by El Dareer (1982) shows that more than 98% of Sudanese women have had this ritual surgery, 12% with Type 2, and 83% with Type 3.

Investigators Raquiya Haji Dualeh Abdalla, Olayinka Koso-Thomas, and Daphne Williams Ntiri found that in some African countries, most young girls between infancy and 10 years of age have had Type 3 circumcision. These and other investigators have discovered that traditional practitioners often use sharpened or hot stones, razors, or knives, frequently without anesthesia or antibiotics (Abdalla, 1982; El Dareer, 1982). In many communities, thorns are used to stitch the wound closed, or perform the infibulation, and a twig is inserted to keep an opening. The girl's legs may be bound for a month or more while the scar heals (Abdalla, 1982; El Dareer, 1982).

A series of pioneering studies conducted in the Sudan by El Dareer (1982), in Sierra Leone by Koso-Thomas (1987), and in Somalia by Abdalla (1982) document that female genital cutting harms in many ways, having both short- and long-term complications. Kopelman (1994, 1997) shows later studies confirm their findings. The operation causes immediate problems that can even be fatal. They find initial problems are pain, bleeding, infection, tetanus, and shock. The degree of harm correlates with the type of circumcision. El Dareer found that bleeding occurred in all forms of circumcision, accounting for 21.3% of the immediate medical problems; infections are frequent because the surgical conditions are often unhygienic. She also found that the inability to pass urine was common, constituting 21.65% of the immediate complications.

El Dareer found that these rites cause many long-term medical complications, including difficulty in the consummation of marriage and hazardous labor and delivery. Urinary tract infections are another long-term complication that 24.5% of women recognized as caused by these rites, and 23.8% recognized that the rituals has caused suffering chronic pelvic infection. The published studies by investigators from the regions where these rituals are practiced uniformly find that women expressed similar complaints and had similar complications from female genital mutilation: at the site of the surgery, scarring can make penetration difficult and intercourse painful; cysts may form, requiring surgical repairs; a variety of menstrual problems arise if the opening is left too small to allow adequate drainage; fistulas or tears in the bowel or urinary tract are common, causing incontinence, which in turn leads to social as well as medical problems; maternal-fetal complications and prolonged and obstructed labor are also well-established consequences (El Dareer, 1982; Koso-Thomas, 1987; Abdalla, 1982; Thompson, 1989).

As high as the rate of these reported complications are, investigator El Dareer believes that the actual rates are probably even higher for several reasons. First, female genital cutting, although widely practiced, is technically illegal in many of these regions, and people are reluctant to discuss illegal activities. (These laws are often the unenforced remnants of colonial days.) Second, people may be ashamed to admit that they have had complications, fearing they are to blame. Third, some women believe that female circumcision or infibulation is necessary for their health and well-being and may not fully associate these problems with the surgery. They assume that their problems would have been worse without it. Of course, many other women, as these studies show, are well aware of the complications from these rituals.

II. ASSESSING REASONS FOR FEMALE GENITAL MUTILATION

Proponents of female circumcision defend these rituals as useful ways to promote many important goals. According to five independent series of studies conducted by investigators from countries where female circumcision is widely practiced including El Dareer, Koso-Thomas, Abdalla, and Ntiri, the primary reasons given for performing this ritual surgery are that it (1) meets a religious requirement, (2) preserves group identity, (3) helps to maintain cleanliness and health, (4) preserves virginity and family honor and prevents immorality, and (5) furthers marriage goals including greater sexual pleasure for men. El Dareer conducted her studies in the Sudan, Koso-Thomas in and around Sierra Leone, and Abdalla in Somalia. They argue that the reasons for continuing this practice in their respective countries rest on ignorance about health, reproduction, and sexuality, and thus these rites fail as means to these ends. These investigators, who come from cultures practicing female genital mutilation, point out many factual errors and inconsistencies in peoples' beliefs about the procedure and their goals they believe these rites serve. This serves as a basis for their moral judgments condemning these practices.

A. Meets a Religious Requirement

According to these studies, the main reason given for performing female circumcision/genital mutilation is that it is regarded as a religious requirement. Most of the people practicing this ritual are Muslims, but it is not a practice required by the Qur'an (El Dareer, 1982; Ntiri, 1993). El Dareer writes: "Circumcision of women is not explicitly enjoined in the Koran, but there are two implicit sayings of the Prophet Mohammed: 'Circumcision is an ordinace in men and an embellishment in women' and, reportedly Mohammed said to Om Attiya, a woman who circumcised girls in El Medina, 'Do not go deep. It is more illuminating to the face and more enjoyable to the husband.' Another version says, 'Reduce but do not destroy. This is enjoyable to the woman and preferable to the man.' But there is nothing in the Koran to suggest that the Prophet commanded that women be circumcised. He advised that it was important to both sexes that very little should be taken." Other Muslims challenge the authenticity of even these comments, arguing that the Prophet did not approve of female genital cutting because he did not have it done to his wives or daughters. Female circumcision/ genital mutilation, moreover, is not practiced in the spiritual center of Islam, Saudi Arabia. Another reason for questioning this as a Muslim practice is that clitoridectomy and infibulation predate Islam, going back to the time of the pharaohs (Abdalla, 1982; El Dareer, 1992).

B. Preserves Group Identity

According to anthropologist Scheper-Hughes, when Christian colonialists in Kenya introduced laws opposing the practice of female circumcision in the 1930s, African leader Kenyatta expressed a view still popular today: "This operation is still regarded as the very essence of an institution which has enormous educational, social, moral and religious implications, quite apart from the operation itself. For the present, it is impossible for a member of the [Kikuyu] tribe to imagine an initiation without clitoridectomy . . . the abolition of IRUA [the ritual operation] will destroy the tribal symbol which identifies the age group and prevent the Kikuyu from perpetuating that spirit of collectivism and national solidarity which they have been able to maintain from time immemorial" (Scheper-Hughes, 1991; p. 27). In addition, the practice is of social and economic importance to many women who are paid for performing the rituals (El Dareer, 1982; Koso-Thomas, 1987; Abdalla, 1982; Ginsberg, 1991).

Drs. Koso-Thomas, El Dareer, and Abdalla agree that people in these countries support female circumcision as a good practice, but only because they do not understand that it is a leading cause of sickness, or even death, for girls, mothers, and infants, and a major cause of infertility, infection, and maternal-fetal and marital complications. They conclude that these facts are not confronted because these societies do not speak openly of such matters. Abdalla writes, "there is no longer any reason, given the present state of progess in science, to tolerate confusion and ignorance about reproduction and women's sexuality" (1982; p. 2). Female circumcision is intended in these cultures to honor women as male circumcision honors men, and members of cultures where the surgery is practiced are shocked by the analogy of clitoridectomy to removal of the penis (El Dareer, 1982).

C. Helps to Maintain Cleanliness and Health

The belief that the practice advances health and hygiene is incompatible with stable data from surveys done in these cultures, where female genital mutilation has been linked to mortality or morbidity such as shock, infertility, infections, incontinence, maternal-fetal complications, and protracted labor. The tiny hole generally left for blood and urine to pass is a constant source of infection (El Dareer, 1982; Koso-Thomas, 1987; Abdalla, 1982; Ntiri, 1993). Koso-Thomas writes, " As for cleanliness, the presence of these scars prevents urine and menstrual flow escaping by the normal channels. This may lead to acute retention of urine and menstrual flow, and to a condition known as *hematocolpos,* which is highly detrimental to the health of the girl or woman concerned and causes odors more offensive than any that can occur through the natural secretions" (1987, p. 10). Investigators Dirie and Lindmark completing a recent study wrote: "The risk of medical complications after female circumcision is very high as revealed by the present study [conducted in the capital of Mogadishu]. Complications which cause the death of the young girls must be a common occurrence especially in the rural areas. . . . Dribbling urine incontinence, painful menstruations, hematocolpos, and painful intercourse are facts that Somali women have to live with—facts that strongly motivate attempts to change the practice of female circumcision" (1992, p. 482).

Although promoting health is given as a reason for female genital mutilation, many parents seem aware of its risks and try to reduce the morbidity and mortality by seeking good medical facilities. Some doctors and nurses perform the procedures for large fees or because they are concerned with the unhygienic techniques that traditional practitioners may use. In many parts of the world, however, these practices are illegal and medical societies prohibit doctors and nurses from engaging in them even if it might reduce morbidity and mortality over the short term.

D. Preserves Virginity and Family Honor and Prevents Immorality

Type 3 circumcision is used to keep women from having sexual intercourse before marriage and conceiving illegitimate children. In addition, many believe that Types 2 and 3 circumcision must be done because uncircumcised women have excessive, or uncontrollable sexual drives. El Dareer, however, believes that this view is not consistently held in her culture, the Sudan, where women are respected and men would be shocked to apply this sometimes-held cultural view to members of their own families.

Beliefs that uncircumcised women have uncontrollable sexual drives, moreover, seem incompatible with the general view, which investigators El Dareer, Koso-Thomas, and Abdalla found was held by both men and women in these cultures, that sex cannot be pleasant for women. Investigators also found that female circumcision and infibulation was no foolproof way to promote chastity. These procedures can even lead to promiscuity because they do not diminish desire or libido even where it makes orgasms impossible (El Dareer, 1982). Some women continually seek experiences with new sexual partners because they are left unsatisfied in their sexual encounters (Koso-Thomas, 1987). Some even pretend to be virgins by getting stitched up tightly again (El Dareer, 1982).

E. Furthers Marriage Goals

Those practicing female genital cutting not only believe that it promotes marriage goals, including greater sexual pleasure for men, but that such practices deprive women of nothing important, according to investigator Koso-Thomas. El Dareer and Abdalla also found widespread misconceptions that women cannot have orgasms, sex cannot be directly pleasing to women, and that their sexual pleasure comes only from knowing they contribute to their husbands' enjoyment. To survive economically, women in these cultures must marry, and they will not be acceptable marriage partners unless they have undergone this ritual surgery. It is a curse, for example, to say that someone is the child of an uncircumcised woman. The widely held belief that

infibulation enhances women's beauty and men's sexual pleasure makes it difficult for women who wish to marry to resist this practice.

For those who are not from these cultures, beliefs that these rites make women more beautiful are difficult to understand, especially when surveys show that many women in these cultures attribute to infibulation their keloid scars, urine retention, pelvic infections, puerperal sepsis, and obstetrical problems. Even some people from within these cultures, such as Koso-Thomas, have difficulty understanding this view: "None of the reasons put forward in favor of circumcision have any real scientific or logical basis. It is surprising that aesthetics and the maintenance of cleanliness are advanced as grounds for female circumcision. The scars could hardly be thought of as contributing to beauty. The hardened scar and stump usually seen where the clitoris should be, or in the case of the infibulated vulva, taut skin with an ugly long scar down the middle, present a horrifying picture" (Koso-Thomas, 1987, p. 10).

The investigators who conducted these studies believe that education about these misconceptions may be the most important means to stop these practices. Some activists in these cultures such as Toubia and Abdalla want an immediate ban. Others encourage Type 1 circumcision (removal of the clitoral hood) in order to "wean" people away from Types 2 and 3 by substitution. Type 1 has the least association with morbidity or mortality and, if there are no complications, does not preclude sexual orgasms in later life. The chance of success through this tactic is more promising and realistic, they hold, than what an outright ban would achieve; people could continue many of their traditions and rituals of welcome without causing so much harm (El Dareer, 1982). Other activists in these countries, such as Raquiya Abdalla, object to equating Type 1 circumcision in the female with male circumcision: "To me and to many others, the aim and results of any form of circumcision of women are quite different from those applying to the circumcision of men" (1982, p. 8). Nahid Toubia also objects because Type 1 circumcision causes considerable, albeit unintended, harm to the clitoris.

III. THE DEBATE OVER ETHICAL RELATIVISM AND CROSS-CULTURAL MORAL AUTHORITY

People from cultures practicing genital cutting regard condemnation by other societies or international groups as irrelevant, misguided, or cultural imperialism. They generally believe that outsiders cannot and should not pass moral judgments on their rituals. There is support for this view in some versions of ethical relativism, a theory that one culture has no moral authority for criticizing another because to say that an act is right means that it has social approval, and that an act is wrong means that it has social disapproval. In contrast to this version of ethical relativism, many moral traditions acknowledge a common basis for some intercultural discussions that have moral authority. For example, shared medical findings contradict beliefs that the practice of female genital mutilation enhances fertility and promotes health, that women cannot have orgasms, and that allowing the infant's head to touch the clitoris during delivery causes death. Kopelman argues that such medical information offer an opening for genuine cross-cultural discussion or criticism of these rites.

In contrast to ethical relativism, theorists may take one of several general positions about the meaning of right and wrong. They may hold that rightness and wrongness are the same in some ways but not in others for different cultures; that they depend upon something in human nature, the natural order of things, or the human condition; or that they are unchanging, either in form or substance, for all people. Defenders of ethical relativism, on the other hand, hold to a skeptical position that such knowledge is not possible. We consider some key points of this debate, after beginning with clarification of the form of relativism that is under consideration.

A. Forms of Ethical Relativism Supporting Female Genital Mutilation

Many social scientists and philosophers defend a form of ethical relativism, holding that something is right means that it has cultural approval, and wrong if it has cultural disapproval. On this view, if female genital mutilation has cultural approval it is right, and where it is disapproved it is wrong. This is not to say, of course, that all defenders of this version of ethical relativists approve of female genital mutilation. Many do not, but their disapproval, they would say, stems from their own cultural beliefs which have no moral authority anywhere else. For example, anthropologist Scheper-Hughes writes, "I don't like the idea of clitoridectomy any better than any other woman I know. But I like even less the western voices of reason [imposing their views]" (1991, p. 27). Philosopher Bernard Williams defends one such version of ethical relativism when he argues that moral knowledge must be inherited by

people within particular cultural traditions that have objectivity only within those cultures. Anthropologists Faye Ginsberg and Nancy Scheper-Hughes point out that ethical relativism has held an important place in anthropology despite the uncomfortable consequence that its approval within certain cultures means that practices like female circumcision are right within these cultures.

"Relativism" however is used in many ways, and not all usages entail this controversial view. Anthropologists such as Richard Shweder admit the terms *cultural relativism* or *ethical relativism* are not used consistently by anthropologists. Often relativism is presented as the only alternative to clearly implausible views such as unqualified absolutism and cultural imperialism; sometimes relativism is used to stress obvious points that different rankings and interpretations of moral values or rules by different groups may be justifiable. Relativism may also be used to highlight the incontrovertible influence of culture on moral development, reasoning, norms, and decisions. It may also be used to show, what is surely true, that in some cases decisions about what we ought to do depend on the situation—for example, that it may not be wrong to lie in some cases.

These versions of relativism are not controversial or in dispute herein, so the following comments do not apply to these versions of relativism. Many who call themselves "relativists" believe *some* cross-cultural moral judgments have moral force. Generally they wish to underscore the role of culture in shaping our moral judgments, showing why it is dangerous to impose external cultural judgments in haste, or stressing that there is often a link between established so-called rational, moral theories and oppression. For example, moral philosopher Susan Sherwin maintains that "normative conclusions reached by traditional theorists generally support the mechanism of oppression; for example, by promoting subservience among women" and concludes, "Feminist moral relativism remains absolutist on the question of the moral wrong of oppression but is relativist on other moral matters" (1992, pp. 58, 75). She uses this form of relativism to argue that female circumcision is wrong. Since her version of relativism permits intercultural assessments with moral authority based upon oppression, however, it is not relativistic in the sense under consideration herein.

In contrast, the distinctive feature of the version of ethical relativism giving theoretical support to defenders of female genital cutting is the skeptical position that one can *never* make a sound cross-cultural moral judgment, that is, one that has moral forces outside one's culture. Defenders such as philosopher Bernard

Williams and anthropologists Faye Ginsberg and Richard Shweder regard their view to be the consequences of a proper understanding of the limits of knowledge. This version of ethical relativism is false if people from one culture can *sometimes* make judgments about actions in another society that have moral authority. Many attacks have been made on the skepticism underlying such ethical relativism (Sober, 1991).

The controversial version of ethical relativism entails that to say female genital cutting is approved in a culture means it is right, and wrong where it is disapproved. To some, this very consequence is sufficient proof that ethical relativism is false. People's intuitions, however, are not convincing to those who disagree; so we need arguments to show the implausibility of ethical relativism and its denial of genuine moral cross-cultural discussions of such topics as oppression, torture, and human rights violations.

Critics of ethical relativism point out that we seem to share many goals and methods of discovery, evaluation, and explanation that can be used to help assess moral judgments. For example, we used shared methods of medical research in evaluating the morbidity and mortality associated with female genital mutilation. We also use shared methods when we translate, debate, deliberate, analyze, negotiate, and use technology. To do these things, however, we must first have agreed to some extent on how to distinguish good and bad methods, research, science engineering, and medicine, and what constitutes a good or bad translation, debate, deliberation, criticism, negotiation, or use of technology.

These shared methods help us evaluate moral judgments from one culture to another in a way that sometimes has moral authority. Moral judgments should be consistent with each other and with the best available information. For example, stable medical evidence discredits beliefs found by Koso-Thomas (1987, p. 10) that "death could result if, during delivery, the baby's head touches the clitoris," and by Abdalla (1982, p. 16) of the utility of regional practices of putting "salt into the vagina after childbirth … [because this] induces the narrowing of the vagina … to restore the vagina to its former shape and size and make intercourse more pleasurable for the husbands."

As we saw in the last section, some moral claims can be evaluated in terms of their consistency with each other or as means to goals. It seems incompatible to promote both maternal-fetal health as a good, and to elect practices imperiling mothers and infants. We need not rank values similarly with people in another culture, or our own, to have coherent discussions about casual relationships, such as what means are useful to promote

ends of maternal-fetal safety. Even if some moral or ethical (I use these terms interchangeably) judgments express unique cultural norms, then critics argue they may still be morally evaluated by another culture on the basis of their logical consistency and their coherence with stable and cross-culturally accepted empirical information.

We also seem to share some moral values, goals, and judgments such as those about the evils of disabilities, untimely death, unnecessary suffering, lost opportunities, the importance of family, the need for food and shelter, the duty to help children, and the goods of promoting public health and personal well-being. These common goals are reflected in the reasons given by men and women who practice female circumcision/genital mutilation in their communities. Although we disagree about the means to these goals, they may offer a basis for genuine moral discussions between cultures. The form of relativism under consideration denies this, and that is why it offers theoretical support to the view that people outside a culture have no basis for criticism of it. We now consider some features of the debate between those who accept such relativism and those who reject it.

B. The Debate

Examination of the debate concerning female circumcision helps us assess the plausibility of certain versions of ethical relativism since the practice has wide support within these cultures and is condemned outside them. For example, when international agencies such as UNICEF or the WHO condemn female genital mutilation, do they merely express a cluster of particular societal opinions that have no moral standing in other cultures?

1. Do We Have Shared Methods to Assess False Beliefs and Inconsistencies in Moral Judgments?

Critics of the version of ethical relativism under discussion argue that a culture's moral and religious views are often intertwined with beliefs that are open to rational and empirical evaluation and this can be a basis of cross-cultural examination and intercultural moral criticism. Defenders of female circumcision/genital mutilation do not claim that this practice is a moral or religious requirement and end the discussion; they are willing to give and defend reasons for their views. For example, advocates of female circumcision/genital mutilation claim that it is a means to enhance women's health and well-being. Such claims are open to cross-cultural examination because facts can be weighed to determine whether these practices promote the ends of health or really cause morbidity or mortality. Beliefs that the practice enhances fertility and promotes health, that women cannot have orgasms, and that allowing the baby's head to touch the clitoris during delivery causes death to the baby are incompatible with stable medical data. Thus, shared medical information and values offer an opening for genuine cross-cultural discussion or criticism of the practice.

Defenders of ethical relativism could respond that we do not *really understand* their views at all, and certainly not well enough to pick them apart. The alleged inconsistencies and mistaken beliefs we find do not have the same meaning to people raised in the culture in question. In short, some defenders of ethical relativism argue that we cannot know enough about another culture to make any cross-cultural moral judgments. We cannot really understand another society well enough to criticize it, they claim, because our feelings, concepts, or ways of reasoning are too different; our so-called ordinary moral views about what is permissible are determined by our upbringing and environments to such a degree that they cannot be transferred to other cultures.

Philosophers Elliott Sober and Loretta Kopelman point out that there are two ways to understand this objection. The first is that nothing counts as understanding another culture except being raised in it. If that is what is meant, then the objection is valid in a trivial way. But it does not address the important issue of whether we can comprehend well enough to make relevant moral distinctions or engage in critical ethical discussions about a universal human right to be free of oppression.

The second, and nontrivial, way to understand this objection is that we cannot understand another society well enough to justify claiming to know what is right or wrong in that society or even to raise moral questions about what enhances or diminishes life, promotes opportunities, and so on. Yet we think we can do this very well. We ordinarily view international criticism and international responses concerning human rights violations, aggression, torture, and exploitation as important ways to show that we care about the rights and welfare of other people, and, in some cases, think these responses have moral authority. Travelers to other countries, moreover, often quickly understand that approved practices in their own country are widely condemned elsewhere, sometimes for good reasons. For example, U.S. citizens traveling to other countries may be surprised to find considerable criticism for actions or omission approved of at home; they may learn the

U.S. population is condemned for consuming a disproportionate amount of the world's resources.

People who deny the possibility of genuine cross-cultural moral judgments must account for why we think we can and should make them, or why we sometimes agree more with people from other cultures than with our own neighbors about the moral assessments of aggression, oppression, capital punishment, abortion, euthanasia, rights to health care, and so on. International meetings also seem to employ genuinely cross-cultural moral judgments when they seek to distinguish good from bad uses of technology, promote better environmental safety, health policies, and so on.

2. How Do You Count Cultures?

Critics hold that debate over female genital mutilation illustrates a difficulty for defenders of this version of ethical relativism concerning the problem of differentiating cultures. People who brought the practice of female circumcision with them when they moved to another nation, still claim to be a distinct cultural group. Some who moved to Britain, for example, resent the interference in their culture represented by laws that condemn the practice as child abuse (Thompson, 1989). If ethical relativists are to appeal to cultural approval in making the final determination of what is good or bad and right or wrong, they must tell us how to distinguish one culture from another.

How exactly do we count or separate cultures? A society is not a nation-state, because some social groups have distinctive identities within nations. If we do not define societies as nations, however, how do we distinguish among cultural groups, for example, well enough to say that an action is child abuse in one culture but not in another? Subcultures in nations typically overlap and have many variations. Even if we could count cultural groups well enough to say exactly how to distinguish one culture from another, how and when would this be relevant? How big or old or vital must a culture, subculture, or cult be in order to be recognized as a society whose moral distinctions are self-contained and self-justifying?

A related problem is that there can be passionate disagreement, ambivalence, or rapid changes within a culture or group over what is approved or disapproved. According to ethical relativism, where there is significant disagreement within a culture there is no way to determine what is right or wrong. But what disagreement is significant? As we saw, some people in these cultures, often those with higher education, strongly disapprove of female circumcision/genital mutilation and work to stop it (El Dareer, 1982; Koso-Thomas,

1987; Abdalla, 1982). Are they in the same culture as their friends and relatives who approve of these rituals?

It seems more accurate to say that people may belong to various groups that overlap and have many variations. Members of the same family may belong to different professional groups, religions, or marry into families of different racial or ethnic origins. To say we belong to overlapping cultures, however, makes it difficult for ethical relativism to be regarded as a helpful theory for determining what is right or wrong. To say that something is right when it has cultural approval is useless if we cannot identify distinct cultures.

3. Do We Have Some Shared Values?

People from different parts of the world seem to share *some* common goals like the desirability of promoting people's health, happiness, opportunities, and cooperation, and the wisdom of stopping war, pollution, oppression, torture, and exploitation. These common values help to make us a world community. By using shared methods of reasoning and evaluation, critics argue we can discuss how these goals should be implemented. We use these shared goals, critics argue, to assess whether genital cutting is more like respect or oppression, more like enhancement or diminishment of opportunities, or more like pleasure or torture. Genuine differences among citizens of the world exist, but arguably we could not pick them out except against a background of similarities. Highlighting our differences presupposes that we share ways to do this.

Defenders of the version of ethical relativism under consideration, argue that cross-cultural moral judgments lack genuine moral authority and perpetuate the evils of absolutism, dogmatism, and cultural imperialism. People rarely admit to such transgressions, often enlisting medicine, religion, science, or the "pure light of reason" to arrive at an allegedly impartial, disinterested, and justified conclusion that they should "enlighten" and "educate" the "natives," "savages," or "infidels." Anthropologist Scheper-Hughes and others suggest that, in arguing that we can make moral judgments across cultures, we are thereby claiming a particular culture knows best and has the right to impose its allegedly superior knowledge on other cultures.

Critics of ethical relativism reply that to judge another culture in a way that has moral force does not entail that one culture is always right, absolutism is legitimate, or we should impose our beliefs on others. Relativists sometimes respond that even if this is not a strict logical consequence, it is a practical result. Philosopher Susan Sherwin writes, "Many social scientists have endorsed versions of relativism precisely out of their sense that the alternative promotes cultural dominance. They may be making a philosophical error in drawing that conclusion, but I do not think that they are making an empirical one" (1992, pp. 63–64).

4. Does This Form of Relativism Promote or Avoid Oppression or Cultural Imperialism?

Defenders of this version of ethical relativism, such as Scheper-Hughes, often argue that their theoretical stance is an important way to avoid cultural imperialism. Kopelman, in contrast, believes it promotes rather than avoids oppression and cultural imperialism. This view, she argues, entails not only the affirmation that female genital cutting is right in cultures where it is approved, but the affirmation that anything with wide social approval is right, including slavery, war, discrimination, oppression, racism, and torture. That is, if saying that an act is right, means that it has cultural approval, then it follows culturally endorsed acts of war, oppression, enslavement, aggression, exploitation, racism, or torture are right. The disapproval of other cultures, on this view, are irrelevant in determining whether acts are right or wrong. Accordingly, the disapproval of people in other cultures, even victims of war, oppression, enslavement, aggression, exploitation, racism, or torture does not count in deciding what is right or wrong except in their own culture.

Kopelman argues that on this version of ethical relativism, objections by people in other cultures are merely an expression of their own cultural preferences, having no moral standing whatsoever in the society that is engaging in the acts in question. Kopelman argues this leads to abhorrent conclusions. If this theoretical stance is consistently held, she argues, it leads to the conclusion that we cannot make intercultural judgments with moral force about *any* socially approved form of oppression including wars, torture, or exploitation of other groups. As long as these activities are approved in the society that does them, they are right. Yet the world community believed that it was making important cross-cultural judgments with moral force when it criticized the Communist Chinese government for crushing a prodemocracy student protest rally, the South Africans for upholding apartheid, the Soviets for using psychiatry to suppress dissent, and the slaughter of ethnic groups in the former Yugoslavia and in Rwanda. In each case, representatives from the criticized society usually said something like, "You don't understand why this is morally justified in our culture even if it would not be in your society." If ethical relativism is plausible, these responses should be as well.

Defenders of ethical relativism may respond that cultures sometimes overlap and hence the victims' protests within or between cultures ought to count. But this response raises two further difficulties. If it means that the views of people in other cultures have moral standing and oppressors *ought* to consider the views of victims, such judgments are incompatible with this version of ethical relativism. They are inconsistent with this theory because they are cross-cultural judgments with moral authority. Second, as we noted, unless cultures are distinct, this version of ethical relativism is not a useful theory for establishing what is right or wrong.

Relativists who want to defend sound social cross-cultural and moral judgments about the value of freedom, equality of opportunity, or human rights in other cultures seem to have two choices. On the one hand, if they agree that some cross-cultural norms have moral authority, they should also agree that some intercultural judgments about female circumcision/ genital mutilation also may have moral authority. Sherwin is a relativist taking this route, thereby abandoning the version of ethical relativism being criticized herein. On the other hand, if they defend this version of ethical relativism yet make cross-cultural moral judgments about the importance of values like tolerance, group benefits, and the survival of cultures, they will have to admit to an inconsistency in their arguments. For example, Scheper-Hughes advocates tolerance of other cultural value systems. She fails to see that claim as being inconsistent. She is saying tolerance between cultures is *right,* yet this is a cross-cultural moral judgment using a moral norm (tolerance). Similarly, relativists who say it is *wrong* to eliminate rituals that give meaning to other cultures are also inconsistent in making a judgment that presumes to have genuine cross-cultural moral authority. Even the sayings sometimes used by defenders of ethical relativism—such as "When in Rome do as the Romans"—mean it is *morally permissible* to adopt all the cultural norms whatever culture one finds oneself (Scheper-Hughes, 1991). Thus, it is not consistent for defenders of this version of ethical relativism to make intercultural moral judgments about tolerance, group benefit, intersocietal respect, or cultural diversity.

Kopelman argues that given these difficulties, the burden of proof is upon defenders of this version of ethical relativism. They must show why we cannot do something we think we sometimes ought to do and can do very well, namely, engage in intercultural moral discussion, cooperation, or criticism and give support to people whose welfare or rights are in jeopardy in other cultures. Defenders of ethical relativism need to account for what seems to be the genuine moral authority of international professional societies that take moral stands, for example, about fighting pandemics, stopping wars, halting oppression, promoting health education, or eliminating poverty. Responses that our professional groups are themselves cultures of a sort, seem plausible but incompatible with this version of ethical relativism, as already discussed. Some defenders of ethical relativism object that eliminating important rituals from a culture risks destroying the society. Scheper-Hughes insists that these cultures cannot survive if they change such a central practice as female circumcision. This counterargument, however, is not decisive. Slavery, oppression, and exploitation are also necessary to some ways of life, yet few would defend these actions in order to preserve a society. El Dareer responds to this objection, moreover, by questioning the assumption that these cultures can survive only by continuing clitoridectomy or infibulation. These cultures, she argues, are more likely to be transformed by war, famine, disease, urbanization, and industrialization than by the cessation of this ancient ritual surgery. A further argument is that if slavery, oppression, and exploitation are wrong whether or not there are group benefits, then a decision to eliminate female genital mutilation should not depend on a process of weighing its benefits to the group.

It is also inconsistent for such relativists to hold that group benefit is so important that other cultures should not interfere with local practices. This elevates group benefit as an overriding cross-cultural value, something that these ethical relativists claim cannot be justified. If there are no cross-cultural values about what is wrong or right, a defender of ethical relativism cannot consistently say such things as "One culture ought not interfere with others," "We ought to be tolerant of other social views," "Every culture is equally valuable," or "It is wrong to interfere with another culture." Each of these claims are intercultural moral judgments presupposing authority based on something other than a particular culture's approval.

IV. CONCLUSION

Those who practice female genital cutting try to promote people's fertility, cleanliness, sexual pleasure, health and well-being; yet it is a leading cause of disability, death, and disease among mothers, infants, and children. Studies from these cultures by their own investigators show these rites cause difficulty in consummating marriage, infertility, prolonged and obstructed labor, and increased morbidity and mortality. These procedures were found not only to increase disease, disability and death, but strain the overburdened health care systems in these developing countries. These investigators draw upon interculturally shared methods of discovery, evaluation, and explanation in concluding that female genital mutilation fails as a means to fulfill many of the cultural goals for which it is intended. Science and medicine include values that are intercultural. They are practiced by people within these cultures, and enables these investigations to conclude these practices are harmful and therefore wrong.

The critique of the reasons given to support female circumcision/genital mutilation in cultures where it is practiced seems to reveal many ways to enter the moral discussions of these and other practices. We can use common needs, goals, and methods of discovery, reasoning, and evaluation to do this. Although many values are culturally determined, and we should not impose moral judgments across cultures hastily, we sometimes seem to know enough to condemn practices such as female genital mutilation, war, pollution, oppression, injustice, and aggression. Ethical relativism challenges this view, but a substantial burden of proof falls upon upholders of this moral theory to defend their skeptical position and show why criticisms of other cultures always lack moral authority. Because of the hazards of even Type 1 circumcision, many groups, including the WHO and the AMA, want to stop all forms of ritual genital surgery on women. Unenforced bans have proven ineffective, however, since this still-popular practice has technically been illegal in most countries for many decades. Other proposals by activists in these regions focus on fines, and enforcement of meaningful legislation, but education of the harms of genital cutting and infibulation may be the most important route to stop these practices.

Also See the Following Article

MORAL RELATIVISM

Bibliography

Abdalla, R. H. D. (1982). *Sisters in affliction: Circumcision and infibulation of women in Africa.* London: Zed Press.

Dirie, M. A., & G. Lindmark (1992). The risk of medical complication after female circumcision. *East African Medical Journal* 69, 9, 479–482.

El Dareer, A. (1982). *Woman, why do you weep? Circumcision and its consequences.* London: Zed Press.

Ginsberg, F. (1991). What do women want?: Feminist anthropology confronts clitoridectomy. *Medical Anthropology Quarterly* 5, 1, 17–19.

Kopelman, L. M. (1994). Female circumcision/Genital mutilation and ethical relativism. *Second Opinion* 20, 2, 55–712. Portions of this discussion were adapted from this article.

Kopelman L. M. (1997). Medicine's challenge to relativism: The case of female genital mutilation. *Philosophy of Medicine and Bioethics in Retrospect and Prospect.* R. A. Carson and C. R. Burns (Eds.). Vol. 50 in *Philosophy of Medicine Series*, pp. 187–202.

Koso-Thomas, O. (1987). *The circumcision of women* London: Zed Press.

Ntiri, D. W. (1993). Circumcision and health among rural women of southern Somalia as part of a family life survey. *Health Care for Women International* 14, 3, 215–216.

Scheper-Hughes, N. (1991). Virgin territory: The male discovery of the clitoris. *Medical Anthropology Quarterly* 5, 1, 25–28.

Schroeder, P. (1994). Female genital mutilation—A form of child abuse. *New England Journal of Medicine* 331, 739–740.

Sherwin, S. (1992). *No longer patient: Feminist ethics and health care.* Philadelphia: Temple University Press.

Shweder, R. (1990). Ethical relativism: Is there a defensible version? *Ethos* 18, 205–218.

Sober, E. (1991). *Core Questions in Philosophy.* New York: Macmillan.

Thompson, J. (1989). Torture by tradition. *Nursing Times* 85, 15, 17–18.

Toubia, N. (1994). Female circumcision as a public health issue. *New England Journal of Medicine* 331, 712–716.

Williams, B. (1985). *Ethics and the limits of philosphy.* Cambridge, MA: Harvard University Press.

FEMINIST ETHICS

Rosemarie Tong
Davidson College

I. Feminine Approaches to Ethics
II. Maternal Approaches to Ethics
III. Political Approaches to Ethics
IV. Lesbian Approaches to Ethics
V. Applications of Feminist Ethics
VI. Conclusion

GLOSSARY

ethics A systematic attempt to understand moral concepts such as right, wrong, permissible, ought, good, and evil; to establish principles and rules of right behavior; and to identify which virtues and values contribute to a life worth living.

feminism A political, economic, cultural, and social movement aimed at eliminating systems, structures, and attitudes that create or maintain patterns of male domination and female subordination.

gender A social term denoting the traits, behaviors, and identities that a culture associates with being female or male; females exhibit "feminine" traits and males exhibit "masculine" traits.

sex A biological term denoting the chromosomal structure of a human being. An XX chromosomal structure is female, whereas an XY chromosomal structure is male.

sexual preference A choice made by individuals to have sexual relations with members of the other

sex (heterosexual), the same sex (homosexual or lesbian), or both sexes (bisexual).

FEMINIST ETHICS is an attempt to revise, reformulate, or rethink those aspects of traditional Western ethics that depreciate or devalue women's moral experience. Among others, feminist philosopher Allison Jaggar faults traditional Western ethics for failing women in five related ways. First, it shows little concern for women's as opposed to men's interests and rights. Second, it dismisses as morally uninteresting the problems that arise in the so-called private world, the realm in which women cook, clean, and care for the young, the old, and the sick. Third, it suggests that, on the average, women are not as morally developed as men. Fourth, it overvalues culturally masculine traits like independence, autonomy, separation, mind, reason, culture, transcendence, war, and death, and undervalues culturally feminine traits like interdependence, community, connection, body, emotion, nature immanence, peace, and life. Fifth, and finally, it favors culturally masculine ways of moral reasoning that emphasize rules, universality, and impartiality over culturally feminine ways of moral reasoning that emphasize relationships, particularity, and partiality.

Feminist ethicists have developed a wide variety of approaches to ethics, including those labeled "feminine," "maternal," "political," and "lesbian." Each of

Encyclopedia of Applied Ethics, Volume 2
Copyright © 1998 by Academic Press. All rights of reproduction in any form reserved.

261

these *feminist* approaches to ethics highlights the differences between men's and women's respective situations in life, biological and social; provides strategies for dealing with issues that arise in private as well as public life; and offers action guides intended to undermine rather than bolster the present systematic subordination of women (A. Jaggar, 1991. In *Feminist Ethics* (C. Card, Ed.). Univ. of Kansas Press, Lawrence). Considered together, the overall aim of all these feminist approaches to ethics is to create a gender-equal ethics.

I. FEMININE APPROACHES TO ETHICS

Biological and/or social differences between men and women are the foundation of men's and women's respectively different styles of moral reasoning, behavior, and identity, according to those formulating feminine approaches to ethics. For example, moral psychologist Carol Gilligan maintains that because women have traditionally focused on others' needs, they have developed a language of care that stresses the importance of creating and maintaining intimate human relationships. In contrast, because men have traditionally devoted themselves to the world of enterprise (business, medicine, and law), they have developed a language of justice that emphasizes the use of mutually agreed upon rules. Gilligan also maintains that widely accepted scales of moral development—for example, Lawrence Kohlberg's Six-Stage Scale—are attuned to the voice of justice but not of care. For this reason, those who speak the language of care (primarily women) rarely climb past Kohlberg's Stage Three ("the interpersonal concordance or 'goodboy–nice girl' orientation"), while those who speak the language of justice (primarily men) routinely ascend to Kohlberg's Stage Five ("the social contract legalistic orientation") or even Stage Six ("the universal ethical principle orientation").

Gilligan's ethics of care is feminist because she insists that women's morality of care is no less valid than men's morality of justice: all human beings should be both caring *and* just. Thus it concerns Gilligan that men seem far less willing than women to embrace the moral values associated with the opposite sex. She suspects that this reluctance on men's part is rooted in Western culture's continuing disrespect for so-called effeminate men.

Even more than Gilligan, Nel Noddings, a philosopher of education, argues that ethics is about caring relationships between individuals. There are, she says, two parties in any relationship: the one caring and the cared for. In the ideal, the dynamic of care consists of the one caring being emphatically engrossed in the cared for as a person, and the cared for recognizing and gratefully responding to the one caring's attention by "turn[ing] freely towards his own projects, pursu[ing] them vigorously, and shar[ing] his accounts of them spontaneously" (N. Noddings, 1984. *Caring: A Feminine Approach to Ethics and Moral Education,* p. 9. Univ. of California Press, Berkeley).

Noddings' feminine ethics of care is feminist because it underscores the differences between men's and women's typical styles of moral reasoning. Although women are just as capable of deductive-nomological moral reasoning as men are, Noddings claims that, far more than men, women prefer to consult their "feelings, needs, impressions, and ... personal ideals" when they make moral decisions (Noddings, 1984, 5). Another reason to view Noddings' feminine ethics of care as feminist is that she provides strategies for dealing with many private or domestic issues, including the care of children, animals, plants, possessions, and ideas.

Whether Noddings' feminine ethics of care is also *feminist* in the sense of subverting the systematic subordination of women is less clear. Although Noddings insists that care giving is a fundamental *human* activity, virtually all of the caregivers Noddings describes are women, some of whom seem to care too much—that is, to the point of imperiling their own identity, integrity, and even survival in the service of others. Moreover, although Noddings claims that the one caring needs to care for herself, she often conveys the impression that self-care is morally legitimate only insofar as it enables the one caring to be a better carer. Finally, Noddings suggests that relationships are so important that "ethical diminishment" is almost always the consequence of breaking a relationship—even a destructive one. For all these reasons, some feminist critics of Noddings urge her to take seriously Sheila Mullett's warning that women should engage only in the kind of care that "takes place within the framework of conscious-raising practice and conversation" (S. Mullett, 1989. In *Feminist Perspectives: Philosophical Essays on Method and Morals* (L. Code, S. Mullett, and C. Overall, Eds.), pp. 119–120. Univ. of Toronto Press, Toronto).

II. MATERNAL APPROACHES TO ETHICS

Closely related to feminine approaches to ethics are maternal approaches to ethics. Virginia Held, Sara Ruddick, and Caroline Whitbeck stress that, in the course of their ethical deliberations, all moral agents should use the concepts, metaphors, and images associated with the practice of mothering. They claim that, as mothers proceed in rearing their children, they typically manifest a type of "maternal thinking" that constitutes human moral reasoning at its best. In Ruddick's estimation, if we all thought like mothers think about their children's individual well-being and social acceptability, we could help each other transform our adversarial and competitive public world into a harmonious and cooperative one.

Maternal approaches to ethics are feminist not only because they value maternal thinking but also because they provide strategies for dealing with issues that arise in the private or domestic realm—for example, how to avoid the kind of psychological and physical exhaustion that contributes to violence in the home. It is not as clear, however, that maternal approaches to ethics help subvert the systematic subordination of women. Ruddick herself notes that her emphasis on mothers could be misread as (1) an unwarranted idealization of mothers as saints who attend to their children's needs no matter the costs to themselves; (2) a privileging of *biological* mothers as the "best" kind of mothering persons; and (3) a presentation of a certain kind of mothering— the kind white, heterosexual, middle-class women exhibit—as somehow better than the kind of mothering some minority women are forced to do in extremely oppressive circumstances. Unless maternal thinkers carefully stipulate their novel use of the term "mother," the mother–child relationship might lead all human beings, but especially women, down some disempowering rather than empowering moral pathways.

III. POLITICAL APPROACHES TO ETHICS

More than feminine and maternal approaches, political approaches to ethics offer action guides aimed at subverting rather than reinforcing the present systematic subordination of women. Liberal, Marxist, radical, socialist, multicultural, global, and ecological feminists have offered different explanations and solutions for this state of affairs. Likewise have existentialist, psychoanalytic, cultural, and postmodern feminists. Proponents of these varied schools of feminist thought maintain that the destruction of all systems, structures, institutions, and practices that create or maintain invidious power differentials between men and women is the necessary prerequisite for the creation of gender equality.

Liberal feminists charge that the main cause of female subordination is a set of informal rules and formal laws that block women's entrance and/or success in the pub-

lic world. Excluded from places such as the academy, the forum, the marketplace, and the operating room, women cannot reach their potential. Women will not become men's equals until society grants women the same educational opportunities and political rights it grants men.

Marxist feminists disagree with liberal feminists. They argue that it is impossible for any oppressed person, especially a female one, to prosper personally and professionally in a class society. The only effective way to end women's subordination to men is to replace the capitalist system with a socialist system in which both women and men are paid fair wages for their work. Women must be men's economic as well as educational and political equals before they can be as powerful as men.

Disagreeing with both Marxist and liberal feminists, *radical feminists* claim that the primary causes of women's subordination to men are women's sexual and reproductive roles and responsibilities. Radical feminists demand an end to all systems and structures that in any way restrict women's sexual preferences and procreative choices. Unless women become truly free to have or not have children, to love or not love men, women will remain men's subordinates.

Seeing wisdom in both radical and Marxist feminist ideas, *socialist feminists* attempt to weave these separate streams of thought into a coherent whole. For example, in *Women's Estate*, Juliet Mitchell argues that four structures overdetermine women's condition: production, reproduction, sexuality, and the socialization of children. A woman's status and function in *all* of these structures must change if she is to be a man's equal. Furthermore, as Mitchell adds in *Psychoanalysis and Feminism*, a woman's interior world, her psyche, must also be transformed, for unless a woman is convinced of her own value, no change in her exterior world can totally liberate her.

Multicultural feminists generally affirm socialist feminist thought, but they believe it is inattentive to issues of race and ethnicity. They note, for example, that U.S. "white" culture does not praise the physical attractiveness of African-American women in a way that validates the natural arrangement of black facial features and bodies, but only insofar as they look white with straightened hair, very light brown skin, and thin figures. Thus, African-American women are doubly oppressed. Not only are they subject to gender discrimination in its many forms, but racial discrimination as well.

Although *global feminists* praise the ways in which multiculturalist feminists have amplified socialist feminist thought, they nonetheless regard even this enriched discussion of women's oppression as incomplete. All too often, feminists focus in a nearly exclusive manner on the gender politics of their own nation. Thus, while U.S. feminists struggle to formulate laws to prevent sexual harrassment and date rape, thousands of women in Central America, for example, are sexually tortured on account of their own, their fathers', their husbands', or their sons' political beliefs. Similarly, while U.S. feminists debate the extent to which contraceptives ought to be funded by the government or distributed in public schools, women in many Asian and African countries have no access to contraception or family planning services from any source.

Ecofeminists agree with global feminists that it is important for women to understand how women's interests can diverge as well as converge. When a wealthy U.S. woman seeks to adopt a child, for example, her desire might prompt profiteering middlemen to prey on indigent Asian or African women, desperate to give their yet-to-be-born children a life better than their own. Ecofeminists add another concern to this analysis: In wanting to give *her* adopted child the best that money can buy, an affluent woman might not realize how her spending habits negatively affect not only less fortunate women and their families, but also many members of the greater animal community and the environment in general.

Departing from these inclusionary ways of understanding women's oppression, *existentialist* feminists stress how, in the final analysis, all selves are lonely and in fundamental conflict. *In The Second Sex,* Simone de Beauvior writes that, from the beginning, man has named himself the Self and woman the Other. If the Other is a threat to the Self, then woman is a threat to man, and if men wish to remain free, they must not only economically, politically, and sexually subordinate women to themselves, but also convince women they deserve no better treatment. Thus, if women are to become true Selves, they must recognize themselves as free and responsible moral agents who possess the capacity to perform excellently in the public as well as the private world.

Like existentialist feminists, *psychoanalytic* and *cultural feminists* seek an explanation of women's oppression in the inner recesses of women's psyche. As they see it, because children are reared almost exclusively by women, boys and girls are psychosocialized in radically different ways. Boys grow up wanting to separate themselves from others and from the values culturally linked to their mothers and sisters. In contrast, girls grow up copying their mothers' behavior and wanting to remain connected to them and others. Moreover, because of the patriarchal cues they receive both in and outside the home, boys and girls come to think that such "masculine" values as justice and conscientiousness, which they associate with "culture" and the public world, are more fully *human* than such "feminine" values as caring and kindness, which they associate with "nature" and the private world.

In the estimation of many psychoanalytic and cultural feminists, the solution to this dichotomous, women-demeaning state of affairs rests in some type of dual-parenting arrangement. Were men to spend as much time fathering as women presently spend mothering, and were women to play as active a role in the world of enterprise as men currently do, then children would cease to associate authority, autonomy, and universalism with men, and love, dependence, and particularism with women. Rather, they would identify all of these ways of being and thinking as ones that full persons incorporate in their daily lives.

Finally, as *postmodern feminists* see it, all attempts to provide a single explanation for women's oppression not only will fail but should also fail. They *will* fail because there is no one entity, Woman, upon whom a label may be fixed. Women are individuals, each with a unique story to tell about a particular self. Moreover, any single explanation for Woman's oppression *should* fail from a feminist point of view, for it would be yet another instance of so-called "phallogocentric" thought, that is, the kind of "male thinking" that insists on telling as absolute truth *one* and *only* one story about reality. Women must, in the estimation of postmodern feminists, reveal their differences to each other so that they can better resist the patriarchal tendency to center, congeal, and cement thought into a rigid "truth" that always was, is, and forever will be.

IV. LESBIAN APPROACHES TO ETHICS

Lesbian approaches are to be distinguished from feminine and maternal approaches to ethics on the one hand and from political approaches to ethics on the other. Lesbian ethicists, like Sarah Lucia Hoagland, generally regard feminine and maternal approaches as espousing types of caring that contribute to women's oppression. They insist that lesbians should engage only in the kind of caring that does not bog down in a quicksand of female duty and obligation from which there is no escape. Lesbian ethicists also take exception to those political approaches to ethics that represent heterosexual relationships as ethically acceptable even in a patriarchal society. As they see it, separation from men is the only course of action for women who wish to develop themselves as truly free moral agents.

Although lesbian ethicists believe that heterosexual women, and even some men, can, and perhaps should, learn from lesbian ethics, they do not believe it is their responsibility to share their insights with men or even with heterosexual women. Rather, they believe it is their calling to create moral meanings and values for lesbians only, leaving it to nonlesbians to create their own moral meanings and values.

V. APPLICATIONS OF FEMINIST ETHICS

Feminist ethicists do not propose uniform answers to the kind of moral problems women typically face. However, there are some key concepts that most feminist ethicists do employ. Whether they are analyzing issues related to sexuality and sexual preference, reproduction, family structure, or work, feminist ethicists are apt to stress one of the following concepts: choice, control, or connection.

A. Sexuality and Sexual Preference

Many feminists claim that, in order to secure men's approval and support, women have struggled to shape their bodies to fit the contours of an androcentric ideal of female beauty. Women have dieted to the point of developing eating disorders like anorexia (self-starvation) and bulimia (binging and purging). They have had multiple cosmetic surgeries, often risking their health in the process. Worse yet, mothers have participated in binding their daughters' feet, or in breaking their ribs with whalebone corsets, or in mutilating their genitals—all in the name of male sexual pleasure. Saddened by the ways in which women have harmed themselves and each other to meet men's sexual needs, these feminists urge women to refuse to forsake their naturally given bodies and faces.

Other feminists claim that cultural ideals of beauty are not necessarily androcentric, and that just because a woman diets, wears make-up, or has a face-lift does not mean she is obsessed with looking like a top fashion model. On the contrary, she might simply be a woman who wishes to look her personal best, and sees no reason not to do so provided that she does not harm herself or others in the process. These feminists insist that women should feel free to perfect their bodies as well as their minds if doing so increases their self-esteem and self-confidence.

To the degree that feminists have expressed considerable disagreement among themselves about how healthy or pathological it is for women to focus on their physical appearance, they have tended to agree that male sexual violence against women is not only widespread but also almost always about power. Despite their uniform opposition to male sexual violence against women, however, feminists have expressed differing views about what it is and how best to combat it.

For example, some feminists insist that whenever persons with unequal power in the workplace or academy have sexual relations the term "sexual harassment" is applicable. As they see it, it is virtually impossible for the less powerful party not to feel that she (he) *has* to have sex with the more powerful person. Other feminists disagree. They fear that an important distinction between sexual harassment and sexual attraction is dissolving—that there can be genuine love between some employers and employees and some professors and students, for example.

Feminists also debate the meaning of the word "rape." Some feminists stress that acquaintances or dates that force themselves upon women are no less deserving of the label "rapist" than strangers who do so. The fact that a woman knows her rapist, has consumed drugs or alcohol with him, or has previously permitted him certain "liberties" with her body does not change the meaning of her "no, stop" to "yes, go." Other feminists, in contrast, believe that women have to be clearer about their sexual needs or wants. As they see it, when a woman gives a man mixed signals about her desire for sexual intercourse, he might *justifiably* interpret her hesitation to mean "yes" after all. These same feminists are also willing to consider that what some women call "date rape" is really only their morning-after reaction to a regretted act of consensual sexual intercourse.

Another sexual violence issue feminists debate is how to best end the cycle of violence that energizes woman battering. Some feminists believe that because women are socialized to blame themselves for everything that goes wrong in their relationships and to "forgive and forget" harms perpetrated upon them, it is crucial that women not give their batterers "another chance." These feminists think that the law should deal with woman batterers in the same way that it deals with anyone who batters another person. In contrast, other feminists maintain that battered women should be the ones to decide whether punishment or treatment is the most appropriate remedy for the men who beat them. They reason that, provided a battered woman is receiving the kind of strengthening counseling she needs for proper self-esteem and self-respect, she should have the option of giving her batterer a chance to salvage his relationship with her.

Given the extent of male sexual violence, it is not surprising that feminists have often questioned whether sexual relations between men and women serve women's best interests. Some feminists claim that heterosexuality is an institution that not only gives men a "right" to women's bodies but also deprives women of the possibility of being lesbians. As these feminists see it, given the intensity of the mother–daughter bond and the tendency of women to establish close emotional friendships with women, there is reason to think that had men not used their power to compel women to love them first and foremost, many women would have chosen women as their primary love objects.

Although it would seem that women can be what lesbian Adrienne Rich terms "woman-identified" without being lesbian, some feminists maintain that, in order to be fully feminist, a woman must be a lesbian even if she is not "naturally" sexually attracted to women. Therefore, if a heterosexual woman wishes to be fully feminist, she must try not only to refrain from sexual relationships with men but also to orient her sexual desires toward women. Other feminists believe that heterosexuality and feminism are compatible, provided that heterosexual women engage in heterosexual relations on their own terms. As these feminists see it, many women have male partners who treat them as full human persons. Not only do these men view their female partners as their social, political, and economic equals, they also view them as their sexual equals—that is, as persons whose sexual needs and desires are just as important as their own.

B. Reproduction

Feminists have expressed a wide range of opinions on the reproduction-controlling technologies (contraception, sterilization, and abortion) and the reproduction-assisting technologies (artificial insemination, *in vitro* fertilization, and surrogate motherhood). Many feminists emphasize that unless a woman can control her reproductive density, she will not be able to pursue her personal and professional interests as successfully as a man can. Thus, laws that prohibit contraception, sterilization, and abortion must be fought, and policies that limit access to these technologies must be challenged. To tell women that they have a right to abort their fetuses, for example, but that no one has a duty to fund or perform abortions is to provide women with a hollow "right."

Conceding that the reproduction-controlling technologies have benefitted many women, other feminists note that these same technologies have probably harmed at least an equal number of women. A woman may "choose" to have an abortion, but only because she lacks the means to raise a child she would very much like to have. Or a woman may "choose" to be sterilized simply because she cannot tolerate the physical and psychological side effects of the few contraceptives currently on the market.

Feminists also disagree about women's use of the new reproduction-assisting technologies. Some feminists believe that these technologies are beneficial because they increase women's reproductive choices. As they see it, provided that they know the risks as well as the benefits of these technologies, women, especially infertile women, should feel free to use the services of gamete donors and even surrogate mothers. They should not be judged on how much of their funds they spend on costly fertility treatments, including those offered by *in vitro*-fertilization clinics.

Other feminists believe that the new reproduction-assisting technologies are harmful because they segment and specialize reproduction as if were just another mode of production: One woman provides the egg; another woman gestates the embryo; and still another rears the child once it is born. The same feminists note that, increasingly, pregnant women are instructed to eat healthy diets, to exercise, to forsake licit and illicit drugs, and, if necessary, to submit to cesarean sections so that their children will be born mentally and physically healthy. They are also urged to screen their fetuses for a variety of genetic diseases and defects, and to abort or genetically alter the unhealthy ones. Finally, they are told that women who, because of the way they conducted their lives during their pregnancies, give birth to a diseased or defective child risk being charged with fetal abuse or neglect.

C. Family Structure

Many feminists resent the kind of family structure that consists of a working father, a stay-at-home mother, and one or more children. They argue that in addition to confining women to activities associated with cooking, housecleaning, and child care, this type of family structure alienates men from their children. Men are banned from the nursery and women are locked out of the worlds of medicine, business, law, and so on. As a result, men and women become half-persons. Women are either not permitted or not encouraged to develop their intellectual skills, and men are either not permitted or not encouraged to develop their emotional skills.

Convinced that the only effective way to enable women and men to become full persons is to eliminate the family structure as it has been constituted under patriarchy, many feminists have pressed for the development of family structures other than the traditional "nuclear family" consisting of a heterosexual couple and their biological children. These feminists maintain that society should bolster rather than undermine single-parent families (especially female-headed ones), lesbian (and gay) families, and extended families in which several generations of biologically related adults and children live together.

Another group of feminists claim that the families just described are not genuine *alternatives* to the nuclear family since they mirror the values of the traditional nuclear family. Thus, in the estimation of these feminists, society should support the growth of so-called family communities in which a number of adults (some heterosexual and others lesbian or homosexual; some married and others single; some with children and others without children) intentionally develop a lifestyle that eliminates child-rearing inequalities between men and women, the sexual division of labor, the sexual exclusivity of couples, and parental possessiveness of children. In such family communities, children would have as much power as adults, homosexuals and lesbians would have as much sexual freedom as heterosexuals, people of color would be accorded as much respect and consideration as white people, and everyone would share their economic resources communally.

A final group of feminists remain unconvinced that the traditional nuclear family is unreformable. As they see it, *less* than two parents is not necessarily good for children. If gender equality is the aim of feminism, then boys and girls should probably be raised by both a man and a woman. Moreover, *more* than two parents is not necessarily good for children as anyone who has reared an adopted child or a step-child knows. Although it is wrong to view children as putty, to shape in one's own image and likeness, these feminists suggest that intense parent–child bonds—a sense of belonging to each other on account of nature (genetics) as well as nurture (environment)—can be a source of great strength. Finally, these feminists maintain that sexual exclusivity, especially within marriage, probably serves women's interests better than sexual libertarianism.

D. Work

Feminists have mixed feelings about women's increasing success in the workplace. Some feminists point with pride to the fact that affirmative action policies have enabled women in large numbers to enter previously male-dominated professions and occupations. Other feminists note that the women who do the best in the public world do so because they adopt "male" ways of thinking and acting there. Thus, they express disappointment that women have not used "female" ways of thinking and acting to transform the competitive world of enterprise into a cooperative one in which people play to each other's strengths and minimize each other's weaknesses. Yet other feminists observe that it is not enough for women to enter the public world of work; men need to assume their fair share of domestic and parental responsibilities in the private world. Without household and child-caring assistance from their partners or hired domestic help (a definite luxury), many women find themselves working an exhausting "double day": one at the workplace and one in the home. Thus, these feminists conclude that if men can have it all—career and family—without exhausting themselves in the process, justice demands the same state of affairs for women.

A final group of feminists emphasize that not all women *want* to work outside the home. These feminists note that work means different things to different kinds of women. For rich, well-educated women, work is a creative outlet or a source of power, in some cases satisfying enough to substitute for an intimate family life. For poor women, who have always had to toil, work means sweating in factories or doing rich women's laundry. Such women dream of being suburban housewives—of having time to play with their children and to chat with their friends. Moreover, many women, irrespective of their class status, think that housework, and particularly child care, is a responsibility that demands the *full-time* attention of at least one parent. Women who wish to assume this responsibility should feel free to do so. Their choice is just as legitimate as the choice of a full-time career woman or a woman who combines career and family responsibilities.

VI. CONCLUSION

Although feminist approaches to ethics are all women-centered, they do not impose a single normative standard on women. Rather they offer to women a variety of accounts that validate woman's moral experience, but in a way that points to the weaknesses as well as the strengths of the values and virtues culture has traditionally labeled "feminine." In addition, they suggest to women a variety of ways to work toward the one goal that is essential to the project of feminist ethics, namely, the elimination of gender inequality.

Although feminists' different interpretations of what constitutes a voluntary and intentional choice, an illegitimate or legitimate exercise of control, and a healthy or a pathological relationship reassure the intellectual and moral community that, after all, feminism is not a monolithic ideology that prescribes one and only one way for *all* women to be, this variety of thought is also the occasion of considerable political fragmentation among feminists. Asked to come to the policy table to express *the* "feminist" perspective on a moral issue, all that an honest feminist ethicist can say is that there is no such perspective. Yet, if feminists have no clear, cogent, and unified position on a key moral issue, then a perspective less appealing to women may fill the gap. Although it is crucial for feminist ethicists to emphasize, for example, how a policy that benefits one group of women might at the same time harm another group of women, it is probably a mistake for feminist ethicists to leave the policy table without suggesting policies that are able to serve the *most* important interests of the *widest* range of women. For this reason, many feminist ethicists believe that, over and beyond their commitment to eliminating gender inequality, feminists need to develop a mutually agreeable methodology that will permit them to achieve a consensus position on many, if not all, the moral issues related to women. Feminist ethicists have a moral duty first to listen to each others' differing points of view, and then to develop policy recommendations that, despite their shortcomings, will nevertheless help inch as many women as possible toward the goal of gender equality with men.

Also See the Following Articles

BIRTH-CONTROL TECHNOLOGY • GENDER ROLES • FAMILY, THE • FEMINIST JURISPRUDENCE • REPRODUCTIVE TECHNOLOGIES • SEXUAL HARASSMENT • WOMEN'S RIGHTS

Bibliography

Gilligan, C. (1982). "In a Different Voice." Harvard Univ. Press, Cambridge, MA.

Held, V. (1987). Feminism and moral theory. In "Women and Moral Theory" (Kittay E. and Meyers, D. Eds.). Rowman & Littlefield, Savage, MD.

Hoagland, S. L. (1989). "Lesbian Ethics." Institute of Lesbian Studies, Palo Alto, CA.

Jaggar, A. (1991). Feminist ethics: Projects, problems, prospects. In "Feminist Ethics" (Card, C. Ed.). Univ. of Kansas Press, Lawrence, KS.

Mullett, S. (1988). Shifting perspectives: A new approach to ethics. In "Feminist Perspectives: Philosophical Essays on Method and Morals" (Code, L. Mullett, S. and Overall, C. Eds.). Univ. of Toronto Press, Toronto.

Noddings, N. (1984). "Caring: A Feminine Approach to Ethics and Moral Education." Univ. of California Press, Berkeley, CA.

Rich, A. (1970). "Of Woman Born." Norton, New York.

Ruddick, S. (1989). "Maternal Thinking: Toward a Politics of Peace." Beacon, Boston.

Tong, R. (1982). "Feminine and Feminist Ethics." Wadsworth, Belmont, CA.

Whitbeck, C. (1984). The maternal instinct. In "Mothering: Essays in Feminist Theory" (Trebilcot, J. Ed.). Rowman & Allanheld, Totowa, NJ.

FEMINIST JURISPRUDENCE

Katherine O'Donovan
University of London

GLOSSARY

autonomy The principle that individual human beings should maintain control of their person and their activities, independent of others or of the society in general.

common law A body of legal principles and concepts developed over time by the precedent of earlier court decisions; contrasted with *civil law* in which the basis is a formal code or set of statutes.

consciousness raising In general, a process in which a person, typically in a group setting, brings to mind certain personal experiences with the goal of recognizing that these experiences are part of a general pattern in society; specifically, such a process in which a woman recalls personal experiences that demonstrate a condition of sexual inequality within the society.

ethic of care The principle that women have a distinctive concern for the welfare of others, and that a conception of justice based on this concern will seek to identify the best possible outcome for all involved, rather than trying to identify which one of competing interests should take precedence.

gender The social and legal characteristics of a person, culturally ascribed to the person's identity as female or male. Contrasted in this sense with sex, a biological identification, although some authors use *gender* in this sense and *sex* in the social sense.

natural law The principle that there is a higher code of moral behavior that is above, and that on occasion may be in conflict with, the common law or civil law of a given society.

patriarchy A system or society in which males occupy a superior position and females are considered subordinate.

polis A Greek term meaning "city," used to identify the sphere of public life, citizenship, and government, as distinguished from *oikos*, the private sphere.

sex The biological identify of an organism as female or male, in terms of reproductive function.

EQUALITY OF ALL PERSONS under and before the law is the justification for subjection to the rule of law. It would seem that this proposition is the central tenet of modern legal systems. Yet postwar feminist theory (the second wave) has challenged the placement of the sexes within the legal system itself. The term feminist jurisprudence has been given to the ensemble of theories, research, and writings concerned with critiquing legal assumptions about, and treatments of, women. This critique concerns the legal system at a number of levels. It takes up topics as diverse as abortion, abuse, bastardy, cohabitation, lesbianism, marriage, prostitution, rape, and sexual intercourse. It examines concepts such as bodily integrity, consent, equality, gender, ownership, possession, private, public, sex, and silence. Of greatest significance for traditional jurisprudence are the epistemological and ontological challenges to definitions and theories long established. In its emphasis on experience, and its development of its own methodologies, feminist jurisprudence positions itself outside the mainstream, or "malestream." It acknowledges subjectivity. The traditional law question is "what is law?" The object of this question is to elucidate the nature of law. Feminist jurisprudence does not attempt to answer this question directly, but rather turns the question to "how is law experienced by women as legal subjects?" This places feminist jurisprudence within an empirical and interpretative framework. In recent years feminist jurisprudence has extended its interests ingender in order to problematize masculinity and maleness. In particular, the poststructuralist critique has illuminated how femininity is defined negatively against masculinity.

I. HISTORICAL AND CONTEXTUAL LOCATION

A. The Jurisprudential Tradition

Jurisprudence has been routinely concerned with the question "what is law?" Within the *common law* tradition the great debate has been between positivists and natural lawyers. *Positivists* define law as the command of human beings. They call on authority of king, state, elected democracy, and a hierarchy of laws, leading to a basic law to answer the question of the nature of law. *Natural lawyers* have called on nature and divinity. Whereas the former see virtue as lying in obedience to law, the latter allow that there are occasions when obedience to human laws may be overridden by adherence to natural law.

The perspectives of the majority of those governed by law have not formed part of the traditional jurisprudential tradition. Obedience of citizens has been a matter of debate, but this has taken place in the context of discussion of just and unjust laws. These debates occur on a highly abstract plane, and are based on absolutist assumptions about justice. Is what is just absolutely clear? If this were so there would be no place for moral philosophy. Is what is unjust to one subject just to another? Is perception of justice linked to one's status and experience? Feminist jurisprudence attempts to answer such questions from an experiential point of view.

Emphasis is placed on persons as embodied and situated selves. The abstraction of concepts such as the "subject" or the "citizen" is challenged within feminist theories. Thus, the analysis of law and legal concepts is from historical, sociological, and critical perspectives.

The definition of law, which has been the central question of jurisprudence for centuries, does not preoccupy feminist jurisprudence. Because the latter is based on lived lives, attempts to understand what law is start from interpretation and critical theory. The definitional question is critiqued as overly abstract. In general, feminist theory looks to the concrete. Understanding of law may emerge from an examination of women's perspectives on law, but not from traditional jurisprudential methods of definition, categorization, conceptual analysis, elucidation, and the drawing of distinctions. In this feminist jurisprudence challenges traditional philosphical thinking.

B. Methods, Concepts, and Categories

1. Consciousness Raising

Feminist jurisprudence grew out of a political movement for the equality of the sexes. That connection with political activism is highly influential. The established *method* of feminism is *consciousness raising*. This method encourages women to recall their personal experiences of subjection. Such experiences are set within a major premise of equality of the sexes as an ideal. In a legal setting unequal treatment by the law itself and by legal institutions is called upon as illustration. There are two aspects to this. First, the question "why should women be treated differently from men?" Second, the question "why should women not have their particular circumstances acknowledged by law?" The second question assumes what the first question asks, in that it accepts that law does distinguish the sexes. This has led to statements that law is gendered, or that law is sexed. The particular circumstances called upon in the second question may be social, political, and biological. Statements that law is gendered, or that it is sexed, lead to definitional difficulties.

A distinction between sex and gender has been central to feminist legal work. Initially sex was defined in terms of biological difference. Gender was distinguished as the social and legal consequences of sex. However some feminist writers give precisely the contrary meanings to these terms. The significance is the distinction between biology and environment. In this article the terms are avoided where possible. However, where they are used it is in reporting the views of scholars.

2. Breaking the Silence

Another method is named as *breaking the silence*. The silence of law about matters that concern women's lives, and where women may experience hurt or harm, is critiqued. Bringing sources of pain, and a sense of injustice, into the open begins with consciousness raising. Speaking and writing about injuries unrecognized by law, creates the possibility of new causes of action, new remedies, new laws, and the extension of old laws. This has happened, for example, with sexual harrassment as a cause of action. In jurisprudential writings the criticism of the noninvestigation of this silence forms part of a more general critique of the questions that jurisprudence has traditionally chosen for focus.

3. Sexing the Subject of Law

Sexing the subject is a method specific to feminist jurisprudence. Who is the person seen by law? Does that person have an identity? What is the identity of that person? Is that person male or female? The aim of these questions is to point up the limitations of abstraction. In the terms of feminist jurisprudence the legal subject is conceived by men and is male. The "sexing" methodology has been criticised by Nicola Lacey as reinforcing what it intends to critique. For, unless care is taken in the analysis of law's subjects, charges of essentialism may be brought. Feminism set itself against limits on women's epistemological and ontological capacities. In this it has been anti-essentialist. Furthermore, one of the criticisms of the jurisprudential tradition has been of its methodology as essentialist.

Identifying women with what is excluded from law's domain is a dangerous strategy. Does exclusion occur because of inability to see women as additional or alternative subjects? It this is so, then equality as an ideal can be called upon as a basis of critique of existing laws or of legal philosophy. Does exclusion occur because the matter of concern to women is defined as not properly within law's dominion? If so, the question becomes one of power of definition and delineation of scope.

Conceptual analysis in jurisprudence owes much to the linguistic analysis deployed by certain philosophers. This form of analysis intends to elucidate a concept in order to gain understanding of the thing analyzed. Feminist jurisprudence starts from a different place, that of challenging both concepts and methods as exlusive and based on a male subject. So feminist jurisprudence has to recognize the place where women are now—known from experience and the "sexing" methodology—with the ideal of limitless ontological possibilities.

Analysis of the person seen by law and the identification of that person as sexed and gendered is central to feminist jurisprudence. Differentiation of persons within the general category of legal subject is significant. But what is the basis of differentiation? In feminist work sex and gender have been developed as categories. Why not focus on abilities, age, class, ethnicity, origins, race, interests, bodily capabilities, and family responsibilities? Once differentiation enters into jurisprudential discourse, scholars become aware that each subject may have a number of different identities.

Questions of identities and standpoints on justice reopen debates about generality and particularity in law. A series of questions arise. Does law's legitimacy depend on its generality? How can law claim generality if it is written and passed by a particular class of subjects? Does recognition of differentiation amongst its subjects detract from law's claim to generality? When are bodily differences a relevant basis for differential laws? These questions are not new, but have been given fresh life by feminist challenges to male domination. The questions do not stop there. Do all women share certain interests? Are these outweighed by classes and categories within womanhood?

Attacks on the unified legal subject comes from several directions. Denial that such an abstract subject is possible is one position. Acknowledgement of law's representation of such a unified subject, combined with arguments that this subject is a middle-class male of European origins is another. Plurality of legal subjects, according to differences such as sex and gender, is a third.

4. Acknowledging the Writer's Subjectivity

The feminist emphasis on experience and subjectivity has a number of methodological and substantive consequences. The critique of traditional jurisprudence as adopting an Olympian stance that claims not only objectivity and neutrality, but also truth, is based on arguments about partiality and omission. If traditional jurisprudence is criticized as ignoring women's experiences and subjectivities, might not feminist jurisprudence be open to similar charges in relation to other silences? Various ways around this difficulty are proposed. The claim has been made that the excluded have a greater claim to represent the truth because they see things from the vantage point of the dominant, with whom they have to cope, and also from the vantage point of the subordinated. Feminist writers acknowledge the limitations of experiential methods and of the writer's subjectivity. The recognition of one's own position inevitably leads to denials of claims to total truth. Partiality as a concept returns to its etymological origins. Katherine Bartlett advocates "positionality," a place in which both the existence and contingency of empirical truths, knowledge, and values are acknowledged. The positional knower conceives of truth as limited by perspective, and therefore situated. From thence insight is gained into the partiality of other points of view. How then are partial truths to be brought together? To Bartlett this is not a meaningful question. For her a continued engagement with others in a critical quest to seek further partial knowledge will, in itself, lead to transformation. "Feminist doing is, in this sense feminist knowing."

II. DEFINITIONAL PROBLEMS

A. What Is the Definition of Feminist Jurisprudence?

Feminist jurisprudence is distinguished from other schools of jurisprudence by its concern with women as legal subjects, by its methodologies, by its critical stance. But does it offer a theory? To ask such a question is to mistake the nature of what is under discussion. For feminist jurisprudence has been characterized by inquiry and exploration and fluidity, as scholars have entered into conversation with one another in an attempt to discover the sources of legal divisions and differences between the sexes. It is premised on an assumption of the subordination of women to men, it asks why that should be, how it is maintained, and whether it can change.

The term has been traced to an intervention by Ann Scales at a conference at Harvard Law School in 1978, and to her article of 1981. There is no standard definition, but some analysts impose a structure on feminist jurisprudence as united by a belief that society and the legal order are patriarchal. The difficulty with this is that patriarchy is neither necessarily nor sufficiently about sex and gender; it is also about age and hierarchy. Metaphors of a mother with many children, or a house with many rooms have been used in description. These catch the idea of debates within the family of feminist jurisprudential writings.

B. What Is the Scope of Feminist Jurisprudence?

Wishik demonstrates the experiential nature of feminist jurisprudence in her suggestion that it poses the following seven questions:

1. How does legal doctrine and process address women's experience of the life situation?
2. What are the assumptions, assertions, definitions, and descriptions contained in law that have a bearing on the gendering of its subjects?
3. Is there a mismatch between the life experiences of women and their gendering in legal doctrines and processes?
4. What patriarchal interests are served by the distortions and mismatches between women's experiences and the law?
5. Can law be changed to reflect women's experiences? What will be the effects of the proposed reforms on women's lives?
6. What would an ideal world offer in terms of law to women?
7. How can the move from current actualities to an ideal world be achieved?

There is a utopian element to feminist jurisprudence as recognized by Drusilla Cornell. However, the reconstructive phase has run into the problem of a plurality of legal subjects, identified *supra*. The strength of feminist jurisprudence has been analysis and deconstruction, particularly in postmodern writings. However, liberal reformers have achieved changes in legal doctrine, for example in laws relating to marital rape, abuse, defences to homicide, and the structuring by law of women as the dependents of men.

C. Other Definitional Problems

A distinction between sex and gender has been central to feminist legal work. Initially, sex was defined in terms of biological difference, in particular women's abilities to gestate, give birth, and lactate. Gender was distinguished as the social and legal consequences of sex. Not all writers accept this, and some use these words in the opposite fashion. The significant point is to distinguish between biology and environment. This is generally accepted as a useful analytical tool. Arguments that both sex and gender are socially constructed illustrate the contingency of culture and social meaning. The distinction between biology and environment is not necessarily undermined by arguments about contingency.

The assertion made by some feminist legal scholars that law is male contains its own internal difficulties. This assertion may concern law making, content, interpretation, method, process, and personnel. It may be intended to as a reflection on the identities of lawmakers and interpreters, the historical processes by which legal doctrine has been established. But does such an assertion not reinforce the very categories feminism sets out to destabilize? If the historical context is clarified is this problem avoided? Is it possible to record and give witness to law as sexed and gendered without making a positive statement?

Further versions of the identity of law assert that law is sexed or gendered. Insofar as such statements reflect deconstructive methodologies such as sexing the subject, or acknowledging subjectivity, *supra*, they may further understandings. But the ascription of a male body to law, as may be done if the "sexing" methodology is not carefully delineated, may give rise to the criticism of this as essentialist. Keeping methodology and substantive argument apart is necessary to avoid such a criticism.

Poststructuralists focus on differences among subjects and how they are constructed in terms of oppositions, rather than on structures as givens. The positioning of difference within postmodern legal feminism does not depend on the definition of essential aspects of what is termed feminine or masculine. The nature, characteristics, and qualities of the differentiated are not presented in essentialist terms, but in terms of difference. Mary Joe Frug rejects the search for law's subject implicit in the "sexing" methodology discussed *supra*. Frug critiques arguments which rely on the category "women," on the grounds of differences within that category. Her position has, in turn, been criticized as overlooking the stategic purposes for which such a category is useful.

Postmodernists argue that discourses are various, varied, nonhierarchical, and mutable. Dichotomizing and opposing discourses, a feature of modernity, are identified with gender. Yet, in making such points, postmodernists have to draw on earlier discourses. Contrasting two essentialist arguments as a form of criticism draws the writer into contrasting her position of fluidity with an essentialist position. Thus, unless great care is taken, the writer may perform what she critiques; that is, she may seem to accept the very categories she is critiquing. To point to law as having a largely male identity does not necessarily commit a writer to an essentialist position on sex and gender. It is possible to locate the ideal of a male identity contextually and historically.

D. Feminist Jurisprudential Taxonomies

Attempted taxonomies of feminist jurisprudence identify four schools: liberal, radical, cultural, and postmodern. The *liberal* school is defined as concerned with equality, as advocating the treatment of women on a par with men. Critics of liberal feminism see a procrustean bed into which women have to fit. This may be an oversimplification of what theorists have argued. Do women want to be surrogate men, or do they want their differences from men recognized? Does a seemingly gender-neutral standard mask inequality? Are there standards that are applied differentially according to gender? Are clearly differentiated standards based on gender appropriate in certain legal areas?

Scholars are united in their criticisms of traditional interpretations of the concept of equality. Treating like alike benefits women who satisfy the assumed normality of the male model and excludes those unable to conform. This has been a major criticism of antidiscrimination legislation in which a claim has to based on comparison of the complainant with a comparator of the other sex. This enshrines a single standard for all regardless of situation, and equal opportunity as the concept of equality.

Radical feminists reject traditional equality discourse and the approach of antidiscrimination legislation. Their analysis is centered on the concept of patriarchy. However, they retain the notion of equality in another form. Catherine MacKinnon argues that inequality and dominance are concepts that elucidate feminist jurisprudence. Rather than accepting a neutral standard, courts should look behind for the inequality it masks. The sources from which this inequality stems are irrelevant. Standards may be unequal, they may mask situational inequality, or they may be applied unequally. Gender equality is concerned with subordination and domination. Women's standpoint on subordination is the starting point. MacKinnon criticizes theorists whose empirical work emphasizes differences between women and men as adopting a male standpoint. Her criticism, in part, is that such work assumes the male as the norm. She, in turn, has been criticized for an essentialist view of women and men, for presenting women as victims, and for denying women's agency.

A major debate has taken place between *cultural feminists* and Catherine MacKinnon. The argument that women have their own culture based on an *ethic of care* is made by Carol Gilligan. Her research on children reveals that, whereas girls play cooperative turn-taking games in which rules are not elaborated and litle adjudication is required, boys compete, are governed by rules, and have processes for dispute adjudication. Gilligan's work on conceptions of morality among adults notes two styles of justice: the first, mainly associated with men, is primarily about competing rights, with formal and abstract rules; the second, mainly associated with women, is concerned with providing an optimum outcome for all individuals involved. MacKinnon denies that the voice associated with women by Gilligan is women's authentic voice. In her view this theory neglects to explain *why* certain values are held by women. Subordination is the reason she supplies. Despite her acceptance of the attraction of the ethic of care, she argues that the identification of women with these values is because of their powerlessness, and because men value women who care for them. Women's authentic voices will not be heard until subordination is ended.

Cultural feminists use argument about equality to validate difference within equality. Robin West argues that the human being seen by law is an atomic individual, unconnected to others. Thus it is that legal theory is male. Feminist jurisprudence will take account of women's connectedness to others through pregnancy, breastfeeding, and heterosexual intercourse. Legal concepts and processes will be reconstructed to include the connectedness viewpoint, and experience. Other writers have criticized West's theory as essentialist.

Postmodern legal feminists use the concept of equality strategically and plurally. Equality is positioned as an idea that drive the engine of modernity. It is a unifying concept, but its universalism is suspect. Is it possible to posit a theory of equality from which all women will benefit? Given that postmodernists see a plurality of legal subjects, overlapping identities, and various and varying experiences, does equality remain useful? A rhetorical and strategie use of the concept of equality has been deployed by feminist jurisprudence in analysis and in advocating change, so its continued use seems likely.

Taxonomies based on the development of feminist jurisprudence see theory as having developed through three positions: Law is sexist; law is sexed male; law is culturally gendered. These movements of theory demonstrate the fluidity of feminist discussions and can be viewed as a source of strength.

III. MAJOR DEBATES

A. Equality and Difference

Debates about equality and difference remain central to feminist jurisprudence. From the mid-1960s antidiscrimination legislation came under discussion as a means of effecting equality between men and women. Law reform took place in many of the Western democracies with a view to remedying historic abberations. Anti-

discrimination legislation soon developed its critics. The legislation is perceived as defective in that it deliberately omits the private sphere (see *infra*). It is marked by an uneasiness at interference in the market, and by qualifications and exceptions. Nevertheless, this legislation marked a radical departure from the past in which discrimination as a wrong was unknown.

Some of the doubts about antidiscrimination legislation relate to the question "equal to what?" Empirical evidence is that many women cannot, or do not wish, to conform to a male norm. Standards that are appropriate for men may not be appropriate for women. Feminist jurisprudence set itself the task of reconceptualizing equality in such a way as to allow for difference.

Identity and difference have other resonances in feminist jurisprudence, as discussed (*supra*) in relation to difference feminism. Identity can be presented as defining itself, *either* by what one has in common with others of the same sex or gender, *or* by the counterposition of those elements by which one differs. Thus, the definition of self may lie precisely in difference from others. Sex and gender as paradigm cases of oppositions and difference have been linked to theories of language, and psychoanalysis. Simultaneously, there is the realization expressed by Nicola Lacey, "that there is, by definition, no language unmarked by gender configurations of power.

B. Public and Private

The distinction between public and private spheres of life has been a major theme in feminist jurisprudential analysis. In Greek thought the *polis*, or public sphere, was distinguished from the *oikos*, or private sphere. The *polis* was the place of citizenship, democratic governance, and the location of freedom and equality. Women, aliens, and slaves were not eligible for membership. The *oikos* was the place of domination by the master, a realm of inequality, subordination, and unfreedom. There was a perceived symbiosis between these two spheres, as the master's freedom to participate in the *polis* was predicated on the *oikos* as a realm of necessity.

In feminist jurisprudence the public domain is presented as the place of law, state, politics, commerce, individualism, and men. The private domain is the place of family, the reproduction of children, domesticity, emotion, and women. The setting up of these dichotomies is historical, but is also a methodological device. Questions are then asked. Why is the private unregulated by law? Is the private defined as that which is not to be legally regulated? Is it of the nature of the private that law should not enter in? What then of law's protective functions in relation to children and the powerless? Is the public the place of legal and social power? Does legal theory assume that the state delegates its power to the husband and father in the private sphere? If so what is the curb on that power?

One of the earliest maxims of the feminist movement that was reborn in the 1960s was that the personal is political. This contained the idea that private and personal lives are just as political as lives in the public sphere. Arguments called on empirical evidence of abuse, marital rape, legal and economic policies that subsumed a wife into her husband's dependent, in support. This strengthened the questioning of nonregulation by law of the area of life it defined as private. Is nonregulation definitive of the private? Does the private preexist its delineation as nonlegal? Is the private brought into being by law's declaration of its extralegal status? As is evident, these questions reveal the circular nature of arguments about the private sphere.

Circular arguments about the private can be avoided by eliminating the question of the regulatory/nonregulatory aspect. Feminist legal scholars argue that the binary opposition of regulation/nonregulation is false. The regulated area may be roughly equated with the public, and the nonregulated area with the private. The boundaries are not fixed and legal history is evidence of constant shift. From law's absence from the private it does not necessarily follow that the private is unregulated. The very definition of an area as "not the law's business," is a form of regulation. What does it mean to say that an area of life, such as the private, is extralegal? Who has power in the private sphere? How is it regulated? Is nonregulation by law a code for saying that law will provide no remedies for harms suffered in the private sphere? O'Donovan argues that the characterization of the family as a sphere unregulated by law is a misunderstanding of power, and of the power that fills a space taken by law as regulated.

C. Family, Sexuality, and Reproduction

Autonomy is a central concept in discussions of the personal life in feminist jurisprudence. Much of the argument has been that the law denies autonomy to women in control over their sexuality and bodies. This critique upholds autonomy as a standard, and a good. It goes further in condemning forced sexual activity, physical abuse of one person by another, and the idea that marriage means ownership of a woman. The role that law plays in denying autonomy over their bodies to women is complex.

The idea that husband and wife are one person in law leads to the conclusion that a husband cannot be charged with the rape of his wife, Notwithstanding that his actions fulfill the legal requirements for such a charge. This idea has been overturned in most common law jurisdictions by legislation. More complex are the critiques in which the legal perspective is denoted male, as for example, in the legal definition of sexual intercourse as penetration of the vagina by the penis. Legal regulation of sexuality is shown by Sheila Duncan as constructing the male subject and excluding the woman as *other*. A subtle deconstructive analysis of the choices of terms and emphases by lawmakers brings out the hidden meanings the law contains. Much of this work can be placed as critique of legal culture as stemming from a male perspective.

Autonomy is a concept used in ethical theory. Distinctions are made between strong and weak autonomy according to subjectivity, but the concept as integral to the human being is not questioned. Critiquing laws and legal doctrine as denying autonomy to a class of adult persons because of gender and/or marital status is consonant with general ethical theories. Questions do remain. Under what circumstances does law consider a person to lack autonomy? Is it ethical to override autonomy? Are the interests of third parties of significance in decisions to override autonomy? Feminist jurisprudence focuses on the relevance of gender to these questions. These questions are gendered when issues of conception, birthing, and abortion arise. Opinions differ as to whether general principles of autonomy should be applied, or whether gender gives these questions a special status.

Of particular interest are the ethical underpinnings of the critique of law. To a certain extent law is indicated as not providing the equality it promises. But there are other assertions in the feminist positions; that all human beings deserve respect; that one person cannot be owned by another; that autonomy over one's body means personal choices. Most recently the concept of "bodily integrity" has been used to contain these ideas.

D. Law's Siren Call

The power of law, not least in its representations of women had lead to calls for resistance to that power. Carol Smart argues that law has delivered little to feminists and that their focus should be elsewhere. She points to legal reformist strategies that have created conditions that have been used against women's interests and provides examples of reforms with unforeseen consequences. Smart's rejection of law and her view of its overinflated view of itself leads her to argue for a decentering of law. This is based on her belief that law's power closes, and her view of its high status in the establishment of knowledge and truth. But if law is so powerful and controlling, this argument might support the work that challenges this power and status, particularly that using feminist methodologies.

Nicola Lacey is less pessimistic than Smart, seeing a place for reformism and utopian imaginings, despite an awareness of the interrelationship of the legal with economic, social, and political relations. It is self-evident that Smart's theory is based on a particular definition of law. Lacey's disagreement is not just about definitions of law, but over Smart's own closure of possibilities. Leaving space for a world of genuine equality, for utopian imaginings, is part of the feminist dream.

IV. FEMINIST JURISPRUDENCE AS ETHICS

The concept of equality, however defined and interpreted, is central to feminist jurisprudence. As has been shown above, this has generated continuing debates. Equality describes a state of affairs, but also serves as an ideal in certain legal discourses. Much of feminist writings, from whichever school, calls on equality as a benchmark against which to measure women's inequality. But what is that benchmark: Is it comparative? Is it relational? Is it an impossible ideal? As we have seen above, conceptions of equality vary and this variation has led to disagreements. Does equality give guidance to feminist scholars, other than as a form of rhetorical critique of law, or as an ideal? Just as feminists have asked the question, "Whose justice?" or "Whose community?" so, too, they ask the question "Whose equality?"

Equality plays an important part in the justification of the legitimacy of the rule of law. It functions as a description of an actual state of affairs: "equality under the law." This serves to justify regulation, coercion, and punishment. It is not intended as a statement of material or substantive equality. When law is taxed with differential treatment of its subjects according to sex or gender, or as written from a male point of view, or as gendered male, this is an attack on its legitimacy. For it is on its claim to objectivity and neutrality that law's self-justification depends.

By exposing law's biases feminist jurisprudence makes a claim that law does not live up to its promises. In this, and in its claim to equality, feminist jurisprudence claims a moral position. A difficulty then arises.

Is a further claim being made that it is possible for a bias-free, objective, and neutral legal system and laws to exist? In accusing law of failing to deliver what it promises, is there a suggestion that such promises *can* be delivered in an ideal system? At this point the skepticism of postmodern legal feminism concerning equality and the legal subject opens up new issues. In particular, assertions about the absence of a single legal subject and about overlapping and multiple identities create problems for feminist jurisprudence itself.

Liberal feminism has turned liberalism's arguments back on liberalism. This has been a successful enterprise in that legal reforms have followed. But this is an argument that remains within liberalism in that it presupposes an ultimate universal standard that is not lived up to. Whether this standard is put in terms of "keep your word," or "be consistent," or "law applies equally to all," or in terms of delivering the equality that has been promised, it is not only a moral standard, but it also is based on a premise of universalization. If universalization is not possible, as many feminists have argued, or if it is a mask for power, then the enterprise of turning liberalisms arguments back on liberalism cannot succeed. It is this difficulty that has lead to the adoption of theories that acknowledge the partiality of perspectives and that posit that understandings are continual, contingent, revisable, and not fixed.

Can law cope with multiple legal subjects? Legal positivism cannot cope with the denial of a clear legal subject and with fluidity. Law requires clear lines, certainty, and feminist jurisprudence is subversive of this in its emphasis on contingency, change, plurality and differences. It encourages ontological challenge to the self, a general flourishing of subjectivities. Is it open to challenge as exclusive, nonrepresentative, unable to represent plural subjectivities? Attempts are made to answer this question in the methodologies outlined, *supra*, and in the very movement of theory itself. Internal arguments about exclusion share a common concern that this is undesirable. Within feminist jurisprudence there is an explicitly agreed starting point of the values of understanding, mutual respect, and empathy.

An ethical stance of concern with the *other* creates space for the concerns of women to be heard. But are there women who are silent? Are there women who are silenced? Are there women who cannot speak because they lack language? Are there women who are speaking in their own languages whom we cannot hear? Are there women who raise their particular concerns but who are ignored as illegitimate or outside the law? These are questions that feminist jurisprudence is beginning to address.

Also See the Following Articles

AUTONOMY • CITIZENSHIP • FEMINIST ETHICS •
LIBERALISM • PATERNALISM • POSTSTRUCTURALISM •
SEX EQUALITY • SEXISM

Bibliography

Frug, M. (1992). *Postmodern legal feminism.* New York and London: Routledge.

Gilligan C. (1982). *In a different voice.* Cambridge, MA: Harvard University Press.

Lacey N. (1995). Feminist legal theory beyond neutrality. *Current Legal Problems,* **48**, 1.

MacKinnon, C. (1987). *Feminism unmodified.* Cambridge, MA: Harvard University Press.

O'Donovan, K. (1985). *Sexual divisions in law.* London: Weidenfeld and Nicholson.

Owens, R., & Naffine, N. (Eds.). (1997). *Sexing the subject of law.* Australia: Law Book Co. Australia.

Smart, C. (1989). *Feminism and the Power of Law.* London: Routledge.

FETAL RESEARCH

Robert H. Blank
University of Canterbury

GLOSSARY

embryo Developing human organism prior to body definition at approximately 6 to 8 weeks after fertilization.

ex utero Outside of the uterus.

fetal tissue transplantation Use of fetal tissues for therapy through transplantation to affected organs.

fetus Developing human organism after body definition from approximately 9 weeks to term.

in utero In the uterus.

neural grafting Transplantation of tissue into the brain or spinal cord to treat neurological disorders.

preimplantational embryo Embryo after fertilization but prior to implantation and formation of placenta.

FETAL RESEARCH encompasses a broad array of research and potential clinical applications. Research can be conducted on the preimplanted embryo, on fetuses in the uterus prior to elective abortion, on previable fetuses after abortion, or on dead fetuses. Clinical applications using fetal or embryonic matter such as tissues, cells, or organs represent another form of experimentation incorporated under the definition of fetal research. Issues arise concerning the moral status of the fetus or embryo and the use of aborted fetuses or preimplantation embryos for research or experimentation. Questions also center on who may consent for the use of fetal materials, in what circumstances the abortion procedure can be modified to meet the needs of the research or transplantation procedures, and what type of compensation, if any, should be allowed for fetal tissues. As a result of these issues, fetal research has been elevated to the public agenda and has become a highly volatile moral and political issue.

I. TYPES OF FETAL RESEARCH

One of the problems in analyzing fetal research is that it encompasses a broad variety of types. One important distinction is that between investigational type research that is not beneficial to the fetus and therapeutic research that is possibly beneficial to the fetus but more likely to be beneficial to future fetuses. Another key distinction centers on the stage of development of the human organism when the research is conducted, from preimplantation to late fetal stages. The general sources of fetal material include tissue from dead fetuses; previable or nonviable fetuses *in utero*, generally prior to an elective abortion; nonviable living fetuses *ex utero;* fetal tissue transplantation research using tissue from dead fetuses; and embryos, *in vitro* and preimplantation. Although the variety of potential uses of fetal tissue is virtually unlimited, five areas are summarized here.

A. Fetal Development Studies

The first category of research deals with investigations of fetal development and physiology. The purpose of this research is to expand scientific knowledge about normal fetal development in order to provide a basis for identifying and understanding abnormal processes and, ultimately, curing birth deformities, or treating them *in utero.* These studies primarily involve autopsies of dead fetuses. However, studies of fetal physiology include the fetus *in utero* as well as organs and tissues removed from the dead fetus. In some instances, this research requires administration of a substance to the woman prior to abortion or delivery by caesarean section. This is followed by analysis to detect the presence of this substance or its metabolic effects in a sample of umbilical cord blood or in the fetal tissue. This research also advances knowledge of fetal development *in utero* by monitoring fetal breathing movements. Fetal hearing, vision, and taste capabilities have been documented by applying various stimuli to the live fetus *in utero.* In addition, some physiological studies utilize observation of nonviable but live fetuses outside the uterus to test for response to touch and for the presence of swallowing movements.

B. Fetal Diagnosis Research

A second type of research focuses on the development of techniques such as amniocentesis to diagnose fetal problems. The initial research was conducted primarily on amniotic samples withdrawn as a routine part of induced abortion to find the normal values for enzymes known to be defective in genetic disease. Once it was demonstrated that a particular enzyme was expressed in fetal cells and normal values were known, application to diagnosis of the abnormal condition in the fetus at risk was undertaken. Recent prenatal diagnostic research on fetuses involves extension of diagnostic capacities to additional diseases, development of chorionic villus sampling, and attempts to detect fetal cells in the maternal circulation.

Research has also been directed toward techniques that allow the identification of physical defects in the developing fetus. Ultrasound, alpha-fetoprotein tests, amniography, tests for fetal lung capacity, and a variety of techniques for monitoring fetal well-being or distress are recent products of this category of fetal research. In each case, following animal studies that indicated the safety and efficacy of the procedure, human fetal research was conducted in a variety of settings. Fetoscopy, for example, because of the potential risk to the fetus, was developed selectively in women undergoing elective abortion. The procedure was performed prior to abortion and an autopsy was performed afterward to determine its technical success.

C. Pharmacological Studies

A third area of fetal research involves efforts to determine the effects of drugs on the developing fetus. These pharmacological studies are largely retrospective in design, involving the examination of the fetus or infant after an accidental exposure. For instance, all studies on the influence of oral contraceptives or other drugs on multiple births or congenital abnormalities have been retrospective, as were most studies of the effects on the fetus of drugs administered to treat maternal illness during pregnancy. In these designs, no fetus was intentionally exposed to the drug for research purposes. However, some pharmacology research involves intentional administration of substances to pregnant women prior to abortion in order to compare quantitative movement of these agents across the placenta as well as absolute levels achieved in fetal tissues. These studies serve as guidelines for drug selection to treat intrauterine infections such as syphilis by examining the dead fetuses after abortion and demonstrating the superiority of one drug over another.

D. Embryo Research

The availability of human embryos for research purposes followed the development of *in vitro* fertilization (IVF). In 1982, Steptoe and Edwards, who 4 years earlier reported the first birth through IVF, announced plans to freeze "spare" embryos for possible clinical or laboratory use. Theoretically, fresh or frozen spare embryos could be augmented by the deliberate creation of embryos for research where donors consent to have their gametes or embryos used in this way. There is considerable hesitancy to move to the deliberate production of embryos for research even though this might be the only way to satisfy expanding research needs.

Although assisted reproduction technologies are all experimental at some stage and thus might be described as research, there are many nonclinical applications that clearly fit a research paradigm. Among the many nonclinical uses of human embryos are to (1) develop and test contraceptives; (2) investigate abnormal cell growth; (3) study the development of chromosomal abnormalities; (4) conduct implantation studies; and (5) initiate cancer and AIDS research. Potential genetic uses of the embryos include (1) attempts at altering gene structures; (2) preimplantational screening for chromosomal anomalies and genetic diseases; (3) pre-implantation therapy for genetic defects; and (4) development of characteristic selection techniques including sex preselection. At some stage research on artificial placentas will be dependent on the availability of human embryos.

E. Fetal Tissue Transplantation

A final area of fetal research involves the use of fetal cells for transplantation. Unlike other areas of fetal research where the tissue is used to develop a treatment that might help future fetuses, in fetal transplantation research the tissue is the treatment used to benefit an identifiable adult patient. Although some persons see no ethical difference between the transplantation of adult organs and that of fetal tissues to benefit individual recipients, others contend that the use of fetal tissue for this purpose is ethically questionable because there are no possible benefits to particular fetuses or to future fetuses.

Despite the ethical controversy surrounding the use of fetal tissue discussed in Section IV, many scientists consider it to be well-suited for grafting. In contrast to adult tissue, fetal tissue cells replicate rapidly and exhibit tremendous capacity for differentiation into functioning mature cells. This capacity is maximal in the early stages of fetal development and gradually diminishes throughout gestation. Moreover, unlike mature tissue, fetal tissue has been found to have great potential for growth and restoration when transplanted into a host organism. Nutritional support provided by blood vessels from the host is readily accepted and likely promoted by fetal tissue.

In animal experiments, fetal tissue has displayed a considerable capacity for survival within the graft recipient. Fetal cells also appear to have increased resistance to oxygen deprivation, which makes them an especially attractive source of transplant material. Furthermore, fetal cells are easily cultured in the laboratory, thus allowing development of specific cell lines. They are also amenable to storage via cryopreservation, and because of their immunological immaturity fetal cells are less likely than adult cells to provoke

TABLE I

Clinical Conditions and the Types of Human Fetal Tissue Transplanted

Condition	Tissue
Acute leukemia	Liver
Addison's disease	Adrenal
Aplastic anemia	Liver
Bare lymphocyte syndrome	Liver
DiGeorge's syndrome	Thymus
Huntington's disease	Neural
Juvenile diabetes	Pancreas
Metabolic storage disorders	
Fabry's disease	Liver
Fucosidosis	Liver
Gaucher's disease	Liver
Glycogenosis	Liver
Hunter's disease	Liver, fibroblasts
Hurler's disease	Liver, fibroblasts
Metachromatic leukodystrophy	Liver
Morquio Syndrome, type B	Liver
Niemann-Pick types A, B, C	Liver
San Filippo syndrome, type B	Liver
Parkinson's disease	Neural, adrenal
Radiation accidents	Liver
Schizophrenia	Neural
Severe combined immunodeficiency	Liver and thymus

Source: Vawter, D. E., (1993). "Fetal Tissue Transplantation Policy in the United States." *Politics and the Life Sciences,* 12, p. 80.

an immune response leading to rejection by the host organism.

Although most applications of fetal tissue transplantation are highly experimental, the potential use is significant (Table 1). The only proven effective treatment to date is the use of fetal thymus transplants for the rare DiGeorge's Syndrome, which has been standard treatment for over 20 years. Also, despite less than encouraging success to date, fetal pancreatic tissue transplants for juvenile diabetes are seen as promising. Fetal liver cells have been transplanted to patients with aplastic anemia with reasonable success, although clinical trials and more research are needed to ascertain the mechanism for recovery of these patients. Other potential applications of fetal liver tissue transplants include bone marrow diseases such as severe combined immunodeficiency and acute leukemia, where HLA-matched donors are unavailable; an array of inherited metabolic storage disorders; and radiation accidents.

II. STATUS OF THE FETUS

At the center of the controversy over fetal research is disagreement over the moral and legal status of the fetus. There is evidence that abortion politics has had a stifling effect on many areas of this research. Because in the United States federal funding of basic research, largely through the National Institutes of Health, is important, recent restrictions on specific types of fetal/embryo research have raised questions concerning their long-term impact on reproductive science and health.

Because the fetus is unable to consent to being a research subject, there is concern over what type of consent and by whom is sufficient. There are also questions as to what types of fetal research ought to be pursued, how to balance research needs with interests of the pregnant woman, and the proper ends of such research. Fetal research has surfaced periodically on the political agenda for two decades and has been addressed in the United States as an issue by national and presidential commissions, Congress, and many state legislatures.

Although the context of fetal research results in various shadings of support and opposition for particular applications, in general there are two major sides in the debate. On the one hand, the research community and its supporters argue that research using human fetal and embryonic materials is critical for progress in many areas of medicine. By and large they recognize no moral objections to using fetal tissues from electively aborted fetuses for basic research and transplantation, and they cite an array of areas where significant contributions can be made.

On the other hand, critics argue that research using aborted fetuses will give abortion greater legitimacy and encourage its use in order to aid research and/or individual patients. They contend that use of embryos and fetuses for research exploits them as the means to another person's ends and reduces them to biological commodities. Moreover, other interests not fully opposed to such research express concern over potential commercialization and payment questions, the ownership of fetal materials, and the need to delineate boundaries for acceptable uses of fetal material.

III. THE POLITICS OF FETAL RESEARCH

A. National Commission

Fetal research first appeared on the national policy agenda in the early 1970s after widely publicized exposés on several gruesome experiments conducted on still-living fetuses. In response Congress passed the 1974 National Research Act (Public Law 93-345) which established the National Commission for the Protection of Human Subjects of Biomedical and Behavioral Research, whose first charge was to investigate the scientific, legal, and ethical aspects of fetal research. The statute also prohibited all federally funded research on fetuses prior or subsequent to abortion until the commission made its recommendations and regulations were adopted.

In 1975 the commission issued its recommendations, which set a framework for the conduct of fetal research. In 1976 regulations for the federal funding of such research were promulgated (45 CFR 46.201-211) and are still in effect. Under the regulations, certain types of fetal research are fundable, with constraints based on parental consent and the principle of minimizing risk to the pregnant woman and the fetus. With respect to cadaver fetuses the regulations defer to state and local laws in accordance with the provisions of the Uniform Anatomical Gift Act. Fetal cadaver tissue is to be treated the same as any other human cadaver.

With respect to research on live fetuses, the regulations provide that appropriate studies must first be done on animal fetuses. The consent of the pregnant woman and the prospective father (if reasonably possible) are required, and the research must not alter the pregnancy termination procedure in a way that would cause greater than "minimal risk" to either the pregnant woman or the fetus. Moreover, researchers must not have a role in determining either the abortion procedure or the assessment of fetal viability. Where it is unclear whether an *ex utero* fetus is viable, that fetus cannot be the subject of research unless the purpose of the research is to enhance its chances of survival *or* the research subjects the fetus to no additional risk and its purpose is to develop important, otherwise unobtainable, knowledge. Research on living, nonviable fetuses *ex utero* is allowed if the vital functions of the fetus are not artificially maintained. Finally, *in utero* fetal research is permissible if it is designed to be therapeutic to the particular fetus and places it at the minimal risk necessary to meet its health needs, or if it imposes minimal risks and produces important knowledge unobtainable through other means.

B. Federal Regulations

In 1985, Congress passed a law (42 U.S.C. 289) forbidding federal conduct or funding of research on viable *ex utero* fetuses with an exception for therapeutic research or research that poses no added risk of suffering, injury, or death to the fetus *and* leads to important knowledge unobtainable by other means. Research on living fetuses *in utero* is still permitted, but federal regulations require the standard of risk to be the same for fetuses to be aborted as for fetuses that will be carried to term.

In 1985, Congress also passed legislation (42 U.S.C. 275) creating a Biomedical Ethics Board whose first order of business was to be fetal research. In 1988, Congress suspended the power of the secretary of the Department of Health and Human Services (HHS) to authorize waivers in cases of great need and great potential benefit until the Biomedical Ethics Advisory Committee conducted a study of the nature, advisability, and implications of exercising any waiver of the risk provisions of existing federal regulations. However, in 1989 the activities of the committee were suspended, thereby leaving the question of waivers unresolved.

Federal regulations on fetal research, then, appear to be quite clear in allowing funding within the stated boundaries. However, in two key areas—embryo research and fetal tissue transplantation research—federal funding was in effect prohibited. The de facto moratorium on embryo research existed between 1980 and 1995. One of the provisions of the 1975 regulations prohibits federal funding of research involving the embryo entailing more than minimal risk unless an Ethics Advisory Board (EAB) recommends a waiver on grounds of scientific importance. The EAB was chartered for this purpose in 1977, first convened in 1978, and in May 1979 recommended approval for federal funding of a study of spare, untransferred embryos. However, in September 1980, Department of Health, Education, and Welfare (HEW) Secretary Patricia Harris allowed the charter of the EAB to expire. Although some observers have speculated that Harris did so to avoid overlap with the planned presidential commission, others concluded that she instead did so out of opposition to federal funding of IVF research. According to them, Harris was fully aware that the EAB was the only lawful body that could recommend waiver of minimal risk in research.

Although NIH directors throughout the 1980s called for a recharter of the EAB, no HHS secretary took action until 1988. Under pressure from Congress, Robert Windom, assistant secretary for Health, announced that a new charter was to be drafted and a new EAB appointed. The draft charter was published in the *Federal Register* as required by law and the charter was approved by HHS secretary Otis Bowen shortly before he left office. The incoming Bush administration, however, never acted and the EAB was not reestablished. As a result, the moratorium on federal funding of all human embryo research, including IVF and other assisted reproduction techniques, continued. According to the Institute of Medicine, this moratorium severely hampered progress in medically assisted reproduction. In 1994 the Human Embryo Research Panel, set up by the National Institutes of Health, recommended federal funding of certain types of embryo research. The recommendations have not yet been acted upon, in part because of resistance in the U.S. Congress.

C. State Regulations of Fetal Research

As with federal activity in fetal research, state regulation was largely a response to the broad expansion of research involving legally aborted fetuses after *Roe v. Wade* [410U.S.113 (1973)]. Table II shows those states with current statutes restricting fetal research. Many of these laws were enacted by conservative legislatures as an effort to foreclose social benefits that might be viewed as lending support to abortion. Of the 25 states with laws specifically regulating fetal research, 12 regulate only research concerned with fetuses prior or subsequent to an elective abortion, and most of the statutes are either part of or attached to abortion legislation. Moreover, of the 13 states that apply more general regulations, 5 impose more stringent restrictions of fetal research in conjunction with an elective abortion.

Under state law, research on fetal cadavers is regulated through the Uniform Anatomical Gift Act (UAGA), which has been adopted by all 50 states. However, some states have excluded fetuses from the UAGA provisions, and others regulate it through fetal research statutes. Although a total of 45 states permit the use of tissues from elective abortions, 14 have provisions regulating research involving fetal cadaver tissue that deviate from the UAGA either in consent requirements or in specific prohibitions on the uses of such tissue. Five states currently prohibit any research with fetal cadavers except for pathological examinations or autopsies. Of these, 4 apply prohibitions exclusively to electively aborted fetuses.

State laws regulating research on live fetuses (*in utero* or *ex utero*) generally constrain research that is not therapeutic to the fetus itself. Because these state laws were adopted in the context of the abortion debate, the primary focus is on research performed on the *ex utero* fetus. Twenty states regulate research on *ex utero* fetuses, while 14 regulate research on *in utero* fetuses. Although the specifics of the prohibitions and the sanctions designated differ by state, most would appear to prohibit research involving transplantation and nontherapeutic research.

TABLE II

State Statutes Regulating Fetal Research

State	Regulates use of fetal cadavers	Prohibits nontherapeutic research on fetus		Prohibits sale of fetal tissue	May restrict preembryo research
		live *ex utero*	live *in utero*		
Arizona	X	X			X
Arkansas		X		X	X
California		X		X	X
Florida		X	X	X	X
Illinois	X[a]			X	X
Indiana	X	X			
Kentucky		X		X	X
Louisiana		X[b]	X	X	X
Maine		X	X	X	X
Massachusetts	X	X	X	X	X
Michigan	X	X	X	X	X
Minnesota		X	X	X	X
Missouri		X	X	X	
Montana		X			
Nebraska		X		X	
Nevada				X	
New Mexico		X	X	X	
North Dakota	X	X	X	X	X
Ohio	X	X		X	X
Oklahoma	X	X	X	X	X
Pennsylvania	X	X	X	X	X
Rhode Island	X	X	X	X	X
South Dakota	X[c]	X[c]	X		
Tennessee	X[c]	X[c]			
Utah			X	X	X
Wyoming		X		X	X

Source: Adapted from OTA (1990). "Neural Grafting: Repairing the Brain and Spinal Cord," pp. 133–134. Government Printing Office, Washington, DC.

[a] Federal District Court ruled this law unconstitutional.

[b] Statute found unconstitutional in *Margaret S. v. Edwards* (1986).

[c] Requires consent.

Another restriction imposed by some of the fetal research statutes addresses concerns over remuneration for fetal materials or participation in research. At present at least 16 states prohibit the sale of fetal tissue, 7 for any purpose and 9 specifically for research purposes. Importantly, some of these restrictions apply only to elective abortions, not spontaneous abortions or ectopic pregnancies. In some states the penalties for violation are quite high. For instance, selling a viable fetus for research in Wyoming is punishable by a fine of not less that $10,000 and imprisonment of 1 to 14 years.

IV. THE CONTROVERSY OVER FETAL TISSUE TRANSPLANTATION

Although fetal research has been embroiled in controversy for two decades, the recent debate has focused on the use of fetal tissue for transplantation research. As noted earlier, while the case can be made that much fetal research leads to knowledge and treatment that may benefit fetuses, transplantation of fetal tissue will benefit primarily adult patients. Because of the important political implications and ethical dimensions raised by transplantation and because it so vividly raises questions of consent and rights, this section examines in more detail this one area of fetal research and the political context of the debate.

A. Controversy over Source of Fetal Tissue

The major policy issue surrounding neural grafting using fetal central nervous system (CNS) tissue centers on the use of fetal tissue in transplantation research. Four possible sources of fetal tissue are:

1. Spontaneous abortions
2. Induced abortions on unintended pregnancies
3. Induced abortions on fetuses conceived specifically for research or therapy
4. Embryos produced in vi. ɔ

A dependence on spontaneously aborted fetuses for research is impractical because of the limited number available, the inability to control the timing, and the fact that fetal tissue is fragile and deteriorates quickly after the death of the fetus. The major supply of fetal tissue, therefore, is likely to come from induced abortions on unwanted pregnancies. Instead of discarding or destroying the tissue, it is retrieved for research or transplantation. If even a small percentage of women elected to donate fetal tissue for research, the million and a half elective abortions performed in the United States each year would appear to be more than adequate to meet most research needs.

Unlike the use of fetuses spontaneously aborted, however, dependence on elective abortions as the primary source raises vehement objections on moral grounds by groups opposed to abortion. Other serious questions are raised when the research or therapy needs affect the timing and method of abortion, or if pressures are placed on the women undergoing the abortion to consent to donation. To ensure against the latter, most observers recommend that the decision to terminate a pregnancy be made separately from the consent for fetal research.

An even more troublesome source of fetal material might arise if a human fetus is conceived specifically for the purpose of aborting it for research or therapy. Although there is no documented evidence that this has happened, in at least two cases women have asked if they could become pregnant to produce tissues or organs for another person. In one case, the daughter

of an Alzheimer's patient asked to be inseminated with the sperm of her father and, at the appropriate stage, to abort the fetus to provide her father with fetal neural tissue for transplantation. Although there is no evidence at present that this is technically possible, and the women's request was denied, this case demonstrates a possible demand for such applications. Similarly, another woman requested that her midterm fetus be aborted and the kidneys be transplanted to her husband who was dying of end-stage renal disease. There is also concern that increased pressures for fetal tissue could lead to a marketplace for this scarce resource which, in turn, could lead to exploitation of poor women (in the United States or elsewhere) paid to conceive solely to provide fetal materials, even if the practice were illegal.

The fourth source of human cells or tissue comes from embryos produced through IVF. Again, the situation is clouded by the need to distinguish between those embryos deliberately created for research purposes and those untransferred embryos remaining after IVF of multiple ova. Although persons who believe that life starts at conception are likely to oppose any use of human embryos for research purposes, many supporters of the use of spare embryos find the production of human embryos specifically for research unacceptable. Questions of consent, ownership, and payment are common to both categories.

B. Interim Moratorium on Fetal Tissue Transplantation Research

In March 1988, in response to a growing political controversy surrounding the publicity over Mexican and Swedish attempts at grafting fetal CNS tissue into Parkinson's patients, Robert Windom, assistant secretary for Health, imposed a moratorium on federal support for fetal tissue transplantation applications, pending a report from a special panel he directed NIH to convene in order to answer ethical and legal questions posed by a proposal for transplanting fetal brain tissue into patients with Parkinson's disease. In September 1988, the Human Fetal Tissue Transplantation Research Panel recommended that funding be restored and concluded that such research is "acceptable public policy." In order to protect the interests of the various parties, the panel recommended guidelines to prohibit financial inducements to women; prohibit the sale of fetal tissue; prevent directed donations of fetal tissue to relatives; separate the decision to abort and the decision to donate; and require consent of the women and nonobjection of the father.

In December 1988, the NIH Director's Advisory Committee unanimously approved the special panel's report without change and recommended that the moratorium be lifted. The committee concluded that existing procedures governing human research and organ donation are sufficient to regulate fetal tissue transplantation. In January 1989, James Wyngaarden, the Director of NIH, concurred with the position of the Advisory Committee and transmitted the final report to the assistant secretary for Health. The report languished in the department without action until November 1989, when Secretary Louis Sullivan announced, in direct conflict with the recommendations, an indefinite extension of the moratorium.

C. Congressional Action

In April 1990, the U.S. House of Representatives Committee on Energy and Commerce's Subcommittee on Health and the Environment held hearings on human fetal tissue transplantation research. In July 1991 the House passed HR 2507, which would have limited the authority of executive branch officials to ban federal funds for areas of research. In May 1992, the House voted to approve the language of the conference committee, which included privacy and consent provisions added by the Senate, and it sent the bill to the president for a certain veto. In anticipation of a likely override of his veto, President Bush issued an executive order directing NIH to establish a fetal tissue bank from spontaneously aborted fetuses and ectopic pregnancies, even though there was little evidence that such a bank could provide sufficient amounts of high-quality tissue for transplantation.

The political controversy continued in June 1992 when a compromise bill was introduced in both houses. This bill in effect gave the administration 1 year to demonstrate that the tissue bank would work. If researchers were then unable to obtain suitable tissue from the bank within 2 weeks of a request, they could obtain it from other sources, including elective abortions. In October 1992, a Senate filibuster by opponents of fetal research ended attempts at passage, leading majority leader Mitchell to vow that the bill would be the first order of business when the Senate reconvened in 1993. On January 23, 1993, on his second day in office, President Clinton as expected issued an executive order that removed the ban on the funding of fetal tissue transplantation research.

D. Issues in Fetal Tissue Transplantation

Despite the President's action opening the way for public funding of fetal tissue for transplantation research, many legal and ethical issues remain. These issues include:

1. The determination of fetal death
2. The distinction between viable and nonviable fetuses as tissue source
3. The suitability of federal and state regulations and guidelines on the use of fetal tissues
4. Issues surrounding the procurement of fetal tissue, specifically who consents, the procedures for consent, the timing of consent, what information must be disclosed, and who seeks consent
5. Questions as to permissibility of altering routine abortion methods or timing in the interest of increasing the yield of fetal tissue suitable for research or transplantation
6. Quality control of fetal tissue, including screening of tissue and storage procedures
7. Issues surrounding the distribution system, including financial arrangements between physicians performing abortions and researchers using tissues, payment for cell lines, and the legality of designated recipients by the tissue donors

Contention over these issues is bound to intensify as the amount of transplantation research increases and the need for fetal tissue expands, particularly for issues 4 and 5.

1. Consent for Use of Fetal Tissue

The question of individual rights is clearly present in the debate over procurement of fetal tissue. Does a woman who decides to abort the fetus maintain any interests in the disposal of the fetal cadaver? In those states that include fetal cadavers under UAGA, proxy consent is required. The most logical proxy is the pregnant woman. Not only is she the next of kin, but the privacy argument suggests the woman's right to control her own body and its products. Observers argue that to deny the woman the opportunity to veto the use of fetal remains for transplant research or therapy denies her autonomy and that consent, therefore, must be obtained to protect the interests of the women. Following this approach, the NIH fetal tissue transplantation research panel concluded that maternal consent is essential prior to the use of fetal cadavers for research.

In contrast, others argue that through abortion the woman abdicates responsibility for the fetus and that as a result there is no basis for seeking her consent concerning the disposition of the fetus. Once abortion has taken place the tissue is no longer part of the woman's body; therefore her claim to the use of tissues from her body carries little weight. Furthermore, since the woman clearly does not intend to protect the fetus it is inappropriate for her to act as a proxy.

Another argument against requiring maternal consent is that such a requirement may be an unwelcome intrusion upon a woman already facing a tortuous decision in the abortion. For instance, in *Margaret S. v. Edwards* [794 F.2d 994 (5th cir. 1986)] the U.S. Fifth Circuit struck down a Louisiana regulation that required the woman's consent for the disposal of the dead fetus. The court noted that informing a woman of the burial or cremation of the fetus intimidated pregnant women from exercising their constitutional right or created unjustified anxiety in the exercise of that right (at 1004). For the sake of reducing a woman's emotional burden and preventing harm to the woman, the court ruled that the woman need not be informed of, nor consent to, the disposal of the fetus.

One might ask whether informing a woman that her aborted fetus may be donated for research is potentially unwelcome information. Although some women might find it an intrusion, others may welcome the opportunity to specify donation for that purpose. The dilemma is that while the UAGA and state statutes require the woman's informed consent in order for her fetus to be a legal donation, *Margaret S.* suggests that this requirement may intrude upon her abortion decision and thus be unconstitutional.

Robinson [The Moral Permissibility of In Utero Experimentation. *Women and Politics* 13, 19–31 (1993)] raises an interesting issue surrounding a woman's decision regarding abortion once she has consented to *in utero* research on the fetus is whether the woman should be able to change her mind about the planned abortion once the experiment on the fetus has began. If yes, the woman's autonomy is ensured at the cost of potentially severe harm to the fetus. If no, limits on her autonomy are accepted in order to prevent possible harm to the fetus. Robinson argued that in this situation, the woman should not be permitted to change her mind once she has begun participation in the experiment—the woman has freely chosen to limit her own autonomy when she agrees to *in utero* experimentation and should be clearly told that she is making an irrevocable decision. This is the case in any abortion where there is at some time a point of no return—this point simply comes earlier in the process when the experiment starts. In either case, even if the fetus were to survive, it would have likely suffered great harm needlessly. Whether one agrees with Robinson's conclusion or not, this scenario reiterates the need for full and informed maternal consent prior to any experimentation on the fetus.

2. Modifications of Abortion Procedure

Another concern in fetal research, especially in grafting procedures where the pressures to obtain tissue of the most appropriate gestational age and optimal condition for transplantation are strongest, is whether the pregnant woman's medical care can be altered in order to meet research purposes. Although some observers approve of modifications in the abortion procedure if they pose little risk for the woman and she is adequately informed and consents, no one has publically advocated changing abortion procedures that entail a significant increase in the probability of harm or discomfort to the woman. At this stage there is general agreement that the means and timing of abortion should be based on the pregnant woman's medical needs and not on research needs. The Fetal Tissue Transplantation Research Panel made this requirement a high priority.

However, the difficulty of ensuring cooperation from abortion clinics and obstetricians in making fetal tissue available for research, attributed in part to reluctance to meet the additional time and resource requirements, has raised concerns for maintaining an adequate supply of fetal tissue. Moreover, the availability of RH-486 and other abortifacients in the near future might diminish the supply of usable fetal tissue at a time when demand might increase should fetal tissue prove to be a successful treatment for a common disease. Despite near consensus that fetal tissue procurement should not pose significant risk to the pregnant woman and that procedural protections must be in place, pressures for an expanding supply of usable fetal tissue demands vigilance to minimize abuses.

V. FETAL RESEARCH AND ABORTION

The ongoing debate over whether the use of fetal tissue from elective abortion encourages or legitimizes abortion will continue to be unresolved. Persons opposed to abortion will continue to oppose the use of fetal tissue altogether or from all but spontaneous abortions and ectopic pregnancies. The arguments that fetus research devalues the fetus and amounts to use of the fetus as the means to another's ends are strongly rooted in the antiabortion position, and arguments of the good derived from such research are unlikely to sway strong opponents. There is no evidence that the use of fetal tissue will encourage women who are ambivalent about the abortion choice to have one, and most experts believe it will not do so.

It is reasonable to establish procurement procedures that remove to the maximal extent possible any likelihood of encouragement or pressure on the women to abort in order to provide fetuses for research or transplantation. Precautions to this end include distancing the abortion choice from the consent for research by prohibiting abortion clinic personnel from even discussing donation until after the woman has formally consented to abortion. The separate consent for fetal donation might even follow the abortion procedure in those situations where possible. Procedures should also require that the woman be fully informed of any risks to her privacy or well-being associated with donation of the fetal tissue and of any interest the abortion provider might have in her donation.

Furthermore, in order to reduce the presence of any coercion of women into conceiving and aborting in order to provide fetal tissue to benefit identifiable others, specification of tissue recipients, including the woman herself, should be prohibited. Payments to women who abort, including compensation for the cost of the abortion procedure, should be prohibited. To further reduce the profit motive in the disposition of fetal remains, payments to doctors, clinics, and other parties involved in the abortion procedure should be prohibited. Fetal materials for research should be distributed through public registries established to distribute them on a nonprofit basis once fetal tissue transplantation needs expand. As noted by Vawter: "Appropriate guidelines for fetal tissue procurement are necessary to replace the inadequate practices currently in widespread use so that fetuses and the women asked to donate tissue after elective abortion receive the respect and protection owed them" (Vawter, D. E. (1993). "Fetal Tissue Transplantation Policy in the United States." *Politics and the Life Sciences, 12,* 79–85.). Although this will not defuse the debate over fetal research nor eliminate the need for continued vigilance, it seems to represent the best balance of the competing interests.

VI. CONCLUSIONS

Clearly some important areas of fetal research have been explicitly constrained on political rather than scientific grounds. The presence of abortion politics continues to exert strong influence on research funded by the government across a wide range of substantive areas. In the process, long-term scientific goals are being compromised by immediate, pragmatic political objectives. Given the sensitivity of human embryo and fetal research and its interdependence on abortion, this should not be surprising. This research will continue to elicit intense opposition and support, thus placing it well within the political agenda throught the 1990s. Fetal research policy raises moral red flags for many persons. In contrast, research on human embryos and fetal tissue transplantation promise significant advances in our understanding of the human condition and represent potentially revolutionary treatment options.

Also See the Following Articles

ABORTION • AUTONOMY • EMBRYOLOGY, ETHICS OF • HUMAN RESEARCH SUBJECTS, SELECTION OF • RESEARCH ETHICS

Bibliography

Andrews, L. B. (1993). Regulation of experimentation on the unborn. *Journal of Legal Medicine, 14,* 25–56.

Donovan, P. (1990). Funding restrictions on fetal research: The implications for science and health. *Family Planning Perspectives, 22,* 224–231.

Fletcher, J. C. (1993). Human fetal and embryo research: Lysenkoism in reverse—How and why? In "Emerging Issues in Biomedicine" (R. H. Blank and A. L. Bonnicksen, Eds.), Vol. 2. Columbia Univ. Press, New York.

Mullen, M. A. (1992). "The Use of Human Embryos and Fetal Tissues: A Research Architecture." Royal Commission on New Reproductive Technologies, Ottawa.

Office of Technology Assessment (1990). "Neural Grafting: Repairing the Brain and Spinal Cord." Government Printing Office, Washington, DC.

Stein, D. G., and Glasier, M. M. (1995). Some practical and theoretical issues concerning fetal brain tissue grafts as therapy for brain dysfunction. *Behavioral and Brain Sciences, 18,* 36–45.

Vawter, D. E., Kearny, W., Gervais, K. G., *et al.* (1990). "The Use of Human Fetal Tissue: Scientific, Ethical, and Policy Concerns." Center for Biomedical Ethics, Minneapolis.

FETUS

Norman Ford
Caroline Chisholm Centre for Health Ethics

I. Formation of the Human Fetus
II. Fetal Losses
III. Human, Individual, and Personal Status of the Embryo and Fetus
IV. Moral Respect Due to the Human Embryo and Fetus
V. Abortion
VI. Ethical Issues in Fetal Therapy

GLOSSARY

blastocyst A hollow ball of cells filled with fluid that is formed about 4 days after fertilization and prior to implantation.

chimera An organism with different cell populations derived from different zygotes or embryos.

chromosomes Threads of DNA that transmit genetic information through genes spaced along their entire length.

DNA Deoxyribonucleic acid, the main constituent of chromosomes and the basis of the genetic code.

embryo A term for the developing human being during the first 8 weeks after fertilization.

fertilization The process that begins when a sperm contacts the plasma membrane of an egg and that is completed at syngamy some 24 hr later.

fetus A term for the developing human being from the 9th week of development after fertilization.

gene The basic unit of inheritance.

genome The complete set of hereditary factors contained in the chromosomes.

hematopoietic Pertaining to the formation of blood cells.

hydrocephalus Dilation of the cerebral ventricles and skull with cerebrospinal fluid.

hydronephrosis Distension of the renal pelvis and calices with urine due to obstruction of the ureter.

primitive streak A piling up of cells on the caudal end of the embryonic disk, providing the first evidence of the embryonic axis.

syngamy The mingling of the male and female chromosomes during fertilization to form the zygote.

totipotency The potency or capacity of a cell or cluster of cells to produce the whole fetus.

trophoblast The peripheral cells of the blastocyst which attach the embryo to the uterine wall and become the placenta and membranes that provide nutrients to the fetus.

zona pellucida A noncellular casing containing the egg, zygote, and early embryo.

zygote The fertilized egg; the cell formed by the fusion of sperm and egg.

THE HUMAN FETUS has given rise to many debates over its human, individual, and personal status. With the advent of artificial reproductive procedures we now know much more about its formation, fueling these debates whose outcomes will decide the moral respect due the embryo and fetus. Religious, traditional, and secular ethics differ considerably in their opinions. This is exemplified in different attitudes to abortion. There is, however, more agreement between mothers and health care professionals on the ethical issues that arise in fetal therapy, fetal surgery, and fetal transplants. This article discusses some moral issues that arise concerning the human fetus in contemporary society.

I. FORMATION OF THE HUMAN FETUS

Fertilization takes place when sperm and egg fuse to form a new cell, an embryo or zygote (from the Greek *zygotos,* meaning "yoked together"). This occurs as the 23 maternal and 23 paternal chromosomes mingle at syngamy, some 22 hr after sperm penetration. Along the 46 chromosomes up to some 100,000 genes are located at specific sites. Genes have encoded instructions for the synthesis of specific proteins that make up all the structures, organs, and tissues of the human individual. At fertilization the individual's genetic complement is determined for life.

The zygote divides into two cells, these into four cells, these into eight, and so on. As cell multiplication proceeds, cell differentiation begins. The genes of the embryo's outside cells are first selectively activated to synthesize proteins for the formation of the trophoblastic cells of the blastocyst, which by this stage is a primitive embryonic organism. Trophoblastic cells are the precursors of extraembryonic tissues and the placenta, while the progeny of the inner cells give rise to the fetus. The blastocyst implants into the mother's womb from Days 6 to 13. Prior to this, the embryo is referred to as a "preimplantation embryo," which was eventually shortened to "preembryo" and began to be used to signify that an embryo was not really formed until implantation was completed. During this period the embryo for the most part lives on the nutrients within each cell. Successful implantation is necessary for the embryo to obtain nutrients from the mother for survival. By this stage the primitive streak is formed, indicating the embryo's craniocaudal axis and the individual's earliest body plan. This is also referred to as individuation and is the last stage at which identical twins can be formed if two primitive streaks appear. Birth is sometimes given to two-headed babies, conjoined twins, and very rarely a one-headed baby with two bodies.

From this stage organogenesis rapidly proceeds, and by the beginning of the 4th week the cardiovascular system has begun to function and to supply nutrients to the developing embryo. By the end of the 8th week the beginnings of all essential external and internal structures are formed. From the 9th week fetal life begins as growth and development continue. Fetal life ends with birth, death in the womb, miscarriage, or induced abortion.

II. FETAL LOSSES

Research shows that the total embryonic and fetal losses in detected pregnancies from the blastocyst stage to 28 weeks are at least 30%. This excludes undetected losses in the first 5 or 6 days after fertilization. The loss of clinically recognized pregnancies from 5 to 6 weeks after the last menstrual period to Week 12 is about 15%. About 5% of all clinically recognized pregnancies are affected by a chromosomal abnormality, and this presumably accounts for over 30% of all spontaneous embryonic and fetal deaths. Cigarette smoking is known to increase miscarriages by at least 25% and the risk of underweight babies at birth by a higher percentage. Other causes of fetal deaths include the effect of maternal age on ova, nutrition, vitamin deficiencies, excessive intake of alcohol, abuse of drugs, maternal health, cardiac disease, infections, endometriosis, viruses (e.g., congenital rubella), stress, and immunological abnormalities leading to rejection and fetal growth retardation.

III. HUMAN, INDIVIDUAL, AND PERSONAL STATUS OF THE EMBRYO AND FETUS

A. A Human Being Is Not Necessarily a Person

For the philosopher Peter Singer a *human being* begins at conception as a member of the species *Homo sapiens.* Michael Lockwood says a fetus could not be a human being before the brain is sufficiently developed to sustain one's identity as a human being with a capacity for consciousness. Michael Tooley, Singer, and Lockwood follow the definition of *person* given by John Locke (d. 1704) as "a thinking intelligent being, that has reason and reflection, and can consider itself as itself, the same thinking thing, in different times and places; which it does only by that consciousness which is inseparable from thinking, and, it seems to me, essential to it." (*Essay Concerning Human Understanding,* Book 11, ch. 27, para. 9.) On this score a fetus could not be a person until well after birth when it becomes possible to have a minimal understanding of oneself, one's interests, one's future, and one's desires.

The rationale underpinning this view is that reality

may be reduced to matter and material energy. This would rule out a spiritual or immaterial soul accounting for a rational nature in a fetus and an adult. On this view rationality and personhood could not be predicated of a human being until there were signs of the acquired capacity for the exercise of some minimal rational activities some time after birth.

B. A Human Individual Is a Person

Some hold that it suffices to be a human being, i.e., a living individual with a human nature, to be a person, even before the onset of the age of reason. In coming to this conclusion, they rely on the classic definition of a person given by Boethius along Aristotelian lines and expressed by Aquinas: "The term 'person' signifies something complete, subsisting in its own right, in a rational nature. (*Summa Theologiae,* 111, Q16, art. 12 ad 2.)" Human nature enables human fetuses to develop to the stage where, without ceasing to be substantially the same living beings, they can exercise rationally self-conscious and free acts. In this view the spiritual soul accounts for the human individual's rational nature and personhood from its inception.

1. The Human Individual already Formed in the Zygote

Many hold that once a new cell is formed by the fusion of sperm and egg a human individual is already formed, because the adult develops from the zygote in a continuous, coordinated biological process. The newly constituted genome in the zygote, by interaction with the maternal environment, directs purposeful development, differentiation, and growth of the one and same living individual. The genetic identity of the adult is practically the same as that of the zygote. The zygote possesses the active potential to develop and grow into an adult, given the right environment and suitable conditions. The same zygote seems to organize itself into an embryo, a fetus, an infant, a child, and an adult without ceasing to be substantially the same living individual. Extraembryonic tissues, membranes, and the placenta are temporary, but constituent, organs *of* the fetus which become redundant and are discarded after birth. This seems to indicate that the zygote or fertilized egg is an actual human being or individual, not a potential human individual. Once the human individual is formed at fertilization, it has been argued that there are reasonable grounds to believe that the immaterial soul or life-principle is created within the zygote to complete the formation of a natural person, though obviously there could be no empirical evidence for the soul's creation.

In the case of twinning at the two-cell stage the human individual formed in the zygote could continue and a new human individual could begin. This would resemble the case of a plant retaining its identity when a slip is cut off and planted in the soil to give rise to a new plant. Alternatively two new human individuals could begin with twinning at the two-cell stage.

2. The Human Individual Formed at the Primitive Streak Stage

Others view things differently. The fact that the genetic identity of the human individual and adult is formed in the zygote does not prove that the human individual is already formed. Identical twins may be formed from the zygote, but they are two human individuals. It would be hard to accept that the first human individual continues despite the loss of half of its mass by fission to one of the first two identical cells. One reply given to this difficulty cites the example of a new plant originating from a slip taken from a parent plant. This reply lacks realism because the capacity for regeneration of a part of a plant and the formation of twins from a zygote are not the same.

In the normal situation when twinning does not occur, at the two-cell stage each of the two contiguous cells seem to be distinct individual cells. Each begins with its own life cycle and has its own nutrients for sustaining its life and energy needs. The zona pellucida which is secreted by the egg and encases the cells is composed of nonliving glycoproteins in a noncellular form. The first two cells, even if interacting, seem to be two entities, not a two-cell individual. The same applies to the four-cell embryo. The human individual appears to be formed after the zygote stage even though the genome in the zygote has a natural capacity for cell multiplication and differentiation to form one or more human individuals.

The totipotency of the first four cells gradually gives way to the pluritotipotency of groups of cells, e.g., half of an eight-cell embryo. At the eight-cell stage, cells are not committed to any specific pathway of development. The first cells to differentiate are those destined to form extraembryonic tissues. It is only at the primitive streak stage that specific cells are destined to form the entire embryo and fetus. This means the genes in the cells within the zona pellucida are not yet sufficiently activated to form one integrated living body. These cells first multiply and then differentiate as they gradually undergo restriction of developmental potency. As further evidence of this, single cells taken from four-cell white, black, and brown sheep embryos that are put in an empty zona pellucida and then placed in a recipient ewe give rise to a single white, black, and brown chimeric sheep, which did not begin at fertilization. The cells of genetically dissimilar embryos collaborate to form an individual chimeric sheep. This suggests that genetically similar embryonic human cells *normally* do the same and that purposeful development occurs *between* cells rather than *within* a multicellular individual.

Normally only one primitive streak is formed about 14 days after fertilization, but two may occasionally be formed to give origin to identical twins from within the existing embryonic organism. When two primitive streaks are formed identical twins result. If the streak forks at the top a two-headed fetus is formed. Conjoined twins are formed if the primitive streak does not replicate completely. If the primitive streak only forks at the bottom an individual is formed with one head and two bodies. The primitive streak marks the formation of a new multicellular human individual with a definitive craniocaudal body axis and bilateral symmetry. The previous rudimentary human organism would function as an extraembryonic organ (placenta) and tissues for the fetus. It is argued there would be no difficulty for a new organization of cells to form a new individual at the appearance of the primitive streak. By then its developing cells would be integrated and subordinated to form a single organic body which would continue as the same living body through all subsequent stages of development and growth. A new human individual would begin once the cells of the embryonic organism form one living body, actuated by a spiritual life-principle created by God within the previously existing organism.

The potency for identical twinning is lost after the primitive streak stage because differentiation has progressed to the point of forming a definitive individual. In other words, one or more definitive human individuals could not be formed before the late blastocyst as a whole loses its pluritotipotency. With the appearance of the primitive streak the definitive embryo is unitotipotent with the active potency to continue development as the same human individual, whereas earlier, a separated totipotent part could form another human individual. Instead of viewing development in the first 2 weeks after fertilization as development of the human individual, it seems preferable to interpret the process as one of cell multiplication and development *into* a human individual—the *synthesis* of an embryonic human individual. If this is so, it would be better to use the term "pro-embryo" rather than "preembryo" to refer to the first cells and the blastocyst.

IV. MORAL RESPECT DUE TO THE HUMAN EMBRYO AND FETUS

A. Theological Reasons

Believers in God find ample grounds in biblical theology to make a strong moral case for showing absolute respect for human life from conception since human life and its formation are exclusively in the hands of God as Creator. God alone, and not human parents, has dominion over human life from its very beginning. The Bible does not differentiate between personal, preindividual, and prepersonal life since all human life is portrayed as belonging to God in a special way. From early Christian times human life has been regarded as sacred and morally inviolable from conception, even when it was assumed that ensoulment could not take place before several weeks after conception. While absolute respect imposes a duty of reasonable care and always rules out intentional assault, it does not require taking unreasonable risks or measures in the circumstances to save the life of a fetus. This is the context for understanding fetal rights.

B. Argument Based on the Human Embryo as a Person

As stated above, moral respect is claimed for the human embryo on the grounds that it already is, or almost certainly is, a human individual and a person. This view is shared by many theists and endorsed officially by Catholic teaching. This view relies on the embryonic human individual being constituted into a person through the creation of a spiritual soul as its life-principle and basis of its rational nature. There would be no need to await the onset of rationally self-conscious acts for the human embryo and fetus to be a person. Where there are doubts about the individual and personal status of the human embryo, the benefit of any reasonable doubt should rightly be given to the embryo.

C. Argument Based on the Human Embryo as a Potential Person

Many hold that an embryo is a potential person, not an actual person, and so does not warrant moral respect unless it remains the same numerical being on becoming a person. Others believe respect should be shown to a nonpersonal early embryo which, on account of its genetically human life and genome, has the inherent developmental potential to become a human individual and person, thanks to the support of the mother's favorable uterine environment. It is claimed that this intrinsic potency and proximity to becoming an actual human individual and person suffice to establish a duty of moral respect. This claim is greater when it is coupled with a belief in the sanctity of the formative process established by God. In this view, regardless of personhood, human life itself suffices for the embryo's claim to special moral significance and due moral respect. Even a corpse is shown respect as a former person.

D. Other Reasons for Respecting the Human Fetus

Those who do not believe the fetus is a person because it has no interests or desire to live do not grant it any personal rights. There would be no intrinsic moral grounds to respect a human fetus prior to sentience. The fetus, however, would acquire some, but not absolute, moral status once the capacity to experience pain was acquired—possibly by about 18 weeks gestation. Its first interests would be to avoid the experience of pain and enjoy pleasure—its only intrinsic title to respect. This status would be shared with other mammals with a capacity to feel pain.

Others who do not believe the human fetus is a person with any rights hold that the fetus warrants some special moral consideration simply because it is wanted by its parents who wish to prevent any harm to the fetus and to the future person it will become. Others may be emotionally distressed at the thought of harm being inflicted on a fetus. Others again use the argument of distress to save the mother from continuing an unwanted pregnancy. When balancing benefits and harms to determine the moral respect due to the mother and fetus in the context of feelings and emotions, utilitarian criteria would need to be applied fairly, and to some extent would be influenced by prevailing community attitudes.

V. ABORTION

Those who do not believe a fetus is a person or a human being hold that abortion would be morally permissible for a proportionate benefit for the mother provided that the fetus was spared any strictly unnecessary pain. On the other hand, as we have already seen, those who believe on one or more grounds in the sanctity of human life from conception take an absolute stand against *di-rect* abortion, i.e., an action which of itself and by intention terminates the life of the unborn child, irrespective of any severe abnormality, by surgical or pharmacological assault or by the removal of a fetus from the womb before the infant is mature enough to sustain life. On this view, a pregnant woman would have a duty of care, even legally enforceable, to protect the fetus within her body from intentional assault. This would also apply to cases of higher order multiple pregnancies. They find it anomalous that one's right over one's body is interpreted to include the deliberate termination of the life of another innocent and defenseless human being namely that of the unborn child.

What has been said so far does not conflict with the proper application of the principle of double effect to allow a life-saving procedure for the mother even though a nonviable fetus has to be removed from the womb. In the case of a cancerous womb, a hysterectomy is performed to save the mother's life even though the loss of the life a previable fetus is foreseen, but not directly intended. This case is often referred to as a justifiable indirect abortion. For proportionate reasons a person may posit a morally good or even indifferent action in order to bring about a good effect even though one foresees that as an incidental, but nevertheless unintended, consequence, an innocent human life may be lost.

Intention is to be accorded due relevance in moral analysis. Those who subscribe to consequentialism judge the morality of actions by their outcomes. If in doing a procedure to save the mother's life the loss of life of the fetus is inevitable, they hold it would be morally indifferent whether the fetus was deliberately killed or allowed to die of prematurity. Others see an enormous moral difference between direct, intentional and unintentional or indirect causing of death that allows the action in the one case but not in the other. Thanks to medical advances, the life of the mother can almost always be saved without even need of indirect abortion.

VI. ETHICAL ISSUES IN FETAL THERAPY

A. Mother Primarily Responsible for Her Fetus

The pregnant woman is the natural trustee of her unborn child and so is primarily responsible for making decisions regarding reasonable care for her unborn child with the assistance of health care professionals. The mother would normally be morally bound to accept any reasonable therapy her fetus may require. She should give due weight to the opinions of the father and the medical team, especially if her condition makes it difficult for her to understand or evaluate all the likely risks. In the final analysis, it is normally her responsibility to make the decision to accept or reject medical treatment for her unborn child after having been informed of the relevant risks and implications for herself, her child, and her family.

The unborn child does have a moral right to simple life-saving or life-enhancing therapy such as a blood transfusion for Rh incompatibility. The doctor, on the other hand, is the mother's agent and is bound to care for her fetus on behalf of the mother. Her informed consent is normally a necessary condition for any therapeutic intervention by the doctor. She may have a duty to permit reasonable fetal therapy but this does not imply that doctors or the state are morally entitled to force competent pregnant women to take medications or undergo invasive fetal therapies against their will, even for a life-threatening defect for which a simple therapy is readily available. The law should not permit intentional assault on the mother, by way of fetal surgery, to uphold a fetus' rights. Maternal–fetal conflicts are better resolved by discussions involving both parents, close friends of the mother, and perhaps consultation with other suitable persons such as a counselor, a pastor, or a psychologist. As a matter of public policy it would be in the best interests of the unborn if mothers' personal autonomy was respected rather than run the risk of pregnant women in need of help being afraid to consult their doctors. It would be different in the case of an infant since no invasive intervention on the mother would be required. Doctors should be legally bound to give blood transfusions to save the lives of infants even if their parents refuse consent.

Most mothers accept doctors' suggestions for fetal therapy, especially when the treating team agree it is warranted and the maternal risks are only slight. This is not bowing to doctors but wisely allowing themselves to be persuaded by the unanimous considered professional judgment of the medical team. It should be pointed out to mothers that choices involving some risk to themselves may be more than balanced by their unborn children's greatly enhanced prospects for a normal life. Successful fetal therapy greatly lessens the hardships of raising children with less serious disabilities or even without any malformations.

Doctors should not be surprised if some mothers do not accept their advice. Mothers as well as doctors have to be satisfied beyond reasonable doubt that decisions to proceed with any fetal therapy are morally permissible. A medical evaluation of slight maternal risk involved in a therapy might not appear slight to a mother whose perspective includes her fears, anxieties, and family situation. Women differ in their reactions to the facts and the risks involved, and consequently in good faith make different evaluations and decisions in similar cases.

B. Doctor's Responsibility to Assess All Risks and Benefits

Fetal therapy is a highly specialized field of medicine where it is becoming increasingly more difficult to apply the general principle of the duty of reasonable care in the context of the maternal–fetal unit. The drawing of the line between when fetal therapy should or should not be offered is one of the most agonizing moral dilemmas that doctors and pregnant women have to face. It can be equally difficult to determine which therapy is the best in the circumstances and when the right time for it is. More than one evaluation of the risks by doctors and the mother could be reasonable without one or the others being unreasonable. In the area of fetal therapy rarely is there only one correct medico-moral answer. Often the therapy adopted may be selected from a range of reasonable options. The community should allow doctors all the necessary freedom to follow their own professional judgment in assessing risks and benefits in clinical practice. Medicine is not an exact science. Errors may be made in good faith without any suggestion of incompetence or the need of actions for negligence. Creating a climate where doctors are unreasonably fearful of being sued for damage hinders the making of good clinical decisions to the detriment of the common good of the community. Unduly protecting oneself from litigation should not be part of the exercise of medical discernment. Fetal therapy is an area of medicine where concrete answers cannot always be given in advance since general medical and ethical principles need to be applied in each case, with a keen eye to the likely short- and long-term consequences of intervention on the fetus, the mother, and the family.

Successful fetal therapies require accurate diagnoses and knowledge of the relevant fetal pathophysiology in each case. This requires a careful evaluation of the fetus in addition to a precise anatomical definintion of the malformation under consideration. Since it is known that malformations often occur as part of a syndrome, a search for associated abnormalities would be necessary to avoid delivering a neonate with one anomaly corrected but still affected by another unrecognized lifelong severely disabling abnormality. The timing of the intervention should not be so early as to endanger the fetus nor so late as to make it futile. It is important to save the mother being subjected to unnecessary invasive fetal therapies. Most fetal defects or anomalies are best treated after birth by the appropriate medical and/or surgical therapy. Other defects detected *in utero* may require inducing premature delivery if continued gestation would have a progressive ill effect on the fetus or if correction of the defect was best left to after birth. Naturally the fetal age selected for premature delivery and treatment ought to be whatever is in the best interests of the mother and the fetus. Others again may be best managed after elective cesarean delivery.

Consultation among colleagues may facilitate the task of assessing the risk of harm to the fetus resulting from fetal therapy against the burden of malformation for a lifetime if no treatment is given. The probability of success would need to be sufficiently high to justify fetal therapy where the risk to the life of the fetus was substantial. A doctor may accept a colleague's alternative medical opinion but not if the advice is believed to be medically unsound. In no circumstances, not even at the request of the mother, should doctors act against their conscientious judgment by giving fetal treatment that is not in the best interests of their patients—the pregnant woman and her fetus. At times mothers or family members ask for unwarranted treatment for peace of mind in the hope that doctors will somehow put things right. Doctors may need to reassure them that no intervention is in the best interests of mother and fetus. It is often a matter of recognizing their heartfelt cry of anxiety and a perplexed conscience expressed in such requests rather than merely heeding the spoken words. Informed consent before medical treatment should not be confused with subordinating professional medical practice to unwarranted therapies.

C. Fetal Surgery

Antenatal diagnosis now enables many conditions to be diagnosed by Week 10. Medication can be given directly to the fetus or indirectly via the mother to treat certain conditions. Fetal surgery may soon become part of contemporary medical practice. Fetal incisions heal without leaving scars and there are biological and immunological advantages for using fetal tissue in transplantation. Fetal surgery is performed to correct lethal defects in organs, which if repaired, would be able to develop normally and give the fetus a chance to survive after birth. Fetal surgery should probably only be used for life-threatening conditions with every precaution

taken to safeguard the life and interests for both the mother and the child, who is normally delivered by cesarean section following fetal surgery.

Fetal urethral obstruction impedes the development of the fetal kidneys and the passing of urine into the amniotic sac. This creates a build-up of fluid inside the fetal body instead of in the amniotic sac. The swallowing of amniotic fluid is necessary for fetal lung development. Unless treatment is given the fetus dies of lung prematurity after birth. If both kidneys are damaged it may be necessary to decompress the fluid by a catheter shunt introduced through the skin by sonographic guidance or by open surgery to create an opening in the bladder. An argon laser probe has been successfully used to burn two small openings through the abdominal wall into the bladder for the immediate release of urine into the amniotic cavity.

Although most fetal defects are better treated after birth, there are some abnormalities which warrant surgery *in utero*, subject to some ethical provisos. The services of a multidisciplinary team should be available, including a perinatal obstetrician, an ultrasonographer, a neonatologist, a pediatric surgeon, and a geneticist. Discernment is needed to keep within the bounds of the duty of reasonable care. It would not seem morally necessary to perform fetal surgery to save a child with a severe enduring defect who otherwise would have died naturally. In general, fetal surgery should only be used for singletons. Guarantees are needed to see that the mother's consent is truly informed and free, and preferably with the involvement of the woman's partner, family, doctor, and counselor. A doctor should act as the advocate of the fetus and follow up opportunities should be required. One needs to ask how certain and great the benefit of surgery would be for the fetus, how harmful it would be for the mother, and what would be the net gain or loss by delaying it until after birth.

Fetal surgeons should be cautious and only routinely provide surgery for a few well-diagnosed and selected anomalies. They should review their work and shelve surgical procedures for conditions found to have poor outcomes. At the same time it would not be unjustified in some circumstances to attempt an innovative therapeutic fetal surgical procedure when the use of other reliable remedies is not appropriate to save the life of the fetus. Improved techniques, skills, and knowledge of fetal pathologies result from the judicious practice of fetal surgery for the benefit of all defective fetuses. Clearly nontherapeutic fetal research that risks causing harm to the unborn child is unethical even if it is done with the consent of the parents. Whenever it is a case of experimental surgery in search of a subject it should not proceed.

Fetal surgery is ethical provided that it is directed to improving the health of the fetus and the risks of intervention are not disproportionate to the integrity, health, and life of the mother and fetus compared to withholding treatment until after birth. It may significantly lessen degrees of disability and suffering and the need for some therapies for a lifetime. Consider the risks of a fetus with urethral obstruction and severe bilateral hydronephrosis. It would be necessary to weigh the risks of probable correction against the trauma of surgery for the mother, and not only neonatal death or severe disability from renal or pulmonary failure, but also the emotional and financial burden of prolonged, burdensome, costly, and sometimes unrewarding treatment of chronic renal failure. It would be pointless to treat *in utero* obstructive uropathy if the kidneys were already ruined or to attempt surgery for hydrocephalus once irreversible brain damage had been caused.

In all cases it needs to be determined whether fetal surgery to correct a malformation is objectively proportionate to the prospects for improvement, taking into account all the risks involved for the mother and her fetus. The possible benefit to be derived from the surgery would depend on the severity of the malformation, its likely degree of correction, and the prospects for survival without severe and painful disabilities and the need of ongoing treatment. In a case of obstructive hydrocephalus, if the choice were between, on the one hand, no intervention and certain severe cerebral palsy and a premature death or, on the other, intervention with a poor chance of correction, leaving an infant with cerebral palsy without any possibility of exercising rational self-conscious acts and some risk of loss of life, all other things being equal, the balance would likely favor nonintervention. In a case of confirmed congenital diaphragmatic hernia it has to be judged whether no intervention would result in a high risk of loss of life or whether correction would allow the lung to grow enough to support life after birth.

Fetal surgery, by focusing attention on the fetus as the subject of therapy, may raise timely questions in the public conscience on the moral status of the fetus as an unborn patient, if not as a person in the legal sense. It is anomalous to find some doctors saving fetuses as unborn patients while others are terminating their lives during abortions. This highlights the inadequacy of the value of life depending on choice.

At the present state of the art, fetal surgery is generally a medico-moral option, not a mandatory procedure.

Unless expertise in fetal surgery improves, it should normally be regarded as a disproportionate rather than a proportionate means of medical treatment to save life and improve the quality of life. Fetal surgery needs to be justified in the sense that the normal presumption favors postnatal treatment. At times it is preferable to let death occur by allowing nature to take its course than to intervene and prolong a life of suffering and distress. It would be better not to intervene if it was known it would most likely result in a life of pain or in a permanent vegetative state.

D. Somatic Gene Therapy by Fetal Stem Cell Transplantation

Blood disorders due to malformation of hemoglobin in the bone marrow and immunodeficiences are inherited genetic defects which are currently treated postnatally by transplanting healthy donor bone marrow cells to the bably. Bone marrow contains hematopoietic stem cells which are capable of specializing further to become blood cells. The progeny of the donor's normal cells colonize the recipient's organism, and once engraftment has occurred, may make up for the genetic defects in its cells and thereby correct the anomaly. This raises therapeutic possibilities for fetal stem cell transplantation and fetal somatic gene therapy for diseases which can be diagnosed and treated to prevent irreversible harm before birth.

Infants and children often are unable to be treated once a disease has progressed beyond a certain point. There would be advantages if fetal transplantation could be done as early as possible in gestation before the fetal immune system is developed, i.e., before the fetus is able to recognize transplanted tissues as foreign and try to reject them. This would decrease the need for immunosuppression with its risks for the baby after birth. It would be even better if early fetal donor cells could be used because they engraft more readily. There would be little risk of rejection of the bone marrow cells by the host if they were derived from a preimmune, recently aborted fetus, and less risk of graft-versus-host disease after transplantation. The effect would resemble the permanent chimerism that naturally occurs in twins who share a common placental circulation.

Cellular transplantation may obviate the need for whole-organ transplants in some instances. A case in point would be therapy for a fetus whose liver had a metabolic disease which could be corrected by cellular transplantation as an alternative to hazardous organ transplants after birth. These hazards include difficulties in finding suitable organ donors, graft-versus-host disease, and the need for immunosuppression for life. When the technology is developed further, fetal cells from cord blood may be cultured to provide a supply of cells suitable for transplantation as fetal therapeutic needs arise. An adult's stem cells are not immunologically competent and could also be transplanted to a fetus to induce tolerance so that postnatal kidney or liver organ transplantation could safely be done.

All the ethical conditions for fetal therapy mentioned earlier would apply to the use of fetal cells or tissues for the treatment of a defective or diseased fetus by transplantation *in utero*. Sufficient guarantees of success would need to be had from research with animal models before moving to clinical practice. It may be ethical in the appropriate circumstances to treat a fetus by transplantation of fetal or adult stem cells. Moral principles require the same respect be given to the life and dignity of both mothers and fetuses, the donor, and the recipient. The mother's informed consent would first be required. Usually this would not be problematic as the transplantation of fetal cells is far less invasive and risky than fetal surgery. Though this need not necessarily be the case, the mother would have a right to a moral objection to refuse to allow her fetus to be treated by the transplantation of cells or tissues derived from a direct abortion. Likewise medical and nursing staff may claim the right to the same objection. According to the circumstances, suitable cells harvested from a source beyond moral reproach may be required for use. This may not be practical as tissue from a miscarriage or from a fetus after a hysterectomy may not be viable.

Moral respect for the donor fetus absolutely demands that cells or tissues not be harvested for therapeutic purposes before it is certain the fetus is dead, irrespective of the stage of development or whether the fetus came from a miscarriage or a direct abortion. Transplantation does not justify the killing of a live fetus. Informed consent is also required of the donor's mother if the tissue is to be used for the benefit of a third party for therapeutic or research purposes. When fetuses are obtained in a medical environment from a miscarriage or an indirect therapeutic abortion, the mothers' rights to determine how their deceased unborn babies should be disposed of remains intact even though it has seldom been claimed until recently.

A major ethical objection to the use of fetal tissue for transplantation is its link with direct abortion when this is the source of the cells or tissue. It would be unethical to have an abortion or to persuade a woman to have one to obtain fetal cells for a therapy. This objection would also apply to a mother who becomes pregnant to abort her fetus so that its tissue could be used for an older sibling. It is clearly unethical for the perpetrator of an immoral deed to profit from it, but not necessarily for others who were not party to the immoral deed. There is no intrinsic moral objection to the therapeutic use of organs from murder victims nor for undertakers to profit from burying murder victims. In principle the use of aborted tissue need not per se imply approval of abortion nor complicity with the institution where the abortions are performed. The moral problem is to find a way to prevent collusion between abortion and the use of aborted fetal tissue. A barrier is needed to morally separate to the community's satisfaction the therapeutic use of tissue from direct abortions. Opinions are divided as to whether this is possible to achieve.

Some believe the morally required separation between consent for abortion and the therapeutic use of aborted fetal tissue is possible. There should be no direct or indirect financial advantages nor other inducements offered to the pregnant woman nor the abortion clinic in exchange for consent to allow the aborted fetal tissue to be used. People who need fetal organs, or their agents, should not contact potential donors to avoid exercising any influence on the decision to abort. The user of the tissue must not influence in any way the timing nor the method of abortion to better suit therapeutic purposes. The management of a pregnancy after the decision to abort must not depend on what best suits the purposes of transplantation. The donor should not have any control over the specific use of tissue donated for medical use or knowledge of its beneficiary. This would include renouncing any financial benefits that could arise in the future from the production of a cell line.

Once transplantation techniques have been perfected and the demand for fetal tissues increases, an independent agency would need to be established to arrange the transfer of tissues from aborted fetuses to those who use the fetal tissues or to fetal tissue banks. The transfer of any necessary medical or genetic information about the mother and fetus should be done only through this intermediary. It is claimed this would guarantee the morally required separation between the users of fetal tissue and the mother's decision to have an abortion and the abortion providing clinic.

There would be, however, the problem of the general knowledge in the community that fetal tissue from direct abortions was being used for the benefit of third parties. It is far from convincing to conclude this arrangement would unduly influence women to have abortions. Legal abortions have been available long before the therapuetic use of fetal tissue began. Powerful personal factors influence a woman's decision to have an abortion—not the abstract consideration of generosity for the benefit of anonymous patients, be they the fetuses of unknown pregnant women or patients with Parkinson's disease.

Those who are morally opposed to abortion do not believe a moral barrier could be raised between the abortion and the decision to make use of a policy designed to make aborted fetal tissue available for therapeutic purposes. The decision to use aborted tissue obtained under this policy implies condoning future abortions on the part of the tissue provider and the recipient. This collaboration would be morally indistinguishable from collusion with abortion and the reduction of some human being as a mere means for another's benefit. It is one thing to use aborted tissue in an emergency situation, but quite another matter to institutionalize and regulate its practice.

Also See the Following Articles

ABORTION • EMBRYOLOGY, ETHICS OF • FETAL RESEARCH • GENE THERAPY • GENETIC ENGINEERING

Bibliography

Baird, R. M., and Rosenbaum, S. E. (Eds.) (1993). "The Ethics of Abortion: Pro-Life vs Pro-Choice." Prometheus, Buffalo, NY.

Brock, D. J., Rodeck, C., and Ferguson-Smith, F. A. (Eds.) (1992). "Prenatal Diagnosis and Screening." Churchill Livingstone, Edinburgh.

Castaldo, P. J., and Moraczewski, A. S. (Eds.) (1994). "The Fetal Tissue Issue: Medical and Ethical Aspects." The Pope John Center, Braintree, MA.

Evans, M. I., Dixler, A. O., Fletcher, J. C., and Schulman, J. D. (Eds.) (1989). "Fetal Diagnosis and Therapy: Science, Ethics, and the Law." Lippincott, Philadelphia.

Ford, N. M. (1988). "When Did I Begin? Conception of the Human Individual in History, Philosophy and Science." Cambridge Univ. Press, Cambridge, UK.

Harrison, M. R. (1993). Fetal surgery. *Western J. Med.* 159, 341–349.

Harrison, M., Golbus, M., and Filly, R. (1990). "The Unborn Patient: Prenatal Diagnosis and Treatment," 2nd ed. Saunders, Philadelphia.

Heaney, J. H. (Ed.) (1992). "Abortion: A New Generation of Catholic Responses." The Pope John Center, Braintree, MA.

Keeling, J. W. (Ed.) (1993). "Fetal and Neonatal Pathology," 2nd ed. Springer-Verlag, London.

Reece, A. *et. al.* (1995). "Handbook of Medicine of the Fetus & Mother." Lippincott, Philadelphia.

Singer, P. (1993). "Practical Ethics," 2nd ed. Cambridge Univ. Press, Cambridge, UK.

FREEDOM OF SPEECH

Larry Alexander
University of San Diego

GLOSSARY

autonomy The condition of being self-governing.
compossible Describing the ability of individuals' rights to coexist without conflicting in any possible situation.
consequentialist Referring to theories of ethical justification that base ethical assessment of acts exclusively on their consequences.
deontological Referring to theories of ethical justification that base ethical assessment on features of acts other than and in addition to their consequences.
incidental restrictions Restrictions on speech that are not aimed at its communicative aspect.

FREEDOM OF SPEECH is widely held to be a moral right and almost as widely recognized as a legal right. It was defended by John Milton in the 17th century and enshrined in the Constitution of the United States in 1791 as part of the First Amendment. Some form of recognition of freedom of speech is expressed in almost every modern constitution and international protocol regarding human rights. Yet, as revealed by the jurisprudence under the First Amendment of the United States Constitution—which is by far the most developed free speech jurisprudence—and the enormous body of philosophical and legal commentary on freedom of speech, the justification(s) for and the contours of freedom of speech are much mooted. Moreover, there are some, even in liberal democracies, who deny any special importance to freedom of speech, and there are others who deny its coherence as a concept.

I. THE SCOPE OF FREEDOM OF SPEECH: WHAT IS "SPEECH"?

Freedom of speech has always been thought to cover more than what is literally speech, that is, spoken language. For example, no one disputes that it covers written language as well as spoken language. Moreover, it is difficult to see how it could be withheld from sign language, pictographs, pictures, movies, plays, and so forth, and indeed the legal protection afforded freedom of speech has been extended to all of these media of communication and expression, as well as to abstract artistic and musical performances. Usually, then, freedom of speech refers to—and is frequently referred to as—freedom of expression or freedom of communication.

It is a commonplace to distinguish between "speech" and "symbolic speech." As the previous paragraph should make clear, however, that distinction is illusory. All speech employs symbols, whether they be sounds, shapes, gestures, pictures, or any other tangible medium. There is thus no such thing as nonsymbolic speech; there is only speech that employs symbols that are less or more conventional. The same point also applies to any purported distinction between speech and "conduct" or "action." All speech requires conduct of some sort, and any conduct can be communicative. The conclusion to be drawn is that freedom of speech should be thought of as freedom of communication.

II. WHO HAS THE RIGHT TO FREEDOM OF SPEECH?

It is most natural to think that if there is a right to freedom of speech, it must be the right of the speaker. Thus, when the government threatens S with punishment if he attempts to give certain information to A, we are tempted to regard this as a violation of S's right to freedom of speech.

On most accounts of why freedom of speech should be protected, however, it is A's freedom of speech that is violated whether or not S's freedom of speech is also violated. For assume that S is the author of a book and is now dead (or the citizen of a foreign country). He has no freedom of speech now in A's country. If A's government is violating anyone's rights by prohibiting the dissemination of S's book, it is A's (the audience's) rights. Moreover, if A's government prohibited A from watching sunsets because it feared A would be inspired to have subversive thoughts, freedom of speech would arguably be implicated, *even though there is no speaker*.

In suggesting that the right to freedom of speech is best thought of as belonging to the audience, I do not mean to imply that people have a claim right against the government or anyone else that they be spoken to or provided with information. If the right of freedom of speech ultimately belongs to the audience, it is in the form of a right not to be prevented from obtaining information or ideas that are otherwise available to it.

In saying that free speech is best thought of as a right of the audience, I also am not saying that speakers have no standing to object to having their speech suppressed. Frequently it will best serve the audience's right to hear if speakers are given a derivative right to speak. Indeed, in most cases where government interdicts a communication between a willing speaker and her audience, the speaker will be in the best position to assert the right to freedom of speech, both because the audience may be unaware of the attempted communication and because the audience's right depends upon the speaker's being willing to speak. (The right is not a claim right against the speaker that she speak.)

III. WHAT ARE THE JUSTIFICATIONS FOR FREEDOM OF SPEECH?

There are numerous theories regarding the justification(s) for freedom of speech. Each theory produces a different conception of what freedom of speech encompasses and when it is violated. I shall lump the theories into four broad groupings.

A. Consequentialist Theories

1. The Search for Truth

One common justification advanced on behalf of freedom of speech is that such freedom is instrumental to the discovery of truth. Freedom to disseminate new information and to criticize prevailing views is necessary for eliminating misconceptions of fact and value.

Although this justification is frequently criticized as resting on a philosophically naive realist view about facts and values, that criticism is off the mark. The justification for free inquiry as a means for discovering truth is not tied to any particular metaphysical view about fact or value.

The real problem with this justification is not in what it assumes about the nature of truth but in what it assumes is the best procedure for obtaining truth. In domains in which obtaining truth is the principal value—for example, in legal proceedings—speech is regulated and circumscribed. Even in the area of scientific inquiry, professional journals refuse to publish claims that the editors believe are not properly substantiated, and faculties and laboratories refuse to employ those who hold what in the opinion of the faculties and laboratories are outlandish views.

Moreover, it is a mistake to assume that truth is something quantifiable, so that we can assess alternative regimes based on how much "truth" each produces. There is no *single thing* called Truth that we can obtain, either absolutely or in varying degrees. To ask whether a regulation promotes or impedes Truth is to ask a question that is essentially meaningless, like asking how many individual things there are in the universe. All regulations, and all failures to regulate, produce different environments, and each environment reveals some truths and obscures others.

Of course the truthseekers might want to see the question posed differently. Instead of posing the question in a way that invokes Truth, one might pose a specific truth-seeking question: whether a specific regulation promotes or impedes a scientific truth.

One should concede that there are specific truths—"right answers" to specific truth-seeking questions. One should concede that some of those specific truths can be viewed as particularly important to obtain. These concessions having been made, it would follow that if (1) a governmental regulation interferes with the search for the answer to a particular question—a particular truth—and if (2) obtaining the answer to that particular question is viewed as very important, then (3) the regulation is unjustified unless (4) the other values served, or "truths" revealed, by the regulation are equally as important as obtaining the answer to that particular question.

For example, one might believe that forbidding the publication of the *Pentagon Papers* substantially obstructs the search for the truth about U.S. involvement in Vietnam, and that the "truths" and other values served by keeping the *Pentagon Papers* secret are less important than the truth about that involvement. If one subscribes to this belief, then one will condemn any attempt to restrain the publication of the *Pentagon Papers*, even though, because of other values that would be implicated, one might not allow citizens to search the Pentagon looking for those papers, or one might punish those whose thievery was responsible for their publication.

The problem with the "quest for truth" as a theory of free speech in the "specific truths" sense is that one cannot extrapolate from the quest for specific truths to any recognizable general theory of free speech. The quest for specific truths demonstrates only that some speech does help answer some questions that are relatively important, and that regulation of speech sometimes will be unjustified. Other speech contributes little toward answering some questions; some activities other than speech contribute a great deal toward answering some questions; and answering some questions is less important than, and occasionally is downright destructive of, other values that even avid specific-truth seekers would want to protect or maximize.

2. Maximization of Other Values

There are other values besides Truth that freedom of speech might advance. These values are various; they include individual self-rule, individual self-develop-ment, and political self-rule. To the extent that we can characterize these theories as based on the general value of autonomy, they seek to maximize autonomy rather than to treat it as some absolute or near-absolute side constraint.

The autonomy these theories seek to maximize, however, is not affected only by regulations aimed at communicative impact, that is, by regulations designed to prevent audiences from learning certain information or hearing certain arguments or opinions. Autonomy also is affected by any regulation that affects the information and opinions one receives—that is, by all governmental regulations. All of government's regulations—those affecting access to information; access to the indefinite diversity of the media of communication; access to private property in others' possession that may be useful for communicating generally, certain ideas, or in a particular form—affect the ideas that individuals receive. Hence, *all* government regulations influence individuals' self-rule and self-development. And, of course, the interests that government balances against speech—such as security of person, security of property, and protection of privacy—all affect autonomy values.

Thus, these consequentialist theories all require some sort of balancing mechanism. Balancing is required so that government can, for example, decide whether allowing Able to burn Baker's dollar bill without Baker's consent (in order, say, to protest inflation in front of a particular audience and with a particular communicative effect) advances autonomy more than not allowing Able to do so (with the resulting benefits of protecting security of property while permitting whatever speech would result if property allocations were undisturbed, and so forth).

Consequentialist theories require that speech be assigned a "proper value" in furthering autonomy. They likewise require that other values be assigned "proper weights" relative to autonomy. Surely "speech" has some value, and surely the value of "speech" varies with its truth, its importance, and so forth. Therefore, these theories require some government agency—ultimately courts or legislatures—to assess speech for its truth, importance, and so forth, as well as to balance the value of "speech" against other values.

None of these theories justifies the special treatment of "speech" as distinguished from other activities that contribute to autonomy. None of them justifies distinguishing courts from primary governmental decision makers, either by treating courts as more trustworthy balances or by recognizing a special need for a second opinion from the courts with respect to "speech" but not with respect to other activities. None of these theories even presents a comprehensive scheme for balancing speech against other activities that contribute to autonomy. None of them, indeed, presents a comprehensive scheme for balancing "autonomy" against other values.

B. Democratic Theories

Freedom of speech is usually thought of as a right to be asserted against the government, even when, as, for example, in the United States, that government is democratic in nature. Yet a very prominent group of justificatory theories of freedom of speech find the central justification of that freedom to be its affiliation with democratic decision making. One idea is that democratic decision making requires an informed citizenry, and an informed citizenry requires freedom of speech. A separate idea is that democratic (in form) decision making is legitimate (and truly democratic) only if public opinion is not itself shaped by the government.

Versions of democratic justifications of freedom of speech vary in scope. Some versions are very narrow, treating freedom of speech as concerned only with communications about governmental policies and personnel. Others are much broader, arguing that informed self-rule requires protection of scientific, literary, artistic, and other types of speech along with the overtly political. The broadest of these theories are operationally indistinguishable from either those which justify freedom of speech as maximizing autonomy, as already discussed, or those which justify it as a deontological side constraint, as discussed further on.

The problem with justifying freedom of speech by its relation to democratic decision making is that both being democratic and being informed are matters of degree. A regime that protects freedom of speech from democratically passed restrictions is in one sense—an informed citizenry—more democratic, and in another sense—democratic laws are struck down—less democratic, than a regime in which democratic decision making is unlimited. Moreover, no citizenry is ever perfectly informed about anything; all information about some things comes at a cost, including the cost of displacing information about other things, and all laws, including laws restricting freedom of speech, bring some new information and opinions into the world at the same time that they eliminate other information and opinions.

C. Deontological Theories

The last group of justificatory theories view freedom of speech as justified, not by its ability to maximize some value such as truth or autonomy, and not by its association with a particular form of government, but by an argument from an asserted moral right not to have government prevent people from having certain ideas because of its fear that they will not respond to those ideas appropriately. The right is deontological in character. Its recognition is not something to be maximized. Rather, it is a side constraint on government's action.

These deontological theories logically require that we look not at government's laws per se, but at government's reasons for enacting those laws. If the reasons are to prevent people from having certain ideas, then freedom of speech is implicated, even if there is no act of communication in the normal sense. Thus, a law banning rallies in residential neighborhoods because of concern with noise or traffic would not implicate freedom of speech under these theories. On the other hand, a law banning toy soldiers based on a concern about creating positive views of militarism would. The root idea is that people have a right that government not take action predicated on its concern that they may otherwise possess ideas that they will act on in harmful ways.

D. Other Theories of Proscribed Government Motives

A final group of theories would have us look at government's reasons for acting, not because people have a deontological right that government not concern itself with their thoughts, but because it is improper for other reasons or dangerous for government to be permitted to act on its views about the worthiness or harmfulness of ideas. Some of these theories are deontological in form, positing, for example, a duty on government to treat ideas with equal respect. Others are consequentialist in orientation, arguing that government is more likely to overestimate the benefits and underestimate the costs of trying to affect what people think through coercion.

Some of these motive theories would have courts ferret out the forbidden motives behind laws directly. Others would have the courts do so indirectly, through various presumptions and burdens of proof. Some, indeed, find the first amendment jurisprudence in the United States most explicable on this latter basis.

IV. THE MAJOR CLASSIFICATIONS OF GOVERNMENT ACTS IMPLICATING FREEDOM OF SPEECH

A. Laws Directed at the Content of Speech

At the core of freedom of speech is a concern over laws directed at the content—the communicative impact—of speech. If any type of law violates freedom of speech, it is a law that picks out certain ideas and prohibits or restricts their communication.

Nonetheless, even laws aimed at interdicting the communication of certain ideas are frequently deemed not to violate freedom of speech. To understand why, it is most useful to examine the linkage between the communication of the idea and the ultimate harm that is the government's concern.

1. Harms That Government May Not Legitimately Seek to Prevent

Freedom of speech itself is usually deemed to make certain "harms" matters with which government has no legitimate concern. For example, government has no legitimate concern with whether people think well of it. Nor does government have a legitimate concern with the religious and political ideas and values of its adult citizens, or their cultural tastes, at least not to the extent that would license governmental attempts to suppress communication.

2. Harms Caused in Two Steps

Frequently when government suppresses speech based on its content, it is seeking to prevent a harm that it may legitimately attempt to prevent. Thus, if S incites A to kill government officials, the government may legitimately prevent A from doing so, and punish A if he attempts to do so.

Here, the ultimate harm that the government may legitimately prevent—killing government officials—is connected to the inciting speech in two steps: The inciting speech communicates the idea to A, and A then decides to act on the idea. The question for freedom of speech is whether the government may seek to prevent the harm more effectively by targeting the first step in addition to the second step.

Laws against inciting or soliciting crimes, advocating the overthrow of the government by force, provoking another to fight, revealing information useful to domestic terrorists or other criminals, and the like are examples of laws suppressing speech based on its content in order to prevent a harm that requires a still further step. The free speech jurisprudence of the United States was largely developed in response to laws of this type, at least into the 1960s.

3. Harms Caused in One Step

Frequently, once information has been communicated to A, there is nothing further the government can do to prevent harm, either because mere possession of this information by A is itself harmful, or because, although the harm will not eventuate without further action by A, government cannot legitimately prevent that further action.

Examples of such harms caused by the content of speech are numerous. They include revelation of secret, confidential, or private information; defamation; infringement of copyright or other property interests in speech; offense; interference with a fair trial; coercion; deception; assault; and adverse effects on the morale or efficiency of governmental operations. (The content of speech can bring about these last harms by causing friction among government employees, causing loss of confidence in government employees among the public clientele, or revealing disloyal or inappropriate attitudes of public employees.) In each of these cases, the question is whether the speech interests of S and A override the competing values.

B. Incidental Restrictions on Speech

Laws directed at the content of speech obviously raise freedom of speech issues. But such laws are not by any means the exclusive determinants of what gets said, by whom, to whom, and with what effect. Indeed, *all laws* have effects on what gets said, by whom, to whom, and with what impact. That is, all laws have information effects.

Thus, arguably the domain of free speech includes not only restrictions on obstructing traffic while speaking or demonstrating, using amplifying devices in residential neighborhoods, posting signs on utility poles, burning draft cards, or sleeping in parks, but also includes tort, contract, and property law, the tax code, and the multitude of criminal and regulatory laws and administrative regulations. For example, laws determining who owns what property under what restrictions or the price and availability of various resources will also determine what gets said, by whom, to whom, and with what effect—that is, the laws will have information effects. A change in the laws of any region of the corpus juris will have information effects. Laws equalizing income would surely have dramatic information effects. Any law, however, and any change in law, will have cognizable effects which will translate into information of some kind.

The courts of the United States have treated some incidental regulations of speech as raising free speech issues, though the jurisprudence has been murky, the number of cases finding free speech violations few, and the choice of which laws to review apparently unprincipled. There is a reason for these problems. If all laws have information effects, then all alternatives to those laws will also have information effects. For example, the setting of the marginal tax rate affects my income, which, if greater, I might devote to increased speaking. The courts could rule that if the government's interest in the present rate is not significant, and the rate adversely affects my speech, the government must abandon that rate in favor of another rate. But any other rate the government chooses will affect somebody's speech—it may result in lower transfer payments, adversely affecting the communication between poorer speakers and their audience—and, thus, *it* will have to serve a significant interest as well.

If all laws—and therefore all alternative sets of laws—have information effects, then courts assessing such laws in terms of freedom of speech need some Archimedean point from which to evaluate such laws and sets of laws. But if freedom of speech functions principally as a bar to government's imposing an evaluation on the content of speech—and since courts are part of the government—freedom of speech arguably and paradoxically requires the courts to forgo reviewing incidental restrictions on speech, even though incidental restrictions have far more important information effects than content restrictions.

Such a conclusion is consistent with the deontological justifications for freedom of speech. They make freedom of speech an issue when and only when government's acts are motivated by government's desire to keep audiences from having certain information or ideas. On the other hand, consequentialist and democratic justifications would arguably require evaluation of information effects across the board, regardless of the type of law (content-directed or incidental restriction) in question.

C. Government Speech and Subsidies of Private Speech

Another area where freedom of speech is arguably implicated is where the government itself "speaks." That area includes not only such acts as government's issuing pamphlets describing laws and programs and government's advertising opportunities in government employment and the military, but also government's running the public schools and universities. Still more broadly it includes government's subsidizing those private speakers who deliver government's message, so long as we are dealing with a true subsidy rather than a penalty on those who refuse to deliver the message.

Some believe that the principle of freedom of speech renders all or some of these acts illegitimate. Others believe that such acts are entirely consistent with freedom of speech. The latter argue that freedom of speech is restricted to coercive government action. The former respond that government action is always coercive in that it involves resources involuntarily extracted from the citizenry that could be devoted to alternative communication and information.

D. Private Suppression of Speech

Although as a legal matter freedom of speech is usually concerned with laws and other governmental acts, it is common to refer to freedom of speech in purely private contexts as well. Thus, if our (private) employer forbids us to discuss politics on the job, or asks us to donate to her political party if we wish to be promoted, we are quite likely to argue that such directives violate our freedom of speech—so, too, if a private residential organization refuses to let pamphleteers enter a gated community, or if a private shopping center bans petition gathering from its premises.

Under the deontological justification theories, the question is whether the private employer or landowner is exercising *its* rights. If so, then, assuming deontological rights are compossible, it is not violating any free speech rights. Of course, it may be acting wrongly even if within its rights. And the autonomy value that lies behind the deontological right of freedom of speech may explain the wrongness even if it does elevate it to the level of rights violation.

The consequentialist theories would not in principle exempt private speech suppression from their purview. Indeed, if the private speech suppression is permitted by law, then *its* free speech status is really just another way of putting the status of those laws that permit it, a matter already touched on in the section on incidental restrictions on speech.

Also See the Following Articles

AUTONOMY • CENSORSHIP • CONSEQUENTIALISM AND DEONTOLOGY

Bibliography

Alexander, L. (1993). Trouble on track two: Incidental regulations of speech and free speech theory. *Hastings Law J.* **44**, 921–962.

Garvey, J., and Schauer, F. (1996). "The First Amendment," 2nd ed. West, St. Paul, MN.

Kagan, E. (1996). Private speech, public purpose: The role of govern- mental motive in first amendment doctrine. *Univ. Chicago Law Rev.* **63**, 413–517.

Post, R. (1995). Recuperating first amendment doctrine. *Stanford Law Rev.* **47**, 1249–1281.

Schauer, F. (1992). Uncoupling free speech. *Columbia Law Rev.* **92**, 1321–1357.

Sunstein, C. R. (1993). "Democracy and the Problem of Free Speech." The Free Press, New York.

FREEDOM OF THE PRESS IN THE USA

Stephen Klaidman
Kennedy Institute of Ethics, Georgetown University

GLOSSARY

communitarian Someone who believes that the rights of the community should generally be given preference over the rights of individuals.

deontology The doctrine that some acts are morally required, irrespective of their consequences.

libertarian Someone who believes that the rights of individuals should generally be given preference over the rights of the state.

utilitarianism The doctrine that morality is most effectively calculated from consequences.

NO CONTEMPORARY EVALUATION of the roles and responsibilities of the American news media is possible without revisiting core historical issues: the social, philosophical, and legal content of freedom of speech and of the press. This is so because many of the most important unresolved questions having to do with press freedom in the age of megamedia corporations and satellite feeds are left over from the age of printer-publishers and

political pamphleteers. We are still groping, for example, to discover the moral and legal limits of inquiry in reporting on public persons. We have no settled idea of what values, if any, ought ever to prevail in a conflict with the right to free speech or freedom of the press. We have no clear conception of whether the press has specific moral obligations to provide public benefits or to avoid harms to the general public or to particular individuals. And it remains unresolved precisely what is meant by the language in the First Amendment to the Constitution that says "Congress shall make no law abridging ... the freedom of the press."

The debate about what the media ought and ought not do is sometimes framed as a conflict between libertarian and communitarian perspectives on the problem of freedom of the press. For libertarians, press freedom is as much a vehicle for individual self-expression as it is an instrument for informing the public. The fact that it provides an opportunity for individuals to realize their human potential by the relatively uninhibited expression of opinions and ideas is seen as central to its value. It is viewed as an extension of a fundamental right to self-expression recognized in the free-speech clause of the First Amendment. Communitarians value press freedom principally because it encourages an open exchange of ideas, opinions, insights, and information, and such an exchange is essential to the functioning of a representative democracy in which the people regularly choose their own leaders and have additional means of influencing public policy. Because libertarians place an extremely high value on individual expression and the rights of the individual generally, they are more likely to be absolutists about press freedom. Communitarians, who are more concerned with the general welfare than with individual liberty, are more often inclined to balance the social worth of press freedom against competing social values such as national security, privacy, and fair trial.

It is central to this discussion that the First Amendment treats freedom of the press as distinct from freedom of speech. The amendment's specific recognition of the press, and much of the surrounding debate, reflects the framers' opinion that the press is something other than just a vehicle for self-expression. If that were not so, the press clause would be redundant. It is true that in the 18th century the American press was a highly politicized vehicle for often scathing self-expression that could be exercised by anyone who owned or had access to a small print shop. James Madison and his colleagues shared the views of Milton, Bentham, and Hume on freedom of expression for individuals, and they respected the rights of all citizens to publish broadsheets and pamphlets venting their personal views. But it is clear from the debate surrounding press freedom in colonial America that the extraordinary protection the press was granted under the law derived mainly if not exclusively from its value to society as a disseminator of news and opinion.

Madison, the principal drafter of the First Amendment, viewed the press as a social institution whose free and independent existence was a condition of democracy. Nevertheless, it is not self-evident from the 18th-century debates that Madison, Thomas Jefferson, or any of their contemporaries believed that press freedom had to prevail every time it clashed with the imperatives of other valued social institutions. Jefferson characterized the importance of the press as it was understood by 18th-century American democrats in its most memorable form:

> The basis of our government being the opinion of the people, the very first object should be to keep that right; and were it left to me to decide whether we should have a government without newspapers, or newspapers without a government, I should not hesitate a moment to prefer the latter.

> (letter to Col. Edward Carrington, 16 Jan. 1787)

The role Jefferson envisaged for the press was to provide the people with the information they needed to reach informed conclusions about the nation's business.

However, Jefferson, like the First Amendment, was silent on the question of the responsibility of the press. And neither he nor Madison had much specific to say about balancing press freedom against other values, in either moral or legal contexts. It has been left to the philosophers and lawyers of succeeding generations to sort out these questions. Law professor Paul A. Freund, put it this way:

> Whatever the philosophic bases for freedom of expression—whether as an indispensable means to the discovery and spread of truth or as a fulfillment of the human vocation to seek to persuade, to inform, to entertain, and to astonish one another—the freedom is, as I have said, defeasible in smaller or larger measure. To regard it as never requiring accommodation with the interests of integrity, security, personal reputation, and human dignity would be to take part of the values of life—however grand a part—in place of the whole, in the realm of public policy to commit the offense of political synecdoche.

> (Autumn 1975. *Am. Scholar,* 546)

Much of the rest of this chapter is devoted to specifying and defining some of the responsibilities of the American press, specifically in its role of reporting news in contrast to providing a forum for opinion. But first let us briefly outline some principles involved in dealing with conflicts between press freedom and other values. To do that, it is essential to distinguish between conflicts that arise in law and those that, because they raise no legal questions, arise in a strictly moral framework.

I. DEALING WITH CONFLICTS BETWEEN PRESS FREEDOM AND OTHER VALUES

Because democratic societies, if they are to function, must vigorously protect individual liberty to speak and promote a free flow of information and opinion, the law must provide a high degree of protection to all forms of speech, including, of course, the form exercised by the press. This protection of expression is especially important because what seems true today may seem false or even invidious to the well-being of society tomorrow, and what seems true and fair to one thoughtful, intelligent person may seem false, scurrilous, or both to another. One way to grasp the point is to consider the history of split decisions on the Supreme Court and to recognize the great dissenting opinions among them that subsequently became law (A. Barth, 1974. *Prophets with Honor.* Knopf, New York).

Although most Americans are not so naive as to believe that in the marketplace of ideas truth always drives out falsehood, at least not in a timely fashion, they have found no better way to test ideas and opinions than to let them circulate freely. It is a matter of societal consensus in the United States, therefore, that no matter how unpopular the ideas or opinions being expressed, they are entitled to the full protection of the law. This broad consensus, however, is a mid-20th-century phenomenon, and it is not without exceptions that remain unsettled in law, such as expressions of obscenity in some circumstances. This legal presumption in favor of free speech and press freedom does not mean that journalists have a moral right to speak, broadcast, or publish without consideration for competing values or the consequences of their actions. No utilitarian calculus would support such a view, and the best-known of all deontological theories, Kant's, is of little use when moral imperatives collide. The British philosopher Isaiah Berlin offered this context for considering what happens when values clash:

> What is clear is that values can clash—that is why civilizations are incompatible. [Values] can be incompatible between cultures, or groups in the same culture, or between you and me. You believe in always telling the truth, no matter what; I do not, because I believe that it can sometimes be too painful and too destructive. We can discuss each other's point of view, we can try to reach common ground, but in the end what you pursue may not be reconcilable with the ends to which I find that I have dedicated my life. Values may easily clash within the breast of a single individual; and it does not follow that, if they do, some must be true and others false. Justice, rigorous justice, is for some people an absolute value, but it is not compatible with what may be no less ultimate values for them—mercy, compassion, as arises in concrete cases. . . . Some among the Great Goods cannot live together. That is a conceptual truth. We are doomed to choose and every choice may entail an irreparable loss.
>
> (March 17, 1988. *N.Y. Rev. Books,* 15)

Sir Isaiah has simply stated the human condition: life is about hard choices. Press freedom is a cardinal social value, but there are times when it must compete with other cardinal values, and times when it should yield. As Sir Isaiah's argument suggests, value disputes cannot be resolved by rules of thumb. Because values are fundamental beliefs, it is no simple matter to weigh one against another. Yet that is what must be done. For example, intuitively, it sounds right to say that press freedom should give way when innocent lives are at stake. But suppose the life at stake is that of a clandestine agent on a mission in a foreign country that violates U.S. law, and the risk of the agent's being killed if a story is broadcast or published can be calculated at about 10%. Similarly, when it appears that someone's right to a fair trial would be prejudiced by disclosure of certain information, should not the press withhold that information? Maybe, but what if the information is verifiably true and the result of not publishing it is likely to be that a murderer who has threatened to kill 10 other people will go free?

Morally it makes no sense to hold out press freedom as an absolute value, because it will inevitably clash with other values that have equally good or, rather, equally poor claims to being treated as absolutes. The question of how much freedom the press should be given under the law, however, is somewhat more complicated. Because it is often difficult or even impossible to calculate the relative benefits and harms of publishing or broadcasting specific pieces of information, because the suppression of free expression is such an obvious and important harm, because the circulation of information is such an obvious and important good, and because the temptation on the part of the powerful to suppress information that is contrary to their interests is so strong, a potent argument can be made against imposing any legal restrictions on the press. Yet many who are otherwise avid First Amendment absolutists do not argue against a ban on publishing information about the movement of troop ships in wartime, to cite a classic example. And many who are virtual First Amendment absolutists would ban the publication of child pornography.

A more difficult case, recently decided by a federal appeals court, involved the delivery of classified photographs to a British military publisher by a U.S. Navy analyst (*U.S. v. Morison,* U.S. Court of Appeals for the Fourth Circuit, Richmond, VA). In 1984 Samuel Loring Morison turned over to Jane's Publishing Company, for whom he did freelance work, three secret spy satellite photographs of the Soviet Union's first nuclear aircraft carrier, which was under construction at a Black Sea shipyard. In 1985 Morison was convicted by a federal court in Baltimore of theft of government property and espionage (*U.S. v. Morison,* U.S. District Court, Baltimore, MD). A three-judge appeals panel unanimously upheld the verdict in April. Morison was not convicted as a journalist, which he was in his freelance role for Jane's, but as a government employee; as a result the appeals court's main opinion by Judge Donald Stuart Russell declared the First Amendment essentially irrelevant to his defense. It is true, nonetheless, as Judge J. Harvie Wilkinson III pointed out in a concurring opinion, that the First Amendment interests in the case were not "insignificant" because "criminal restraints on the disclosure of information threaten the ability of the press to scrutinize and report on governmental activity."

The *Washington Post* wrote in an editorial, "Surely the government has a right—even an obligation—to protect the kind of national security information that could, if secretly slipped into the hands of a foreign power, harm the nation. . . . But never before has anyone been convicted of espionage for giving secret information to the press." The *Post's* conclusion was, "The ruling . . . should be overturned by the full court of appeals or the Supreme Court" (6 April 1988. *Washington Post*, A-24). The Morison case represents a clear-cut clash between two values: the government's right to protect secrets essential to the national security and the press's need for a broad mantle of protection under which it can report freely on issues that might be improperly classified and about which the public might have a need to know. (The Soviet Union already had had the manual for the KH-11 spy satellite in question "secretly slipped into [its] hands," so it seems unlikely that Morison's breach of security had grave implications. The precedent set by the court, however, could significantly influence future rulings in cases involving all classified information.)

The *Post* argued that, because the Morison decision has the potential for chilling reporting on classified matters, it should be reversed. But the *Post's* argument does not come to grips with the central issue. The photographs Morison provided to the British publisher were printed in *Jane's Defence Weekly*, a publication readily available to anyone who cares to buy it, and subsequently some of them were published in several general circulation newspapers. It is possible, therefore, even if in this specific instance it might not be likely, that Soviet analysts, by studying the photographs in the journal, might have learned something detrimental to U.S. security interests. It is logical to wonder, therefore, how great the difference would be if the information were "secretly slipped into the hands of" the Soviet Union? In either case the potential might have existed to compromise national security.

At the same time, it seems equally clear that an all-encompassing legal ban on government employees' disclosing classified information would have an undue chilling effect on the free flow of information. One solution could be narrowly drawn legislation that specifically bans what Morison did, that is, make available for publication (or broadcast) photographs (or information) that compromise U.S. intelligence sources. But it will not do to imply that whenever there is a possible chilling effect, the real conflict of values involved need not be addressed at all.

Therefore, although there is a strong historical and philosophical case for giving freedom of speech and freedom of the press extraordinary protections because of their intrinsic value, and their value as a precondition to many other freedoms, the case for protecting them absolutely is unsustainable. Even as staunch a defender of free speech and free press as the philosopher Alexander Meiklejohn wrote,

> No one can doubt that, in any well-governed society, the legislature has both the right and the duty to prohibit certain forms of speech. Libellous assertions may be, and must be, forbidden and punished. So too must slander. Words which incite men to crime are themselves criminal and must be dealt with as such. Sedition or treason may be expressed by speech or writing. And, in those cases, decisive repressive action by the government is imperative for the sake of the general welfare. All these necessities that speech be limited are recognized and provided for under the constitution.

(1948. *Free Speech*, p. 18. Harper & Brothers, New York)

Although debate continues about whether the First Amendment was meant to be as absolute as its language suggests, there is fairly widespread agreement that anything that does not constitute a "clear and present danger" to the national security, with the emphasis on "clear and present," may be published. Punishment, if any, is to be meted out after the fact. The judicial history supporting this view runs through a series of Supreme Court cases known to First Amendment scholars as *Schenk, Abrams, Near,* and the *Pentagon Papers* cases, to name perhaps the best-known among them. There are those who argue as well that even penalties after the fact are an unwarranted encroachment on press freedom, but that remains a minority position. Here again it is important to note that the legal right to publish provides no moral sanction for publishing.

To make the transition from legal rights to moral

duties is, in effect, to introduce the subject of responsibility. If the press has the *right* to publish just about anything in just about any fashion, *responsibility* entails making choices about what to publish and in what fashion. It seems a truism to say that the press ought to be responsbile. Yet Alan Barth, one of the most thoughtful journalists and civil libertarians of our time, calls it into question. Barth wrote,

> Now, a press which enjoys such independence of the government [as the American press does] is, almost by definition, in some degree irresponsible. And no one ought to be surprised if it behaves at times altogether irresponsibly. A measure of irresponsibility was the price which had to be paid—and which the Founders were quite prepared to pay—for the independence without which the press could not discharge its vital function.
>
> A great deal has been said in a great many lectures by a great many eloquent lecturers concerning the irresponsibility of American newspapers. I do not propose to add to that indictment.... On the contrary, I mean to raise a rather different question for your consideration. I want to ask—and not altogether rhetorically by any means—whether the press in the United States today has not become excessively *responsible,* whether it has not, in fact, to an alarming degree, become a mouthpiece and partner of the government, rather than a censor.

> (1984. In *The Rights of Free Men* (J. E. Clayton, Ed.), pp. 292–293. Knopf, New York)

Barth's concern is not idle, but his language might be misunderstood outside the culture of journalism. If I understand correctly, what he means by "excessively responsible" is too careful, or too easily co-opted by official sources. In other words, if the press is too docile, it is unlikely to fulfill its responsibility as a watchdog of government. Nowhere, however, does Barth argue that the press *ought* to be irresponsible. He saw some degree of "irresponsible" conduct as an unwelcome but unavoidable side effect of doing what the press does in the circumstances in which the press does it. He had a clear personal sense of what it meant to be a responsible journalist and practiced his craft accordingly. What follows is an attempt to define responsibility in American journalism in a way that would satisfy the exacting criteria of a journalist of the probity and intelligence of Barth. The following criteria are ideals in the sense

that they do not reflect commercial pressures exerted on newsrooms in the highly competitive media marketplace. They are, however, attainable, at least in print journalism. Many reporters and editors meet them regularly.

II. RESPONSIBILITY OF THE PRESS

Responsibilities in journalism, or in any profession for that matter, fall into two categories: role responsibilities, that is, those that go specifically with the calling, and general moral responsibilities such as fairness and telling the truth. Role responsibilities, of course, vary by definition. As for general moral responsibilities, some are more relevant to certain professions than to others. For example, the duty of beneficence, to do good, specifically and concretely, seems more applicable to medicine than to journalism. What follows are a brief description of the role responsibilities of journalists and an effort to give content to the most relevant general moral responsibilities.

The press, as has already been indicated, is both an outlet for expression and a means of circulating news, ideas, opinions, and other kinds of information. But it is as a disseminator of information, not as a vehicle for anyone's self-expression, that the press has been given explicit constitutional protection, and therefore it is from this role that responsibility most directly flows. When the two values clashed, the issue was decided by the Supreme Court. A political candidate's suit to force a newspaper to publish a reply to editorials criticizing his record was denied. The court ruled that the newspaper was not obliged to give him access to its columns (*Miami Herald Publishing Co. v. Tornillo,* 1974). Chief Justice Warren Burger wrote the following opinion for the Court:

> A newspaper is more than a passive receptacle or conduit for news, comment, and advertising. The choice of material to go into a newspaper, and the decisions made as to limitations on the size and content of the paper, and treatment of public issues and public officials—whether fair or unfair—constitute the exercise of editorial control and judgment. It has yet to be demonstrated how governmental regulation of this crucial process can be exercised consistent with First Amendment guarantees of a free press as they have evolved to this time.

> (*Tornillo,* 1974)

The ruling denies access to someone seeking to be heard with the underlying purpose of protecting the press's ability to inform people without inhibition about all the matters that are material to their concerns as citizens. From such powerful protection of the prerogatives of the press flows a profound responsibility to report on these matters in a way that meets the public's needs. What are these needs? In asking whether "the news as we experience it [is] promoting democratic liberty?" William Henry III suggests an answer (Spring 1987. *Gannett Center J.,* 114). But the formulation is vague. It can be made concrete by specifying the informational requirements of an idealized reader or viewer who represents the public. The section that follows attempts to do that and thereby to give content to the fundamental responsibility of the American press. Although it is not a verbatim account, it is based substantially on my earlier research with Tom L. Beauchamp published in a volume titled *The Virtuous Journalist* (1987. Chap. 2. Oxford Univ. Press, New York).

III. THE REASONABLE READER

As a rough standard, what the press collectively has a duty to report is correlated with what the public has a need to know. In reflecting on how the press can meet that standard, it is useful to draw on a legal model known as "the reasonable person," which for purposes of greater specificity can be transformed into a model called the reasonable reader or viewer. This model is designed to incorporate the common body of assumptions that members of a society make about their fellow citizens in order to cooperate efficiently. The reasonable person is never to be understood as either a specific person or an average person. In the words of William Prosser, "he is a prudent and careful man who is always up to standard. . . . He is a personification of the community ideal of reasonable behavior (1971. *The Law of Torts,* 4th ed., p. 151. West, St. Paul, MN). Under a standard such as this, a journalist can be found negligent even if the information provided is well within the bounds of accepted professional practice.

As this suggests, the reasonable reader standard is to be understood from the point of view of a reader's needs for information rather than from the perspective of routine media practices. The reasonable reader is the community ideal of an informed person with informational needs that the so-called "quality," general news media are designed, or at least ought to be designed, to serve. This general model provides a guide for establishing standards of completeness, accuracy, under-standing, and objectivity that are intended to yield, within attainable limits, useful, fair, and impartial journalism.

To make the concept more concrete, consider this question. In a first story about the 1979 nuclear accident at Three Mile Island in Pennsylvania, what would the reasonable reader living in California need to know and have a right to expect from a local California newspaper? Initially, there is a need to know what happened and what is known about the safety, health, and economic implications of the event. The reasonable reader would not be interested in the press's comparisons of the event to a contemporaneous film (*The China Syndrome*) that treats the subject of a nuclear accident in fictional form. But the reader would need to know how much risk was associated with the accident and whether there were similar nuclear plants located in the reader's area. As the story develops, more information will be needed about how the utility and the government were handling the aftermath of the accident, what had been learned about how the accident happened, how it could be expected to affect the physical and mental health of persons living in the area, and what implications the accident had for the nuclear power industry. As is always the case with an unfolding event or series of events, it would take more than one story to meet the reasonable reader's needs. Follow-up stories should continue to appear as long as those needs remained unmet.

A. Completeness

Given the constraints of print and even more so of electronic journalism, any standard of completeness must be reasonably flexible. If the concept of completeness is viewed as a continuum with "no truth" at one end and "the whole truth" at the other end, the threshold standard that journalists should satisfy is the point along the continuum marked "substantial completeness." This would be the point at which a reasonable reader's need for information would be satisfied. A decision about where to situate substantial completeness on the continuum depends on practical, institutional, moral, political, and policy considerations. Providing substantially complete coverage means that within the constraints of these competing values, as well as the availability of staff, space, and other resources, and the accessibility of sources and documents (a professional level of resourcefulness in uncovering information is assumed), a news organization would, over the course of its coverage, publish enough information to satisfy the needs of an intelligent nonspecialist who wanted to evaluate the situation.

B. Understandability

Completeness is not enough, however. News reports must meet several other tests to fulfill their responsibility. Among other things, they must be understandable to the reasonable reader. As with the whole truth, complete understanding, in some senses, is an unattainable ideal. A person could be said to understand a situation or event fully only if that person were to grasp all relevant propositions or statements that accurately describe events that are reported, as well as their possible outcomes or consequences. What journalism can legitimately be expected to produce is, of course, far short of this ideal. Moreover, even if news organizations could provide all the information that was relevant and material to all of the stories published and broadcast, that amount of information would overwhelm rather than inform readers and viewers. The goal should be substantial understanding. In addition to providing the vital facts clearly, a story that strives to promote substantial understanding should leave out the irrelevant and trivial; should make clear what relevant facts are not known; should set new facts in an appropriate context; and, especially in complex technical stories, should begin at a point that is sufficiently elementary for the intended audience and frame information in a way that is neutral rather than encouraging, unintentionally or otherwise, a particular reader response.

C. Objectivity

Stories written for the reasonable reader must also strive to be objective. According to the *American Heritage Dictionary of the English Language,* objectivity entails being "uninfluenced by emotion or personal prejudice." It is, of course, unrealistic to expect even the most objective persons to be totally uninfluenced by these sources. Nevertheless, although a reporter might be motivated to pursue a story from a tangle of emotion and reason, it is possible in the writing and reporting to distinguish personal attitudes, religious or political dogma, and so forth from facts and justified beliefs. This statement does not mean that such facts and beliefs are not subject to legitimate dispute, but rather that, in reporting news, journalists should strive to identify disputed areas even when they personally favor one side over another. In other words, in the American context, reporting on the news ought not be politicized, ideological, or in any way polemical. News stories

should be written and organized so as not to suggest or express a preference for one set of values over another.

Objectivity does not, however, require the mindless balancing of viewpoints when the preponderance of evidence is heavily weighted in one direction. Similarly, objectivity is a journalistic responsibility in the selection of stories to be published in the main news section of a newspaper or aired during the main portion of a network news program. Generally speaking, priorities should be assigned according to criteria having to do with the public's need to know in areas bearing on important matters such as political choice and public health.

D. Accuracy

Finally, the reasonable reader demands accuracy from journalism. To be accurate means to present as facts only that information for which there is good and sufficient evidence. If, after checking the evidence, a reporter or editor remains even minimally doubtful about the accuracy of the information, that doubt should be incorporated into the story if the information is used. Accuracy also requires precision in such things as quotation, paraphrasing, and description. And proper attribution is a hallmark of accurate reporting. Reporters usually should describe without attribution only what they have witnessed and what is common knowledge; one possible exception is the reporting of an event that was witnessed by a trusted colleague.

Attribution, of course, does not authenticate information. It only lets the reader or viewer know its source and therefore what bias if any it might reflect. The duty to be accurate and the constraints of the fast-moving world of journalism are often incompatible. As a result, it would be foolish to think that mistakes will never be made. But a high standard of accuracy is consistent with the importance of the role assigned to journalism in America. The best journalists take this test daily and pass it with remarkable regularity.

By serving the reasonable reader as indicated, and by providing space or air time for the circulation of diverse opinions, print and broadcast media fulfill their role responsibly. And, as a result of aspiring to this level of journalism, they are likely to provide coverage that is maximally fair and minimally biased. In so doing, however, they do not necessarily meet all their responsibilities. The media may have a duty to perform public services that go beyond the mere provision of information that is deemed newsworthy. For example, newspapers may have a responsibility to publish the telephone numbers of hot lines for information on AIDS or drugs.

And some television news organizations, such as WJLA-TV in Washington, intervene on behalf of citizens frustrated by government bureaucracy.

Is there a duty to weigh harm to the public, sources, and subjects of stories against the benefits of publishing or broadcasting? Suppose, for example, that a newspaper learns that a public figure had a single homosexual encounter five years before he was elected to office and seven years before his marriage. Publishing the story could wreck both his marriage and his career. Should the paper publish it? And finally, what about accountability? Because the American media are so protected and privileged, are they, as a result, essentially unaccountable? The industry argues that the media are ultimately accountable to readers and viewers who can buy another paper or flick the TV dial to another channel. But given the patterns of media ownership in America, with most cities limited to a single newspaper that very likely is chain-owned, it is fair to ask just how much *accountability* is likely to be imposed at the newsstand. Similarly, it is obvious to people who follow network news coverage that the evening TV news programs are so much alike that little real accountability can be enforced in the living room either.

I think that the media have a duty to perform public services, to avoid harms that are greater than the correlative public benefits, and to be accountable. Space does not permit a full explication of these views, but the main points are briefly summarized in the section that follows.

E. Public Service

The record in support of a public service role for the press goes back at least to the 18th century. In making its case for independence, the Continental Congress offered the following rationale for an independent press:

> The importance of this [press freedom] consists, besides the advancement of truth, science, morality and arts in general, in its diffusion of liberal sentiments on the administration of government, its ready communication of thoughts between subjects, and its consequential promotion of union among them.

(quoted in L. W. Levy, 1985. *Emergence of A Free Press,* p. 174. Oxford Univ. Press, New York)

In modern times, the American Society of Newspaper Editors (ASNE) says in its statement of principles that "the primary purpose of gathering and distributing news and opinion is to serve the general welfare by informing the people and by enabling them to make judgments on the issues of the time" (as printed in J. L. Hulteng, 1981. *Playing It Straight,* p. 85. American Society of Newspaper Editors, Chester, CT).

Both these quotations relate to promoting the public good, or the general welfare, as the ASNE statement puts it. And they both tend to support the thesis that the implicit contract between the press and society, on which the privileges of the press are based, extends to providing adequate information to the public in spheres other than politics. The measure of the adequacy of the information published and broadcast is the degree to which it promotes autonomous deliberation and choice. That standard would indicate a duty to publish hotline numbers when they would facilitate choice, but no duty to intervene directly in disputes between citizens and government.

F. Doing Harm

The question of doing harm in journalism is more complex than the question of what public services the press has a responsibility to perform, because some public benefits of reporting news entail harms. Moreover, the benefit might be marginal or ambiguous and the harm significant and concrete. For example, exposing the fact that a Supreme Court nominee has smoked marijuana during his tenure as a law professor or that a candidate for president has jeopardized his campaign by spending time in compromising circumstances with a woman who was not his wife harms the nominee and the candidate, but some observers find the benefits questionable. From their perspective, reporting of this kind might even hurt the public by denying qualified persons the opportunity to serve in public office. It might also be that some harms are deserved, resulting more from the act itself than from the fact that the act was reported in a newspaper or on television.

A principle is needed to help determine in what circumstances, if any, press freedom should be overridden to avoid harm. That principle is provided in John Stuart Mill's monograph, *On Liberty* (1955. Henry Regnery, Chicago). Mill's harm principle says, in effect, that a liberty may be restricted if the harm caused outweighs the value of that liberty. There are many ways to define harm, but the philosopher Joel Feinberg has devised one that works well for journalism. Feinberg proposes that a harm is something that thwarts, defeats, or sets back an interest such as that which one might have in property, privacy, confidentiality, friendship, reputation, health, or career (1984. *Harm to Others,* pp.

34–35. Oxford Univ. Press, New York). Taken together, the ideas of Mill and Feinberg provide a conceptual framework for weighing harms against the benefits provided by a free press, but they are no help in determining whether a specific harm outweighs a specific benefit.

In an ideal world, there would be a formula that a journalist working on deadline could use to decide whether to include in a story a paragraph with some news value that might harm someone. There is no formula, but there are ways to think about whether potential benefits outweigh potential harms. For example, invading the privacy of a public official to report on matters relevant to the carrying out of his or her public responsibilities would be a more justified harm than invading the privacy of a mother to report on the death of her child in an accident. This is so partly because, by accepting public office, the official has given up part of his or her claim to privacy and partly because the public has a legitimate need to know about matters relevant to the carrying out of official duties. The mother, in contrast, has a full claim to privacy, and there is no compelling need for the public to know how she feels in her time of grief.

Not every case is so clear-cut, however. Suppose a reporter invades the privacy of a reclusive actress to report on her affair with the husband of her best friend. Does her right to privacy outweigh the interest of her fans in reading about the affair? The trade-offs in matters of this kind are not peculiar to journalism, so I will not belabor them here. The main point is that there is a benefit–harm equation and responsible journalism entails taking it into account.

G. Accountability

Finally, there is the conflicted question of accountability in journalism. To be both free and accountable is the democratic ideal, but like most ideals it remains distant from reality. Journalism in the United States is not absolutely free, but it comes a lot closer to being absolutely free than it comes to being absolutely accountable. Journalists are sometimes co-opted through cleverness or flattery by their governmental adversaries, but they are rarely if ever deterred from publishing or broadcasting for fear that they will have to give an account of their actions afterward. Because Congress is permitted to "make no law abridging the freedom … of the press," the government has little power to make the press accountable, which, given the potential for abuse of that power, is as it should be. The press is even less accountable than the liberal professions, which, although self-policing in many areas, also are subject to licensing restrictions. The print press in America is not licensed, nor should it be, especially because the government could use the licensing process as an instrument to enforce accountability. (The knotty problem of broadcast licensing in the cable and satellite age is beyond the scope of this article.)

In the end, the press remains accountable to the public because it is privileged and protected so that it can serve the public. Because the press is the public's surrogate for keeping tabs on the government, it stands to reason that it would be inappropriate for the government to enforce press accountability. Who, then, is to do it? The answer is some combination of the press itself, monitoring bodies not dissimilar to the defunct National News Council composed of media and public members with power to publicize their findings but not to punish offenders, and the public, by exercising its right to switch channels or newspapers.

A more fundamental question is, What does it mean for the press to be accountable? To be accountable is to be answerable to someone or some group to whom accountability is legitimately owed. Press accountability therefore cannot be satisfied by providing space for letters to the editor or by running an ombudsman column that criticizes the paper's coverage. It requires explanations and justifications of why controversial stories were reported as they were, why an unidentified source was allowed to malign a public figure, and so on. Traditionally the American media have feared any formal structure of accountability as the first step on a slippery slope toward media regulation. In fact, however, the opposite might be true. A media-supported mechanism of accountability would more likely serve to defuse media bashers and enhance media credibility than to promote a trend toward control of the press by outsiders, governmental or otherwise.

IV. CONCLUSION

This article does not attempt to present a comprehensive account of the role and responsibility of the press in the United States. To do that would require a substantial book. It is only an effort to suggest some essential elements of that role and responsibility. Nonetheless, it stands to reason that if journalists seek to serve the reasonable reader in some of the ways described here and to reflect on questions of harm and public benefit, and if they consider themselves accountable to the public, much else will take care of itself.

Also See the Following Articles

CENSORSHIP • NATIONAL SECURITY ISSUES • PRIVACY
VERSUS PUBLIC RIGHT TO KNOW

Bibliography

Dickerson, D. L. (1990). "The Course of Tolerance: Freedom of the Press in 19th Century America." Greenwood, New York.
Garry, P. M. (1990). "The American Vision of a Free Press: An Historical and Constitutional Revisionist View of the Press as a Marketplace of Ideas." Garland, New York.
Leahy, J. E. (1991). "The First Amendment, 1791–1991: Two Hundred Years of Freedom." McFarland, Jefferson, NC.
Lichtenberg, J. (ed.) (1990). "Democracy in the Mass Media: A Collection of Essays." Cambridge Univ. Press, New York.
Miller, W. L. (ed.) (1995). "Alternatives to Freedom: Arguments and Opinions." Longman, New York.
Murphy, P. L. (1992). "The Shaping of the First Amendment, 1791 to the Present." Oxford Univ. Press, New York.
Powe, L. A., Jr. (1991). "The Fourth Estate and the Constitution: Freedom of the Press in America." Univ. of California Press, Berkeley.
Wilkinson, F. (1992). "Essential Liberty: First Amendment Battles for a Free Press." Columbia Univ. Graduate School of Journalism, New York.

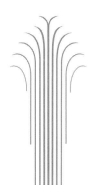

FREUDIANISM

Tadeusz Szubka
The University of Queensland

I. Freud's Theory of Mind
II. Superego and Morality
III. The Significance of Freudianism
   for Moral Theory

GLOSSARY

ego The mostly conscious part of the mind that tries
to meet and suppress the demands of the id, considering the constraints imposed by the external world.

id The most basic and primitive part of the mind; the
repository of the instincts and psychic energy, as well
as of the mental states removed from consciousness.

Oedipus complex The ambivalent attitude of the child
toward its parents that consists of being sexually
attracted to one of them and perceiving the other
one as the rival. Named by reference to the ancient
myth of King Oedipus who killed his father and
married his mother.

superego The part of the mind that consists of various
norms and prohibitions acquired in the course of
parental upbringing and social interaction. Its main
role is to oversee and judge the activities of the ego,
as well as to provide it with a range of ideals.

unconsciousness A collection of content-bearing mental states, processes, and events that play an important role in a person's conscious life, but are
acknowledged by their possessor with great difficulty
and, in many cases, recognized only through symptoms by a professional psychologist or psychiatrist.

FREUDIANISM is a general view about the nature of
human mental life, insisting on its unconscious and
sexual roots, put forward by the originator of psychoanalysis, Sigmund Freud (1856–1939), and developed
in various directions by his successors. Although the
idea of unconscious psychological states is not, strictly
speaking, an invention of Freud (one can trace its history back at least to G. W. Leibniz), he was certainly
the first thinker who made such a powerful and influential use of it. Freudianism, as both a psychological
theory and a method of psychotherapy, has been and
still is the subject of vigorous controversies. For some
it is the doctrine that drastically transformed and expanded our unstanding of human mind; for others it
is an example of a decadent and deeply flawed research
program, or perhaps even a pseudo-scientific theory
without any significant empirical support. Nevertheless
one could hardly question its massive impact on the
humanities, the social sciences, and popular culture. It
is also of great importance for philosophy, including
moral theory.

I. FREUD'S THEORY OF MIND

According to Freud the mental life of a person is like
an iceberg. Just as the visible part of a floating iceberg

is only a small fraction of it, so our conscious mental states are only a small part of our whole mental life, which is mostly unconscious. Granting this, one would have to deny the assumption quite often made by psychologists and philosophers that the essential and constitutive feature of the mental is its conscious character. In other words, one would have to deny that being in a mental state means, among other things, that a person is aware of its occurrence. Since apparently it is not a necessary or conceptual truth that any mental item is conscious, the hypothesis of unconscious mentality cannot be dismissed as self-contradictory. Moreover, in Freud's view, the evidence confirming the hypothesis is overwhelming and relatively easily available. The unconscious stream of our mental life manifests itself in some way in our dreams, and its existence and impact seem to be the only plausible explanation of numerous pathological cases (neurosis, schizophrenia, and the like), as well as of various puzzling occurrences in the conscious mental life of normal ordinary persons (slips of tongue, unexpected forgetting, and the like).

But what exactly are the unconscious mental or psychological states and what are their essential features? Freud thought of them very often as states that had been originally conscious, but for various reasons and by various mechanisms were subsequently repressed and moved beyond the boundaries of consciousness. In *The Ego and the Id* (1923) he explicitly claims, "Thus we obtain our concept of the unconscious from the theory of repression. The repressed is the prototype of the unconscious for us" (1953–1974. *The Standard Edition of the Complete Psychological Works of Sigmund Freud* (J. Strachey *et al.,* Eds), vol. 19, p. 15. Hogarth, London). This then suggests the following provisional characterization of unconsciousness: it is the part or dimension of the mind that consists of those mental states that were conscious, but have ceased to be so in virtue of a repression mechanism. However, such an account of unconsciousness would be exposed to the charge of arbitrariness if it were not extended in order to admit the existence of unconscious mental items that have not yet been made conscious but which could become conscious in particular favorable circumstances. Nonetheless even that extension gives us a rather weak notion of unconsciousness, since a state is considered to be mental and unconscious due to its standing in the relation of past, future, or merely possible manifestability to consciousness. There is some evidence that Freud endorsed also (and was followed in that more decisively and explicitly by M. Klein and others) a much stronger notion of unconsciousness, allowing to count as unconscious and mental even states

that could not become conscious, or at least could not become conscious without undergoing a radical transformation or losing their original identity. But then the pressing question arises of how to distinguish such strongly unconscious mental states from ordinary physical states.

One cannot repudiate this question by observing that freud was an advocate of materialism or physicalism, according to which every mental state, whether conscious or not, is identical with a physical state. First, the actual views of Freud on the matter, although obviously much closer to materialism than dualism, are more complicated. They could be perhaps better described as a form of the double-aspect theory that takes mental states to be an aspect of certain physical or, more specifically, neurophysiological states. But, second, even if Freud's position did indeed amount to a version of strong or reductive materialism, the above question could be easily rephrased as follows: which class of physical states may be justifiably referred to as the class of unconscious mental states?

The most plausible answer to this question, it seems, is to give an account of unconscious mental states by invoking the notion of content, and to say that they are states possessing content (or, more cautiously, states of such a complexity that, according to ordinary standards, the ascription of content to them is reasonable), in virtue of which they exercise an influence on conscious occurrences. This account would be hardly illuminating without clarifying what is meant by content. But that is a contentious and difficult issue. For the present purpose it should be sufficient to say that content is generally ascribed to states like sensations, beliefs, and desires.

The metaphor of the iceberg previously mentioned need not be taken too literally. Although it gives a good picture of the proportion between conscious and unconscious mental life, it may also suggest that the unconscious is relatively homogeneous and located, as it were, in one place. But nothing could be more false in light of Freud's views on the structure of mind, developed in detail mostly in his later writings. He holds there that our mental life is the result of the interplay of three constituents or systems: the id, ego, and superego.

The id is the most basic and primitive part of our mind, and is the repository of the instincts forming our life, as well as of the repressed mental states, that is, those removed from consciousness. The instincts should not be understood in this context as mere brute physical or biological forces, but as a physical representation of a biological source of stimulation, lying on the frontier between the physical and the mental. They are ultimately reducible to two opposing drives, Eros and Thanatos, that is, the life and death instincts. The id is in their service and aims at their satisfaction irrespective of the constraints and demands of external reality. It thus behaves according to what Freud calls the pleasure principle. The id is entirely unconscious. In contrast, the ego is for the most part conscious and tries to meet and suppress the demands of the id, taking into account the constraints imposed by the external world, including other people. It acts in accordance with the reality principle. Although the ego gets its power or energy from the id, it is to some extent able to control it. This control is very often exercised in conjunction with the third mental system, the superego, which consists of ideals and moral norms acquired in the course of social development and education.

II. SUPEREGO AND MORALITY

The superego is formed in early childhood when parents impose on their children certain rules of behavior by rewarding actions which they consider appropriate and good, and punishing those which they take to be inappropriate and bad. At the bottom of this process are the dynamics of sexual desire and the child's ambivalent attitude toward the parents, called by Freud the Oedipus complex. The attitude is ambivalent since the child seems to both love and hate the parents. In *Five Lectures on Psycho-Analysis* (1909) Freud gives the following general description of this complex:

> The child takes both of its parents, and more particularly one of them, as the object of its erotic wishes. In so doing, it usually follows some indication from its parents, whose affection bears the clearest characteristics of a sexual activity, even though of one that is inhibited in its aims. As a rule a father prefers his daughter and a mother her son; the child reacts to this by wishing, if he is a son, to take his father's place, and, if she is a daughter, her mother's. (*Standard Edition,* vol. 11, p. 47)

In the case of boys this wish takes the form of a desire for the sexual intimacy with the mother and for the death of the father. In the case of girls this is supposed to be the reverse: a desire for the sexual intimacy with the father and for the death of the mother. Strictly speaking this is the way in which the so-called positive form of the Oedipus complex is manifested. In its negative form, not so uncommon and usually coexisting

with the positive one, the child loves the parent of the same sex and hates the parent of the opposite sex. The Oedipus complex exercises a strong influence on the child between the third and fifth year of its life, then enters a long period of latency, and strikes with a new force at puberty. Why and how is the complex overcome and what are the consequences?

First, there are internal factors in this process. The child feels its total dependence upon the parents, and so the hostility toward them seems to be out of place. Moreover, if the child is the subject of both forms of the Oedipus complex, it has conflicting attitudes toward each parent and tries to remove this conflict. A special significance should be also attached here, especially in the case of boys, to the castration threat: the anxiety of the child that he may lose his penis when the father notices his sexual attraction for the mother coupled with his hostility toward the father. Second, there are also some external factors of this process. They amount to the prohibitions by means of which parents modify the spontaneous behavior of their children.

These external factors play an essential, and arguably the most important, role in the emergence of the superego, described by Freud as the heir of the Oedipus complex and the psychoanalytical equivalent of the traditional notion of conscience. The superego is formed when the parental prohibitions and demands enter the child's mind so deeply that they begin to be taken as an integral part of its own psyche, that is, when they become internalized. For the most part the superego acts as a severe and harsh judge or critic of the ego's attempts to meet various instinctual demands of the id, forbidding or condemning certain actions, causing the feeling of guilt, etc. In pathological cases, which suggested to Freud the hypothesis of the existence of superego, the patients suffered from the delusions of being constantly observed and judged, and in the course of depression attacks they condemned themselves for almost everything that they had done in the past. However, sometimes the superego functions in a different way: it sets up an ideal the ego wants to follow—it points out a possibility to which the ego aspires.

Taking into account these two roles of the superego, Freud defines it in *New Introductory Lectures on Psycho-Analysis* (1933) as "the representative for us of every moral restriction, the advocate of a striving towards perfection," and adds immediately that this is "as much as we have been able to grasp psychologically of what is described as the higher side of human life" (*Standard Edition,* vol. 22, p. 67). Since the essence of "the higher side of human life" seems to be the demands of morality, one can say that Freudianism identifies the moral sense with the superego. But there is one significant disanalogy between the notion of superego and the traditional concepts of moral sense or conscience. Unlike the latter the superego acts very often in an unconscious way: it manifests itself as an irresistible pressures exercised upon the ego from above, parallel to the drives or instincts influencing the ego from below, that is, from the id. As a matter of fact, the superego and the id are merged through the Oedipus complex.

Freud seemed to accept the widely held general conception of morality, according to which only those actions can be counted as fully moral that are motivated not by self-interest, but rather by a sense of obligation or duty. He believed that to some extent the commands of the superego can be taken as moral in this sense. Moreover, it would be too hasty to maintain that he nonetheless radically diverged from this conception by making the demands of parents the ultimate source of morality. It would be too hasty, since Freud clearly suggested that the child's superego is constructed not on the model of its parents, but rather out of the parents' superegos. Of course, the latter superegos were formed out of the superegos of the parents of those parents, and so on. This means that the superego is the repository of traditional values and norms, transmitted from generation to generation.

But there is a point at which Freudianism certainly parts company with the traditional vision of morality. An important element of the latter is the belief in the prospect of attaining moral perfection and harmony. Freud was skeptical about that and thought that the struggle between the superego as an ideal and the superego as a judge or critic would never be terminated. In other words, when a person has successfully realized a particular moral ideal or has come close to realizing it, the superego will immediately replace it with another ideal more stringent and difficult to attain. This in turn will allow the superego in its critical function to produce a whole range of condemnatory moral judgments and a feeling of moral failure. As this may lead to many pathological distortions of personality, Freud recommended that we should give up the idea of achieving moral perfection and harmony, and instead try rather to weaken the superego to some reasonable extent. Hence he was in favor of more lenient parenting and more liberal social norms of behavior.

III. THE SIGNIFICANCE OF FREUDIANISM FOR MORAL THEORY

Freudianism seems to be pertinent to moral theory in at least three crucial issues: the objectivity of morality,

the nature of moral motivation, and the relationships between gender and morality.

Concerning the objectivity issue, Freudian views admit two radically different interpretations. According to the first (favored, among others, by R. Wollheim and R. Rorty), Freud has decisively shown that morality does not reflect some transcendental order, and its demands arise out of human psychology and not out of a supposedly objective hierarchy of values. The most fundamental and basic part of human psyche, the id, knows no judgments of value—no good or evil. Moral norms are created in response to sexual drives and aggression directed at others, and what is considered to be a moral sense or conscience is merely a result of the complex processes of introjection and projection. In other words, the so-called moral order is nothing more than a relatively stable outcome of the struggle between various parts of human psyche and conflicting interests of individuals constituting a given society. Hence a system of morality is justified, if at all, not by its correspondence to the preexisting reality, but by bringing about a state of social equilibrium. In this respect, the advocates of this interpretation continue, Freud followed and developed in a highly original way the genealogical account of morality proposed by F. Nietzsche.

But Freudianism also allows a more objective account of morality (as has been pointed out recently by M. Cavell and others). In accordance with that interpretation we should draw the following lesson from Freud's developmental theory of mind: the human psyche constitutes itself in a long process whose essential phase is recognition of other humans and their demands—in the first instance, those with whom we are connected by some kind of primitive emotional bond. On this view the Oedipus complex that gives rise to the superego should be conceived not as something to be explained merely in terms of completely subjective and mostly unconscious happenings, but mainly as the child's full entrance into intersubjectivity, that in turn is a necessary condition for having a conscious mind and entertaining thoughts. In addition, the primitive acts of emotional recognition are not to be taken as a combination of genuinely objective knowing with projective valuing, as the latter can also be an objective discovery of some aspects of reality. but how, one may wonder, does one develop from the highly idiosyncratic and personal relationships or attitudes of the child a set of abstract moral norms binding human beings as human beings or persons as persons? It seems that the only available answer for the advocate of Freudianism would be to say that as soon as these relationships or attitudes are internalized they lose their particularity and become more abstract, and hence applicable to other, relevantly similar situations. However, it is contentious and doubtful whether one can give a satisfactory account of those universalizing mechanisms without essentially revising the framework of Freudian doctrine.

It has been emphasized (most notably by S. Scheffler) that Freudianism is able to give a very plausible naturalistic account of moral motivation. There are several reasons why this is so. First, according to this doctrine the human psyche is a structure of considerable complexity, and that makes it possible to show how moral motivation arises out of the interplay between the central elements of the structure. Second, it provides us with a rather convincing story about how the impulse to restrain oneself, apparently crucial for most accounts of moral motivation, emerges gradually out of a conflict between powerful amoral drives directed at others and a wish for self-preservation and survival. Third, it explains various distortions and deformities of moral motivation, as well as its fragility, by revealing its dependence on highly contingent features of the child's environment and upbringing, and by showing how having the appropriate moral motivation leans on a delicate balance among powerful psychic forces.

However, is Freudianism able to incorporate and give a naturalized sense to the traditional distinction between motivation from a sense of duty (authoritative motivation) and motivation from sentiment or desire (desire-based motivation), or to put in a slightly different way, between the categorial and the hypothetical imperative? For an advocate of the traditional conception of morality this is the crucial question, since in light of it only motivation of the first kind deserves to be called moral. The answer of those closely following Kant in the elaboration of the distinction is negative: authoritative motivation comes from reason alone and is not contaminated by natural considerations (and is very often even opposed to them); hence any project of deriving it out of our psychological nature is doomed to failure.

However, those who find such an uncompromising Kantianism untenable may come to the conclusion that Freudianism can give a perfectly legitimate sense to this distinction. After all, the fully formed and established superego is the source of moral motivation in the traditional sense (Freud himself referred to it as the source of the categorical imperative). For instance, for someone with a particular superego, the fact that a given act will fulfill a promise constitutes an adequate motivating reason to perform it. The motivation for action in this situation will be simply the recognition of this fact, without any additional and independent desire (e.g.,

the desire to be seen by others as a dependable person). The act will be performed out of sense of duty or obligation. One can object to that construal by insisting that the superego has been formed in response to a range of instinctual sexual drives and certain desires (fear of parental anger, the need to restrain its own aggressiveness, etc.), so contrary to the *prima facie* appearance, the act in question (and all other acts, for that matter) is ultimately motivated by particular desires. Moreover, in almost every case an act will be accompanied by a universal fear of the authoritative and harsh superego. The obvious reply to this objection would be to remark that the latter is not present in the case of persons whose superegos are perfectly integrated into their personality, and that the general and largely unconscious reasons for acquiring the superego cannot be reckoned as the motivation of a particular action.

Therefore the original supposition that Freudianism offers a sophisticated naturalistic construal of moral motivation that admits the distinction between desire-based and authoritative motivation remains undefeated. But, of course, one has to remember that Freudianism is capable of accommodating only a part of our traditional understanding of morality, especially if we think that Kantianism is a very intuitive and plausible elaboration of this understanding. It should be noted that the aim of the distinction between the categorical and the hypothetical imperative was also to separate the considerations that provide reasons for and are able to motivate any rational person from those that do not. Certainly, the Freudian construal of the distinction does not capture the latter contrast. It does not take authoritative or categorial motivation to be the motivation of any rational person, but merely of those persons who have the superego of a certain kind. So the Freudian naturalized authoritative motivation is essentially conditional and lacks the feature of unrestricted universal appeal.

One of the central problems for Freudianism is establishing to what extent the sexual differences between boys and girls, or between men and women, have on the human mind, especially its superego, and thereby on morality. The problem is widely discussed by current feminist literature. At the focus of attention are particularly Freud's speculations on the way in which the Oedipus complex is formed in girls, and how they manage to suppress it. Freud thought that girls suffer from the castration complex, which manifests itself as envy for the penis, and that they cannot successfully overcome the Oedipus complex, since in their case there is no castration to fear. Hence they are not able to form the same strong superego as men and enter the adult life with infantile relics. Provided that there is indeed a close connection between the superego and a moral sense or judgment, many feminist critics argue that Freudianism is committed to the unacceptable claim that women are inferior moral agents less capable of being authoritatively motivated and more often driven by conflicting or uncontrolled emotions. Freud, as was already noted, did not hold that a stronger superego provides us with a better moral sense and superior morality. He held quite the opposite: some weakening of the superego is a necessary condition of enjoying a healthy mental life and undistorted moral sense. Moreover, given all of Freud's ideas concerning various forms of the Oedipus complex, along with his conjecture about the primary bisexual dispositions of every human being, it is highly implausible to ascribe to him a grossly simplifying view that there are two essentially different and fixed kinds of mentality: feminine and masculine. Admittedly, in his popular writing and private correspondence Freud made some remarks about women and their social role that were expressions of common opinions and prejudices held in his times. But as long as they are not entailed by his psychoanalytical theories, there is no substantial reason why Freudianism as a doctrine has to be associated with them.

Also See the Following Articles

MORAL DEVELOPMENT • PSYCHIATRIC ETHICS

Bibliography

Cavell, M. (1993). "The Psychoanalytic Mind: From Freud to Philosophy." Harvard Univ. Press, Cambridge, MA.

Chodorow, N. J. (1994). "Feminities, Masculinities, Sexualities: Freud and Beyond." The Univ. Press of Kentucky, Lexington.

Deigh, J. (1996). "The Sources of Moral Agency: Essays in Moral Psychology and Freudian Theory." Cambridge Univ. Press, Cambridge.

Freud, S. (1953–1974). "The Standard Edition of the Complete Psychological Works of Sigmund Freud" (J. Strachey et al., Eds.), 24 vols. Hogarth, London.

Kitcher, P. (1992). "Freud's Dream: A Complete Interdisciplinary Science of Mind." The MIT Press, Cambridge, MA.

Lear, J. (1990). "Love and Its Place in Nature: A Philosophical Interpretation of Freudian Psychoanalysis." Farrar, Straus, & Giroux, New York.

Neu, J. (Ed.) (1992). "The Cambridge Companion to Freud." Cambridge Univ. Press, Cambridge.

Scheffler, S. (1992). "Human Morality." Oxford Univ. Press, New York.

Wollheim, R., and Hopkins, J. (Eds.) (1982). "Philosophical Essays on Freud." Cambridge Univ. Press, Cambridge.

FRIENDSHIP

Laurence Thomas
Syracuse University

GLOSSARY

companion or character friends Especially close friends whose trust of one another and self-disclosure to one another are exceedingly high.

Kantian morality The idea that there are absolute rights and wrongs, and that persons act from the motive of moral duty if and only if they are motivated purely by the rational concern to do what is morally right. One of the cornerstones of Kantian morality is the Categorical Imperative, of which there are three formulations. The most famous formulation says that in our actions we always should treat the humanity in ourselves and others as an end and never as a means only.

self-disclosure The act of revealing to a person information about oneself that is of a particularly personal nature. Especially close friends engage in mutual self-disclosure. Self-disclosure between friends often involves the highest level of trust. It is possible to self-disclose information to a person which the individual already knows. The self-disclosure is still significant, because it is only with the self-disclosure that one opens up to the other and makes the other a part of one's life.

trust The willingness to be vulnerable to a person and the belief that the individual will not harm one although she or he could do so with impunity. Trust can be reasonable or unreasonable.

IN IMPORTANCE, FRIENDSHIP is rivaled, if at all, only by romantic love. And some would finesse the difference between the two by insisting that romantic love is at its best only when the lovers are also the best of friends. Aristotle observed that a life without friendship was an incomplete life, though a person possessed all the riches in the world. Two thousand years later, Aristotle's observation still strikes a responsive chord in our hearts.

Although there is, these days, a rather loose use of the word friend whereby people who barely know each other might refer to one another as friends (bar scenes come quickly to mind here), absolutely no one is oblivious to the difference between, at one end, friends who are mere acquaintances or who interact socially from time to time—casual friends, let us say—and, at the other end, friends who constitute a deep friendship—that is, individuals who are the best of friends. Aristotle's observation, of course, is about deep friendships, commonly referred to in the philosophical literature as character or companion friendship. No one today would be inclined to think that his observation applies equally well to individuals who are casual friends. In fact, the term friendship, itself, is generally reserved for individuals who are the best of friends. Thus, while we may use the casual sense of the word friend in ordering another beer for the person whom we have just met and with whom we are enjoying a conversation, it will most likely take more than the animated conversation that is taking place before we think of ourselves as having a friendship with that person. Common wisdom has it that casual friends are easy to come by, whereas companion friendships are rare.

I. FEATURES OF COMPANION FRIENDSHIP

What are the features of companion or character friendship that so recommends this relationship to our lives? It is illuminating to listen to how people describe their best friend. Let Leslie and Marion, who may be female or male, be companion friends. Here are several commonplace claims: "We always spend lots of time together." "Leslie would do anything for me." "I could tell Leslie anything, for no one understands me like Leslie does." "We often know how one another feels without having to say much of anything." Even if there is some hyperbole here, the fact that people express their feelings in such strong terms is itself significant. These claims speak to four very important things. Respectively, they are delight in one another's company, aid, self-disclosure, and understanding. Let me comment briefly upon each one.

Deep friends take enormous pleasure in one another's company, as is beautifully described by St. Augustine. Sometimes friends want to be in the proximity of one another even as they engage in different activities. Just knowing that the other is near by—within room's reach, say—is often satisfying. Interestingly, in spite of the many obvious differences between the parent–child relationship and friendship, we have with this observation about friendship a striking similarity, for the young child takes enormous comfort in knowing that its parents are nearby even as she or he engages in independent exploration.

Turning to the next consideration, we expect our close friends to be willing to aid us in ways that go significantly beyond what the morally decent person might do. While this includes material aid, such aid is rarely the centerpiece of companion friendship, which is in keeping with Aristotle's observation that a person who has everything still needs friendship. Once material aid is set aside, the primary way in which companion

friends aid one another comes through self-disclosure and understanding. Still, there are obligations of friendship which do not seem to have their source in the demands of morality. Character friends can make demands on one another's time that no casual friend could make, which is very much in keeping with the first observation. Indeed, even if a casual friend were to make an appearance during a person's time of need, the appearance would not have the same comforting results as that of a character friend, although the individual's showing up would be profoundly appreciated. From the other direction, deep friendship pushes the limits of morality without actually encouraging moral slothfulness. It goes without saying that heinous acts of immorality cannot be justified in the name of friendship. But between heinous acts of immorality and complete moral rectitude, there is a lot of moral space. And we might tolerate a deep friend's impropriety, though we would never tolerate a like impropriety from a stranger. I shall say more about this in Section IV. However, the point leads us to the topics of self-disclosure and understanding.

Companion friends know things about one another that others do not know, because companion friends self-disclose personal information about themselves to one another. Now, while telling someone personal information about oneself is obviously a way of self-disclosing, it is not the only way. We may do so indirectly. Companion friend Marion may know enough about Leslie that a piece of behavior on Leslie's part which is of little significance in the eyes of others is quite revealing in the eyes of Marion. And Leslie may so behave in front of Marion and others fully cognizant of the fact that Leslie, and no one else, will draw an inference about his personal life that is very poignant, indeed.

Now, there is a fundamental difference between understanding why a person behaved in a certain way and justifying that behavior. In many cases, we expect our companion friend to understand why we made our mistakes even if our behavior cannot in any way be justified. It is this consideration, I want to say, that explains the willingness of friends to engage in self-disclosure. Suppose that Leslie had an extramarital affair. She may self-disclose this to Marion, not with the thought that Marion will see her as not having done wrong, but with the sense that Marion will understand how she might have succumbed in this way. Two general points about human beings are quite relevant here. One is the ever so obvious but far from trivial truth that no one is infallible. The other is the truth that there can be better and worse explanations for even the wrongs that we do. One kind of explanation—which I shall call an excoriating one—reveals us to be utterly indifferent to the wrong that we do. Another kind of explanation—which I shall call an ameliorative one—reveals us to be concerned to do what is morally right but momentarily lacking in moral fortitude. One of the important ways in which companion friends exhibit understanding is that they help us to construct sound ameliorative explanations of our mistakes. Thus, in the case of Leslie's affair, if the available facts supported an ameliorative explanation, Leslie could count on Marion to see this or to help her in constructing such an explanation. It is most significant that persons are sometimes in need of help in constructing an ameliorative explanation concerning a moral failure on their part. In some cases, surely, this is because sometimes we are so stunned and overwhelmed by our mistakes that we lose our perspective.

Summing up, then, the deep, deep trust between character friends manifests itself not only in the high level of self-disclosure between character friends, but also in the conviction that each will endeavor to portray the other in the best moral light. Although such portrayals to third parties may come naturally to mind, the fact of the matter is that often enough a character friend does an invaluable task in portraying the other to himself.

While I do not want to enter into a discussion of the difference between ties of friendship and romance, it will be useful to conclude this section with a remark that speaks to the relative importance of self-disclosure vis-à-vis the sexual bonding that we associate with romance.

It is commonplace to say that sexual bonding is the deepest form of bonding that two human beings can experience, and the ultimate form of self-disclosure. But is this really so? Notice that the person who knows the most about us need not be our sexual partner. In fact, we can have ever so meaningful sex with a person and yet be deeply afraid of self-disclosing things about ourselves to that person. Sex at its best invariably involves a certain kind of affirmation and trust. Yet, sex at its best is nothing like the window to our soul that significant self-disclosure is. If a woman should self-disclose to her lover that she was repeatedly raped by her father when she was age 6, she will have displayed a level trust in her lover that has no equal in the sexual realm. Self-disclosure at its best is anchored in a profound trust, and no other form of social interaction seems to be tied to this level of trust. And if trust is rightly thought to constitute a form of bonding, then suffice it to say that the rich bonding that sexual intercourse yields neither equals nor necessarily serves as a precursor to the bond of trust cemented by self-disclosure.

II. SELF-DISCLOSURE, CHOICE, AND SELF-KNOWLEDGE IN FRIENDSHIP

What underlies these three aspects of companion friendship—aid, self-disclosure, and understanding? No doubt an answer that comes readily to mind is that companion friends deeply love one another. While that is certainly true, love cannot be the answer to the question just posed. To be sure, we are generally willing to aid those whom we love. However, self-disclosure and understanding do not follow simply in love's wake, as the parent–child relationship readily reveals. Parents and children often go to great lengths to hide important aspects of their lives from one another, although the love between them is extraordinary. Or, there can be deep, deep failures of understanding between the two.

Nowadays, a classic example would be the child who is gay or dating a member of a different ethnic group. It is common enough for such a child, who has no doubt whatsoever about the enormous love which his parents have for him, to say that it would hurt his parents enormously if they knew that he was gay or dating an X (a member of a different ethnic group). Or, to go in the other direction, adult children who love their parents dearly may nonetheless be unable to understand why their parents are getting a divorce—so much so that the children actually become angry at the parents. By contrast, friends of the parents may understand all too well why the parents are divorcing.

It might seem appropriate to respond here that the love between parent and child is in a category unto itself. So the fact that self-disclosure and understanding do not follow simply in the wake of this love tells us nothing about the character of love outside of that context, the love of friendship in particular. There is a fundamental insight here that needs to be brought into sharper focus.

A significant asymmetry between the love between character friends on the one hand, and the love between parent and child on the other, is choice. We choose a friend because we find her or his character appealing to us, whereas we choose neither our parents nor our children at all. To be sure, we choose to have children, but that is very different from choosing the child itself. And while adopting a child is, indeed, an instance of choosing a child, infant adoptions still represent choosing a substantially unknown entity, in terms of both physical and, in particular, character development, for it is impossible to extrapolate from an infant child's appearances and behavior what its appearance and character will be when it is a 10-year-old child. However, although we choose neither our parents nor our children, the general thought is that parents should love their children regardless of the children's behavior and children should likewise love their parents. It would almost never be argued that a person's moral character has become so heinous that the person's parents or children are morally blameworthy for maintaining their love for him, although it may be understandable that they cease to love the person.

We may think of the love between child and parent as purely role-based: "X has the role of being child of so-and-so," or "X has the role of parent of so-and-so." By contrast, we may consider the love between character friends as choice-based, where the choice is based upon the person's character. Thus, even if Marion and Leslie represent companion friendship at its very best, they would not have been open to moral criticism merely on account of not having become companion friends. And if both were morally decent individuals when they became companion friends, and Marion, say, changed for the worse, embarking upon a life of crime, we would expect the companion friendship, and so the love, between them to end. More precisely, we would expect Leslie to move on. And if she did not, the explanation, "We are companion friends," would neither seem convincing nor strike us as appropriate, whereas "That is my child" or "That is my parent" would be both convincing and appropriate in a parallel situation.

The only other form of love that also seems to be purely role-based is sibling love, though I suspect that its force, at least socially, is not equal to the love between parent and child. Many ancient texts which speak to the importance of honoring the father and mother and to the importance of caring for children say nothing about sibling relations, save that there should not be sexual intercourse between them. It is hardly accidental, I suspect, that we have role-based love only in the context of biological ties (or their social analogue, as with adoptions and children raised as siblings), for the nature of biological ties (1st or 2nd cousin to X, child/parent of X, and so on) is absolutely unalterable by social conventions and is extinguishable, if that is the word for it, only by death (it being only upon X's death that a person who was the child/parent or cousin of X is no longer that). Religion has often sought to turn marital love into purely role-based love. Yet, it concedes from the outset the relevance of behavior, since religion

has generally regarded infidelity as suitable grounds for divorce.

In any event, one would expect a love that is choice-based, where the choice is based upon the person's character, to be tied to understanding and self-disclosure, whereas one would expect these two features to play a significantly subordinate role in a love that is role-based.

Whenever one makes a choice, one can ask whether it was a good one. This is so even in matters of little or no consequence. Suppose I decide to try a new ice cream flavor and from the list of flavors which I have not yet tasted I request coconut apple. I will consider myself to have made a very good choice if I like it enormously, a bad choice if I really dislike it, and a so-so choice if I find it more or less satisfactory. In terms of significance, clearly, the choice of a companion friend is on a much higher plane. Moreover, one wants to make a good choice from the very start. This requires having some insight into the person's character that goes beyond the person's public self-presentation, which is usually what first catches our attention.

Typically, character friendships have their beginning in a conversation that focuses on something important which is of mutual interest to the individuals involved. They find either that they have similar views or that their disagreements are remarkably constructive. In either case, both find each other quite appreciative of one another's views. After all, people with similar views can learn a lot from one another.

With a companion friendship in-the-making, a conversation will often have what I shall call a distant self-disclosure. On the one hand, a distant self-disclosure is revealing without leaving the speaker particularly vulnerable or requiring supportive behavior on the part of the listener. On the other, a distant self-disclosure often allows ample opportunity to gauge the listener's reaction and understanding of the matter. An example of a distant self-disclosure would be that 20 years ago one smoked marijuana to get through a certain crisis, or that while in the army as a teenager one engaged in a certain form of criminal behavior. With a companion friendship in place, the self-disclosures will invariably cease to be distant.

At this juncture, it is worth mentioning another observation by Aristotle, namely that having a companion or character friend is rather like having another self for a friend. What Aristotle most certainly did not mean is that companion friends are mutual sycophants merely parroting one another's sentiments. For the author who observed that a life without friendship was incomplete surely did not think that what made a person's life incomplete is that he lacked someone who merely parroted his views. The best way to appreciate Aristotle's second observation is to consider the difference between honesty and self-honesty.

A person can be honest in his remarks without telling the entire story. Suppose a student asks me about how well he performed on his essay. I answer honestly if I truthfully tell him that he did not do well and that his paper actually needs enormous work if it is to measure up. I answer honestly, although my considered judgment is that his essay was the worst that I had read in 20 years. Honesty does not require me to add this further assessment. In fact, many would regard my doing so as rather mean-spirited. Most questions have a point to them, and in many cases that point can be spoken to, and so the question can be answered honestly, without offering a full description of things. If you merely ask me was John home last night, I answer honestly if I truthfully tell you that he was not, although I also know that he spent the night at someone's house having an affair. If you are his lover, then the question immediately becomes more complicated. When a lover asks that question, the point is rarely innocuous. Then, an honest answer depends, in part, on the kind of information about John that I realize you correctly take me to have about him. Things can get very complicated here. For I may know that the point of your question is whether John was out having an affair; what is more, it may be that it is entirely by accident that I know that he was (say my cordless phone picked up the conversation as the matter was being discussed). Finally, I may know that you do not really expect me to know the answer, but that you were merely asking me in desperation (I could have been just about anyone). Fortunately, this matter need not be settled here, since offering an account of honest behavior is not the aim of this essay. Yet, this last discussion nicely leads us to the topic of self-honesty.

As a purely conceptual matter, it is not true that a person always knows more about himself than another does. For instance, a person can be infatuated with another or depressed and not realize it, though someone else does. What self-honesty requires, however, is not that a person know more about himself than anyone else, but that he acknowledges to himself his beliefs and feelings such as he understands them to be, regardless of how pleasant or unpleasant they are (where beliefs and feelings are understood to cover intentions, motivations, and emotions). While self-honesty is perhaps easier to achieve than honesty, self-honesty is by no means an inevitable feature of life, as the phenomenon of self-deception makes abundantly clear. And short of out-

right self-deception there are a multitude of ways in which a person can avoid giving full acknowledgment to his beliefs and feelings. Self-honesty, then, is no small accomplishment, often calling for a certain level of courage.

It is in this light that we should understand Aristotle's claim that a character friend is rather like another self. Imagine a person who is masterfully self-honest. If that person has a character friend, then the extent to which that person will be forthcoming in discussions with her character friend will approach the level of self-honesty that she has attained in her life. Bearing in mind that an honest answer often does not require a full description, then the idea here is that with one another character friends are forthcoming about themselves in ways that significantly exceed the demands of honesty alone. What is more, the character friend will play an active role in getting the other to appreciate her own actions or those contemplated; and this, in turn, will be part of the reason why the other is forthcoming.

So, to recall our two companion friends, Marion and Leslie, if the next door neighbor were to ask Leslie about the banquet for her 25th reunion, a perfectly honest answer could be that she had a great time and reacquainted herself with a number of former classmates. Leslie is not being dishonest by failing to add that she ran into an old flame and there were sparks again. Nor is Leslie being dishonest if she fails to add this when Marion asks her about the banquet. All the same, in responding to Marion, not only would it be quite natural for Leslie to add this, Marion would be unpleasantly surprised if she learned of this from someone else other than Leslie. Of course, Leslie need not tell the whole story right at that moment. Or, if the inquiry about the reunion banquet is made in a public setting, a piece of nonverbal behavior or a code word may accompany Leslie's reply that signals to Marion, and no one else, that there is more to the story. But Marion remembers just how painful Leslie's relationship with that old flame was, and when they have a chance to discuss the matter in private, Marion forcefully reminds Leslie of this, which proves to be another instance of why Leslie is so grateful for their friendship.

Thus, insofar as companion friends are mirrors to one another's soul, a gloss is in order. Contrary to what the metaphor of a mirror perhaps unwittingly invites, companion friends are far from passive in the role which they play in one another's life. A mirror reflects, but the verb "to reflect" has two meanings, one of which pertains to the reasoning that is involved in weighing considerations. Character friends, then, are not just mirrors, but mirrors of insight into one another's soul, thereby helping each other to live up to her or his moral ideals and, at least from time to time, improving upon those ideals. Understanding the mirror metaphor in this way is in keeping with the idea that character friends help one another to see whether an excoriating or ameliorative explanation applies to a serious moral failing. And if an excoriating explanation holds, a character friend will make the case without in any way being self-righteous.

Now, these last remarks speak to the question of what is the gain in having a friend where the level of self-disclosure would invite the idea that the friend is rather like another self? The gain is moral and personal flourishing, an essential ingredient of which is the practical knowledge to interact in the social world in just the right way, given who one is. Consider that a person with all the theoretical knowledge in the world concerning what pregnancy is like does not, thereby, have any practical knowledge about the matter. To have practical knowledge here, there is one, and only one, thing that will do, namely having been pregnant.

To live well is not just to have theoretical knowledge about what is morally right and wrong and personally good or bad for one, but practical knowledge about such matters. And that knowledge is unattainable in the absence of social interaction. But this does not require that one interact with everyone, but only with the right individuals. And no one is better placed for such interaction than a friend who is rather like another self. Let me explain, starting with an illustration.

No matter how well one rehearses a speech that one is going to give, that will never be tantamount to actually giving the speech. A speech that has only been rehearsed can always be revised, whereas a speech that has been given can never be rendered a speech that has not been given. It is only in giving the speech that one can feel, say, either relief (or pleasure) for having gotten that out of the way (for having done a wonderful job) or regret for not having gotten things just right. Quite simply, feelings developed in isolation are characteristically too much infected by our hopes and fears. What is more, no matter how self-aware we are concerning the impact which our behavior has upon others, there is no substitute for the actual reactions of others—their praise, criticism, or even indifference, which in some instances can be more haunting than criticism.

Companion friendship often provides the much needed social space between words rehearsed and words spoken to their intended hearer. To our companion friends, we express our feelings about people and situations in ways that we would never express to others, and often enough it is only in so doing that often we learn or appreciate more fully that, indeed, we should never express our feelings in those ways to others. A remark may prove too hostile or too familiar. Sometimes the friend draws this to our attention; sometimes merely uttering the remark to the friend suffices for us to see this. Expressing our most intimate feelings with our companion friend and matching our feelings with theirs is an indispensable moral exercise. This moral exercise yields insights that cannot be had in any other way, even by self-reflection at its very best. Because, as a result of self-disclosure, companion friends have a commanding perspective of one another's life, they are in the position to offer advice, constructive criticism, and running commentary that is profoundly informed, but yet has distance from the person's life. Even as having a character friend approximates having another self, the fact remains that the friend's feelings and reactions will always be those of another person, and self-knowledge, for all of its importance and significance, is no substitute for the knowledge that is given by another's feelings and reactions.

Of course, the very fact that a deep friend so identifies with us can itself be a reason to seek the reactions of others, since we expect that our friend will readily grasp the proper point of our endeavors, and what may rightly be of concern to us is whether those who take no interest in our endeavors, as such, will readily enough correctly grasp the point of our endeavors. A striking difference between companion friendship and the parent–child relationship comes to mind here. It is that in general companion friends never seek the kind of independence from the opinions of one another that children often seek from their parents. At least part of the explanation for this is that, in the eyes of the child, even an adult child, the opinions of parents never entirely lose their authoritative force, owing to the authority that parents properly have over their child in its youth, whereas from the start friends do not have authority over one another, although they certainly have considerable influence with one another. This points to the subtlety of social interaction. A friend's influence can be utterly considerable, making all the difference in what we do; yet we may find this infinitely preferable to even the mere vestiges of authority that remain with our parents. And this, I suspect, is because moral behavior and related concerns are one of the central aspects of friendship, a topic which I take up next.

III. FRIENDSHIP AND THE TENSIONS OF MORALITY

We can quickly get at some of the issues that arise concerning friendship and morality by looking at a particular reading of morality that no doubt has its inspiration in Kantian thought. The view is that a person is not entitled to set aside the demands of morality when it comes to his own behavior. What is morally required of others, in a given set of circumstances, is no less required of that person in like circumstances. Thus, if a person finds $10,000, and morality requires that anyone who finds $10,000 should report the discovery, then that person is not morally permitted to regard his circumstances as different and not report the loss. While technical maneuvers can be made regarding what counts as similar circumstances, the general insight seems relatively secure.

Now, everyone knows that they commit moral errors, including egregious ones from time to time. Some who make egregious moral errors engage in quite substantial acts of self-flagellation. And as I noted in Section I, it sometimes happens that people fail to construct the veritable ameliorative explanation for their moral failure, thinking much worse of themselves than the circumstances warrant. These situations are common enough, though perhaps most people do not react to their grave moral failures in this way.

In most instances, people feel terribly guilty for a period of time, and then get on with living their lives. Rarely do people subject themselves to any of the excoriating blame to which they subject others who make similar gregious moral errors. This is often the case even among people who are quite demanding of themselves (at least when the moral error does not yield lasting damage). While, in the case of people who are morally demanding of themselves, there are a number of explanations for this that operate in concert, I shall focus upon self-knowledge. Having committed an egregious moral error, a person who is morally demanding of herself may have such a poignant sense of moral failure that, with good reason, she is certain that she will never commit that error again. This person would gain very little from acts of self-flagellation. Self-knowledge enables the person to put the wrong behind him without, in any way, condoning the wrong that he has done. Incidentally, this brings out that, in some though hardly all cases, the value of the institution of punishment may lie more in the role it plays in the public's eye than the good that it does for the person being punished.

At any rate, there is another side to the coin of self-knowledge, perhaps a more slippery side. Suppose that what makes a piece of morally objectionable behavior particularly so is that it is done for ignoble reasons, say, a married person's having an affair to test her or his sexual prowess. But suppose that Johnson recently had an affair because her husband has been completely paralyzed for 10 years. Johnson could say, with some justification, that while having an affair is morally wrong, her reason for doing so is considerably less open to moral criticism than numerous other reasons which people give for having an affair; and let us also suppose that she rightly holds that but for the circumstances of her husband's permanent physical impairment she would have done no such thing, since she dearly loves her husband. Accordingly, she may be able to forgive herself for having deliberately done what she regards and continues to regard as morally wrong, for she thinks that if ever it were understandable that a person had an extramarital affair, it is so in her case. Whether in the end Johnson is open to the same level of moral criticism as is any other person who has an affair is a matter that I shall not discuss. What I mean to be drawing attention to is that as people view their personal lives, a Johnson-like line of reasoning is often deemed efficacious to permit moral self-pardoning: X is morally wrong, but I committed X for reason R, and R is a considerably less morally objectionable reason for X-ing than most other reasons why people X; indeed, doing X for reason R is forgivable.

We should be clear about what has been claimed here. I have not argued that people are naturally inclined to be more forgiving of themselves than of others, although that may be true generally. Instead, the claim is that owing to self-knowledge, a person has access to exculpatory reasons for his morally inappropriate behavior which are not readily available to others, and the problem is that a person might succumb to rationalization, taking something as an exculpatory reason when (reflection would reveal that) it is no such thing. The idea here is that because a person knows himself well, he is aware of the kind of reasons that will work for him, psychically, to get him to assuage his conscience.

No doubt one can immediately see the relevance of the prceding discussion to the issue of friendship and morality. Companion friends have enormous knowledge of one another's lives. The point I wish to make, which surely has been anticipated, is that from the standpoint of moral assessment, the knowledge which friends have of one another functions in roughly the same way as self-knowledge does in the individual case.

Returning to companion friends Leslie and Marion, I offer a two-step example of a moral wrong, speaking first to the case where a person is too self-critical and then to the case where a person perhaps has an exculpatory reason.

Leslie may know that Marion had an affair with a 26-year-old student who had been pursuing him, and that Marion is so devastated over the fact that he did this that nothing good whatsoever would be gained by reporting Marion—a brlliant instructor—to the administration, which Leslie has done in other cases. In tears, Marion tells Leslie that he is so terribly ashamed of himself—that not having ever done such a thing before had been a tremendous source of moral pride. In fact, Marion has written his letter of resignation. To now give this example the flavor of the previous Johnson scenario, Leslie may also know that were it not for Marion having just lost both of his parents, he would never have been so emotionally vulnerable as to succumb to such a thing, for Leslie knows that the opportunity (with others) has forcefully presented itself on numerous occasions. I am supposing that in the first instance Marion has no exculpatory reason for his inappropriate behavior, but that he does in the second one. Without adding the loss of parents, Leslie may know that Marion is profoundly sincere and remorseful for what he has done, and from past experience Leslie may know that when Marion exhibits such profound remorse over some behavior the chances of Marion's engaging in that behavior again are next to zero. To be sure, Leslie could scold Marion for having done this thing and file a report against Marion, but I trust that, as I am telling the story, filing a report would hardly seem to serve any purpose. Moreover, I trust that scolding him would seem pointless as well, for the issue is not one of Marion failing to have the appropriate moral ideal here; nor is it one of his failing to have and show appropriate remorse for his wrongdoing. Accordingly, would it not be far more natural for Leslie to want to comfort Marion, to let him know that this one mistake does not render him morally bankrupt, to point out that many a person would have succumbed much earlier on to the student's advances, and so on. In fact, were Leslie to scold Marion as if Marion were but a lecher we might think that Leslie was being rather harsh.

So without adding the loss of parents to the scenario, Leslie's posture is not that Marion has an excuse for his impropriety, but one of understanding without condoning. If we add the loss of both parents, then Leslie's posture becomes all the more one of understanding without condoning. The difference is that in one case the understanding is tied to the simple truth that even

morally decent human beings are fallible, whereas with the addition of the loss of both parents, the understanding is also tied to the realization that a traumatic emotional loss can render a person extremely vulnerable emotionally. Of course, the tragic loss of parents or not, Leslie could rightly insist that, in having that affair with that 26-year-old, Marion had violated a most important principle of the academy. But, given Marion's character and Leslie's familiarity with it, I trust that, even without this addition, such a stance on Leslie's part reeks of fulsome moral self-righteousness rather than a justified invocation of moral standards, which is not to say that we have self-righteous behavior whenever a friend holds the moral line with a friend. By contrast, were the offender simply another member of the faculty, we would not expect Leslie even to attempt to be as understanding, although this other faculty member could be just like Marion in every way.

Of course, we can be horrified that a friend behaved in a certain way, especially if the person's behavior reflects negatively upon us. In any case, such behavior usually has to be particularly egregious in some way. The very wrongdoing itself goes beyond the pale or, for instance, the act showed a flagrant indifference to the feelings of others. Suppose everyone in a room failed a most important examination, save one's friend. Or suppose that she passed the examination and it is announced that a person's mother just passed away. In either context it would be most inappropriate for her to make much of her success, perhaps saying nothing unless she is directly asked about her performance on the examination, although she is rightly proud of this success. It is important to bear in mind the difference between explaining a friend's behavior and apologizing for it. Others may find our friend's behavior strange, whereas we appreciate and admire it. Here, we do not apologize for how she behaves, since we do not concede any inappropriate behavior on her part; indeed, we may chastise others for being judgmental. We apologize for inappropriate, especially wrongful, behavior, and for reasons that I shall give below in this section, occasions of this sort should be few and far between.

We are now in the position to appreciate more fully the claim made in the introduction that friendship pushes the limits of morality. Limiting ourselves to innocent people who have been wronged, it is natural for morally decent persons to experience, on behalf of the victim, indignation toward the perpetrator of the wrongful behavior. And if the victim is a companion friend, then it is common enough to experience enormous resentment as well toward the perpetrator. But here is the rub. When the perpetrator turns out to be a companion friend, we do not experience a like level of indignation toward the friend—certainly not immediately and often never—on behalf of the innocent victim. On the contrary, as I have indicated with the example of Leslie and Marion, we seek to understand the friend's behavior, to put his wrongdoing in perspective, with the result being that the innocent victim fails to receive his moral due, if you will, in terms of our moral reaction to his having been wronged. This is of enormous significance because if indignation and resentment motivate us to press for what is right on behalf of those who have been wronged, then friendship can be a substantial barrier in this regard, when the wrongdoer is a deep friend.

Another way of getting at the tension between morality and friendship is by looking at the phenomenon of loyalty in friendship. In moral theory, objectivity and impartiality are highly valorized. A wrong is a wrong whether it is done by a friend or a stranger. But this kind of moral stance can be at odds with the demands of loyalty in friendship. Although as with honesty, kindness, and so on, a person can certainly be loyal to a fault, merely being willing to plant one's feet firmly on the soil of available circumstantial evidence is not generally a sign of loyalty, as one can presumably expect that of anyone. If the loyal soldier is one who, up to a point, continues to stand by his captain even when the evidence on the battlefield would point to her defeat, then a loyal friend, presumably, is one who holds fast to the belief that his friend is of good character, even though strong circumstantial evidence would suggest otherwise. As a result of loyalty, not only does a friend give the benefit of the doubt to a friend when it would be reasonable for a stranger not to, but a friend will often distance her- or himself from reasonable acts of public criticism of a friend. Of course, it is arguable that anyone should be given the benefit of the doubt where this is possible. Perhaps. But the point is that the motivation to do so would seem to be anchored in loyalty rather than morality.

All the same, none of previous discussion should be mistaken for the view that friends are tolerant of moral squalor on one another's part. I have not made any such claim; nor does a claim of this sort follow from what has been said, including the remarks about loyalty, for a quite loyal friend may nonetheless be concerned to get at the very truth of the matter. Without ever engaging in anything like a display of righteous moral indignation toward a friend on account of the wrong that he has done to an innocent person, one can take a very hard moral stance with him on account of the wrong that he has done. One can indicate the pain that

his wrongdoing has caused one, because one has held him in such high moral esteem. One can go on to express how such wrongdoing even jeopardizes the friendship, if only because one does not want to be associated with a person who so behaves. Still, this will be very different from acting on the victim's behalf against the friend. Except incidentally, an argument that a friendship has been jeopardized by wrong done to another leaves unaddressed the harm that the innocent person has suffered.

The reader will notice that I have been careful not to offer an assessment of whether there should be this tension between friendship and morality. There are those who would insist that all personal relations, no matter what level of affection they may attain, are properly subsumable under the principles of morality. All that I want to say here is that this view of the priority of the right cannot, it seems, be squared with the psychological makeup of human beings, where profound ties of affection are involved. Within a rather wide range, a person would have to be capable of extraordinary compartmentalization in order to be capable of responding to a friend's wronging of an innocent third party with the same kind of wrath and resentment with which he would respond to any stranger's wronging of an innocent third-party. And such compartmentalization does not make for a psychologically healthy self nor for wholesome friendship. In the *New Testament,* there is the saying that love hides a multitude of faults. Taken literally, this may be far too strong. But a gloss on this saying would be that love carries in its wake an understanding of the faults of others that is rarely achieved in its absence. And the psychology of understanding a person for whom one has great affection may be such that, up to a point, any rate, it calms the storm of moral indignation that we would otherwise have.

On the other hand, our understanding of the wrongdoing of a friend would seem to hit a most impenetrable wall when we turn out to be the victim of the friend's wrongdoing. This should come as no surprise. This is because if anyone should be fortified with reasons not to harm us, a character friend should. Not only are there the ever-present moral considerations, which should be reason enough, but there is the love of the friendship itself, which one supposes should serve as a fail-safe measure. When we are wronged by a friend, the question is never simply, "How could you have done that?" Rather, it is, "How could you have done that to *me?*" What cries out for an explanation is not as much the wrongdoing as it is the target of the wrongdoing. These considerations indirectly complement our preceding discussion. In friendship, we expect love to reign and to govern interactions to a degree that far exceeds the demands of morality. This love should serve as a safety net for us against even the very temptation to wrong us, and it should give us understanding in many instances where morality would render a verdict of guilty.

In bringing this section to a close, let me return briefly to the subject of friendship and moral squalor. As I have indicated, the tension that I have spelled out between morality and friendship does not entail that companion friendship is a matter of tolerating moral squalor. On the other hand, companion friends tend to maintain the same level of moral rectitude in their lives, whatever that level might be. Thus, take two companion friends at the same level of moral rectitude. If one became a more morally upright person than the other or, conversely, one became a more ignoble person than the other, then either the friendship would terminate or the other friend would change accordingly. There are two reasons why this is so.

One of these has to do with the importance of self-disclosure between friends. In general, aside from matters involving counseling, we are uneasy self-disclosing to people whom we regard as morally superior to us because it is simply impossible to avoid the feeling that the person is sitting in judgment of us, although the friend may assure us that nothing of the sort is going on. The second reason is related to the first.

While saints and heroes are a wonderful reminder of the potential for goodness that exists in human beings, the fact remains that most us of are neither, nor are we much concerned to be either. Most of us are rather content to be ordinary human beings with, if at all, moments of excellence here and there. More poignantly, most of us are inclined to think that this is all that can be rightly expected of us; hence, it is unreasonable to expect people to realize their full moral potential. If two individuals start at the same level of moral rectitude and one goes on to a much higher level, then this becomes, as it were, a moral challenge to the other friend, which he must either accept or decline—for if one could have made the change for the better than the other could have as well, since they supposedly had the same kind of moral timbre. On the other hand, if one descends to a much lower level of moral rectitude, then in addition to the problem of self-disclosing which the person who has descended will have, the one who has not descended will find the friendship increasingly unsatisfying.

On the one hand, there will be the tensions that come with having a close friend who constantly engages in moral behavior that one finds unacceptable. If the friend does not make a turnaround in his behavior, then one loses one's moral leverage with that person, since he can rightly point out that his behavior is no different from that which one has been tolerating all along. To be sure, one can talk about limits having been reached, and so on. But to make this move is, in effect, to issue an ultimatum: change or lose a friend. On the other hand, there will be the issue of one's own moral reputation, which will become sullied by association: either one engages in certain immoral behavior or one is tolerant of it in (at least certain) others. Either way, one's reputation has been sullied, though undoubtedly more so in the first instance. But the second instance is hardly trivial; to be known as one who is tolerant of such-and-such immoral behavior when committed by X and Y is invariably to lose one's moral leverage with others. Thus, the one who sustains the level of moral rectitude with which the two parties started their friendship will become disenchanted with the friendship.

I have not addressed the topic of friendship where both individuals are immoral. This case raises special problems insofar as immoral persons can be viewed as egoists. How can two people, each of whom is primarily concerned with promoting only her or his self-interests, have genuine affection for another? And if each claims that the other is an exception, what reason does the other have to place much confidence in this claim. I shall not pursue these issues except to note that if there can be genuine friendship among the immoral, the argument in the preceding two paragraphs concerning the importance of parity of moral rectitude between friends applies equally well to such cases. Just as moral goodness admits of considerable range, so does moral badness. And the absence of parity pertains to there being a significant distance in quality between the moral character of two people, a distance which can be anywhere along the spectrum of moral goodness and badness. So suppose that Leslie and Marion are both immoral friends who engage in the immoral behavior of defrauding the elderly, but that, after awhile, Leslie moves on to murder. If Marion were to protest that Leslie had gone too far, Marion's protest would make sense notwithstanding the fact that Marion's own moral behavior is quite reprehensible.

IV. CONCLUSION: FRIENDSHIP AND THE IDEAL SOCIETY

As a most fitting way of bringing this essay to a close, the preceding discussion suggests a very profound way in which friendship can push morality to its limit. If the account just sketched of the equality of moral rectitude between friends is correct, then a most interesting question arises, bearing in mind just these considerations: Might a person refrain from becoming a morally better person in order to maintain a friendship with a person, where the friends are morally decent to begin with? Could the good that flows from a friendship be preferable to the good that flows from being a morally better person? In *The Politics,* Aristotle observed that those who have no need of others are either gods or beasts. So we can ask whether a person could have a proper understanding of the value of others if she or he were prepared to forsake all ties of human affection in the ascent toward moral perfection. It is difficult to see how such a person could. Alas, it would seem that if a friendship is rich enough then morality's claim to continual moral self-development may, at some point, fall upon deaf ears. None of this may be justified; but, alas, it may all be more understandable than we had been inclined to suppose. And if so, then Aristotle's observation about friendship may be so enduring because it speaks to a deep deep insight concerning what it is like to be a human being: Even with all the riches in the world a life without friendship is incomplete. Why? Because neither morality nor all the riches in the world can take the place of the affirmation, the understanding, and the reflection of ourselves that we all need from time to time in order to flourish and which companion friendship—that is, friendship at its best—affords us. I have not argued that the affection and affirmation of friendship is always preferable to moral betterment. Rather, I have challenged the converse, namely that moral betterment is always preferable to these things. Although there are few, if any, instances when a person might be open to criticism for eschewing friendship in order to achieve moral betterment, I have suggested that in view of the nature of human psychology, it is untenable to hold that in choosing friendship over moral betterment a person is thereby, and always, open to moral criticism. The quality of some friendships may be worth the trade-off. Thus, we may find in friendship a formidable challenge to moral perfectionism, understood as the idea that human beings should have as their sole goal the moral perfection of their lives.

So to conclude with a most speculative remark regarding a society replete with friendship at its best, this society would be an association of individuals for whom each serves as a mirror of insight for another, who in turn serves as a mirror of insight for that person. Accordingly, even if each friendship in and of itself does not represent a life of morality at its best, this association of individuals taken together would nonetheless yield an outcome, among individuals who are neither gods nor beasts, whereby the quality of the whole of moral life in society would nonetheless achieve a moral good that could never be reached by single pairs of friends living in isolation of one another.

Acknowledgments

I thank Michele Moody-Adams, Neera Kapur Badhwar, Lawrence A. Blum, David Kim, Alasdair MacIntyre, and Howard McGary for their instructive comments upon earlier versions of this essay.

Bibliography

Badhwar, N. K. (Ed.) (1993). "Friendship: A Philosophical Reader." Cornell Univ. Press, Ithaca, NY.

Badhwar, N. K. (1996). The limited unity of virtue. *Nous,* **30,** 306–329.

Blum, L. (1980). "Friendship, Altruism, and Morality." Routledge and Kegan Paul, London.

Cooper, J. M. (1980). Aristotle on friendship. In "Essays on Aristotle's Ethics" (A. Rorty, Ed.). Univ. of California Press, Berkeley.

MacIntyre, A. (1981). "After Virtue: A Study in Moral Theory." The Univ. of Notre Dame Press, Notre Dame, IN.

Railton, P. (1984). Alienation, consequentialism, and the demands of morality. *Philos. Public Affairs* **13**(2), 134–171.

Schwarzenbach, S. (1996). On civic friendship. *Ethics* **107**(1), 97–128.

Sherman, N. (1989). "The Fabric of Character: Aristotle's Theory of Virtue." Oxford Univ. Press, New York.

Stocker, M. (1990). "Plural and Conflicting Values." Clarendon Press, Oxford.

Thomas, L. (1989). "Living Morally: A Psychology of Moral Character." Temple Univ. Press, Philadelphia, PA.

GAIA HYPOTHESIS

Andrew Brennan
The University of Western Australia

GLOSSARY

biodiversity One common measure of biodiversity combines richness of species with evenness of distribution of individual organisms among the species. A community with many species represented by only a few individuals would be regarded as rich, but not very diverse, for the rarer species would be easily lost.
biosphere All living things, and communities of life, on the earth's surface.
community A biological community is usually (and inadequately) defined as an assemblage of species populations that are (a) located together in space and time, (b) linked by relations of feeding, decomposition, biological productivity, and so on, and (c) historically distinct from other communities.
ecosystem A biological community together with the nonliving (abiotic) material from its environment cycled and used within the community.
Gaia The ancient Greek goddess of the earth.
Gaia hypothesis In its original form, the proposal that the biosphere, atmosphere, oceans, soil, and rocks of the earth constitute a self-regulating system that maintains the conditions necessary for life.

geophysiology Lovelock's proposed name for a science that embraces ecology, geochemistry, and geophysics (also known as Gaia science).
richness The greater the number of different species in a biological community, the greater its richness.
rock cycle Popular name for the changes in, and cycling of, rock, which occurs as a result of forces such as continental drift, earthquakes, and volcanic activity.

THE GAIA HYPOTHESIS is that the earth's crust, along with its oceans, atmosphere, and biosphere is one system. This great structure is self-sustaining and self-regulating. In particular, Gaia regulates those features critical for the maintenance of life—the oxygen content of the atmosphere, the salinity of the seas, mean surface temperatures, atmospheric pressure, and so on. According to Lovelock, instead of thinking of ourselves as living on an inert planet that "supports" a biosphere, we should think of the whole earth as a single large "superorganism." Its parts include rocks and structures studied by geology as well as the living communities and the elements—carbon, nitrogen, and so on—cycled through them.

I. THE HYPOTHESIS AND ITS HISTORY

The theory that earth is a single living organism has its origins in the work of the eighteenth-century Scottish geologist, James Hutton. He was the first person to propose that the planet's crust is a kind of physiological system. The rock cycle, for example, redistributes and changes material belonging to the mantle, crust, and surface of the earth. By studying rocks we discover that over enormous spans of time mountain ranges grow and disappear, valleys form and close, and coasts advance and recede in a process of endless change. The movement of water from sea to land and back again, and the recirculation of nutrition through the soil was Hutton argued, akin to the circulation of blood and nourishment in the living body.

Following Hutton's inspiration, James Lovelock in 1988 proposed to use the term "geophysiology" as a substitute for what he had earlier called "Gaia science." Lovelock's central ideas of Gaia science had been anticipated not only by Hutton but also by Russian theorists in the late nineteenth and early twentieth centuries. It was V. I. Vernadsky who adapted and developed Eduard Suess's concept of "biosphere" to apply not just to living things and processes but also to "the area of the Earth's crust occupied by transformers which convert cosmic radiation into effective terrestrial energy." Even in his early work, Lovelock counted the rocks, air, and oceans as part of Gaia. Indeed, in a striking comparison, he points out that just as the dead heartwood of a tree carries the history of its earlier growth, so the atoms of rocks deep in the magma come from the ancestral life that once existed on the planet's surface. If we regard trees as living organisms, then the planet can also be regarded as a living thing—Gaia.

In his first book, *Gaia: A New Look at Life on Earth,* Lovelock argued that if the level of atmospheric oxygen increased even by a small amount, the next lightning strike in a dry forest would result in a massive conflagration. If the salinity of the sea were to rise or fall more than a small amount, many fish species would go extinct. The mechanisms determining the levels of salt in the sea and oxygen in the atmospheres maintain stability despite fluctuations in the amount of fresh water pouring into the sea each year and variations in the extent of oxygen-producing vegetation. The result is an appearance of design: the temperature of the earth, the salinity of the seas, and the composition of the atmosphere look as if they are designed to support life.

In his early work, Lovelock speculated that living organisms themselves strive to maintain the conditions that support their continued existence. This led to criticisms from biologists, such as Ford Doolittle and Richard Dawkins, who pointed out that evolutionary biology can explain the appearance of design in nature by reference to blind forces of natural selection operating over vast timescales. If, as Dawkins speculated, living things are survival machines constructed by genes, there is no room for the further hypothesis that living things operate according to a higher purpose—the maintenance of stable conditions for the production of more living things.

In his response, published in 1988 as *The Ages of Gaia,* Lovelock developed and refined his account. He removed any hint of purpose from the theory and argued that it was complementary to evolutionary theory. A major achievement of this later work was to show, by means of a species of simple "daisyworld" models, that an imaginary planet can maintain a relatively constant temperature in the face of increasing solar radiation through the "struggle for existence" among daisies of different shades of color.

The daisyworld models revealed two things. First, that living things in competition with each other for space to grow can work like a thermostat controlling the overall temperature of their planet. In this way, Darwinian biology is incorporated into the theory, not excluded by it. Second, the models provided a possible answer to the question: why is there an increase in biodiversity over time? Increasing biodiversity will ensure greater resilience and sophistication of the temperature-controlling mechanism in the face of fluctuations in solar radiation (see more below). In principle, the same story can be thought to apply to mechanisms regulating other important conditions. This would include, for example, the availability of elements essential for the growth and maintenance of living things as well as the factors that ensure relatively constant proportions of atmospheric gases.

II. EVIDENCE FOR LOVELOCK'S THEORY

The salinity of the seas and the proportion of oxygen in the atmosphere appear to have remained relatively constant over millions of years. What is the explanation for this? As a consultant for NASA in the 1960s, Lovelock predicted that Mars does not at present support life. Like Venus, the atmosphere of Mars is in chemical equilibrium, with carbon dioxide predominating and nitrogen levels of less than 4%. Earth's atmosphere is far from chemical equilibrium, with carbon dioxide at minimal levels, nitrogen predominating, and oxygen at around 21%. Small perturbations in the proportion of oxygen would lead to disaster as far as many forms of life are concerned.

Oxygen itself started to accumulate in the atmosphere as a polluting gas more than 2 billion years ago as a waste product of cyanobacteria. In Western Australia rocklike stromatolites formed by colonies of these photosynthesizing bacteria can still be found. According to Lovelock and his collaborator Lynn Margulis, the changing nature of the atmosphere forced diversification of life away from that based on nonnucleated (prokaryotic) cells to the eukaryotic, nucleated cell on which plant and animal life is based. The prokaryotes did not die out. They survive in our intestines and in the mud where they are safe from oxgyen. According to Lynn Margulis, some of them evolved into the organelles of the complex eukaryotic cells within whose walls they were safe from the slowly accumulating oxygen. Here is a case where massive "pollution" led to a major change in the nature of life on earth and the emergence of new families of species.

Most biological and ecological theory focuses on competition as the force that drives evolution. However, if Margulis's story about the evolution of the eukaryotes is accepted, it appears that the evolution of life can depend on cooperation, or symbiosis, as much as on competition. In the last two decades, the bacteria and related microorganisms have been subject to intensive study and reclassification. None of these changes threatens the plausibility of the suggestion that cooperation may be just as fundamental as competition in explaining the nature of life on earth. It is important, however, to keep a clear distinction between the speculations about cell evolution and the more firmly based hypotheses that claim that competition in the daisyworld models serves to inhibit change (at least for a time) in the parameters critical for maintaining life at a given level of organization.

In one daisyworld model, there are two kinds of plants only—black and white daisies. Each species can only survive at temperatures above 5°C and below 40°C. Over a long period, the sun of daisyworld is heating up. In the beginning, the surface temperature of the planet is cool, and the black daisies germinate and grow slowly. Being darker than the soil, the spread of the black daisies produces higher temperatures on the parts of the planet on which they are established. The warmer conditions favor more rapid germination and faster growth, so the black daisies spread more rapidly. This leads to more absorption of solar energy and a generally warmer planet.

After a long time, the hot spots created in dense areas of black daisies inhibit further daisy growth. As the sun gets progressively hotter, the white daisies begin to have an advantage. They reflect more of the sun's heat away from the surface of the earth producing conditions favorable to longer life for them and their offspring and better chances for seeds to germinate. Black daisies start dying out, as the whites win in the struggle for existence. At the global level, the success of the white daisies means that the average surface temperature of the planet does not increase. Instead, there is a roughly constant temperature maintained during the changes in daisy populations.

From the point of view of the daisies, this is just a struggle for survival between two species with different pigmentation and similar temperature tolerances. But from the point of view of the planet, the change from black to white dominance has preserved a relatively stable mean temperature. No daisy, or population, intended to achieve this result. So, despite the appearance of design, there is no need to attribute purpose at any level in the daisyworld system. To make his models more realistic, Lovelock next introduced two further features. First, there were more shades of daisies. Next, he envisaged recurring plagues that destroy a given proportion of the daisies at regular intervals. The results showed even more sophisticated temperature regulation. Suppose there are 10 species of differently shaded daisies, and 10% of them are wiped out by plagues every so often. Lovelock demonstrated that in such a scenario oscillations in overall temperature after each plague are rapidly damped down.

The daisyworld models strongly suggest that plant diversity will help to maintain relatively constant levels of critical atmospheric gases, stable global temperatures, and so on. It is notable that the earth has supported life for approximately 4 billion years, during which time the sun's luminosity has increased by around 30%. The evidence available suggests that, just like the daisyworld, earth has maintained relatively stable mean temperatures over much of that time thanks to the changing distribution and diversity of living species themselves. The simple daisyworld models provide a persuasive case for the Gaia hypothesis. If correct, this means that the environment does not simply put selectional pressure on organisms, but their behavior in turn also affects the nature of that environment itself.

III. GEOPHYSIOLOGY AND SCIENCE

Gaia science has suffered a similar fate to systems theory by being marginalized in main-line science. Typical textbooks in ecology ignore it. By contrast, some popular publications have put geophysiology and related ideas before a general audience, including educators.

Two particularly popular and influential works, both published by Pan Books in the late 1980s are *The Gaia Peace Atlas* and *The Gaia Atlas of Planetary Management*.

In recent years there has been a tendency for ecology to focus on the actions of communities and populations instead of ecosystems. When the interactions between a population and its changing environment are discussed, this is generally limited to describing deposition of plant litter, defecation, siltation, and the like as the major way in which communities of organisms can change their environment. The claim that natural selection favors the organisms that are better adapted to environmental conditions is often stated. But, although the Gaia hypothesis accepts this as a correct statement, it is also regarded as incomplete.

Lovelock diagnosed the situation in this way:

> Because of the tribalism that isolates the denizens of the scientific disciplines, biologists who made models of the competitive growth of species chose to ignore the physical and chemical environment. Geochemists, who made models of the cycles of the elements, and geophysicists, who modelled the climate, chose to ignore the dynamic interactions of the species.

To overcome such tribalism, biologists would have to note that evolutionary explanations are adequate only up to a point, and ecology would have to recognize that the explanation for biodiversity is to be found by taking species and their physical and chemical environments as constituting a single system (see Thompson, 1987, for a series of essays by scientists committed to rejecting tribalism).

One possible motive for scientific and philosophical distrust of the science of geophysiology might be a worry that Lovelock's original program was reductionist. This may seem an odd charge to level at an explicitly holistic theory that criticized the reductionism of conventional science. But there can be holistic reduction. When features of life on earth are explained by reference to Gaia, the behavior of parts is being interpreted in terms of the behavior and function of the whole. To do this for all features of the parts is just as reductionist as to attempt to explain all aspects of the whole purely in terms of aspects of its components.

IV. GAIAN ETHICS

Despite the importance of geophysiology, philosophy has followed the scientific mainstream in giving scant attention to Lovelock's work (but see Brennan, 1988, for one exception). A few articles have discussed the prospects for Gaian ethics, the most interesting being by Stephen Clark. According to Clark, the theory gives a grounding for an environmental ethic. Gaia herself is a magnificent thing—the world's most distinguished subsystem. Part of this magnificence is a matter of aesthetics; Clark avoids pinning any kind of inherent, or intrinsic, moral value on Gaia. Each of us, he says, carries a small portion of value for larger systems, including ultimately Gaia herself. Given that individual living things have value, then our existence as parts of Gaia raises the following question for us: what should we do to maintain the value of the whole system to which we belong?

Clark endorses a form of holism in which individuals are reflected in, and in turn reflect, the larger systems that maintain life on earth. Their relation to the environment is not just a question of prudence or aesthetics, but also a question of ethics. Our relationship to Gaia may require some sacrifices on our part to maintain the planetary superorganism in a state of good health. Such a version of Gaian ethics can motivate the same kind of respect for nature advocated by followers of "deep" green perspectives and ecofeminism.

Like other holistic theories, Clark's takes cooperation and symbiosis as natural models for human moral behavior. Other theorists, notably some biologists and economists, see apparently cooperative behavior as best explained by underlying selfishness. For Richard Dawkins, for example, altruism is a survival strategy for "selfish" genes. Similarly, some economists would define altruistic behavior as, ultimately, a kind of self-benefiting behavior (the altruist is the person who gets good feelings, as it happens, from helping others). These latter treatments either redefine the notions of altruism and selflessness, or try to show, more modestly, that the fundamental motives to which everything else reduces, are ones of selfishness or self-interest.

It would be wrong to conclude, however, that geophysiology is different from economics and molecular biology in emphasizing cooperation over competition. Indeed, additional argument is necessary to link Gaia science with any particular moral point of view. This can be strikingly illustrated by comparing Clark's conclusions with those of Lynn Margulis and Dorion Sagan. They argue that it is an open question whether the planet is sick:

> If global biospheric relations are undergoing a major reorganization due not so much to the interference of humanity (this would . . . be the

epitome of the shallow ecological view, since it keeps people apart from nature) but rather the development within the biosphere of the human phenomenon, it is perfectly natural for us as sentient beings to feel distress in the presence of such changes. What is in question, however, is the assumption that we know that the planet is sick and can fix it by bringing it to some sort of environmental stasis. Without being dismissed as technophiliac, we would like to suggest that the decline in species diversity may be balanced by an increase in technological diversity—a trade-off that may ultimately enhance the longevity of the biosphere.

What can account for two so radically different prescriptions? Clark supports a reduction in our interference with natural processes, while Sagan and Margulis seem to see human pollution and appropriation as perhaps a further stage in the evolution of Gaia.

One way to understand the issue is to consider whether human beings are part of nature, or radically separate from it. The success of naturalistic science has encouraged the cancellation of distinctions between humans and nature, and between culture and nature. Sagan and Margulis seem to accept that human behavior takes place wholly within nature: we are just one species among millions of others. By contrast, for Clark, there may be a cultural and moral question posed for us as beings that are different from the rest of nature. We have the capacity for making free choices in the light of reason—a capacity that cannot be reduced to biological features, and a capacity that is only dimly mirrored, if present at all, in the higher animal species.

For the naturalist, the space for moral choice is relatively limited. For the thinker who rejects the reduction of human capacities to biological functions, and for whom humans are morally and intellectually unique among species, the space for moral choice is relatively large. The naturalist sees what choices we have as taking place within the systems described and structured by geophysiological theory. By contrast, the nonnaturalist sees Gaia science as describing a nature that is apart from humans. As a result, the nonnaturalist regards the findings of Gaia science as posing a moral question that is difficult for the naturalist to recognize.

V. CONCLUSION

The existence of these two approaches to the status of humans and nature provides one explanation of why

accepting the legitimacy of geophysiology as a branch of science does not translate into automatic moral agreement on conservation goals. If we are part of Gaia, then we may be like the cyanobacteria, whose waste material provoked the emergence of more complex forms of life. Whether our pollution and destruction of ecosystems produces fruitful changes or not, our roles as parts of Gaia is a legitimate subject of geophysiological study. If we are separate from Gaia, then our pollution and destruction is an object of moral, aesthetic, and spiritual concern.

This particular problem reflects a wider puzzle for the whole project of contemporary environmental ethics. The question of whether humans are best regarded as part of nature, or as separate from it, is perhaps the key issue dividing various thinkers in the field. It is tempting in such cases to look for a synthesis between the opposing views. This would reveal the ways humans are, and the ways in which they are not, part of nature. The present hegemony of scientific materialism, and the almost unquestioned acceptance of physicalism among the majority of contemporary philosophers and scientists, makes the systematic quest for such a synthesis a difficult undertaking.

Geophysiology provides a number of different natural models for human moral behavior. While evolutionary theorists emphasize fitness in the "struggle for existence," and some molecular biologists stress the "selfishness" of genes, Gaia science leaves a place for cooperation as a fundamental process in explaining the evolution of some aspects of biological complexity. Additionally, instead of seeing life as an adaptation to fixed geochemical conditions, it depicts the living world as involved in constant exchange with the nonliving, a result of which is the striking disequilibrium conditions that mark out Earth as the only "living planet" in the solar system. How geophysiological theories will be woven into future ethical and cultural ideas is a matter of speculation. Given its impact on popular thought, it is likely to find further niches in conservationist thinking and environmental ethics.

Also See the Following Articles

BIODIVERSITY • DEEP ECOLOGY • ECOLOGICAL BALANCE • SPECIESISM

Bibliography

Brennan, A. (1988). *Thinking about nature*. London: Routledge.
Clark, S. R. L. (1983). Gaia and the forms of life. In Elliot, R., & Gare, A. (Eds.), *Environmental philosophy*. Milton Keynes: Open University Press.

Dawkins, R. (1989). *The extended phenotype*. Oxford: Oxford University Press.

Gould, S. J. (1996). *Nature's grandeur*. London: Jonathan Cape.

Lovelock, J. E. (1979). *Gaia: A new look at life on earth*. Oxford: Oxford University Press.

Lovelock, J. E. (1988). *The ages of Gaia: A biography of our living earth*. Oxford: Oxford University Press.

Plumwood, V. (1993). *Feminism and the mastery of nature*. London: Routledge.

Sagan, D., & Margulis, L. (1993). God, Gaia and biophilia. In Kellert, S. R., and Wilson, E. O. (Eds.), *The biophilia hypothesis*. Washington, DC: Island Press.

Sylvan, R. & Bennett, D. (1994). *Greening ethics*. Cambridge: White Horse Press.

Stark, O. (1996). *Altruism and beyond*. Cambridge: Cambridge University Press.

Thompson, W. I. (Ed.). (1987). *Gaia: A way of knowing*. Great Barrington, Mass.: Lindisfarne Press.

GAMBLING

Valerie C. Lorenz
Compulsive Gambling Center, Inc.

"In the world of sport all men win alike
but lose differently; and so gamblers are rated,
not by the way in which they win,
but by the way in which they lose.
Some men lose with a careless smile,
recognizing that losing is a part of the game;
others curse their luck and rail at fortune;
and others, still, lose sadly; after each
experience they are swept by a wave of reform;
they resolve to stop gambling and be good...

Those in the first class are looked upon with admiration;
those in the second class are merely commonplace;
while those in the third are regarded
with contempt."

JAMES WELDON JOHNSON
The Autobiography of an
Ex-Coloured Man, 1912

GLOSSARY

bailout Relieving the compulsive gambler of a financial or emotional burden on the promise to stop gambling.

cannibalizing A term popularized in the past decade to indicate money formerly spent on one form of activity or product which is now spent on something else, as money spent typically on restaurants is now spent on casino gambling.

chasing Increasing one's wagers in a desperate attempt to regain past losses, as in "chasing one's losses."

compulsive gambler A popular term for pathological gambler.

criminal gambler A gambler who typically has a long history of illegal activities, including that of gambling-related activities, such as bookmaking, running an illegal gambling game or activity, or loan-sharking.

gambling Wagering or betting something of value, usually money, on an activity which is predominantly chance, in the hopes of gaining something of larger value.

gaming The English word for gambling some 200 years ago, and a preferred term by the casino industry, worldwide, to describe casino gambling.

pathological gambler An individual suffering from a diagnosable and treatable psychiatric disorder associated with excessive and chronic gambling, adversely affecting that individual's health, family, work, and social life, most often ending in financial ruin, criminal activity, and suicidal tendencies, and who is unable to control that gambling and related behavior.

problem gambler An individual who may gamble excessively or with money and time better spent otherwise, but who maintains a modicum of control over the gambling.

professional gambler An individual who earns his livelihood from gambling, such as a poker champion, and who remains in control of the gambling.

social gambler An individual who gambles for recreation, with control of the amount of time, money, and frequency spent on gambling,

wagering The same as "gambling" but a term preferred in the horseracing industry.

GAMBLING is risking something of value on an activity that is primarily chancy, in the hopes of realizing a profit. It has existed in virtually every society since prerecorded history. It has been incorporated into local customs and rites of passage through the ages.

I. GAMBLING, HISTORICALLY AND UNIVERSALLY

Gambling has its own groups which prefer different forms of wagering and is beset with its own forms of discrimination, often based on sex, age, and social class. One can place a wager on virtually anything, although certain forms of gambling have become ritualized and legitimized. This is not to say that all gambling is honest or legal; indeed, illegal forms of gambling, swindling, and cheating on games are as commonplace today as they were in yesteryear. Gambling historically has been associated with crime, political corruption, and positive and negative economic and social impact.

Universally and historically, gambling has had its strong advocates and its forceful opponents. Through-

out the debates, gambling has proven its durability by its appeal to fantasy, riches, and moments of grandeur. Currently promoted as a "painless tax," it has made millionaires of some, while resulting in personal ruin, crime, and devastation for others.

Today the progambling movement is mounting an all-out effort as the antigambling forces are gaining in strength and numbers.

A. Historical Gambling

Gambling is found in mythology among the Greeks, Romans, and Egyptians. The Greeks thought that gambling was invented by the gods. Aphrodite, the Goddess of Love, is known to have gambled on knucklebones with the god Pan. These knucklebones, or astragals, were thrown from a cup and became the forerunner of dice and dominoes, which are also referred to as "bones." Astragals were also used by the Greeks to divide the universe, just as lots were drawn at the foot of the cross for Christ's robes, for the division of land, and for the position of rank.

In mythology it is written that Mercury "played at tables" with the Moon. The Goddess of Fortune was lured into the arms of the God of War, and had a child named Gaming, which could be pleased only with cards, dice, or counters.

In the *Book of the Dead*, the souls of ancient Egyptians had to pass several tests before they could enter the Blessed Fields of the Dead where they could enjoy afterlife with such pleasant diversions as the game of senat, the forerunner of backgammon.

Implements and paintings found in tombs and in archeological digs attest to gambling's existence in antiquity. The earliest known board game was made of clay and ivory and was found to date to approximately 4000 B.C. in upper Egypt, although presumably games made of mud and wood may have been played in Egypt and parts of Africa prior to that time. Early board games were also found in Iraq, dating from 3000 B.C., and in Israel, dating to about 2000 B.C. A senat board dating to 1500 B.C. is housed in the Louvre.

Although it is popularly believed that Palamedes invented dice during the 10-year Trojan War, astragal cubes made from dog or sheep bones predate those found in Troy.

Loaded dice were buried with the Pharaohs in the pyramids upon their death, testifying not only to the existence of gambling, but also to cheating among Egyptians. Gambling has always had its problems.

The results of excessive gambling are as ancient as gambling itself. The Emperor Domitian gambled without cessation on a daily basis. Children played dice in imitation of their elders, and Juvenal laments about "the madness of games of chance." Tacitus, the Roman historian, wrote about the old Germans, who would "stake their freedom and even their life on the last throw of the dice."

In China, for centuries gambling was viewed as the principal cause of disputes and family disharmony, even over opium addiction and drunkenness.

In more current times the Communist Party attempted to suppress gambling; however, in 1981 gambling was so widespread in China that peasants neglected the spring planting in favor of betting. Operators of gambling dens were rebuked for swindling the people of their property and disturbing the social order.

In England, too, gambling became a social pathology many years ago. In the 14th century Geoffrey Chaucer wrote, "gambling is the very mother of all lies," and during the 19th century many English aristocrats were known to have lost their lands and their titles, causing the monarchy to forbid the importation of playing cards from Italy.

B. Gambling in the Colonies

The United States is no stranger to gambling. It is conceivable that Columbus brought playing cards to the western hemisphere in 1492, and it is known that the early European settlers brought gambling paraphernalia and traditions with them. They quickly learned of native American gambling.

Gambling is inherent in virtually all native American tribes. It can be found in tradition, legends, mythology, and art. Their mythology suggests that gambling was a most popular activity. It shows a linkage between the supernatural and games of chance, just as it did in other cultures.

Among native Americans, gambling was divided into games of physical skill, games of strategy, and games of chance. Games of physical skill included foot races, horse races, and athletic contests demonstrating hunting and warrior skills. The games of chance included dice games, hand games, and stick games. Games of warring skills or hunting were restricted to young males, while dice games or stick games were often limited to the women.

Gambling usually involved very high stakes. Gambling rewards were blankets, jewelry, weapons, livestock, and, on occasion, the wife.

Cheating was common, thus much of Indian gambling was tightly controlled through customs, rituals, and superstitions. Among the Yakima, where betting

was particularly heavy, the economic status of the players and the lifestyle of individuals could be altered quickly and dramatically through gambling wins or losses.

Among the Mohave, gambling had strong sexual connotations, and although stakes among the Mohave included one's wife, one's own life or blood relatives could not be used as stakes. Among the Pomo there is evidence of professional gamblers who required a lifetime apprenticeship to improve the skills of gambling and to learn the myths and traditions associated with gambling.

C. Gambling and Crime

America's oldest means for the quick raising of money was through local lotteries. Familiar with European lotteries, the early settlers implemented local lotteries to support construction of buildings, roads, and bridges. Lotteries helped support local government, Harvard and Princeton University buildings, and churches. Lotteries established by the Continental Congress financed the Revolutionary War and the expansion of the new colonies. Lotteries became so commonplace that in 1831 eight states operated over 400 lottery games, with sales being more than five times the federal budget for that year.

However, lotteries were also easy prey for swindlers and cheats, often leading to skimming and corruption of public officials. Government reform, under the leadership of President Andrew Jackson, became synonymous with lottery reform and eventual abolishment of the lotteries.

Other than lotteries, most forms of gambling in the early years of the United States appear to have been honest. This changed as the frontier expanded. The desire for work and for gold was matched only by the frontiersman's loneliness and lack of opportunity for more varied activities. Gambling became commonplace, and with it, cheating; indeed, the earliest other evidence of illegal gambling appears to be found in the mid-1800s among riverboat gamblers and frontier saloon gamblers.

The riverboat gambler, usually described as a fancy dude with a diamond stickpin and smoking a large cigar, often had to make a hasty exit from the riverboat prior to docking to avoid capture by the sheriff on land or to avoid capture by a victim on the boat. Evidence of other cheating is found even in unexpected places, as the following epitaph on a tombstone attests: "Played five aces, Now he's playing a harp."

Three-card monte players, who were "the most brazen tricksters on the Western rivers" during the 1850s, can still be found on busy street corners in urban areas today.

Illegal numbers rackets became widespread, particularly among urban African-Americans and the Irish, and later among Hispanic groups. Numbers gambling was serious business. Among African-Americans, the numbers were associated with dreams, anecdotes, and verses with numerical themes. Numbers wagering was a means of supplementing one's income, while providing an opportunity to participate in the social activities surrounding the "numbers man." Sociologists consider numbers and lottery gambling among the poor as the most prominent financial adaptation of the culture of poverty. Among many urban blacks, lottery or numbers gambling is viewed as a rational economic activity.

Two groups of gamblers emerged, both often the focus of Victorian-era moralists. One was termed the confidence man, the predatory card shark who learned quickly how to manipulate and exploit the gullible and unwary. The second group was composed of the gamblers, those who could afford to while away their time and money, and those who either desperately sought to contribute to their meager incomes or succumbed to the lure of "something for nothing." Those in the second group were considered degenerates who failed to contribute to their communities and who brought themselves and their families to despair and ruin, often committing crimes in the process.

A hundred years ago New York City had over 2500 illegal gambling houses. While some were opulent casinos, open only to the elegant and the aristocratic gamesters, others thrived on violent gambling, such as betting on boxing, cock fights, and rat baiting (starving rats for several days and then setting them against each other in a box, betting on which would survive).

Geographic differences in gambling became part of the American character. New Orleans has long been a hub of gambling. At the turn of the century there were over 2000 gambling houses in New Orleans lined with slot machines, from the garish to the elegant. Corruption of public officials and crime was rampant. New Orleans earned the dubious distinction of being the sin city of the country.

During the 20th century, however, the most prevailing connection between gambling and crime came about as a result of the association between organized crime mobster Benjamin "Bugsy" Siegel and the casinos in Las Vegas. This quickly spread to other casinos, and not until the mid-1970s did the casino industry make a deliberate effort to sever its relationship with elements of organized crime in order to expand to Atlantic City and the East Coast. Nevertheless, evidence of connection with organized crime associates, directly or indirectly, and evidence of political corruption, such as in Louisiana in 1996, continue to plague the casino industry.

D. Expansion of Gambling in the United States Today

The Depression of the 1930s may be considered a major contributing factor in the expansion of gambling in the United States. Brought to the point of personal ruin, many Americans began to put an inordinate emphasis on money. Business became rooted in the "bottom line" of profits. Economic turmoil in the 1970s was compounded by citizens' outrage against increased taxes. Legislators were looking for painless means to meet government expenditures. The Civil Rights Act and Women's Liberation Movement, providing freedom of movement and greater economic parity for women and minorities, are also contributing factors. Technical advances, through computers and communications, including the media, catapulted a slow industry into a race to be the first, the biggest, and the best.

1. Casinos

Casino gambling, long the main industry of Nevada, particularly in Las Vegas and Reno, began its expansion in 1976, when New Jersey voters approved casinos in an effort to revitalize the dying beach resort town of Atlantic City. Opened in 1978, Resorts International Casino won over $1 million the first day of operation. It repaid its entire capital venture of $77 million within the first year of its opening. Atlantic City itself, in the meantime, remains an embarrassment to the casino industry, as housing, jobs, and renewal plans remain unmet, while hints of association with organized crime and political corruption continue to surface.

Casino expansion received unparalleled support when Congress passed the Indian Gaming Regulatory Act of 1988. Within 10 years this led to expansion of bingo and casino gambling on Indian reservations. Promoted as providing a means for economic development and land acquisition, small reservations became hubs of casino gambling almost overnight. Now legal in 23 states, the tribes have had varying success. While some are highly profitable economically, others have fared poorly in contracts with casino management companies.

Socially, on some reservations the casinos are seen as the cause of a breakdown of tribal unity, leading to warring factions, accusations of corruption and mismanagement, and a violation of Indian culture and Indian ways. Murder, theft, indictments, and gambling addictions have followed.

Las Vegas has long been the casino capital of the world. As gambling increased, Vegas casinos offered a variety of designs consistent with expansion, local needs, and opportunities. These land-based casinos have provided entertainment by superstars—singers, dancers, actors, and comedians of renown. The dancers are highly skilled, the choreography is superb, costumes are opulent, and shows tend to leave the audience enthralled. Often the entertainment was the main attraction for old and new patrons.

Casinos have also added other attractions, for example, holding championship poker tournaments and championship boxing fights. Side offers are boutiques, jewelry stores, and souvenir shops. Personal services are readily available, alcohol beverages are offered free of charge to players, and the atmosphere has become one of comfort and attention, with free rooms, services, meals, champagne, and limousines for the high rollers.

Competition due to expansion has forced dynamic changes in types of casinos, locale, and organizational structure. Theme park- and frontier-type casinos tend to offer gambling 24 hr a day.

a. Theme Park Casinos

Las Vegas has always been in the forefront of "theme parks" which focus on a central theme, such as filmmaking or New York City. These theme park casinos cater to the entire family and promote gambling as family entertainment. The industry plans to continue with such theme parks, with more emphasis on attracting the entire family, thus hoping to establish a younger and longer-lasting clientele.

b. Frontier Casinos

In 1988, Deadwood, South Dakota, voters elected to allow frontier saloon-types of casinos, hoping to raise enough revenues to improve its water and sewer system. Within a few years the city had nearly 100 saloon casinos. Virtually all former businesses in the town have closed, and the entire character of the once sleepy mining town is now one of a bustling casino frontier town. While some of the casinos have failed, others are thriving economically.

c. Riverboats

Mississippi riverboat nostalgia has led to cruising and noncruising types of riverboats since the late 1980s. Some noncruising riverboats have the capability of moving, but typically do not, because river currents are too fast, thus rendering the boat unsafe for cruising. Docksides are casinos on barges which are not capable of moving. The legal criterion is that the gambling floor space must be on water rather than on land.

These riverboats range from the elegant, with dance reviews, comedy acts, big-name entertainers, and high-stakes baccarat and other table games, to those with low ceilings, fast food, and primarily video gambling machines.

Current practice is for riverboats to slowly cruise a short distance from the shore, and return after a two-hour time period. They generally operate 12 hours per day.

d. Dockside Casinos

Similar in design to cruising riverboats, dockside casinos are stationary, affixed to the local dock or piers. The appeal is in its continuous access to patrons, since it is not away, cruising on the river.

e. Charitable Casinos

Another version of casinos are those operated by non-profit groups, such as firehouses and veterans organizations. They often are limited to certain types of gambling, such as blackjack tables. Their operating times are limited in number of hours or days they may provide gambling opportunities, and a specified percentage of revenues must be donated to charities.

Due to the rapid expansion of casino gambling, it is conceivable that a transition period will emerge during which the quality of entertainment, management, and expertise of casino personnel, such as dealers and pit bosses, will fluctuate and profits will waver, until a new equilibrium has been established.

2. Horseracing

Horseracing in the United States is as old as native American tribes, and its popularity quickly expanded with the growth of European migration. The first regulated race was sponsored by the governor of New York in 1665. By the early 1700s, Virginia, Maryland, and New York each had several race tracks. Favored by the aristocracy of early settlers, it was the gentlemen's form of entertainment. Only the gentry were allowed to wager on horses, while the poor were expected to indulge their fancies in other activities, such as shooting craps outside the track. It was not unusual for Congress to lack a quorum because its members were at the race track.

The Victorian era in the United States was a period of great horses and even greater gamblers. John "Bet-a-Million" Gates ranked equal to Payne Whitney, who lost a quarter of a million dollars at one time. The Kentucky Derby and the Preakness became famous horse races enlivened by parades and week-long festivities.

After the Depression, 21 states offered legal horse racing. Today, the horseracing industry has expanded to 33 states, complete with simulcasting at the track and at off-track betting parlors. Initial trials are being made to permit horserace betting from the home, through preestablished credit lines. Since the mid-1990s, the horseracing industry has expanded its gambling opportunities by offering slot machines or video gambling devices at race tracks and OTBs.

At one time viewed as a highly romanticized form of entertainment, in more recent years horseracing has dropped in popularity, its appeal diminished by virtue of cannibalization by other forms of gambling. Costs have gone up and purses are down at race tracks, while at casinos many forms of gambling and entertainment abound.

3. Bingo

In the 1950s a major expansion of gambling was in the form of bingo, which was seen as a means of raising funds for charitable organizations, such as churches and schools. Technically illegal, this type of gambling activity was overlooked by law enforcement because of the benign nature of the game and the operators. However, in the 1970s states began to legalize bingo games in response to charges of selective law enforcement. New bingo laws resulted, permitting bingo gambling for charitable purposes, typically for a limited number of hours or for a certain number of days.

The laws also led to the establishment of bingo parlors, often open 12 or more hours per day. These bingo parlors frequently offer side games, such as instant lotteries and pulltabs. Bingo parlors are also found on Indian reservations. Most jackpots are prizes of several hundred dollars, although pari-mutuel bingo prizes can be greater than a million dollars.

When not run by nonprofit agencies, bingo parlors are owned by private entrepreneurs. Regulation or law enforcement was minimal until recently, when it was discovered that some bingo parlors were found to be skimming profits and to have associations with organized crime rings.

4. State Lotteries

Throughout their history, lotteries have had their strong advocates and even stronger opponents. Lotteries continue to be viewed by many as a pernicious form of gambling, preying on the weak and needy, and on those who can least afford to play.

Banned by state after state during the 1900s, lotteries made a comeback, once again due to economic privations, starting in New Hampshire in 1964. This quickly expanded across the country, resulting in lotteries in 37 states and Washington, DC, by the year 1996. This includes scratch-offs, Pick 3 and Pick 4 games, five-number and six-number lotto, and video lottery terminals. Drawings are on a daily basis, and in some states twice a day. State lotteries offer 6-month subscriptions, and are attempting to establish credit lines, so that lotteries can be purchased from one's home over the telephone. Currently two multistate lotteries exist, and a national lottery is being explored. International lotteries are close to implementation.

Another lottery game is Keno, in which players select from 80 numbers their hoped-for winning numbers. Legal in Las Vegas casinos, since 1990 Keno has also become associated with state lotteries. Keno typically is available for 18 hours per day, with winning numbers drawn every 5 minutes. A clock counting down the minutes and seconds left for the next play contribute to the gambler's sense of urgency and action to play. Keno games are typically found in the same locations that sell lottery tickets.

A current development in lotteries is that of video lottery terminals (or VLTs). These are similar to electronic video games, with poker, blackjack, roulette, dice, horse racing, bingo, and Keno games. They are owned and operated by state lotteries.

Prior to the vast expansion of legalized gambling in the United States, lottery players tended to be lower in education and income than race track or casino gamblers. However, as the gambling industry continues to spread and be readily accessible to all groups of people, this trend may change.

Lottery advertising has come under particular public scrutiny for a number of reasons. State lotteries have been termed "governmental bookmakers" who prey on the poor and subject them to unfair taxation. Lottery advertising has been the object of much public criticism for giving false impressions of the potential for winning or of the actual prize. A million dollar jackpot in the typical state lottery, for instance, is not paid out in full, as it is in Canada, but rather it is paid out in annual installments over 20 years. Another discontent about lottery advertising is its tendency to promote all forms of gambling, since it has themes of slot lots, sports betting, or card playing. Is it a proper function of state government to promote gambling per se? Lottery advertising has repeatedly been condemned for targeting certain groups, such as children or the elderly, while praising the benefits of lottery proceeds through emotional appeals, namely, the elderly, education, the handicapped, or neonatal care.

The Iowa State Lottery was the first public or privately owned gambling enterprise to express concerns about compulsive gambling. In 1985 it dedicated one-half of 1% of its sales (over $1 million) to combat gambling addiction. Since then, other state lotteries have contributed varying levels of support.

5. Slot Machines and Electronic Video Games

Slot machines were first brought to the United States in 1901. These were mechanical devices with levers and reels, typically with fruits and symbols designating winning combinations. Starting out as penny or nickel slots, these machines expanded to dimes, quarters, and silver dollars. Players could chose to play one coin or up to three for any one play. Prizes were based on the number of coins inserted and on the depiction of the reels.

With the expansion in the 1970s of the computer age and technical advances, some of these slot machines were converted to electronic video gambling machines. The first of these machines typically displayed casino cards games, such as poker or blackjack. Advances led to other designs, such as one-liners to eight-liners, using bars or similar symbols. A more recent design is one which is similar to the old mechanical slot machine, and is referred to as a "fruit machine." These video games were generally preferred by lower-income gamblers and those with a high school education or less. The eight-liners were preferred by males, while the fruit machines generally hold more appeal for women or the elderly. Today their appeal is democratic.

Video gambling machines are legal in seven states, with expansion being planned in other states. The first machines were quarter machines, and a player could wager one to five coins or credits, doubling or redoubling a play. Current machines accept paper currency and credit cards to hasten the play and amount to be wagered. The casino industry uses plastic cards inserted into the machines to "track" the players, learning which games the player prefers and how much is wagered.

6. Other Gambling

Some states offer dog racing, although this is not a particularly appealing form of gambling for most Americans. Dog or greyhound racing has long been opposed by animal rights groups protesting cruelty to animals, particularly in the training of race dogs and in their extermination when they are no longer useful for racing. Mechanical rabbits are now used in training. As horseracing and other forms of gambling spread across the United States, conceivably so will dog racing.

Florida has had ostrich races, and several states offer jai alai. Only Nevada currently has legal sports betting, at its casinos. However, this too is expected to expand to other states, either within the casinos or as a separate legal gambling enterprise.

As of 1996, 48 U.S. states had some form of legalized gambling. Of these 46 have bingo; 37 states and Washington, DC, have lotteries; 33 states have horseracing; 25 states have various forms of casino gambling; 11 states have dog racing; and seven have legal video slot machines. Only Hawaii and Utah have no legal gambling. Nevertheless, the casino gaming industry is attempting to reverse this status, and illegal gambling is widespread in Hawaii.

7. Illegal Gambling

Illegal gambling is as pervasive as ever, if not more so, in spite of the expansion of legal gambling. In the past, illegal gambling was estimated to exceed that spent on legal gambling. With the current increase of legal gambling, however, it is more likely that the amounts spent on legal and illegal gambling are more equal.

The most prevalent type of illegal gambling is sports betting. Once accessible virtually only to adult males, it has become commonplace in high schools and colleges, is found in office pools, bars, and clubs, and is associated with bookmakers of all types, ranging from friendly neighborhood bookies to organized crime figures. Bookmakers are closely associated with loansharks, who have a reputation for forceful collection strategies, often leading to desperate acts by losing gamblers.

Illegal video gambling machines are to be found across the United States in neighborhood bars, restaurants, bowling alleys, and small businesses. Video machine players tend to be blue-collar workers, male and female, typically in their thirties or forties.

Illegal numbers games, historically a social function of the African-American community and Hispanic and Irish groups, are now prevalent across the country. The appeal lies in the availability of credit and the initial smaller amounts required to play. Another incentive is that winners do not pay taxes on their returns.

After-hours clubs, typically offering poker games or blackjack and craps games, are found everywhere. After-hours clubs may be an extension of legal gambling after closing time, or may be run by neighbors as private card games, or may be operated by organized crime figures.

Dice, found in bars, clubs, homes, and street games, are more often associated with minority groups and male gamblers.

While states had hoped that the legalization of gambling would cut down on illegal gambling, the reverse appears to be more accurate. As legal gambling has become more widespread, so has illegal gambling.

II. PROGAMBLING INTERESTS

The United States has experienced repeated progambling and antigambling movements, and in the 1990s saw a major confrontation between these two forces.

A. Political Expansion Tactics

In the 1970s Las Vegas casino interests, hoping to expand their gambling outlets, looked to the East Coast, initially to Miami, Florida, as a possible site. Miami was a tourist city, had many retired citizens with strong financial status and much leisure time, while the city had economic need. However, the community was, and still is, opposed to casino gambling there and defeated all legislative efforts for the establishment of casinos.

The casino industry then turned to Atlantic City, New Jersey, a city of urban blight and decay. Politically, the casino industry promised sufficient revenues to ensure the physical rehabilitation and economic revival of Atlantic City. New Jersey voters anticipated that housing and infrastructure would be built up and that tax revenues would combat the many problems associated with the influx of large numbers of tourist. To date, unfortunately, little has been done to revitalize the city itself, crime has risen, and economic ruin and unemployment are high. The casino industry looks at Atlantic City as "an error made and to be avoided in the future."

The casino industry, and now vis-a-vis its American Gaming Association, promises economic advantages through casino expansion by virtue of increased jobs, tax revenues, and sales from tourism. These are strong enticements for legislators, who resist tax increases. When legislative approval fails, the gaming industry tends to take the issue to statewide referendum, thus giving the citizens of the state the choice. In more recent years, individual casinos have targeted specific counties where they wish to establish themselves as a means of breaking through the no-casino barrier. Since 1995, the casinos have found it expedient to link up with other gaming industries, such as the racetracks or state lotteries, to bring casino gambling into new territories.

Some of these efforts failed. The racetrack industry then proclaimed that cannibalization of racetrack dollars, due to many other forms of gambling, was causing serious economic hardships in its industry and predicted that without state support thousands of jobs would be lost (specifically, 20,000 jobs would be lost in Maryland). The industry convinced one state legislature, Delaware, that video gambling machines at the tracks or OTBs would prevent this economic upheaval. While this appears to have saved Delaware racing, bringing in better horses and bigger purses, the competition has resulted in lower racetrack attendance and in revenue losses in nearby states. Further complications may develop as gambling machine manufacturers ally with the racetracks in direct competition with casinos and as both attempt to forge alliances with state lotteries.

B. Gaming Industry Response to Compulsive Gambling

The antigambling, or antiproliferation of legalized gambling, movement took root in May 1995 when economists, crime commissions, and religious and community leaders combined forces and created the National Coalition Against the Proliferation of Legalized Gambling.

Mental health advocates joined, not necessarily to support antigambling efforts, but to speak out about gambling addiction. Research studies from state task forces, universities, and state lotteries identified a growing trend of compulsive gambling across the country.

For many years, the casino industry, state lotteries, and racetracks denied the existence of compulsive gambling. Casino explanations suggested that only gamblers from out of state could become addicts: local residents were accustomed to gambling. State lottery staff insisted that "lottery games are too passive, they can't become addictive." Racetracks generally ignored all references to compulsive gambling. Fighting the antigambling interests, casinos became particularly vocal, with protestations in the form of, "Why deny those who enjoy it?" or "It's only a small percentage of people who can't control themselves" or "It's not our responsibility."

Citizens and legislators became more adamant, forcing the casino industry to change its tactics. The casino response became, "There is so much gambling already, casinos will not increase the number of compulsive gamblers" and "It is immoral to deny establishment of casinos when a state already has other forms of gambling, such as a government lottery. This is government denying private interests."

Currently, casinos are suggesting that they are doing something about problem gambling, and that they can work together with compulsive gambling agencies, or can serve a good cause by helping the needy and the poor.

State lotteries have followed similar persuasions. Although the Iowa State Lottery has granted 0.5% of its earnings for compulsive gambling assistance since 1985, and the Texas State Lottery legislation allocated $2 million per year for such purposes, only a handful of other state lotteries have taken a preventive posture by funding a stateside compulsive gambling crisis line or developing a brochure for lottery vendors. Further expansion will require studying the cannibalization of gaming enterprises and profits, developing accurate profiles of industry growth and impact on local businesses and communities, and addressing the previously mentioned negative economic and social concerns.

III. ANTIGAMBLING CONCERNS AND EFFORTS

A. History

The Bible has many references to the drawing of lots and similar forms of gambling. Theologians and moralists have taken a stand on the issue of deity and gambling. Nowhere in the Bible does it state, "Thou shalt not gamble," yet the Bible presents a moral ideal for man's conduct in relationship to his fellow man.

The expansion of gambling, associated with crime, corruption, and addiction, has put religious organizations in a moral dilemma. They need revenues to support churches and parochial schools, yet these have often been funded by gambling revenues through weekly bingo games or special fundraisers such as casino nights or festivals, where gambling games are prevalent.

B. The Moral Issue

Church leaders face the questions of whether gambling is a sin or is immoral, and if so, why do we condone gambling in our church or our community?

The antigambling movement was particularly strong during the 19th century, espousing the lack of virtue in the gamester, the villain who would profiteer from the weaknesses of others, and the infidel who sought instant gain without the merit of hard-earned labor. Gambling was a violation of the mores and morality of the times.

Gambling was also viewed as a loss of character, with intelligent decision making being turned over to blind chance. It was viewed as destroying the individual's responsibility to his family, the family's to the community, and the community's to the government. A government basing economic stability on a game of luck was a government lacking in rationality of reason, confidence in its leaders, and concern for its citizens.

Gambling, in short, was seen as encouraging a something-for-nothing attitude, and as fostering materialism, an attitude of "all for me" rather than "what can I do for others?" The "why work when you can play?" lottery advertisement is tantamount to government's failure to support the intrinsic value of work, violates the work ethic, and is in direct conflict with parental efforts to install individual and community values in their young.

C. Economic Morality

Gambling is viewed by the antigambling movement as "economic immorality." Gambling is presented as preying on the poor, since more poor people play the lottery, and poor people spend a larger percentage of their income on lotteries. Lotteries are thus viewed as a regressive tax on the poor, and it is immoral for a government to exploit the less fortunate of its citizens to support the rest.

Gambling is also seen as economically immoral because money spent on gambling is money not spent elsewhere—on business, in shops and restaurants, or on groceries. Gambling fails to produce new wealth for a community, and is therefore seen as an economic parasite. Those businesses within a 50-mile perimeter of casinos tend to fare poorly after casinos come to the community.

D. Quality of Life Issues

Parents attempt to teach their children self-discipline and patience. Gambling, on the other hand, represents depending on chance and desiring instant gratification. Gambling is said to destroy character, rather than building it.

The gaming industry insists that people will gamble, so why not legalize it and tax it, thus benefiting the state? The response by the antigambling forces is that "two wrongs don't make a right."

The church and ethicists historically have considered gambling to be predatory upon the family. Gambling is viewed as robbing the family of the time that children need from the parent to teach and guide them, and to nurture and protect them. Gambling losses can rob the family of its basic necessities, which leads to family arguments. Through gambling, the basic unity and peace of the family may be destroyed.

Fueling the outrage of the antigambling movement is the expansion of gambling into the home. Department stores and dime stores now sell handheld video gambling games, marked as appropriate "for ages 5 and up." Toy stores are selling pint-sized slot machines, with symbols of puppies and kittens, in place of the more traditional cherries. Video stores display gambling games in the family section for family entertainment.

The antigambling movement was successful in defeating gambling initiatives in nine states in 1996, and will continue to escalate its efforts. It is apparent that the strong progambling movement and the rapid expansion of gambling are nearing their peak.

Gambling debates will continue in the present, as they have in the past, only stronger and louder. Once viewed as sinful and immoral, it has evolved from illegal to legal, from economic savior to economic ruin, from gambling to gaming, from recreation to family entertainment, and from being promoted as an act of social responsibility and doing something for a good cause to the "Addiction of the Nineties" and a surging antigambling movement.

IV. PATHOLOGICAL GAMBLING

For some, social gambling leads to compulsive gambling, with its inherent financial ruin, family devastation, poor health, crime, and suicide attempts. In 1976, after a comprehensive four-year study, the U.S. Commission on the Review of the National Policy Toward Gambling determined that about 1% of the adult population in the United States could be pathological gamblers. The commission found that the incidence of pathological gambling in Nevada, at that time the only state to have widespread legal gambling, was more than double that of anywhere else.

Since the expansion of legalized gambling, the incidence of adult pathological gambling has increased to as much as 5.4% in some states. The incidence of adolescent gambling, nil in 1976, has increased to as much as 11% in various states.

A. Definition

Social gamblers have control over the amount of money they are willing to gamble and lose, the amount of time spent on gambling, and the frequency of their gambling.

Pathological gamblers (more commonly referred to as compulsive gamblers) do not have this control. They attempt to set limits, but lack the appropriate coping skills and support base to abstain from gambling.

Professional gamblers, such as stock brokers or card dealers in a casino, earn their livelihood from gambling. Their reasons for gambling differ from those of the compulsive gambler. They learn from their experiences and maintain control over their gambling. However, due to their ongoing involvement in gambling, they are more at risk of succumbing to the addiction than a social gambler. Whereas the nonaddicted professional gambler will learn from experience, the compulsive gambler does not. Instead, the gambling addict will repeatedly resort to irrational behaviors, especially under times of stress.

Individuals involved in illegal gambling, such as bookmakers, are also somewhat more at risk of becoming addicted than the social gambler. It is not unusual for a sports bettor/compulsive gambler to become a bookmaker in an attempt to gain money in support of his addiction. It would be highly unlikely for a bingo addict to become a bookmaker.

Any form of gambling may lead to addiction, whether it is a card game, lottery tickets, bingo playing, or betting on pool, sports, horses, or the toss of a coin. Certain forms of gambling, though, in the past had greater appeal to specific groups (although this is rapidly changing with the expansion of gambling): middle-aged, middle-income males gambled at race tracks and casinos; males of all ages preferred betting on sports; and lower-income people of all ages preferred slot machines or video gambling machines, or less expensive forms of gambling such as lotteries, bingo, and numbers. While subgroups are currently showing preferences, it is anticipated that all forms of gambling will become universally preferred by compulsive gamblers, assuming that access is equally available.

What remains constant is that the compulsive gambler is someone whose gambling has become chronic over time, with progressively larger amounts of money and for longer periods of time, so that it disrupts or compromises the gambler's occupational, family, or social pursuits to the point of financial indebtedness, a broken home, poor health, the commission of crime, and suicidal tendencies.

Current research indicates that while gambling is more prevalent among males than females, pathological gambling is a psychiatric disorder without boundaries of socioeconomic status, race, ethnicity, sex, religion, or age. The largest age group of those in their mid-forties, as was the case 20 years ago, has been replaced with that of early twenties and adolescents.

B. Theoretical Framework/Contributing Factors

No single theory fully describes pathological gambling; rather, elements of several theoretical frameworks apply to pathological gambling. These theoretical orientations continue to be researched as the incidence of compulsive gambling increases.

Initially gambling as play was a model applicable to social gambling, as a precursor to pathological gambling. Gambling was viewed as a form of entertainment, a means to relax and divert from life's pressures. Gambling as an economical model was espoused, suggesting that gamblers needed to improve their money management skills. While not quite accurate, concepts of the theory can be useful in developing budgets and restitution plans and in teaching responsible money management.

The link of biological factors to pathological gambling may be accurate. Evidence suggests that a low serotonin level leads to depression; gambling serves as a form of self-medication to alleviate this depression. Recent research also suggests a genetic link.

The medical model is appropriate, since medical treatment is often necessary in addition to psychiatric therapy. Many compulsive gamblers suffer from a variety of psychosomatic symptoms, such as chronic headaches or migraines, upper and lower back discomfort and muscle tenseness, gastrointestinal complications, chest or heart pains, eating disorders, and sleep disturbances.

Social learning theory espouses the imprinting of family values and behaviors, with a lack of appropriate nurturance and guidance leading to poor coping, communication, and conflict resolution skills, and poor emotional development. Family systems theories also apply, since evidence suggests that pathological gambling, or related addictions and disorders, tend to be consistent among generations of family members.

The psychoanalytic model holds that pathological gambling is a response to a unipolar dysphoric mood state, often acquired in early childhood due to emotional trauma or deprivation. This fosters low self-esteem and the development of defense mechanisms to cope with life.

Addictions theories contribute to the overall understanding of compulsive gambling and must, along with other theories, be considered in treatment, especially as compulsive gamblers are coaddicted or may have cross-addicted from other substance or behavioral abuses or dependencies. Some 30–40% have a past or present alcohol problem.

The progression of pathological gambling is similar to that of other addictions, in that the gambling becomes chronic and progressive, tolerance levels are built up, the addict does not consider the consequences of the gambling, there are repeated urges and cravings to gamble, attempts at abstinence results in withdrawal symptoms, and there are repeated slips and relapses.

Whereas pathological gambling has been termed the "Addiction of the Nineties," it is also responsive to appropriate treatment and suggests a high positive treatment outcome or recovery. The treatment philosophy in the United States is that of total abstinence as espoused by Gamblers Anonymous. This belief is not shared in other countries, such as Australia or Germany, but at this time there is no evidence to suggest that controlled gambling is a viable alternative for the individual diagnosed as a pathological gambler.

C. Impact on the Compulsive Gambler

The pathological gambler's initial area of impact is that of severe loss of monies and indebtedness. Debts equivalent to an annual salary are the norm for lower-income gamblers. Those with higher incomes may be several millions of dollars in debt. Bankruptcy may be the only option of economic survival.

Compulsive gamblers as a rule are high achievers, and tend to be outstanding employees, often winning many awards or commendations for outstanding work performance. However, as the gambling addiction progresses, work productivity may deteriorate to the point of the person's being terminated from employment or of losing his own business.

Social interactions cease, both because the compulsive gambler is too involved in the gambling or in the need to obtain money for gambling, and because friends and associates distance themselves from the gambler to avoid being coerced into giving the gambler another loan or being told another lie.

Virtually all compulsive gamblers resort to some form of illegal acquisition of funds in order to support their habit. Teenagers steal from family members, those with access to company funds find weaknesses in accounting systems and embezzle from their employers, and most write bad checks or abuse credit cards. Nonviolent crimes of a financial nature account for perhaps 90% of the criminal activities of a compulsive gambler, although street crimes, drug selling, and prostitution may become more frequent as the illness strikes a more democratic population base of gamblers. About 25% to 30% of compulsive gamblers are charged with criminal violations, and about 15% end up being incarcerated.

Not surprisingly, many compulsive gamblers become seriously depressed and suicidal. Studies indicate that two out of three compulsive gamblers have repeated suicidal thoughts leading to suicidal intent. Most attempt suicide through automobile accidents. Those with military or law enforcement training are more likely to use a weapon, such as a gun. Coaddiction to alcohol is particularly common among those with a military background while others may turn to marijuana or cocaine.

D. Impact on the Family

Depression is not restricted to the gambler. Spouses, parents, and children of the gambler may also become seriously depressed or suffer from various forms of anxiety. They, just like the gambler, may resort to excessive use of alcohol, prescribed drugs, marijuana or cocaine, food, or cigarettes to alleviate their discomfort.

Wives of compulsive gamblers report taking their anger and frustrations out on their children, often becoming physically abusive as well as verbally abusive. Teenaged children often become depressed or truant, and do poorly in school. Parents of the gambler may obtain second mortgages on their homes to pay off the gambler's debts. Emotional coverups and financial bailouts are the norm, rather than the exception, thus involving myriad family members in the related gambling activities.

Frequent evictions and moves, doing without utilities such as heat, electricity, or phone, and going without food, medicine, or clothing are common consequences suffered by compulsive gamblers and their family members. Not surprisingly, these homes are fraught with anger, fear, arguments, and isolation. Marital separations are commonplace, although divorce can be avoided if the gambler seeks help in time. Infidelity is rather rare, although sexual estrangement may continue for many years after abstinence, if no professional counseling is sought. The lack of trust, poor communication skills, and vulnerability to rejection interfere with emotional closeness and trust.

E. Treatment

In most instances, all family members need some level of support, whether this be professional counseling or 12-step program intervention. Residential or inpatient treatment for the compulsive gambler is dependent upon the severity of comorbidity, such as suicidal or homicidal thoughts; delusions, paranoia, depression, or anxiety; other addictions; repeated relapses; or ongoing

commission of crimes. The length of stay for residential treatment varies with each individual, based upon motivation, acceptance, and assimilation of treatment concepts, and appropriateness and quantity of treatment offered. A typical residential stay is for 4 weeks.

Outpatient treatment typically is at a less intensive level and includes aftercare and relapse prevention treatment. Duration of outpatient treatment varies with the individual gambler, although 6 months to 2 years is fairly common.

Treatment for compulsive gambling may consist of individual, group, marital, or family therapy. The orientation may be psychodynamic, cognitive/behavioral, or eclectic. It may be augmented with adjunctive or expressive therapies, such as movement or occupational therapy, art therapy, acupuncture, or biofeedback. Addiction education and 12-step counseling are found in most compulsive gambling treatment programs. Spiritual counseling, budget and financial management training, stress management, relaxation training, assertiveness skill building, conflict resolution, or anger management training are all appropriate forms of therapy for compulsive gambling treatment.

Peer support for the compulsive gambler is found in groups such as Gamblers Anonymous, Bettors Anonymous, and Rational Recovery. Family support is available also through 12-step groups such as GamAnon or GamAteen. Unfortunately, these are rather limited in numbers at this time, with some states not having any such chapters.

F. Treatment Concerns

Not only are 12-step support groups such as Gamblers Anonymous and GamAnon limited in numbers, but often they are unaccessible or beyond reasonable travel distance for an affected person.

Neither professional nor self-help group support is available for those compulsive gamblers who are incarcerated due to gambling-related criminal activities. Ironically, many of these gambler/inmates gamble while in jail and continue to gamble and repeat their criminal activity upon release from jail. Abstinence is generally of short duration if the gambler has not sought professional treatment or 12-step support.

Until early 1990, access to treatment was somewhat limited due to lack of availability of a treatment program or because the compulsive gamblers lacked health insurance or money to pay for treatment. Since then, however, government's efforts to curb health care costs have resulted in the concept of "managed care." Managed-care companies review all claims for treatment, and invariably became involved in decisions about the proper treatment of the patient. Managed-care companies tend to minimize payments to providers. They typically deny access to providers outside of their own network, and they often deny the level of care sought by the provider and limit the amount of treatment deemed necessary. This results in patient frustration, and poor treatment outcome and eventual relapse. This is a battle currently being fought between providers and managed-care companies at the expense of the gamblers and their family members who seek to recover from their illnesses. In the interim many compulsive gambling programs were forced to discontinue services.

V. PUBLIC POLICY AND GAMBLING

Historically and currently the United States has failed to develop a comprehensive public policy on gambling. More typically it has responded to economic crises with the legalization of some form of gambling affixed with local appeal. State governments have failed to consider just how far gambling should be allowed to infuse itself into the economic, political, and social fabric of its communities, and who shall own the game or run the game, for how long, where, and for whom. Advertising criteria and age of minority are inconsistent within states and across states. Concerns about gambling addiction, prevention, and treatment have been minimal and inconsistent.

A. Regulation

Attempts have been made to regulate existing forms of gambling, such as state lotteries, casinos, and racetracks; however, much of this is focused on prevention of cheating and prevention of grifting games or fixing races. Little effort is spent on enforcing rules, such as barring minors from gambling and Atlantic City casinos are routinely fined for permitting minors to gamble. Some casinos encourage attendance of minors in their casinos, if not actual gambling. A recent research study on Massachusetts lottery outlets found that 48 of the 50 outlets sold lottery tickets to minors.

Another area requiring regulation is that of extension of credit. Casinos have fought for many forms of credit extension, such as establishing credit lines, granting of chits, and the use of automatic teller machines at central locations, and now offer credit card outlets on video gambling machines.

Lotteries and racetracks have established home credit in some locales, and expansion is predictable.

Credit card companies are accepting credit cards for lottery purchases and at casinos. Internet gambling is totally unregulated. All of this can lead to rapid overextension of credit, an inability to make payments, an increase of bankruptcies, and for some a greater likelihood of succumbing to gambling addiction.

Other regulations may be a fact of law; however, often these regulations are not enforced. One such area is that of association with organized crime elements. This continues to plague the casino industry, and to a lesser extent the bingo and racetrack industry.

Public policy is needed to determine how much gambling should exist in any given state or in the country as a whole. Does a state, for instance, want or need a state lottery, and if so, how many instant games shall there be? How many lotto drawings per week shall be legal? Should the state lottery also operate Keno, and if so, for how many hours per day? If the state has a lottery, shall it also operate video lottery terminals, and how many terminals at how many locations, offering which games, and should these be associated with racetracks or remain independent of other gambling establishments?

Similar questions can be asked of any other type of gambling, such as horseracing, dog racing, casinos, and bingo parlors. How many racetracks should be in any given state, how long are the hours of operation, and will there by off-track betting parlors, with simulcasting races from across the country? Some racetracks also simulcast sports games, which leads to sports betting, both legal and illegal.

The horseracing industry, in a steady period of decline over the past decade, is attempting to revitalize its industry by becoming slot machine parlors. The casino industry has bought some racetracks and placed slot machines in these locations. In 1996 Delaware racetracks had some 12,000 video gambling machines. Maryland racetracks are lobbying heavily for 15,000 slots or video gambling devices which they consider vital to their ability to compete. Who will own these machines, distribute them, regulate the payoff, and be responsible for the financial accounting—the slot machine manufacturer, racetrack, or state lottery? The question of length of time that racetrack/slot machine parlors shall remain open within a given 24-hour period needs to be established by comprehensive policy.

Race tracks are usually open for 3 to 4 hours, while casinos operate round the clock. Might a case be made for discrimination or unfair competition if a casino is open 24 hours, while the race track is open 12 hours?

B. Crime

Financial accountability has long troubled the gambling industry, especially in charitable or nonprofit gambling enterprises. Records are incomplete and inaccurate, and violations are not actively pursued by law enforcement or state prosecutors. Many abuses have been found in so-called "charitable" gambling parlors, such as fraternal clubs or associations operating slots or casinos. Skimming, underreporting of revenues, and failing to make appropriate donations to the local community or charity are commonplace.

Historically, too, gambling violations tend to be ignored. Gambling crimes are viewed as "victimless crimes" and thus tend to be neither actively pursued nor harshly punished by the courts.

C. Cannibalization

Another troubling issue is that of cannibalization of funds from one business or industry to another, at the expense of the latter. As state lotteries, casinos, and racetracks expanded, gambling dollars became more scarce. Monies formerly spent in local restaurants and shops, on goods and services, are now being diverted, so that these businesses suffer economic losses. This results in layoffs and unemployment, increased debts and bankruptcies, and the accompanying social service costs.

The gaming industry, too, is concerned about cannibalization, and is countering this by expanding its products: racetracks have slot machines, bingo parlors are also selling lottery tickets, lotteries are expanding into the home credit market—with more games, higher prices, and for longer hours—and video lottery terminals provide many games, including Keno, poker, and blackjack.

Indian reservation gaming is still relatively new, but already there have been major incidents of association with organized crime, misrepresentation in contracts, cries of discrimination, and tribal friction within the reservation and between reservations. Not surprisingly, native Americans, already suffering from a high degree of alcoholism, are now cross addicting to compulsive gambling, while treatment and prevention have yet to be implemented.

D. Advertising

Gambling advertising, especially that of state lotteries, is coming under increasing scrutiny. Misrepresentations, such as "Everybody wins," are dishonest. Others are unethical. One state lottery's slogan near a college campus read, "Be a millionaire before you graduate." A Washington, DC, lottery campaign boasted to tourists crossing into the District of Columbia, "Now that you have arrived, buy a lottery ticket." This leaves a questionable impression on tourists and foreign visitors as to the priorities of the nation's capital.

State lotteries do not simply promote their own lotteries—they promote all forms of gambling by virtue of such formats as Aces High, Blackjack, Slot Lots, and sports themes. The Vermont lottery promoted itself on a deck of cards, displaying horseshoes. The Maryland State Lottery gives out key chains with a penny and a horseshoe on it. State lotteries are also using depictions of pirates, Batman, Superman, or marbles, thus appealing to children of young age.

Other offensive advertising found ubiquitously is that of exploitation of children, the aged, or the infirm. The advertisements depict themes of healthy babies or children able to go to school because parents buy state lottery tickets. New Jersey lottery advertising depicted a handicapped man in a wheelchair. Many promote lotteries on the premise that funds will go for services for education, the elderly, the poor, or the environment. In one state government office, a small vendor displayed 13 lottery posters.

"Buy American" is not a state lottery policy. Consider the Vermont Lottery—its deck of cards was printed in Canada, yet the lottery was established because the state needed additional revenues.

Ethical standards of the advertising industry are routinely ignored in state lottery advertising. State regulations do not exist or are inadequate.

E. Government Dependence on Gambling Revenues

The casino industry has experienced repeated failures in the past decade, resulting in delayed openings, casino closings, or bankruptcies. Since both local and state governments depend on gambling revenues, an argument can be made that gambling-induced revenues provide a rather unstable support and inconsistent source of funds for governmental budgets.

More recently, economic studies indicate that for every dollar spent on gambling, $3 are lost. Compulsive gambling alone costs the state of Maryland $1.5 billion a year in lost work productivity and monies that are abused, such as through fraud, forgery, embezzlement, or failure to pay state taxes. The profits of the state lottery, charitable casinos, or racetracks cannot offset these costs.

States are forming task forces to explore the impact of gambling and lack of gambling within their boundaries. The gaming industry presents expensive brochures and billboards to the public while lobbying legislators and policy makers. This is countered by the antigambling movement through its voices and numbers.

Congress has passed legislation to establish a commission to study the impact of gambling on the nation. The first Commission member appointed was the executive director of a highly successful Las Vegas casino. Three others with close ties to Vegas or Atlantic City gambling were also appointed, as were a radiologist, professor, Native American tribal leader, president of a Christian family group, and a former lieutenant governor. Neither an ethicist nor a compulsive gambling expert was chosen. Only time will tell how objective these findings will be and what recommendations will be made.

Also See the Following Article

VICTIMLESS CRIMES

Bibliography

Abt, V., Smith, J., & Christiansen, E. (1985). *The business of risk: Commercial gambling in Mainstreet America.* Lawrence, KS: Univ. of Kansas.

Chafetz, H. (1960). *Play the devil: A history of gambling in the United States from 1492 to 1955.* New York: Potter.

Clotfelter, C. T., & Cook, P. J. (1989). *Selling hope: State lotteries in America.* Cambridge, MA: Harvard Univ. Press.

Custer, R. C., & Milt, H. (1985). *When luck runs out.* New York: Facts on File.

Dombrink, J., & Thompson, W. N. (1990). *The last resort: Success and failure of campaigns for casinos.* Reno, NV: Univ. of Nevada Press.

Eadington, W. R., & Cornelius, J. A. (Eds.) (1991). *Gambling and public policy: International perspectives.* Reno, NV: Univ. of Nevada, Institute for the Study of Gambling and Commercial Gambling.

Geisler, N. L. (1990). *Gambling: A bad bet.* Old Tappan, NJ: Revell.

Heineman, M. (1992). *Losing your shirt: Recovery for compulsive gamblers and their families.* Minneapolis, MN: CompCare.

International Gaming and Wagering Business Magazine, various issues. Monthly trade journal of the gambling industry.

Journal of Gambling Studies, various volumes. New York: Human Sciences.

Lesieur, H. R. (1984). *The chase: Career of the compulsive gambler.* Cambridge, MA: Schenkman.

Lorenz, V. C. (1993). Using rational-emotive therapy in treating pathological gambling. In Dryden, W. & Hill, L. K. (Eds.) (pp. 72–90). *Innovations in rational-emotive therapy.* Newbury Park, CA: Sage Publications, Inc.

Rose, I. N. (1986). *Gambling and the law.* Hollywood, CA: Gambling Times.

Rosecrance, J. (1988). *Gambling without guilt: The legitimation of an American pastime.* Pacific Grove, CA: Brooks-Cole.

Thompson, W. N. (1994). *Legalized gambling: A reference handbook.* Santa Barbara, CA: ABC-Clio.

U. S. Commission on the Review of the National Policy toward Gambling (1976). *Final report: Gambling in America.* (4 vols.). Washington, DC: U.S. Government Printing Office.

GAME THEORY

Guillermo Owen
Naval Postgraduate School

GLOSSARY

complete information A situation in which a player knows all the laws of the game she is playing.

matrix game A finite two-person zero-sum game in normal form.

mixed strategy A randomization scheme for choosing among a player's pure strategies.

Nash equilibrium An *n*-tuple of strategies such that no player can gain by a unilateral change.

NTU game One in which utility is not freely transferable.

optimal strategy A strategy which guarantees the value.

perfect information A situation in which a player knows all moves that have been made.

saddle point An entry (in a matrix) which is the smallest in its row and the largest in its column.

strategy A rule that tells a player what to do at each position.

threat strategy A strategy to be used in case of no agreement.

TU game One in which utility can be freely transferred among coalition partners.

value In a matrix game, a quantity which the maximizer can ensure herself of winning; the minimizer in turn can ensure himself against losing more than that quantity.

zero-sum game One in which the sum of payoffs to all players is always zero.

GAME THEORY is the mathematical study of situations of conflict of interest. As such it is applicable to parlor games (hence its name), but also to military and economic situations, and, to a lesser extent, to situations in other social sciences. Game theory studies three general phases in the process of interaction: the choice of *strategies*, the formation of *coalitions*, and *bargaining* within coalitions.

As concerns ethics, game theory is useful as an arbitration technique for bargaining problems (Section IV) and, in distributive justice, for allocating the gains from cooperation (Section V). Conversely, it can be used to design rules (e.g., assignment of weights for voting in a parliament whose members represent constituencies of different sizes) so that normal play of a game will lead to a "fair" outcome.

I. REPRESENTATION OF GAMES

Games are represented in several ways. Among these are the *extensive* form, the *normal* form, and the *characteristic* function.

A. The Extensive Form

The extensive form of a game is a tree (graph) which exhibits the logical sequence of moves in a game, showing the order in which players move, the information they have when making a move, and, for chance moves, the associated probabilities.

Example 1—Matching Pennies

Player I chooses either H (heads) or T (tails). Then Player II, in ignorance of I's choice, chooses either H or T. Now, if both choose H, I pays $3 to II; if both choose T, I pays $1 to II. Otherwise, II pays $2 to I.

This game is represented by the tree in Figure 1. The game starts at vertex A, which "belongs" to Player I. From here, I's choice leads to either B or C, both of which belong to Player II. The shaded area joining these two vertices is used to represent II's lack of information: when he moves, he knows he is at one of these two vertices, but cannot distinguish between them. Technically, vertices B and C belong to the same *information set*. From either of these, II has two alternatives, H and T. After this, the game terminates at one of the vertices, D, E, F, or G. A vector with two components is assigned to each of the terminal vertices: these are the payoffs. For example, the $(-3, +3)$ assigned to vertex D means that Player I loses $3 and II wins $3.

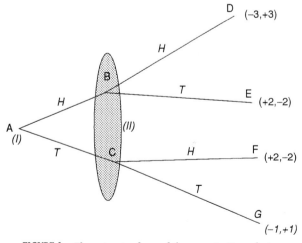

FIGURE 1 The extensive form of the game in Example 1.

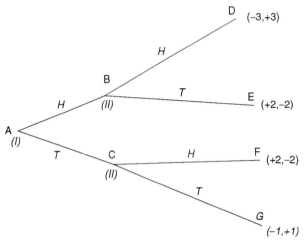

FIGURE 2 The extensive form of the game in Example 2.

Example 2

Consider the same game as in Example 1, with the sole change that Player II is allowed to make his decision after seeing what Player I has chosen. All else is as in Example 1.

This game is shown in Figure 2. The only difference lies in the fact that vertices B and C are not in the same information set; in this game, Player II can distinguish between them.

In Example 2, note that all information sets consist of a single vertex. In such a case, the game is said to have *perfect information*. The game in Example 1 does not have perfect information, nor does the one in the following Example 3.

Example 3—Rudimentary Poker

Chance gives Player I either a high card (H) or a low card (L), with probabilities of 0.2 and 0.8, respectively. Player I, seeing the card, can bet (B) or pass (P).

If Player I passes, the game terminates immediately. Player II pays $1 to I if I has H, while I pays $1 to II if I has L. If Player I bets, then II can call (C) or fold (F). If player II folds, then he pays $1 to player I. If II calls, then II pays $3 to I if I has H, and I pays $3 to II if I has L. Recall that, in deciding to call or fold, Player II knows whether I has bet or passed, but not whether she is holding H or L.

This game is represented in Figure 3. Note that at the chance move, the probabilities are specified; we assume that both players know the probabilities. Any attempt to change the probabilities (e.g., by stacking the deck) is considered cheating and is illegal. Note

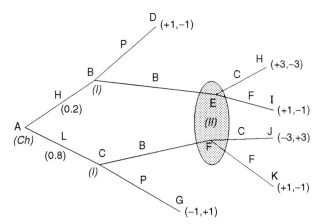

FIGURE 3   The extensive form of the game in Example 3.

also that two vertices (E and F) are in one information set; hence Player II's information is imperfect.

B. The Normal Form

While the extensive form representation of a game gives us a very good description of the actual play of a game, it is easier to analyze the game (as regards maximizing winnings) with the normal form. This is based on the notion of a *strategy*.

A strategy for a given player is a comprehensive set of rules telling a player which alternative to choose in each information set. Note that a strategy may be good or bad, and that the rules which make up a strategy do not have the force of laws: a player may disregard such a rule if she so wishes.

To go back to Example 1, we see that Player I has one information set (vertex A) with two alternatives. Thus she has two strategies, H and T. Similarly, Player II, with one information set (B and C) and two alternatives there, has two strategies, also called H and T.

In Example 2, Player I has once again two strategies, H and T. Player II, however, has two information sets, with two alternatives in each. Thus player II has four strategies: HH (always call H), HT (call H at B, call T at C), TH (call T at B, call H at C), and TT (always call T).

In Example 3, Player I has two information sets, with two alternatives at each, and thus four strategies: BB (always bet), BP (bet at B, pass at C), PB (pass at B, bet at C), and PP (always pass). Player II has only the two strategies, C and F.

In a given game, suppose each player has chosen a strategy. If the game has no chance moves, the several players' strategies will entirely determine the course of play, and hence the outcome and payoff of the game. In a game with chance moves, the outcome will also depend on the chance moves. By hypothesis, however, the probabilities at the chance moves are well determined. Hence a choice of strategies will determine, up to a probability distribution, the outcome of the game. It is thus possible to calculate the mathematical expectation of the payoff. In other words, the expected payoff of the game is a function only of the strategies used by the players. This function, usually shown as a table or matrix, is the *normal form* of the game.

The normal form of the game in Example 1 is the matrix

$$
\begin{array}{c c c}
 & H & T \\
H & (-3, 3) & (2, -2) \\
T & (2, -2) & (-1, 1)
\end{array}.
$$

By convention, in two-person games, the normal form is a matrix, with rows representing Player I's strategies columns representing those of Player II.

The game of example 2 is represented by

$$
\begin{array}{c c c c c}
 & HH & HT & TH & TT \\
H & (-3, 3) & (-3, 3) & (2, -2) & (2, -2) \\
T & (2, -2) & (-1, 1) & (2, -2) & (-1, 1)
\end{array}.
$$

It may be noted that, at each cell of the matrix, the sum of the two entries is equal to 0. The reason for this is that, in each of our examples, money is transferred directly from one player to the other without any external credits or debits for either player. Such games (where one player loses whatever the other one wins) are known as *zero-sum games*. In a two-person zero-sum game, it suffices to show the first player's payoff, since the payoff to the second player is always its negative. Thus, the normal form of a finite two-person zero-sum game is a matrix whose entries are, by convention, the payoffs to Player I.

In the game of Example 3, suppose Player I chooses BB (always bet) while Player II chooses C. In that case, Player I has a 0.8 probability of losing $3, and a 0.2 probability of winning $3. Thus I's expected payoff is $0.8(-3) + 0.2(3) = -1.8$. Other payoffs are calculated similarly, giving us the normal form

$$
\begin{array}{c c c}
 & C & F \\
BB & -1.8 & 1 \\
BP & -0.2 & -0.6 \\
PB & -2.2 & 1 \\
PP & -0.6 & -0.6
\end{array}.
$$

We postpone discussion of the characteristic function until treatment of cooperative games with three or more players.

II. TWO-PERSON ZERO-SUM GAMES

As just discussed, these games represent a closed system: whatever one player wins, the other player loses. In the finite case, such a game is represented by a matrix. If Player I has m strategies, while II has n strategies, then the normal form is an $m \times n$ matrix A, where a_{ij}, the entry in the ith row and jth column, is the payoff to Player I if she uses her ith strategy while II uses his jth strategy. The game is a *matrix game*.

A. Saddle Points

Now, Player I wishes to maximize, and Player II to minimize, the payoff. For Example 1, the normal form (abbreviated) is

$$\begin{array}{c} \\ H \\ T \end{array} \begin{array}{c} \begin{array}{cc} H & T \end{array} \\ \begin{pmatrix} -3 & 2 \\ 2 & -1 \end{pmatrix}, \end{array}$$

and it may be seen that there is no strategy that can be considered truly "good": whatever one player chooses, the other can win by simply "guessing correctly." Thus if I choses H, then II can win by choosing H; but if so then it would be better for I to choose T; but then it would be better for II to choose T; but then it would be better for I to choose H; etc. Thus it is not clear what should be done in this game.

Contrast this with the game of Example 2, whose matrix is

$$\begin{array}{c} \\ H \\ T \end{array} \begin{array}{c} \begin{array}{cccc} HH & HT & TH & TT \end{array} \\ \begin{pmatrix} -3 & -3 & 2 & 2 \\ 2 & -1 & 2 & -1 \end{pmatrix}. \end{array}$$

In this game Player II has a "sure thing" strategy in HT. Whatever Player I chooses, II does at least as well with HT as with any other strategy. Thus II should always use HT. Given that II will choose HT, Player I should choose T as this minimizes her losses.

Example 4

Consider the following matrix game:

$$\begin{array}{c} \\ D \\ E \\ F \end{array} \begin{array}{c} \begin{array}{ccc} A & B & C \end{array} \\ \begin{pmatrix} 4 & 1 & -3 \\ 5 & 2 & 4 \\ -1 & 0 & 6 \end{pmatrix}. \end{array}$$

In this game, there is no "sure thing," in the sense of a strategy (for either player) which is always better than anything else. Rather, we analyze the game as follows:

If Player I is cautious, then, in using any strategy, she will worry about the worst that can happen to her. This "worst" is represented by the smallest entry in each row, namely -3 for D, 2 for E, and -1 for F. Thus caution suggests using row E.

Suppose, however, that Player II figures out what Player I is thinking (i.e., using row E). Then he would use column B as this minimizes the payoff in row E. But, if II is using B, this is all the more reason for I to use E (as this maximizes the payoff in column B). Thus, the pair of strategies (row E, column B) presents a very stable type of equilibrium. The value of 2 at their intersection, which is both the smallest entry in its row and the largest entry in its column, is a *saddle point*.

Definition 1

In a matrix game A, the entry a_{kh} is a saddle point if, for each $i = 1, \ldots, m$,

$$a_{kh} \geq a_{ih}$$

and, for each $j = 1, \ldots, n$,

$$a_{kh} \leq a_{kj}.$$

If a matrix game has a saddle point a_{kh}, then this saddle point is a very satisfactory *solution* for the game. In fact, by using the kth row, Player I expects to win at least a_{kh}; by using the hth column, Player II expects to lose no more than this same amount. We say then that a_{kh} is the *value* of the game, and the two strategies (row k, column h) are *optimal strategies*. In case of more than one saddle point, the following theorem is helpful:

Theorem 1

Let the matrix game A have saddle points at a_{kh} and at a_{ij}. Then $a_{ij} = a_{kh}$, and, moreover, the entries a_{kj} and a_{ih} are also saddle points.

The importance of Theorem 1 lies in the fact that (1) players have no incentive for trying to change from one saddle point to another, and (2) if the two players try for two different saddle points, the outcome will nevertheless be a saddle point.

B. Mixed Strategies

While saddle points represent a very satisfactory solution for matrix games, the fact remains that, in general, such games need not have saddle points. (Note Examples 1 and 3 for games with no saddle points.) In such a case, it seems that the winner will be the one who can think one step further than the other player. ("He bluffed last time, so he will expect me to call this time, and therefore he will not bluff, so I should fold if he bets. But perhaps he knows that I am thinking this, and will bluff again, so I should call his bet. But perhaps he is thinking this, too, so . . . .") Unfortunately, thinking two steps (instead of one) further ahead than the other might well lead to defeat. Rather than this attempt at outguessing, mathematicians have developed the idea of a *mixed strategy*.

Consider once again Example 3. The first thing to notice is that there is no point in using either row 3 (PB) or row 4 (PP). In fact, BB is always at least as good (for Player I) as PB, and somethimes better, while BP is always at least as good as PP, and sometimes better. This says quite simply that Player I should always bet on a high card. The question is whether she should bet (bluff) or pass on a low card. As mentioned above, it is important for Player I to keep her opponent guessing.

To keep Player II from outguessing her, Player I might well decide to choose her strategy at random, i.e., in case she receives L, she might flip a coin and bluff if the coin comes up heads, or pass if the coin comes up tails. In fact this is a possibility, but it effectively seems to take away any "free choice" that Player I might have. Moreover, it is not clear why bluffing exactly half the time should be particularly good.

It turns out that, in this game, Player I's best choice—in a way to be explained shortly—is to bluff one-eighth of the time, i.e., always bet if she has H, and, with L, bet with probability 0.125. Note that, in this way, she does not really give up her free choice—she chooses the probability, 0.125, in a rational way, and then lets a randomization device tell her what to do. More precisely, she chooses among her four strategies through a random mechanism which assigns probabilities 0.125, 0.875, 0, and 0 to them. This is a mixed strategy. We will use the term *pure strategy* for the rows and columns of the matrix (i.e., for what we have up to now called strategy).

Definition 2

In an $m \times n$ matrix game, a mixed strategy for Player I is a randomization scheme over that player's pure strategies, or equivalently, a vector $\mathbf{x} = (x_1, \ldots, x_m)$ with nonnegative components which add up to 1. Similarly, a mixed strategy for Player II is a vector $\mathbf{y} = (y_1, \ldots, y_n)$ with nonnegative components that add up to 1.

Essentially, the rationale for mixed strategies lies in the fact that Player II might be able to reproduce (in some way) Player I's thinking process and thus might be able to guess I's mixed strategy. However, II will not know what Player I actually does since this depends on a random mechanism. Similarly, I can guess II's mixed strategy but not his actual choice of action.

Assuming Player I uses the mixed strategy $\mathbf{x}$, while II uses $\mathbf{y}$, then under the assumption of independence (these two randomization schemes are carried out independently of each other), the expected payoff will be

$$\sum_{i=1}^{m} \sum_{j=1}^{n} x_i a_{ij} y_j,$$

or, in matrix notation, $\mathbf{x}^{\mathrm{T}} A \mathbf{y}$.

Now, Player I will try to choose $\mathbf{x}$ (among all her mixed strategies) so as to maximize $\mathbf{x}^{\mathrm{T}} A \mathbf{y}$, while II will try to choose $\mathbf{y}$ so as to minimize this same product. We then define saddle points in mixed strategies in terms of the expected payoff, i.e.,

Definition 3

A pair of mixed strategies $\mathbf{x}^*$ and $\mathbf{y}^*$ form a saddle point for game A if, for any mixed strategy $\mathbf{x}$ of Player I,

$$\mathbf{x}^{*\mathrm{T}} A \mathbf{y}^* \geq \mathbf{x}^{\mathrm{T}} A \mathbf{y}^*$$

and, for any mixed strategy $\mathbf{y}$ of Player II,

$$\mathbf{x}^{*\mathrm{T}} A \mathbf{y}^* \leq \mathbf{x}^{*\mathrm{T}} A \mathbf{y}.$$

In Example 3, the pair of strategies $\mathbf{x}^* = (0.125, 0.875, 0, 0)$ and $\mathbf{y}^* = (0.5, 0.5)$ is a saddle point, with $\mathbf{x}^{*\mathrm{T}} A \mathbf{y}^* = -0.4$. To see this, note that, against either one of Player II's pure strategies, $\mathbf{x}^*$ gives an expected payoff of -0.4. Since any mixed strategy of Player II simply chooses one or the other of these two with certain probabilities, it follows that the expected payoff, if I uses $\mathbf{x}^*$, will be -0.4, no matter what mixed strategy II uses. Similarly, against Player I's four pure strategies, $\mathbf{y}^*$ gives expected payoffs of -0.4, -0.4, -0.6, and -0.6, respectively. Since none of these gives I a better payoff than -0.4, none of her mixed strategies can give a better expectation. This quantity -0.4 is the *value* of the game.

C. The Minimax Theorem

The question obviously arises as to the existence of saddle points in mixed strategies. The following theorem, due to J. von Neumann, is probably the most important in game theory:

Theorem 2 (The Minimax Theorem)

Any matrix game has at least one saddle point in mixed strategies.

If $(\mathbf{x}^*, \mathbf{y}^*)$ is a saddle point for game A, then the strategies $\mathbf{x}^*$ and $\mathbf{y}^*$ are said to be *optimal strategies*, while the quantity

$$v = \mathbf{x}^{*\mathrm{T}} A \mathbf{y}^*$$

is the *value* of the game. There may be several saddle points, but a theorem similar to Theorem 1 guarantees that the value is unique. A *solution* of the game is a triple $(\mathbf{x}^*, \mathbf{y}^*, v)$.

It may be that the game has a saddle point in pure strategies. If so, Theorem 2 is still true because a pure strategy can always be thought of as a (degenerate) mixed strategy: one that assigns probability 1 to one of the pure strategies, and 0 to all others. Thus, the game of Example 2 has the optimal strategies $\mathbf{x}^* = (0, 1)$ and $\mathbf{y}^* = (0, 1, 0, 0)$ and value $v = -1$.

For Example 1, the reader can verify that the solution is $\mathbf{x}^* = (0.375, 0.625)$, $\mathbf{y}^* = (0.375, 0.625)$, and $v = 0.125$.

While the mimimax theorem guarantees the existence of optimal strategies and a value, the problem of computing these remains. There are two well-known techniques for this. One is based on linear programming: the optimal strategies are solution vectors for a pair of mutually dual linear programs. The other technique, known as *fictitious play*, assumes that two players play the same game a large number of times; each keeps track of his or her opponent's past choices, and at each iteration, uses the pure strategy which will do best against the opponent's empirically observed strategy. A theorem due to J. Robinson shows that under such assumptions, the empirically used strategies of both players will converge to optimality.

D. Infinite Games

Where each player has an infinite number of pure strategies, it is still possible to define mixed strategies and optimality. Unfortunately, the minimax theorem will not always hold for such games, and where it holds, computation of the optimal strategies may be quite complicated. We will not discuss such games here.

III. GENERAL-SUM NONCOOPERATIVE GAMES

As opposed to Section II, we consider here games in which either the sum of the payoffs is not zero or there are more than two players. For these games, cooperation may or may not be allowed. We discuss first the noncooperative case.

The number of players may be any integer $n \geq 2$; we will label them $1, 2, \ldots, n$, and let N be the set of these players.

A. Nash Equilibria

In normal form, each player, j, has a strategy set which we denote by Γ_j. A game is represented by n payoff functions π_j, defined for n-tuples of strategies. Thus, if $\sigma_1, \ldots, \sigma_n$, are strategies for players $1, \ldots, n$, respectively, then

$$\pi_j(\sigma_1, \ldots, \sigma_n)$$

is the payoff to player j $(1 \leq j \leq n)$ for this choice of strategies. As usual, we assume each player wishes to maximize his payoff.

In this case, the analogue to the saddle point is known as a *Nash equilibrium* (after J. Nash). Specifically,

Definition 4

For an n-person game with payoff functions π_j, the n strategies $\sigma_1^*, \sigma_2^*, \ldots, \sigma_n^*$, form a Nash equilibrium if, for each player j $(1 \leq j \leq n)$, and each strategy $\tau \in \Gamma_j$,

$$\pi_j(\sigma_1^*, \ldots, \sigma_j^*, \ldots, \sigma_n^*) \geq \pi_j(\sigma_1^*, \ldots, \tau, \ldots, \sigma_n^*).$$

(On the right-hand side of this last inequality, it is understood that only the single term σ_j^* has changed, to be replaced by τ.) Thus, no player can gain by a unilateral change of strategies.

Example 5—The Battle of the Sexes

Player I (a woman) and Player II (a man) wish to go to either a hockey game (G) or the ballet (B). Player I would prefer the game; II prefers the ballet. However, both wish to be together and will derive no utility from going to either event alone. We represent this game by

$$
\begin{array}{cc}
 & \begin{array}{cc} \text{G} & \text{B} \end{array} \\
\begin{array}{c} \text{G} \\ \text{B} \end{array} & \begin{pmatrix} (3, 1) & (0, 0) \\ (0, 0) & (1, 4) \end{pmatrix},
\end{array}
$$

where, as usual, Player I chooses the row and II the column. In each case, the first component is the payoff to I, and the second the payoff to II. It may be seen that this game has two Nash equilibria, consisting of the strategy pairs (G, G) and (B, B).

Example 6—The Prisoner's Dilemma

In this game, due to A. W. Tucker, Players I and II are prisoners, suspected of a particular felony. The prosecutor, having no hard evidence, must hope that they will confess. He therefore offers each of them a deal.

If neither confesses, both will go to jail on minor charges. If both confess, both will receive medium sentences. If only one of the two confesses, then the one that confesses will be given a suspended sentence, and the other will receive a severe sentence.

For this game, the prisoners both have the strategies confess (C) or do not confess (D). (The prosecutor is not considered a player.) The game can then be represented by

$$
\begin{array}{cc}
 & \begin{array}{cc} C & \quad\quad D \end{array} \\
\begin{array}{c} C \\ D \end{array} & \begin{pmatrix} (-5, -5) & (0, -10) \\ (-10, 0) & (-1, -1) \end{pmatrix}.
\end{array}
$$

This game has the unique equilibrium (C, C). The reason for this is that for each player, C is always better than D, *whatever the other player does*. Hence both will, presumably, confess. (This although both will be better off if neither confesses!)

Example 7—Cournot Oligopoly

Assume there are n producers of a homogeneous good. Each firm, i, chooses the quantity q_i it will produce. The market price p of the good will depend on the total quantity produced by the n firms. Each firm wishes to maximize its profits, defined as revenue minus costs, where revenue is the product pq_i.

In the simplest case, we assume that the inverse demand function is linear, given by $p = A - Q$, and that each firm's costs are zero. Then firm i's profits are $\pi_i = (A - Q)q_i$, where $Q = \sum_j q_j$.

For this game, an equilibrium (here a Cournot–Nash equilibrium) is obtained by differentiation, maximizing each function π_i with respect to the corresponding q_i. This equilibrium gives us $q_i = A/(n + 1)$ for each firm. All firms produce the same amount, with total production $Q = An/(n + 1)$, and market price $p = A/(n + 1)$. Profits for each firm will be $\pi_i = A^2/(n + 1)^2$.

In all three of Examples 5, 6, and 7, Nash equilibria (in pure strategies) exist. In general this is not so. It turns out, however, that, when mixed strategies are allowed, equilibria do exist. The following theorem is due to Nash.

Theorem 3

Any finite n-person game will have at least one equilibrium n-tuple of mixed strategies.

This is an existence theorem, based on a fixed-point argument, and calculation can be quite complicated. For two players, a clever technique due to C. E. Lemke and A. Howson is frequently used; for three or more, an approximation technique due to H. Scarf is extremely complicated but is the only available method.

More troublesome than the problems with computation of Nash equilibria is the fact that these tend to exhibit pathologies which never occur with matrix games. For one thing, Example 5 shows that no analogue of Theorem 1 holds, even for two-person general-sum games. The given game has two equilibria, but payoffs at both equilibria are different; thus, there will be attempts by the two players to steer the game toward one or the other of the two equilibria. Moreover, if player I tries for one equilibrium, say (G, G), while II tries for the other equilibrium (B, B), the result will be the "disaster" (G, B). There seems to be no way to choose between the two equilibria. A third equilibrium, in mixed strategies, is very unsatisfactory.

Even in cases where there is only one Nash equilibrium, as in Example 6, this equilibrium may be unsatisfactory. In fact, both players will do much better if they both employ their nonequilibrium strategy, D. There is no way that the theory of Nash equilibria can solve this problem.

IV. TWO-PERSON COOPERATIVE GAMES

Where cooperation is permitted, much of the interest is centered on the bargaining process that takes place prior to cooperation. This is best studied in the two-person case, where the distraction of alternative coalitions is avoided.

A. Nash's Bargaining Model

In this model, also due to Nash, two players are to divide a "pie" (some asset). If they can come to an agreement, this will take effect. Otherwise, neither will receive anything.

A game such as this is represented by a set S in two-dimensional space, the set of *feasible points*: if the point with coordinates (u, v) lies in set S, then Players I and II can, if they so agree, obtain utilities of u for Player I and v for II. It is usually assumed that S is closed and bounded above (so that infinite amounts of utility are impossible). It is also assumed that S is convex (this is a realistic assumption since, given any two outcomes, the players are allowed to randomize between them). Apart from this, a *conflict point* (u_0, v_0) is given: in case the two players cannot agree, they will receive u_0 and v_0, respectively. The conflict point will also lie in the set S, since the two players may, if they wish, "agree to disagree." We wish, now, a *general bargaining rule* which will assign, to each such problem, a feasible point (u^*, v^*) as a solution.

Nash lays down four axioms that the bargaining rule should satisfy. These axioms, explained further on, are Pareto-optimality (N1), independence of irrelevant alternatives (N2), invariance under linear transformations of utility (N3), and Symmetry (N4).

N1 states that if point (u^*, v^*) is the solution to a problem with feasible set S, then there can be no point (u, v) in S such that either $u > u^*, v \geq v^*$, or $u \geq u^*$, $v > v^*$.

N2 is a rather technical axiom which states, essentially, that if point (u', v') is chosen rather than (u'', v'') for a given problem, then enlarging the feasible set (by adjoining new alternatives), and keeping the same conflict point, can never lead us to choose (u'', v'') over (u', v').

N3 is based on the idea that each individual's utility is subjective, and that there is no interpersonal comparison of utility. Moreover, each individual's utility scale is subject to linear transformations (much in the way that temperature can be measured either in the Celsius or in the Fahrenheit scale). Thus the same real-life problem has many different mathematical representations. The axiom states that the solution point should have the same real-life interpretation for all representations of the same real-life problem.

N4 states, essentially, that if the problem is symmetric (in the sense that whenever a point (u, v) is feasible, then so is (v, u), and that $u_0 = v_0$), then the solution point must satisfy $u^* = v^*$. We then obtain the following:

Theorem 4

There is a unique bargaining rule which satisfies Nash's four axioms. This rule chooses the point (u^*, v^*) so as to maximize the product

$$g(u, v) = (u - u_0)(v - v_0)$$

of the increments of the utilities, subject of course to the constraint that the point must lie in S (and, in fact, in the part of S "above and to the right" of the conflict point).

Example 8

Players I and II are to divide the sum of \$100. Player I's utility is linear with money, i.e., her utility for x dollars is equal to x. On the other hand, player II's utility for y dollars is only $y^{1/2}$. If they cannot come to an agreement, neither will receive anything.

In this case, the conflict point is $(0, 0)$. If Player I receives x dollars, then her utility is $u = x$, while II's utility is $v = (100 - x)^{1/2}$. Thus, in an agreement, u and v satisfy the equation

$$u + v^2 = 100.$$

We look then for the point which maximizes the product uv. Some calculus tells us that the maximum is at $v^* = 33.3^{1/2}$ and $u^* = 66.7$. Thus Player I should receive \$66.7, while II receives only \$33.3. While this division looks strange, the point is that, because of II's utility function, the \$33 which he gets represents more utility to him than the \$66.7 which he does not get. This gives a bargaining advantage to Player I, and she can use it to get a larger share of the \$100.

B. Threats

One problem with the model above lies in the determination of the conflict point. In Example 8, the situation is deliberately kept simple: failure to agree reduces each player to the status quo. In general, of course, the situation can be much more complicated. Consider a situation in which Player I is a law-abiding citizen, walking along a lonely street, while Player II is an armed robber. The two will "bargain" over I's wallet, and, if no agreement is reached, Player I may find herself much worse off than at the status quo. Player II, by wielding a gun, has changed the conflict point from $(0, 0)$ to, say, $(-500, -10)$. At the new conflict point Player I loses a lot; II also loses something as he would prefer to get the wallet without need for violence.

Some further points should be made here: (a) Player II may have several different threats; (b) Player I may herself have some available threat(s); and (c) in any case, it is not clear that the players will carry out their threats.

To take threats into consideration, Nash modified his model. In this new model, each player has finitely many threats (threat strategies). If Player I uses her strategy σ_i while II uses his strategy τ_j, they receive utilities of a_{ij} and b_{ij}, respectively. Thus the game is represented by two matrices A and B (payoffs to the two players in case of conflict) and a set S of feasible points. It is assumed that all points (a_{ij}, b_{ij}) lie in S. S might, however, be much larger than the convex hull of these conflict points.

Nash now assumes that the bargaining will go as follows:

1a. Player I chooses a (mixed) threat strategy, $\mathbf{x}$.
1b. Player II, in ignorance of $\mathbf{x}$, chooses a threat strategy, $\mathbf{y}$.
2. The two players, knowing both $\mathbf{x}$ and $\mathbf{y}$, bargain (look for a point of S on which they might agree). If they cannot agree, then they *must* use their threat strategies, obtaining (expected) payoffs of $\mathbf{x}^T A \mathbf{y}$ and $\mathbf{x}^T B \mathbf{y}$, respectively.

Applying Nash's previous model to this last bargaining step, we come to the conclusion that Players I and II will choose that point $P^* = (u^*, v^*)$ which maximizes the product

$$(u - \mathbf{x}^T A \mathbf{y})(v - \mathbf{x}^T B \mathbf{y}),$$

subject of course to the constraints that $(u, v) \in S$ and $u \geq \mathbf{x}^T A \mathbf{y}$, $v \geq \mathbf{x}^T B \mathbf{y}$.

Since P^* depends on the threat strategies $\mathbf{x}$ and $\mathbf{y}$, it follows that Player I should choose $\mathbf{x}$ so as to maximize u^*, while II chooses $\mathbf{y}$ so as to maximize v^*. Now (u^*, v^*) lies on the Pareto-optimal ("northeast") boundary of S, which means that as u^* increases, v^* decreases, and vice versa. The situation then is very similar to that for matrix games: there exist *optimal threat strategies* and a *bargaining value* for such games. Computation of these is generally based on the solution of a sequence of related matrix games, each of the form $A - kB$.

It should be noted that this model assumes that players *will* use their threat strategies if no agreement is reached. It is not clear just how this can be enforced. No generally accepted theory is currently available to deal with unenforceable threats.

V. n-PERSON GAMES

We consider now cooperative *n*-person games, where $n \geq 3$. The point here is that players will typically have several alternative coalitions. Thus bargaining within a coalition must be made with these competing alternatives in mind.

A. The Characteristic Function

The theory developed by J. von Neuman and O. Morgenstern assumes a finite set $N = \{1, 2, \ldots, n\}$ of players. A *coalition* is any nonempty subset of N (including N itself and all the one-player sets). An assumption is now made that, if a coalition S forms (or even if its members merely discuss this idea), it must consider the possibility that the remaining players—the complementary coalition $N - S$—will form. Thus S will find itself playing a two-party game against $N - S$. Still another assumption says that utility is directly transferable (at a one-for-one rate) between members of a coalition, so that all that matters at this point is how much total utility S will gain. (Side payments within S will then adjust the several members' shares.) This is generally known as the TU (*transferable utility*) case.

If the *n*-person game is zero sum (the sum of payoffs to all players is zero) or at least constant sum, then the game between S and $N - S$ can be solved as in Section II, with S as maximizer and $N - S$ as minimizer. Let $v(S)$ be the value of this game.

If the *n*-person game is not constant sum, then the two-party game will be a bimatrix game as in Examples 5 and 6. In this case the situation is not quite as clear as before; nevertheless, we will define $v(S)$ as the largest amount (of utility) which S can guarantee for its members *no matter what $N - S$ does*.

We call $v(S)$ the *worth* of coalition S. The function which assigns to each subset S of N its worth $v(S)$ is the *characteristic function* of the game.

Example 9

In a game with three players, there is a trunk full of precious objects, valued at 1000 units. The trunk is too heavy for one person to lift, but any two of the three players can lift it together—and they will then be in possession of the trunk.

In this case, we have $N = \{1, 2, 3\}$, and

$$v(\{i\}) = 0 \qquad \text{for } i = 1, 2, \text{ or } 3$$

$$v(S) = 1000 \quad \text{for any } S \text{ with two or three players.}$$

By convention, we also have $v(\phi) = 0$ (ϕ being the empty set).

Example 10

A woman (Player I) has a horse which she wishes to sell. She has no use for it. There are two possible buyers,

Players II and III. Player II values the horse at 1000 units, while Player III values it at 500 units.

In this case, a single player can produce no utility. Neither can the coalition {2, 3}. On the other hand, the coalition {1, 2} can produce a total of 1000 units of utility, to be divided among them as they wish. (If Player I sells the horse to II, I's profit is then the price she receives for the horse, while II's profit is 1000 minus the price he pays. Their total profit is then 1000.) Similarly, {1, 3} can produce 500 units of utility. This game has the characteristic function

$$v(\{i\}) = 0 \quad \text{for } i = 1, 2, 3$$

$$v(\{1, 2\}) = 1000$$

$$v(\{1, 3\}) = 500$$

$$v(\{2, 3\}) = 0$$

$$v(\{1, 2, 3\}) = 1000.$$

Given the characteristic function of the game, we look for a way to distribute the amount $v(N)$ which is the total utility available to the set of n players. Assuming that no player will accept less than what he can guarantee in the worst of cases, we define an *imputation* as a vector $\mathbf{x}$ with n components such that

$$x_i \geq v(\{i\}) \quad \text{for all } i \in N$$

$$\sum_{i \in N} x_i = v(N).$$

Thus, imputations are possible payoff vectors—allocations to the n players of the total amount $v(N)$.

In Examples 9 and 10, notice that the imputation set in each case is the set of all vectors with three nonnegative components adding to 1000. In this, the games are similar, but as we shall see, they are quite dissimilar in other ways.

B. The Core

Given a game in characteristic function form, $\mathbf{v}$, we know its imputations. We still require some way to determine which imputations are in some way "better" or "more stable" than others. We base this on *domination*. An imputation $\mathbf{x}$ dominates another, $\mathbf{y}$, if there is some coalition S such that (a) all members of S prefer $\mathbf{x}$ to $\mathbf{y}$, and (b) S is strong enough to obtain $\mathbf{x}$. Mathematically this means that $x_i > y_i$ for all $i \in S$, and $\sum_{i \in S} x_i \leq v(S)$. Then, the *core* of a game is the set of all undominated imputations.

In Example 9, the core is empty. For, let $\mathbf{y} = (y_1,$ $y_2, y_3)$ be an imputation. The three components of $\mathbf{y}$ add to 1000, and thus at least one of them is positive. Assume that $y_1 > 0$. Then $\mathbf{x} = (0, y_2 + y_1/2, y_3 + y_1/2)$ dominates $\mathbf{y}$ (with $S = \{2, 3\}$). Similarly, all imputations are dominated, i.e., the core is empty.

In Example 10, the core is nonempty; it consists of all imputations of the form $(x_1, 1000 - x_1, 0)$, where $500 \leq x_1 \leq 1000$. This says that Player I will sell the horse to II; the price cannot be more than 1000 since the horse is only worth 1000 units to II. On the other hand, the price must be at least 500 units as, below 500, Player III will bid so as to raise the price.

C. The Shapley Value

While the core is an intuitively appealing solution concept for n-person games, we note that in many cases it will be empty. It also fails to take certain possibilities into account. In Example 10, e.g., the two buyers might collude so as to bring the price of the horse below 500 units: Player III realizes he will be outbid anyway, so he agrees to stay out of the bidding for a price (a side payment from II), and so an outcome such as (300, 600, 100), although not in the core, is not out of the question. For these reasons, theorists have looked at alternative solution concepts. Perhaps the best known one is the *value*, or *power index*, due to L. S. Shapley.

Given an n-person game $\mathbf{v}$, Shapley looks for an outcome $\Phi[\mathbf{v}]$—a vector with n components—which says what each player might reasonably expect to obtain in the game. His approach is axiomatic, based on the idea that two games (with the same players) can be added to give another game. He then gives four axioms that the value rule Φ should satisfy: efficiency (S1), dummy exlusion (S2), symmetry (S3), and additivity (S4).

Of these, S1 says that all players together should receive the amount $v(N)$. S2 says that a player who contributes nothing—good or bad—to any coalition, will receive nothing. S3 says in effect that if $v(S)$ depends only on the number of players in S, then all players in the game should receive the same amount. Finally, S4 says that the value $\Phi[\mathbf{v} + \mathbf{w}]$ of the sum of two games is equal to the sum $\Phi[\mathbf{v}] + \Phi[\mathbf{w}]$ of the values of the two games.

We then obtain the following theorem:

Theorem 5

There is a unique value rule, defined over the space of all n-person games, satisfying the axioms S1–S4. This rule Φ gives to player i in game $\mathbf{v}$ the amount

$$\Phi_i[v] = \sum \frac{(s-1)!(n-s)!}{n!}\,[v(S) - v(S - \{i\})],$$

where the summation is taken over all coalitions S with $i \in S$, and s is the number of elements in set S.

As may be seen, the value assigns to Player i a weighted average of her *marginal contributions* $v(S) - v(S - \{i\})$ to the several coalitions she may join (cf. the usual economic idea of paying factors of production according to their marginal product).

In Example 9, it is no great surprise that the value is (333.3, 333.3, 333.3). In Example 10, the value is (583.3, 333.3, 83.3). Note that Player I—as the only seller, with two buyers—is in a position to obtain most of the profits. Note, however, that Player III gets something—he is not quite so helpless as the core analysis above would have us believe.

D. Other Solution Concepts

The core represents a very strong type of stability, which need not exist; the Shapley value gives us a kind of expectation which does not take into account prior relations among the players. Thus, other solutions concepts have been proposed, some looking for a weaker type of stability, and others perhaps looking for the outcome of a single play, or taking prior agreements among the players into account. We mention only a few of these.

Von Neumann and Morgenstern developed *stable sets* which represent "standards of behavior." A set V of imputations is stable if (a) no imputation in V dominates another, and (b) every imputation outside V is dominated by at least one in V.

R. J. Aumann and M. B. Maschler developed *bargaining sets*, based on the idea that, in a coalition, some players may *object* to a payoff if they feel that others in the coalition are receiving too much of the coalition's profits. The objected players may be able to show, by means of a *counterobjection*, that they can protect their share. A payoff vector is in the bargaining set if, for any objection, there is a counterobjection.

Other solution concepts include the *kernel*, due to M. B. Maschler and M. Davis, and the *nucleolus*, due to D. Schmeidler. Modifications of the Shapley value, using information about some players' relationships to others, have been suggested. Chief among these are one by R. Myerson and another by G. Owen.

VI. MODIFICATIONS OF THE GAME MODEL

A. Games with Nontransferable Utility

As mentioned in Section V.A., von Neumann and Morgenstern's theory is based on the assumption that utility is freely transferable (at a one-for-one rate) between members of a coalition. In real life this may not be possible, either because there is no perfect "money" (to be identified with utility) or because rules (e.g., antitrust laws) forbid it. Theorists have therefore developed a model for games without side payments (the NTU case). In these games, $v(S)$, rather than a single number, is a set in s-dimensional space—a generalization of the two-dimensional sets discussed in Section IV.A. It is possible to define imputations, dominations, and the core for these games. Attempts have been made to generalize other concepts—mainly the value and the bargaining sets—but no generalization seems as satisfactory as the original (TU case) concepts.

B. Games with Incomplete Information

Game theory usually assumes that the players have *complete information* as to the game they are playing—e.g., they know the strategies available, the probabilities at chance moves, and the payoff functions. In practice this need not be so. Thus theorists (J. C. Harsanyi, R. J. Aumann, and M. B. Maschler among them) have studied situations in which the players have subjective probabilities as to the games they are playing. Aumann and Maschler have studied the problem faced by a player who wishes to use private information but fears that its use may reveal this information to an opponent, and the dual problem faced by a player who wishes to elicit information from an opponent's moves.

Bibliography

Aumann, R. J., Maschler, M. B., & Stearns, R. E. (1995). *Repeated games with incomplete information.* Cambridge, MA: MIT Press.

Harsanyi, J. C. (1977). *Rational behavior and bargaining equilibria in games and social situations.* Cambridge: Cambridge Univ. Press.

Luce, R. D., & Raiffa, H. (1957). *Games and decisions.* New York: Wiley.

Owen, G. (1995). *Game theory.* San Diego: Academic Press.

van Damme, E. (1987). *Stability and perfection of Nash equilibria.* Berlin: Springer.

von Neumann, J., & Morgenstern, O. (1944, 1947). *The theory of games and economic behavior.* Princeton, NJ: Princeton Univ. Press.

GENDER ROLES

Gillian Howie
Liverpool University

I. Essentialisms
II. Acquisition Theory
III. Ethics of Sexual Difference

GLOSSARY

gender Any of two or more subclasses that are partly arbitrary and partly based on distinguishable characteristics such as sex; the assignment on the basis of sex of two or more different series of personality traits. These are thought to be mutually exclusive.

gender role The allocation on the basis of sex of different categories of those activities considered to be useful or necessary for the sustenance and improvement of living; also, the attitudes and behaviors members of society are supposed to enact. The United Nations Conference on Women in Copenhagen in 1980 concluded that women do between two-thirds and three-quarters of the work in the world, produce 45% of the world's food, earn 10% of the world's income and own less than 1% of the world's property.

identification Psychological term designating the internalization of expectations, behaviors, models.

identity (i) Object identity: continuation through time and space; (ii) subject identity: where something remains the same throughout change and alteration. This can be either primary sexual characteristics (scientific arguments) or qualities such as rationality. The concept of subject identity also involves the concept of identification.

norm Shared rules of behavior.

role The expected behavior associated with any given status. Roles are defined and structured around the privileges and responsibilities that the status is seen to possess (e.g., mother as status, role is nurturer, father as status, role is breadwinner).

sex The biological aspects of an individual; i.e., chromosomal, hormonal, anatomical, reproductive, and physiological attributes.

sexism Discrimination on the basis of sex; specifically, the investment of the male sex and masculine character traits with higher value than the female sex and feminine traits.

sexual dimorphism The separation of individuals into two distinct types, based first on biological distinction then on psychological traits.

sexual identity An identity that is held between sex, gender, gender role, and sexual orientation.

sexual orientation The manner in which individuals experience sexual pleasure or arousal, usually considered to be between types rather than within the same type.

THE CONCEPT OF GENDER ROLE refers to the allocation of different categories of activities considered to be useful or necessary for social production or reproduction. This allocation is made according to sex because types of work are identified with certain behavioral characteristics or dispositions (gender) and these behavioral traits or characteristics (gender) are thought to be caused by primary or secondary sexual characteristics (sex). Because this definition concerns the allocation of socially useful labor, we are assuming that a gender role is a social role. So, we could define "mother" as a social status and "mothering" as a social role that is sex-specific. The next step is to analyze what "mothering" denotes. We find that the term denotes varied tasks, including nurturing, emotional support, and the provision of domestic labor. The main point of contention is whether or not these tasks are performed by one sex rather than another because this sex is predisposed to behave in ways that are consistent with the (successful) performance of the role. There are three questions. First, is it the case that diverse activities can be gathered together as definitional of certain roles? (To mother is to nurture, to nurture means to give emotional support, to father means to provide, to provide means to struggle in competition for primary goods.) Second, is it the case that there are two classes of individuals, identifiable by primary sexual characteristics, who have distinct or dimorphic patterns of behavior? Third, if it is the case that there are two classes of individuals with dimorphic patterns of thinking or behaving, are the behaviors causally related to primary or secondary sexual characteristics (naturalism/essentialism)? Or are these patterns learned (social acquisition theory)?

I. ESSENTIALISMS

A. Ontology

Essentialist arguments, in all permutations, maintain that the classifications "male" and "female" are a conceptual discrimination within an original type "human." This is based on the belief that all instances share a common feature (whatever it is to be human). The further discrimination into two classes is premised on the belief that there are irreducible differences between men and women and that within each class there are enough similarities to justify dimorphic classification. We classify things by making judgments concerning identity and difference: Is x the same as, or relevantly similar to, y? How do instances x and y differ from instance s? The classification of individuals into two classes would need to be based on the idea that all men share the same property or characteristic that defines them essentially as men and all women share the same

property or characteristic that defines them as women. These qualities or characteristics would have to be (i) identifiable and (ii) different between classes. Modern science, while appearing to eschew the notion of essential properties, works with a taxonomy that separates things into classes according to a decision as to what counts as a "real" or "deep" explanation for a thing's behavior or difference from another thing and what is merely trivial or nonexplanatory.

I will now investigate sex–gender taxonomies presented in biology, physiology, and sociobiology to see whether the classifications can be justified as "deep" explanations for apparent differences.

1. Essentially Different

a. Biology

If it is sex that explains dimorphic classification, then we need to investigate what is meant by an individual's sex. Basically, sex is defined in terms of gametes or germ cells that an animal produces. If the gamete is large, contains food, and is immobile, it is called an egg cell and the animal is defined as female. An animal that produces a gamete that is small, contains no food resources, and is mobile is classified as male. All cells in a woman's body, except the egg cells, contain two XX chromosomes and all cells in a man's body, except sperm cells, contain an XY chromosome. In germ cells only half the chromosomes are present. The female cells contain one X chromosome and the male cells might contain either an X or a Y. These join together and form a fertilized egg that is either XX or XY. The Y chromosome is critical for the embryonic gland to develop into a testes, which will then secrete two hormones: testosterone and an undetermined substance. The secretion of these two hormones stimulates a specific development of internal ducts. Where there is a second X chromosome, the internal duct will continue to develop. Both male and female external genitals develop from an undifferentiated structure. If the androgen dihydrotestosterone is secreted by the mother, during the third and fourth months of pregnancy, a penis and scrotal sac will be formed; otherwise a clitoris and labia will develop. Prenatal testosterone effects the onset of puberty. Where it is present puberty will be delayed and this is taken to explain why girls "mature" earlier than boys. There are three sex hormones that trigger puberty: testosterone in boys, oestrogen and progesterone in girls. The first causes the development of secondary sexual characteristic such as muscular development, deepening voice, growth of skeletal size, capacity to carry blood to the heart. The second causes secondary sexual characteristics such as breast development and the onset of the menstrual cycle. Female pubic hair and axilla are produced by adrenal androgens. Androgens are hormones produced in both sexes by the adrenal gland situated above the kidneys. Ovaries and testes each produce all the other hormones to a greater or lesser extent.

It is clear that there is dimorphic organization of primary characteristics, although there is great variety within each class and that there is a connection between primary and secondary sexual characteristics. For three reasons it would be unsound to infer from these secondary characteristics an explanation for different behaviors. The first reason is that there is general problem with *reductionism*. It could be argued that the attempt to explain phenomena in one field of study (social behavior) in terms of a more fundamental science (here biology) misses too much in its translation from one language (a description of social behavior) into the supposedly more fundamental language (biological descriptions). The second is a problem of induction: we are dealing with very general classes within which there is great variety. It would be unsound to take one example and infer certain things about that according to a very general taxonomy. The third point is that theoretical taxonomies or principles of classification are organized according to assumptions that may say more about the scientist, and his or her social location, than about the material in question. One of the few things that might follow from biology is that because testosterone is an anabolic, men will be, on average, more suited for heavy, or physically demanding, activities. But because we are dealing with generalities, there can be no legitimate reason that would justify the exclusion of all women from such activities. The criteria for inclusion should be specific to the activity rather than premised on general assumptions concerning sex. It should also be noted that cultural exclusion, such as from sporting activities, restricts activity and training and thus accentuates average sex differences, physical strength, stamina, and speed, which then appear to confirm the original hypothesis.

b. Physical Theories

Because it is thought by some that our responses to stress, our mood disorders, our "madness," our sexual orientations and our "deviant" or "criminal" behavior are caused by features of the brain, an attempt is made to reduce complex behaviors and mental states to brain states and brain states to different chemistries. Characteristics and behaviors are separated into two and assigned to the different sexed bodies. These characteristics range from aggression, violence, and computational skills in men, to emotional instability, linguistic competence, and sociability in women. Because it is impossible to "see" the causal connection, a scientist will examine behaviors, alter chemistries of experimental groups, and study "deviancies."

We can break the proposition that males are more aggressive than females into two parts: (a) on average males are more violent than females; (b) the best explanation for this is that there is a one-way causal relationship between testosterone and aggressive behavior. We would first have to define what we mean by aggression: are we referring to injury actually inflicted, to the intention to inflict injury, to the emotion behind the act, or to verbal or physical aggression, and do we believe that aggression and violence are synonymous terms? We might also ask further questions. For example, is aggressive behavior a response to a hostile environment? After clarifying our initial definitions and beliefs, we might accept (a) as applicable to *Homo sapiens*, men are more aggressive in general than women, but even then we are not pressed to accept (b). The argument that there is a one-way causal relationship emerges from various cross-species studies. These studies have only concentrated on very specific control groups and due to this the inference is at best unproven. In addition there have been many studies providing contradictory evidence. Finally, there are studies that demonstrate that physiological and psychological events are not in a one way causal relationship. It is the case, though, that masculinity has always been associated with aggression and aggression with dispositions to be active, and this has been used to explain why men "succeed" in the "public" sphere and why women need protecting (by a man from other men) or why distinct gender roles are performed by the two sexes.

c. Sociobiology

The basic argument from sociobiology is that current gender roles are adaptive features resulting from natural selection during hominid evolution. There are two primary questions asked by sociobiologists: Why did sexual reproduction occur? Why two distinct individuals? The answer is usually that variety and adaptability are useful evolutionary developments. If this is the case then a third question arises: what is it that introduces variety in sexual reproduction? Darwin's theory (1871) ran like this: (i) all organisms must reproduce; (ii) all exhibit hereditary variation; (iii) hereditary variation differs in its effect on reproduction; (iv) variations with favorable effects on reproduction will succeed. Thus, according to Darwin, reproduction was the means of special variation and sexual reproduction introduced that variation. Sexual selection was the principal motor of selection within a species. He described this motor as being driven by the principles of desire for access to the female and sexual jealousy. Such arguments are not far removed from recent presentations. Trivers argued that sexual selection can be viewed as a consequence of different sized gametes. Male reproductive success would not be limited by the amount of energy required to produce its gametes, because the male gamete is small, but it would be limited by the male's ability to fertilize a female. The female's reproductive success would be limited by the production of gametes because female gametes are large and energy-consuming. Two main dimorphic patterns of behavior were said to follow: (i) males will compete for access to females, who in turn seek out the fittest mate; (ii) females invest more in gametes and consequently in offspring. This argument would stand a chance of working only if it could be shown that females invest more energy in producing gametes than do males. However, males produce many more gametes than females and thus nothing is proved. Others argued that men and women inherit different biogrammers: genetically based programs that predispose individuals to behave in distinct ways. While these are not absolutely fixed, to be consistent with the evolution argument, they change slowly and change ought not be brought about by "unnatural attempts" of either sex to challenge existing roles.

The two principal tenets of sociobiology are that (i) all social behavior has a biological explanation and (ii) this biological basis is genetic: the encoding of features that have been selected during evolution. The main problem is to demonstrate what actually can be explained in this way and to offer convincing criteria for choosing the "best" of competing genetic stories. Unfortunately, sociobiology too often falls into a naturalism. *Naturalism* is the theory that nothing resists explanation by natural sciences and there is often an additional connotative sense that there is a "natural order." For example, homosexuality is unnatural, and it is natural for men to have many sexual partners and unnatural for women to do so. But for many sociobiologists, current social organization the nuclear family, the expectation of female sexual "purity" and specific parental roles, can all be explained according to these argumentative steps.

d. Reproduction

From the simple fact that some, although not all, women carry a fetus to term and that some of these, although not all, breastfeed many other facts are said to follow. These include emotional–cognitive differences between the sexes, sex-based assignments of roles, duties, and labor, and the naturalness of the family unit. Otherwise put, the fact that a woman is a mother means that she has carried a fetus to term, but does it mean anything in terms of consequent roles?

Firestone (1970) argued that sex or gender roles are a consequence of different roles in sexual reproduction. The economic–cultural class system developed from this more original sex-based division of labor. To remove the conditions for the "sexual caste system" would thus require women to be released from their biological role in reproduction. Where Firestone called for a sexual revolution to "seize the means of reproduction," neither Dworkin nor Corea shared her optimism: which means that they were more skeptical about the possibilities afforded by reproductive technology. Others argued that the sexual caste system is not a natural consequence of biological roles but is a consequence of men's desire to control women's reproduction. O'Brien explained this desire as an effect of the fact that men are alienated from the act of giving birth. Separated from the act of creation, men wish to control it and need to do this if they are to establish the grounds for patrilineage. So, it was this attempt to control sexual reproduction that resulted in the dimorphic classification and definition of gender roles. The consequence of this was a specific arrangement of social life: into *public* and *private* spheres where the private was organized as a family unit. The head of this unit was male and publicly active, while the woman was subservient to, and usually economically dependent on, the male head and performed domestic chores. Echoing the above, Rich argued that men experience jealousy and fear the "power of the mother." As a result they strive to curtail the authority of women and to wrest birthing practices from the hands of women.

While Firestone accepted that there were natural, if unpalatable, consequences of biological roles in reproduction, O'Brien argued that relations of reproduction are social and have little to do with biology. Pursuing this line, Oakley asked whether there is a natural disposition "to mother." She argued that the supposed psychological and emotional disposition to reproduce, and then to mother, (for example, the concept of the biological clock), are an effect of an already established sexual caste system: an oppressive system that circulates myths relating to parenting. There are three prevalent myths. The first is the assumption that all women need to mother, the second is the belief that all mothers need their children, and the third is that all children need their mothers. Taken together, these myths tie complex social caretaking arrangements to simple biological facts.

2. Essentially the Same

As a refutation of such sex-based allocation, many theorists and philosophers have argued that men and women are identifiably the same: free rational agents. Personality or behavioral traits, identified as gender, can be classified as accidental or contingent. Following this line of reasoning, it is possible to argue that no dimorphic division of labor could be justified in terms of primary sexual characteristics and that even when it might be appropriate, the field of application is extremely narrow. Thus, Wollstonecraft allowed the argument that the status "mother" was a reasonably sex-based assignment but denied claims that women ought to be excluded from educational institutions or from political organizations. This is because, where these latter are concerned, it is rationality that is the relevant characteristic: a property that men and women share. Although these arguments undoubtedly were made by countless women through the centuries, it was not until Seneca Falls Convention and the Declaration of Sentiments (1848) that they were formalized into a political doctrine. This was therefore a direct challenge to the assignation of particular responsibilities and duties associated with status.

II. ACQUISITION THEORY

A. Psychology

If we define gender in terms of behavioral traits, dispositions, and expectations, and sex as the body, and if we reject essentialist arguments, then we require an explanation for why one group of traits can be identified with one type of body and the other group with the other type. One explanation uses the psychological concept of "identification." *Identification* is a psychological term designating the introjection of various beliefs, values, and role models. Taken together, these provide the conditions for the cognitive, emotional, and motivational responses within a person. The assumption is that men and women undergo similar psychological processes and because of this display different behaviors. The argument is that these behaviors fall into two distinct groups and that the infant learns which group is suitable by associating them with an adult and then after judging which adult is most like her- or himself, imitates behavior or uses imitated values and beliefs as organizational principles of behavior. The first judg-

ment of similarity is considered to be premised on the identified sex of primary carers. Thus, the psychological process of identification concludes with an identity holding between the child's sex, gender (behavioral traits), expectations of gender role, and sexual orientation. The principal point of contention is whether the infant identifies with the same-sex parent because it first recognizes its own sex or whether such identification is the end result of a process that includes rewards and punishment for appropriate behavior. If the first is taken to be the case then the child would be first aware of sex categories, this would lead it to identify gender behavior with appropriate sex and a final identification with the same sex parent. Piaget explained that the latter must be the case because an infant is incapable of ascribing permanency to physical objects, including itself. It is only when it develops an awareness of gender-specific behaviors that it has the cognitive ability to grasp the specificity of sex. This would mean that same-sex identification is the result of a process that includes the recognition of different ways of behaving and the application of this to itself. In order to explain why a child might identify with a specific pattern of behavior Mischel argued that the child is rewarded or punished for appropriate or inappropriate behavior and it learns to behave in a way that wins it approval. Thus, a child's gender behavior, and its self-identification with the same-sexed parent, is the result of corrective training.

The psychological concept of identification is proposed as an explanation for a child adopting and demonstrating traits and behaviors congruent with its sex. Again, this would be fairly anodyne if it were merely descriptive. However, the proposition that men and women have differing emotional–cognitive dispositions has been used by philosophers such as Rousseau to justify the exclusion of women from the body politic and used by those in authority to justify the exclusion of women from public office, from certain types of work, and from educational institutions. Here I will outline the argument that men and women have different *ethical sensibilities* due to early psychological development.

Kant defined enlightenment or *maturity* as the ability to use one's reason without the guidance of another and this, he stated, was a prerequisite for moral judgment. If we were to argue that maturity thus requires the individual to be "field independent," in other words, to be able to separate oneself from one's context and personal relationships, and if we were to argue that this ability to separate oneself from one's environment was the result of a psychological process involving detachment from one's parental figures, and if we were to argue further that this psychological process was different for girls and boys, we would have good reason to assert different "maturities" or at least different levels of maturity. The reason why moral judgment appears to require such "field independence" is that it involves the universal application of rules according to which particular instances are judged. Now, if it is claimed that a boy, because he identifies with a parental figure who is either absent or who is not his most immediate caregiver, would have to learn to distance himself from his emotions and that girls do not have this distancing experience due to the fact that they identify with their most immediate caregiver, then we would also have good reason to argue that men and women have different ethical sensibilities because maturity, or field independence, is a prerequisite for moral judgment.

This was the crux of the argument between Kohlberg and Gilligan. Gilligan, accepting largely Kohlberg's reasoning, argued that girls, because they do not suffer such detachment, are able to introduce into ethical judgment a finer sense of other people, to understand the complexities of emotionally demanding situations, and to reason from specific contexts. She argued that Kohlberg's morality of justice was premised on the idea that one ought to approach all people as rights-bearing individuals and that moral dilemmas could be resolved by applying universal moral principles. Against this, she posited a morality of care and responsibility. Moral dilemmas, she argued, were context-specific and were to be solved through a process of induction. Such inferences would require an understanding that each individual is situated within a web of relationships that brings with it a set of demands, needs, and interests. To understand this, she claimed, one would require the ability to empathize and to feel compassion. These are not the values of field independence and a mature moral voice would thus not be of the type outlined by either Kant or Kohlberg.

There are four main points to make concerning the above analysis of cognitive development and moral judgment. The first is that the methodology in both cases has been severely criticized and the statistical evidence is weak. The second point is that, and this can be witnessed most clearly with Kohberg's work, the theoretical assumptions that gave direction to the methodology were inherited from a tradition that presumed dimorphic behavior, development, and abilities. There are striking parallels with social anthropological assertions relating to masculinity, maturity, and field independence. Following from this, the hypothesis that maturity, as a psychological process, coincides with proper moral judgment, premised on rights and auton-

omy, needs itself to be contextualized as ancient and medieval moral systems were quite different. Hence, the Kantian system should neither be taken as a historic (Kohlberg) nor essentialized as male (Gilligan). The final point is that, unless one argues independently for an essentialist hypothesis, all one has proved, if the evidence could be taken seriously, is that men and women display, on average, dimorphic traits. Such evidence is neither confirmation for a hypothesis concerning field dependence or independence and early psychological experience, nor is it a secure basis for inferences concerning sexed ethical sensibilities.

B. Psychoanalysis

It was with Freud that the centrality of sexuality as an organizing principle in mental life came to the fore. He proposed that adult *heterosexuality* is the end result of a series of psychological events, the experiencing of which organizes infant sexuality from a state of polymorphous perversity to an adult libidinal state. Instincts, according to Freud, have their origin in the human body and have sources of excitation in erogenous zones. These zones, and stages of development, were classified into three: the oral stage, the anal stage, and the genital stage. The seduction fantasy was adopted early in Freud's writings (1895–1897) to signify an actual traumatic sexual scene—the first stage of seduction was believed to occur before the child was conscious of its sexuality. The memory was not repressed until it was subsequently triggered and imbued with full sexual connotation. In a letter to Fleiss (1897) Freud retreated from this position and from then the phantastical nature of the memory was stressed and developed into the theory of the *Oedipal complex*. The phantasy, however, does still, for Freud, have a basis in reality: not the reality of child abuse (seduction) but the reality of the child's sexual desires for its parents.

Freud's theory of psychosexual development may be described in this manner. When the boy reaches the phallic, or genital stage, he desires his mother to satisfy all his erotic needs and begins to view his father with antagonism because his exclusive enjoyment is hindered by paternal intervention. These feelings of antagonism are muted by the child's desire to win love from his father. In order to do this, the boy situates himself beside his mother and, in competition for his father's affection, experiences antagonism towards her. But the partial hatred felt toward the father results in a fear of punishment. This is conceived in terms of denial. The most horrific form of denial would be the loss of his favorite "plaything": his penis. The boy reacts to this fear of castration by completely withdrawing from his mother. He then enters a period of sexual latency. The castration complex is overdetermined by the fear that love may be lost from the father, compounded by a general vulnerability of a fragile ego attempting to survive and negotiate the demands of an external world. Sexual latency is a method of self-protection, but the repressed instincts will surface later on. During puberty the Oedipal complex once again resurfaces and its successful resolution relies on the boy being able to choose a woman other than his mother as a love object. Overcoming castration anxiety is the final step. The boy understands that although his penis is smaller than his father's, it is not a sign of inferiority but a stage in his natural development. Although he cannot "have" his mother in the same way as his father, he learns to wait his turn. By doing this, the ambivalence within the notion of identification is taken to be resolved: he is like his father but not yet the same.

Freud was less confident with his description of female psychosexual development. Because his working assumption was that there is no pre-Oedipal difference of erotic organization between the sexes, he had to explain why the girl, without a penis, with no threat of castration, would detach her erotic love choice from her mother and then reestablish a maternal bond based on identification. His solution is that during the phallic phase the girl, on seeing male genitalia wonders why hers are absent. She makes sense of this by deciding that she is already castrated. Casting her gaze at her mother, finding her too castrated, she turns to her father in anger. This foundational penis envy becomes erotically transformed into the desire to give her father a child. Unfortunately, this leaves the girl in an ambiguous position. Identification with the mother would be permeated by the low opinion formed with the discovery of her lack. Additionally, there lies a fundamental conflict in her superego, which is the harbinger of social mores and values, and her own ego ideal. If, in order to overcome her penis envy, she were to identify with her mother, of whom she has such a low opinion, and adopt a passive position, there would be conflict with her own ego ideal. But, to retain a picture of herself as "active," a picture that would please her ego ideal, she would need to deny the fact that she "lacks" a penis.

In the phallic, or genital, stage both girl and boy have a "masculine" attitude, which means that both wish to penetrate: to be active. But it is also the case that both take an erotically passive, feminine, position to the father: desire to be penetrated. This is further complicated by the desire to be penetrated by the mother and to penetrate the father. Thus the Freudian Oedipal complex requires the concept of *bisexuality* in order to explain the oscillation between father and mother, the active or passive positions taken in relation to them and cross-identifications. However, these identifications finally come to a halt and the correct ones are the foundation for mature heterosexuality. Both boys and girls recognize the penis as the symbol of activity and passivity and castration anxiety is essential if the boy is to separate from his mother and to identify with his father. "The antithesis runs: male genital organ or a castrated condition not until completion of development at the time of puberty does the polarity coincide with male and female. In maleness is concentrated subject, activity and the possession of a penis; femaleness carries over the object and passivity. The vagina becomes valued henceforth as an asylum for the penis; it comes into the inheritance of the mother's womb." (SE XIX). At root a biological essentialism permeates Freud's work, linking mature adult sexuality to heterosexuality, to positions of activity and passivity, and ultimately to penetration. A man is masculine, active, and subject when he penetrates, a woman is feminine, passive, and object when she "is penetrated." This seems to be simple equation between grammatical convention, subject-verb-object, and the prejudice that sexuality is by definition an action and the action "penetration."

This biological essentialism has been challenged by feminist theorists. Friedan argued that one must understand psychoanalysis as a cultural practice. Psychoanalysis, as any science, is a series of assertions formed into a hypothesis designed to explain specific phenomena with an expectation that future phenomena will confirm the hypothesis. However, confirmation within psychoanalytic practice depends on the successful resolution of deviant and newly diagnosed "neurotic" and "psychotic" behavior. Firestone, who disagreed with Friedan on a number of points, argued that the effect of successful therapy was to reconcile women to the ideology of femininity and to the structures of patriarchy. Friedan and Firestone disagreed over the truth of the claim that sexuality is central in the organization of mental life. For Friedan this concentration on sexuality is a facet of the "feminine mystique," which encourages women to be overly concerned with the "private" self.

Other theorists view psychoanalytic theory in a more positive light because it begins to investigate how social beings emerge from biological ones and thus opens a series of questions concerning the unconscious, desire, and the construction of sexuality. Horney argued that women do feel inferior to men and that this is not the result of "penis envy" but the consequence of their actual social subordination. She further suggested that patriarchal culture defines the concept of the feminine (passive, masochistic, narcissistic) and that the infant learns to accommodate her subordination by identifying with the feminine. This attempt to accommodate a position of subordination explains, for Thompson, why women have weaker egos than men—an effect of constant deferral to male authority. One overall criticism of psychoanalytic feminism is that it tends to posit universal psychic structures and symbolic systems and avoid empirical analyses of the cross-cultural and historically changing material conditions of women's oppression.

C. Socialization

So far we have been examining how, if one rejects essentialist or scientific explanations for dimorphic behavior or character traits, one can explain why and how individuals adopt or acquire gender-specific roles. Another dimension to this question relates to the way that tasks are organized and become definitional of the role. Under the general description "socialization" many theorists have argued that individuals are socialized in such a way that they will perform the designated roles. The above question, "how does that socialization take place," remains but now we also need to examine why the roles exist in the form which we encounter.

1. Social Stability and Gender Role

It has been argued that the way in which we assign tasks within the family ensures a stable family unit and that this is the foundation for a stable social organization. The theory developed by Parsons and Bales posits two principal sets of tasks in the family: the provision of emotional support and the provision of primary goods. It also posits a distinction between individuals in terms of their dispositions or orientations. One group of individuals, the argument runs, has an *expressive orientation* and the other an *instrumental orientation*. The former fits nicely with the expressive role in the family and women, who according to Parsons, have an instinct to nurture as a result of their biologically based role in sexual reproduction, are thus ideally suited to perform the expressive role in the family. Men, on the other hand, due to their physiology, have an instrumental orientation that fits nicely with the role relating to the provision of primary goods. If the two sexes adopt these gender-specific roles, then social harmony can be ensured. Similarly, but without eulogizing the role of the family, Bloom argued that it is the case that instrumental, or goal-oriented activity, dominates the "public"

world of paid employment and, he argued, it is also the case that instrumental rationality, which entails efficient task-oriented activity, can brook no slack or compassion. Because of this an emotional outlet is required and this is provided by the family, more specifically by women—so men and women have to be socialized in different ways. The thesis, then, is that behaviors and characteristics, known as gender, are the result of a process of socialization, the purpose of socialization is to ensure that two different roles, with very different requirements, can be performed successfully, and the tasks are organized into the roles, known as gender roles, to guarantee social stability.

There are four principal criticisms of both positions. First, it is clear that labor is performed in both spheres. If one wishes to press a distinction in methodology then a further argument needs to be made: for *domestic labor* is as much task oriented as economically rewarded labor. Second, neither theory leaves room to explain the psychosexual effects of structural male unemployment. The third point is that it has never been the case, and it is less so now than ever, that women have only undertaken domestic labor. The final point is a general criticism of the claim that mind states differ between men and women. No social psychologist has been able to prove conclusively the fact of dimorphic patterns of emotional–cognitive states or behavior. The Parson-Bales thesis elaborates the conditions of social organization in terms of primary sex characteristics. Bloom's thesis explains sex-based division of labor in terms of the social conditions of labor. The point left unaddressed by the first is that "masculine' and "feminine" traits are valued differently and that the "task-oriented" activities involve access to the "public" world of power, both economically and politically. The point left unaddressed by the second is an explanation for why men and women, as two distinct groups, are assigned different roles and values. In order to understand how dimorphic roles guarantee social stability, one must also understand that the concept "gender role" designates tasks and behaviors that might or might not command respect and power, and one must also understand that at root we are dealing with the organization of behaviors between the sexes.

To return, for a moment, to the question relating to the process of socialization, we could argue that as soon as the child learns linguistic discrimination and learns the conceptual schemes culturally prevalent, she or he has already been socialized. Symbolic agents and representations of many varieties play their part in forming the infant's understanding of her- or himself and the world. The main question is whether these *symbolic systems* involve beliefs, representations, images, and institutional practices that keep existing sex–gender role systems in smooth operation and whether this benefits or advantages one sex over the other. According to the feminist theory of *patriarchy*, from foot-binding to stilettos, from exogamy to the marriage contract, from religious presentations of women as mothers or whores, to explanations and justifications of rape, from sexual harassment to "domestic" violence, from genital mutilation to cosmetic surgery, the issue is one of power exerted by men over women. Sexual domination, stated Millett is so universal and ubiquitous that it *appears* to be natural. Further, she argued, these power differences between men and women, are institutionalized and the institutions establish and then endorse these differences by ensuring that men and masculine roles are always dominant. These institutions present a picture of gender behavior that reflects and is reflected by all forms of mainstream cultural *representation*: representations that appear to describe behavior but that, in fact, prescribe types of suitable behavior and values. These values and expectations are internalized by each child beginning with experiences in the family. This "interior colonization" results in the girl child feeling low self-esteem, self-hatred, and an acceptance of her inferiority. In summation: patriarchy can be defined as the set of systems, practices, institutions, and symbolisms that always have and still do, organize the domination of one group, or class, over another. The idea of men and women as distinct classes is echoed by Dworkin, Firestone, and French, who all argued that women are not valued as individuals but as members of a class that serves men both sexually and socially.

2. Social Reproduction and Sexual Reproduction

The above theorists of patriarchy thus believe that social stability is a function of power differences between two classes: men and women. They also believe that behaviors and tasks are organized in a way that will benefit all men. The ideas that power relations between men and women are the condition for all other relations of power and that men and women are two distinct classes are rejected by socialist or Marxist feminists. In a nutshell the problem is how to explain the relation of production to reproduction: whether women's subordination to men is an effect of economic dependency, a dependency that is the result of women's role in sexual reproduction, a role that is required by capitalism or whether economic dependency is another facet of a more general system of male power and that this might or might not coincide with a specific organization of

labor defined as *capitalism*. We have already defined patriarchy as the set of systems, institutions, and symbolisms that organize the subordination of one class, women, to another, men. Capitalism has been defined as the organization of production for profit, where one class, the bourgeoisie, extracts surplus labor from another class, the proletariat. *Dual systems* theorists argue that patriarchy and capitalism are two distinct systems that intersect. *Unified systems* theorists argue that capitalism and patriarchy can be seen as a set of social relations and therefore that one conceptual scheme is adequate.

Mitchell contended that the two systems are theoretically irreducible. Her argument is that women's relation to production, low pay, part-time work, and economic dependency is a cause of oppression but that this operates in tandem with biosocial considerations and more general ideas circulating in society concerning masculinity and femininity. These ideas are buried deep within each individual psyche and if we were to alter the relations of production we would still be left with the ideological system. Hartmann, another dual systems theorist, developed a materialist account of patriarchy and was concerned by the fact that if we reduce all power relations to relations of production we miss the point that all women are oppressed by men—whether the women are economically productive or unproductive. Hartmann described patriarchy as a set of material relations that allows men to control women's labor power. These material relations are made possible by the interdependence and solidarity of men, and they enable men to dominate women, to exclude women from positions of public power, and to control women's sexuality. These material relations have altered throughout history and today could be described as capitalistic patriarchy. The interests of capitalism and patriarchy, she concluded, are different, they have been in conflict but they are now in harmony. The former is designed to extract surplus labor from workers and the latter is motivated by male desire to control women.

Young, on the other hand, believed that the very categories of analysis used by dual systems theorists were misguided. Women, she argued, are not oppressed as women within the family and as workers within the economy but are oppressed as women workers—capitalism is at its core gender biased. By investigating the gendered nature of the division of labor one can detect how capital requires for its smooth operation a reserve pool of cheap, often casual or part-time, female labor, unpaid domestic work, and efficient sexual reproduction. Developing this insight, Jaggar suggested that political theory ought to expand the notion of relations of production to include the idea of sexual reproduction because capitalism requires a specific organization of sexual reproduction. Thus, sexual reproduction takes its place alongside the production of commodities as the primary site of empirical analysis. With the idea that relations of production and reproduction constitute the conditions of social experience, Vogel argued that in order for capitalism to reproduce itself, the conditions for production must themselves be reproduced. This means that labor power must be made available, which means, in effect, that sexual reproduction is an essential component of social reproduction. The idea of social reproduction covers both the "production" of new labor and the appropriate socialization of that labor. Women fulfill a dual role in the social system because they are economically productive and sexually generative. But, importantly, this is a source of contradiction: when a woman is reproductively active, her economic productivity is temporarily reduced. This contradiction is resolved, according to Vogel, in three ways. First, the form of economically productive labor undertaken by women allows for great flexibility. Second, the fact that the male wage was supposed to be a family wage factored in women's economic dependency and made the form of female labor appear to be more acceptable. Finally, the ruling class enlists the support of working-class men to ensure that when a woman is less economically active she "freely" performs the necessary domestic labor required to guarantee the maximum economic labor from men. Men consent to the general system, which in effect also exploits them, partly because they reap sex-based rewards: sanctioned advantage (economic privilege) and sanctioned domination (patriarchal authority). Vogel's account then allows the fact of sex-specific oppression within a general framework of economic exploitation. The *family* unit can be analyzed in terms of how it maximizes available labor and as a structure that reproduces new labor. The maintenance of sex-based labor roles, within and reproduced through the family, allows capitalism to reproduce itself. Thus the idea of a natural "gender role" is ideological in the sense that these relations are contingent on a form of social and economic (re)production but also have their basis in a factual division of labor.

3. Social Stability and Subject Identity

Given the above analysis, it seems strange that women not only consent to performing their roles but sometimes want to behave in ways that are to their detriment. MacKinnon, a dual systems theorist, argued that sexuality is a social process, general yet specific to certain historical and social moments. She made two main points. First, a "woman" must learn to have sex in order to become a woman, "woman" as gender comes through the experience of, and is the condition for, "having sex." In order to "have sex" one must be desirable and there are specific codes of desirability that one must learn and introject. The second point involves an analysis of what counts as desirable. By examining presentations of desirable women, MacKinnon concluded that a woman's sexuality is constructed for men and that this involves the woman displaying characteristics that support men's assumed dominance. Thus, she argued, learning how to be a woman means learning that one is defined by what men count as desirable: subservience, vulnerability, passivity. A woman's sexuality then always embodies power: a compulsory heterosexuality and a mature woman is one who can be described as feminine, which means displaying traits or behavior that support male dominance.

Sex refers to the biological aspects of an individual. Gender refers to two different personality types and consequent abilities. Sexual orientation refers to the manner in which individuals experience sexual pleasure or arousal. The naturalist assumption is that sex, the body, remains fundamentally the same throughout alteration and that there is a causal, physical link between behavior or psychology and primary sexual characteristics. A particular individual who either does not act out the expected role, or is sexually oriented to someone of the same sex, is considered deviant: the explanation for this deviancy is given in terms of physiology or psychology and treatment is made available. An alternative to this naturalist account is the argument that the congruence of sex, gender, and sexual orientation is an effect of socialization. One could argue that what is transmitted through a series of codes, representations, sanctions, and prohibitions is the basis for an appropriate emotional–cognitive situational response: that according to one's body (sex) there are appropriate ways of behaving, expectations, and sexual responses. The implication is that identity between sex, gender, and sexuality is the consequence of various processes, that to gain the status "man" or "woman" one must learn how to behave in an appropriate fashion and that men and women occupy different positions in the symbolic system. So, to return to the question of how this guarantees social stability we can make a number of points. First, to be a "grown-up" means to be locked into a system where we actually desire things that will, in effect, maintain the current social organization. Second, the congruence of sex, gender, and sexual orientation is the result of various processes that secure these desires and behaviors. Third, our sense of who we are depends on these beliefs, desires, and behaviors. Fourth, if it is the case that roles are structured so that one group has power over the other, and if it is the case that the power of one group depends on its power over the other, then social stability is premised on the subjection of women. Finally, in conclusion, the naturalist explanation of gender behavior can be held to account for mystifying relations of power.

4. The Meaning of Masculinity and Femininity

MacKinnon's argument that to be a woman is to be someone who reflects men's desires, that the feminine is always *the other* to masculinity, is a common one. From de Beauvoir's *Second Sex* (1953) and Greer's *Female Eunuch* (1970), feminist theorists have demonstrated that women are expected to reflect men back to themselves "at twice their natural size": that a woman is the mirror that men hold up in order to see themselves in their full glory. A difficult, but important, conceptual distinction can be drawn between representation and women's experience. Spender detailed how women's labor, be it cultural, political, or economic, has been overlooked and has thereby disappeared from historical narratives. Later, she added that control is also exercised through the very medium of language, which is not a neutral medium of communication. Daly elaborated this "grammar of oppression" by examining how values are transmitted, encoded, or connoted through language. This is a similar investigation to those undertaken by Millett, who analyzed forms of representation in literature, Mulvey, who analyzed the presentation of the feminine in film, and Dworkin, who examined the structuring of sexual responses. Because the actual history of women has been excluded from historical narrative, and because the way in which women understand or interpret their experience occurs through language, we can see the central importance of linguistic analysis for grasping how women's self-understanding is constructed.

For writers such as Kristeva, Irigaray, and Cixous male control over language is not merely a question of meaning but central to all its structures (see Moi, T. (1985). *Sexual/Textual Politics*. London: Routledge). Different characteristics and connotive senses are hierarchically organized. This can be most clearly seen in essentialist arguments and psychological and psychoanalytic explanations for role adoption. In all such theories the active principle, rationality, and maturity are associated with men and the passive principle, emotional states, and immaturity with women. These terms have value: the masculine is valued over and against the feminine. The point made by *poststructuralist* feminists is that the meaning of masculinity depends on its difference from the feminine. A deconstructivist reading attempts to subvert the hierarchy and to demonstrate the relation of dependency. Although Irigaray, Cixous, and Butler speculate about the psychological origins of this desire, drawing mainly from Lacanian psychoanalysis, most agree that such speculations are hypotheses that will, almost inevitably, repeat cultural myths.

III. ETHICS OF SEXUAL DIFFERENCE

If ontology is an investigation into the types of things in the world, if it is concerned with "natural kinds," and if we organize our conceptual scheme according to the types of things that we think exist, then we must analyze our original ontological assumptions to see whether the idea of a "natural kind" is appropriately applied to gender or sex.

A. Political Categories and Gender

Early feminists accepted natural kind arguments and believed that the human being has a property or quality that defines it as the type of thing that it is: rationality. For them this was the foundation for ethical and political value. The relevant characteristic, or property, for participation in the decision-making process is rationality, definitional of humanity, so universal rights could be placed high on the political agenda. Distrust and disappointment with the political gains of the first stage led feminists to rethink the scope of the argument. Armed with their analyses of the family, cultural representations, and sexuality, second-stage feminists argued that political gains of equal rights were mere chimera because patriarchal structures and values had been left in place. These structures defined the roles and values accorded to men and women, the masculine and the feminine. Thus, the term "feminine" does not designate natural dispositions, traits, or qualities and "woman" does not refer to an original natural kind. The political slogan "equal but different" is obviously mystifying if the masculine is valued over the feminine and men are guaranteed sanctioned advantage and domination. The structures themselves would need to be revised according to different values. Millett argued that separate masculine and feminine subcultures needed to be integrated and that this would lead to the birth of the *androgynous* person: an individual who combined the most positive traits and characteristics previously given dimorphic classification. This integration, according to French, would be necessary to avoid the catastrophic consequences of a social system organized according to destructive and aggressive values. The problem that emerges is how to value either masculine or feminine traits that are internal to a system that subjugates women: to value "the feminine" means to value something that has already been defined by the system. French believed that because patriarchy distorts masculine traits we would need first to supply positive referents to make a positive description of masculinity meaningful. The concern was that the idea of androgyny was another product of a system that would in effect only value specific traits, behaviors and actions. Aware of this definitional bind, Daly returned to a more *gynocentric position*: placing feminine values at the center. Daly argued that given the construction of gender no absolutely positive trait can be rescued and therefore what we need is a transvaluation of all values: a "no" to the values of the morality of victimization and a "yes" to the values of the "ethics of personhood." This transvaluation of all values leads to a thorough revision of meanings and connotive senses and thus to a different political imagination. The intent was to "empower women," to enable women to think of themselves and to experience the world outside the limits of patriarchal definitions. Examples to fire the political imagination of women are already present: for example the "wild woman" and "the hag." The *postmodernists*, who refined the conceptual and linguistic analysis, recognized that one cannot think outside the constraints of language. The challenge was to think, or to represent, subjectivity without the binds of conceptual hierarchies. They developed a way to write from the body—a procedure designed to demonstrate the vagueness or fluidity of conceptual discrimination and to allow unconscious desires to surface. A further refinement has occurred. The argument is that the political demand to recognize equality, or to value difference between men and women, is premised on an original ontological assumption that the concept "human" has referential sense. If subject identity is not stable, if it cannot be defined according to the property of rationality or by its physical makeup, then how we identify ourselves, who we identify with, and how we are identified can shift and alter throughout time. Further, if we separate sex from gender and from sexual orientation, and if we experiment with behaviors, then we can demonstrate that it is not a necessary fact that an individual with a sex will behave in specifiable ways. By using images, which are not drawn from the maze of dualisms currently circulating, imaginations might be fired to think beyond current

limits. This would also require us to revise our basic political categories and thus to rethink the purpose of political action. The two, often intersecting, theories that use these ideas are *queer theory* and *cyborg feminism*.

B. Power and Gender Roles in the Twenty-First Century

Whether one accepts a dual or unified systems analysis, it is the case that as we approach the twenty-first century, various changes in the division of labor have occurred. Within the developed world, old-style working practices have been replaced by new, flexible employment practices. This has been called the *feminization of labor*. There are two explanations for this. One, from Handy, is that flexible employment requires the skills and abilities associated with 'the feminine' (1994. *The Empty Raincoat*. London: Hutchinson). These include computer literacy and keyboard manipulation skills rather than heavy manual work, the ability to negotiate rather than to confront, the ability to be multitasked rather than monolinear, the ability to work in teams rather than as a competitive individual. Men have the option to learn these qualities and behaviors or to face long-term unemployment and economic dependency. Another explanation is that flexible working practices are employment strategies designed to extract the maximum amount of surplus labor and that these coincide with the type of labor practices historically assigned to women. Again men have two options. They can either reconcile themselves to the fact of short-term, part-time, contracts or suffer the consequences of unemployment. Whatever the explanation, the feminization of labor has begun to shift the balance of economic power. Cultural representations and meanings have become a primary site of struggle as men and women come to terms with the fact that not only have roles altered but also representations are so firmly out of kilter with women's experiences and expectations that the contradictions, outlined by Vogel, have emerged into the clear light of day. One response to this was the, now virtually defunct, man's movement: a reassessment of the concept of masculinity, roles and expectations by men. Another response has been the declaration of the postfeminist era. A third response has been a number of warnings relating to a "backlash." Cocks argued that the decline in traditional patriarchal power within the family has been accompanied by a rise in "phallic" power, sexual domination, the feminization of poverty, and a resurgence of the moral voice blaming economic woes on working women and calling for a return to family values. The contradictions however need to be seen in context, with the UN figures outlined earlier illustrating just how little real economic power has shifted.

Also See the Following Articles

FAMILY, THE • FEMINIST ETHICS • FEMINIST JURISPRUDENCE • FREUDIANISM • MARX AND ETHICS • POSTSTRUCTURALISM • SEXISM • SEXUAL ORIENTATION

Bibliography

Alcoff, L., & Potter, E. (1993). *Feminist epistemologies.* London and New York: Routledge.

Butler, J. (1990). *Gender trouble: Feminism and the subversion of identity.* London and New York: Routledge.

Humm, M. (1989). *The dictionary of feminist theory.* London and New York: Harvester.

Tong, R. (1989). Feminist thought: A comprehensive introduction. Sydney and Wellington: Unwin Hyman.

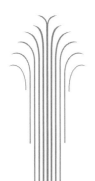

GENE THERAPY

Adam M. Hedgecoe
University of Central Lancashire

I. Introduction
II. Definitions and Distinctions
III. Pragmatic Concerns
IV. Arguments in Favor of Gene Therapy
V. Arguments against Gene Therapy
VI. Conclusions

GLOSSARY

DNA The basic material of inheritance.
genome The total set of genes in any one person's body.
germ-line gene therapy Interventions on a person's genome that will be passed onto future generations.
in vitro **fertilization (IVF)** The fertilization of an ovum outside the body before reimplantation ("test-tube" baby).
somatic gene therapy Genetic interventions that do not affect future generations.

GENE THERAPY is the use of genetic information to intervene in the DNA of a human cell to relieve the symptoms and prevent the causes of diseases with a genetic component. The obvious candidate diseases are those which run in families, such as sickle cell anemia and Huntington's disease, although many other diseases have been cited as possible candidates for treatment, including complex disorders such as cancer and even

HIV/AIDS. The ethical concerns about gene therapy center around the fact that such treatment can have direct and permanent effects on future generations, as well as on the fact that changes are made at a very "basic" biological level.

I. INTRODUCTION

Gene therapy is one of the areas of greatest ethical concern in modern genetics. It is also novel in that it is one of the few cases where large-scale debate of the ethical considerations has taken place well before the technologies concerned have become available on anything but a very experimental level. Although debate about other issues in genetics, such as screening and counseling, has taken place, this has occurred either after technologies have been developed or at the same time. Gene therapy is one of the first chances to allow ethical debate to shape and contribute to a technology from the very first stages of its development.

Despite its highly novel nature, there has been a great deal of commercial and public interest in gene therapy because it is seen as having such great potential for curing disease. It is suggested that because it attacks the genetic cause of diseases, gene therapy is far more beneficial than current treatments which only deal with the symptoms and which are far less specific. Gene therapy holds out the promise of permanently eradicating diseases which have plagued humans for millennia.

The aim of this entry is to present the various types

of gene therapy and to outline the ethical arguments both in favor of and against its development and use. This means that this entry will *not* address ethical issues associated with gene therapy but which are not specific to it; these include objections to embryo experimentation, abortion, and biotechnology as a whole. All these areas are relevant, especially to the experimental development of gene therapy, but to include them would overlap with other entries. An example of one relevant area of discussion is that of cloning. At the end of February 1997, it was announced by scientists in Scotland that they had successfully cloned an adult sheep, producing an identical (though younger) copy, called Dolly. Although cloning of mammals had taken place at the embryonic stage (by splitting an embryo—inducing identical twins in short), the cloning of an adult, i.e., taking cells from an adult mammal and producing a clone from them, had never been done before. As a result, a great deal of interest and concern was generated worldwide over the possible (future) application of these techniques to humans. Although these issues have concerns in common with gene therapy (such as interfering with nature or affecting future generations againt their will), it is important that they be separated from gene therapy. We do not need clones to have effective gene therapy (though they might conceivably be useful in experimental tests), nor do we need gene therapy to produce clones.

II. DEFINITIONS AND DISTINCTIONS

A. Somatic Gene Therapy

This form of therapy has been carried out already and is the simplest and least controversial form of gene therapy. It involves acting on the DNA contained in a person's body, or "somatic" cells; this means that any changes produced by the therapy will be limited to that patient, i.e., changes will not be transferred to the patient's children.

In 1993, experimental trials were run in London on a somatic gene therapy for cystic fibrosis (CF). This involved patients inhaling a fine spray which was composed of fatty packets called liposomes. Inside each of these was a copy of the gene which cystic fibrosis sufferers lack. This gene was inserted into the lining of the nasal passage by the liposomes. Once in the body, it was hoped that the gene would start to produce copies of the protein which is missing in CF patients and which contributes to their breathing difficulties. This trial followed the now standard approach to somatic

gene therapy, which is to use a vector, in this case liposomes, to carry the target gene into the body where it is hoped that it will produce the missing protein. In trials carried out at the same time in the United States, scientists used an adenovirus (the same type of virus as the common cold) to insert genes into the lungs of CF patients. The viral vector was more efficient at transferring the genes into the patient than the liposome method, but led to more side effects.

The first ever effective gene therapy, carried out in 1990 in the United States, involved the immune deficiency disease "ADA deficiency." In this case, scientists removed some of the white blood cells from a young girl's body, inserted new copies of the ADA gene into the cells, and then put the cells back into the girl's body with a transfusion. The modified cells were able to manufacture the missing chemical, ADA, and the girl's immune system improved remarkably. In many ways, these descriptions of somatic gene therapy make it sound very much like any advanced medical procedure, and indeed, that is the way it is viewed by the majority of those people working in the field and those who are concerned with the ethics of such experiments. Somatic gene therapy, because changes are limited to the initial patient, and because they are not passed down to later generations, is not generally seen as ethically problematic.

B. Germ-Line Gene Therapy

Germ cells are those cells found in the ovaries and testes of humans that give rise to sperm and ova. These are the cells that germ-line gene therapy would act upon. The theory is that at a very early stage of an individual's development, perhaps even before conception, changes could be made to a person's genome that would have an effect on every single cell of their body (since all other cells would develop from those early ones) and upon children that they have (and upon all subsequent generations). Any change made to a person's genome using germ-line gene therapy would have long-term, and possibly unpredictable, effects. At the moment, germ-line gene therapy is not even at an experimental stage, there is a worldwide ban on its development, and ethical debate about its acceptability has been increasing.

Very closely linked to germ-line gene therapy, in fact one might almost call it passive germ-line therapy, is the technique of selective implantation in *in vitro* fertilization (IVF). This technique does not directly act on the genome like germ-line gene therapy, but produces the same results. By using genetic screening, it is possible for couples undergoing IVF to select embryos to implant which are free from disease genes (for example, if their families have a history of muscular dystrophy). This would produce a child without the gene for that disease, just as germ-line gene therapy would. This technique is already available and being used by some hospitals, yet although there has been ethical discussion of it, it has not really been of the same tenor as that around germ-line therapy. The point is that if both selective implantation and germ-line therapy produce the same results, are they ethically different, and if they are different, then there must be something ethically significant about directly acting on and manipulating a person's DNA, which is not the case in simple selection.

C. Therapy vs. Enhancement

The final distinction to draw is between genetic technologies used as a form of medical therapy and those same techniques used to enhance the abilities and characteristics that persons already have. For example, gene therapy might be used to increase the height of children with growth hormone deficiency to that of the norm in the population. This would count as therapy. But the same (or similar) techniques could be used to increase the height of a normal child so that they were of above average height. This would be enhancement of characteristics. These possibilities have raised fears of "designer babies" and are felt to produce some of the strongest arguments against gene therapy, or specifically, germ-line gene therapy, since the general view is that effective enhancement treatment would have to act on the germ cells.

As the above example suggests, the line between therapy and enhancement is far from clear, and for some this has led to the conclusion that any form of germ-line therapy, however well intentioned initially, will inevitably lead to the development of enhancement technologies. Such "slippery slope" arguments are often used to oppose germ-line therapy as a whole.

III. PRAGMATIC CONCERNS

When one looks at the ethical debate surrounding germ-line gene therapy, two distinct types of argument can be distinguished: the practical difficulties and the categorical objections. The former are often presented as if they are a final and definite proof of the ethical wrongness of germ-line gene therapy, but in effect, they are merely the normal pragmatic concerns that surround any new technology. For example, the committee set up by the UK government to look at gene therapy (the Clothier Committee) offers only practical, safety-based objections to germ-line therapy: "there is at present insufficient knowledge to evaluate the risks to future generations . . . [and] therefore . . . gene modification of the germ line should not yet be attempted" (C. Clothier *et al.*, 1992. *Report of the Committee on the Ethics of Gene Therapy* (p. 18). London: HMSO). The practical problems stem from the fact that gene therapy deals with systems in the body that are still largely unknown and unpredictable, and in the case of germ-line therapy, many of the effects of the treatment will not be known for a long time (many generations perhaps). But these are the sorts of problems associated with most new medical treatments. Before we make widespread use of heart surgery, we would want to make sure that the techniques used were as safe as possible, that there were no unforeseen side effects, and that we understood as much as possible about the parts of the body that might be effected by such treatment. The same holds true for gene therapy (of whatever type). The U.S. cystic fibrosis trials were stopped because of patient reaction to the virus used as a vector; this does not necessarily mean that such treatment is unethical, merely that all such experiments must be carried out with great caution. This is what we would expect from responsible medical science.

The pragmatic difficulties with somatic gene therapy are manifold. Even if safe vectors can be discovered (and there is some concern over the use of viruses in gene therapy, because of their tendency to mutate and change), the actual insertion of the new DNA into the patient's cells is still very haphazard. At the moment, there is no sure way of getting the new DNA to "slot into" the correct place in the patient's genome. There is the possibility of disrupting the working parts of the genome, and even of triggering cancer. With germ-line gene therapy any effects on an individual treated in this way would transfer into their children and even later generations. But of course the possibility is that many of the side effects might never be revealed *until* those later generations are born. Does this place an impossible burden of proof on germ-line gene therapy? Is it possible that we will never know, to a reasonable, acceptable level of doubt, whether such treatment is actually "safe"? Such doubts should certainly be considered. Perhaps germ-line gene therapy will never be safe to use, but it is important to note that this is not a categorical ethical objection to germ-line gene therapy, but depends upon empirical results of its efficacy and safety. There may come a time in the future when we have to accept that germ-line therapy is safe, or at least as safe as some other medical techniques. It may be unethical to use a treatment that is not tested and safe, but when such a treatment becomes safe, can we still call it unethical? The answer from the second type of objection raised against germ-line therapy, categorical objections, is that it remains unethical.

In the following discussion of gene therapy, most of the issues will be concerned with germ-line therapy and the categorical objections to it that have been raised. As has already been suggested, the ethical problems associated with somatic gene therapy are similar to those issues related to organ transplants and other current medical procedures; i.e., they stem from practical concerns about the treatment's safety. Germ-line therapy is far more ethically problematic, whatever the state of its practicality and safety. It must also be borne in mind that gene therapy may turn out to be safe, but ineffective, or even safe, but too expensive to realistically develop into a standard technique. These points have their own ethical issues (such as distribution of limited resources), but these will not be addressed here.

IV. ARGUMENTS IN FAVOR OF GENE THERAPY

A. Beneficence

This is the idea that doctors should not just "do no harm" (nonmaleficence) but should also actively strive to benefit their patients. Thus, if a doctor knows that by using germ-line therapy he or she can ensure that the child who is born does not have a particular disease, the duty of beneficence would seem to require that the doctor carry out this form of therapy. Put another way, if the doctor knows that there is a high chance of any child born to a particular couple suffering from a disease (for example, if they are both cystic fibrosis sufferers), then we might hold the doctor responsible in some way if he or she allows a child to be born with that disease, when the means of preventing it are available.

Although this might appear a clear case of the duty of beneficence coming into play, it has to be noted that it extends the limits of this duty a little more than is normal. Doctors are normally required to "do good" to current patients, but germ-line gene therapy involves doing good to a person who is not yet even in existence (even if one counts personal existence as starting at conception, the fact that germ-line therapy may operate *before* conception still means that there is no person in existence at the time of action). Thus the responsibility of doctors is spread to people who do not exist. For

some this might not be problematic. Perhaps we are all felt to have some sorts of duties toward future generations (with regard to natural resources, for example), and this extension of beneficence might been seen in a similar light. There is even a precedent in that doctors inoculate women against German measles/rubella to prevent them catching it during pregnancy and harming their child. This could be seen as analogous to germ-line gene therapy. Others may not be convinced, perhaps feeling unease at the shift in emphasis in medicine, which has traditionally is concerned with treating the sick in the population. Germ-line gene therapy could be seen as a way of, instead, preventing the sick from joining the population in the first place.

B. Consequences

This broader position holds that ethical actions are those that produce the best consequences (however best is measured; traditional utilitarian calculations use "happiness"). The argument would follow that the use of germ-line therapy would produce an increase in happiness in the future, with less people suffering from disease, and therefore it should be used. Against these obvious benefits are questions about whether people in the future, if they know they are the product of genetic engineering (of some form), might not suffer psychologically or feel less human because of the action that was taken at such a early stage in their life. This then has to be measured against how "happy" they would feel if they were left alone and developed the disease that germ-line therapy could have prevented. These are speculative questions, hindered by difficulties of comparing people with nonexistent persons ("persons they might have been"), and as such are very hard to answer one way or another. But these are the sorts of issues that need to be considered before one can decide whether germ-line gene therapy is ethical or not.

C. A Duty to Enhance?

John Harris has suggested that if the technology exists, then we should use germ-line therapy to enhance future generations. His analogy is with schooling. If we are prepared to pay large sums of money to ensure that our children get the best education possible, to make them as intelligent as possible, then why should we not use germ-line treatments to enhance their intellectual capabilities as well? "If the goal of enhanced intelligence . . . is something that we might strive to produce through education . . . why should we not produce these goals through genetic engineering?" (J. Harris, 1992. *Won-*

derwoman and Superman (p. 142). OUP). The "why not's" to this question will be presented in the next section, but it is enough at this point to note that as in the case of selective implantation of fetus, this is a case where germ-line therapy reaches the same results as another, less controversial technique. If there is something ethically wrong with germ-line therapy, then it must intrinsically have to do with its direct action upon human DNA, rather than its end results.

V. ARGUMENTS AGAINST GENE THERAPY

A. Right to an Unaltered Genome

It has been suggested that every human being has a right not to have their genome altered by other humans. Germ-line gene therapy would alter human genomes (though somatic therapy would not), and therefore germ-line gene therapy is unethical. This argument has the advantage of being rooted in the language of human rights, which is widely recognized as voicing valid ethical concerns (we think of the UN Universal Declaration of Human Rights as outlining ethically ideal behavior for governments, for example). But this right is certainly not one of the "traditional" rights debated over time (for example, the American right to "life, liberty and the pursuit of happiness"). On what basis do we gain such a right? It is not at all clear. Perhaps it is on the basis of human dignity (see next section). Another difficulty is the idea of a nonexistent person having rights (which is very controversial). While people who complain about their being treated with germ-line gene therapy would be rational beings, the same cannot be said for them when their right was infringed, i.e., just after (or before) their conception. They did not actually have that right at that time, since they did not exist; therefore it is hard for them to complain about infringements of rights they did not have.

The right to an unaltered genome is problematic in other ways since, following the ideas of Derek Parfit, we can say that almost everything we do alters our offspring's genome, the most obvious being our choice of sexual partner. When we choose the person we want to be a parent with, we are automatically making decisions about the genome of our offspring. How is germ-line gene therapy different? If it is different, then this difference must lie in the actual process of the therapy, rather than in the fact that the offspring's genomes are different to how they might otherwise be. The problem is, can we even describe this as "altering" a person's genome? is it not better described as affecting the characteristics that person will have? The same description could be applied to germ-line gene therapy, certainly that type which operates on sperm or ova (i.e., before conception, before any possible person exists), and perhaps, if we do not count a fertilized ovum as a person, germ-line therapy as a whole. Can a person describe themselves as having an altered genome, when in fact what happened was that their parents chose the characteristics that they would have? Does this make an ethical difference? It certainly makes germ-line gene therapy closer to selective implantation and IVF in ethical terms.

B. Human Dignity

A related objection to germ-line gene therapy is that it offends against human dignity, an idea derived from Kant, specifically his categorical imperative that we should always treat people as ends in themselves and not merely as means to an end. Yet it is hard to see how seeking to cure people, or more accurately, prevent them from developing disease, is treating them as means to an end. What end is it that we are treating them as a means to? Perhaps it could be claimed that the end is one of a healthy society, and using the therapy is treating people as merely a means to this end. But then surely this is true of all medical treatment. Rather, medicine is administered to treat individuals, to make individuals better—a side effect is the improved health of society as a whole. Proponents of the human dignity argument have to show why trying to prevent someone getting a disease is not treating them as an end in themselves.

Of course, such a case can be made for *experimental developments* of gene therapy, where the patients are, to some extent, human guinea pigs. In this case, it could be claimed that use of (experimental) germ-line gene therapy treats people as means to an end (that end being experimental results) rather than ends in themselves and could thus be seen to act against human dignity. Perhaps such arguments could be used against the development of germ-line therapy; even if the use of such therapy is ethical, its development is not. The trouble with this position is again the similarity to standard medical treatments. Were these considered as acting against human dignity when they went through experimental testing?

C. Naturalness

Is gene therapy "unnatural," and if so, does this make it unethical? It is difficult to know exactly what is meant when it is claimed that gene therapy is unnatural or "against nature." Certainly it does not occur in the natural world, but then this is true of much that human beings do and build. Perhaps it is rather that such claims of unnaturalness express a deep unease with technologies that act at such a very basic level. The actual DNA that is inserted into a patient's body or genome during gene therapy is as natural as the DNA that it is replacing or overriding. While it may be true that gene therapy thwarts the "natural course of events," this is also the case with taking aspirin, stitching a wound, or administering the kiss of life. All medical treatment effectively acts against the natural course of events. In some ways, that is what medicine is for.

D. Playing God

Ruth Chadwick has suggested that when the term "playing god" is used in moral arguments, it can mean two separate things, depending on the context. In the first case, it is a warning to decision makers that they are not infallible, that they can make mistakes, and that they are not omniscient and divine. The second way is as a warning of unease and disquiet about a particular course of action being taken—that human beings might be going too far and risk unforeseen consequences and disaster. Both of these interpretations are useful for informing our decisions about germ-line gene therapy, but neither of them provides a categorical opposition to it. The first meaning brings us back to the practical problems associated with gene therapy. We must know that it is safe (however that is defined in this context), and that decisions we make about its use are always open to question. The second meaning is useful as counsel, in warning us that we must be cautious in our use of the new technology, not just in terms of physical risk but the changes that it may bring about in our perception of ourselves and our children (and their self-perception). "The playing-God objection is more than mere rhetoric, but less than an argument against a particular course of action. As a counsel it has some value" (R. Chadwick, 1989. Playing God. *Cogito,* Autumn, p. 193).

E. Consent of Future Generations

This argument rests on the premise that the use of germ-line gene therapy involves making decisions about the lives of future generations that they have no say in (for obvious reasons, they do not exist yet). We may be doing things to them that they, if they had the choice,

would not want done to them. We cannot tell what future generation, perhaps thousand of years hence, would want us to do for them. Who knows what sort of people or society might exist then or what its values will be. It is unethical for us to make decisions on their behalf.

This argument can be used with quite some strength against those who favor allowing genetic *enhancement* for future generations, perhaps for things such as height, body shape, and hair color; these are things we cannot really make anything more than a vague guess about with regard to their desirability for future generations. It is less effective against the use of germ-line gene *therapy* since we already make decisions concerning the health of future generations, and these are not regarded as very difficult to make. The most obvious example is the one of toxic or nuclear waste. When there are fears about deep-sited nuclear waste dumps, these are rarely about current populations. Such claims are usually made on behalf of future generations, and so they should be. It will not effect me if highly radioactive plutonium is placed at the bottom of a mine shaft in containers that allow radioactivity to leak out into the atmosphere and water table in minute quantities. It may not even effect my grandchildren, but it could possibly effect later generations that are born long after my death. The same argument can be made for genetic risks. The fact that I am a carrier for a lethal genetic disorder may not affect me (since I am only a carrier), but it could, at some unspecified time in the future, effect future generations. Just as we think we should protect future generations from the foreseen harm resulting from nuclear waste, the same argument can be made that we should protect them from the foreseen harm resulting from bad genes. It is hard to argue that we do not really know what future generations want with regard to health, certainly in terms of serious genetic disease.

E. Eugenics

One concern of opponents of germ-line gene therapy comes from the historical precedents that have been set by people trying to affect human inheritance and health. The word that is used is "eugenics," which literally means "well born" and which was adopted by a movement in the United States and United Kingdom (and whose ideas were later picked up by the Nazis in the 1930s Germany) which at the turn of the century tried to improve society by breeding out of the population undesired traits. Much of the rhetoric used was racist, and many of the actions carried out in the name of eugenics, such as the forcible sterilization of thousands of people in 1920s America, are now looked on with horror. The argument goes that germ-line gene therapy is eugenics by other means, or, at the very least, it has the potential to descend into the same sort of mistakes as the original eugenics movement.

This argument has a great deal of emotional impact due to the distaste in which the original eugenics is held, but there are important differences between eugenics and the widespread use of germ-line gene therapy. The most obvious is the involvement of the state and the involuntary nature of much of eugenics. But germ-line therapy is conceived of within the framework of modern medicine, with its emphasis upon individual decision making and patient autonomy. It is not suggested that germ-line gene therapy would be applied against parent's wishes, to force them to have healthy children, though of course it is possible that a subtle form of social pressure and drive to conform could arise if germ-line therapy became freely available. Supporters of germ-line therapy have pointed out that eugenics is concerned with preventing the disabled from reproducing, while germ-line therapy is concerned with preventing couples from producing sick and disabled children. This leads into a related claim which is often voiced by disabled people and their support groups, that the use of germ-line therapy to prevent disablement and disease is in effect devaluing those people who currently have those disabilities and diseases, a way of saying they are less important, what has been called the "expressivist objection" (A. Buchanan, 1996. Choosing who will be disabled: Genetic intervention and the morality of inclusion *Social Philosophy and Policy,* **13**(2), p. 28). While this is an understandable reaction, it is hard to make this accusation stick.

> In advocating the use of genetic science to reduce disabilities one *is* saying that avoidable disabilities ought to be avoided, and that in that sense one *is* saying that our world, in the future, should not include the existence of so many people with disabilities. But it is not the people who have disabilities that we devalue; it is the disabilities; and one need not and should not wish to reduce the number of people with disabilities by taking the life of any person who is disabled.
>
> (BUCHANAN, 1996, 32–33)

Some people have argued that we have to accept the fact that selective implantation and germ-line gene therapy will lead to a form of eugenics, what has been labeled as "utopian eugenics" (P. Kitcher, (1996). *The lives to come.* New York: Simon & Schuster).

F. Broader Consequences

The previous objections are all put in categorical terms in that they attempt to show that germ-line gene therapy is wrong for a single specific reason. Although all these objections have their points, it is not clear that they are overly persuasive. The best case against germ-line theory may in fact lie in looking at the possible consequences of germ-line therapy on future society. The most obvious area of concern is access to these new technologies. They are likely to be very expensive, and certainly when first available. Is there not a real risk that germ-line therapy will reinforce economic differences within society? If such treatments are only available to the very wealthy, huge disparities in wealth could be added to by disparities in health. While this may already be the case to some extent, it is valid to ask whether we would want to introduce technology which will increase such differences even further. Such concerns are outside the simple risk assessment of whether gene therapy is safe in purely medical terms and questions of whether these technologies will have a detrimental effect on society. As consequencialist arguments, these would of course have to be considered against similar arguments in favor of germ-line gene therapy, with its effect on individual health.

VI. CONCLUSIONS

Gene therapy is one of the areas of greatest ethical interest in genetics, but there is a great deal of speculation about the actual practicality of these technologies. Nevertheless, it seems likely that at least some forms of somatic if not germ-line gene therapies will be developed in the future. In some ways the ethical issues associated with these technologies are nothing new, with comparisons being drawn to other novel medical techniques. In other respects germ-line gene therapy presents us with new problems, because of its long-term, unpredictable impacts on future generations, and its involvement with very basic elements of life. Many of the objections to germ-line gene therapy which are normally made rely on categorical opposition, saying that there is something uniquely wrong about germ-line gene therapy because of the actual direct intervention in the genome. It is not clear how germ-line therapy differs from other medical treatments currently available. Stronger objections to germ-line therapy rely on analysis of the possible consequences on society of such technologies and the wider dangers that exist. What is clear is that the issues raised by gene therapy will continue to be debated as genetic technologies advance.

Also See the Following Articles

ABORTION • EUGENICS • FETAL RESEARCH • GENETIC ENGINEERING • GENOME ANALYSIS • REPRODUCTIVE TECHNOLOGIES • SLIPPERY SLOPE ARGUMENTS

Bibliography

Anderson, W. A. (1990). Genetics and human malleability. *The Hastings Center Report,* **20**(1), 21–24.

Munson, R., & Davis, L. (1992). Germ-line gene therapy and the medical imperative. *Kennedy Institute of Ethics Journal,* **2**(2), 137–158.

Reiss, M., & Straughton, R. (1996). *Improving nature? The science and ethics of genetic engineering.* Cambridge: Cambridge Univ. Press.

Wachter, M. (1993). Ethical aspects of human germ-line gene therapy. *Bioethics,* **7**(2/3), 166–177.

GENETIC COUNSELING

Angus Clarke
University of Wales College of Medicine

GLOSSARY

carrier testing The identification of healthy (unaffected) carriers of a genetic condition. This applies particularly to carriers of autosomal recessive diseases, who have one faulty copy and one intact copy of the relevant gene; to female carriers of sex-linked disorders, to whom the same applies; and to carriers of balanced chromosome rearrangements who are generally unaffected themselves but who may transmit to their children an unbalanced set of chromosomes (with a deficiency of some, and an excess of other, chromosomal material).

chromosome A physical structure that carries genes through the processes of cell division and that is involved in the coordination of gene expression in the cell nucleus. There are 23 pairs of chromosomes in each cell of the human body, with one copy of each chromosome being derived from each parent. Twenty-two of the 23 pairs of chromosomes are the same in males and females—the autosomes. The twenty-third pair consists of the sex chromosomes, X and Y. The X chromosome contains many genes that relate to a wide range of body functions.

directiveness A style of genetic counseling that leads clients to make specific decisions, often in relation to reproduction. Directiveness may be a conscious policy, where the counselor frankly recommends what she thinks is best for the client, or it may be the result of subtle, implicit attitudes held by the counselor.

DNA (deoxyribonucleic acid) A linear molecule composed of a backbone of alternating ribose (a 5-carbon sugar) and phosphate groups with one of four bases attached to each ribose element. The molecule adopts a helical configuration, and the bases— adenine, guanine, cytosine, thymine—project inwards towards the longitudinal axis. Two such linear molecules, oriented in opposite directions, interlock to form a double helix molecule in each chromosome.

gene A coded message that instructs the body as to how to develop and function. Genes generally come in matching pairs, with one of each type coming from each parent in the sperm and the egg. Each cell in the body contains an entire set of genes, which are copied every time a cell divides. There are many thousands of different genes, which are too small to be visible even under a microscope. Genes are organised along the length of the chromosomes, rather like beads on a length of string. If one copy of a gene is faulty—is disrupted by a mutation—this will often cause no problems, as long as the other copy of the same gene is intact; this type of gene defect is termed **recessive**, and an individual will only be affected if they have inherited a faulty copy from both their parents (who may be affected by the condition or who may be unaffected carriers). If a single faulty copy of a gene is sufficient to cause disease, then the faulty gene is said to be **dominant**. An individual will have this type of gene defect either if one of their parents is affected and has transmitted to them their faulty copy of the gene, or if a new mutation occurred in that gene in the production of either the egg or the sperm that went to create them.

multifactorial conditions Also known as polygenic or complex traits, these are characteristics or diseases that are not simply determined by the copies of a single gene present in an individual, but are influenced by multiple genetic factors and often also by other, nongenetic circumstances—by environmental conditions or by chance. A single genetic factor may modify susceptibility to a disease but could not be said to cause it or to determine its development.

predictive genetic testing The identification of healthy individuals as likely or inevitable to develop a specific genetic disease. Such testing may be carried out to identify those likely to benefit from surveillance for the early detection of tumors (in family cancer syndromes), or may be carried out at the request of individuals at high risk of developing an untreatable, late-onset condition (such as Huntington's Disease) in order to clarify their genetic status and thereby enable them to make important life decisions with full information.

screening test A test applied to an entire population or a subpopulation, rather than to individuals or specific families, and which may not be of very great sensitivity or specificity. Screening tests are usually offered pro-actively by health professionals to large groups of people who individually have a small chance of being identified as affected or at risk of problems—e.g. to all newborn infants, to all pregnant women.

susceptibility testing Testing an individual for their inherited susceptibility to a multifactorial disorder. Such testing is not able to predict whether a person will or will not develop a condition, but will merely indicate their relative risk—whether their chance of developing the condition is average, somewhat greater than average or somewhat less. Some of those at high risk will escape the disease, and some of those at low risk will develop it.

GENETIC COUNSELING is a process of communication between clients and professionals. Clients have questions or concerns about a disorder in their family that is, or may be, genetic in origin, and they put these to the professionals, who attempt to clarify the situation as far as possible. The focus of the consultation may be on:

1. Establishing a diagnosis of the condition in the family
2. Finding out more about the condition, i.e., what the future may hold for affected individuals
3. Considering who else in the family may also come to be affected
4. Considering who could have affected children, and how this may be avoided
5. Discussing the treatments available for affected individuals, and whether or not complications can be treated more successfully if they are diagnosed early by a program of surveillance
6. Considering the likely emotional impact on the client and on other family members of the various possible outcomes of any genetic test that the client may take, whether it is a predictive test, a prenatal diagnostic test, or a test of carrier status

The extent to which the concerns of a client will focus on any one of these areas will vary enormously, depending upon the prior experience and knowledge of the family members, the nature of the disorder in question, and numerous other factors. There are certain tasks, however, that will frequently be required of any genetic counselor, and these can be summarized as (i) listening to the client, (ii) establishing or confirming the diagnosis of the condition in the family, (iii) communicating information to the client, (iv) scenario-based decision counseling, and (v) providing ongoing support to the client and family. It may be helpful next to put some of these genetic counseling activities and tasks into context.

I. THE SCOPE OF GENETIC COUNSELING

Listening to the client has to be the first task of genetic counseling, to find out what questions and concerns the client has, and what she already knows. It is otherwise impossible to provide the appropriate information for the client in a comprehensible form that the client can incorporate into her decision making. Furthermore, the doctor who has referred the client may have an expectation of genetic counseling that differs from the client's, and the genetic counselor must not fulfill the doctor's expectations at the expense of the client, as when the referring doctor expects the genetic counselor to instruct a couple to have no more children.

Diagnostic questions will often predominate when a child has multiple unexplained developmental difficulties and/or physical anomalies. Do the child's problems amount to a specific condition—a pattern or "syndrome"—or have they occurred together in the child by chance? It may be possible to identify a genetic cause for such a child's problems, although often it is not. Clinical experience and expertise will be required for this component of genetic counseling. Sensitivity to the needs of the clients is required when, for example, parents have been unable to accept the serious nature of their child's developmental difficulties—they may not be ready to accept certain genetic diagnoses.

Some clients wish to discuss the consequences of the condition that has been diagnosed in their family. What does the future hold for the affected person? How will the illness progress? What implications are there for other family members? Who else may come to be affected in the future, or who may have affected children? Will the client's future children be at risk of developing the same condition? If so, is it possible to perform prenatal diagnosis with the selective termination of affected fetuses? May other members of the family be unaffected carriers of the condition, with a risk of having affected children? For some clients, a simple explanation of the mode of inheritance of the condition may answer most of their concerns, while others may wish to have much more detailed information about the likely course of the illness.

If affected individuals are likely to develop serious complications from their genetic condition, are there useful methods of surveillance that can identify these complications at an early stage and improve the outcome through better treatments? In family cancer syndromes, can tumors be detected early and treated better as a result, or can surgery be offered to reduce the risk of malignancy? Under conditions that predispose one to cardiovascular disease, can a catastrophe be prevented or deferred by control of blood pressure or by a surgical intervention?

The emotional impact of the condition on members of the family will often need to be considered in a genetic counseling consultation. Where reproductive decisions or predictive testing decisions are to be made, however, these may need to be considered with special care and in a systematic way. For example, in the context of someone weighing whether or not to proceed with predictive testing for a disorder with a bleak outlook—e.g., for a neurodegenerative disorder such as Huntington's disease (HD)—it may be helpful for them to be invited to consider the likely impact on themselves and on other members of their family for each possible outcome of the counseling process. How will they and the others respond if (i) they choose not to proceed with testing, and thereby retain uncertainty but also hope? (ii) they proceed with testing and are shown to have the disease-causing HD gene allele? or (iii) they are tested and are shown not to have the disease-causing HD gene allele? Although this last outcome is obviously the preferred one, such favorable results may still cause much distress to the individual and serious difficulties within families. Comparable consideration of the various possible outcomes for the client and for the family may also be helpful when a client is deciding whether or not to embark upon prenatal diagnosis. This type of discussion can be termed scenario decision counseling.

Finally, it may be appropriate to maintain occasional contact with a family over a period of years. If the condition that affects a child has not been identified, it may be helpful to reassess the diagnosis at intervals. If an adult at risk of developing a late-onset condition has decided not to undergo predictive genetic testing, then they may find it helpful occasionally to reassess their family situation—and the reasons that counted for and against testing. It may also be appropriate to maintain contact with those at risk of developing such diseases, so that they have an opportunity to discuss the difficulties of their situation—living under the cloud of a genetic disease—and so that appropriate interventions can be offered if they develop signs of the condition. Those clients at risk of carrying a recessive or sex-linked disorder may also wish to maintain contact so that they can discuss the issues when it feels most relevant, and so that they can be offered the most appropriate carrier or prenatal diagnostic testing available. In families where several generations have carried or been affected by a genetic condition, it may be helpful to maintain contact so that the younger generation can be offered counseling when they judge it to be relevant to themselves.

II. GENETIC TESTING AND GENETIC SCREENING

Genetic testing may be carried out in many different contexts. It is helpful to distinguish these contexts because the ethical issues that arise can be very different. Genetic testing can be offered to individuals because of their specific family histories or other circumstances, or it can be offered to large groups, to populations or subpopulations (e.g., all newborn infants or all pregnant women). The first type of testing is specific to the individual or the family context; the second type of testing is termed population screening.

Genetic testing (of the individual in their family context) and genetic screening (offered to a large population group) can also be categorized as predictive or reproductive. Reproductive testing can take the form of carrier testing, to identify healthy carriers who may have children affected by genetic disease in the future, or prenatal testing carried out during pregnancies to identify those in which the fetus is affected by a genetic condition. Genetic testing of the individual can also be diagnostic; this context arises when the patient has signs or symptoms of disease, and so is not applicable to population screening programs.

A. Predictive (Presymptomatic) Genetic Testing

This type of test is carried out on individuals known to be at risk of a serious genetic disease because other members of their family are affected. There may be definite health benefits from such testing if complications of the disorder can be managed better when they are identified early. In some family cancer syndromes, for example, the early detection of tumors improves the outcome, and so the identification of those at risk of the tumors helps in coordinating surveillance. Furthermore, those at risk of being affected but who are shown not to carry the relevant faulty gene are spared the costly and troublesome surveillance process.

For other diseases, however, testing may give knowledge and hence relieve uncertainty, but without leading to any improvement in the course of the illness. Particularly for these conditions, such as the neurodegenerative diseases where presymptomatic diagnosis does not improve prognosis, it is important to ensure that those who seek testing have thought through the practical and personal consequences. To this end, many centers have adopted protocols for counseling individuals seeking such tests.

B. Diagnostic Genetic Testing

This test is carried out when an individual presents to a doctor with signs or symptoms of a disease that may be genetic in origin, and genetic tests are employed to clarify the cause of the illness. Genetic disease may be diagnosed by more traditional tests, such as muscle biopsy (for Duchenne muscular dystrophy) or renal ultrasound scan (for polycystic kidney disease), but molecular genetic tests are being used increasingly to diagnose (or exclude) symptomatic genetic disease.

When a patient is found to have a genetic condition, there may well be implications for other members of the family. When the condition comes to light inadvertently there is little chance to prepare the patient or the family for this possibility. But if the possibility of a serious genetic disorder is acknowledged early in the diagnostic process, it may be helpful to raise this with the affected individual and/or other members of the family before the tests are carried out.

If the doctor knows that the patient has a family history of a genetic disorder, and if this could account for the patient's problems, then the tests may be focused more rapidly on the relevant inherited condition. This may be more efficient, although there is also a chance that a treatable, nongenetic condition may fail to be diagnosed in someone whose problems are attributed too readily to the familial disorder. In someone at risk of Huntington's disease, for example, a complaint of forgetfulness or lethargy could be caused by another illness (depression, perhaps) and may respond well to appropriate treatment—even in the presence of the HD gene mutation.

C. Newborn Screening

Presymptomatic genetic screening is also carried out in many countries on newborn infants. This is not usually controversial from an ethical perspective because the goal of most such screening programs is to identify infants who will benefit very substantially from early diagnosis and treatment. This is certainly the case with respect to phenylketonuria (PKU) and congenital hypothyroidism, and may also be true for certain other metabolic disorders, sickle cell disease, and cystic fibrosis (CF).

Screening to identify infants affected by Duchenne muscular dystrophy (DMD) is more controversial because there is no effective treatment for DMD and so its early diagnosis provides little benefit to the affected boy. DMD is a lethal, sex-linked disorder affecting 1 in 3500 infant males and is often not diagnosed until 3–6 years of age. The potential benefits of early diagnosis include the avoidance of a prolonged and distressing diagnostic process and providing the opportunity for the extended family to seek genetic counseling and, perhaps, prenatal diagnosis in future pregnancies. There are potential problems too, however, including the difficulty of ensuring adequate informed consent for such testing, the distress caused by the imposition of such unwelcome knowledge some years earlier than would otherwise have been the case, and the possible disruption of family relationships as a result. This is a good example of an ethical issue that cannot be resolved *a priori* but requires a careful evaluation of such a screening program in operation.

The concerns about possible harmful effects of newborn screening for DMD apply *a fortiori* to screening for fragile X syndrome, the commonest familial form of learning difficulties and mental handicap. This affects about 1 in 2000–2500 boys and rather fewer girls. In addition to the problems already suggested is the potential danger that labeling a child as being affected by fragile X will lead to his educational problems being exacerbated by diminished expectations from his earliest days—a self-fulfilling prophecy.

D. Susceptibility Screening and Commercialization

Screening for genetic susceptibility to common disorders is not yet a reality, but it is expected to become available over the next 5–10 years. In the past, most genetic research has focused on the understanding of conditions inherited as simple, Mendelian traits (i.e., single gene disorders). Over the past few years, the genetic dissection of more complex, polygenic diseases has begun. Already, the localization of many loci contributing to juvenile- and maturity-onset diabetes, raised blood cholesterol level, hypertension, Alzheimer's dementia, and several types of cancer has been achieved. The search for these genetic factors and others involved in psychiatric disease, alcohol tolerance and dependence, personality traits, and "intelligence" are being pursued by numerous academic and commercial research groups.

While the primary scientific motivation for this research is to improve our understanding of the disease mechanisms and thereby open up new possibilities for therapy, there will be strong professional and commercial pressures to apply this knowledge so as to identify individuals at high or low risk of these common diseases. This may be justified when it leads to health benefits from useful clinical interventions or lifestyle changes, but there are real possibilities of causing harm by such susceptibility screening in the absence of useful treatments or prevention. Individuals identified as being at high risk of a disease will often feel distress and anxiety. They may also respond fatalistically by indulging in a high-risk lifestyle (e.g., smoking or consuming more cholesterol), while those given a low risk of disease may behave in the same "unhealthy" way if they feel themselves to be invulnerable. Such paradoxical responses that worsen the outlook for individuals in the high- and low-risk groups have been observed after cholesterol screening programs. Other possible difficulties include the consequences of labeling a healthy person as "sick," as when asymptomatic individuals identified as hypertensive adopt the sick role. Regulation of the commercial promotion of such tests and the development of minimum standards for the associated counseling will be necessary, but may not be sufficient to prevent these problems.

One particular concern about susceptibility screening is that it may undermine collective public health measures to improve the welfare of society, such as attending to public policy on housing, food, education, transport, and safety in addition to health. Because each person will be able to tackle the risk factors peculiar to themselves, the political will to tackle these issues collectively may dwindle whereas such a collective approach may be the most efficient way of improving everyone's life and health. Furthermore, collective approaches may be the only means of helping the most vulnerable groups in society.

E. Cascade Carrier Testing

When one member of a family has been identified as a carrier of a genetic disorder, the question arises as to whether any other members of the family may similarly be carriers. Such testing of the relatives of a gene carrier for some genetic disorder is termed cascade testing.

This situation arises in families with autosomal recessive disorders, sex-linked (X chromosome) disorders, and balanced chromosome rearrangements that do not cause disease in the carrier but which may cause serious problems in the carrier's future children. A child will only be affected by an autosomal recessive disease if both parents are carriers, but may be affected by a sex-linked disease (if male) when the mother is a carrier or by an unbalanced chromosome translocation if either parent carries the balanced translocation. The carrier status of one family member may have come to light because an affected child has been diagnosed in the family, or if the genetic testing has been carried out as part of a population screening program, or because the genetic tests were being performed for some other reason (e.g., prenatal diagnostic testing for some other condition).

The term cascade testing may also be applied in the context of autosomal dominant disorders in which serious complications of the disease may develop in a carrier of the faulty gene without any prior indication of the person being "at risk." This applies in some of the familial cancer syndromes, where family members may be at risk of malignant tumors in the colon, breast, thyroid gland, or other organs. Knowledge of a person's risk status allows him to take preventive action or to be screened regularly to detect complications and optimize treatment. Tracking the condition back through the family in a cascading fashion allows other family members to be alerted to their risk of complications.

The attitude of family members to the offer of cascade testing will vary greatly, depending upon their experience of the disorder, the chance of their developing the disease or of having an affected child themselves, and other factors. The healthy sibs of individuals with cystic fibrosis can find the process of carrier testing to be disturbing; the best age at which to offer carrier testing in these circumstances is controversial. Members of an extended family may have lost touch with each other, and it can be both practically difficult and emotionally distressing to reestablish family contact under the cloud of a genetic disease.

To what lengths should families be expected to go to pass on genetic information to their relatives? This will depend in part upon the probability of the relatives being carriers of the disorder in question, and upon the chance of this being significant for them (the risk of a future child being affected, or of a gene carrier developing a complication of the disease), as well as on the feasibility of establishing contact. The nature of the obligation to share some types of genetic information with relatives is discussed further on.

F. Population Carrier Screening

This is genetic testing to identify healthy carriers of autosomal recessive diseases from among the general population or a specific subgroup. This type of testing is offered to individuals with the standard, population risk of carrying the disorder in question rather than to those with a family history of the condition. Thus, testing the general public in Britain would identify about 1 person in 25 as a healthy carrier of a disease-causing allele at the cystic fibrosis gene locus. Testing individuals with a history of CF in their close family would

identify a much higher proportion of carrier individuals than this, and would amount to cascade testing.

One important difference between family-based genetic testing and population-based genetic screening is that population screening is offered proactively by health professionals (or commercial organizations) to individuals who had not previously decided to seek testing. They will often have no personal knowledge of the disease in question, and a positive test result—showing that they are carriers—may never have any implications for their own health or the health of other family members, because few of their partners will be carriers. Many more individuals will be identified as carriers than there are carrier couples, so for most identified carriers the process of counseling and testing may complicate their family lives and reproductive decisions without it yielding any "benefit." The screening may introduce anxiety into the lives of many without delivering clear health benefits. There is evidence that some carriers of recessive disorders identified in population screening programs can have misunderstandings about their carrier status with inappropriate concern about their own future health and confusion about the implications of their test result. What benefits to some carriers would justify these concerns among others? How should society decide its collective response to such questions?

It is known from pilot studies of CF population carrier screening in Britain, Europe, and North America that the way in which the offer of screening is made has a great influence on the proportion of people who accept the offer. As many as 70–95+% of individuals will agree to testing if it is offered in person to those attending a health center or antenatal clinic and if it is available on the spot without inconvenience; if the offer is made by mail, or if a specific visit to the clinic must be arranged, then the rate of uptake of the test is much reduced (10–15%). This suggests that the high uptake rate that prevails in some circumstances reflects the compliance of an apathetic public in the face of professional enthusiasm. If health professionals, society, or commercial interests decide it would be advantageous for population screening to be introduced on a wide scale, it seems that it would be possible to adjust the numbers of those "choosing" to be tested to suit the interests of those offering the test. Given this, to what extent can people's decisions to accept the offer of such screening be considered to reflect their "true" wishes and their "adequately informed" consent?

Another important fact relating to population screening is that the frequency of carriers for many recessive disorders varies between populations (ethnic groups).

It may therefore seem appropriate for carrier screening programs in multiethnic societies to be targeted toward those of particular ethnic backgrounds. This can cause problems, however, if one racial group (more prone to a specific disease) is subject to discrimination and stigmatization at the hands of a different, socially dominant group. Identification as a carrier of sickle cell disease, for example, added to the burden of racial discrimination already being experienced by black people in the USA during the 1970s when legislation to promote carrier screening among black people was abused in relation to employment and insurance.

G. Prenatal Diagnostic Testing

This test is offered to women or couples whose pregnancies are known to be at increased risk of a genetic disorder or congenital anomaly, because of specific grounds for concern about the health of their fetus. This will be based either on a family history of a genetic condition or on some prior evidence from the pregnancy suggesting the possibility of a problem. Such evidence might include an ultrasound scan suggestive of a chromosomal anomaly or an increased probability of Down's syndrome calculated from maternal age and serum screening. Where there is a family history of the disorder in question, the couple is likely to have some experience or knowledge of the relevant condition. The genetic counselor will still need to explore the couple's level of knowledge and understanding, but this is likely to be much higher than for women entering routine population screening programs.

Diagnostic testing usually provides a definitive result, confirming that the fetus either does or does not have a specific disorder. Molecular genetic (DNA) and cytogenetic (chromosome) testing usually achieve this, although a small proportion of results may be of uncertain significance. If a few cells with a cytogenetic anomaly are identified from amniocentesis or chorionic villus sampling (CVS) while most cells are normal (chromosomal mosaicism), then this may be relevant to the fetus, may represent an anomaly confined to the placenta or fetal membranes, or may have arisen as an artifact in the cells cultured in the genetics laboratory. A further invasive (and therefore hazardous) diagnostic procedure may then be needed if the significance of the finding is to be established.

Another type of difficult result is the finding of an unanticipated anomaly—an incidental finding rather than the condition that was being sought. This often results in difficult counseling scenarios, as regularly happens when a case of sex chromosome aneuploidy

is diagnosed. In these conditions, when there is only one sex chromosome (Turner syndrome with one X chromosome) or when there are additional sex chromosomes, the outlook for the future child may be much less serious than with many other chromosomal disorders. For example, a child with Turner syndrome is likely to be of short stature and to have delayed puberty, but these problems can be treated. A minority of affected girls will require cardiac surgery but the outlook for them is usually very good. The affected girl will be infertile, but not mentally or physically handicapped. Despite the relatively less serious of these problems, many fetuses with Turner syndrome are terminated. Factors influencing the decision include the specialty of the doctor who discusses the chromosome results with the woman—there are fewer pregnancies terminated if the woman discusses the results with a clinical geneticist rather than with an obstetrician. Being told that the chromosome result is abnormal can lead some women/couples to make a rushed decision to terminate their pregnancy even though the condition diagnosed is not the condition for which prenatal diagnosis may have been performed. Such women can regret their decision when they subsequently learn more about the condition. Being given more information about the chromosome anomaly at the time of the initial giving of the results can help some couples to pause and reflect instead of proceeding immediately to a termination.

Some of these problems can be avoided if the possibility of unusual results, of either uncertain significance or indicating relatively minor anomalies, is explained to the woman/couple in advance of the test being performed. This may make it easier for the woman to defer a decision about termination in the event of such a result until she has sought further information or advice. These considerations serve to emphasize the importance of women being offered full information and the opportunity to consider the implications of testing before they make any decisions about prenatal screening or diagnostic testing. For consent to prenatal testing to be meaningful, it must include an adequate delay between the offer of testing and the test itself to permit the woman to reflect, to discuss the issues with friends and family, and to request further information.

H. Antenatal Screening for Genetic Disorders and Malformation

This is offered to most pregnant women in developed countries, and also to many women in developing countries. There are five types of genetic screening tests to mention in this context.

1. Amniocentesis entails taking a sample of the fluid from around the fetus. This is usually performed at about 16 weeks of gestation and permits the chromosomal analysis of cultured cells from the fluid. This may be carried out in the context of a couple's high risk of genetic disease or as part of a screening program aiming to identify (and terminate) Down's syndrome fetuses. Amniocentesis can result in an increased risk of miscarriage in the pregnancy (the increase in risk being 1 in 100 to 1 in 150).

2. CVS is a similar invasive test with a slightly higher associated risk of miscarriage (about 1 in 50). It entails removing a sample from the developing placenta, and can be performed from about 10 weeks of gestation.

3. Maternal serum screening is carried out on a blood test from the pregnant woman; the level of particular materials in the serum (notably alpha-fetoprotein and beta-HCG) gives some indication of the probability that the fetus has Down's syndrome; this is interpreted along with the age-dependent risk of Down's syndrome to give a combined probability. Women whose pregnancies have a chance of having Down's syndrome of greater than 1 in 200 to 1 in 250 are often then offered amniocentesis as a diagnostic test.

4. Fetal ulstrasound scanning may be offered at several stages in pregnancy, but fetal anomaly scans are frequently performed at 18 weeks of gestation. These scans are very effective at identifying structural anomalies such as spina bifida, and scans earlier in pregnancy will also identify many pregnancies with chromosomal anomalies.

5. There are newer techniques of prenatal screening being devised, such as the sorting of fetal cells from a maternal blood sample. The sorted fetal cells can be subjected to genetic tests without putting the pregnancy at risk. The development of such techniques will clearly be a great benefit to high-risk families who want prenatal diagnosis for serious genetic disorders. They may result in less positive consequences for some women, however, such as those who would prefer not to have prenatal diagnosis at all but who decline the offer of the current, invasive tests on the grounds of the associated risks of miscarriage. Such women may find it harder to decline testing in the future.

Because ultrasound scans may also be used for other purposes in the management of a pregnancy, fetal anomaly scans are often performed without the woman fully appreciating the purpose of the scan. Worse, scans may be regarded as a means of promoting maternal "bonding" with the fetus. The irony of this becomes apparent when such "bonding" is rudely shattered if a congenital anomaly is identified and staff suggest that the mother should consider a termination of the pregnancy.

The major ethical issues arising in the context of prenatal screening concern the social nature of the screening program as opposed to the individual focus of prenatal diagnosis arising within known high-risk families. First, because such screening programs are offered to the whole population of pregnant women, inadequate attention may be paid to the nature of the consent obtained before women participate in the screening. The offer of screening may become routine and staff may exert pressure on women to comply with the policy of the clinic instead of encouraging women to consider the issues and weigh the potential advantages and disadvantages of screening for themselves as individuals. There is ample empirical evidence that such unsatisfactory practices are widespread.

Secondly, there is the question of equity of access to screening tests. Access to, and uptake of, most health services is greater in the professional and middle classes than in the working class and in some ethnic minority groups. Is this also true for prenatal screening programs? If so—as often is the case—this could lead to a higher incidence of genetic disorders being found in working class communities, those sections of society with the least independent resources to cope with such problems. The higher mean maternal age in the higher social classes may in part counter this effect because Down's syndrome births will accordingly be more frequent, but in so far as prenatal screening is a benefit it should be equally accessible to women from all social groups.

Third, there is the question of how society comes to decide which possible screening test should be offered. There have been two routes to the introduction of new prenatal screening tests. Fetal ultrasound scanning, although unevaluated, was introduced piecemeal by enthusiastic professionals. The technology—the scan machines—are readily available because they are used for many other purposes apart from fetal anomaly scans, and these scans are popular with many clients and professionals, so that it would now be difficult to provide antenatal care without offering them.

Maternal serum screening to identify pregnancies with an increased risk of Down's syndrome has been more controversial, but has become effectively entrenched in much of Britain through the concerted efforts of professional and commercial interests to persuade pregnant women (service users), obstetricians (service providers), and health authorities (the purchasers of health services) of its worth. Similar efforts by interested parties in Europe and North America have led to similar situations. Indeed, in California it is mandatory for physicians providing antenatal care to offer serum screening to every pregnant woman. Such serum screening programs are backed up by amniocentesis as a diagnostic test, with the specific goal of reducing the birth incidence of Down's syndrome. These efforts have largely succeeded, despite objections that the problems caused by these screening programs have largely been ignored. The principal argument put forward to justify such screening for Down's syndrome is that screening costs the health services less than providing care for live-born affected children. This justification would be acceptable in a business venture, but is not the standard justification for items of health care.

This discussion leads on naturally to the central ethical question arising in prenatal diagnosis of genetic conditions: how "severe" does a disorder have to be for it to justify the termination of an otherwise wanted pregnancy? It is possible for a society to legislate to draw up a list of conditions that are acknowledged as being sufficiently severe to permit prenatal diagnosis and possibly a termination of pregnancy. It is also possible for society to permit whatever a woman and her physicians agree together as appropriate (as effectively is the case in Britain). Practice in USA differs between the private sector and the public sector supported by federal funds: there are constraints in the public sector that prevent the termination of pregnancy even being discussed in many publicly funded clinics.

From the perspective of a clinical geneticist, it is possible to respond differently in the two distinct contexts of prenatal diagnostic testing and of population screening. In the case of a family with intimate knowledge of a genetic condition, who have sought out genetic counseling because they fear a recurrence of the disease, it would be difficult for a professional, or for society, to refuse the request for prenatal diagnosis when the family has agonized over this very issue, perhaps for years. Complying with the family's wishes will probably lead to fewer "casualties" than any other policy, as long as the counselor ensures that the family has a good understanding of their genetic situation and of the testing process. But screening programs are very different, because they touch the lives of so many individuals—not just those few at very high risk of problems. Accordingly, even a low incidence of iatrogenic complications resulting from the screening program may dwarf the potential benefits. And when one considers that there is real disagreement within society over whether or not Down's syndrome or spina bifida—the two principal conditions identified by antenatal screening—are suf-

ficiently serious to justify the termination of pregnancy, it can be appreciated that a permissive approach to prenatal diagnosis can reasonably coexist with a skeptical approach to prenatal screening programs.

III. THE GOALS OF GENETIC COUNSELING

There are many possible goals of genetic counseling, which can be approached from the perspective of the individual client or of the population served by a genetic counseling service. In examining the effectiveness of a service both perspectives may need to be evaluated, but it is important to decide which is dominant. If the principal goal is the avoidance of suffering, should this be assessed by in-depth interviews with individuals and families, or by counting the births of affected children? The aim of defining the goals of genetic counseling is to enable the effectiveness and quality of genetics services to be examined, and this will have important implications for the nature of the services provided.

Measures of individual client outcomes may assess information retained by the client (e.g., the mode of inheritance, likely medical complications, or the risk of future children being affected by the condition under consideration), the influence on reproductive plans, the influence on reproductive behavior, or client satisfaction with the service provided. None of these measures is very suitable, however, because they prejudge the reasons for seeking genetic counseling and how information gained in such counseling should be used. Thus, information about reproductive risks may well be sought by the client, but may not be remembered in the form in which it was given to them but in a simpler, binary form of the risk being either acceptable or unacceptable. Again, some clients are seeking a diagnostic label for the condition in their family, or an explanation for the problems faced by their child, and have no plans for further children—the focus on reproductive plans or behavior would be inappropriate for them.

A focus on client satisfaction may at first seem more attractive, but it too is problematic because many clients will be given unwelcome information in genetic counseling, and their dissatisfaction with the information may lead them inappropriately to express dissatisfaction with the service. Also, they may have unrealistic expectations of the service; diagnostic certainty may simply be unattainable in their family circumstances. Another approach to the assessment of genetics services is to develop a measure of satisfaction that will not be so distorted by this problem of "blaming the messenger"; this could take the form of a retrospective assessment of satisfaction with the service provided, once the client has sufficient experience to know what expectations of the service would have been reasonable.

Measures of population outcomes for genetic counseling and screening have also been proposed. In effect, are the births of children affected by serious genetic disorders decreased when genetic counseling services are provided? This approach to measuring the impact of genetics services ignores the impact of the service on individual clients and is really seeking to justify expenditure on genetic services on the grounds that they save money—there are fewer individuals born who will be a burden on the taxpayer through provision for their health, social, and educational needs.

There are two principal grounds for rejecting this approach. First, because it is profoundly disrespectful to so many people with genetic conditions, suggesting that their lives are not worthwhile and that they are merely a burden to their fellow members of society. Many individuals with genetic disease and congenital malformations do support the availability of prenatal diagnosis for "their" conditions, but the widespread promotion of screening to prevent the birth of people like themselves can still have very negative effects on their feelings of self-worth—and there are many individuals with Down's syndrome or spina bifida, for example, who are advocates for the rights and worth of people with these conditions. Second, if society decides to provide genetic counseling services simply on the grounds that it saves money in the long run, then any process of audit of the service that seeks to maximize the "benefits" to society—the savings—will lead to pressure on service providers to pay less attention to individuals who are seeking only explanations, and to present the reproductive options to those considering further children in such a way that they minimize the chance of an affected child being born. In such circumstances, genetics services may be led toward a frankly eugenic role in which they would be held accountable for an "excessive" number of births of affected children in their areas. This may appear to be alarmist fantasy, but it is already happening in China; market forces could lead to a similar result in other countries if the state or private health insurance corporations refused to make adequate provision for children with "potentially avoidable" conditions. It could even be argued that the provision of care for individuals with genetic disease and disability is currently inadequate even in many developed countries.

An attempt has been made by B. Modell and A. M. Kuliev to bridge the gap between measures of individual and population outcomes in genetic counseling through a focus on "informed reproductive decisions." This approach is attractive in many ways, but depends upon the notion of "informed reproductive decision" being both easily measured and intellectually coherent. Unfortunately, many informed reproductive decisions would escape measurement in practice (e.g., decisions to have no further children), and many such decisions would have little relevance to medical care but really reflect social pressures. For example, there are many "informed reproductive decisions" facilitated by medical technology around the world each year which lead to the termination of female fetuses on social, not medical, grounds. To define "informed reproductive decisions" as the goal of genetic counseling is to evade the value-laden question as to which of the possible reproductive decisions that could be made are the desirable ones.

In summary, the goals of genetic counseling can be viewed from individual or population perspectives. The goals of genetic screening programs must almost inevitably be viewed from the population perspective, and these can be considered under three categories. Screening programs may be justified by appeal to (i) the avoidance of human suffering, which is not controversial unless it also leads to the avoidance of particular types of people (those with Down's syndrome, for example, or women); (ii) the promotion of informed reproductive choices; or (iii) the most effective use of limited resources. As already discussed, the goal of a screening program is important because it has implications for the ethos of service delivery, and hence for the personal experiences of those individuals offered screening.

IV. AUTONOMY, INFORMED CONSENT, AND "NONDIRECTIVENESS"

The eagerness of clinical geneticists to escape from the aura of negative emotions surrounding their past involvement in the eugenic movements in Germany, the USA, Britain, and other countries has led us to reject any suggestion that we might encourage, persuade, or lead our clients to make specific reproductive decisions. As a professional group, genetic counselors have accordingly espoused "nondirectiveness." It is our task to present clients with the information they seek, and we thereby assist them in the process of making their personal reproductive decisions, but it would be unacceptable for us to impose a decision on our clients, however subtly. Indeed, any suggestion that we might be even unintentionally directive, as a profession, can provoke fierce objections.

The eugenic past doubtless accounts for the vehemence of the feelings in support of "nondirectiveness," but there are other grounds for the adoption of this slogan. First, there is the current enhanced respect for autonomy as one of the cardinal principles of health care ethics, with less support for paternalism. Second, there is the usefulness for counselors of some detachment from the decisions made by their clients. This affords relief from the emotional burden of clients' decisions—whether in predictive testing or decisions relating to prenatal diagnosis and the termination of pregnancies. And it also simplifies the legal aspects of genetic counseling practice. As long as "the relevant facts" have been presented, then it is the clients who carry the emotional and the legal burdens.

What are the relevant facts here? How "informed" is "informed consent"? The level of technical facts provided is only one aspect of this question, and can usually be resolved in a discussion between the client and an adequately informed counselor. It would not be possible for a genetic counselor to describe in detail every possible outcome of a prenatal diagnostic test, but it is feasible for them to outline the range of possible outcomes and the range of possible consequences. Thus, it is possible to explain that results may not be simply "normal" or "affected," but fall into a "gray area"—unclear or unanticipated. The possible consequences of the decisions being made by the client can be explored in a technical sense and also in terms of their personal meaning for the client and the emotional impact of the test results on her and on her relationships with her family and friends. At entry to maternal serum screening for Down's syndrome, therefore, the possibility of the test leading toward a termination of the pregnancy should be mentioned, and the client's likely reactions to this prospect can be considered. To gloss over these aspects of an important decision could result in the client making a decision that was inadequately informed.

The claim that genetic counseling should be nondirective is comprehensible; the claim that it is so in practice, however, is somewhat ingenuous. While the genetic counseling of individuals and families may often contain no "directiveness"—it may not be related to decision making at all—there is a clear message conveyed to society at large from the existence of genetic counseling clinics and—a fortiori—from the existence and operation of antenatal genetic screening programs. The existence of genetic counseling clinics conveys the message that health professionals, and perhaps society at large, consider it reasonable—even desirable—for individuals to make rational reproductive decisions in the light of information concerning the possible outcomes of future pregnancies. Society, in a sense, has set up genetic counseling to combat genetic fatalism as well as the fear of genetic risks. Most genetic counselors would defend this stance, and would willingly argue against fatalism with respect to genetic disorders. But genetic counseling is not neutral in relation to this issue.

This argument applies more powerfully in relation to genetic screening programs, because the very existence of a screening program amounts in effect to a recommendation that the testing thereby made available is a good thing. Health professionals and society would hardly establish and promote antenatal screening for Down's syndrome unless they wanted people to make use of it—the existence of such a program is an implicit, but powerful, recommendation to accept any screening offer made. Screening programs, therefore, simply cannot be nondirective. Health professionals may respect the decisions of those who decline the offer of screening, not coercing them into compliance, but those who decide against participation will carry a label of social deviance unless great efforts have been made to avoid this. In practice, at least some of the personnel offering such tests are likely to regard those who decline screening as irritating, if not irresponsible, and to make this clear to their "clients."

Another issue is whether or not clients want genetic counseling to be nondirective. There are some clients who would actively prefer their genetic counselor to provide guidance as to what course of action to follow. Given that many genetic decisions are difficult and involve choosing between two or more options, all of which entail unhappy long-term consequences, this is thoroughly understandable. It is the client, however, who will have to live with the emotional consequences of their decision in the long term—perhaps with childlessness, with regret at having had a termination of pregnancy, or with an affected and suffering child—and most genetic counselors are unwilling to accept the burden of explicitly sharing such responsibilities, quite aside from medicolegal considerations.

Finally, there are circumstances in which genetic counselors are expected at least to attempt to persuade their clients to take one course of action rather than another—to share information about the genetic condition in their family with other family members. This is discussed further on.

V. CONFIDENTIALITY AND GENETIC PRIVACY—WITHIN THE FAMILY

Genetic information is intensely personal, relating as it does to a person's very biological existence as an individual. It would therefore seem reasonable to treat it with the greatest respect as private and confidential, not to be divulged to others without consent except in the most exceptional of circumstances. On the other hand, genetic information is usually—by its very nature—a family concern. We share our genes with other members of our biological family. Should we not then share information about our genes with them, at least when it might be of any relevance to decisions they might make about their health care, their reproductive plans, or other life decisions?

Even when family members have lost affection for each other or have strayed apart geographically, they are usually willing to share personal information with other family members when it could be helpful to them. If an individual is at first reluctant to contact other family members, the thought that they could be held morally responsible for future problems in the family is usually enough for them to change their minds. Few would wish to be blamed for another member of their family suffering from an avoidable cancer or preventable heart disease, for example, or for the birth of a child affected by a severe genetic disease or set of malformations.

Occasionally, however, an individual will refuse to make contact with family members about a condition that could well be relevant to their welfare. What should health professionals do in such circumstances? One response in certain British reports has been the suggestion that the professionals should breach confidentiality and pass on the information to other family members without the consent of the first individual. While it is difficult to rule out this course for all circumstances, there are good grounds for caution about even drawing up proposals to define the circumstances in which confidentiality can be breached in this way.

First, the Hippocratic origin of medical confidentiality has served the public and the profession well, and any grounds for breaching it must be very strong; any harm to be prevented in this way would have to be a very serious harm and not just a vague possibility or something that is likely to happen regardless.

Second, the mere existence of guidelines for breaching confidentiality will have an effect on the trust placed in genetic counselors by clients. Many clients may decide not to seek a referral to the genetics service at all, or might give misleading information about their family history that would make the interpretation of their genetic situation much more difficult. This could interfere in many consultations because many clients initially have doubts about the motivation and integrity of the genetics staff and gain confidence in genetic counseling services over time. Damage could result from this interference in many more families than the very few where respecting confidentiality appears to be a problem now.

Third, families in which information is shared without persuasion or coercion being applied may be strengthened by the process; the opportunity for this will diminish if it is known that the relevant family member had no choice about disclosure of the information.

Fourth, the existence of guidelines for breaching confidentiality will lead to an expectation that genetic counselors should trace the members of their clients' families with whom the clients have lost contact. This could evolve all too easily into an unrealistic legal obligation on the counselor to trace families, with genetic services becoming liable for damages if they do not go to great lengths to do so.

VI. CONFIDENTIALITY AND GENETIC PRIVACY—THIRD PARTIES

In what other contexts does the issue of genetic privacy arise? Apart from family members, the principal other parties who might wish to acquire genetic information about an individual are employers, insurance companies, and the state. Employers may wish to select employees who are likely to remain healthy and to have suitable personalities for their work; some employers may also wish to select employees who would be less likely to develop specific occupation-related illnesses. Insurance companies will want to have access to any information about their clients' chances of developing ill health that is available to their clients—otherwise those at high risk of ill health will take out larger policies. The state may wish to gather genetic information on its population for a variety of purposes—such as for planning health services, for restricting immigration to blood relatives, and for forensic purposes.

What is it reasonable to permit these third parties to do?

It could be argued that employers should be free to assess the current health of an employee or a prospective employee by conventional clinical examination, but that tests of genetic susceptibility to future illness should not be imposed as a condition of employment except when public safety depends upon the good health of the employee. Such testing would have implications of much wider scope than just employment, and may relate to other family members, and so should not be imposed by employers. For such testing by employers to be both fair and rational, there would have to be some intervention that could be offered to improve the outlook for an employee identified as being at increased risk of a health problem; knowledge of risk alone would not justify the imposition of testing. If testing could identify those at increased risk of an occupational health hazard—such as exposure to dust or chemicals—then it could be worthwhile as long as it did not substitute for attempts to minimize exposure to the hazard for all employees, and as long as an employee at high risk was offered equivalent work elsewhere, without the hazard. Such testing to identify susceptible employees should not replace safety measures for all; even those at below average risk will still be at risk from exposure to the hazards.

If insurance companies could use genetic information to predict the future illnesses and the likely ages and causes of death of most individuals, then the whole rationale of health and life insurance would be destroyed. Instead, each individual would need to work hard to pay in advance for their likely future health care needs. Only accidents would be insurable. Because the future is unknown, it makes sense now for many individuals to contribute to a common fund to meet the costs of the few individuals or families who have to cope with unforeseen premature death or disease. In so far as our knowledge of the future becomes more certain, the system of social solidarity represented by the insurance industry will be undermined. Our present collective approach to confronting disease and death will be fragmented and individualized. Arguably, we will all be poorer as a result.

At present, such accurate foreknowledge is not available, and in principle it is unattainable because the complexity of our body systems, and the effects of environmental factors and chance, will conspire to prevent it. But it is possible to identify those at high risk for the uncommon single-gene disorders, and it will become possible to assess individual risks of the common diseases such as breast and colon cancer, heart disease, diabetes, hypertension, stroke, and Alzheimer's dementia. How should insurance companies use such data? While a strategy for society's collective response to the future availability of susceptibility testing for the common diseases is being considered, it has been suggested that we must adopt a policy for dealing with the genetic testing issues that are already being confronted in practice—problems with the single-gene disorders. It is necessary for insurance companies to be protected from adverse selection, while not denying the social benefits of insurance to those individuals destined to develop the serious Mendelian disorders. This is particularly true in Britain, where housing is often obtained through a life insurance policy. Here, one interim proposal put forward by Harper has been that insurance companies should not demand that genetic tests be performed at all, and that they should not even have the right to request the results of such tests as have been performed unless the life insurance policy being sought is for an unusually large sum. A similar policy has been implemented in Holland.

A discussion of the rights of the state to gather genetic information on its subjects falls outside the scope of this entry. Suffice it to say that many geneticists are skeptical about the wisdom of entrusting such information to the state when it is understood how easily such data could be obtained illicitly for commercial applications, or how they could even be abused by the state itself.

VII. GENETIC TESTING OF CHILDREN

It is as easy to carry out genetic testing on children as on adults. Sometimes this will be perfectly appropriate, as when a child has presented with symptoms or signs of a disorder that could be genetic in origin. Equally, if a child is at risk of complications from a disease that runs in his family, and if early (presymptomatic) diagnosis may be to his advantage—improving the surveillance for complications if he does have the faulty gene and avoiding the need for it if he does not—then genetic testing will be seen by everyone as helpful. There are circumstances, however, where the issues are more complex. These arise when parents or others request genetic testing for a child as either (i) a predictive test for a late-onset (usually adult-onset) disorder where there is no question of useful medical interventions in childhood, or (ii) a test of the child's genetic carrier status, of possible relevance to the child's future reproductive plans but not to his health in childhood. We are concerned here with the imposition of testing on those children who are not sufficiently mature to request testing in their own right. Although maturity is more difficult to define than chronological age, it is this that is important in ethics and in law.

Predictive tests for late-onset genetic disorders have several potential disadvantages. Identifying a child as destined to develop a serious, late-onset disorder such as Huntington's disease or familial breast and ovarian cancer could affect the child's upbringing and her emotional development. Expectations of the child's future relationships or educational attainments may be altered in such a way as to damage the child's progress, and these altered expectations could act as self-fulfilling prophecies; the child's adult life would then be blighted even more thoroughly than living at risk of the disease would achieve. In addition, the future right of the child to decide for herself about testing—the right to autonomy—and the right of the future adult to confidentiality of the test result have both been abrogated. This is a particular concern when we know that many adults at risk of such disorders choose not to be tested, and that some tested individuals choose not to inform other members of their families about the test results or even the fact of testing.

Against these considerations, the case can be made that children may adjust better to unwelcome genetic information if they find out about it at an early age, and that there is no firm evidence of any harm being done by such testing. On the other hand, while children may adjust well to the knowledge of genetic risk, it may be that individuals cope with unwelcome genetic information more readily if they are actively involved in seeking testing; genetic testing could then be likened to the search by an adopted child for his or her biological parents. Given that young children at risk of Huntington's disease and other such disorders have not been tested, it will of course be difficult to obtain evidence about the long-term consequences of such testing without performing the tests, having decided that the ethical concerns—the abrogation of the child's future rights to autonomy and confidentiality—can be ignored, and then waiting for 20–30 years until the consequences can be assessed.

The arguments in relation to carrier testing in childhood are similar, but the stakes are not so high. The child's future autonomy and right to confidentiality are both lost, but his or her own future health and existence are not affected. What may be affected is the child's emotional development if the parents seek to raise the child in such a way as to influence the child's future pattern of relationships and reproduction. Quite apart from the possibility of such attempts in practice being counterproductive, they may also be emotionally harmful. There is a better chance of obtaining evidence on this point than with predictive testing, because carrier testing for cystic fibrosis has been carried out routinely in many centers since the isolation of the CF gene in 1989 and children in families with balanced chromosomal translocations have been tested since the early 1970s.

Another context in which the possibility of inappropriate genetic testing could arise is in relation to susceptibility screening. There is some evidence that children can be harmed by dietary restriction after cholesterol screening, and similar problems could arise after molecular genetic testing for susceptibility to many common diseases. There may be contexts in which testing for predispositions could be helpful, but inappropriate testing could be a problem if commercial promotion of such tests was targeted toward the testing of children.

VIII. CONCLUSION

Genetic counseling brings together traditional medicine with the "new genetics," and applies them both to the difficult circumstances of those individuals and families who are confronted by the reality of genetic disease. It is therefore not surprising that the ethical issues that arise in this context are so complex. There are other ethical issues generated by the new genetics that have not been considered here, such as the implications of the Human Genome Diversity Project for the members of oppressed ethnic minority groups, and the genetic dissection of individual variation for nondisease traits such as personality attributes and intelligence. These were outside the scope of this entry, but if (when) the future application of such new knowledge to the genetic testing of adults, children, fetuses, and embryos becomes possible, it may be that we will have to confront even more, and more difficult, ethical problems.

Also See the Following Articles

EUGENICS • FETUS • GENETIC ENGINEERING • GENETIC SCREENING • REPRODUCTIVE TECHNOLOGIES

Bibliography

Abramsky, L., and Chapple, J. (Eds.) (1994). "Prenatal Diagnosis: The Human Side." Chapman & Hall, London.

Andrews, L. B., Fullarton, J. E., Holtzman, N. A., and Motulsky, A. G. (Eds.) (1994). "Assessing Genetic Risks: Implications for Health Policy." National Academy Press, Washington, DC.

Annas, G. J., and Elias, S. (1992). "Gene Mapping: Using Law and Ethics as Guides." Oxford Univ. Press, New York/Oxford.

Bekker, H., Modell, M., Denniss, G., Silver, A., Mathew, C., Bobrow, M., and Marteau, T. (1993). Uptake of cystic fibrosis testing in primary care: Supply push or demand pull? Br. Med. J. 306, 1584–1586.

Billings, P. R., Kohn, M. A., Cuevas, M. de, Beckwith, J., Alper, J. S., and Natowicz, M. R. (1992). Discrimination as a consequence of genetic testing. *Am. J. Hum. Genet.* **50,** 476–482.

Bosk, C. L. (1992). "All God's Mistakes: Genetic Counseling in a Pediatric Hospital." Univ. of Chicago Press, Chicago.

Chadwick, R., and Levitt, M. (1996). EUROSCREEN: Ethical and philosophical issues of genetic screening in Europe. *J. Roy. Coll. Phys. London* **30,** 67–69.

Clarke, A. (1995). Population screening for genetic susceptibility to disease. *Br. Med. J.* **311,** 35–38.

Clarke, A. (Ed.) (1994). "Genetic Counseling: Practice and Principles." Routledge, London/New York.

Clarke, A. (1990). Genetics, ethics and audit. *Lancet* **335,** 1145–1147.

Clarke, A. (1991). Is non-directive genetic counseling possible? *Lancet* **338,** 998–1001.

Clarke, A., Parsons, E. P., and Williams, A. (1996). Outcomes and process in genetic counseling. *Clin. Genet.* **50,** 462–469.

Clinical Genetics Society Working Party (1994). The genetic testing of children. *J. Med. Genet.* **31,** 785–797.

Davison, C., Macintyre, S., and Smith, G. D. (1994). The potential social impact of predictive genetic testing for susceptibility to common chronic diseases: A review and proposed research agenda. *Sociol. Health Illness* **16,** 340–371.

Duster, T. (1990). "Backdoor to Eugenics." Routledge, Chapman & Hall, London/New York.

Green, J. M., and Richards, M. P. M. (guest Eds.) (1993). Psychological aspects of fetal screening and the new genetics. *J. Reprod. Infant Psychol.* **11**(1), 1–59 (special issue).

Harper, P. S. (1993). Genetic testing and insurance. *Lancet* **341,** 224–227.

Harper, P. S. (1993). "Practical Genetic Counseling," 4th ed. Butterworth–Heinemann, Oxford.

Kessler, S. (1989). Psychological aspects of genetic counseling. VI. A critical review of the literature dealing with education and reproduction. *Am. J. Med. Genet.* **34,** 340–353.

Koch, L., and Stemerding, D. (1994). The sociology of entrenchment: A cystic fibrosis test for everyone? *Soc. Sci. Med.* **39,** 1211–1220.

Macintyre, S. (1995). The public understanding of science or the scientific understanding of the public? A review of the social context of the "new genetics." *Public Understanding Sci.* **4,** 223–232.

Marteau, T., and Richards, M. (Eds.) (1996). "The Troubled Helix: Social and Psychological Implications of the New Genetics." Cambridge Univ. Press, Cambridge.

Michie, S., and Marteau, T. M. (1996). Predictive genetic testing in children: The need for psychological research. *Br. J. Health Psychol.* **1,** 3–14.

Modell, B., and Kuliev, A. M. (1993). A scientific basis for cost–benefit analysis of genetics services. *Trends Genet.* **9,** 46–52.

Nuffield Council on Bioethics (1993). "Genetic Screening—Ethical Issues." Nuffield Council on Bioethics, London.

Pelias, M. Z. (1992). The duty to disclose to relatives in medical genetics: Response to Dr Hecht. *Am. J. Med. Genet.* **42,** 759–760.

Pokorski, R. J. (1995). Genetic information and life insurance. *Nature* **376L,** 13–14.

Richards, M. P. M. (1993). The new genetics: Some issues for social scientists. *Sociol. Health Illness* **15,** 567–587.

Rothman, B. K. (1988). "The Tentative Pregnancy." Pandora, London.

Royal College of Physicians Committees on Ethical Issues in Medicine and Clinical Genetics (1991). "Ethical Issues in Clinical Genetics." Royal College of Physicians of London, London.

Wertz, D. C. (1992). Ethical and legal implications of the new genetics: Issues for discussion. *Soc. Sci. Med.* **35,** 495–505.

World Federation of Neurology (1989). Research Committee Research Group: Ethical issues policy statement on Huntington's disease molecular genetics predictive test. *J. Neurol. Sci.* **94,** 327–332; (1990). *J. Med. Genet.* **27,** 34–38.

GENETIC ENGINEERING

Matti Häyry and Heta Häyry
University of Helsinki

GLOSSARY

biotechnology The application of biological advances such as genetic engineering to industry.
DNA Deoxyribonucleic acid. Any of the nucleic acids that are localized especially in the cell nuclei and that form the molecular basis of heredity in organisms.
gene The unit of hereditary information, which is in most organisms composed of DNA.
genetic engineering The directed alteration of genetic material, particularly by recombinant DNA techniques.
genome The totality of the chromosomes of a species, including all genes and their connecting structure.
recombinant DNA DNA that is produced technologically by breaking up and splicing together DNA from different species of organisms.

GENETIC ENGINEERING is the science of altering genetic material by intervention in genetic processes to produce new traits in organisms. Humankind has manipulated the qualities of living beings for thousands of years through, for instance, breeding, domestication, and training, but since the 1970s, biologists have been able to bring about considerably more radical and rapid changes by employing recombinant DNA techniques—that is, by isolating and combining the genetic materials of different organisms, frequently across the boundaries of natural biological species.

The practical uses of genetic engineering are expected to be abundant. The manipulation of plants, animals, and bacteria can generate improved crops, inexpensive food products, and more efficient pharmaceuticals, while the genetic alteration of the human constitution can be useful in medicine, especially when it comes to the treatment and prevention of hereditary diseases.

The ethical rightness or wrongness of genetic engineering can be examined from four different philosophical perspectives. From the viewpoint of *positive utilitarianism,* the central question is one of whether the good consequences of gene technology outweigh its costs and undesired side effects. For *teleological* ethicists, the important point is whether the genetic alteration of living beings is regarded as natural or unnatural. *Deontological* moralists, in their turn, stress the necessity of inflexible rules and limits in the regulation of human actions. And *negative utilitarians* emphasize the need of humankind to prevent and to remove unnecessary suffering whenever this is possible.

I. THE CONSEQUENCES OF GENETIC ENGINEERING

A. The Advantages

The advantages of genetic engineering, as seen by its proponents, include many actual and potential contributions to medicine, pharmacy, agriculture, the food industry, and the preservation of our natural environment.

1. Genetic Medicine

Within medicine and health care, the most far-reaching consequences are supposed to follow from the mapping of the human genome, an enterprise which holds the key to many further developments. Accurate genetic knowledge is a precondition for many foreseeable improvements in diagnoses and therapies as well as an important factor in the prevention of hereditary diseases, and possibly in the general genetic improvement of humankind. Provided that such knowledge becomes available, potential parents can in the future be screened for defective genes and, depending on the results, they can be advised against having their own genetic offspring, or they can be informed about the benefits of prenatal diagnosis.

One of these benefits is that an adequate diagnosis may indicate a simple monogenic disease in the fetus which can be cured by somatic cell therapy at any time during the individual's life. Another possibility is that an early diagnosis may reveal a more complex disorder which can be cured by subjecting the embryo to germline gene therapy—this form of prenatal treatment also ensures that the disorder will not be passed down to the offspring of the individual. Even in the case of incorrigible genetic defects the knowledge benefits the potential parents in that they can form an informed choice between selective abortion and deliberately bringing the defective child into existence.

Prenatal checkups and therapies do not by any means exhaust the medical applications of future genetic engineering. Somatic cell therapies are expected to help adult patients who suffer from monogenic hereditary diseases, and the increased risk of certain polygenic diseases can be counteracted by providing health education to those individuals who are in a high-risk bracket. In addition, the purely medical benefits of genetic engineering are extended by the fact that gene mapping will probably prove to be useful to employers and insurance companies as well as to individual citizens. Costly mistakes in employment and insurance policies can be avoided by carefully examining the applicants' tendencies toward illness and premature death prior to making the final decisions.

2. Biotechnology

Gene therapies and genetic counseling are practices which require advanced knowledge concerning the human gene structure. But the genetic manipulation of *nonhuman* organisms in biotechnology can also be employed to benefit humankind. The applications of genetic engineering to pharmacy, for instance, can in the future produce new diagnosing methods, vaccines, and drugs for diseases which have to date been incurable, such as cancer and AIDS. The agricultural uses of recombinant DNA techniques include the development of plants which contain their own pesticides. In dairy production, genetically engineered cows give more milk than ordinary ones, and with the right kind of manipulation the proteins of the milk can be made to agree with the digestive system of those suffering from lactose intolerance. As for other food products, gene technologies can be applied to manufactured substances like vanilla, cocoa, coconut oil, palm oil, and sugar substitutes. And biotechnology can even provide an answer to the growing environmental problems: genetically engineered bacteria can be employed to neutralize toxic chemicals and other kinds of industrial and urban waste.

B. The Disadvantages

The disadvantages of biotechnology, as seen by its opponents, are in many cases closely connected with the alleged benefits. An efficient strategy in opposing genetic engineering is to draw attention to the cost and risk factors which are attached to almost all inventions and developments in the field.

1. Costs and Dangers

One general critique can be launched by noting that the applications of recombinant DNA techniques are enormously expensive. Millions and millions are spent every year by governments and multinational corporations in biotechnological research and development. These resources, opponents of the techniques argue, would do more good to humankind if they were allocated, for instance, to international aid to the Third World.

Another problem is that, despite the undoubtedly good intentions of the scientists, the actual applications of genetic engineering are often positively dangerous. Consider the case of plants which are inherently resistant to diseases, or which contain their own pesticides.

Although there are no theoretical obstacles to the production of such highly desirable entities, corporations—who also sell chemical pesticides—might prefer to market another type of genetically manipulated plant, which is unprotected against pests but highly tolerant to toxic chemicals. The result of this policy would be an increase in the use of dangerous chemicals in agriculture, particularly in the Third World—which is to say that the outcome is exactly opposite to the one predicted by the proponents of biotechnology. Besides, it is quite possible that genetically engineered grains are less nourishing than the grains which are presently grown. If this turns out to be the case, then the employment of biotechnology will intensify instead of alleviating famine in the Third World. And to top it all, genetically manipulated plants may contain carcinogenic agents, and thus contribute to the cancer rates of the developing countries.

An oft-used criticism against agricultural biotechnology is that the introduction of altered organisms into the natural environment can lead to ecological catastrophes. Scientists working in the field of applied biology have themselves noticed this danger, and set for themselves ethical guidelines which are designed, among other things, to minimize this particular risk. But as the opponents of genetic engineering have repeatedly pointed out, not all research teams follow ethical guidelines if the alternative is considerable financial profit.

2. Injustice

Apart from the excessive expenses and the increased risk of physical danger caused by biotechnology, its opponents can appeal to yet another disadvantage, which is related to widely shared moral ideals rather than to straightforward estimates concerning efficiency. Genetic engineering, it can be argued, is conducive to economic inequity and social injustice, both nationally and globally. Even in the most affluent Western societies, gene therapies are too expensive to be extended to members of all classes and age groups. Subsequently, these therapies are likely to become the privilege of an elite, and they will drain scarce resources from the more basic areas of health care provision. In the developing countries, the situation is even more absurd. Medical problems which originally stem from lack of democracy, lack of education, shortages of fresh water, population explosion, archaic arrangements of land ownership, and the like cannot possibly be solved by high-tech Western innovations which can barely be made to work in the most affluent and democratic of countries.

Another type of injustice emerges from the fact that the natural national products of many developing countries are superseded in the market by the biotechnological products of multinational corporations. Genetically engineered substitutes for sugar, for instance, could adversely affect the lives of nearly 50 million sugar workers in the Third World. Biotechnological vanilla could increase the unemployment figures by thousands in Madagascar, Reunion, the Comoro Islands, and Indonesia. And plans to produce cocoa by genetically manipulating palm oil threaten the current export market of three poverty-striken African countries, namely, Ghana, Cameroon, and the Ivory Coast. In all these cases, the profits of multinational Western corporations are clearly and directly drawn from the national income of the developing countries.

Finally, as regards medical biotechnology, there are those who believe that advanced knowledge concerning the human genome will inevitably become an instrument of genetic programming, which in its turn leads to subtle forms of genocide and general injustice. The opponents of gene splicing argue that the development begins inconspicuously with attempts to eliminate hereditary diseases. This practice of what is called "negative" eugenics will, however, soon be followed by more "positive" efforts toward altering the human genome: the inborn qualities of future individuals will first be improved in their own alleged interest, and then, later on, in the interest of society at large. When this development has gone far enough, scientists will also be asked to design special classes of subhuman beings who can do all those occupations which are too dangerous or too tedious for ordinary people. The outcome, according to the opponents of biotechnology, will be something like Aldous Huxley's *Brave New World*.

C. Optimism and Pessimism

Although the expected advantages and dreaded disadvantages of genetic engineering are fairly well publicized, it is difficult to assess objectively what the actual consequences of employing the techniques would be. The outcome depends, namely, upon the social and political setting in which the application takes place. As different groups of people hold different views concerning the structure and dynamics of social and political life, these groups inevitably also disagree upon the consequences of the development of recombinant DNA techniques.

The optimism of the proponents of genetic engineering can be defended by noting that during the last decades nothing particularly alarming has happened in genetics. No bizarre life-forms have been created, and nobody seems to have any major plans to try to improve the human race. Thus, at least the worst-case scenarios involving genetically determined social classes seem, at the moment, farfetched.

On the other hand, it would be naive to believe that the multinational corporations which presently control biotechnological development would voluntarily undertake to further general welfare and global justice. Pessimism in this sense is therefore justified. Doubts are also warranted when they prevent people from believing uncritically what genetic engineers claim about the advantages of the new techniques—applied biologists do, after all, have many vested interests in biotechnology.

The upshot of the disagreement regarding the consequences of genetic engineering is that it is not possible either to justify or to condemn all applications of recombinant DNA techniques in a straightforward positive utilitarian analysis. The benefits are in many cases indisputable, but they are almost always counterbalanced by equally considerable disadvantages. The ultimate moral rightness or wrongness of genetic engineering must, therefore, be determined in the light of other ethical theories.

II. GENETIC ENGINEERING AND UNNATURALNESS

A. The Teleological View

The core idea of teleological ethics is that all beings have a natural *telos*—a goal toward which they are ideally inclined to move or to develop. The telos of human beings is, according to the original Aristotelian reading of the view, a good life in a just society, or, beyond that, intellectual contemplation. Later, Christian interpretations of the theory have stated that the ultimate goal of human beings is an afterlife of everlasting joy.

It is not easy to apply the teleological model in its more philosophical—or theological—forms to the questions of genetic engineering. The link between recombinant DNA techniques and the human good is obscure, and it seems that an accurate view of the consequences of genetics would be required to support an adequate analysis of the connection. On a less philosophical level, however, traces of teleological thinking can be detected in many popular objections to biotechnology, especially in the claim that genetic engineering is unnatural.

B. The View of the German Enquete Commission

The best attempt to formulate and employ the argument of unnaturalness against human genetic engineering can be found in the report of the Enquete Commission to the German Bundestag. In its 1987 report the Commission tackled three questions which are fundamental to the issue, namely, the definition of the natural as opposed to the unnatural, the reasons for preferring naturalness to unnaturalness, and the division of different kinds of biotechnology according to their natural and unnatural characteristics.

As for the question of definition, the development of individual human beings is regarded in the report as natural only if it is not determined by technical production or social recognition. Technological and social processes can, according to the Commission's view, produce only unnatural artifacts.

The value of promoting naturalness and avoiding artificial elements in practices which concern human development is linked in the report with the need to protect the humanity and dignity of human beings. Our humanity, so the Commission asserts, "rests at its core on natural development," and our dignity "is based essentially on the naturalness of our origins." (1988. Prospects and risks of gene technology: The report of the Enquete Commission to the Bundestaq of the Federal Republic of Germany. *Bioethics* 2, 256–263) If technological or social interventions are allowed, then the result is that people will be created by other people, and the Commission regards this possibility with extreme suspicion. Human beings whose existence and personal qualities depend on the planning or caprice of other human beings are not free persons in the full meaning of the term, and their lives lack the individual worth of naturally developed human lives. It is the pure chance of nature that secures our independence from other people, our personal freedom, and our individual worth as human beings.

These considerations lead in the report to the following normative views regarding different kinds of human genetic engineering. First, somatic cell therapies performed on fetuses, infants, and adult human beings are, at the moment, justifiable as experimental treatments, since they are intended to cure only the individuals who are actually being treated. Whether or not such treatments should be abandoned or condoned in the future remains to be judged by their practical success. But the humanity of individuals is not threatened by the use of genetic medicine when the individuals in question have already developed into the beings that they "naturally" are.

Second, the mapping of the human genome is legitimate as long as it is employed to diagnose the need for somatic cell therapies. The potential use of gene maps for other (eugenic) purposes is more controversial. Third, cloning and large-scale eugenic programs must, according to the report, be banned as gross instances of manufacturing people. And fourth, if a strict interpretation is given to the Commission's ideas concerning naturalness, germ-line gene therapies, which are expected to rectify hereditary disorders both in the patients themselves and in their descendants, must also be prohibited. All interventions in the germ lines of individuals diminish, according to the foregoing argument, their independence, uniqueness, and worth as human beings.

C. A Disagreement among the Commission

The opinions among the Enquete Commission diverged, however, regarding the legitimacy of germ-line gene therapies. Only some members of the Commission upheld the strict interpretation of naturalness, while others advanced a more moderate view. The core of the latter, moderate interpretation is that the medical corrections of obvious defects are not unnatural, as they do "not manufacture the human genome capriciously, but measure it against nature, that is, good health." (1988. Prospects and risks of gene technology: The report of the Enquete Commission to the Bundestaq of the Federal Republic of Germany. *Bioethics* 2, 256–263) Illness and suffering can be a part of a person's identity, but if they are prevented before the person even exists, there is no point in maintaining that her or his individuality is unlawfully changed or manipulated. The genetical treatment of early embryos is, so the moderate reading goes, directly comparable to any conventional treatment of fetuses and neonates who cannot give their consent to the procedures.

There are two intrinsic problems within the "moderate" view. First, defining "good health" is not an unambiguous matter, and one could well argue that human caprice always enters germ-line gene therapies through the particular definition employed. Second, the moderates of the Commission seem to assert that eugenic programming can be absolutely prohibited due to unnaturalness even though germ-line gene therapies cannot. This is a highly controversial view which presupposes that a tenable distinction can be drawn between the two practices.

The alleged difference between gene therapies and genetic improvement programs is that the former is aimed at eliminating hereditary diseases while the latter is intended to bring about or intensify some positive qualities in future individuals. This distinction is unclear, as it is obvious that illness may hinder the development of certain positive qualities and promote the development of others. A physically disabling disease, for instance, may prevent the individual from being strong and athletic—which are often regarded as "good qualities"—but it may indirectly promote the individual's willingness to learn cognitive and artistic skills—which are also often considered good.

D. A Critique of the Commission's View

The divergence of opinions within the Commission is an interesting detail, provided that the unnaturalness objection can be regarded as tenable. There are, however, several good reasons for thinking that this is not the case.

First, the argument from unnaturalness seems to apply to many practices which have been traditionally considered quite acceptable. If genetic engineering is to be condemned due to its power to change individuals by technical means, then most medical interventions should be condemned as well. Surgical operations, for instance, often alter people by transforming them from fatally ill patients into perfectly healthy citizens. And changes of personal identity may be even more drastic in the case of radical psychiatric treatments.

Second, the Commission's argument presupposes theoretical elements which are by no means universally accepted. The report's entirely biological view concerning personal identity is a case in point. According to the view, human beings are who they are and what they are almost exclusively owing to the arrangement of their genes. Culture, education, and social environment cannot significantly change the individual's identity, only biotechnology can do that. Very few philosophers today believe that such a strict biological definition of personality and individuality could be credibly defended.

Another presupposition in the report which can be criticized is its underlying view of human freedom and independence. The argument requires that human beings can be free from each other's influence in the sense that people are not "manufactured" by other people. This is obviously true if the manufacturing of people is understood literally: human beings cannot at the moment be mechanically created by each other except in science fiction. But when it comes to less obtrusive types of interaction, it is also true that people simply cannot survive and function without the often restrictive and molding presence of other people. Human freedom without the individual's dependence on others is only an abstraction.

Third, the unnaturalness objection presented in the report rests on the assumption that genetic engineering would undermine the worth, humanity, and dignity of the individuals produced by using the technique. This assumption is not only dubious but it may be positively insulting toward those human beings who will be born in the future genetically altered or cloned, perhaps against prevailing laws. The depth of the actual insult depends upon the interpretation that one gives to the Commission's view.

One possibility is to state that, according to the report, genetically engineered individuals would in fact lack humanity, dignity, and personal freedom because their chromosomes have been tampered with. This line of argument would obviously be unreasonably unfair toward the individuals in question.

Another possibility would be to assume that the Commission does not discuss the objective worth of human life in the first place, but the individual's subjective sense of worth in her or his life. The argument would then be that genetic engineering is wrong because the knowledge of one's "artificial" and "unnatural" origin reduces one's sense of worth and dignity. And yet another possibility is to claim that other people's adverse attitudes will make genetically engineered individuals unhappy.

The remarks concerning attitudes can, no doubt, be valid in predictable circumstances. But since people's attitudes toward themselves and toward others are subject to change, the argument in this form is conditional. If genetically altered human beings can be expected to have difficulties in coping with the question of their origins, then these difficulties may constitute a weak case against germ-line gene therapy, cloning, and eugenic programs. But this does not imply that these practices could be categorically rejected because of the attitudes that people happen to have.

III. DEONTOLOGICAL OBJECTIONS TO GENETIC ENGINEERING

A. The Role of Rules and Limits

The fundamental tenet of deontological ethics is that there are certain things that should not be done whatever the consequences of the omission. Ruth Chadwick has distinguished four different ways to intrepret this tenet. First, deontological ethicists can argue that there are duties which should not be overridden by consequentialist considerations. Second, they can maintain that there are rights which should not in any circumstances be violated. Third, it can be claimed that there are, irrespective of our duties and rights, boundaries which must never be crossed. And fourth, one possible line is to state that certain things count as "playing God" and should not therefore be attempted.

The first three lines of argument have not been fully developed with regard to the morality of genetic engineering, but brief descriptions of their possible characteristics follow in the next three sections. The playing-God argument, however, has been thoroughly analyzed by Ruth Chadwick, and it will be given a more detailed treatment in Section III.E.

B. Duties

What duties can we have with regard to genetic engineering? The fundamental duty postulated by Immanuel Kant, the foremost advocate of the intellectualistic version of deontological thought, is our obligation to treat the humanity in ourselves and in other persons always as an end and never as a mere means. This obligation, which we owe to our fellow humans but not to the members of other species, is based on our nature as rational agents. The way we ought to treat animals, plants, and other life-forms is determined by our duties toward ourselves and other persons, not by their nonexistent worth as ends in themselves.

The difficulties of applying Kant's views to the manipulation of nonhuman beings by recombinant DNA techniques include the fact that he did not clearly specify what our duties as regards animals, plants, and other nonhuman organisms are. He believed that violence and cruelty toward animals set a bad example to our treatment of other people, and that not even inanimate objects should be wantonly destroyed because that would prevent others from making use of them. But how these remarks should be interpreted in the context of genetic engineering in a purely nonconsequentialist analysis remains an unanswered question.

When it comes to the alteration of the human genome, Kant's principle is open to two readings. Many 20th century philosophers have thought that our humanity as persons can be best enhanced by respecting our preferences and freely made choices. If this is true, then somatic cell therapies and also germ-line gene therapies should presumably be condoned whenever the patients themselves decide that these treatments are beneficial to them. But Kant's own interpretation seems to be, rather, that our essential humanity should take priority over our contingent and irrational desires and decisions. Reason commands us to obey the moral law, usually against our own inclinations, and our true humanity can be respected only by protecting our rational nature against our externally generated impulses. This view bears a resemblance to the teleological doctrine, examined in Section II, which emphasizes the immorality of acting in unnatural ways, and it can most probably be criticized along the same lines.

C. Rights

Do individuals have specific rights with regard to their basic biological constitution? Is there, for instance, a right to genetic treatment which is equal to the right to be aided by other medical means? Or do future generations perhaps have a right to the genetic disorders of their ancestors—a right which would cancel the permission of present generations to undergo germ-line gene therapy? And if rights like these do exist, what is their foundation, and how can they be justified?

One answer to these questions can be found by studying the prevailing laws. In the *legal* sense, individuals are endowed with the rights and liberties that can be derived from national and international laws and statutes. But there are two problems with placing too much trust in this solution. First, the legislation concerning genetic engineering has not yet been completed, and it is impossible to foresee what rights individuals will acquire in the process. Second, even if the legislation had been completed, the prevailing laws could be morally condemnable. Lawgivers have been known to pass laws which, in further analysis, have turned out to be counterproductive or conducive to suffering and injustice.

Another possibility is to argue that individuals have *moral* rights which are not necessarily enforced by existing laws but which in the majority of instances should be. The justification for these moral rights can be found in either consequentialist or nonconsequentialist thinking. In the former case, the principles for postulating them are sketched in Sections I and IV. In the latter case, the answers must be mainly sought in natural rights theories, which range from the Catholic teaching of Thomas Aquinas to the libertarian doctrine originated by John Locke and recently revived by Robert Nozick. The Catholic view derives its definition of the concept of "natural" from the essential features of the ideal human being, and it is therefore open to the type of criticism presented in Section II.D. The libertarian view has been, and probably can be, applied only to the economic aspects of genetic engineering, such as the right of individuals to patent life-forms. According to this type of thinking, next to no restrictions should be set on the development and use of biotechnology.

D. Limits

Some people believe that there are limits which should never be crossed by human actions even if these actions cannot be identified as unprofitable, harmful, or unnatural, and even if they do not prevent agents from performing their duties or force them to violate the rights of others. One version of the view states that people are playing God if they cross certain boundaries—this notion is scrutinized in the next section. The only other version that theorists have come up with so far is emotionalistic, and it states that the morality of actions can be determined only by recourse to sentiments. According to emotion-based deontological thinking, if we feel strongly enough that genetic engineering is bad, evil, disgusting, or immoral, it ought to be banned.

The main difficulty with the emotion-oriented model is that it is exceedingly relativistic. In most cases there is no consensus concerning feelings, and many questions remain unanswered. Whose feelings should be respected? Should genetic engineering be banned only if *everybody* feels that it is bad? Or is it sufficient that the *majority* feel that way? Or perhaps prohibitions ought to be employed if a significant *minority* nurtures these feelings? Or should we say that if *anybody* feels this way, biotechnology ought to be rejected? There seem to be no good responses to these queries either at the general level or in the context of biotechnology.

E. Playing God

The argument of "playing God" in medicine has been thoroughly scrutinized by Ruth Chadwick. According to her analysis, the objection that an action is wrong because it is an instance of playing God has two different meanings in two different kinds of setting. In the context of sensitive medical decision making, the point of the objection is that human beings are in no position to decide legitimately about each other's fates on the basis of quality-of-life judgments. In the context of new medical technologies, again, the crux of the argument is that actions describable as playing God can lead to disastrous and unpredictable consequences. These two aspects are both present in certain forms of genetic engineering, such as germ-line gene therapy, and it is therefore useful to take a closer look at Chadwick's account.

1. Sensitive Medical Decision Making

With regard to the decision aspect of the playing-God objection, Chadwick distinguishes three major lines of argument, two of which she finds untenable.

First, the wrongness of playing God can be based on the idea that it is God's prerogative to give life and to take it away. Active euthanasia, for instance, has been attacked by referring to this notion. But the problem here is that no reasonable morality condemns doctors and nurses who do their best to save and prolong lives, although this work can, according to the interpretation, also be described as playing God.

Second, the point of the objection may be that in certain matters the natural course of events should be preferred to human interference. An example of such matters is the reallocation of health through medical decisions. To kill one patient in order to save two others would be the best thing to do in crude utilitarian terms, but it would also be a hideous instance of playing God. In situations like this, so the argument goes, doctors can act morally only by letting nature take its course. The obvious difficulty in this second interpretation is that whatever decisions doctors make, they cannot help playing God in the defined sense. Refusals to alter the "natural" course of events affect the patients and their lives as much as any positive action.

Third, the formulation that Chadwick finds plausible and morally relevant is founded on the equality and limited knowledge of human beings. In matters concerning life and death we may justifiably feel that no one else is qualified to judge whether our lives are worth living. This conviction stems from two factors. On the one hand, it can be argued that every human life has equal value, and that no person or group has the right to make decisions concerning the lives of others on assumptions of inequality. It is not, for instance, justifiable to allocate scarce life-saving medical treatments on the basis of quality-of-life measurements. On the other hand, even assuming that some human lives are more valuable than others, the judgments concerning them may require superhuman capacities. The traditional theological assumption is that while human beings are imperfect and their knowledge limited, God is omniscient. This implies that even if God, as an omniscient being, could pass valid judgments concerning human lives, the comparisons made by human beings would still be mere arrogant instances of playing God.

As Chadwick notes, the playing-God objection may in this third form have some moral relevance as a re-minder of the limits of our knowledge. It may also serve as a warning against employing irrelevant criteria, like life quality, in the inescapable human decisions concerning life and death. But the objection is not by itself sufficiently strong to refute any actual practices, and it cannot be directly applied to genetic engineering, as the persons whose lives are compared, for instance, in decisions concerning germ-line gene therapy, do not exist at the time of the choice.

2. New Medical Technologies

With regard to the technology aspect of the playing-God objection, Chadwick argues that divine omnipotence rather than divine omniscience provides the key to this side of the issue. People who oppose activities like genetic engineering or artificial reproduction typically see these technologies as attempts to rival God's power by trying to create life or life-forms. When it comes to artificial insemination and *in vitro* fertilization, the counterargument can be made, as Chadwick in fact does, that reproductive technology only aims at rearranging materials, not at creating previously nonexistent entities. The same is not, however, quite true with regard to genetic engineering, which may, after all, create completely new life-forms. Admittedly, new life-forms have been created for centuries by animal and plant breeding. But these processes have been relatively slow, and humans have not been explicitly included in the program. The opponents of genetic engineering may wish to argue that there are certain limits beyond which human beings cannot go without unlawfully playing God.

If this idea of fixed moral limits is taken seriously, the next step is to find out where the lines have been drawn and by whom. Chadwick considers three possibilities.

First, playing God can be understood literally as a transgression of the invisible boundaries that separate immortal gods from mortal human beings. People who try to assume the role of gods are guilty of what the ancient Greeks used to call *hybris,* that is, excessive pride. In Greek mythology, overstepping the limits set by a divine will was generally punished in unusual and cruel ways. This literal interpretation of the playing-God objection is clear and intelligible, but its value as a moral guide is suspect. No critical morality can be based on the assumption that divine beings have set us limits which they continuously protect. Even if one believed in the existence of such divinities and in the sacredness of their will, it would be impossible to discover what the chosen deity would want us to do. In fact, one could well argue that the humans who pretend to be acquainted with the divine will are putting themselves in the divine role, and thereby themselves playing God.

Second, the playing-God objection in the context of medical technologies may also be meant to state that the natural environment as a whole sets certain limits to our actions. Humankind has during the last few decades acquired powers which could be used to destroy most of the biosphere. Many people seem to think that genetic engineering is one of these powers, and they fear that, for instance, the release of genetically altered organisms into the environment may have irreversible ecological consequences. Assuming that we are interested in the preservation of the biosphere, this objection against genetic engineering does indeed have some moral relevance. But the problem is that the appeal to consequences, which gives this argument its weight, also deprives it of its categorical disguise. It would, no doubt, be pragmatically unwise to destroy the only environment where we can live at present, but this does not amount to a categorical, or deontological, rejection of genetic engineering. The wrongness of the activity remains conditional upon the consequences.

Third, the limits of playing God can be set by human beings on the ground that certain actions, especially technology-related actions which have never been taken before, are liable to produce unforeseen, unpleasant, and unpredictable consequences. Despite the appeal to consequences, this approach may be genuinely categorical, since no weight is given to the nature of the feared outcome or to the probability or improbability of its occurrence. According to Chadwick, the logic of the playing-God objection here is that the unknown consequences of going beyond (present) human limits cause fear, anxiety, and uneasiness in many people. Some of these people believe that we will be faced with unimaginable disaster if new technologies are implemented. Others may have the feeling, unjustified perhaps but nonetheless painful, that divine retribution will follow the alleged human arrogance. Still others may be worried about the preservation of the current worldview, which may suffer from the breakdown of its customary limits.

None of these negative feelings amounts, by itself, to an independent refutation of new technologies, including genetic engineering. But as Chadwick points out, the appeal to unforeseen consequences may be taken as a counsel advising us to be very careful in assessing certain delicate decisions. If the pros and cons of a given new technology are otherwise equal, the scales can be tipped by the unpleasantness inflicted on people by the mere thought of the innovation.

IV. GENETIC ENGINEERING AND RISK

The concept of risk is one of the most important elements in negative utilitarian analyses of biotechnology. The term, or its linguistic equivalents, can be found in teleological and deontological arguments as well, but the role of risk in these is nullified by the absolute nature of certain perceived dangers.

A. The Risks Involved in Biotechnology

Risk can be defined as the possibility or probability of a loss, an injury, an unwanted outcome, or an undesired result. The main risks involved in genetic engineering are, as the positive utilitarian analysis in Section I partly indicates, the following.

The *release* of genetically altered organisms in the environment can increase human suffering when medical measures are concerned, decrease animal welfare in experiments or through the use of recombinant DNA techniques in breeding, and lead to ecological disasters. The *containment* of biotechnological material in laboratories and industrial plants involves two dangers: first is the possibility of an accidental release, and second is the increased probability with which uncontrolled releases can produce undesired results.

A risk that lies between these "scientifically controllable" dangers and the more indirect political hazards of biotechnology is the probability of inadequate containment and irresponsible releases, which can be prompted by the economic self-interest of research groups and industrial corporations. The difference between this type of risk and the more controlled hazard is that while in the ideal case of balanced decision making the risk lies between the act—of containment or release—and harm, in this case it lies between the agent and the act. What we primarily fear in this case is human weakness or immorality. What we primarily suspect in the case of scientific risk assessment is carelessness or negligence in the calculation of possible outcomes.

The purely social and political dangers of genetic engineering include the possibility of increased economic inequality and the possibility of large-scale eugenic programs and totalitarian control over human lives. The risk in these cases lies clearly between the agents and their actions. If multinational corporations choose to supersede the national products of Third World countries by their own biotechnological substances, millions of workers will in a few years' time be unemployed. And if governments decide to develop racial programs and surveillance systems based upon the achievements of genetic engineering, the undesired outcome is certain, not possible or probable.

In debates concerning the risks of biotechnology the social and political dangers are not discussed as often as the hazards of responsible and irresponsible containment and releases. A partial reason for this can be that economic inequality and totalitarian measures are not seen by all as unwanted, undesired, or evil. Another partial explanation could be that the probability of these outcomes is small, especially in the assessment of particular biotechnological innovations or products. It is difficult to see a connection between, say, a technological process designed to produce inexpensive pharmaceuticals on the one hand, and the emergence of an unjust, totalitarian political order on the other.

B. The Morality of Risk Taking

If risk can be defined as the probability of harm, then how should we define the concept of "acceptable risk," on which analyses of the morality of risk taking often center? Is a risk acceptable if the *probability* of harm is on a reasonable level, or should we require that the expected harm is also tolerable? The quick answer to this question is that the acceptability of a risk is the product of the acceptability of the expected harm and the acceptability of its probability. But acceptability to whom, and when, and on what criteria?

Industrial corporations have a tendency to treat risks as probable costs. This is not always commendable, because some of the harms inflicted by the production and marketing of goods cannot be easily compensated to those whom the harm befalls. When, for instance, the directors and engineers of an American automobile company noticed that they had produced a car which exploded in a rear crash if the speed was right and the left rear blinker was on, they went on to market the model on the ground that the overall economic loss incurred by the expected lawsuits would be lower than the price of repairing the cars. This decision cost many people their lives and caused others inordinate suffering, and although the statistics were correct, the company's policy was clearly immoral. At the very least, the buyers should have been given the chance to decide for themselves whether or not they wanted to take the risk, perhaps by purchasing the car at a lower price. Death and suffering caused by attempts to make an economic profit are not commensurable with the work and capital invested in the enterprise.

How, then, should we define the acceptability of the risks of genetic engineering? The assessment should probably in each case be left to those who can be harmed by the decision in question. Economic risks are acceptable, if they are condoned by the biotechnological corporations and governments who take them. The risks imposed on laboratory personnel by the containment of dangerous materials ought to be evaluated by the laboratory personnel themselves. All other risks involved in genetic engineering are more or less universal, and should therefore be assessed—and eventually accepted or rejected—as democratically as possible.

Scientists, industrialists, and autocratic political decision makers can argue against democratic risk assessment by claiming that their expertise enables them to predict with greater accuracy the consequences of policies. If the choices are left to democratic processes, they say, many good outcomes which would have been perfectly safe fail to come into existence, while many undesired results are brought about by the prevailing lack of knowledge.

What this objection overlooks is that the acceptability of a risk for a given group is not determined exclusively by the facts of the matter, but also by the way the members of the group perceive the facts, and by the way they evaluate them. People cannot fully commit themselves to decisions which are based on epistemic and moral values that they do not share. Thus if anything goes wrong with the predictions of the experts, people feel and are entitled to resent the consequences of the authoritarian choices. The risks taken by experts on behalf of others are therefore unacceptable. But if risk taking is based upon the considered choices of those who can be harmed by the consequences themselves, the situation is different. Even if the undesired outcome is realized, the risk is acceptable, because it is embedded in their own system of ethical and epistemic values.

V. CONCLUSIONS

In sum, the actual consequences of genetic engineering are difficult to assess, and it would therefore be unwise to make decisions concerning the use of recombinant DNA techniques on purely positive utilitarian grounds. The same conclusion applies to teleological objections against genetic engineering, and to most deontological critiques which are based on duties, rights, or absolute limits. The playing-God objection has two conditional readings that can be useful as reminders of our lack of knowledge and our need to respect people's feelings. Probably the best way to evaluate the morality of genetic engineering is to analyze the risks involved in its implementation, but it should be kept in mind that mere scientific risk assessment is not sufficient. When the risk of harm is more or less universal, the acceptability of the risk must be decided as democratically as possible.

Also See the Following Articles

BIOTECHNOLOGY • FETAL RESEARCH • GENETIC RESEARCH • GENOME ANALYSIS • PLAYING GOD

Bibliography

Chadwick, R. (1989). Playing God. *Cogito* 3, 186–193.
Chadwick, R., Levitt, M., Häyry, H., Häyry, M., and Whitelegg, M. (Eds.) (1996). "Cultural and Social Objections to Biotechnology: Analysis of the Arguments, with Special Reference to the Views of Young People." Centre for Professional Ethics, Preston, UK.
Dyson, A., and Harris, J. (Eds.) (1994). "Biotechnology and Ethics." Routledge, London/New York.
Harris, J. (1992). "Wonderwoman and Superman: The Ethics of Human Biotechnology." Oxford Univ. Press, Oxford/New York.

GENETIC RESEARCH

R. O. Mason* and G. E. Tomlinson†
*Southern Methodist University †University of Texas

GLOSSARY

alleles The small sequence differences in DNA that form the genetic material at a particular locus on a specific chromosome and that may be inherited along with different versions of the same gene.

autosome Any chromosome other than a sex chromosome. In humans there are 22 pairs of autosomes.

base pair A bond between two bases or nucleotides. Adenine bonds only with thymine (A-T or T-A) and guanine only with cytosine (G-C or C-G).

bases—nucleotides Elementary units that occur in DNA molecules and determine their specific form. The four kinds of bases are adenine (A), cytosine (C), guanine (G), and thymine (T).

Bayesian analysis A form of probability calculus in which the probability of a hypotheses h being true given the evidence e is that of e, given p, multiplied by the independent probability of h and divided by the independent probability of e. $\text{Prob}(h|e) = \text{Prob}(e|h) \times [\text{Prob}(h)/\text{Prob}(e)]$. In general the increase in probability which a hypothesis gains when its consequences are confirmed by means of a research project is proportional to the improbability that the research study would yield those consequences. Due to Reverend Thomas Bayes (1702–1761).

chromosome The threadlike linear strands of DNA and associated proteins in the nucleus of animal and plant cells that carry the genes and function to transmit the hereditary information. (Each human being has 23 pairs of chromosomes, which are found in every cell of his or her body. One chromosome of each pair comes from each parent.)

DNA Deoxyribonucleic Acid, the primary genetic material of cells. It is composed of four molecules called bases or nucleotides, which, like letters of the alphabet, spell out an organism's genetic information.

DNA sequence The specific nucleotide order of DNA.

dominant Describing a phenotype that requires only a single copy of an altered gene from either parent to manifest its presence. Compare with recessive.

gene A hereditary unit that occupies a specific location on a chromosome, contains the instructions for a given protein, and determines a particular phenotype in an organism. Each gene has a unique DNA sequence and a specific location, called its locus, on a specific chromosome. Genes exist in a number of different forms and can undergo mutation.

genome The set of genes characteristic of each species revealed by the base set of chromosomes, which is species specific. In humans, the genome consists of 23 pairs of chromosomes.

genotype The genetic constitution of an organism or a group of organisms. More precisely, a combination of alleles present at a locus, or a number of loci. Compare with *phenotype*.

locus A place on a chromosome or on a chromosome pair occupied by a gene or by two alleles of the same gene. Loci is the plural of locus.

map To determine the relative position, i.e. locus or loci, of a gene on a chromosome.

mutation A local change in the genetic information carried by DNA or a change in DNA sequence. This change may be responsible for causing a disease.

nucleotides—bases Adenine, cytosine, guanine, and thymine, the four molecules that make up DNA. Nucleotides occur in pairs—base pairs. Adenine always pairs with thymine and cytosine always with guanine.

penetrance The frequency, usually expressed as a percentage, with which a particular geneotype produces a specific phenotype in a group of organisms.

phenotype The observable physical or biochemical characteristics of an organism, as determined by both genetic makeup and environmental influences. Examples include eye color, skin pigmentation, body build, sexual orientation, and observable diseases, for example, breast cancer. Compare with *genotype*.

polymerase chain reaction (PCR) A process developed in the mid-1980s by which a large number of copies of a specific DNA sequence can be produced from very little DNA (less than 0.000000001 grams).

polymorphism The occurrence of different forms, stages, or types in individual organisms or in organisms of the same species, independent of sexual variations. Also called normal variants.

recessive Describing phenotype that requires two copies of an altered gene, one passed on from each parent, in order to manifest itself. Compare with dominant.

GENETIC RESEARCH is undertaken to increase society's understanding of the genetic composition and hereditary nature of organisms, especially human beings; and, it is pursued with the long-term aim of securing improvement in the human condition.

A *gene* is a heredity unit and a unit of information. It is comprised of a sequence of DNA (nucleic acid found in the nuclei of cells) and contains instructions for producing a given protein that, in turn, contributes to a particular characteristic, trait or *phenotype* of an organism. Each gene has a unique DNA sequence and a specific location on specific chromosomes—called its *locus*. The genetic constitution of an organism or a group of organisms is called its *genotype*. The traits that organisms exhibit are called their phenotypes and include characteristics such as eye color, skin pigmentation, body build, and observable diseases, for example, cystic fibrosis, sickle cell anemia, and, in some instances, cancer. More questionably of purely causal genetic origin, but of considerable social concern, are phenotypes involving qualities of temperament and behavior that may be contribute to, on the negative side, feeblemindedness, epilepsy, insanity, alcoholism, prostitution, criminality or poverty, or, on the positive side, high IQs or superior athletic performance.

People, other than geneticists, do not care much about genes per se. They care about phenotypes. Phenotypes are both the subject and the object of many human values. Their presence or absence is consequently a contributor to many ethical issues. Phenotypes are determined by an organism's genotype in conjunction with its environment, although the proportional contribution varies in different situations. For example, current research indicates that cystic fibrosis is almost entirely genetic in origin; 40% of adult onset diabetes cases are perhaps due to genetic predisposition; while AIDS has only a minor underlying genetic component (although recent research indicates that as many as 1 in 100 people may have a mutation of the CCR5 gene that prevents the AIDS virus from docking on it). Research has also shown that genes are not necessarily rigid pieces of information with predetermined outcomes. Changes in their biological, physical, and chemical environment can turn genes on or off, or can change their phenotypic expression during an organism's development process and it does this at various rates. (The frequency within a population that a geneotype is manifested as a certain phenotype is referred to as its *penetrance*.) This has moral consequences: the agents who create the biological, physical or chemical environment may be as responsible for an organism's phenotypes as are its genes.

Many ethical issues also stem from scientific findings about the relationship between a given genotype and phenotype. If a given genotype is necessary and sufficient to bring about a phenotype—as it appears to be in just a very few cases such as cystic fibrosis, Tay-Sachs disease, and the retinoblastoma gene whose alteration leads to cancer—then the relationship is purely *cause/effect*. The moral concerns focus on two issues: how best to treat the genetic cause or how to help the subject live in serenity with the effects. If, however, a genotype is necessary but *not* sufficient to bring about a phenotype—that is, if elements of the organism's environment are coproducers of the phenotype and are actively operative as well—then the relationship is one of *producer/product*. This is the most common relationship. For example, most of the cancer-causing agents, such as those resulting in breast and lung cancer, are of this type. Under conditions of producer/product all of the moral issues associated with social, cultural, and economic environments—such as the availability of medical treatments, of education, of employment, of insurance, or of certain restraints on working conditions—play a crucial role because they also contribute to the production of the phenotype under investigation.

From the standpoint of social values, the fact that the environment plays a role in the production of phenotypes means, among other things, that the grand debate pitting beliefs in genetic determinism—the notion that genes have the power to determine social and personality phenotypes—against those of reactive environmental dogmatism is misplaced. The ethical policies necessary to deal with genotype/phenotype as producer/product relationships must be based instead on a deeper and more complex understanding of the underlying science of genetics and its nuances.

Genetic research, in summary, is the application of the scientific method to the study of four related areas: (1) genes, genetic material, and their mutations in all of the many different forms they may take—that is, genotypes; (2) the phenotypes that are associated with or predisposed by specific genotypes; (3) the effects of different environments on a given genotype that ultimately produces phenotypes; and (4) kinships, the hereditary social groupings or families in which both genotypes and phenotypes are found.

I. A BRIEF HISTORY OF THE RESEARCH IN GENETICS

The modern science of genetics arose in about 1900, with rediscovery of Gregor Mendel's work (circa 1866) on inherited traits. In general, the Mendelian system holds that each inherited phenotype is determined by the combination of two genes, one from each of the parental reproductive cells. A gene may play one of two functional roles: *dominant,* for which only a single copy is needed from either parent to manifest its presence and *recessive,* for which two copies, one from each parent, are required. A recessive gene stems from an *allele* that does not produce a characteristic phenotype or trait when a dominant allele is also present; that is, the recessive is dominated. Thus, a dominant gene

masks the presence of a recessive gene that, in turn, lies "hidden" in the organism's DNA but it still may be passed on to subsequent generations. The hidden gene may be inherited under conditions of dominant susceptibility in which a single copy of an altered gene that is inherited from either parent increases the subject's susceptibility to being affected by a given disease although other events are also required. The breast cancer genes *BRCA1* and *BRCA2* cause a dominantly inherited susceptibility. Many of the ethical issues created by genetics research are founded on distinctions made between dominant and recessive genes, who their carriers are and what the underlying conditions of inheritance might be.

Some very emotional ethical issues depend also on the type of cell affected: *germ-line* or *somatic.* Germ-line cells, also called "gametes," include ovum and sperm cells (or one of their developmental precursors). More specifically, they contain the appropriate chromosomes to make them capable of fusing with similar cells of the opposite sex to produce a fertilized egg. Any genetic alteration that is present in the germline manifests itself in every cell derived from the fertilized egg and, thus, is present in all body cells in the next and potentially subsequent generations. In this way germ-line cells directly effect inheritance. Because future generations—and potentially entire subsequent races of people—may be affected by research on germ-line cells, the ethical issues raised by this line of research are considerable and virtually unprecedented.

On the other hand, there are genetic events that occur at the cellular level in a formed body organ that do not directly affect inheritance. These cells are called somatic, or "body," cells. The ethical issues generated by research on somatic cells, while significant, are similar to those encountered in other areas of medical ethics and bioethics since in a given instance only one individual is primarily affected.

Genetic research into the presence of dominant or recessive genes in either somatic or germ-line cells brings together two steams of scientific inquiry. One is field-based research undertaken without the collection of biological material and in the absence of laboratory analysis. Field methods include research into inheritance and the construction and study of pedigrees consisting of databases and charts of information pertaining to an individual's ancestors. These data sources are used to determine patterns of Mendelian inheritance of identifiable phenotypes, especially of familial diseases.

The other line of inquiry is laboratory based. It includes analysis of several different types of genetic material and different levels, ranging from elemental bases to full genomes. One type of research focuses on *bases* or *base pairs* that reside in genes, which may exhibit sequence differences. These differences are called *alleles* and are located, at the next level of complexity, in *chromosomes* or *chromosomes bands* or *fragments* that are, in turn, contained in *cells*. When a sequence difference has an impact on the phenotype (usually taking the form of a disease) then it creates a *mutation*. Other sequence differences may not have an affect on a phenotype. In this case it is considered a normal variant or *polymorphism*. The genes contained in an organism when considered in their totality are called its *genome*. Information resulting from both field and laboratory studies are then combined with information about an organism's environment. The outcome is used to help geneticists make inferences about relationships between genotypes and phenotypes.

For the most part, some form of *Bayesian analysis* is ultimately used to bring the results of these two lines of inquiry together. Evidence adduced from research studies is used to establish one of two probabilities or likelihoods. One, that of subjects who express a given phenotype also possessing a given genotype—Prob(G | P). For example, current research indicates that of the group of women in the general population who are diagnosed with breast cancer before the age of 35 years the likelihood is approximately 0.10 or 10% that they have the germline BRCA1 mutation on chromosome 17. Second, that subjects discovered to have a given genotype also will manifest a given phenotype—Prob(P | G). For example, women who test positive for the BRCA1 mutation have a lifetime likelihood of contracting breast cancer that may be as high as 0.90 or 90%. These Bayesian-type likelihoods are frequently arrayed by age in morbidity or mortality tables. New research results, including that on the effects on different environmental conditions and different treatments or therapies, are used to "condition"—increase or decrease—these probabilities based on the improbability of obtaining those results. The widespread use of likelihood analysis emphasizes the fact that genetics research is rarely deterministic. An element of uncertainty or risk is almost always present. Consequently the moral judgments made about genetics research must be based on an estimate of risk as well as on notions of good or bad, right or wrong, or just or unjust outcomes.

Three major scientific discoveries have shaped modern genetics research. The first came in 1953 when James Watson and Francis Crick discovered the fundamental structure of DNA—that its strands, connected by hydrogen bonds between pairs of bases, are coiled in a double helix. This was followed during the 1970s with the discovery that strands of DNA can be spliced, recombined and cloned by subjecting them to *restriction enzymes*. These enzymes recognize particular sequences in a piece of DNA and cut it at locations that are within or near those sequences. If the fragments are of appropriate size and character, they can be combined with the DNA of other organisms and the new host can be prompted into making additional copies of *recombinant DNA*. Once a gene is cloned it can be subjected to considerable further research and use to develop diagnostic, predictive, therapeutic, identification, or other techniques. The third innovation occurred during the mid 1980s when Kary Mullis invented a simple but revolutionary technique, known as *polymerase chain reaction,* or PCR, for reproducing billions of copies of a single piece of DNA. In one of many applications, for example, PCR has enabled genome researchers to use short stretches of DNA and merge them together to make genetic linkage maps and a variety of physical maps. PCR together with rapidly increasing knowledge of human DNA has opened up new opportunities for direct diagnosis at the DNA level including genetic tests such as that for cystic fibrosis.

This kind of applied research relies on two general strategies. One is called *positional cloning* and begins with a phenotype (e.g., a disease), finds associations on a map of the genome, from these associations deduces the composition of the causal genes and infers their function from the result. This approach has been used to identify the culprit genes in cystic fibrosis, Huntington's disease, and breast cancer (i.e., BRCA1 and BRCA2). The second is called *functional cloning*. It also begins with a phenotype, but then goes on to determine the chemical functions that give rise to it, deduce the originating gene, and from that infer the gene's location on the genome map. Functional cloning has been used effectively in discovering the genetic basis of sickle cell anemia and thalassemia.

The result of genetic research to date may be summarized in terms of five overarching and significant scientific findings: One, genes are inherited. Consequently, knowledge about family pedigrees makes a difference. Two, identifiable mechanisms exist by which genes figure (either as cause/effect or producer/product) in the determination of all life processes. They do this by directing the synthesis of cell proteins. Three, processes exist by which genetic mutations, either alterations in gene or chromosome structure, may contribute to the production of specific, identifiable phenotypes such as diseases. Four, by means of a technique known as *cloning*—using, for example, PCR technology—multiple copies of a fragment of DNA can be made. This makes it possible to reproduce, manipulate, and study large quantities of a particular genetic material. Five, in some cases—presently and potentially more so in the future—genetic material can be inserted into the body of an organism, including human beings, and thereby used to change that organism's inherited genetic structure, leading also to a change in its phenotypic manifestations. These five findings result in moral and ethical issues that lie at the very heart of all those concerning human life, the human condition, future generations, and the nature of society.

Of particular contemporary interest is the human genome, a collection of about 3 billion base pairs. The entire genome contains about 100,000 genes. The average gene consists of from about 2,000 to 200,000 base pairs. Only one base pair, however, needs to be altered, deleted, inserted, or substituted by another to cause a predisposition to a disease or other phenotypic trait. The human genome is being explored by the Human Genome Project, an ambitious multinational effort to map, sequence, and decipher it in its entirety. It began in October 1990 and is expected to complete its first phase consisting of producing a genetical map, physical location map, and DNA sequence by 2006, or likely earlier, at a total cost of about $3 billion. At this writing about 2700 genes have been successfully mapped. (This out of the 100,000 estimated total and the 6200 actual and putative reported in scholarly publications as reviewed by Victor McKusick. See the *Online Mendelian Inheritance in Man* home page on the World Wide Web.) When the mapping is completed, scientists will have a full characterization of the human genetic complement that is analogous in its informative content and use to the familiar anatomical charts seen in textbooks or hanging on physicians' walls. Just as anatomical charts represent the structural components of the human body and characterize the ways in which human physiology carries out its bodily functions, the human genome map will have several similar uses: to diagnose genetic disease, to identify individuals who are at risk of contracting a genetic disease, and to develop disease prevention therapies.

This line of genetic research is already helping society learn a great deal about the genetic makeup of individuals, especially their propensities to disease or to abnormalities of some kind. Indeed, it is believed that virtually all diseases have a contributory genetic component as well as an environmental component (although the proportions vary for different diseases). That is, diseases result, in part, from misspellings of base pairs. This research is also revealing a startling amount about its possible applications to various types

of medical and health care decisions: diagnosis and prevention, drug therapy, and gene therapy or genetic engineering. Among the broad questions of applied ethics genetics research raises are: Will the genetic information be used for good purposes or bad? What kinds of manipulations, that is, gene therapy, if any, should be permitted? What are the implications for humankind's understanding of ourselves as human beings and of the human condition in general? In order to examine these questions it is instructive to see how they arise during the processes of conducting the research itself.

II. AN OVERVIEW OF THE GENETICS RESEARCH PROCESS

The conduct of genetics research proceeds in several closely related, sometimes overlapping or iterative, processes. In summary, they are as follows: (1) defining the research problem, determining its objectives and allocating resources to it; (2) creating a model or framework within which the research problem can be defined; (3) developing from the model the hypotheses and explanations to be tested or explored; (4) specifying the data that will be required, the number of observations, and their form and precision; (5) identifying the subjects or other sources from whom the data will be collected; (6) specifying the protocols under which the data will be collected; (7) collecting the data according to the protocols; (8) transmitting the data to a central point; (9) analyzing the data; (10) producing the research results; (11) storing the original data and the results, and transmitting them when needed; (12) determining the use to which the results will be put. Critical ethical issues can arise during all of these processes; although, processes 5, 6, 10, 11, and 12 are replete with them.

There are several types of parties who participate in or are implicated by genetics research. Several important ethical relationships are formed between these participants including: scientific investigators to funders; investigators qua teachers to their students; investigators to their staff; investigators qua scientists to their subjects; investigators qua physicians to their subjects (patients), investigators and their peers—individually and as members of professional societies; and scientific investigators and society. Genetic research places considerable stress on each of these relationships and, in some cases, has caused them to be reformulated. Of special importance are the investigator qua physician and/or qua scientist relationships. At the outset of their research some scientists who are searching for genes assume that they have a trivial, if any, (distant at most) relationship with their research subject. Canons of objectivity reinforced this belief. As it becomes clearer, however, that a certain genetic sequence is associated with a particular disease phenotype among their subjects, it is morally more difficult for them to maintain this assumption of independence and separation. Ethical issues such as validation, consent, and disclosure come to the fore, putting the scientist's role values in conflict with those, say, of physician/patient or physician/family relationships.

Some of the fundamental ethical values that are relevant for guiding the conduct of genetics research and forming ethical relationships among its participants include: truthfulness, loyality, trustworthiness and fidelity, stewardship, autonomy, respect for others, validation, nonmalfeasance (do no harm), beneficence, justice, and virtue. Truthfulness—telling the truth consistent with the reality of a situation, is essential for the scientists themselves and it is important for the other participants to remain open to the ideas and conclusions presented by investigators and for approaching the scientific ideal of objectivity by overcoming bias and self-interest. Because the public bases much of its behavior on scientific results, the falsification of results can lead to great harm. Loyalty—to one's profession and its codes of conduct, is essential for building trust. Trust and fidelity—in intentions, reliability, discharging duties and obligations, and honoring of colleagues, is essential for people to have confidence in research results. Stewardship—defined as the researcher's responsibility for safeguarding subjects, resources, institutions, and research data and results, is essential for the enterprise of science to succeed. Autonomy of subjects, patients, and other participants—defined as the ability to be free and self-governing in decision-making, leads to dignity, free inquiry, and creativity among participants and is essential to ensure respect for the dignity of research participants and their uncoerced consent to participate. Respect for others—loving one's neighbors as one loves one's self, is essential for honoring others' autonomy and for giving them their due. Validation—the scientist's dual obligation to make sure that the findings are verified and reproducible prior to publishing and prior to being given to subjects or those who are responsible for their care, is essential for according others respect and for preventing the doing of harm. Nonmalfeasance—avoiding doing harm and placing proper constraints on the power of knowledge, is essential to respect the humanity and dignity of all research participants. Beneficence—providing benefits, balancing benefits against risks, and using science to secure improvement in individuals and society, is an important goal of genetics research in particular and of research in general. It is also a major value of all medical ethics and bioethics. Justice—to see that benefits, costs, and risks are distributed among all participants fairly, is essential for the enterprise of science to fulfill its role in society, especially a democratic society. Virtue—aspiring to be a "good" scientist, characteristics of a moral agent such as courage, temperance, prudence, justice, honesty, and so on, is essential for ensuring that the scientist's motives and character are of the highest moral quality. For example, the most reliable protection for research subjects is provided by researchers who are informed, conscientious, compassionate, and responsible, that is, virtuous.

III. ETHICAL ISSUES ENCOUNTERED DURING EACH RESEARCH PROCESS

A. Problem Definition and Funding

A research agenda is a manifestation of human values. Major ethical questions generated during this stage in genetic research include: Who sets the agenda? What form does it take?

In the early days individual scientists pursuing their own curiosity generally selected the research topics to be studied. As the amount of resources required to conduct both field and laboratory genetics research has increased, however, governments, private foundations, and more recently private business enterprises have played a more central role. In the United States programs managed by the National Institutes of Health (NIH), the Department of Energy (DOE), and the Department of Defense (DOD) have become the primary sources of funds; and, hence, they are highly influential in setting the agenda. In one enlightened set of events, an examination of ethical issues has been a part of the U.S.'s Human Genome Project, funded by NIH and DOE, since its inception. Under the influence of its first director, James Watson, about 3% of its annual budget is devoted to the study of ethical, legal, and social implications under a program whose acronym is "ELSI". (ELSI currently receives about 5% of the budget.) This is one of the first instances in history of a program dedicated to studying the ethical implications and consequences of basic research prospectively and, hopefully, preemptively.

For some specific kinds of genetic diseases, private foundations, such as the American Heart Association,

Muscular Dystrophy Association, and Susan G. Koman Foundation for Breast Cancer, constitute alternative sources of research funding. Each of these foundations funds research aimed at decreasing the mortality and morbidity of given diseases. Both governments and foundations, with input from scientists, however, generally set the overarching agenda and then evaluate individual scientist's project proposals according to the guidelines they establish. The guidelines are usually based on political considerations and personal preferences. Thus, during the process of program guideline development important stakeholders' needs, such as patients with or without a given disease, could be overridden. Moreover, by responding to these programs and their guidelines in order to get support for their research, scientists often must give up research ideas in other areas which they think are more valuable.

For example, a group on concerned families whose members have a history of a disease called dysautonomia found that the affliction was of little scientific interest to researchers. Dysautonomia is degenerative neurological disease that occurs predominantly among Ashkenazi Jews and is currently incurable. Because its affected population was rather small, it did not capture the attention of large public granting agencies. (The disease results from inheriting a recessive gene found in about 1 in 30 Ashkenazis. Thus, the chances both members of an Ashkenazi couple will carry the mutated allele are about 1 in 900 ($1/30 \times 1/30$). Based on Mendel's formula, there is a 1 in 4 chance that each child born to the couple will inherit copies of the gene from both parents and, therefore, will have the disease. This yields an incidence of about 1 in 3600 within the Ashkenazi population.) People of Ashkenazi descent, however, make up a very small percentage of the U.S. population; so, what is a significant incidence of disease for them within their subgroup does not figure so prominently in the concerns for the nation as a whole. This may be one reason why very little research effort was devoted to the disorder. Nevertheless, these peoples' loved ones have been suffering from it; and, this led members of the concerned families to set up the Dysautonomia Foundation to support research into the disease. As of 1996 the markers for the gene have been identified and, if the necessary pedigree information is also available, a prenatal diagnostic test may reveal whether or not the fetus has dysautonomia. Some observers believe that these grassroots efforts make for the most effective and just overall allocation of research resources; others believe that they tend to dissipate valuable resources best used elsewhere.

The dysautonomia case is also an example of the problem of opportunity costs associated with the allocation of research funds and of finding the most effective organizational mechanisms for using them. These questions have been raised in genetics research since the early 1980s when national budget deficits placed political pressure on government allocations. The National Institutes of Health and the Department of Energy currently spend about $200 million annually on genetic research. Continual efforts to cut this budget have resulted in, among other things, an arrangement known as the cooperative research and development agreement (CRADA) between federal agencies and private enterprises. This is a joint agreement in which scientists, often university based, can participate without a legal conflict of interest. Some observers believe, however, that these arrangements divert research efforts away from basic research and redirect them toward producing more commercializable knowledge.

Genetic knowledge bestows power on its possessors. Because of their central role in all life, the results of research in genetics are a source of social and economic power, raising all of the attendant concerns people have about the moral and ethical use of power; and, it is doing this at all societal levels. Nationally, concerns about "Big Brother" have reemerged. As early as 1971 Joseph Fletcher observed of genetic research, "Even though its medical aim were only to gain control over the basic 'stuff' of our human constitution it could no doubt also be turned into an instrument of power" (1971. Ethical Aspects of Genetic Controls: Designed Genetic Changes in Man. *New England Journal of Medicine,* Vol. 285, pp. 776–783). Insurance companies and employers now have the power to select or deselect their customers or employees based on their genetic makeup. Individuals now have the power to select the genetically "best" mate for themselves or for their relatives and to decide whether or not to carry a pregnancy to termination.

Any research project that might serve to redistribute the social balance of power, therefore, should be examined very carefully. Increased private sector involvement is bringing this concern to public attention. As the profit-making potential of genetic tests and therapies has become more evident, commercial diagnostic labs, pharmaceutical companies, and other business firms, both established and newly created, have become a major source of research funding and a major user of research results. By 1994 the pace of research in the biotechnology industry was generating about one new gene or so a day, one new company per week, and one new drug a year for potential use in therapy. In 1996 the biotechnology industry consisted of more then 1300 companies, employed about 100,000 people, had sales of more than $7 billion, and had reached a market capitalization of more than $45 billion. Their total contribution to R&D was about $15 billion and was expected to rise to $50 billion by 2000. This rapid pace of innovation has increased the output of research; but, it has also created puzzling conflicts of interest among researchers, universities, the scientific community, the public, and business.

In a harbinger event, the Biogen Company was set up in early 1980s by Harvard professor Walter Gilbert, a Nobel Laureate and developer of DNA sequencing technology, under the assumption that the commercialization of his research was an appropriate extension of his work as a scientist. This and many other similar events since raise several important questions of ethics. Should the scientific agenda be shifted from seeking basic knowledge (the unversity's traditional role) to seeking commercializable, profitable knowledge (the private sector's role)? Should the public agenda for producing basic knowledge be augmented to include the development and production of usable genetic products that benefit the public? Because most basic research is funded by public tax dollars, the scientific establishment may have an ethical obligation to facilitate the return of the "fruits of their research to the public directly. Ultimately, this raises questions about the ethics of cooperative capitalism. Does competition among scientists working under grants from different companies jeopardize the open and free flow of scientific communization among the scientific community? What are the implications of the commercialization of a scientists' research for their obligations and allegiance to their universities or other employing research organizations? Because universities may also profit from controlling the publication of research, what obligations do they have to ensure the timely dissemination of research results produced by their faculty and staff? And, given that a university's faculty works on industry-sponsored research grants, does this tend to compromise the education of their students and research fellows?

B. Creating or Adopting a Research Model

Knowledge is conditioned by historical and cultural forces. As Thomas Kuhn has pointed out for science in general and Ludwik Fleck for medicine in particular, "paradigms," and all of the hidden, underlying assumptions in the theories or models used in research, are shaped by these social forces. These forces are at work when scientists create the theories, models, or frameworks within which their research problems are to be defined. Because these theories reflect human values, they, therefore, have moral and sometimes far-reaching implications.

During the 1930s, for example, research in genetics was thriving in the Soviet Union. Under the leadership of Academician T. D. Lysenko, head of the All-Union Institute of Genetics and Selection in Odessa, the research was conducted under the Marxist assumption that human beings could be changed by altering society. Furthermore, these newly acquired phenotypes could be inherited by subsequent generations. This Stalin-inspired theory is sometimes called "reactive environmental dogmatism" or the doctrine of acquired characteristics. The theory, which implies that genes are either irrelevant or totally mutable by environmental forces, was applied in 1942 to Russian agriculture with disastrous effects. Following the theory's edicts, Lysenko instructed Siberian peasant farmers to plant winter wheat, which survives only in mild southern climates, in the harsh northern ground, sprinkling the seed among the short, stiff stalks that remained in fields after harvesting the previous season's spring wheat (which only grows during the warmer summer months). The theory implied that the winter wheat would become acclimatized to its new environment and yields would soar. They did not, and a reign of famine ensued.

C. Developing Hypotheses

Whatever theory or model is adopted, it is used to derive the hypotheses and explanations to be tested or explored. Canons of free and open science inquiry require that any hypotheses arrived at this way should be open to investigation. Again, however, social and political forces can intercede. Some hypotheses may be too "hot" or culturally incorrect to study. One such hypothesis stems from the theory of biodeterminism that implies that human intelligence can be meaningfully abstracted and measured by a single number. This measurement can then be used to rank all people and all races on a linear, ratio scale of, as Stephen Jay Gould puts it, "intrinsic and unalterable mental worth." A recent controversial study in this tradition by Hernstein and Murray, entitled *The Bell Curve,* attempts to show that certain races are biologically, and hence genetically, inferior to others. The study has been attacked on moral as well as scientific grounds. Some people believe that it is simply unethical to explore hypotheses and explanations such as these; but, when all genes have been mapped and the gene frequencies present in each of various populations known people will be tempted to make judgments about "good" and "bad" genotypes as they are found in different racial groups. Is this ethically acceptable?

D. Data Specification

Unexpected ethical issues may arise during the process of specifying the kind of data and the number of observations that will be required and their levels of accuracy and precision. The results of research in genetics will be used making medical and policy decisions that affect the lives of people. The geneticist is responsible, in the first instance, for ensuring that the form of the data is analytically appropriate for testing the hypotheses under investigation. This requirement may be difficult to comply with because it may require access to pedigree information or subjects that are unavailable. Next, a decision must be made as to the number of observations to collect. Statistical theory is used to project the minimal number required; but economics and availability always play a pivotal role. It is often the case that the cost of acquiring data increases exponentially with the number of observations, especially after some modest number is exceeded and local availability is exhausted. The judgments researchers make at this juncture may carry many future consequences. Peer review of scientific results is one safeguard against the most disastrous of these consequences; but, it is not infallible.

E. Selection of Subjects

Many human values relate to the subjects that are used for genetics research. The questions—"What research is permissible with certain subjects, especially human subjects?" and "How are subjects to be selected?—are paramount during this phase. Considerations may be divided into three parts: dead material, plants and animals, and human beings. With respect to dead material, many research studies benefit greatly from the use of surgical samples archived in hospital pathology labs. But, this practice violates some peoples's beliefs. In some cultures and among some peoples there is a strong belief that a being's spirit remains intact long after the body has ceased to function. Hence, harm can be done to the organism after it is pronounced dead, unless proper cultural precautions are taken and proper respect is accorded the remains. This concern extends especially to inheritable material such as DNA and is complicated by the fact that the DNA of persons or organisms long deceased can reveal a great deal about them and their descendants, including those still living.

Similar concerns have also been voiced with respect to research using animals as subjects. For example, Peter Singer's *Animal Liberation,* published in 1975, argued for animal rights in research on the basis that they, too, show evidence of suffering, that they are aware of the suffering, and that they are not expendable. Because so much genetics research has been done on fruit flies, mice, nematode worms, and other beings that reproduce rapidly in captivity these are not idle concerns for geneticists.

The selection of human subjects, however, presents the most compelling ethical issues. At this point the genetic researcher's role as a scientist comes into conflict with his role as a physician. As Leon Kass avers, "the physician must produce unswervingly the virtues of loyalty and fidelity to his patient." In contradistinction, the scientist is trying to determine the validity of a formally constructed hypothesis or answer a general scientific question. The ultimate goal of genetics research is to find (1) broad explanations about and (2) therapeutic modalities to treat *anyone* who happens to have certain conditions. Consequently, during a research project a "subject," having been converted from "someone in particular" to "anyone who happens to have this genotype or phenotype," becomes an anonymous "object," essentially a nonperson. This change of status begins as soon as the subject agrees to participate in a research project. Two great moral traditions also come into conflict here. One is Immanuel Kant's view of human beings as bearers of dignity and therefore not to be treated as means only to a researcher's or society's ends. It argues against the "anyone" subject treatment in experiments. The other is the utilitarianism in the tradition of Jeremy Bentham and J. S. Mill that seeks to find the greatest good for the greatest number and, thereby, allows the researcher to make defensible trade-offs among people in its pleasure (benefit)/pain (cost) calculus. Whichever tradition prevails one minimal obligation overrides all others: there is a generally accepted moral imperative not to treat people *solely* as anonymous subjects. This has an important history.

The Nuremberg War Crimes Trials at the end of World War II revealed that prisoners of war and citizens were forced to participate in experiments that either maimed or killed many of them. At Dachau concentration camp, for example, in 1943 the German military placed subjects in very low-pressure chambers and in tanks filled with ice water to determine the limits of their endurance and existence. In other concentration camps subjects were purposefully inflicted with different types of wounds and with malaria, typhus, yellow fever, and other diseases to learn more about the afflictions and their possible treatments. The outrage at these revelations resulted in The Nuremberg Code on 1946, which established that the voluntary consent of a human subject to an experiment was absolutely essential. This was followed by the Helsinki Declarations of 1964 and 1975 which set the following basic principle: Every biomedical research project involving human subjects should be preceded by careful assessment of predictable risks in comparison with foreseeable benefits to the subject or others. Concern for the subject must always prevail over the interests of science and society. Disclosure of the Tuskegee syphilis study and San Antonio contraception study among others in the United States served to reinforce the needs for these codes. In these cases, the researchers' duty of beneficence was obviously violated and the subjects were precluded from achieving any sense of autonomy. These codes require that special attention be given to the selection of children, prisoners, or other people in positions of lesser power as subjects and has led to the development of protocols and principles of informed consent discussed in the next section. While these historical cases seem obviously unethical by modern research standards, similar, although perhaps more subtle, concerns can be raised about contemporary genetics research. For example, should genetic tests be administered to subjects to study diseases for which there is no known intervention?

F. Specifying Protocols for Data Collection

A typical research project involving human subjects and aimed at understanding a specific gene or gene marker might include the following steps. It begins by mailing requests to participate to members of a population chosen for its relevance to the phenotypes or mutations under study. Those who ignore or refuse the request are dropped. Consent (i.e., informed consent) documents are sent to those who agree to participate and a baseline survey is administered to them. Upon receipt of the survey a genetic counseling session is held. Psychological screening at this point may result in some subjects declining to continue, being deferred, or dropped. Blood is then drawn from the subjects thus selected and its DNA is analyzed. In general, two outcomes are possible at this point: The tests reveal that the subject is either a carrier or a noncarrier. Based on the outcome genetic, psychological, surgical, oncological, or other relevant forms of counseling are made available to both classes of subjects. If the experiment involves a therapy, then subjects are assigned, in some cases randomly, to groups, some of which receive the therapy to be tested while the other group receives a placebo or perhaps an unsatisfactory treatment.

The research data generated by projects of this kind should be collected with strict adherence to previously approved protocols, both for animal and human research. While each project presents its own individual problems, the following guidelines should provide some basic protections for the subjects: All subjects receive genetic counseling before and after genetic testing; psychiatric screening typically before and counseling by a family therapist afterward, depending on the results of the tests. Subjects are encouraged to bring a nonkindred support person to the sessions. Strict confidentiality is maintained. DNA analysis is undertaken with constant attention to accuracy by using a clinical diagnostic laboratory approved by an appropriate agency. At any time during the research the subject is free to withdraw (i.e., informed nonconsent). And, most importantly, the subject gives his or her informed consent.

Informed consent involves more than just having subjects sign forms or share with researchers in decision-making processes involving their participation in the research. It should be based on the concept of autonomous authorization by the subjects. Among the criteria for autonomous authorization are: subjects' substantial understanding of the research and its possible harms, benefits and risks; a lack of coercion or control by others (that is, no elements of force, fraud, deceit, duress, overreaching, or other ulterior form of constraint or coercion); and, full compliance with social and legal rules of consent. In order to achieve this the researcher must ensure that each subject satisfies the following criteria: he or she is competent; is disclosed and receives adequate information about the plan of the research; that the disclosure is understood clearly as to what was asserted, the nature of the procedures involved, the foreseeable consequences, and possible outcomes that might follow, and the distinction between being a subject for research and being a patient for health care. So informed, the subject voluntarily agrees to participate according to the plan of the research; gives consent by making an overt decision to participate; and formally authorizes the plan of research. The American Society of Clinical Oncology, for example, recommends that prior to conducting genetic testing the following items should be discussed with each subject:

1. Information on the specific test being performed.
2. Implications of a positive and negative result.
3. Possibility that the test will not be informative.
4. Options for risk estimation with genetic testing.
5. Risk of passing a mutation to children.

6. Technical accuracy of the test.
7. Fees involved in testing and counseling.
8. Risks of psychological distress.
9. Risks of insurance or employer discrimination.
10. Confidentially issues.
11. Options and limitations of medical surveillance and screening following testing.

Regardless of the particular protocol used, it should be evaluated by a group of peers from within the investigator's institution. Since July 1966 all parties receiving funding from NIH have been required to submit their protocols to a panel of peers known as an Institutional Review Board. (IRB) The proposed protocols and plan of research must be described to the IRB so that they can determine the risks to subjects, estimate the likely benefits to both the subjects involved and society at large, and determine whether or not the overall benefits outweigh the risks.

One especially challenging ethical issue for researchers and IRBs to resolve involves deception or intentional nondisclosure of facts to subjects. Many research design plans use techniques such as randomized trials or blind or double-blind treatment in which neither the researchers or the subjects know which particular treatment or "control" group each subject is assigned to. This technique eliminates several major sources of bias and thereby improves the scientific validity of the results. But because the subject is not fully informed, blind experiments may generate subject anxiety or even inflict harm on a subject and they might also compromise the requirement of informed consent. In particular, the researcher qua physician's obligation to provide the very best treatment for his patient comes into conflict with the researcher qua scientist's obligation to produce valid information and make it available for the benefit of society. Only if the researcher is in a state of equipoise—that is, he believes that the severity and likelihood of harm and good are evenly balanced for either treatment—are randomization and blind trials ethically acceptable without dispute. Even if it is decided that it is ethically acceptable to begin a study it may become ethically problematic to continue. This issue of ethical stopping rules is discussed in the next section.

The researchers and their staffs may also be at risk and they deserve as much attention as the subjects. Biological and physical safeguards should be used in all DNA research, especially if new organisms are involved. Biological barriers include bacterial hosts that will not survive in the material being tested and vectors able to grow only in specific hosts. Physical barriers include the use of gloves, goggles, hoods, clean rooms, filters, and other containment technologies. Both types of barriers should be deployed with a set of enforced organizational rules and procedures designed to protect the safety of all research workers. In general, the principles of informed consent indicate that all researchers and their staffs should be fully informed about the hazards involved before they agree to work on a project; they should be properly trained in safety and containment procedures, and they should be monitored throughout the experiment for exposure to dangerous substances and for their general health.

G. Collecting Data According to Protocols

The ethical planning of a research project must be followed by the ethical management of its execution. At a minimum this requires ensuring that the study is run and the data are collected according to the protocols. This means that all researchers and their staffs must have appropriate training and education in ethics as well as in the project's protocols. They must also develop a deep concern for the integrity of the data and for its potential impact on the subjects. Constant monitoring of the subjects and their well-being is essential and this raises the issue of ethical stopping rules. In some kinds of studies, such as those for cancer or AIDS, subjects may exhibit serious side effects and the researcher has to "unblind" the experiment to provide proper treatment. If blind or random assignment is stopped, the scientific value of the study may be lost and the participation of the other subjects wasted. Moreover, the scientist's qua physician's responsibility to the subjects changes dynamically as the results of the experiment emerge. Once a researcher, for example, has formed a view about a new treatment or the condition of a subject—good or bad—should the blindness and randomization be continued? The obligation of beneficence requires that as soon as a researcher believes that he can help the subject he should intercede and provide the help. Trials are, also, usually halted if the data show that there is only a small likelihood, as a function of statistical variation or the standard deviation—say 0.01 or 0.05—that the results are due to chance rather than a true relationship. At this point the efficacy or safety (or lack thereof) of the treatment or the statistical generalizations is established. If there are too few observations made to reach this point then the study will lack statistical significance and scientific validity. However, if more observations are made, say to improve the statistical significance, this will result in delays in making the knowledge available and in securing its benefits.

H. Data Transmission

There is an important intermediate, and often overlooked, step between collecting and analyzing research data. Observations acquired from disparate points must be brought together and delivered to the central point at which they will be analyzed. Also, biological samples, such as DNA, are often shared by more than one investigator and may be examined in different research laboratories within the same or different institutions. This creates a point of vulnerability. Data security and confidentially requirements are in danger of being breached. Consequently, values for accuracy and reliability are important; staff training is essential; and, adequate resources must be allocated to the job.

I. Analyzing Data

There is a temptation for researchers to want to prove their hypothesis and to produce publishable results, perhaps even pathbreaking results. Among other things, receiving substantial project grants and academic promotions depend on it. Consequently the researcher's values for scientific integrity and truthtelling are put to the test. Sometimes the researcher fails. In 1981 in a highly publicized case John Darsee of the Harvard Medical School admitted to falsifying the results in one of his research papers, presumably to continue to get grants and to keep his research scientist job. Subsequent investigations uncovered a troubling fact. Not only had Darsee been dishonest; but, his co-authors and peers had failed to detect the flaws before it was published. They, too, bore a responsibility for scientific integrity and their failure to discharge it seriously compromised the system of guarantorship upon which integrity is based.

These concerns were magnified in a case *The New York Times* questioned might be "A Scientific Watergate?" Thereza Imanishi-Kari of Tufts published a paper in a 1986 issue of *Cell* concerning genetic influences on the immune system that claimed to show that inserting a gene from a foreign mouse into a certain, different strain of mice caused changes in the host mouse's stock of antibodies. Noted geneticist and Nobel laureate David Baltimore was a co-author. Dr. Margot O'Toole, a postdoctoral researcher in molecular biology at Tufts distrusted the results and openly questioned the validity of some of the analysis at the time. For this she was dismissed from her job. The case was brought

to the NIH and reached the floors of the U.S. Congress. Laboratory notebooks of the experiments were subpoenaed by the Secret Service, whose forensic studies of the notebook pages, inks, and counter tapes from assays of radio-labeled reagents tended to support the conclusion that some entries had been wrongly dated and possibly fabricated. The report of an NIH committee in 1990 found Imanishi-Kari guilty of "serious scientific misconduct," stating that she had repeatedly presented false and misleading information. O'Toole was praised for her dedication to the truth, her courage, and for blowing the whistle. But, these findings were appealed and in 1996 a panel of the Department of Health and Human Services ruled that the evidence did not support government's scientific misconduct case. Nevertheless, they found that the paper as a whole was "rife" with errors of all sorts and that Baltimore, although never accused of fabrication, as a co-author must share some of the responsibility.

Vigilance must be constant. Even the most highly regarded researchers can be victimized. Because a junior colleague had fabricated data, Dr. Francis Collins, who heads the Human Genome Project, decided to retract five research papers on the role of a defective gene in producing leukemia. An anonymous peer reviewer's observation that the data "suggested intentional deception" caused Collins to investigate and discover the source of the fabrication. Collins concludes that "there is no fail-safe way to prevent this kind of occurrence if a capable, bright, motivated trainee is determined to fabricate data in a deceptive and intentional way, short of setting up a police state in your laboratory" (quoted from the *New York Times,* November 6, 1996). Collins' timely and full disclosure by means of a "Dear Colleague" letter served to reduce the negative impacts of the falsification.

Two ethical issues are put into relief by these cases: the temptation for scientific misconduct and the responsibility of peers. The guarantor of the results of most scientific inquiry is the agreement of the community of scientists. It is apparent in the Imaishi-Kari case that both her co-authors and the review panel at *Cell* failed to discharge this responsibility, whereas in the Collins case they did, albeit belatedly. This concern has resulted in the NIH and Alcohol, Drug Abuse and Mental Health Administration (ADAMHA) publishing a set of principles of scientific integrity to be given to staff and students at institutions receiving grants and encouraging the delivery of training programs to all researchers. Education in ethics for scientists and staff, whether informal or formal, is essential. Topics to be covered include responsible authorship, responsible reviewership, the recording and retention of data, conflict of interest, issues of human and animal experimentation, and professional standards and codes of conduct. The American Association for the Advancement of Science has also promoted the need for professional standards and codes of conduct.

J. Producing and Publishing the Research Results

The norms of science call for open and free inquiry and the free exchange of information and materials among scientists. This includes publishing results promptly and making them available publicly, usually via academic journals. Individual scientists, however, sometimes have incentives to either delay publication in order to cash in on the findings beforehand or to patent the results. These problems will be exacerbated in the near future. It is likely that genetics research in general and the Human Genome Project in particular will be the source of increasing amounts of basic information that can be used for targeting new drugs and genetic therapies. This will become the mainstay of the pharmaceutical industry. Investment and commercial application of the discoveries often requires protection of the intellectual property rights involved by means of patents. This raises the questions: Who owns the data and the research results: scientists, business, universities, the public, others? Can they be patented? By sequencing any fragments of DNA and relating the results to Human Genome maps it is possible to discover new genes and determine their functions, even if they are arbitrary fragments of genes with no known use. Should an individual or corporation be able to lay claim to any such sequence? In 1991 the NIH filed for four patents for fragments of gene sequences that had been obtained from copies of DNA using rather standard techniques. The applications were rejected by the U.S. Patent Office in part because they failed to meet the main criteria for patentability—innovation or novelty, commercial utility, and being nonobvious. But, as more uses of genetic research become evident, it can be expected that the pressure to patent will continue. The issues of publication and ownership also relate directly to some of the ethical issues that emerge during the storage and retrieval of research information.

K. Storage and Retrieval of Research Information

Several crucial issues arise with respect to the storage and retrieval of genetic materials and research results.

Because genetic materials such as DNA splices or sperm can be used to alter life the highest regard must be given to their security and safety. People will be tempted to use them for purposes other then those intended when they were collected. For example, in a recent case the University of California, Irvine, is being sued because some donors' sperm allegedly was substituted for others. DNA tests on the children conceived in vitro support the allegation. It is contended that the university failed to install adequate security measures.

Respecting subjects' privacy is another issue. Much of the genetically relevant information collected about subjects and the results of studies conducted on them reveals considerable intimacies about the subjects and their families, information people most generally want to keep private. Safeguarding against the unwanted disclosure of private information has always been a problem, even prior to the development of molecular biology. Lay and professional people have always drawn anecdotal conclusions about a person's genotype from the phenotype he or she manifests and from the traits of relatives. The results of the new genetic tests, however, provide far more comprehensive and reliable information about a person than this; and, they can be used for genetic discrimination or stigmatization. Protection against this requires norms of confidentially on the part of researchers. The scientific investigator/subject relationship is akin to the physician/patient relationship. It must be based on trust and a due respect for the autonomy of the subject; not only as a moral obligation, but also because the continuance of the scientific enterprise and the willing participation of subjects requires it. This means that, in general, genetic information should be kept materially secure from an unwanted physical intrusion and institutionally secure from unwarranted acquisition by means of procedures to safeguard confidentiality.

In practice this may be difficult to achieve. Insurers and employers have strong motivations to acquire the data. Even acceding to seemingly appropriate requests can lead to unanticipated disclosures. In one case the attending physician requested genetic information about his patient from members of a genetics research project he knew the patient and her family had participated in. The research team released the information under strictures of confidentiality because they believed that the information would be used to help the patient. The physician accepted the information in good faith and based his diagnosis, in part, on it; but, not fully understanding the consequences of his actions, he recorded the genetic test results in the patient's bedside chart. This made it semipublic information and soon nurses, other medical personal, insurers, and others were privileged to information about the woman that was intended to be restricted only to the physician's and the researchers' eyes.

A similar issue arises when researchers publish their results. Usually group statistics are presented covering a large enough number of subjects to protect their anonymity. But sometimes small samples are used or unique individual cases are discussed using pseudonyms. In these cases, although the researchers attempt to maintain anonymity, it is sometimes possible with the use of little additional knowledge to unveil the subjects' true identity.

A new scientific discipline called "bioinformatics" has been created to meet the technical challenges of storing and sorting genetic information and materials. This discipline, too, must find its ethical base. The fundamental moral quandary facing bioinfomaticians and genetic researchers with respect to the storage and retrieval of genetic information and material is challenging. It pits the researchers' scientific needs to participate fully in the democratization of genetic science and to create a collegial partnership in the production of knowledge—one that may also serve his or her own self-interests for acclaim or promotion—against the subjects' rights to privacy and autonomy.

L. Using Genetic Research Results

The value in genetics research, and hence the source of many of the ethical issues it engenders, lies in the uses to which it can be put, good and bad, just or unjust. The possible applications of the research results are quite numerous and growing rapidly as the pace of research increases. They can be classified into five general categories: diagnosis, prediction, identification, therapy, and enhancement.

1. Diagnosis

Genetic research results are used to develop genetic tests. The diagnostic use of genetic testing occurs either (1) when a particular phenotype is observed, usually a disease or an abnormality, and the investigator wants to determine its genetic origins, that is, its genotype, in the hopes of providing useful information to the patient; or, (2) when a particular individual is asymptomatic but wants to know what diseases he or she may be susceptible to. Fragments of a subject's DNA are isolated and used to determine how the sequence of base pairs he or she carries compare with normal and mutant alleles at the loci from which the fragments were extracted. This information is used to determine

the disease's genetic causes or, when used in conjunction with other diagnostic techniques, to reduce the ambiguity in diagnosis. Diseases such as Tay-Sachs, cystic fibrosis, and sickle-cell anemia can be diagnosed in this way. In all of these clinical symptoms are apparent early in childhood. Diagnostic results may thus serve as the basis for a therapy. While this is a powerful tool the ethical issues it engenders are similar to those addressed by medical ethics in general.

2. Prediction

Prediction involves determining the probability that a particular phenotype will occur in the future given that the subject has been diagnosed as having a specific genotype. Predictive uses of genetic information include protecting individuals from getting illnesses to which they are genetically predisposed and preventing the transmission of genetic predisposition to the next generation. On the surface these are laudable goals but reaching for them also generates several types of difficult ethical issues. First, because the occurrence of a phenotype is the result of the workings of the genotype and the environment as they interact over time, calculating the probabilities and producing morbidity tables is an error-prone activity, potentially leading to harmful, inaccurate conclusions. The likelihood of producing false positives or false negatives is increased. Second, and most significantly, more morally questionable actions stem from prediction than from diagnosis. Genetic predictions play a prominent role in the ethical issues of the use and abuse of genetic testing in the workplace, by insurance companies, for other types of carrier testing, and to make abortion decisions. For example, concern has been expressed that employers will seek genetic information about current or prospective employees and use it to deny them jobs. Similar concerns are expressed that insurance companies will use genetic information to deny people health care or life insurance. In these cases an individual's rights are placed in opposition to those of the employing organization or insurance company.

3. Identification

Polymerase chain reaction (PCR) makes it possible to multiply small quantities of DNA into large quantities relatively easily and inexpensively. This means that DNA samples found in trace materials such as hair, blood, or semen can be reproduced and compared with DNA samples deposited in a master databank and used to identify individuals by means of genetic "fingerprinting." The forensic use of the technique using items picked up at a crime scene is relatively well established.

In fact, judges are being educated in its scientific underpinnings. It is fairly well established that DNA test can be used effectively to exclude an individual from being the person whose DNA was tested; but, because it involves many complex probability calculations and the assumption that a combination of specific repetitive DNA sequences from the person tested is very unlikely to match the DNA of anyone else, an error-free, positive identification is more difficult to obtain. The ethical issues created by forensic use are similar to those found with the use of other criminal evidence generating techniques. The possible use of genetic fingerprinting for other forms of identification raise important ethical issues of informed consent and invasion of privacy. The possibility of abuse of DNA information is one reason many people are leery of contributing to DNA banks and why security and confidentiality are such important factors.

4. Therapy

Genetic research informs and enables two types of therapy: drug and genetic. Drug therapy is primarily used to cure a disease although some drugs are also used as a preventive measure. Drugs are essentially foreign substances that, when introduced into the body, have a biological effect. New drug therapies are developed by figuring out what genotypes are at the root of a particular phenotype. A drug then is developed that targets the relevant genes, or the proteins for which they are the blueprint, and alters or suppresses the genes' activity. Marketing these drugs is a major business opportunity for pharmaceutical firms and this is one of the reasons the firms want to set the research agenda for genetic research and own or control its results. The ethical issues raised by drug therapy, however, are similar to those raised by other forms of pharmacology. Gene therapy, in contradistinction, introduces normal genes into a subject's cell nuclei in order to repair, replace, or compensate for the defective or mutilated allele. These genes may subsequently be inherited by the recipient's offspring. Gene therapy can be used to cure a disease; but, it also creates a temptation to enhance a person's own capacities or those of his or her children. Thus, gene therapy raises many new ethical issues.

5. Enhancement

The broad term used to describe the goal of enhancing the human condition by means of genetic manipulation is called *eugenics*. Positive eugenics uses the results of genetic research to produce people with "superior" phenotypes; negative eugenics seeks to improve the human condition by eliminating biologically "inferior" people or unwanted clusters of phenotypes from the population. Genetic engineering is based on several evolving science-based techniques by which these goals are achieved. In Benedikt Hårlin's words both of these forms of enhancement must be based on crucial scientific and value judgments about what are "normal and abnormal, acceptable and unacceptable, viable and non-viable forms of the genetic make-up of individual human beings before and after birth." In a democratic and market-oriented society many eugenic decisions are made by individuals themselves, resulting in a kind of "homemade" eugenics, one often favoring the wealthy or powerful. In a totalitarian or authoritarian society despots—a Hitler or a Stalin—make the decisions and can result in genocide as well as attempts to create a super race.

The risks in doing this have been captured well by Monette Vaquin: "Today, astounding paradox, the generation following Nazism is giving the world the tools of eugenics beyond the wildest Hitlerian dreams. It is as if the unthinkable of the generation of the fathers haunted the discoveries of the sons. Scientists of tomorrow will have a power that exceeds all the powers known to mankind: that of manipulating the genome. Who can say for sure that it will be used only for the avoidance of hereditary illnesses?"

IV. CHALLENGES TO OUR UNDERSTANDING OF OURSELVES AS HUMAN BEINGS AND SOCIETY

The questions: Who are we as human beings? What is the meaning of life? What is a "good" or "superior" human being? What is a society, a community? What are its members' responsibilities to it? They have motivated much of scientific and ethical inquiry from the beginning. Genetics research brings them even more prominently into the forefront. It promises to take much of the mystery and, perhaps, even the variety out of life. New views of nature are also evolving. Part of the mystery and, hence, motivation, of the human condition is a striving for self-discovery, personal expression, and actualization. We do not know what we might become and many of us have faith that we can shape the process of becoming who we want to be. Genetic research challenges these beliefs. Genetic predispositions—our genotypes, greatly condition our physical makeup as expressed throughout our lives and, to some extent, our traits and characteristics—our phenotypes. All is not in our own hands. But, as the discussion above of the producer/product relationship between genotype/ phenotype describes, all is not out of our hands, either. The issues of applied ethics concerning the creation and maintenance of a nurturing and supporting environment are still with us. The challenges presented by genetics research to applied ethics are to accept with serenity what is out of our ability to change and to have the wisdom and courage to change those things we can that will lead to a healthier society and to not intercede when improvement is not likely to be forthcoming or harms will result.

As the discussion of eugenics suggests, there is a great temptation for members of society to use the results of genetics research to abort or otherwise eliminate human beings or other organisms whose genetic makeup leads to undesirable phenotypes; or, to discriminate against and stigmatize them; or, to use the new genetic technologies to attenuate their effects by means of drug therapy; or to reconstitute a person's or other organism's genome by means of gene therapy or genetic engineering. Some of these actions, such as eliminating fatal inherited diseases, may be morally justifiable. Others, such as using genetic therapy for cosmetic purposes, is likely not. Many such possible actions will remain morally ambiguous.

One crucial element in the moral evaluation of genetics research and its uses is our concept of community. In *Earthwalk,* (1974) Philip Slader draws a key distinction between a network and a community. At one end of a continuum a network is a group of homogeneous individuals who take pride in their commonalities. At the other end is a community, which is composed of a rather heterogeneous group of people—young and old, rich and poor, large and small, sick and healthy, the wise old man, the village idiot, butcher, baker, candlestickmaker and the like. Communities celebrate their differences. And, they draw strength and a sense of individuality from them. The temptation to use genetics research to alter our fates serves to move society from its historical and natural foundations in community toward those of a network. This not only has implications for contemporary moral values, it has implications for the long-term survival of the human species itself, perhaps the greatest value of all. It reduces variety in the gene pool and, thereby, may eliminate a vital, yet currently unrecognized, genetic response to some new environmental force unfolded by Darwinian evolution.

Not only can genetics research lead to a change in the structure of community, it can also lead to a change in an individual's sense of their roles and responsibility to it. Too strong a belief in genetic determinism will cause people to eschew personal responsibility. "My genes made me do it!" The abiding concerns of applied ethics—virtue and good motives for one's actions, compliance with one's duties, and choosing acts that result in the overall greatest social happiness—require that every moral agent assume responsibility for his or her actions. The findings of genetics research in general and of the studies and tests performed on an individual should not be used to rob human beings of that most fundamental of human characteristics—responsibility.

Also See the Following Articles

BIOTECHNOLOGY • EUGENICS • GENETIC ENGINEERING • GENOME ANALYSIS • HUMAN RESEARCH SUBJECTS, SELECTION OF • RESEARCH ETHICS • SCIENTIFIC PUBLISHING

Bibliography

For an in depth treatment of the systems approach to scientific inquiry and of information handling as used in this article see:

Churchman, C. W. (1971). *The design of inquiring systems: Basic concepts of systems and organization.* New York: Basic Books.

Mason, R. O., Mason, F. M., & Culnan, M. J. (1995). *The ethics of information management.* Thousand Oaks, CA: Sage.

Some relevant readings in genetics research include:

Bodmer, W., & Mckie, R. (1994). *The book of man: The Human Genome Project and the quest to discover our genetic heritage.* New York: Scribner.

Cook-Deegan, R. (1994). *The gene wars: Science, politics, and the Human Genome Project;* New York: W. W. Norton.

Kitcher, P. (1996). *The lives to come: The genetic revolution and human possibilities;* New York: Simon & Schuster.

Lyon, J., & Gorner, P. (1995). *Altered fates: Gene therapy and the retooling of human life.* New York: W. W. Norton.

Murphy, T. F., & Lappe, M. A. (1994). *Justice and the Human Genome Project:* Berkeley: University of California Press.

Rosenberg, S. A. (1992). *The transformed cell: Unlocking the mysteries of cancer;* New York: Avon.

Watson, J. D. (1968). *The double helix.* New York: Penguin.

Related readings in medical ethics and bioethics may be found in:

Beauchamp, T. L., & Childress, J. F. (1994). *Principles of biomedical ethics* (4th Ed.). New York: Oxford University Press.

Bulger, R. E. (Ed.) (1993). *The ethical dimensions of the biological sciences.* Cambridge: Cambridge University Press.

Engelhardt, H. T., Jr. (1986). *The foundations of bioethics.* New York: Oxford University Press.

Faden, R. R., & Beauchamp, T. L. (1986). *A history and theory of informed consent.* New York: Oxford University Press.

Kass, L. R. (1985). *Toward a more natural science: Biology and human affairs.* New York: The Free Press.

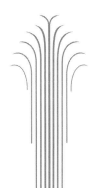

GENETICS AND BEHAVIOR

Garland E. Allen
Washington University

GLOSSARY

genetic marker Any detectable element at the genetic level (chromosome, segment of DNA) that can be followed in successive generations within a breeding group (family lines). Chromosomal markers include particular band patterns, extra segments, knobs, or other distinguishable features of chromosome morphology that can be observed (microscopically); molecular markers can be identified indirectly by extracting and separating components of an organism's DNA (using such separatory techniques as gel electrophoresis). The appearance of markers is correlated with the appearance of phenotypes (see below) in given breeding lines to suggest the possible existence, or location of genes for the trait in question. Markers do not, however, mean that genes for the trait necessarily exist, or are located at the position in the genome occupied by the marker itself.

genome A general term for the totality of genetic information contained within an organism, or a species. Thus, geneticists speak of the genome of a particular individual, meaning the genes carried by that individual, or of a whole population, such as the human genome.

genotype The basic genetic elements (genes, DNA segments) inherited by an individual from its parents and capable of being passed on to its offspring. The genotype is distinguished from the phenotype (see below), or outward appearance of the organism as it develops.

phenotype The appearance of an organism for a given trait (anatomical, physiological, behavioral), produced by an interaction between the organism's genotype and the environment in which the organism developed. Phenotype, as opposed to genotype, cannot be directly passed on to an individual's descendants.

polymorphism The occurrence of varying forms of a trait, gene, or marker within a population. Most complex traits in animal, plant and human populations are polymorphic (in humans, for example, hair color, eye color, blood groups, etc).

BEHAVIOR GENETICS is a field of the biological sciences that seeks to elucidate the genetic, or inherited, components of animal behavior. The field at present encompasses a large group of researchers whose focus is behavior in nonhuman animals, ranging from one-celled protozoa to nonhuman primates. A somewhat smaller group of researchers focuses primarily on hu-

Copyright © 1998 by Academic Press. All rights of reproduction in any form reserved.

man behavior where, for practical and ethical reasons, genetic data cannot be obtained by the usual methods (planned breeding and rigorous control of environmental conditions in which offspring develop).

I. INTRODUCTION

Most workers in the field of behavior genetics, regardless of the organism(s) with which they work, harbor some hopes that their work will throw light on general aspects of human behavior and its origins. However, many are highly skeptical of naive attempts to reason by analogy from other animals to human beings, or to directly apply their findings in non-human species to humans. This schism has plagued the field of behavior genetics for a century or more, and manifested itself overtly in a split within the Behavior Genetics Society (an international professional organization) in 1995. Partly as a result of growing distrust of exaggerated claims for a genetic basis of many human personality and behavioral traits, and partly in protest against remarks made by the president of the Society at the annual meeting in that year (he claimed that behavior genetic studies might well show that African Americans were genetically inferior to Caucasians in intelligence), a number of researchers left the Society to form a new organization that would focus on studies of nonhuman animals. Despite these controversies, however, the field of behavior genetics holds much potential for elucidating the evolution and adaptive significance of behavior in many animal species.

Behavior genetics gains much of its interest and controversy when applied to human behavior for a number of reasons. First, unequivocal data are difficult to come by, and thus require considerable interpretation and qualification. Second, past history has shown that claims about the genetic causes of specific behaviors (usually what were considered undesirable behaviors) have often been put to misuse, as in justification of genocide, or restricting the reproduction of individuals or families claimed to harbor genetic defects in their behavior. Third, claims about the genetic basis of behavior today have obvious and unavoidable implications for social policy. For example, researchers do not study the possible genetic basis of such conditions as alcoholism or manic depression, for purely abstract purposes; the ultimate aim is eventually to reduce the amount of overt alcoholism or depression in society as well as to help individuals who suffer from these behavioral conditions.

However, genetic claims about behavioral (as well as all other) traits have almost always been accompanied by the underlying assumption that what is genetic cannot be changed: "Genes are destiny," as this view is sometimes characterized. Behavior genetic claims thus raise a host of ethical and social issues, all of which revolve around the question of how society should react to individuals diagnosed with any one of a number of behavioral/personality traits that are claimed to have a significant genetic basis. Most importantly, what social or legislative policies should or should not be adopted with regard to the perpetuation of such traits? In the past, it has been claimed that so-called genetically defective individuals should be (1) sterilized, (2) hospitalized, (3) forbidden to marry, (4) refused immigration status, (5) treated with drugs or other external "therapies", and so on. An even deeper question arises about the extent to which social, moral and ethical decisions should be based on genetic (or any scientific) claims. Science may inform by presenting information, but can or should it dictate policy? The complex moral and ethical issues thus raised by behavior genetics, along with its often questionable, or at least highly controversial claims, has raised the question of whether research on such issues (the genetic basis of schizophrenia, criminality, compulsiveness, homosexuality, etc) should be supported at all. There is no agreement on this issue among researchers in the field or among ethicists and specialists in science policy. However, the issue is significant enough that calls for halting such research have been heard in recent years in the United States, the United Kingdom, and Germany. The reasoning behind such claims are discussed in Section IV.

II. HISTORICAL BACKGROUND

The question of why animals behave as they do—the broad similarities within species as well as the differences between species—has intrigued and perplexed naturalists and philosophers for centuries. Hippocrates (460?–377 b.c.) and Aristotle (384–322 b.c.) both wrote on animal behavior, developing the first Western notions of *instinct* as built-in or natural (as opposed to learned) behavior. In the Greek sense, instinct was seen as necessary for the survival of lower animals, but ascending the "Great Chain of Beings," an array of the world's organisms arranged from simplest to most complex showed, that as complexity of animal organization increased reliance on purely instinctual behavior decreased, with learning becoming a more dominant aspect of behavior. For the ancients, humans showed only the most general kinds of instinctual behavior: self-protection and survival, maternal care, and sociality. In Greek terms, human beings were distinguished from other animals by their self-awareness, capacity to learn and engage in abstract thought (their "rational soul" in Aristotelian terms). Conversely, the lower an animal ranged on the "Chain of Beings," the more it relied on instinctual, or built-in behavior.

Among the first and most thorough treatments of instinct theory in terms of natural history can be found in Darwin's *On the Origin of Species* (1859) and (more explicitly) in *The Descent of Man* (1871) and *The Expression of Emotions in Animals and Man* (1872). Darwin emphasized that instincts had to be studied as behaviors arising from at the time unknown, but assumed, biological causes, and that this biological basis was shared by members of a species. Darwin made the further assumption that such behaviors were largely inherited, a view that was necessary for application of his theory of evolution by natural selection to the origin of instinct. According to Darwin, new instincts evolved through the action of natural selection on variations in previously existing instincts. In Darwin's sense, learned behaviors could become instinctual only if they gradually became inherited through repetition and were eventually incorporated into the species' germ plasm (he believed in a form of the inheritance of use and disuse of parts, including behaviors). Darwin also recognized that in higher animals instinctual behavior was often overlain by learned behavior. The adaptive value of instinctual behavior was that it provided an organism with a repertory of immediate, ready-made responses that enhanced its survival without having to go through the sometimes long and haphazard process of learning. At the same time, instinctual behaviors are not easily modified to fit new or complex circumstances; the ability to learn, and therefore modify, behavior to meet new circumstances could thus be seen as, ultimately, a more complex and "advanced" adaptation.

Darwin's ideas stimulated much work on the nature of instinct in the late-nineteenth and especially the twentieth centuries. With the rediscovery of Mendelian genetics in 1900, the study of what has come to be regarded as "behavior genetics" in the modern sense may be said to have begun. Mendel's work provided a predictive and experimentally based system by which to determine the pattern of inheritance of many kinds of traits. Although behavioral traits were not among the first to be examined by the new school of Mendelian genetics, after about 1910 there was a considerable attempt made to apply Mendel's work to a wide

variety of human behaviors. Numerous studies of the genetics of alcoholism, prostitution and sexual immorality, manic depression, criminality, feeblemindedness, musical ability, genius, sea-faringness, and the like abounded in the early decades of the century. Most were based on naive applications of Mendelian principles to family pedigree analyses, but they stimulated a whole movement known as *eugenics*, or the attempt to determine the hereditary basis of human social and behavioral traits with an eye to eliminating "undesirable" and promoting "desirable" traits within society. On these grounds, eugenicists succeeded in passing legislation in many countries of western Europe and the United States that would ban immigration or provide for the compulsory sterilization of individuals deemed genetically defective in a variety of social behaviors.

The rise of *behaviorism* in psychology during the first decades of the twentieth century deflected interest from the study of instinct, focusing rather on learned or conditioned behavior. Behaviorists such as John B. Watson (1878–1958) and B. F. Skinner (1904–1990) assumed that organisms (at least higher vertebrates, including humans) began life with a minimum of inherited behavior, with most of their specific responses being learned by repetitive conditioning. For example, while the general behavior associated with foraging, or search for food, might be called instinctual (animals do not have to be taught to want food and to look for it), the process of finding food on a daily basis, in specific localities, using specific techniques and activities were all learned. Thus, until the 1930s, the study of instinctual behavior in animal models and its possible genetic components, was pursued by relatively few biologists or psychologists.

One of the important developments stimulating work in the genetics of behavior was the growth of a field of biology known as *ethology* in the interwar and especially post-World War II era. Ethology, pioneered by such investigators as Konrad Lorenz (1903–1989) in Germany, Nikolaas Tinbergen (1907–1988) in the Netherlands and later Great Britain, and Daniel Lehrman in the United States, was the attempt to study animal behavior from an observational and comparative point of view, with the aim to understanding the evolution of particular behaviors. Ethologists made detailed studies of animal behavior such as mating, feeding, defense, territoriality, aggression, parental care, among others, and attempted to see how these behaviors evolved from simpler ancestral forms. What ethologists brought to the fore was Darwin's issue of behavior as an inherited, adaptive trait that was capable of modification by natural selection. If this were true, then it was imperative to find out more about the nature of the inheritance of complex behaviors, about which very little was actually known at the time; by making this gap in knowledge so obvious, ethologists stimulated other biologists to search for the genetic basis for specific animal behaviors.

Early attempts to study the genetics of behavior in larger animals such as dogs by American researcher John Paul Scott (b. 1909) were problematic: the behaviors were complex, variable even when environmental conditions seemed stable, and breeding was slow and results inconclusive. Among the earliest successful attempts to work out the genetic basis for a specific animal behavior focused on the social insects. Experiments in the 1950s showed that among honeybees (*Apis mellifera*) there were two different behavioral responses to the death of larva within a cell of the honeycomb (where the larvae normally develop). In one strain (called "hygienic") the workers remove the dead larva and discard it outside the hive; in the other strain (called "unhygienic") workers leave the larvae in the cell to decompose. Crossing purebred hygienic bees (symbolized *hh*) with purebred unhygienic (symbolized *HH*) produced hybrids that were all unhygienic (symbolized *Hh*) but that, when crossed with each other (that is *Hh* × *Hh*) produced an expected Mendelian ratio of three unhygienic (either *HH* or *Hh*) to one hygienic (*hh*) offspring. According to Mendel's principles, unhygienic behavior was said to be *dominant* over hygienic, while hygienic was said to be *recessive* to unhygienic. Further experiments showed that this behavior could be analyzed into two different components: uncapping the cell (taking off the seal from the top) followed by removing the larva. Each of these behaviors appeared to be controlled by a different set of genes: uncapping/nonuncapping, and removal/nonremoval. Work such as this showed clearly that at least some basic animal behaviors could be inherited according to simple Mendelian principles.

In the half century since such work has begun, biologists have elucidated the genetic basis for many instinctual behaviors in organisms as widely diverse as fruit flies (*Drosophila*), spiders, round worms (*Caenorhaabditis elegans*), mice (*Mus*), a variety of birds (especially pigeons) and dogs. With the advent of molecular genetics, the chemical basis of actual genes for some animal behaviors have been localized to specific segments of DAN in the organism's genome. Behavior genetics has thus become a major field within modern biological science.

III. BEHAVIOR GENETICS TODAY: AIMS AND METHODS

The aim of behavior genetics was set forth clearly in the first of the journal *Behavior Genetics* in 1970: "... behavior genetics is simply the intersection between genetics and the behavioral sciences." Although from the beginning, human behavior was considered an important component of the field, many investigators focused their attention on less complex animals, especially the small fruit fly *Drosophila melanogaster*, because so much was known about its genetics. Pioneers in that work included American psychologists-geneticists such as A. Manning and Jerry Hirsch, both of whom carried out breeding and selection experiments on *Drosophila* to study the mode of inheritance of behavior and its modification through selection. For example, Manning (1961) carried out two selection experiments for mating speed in *Drosophila melanogaster*, producing a slow and a rapid strain that were easily distinguishable. Hirsch selected for various behavioral traits over hundreds of generations, producing strains with widely divergent behavior patterns. Such experiments showed clearly that specific behaviors in fruit flies have a distinct genetic component and that the traits can be altered by selection.

The outcome of the earlier work was to show that mating behavior in *Drosophila*, like response of worker bees to dead larvae, consisted of a number of separable components. In the 1980s and 1990s Ralph Greenspan and his associates at New York University have identified some of these components and traced out their neurological and genetic bases (1995). Gene mutations are observed to affect such features of courtship as "mating song," produced as sound pulses when the male flaps his wings in certain rhythms. Males with a mating song gene mutation called *period* flap their wings at different intervals than normal males. The result is that mutant males have less success copulating with females than normal males do. The "song" is just one aspect of a complex courtship ritual that involves specific male and female motions, wing positions, extension of the proboscis (a long feeding device extruded from the mouth), licking of the genitals, and copulation itself. That these individual components can be isolated and studied at the genetic and neurological level demonstrates the power of behavior genetic analysis when carried out under rigorous laboratory conditions.

More recent work has focused on interspecific comparisons in *Drosophila*, again using mating behavior as the prototype. Behavioral hybrids produce courtship responses that are many times intermediate between the two parental species, thereby reducing the number of successful copulations. Such experiments have thrown much light on Darwin's hypothesized mechanism of sexual selection. A variation of natural selection, sexual selection was introduced by Darwin to explain the almost-universal sexual dimorphism (distinct differences), in both physical traits (male–female differences in coloration, plumage in birds, or hair distribution in mammals) and behaviors (maternal behavior in female and territorial behavior in male baboons). Such persistent differences of forms within a species seemed difficult to account for in terms of traditional natural selection. Darwin concluded that females choose among competing males for a partner, selecting the male with the brightest plumage or the most distinct courtship behaviors. Thus, from an original population of showing little or no plumage or courtship behavior, males could gradually evolve distinct male-associated characteristics (comb of the cock, mane in male lions, etc.) that seemed to serve no other function than as a means of attracting the opposite sex. By way of such arguments, behavior genetics, like its ancestor ethology, has always had a close association with evolutionary theory.

Modern-day behavioral geneticists work with a much larger variety of animals than fruit flies and round worms. Many studies have been carried out with mice, especially those laboratory strains whose genetics is thoroughly understood. And despite the difficulty in working with them, dogs continue to be a popular object of behavioral studies. Primates such as chimpanzees or macaques have also been used, though for obvious reasons (like humans they have small numbers of offspring and their gestation periods are long) genetic data are more difficult to come by.

In the past decade behavior genetic research on humans has increased at a great rate, despite the contentiousness and public sensitivity to the issue. Behavior geneticists such as Robert Plomin at Pennsylvania State University and Joel Gelernter at Yale University argue that the field of human behavior genetics has been misrepresented, especially by its critics. They point out that many human behavioral genes, or at least chromosomal or molecular markers (markers are regions of chromosomes or of DNA that appear repeatedly in individuals who exhibit some specific phenotype, or trait; the markers are not necessarily the "genes" for the trait in question, but are simply correlated at the genomic level with appearance of a trait at the organismic level). For example, specific molecular markers have been correlated with Tourette's syndrome (leading to uncontrollable movements and speaking), schizophrenia,

manic depression, alcoholism, attention deficit syndrome (ADS), and homosexuality to name just a few—suggesting that there might be a significant gene or genes somewhere in the region of the marker for these behaviors. Moreover, genetic markers show variability at the marker level just as the behaviors show variation at the phenotypic level (such variations are called polymorphisms, and it is important to correlate polymorphisms in marker and phenotype in making a strong genetic claim). Human behavior genetic researchers emphasize that they do not discount the role of environment, nor the additive effect of many genes impinging on any given behavior. In fact, they make a point of emphasizing that the outcome of any behavioral development in humans (or any other organism) is of necessity the product of genes interacting with environment. They therefore argue that the old nature-nurture dispute is meaningless. All traits, including behavioral ones, are a product of the combined effects of heredity and environment.

IV. RESEARCH METHODS IN HUMAN BEHAVIOR GENETICS

Basic methods of research in human behavior genetics usually begin with a definition of the behavioral trait in question—alcoholism, schizophrenia, violent/aggressive behavior, homosexuality—followed by determining criteria for diagnosis (i.e., guidelines for identifying who does and does not display the condition). For example, in genetic studies of crime and alcoholism, psychiatrist C. Robert Cloninger at Washington University Medical School (St. Louis), used police and temperance board records from Sweden (where good public health records have been kept for many decades) to classify individual subjects as either "criminals" or "alcoholics" or both (he used the existence of three or more citations in the public record to establish that an individual was an "alcoholic" or a "criminal"). Many psychiatrists in the United States and abroad use the American Psychiatric Association's *Diagnostic and Statistical Manual IV* (now in the second version of its fourth edition) as the criterion for diagnosing individuals with one or another mental illness. Behavioral geneticists emphasize that it is necessary to establish unambiguous definitions of traits before setting out to investigate their inheritance patterns.

A second step is to trace the occurrence of the trait in a given family or group of relatives. The traditional method for recording such data is by constructing a family pedigree chart for the trait through as many generations as possible; in more recent times researchers carry out genetic analysis by identifying chromosome or DNA markers. In either case, the presence or absence of the marker is correlated with the presence or absence of the trait in the individual's behavior. For example, the Xq28 region of the human X-chromosome contains many molecular members, some of which have been correlated with homosexual behavior. In a study published by Hamer and his colleagues in 1993, 40 pairs of gay brothers and members of their families were surveyed for particular markers in the Xq28 region; in 33 of the 40 cases the same marker was found. It was not, however, found with such regularity in the x-chromosome of the mothers of these subject-pairs, and has not been unequivocally replicated in other sample sets. It is important to note that markers are not equivalent to genes affecting the trait; they only provide some sort of clue about a region of the chromosome where the gene or genes for the trait might be located. It is also important to note that markers are variable (polymorphic) within a population, just as are phenotypes (including behavior). It is particularly useful in behavior genetics to be able to correlate variations in markers with variations in the behavior in question.

A third component of the method is to analyze statistically the frequency of correlation between marker and visible trait in the family in question, collateral family lines, and in the population at large. A useful tool for this purpose is known as analysis of variance and an associated calculation known as the *heritability* of a trait. While some behavior geneticists today have abandoned heritability, it has been a staple of human behavior genetics for at least a half century or more. Heritability is a technique that attempts to estimate that portion of the phenotypic variation in a population that can be attributed to genetic factors. Thus, a heritability value of 0.8 (=80%) can be interpreted to say that 80% of a given trait could be due to hereditary effects. It does not say that 80% of the trait is genetically determined. The term "heritability" in its technical sense has led to considerable confusion in the literature, both scientific and popular, because it is often interpreted to mean "inherited," as in "trait X is 80% due to genetics and 20% due to environment." Heritability calculations only state that, all other things being equal, a certain portion of the *variance* observed in that trait *can be ascribed* to genetics. It is, of course, the "all other things being equal" part (i.e., knowing the genetic relationships between organisms in the sample, and knowing specific and relevant features of the environment in which the individuals have developed) that is the catch. For hu-

man behavior, the latter set of conditions is particularly difficult to assess with any accuracy (do two children brought up in the same household have the *same* environment? Do children brought up in different households have significantly *different* environments? What counts as significant components of the environment in terms of effects on adult traits?) The statistical analysis part of human behavior genetics has always raised sticky methodological issues.

Finally, once the data are analyzed the behavior geneticist is faced with trying to draw some conclusions about the degree to which a given trait might be affected by some genetic component. This is where even the staunchest behavior geneticist admits there are great pitfalls. The most common is the tendency to overinterpret the data. Are there any genetic effects to be discerned at all? If so, do they appear to be single-gene effects (very few complex traits in humans or any other animals appear to be attributable to single genes), are they additive effects (the presence of two genes yields roughly twice the effect of one) or are they nonadditive (two genes yields three times the effect of one, etc.)? Are the relative comparisons (control groups) available for judging the possible genetic effects in the observed group (for example, if a particular chromosome marker is found in a group of people who show a particular behavioral trait, it would be necessary to know the prevalence of the marker in the general population to draw any conclusion about the possible genetic effects in the observed group)?

V. CRITICISM OF HUMAN BEHAVIOR AND GENETICS RESEARCH

Critics of human behavior genetics such as Jonathan Beckwith of Harvard Medical School, Peter Breggin, Director of the Center for the Study of Psychiatry (Bethesda, MD), or Steven Rose at the Open University in Great Britain, disagree that the findings of behavior geneticists are conclusive in any way. They point to a number of methodological problems that have undermined virtually all studies purporting to have found a genetic determiner for any specific human behavior. The flaws generally fall into the four-point methodological categories discussed above.

First, is the problem of defining human behavioral traits in such a way that they can be diagnosed by any well-trained observer. This becomes difficult, the critics point out, for traits such as criminality, aggressiveness, alcoholism, manic depression, schizophrenia, homosexuality, and many others. These are very complex behaviors and judging whether an individual really fits into the trait category can be quite subjective (was Robin Hood a criminal or a hero when he stole from the rich to give to the poor?) Psychiatrists are debating today whether schizophrenia and manic depression are really different diseases or varying manifestations of the same disease. Furthermore, where some real genetic differences may exist between individuals—for example, the ability to metabolize alcohol rapidly and thus exhibit greater tolerance—is not the same as the social behavior we call "alcoholism." With such wide areas of possible disagreement about what constitutes a particular trait, critics point out that it is no wonder human behavior geneticists have a difficult time even replicating each other's work, much less carrying out a clear genetic analysis.

At the second step—gathering data on families, siblings, adoptees, and so on—critics argue that many human behavior genetic studies are sometimes egregiously faulty. Some have too small a sample size, a special problem for those studies using monozygotic (identical) twins raised apart (Cyril Burt, on whose famous twin studies so much research on the inheritance of IQ has been based, managed after 40 years to accumulate only 53 pairs of twins). One study of homosexuality consisted of a total of seven twin pairs, three male and two female. Even a study of 40 siblings, as in the example of Hamer's research on homosexuality, is tiny by comparison to the number of organisms used in any behavior genetic study of nonhuman animals. Others do not institute proper controls. A recent study by Dean Hamer and his colleagues at the National Cancer Institute, found a genetic marker on the X-chromosome in 33 out of 40 pairs of gay brothers, suggesting to the team that there might be genes located on the chromosome near that marker, predisposing those individuals to homosexual behavior. However, the study did not provide information on whether other brothers (nongay) in the same families did or did not have the marker. If other sons in the families had the marker, the correlation with homosexuality would be meaningless. Other problems with this second step include nonstandardized methods of determining which individuals have the trait in question (different diagnostic procedures/criteria, assessment made under different conditions), and bias in selecting subjects for the study (many studies get their subjects by asking publicly for volunteers, which can bias the results toward individuals who are outgoing personality types and will exaggerate claims about themselves to remain in the study).

Critics also argue that in the third step of human behavior genetics research—introduction of various statistical procedures—researchers often misuse or misapply particular techniques. One of the most commonly misused and misunderstood statistical procedures is that of heritability. As pointed out above, heritability does not mean "inherited," although many behavior geneticists do not make the distinction clear, especially when talking to reporters or giving popular talks. A more common problem, however, is the failure of those using heritability to take into account two underlying constraints on the method. First, any heritability estimate is limited to a given population, in a given environment. Thus, the heritability estimate for a trait in population A cannot be applied to population B, because there is no guarantee that either the genetic or environmental components of the two populations are comparable. Critics point out that Berkeley psychologist Arthur Jensen committed this error in his famous paper of 1969, in which he applied heritability estimates of IQ based on British Caucasian students (population A) to American Caucasian and African American students (populations B_1 and B_2). Such a comparison is invalid by the rules of heritability analysis.

A second assumption of heritability is that all members within a single population (for example, population A) share the same or nearly similar environments. Because heritability as a technique was introduced in the 1930s primarily as an aid to animal and plant breeders, this assumption, under most breeding conditions, was reasonably safe. However, applied to humans—for example, to Caucasian and African American populations in any large American city—the assumption is clearly untenable.

The race and IQ issue that surfaced so dramatically in Jensen's work became a landmark in focusing attention on the potential flaws in work claiming a genetic basis for human mental and personality traits. It came at the time of the great civil rights upsurge in the United States, and claimed to speak directly to public policy issues such as school desegregation, busing, equal opportunity in the workplace, and the like. It pointed up all of the problems inherent in such research, from defining the phenotype (what is "intelligence"?) to the analysis of heritability, on which critics were to focus for years. And of course, its conclusions resurfaced as late as 1994 with the publication of Charles Murray's and Richard Herrnstein's *The Bell Curve,* which based its claim (that African Americans and other minorities were probably never going to have proportional representation in high-paying, high-tech jobs because of their innate—i.e., genetic—limitations) on Jensen's work.

Critics pointed out that the potentially destructive effects of very tenuous conclusions did not justify either funding of the research itself or publication of the results.

It is in the fourth step, or procedure, in human behavior genetics—drawing conclusions from the data—that critics find some of the most flagrant violations of sound scientific procedure. On the one hand the conclusions can sound impressive but can be enormously trivial. As critics have put it, to claim that a particular study shows that genes and the environment interact in producing a particular behavioral trait is such a truism as to say nothing of any interest. *Every* physical, chemical, or biological, trait in every organism is the result of *some* interaction between genetic and environmental components. The important question in any given case is to show how and under what conditions (genetic and environmental) a particular behavioral outcome will result. Few if any human behavioral genetic studies have been able to make such a relationship clear or precise. A second violation is in a sense the flip side of the same coin: overinterpretation of the results of a given study. Both Jensen's study of racial differences in IQ in the 1960s, and Hamer's study of the hereditary component of male homosexuality in the 1990s were guilty of overinterpretation. Whether in the verbal form of "the gene for ..." or "the genes for ...," overinterpretation gives the impression, especially among lay readers, that the biological evidence is much stronger than it actually is. According to most critics of human behavior genetics, given all the problems with carrying out research on this topic, virtually all strong claims are bound to be guilty of overinterpretation.

One aspect of human behavior genetics work that has also bothered critics as well as other members of the scientific community at large, is the tendency to researchers to talk freely, and often in exaggerated terms, to the press. While announcing new scientific findings in press conferences has become more prevalent in all areas of science than it used to be, it is particularly disturbing in areas with considerable political implications. Critics point to the fact that the discovery of a putative gene for "alcoholism" (the D_2, or dopamine receptor locus, on chromosome 11) in 1990 was announced with great fanfare as front-page news in many newspapers and as cover stories for a number of magazines. Failure of other researchers to replicate the study has resulted in ultimate discrediting of the work; announcement of this failure got no publicity at all. Critics argue that those who do work in the area of human behavior genetics should use more than the usual amount of caution in an-nouncing any purported discoveries in the press or in other arenas.

VI. ETHICS AND HUMAN BEHAVIOR GENETICS

As with virtually all areas of scientific research, the nature of claims made and conclusions drawn from specific findings can have profound effects for matters of ethics. In human behavior genetics the effects can be particularly alarming when they affect attitudes toward health care (including mental health), education, official public policy (such as sterilizing or incarcerating persons claimed to be genetically defective), and ultimately, the issue of research involving human subjects. The latter is the most extreme and probably involves the least amount of contention. Especially given the widespread use of human subjects, including identical twins, by the Nazis for genetic studies, the Western scientific community has adopted explicit, and rigorous conditions on the use of humans as subjects for scientific research. For human behavior genetics, this means that the avenues open to animal behavior geneticists—planned breeding and raising of offspring under highly controlled environmental conditions—are not an option. There seems to be little doubt about this issue among either researchers or lay persons.

More problematical are ethical issues raised by overinterpretation of results and the ensuing effect such conclusions—especially when widely disseminated in the press—can have on both public attitudes and policy. Given the fact that still today, to claim that a trait is *genetically determined* (or at least largely so) is to be heard as saying the trait cannot be altered, and suggests only a limited number of options for treating individuals who harbor undesirable traits. Despite considerable exaggeration by some molecular geneticists, gene therapy as a significant remedy of even well-identified genetic traits is at very best a distant hope. Thus, claims by human behavior geneticists that alcoholism, schizophrenia or manic depression, disposition to criminal activity, and attention deficit disorder (ADD) are *genetic* is tantamount to saying that the root cause cannot be changed, only the external manifestations "managed," usually in today's terms by drug therapy, and if that does not work institutionalization and/or sterilization.

These approaches raise a host of ethical issues. First, the very claim that a given behavioral condition is genetic, in the face of so much question and controversy within the scientific community, raises questions about credibility. If the conclusions are so ambiguous, is it ethical to be treating children diagnosed as having ADD, with drugs such as ritalin (that decreases overall metabolic activity) instead of looking to boring, overcrowded school conditions, or problems within the family, as the source of the behavior? Proponents of the genetic point of view, such as Dr. David Comings of the City of Hope Medical Center in California, argue that traditional psychological counseling and other supposedly curative approaches have not worked, and that drug therapy makes the life of the child, his teacher, and his parents much less stressful, and actually increases school performance noticeably. Critics point out, however, that the gene-drug approach ignores problems in the school and home and thus allows the conditions generating ADD to persist—like allowing a person to continue eating a poison while continuing to give them a curative. The problem still remains.

Human behavior genetics raises the difficult ethical issues of where to draw the line between using science to help individuals improve their lives and using science for social control. Even if all the claims of human behavior genetics were taken at face value, the implications of these findings for social policy are not clear. People who are truly genetically defective, it can be argued, deserve more of society's support and resources, not less. But, as critics of the human behavior genetic program point out, at the present time with insurance companies refusing to cover certain conditions because they were acquired before the client took out the policy, genetic arguments can provide an easy way to limit payments. The problem is even more acute when the scientific evidence itself is highly debatable.

According to some of the most extreme critics, the whole focus on genetic explanations is economically driven. At a time when both private corporations and government are cutting back resources (jobs, health care, salaries) providing a medical/genetic explanation for social/behavioral problems provides a cheap solution. Drugs such as ritalin are expensive, but not nearly so much as one-on-one psychological counseling or therapy. Drug therapy is even cheaper than paying people higher wages, increasing (or at least not cutting back) benefits such as health care, or reducing the stress in the workplace by hiring more workers. According to this scenario the funds provided for research into, and popularization of, human behavior genetic work,

only serves as a smokescreen to hide the true causes of widespread mental and personality problems.

From a biological point of view, there is nothing that says that even if a trait is significantly affected by genes, it cannot be changed to some degree. People have genetically determined diseases like diabetes, yet over much of a lifetime it can be managed by controlling diet and taking artificial insulin. People with genetically defective eyesight wear glasses. People with genetically determined brown hair convert it to blonde by hair dyes, and so on. But these are only corrective measures. In addition, biologists now know that all genes are influenced by various environmental factors during embryonic development and to varying degrees throughout the rest of their lifetime. Thus, even if a child inherits a tendency to produce more dopamine receptors than normal, a particular type of home environment can alter the expression of that gene. Genes do not unfold automatically into adult traits, but rather have a range over which their expression is altered by varying environmental factors. Geneticists know very little about the range of most genes, especially putative genes for behavioral traits. Thus, most biologists would warn heavily about relying on genetic claims regarding human social and personality traits as a basis for formulating medical or social policy.

Also See the Following Articles

EUGENICS • GENETIC COUNSELING • GENETIC RESEARCH • GENOME ANALYSIS • RESEARCH ETHICS

Bibliography

Allen, G. E. (1996). The double-edged sword of genetic determination: Social and political agendas in genetic studies of homosexuality, 1940–1994. In V. A. Rosario (Ed.), *Science and homosexualities*, pp. 242–270. New York: Routledge.

Barinaga, M. (1994). From fruit flies, rats, mice: Evidence of genetic influence. *Science* **264**, 1690–1693.

Greenspan, R. (1995). Understanding the genetic construction of behavior. *Scientific American* **272**, 72–78.

Mann, C. C. (1994). Behavior genetics in transition. *Science* **264**, 1686–1689.

McDonald, K. A. (1994, September). Biology and behavior. Social scientists and evolutionary biologists discuss and debate new findings. *Chronicle of Higher Education,* **14**, A10–11; A21.

Plomin, R., Owen, M. J., & Mcguffin, P. (1994). The genetic basis of complex human behaviors. *Science* **264**, 1733–1739.

GENETIC SCREENING

Ruth Chadwick
University of Central Lancashire

GLOSSARY

genetic screening The determination of the prevalence of a gene in an asymptomatic population or population group, where for any given individual there is no reason to believe that he or she has the gene in question. Normally contrasted with the genetic *testing* of an individual for whom there may be some reason to think he or she is at risk, for example, because of family history.

I. CRITERIA FOR THE INTRODUCTION OF GENETIC SCREENING PROGRAMS

In the light of developments in human genome analysis, the prospects for population-wide genetic screening programs are increasingly an issue. The question arises as to when it is worthwhile to introduce a screening program—what criteria have to be met, and in accordance with what principles should it be carried out?

This article will examine these issues with special reference to reports and statements in selected countries on criteria for introduction of a program, criteria for implementation, ethical principles and values appealed to, and social implications considered.

The first thing to note is the definition of genetic screening. The Danish report defines it as the study of the occurrence of a specific gene or chromosome complement in a population or population group (Danish Council, p. 56). The Council of Europe adds that there should be no previous *suspicion* that the individuals have the condition (Council of Europe, pp. 9–10): the Nuffield that there should be no *evidence* that the individual does, thus replacing a subjective test with an objective one (Nuffield Council, 1993, 1.9). There are, of course, different types of screening: neonatal, childhood, adult, preconception, and prenatal. The question arises as to whether the same set of criteria can apply to all of these, but it is not possible in the scope of this article to address all these issues in detail.

What condition(s) is it worth screening for? The Wilson-Junger principles on screening, which were not confined to genetic screening, stated that the condition sought must be an "important problem" (Wilson and Junger, 1968, Principle 1). What counts as important, is, however, a matter of debate. Important to whom?

The Nuffield Council on Bioethics says that at present the "prime requirement" is that the condition sought be a serious disease (para. 3.10). They refer to the

Clothier report's recommendation that the first candidates for gene therapy should be conditions that are life-threatening or seriously handicapping, and for which treatment is either not available or unsatisfactory (Clothier, 1992, para. 8.6). They acknowledge, however, that for screening, the criteria are likely to be wider than that, but that it is difficult to define them precisely. In the light of this they take a negative approach of exclusion rather than inclusion. Screening should not be offered for conditions that, while having a genetic component, are not diseases. The so-called "gay gene" is offered as an example here (para. 10.3). Thus, the criterion of "serious disease" seems to be replaced by "disease."

In attempting to establish what is regarded as serious disease the sociocultural context cannot be ignored. Suppose, however, that what counts as sufficiently serious *has* been agreed. The question then arises as to what benefits should be expected of the program. Wilson and Junger require that treatment be available (Wilson and Junger, 1968, Principle 2). The Nuffield Council lists the availability of therapy as one of six criteria identified as important at the end of its report, while acknowledging that if it is not, it does not mean that screening is not worthwhile (para. 10.21): other benefits can result from screening.

The Danish Council of Ethics recognizes this, in saying that evaluation of a screening program depends on available "scope for action" (p. 50). This could encompass a broader interpretation than simply the availability of therapy, such as the making of reproductive choices and alterations of life-style.

II. IMPLEMENTATION

The Wilson-Junger principles mention that there must be an acceptable test (Wilson and Junger, 1968, Principle 7). This is not emphasized in the Nuffield or Danish reports. Perhaps it is thought that DNA testing can be done in a noninvasive way (e.g., by a mouthwash test) so that it is not necessary to have this requirement. There are still matters of inconvenience to be considered, however.

The predictive power of a given test is important, especially when taking into account whether the benefits of taking the test are likely to make the possible inconvenience worthwhile. It will be especially significant when considering screening for *predispositions* to multifactorial diseases—for example, in a disease that counts as an important problem, and that has a genetic component, but where there is a low concordance rate

between identical twins, such as rheumatoid arthritis. If we know that the presence of a particular gene is a factor, but without a high predictive value, the most we might be able to tell is that someone *without* the gene is very unlikely to suffer from the condition in question. To those people the result of a test might bring considerable relief, but would this be worth doing? Would the criterion of "scope for action" be met? This is not clear. There is a further problem about the extent to which those being screened will understand the drawbacks in predictive power of particular tests.

The Nuffield and Danish reports and the Council of Europe all emphasize the importance of genetic counseling, with an interesting difference of wording. Nuffield and the Council of Europe say that counseling *should* be available (Nuffield, para. 10.5; Council of Europe I.3a); the Danish Council says it *must* be available (p. 66). The Danish Report says that it must be nondirective (p. 66), as does the Council of Europe (I.3a). The Nuffield report, however, recognizes that counseling is unlikely to remain completely neutral and that there are disadvantages in counseling that seems cold and unhelpful (para. 4.21). It may be, then, that there is a shift away from the ideal of counseling as non-directive.

III. SECONDARY FINDINGS

The Danish report says that screening should be so organized as to examine only those factors on which the screening is focused (p. 48), but because it is not possible to exclude secondary findings, they recommend follow-up research to establish what importance such findings have acquired (p. 67). The Council of Europe provides that unexpected findings may be communicated only when they are directly of clinical importance (III.11).

IV. ETHICAL PRINCIPLES

The Danish Council of Ethics gives a detailed exploration of principles, locating the discussion within the general framework of a series of oppositions: private versus public, individual versus society, autonomy versus utility.

Autonomy plays a major role in most if not all discussions of the issues, whether explicitly or implicitly. In the Danish report the duty to help is itself interpreted in terms of autonomy (p. 63), rather than, for example, promoting the health of the individual or the genetic health of the population. In medical practice generally there is a duty to help where possible—in effecting a cure, for example, but the duty to help in genetics is said to be of a different kind because the aim is not to effect a cure but to provide information that may be important in facilitating autonomy. Here autonomy appears to be interpreted in a wide sense: in other words, what is at issue is not self-determination in specific situations of choice, but the empowerment of people to think for themselves and to take charge of their lives. However, there may come a point at which so much information is forthcoming that it undermines rather than promotes autonomy:

> It is perfectly conceivable that the greatest problem will be the volume of accessible information on the individual's personal sphere, in which case respect for the personal sphere will outweigh the motive for helping people achieve greater autonomy. In such situations, the implementation of genetic screening will not be ethically defensible (p. 63).

This is a strong statement. Clearly, in the Danish report, autonomy takes precedence. This is also made clear when it is said that "the overall objective must be to safeguard the individual's autonomy with regard to participation or non-participation" (p. 66). This, however, seems to be a different interpretation of autonomy in terms of self-determination in a specific choice situation—a narrower interpretation. The reasons for this position are connected with values supported in Danish society. Thus it is said that, for example, utilitarianism cannot be the fundamental principle on which Danish society rests (p. 64).

Although the Council of Europe statement and the Nuffield report do not contain such a detailed discussion of autonomy, the principle is implicit in both. The Council of Europe appears to be interpreting it in the narrower way, in saying that provision should be based on respect for the principle of self-determination: this underlies the concern for informed consent therein (II.5). Both the Danish and Nuffield reports also give a central place to informed consent (Danish Council, p. 66; Nuffield Council, Chapter 4), but this is precisely what is going to become increasingly problematic as human genome analysis makes possible broad spectrum screening. There are hints in the Nuffield report of implicit adherence to autonomy in the wide sense. It speaks of "the value to those being screened of the knowledge gained" (para. 10.21). It is said that "the benefits [of screening] should be seen as enabling indi-

vidual to take account of the information for their own lives and empowering prospective parents to make informed choices about having children" (para. 10.21).

The Danish report is unusual in mentioning the duty to help in specific terms, although arguably this is an important factor in considering the moral aspects of screening. If screening is withheld, individuals who could benefit from it are denied those benefits. There are well-known, although contested, arguments to suggest that the duty to help is less stringent or urgent than the duty to avoid harm, and screening has the potential to harm, by raising anxiety, by changing people's self-image, and by paving the way for genetic discrimination. The harm caused by failure to screen, and the harm caused by implementing the screening program, must both be considered in evaluating a proposed program.

The Council of Europe includes a recommendation that there should be equality of access to genetic testing, without discrimination. They mention that financial considerations, for example, are irrelevant (II.4).

It may be possible to monitor equality of access once a program is in place. The problem arises, however, as to considerations of equality in deciding what programs to offer. Arguably, as suggested above, the determination of what counts as an important problem may be influenced by factors such as social class, ethnicity, and sex.

Abby Lippman, for example, has argued that:

> posing "access" as an *isolated* problem [of prenatal diagnosis] may produce failure to grapple fully with the issue of who is or can get tested ... Comparable availability does not automatically lead to equity, especially when individuals start off unequally.

V. SOCIAL IMPLICATIONS

Consideration of equity is one aspect of the social implications of genetic screening. The Nuffield report cites social implications as one important factor to take into consideration, and they figure large in all of the document's genetics. Indeed, this is one area of medicine in which social factors are particularly important, and one perhaps that suggests some tension with relation to autonomy.

The first social consideration concerns the implications for family members. Whereas in bioethics generally most questions have typically been framed in terms of the individual, genetics is concerned with *relatedness*. The Nuffield report says:

> Thus the status of genetic information raises ethical questions that differ significantly from the normal rules and standards applied to the handling of personal medical records (Nuffield, para. 1.10).

Paragraph 10.4 mentions the importance of the implications for family members in informed consent. Para 10.7 provides that the family implications of genetic screening and genetic testing "will sometimes require health professionals to revise the application of the current principles governing the confidentiality of medical information." For the Danish Council the impact of family members is a question for follow-up research. For the Council of Europe, in the case of a severe genetic risk for other family members, consideration should be given to informing them about matters relevant to their health or that of their future children (III.9).

The important question for ethical theory is *how* the family enters the debate. There are various possibilities: as an independent value, as an extension of the ethics of individualism, or as part of a communitarian ethic. The first of these can quickly be disposed of. It is not the integrity of the family itself that is at issue, as it has been, for example, in debates about the well-being of the nuclear family. There are different issues here, and it is worthwhile to try to tease out what they are. Within an individualist ethic, genetic information concerning the person screened may have implications for the life choices of their spouse or genetic relatives. So their autonomy is at stake as well.

Another potential focus of concern, however, is the prevention of avoidable genetic disorders. What is not clear is whether this can or should be understood in an individualistic way or whether some attention to public health genetics is indicated. If the latter is desirable, then the question arises as to whether autonomy alone can do the work required, or whether some kind of communitarian approach is indicated for addressing the issues in genetic screening, which would set limits to the boundaries within which autonomy is exercised. The duty to help, if subscribed to, would also have to be wider than that of facilitating autonomy. The social and political context is crucial here.

One of the most significant social implications of genetic screening is the concept of normality. As the Danish report says:

> Normality is a relative concept, and any health-related examination therefore includes a risk of the examinees feeling or being thought of as abnormal or just plain ill (p. 60).

They call this morbidification and recommend that there should be follow-up to shed light on the individual and society's conception of normality. Some people object to the language of normality and abnormality, suggesting that it is not ethically neutral—in this connection it is of interest that the Nuffield Council uses this terminology (see, e.g., para. 1.1).

The issue of abnormality is related to that of stigmatization, the danger of which is recognized by the Council of Europe (p. 9). The Nuffield report is fairly optimistic about the dangers of stigmatization. They say:

> Such evidence as exists suggests that current genetic screening programs need not result in any significant stigmatization (Nuffield, para. 8.14).

The Nuffield Council may be right to say that previous disturbing precedents arose largely because of inadequate or poorly understood information. The question must be asked, however, about the significance of such factors as the social context, target population and the nature of the disorder in question. It has been argued, for example, that there is a danger of racism in discussions of genetics, in cases where some minority ethnic groups have a higher frequency of a particular gene.

Stigmatization is not, of course, the same as discrimination. Even in the absence of stigmatization, which is defined in the Nuffield report as "the branding, marking or discrediting . . . of a particular characteristic" (para. 8.8), there are fears that individuals may suffer from discrimination in relation to insurance and employment. Hence, recent arguments have turned from arguments about the rights of individuals to know their genetic status (a particular application of claims to have access to medical information about oneself) to arguments for a right *not* to know. One of the implications of such an argument would of course be that they could not be required to undergo testing. On the other hand responses to this argument have included an argument based on grounds of solidarity for a responsibility to share genetic information that can have potentially adverse consequences for other people, and hence a responsibility to know it.

In this particular area the tension between the interests of the individual regarding control of their genetic information and the interests of others in having access to it becomes acute. The potential benefits of greater sharing of genetic information, in terms of the interests of genetic relatives, future people and society as a whole, may be great but the question is whether they are sufficiently compelling to justify the imposition of individual responsibility to share it (cf. Chadwick *et al.*, 1997). The most promising way forward seems to be to attempt to mediate between the interests of the individual and community, via the *encouragement* of sharing of information, rather than by a *requirement*.

VI. OTHER ISSUES

The central questions on which future debate should focus are two: first, to what extent do social values and social inequalities play a part in constructing a genetic condition as serious or important? Second, is there a responsibility to promote the genetic health of the population? This would be a possible interpretation of the duty to help those at risk.

The second question gives rise to worries about the use of screening as a technique of power and surveillance, and concerns about eugenics. Some object to the term "genetic health," on the grounds either of political correctness or of conceptual unclarity. Where political correctness is concerned, there is an issue of whether it is possible to be concerned for the genetic health of the population without adopting discredited eugenic policies—the term "genetic health" might be thought to imply intolerance of imperfection. Arguably, however, if health of the population is a good that public health medicine has a duty to pursue, then why is not genetic health a good that public health medicine has a duty to pursue? Reasons for holding that there is a moral difference are unclear, but the prior question is one of conceptual unclarity. The unclarity relates to the concept "health," however, not the "genetic" element specifically. On one interpretation the content of the purported duty would be to reduce the incidence of genetic disorders, analogously to reducing the incidence of, say, infectious disease. The question is to what extent the goal could be achieved while safeguarding the interests of individuals. The tension is reflected as at deeper level by the theoretical ethical question of the opposition between autonomy and community.

VII. CONCLUSION

The reports and statement considered above take different positions on the ethical question. The Danish Council is very much on the side of autonomy, both local (narrow) and global (wide). The Council of Europe supports autonomy under the guise of self-determination, but shows concern for the interests of other *individuals*, where these interests can be interpreted in terms of clinical benefits. The Nuffield Council supports local autonomy (informed consent) and, arguably, global autonomy, but also takes into consideration the social implications. The question for ethical theory is the extent to which it is possible to mediate between autonomy and community, and in this specific context whether and how it is possible to pursue public health genetics without adopting eugenic policies that are neither morally nor politically feasible.

Also See the Following Articles

EUGENICS • GENE THERAPY • GENETIC COUNSELING • GENETIC TECHNOLOGY, LEGAL REGULATION OF • GENOME ANALYSIS

Acknowledgments

I am grateful to the Commission of the European Communities for funding the EUROSCREEN project of which this work forms a part.

Bibliography

Chadwick, R., *et al.* (Eds.). (1997). *The right to know and the right not to know*. Aldershot: Avebury.

Clothier, C. M. (Chairman). (1992). *Report of the committee on the ethics of gene therapy*. London: HMSO.

Council of Europe. (1992). *Recommendation R(92)3 on genetic testing and screening for health care purposes*. Reprinted in *Bulletin of Medical Ethics* (February 1994) pp. 9–11.

Danish Council of Ethics. (1993). *Ethics and mapping of the human genome*. Copenhagen: Danish Council of Ethics.

Lippman, A. (1994). Prenatal genetic testing and screening: constructing needs and reinforcing inequities. In A.Clarke (Ed.), *Genetic counselling: Practice and principles*. London: Routledge.

Nuffield Council on Bioethics. (1993). *Genetic screening: Ethical issues*. London: Nuffield Council on Bioethics.

Royal College of Physicians. (1991). *Purchasers' guidelines to genetic services in the NHS*. London: Royal College of Physicians.

Wilson, J. M. G., & Junger, G. (1968). The principles and practice of screening for disease. *Public Health Papers,* **34.** Geneva: World Health Organization.

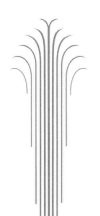

GENETIC TECHNOLOGY, LEGAL REGULATION OF

Tony McGleenan
The Queen's University of Belfast

I. International Regulation
II. National Regulations
III. Discussion

GLOSSARY

DNA (deoxyribonucleic acid) The chemical substance that makes up a gene and that contains an individual's genetic code.
gene The basic unit of heredity, consisting of a sequence of DNA that occupies a particular location on the genome.
genome The total genetic complement of an individual or of a species.
germ line gene therapy A scientific procedure that alters the reproductive cells of an individual thereby altering the genome permanently for future generations.
somatic cell gene therapy A scientific procedure that alters the genetic structure of the ordinary cells of an individual.

GENETIC TECHNOLOGY promises to deliver tremendous health and social benefits to the human race. It may be possible to utilize genetic technology to eradicate some of the major genetic diseases that currently truncate the human life span. Advances in genetic screening and testing will enable us to determine our susceptibility to certain diseases, including some of the major multifactorial diseases such as cancers and heart disease. It may then be possible to make suitable life-style changes in order to minimize the risks from these illnesses. However, alongside these potential benefits, genetic technology also carries tremendous potential for harm. Gene therapy techniques could be used to interfere with an individual's reproductive cells and so alter the genetic composition of generations of offspring. Genetically modified organisms may be accidentally or deliberately released, causing untold environmental damage. Unscrupulous regimes may attempt to link genetic technology with political ideology to create stronger, taller, or more intelligent human beings. Genetic screening techniques could be employed to provide intimate information about individuals that could be used by insurers, employers, or governments to deny basic benefits such as health insurance, life assurance, housing, and employment to those seen as high risk. Prenatal genetic testing could be utilized in order to facilitate the termination of pregnancies where the fetus is found to have less than optimum genetic health. Because of the potential for genetic technology both to benefit and to harm the human race discussions about means of regulating the use of these techniques have begun in many countries. This article examines the different modes of regulation adopted at both international and national level and comments on the trends in genetic regulation.

I. INTERNATIONAL REGULATION

A. International Declarations

1. The Declaration of Inuyama

At the 1991 CIOMS conference on Genetics, Ethics and Human Values the Declaration of Inuyama was formally adopted (CIOMS, 1991). Many of the provisions of the Declaration have gone on to inform other international documents addressing the issues raised by gene therapy. Section 1 of the Declaration affirms the need for gene therapy to conform to the ethical standards of research and for any knowledge acquired by genetic techniques to be used appropriately. It states that somatic cell gene therapy should be approached like any other form of therapy but that any use of genetic technology that is intended to improve or delete aesthetic, behavioral, or cognitive characteristics is prohibited except where such action is associated with the treatment of a disease. Section 6 of the Declaration states that germ line gene therapy should only be acceptable when all risks have been eradicated.

2. The Valencia Declaration

At the Second International Cooperation Workshop of the Human Genome Project the Valencia Declaration was adopted. This stated that somatic cell gene therapy was an acceptable form of treatment for certain diseases. The use of germ line gene therapy was opposed on the basis of the technical difficulties that confronted it and the ethical controversey that surrounded the technique.

3. The Bilbao Declaration

At an international workshop on the legal implications of the Human Genome Project the Bilbao Declaration was formally adopted. This document suggests the introduction of a moratorium on germ line gene therapy until the safety and efficacy of the techniques used can be guaranteed.

B. European Community Regulations

There are many hundreds of regulations, directives, and decisions in European Community law that are directed at the field of genetic technology. However, most of these measures are derivative of a number of key directives that have been adopted in order to ensure a coordinated approach throughout the member states of the European Community to regulation. The most significant European laws to date have involved the development of biosafety directives relating to contained use and deliberate release of genetically modified organisms. These provisions are considered directly applicable in the member states and consequently the national governments must implement the policy, although they retain discretion as to the detail of the legislation. The following directives have been implemented into the national laws of most member states in the European Community.

1. Contained Use Directive 90/219 EC

This directive seeks to prevent environmental damage from accidental release of genetically modified organisms (GMOs) by ensuring harmonization between the laws of the member states that relate to the use of GMOs "with a view to protecting human health and the environment." The directive obliges member states to ensure that all appropriate measures are taken to avoid adverse effects on human health and the environment that might arise from the contained use of GMOs. The directive imposes a significant administrative burden on member states in the interest of biosafety, including reporting requirements and the introduction of guidelines for the safe handling of GMOs. At the end of each year member states are required to inform the European Commission of all instances of the contained use of GMOs.

2. Deliberate Release Directives 90/220 EC

The objective of this Directive is "to approximate the laws, regulations and administrative provisions of the Member States and to protect human health and the environment: when carrying out the release of genetically modified organisms into the environment, when placing on the market products containing, or consisting of, genetically modified organisms intended for subsequent deliberate release into the environment." The directive contains 23 detailed articles that impose a series of conditions upon any researcher who plans to release genetically modified organisms into the environment. Most member states have implemented the contained use or deliberate release directives in some form. One area of controversy in relation to the deliberate release directive is whether it will apply to human beings who have undergone some form of somatic cell gene therapy. Such an interpretation would require the introduction of a significant number of procedural safeguards to the process of somatic cell gene therapy trials. The directive is not explicit on the point of human gene therapy. The definition of a genetically modified organism simply states that it refers to "an organism in which the genetic material has been altered in a way that does not occur naturally by mating and/or natural recombination." The legislation contains appendixes that state that the process of genetic modification is not to be taken to include in vitro fertilization. It remains silent however, on the question of human somatic or germ line gene therapy, which could lead to the interpretation that these treatments could come within the bounds of the legislation. The matter has been clarified somewhat by the 1993 marketing authorization directive 2903/93, which states that: "Art 11 to 18 of Directive 90/220 EEC shall not apply to medicinal products for human use containing or consisting of genetically modified organisms." It would appear therefore that the other articles of the directive do in fact apply to human gene therapy trials.

3. Marketing Authorization Directive 2309/93 EC

In 1993 the Council of the European Communities laid down procedures for the establishment of a European Agency for the Evaluation of Medicinal Products. The purpose of this legislation is to introduce a standardized system of regulation of medicinal products. Before any such product can be placed on the market in any member state of the European Community it must receive market authorization from the European Agency. In particular the directive states that where a medicinal product involves a genetically modified organism as defined in 90/220/EEC the application for market authorization must be accompanied by a copy of any written consent from the competent authorities to the deliberate release of the GMO's into the environment; a technical dossier; an environmental risk assessment and the results of any investigations performed for the purposes of research or development. Art 6(4) states that the European Agency has a duty to consult with the biosafety bodies established in the member states and it should draw up guidance for the use of GMOs in humans in concert with such bodies and with other "interested parties." The directive introduces a number of new requirements in the name of "pharmacovigilance." Thus, adverse reactions to any medicinal product authorized for use in the EU must be reported to the Agency.

4. Council of Europe

The Council of Europe has taken an interest in the regulation of genetic technology since the advent of the scientific techniques. In 1982 the Parliamentary Assembly of the Council of Europe issued recommenda-

tion 934 on genetic engineering, which contained a call for the introduction of safeguards into the use of genetic technology. More recently, in June 1990 the Committee of Ministers issued Recommendation R(90) 13, which stated that:

> Governments of member states are recommended to adopt legislation in conformity with a series of fourteen principles, or to take other appropriate measures to ensure the implementation of these principles.

In 1992 the Committee of Ministers again turned to the issue of genetic testing and screening for the purposes of health care and issued Recommendation R(92)3, which advised the governments of member states that in drawing up legislation and policy in the field of genetic screening and testing they should be guided by a series of 14 principles and recommendations.

Various other organs of the European Community have issued official statements or policy documents which relate to the question of genetic technology. In 1989 the European Parliament published a resolution on the ethical and legal problems of genetic engineering which addressed both gene therapy and genetic screening. The Council issued a decision in December 1994 adopting a specific programme of research and technological development in biomedicine and health (Decision 94/913/EC). Part of this program relates to research on the human genome and the decision contains an apparent prohibition on the use of germ line gene therapy. It states that:

> No research modifying of seeking to modify, the genetic constitution of human beings by alteration of germ cells or of any stage of embryo development which may make these alterations necessary, will be carried out under this programme.

Similarly, the Group of Advisers on the Ethical Implications of Biotechnology who report to the European Commission, issued an opinion in 1994 on the ethical implications of gene therapy. This report described the criteria under which somatic cell gene therapy could be undertaken in the United Kingdom and then went on to state that germ line gene therapy was not "at the present time" ethically acceptable.

II. NATIONAL REGULATIONS

A. Australia

The regulation of medical research in Australia adopts the two-tier model of regulation. Overall regulation is coordinated by the National Health and Medical Research Council (NHMRC), a body that was placed under a new statutory framework by the National Health and Medical Research Council Act of 1992. This body supervises all experimentation on human subjects and requires the establishment of Institutional Ethics Committees (IEC) as a precondition for research funding. IECs are required to monitor the progress of the project and to ensure that appropriate procedures for obtaining consent are followed. Unusually for a system of local ethical review, the IECs monitor not only those projects funded by the NHMRC but also projects that are funded internally by the particular academic institution and those that are funded externally by other bodies. For this reason they have been described as the "linchpin" of the Australian system. The National Health and Medical Research Council Act of 1992 established a new regulatory framework and an Australian Health Ethics Committee (AHEC) to which the IECs must report. In the field of gene therapy IECs are guided by the NHMRC Guidance Note 7, introduced in 1987 and modified in 1992, which states that while somatic cell gene therapy is acceptable, germ line gene therapy is not. Somatic cell gene therapy is regarded as experimental treatment and the IEC should satisfy itself that the research is ethical and that the investigators are competent. In 1994 the NHMRC established a centralized Gene Therapy Committee (GTC) closely following the model of GTAC in the United Kingdom and adopting to a large extent the protocols developed by the RAC in the United States. The GTC does not hold public meetings. This two-tier ethical review system is supplemented in the area of safety by the Genetic Manipulation Advisory Committee (GMAC), which supervises the use of novel genetic manipulation techniques and is primarily concerned with the containment of genetically modified organisms in order to prevent the escape of such entities into the environment. Most human gene therapy protocols are exempted from review by GMAC.

Genetic technology is also regulated under the umbrella of assisted conception laws. Australia has a federal and state system of government, and the individual states have opted for slightly different forms of regulation for the new reproductive technologies. Three states, Victoria, South Australia, and Western Australia opted for statutory frameworks. In Victoria the Infertility (Medical Procedures) Act 1984 established a standing committee that operates in effect as a licensing authority. South Australia, under the Reproductive Technology Act 1988, and Western Australia, with the Human Reproductive Technology Act 1991, opted for a more explicit licensing system. In each state an annual license is required that stipulates the conditions that must be met in the use of reproductive technology. Three states, Queensland, Tasmania, and New South Wales opted for a system of self-regulation rather than a statutory framework. This patchwork, system of assisted conception regulation is currently being reviewed by the AHEC, which aims to develop a set of national guidelines that could be administered by an independent national body.

B. Austria

The Austrian government enacted in July 1994 the Gene Technology Law *Genetechnik* Federal Law BGB 510/ 1994. This is a broadly based piece of legislation that regulates all work with genetically modified organisms and the use of genetic testing and gene therapy in human beings. Section 1 states that the aims of the legislation are first to protect the health of humans and their descendants from damage that may be caused by manipulation of the human genome, by genetic analysis, or by the impact of genetically modified organisms. Second, the legislation is intended to support the application of genetic technology for the sake of human well-being by creating a legal framework for research, development, and application of genetic technology. Section IV of the Act applies to the use of gene analysis and gene therapy techniques in human beings. Section 64 of the Act contains a direct prohibition of intervention in human reproductive cell lines; thus germ line gene therapy is clearly prohibited.

Section 65 of the Gene Technology Law deals in some detail with the issues arising from genetic screening and testing technology. The law states that genetic testing or screening can only be carried out at the request of a doctor specializing in medical genetics. The analysis cannot be performed without the written consent of the patient. Prenatal genetic screening must only be carried out where it is medically necessary to do so. Under section 70 of the Act the doctor carrying out the analysis is required to advise the person whose DNA is being analysed to inform relatives of the test where the testing of relatives would verify the diagnosis, or where it is believed that there will be a risk for the relatives of the individual. The legislation also contains substantial provisions on the storage and protection of data derived from genetic screening.

C. Belgium

Although, like many other nations, Belgium does not have a specific genetics law it was one of the first nations to attempt to address the problems that might arise from genetic technology in that it established a Higher Council on Human Genetics in 1973. More recently the Crown Order of December 14, 1987, established explicit standards for the operation of centres for human genetics. In the Law of June 25, 1992 the Belgian government precluded insurance companies from requesting or using genetic information in their determinations of life insurance contracts.

D. Canada

The use of gene therapy in Canada is largely supervised by the Canadian Medical Research Council (MRC). The use or development of germ line gene therapy is completely prohibited. The MRC does permit the use of somatic cell gene therapy provided that:

- The disease is attributable to a single gene disorder.
- The genetic anomaly must give rise to a seriously debilitating disease or premature death.
- The disease cannot be successfully treated by any other method.

These guidelines were drawn up by the MRC in 1987 and were accompanied by a recommendation that a National Committee for the Examination of Gene Therapy should be established. In 1993 the Royal Commission on New Reproductive Technologies also recommended that all gene therapy protocols should be evaluated by a national assessment committee.

A new legislative initiative to regulate genetic technology in Canada was introduced in the House of Commons in June 1996. This followed the recommendations of the Final Report of the Royal Commission on New Reproductive Technologies. The Human Reproductive and Genetic Technologies Act will be the first stage of a regulatory framework which will also include a national agency, operating at federal level, which will develop national standards for the use of genetic materials, issue licenses and ensure compliance with the legislation. Section 3 of the Act states that the objectives of the legislation are to:

> protect the health and safety of Canadians in the use of human reproductive materials for assisted reproduction, other medical procedures and medical research; to ensure the appropriate treatment of human reproductive materials outside the body in recognition of their potential to form human life; and to protect the dignity of all persons, in particular children and women, in relation to uses of human reproductive materials.

The Act itself prohibits 13 practices which are set out in Section 4 of the proposed legislation. Among the prohibited practices are sex selection for nonmedical purposes, commercial sale of eggs, sperm or embryos, germ line genetic manipulation, cloning of human embryos, commercial surrogacy, research on human embryos later than 14 days after conception and the creation of embryos for research purposes only.

The second stage of the legislative program is a proposed federal regulatory framework that would supervise practices that were not explicitly prohibited under the Act but that were still considered to pose ethical concerns. It is proposed that a national agency will be established to report to Parliament through the Minister of Health. The agency would approve licenses, inspect facilities, and ensure compliance with the regulations contained in the Human Reproductive and Genetic Technologies Act.

E. Denmark

The Danish Law 353 of June 3, 1987, established the Danish Council of Ethics, which has produced several significant reports on the area of genetic technology. In 1989 the Danish Council produced a report on the protection of human gametes, fertilized ova, embryos and fetuses that argued for a prohibition on germ line gene therapy. The report was more accommodating toward somatic cell gene therapy, although the Danish government stated that any such intervention would only be tolerated if it could be shown that there was no danger that somatic cell therapy could alter the germ cells.

F. Finland

In 1995 Finland passed the Gene Technology Act (337/1995). The aims and scope of this legislation are established in Section 1 which states:

> The aim of this Act is:
> 1. To promote the safe use and development of gene technology in a way that is ethically acceptable; and
> 2. To prevent and avert any harm to human health, animals, property or the environment that

may be caused by the use of genetically modified organisms.

The operation is supervised by the Finnish Ministry for Social Affairs and Health insofar as it relates to general matters potentially affecting human health. It is jointly controlled by the Ministry of the Environment, which has jurisdiction over those aspects of genetic technology and genetically modified organisms that may have some impact on the environment. In addition, the legislation establishes a broader regulatory framework through the introduction of a Board for Gene Technology. The details and functions of this board are more fully established in the Gene Technology Decree (821/1995) of May 24, 1995, which provides that, inter alia, the Board shall act as a registration authority, that it should review on a case by case basis the initial use of any new genetically modified organisms, that it should provide guidelines for institutions engaged in genetic technology research or production, that it has the power to impose sanctions on institutions using genetically modified organisms under Section 22 of the 1995 Act and that it should have responsibility for the contained use and deliberate release of genetically modified organisms.

In addition to the Gene Technology Board, Section 6 of the Act also makes provision for the utilization of such "expert authorities and institutions" as may be specified by decree. This is developed in the Gene Technology Decree, which lists five expert authorities and four expert institutions.

G. France

France has developed one of the most comprehensive systems of regulation of genetic technology. This reflects the fact that the issues relating to genetic technology have provoked a considerable degree of public interest and debate within France. A number of influential reports on the issue of genetic technology have emanated from France including the Lenoir Report, the Serusclat Report, the Bouliac Report, and the Matie Report. The *Comite consultif national d'ethique pour les sciences de la vie et de la sante* (CCNE) has twice reported on the questions raised by genetic technology. In 1990 the CCNE formally prohibited all forms of germ line gene therapy and limited the use of somatic cell gene therapy to monogenic heriditary disease with a grave prognosis. The permissible scope of somatic cell gene therapy was extended by a second opinion of the CCNE in 1993 that stipulated five requirements

which must be met before any form of somatic cell gene therapy could go ahead:

1. Any procedure designed to change the physical or mental characteristics of an individual, except in the case of serious disease, is prohibited;
2. Somatic cell gene therapy trials must be preceded by adequate prior examination of animals to determine the effectiveness and safety of the techniques;
3. Somatic cell gene therapy may only be used in individuals suffering from a condition for which there is no available effective treatment and the prognosis for which is sufficiently serious to warrant the potential risks;
4. The results of all research must be monitored for scientific and technical validity and by the CCNE for ethical standards;
5. Any information about the potential for the research must be released with objectivity, restraint and realism to avoid unduly heightened expectations.

In addition to the CCNE two other bodies are concerned with the regulation of genetic technology in France, the *Commission de Gene Genetique* (CGG) and the *Commission de Genie Biomoleculaire* (CGBM). These two bodies are charged with ensuring compliance with the EC directives on controlled use and deliberate release. They in turn report to the *Agence du Medicament*, which has two commissions with competence in this area, the Commission on Viral Safety and the Commission on Clinical Trials. These commissions are directly connected and report to the French Minister for Health. In common with the two-tier system operated in many countries, the French also have local ethical review which takes place under the auspices of *Comite Consultif de Protection des Personnes se pretant a des Recherches Biologiques*.

H. Germany

There are at least three areas of law which regulate genetic technology in Germany. First, the use of genetically modified material is regulated by the *Arzneimittelgesetz* (AMG) (The Law of Medical Drugs). Sections 40–42 of the AMG regulate the safety of the patient who is undergoing any form of medical treatment. The AMG requires that a local ethical committe give approval to any clinical trial. The law requires that the patient consent to the intervention having been informed of the nature and effect of the treatment. The patient must be insured and has the right to be compensated for any damage that occurs as a consequence of the treatment.

Of perhaps greater importance is the more controversial *Embryonenschutzgesetz* (ESG) (Embryo Protection Law). As with the United Kingdom's Human Fertilisation and Embryology Act, the ESG states in Section 5 that the alteration of human germ line cells is a criminal offense. The ESG differs from similar legislation in other states insofar as it introduces an element of intent. Thus, where the germ line alteration is unintentional, for example, as a consequence of radiation treatment or chemotherapy, the action does not fall within the prohibition in Section 5. While this may appear to be a sensible rule it has given rise to controversy as it would appear to permit unintentional germ line gene therapy that occurred during the development of somatic cell gene therapy techniques.

The use of genetic technology in Germany is also circumscribed by the relatively rigid rules of the German medical profession. Most significant among the rules that have been developed by the German medical profession is the principle that a physician need not seek full legal and ethical approval for the "single attempt to heal." Thus an exception is made to the normally very rigid codes of practice where the treatment in question is an experimental treatment carried out as a matter of last resort.

Also of importance is the *Gentechnikgesetz* (GTG) (The Law on Genetic Technology). This law does not refer directly to the use of genetic technology on human beings but is, rather, a biosafety measure designed to comply with the requirements of European Law. Before any clinical trial involving genetically modified material can begin the safety of the proposed procedure must be assessed by the Central Commission for Biological Safety.

I. Italy

No specific legislation has been adopted in Italy to address the issue of gene therapy. The EC contained use and deliberate release directives apply and oversight of genetically modified material is carried out by the *Commissione Unica del Farmaco* of the Italian Ministry of Health. Some regional laws have been enacted in the area of genetic screening and counselling. For example in Fuili-Venezia Guilia Regional Law 49 enacted on June 24, 1993, sets out provisions on the need for genetic counselling before conception and prenatal diagnosis.

J. Netherlands

Genetic screening has been regulated in the Netherlands since 1992 when the *Staatsblad van het Koninkrijk der Nederlanden* (Population Screening Act) was enacted. This law requires that the minister approve any genetic screening program before it is implemented and requires that he be advised on the matter by the Health Council. The Act defines population screening in broad terms as "a medical examination which is carried out in response to an offer made to the entire population or to a section thereof and which is designed to detect diseases of a certain kind or certain risk indicators either wholly or partly for the benefit of the persons to be examined." A license for the screening program will be refused if it is scientifically unsound, if it conflicts with statutory regulations, or if it involves risks that outweigh the likely benefits. Following the implementation of this law the Health Council of the Netherlands published a report from the Committee on Genetic Screening. This report states that screening should not necessarily be restricted to certain categories of serious genetic disease but rather takes the view that the provision of comprehensible information is essential to maintain the autonomy of the individual.

In the area of gene therapy legislation was introduced in 1993 to implement the EC directives on genetically modified organisms into Dutch national law. The Dutch Health Council reported on the issue of gene therapy in 1989 and found that somatic cell gene therapy was an acceptable experimental procedure which could be undertaken provided the following safeguards had been met:

- The protocols must be approved by the Central Committee on the Ethics of Medical Research;
- The procedures must be monitored to ensure that they comply with the terms of the submitted protocol;
- The protocols will be the subject of specific requirements in relation to the scientific value and safety of the project.

Germ line gene therapy was also considered by the Health Council and they recommended that a moratorium on germ line research be introduced because of the unduly high risks posed by the technique.

K. Norway

In August 1994, the Storting passed one of the more restrictive laws relating to the regulation of genetic technology. The preamble to the Act Relating to the Application of Biotechnology in Medicine (1994) states that:

> The purpose of this Act is to ensure that the application of biotechnology is utilised in the best interests of human beings in a society where everyone plays a role and is fully valued. This shall take place in accordance with the principles of respect for human dignity, human rights and personal integrity and without discrimination on the basis of genetic background based on ethical norms relating to our western cultural heritage.

Section 7 of the Act deals directly with the issue of gene therapy and states that the human genome can only be altered for the purpose of treating serious disease or preventing serious disease from occurring. In common with many other regulations it states that germ line gene therapy is prohibited. In addition to the terms of the legislation the Act also requires that no treatment involving gene therapy can go ahead without first obtaining permission from the Ministry of Health, which has constituted a Biotechnology Advisory board. The Norwegian statute also refers to the issue of genetic testing in Section 6. Genetic testing is permitted although Section 6(2) states that it may only be carried out when there is a clear diagnostic or therapeutic objective. Perhaps, more importantly, given the dangers of genetic discrimination, Section 6(7) of the Act states that "it is prohibited to request, receive, possess or make use of genetic information concerning an individual that results from a genetic test." Similarly it is illegal to inquire as to whether or not a genetic test has actually been carried out.

L. Sweden

In Sweden genetically modified material, which would include the type of products to be used in gene therapy, fall into the category of drugs, and are therefore regulated under the Swedish Medical Products Agency. Under the Law 114 of March 1991 *Svensk forfattningssamling*, authorization is required before investigations or testing of DNA can be carried out. Under Law 115 of March 1991 this body must give its approval to any somatic cell gene intervention. This law states that experimentation on fertilized oocytes must not have the objective of developing methods of "causing heritable genetic effects." Approval is also required before any genetic testing is carried out for diagnostic purposes. In addition to the national body Sweden has also devel-

oped a system of regional advisory ethics committees which assess the scientific validity of research protocols.

M. Switzerland

Switzerland, perhaps uniquely, has actually amended the Federal Constitution by the insertion of a new Section 24, which states that:

> Man and the environment are protected against the abuse of genetic engineering and reproduction technology.

The amendment states that interventions that affect the genetic heritage of human gametes are not permissible; that the germ lines of nonhuman species should not be transferred into human beings; that human germ line cells should not be the subject of commercial transactions, and that an individual's genetic composition may only be analyzed, recorded, and disclosed with their consent.

In addition to this constitutional regulation, individual cantons have also enacted laws that impact on the field of genetic technology. A directive issued in the canton of Basel-land in 1987 relating to the use of in vitro fertilization techniques provides that interventions on the genetic material of human cells is to be prohibited. In April 1994 the canton of Geneva passed regulations on clinical research involving interventions in the field of human genetic manipulation. This legislation requires that research in the field of genetic manipulation is to be undertaken solely under the auspices of Geneva University or a body of similar academic standing, and stipulates conditions that must be met by research protocols contemplating the use of genetic manipulation techniques. Since 1993 the Regulation for Intercantonal Control of Medicinal Products has been in force. Currently, drug and clinical trials are regulated at cantonal level but the new regulation harmonizes the regulatory procedure and defines the tasks of the local ethical committees. This regulation closely affects the development of gene therapy trials in Switzerland.

The issues of contained use and deliberate release of genetically modified organisms into the environment are addressed in the Law on Environmental Protection, which in conjunction with the Law on Epidemics has led to the establishment of an Expert Commission for Biosafety. These two laws and the Commission are to come into force in 1997.

The use of genetic technology in Switzerland is also constrained by the guidelines of two national bodies in the Swiss Academy of Medical Sciences (SAMW) and the Swiss Commission for Biological Safety (SKBS). The SAMW guidelines require that any research project involving human beings must gain the approval of an ethics committee before proceeding. The SAMW is not a state body and this system of regulation is a voluntary one except in those cantons where the guidelines have been incorporated into legislation. The SAMW has considered that genetic technology poses such significant problems that a special subcommitte on gene therapy has been established.

While ethical oversight is mainly the preserve of the SAMW, issues of safety are considered by the SKBS. This organization registers the interests of researchers and in 1992 issued Guidelines for Work with Genetically Modified Organisms to researchers planning to submit a protocol involving genetic technology. These guidelines are broadly based on the Points to Consider documents developed by the United States National Institutes of Health. The SKBS is organized along the lines of the RAC in the United States and it is intended that by 1997 the SKBS will become a Federal Expert Committee. The current procedure for the submission of a gene therapy protocol in Switzerland is that first of all the protocol submitted to the SKBS should conform with the NIH Points to Consider document. Within three months an expert subcommittee of the SKBS should review the protocol. The applicant should then inform the cantonal authorities while the project is submitted to a local ethics committee. The SKBS informs both the federal authorities and the public of its findings. A duty is imposed upon the researcher to report any adverse findings to the SKBS along with a duty to submit a final report.

N. United Kingdom

In the United Kingdom regulatory mechanisms, both legislative and procedural, have been established in a number of areas that relate directly and indirectly to the use of genetic technology. In each of these areas the regulatory framework has been set up following the publication of a government report.

In 1984 the Warnock Committee was established to consider the ethical issues arising from the development of in vitro fertilization techniques. The Committee reported in 1985, and the findings of this report were finally embodied in the Human Fertilisation and Embryology Act 1990, which established a regulatory body, the Human Fertilisation and Embryology Authority, to operate a licensing scheme for IVF treatment centers. The act is a significant piece of legislation for many reasons, but in the area of genetics it explicitly addresses the question of germ line gene therapy. Section 3(3)(d) of the Act states that:

> A licence cannot authorise ... (d) replacing the nucleus of a cell or embryo with a nucleus taken from a cell of any person, embryo or subsequent development of an embryo.

However, despite this apparently rigid prohibition the licensing authority still retains a degree of discretion as to what type of procedures it is prepared to authorize.

The issue of gene therapy was explicitly addressed by a House of Commons Committee chaired by Sir Cecil Clothier. In common with similar studies elsewhere, the Clothier Committee concerned itself primarily with the dichotomy between germ line gene therapy and somatic cell gene therapy, concluding that germ line gene therapy was unacceptable. It recommended that somatic cell gene therapy be permitted as it posed no new ethical problems, but included the caveat that it should be considered an experimental procedure and thus be subject to higher standards of scrutiny than an ordinary medical treatment. The major practical recommendation of the report was to set up the Gene Therapy Advisory Committee (GTAC), a nonstatutory committee charge with reviewing the ethical acceptibility of proposals for gene therapy. Despite the terms of reference of the GTAC, it would appear that, like many similar bodies, it concerns itself more with the scientific merit of gene therapy protocols than with the ethical acceptability of the proposals (Gene Therapy Advisory Committee, First Annual Report, 1995).

The entire field of genetic technology was surveyed by the House of Commons Select Committee on Science and Technology in a report published in July 1995 (HMSO, July 1995). This report examined the ethical issues arising from genetic technology and made a number of criticisms of existing procedures. It recommended the setting up of a Human Genetics Commission to regulate the advance of genetic technology. Arguments for national bodies have been made elsewhere and the proposal has obvious attractions. There have also been arguments generally in the United Kingdom for the replacement of the LREC system with a national ethics review board that could scrutinize the ethical implications of research while perhaps leaving the scrutiny of the research methodology to a local group.

However, rather than establish a Human Genetics Commission with full powers to investigate the application of genetic technology and with a budget to pursue proactive research in the area, the Department of Health decided to establish an advisory subcommittee to provide advice relating to genetic testing and screening. This committee is to be chaired by Rev. Dr. John Polkinghorne, who had previously chaired another committee of inquiry into the use of fetal tissue. This committee has advisory powers only and operates exclusively under the auspices of the Department of Health.

O. United States

Many of the components of the United States approach to the regulation of genetic technology have been emulated and implemented elsewhere. Indeed, this has happened to the extent that there are calls for the American model to become the standard for a harmonized global system of regulation.

Gene therapy protocols are the subject of regulation by two national and one local body. The national bodies are the Food and Drug Administration (FDA) and the Recombinant DNA Advisory Committee (RAC) of the National Institutes of Health (NIH). The FDA is charged with reviewing all new and investigational gene therapy protocols that take place in the United States. This work is done at the Center for Biologics Evaluation and Research (CBER). The RAC has a somewhat different ambit in that it is charged with reviewing all gene therapy protocols that use NIH funds. The RAC is a multidisciplinary body made up of scientists, physicians, lawyers, and ethicists that holds its meetings in public. At local level all uses of gene therapy must gain the approval of an Institutional Review Board (IRB).

The process has recently been streamlined with the introduction of a consolidated review system. Thus a project that is publicly funded is first assessed to determine whether it is a novel protocol. If it is a new technique, then the application must go to both the RAC and the FDA. If, on the other hand, the technique is not new than the review process is deferred by the RAC and oversight is carried out by just the FDA. Currently, most of the United States gene therapy protocols follow this procedure.

If the application is novel and approval is obtained from the FDA and RAC then the investigators also need FDA approval of an Investigational New Drug (IND) in order to be exempt from the FDA premarket licensing requirements. The IND approval is obtained after review by a team of experts who either give permission to proceed or put the application "on hold." The team is made up of a primary product reviewer, a pharmocology and toxicology reviewer, a clinical reviewer, and any other consultants who are considered to be necessary. The investigators are informed of the concerns that led

to the imposition of the "hold," and if these concerns are addressed, then the study may proceed. Typical concerns that would arrest a trial would be that there is an unreasonable or significant risk, or that the reviewers have not been presented with sufficient information to assess the risk. Once the protocol is given permission to proceed, any adverse events that occur must be reported to the FDA. In addition, there is a duty to submit an annual report on the progress of the research.

Clinical trials in the United States are separated into three phases. Phase I trials involve the initial introduction of a product into humans in order to determine safety and toxicity with increasing doses. Phase II trials seek to determine short-term side effects and risk as well as evaluating the efficacy of the product in a more controlled study. Phase III trials are expanded trials that are designed to gather additional information on efficacy, safety, and toxicity so that an overall risk to benefit analysis can be made.

The RAC system of review has proved to be popular because of the transparency and consistency of its processes. However, it is not without defects. It is limited to reviewing proposals that are funded by the NIH, and cannot therefore exercise jurisdiction over externally funded research. In addition, the RAC is itself a subcommittee of the NIH and there is therefore a possible conflict of interest in that the NIH is both the instigator, funder, and regulator of research.

III. DISCUSSION

The international community of legislators has responded with commendable speed to the perceived threats of a technology that is still in its infancy. The timely introduction of a panoply of different forms of legislation illustrates that interference with the human genome is a concept that provokes deep concerns. Given the substantial jurisprudential and cultural differences that exist between national legal systems, there would seem to be a remarkable degree of homogeneity among the legislative responses. However, this confluence of opinion cannot in itself be taken to imply that the legislative responses that have appeared to prevail are in fact the best means of minimizing the dangers of genetic technology, nor that these responses are philosophically sound. Legislation that introduces procedural safeguards without some substantive basis or ethical underpinning may prove only to be of value in the short term. Procedural safeguards, and "soft" regulatory systems generally, are dependent on those who supervise the licensing procedures. The bodies that oversee these procedural safeguards are often made up largely of individuals sympathetic to the practices in question, in this case scientists. There is then a possibility that the regulatory system will not be applied as rigorously as might have been anticipated by those who designed the system.

Having catalogued the regulatory responses of some countries at the leading edge of genetic technology it is possible to discern a number of common trends. First, in relation to gene therapy, many of the countries have opted for the two-tier, method of ethical oversight. This typically involves a local research ethics committee reviewing the proposed protocol as if it were any other clinical trial. The role of these local bodies differs slightly in the various countries, but generally they are tasked with assessing the ethical and scientific merit of the protocols. The argument for doing this at a local level is that there may be localized cultural difficulties with carrying out such research in a particular area and that community representatives should have some form of input into the process.

The second tier involves review at national level. In the United States, United Kingdom, and Australia this is carried out by a national committee of experts who meet to discuss approval for specific genetic manipulation projects. These committees tend to be scientifically dominated, despite the fact that their remit is usually confined to the assessment of ethical issues related to the project and that the assessment of the scientific merit of the procedure tends to form a separate part of the review process. The tendency to overlap and to overemphasize the need for scientific appraisal of gene therapy proposals, often at the expense of more rigorous ethical review, is one of the shortcomings of many of the two-tier systems of ethical review.

Another recurring feature of the regulatory landscape is that many of the countries have opted, often at an early stage in the regulatory debate, to utilize assisted conception legislation as a means of regulating genetic technology. This is true of Australia, Germany, the United Kingdom, and Sweden. One weakness of this approach is that assisted conception laws were drafted as a specific response to the advent of in vitro fertilization techniques in the late 1970s and early 1980s. While such legislation often refers to the need to avoid interference with the reproductive cell lines of human beings, the provisions relating to genetic technology tended to be introduced as amendments in response to rather vaguely drawn concerns about the advent of "designer babies." As such, many of these measures may be of limited efficacy in relation to regu-

lating the reality of germ line or enhancement gene therapy techniques.

The legislative responses to gene therapy are almost unanimous in their adoption of the somatic cell/germ line dichotomy. This split has been in evidence from the earliest reports and inquiries into the issue of gene therapy such as the Declaration of Inuyama and the Clothier Report. In most instances it has been argued that somatic cell gene therapy poses no new ethical problems, but should be regulated as if it were an experimental treatment. Germ line gene therapy is seen to pose too many risks both in terms of biosafety and in terms of potential damage to future generations. There are a few exceptions. The Netherlands for example, has rejected this rigid approach to germ line gene therapy and appears to recognize that there may in fact be good reasons for permitting limited use of such techniques. However, attractive the distinction between germ line gene therapy and somatic cell gene therapy might appear to regulators and legislators, the distinction between the two may not be as scientifically, or indeed, ethically sustainable as was once thought. An outright prohibition on germ line gene therapy seems to be a measure that will come under increasing strain as techniques are developed that will make it safe and as public demand for such an apparently "magic bullet" therapy grows.

The two-tier method of review and the FDA/RAC model developed in the United States and much copied elsewhere is based on a case-by-case review system. There are inherent dangers built into such a system of operating. While dangers of a slippery slope that will take us into the realm of supermen and wonderwomen are probably greatly exaggerated it is possible that the case-by-case system of ethical review is more likely to move the regulatory system in a liberal direction as fine distinctions and comparisons are made and as a body of regulatory "precedent" develops over time. This is not to argue that moving in a liberal direction is necessarily a bad outcome but rather that without a coherent agreement on the underlying ethical principles which govern gene therapy research it will be difficult to prevent this form of regulatory "creep."

Despite the considerable degree of legislative effort and energy that has been expended on this topic there is still only a very small amount of legislation that has been drafted specifically to tackle the problems of genetic technology. Perhaps genetic technology does not pose problems of such a difficult nature that they require a specific legislative response. Alternatively, there may not be the will or the energy within the various legislatures to tackle the complex moral issues that genetics can raise. Much of the regulation of genetic technology that does exist tends to come under the umbrella of broader measures intended to tackle issues such as assisted conception or reproductive technology. One consequence of this lack of topic specific legislation is the degree of overlap that tends to occur between the regulation of genetic technology as it is applied to human beings and the broader regulation of biotechnology and the use of genetic technology in agriculture and industry. This is perhaps most pronounced in Europe where there are EC directives relating to the use of "genetically modified organisms" alongside existing national legislation on biosafety or reproductive technology. The overall effect can be to confuse rather than to clarify the situation. A further weakness of the current approaches to the regulation of gene therapy is that there is little evidence of the regulatory mechanisms pursuing a proactive research agenda. The scientific developments are constantly progressing and consequently an onus lies upon the regulatory systems to at least keep pace with, and preferably to anticipate future developments.

The examination of the national responses to the problems posed by genetic technology also appears to reveal a disproportionate weighting of legislation in the area of gene therapy and a relative dearth of regulation in the area of genetic screening. While the possibility of manipulating genetic material for therapeutic purposes tends to capture the headlines and the imaginations of legislators, it is the arguably less newsworthy issue of genetic analysis by screening and testing that poses the more immediate dangers. Gene therapy techniques may pose dangers for the future, but genetic screening and analysis poses immediate problems of discrimination and invasion of privacy. Surprisingly, there has been little direct regulatory response to this issue. Many countries have enacted disability discrimination legislation, and others have introduced measures that seek to safeguard the methods of storage of genetic test samples and results. The Austrian legislation, for example, contains detailed provisions on the storage of genetic information. The Ethical, Legal and Social Implications (ELSI) research group of the Humane Genome Project has drafted a model Genetic Privacy Act that directly addresses some of these problems. These regulatory responses share a common basis in that they follow the procedural model of regulation by introducing safeguards to minimize access to information.

Also See the Following Articles

EMBRYOLOGY, ETHICS OF • EUGENICS • GENE THERAPY • GENOME ANALYSIS • REPRODUCTIVE TECHNOLOGIES

Bibliography

(1994). Bilbao Declaration 45(2) International Digest of Health Legislation 234–237.

Billings, P., & Beckwith, J. (1992). Genetic testing in the workplace: A view from the USA. *Trends in Genetics,* **8.**

Chalmers, D. (1994). Institutional ethics committees and the management of medical research and experimentation. 3 *Australian Health Law* 37.

Cohen-Haguenauer, O. (1995). Overview of the regulation of gene therapy in Europe: A current statement. *Human Gene Therapy,* **6,** 773–785.

Council for International Organisations of Medical Sciences. (1991). The Inuyama declaration. In Bankowski, Z., Capron, A. M., (Eds.) (1991). *Genetics, ethics and human values: Human genome mapping, genetic screening and gene therapy.* Proceedings of the XXIVth CIOMS Round Table Conference. CIOMS, Geneva, pp. 1–3.

Fletcher, J. C., & Anderson, W. F. (1992). Germ line gene therapy: A New Stage of Debate. *Law, Medicine and Health Care,* **20,** 26–39.

Gene Therapy Advisory Committee. (1995, March). *First Annual Report.* Department of Health.

Gene Therapy Advisory Committee. (1996, April). *Second Annual Report.* Department of Health.

Kielstein, R., Sass, H. (1992). Right not to know or duty to know? Prenatal screening for polycystic renal disease. *Journal of Medicine and Philosophy,* **17,** 395

Lappe, M. (1991). Ethical issues in manipulating the human germ line. *Journal of Medicine and Philosophy,* **16,** 621.

Matthewman, W. D. (1984). Title VII and genetic testing: Can your genes screen you out of a job? *Howard Law Journal,* **27,** 1185.

Medical Research Council of Canada. (1990). *Guidelines for Research on Somatic Cell Gene Therapy in Humans.* Subcommittee on Human Gene Therapy, Recombinant DNA Advisory Committee. National Institutes of Health. Points to Consider in the design and submission of protocols for the transfer of recombinant DNA into the genome of human subjects. *Human Gene Therapy,* **1,** 93.

McGleenan, T. (1995). Human gene therapy and the slippery slope arguments. *Journal of Medical Ethics,* **21,** 350.

Rothstein, M. A. (1991). Discrimination based on genetic information. *Jurimetrics Journal,* **33,** 13.

(1991). Valencia Declaration on Ethics and the Human Genome Project 42, (2) *International Digest of Health Legislation,* **42,** 2, 338–339.

Walter, L. (1991). Human gene therapy: Ethics and public policy. 2 Human Gene Therapy, **2,** 115.

Zimmerman, B. K. (1991). Human germ line gene therapy: The case for its development and use. *Journal of Medicine and Philosophy,* **16,** 593.

GENOME ANALYSIS

Adam M. Hedgecoe
University of Central Lancashire

GLOSSARY

big science A popular term for large-scale, very expensive projects that usually involve large installations or equipment, or more rarely, a large number of smaller, less expensive research centers.

DNA Deoxyribonucleic acid, the material contained in all living things that makes up a gene and that contains an individual's genetic code.

gene The basic unit of heredity, consisting of a stretch of DNA that carries instructions telling the body how to make a particular protein.

geneticization The process by which diseases (especially in humans) and behaviors are described and understood in genetic terms.

genome The sum total of all genes carried by any individual organism or species.

Human Genome Diversity Project A contemporary research effort aimed at describing the genetic differences and similarities of various human populations or ethnic groups.

Human Genome Project The attempt to analyze and identify all the genes, and sequence all the DNA present in human beings.

mapping A generic term used to describe the activity of finding out the position of various genes in the genome.

reductionism The increasingly fine-tuned analysis of scientific processes, "reducing" the explanation of processes to smaller scale.

sequencing The act of determining the exact molecular sequence of genetic material.

GENOME ANALYSIS is the investigation into the genetic information carried by individual living things. This information is of great interest to scientists, doctors, and other experts, and the ethical aspects of its application are huge. There are also ethical issues involved in simply investigating the genome, irrespective of the use to which the information produced is put.

Large amounts of money are currently being spent on the Human Genome Project, the international effort to discover everything about the human genome, and it is expected that the final results, with a complete description of the human genome, will be available by the early years of the next century. Thus, there is urgent need to address the ethical issues raised by genome analysis.

I. INTRODUCTION

The aim of this article is to present the ethical issues associated with the investigation, analysis, and discovery of information present in the human genome, that is, the sum total of genetic material carried by any one person. The concentration will be on human genetics, because although some of the issues are related to analysis of the genomes of other species, these problems are most acute when seen in the context of humankind.

The first difficulty with this aim is the fact that much of the ethical writing on genetics is associated with the *use* of genetic information discovered in the analysis of the genome (e.g,. genetic testing and health insurance, gene therapy, etc.) rather than the simple fact of the discovery of that information in and of itself. Quite often, genomic analysis is not felt to be ethically difficult, only the consequences of its information. For example, the Declaration of Inuyama of the Council for International Organizations of Medical Sciences, states that "efforts to map the human genome present no inherent ethical problems." But others have rejected this viewpoint, making clear that "Gene Mapping is in itself problematic and of concern in ways that ongoing research on the social, legal, and ethical consequences of the information deriving from genome projects cannot address." (A. Lippman. (1992). Led (astray) by genetic maps: The cartography of the human genome and health care. *Social Science and Medicine,* 35 (12), 1469–1476). This article will outline those instances when human genome analysis *is* ethically significant in itself. This article will concentrate on the huge, multinational program known as the Human Genome Project (HGP) as the best-known example of genome analysis, but as will hopefully become clear, many of the ethical issues associated with genome analysis are not limited to large-scale projects like the HGP, but also to the idea of genome analysis itself.

II. TECHNIQUES OF ANALYSIS

The human genome is often described as a "blueprint" or a "book" that lists the secret of humanity, but the analogy most used in the actual science of molecular biology is that of "mapping." The four ways of analyzing a genome are genetic mapping, physical mapping, cDNA mapping, and DNA sequencing, and these can be seen as four separate scales or levels of resolution with which to look at a genome.

A. Genetic Mapping

Genetic mapping (also known as genetic linkage mapping) shows the relevant locations of specific DNA markers along a chromosome. These markers are either active DNA regions (i.e., genes, or "exons") or areas for which no particular use has been discovered ("junk" DNA, or "introns"). These markers are used to trace the familial variations of various observable ("phenotypic") characteristics, whether they be diseases or physical characteristics such as eye color. When genes are passed from parents to children, the process involved may split up any two markers on the same chromosome; the closer the markers are together the less likely they are to be split up, and so the rate at which various markers occur can be used as a means to estimate the distance between markers on a chromosome. Thus, even if the actual gene for a particular disorder is not known, it is possible to identify those markers that are normally associated with it (and that do not occur in individuals without that disorder), and thus a test for genetic diseases can be produced.

B. Physical Mapping

The lowest resolution physical map is the chromosomal map, which assigns genes and other identifiable DNA fragments to their various positions on the chromosome, with the distance between fragments measured in base-pairs, which are the combinations of the four chemicals that make up the "rungs" of DNA's double helix structure. Beyond these lower resolution maps, there are high resolution methods that can allow the identification of DNA pieces in stretches of genome measuring only 10,000 base-pairs long.

C. cDNA Mapping

The complementary (cDNA) map includes only the expressed regions of DNA; that is, it includes only the genes, without the interspersing junk DNA. Because these maps represent only that DNA that codes information, they are felt to be useful in the identification of those genes responsible for disease causation.

D. Sequencing All the DNA

The ultimate map of a genome involves "sequencing" it; determining the exact sequence of base pairs along each chromosome. This involves techniques of purification and separation of DNA sequences and in the future will use cloning techniques and PCR (polymerase chain reaction, a means of "amplifying" quantities of a particular DNA stretch).

III. THE HUMAN GENOME PROJECT

All these techniques are currently being used in the HGP. This has variously been described as "a biological moonshot," producing the "Rosetta stone for studying human biology" and reading the "book of man." Once past all the hyperbole, the HGP is still an extremely impressive undertaking. In 1988 estimates were that it would cost $3 billion in total. In 1995 this was estimated at only $200 million and the project is expected to be completed between 2001 and 2003. Originally conceived of in the mid to late 1980s, the HGP only really began producing results in the 1990s, but the developments of sequencing technology and knowledge about human genetics has developed at a far faster rate than many people expected, resulting in downward revisions of the end date of the project. The HGP is overseen by the Human Genome Organization (HUGO), which has the responsibility for disseminating new information and for coordinating the research efforts of teams in the various countries taking part.

Although the HGP is "only" genome analysis on a grand scale, there are ethical issues that relate to it, and not to genome analysis itself. These are to a large extent a result of the sheer size of the HGP and the criticism that such "big science" arouses.

A. Big Science

Although there seems to be no cut-off point in terms of cost between big science and the rest of science, most commentators would agree on examples of the former if presented with them. Often they involve large, expensive installations or equipment. Examples of this sort might include the CERN accelerator near Geneva used for investigating subatomic particles, or the Hubble telescope launched by NASA. The HGP is a different sort of big science, because it is not about one large installation, carrying out all the genome analysis work, but a network of mainly preexisting labs and centers, scattered around the world, supported by funding from their own countries. Thus it is the overall cost of manpower, new computer banks to store the information, and personnel costs that raise criticisms. The arguments against big science suggest that large sums of money are spent, largely

inefficiently (due to the large bureaucracies generated), on scientific topics that may turn out to be just a "fad"; this money could be redistributed to other, smaller-scale projects with greater effect. Those in support of the HGP cite it as the only means by which such a massive undertaking could be completed; the human genome is so immense that only an equally huge project could analyze it properly. In many ways, the HGP is only "big" in comparison with the size of studies that are normally carried out in the biological sciences. For example, in 1991, the U.S. government spent $136 million on the HGP; but in comparison with the average U.S. $300 million (on average) spent on the development of a single pharmaceutical (bearing in mind the potential benefit for human health that the HGP embodies) it seems rather small.

In fact, the case could be made that objections to the HGP on the grounds that it is too big are not really ethical at all. It is not that most critics are suggesting that the money be spent on an activity such as feeding the Third World, or increasing welfare benefits. They would prefer that the money be spent on other areas of biology or science. Thus, the concerns raised are mainly ones of efficiency and effectiveness, rather than inherently ethical.

B. Access to Information

The problems that still remain concern access to, and the ownership of, the information that results from the analysis being carried out. Although public funds are going into the HGP, so is money from private firms, especially pharmaceutical companies. The issue then arises of who should be allowed access to which data. At the beginning of the project, James Watson, then head of the U.S. NIH/DoE genome project, threatened to withhold access to genomic information from the Japanese, unless they in turn allowed others access to their own research. While there was some sympathy for this position, criticism was voiced by those who felt that the human genome is a world resource, and not the property of any one person or organization to control. At a more practical level, doubts have been raised about the point of an international collaborative project, if the results are subject to government imposed scrutiny. There is a history of political use of scientific information, such as the U.S. National Library of Medicine denying Soviet users access to the Genbank and PIR databases during the Soviet invasion of Afghanistan. The initial result of the U.S. threats was wider interest in funding the HGP, so perhaps it could be said that they were successful; in the long term, such a tactic could be counterproductive leading to tit-for-tat denials by national governments.

At the level of personal ethics, individual researchers may have an interest in delaying publication of information for a period of time, to enable their own research to progress, while denying others the chance to catch up. This would seem to breach the generally accepted ethical requirements for researchers to share data with others, especially in those cases where public funding is involved.

More recently, the issue of access has arisen, not in terms of national efforts but with the increased commercialization of the HGP. The best-known example is that of The Institute for Genomic Research (TIGR), which has a large database of expressed sequence tags (EST). These are short stretches of DNA associated with particular genes, which can be used to identify the postion of genes on any stretch of DNA far quicker than with other methods. TIGR originally tried to patent these ESTs, but was told by the National Institutes of Health that because they were not useful in and of themselves, they were unpatentable. TIGR then agreed to allow other researchers to access the database and its 160,000 ESTs, but on the one condition that if any marketable product was produced as a result of the use of the ESTs, then TIGR, or rather its commercial arm, Human Genome Sciences (HGS), and its partner and financial backer, SmithKline Beecham, would be allowed first refusal on marketing that product. This idea produced alarm in the scientific community, which had assumed that the information was to be made available with no conditions attached. It has been stated that because researchers need access to other DNA sequences in order to compare the accuracy of their own research, the denial of access to such a large database will impede the overall progress of the HGP. TIGR's reply is that they have to maintain some sort of control over their work in order to justify the huge investments made by SmithKline Beecham, and that by not publishing their database, they are allowing people who do discover something useful via one of the ESTs to patent it, because such information would not be in the public domain and thus not infringe the "unobvious" requirement of patentability. Whether or not TIGR's actions are ethical, the fact remains that the Human Genome Project seems likely to become more and more commercialized, as large pharmaceutical firms invest in sequencing laboratories. This in turn will have an effect on researchers' personal ethics, as they try to balance a "scientific duty" to publish their work, and the commercial need for trade secrecy.

IV. UNESCO DECLARATION OF THE PROTECTION OF THE HUMAN GENOME

As a result of general concern about developments in human genetics, UNESCO set up (in 1993) an International Bioethics Committee, which has published several papers. Its main work involved drafting the Declaration on the Protection of the Human Genome and Human Rights, which aims at guidelines that should be borne in mind by those who are carrying out research into the Human Genome Project, although its overall remit is much broader.

The document itself contains 23 articles, starting with the proclamation that "the human genome is the common heritage of humanity." This is an important step, because this is a very public expression of what is considered ethical in the realm of genetic investigations. The declaration then goes on to outline acceptable research behavior in the areas that relate to genetic therapy, screening, and genetic privacy. Criticism has been voiced about the thinking behind such a declaration and the wording used to express these thoughts.

One question arises with the reference to the genome as "common heritage of humanity." The explanatory notes to early versions of the declaration make explicit reference to international treaties that have been drawn up, comparing the genome to such *limited* resources as the seabed. But the appropriateness of this comparison has been questioned; the human genome (either in its material form, or in terms of the information it contains) cannot be used up in the same way as more "traditional" resources such as fossil fuels or mineral deposits, so the exact reasoning behind this link remains unclear. Similarly, confusion rests on the assumption that the human genome is in *need* of protection; from whom or what is not made clear. While the originators of the declaration may have felt that its content was relatively straight forward, it can be argued that it rests upon certain assumptions (such as "the human genome is a finite resource") that are not at all certain. Certainly, if the human genome *is* a resource that belongs to the whole of humanity, this raises questions about whether it is right that private companies should be involved in the HGP, or, separately, whether they should be allowed to profit from the work they do. It also leads us to ask, who should fund the HGP, one answer being all those countries that can afford to, although we could also insist that this does not exclude those who cannot afford it, from benefiting from the results of the research. But whatever queries there may be over the actual semantics of the Declaration, that such a document has been drawn up highlights the fact that investigations into the human genome raise ethical issues, independent of the use to which genetic information is put.

V. THE HUMAN GENOME DIVERSITY PROJECT

Initially proposed by several American academics in 1991, this project had not started by 1996, despite being supported by HUGO since 1994. This delay was largely due to ethical concerns. The Human Genome Diversity Project (HGDP) aims to help us "find out who we are as a species" by preserving cells from various ethnic groups and aboriginal populations around the world, to give students of human genetics access to various exotic gene pools. This work is also of interest to anthropologists, epidemiologists, and even linguists. It has produced ethical questions of its own and has led to a great deal of controversy.

A. Rationale for the HGDP

The proposers of the diversity project claim that however useful the HGP is in refining genetic analysis techniques and information storage systems, its one Achilles heel is that it is explicitly mapping a single genome (not the genome of any one individual, but a combination of genomes). Thus it ignores one of the most interesting aspects of human genetics, the variation between populations. Each of our genomes is a unique product of cultural, environmental, and historical factors, many of which we share with people who have the same history that we do. Thus there are genetic variations between different ethnic groups, or populations. As well as the more academic interest in genetic variation, there is the practical fact that by finding out why some groups are genetically different from others, we will discover more about diseases prevalent among particular groups and thus help forward the HGP's stated aim of improving knowledge about human health.

B. Methods

The HGDP requires that between 400 and 500 ethnic groups, or "populations" should be identified to represent humanity. Preferential treatment would be given to those populations that conformed to one or more of six criteria, ranging from those with the best knowledge of processes that impact on their genetic composition, through those populations that might be most useful in identifying specific genetic diseases, to those that are in danger of losing their genetic, cultural, or linguistic uniqueness. This last criteria means that a great number of indigenous populations are suitable for sampling in the HGDP, and this has raised a number of ethical problems (see below). There are three types of sampling that will be carried out on the populations identified. A large number of genetic markers (150) from single individuals or a smaller number from between 20 and 25 individuals. In both cases they will denote blood that will then be transformed into "immortal" cell lines that will preserve the biological material for indefinite periods of time. A larger number from each population (100–200) may donate some blood and other material (such as hair tissue) that will be used for studies using larger numbers, but with finite material. The total estimate was at first put at between $25 and 30 million for 5 years; this is about 1% of the projected total cost of the HGP as a whole, and it is claimed that bearing in mind the usefulness of the information produced, this should not be regarded as excessive by any means.

C. Benefits

There are four keys areas of research that will benefit from the HGDP:

1. The Origin of Modern Humans

HGDP information will help researchers trying to determine whether humans evolved in Africa and then migrated (the "Out of Africa" thesis), or developed simultaneously across the globe. The information gathered would also shed light on more recent migrations (such as the spread to the Americas) and support archeological evidence that is, at the moment, indeterminate.

2. Social Structure

Anthropologists will gain important clues about mating patterns (such as whether males or females leave the tribe to mate) from DNA samples. Because Y chromosomes are only found in males, it is hoped that the "route" taken by particular DNA can be traced.

3. Adaptation and Disease

Perhaps the most obviously "useful" reason for the HGDP is that the information gained will show whether variations in disease patterns between various populations are due to adaptation to local conditions or merely random changes in genetic make up.

4. Forensic Anthropology

This will add to our sum of knowledge about simply knowing which population is where, and how populations differ from each other.

D. Criticism of the HGDP

1. Racism

Critics of the HGDP claim that it is applying modern technology to an outmoded concept, that of "race." Anthropologists have questioned the central assumptions of the project, that isolated populations are genetically discrete, that human groups are defined solely in terms of genetics, and that genetic differences between groups are greater than those between individuals. There are worries that by focusing on race, however scientifically defined, the HGDP may inadvertently foster racist attitudes. A UNESCO subcommittee set up to examine this issue found that it is not necessarily the case that the supporters of the HGDP are racists (although this claim *has* been made by some indigenous peoples) but that they are naive in not accepting the dangers that their research may produce. This is denied by the HGDP researchers themselves, who claim they are aware of the risks, and that their work is in fact more likely to *reduce* racism, by exposing the scientific fallacy of racist doctrine, than to encourage it. This case has been put very strongly by Luca Cavalli-Sforza, one of the founders of the HGDP, who states "there is no documented biological superiority of race, however defined. Nowhere is there purity of races . . . No damage is caused to humans by racial mixture . . . In fact, the concept of race can hardly be given a scientific, careful definition." (Cavalli-Sforza L. (1994, September 12). *The Human Genome Diversity Project: Address to a Special Meeting of UNESCO. Paris*). The question still remains, though, whether the information resulting from the HGDP could be used by those with less concern for scientific facts, and more dangerous motives.

2. Informed Consent

The leaders of the HGDP intend to enforce the requirement of informed consent when collecting the genetic material, but this has run into objections from indigenous peoples' groups, on both conceptual and practical grounds. Individuals who work with native populations have questioned whether proper *informed* consent can be obtained in the short time envisaged by the HGDP teams. It can take anywhere from 6 months to 5 years for even a minority of individuals to achieve levels of understanding that would normally be considered acceptable. The conceptual difficulty rests on the question of who is justified in giving consent? Although individuals are donating material, the information sought is exclusive to the ethnic group concerned (that is the raison d'être of the HGDP after all). Who then should give permission? The individuals, the whole ethnic group, a majority or a representative (such as a chief, or tribal council). Native rights groups have attacked the HGDP on the grounds that it has failed to address these issues adequately.

3. Patenting, Profiting, and Ownership

The ownership of genetic material and information is highly controversial anyway, but it has added overtones in the realm of human diversity. A great many objections have been raised to the suggestion that scientists from the developed world will take genetic material from indigenous people, isolate important genes from it, and then make a profit out of any products that are developed. Discussions about this took place in March 1995 as the United States issued a patent on genetic material taken from a member of the Hagahai people from Papua New Guinea; the material is useful in detecting HTLV-1-related retroviruses. Although this research was not connected to the HGDP and the Hagahai are not on the provisional list of candidate populations for it, opponents of the HGDP, now dubbed the "Vampire project," suggested that the HGDP would merely continue the same practices, except on a larger and far more organized scale.

This has been explicitly rejected by the leaders of the HGDP, who claim that no commercial use can be made of indigenous genetic material without the express permission of regional committees that represent all interested parties in the project (including the sampled populations). Moreover, any money gained from these products will be shared with the indigenous groups, either as direct royalties, or as funds distributed by a neutral external body.

4. Genetic Imperialism

The above complaints combine to form the objection that the HGDP is just the latest in a long line of various forms of colonization, exploitation, and imperialism, carried out by the Western world upon developing countries. In previous times the object of colonization was the land where the indigenous peoples lived. Today, it is their genetic material. This position is eloquently outlined by Aroha Te Pareake Mead, of the Indigenous Peoples' Biodiversity Network, who states "For Maori, and many others, the human gene is geneology . . . It is difficult to articulate the degree to which indigenous and Western scientific philosophies differ on such a fundamental point . . . but . . . it is the difference in understanding of the origin of humanity, the responsibility of individuals and the safety of future generations which sits so firmly at the core of indigenous opposition to the HGDP . . . This type of research proposes to interfere in a highly sacred domain of indigenous history, survival and commitment to future generations" (Mead, A. (1995), Correspondence: Response to Draft UNESCO Bioethics Paper). Such objections would appear to be at a ethical level far removed from the practical difficulties of ensuring that proper informed consent is achieved for all participants in the project, and it is not clear how the supporters of the HGDP intend to respond to such criticism.

VI. GENETICIZATION

Criticism of genome analysis is not limited to large-scale, international projects like the HGP and HGDP. The very act of sequencing a genome, it is claimed, whatever the information it contains is used for reinforces certain beliefs about human genetics and encourages "geneticization." This "refers to an ongoing process by which differences between individuals are reduced to their DNA codes, with most disorders, behaviors, and physiological variations defined, at least in part, as genetic in origin . . . Through this process, human biology is incorrectly equated with human genetics, implying that the latter acts alone to make us each the organism he or she is." (Lippman, A. (1991) Prenatal genetic testing and screening: Constructing needs and reinforcing inequalities. *American Journal for Law and Medicine,* 17(1&2), 15–50). Genticization is a form of scientific reductionism, in that it describes events at a higher level (that of physiology or psychology) in terms of a lower one, molecular biology. Much of force of this reductionism is a result of the information to which genetic material might or will be put to use when it becomes available (such as genetic tests by health insurers), but much of it can also be traced back to the language used to describe the Human Genome Project in particular, and genome analysis in general.

A. Mapping

Genome analysis aims to produce maps, of varying scales. The image of the map is a particularly powerful one, especially as we no longer expect to see "here be dragons" but rather "X marks the spot." Modern maps are held to be definitive indicators of the absence or presence of an object, whether it be a road, a stream, or a gene "for" a disease. The mapping metaphor currently at use in molecular genetics suggests a degree of certainty and clarity about genetic information that is not reflected in terms of actual results. Abby Lippman has criticized the use of such metaphor (and its attendant correlate, the "blueprint"); "Mapmaking, whether of the body or of the earth is as much political and cultural as it is 'scientific'. It is a social activity . . . because it is an expression of and influence on social values . . . geneticization gives mapmakers . . . tremendous power . . . for defining how we think of ourselves and others and for determining who will manage us as individuals and as a society" (Lippman, 1992). She proposes an alternative metaphor, taken from management theory, that of the organogram, the bureaucratic design of an organization. This would at least have the advantage of obviously displaying its limitations, which cannot be said for maps.

B. Genetic Stories

Mapping is just one of a range of stories that are told by scientists, doctors, and politicians about genetics. These stories are also told by members of the public; the gene is no longer just a scientific entity. As Dorothy Nelkin and Susan Lindee have documented, the image of the gene and DNA's double helix permeate popular culture with a variety of images; "Geneticists also refer to the genome as the Bible, the Holy Grail and the Book of Man. Explicit religious metaphors suggest that the genome . . . will be a powerful guide to moral order." They warn that "the images and narratives of the gene in popular culture reflect and convey a message that we will call genetic essentialism [geneticization]" (Nelkin D., & Lindee, M. S. (1995) *The DNA Mystique: The Gene as a Cultural Icon.* New York: Freeman). The main objection to such use of language is not that there is an explicit plan to promote a genetic view of the world. Rather, the position is that the exciting and groundbreaking work currently being carried out in the area of human genetics reinforces geneticization as a side effect of the production of genetic information, regardless of the actual use to which that information is put. Proponents of this position do not object to genome analysis as it *might* be carried out, but in the way it is currently carried out. There might be ways of investigating the human genome and publicizing this information that would not enforce an overly genetic view of the world.

VII. CONCLUSION

Genome analysis, especially in the form of the Human Genome Project, holds great potential for our understanding of ourselves of disease and of life itself, but the concept of genome analysis is an extremely potent one. The language used and the images presented carry with them the potential to reinforce an extremely limited view of what human beings are, and with it the possibility of harmful application of genetic information. It is not that the ethical problems associated with genome analysis *have* to be so. With awareness of how powerful genes are in people's minds and in our culture, their actual power and use can be controlled.

Also See the Following Articles

GENETIC RESEARCH • GENETIC TECHNOLOGY, LEGAL REGULATION OF • INDIGENOUS RIGHTS • INFORMED CONSENT • RESEARCH ETHICS

Bibliography

Hubbard, R., & Wald, E. (1993) *Exploding the Gene Myth.* Boston: Beacon Press.

Macer, D. (1991). Whose genome project?. *Bioethics,* 5(3), 183–211.

Marteau, T., & Richards, M. (1996). *The troubled helix: Social and psychological implications of the new human genetics.* Cambridge: Cambridge University Press.

Mauron, A. (1995). HGP: The Holy Genome Project? *Eubios Journal of Asian and International Bioethics,* 5, 117–119.

UNESCO IBC (1995). Preliminary draft of a universal declaration on the human genome and human rights.

UNESCO IBC (1995). Report on bioethics and population genetics research.

GOVERNMENT FUNDING OF RESEARCH

Rudolph J. Marcus
Ethics Consultant

GLOSSARY

extramural research Research funded by a government agency at institutions outside its administrative control.

intramural research Research funded by a government agency in its own laboratories.

peer review The existing system by which applications for research support and manuscripts for publication are read and evaluated by anonymous reviewers.

recuse, recusal The act of standing aside from decision making in specified cases in which one might be considered to be possibly prejudiced, unduly influenced, or otherwise compromised. Each instance of recusal is usually defined in writing and approved by superiors and ethics officals.

referee The anonymous reviewer in a peer review process.

semi-Socratic method A discussion and learning modality in which responses to a leader's questions are augmented and corrected, if necessary, only by further questions rather than by authority, argument, or majority vote.

NO GOVERNMENT is likely to have sufficient funds to fill the perceived needs of all researchers. Dealing ethically with the allocation of limited funds involves two problems. One is to provide an equal opportunity of competing for government research funds, sometimes called a level playing field. Another is to legitimize uneven shares of research resources. That applies as much to resources such as research time, laboratory and desk space, and publication of results as it does to research funds. This chapter is about means of leveling the playing field for, and of legitimizing uneven distribution of, government funds for research.

I. INDIVIDUALS, LAWS, AND CODES

RESEARCHERS are subject to codes that regulate professional practice; those are a means of leveling the playing field. Government employees are subject to laws intended to level the playing field. Do those laws and codes give the same cues to full-time and part-time, permanent and temporary, government researchers? Are the laws that apply to all government employees compatible with the codes of professional practice that apply to researchers?

Each government agency that funds extramural re-

Encyclopedia of Applied Ethics, Volume 2

search has employees, consultants, and advisers with research experience who divide and assign research funds. These full- and part-time employees are charged with leveling the playing field and with legitimizing uneven shares of research resources. In some government agencies researchers split their time between doing intramural research and funding extramural research. That practice seems to be declining because of its inherent conflicts of interest.

Like all researchers, each intramural researcher would like to obtain as much money as each feels one needs for one's research. Each one who funds extramural research would like to obtain the maximum amount of funding for the research programs that are in one's charge. The constraints to those desires are those same laws and professional codes.

I have spent decades in both positions, first as an extramural researcher funded by the government, and then as a government employee responsible for dividing and assigning government money for research. In this article, I am writing from personal experience about the laws and the professional codes, their overlap and their differences, and how I have seen the differences handled. I am writing about individuals, laws, and codes, and not about abstract or philosophical ethics.

II. LEVELING THE PLAYING FIELD; CODES OF ETHICS

There are four codes that prescribe behavior expected of researchers on the public payroll. These four codes are listed in Table 1. First of all, because those researchers grew up and are still practicing within their own culture, the moral code of their culture is ingrained in them. They are employees or contractors of a government agency, so that they are subject to the ethics code of that governmental entity. As professionals they are subject to the ethics code of the licensing board or professional society of their particular discipline. Fi-

TABLE 1

Various Ethics Codes and Their Nature

Code	Nature	Origin and enforcement
Moral	Written	Societal
Government	Written	Legal
Professional	Written	Licensure or membership
Research process	Unwritten	Self-enforcing

nally, as researchers they are subject to a code of research ethics. Those four codes will now be discussed in detail.

A. Moral Code

In Western civilization, the code of ethics is expressed in statements such as those of the Ten Commandments. All of us who have grown up in that culture, whether we are believers or not, judge ourselves and others by that standard, consciously or unconsciously.

This code is written, and its enforcement is by society at large as well as by the unconscious of the individual. (The ethics codes of indigenous populations are often more holistic than the Ten Commandments. They are usually not written or collected in one corpus. They are not now enforced, or are even actively suppressed, by the dominant society at large.)

"Unconscious enforcement" means that the individual who contravenes one of the Commandments might feel guilty, or point the finger at others to hide one's own contravention, or make a sport out of trying to get away with as much as possible, and so on. The Bible states the Ten Commandments in various places, the earliest of which is Ex. 20:2–17.

Which Commandments apply particularly to researchers? "You shall not kill" (v. 13) has been of crucial importance in discussions of the ethics of armament research, particularly nuclear weapons and even nuclear energy, the ethics of using animals as research subjects, and the bioethics of abortion, triage, and assisted suicide. It also expresses a caution about certifying or marketing drugs, foodstuffs, or agricultural chemicals that might endanger human, fetal, or animal life. The same caution applies to environmental consequences of emissions from generating or manufacturing processes.

"You shall not steal" (v. 15), "you shall not bear false witness" (v. 16), and "you shall not covet" (v. 17) apply to the dealings of researchers with their colleagues and competitors in publication, refereeing, patenting, and the like. They also apply to government employees who choose, supervise, and fund extramural research.

B. Governmental Code

The ethics codes of governmental agencies are generally written and are legally enforceable. In the United States, the federal government, some states, and very few counties and cities have ethics codes. The Federal ethics code is a part of the U.S. Code of Law (Title 18, USC, and Executive Order (E. O.) 12731). The executive order (included as Box 1) specifies six forbidden activities (subsections b, c, d, f, g, and j) and seven mandated activities (a, e, h, i, k, l, and m) in addition to three mandated behaviors (k, l, and n). Possible consequences of violations include admonishment, reprimand, suspension without pay, prison, fine, and dismissal. Let us look at these clauses in more detail.

Box 1

U.S. Federal Code of Ethics (E.O. 12731)

Part I—Principles of Ethical Conduct

Section 101. *Principles of Ethical Conduct.* To ensure that every citizen can have complete confidence in the integrity of the Federal Government, each Federal employee shall respect and adhere to the fundamental principles of ethical service as implemented in regulations promulgated under sections 201 and 301 of this order:

(a) Public service is a public trust, requiring employees to place loyalty to the Constitution, the laws, and ethical principles above private gain.

(b) Employees shall not hold financial interests that conflict with the conscientious performance of duty.

(c) Employees shall not engage in financial transactions using nonpublic Government information or allow the improper use of such information to further any private interest.

(d) An employee shall not, except pursuant to such reasonable exceptions as are provided by regulation, solicit or accept any gift or other item of monetary value from any person or entity seeking official action from, doing business with, or conducting activities regulated by the employee's agency, or whose interests may be substantially affected by the performance or nonperformance of the employee's duties.

(e) Employees shall put forth honest effort in the performance of their duties.

(f) Employees shall make no unauthorized commitments or promises of any kind purporting to bind the Government.

(g) Employees shall not use public office for private gain.

(h) Employees shall act impartially and not give preferential treatment to any private organization or individual.

(i) Employees shall protect and conserve Federal property and shall not use it for other than authorized activities.

(j) Employees shall not engage in outside employment or activities, including seeking or negotiating for employment, that connect with official Government duties and responsibilities.

(k) Employees shall disclose waste, fraud, abuse, and corruption to appropriate authorities.

(l) Employees shall satisfy in good faith their obligations as citizens including all just financial obligations, especially those—such as Federal, State, or local taxes—that are imposed by law.

(m) Employees shall adhere to all laws and regulations that provide equal opportunity for all Americans regardless of race, color, religion, sex, national origin, age, or handicap.

(n) Employees shall endeavor to avoid any actions creating the appearance that they are violating the law or the ethical standards promulgated pursuant to this order.

The executive order states that public service is a public trust (subsection a). For a Federal employee, there is only one master and that master is the employer. The standards and ethics of an employee's profession are to be disregarded when they conflict with the standards and ethics set by the employer. Because there is only one master, there may be no conflict of interest. It is forbidden to use public office for private gain (a, g), and a number of clauses specify what "private gain" might be. The employee must not accept gifts (including free lunches) (d) and may not accept outside employment (including honoraria for speeches) (j, d). The employee may not further private interest (the employee's own interest, or the interest of others) by use of information acquired in the course of government employment (c). Think of the information acquired by reading a research proposal or a progress report, and you get an idea of how easily the forbidden conflict of interest may arise. Reviewers involved in peer evaluation of research proposals are now required to file nondisclosure statements.

Three behaviors are specifically mandated. The Federal employee must satisfy a citizen's obligations (I). Thus, a Federal employee who is convicted of tax violations may lose his or her job as well. Similarly, the federal government will not ask that an employee be excused from jury service—I have done necesary work each night after jury service myself because of this clause. "Whistle-blowing" on waste, fraud, abuse, and corruption is another mandated behavior (k). Finally, a "Caesar's Wife" clause (n) is used in cases where an ethics violation is hard to prove, but the resultant publicity is deemed harmful to the government or to the morale of other Federal employees. It is a rule that is invoked frequently for the convenience of the government when violation of a more explicit rule would be hard to prove.

C. Professional Code

A third type of ethics code is the kind promulgated for a particular profession, usually by its state licensing board or professional society. These codes are written. In contrast to the moral and government codes of ethics discussed above, there is almost no legal or moral enforcement of these professional codes of ethics. Withdrawal of license or stripping of professional society membership occur most rarely because of reluctance of one practitioner to testify against another practitioner.

The code of ethics of the American Chemical Society (ACS) (reprinted in Box 2) is an example of this type of code. It lists a chemist's responsibilities to public, science, profession, employer, employees, students, associates, clients, and the environment. It calls upon the chemist to serve the public interest and welfare, to further the knowledge of science, and to share ideas and information. The chemist is to be mindful of the health of co-workers, consumers, and community, and to anticipate the environmental consequences of his or her work. That sounds like the "only one master" of the Governmental Code (II.B).

On the other hand, the ACS code of ethics wants the chemist to protect the legitimate interest of employers and to respect confidentiality with respect to clients. Here the ACS code introduces a second master. The possible conflicts of interest arising from the introduction of a second master are not recognized by the ACS code. As a matter of fact, the ACS code then says that "conflicts of interest are incompatible with this Code."

At some point a chemist will have to choose between "share ideas and information" and "respect confidentiality." That will be an ethical choice for which the code does not give the chemist any guidance. Often, contractual arrangements between sponsor and researcher specify what may be shared and what shall remain confidential. Even then, different interpretations of the contract or unforeseen research results require ethical choices by sponsor and researcher.

Fabrication, falsification, and plagiarism are stated to be incompatible with the ACS code. These subjects rank high in the final code of ethics, the research code, which is discussed in the next section.

Box 2

American Chemical Society (ACS) Code of Ethics

(Copyright 1994, American Chemical Society. Reprinted by permission of the American Chemical Society)

The Chemist's Code of Conduct

The American Chemical Society expects its members to adhere to the highest ethical standards. Indeed, the federal Charter of the Society (1937) explicitly lists among its objectives "the improvement of the qualifications and usefulness of chemists through high standards of professional ethics, education, and attainments ..."

Chemists have professional obligations to the public, to colleagues, and to science. One expression of these obligations is embodied in "The Chemist's Creed," approved by the ACS Council in 1965. The principles of conduct enumerated below are intended to replace "The Chemist's Creed." They were prepared by the Council Committee on Professional Relations, approved by the Council (March 16, 1994), and adopted by the Board of Directors (June 3, 1994) for the guidance of Society members in various professional dealings, especially those involving conflicts of interest.

Chemists Acknowledge Responsibilities to:

• The Public
Chemists have a professional responsibility to serve the public interest and welfare and to further knowledge of science. Chemists should actively be concerned with the health and welfare of co-workers, consumers, and the community. Public comments on scientific matters should be made with care and precision, without unsubstantiated, exaggerated, or premature statements.

• The Science of Chemistry
Chemists should seek to advance chemical science, understand the limitations of their knowledge, and respect the truth. Chemists should ensure that their scientific contributions, and those of their collaborators, are thorough, accurate, and unbiased in design, implementation and presentation.

• The Profession
Chemists should remain current with developments in their field, share ideas and informa-

tion, keep accurate and complete laboratory records, maintain integrity in all conduct and publications, and give due credit to the contributions of others. Conflicts of interest and scientific misconduct, such as fabrication, falsification, and plagiarism, are incompatible with this Code.

- The Employer

Chemists should promote and protect the legitimate interests of their employers, perform work honestly and competently, fulfill obligations, and safeguard proprietary information.

- Employees

Chemists, as employers, should treat subordinates with respect for their professionalism and concern for their well-being, and provide them with a safe, congenial working environment, fair compensation, and proper acknowledgment of their scientific contributions.

- Students

Chemists should regard the tutelage of students as a trust conferred by society for the promotion of the student's learning and professional development. Each student should be treated respectfully and without exploitation.

- Associates

Chemists should treat associates with respect, regardless of the level of their formal education, encourage them, learn with them, share ideas honestly, and give credit for their contributions.

- Clients

Chemists should serve clients faithfully and incorruptibly, respect confidentiality, advise honestly, and charge fairly.

- The Environment

Chemists should understand and anticipate the environmental consequences of their work. Chemists have responsibility to avoid pollution and to protect the environment.

D. Research Process Code

A research process code of ethics is not written and is certainly not compiled in any universally accepted document like, say, the Hippocratic oath is for physicians. An iconoclastic attempt to redefine such a code has been made by Woodward and Goodstein (1996). Yet practicing researchers are aware of the existence of such a code and know that it is self-enforcing. Self-enforcement is seen when violations of this unwritten code are detected during the refereeing process for publications and grants, and during the examining process for patents. Similarly, self-enforcement is seen when violations are detected in evaluations by peers for tenure and for promotion. Papers published in the technical literature are subject to self-enforcement of the research process ethics code by comments and corrections published in the literature by other workers. Similarly, lack of replication of published results, or failure to build on published work, is sometimes traced to conscious or unconscious violations of the research process ethics code. Even with all of this often slow and indirect self-enforcement, many researchers have experienced significant infractions of this code with respect to their own work or work in their particular area.

Honesty in obtaining and reporting data is a primary component of this unwritten code (compare the "falsification and fabrication" in the ACS code above). The avoidance of experimental artifacts and an examination of all possible explanations for an experimental observation are part of that honesty (polywater and cold fusion are recent examples in chemistry). Publication of results, rather than hiding or withholding them, is required by this code. Enough different literatures exist, such as journal, classified, company, and patent literatures, so that any security or commercial secrecy requirements can be satisfied. The current (1997) publicity furor about withholding information on the addictiveness of nicotine is an example of the large-scale effect that self-enforcement of the research code of ethics can have.

Acknowledging the contributions of co-workers, of parallel efforts, and of previous work is another strand of this code. This is stated in a number of different ways in the ACS code. It is also the research process code equivalent of the stealing, coveting, and bearing false witness prohibitions from the moral code. Finally, the research process code asks for an awareness by the researcher of the built-in design and practice quirks of the research process.

Examples of such quirks would include the "Noble Scientist's little hypocrisies" (Goodstein, 1992), the observer being part of the observing instrument, the deceptive ease of getting the desired result, and the existence of paradigm paralysis (a catchy term used by management consultant Joel Barker, building on *The Structure of Scientific Revolutions* by Thomas Kuhn).

III. LEGITIMIZING UNEVEN SHARES OF RESEARCH RESOURCES: PEER REVIEW

Peer review plays a large part in the funding of research and in the publication of research results. Normal practice is that referees of manuscripts for publication, and evaluators of proposals for research grants or contracts, remain anonymous. Anonymity is supposed to encourage franker evaluation. That in itself is an ethical problem. Would you say something behind a researcher's back that you are not willing to say to that researcher's face? I have always written my reviews in the same way in which I would have made my comments to that researcher's face.

The supposed anonymity of referees and reviewers is a pretense anyway. The number of equals in a researcher's speciality is small enough so that they all know each other. They will have reviewed each other's work many times and know each other's styles. The author of a research proposal or manuscript will often be asked for the names of appropriate referees. I have usually identified the anonymous reviewers of my papers quite easily.

Confidentiality of manuscripts or research proposals is the ethical foundation of the peer review system. Competitors are not supposed to know discoveries described in a manuscript until it appears in print. Research proposed must remain confidential if the peer review system is to function. How to maintain this confidentiality when referees or reviewers, and authors of a paper or research proposal, are colleagues in the same small subspeciality is a major ethical problem. Outside readers of research proposals for some U.S. government agencies are now required to file nondisclosure documents with respect to those proposals. The dollar cost of a single violation of peer review confidentiality is shown by the just-reported settlement of a 12-year-old suit. Patents gained through the breach of confidentiality were turned over to the complainant, who also received a $21 million payment (Marshall, 1996, and Kirschner, 1996).

A. Skewing the Peer Review System

The selection of referees for manuscripts, or of reviewers for peer evaluations of research proposals, poses yet another ethical choice. Journal editors and extramural research administrators are likely to know, or can easily find out, who is on whose side in a small subspecialty. Should they be inclined to do so, they can easily choose reviewers who will favor a given manuscript or proposal, or reviewers who will tear the proposal to pieces. Similarly, research proposals that hint at the possibility of new paradigms are particularly vulnerable to the selection of readers who are firmly stuck in the customary paradigm.

In the United States, government agencies are required to advertise research areas that they are funding. These advertisements are called "Broad Agency Areas" (BAAs). They contain explicit evaluation factors and often even the weights assigned to each of these factors. The BAAs of some agencies even have a source selection evaluation plan that prescribes selection officials, review boards, evaluation panels, forms to be submitted, and so on. The description of research areas, and evaluation processes prescribed, can easily be manipulated by the writers of these documents so as to skew the selection toward certain desired recipients. That is an ethical problem in two ways. The intent of leveling the playing field may be negated. Also, the whole process of managing an extramural research program has become so cumbersome that manipulation can easily replace straightforwardness as a way of life.

B. Research Funding without Peer Review

There are also research projects that are funded without peer review. In all countries with a parliamentary system, research appropriations may carry "earmarks" for specific projects by named institutions and/or named investigators. In the United States, this is referred to as "pork-barrel funding" or just "pork" for short. It is a practice that again defeats the intent of leveling the playing field. In addition, the practice reduces the amount of money available for distribution through the peer review system. Even if the appropriation does not carry an earmark, legislative intent for specific projects at specific institutions or by specific investigators may be indicated through comments at committee hearings or on the floor of the legislative body. The ethical dilemma for the extramural research administrator then is one of adhering to the peer review system and courting legislative displeasure, or of following legislative intent and thereby unleveling the playing field. Those are difficult choices because they may involve more than just individual moral choice. The administrator may not only endanger his or her own career, but also the economic well-being of his or her family and the prosecution of highly desirable research objectives.

IV. THE TWO HATS—A USEFUL METAPHOR

A. Origin and Definition of the Two Hats

A "two-hats" picture may illustrate the possible conflicts of employees who are subject to more than one code of ethics. The metaphor comes out of a discussion at the 1996 annual meeting of the Association for Practical and Professional Ethics. Roger Boisjoly, an engineer working on O-ring development and testing of space shuttle launchers, recounted the final conversation between contractor and NASA teams about the decision to launch the space shuttle *Challenger* (Boisjoly, 1996). The NASA team asked whether the contractor team foresaw any problems with a launch at low temperatures. The contractor engineers recommended against a launch because fuel leakage had been known to increase with decreasing temperatures. At that point the head of the contractor team asked for a 5-minute recess, during which he told the engineering spokesman: "Take off your engineering hat and put on your management hat." Because contractor management was then negotiating a multiyear contract renewal with NASA, "putting on the management hat" meant acceding to NASA management's strong desire for a launch the next day. When the conversation resumed after the 5-minute recess, the engineering spokesman reversed his engineers' recommendation against the launch. *Challenger* exploded 73 seconds after lift-off the next day, killing all crew members and a teacher, the first nonastronaut space shuttle passenger. In addition to the deaths, the NASA space shuttle program was set back by years and hundreds of million dollars.

In the discussion following Boisjoly's recounting of this incident, it developed that every researcher wears two hats, starting about 5 years after graduating and entering the work force. In industry, the two hats are "promote and protect the legitimate interests of their employers" and "serve the public interest and further knowledge of science," to use the words of the ACS code of ethics. In government, the two hats are public administrator and research administrator. The main question is how to wear both hats at the same time.

Wearing the two hats at the same time does not necessarily have to result in forsaking professional ethics. A case in point was the flawed joints in the Citicorp Center building in New York, at that time the seventh-highest building in the world (Morgenstern, 1995; Marcus, 1996). Hurricane season was approaching, a 1-in-16 probability of joint failure in a hurricane had just been discovered, professional reputations and millions of dollars in damages were at stake in addition to the lives of occupants and people on the ground. Yet in that case the ethical decision for disclosure was made and repairs were accomplished in time without alarming occupants and community. There was no damage to professional reputation, and money damages were limited to the amounts covered by insurance.

B. Tricks of the Trade

Every researcher aware of his or her double-hatted position develops individual ways of dealing with that situation. Of my 40 double-hatted years, 20 were spent in a government agency, making site visits that determined who received research grants. Tricks of the trade that I used in dealing with that situation should therefore be viewed as descriptive rather than prescriptive.

The first need is continued awareness of the two hats one is wearing, and not to let them get amalgamated. One way of doing that is to talk to researchers rather than only management at client institutions (contractors, grantees, grant applicants) and to talk to them, as much as possible, as a fellow researcher. If a niggling contract detail was asked about, I said: "Have your bean counter call my bean counter," which neatly separated the two hats. Visiting researchers as a fellow researcher was particularly annoying to the U.S. State Department (foreign ministry) during my 2 years in Japan, because the State Department preferred ministry-to-ministry contacts to individual-to-individual contacts.

While contract negotiations and grant awards must be handled at arm's length so as to assure a level playing field for all possible applicants, it is possible to ask applicants as a fellow researcher: "What is the art or science that you really want to do?" The research administrator gets an explanation that is not in the papers at hand, and the applicant realizes that the application is not as clear as it needs to be.

On the other hand, an applicant or the applicant's institution often tries to muddy the waters between those two hats by asking for the likelihood or probability of being funded before the funding decisions are made or announced. Such inquiries are often reasonable; a good post-doc has applied and would be hired if funding were likely, or possible funding is a factor in tenure or promotion decisions, or in cutbacks in industry. There can be much unhappiness if the ethics codes are not strictly followed in such cases. The best answer I have found when pressed is: "If you need an answer right now, the answer is 'no.'"

"Furthering no private interest with Government information" (Section 101c, Box 1) is a vexing question for government research administrators who read dozens of research proposals and even more progress reports each year, to whom research results are confided years before they appear in the technical literature, and who are recipients of trial balloons that may never become formal research proposals. The examples of "furthering private interest with government information" in the public press are usually stock market sales or purchases made on the basis of information that is not available generally. What private interest might be furthered with information gleaned from research proposals or reports? Sure, the research administrator might use knowledge gained that way to further her or his personal research, although that does not seem to be a frequent occurrence. However, "private interest" has been interpreted as not only the government administrator's private interest, but the interest of any party other than the government.

Consider now the research administrator who hears that a testing procedure or a chemical synthesis delays research progress in Laboratory A, and who remembers hearing that Laboratory B, doing different research, developed that test or synthesis months ago. Laboratory B's test procedure or synthesis may be months away from publication, or may even be too peripheral to their interests for publication. It is Laboratory A's private interest that would be furthered if the government research administrator told them about the test or synthesis developed by Laboratory B. Yet "furthering knowledge of science" from the ACS code, and the desire to save money and time for the government and the taxpayer, demand that the private interest of Laboratory A be furthered.

The pragmatic solution that I used was to create frequent occasions at which grantees in particular subspecialties could mingle and exchange such problems and solutions themselves. A few hints on making such meetings productive:

— Each series of meetings is focused on one research area, so that participants get to know each other and they speak the same language.
— Gordon Conference rules are followed; the meetings are off the record, nothing that is said may be quoted, and the meeting may not be cited as a reference.
— Meetings are limited to 1 day; people will come to a 1-day meeting, even if it is 14 hours long, who would not come to a multiday meeting.
— Principal investigators had to attend if they wanted work of their grants to be discussed.

— Everyone presents; no one just sits there and absorbs.
— Long coffee breaks and meals together are the places where most of the nitty-gritty information is exchanged.
— Meeing sites are rotated so that the various laboratory setups could be shown, and local students could attend the meeting.

V. ETHICS AND PRODUCTIVITY

A. Definition and Example

It should be obvious by now that positive results can flow from wearing those two hats at the same time. Ethics is not just a matter of keeping ones' nose clean; it can also be productive for the individual who practices it, the public that employs the individual, and the research community that the individual serves. Consider the example cited in a recent *Science* guest editorial (Fink, 1996). "Without the intervention of a government research administrator, the hepatitis B vaccine would have been delayed by 2 years and millions of lives would have been lost." The National Science Foundation (NSF) administrator, wearing his research administrator hat, heard that one of his grantee's experiments on a National Institutes of Health (NIH) grant were being thwarted by NIH safety rules then in effect. Wearing his government administrator hat, he identified a loophole; NSF was not constrained by the NIH safety rules. He authorized the thwarted experimentation on the NSF grant, with the resultant savings of years and lives. The NSF administrator wrote later about his motivation in doing so: "I learned that if you were a little aggressive, had confidence in your scientific judgment and exercised some imagination, you could get lots done within the system to catalyze science."

Everyone of us who has worn those two hats at the same time knows that opportunities for similar interventions arise every month. Not all of them have spectacular, life-saving results, but all of them are equally satisfying in the successful wearing of two hats at the same time.

Another example of productive ethics in wearing the two hats was the advice that I received from a superior several levels above me in the hierarchy. I had told him about a new initiative that I was going to start. His response was: "You are going to do it anyway, aren't you, because you feel it's the right thing to do? Then why tell me beforehand? If I say no, and you do it anyway, then you are in trouble unnecessarily."

B. Keeping Both Hats Viable

An important aspect of wearing the two hats at the same time is to keep one's self-respect as a researcher. It is vital to do some research of one's own, even if one has to work some evenings or weekends to do it. It may be necessary to shift from a large research team to individual work, or from laboratory work to desk work, in order to do that. It may be necessary to do one's own writing instead of signing off on an assistant's draft. A paper published now and then does wonders for one's own scientific confidence. Also, it maintains one's own credibility in the research community with which the government research administrator deals every day. Participation in professional society activities is another way of maintaining self-respect. There are many committee, board, and governance positions in professional societies that are not in conflict with one's government administrator hat, and where one can see and be seen by one's fellow researchers. Participation in research community activities gives the government research administrator solid ground to stand on when an ethics conflict arises between the two hats that the administrator wears.

VI. WHEN AND HOW ETHICS CHOICES CAN BE MADE

Up to now the choices posed by obeying the various laws and codes have been discussed. Obviously, any law or code must be general, and cannot describe every ethical conflict in which the government research administrator may find oneself. An example of an ethical conflict is a relationship with a fellow researcher that slowly ripens into friendship. At some point the government administrator may have to recuse oneself from dealing with the new friend's application for research funds, even applications in fields completely different from the administrator's own field of research, or even from dealing with all applications from the friend's university or industrial organization. This section will describe the resources that exist to guide the government administrator when these or similar lacunae are encountered. The main point is that when the written guides fail, there are unwritten guides within oneself that can be activated and can be clearly heard.

A. Ethics Training for Government Research Administrators

Ethics training and yearly refresher training for government administrators have been mandated for some time. Often such training consists of a recitation of the ethics code, and is considered boring, insulting, and degrading by those forced to attend. Discussion among attendees is provoked only occasionally when interesting case studies are provided.

Ethics training for government research administrators seldom mentions the other ethics codes by which researchers are bound because the government ethics code is founded on the "only one master" principle. For that reason the question of how to work with the opposites—called "wearing two hats at the same time" above—is often not discussed in government ethics training.

B. Opposites

Many of these opposites, listed in Table 2, have been discussed previously in this chapter. "Public welfare" and "interest of employer" are opposites in the ACS code. "Engineering hat" and "management hat" are both worn by researchers after they have worked in industry for about 5 years after their last academic training. "Research administrator" and "public administrator" similarly are concurrent functions of government researchers about 5 years after their last academic training. "Professional obligation" is laid on researchers by the research process code and their professional society code; government researchers are legally bound by "government employee regulation" as embodied in Title 18, U.S. Code and Executive Order 12731. Rohr (1996) sees "effectiveness" as a positive imperative in codes other than the government's; Rohr calls the government code a "political imperative." Similarly, Rohr argues that the professional codes (research process code and professional society code) encourage "decision-mak-

TABLE 2

Opposites

Public welfare	Interest of employer
Engineering hat	Management hat
Research administrator	Public administrator
Professional obligation	Government employee regulation
Effectiveness	Political imperative
Decision-making	Avoidance

ing," whereas the government code encourages "avoidance" of decision-making.

C. Effective Training

With this analysis of the various codes, what kind of ethics training might get attention and be effective? The purposes of such training should go far beyond just the contents of the codes. All of us who are subject to the codes need to know that both of the opposites on each line of Table 2 are present and required in each action by the government research administrator. We need to learn not to choose one of those opposites and to belittle the other one. The most effective training is that which lets us know that each of the opposites that make up a pair are parts of oneself, and that both opposites of each pair can be contacted and consulted within oneself (Marcus, 1996b).

That kind of training uses case studies that show the disanalogy between the "real" and the moral world (I have not found the source of that useful phrase). In the semi-Socratic method of working with case studies, the case is the authority in the center of the discussion circle, and participants in the discussion circle speak to the leader's questions about the case. The responses asked for are perception, feeling, and personal experience, rather than just analysis.

The procedure for working out an ethics conflict in an actual work situation is similar. The ethics conflict, just like the case study, is the authority in the center of the discussion circle. All parties to the conflict need to be called to the discussion circle, in person or in visualization/dialog. The question is what opposites are involved, and how can I, the researcher with the ethics conflict, live with those opposites, knowing that those opposites are part of the whole that makes up oneself as well as the outer situation?

Also See the Following Articles

CONFLICT OF INTEREST • CODES OF ETHICS • RESEARCH ETHICS • RESEARCH METHODS AND POLICIES • SCIENTIFIC PUBLISHING

Bibliography

Boisjoly, R. (1996). *The Space Shuttle Challenger disaster: A paradigm for changing workplace/career ethics.* 1996 Annual Meeting of the Association for Practical and Professional Ethics, Paper IIIA.

Fink, G. R. (1996). Bureaucrats save lives. *Science* 271, 1213.

Goodstein, David (1992, March 2). What do we mean when we use the term 'science fraud'? *The Scientist,* p. 11.

Kirschner, E. (1996, November 11). Biotech firms settle suit charging data theft by peer reviewer. *Chem. Eng. News,* p. 9.

Marcus, R. J. (1996a, March 11). Ethical considerations. *The New Yorker,* p. 14.

Marcus, R. J. (1996b). *Mythological stories as case studies for teaching scientific ethics.* 1996 Annual Meeting, Association for Practical and Professional Ethics, Paper II H. 1.

Marshall, E. (1996). Battle ends in $21 million settlement. *Science* 274, 911.

Morgenstern, J. (1995, May 29). The fifty-nine story crisis. *The New Yorker,* p. 45.

Rohr, J. (1996). *The dilemmas of administrative ethics.* 1996 Annual Meeting of the Association for Practical and Professional Ethics, introductory talk for Public Service Ethics and the Public Trust miniconference.

Woodward, J., & Goodstein, D, (1996). Conduct, misconduct, and the structure of science. *American Scientist* 84[5], 479–490.

GREEK ETHICS, OVERVIEW

Christopher Gill
University of Exeter

I. Early Greek Thought
II. Socrates, Plato, and Aristotle
III. Hellenistic Philosophy
IV. Later Antiquity
V. Conclusions

GLOSSARY

character (*ēthos*) Stable pattern of motivation and emotion; central to Greek conception of virtue.

dialectic Systematic argument or debate, taken to be the normal mode of reflection in Greek philosophy.

happiness (*eudaimonia*) Widely supposed in Greek thought to be the overall goal (*telos*) of a human life; also often identified as the (overall) good (*agathon*).

indifferents Technical term in Stoic ethics for things other than virtue conventionally supposed to be good, e.g., health, social status, and wealth.

psyche (*psuchē*) Greek term signifying life/mind/soul/personality.

virtue (*aretē*) Excellence of character and life; together with "happiness," the key notion in Greek ethical philosophy.

GREEK ETHICS is taken here to mean the ethical thought of ancient Greece, in the period from the 8th century B.C. to the end of antiquity (ca. 5th century A.D.). Greek thought, together with Christianity, has been a key influence on the development of Western ethical thought and is still regarded as being of the highest philosophical importance. This article outlines the main features of Greek ethical thought, focusing on the question of how far this contained what we might call "applied ethics." For this purpose, we can demarcate four broad phases of Greek thought, in each of which the question of "applied ethics" takes a rather different form. (1) Greek thought prior to the demarcation of ethics as a distinct area of philosophy, including Presocratic thought and the sophistic movement down to the late 5th century B.C. (2) The emergence of ethics as a distinct area through the work of Socrates, Plato, and Aristotle (5th–4th century B.C.). (3) The systematization of branches of philosophy in later Greek (Hellenistic) philosophy, especially Stoicism, and the associated demarcation of "practical ethics" (the closest ancient analogue to modern applied ethics). (4) Ethical philosophy in late antiquity, including Neoplatonism, and the interplay between Classical thought and Christianity.

In modern Western thought, applied ethics is typically understood as an organized communal response to perceived personal and social problems, especially those brought to light in certain professional areas, such as medicine or law. Although we do not find in ancient Greece an exact equivalent for this conception, or for its cultural context, there are two recurrent features of Greek thought that are especially relevant. One is the tendency for social problems to give rise to (more or less public) argument and debate, including debate about fundamental ethical questions and principles. Another is the belief that properly conducted debate, issuing in well-reasoned conclusions, provides an authoritative basis for resolving practical problems and shaping people's lives. The practical outcome of ethical reflection is conceived either as (sometimes utopian) programs for large-scale social change or as advice to individuals on how to direct their lives.

I. EARLY GREEK THOUGHT

A. Traditional Thought: Homer

The first surviving Greek text, Homer's *Iliad* (ca. 8th century B.C.), exemplifies certain general characteristics of Greek thought which also figure in subsequent ethical theory. The wrath of Achilles, caused by the breakdown in cooperation between Achilles and his fellow chieftains, stimulates, especially in Book 9, reflective debate about ethical questions. These include that of the basis of cooperative relationships, the justification for breaking social bonds, the best form of a human life, and the grounds for dying for others. Also characteristic of later Greek thought is that these questions are not taken to be settled by an appeal to authority, whether human or divine. Rather, the ethical status of human (political) and divine authority is one of the questions raised through the medium of this epic poem. There is an obvious contrast on this point with the Judeo-Christian tradition, especially as expressed in the Old Testament, in which the idea of God as an ultimate moral authority, and as the source of determinate moral rules (e.g., the Ten Commandments), is fundamental.

The *Iliad* also gives rise to an issue much discussed by scholars in recent years, that of the nature and development of Greek ethical attitudes as expressed in literary forms and social practices. Earlier scholars tended to characterize early Greek ethics as based on a socially derived sense of shame and honor, and as developing only later, if at all, a more inner sense of guilt and moral responsibility. Some recent work (notably by Bernard Williams) has argued, by contrast, that, from the *Iliad* onward, Greek ethics places value on the internalization of social principles (on making shame and honor integral to one's character); value is also placed on reflective debate about what what these social principles should be. A related idea, also expressed in the *Iliad,* is that emotions and motives

are properly modified by such debate, and that they should not, therefore, be rigidly subject to conventional social rules. These poetic ideas prefigure the themes of much later Greek philosophy: that virtue centers on character shaped by one's ethical community, and that dialectical debate properly determines norms for character as well as action.

B. Presocratic Philosophers

Characteristic of the earliest Greek philosophers (whose work survives only in fragments) is that they discuss ethics only as part of their highly speculative accounts of nature and reality as a whole. For instance, Anaximander (ca. 610–540 B.C.) analyzes the natural world in terms of retribution and injustice, and Empedocles (ca. 493–433 B.C.) does so in terms of alternating patterns of love and strife. For Heraclitus (late 6th–early 5th century B.C.), the *logos* ("reason") is at once the basic principle of nature, ideal law, and rationality. Sometimes explicit in their thought (e.g., that of Xenophanes, 6th century B.C., or Anaxagoras, ca. 550–428 B.C.), and sometimes implied, is a critique, or rethinking, of the traditional, anthropomorphic Greek religion to match their rethinking of nature. The application of the principles emerging from their work takes two main forms. The thinkers sometimes advocate (at least by implication) the adoption of the state of mind and character which corresponds to the underlying pattern discerned in nature. This advice is mostly given to individuals (e.g., the named addressees of the thinkers' works), who are urged to adopt this pattern for themselves. However, Pythagoras (6th century B.C.) apparently saw his theory as providing the basis for a political and ethical community (in Croton, South Italy). "Harmony" was conceived both as a cosmic principle (analyzable by number theory) and as an ethical norm for diet, daily life, and social relationships.

C. The Sophists

A feature of the second half of the 5th century B.C., especially in the economically flourishing democracy of Athens, was the growing professionalization of branches of knowledge and education, including the skills of rhetoric (public persuasion) and medicine. Key figures in this process were itinerant teachers of rhetoric and other skills ("sophists") who received fees for their teaching. The conflict and debate associated with this process are presented vividly (though from strongly partisan standpoints) in, for example, Aristophanes' comic play *Clouds* (423 B.C.) and Plato's *Gorgias* and *Protagoras* (early 4th century B.C.). A central issue was whether authority in transmitting ethical beliefs belonged to the family and the community of the city-state as a whole or to experts in, for instance, rhetoric, argument, or natural science. There was also competition between different forms of expertise about which one played the most important role in this process. This debate is analogous with one of those associated in modern times with "applied ethics," namely that of the relationship between professional expertise and the ethical standards of the community. In *Protagoras,* Plato ascribes to Protagoras (ca. 485–415 B.C.), a leading teacher of rhetoric, what might be called a "communitarian" position on ethics, according to which justice and the other virtues are developed, in any given community, by public and private discourse; the expert's role is limited to facilitating this process. (For the contrasting status given by Plato's Socrates to dialectical expertise, see Section II.A.) Plato's *Gorgias* centers on the related question of whether techniques of discourse, such as rhetoric and dialectic, are value-neutral instruments or whether the techniques in themselves necessarily carry implications about the ends to which they should be used.

The 5th to 4th centuries B.C. also saw the emergence of the Hippocratic and other schools of medicine, and, in the Hippocratic Oath, one of the first surviving Western formulations of "professional ethics." Doctors, like other claimants to wisdom, took part in public debates about nature (including human nature), environmental influences on social character (e.g., *Airs, Waters, Places*), and the status of their expertise. However, the professional status and techniques of medicine in antiquity were too insecure and disputed to generate analogues for the issues about ethics and medical science (e.g., about artificial insemination or genetic engineering) which are central to modern debate. An issue which recurs in different contexts throughout this period (and which also takes up questions raised by the Presocratics) is that of the relationship between nature (*phusis*) and law or ethical conventions (*nomos*). Among the positions advanced are (1) that human nature and desires are inherently in conflict with ethical principles and laws; (2) that morality is the product of an implied "social contract," adopted as a second-best to the pursuit of self-interest; and (3) that human nature, if properly understood, is functionally adapted to develop toward virtue. This debate persists in subsequent Greek ethical theory,

in which Plato, Aristotle, and the Stoics adopt versions of the third position.

II. SOCRATES, PLATO, AND ARISTOTLE

A. Socrates

Socrates (469–399 B.C.) had a crucial role in the history of Greek ethics in that the scope of his interests defined, in effect, what "ethics" meant in Greek philosophy. His basic question is "how should one live?" More specifically, he is presented as asking what virtue (or a given virtue) is, how it is acquired, how it affects action and feeling, and whether it constitutes happiness. Socrates is presented, especially in Plato's early dialogues, in Aristotle, and to a lesser extent in Xenophon, as practicing a distinctive method of systematic questioning (dialectic) conducted with one person at a time and designed to produce a logically consistent set of beliefs. By implication, Socrates claimed that ethical virtue depends on expertise in this form of dialectic. The so-called "Socratic paradoxes" which recur in his arguments (virtue is knowledge, virtue is one, and no one does wrong willingly) can be understood as meaning that there is a direct correlation between (this type of) dialectical expertise and ethical virtue.

This approach to ethics (which can be contrasted with the more "communitarian" position associated with Protagoras, Section I.C) was highly controversial, and may have contributed to Socrates' trial and execution by the Athenian state in 399 B.C. (on the charges of "corrupting the young and not worshipping the gods the city worships"). On the other hand, Socrates seems also to have assumed that such dialectical expertise is, in principle, open to everyone, and that his method consisted simply in articulating ethical assumptions implicitly held by all human beings. Indeed, he claimed that he "knew nothing," and that his dialectic served simply as the vehicle for this articulation of shared (consistent) human beliefs. Unlike the sophists, he charged no fees and did not undertake to teach a technique. The question of whether Socrates' dialectic does or does not imply a determinate set of doctrines, and does or does not claim to achieve knowledge, has been a matter of dispute since antiquity. What is undisputed is that his approach represents in an extreme form a position sometimes found elsewhere in Greek thought—that the "application" of ethics is inseparable from reflective ethical enquiry, or in Socratic terms, "the unexamined life is not worth living" (Plato, *Apology* 38a).

B. Plato

Although Socrates wrote nothing, Plato (ca. 429–347 B.C.) conducted philosophy (in part) through writing dialogues, combined in later life with dialectical teaching in the philosophical "school" (study or research center) that he founded, the Academy. Plato's early dialogues represent Socrates' distinctive method of dialectic. Since all the dialogues are more or less fully fictionalized, and Plato was a highly creative philosopher, we cannot draw a sharp distinction between Socratic and early Platonic thought. In the middle-period dialogues (e.g., *Phaedo, Symposium, Republic*), Plato is generally supposed to have pursued the implications of Socrates' arguments and methods further than Socrates himself did. In the late dialogues, Plato seems to have reexamined the theories of the middle period and either extended or modified these, partly as a result of expanding the scope of his philosophy beyond the ethical concerns that are dominant in the early and middle dialogues. Although the middle and late dialogues contain more constructive argumentation than the early ones, Plato's continued use of the form of the Socratic dialogue raises the question (as in the case of Socrates) of whether his philosophical activity is conceived by him as a continuing search or as achieved understanding.

Central to the middle-period dialogues is the exploration of Socrates' claim that virtue depends on dialectical expertise. A key idea in this exploration is the contrast between belief/opinion (based on social communication) and knowledge (based on philosophical argument). A related contrast is that between particulars (individual objects and qualities) and Forms (ideal or objective realities). A recurrent theme is that dialectically based understanding provides objective knowledge of what is really or essentially just or good (the Forms), whereas social communication merely provides subjective, localized opinions (that this or that act is just or good). This way of analyzing Socrates' claim is coupled in Plato's middle period with exploration of the psychological implications of the claim. The Socratic idea that knowledge carries with it correlated actions and feelings (that no one does wrong willingly) is developed into more complex ideas about the relationship between body and psyche, and between the parts of the psyche. One such idea is that the achievement of postdialectical knowledge depends on (but also enhances) a cohesive, "harmonized" relationship between the parts of the psyche, in which the other parts are persuaded to accept the rule of reason.

The *Republic* contains the fullest discussion of these ideas; it also outlines the political preconditions for the achievement of these ideal types of knowledge and character. These preconditions center on a two-stage educational program (for the guardians of the ideal state) which combines the Socratic ethical approach with a version of the communitarian one. The guardians' attainment of postdialectical knowledge and the corresponding psychic state depends on the previous (childhood) shaping of their beliefs and emotions by their community. The second stage of their education converts these prereflective beliefs into objective knowledge, culminating in knowledge of the Form of the Good. The knowledge thus achieved provides the basis for the prereflective belief structure of the community. Plato's last work, the *Laws*, takes this version of a communitarian approach to ethics still further. It pursues the idea that a good community is one in which the beliefs and desires of the whole citizen body are correctly shaped by public persuasion and social institutions, though it retains the idea that a minority of the citizens must also be able to understand through dialectic the truth of the community's informing beliefs.

Plato's dialogues offer differing indications about the way in which these ethical and political ideals could be realized. The *Phaedo* and *Symposium,* for instance, suggest that it is only by adopting the philosopher's pursuit of objective truth (the Forms) as one's overriding goal that one can make progress toward achieving real virtue in character, action, and relationships. In a late dialogue, the *Philebus,* which offers a more subtle and metaphysically complex account of the relationship between knowledge and pleasure in the good life, it is also left to each individual to apply the outcome of the argument. The question of how one should try to put into practice the ideas of the *Republic* or *Laws* is more open to debate. For one type of interpretation, these dialogues present constitutional blueprints which Plato would have liked to put into political practice (as Protagoras, apparently, drew up a law code in 444 B.C. for Thurii, a newly founded city-state). Some support for this idea comes from two of the letters ascribed to Plato in antiquity, the Second and the Seventh. For another type of interpretation, these dialogues present normative ideals, which are designed to shape ethical and political debate and life conducted in very different circumstances from those described in the dialogues. At least one passage in the *Republic* strongly supports the latter view that the ideal state provides an ethical pattern "in heaven" for each of us to establish within ourselves (592b). Broadly similar issues are raised by other ideal constitutions in Greek philosophy, including Aristotle's *Politics* 7–8, and two works called *Republic* by the Stoics Zeno and Chrysippus.

C. Aristotle

Aristotle (384–322 B.C.) was Plato's pupil for 20 years and later set up his own school, the Lyceum or Peripatos; the surviving works, including the *Eudemian* (EE) and *Nicomachean Ethics* (NE), are based on his lectures in the school. Although those works seem not to have been available in the early Hellenistic period, his ethical approach was maintained in his school and was influential in determining the general form of subsequent Greek ethical theory. The fundamental issue (derived from Socrates' characteristic questions) was this: how should we shape our life as a whole; that is, what should we take as our overall goal (*telos*)? The goal was generally assumed to be happiness (*eudaimonia*) or (regarded as the same thing) the good (*agathon*); debate focused on what "happiness" was. For Aristotle, as for Plato in the *Republic,* the answer was that it was virtue (*aretē*), or more precisely, "life according to virtue," and, more precisely again, "according to the best and most perfect [or complete] virtue" (NE 1.7). However, for Aristotle (by contrast with the stoics) this does not mean that "external" goods such as health, wealth, and social position are without any importance in determining one's happiness (NE 1.8–11).

Virtue is defined partly in terms of psychological capacities and functions, and partly in terms of modes of action and social behavior. Aristotle distinguishes between virtue of character (*ēthos*) and that of intellect (*dianoia*), though seeing these as partly interdependent. Ethical or character virtue (from whose name, *ēthikē aretē*, the category of "ethics" was derived) is defined by the fact that the virtuous person does virtuous acts because of a combination of correct (and stable) motivation ("character") and correct practical reasoning. The virtuous person is motivated to act virtuously "for the sake of the fine" (*to kalon*) or "for its own sake" (taken to be the same). His or her motivation and action hits the "mean" between defective extremes. The failure to develop ethical virtue results in a character and life that display either defectiveness/vice (*kakia*) or the "weakness of will" of those for whom virtuous patterns of desire and emotion have not become integral to their character.

Although Aristotle demarcates ethics as a separate area of theory, he also stresses that its ultimate aim is practical: "we enquire not to know what virtue is but to become good people" (NE 2.1). This view is characteristic of Greek ethical philosophy; hence, the modern distinction between ethics and metaethics (or between theoretical and applied ethics) goes against the grain of much Greek thinking. The interplay between practical and theoretical aspects of virtue for Aristotle can be defined, in part, by the way in which, like Plato in the *Republic* and *Laws,* he combines communitarian and dialectical approaches to ethics. Aristotle stresses that effective ethical reflection needs to be based on the prereflective shaping of dispositions through the beliefs and practices of one's family and community. (By contrast with Plato in the *Republic,* Aristotle seems to think that this process can occur in conventional societies, and not just in a community based on ideal knowledge.) Many of the virtues discussed by Aristotle, including tact, generosity, and magnanimity, are those recognized in conventional Greek ethics. This feature of Aristotle's thought is contrasted favorably by some modern thinkers (including Alasdair MacIntyre and Bernard Williams) with the grounding of ethics on abstract norms such as rationality and benevolence in much modern theory. Part of the practical outcome of ethical enquiry, for Aristotle, lies in enabling an engaged member of his or her community to gain a better understanding of the conception of "virtue" implied in its belief structure.

On the other hand, Aristotle also sees ethical reflection as revising, rather than simply codifying, conventional attitudes. For instance, his account of friendship does not simply offer a new analysis (in terms of virtue, as distinct from utility) of the conventional ideal (which is that of loving the friend "for the other person's sake") (NE 8.3–8.5)). He also presents this ideal, controversially, as a means of virtuous self-love and of extending one's own (virtuous) existence, and thus of contributing to one's happiness (NE 9.4, 9.8, 9.9). His most controversial move, in NE 10.7–10.8 (though not in EE), is that of presenting contemplative, rather than practical and ethical, virtue as the highest realization of human (or "divine") happiness. Some modern scholars claim that this move is inconsistent with the presentation of ethical virtue as the chief element in human happiness elsewhere in the ethical treatises. Others, however, argue that it is consistent with the ranking of contemplative wisdom above practical wisdom in NE 6.7 and 6.13, as well as with Aristotle's metaphysical conception of god. Another area of current controversy is whether the appeal to the notion of "human" or "divine" nature (NE 1.7, 10.7–10.8) constitutes a move within ethical theory or an attempt to ground ethics on a metaphysical account of reality. On either view, however, Aristotle's move in NE 10.7–10.8 illustrates both his dialectical revision of conventional thought and the practical outcome of reflection (in that he commends a specific conception of the overall goal by which to shape one's life).

III. HELLENISTIC PHILOSOPHY

A. General

In the Hellenistic Age (323–31 B.C.), and under the Roman Empire (31 B.C. onward), there are two important developments in Greek ethical thought. One is that philosophical debate becomes centered on the positions of the various schools (the Academy, Lyceum, Epicurean, or Stoic) and that ethics is treated as part of the integrated system adopted by each school. The other recurrent idea is that adopting any one of these systems carries with it a distinctive way of life and pattern of character. Spelling out the form of life implied by each system is described as "practical ethics"; this work is also characterized as providing "therapy" for the sicknesses which are the outcome of living by purely conventional beliefs. The main ethical positions of the Hellenistic schools are presented in Sections B–D; the practical implications of these positions are examined in Sections E and F. Whereas Plato's dialogues and Aristotle's school texts have survived in considerable quantity, the works of the most important and innovative Hellenistic philosophers survive only in fragments and quotations. However, later Greek and Roman writings (especially from the first centuries B.C. and A.D.) enable us to reconstruct the main features of Hellenistic ethical theory and their thinking about the application of these theories.

B. Stoicism

Stoicism evolved as a system under successive heads of the school, especially Zeno (334–262 B.C.) and Chrysippus (ca. 280–206 B.C.), though retaining a set of core positions. In ethics, Stoics maintain in a strong form the thesis also adopted by Plato and Aristotle that virtue constitutes happiness. The Stoic claim is that virtue is not just the chief goal of a life, but the only good; by contrast with Aristotle, who allowed that, for instance, health and property count as "external goods" (NE 1.8–11), the Stoics describe these as "matters of indifference" in comparison with virtue. However, most Stoics allow that such things are, at least, "preferable," and that selection between indifferents (though not the pursuit of them for their own sake) is the only way to make

progress toward complete virtue (or "wisdom"). The latter is a state of character and way of life grounded on full understanding of what "virtue" is and of the fact that it is the only good.

The Stoics see ethics as closely integrated with logic and physics (study of nature) in a three-part philosophical system. Like Aristotle (NE 1.7), the Stoics claim that the life according to virtue is natural for human beings, and that the progressive recognition of the naturalness of the virtuous life is a crucial element in making ethical progress. There is currently dispute among scholars as to how far the recognition of the ethical significance of nature belongs to the sphere of ethical philosophy, and how far it belongs to the integrated understanding of ethics and physics (and logic). The doctrine of *oikeiōsis* ("appropriation" or "familiarization"), the idea that humans naturally develop toward the recognition that virtue is the only good, seems to fall centrally within the sphere of ethics. Also part of this doctrine is that human beings develop naturally from wanting to benefit only those close to them (family and friends) to wanting to benefit other human beings as such (as fellow rational animals). However, the understanding of the way in which the universe constitutes a rational, providentially ordered whole seems to require an integrated grasp of physics and ethics. The ideal normative figure in Stoicism, the "wise person" or "sage," combines this understanding with a recognition of the providential character of all events (including apparent misfortunes), and a correspondingly dispassionate attitude toward such events (see Section III.E).

C. Epicurus

Epicurus (341–271 B.C.) stands apart from Plato, Aristotle, and the Stoics in seeing the goal of life as pleasure rather than virtue. (In this respect, he developed the theory of Democritus, born mid-5th century, that "cheerfulness" was the goal, just as he also developed Democritus' atomic theory of matter.) However, Epicurus' aim, like that of most other Greek thinkers, was to identify as the goal a certain character and mode of life; the Cyrenaics, by contrast, saw the goal as simply maximizing episodes of pleasure. For Epicurus, pleasure is defined negatively, as the absence of physical pain and emotional disturbance. He also distinguishes between types of desire (natural, necessary, nonnecessary) and types of pleasure (kinetic and static) in order to characterize those desires and pleasures (natural and necessary, static) which are characteristic of the truly pleasurable life. Like the Stoics, Epicurus supposes that an understanding of human nature and the nature of the universe plays a crucial role in producing happiness. Such an understanding can free people from false or empty desires (such as for wealth or political power) as well as from misguided fears (above all, fear of death). The recognition that the universe functions by purely natural causes, without divine intervention (even of a providential kind), and that death is simply the decomposition of a certain set of atoms should free people from fear of divine interference in life or after death.

Epicurus' positions on virtue, friendship, and justice (central topics in Greek ethics) are more complex, and closer to other schools, than they seem at first. Although virtue is seen as purely instrumental to the overall goal of pleasure, it is also described as "inseparable" from the pleasant life. Although friendship is valued as a way of providing mutual assistance and pleasure, the friendship so valued is that in which we love our friends as ourselves. For Epicurus (by contrast with the Stoics), justice is taken not to be an objective ethical norm, but only "a guarantee of utility with a view to not harming another and not being harmed." However, the ideal Epicurean community will be one in which "everything will be full of justice and mutual friendship" because a correct grasp of the goal of life makes unjust action unnecessary. (See A. A. Long and D. N. Sedley, 1987. *The Hellenistic Philosophers,* 2 vols. Sect. 22, esp. A, E–I, O, S. Cambridge Univ. Press, Cambridge.) Implied in all these points is that a proper understanding of Epicurean philosophy carries with it a revised conception of what virtue, friendship, and justice mean, and of how they contribute to happiness.

D. Skepticism

This position, attributed to Pyrrho (ca. 360–270 B.C.), was adopted by leading figures in Plato's Academy from the mid-3rd to the 1st centuries B.C., who saw it as an extension of the Socratic conception of philosophy as an unending search for truth (see Section II.1). Sextus Empiricus (2nd century A.D.) provides the fullest surviving statement of the position. Ancient skeptics deny the possibility of gaining knowledge, as distinct from receiving "appearances" about how the world looks or forming beliefs that do not constitute knowledge. The recognition that knowledge is unavailable is thought to lead to "suspension of judgment" and so to provide freedom from emotional disturbance. This is because one escapes from the distress of trying to reconcile the (dogmatic) claim to knowledge with the contradictions that inevitably arise on any topic. Also, one achieves "moderate feeling" through not claiming to have knowledge about what is good or bad and therefore not having

the intense emotional reactions that result from this supposed knowledge. Unlike modern skepticism, which is often seen as a purely theoretical position, not affecting practical life, the ancient skeptic maintained that this position (like those of the other schools) changed one's entire character and way of life.

E. Practical Ethics and Therapy

A prominent idea in Hellenistic thought is that philosophy should spell out the practical implications of its ethical theories and the kind of "therapy" it can offer both to adherents of the systems and to those not (or not yet) committed to any one system. Much Roman ethical philosophy, which is based largely on Hellenistic theory, centers on this idea. This is true, for instance, of Cicero's (106–43 B.C.) *On Duties, Tusculan Disputations* 3–4 and Seneca's (ca. 4 B.C.–65 A.D.) *Moral Epistles, On Benefits,* and *On Anger.* Seneca writes as a committed Stoic, Cicero as an Academic skeptic (or at least an independent-minded thinker), not committed to any one position but strongly attracted to Stoic ethics. It is also true of much Greek work from this period, including the *Discourses* of the Stoic Epictetus (ca. 55–135 A.D.) and the moral essays (*Moralia*) of the (broadly) Platonic thinker Plutarch (ca. 50–120 A.D.). The analogy between philosophy (for the mind or character) and medicine (for the body) is developed extensively in this connection. For instance, Philo of Larisa (ca. 110–79 B.C.), a skeptic, subdivides practical ethics into "protreptic" (persuading someone to engage in philosophy), "therapy" (removing the false beliefs which cause distress), and "advice" (giving instructions about how to live), and compares each of these functions to aspects of the work of the doctor. Eudorus (1st century B.C.) and Seneca present comparable typologies of philosophical discourse, based on the idea that there is a close link between the key principles of a given ethical theory and the associated implications for character and action. Epictetus (*Discourses* 3.2.1–3.2.5) defines a three-stage curriculum of practical ethics by which one can systematically examine one's desires, feelings, and social actions, and the logical relationship between one's beliefs, to make sure these are in line with the fundamental principles of Stoic ethics.

There are certain general reasons for the stress on philosophy as therapy and a source of practical advice in this period. By contrast with the communitarian ethical approach noted above, in different versions, in some earlier Greek thought (e.g., Protagoras in Section I.C and Aristotle in Section II.C), Hellenistic philosophy regards conventional ethical discourse as promoting misguided norms for shaping character and action. Stoics stress that the conventional valuation of ethical "indifferents" (e.g., health and wealth) produces "passions," intense emotions expressing incorrect judgments about what is really valuable. Epicureans, similarly, see conventional thought as promoting misguided valuations (e.g., of wealth and power) and fears (e.g., of divine intervention and death) which cause emotional disturbance and so prevent peace of mind. (See Sections III.B and III.C above.) The "therapy" offered by these philosophical systems is, primarily, the removal of the false beliefs developed by conventional societies and of the "sicknesses" of intense or painful emotions and desires produced by these beliefs. Like modern "cognitive therapy," these ancient theories presupposed a belief-based model of human psychology (a connection explored in recent work by Martha Nussbaum). However, the ancient theories laid much greater stress than modern cognitive therapy on the idea that one's overall conception of the good informs one's whole pattern of motivation and action. They also stressed that the only complete therapy lies in achieving the understanding of the truth of this conception of the good which (together with the corresponding character and way of life) constitutes complete "wisdom," as envisaged by each school.

F. Political Theory

A further question about the application of ethical ideas arises in Hellenistic political theory, especially that of the Stoics. In Stoic thought, emphasis is placed on certain general ideals which go beyond conventional political norms, e.g., the brotherhood of humankind, rational or "natural" law, the city of gods and humans, and cosmopolitanism (citizenship of the universe). On the other hand, some Stoics, including Chrysippus, the main theorist of the school, saw ethical development as normally occurring within conventional societies, and apparently offered a theoretical justification for conventional institutions such as private property. Some scholars think there was a shift from an earlier, more radical phase of Stoicism (strongly influenced by Cynicism), expressed especially in Zeno's *Republic,* to a later phase in which Stoic ideals were seen as guiding principles for application within conventional societies. Others think that these ideals were always seen as having the latter function. Some later Stoics, such as Musonius Rufus (ca. 30–101 A.D.), use Stoic principles to argue, against ancient conventions, that men and women are equally capable of developing virtue and of doing philosophy, or to emphasize the conventional basis of the institution of slavery (without arguing for

its abolition). However, a more prevalent tendency is to use Stoic ideals, including those already mentioned, as regulative norms to help people to live virtuous lives in any social and political context. The *Meditations* of Marcus Aurelius (121–180 A.D.), for instance, shows a Roman emperor using ideals such as the brotherhood of humankind and cosmopolitanism to reinforce his dutiful (and largely conventional) practice of his role as emperor. Epicureanism is more consistently opposed to any form of conventional political system, as being necessarily based on false conceptions of what is truly desirable. The community of friends sharing their lives in Epicurus' own Garden served as an ideal model of society, though there is little evidence to suggest that Epicureans succeeded in developing other such communities in antiquity.

A subject of recent debate has been whether the Stoic ideal of rational or "natural" law exercised any significant influence in Roman legal thinking. Cicero, in his *Republic* and *Laws,* sometimes uses this ideal to signify a core of universally valid rules (though he fails to specify their content). This is, broadly, the way that the idea of "natural law," and, subsequently, "human rights," has been used in modern Western thought. Also, the term "natural law" sometimes appears in the writings of Roman jurists from the 2nd to 3rd centuries A.D. Gaius (mid-2nd century) uses it as a synonym for the "law of nations," that is, roughly, international law, by contrast with the "civil law" applying only to Roman citizens. At the start of Justinian's *Digest* (6th century A.D., but based on earlier material), natural law is conceived as a universal norm going beyond both the other categories of law. However, some scholars have pointed out that, in the moral thinking that is embodied in Roman legal writing as a whole, natural law figures much less as a normative idea than, for instance, "fairness" or "good faith." Also, within Stoic thought, natural law signifies an objective norm (whose content is only fully understood by the wise person) and not a determinate body of rules which could guide legal decision making.

IV. LATER ANTIQUITY

In later antiquity, we find a tendency to collect, codify, and comment on previous Greek thought (which was already seen as having reached an exceptional, "classical" status). For instance, two important sources for Stoic ethics are Diogenes Laertius' (ca. 3rd century A.D.) life of Zeno (in *Lives of the Philosophers*) and Arius Didymus' (1st century B.C.) summary preserved in Stobaeus' anthology (5th century A.D.). A related tendency was renewed interest in Plato and Aristotle, and the use of commentaries on their works as a mode of continuing philosophical reflection (by, e.g., Alexander of Aphrodisias, 3rd century A.D., and Proclus, 5th century A.D.). Neoplatonism, one of the more creative philosophical movements in this period is, in effect, a synthesis of Platonic and Aristotelian thought, which especially develops the idealism of Plato's middle period. In the *Enneads,* Plotinus (205–270 A.D.) defines three fundamental levels of reality which are (in ascending order of being and value): (1) the psyche (conceived as nonmaterial), (2) the intellect, and (3) the One (or Good). Plotinus' view is that human beings are naturally disposed to aspire toward the highest possible level of reality, that is, toward psychic rather than material being, intellectual rather than sensual or emotional being, and, finally, a state of union with the One or Good.

Another tendency is the interplay between Greek philosophical ideas, especially Platonic, Aristotelian, or Stoic ideas, and Christian thought. This can already be seen in the New Testament (written in colloquial or *koinē* Greek), especially in John and Paul, and continues in a more fully articulated form through the early Church Fathers to Thomas Aquinas and beyond. The *Confessions* of Augustine (354–430 A.D.), an intellectual and spiritual biography, exemplifies this interplay. Augustine was attracted first by Manicheanism, whose worldview centered on a stark contrast between good and evil (seen as cosmic principles locked in permanent struggle). He then turned to Neoplatonism, for which the universe was a combination of (nonmaterial) being and matter, in which matter was at a lower level than being but was not bad in itself. Finally, he returned to a more theorized version of the Christianity in which he was brought up. In Christian thought (as Augustine understands this) evil is explained by the fact that, although God created the universe, human beings are free to reject God's love, and human sin is redeemed by God's grace, as expressed in the Incarnation. Augustine used Greek thought as part of the means of achieving and defining this worldview (for instance, Neoplatonic thinking about the three forms of reality helped Augustine to analyze the three Persons of the Trinity). But his final account of the ethical relationship between the human and the divine is significantly different from anything in Greek thought.

V. CONCLUSIONS

As well as playing a crucial role in shaping Western ethical ideas, Greek thinkers, especially Plato and Aris-

totle, are still regarded as philosophers whose work is of substantive importance to modern thought. Some current thinkers, notably Alasdair MacIntyre and Bernard Williams, have emphasized the value of Greek, especially Aristotelian, theory as an example of "virtue ethics" (centered on virtue and happiness, not rule following). As noted in Section II.C, they commend the Aristotelian idea that general moral ideas (e.g., "human nature") need to be grounded in dispositions and beliefs developed in ethical communities, rather than treated as foundational without such support, as they are in some modern theories (e.g., Kantian or utilitarian). Recent scholarly work in ancient philosophy has given special attention to Hellenistic ethics and its practical implications. As indicated in Sections III.E and III.F, the Hellenistic conceptions of practical ethics and of philosophy as therapy, and the philosophers' thinking about the role of general norms in shaping social and political life, are complex and sophisticated and are of continuing interest for modern thinking about the application of ethical ideas. Martha Nussbaum, for instance, sees in the Stoic combination of a belief-based psychology and an appeal to universal norms (e.g., natural law) a powerful statement of the idea that philosophy can change attitudes and emotions by revising ideals.

Also See the Following Articles

ARISTOTELIAN ETHICS • CHRISTIAN ETHICS, ROMAN CATHOLIC • EPICUREANISM • PLATONISM

Bibliography

Annas, J. (1993). "The Morality of Happiness." Clarendon Press, Oxford.
Gill, C. (1996). "Personality in Greek Epic, Tragedy, and Philosophy: The Self in Dialogue." Clarendon Press, Oxford.
Irwin, T. (1995). "Plato's Ethics." Clarendon Press, Oxford.
Irwin, T. (1989). "Classical Thought." Clarendon Press, Oxford.
Kraut, R. (1989). "Aristotle on the Human Good." Princeton Univ. Press, Princeton.
Nussbaum, M. C. (1994). "The Therapy of Desire: Theory and Practice in Hellenistic Ethics." Princeton Univ. Press, Princeton.
Prior, W. J. (1991). "Virtue and Knowledge: An Introduction to Greek Ethics." Routledge, London.
Rorty, A. O. (Ed.) (1980). "Essays on Aristotle's Ethics." California Univ. Press, Berkeley.
Vlastos, G. (1991). "Socrates: Ironist and Moral Philosopher." Cambridge Univ. Press, Cambridge.
Williams, B. (1993). "Shame and Necessity." California Univ. Press, Berkeley.

GUN CONTROL

Preston K. Covey
Carnegie Mellon University

GLOSSARY

assault rifle A technical military term derived from a World War II German innovation, the Sturmgewehr ("storming rifle," "assault rifle"). Three features are essential to the assault rifle: (1) selective fire, as between semiautomatic and fully automatic modes; (2) chambering for a cartridge intermediate in case length (and consequent power) between larger battle rifle rounds and submachine gun (pistol) rounds; and (3) relative compactness and light weight.

assault weapon A nontechnical term applied to a variety of repeating pistols, shotguns, and rifles, with the general sense that the firearms in question are useful only for what is termed military or criminal "assault," that is, mass or wanton violence, devoid of any legitimate sporting or defensive function.

automatic firearm A firearm that can automatically reload its chamber after initial manual discharge and continue to fire as long as the trigger is depressed. Such firearms are often called "fully automatic" to emphasize the contrast with semiautomatic firearms. In popular, but not technical, use, the term "auto-matic" often refers to both fully automatic and semi-automatic firearms.

BATF Bureau of Alcohol, Tobacco and Firearms, an arm of the U.S. Department of the Treasury empowered to supervise the production and distribution of firearms; often shortened to ATF.

discretionary licensing A firearm licensing system that imposes criteria such as "good reason" or "special need," allowing for relatively subjective judgment and discretionary latitude as to who qualifies for a license.

gun ban A law or policy that prohibits the manufacture or import, sale or transfer, acquisition, or possession of given firearms for the general population within a certain jurisdiction. Laws that disqualify some identifiable portion of the general population, such as minors or those with felony records, from possessing firearms are not usually referred to as bans because they do not affect the general population.

semiautomatic firearm A firearm that operates automatically to the extent that it can reload its chamber by an automatic process, but which requires that the trigger be released and pressed again for each successive shot.

shall-issue licensing Firearm licensing schemes that, in contrast to typical discretionary licensing regimes, allow far less judgmental discretion on the part of licensing authorities. Typical criteria for shall-issue licensing include being of a certain age, having no record of criminal conviction or involuntary commitment for mental disability, and (for a license to carry a concealed firearm) passing a certified course on relevant law, safety standards, or marksmanship.

GUN CONTROL assumes myriad guises among over 20,000 current laws, the endless array of proposed legislation at all levels of government, evolving case law, administrative policies, consumer-product safety regulations, and novel liability and litigation stratagems. The topic embraces a wide variety of arguable means and social ends and therefore involves a maze of issues. Any instant case of gun control policy serves, in effect, as a rabbit hole leading to an underlying warren of issues: questions of fact, questions of value, and questions of how to try the facts and weigh the values at stake. Consequently, gun control is a matter which few can count themselves for or against simpliciter, notwithstanding the hard and fast battle lines drawn by partisans on either side of the nominal issue. Indeed, the controversy over gun control has been called a "culture war," because it evokes impassioned conflict amongst people's deepest sensibilities and convictions about how best to secure human life and limb, individual liberty, social order, or an appropriate balance of these values. So construed, the controversy over gun control in the United States has few rivals as a potential threat to that very social order or as a challenge to our collective ability to give both the factual disputes and the competing values at stake a fair hearing and trial.

I. THE VARIETIES OF GUN CONTROL

A. Defining Gun Control

Gun control opponents prefer to define "gun control" as proper grip, presentation, stance, sight picture, and trigger control. This quip calls the question of how to parse the ambiguity of "gun control" as it refers to a complex of social policy. "Gun control" as social policy typically refers to law that regulates such specifically firearm-related activities as the manufacture, import, sale, ownership, transport, or carrying of firearms. However, there is more dimension to gun control policy and controversy than statutory law, including constitutional law, case law, and administrative regulations as well as discretionary administrative, judicial and enforcement policies, civil litigation stratagems, and private-sector policies enabled under law. Because generic definitions do not reveal the variegated landscape of either gun control or its attendant controversies, a rough taxon-

omy is helpful. Different types of gun control, as well as their different strategies, give rise to different sorts of controversy.

B. Categories of Gun Control

The following (adapted from Kleck, 1991, see Bibliography) are dimensions along which gun controls can be categorized and which occasion controversy: the type, level, or jurisdictional scope of the agency effecting regulation; the targets of regulation (the gun-related activity, the category of persons or the type of firearm targeted); and the dimensions and degree of restrictiveness of the regulation (from extremely permissive to extremely restrictive or prohibitory).

1. The Agency Effecting Regulation

The type of agency or institution enacting or effecting regulation is typically some level (federal, state, or local) or branch (executive, legislative, or judicial) of government, although private-sector entities (such as businesses, other private institutions, or their agents) can lawfully restrict otherwise lawful gun-related activities (a source of controversy endemic to conflicts among enabling laws).

a. Private-Sector Agency

Private-sector gun control, or lack thereof, as allowed within the law is a salient social concern. For example, when within a year and a half there occurred seven suicides and one murder-suicide with rented handguns at shooting ranges in California, there was an outcry for ranges to stop renting guns. In the absence of a law prohibiting the rental of firearms at shooting ranges, the controversy concerned what the private-sector policy should be. Airlines have policies regarding how firearms are to be declared for transport on passenger airliners, over and above what is required by the Federal Aviation Administration.

More salient examples of private-sector agencies of gun control policy are enterprises (such as pizza chains or delivery services) that prohibit licensed employees from carrying concealed firearms when delivering goods or services, businesses that prohibit concealed carry by licensed customers and employees on their premises, or churches and private schools that have similar policies. Social controversy in such cases arises over whether the law should favor proprietors' rights over those of employees or clientele, whether such discrimination against legally armed citizens is justified, or, conversely, whether citizens should be restrained from being armed on certain premises even when the law generally allows it.

According to the National Institute of Occupational Safety and Health (NIOSH), empirical evidence shows that three of four murdered workers are killed by armed robbers, and that permitting concealed carry by armed license holders not only occasions virtually no wrongful violence, but in fact has occasioned many successful defenses against criminal offenders and probably deters even more such offenses. Nevertheless, many proprietors and clientele of businesses, churches, and private schools object to the very idea of guns kept or carried even for self-defense. Thus cultural attitudes toward guns and gun control run deeper than beliefs amenable to empirical evidence.

b. Government Agency: Level, Branch, Jurisdiction

While the category of gun control that enjoys the widest controversy is highly visible federal gun law, the vast majority of firearms laws are at the state and local level, where more restrictive controls and more intense controversy tend to be found. The multilevel distribution of controls can make for an inconsistent patchwork of laws, which run to such extreme variations as the ban on handguns in Morton Grove, Illinois, and the mandate that every household possess a firearm in Kennesaw, Georgia. The inconsistency of gun laws across jurisdictions is itself a matter of controversy. Control critics argue that it is unfair to treat citizens with similar qualifications differently on account of their location or residency, while advocates complain that controls legitimately established in one area are undermined by "leakage" from more lax jurisdictions. A collateral and more fundamental issue is the proper apportionment of jurisdictional powers among federal, state, and local government.

The Brady Law, requiring a national 5-day waiting period to enable point-of-sale background checks by local law enforcement, has raised issues of states' and local rights against compliance with unfunded federal mandates. Brady is contested on 10th Amendment grounds (that all powers not specifically granted the federal government by the Constitution remain with the states) and, along with the federal ban on so-called assault weapons, has intensified the antifederal sentiments of state- and local-rights partisans (including members of the populist militia movement). Similarly, state preemption laws, which reserve authority for all or certain gun controls to the state legislature, address the pragmatic problem posed by an inconsistent patchwork of laws across localities but run afoul of partisans

of local autonomy (as when, for example, the Pennsylvania General Assembly forced Philadelphia to change from discretionary to "shall issue" licensing for concealed carry).

Inconsistencies among the patchwork of state and local laws thus raise controversies both pragmatic and philosophical. Just as gun control advocates argue that firearms should be uniformly subject to registration as are motor vehicles, for pragmatic reasons (such as to aid criminal investigations), gun rights advocates argue that concealed carry licenses issued by one jurisdiction should be honored uniformly in others, as are drivers' licenses, collateral with the right of self-defense, which presumably knows no borders. The latter right itself is, in turn, contested by certain pacifists and other opponents of the private use of deadly force even in self-defense. For example, some American gun control advocates prefer the policy of England, Canada, and Australia, according to which self-defense is not regarded by the law as a valid reason for owning a firearm.

Here also, state or local jurisdictions with more stringent controls complain that the efficacy of their laws is unfairly undermined by more permissive regimes elsewhere (as when the District of Columbia, which prohibits the sale and acquisition of firearms, suffers "leakage" from nearby Virginia, where sale and purchase are permitted). While the leakage problem affects only certain forms of gun control, such as restrictions on acquisition and possession, it is cited in support of the preemption of state and local authority by uniform federal law. Likewise, rights afforded by federal law can be compromised by state or local policy. For example, federal law allows lawful owners to transport their firearms in their vehicles for purposes of interstate travel to destinations where possession of the firearms is legal.

The patchwork problem is, therefore, compounded by different layers of authority within branches of the federal, state, or local government. For example, the federal judiciary encompasses district and appellate courts (which have made conflicting rulings on the constitutionality of the Brady Law and on challenges to the federal "assault weapon" ban) as well as the Supreme Court, which may, within its discretion, ignore certain constitutional controversies, as it has done regarding the Second Amendment since the 1930s. Enforcement of firearms laws, a crucial dimension of gun control, is conditioned by discretionary policies on the part of U.S. Attorneys, States' Attorneys General, and local District Attorneys as well as by the policies of lower layers of authority within law enforcement agencies and the judiciary.

A case in point is the discretionary executive, enforcement, and judicial policy that determined how lower-echelon BATF officials pursued suspected illegal firearms at the Branch Davidian compound in Waco, Texas, and led a Texas magistrate to issue the ATF agents a warrant on the basis of an arguably dubious affidavit as probable cause. Another example is the policy that led federal agents to entice Randy Weaver into illegally sawing off and selling two shotguns in order to enlist him as an informant and later to mount a siege on his Ruby Ridge home, precipitating a chain of events that cost the lives of Weaver's wife and son and a U.S. marshall, as well as several million tax dollars. The costs of gun-law enforcement initiatives in both the Waco and Ruby Ridge incidents have been characterized as well out of proportion to the initial violations at issue (as one report on Waco noted, "90 People Dead Over Gun Parts"), thus illustrating how lower-echelon enforcement and judicial policies can become a salient dimension of gun control controversies at the national level.

2. The Targets of Regulation

Gun controls can be categorized according to the firearm-related activity, the category of persons, or the type of firearm (or ammunition) being targeted for regulation.

a. Types of Activities

Types of firearm-related activity regulated include use, manufacture and importation (also exportation), transfer (including sale and purchase), transport, and possession (which includes both the "keeping and bearing" of firearms).

i. Use Actual deployment, including the intentional presentation of a gun as well as the firing of a gun for some purpose, is distinguished from the possession or carrying of a firearm. General criminal or civil law covers crimes, torts, or justifications for the use of force (such as self-defense) that happen to involve the use of guns but whose actionable nature is not instrument specific. (For example, general laws defining murder or self-defense are indifferent to whether a gun or some other instrument is used.) "Place and manner" laws specifically regarding where or how firearms may be used provide sentence enhancement for crimes committed with a gun and forbid uses such as the reckless display of a gun or discharging a gun within certain areas.

The most salient type of law governing the use of firearms imposes sentence-enhancement for the commission of certain crimes with a firearm. For example, the Gun Control Act of 1968 made the overt use (or even covert possession) of a firearm in the commission of a federal crime a discrete offense in its own right subject to an additional minimum penalty beyond the sentence prescribed for the primary offense. The Firearms Owners Protection Act of 1986 added serious drug offenses to the crimes that entailed an added penalty in case a gun was used. It also doubled the prescribed penalty for any crime if it was committed with a machine gun or a firearm equipped with a sound suppressor. State and local laws likewise often make the use of a firearm in the commission of certain serious crimes a separate offense entailing an enhanced penalty.

ii. Manufacture and Importation The manufacture of firearms is regulated in a number of respects. A federal license is required for virtually all firearms manufacture and, by federal law, all firearms must be made with unique serial numbers and with a minimum metal content identifying them as firearms. The latter requirement, known as the "plastic gun bun," was motivated by the possibility that firearms technology might someday permit the manufacture of nonmetallic firearms that could not be recognized as such by metal-detection equipment.

Local zoning ordinances can prohibit the manufacture of firearms, as well as commercial sale. Certain states (Hawaii, Illinois, Maryland, Minnesota) and localities (in California) prohibit the manufacture and sale of certain types of firearms, such as so-called Saturday Night Specials.

Unlike manufacture, the importation of firearms is regulated exclusively by the federal government and, like manufacture, requires a federal license. The Gun Control Act of 1968 introduced the "sporting purpose" requirement for purposes of an import ban on "nonsporting" firearms, in particular military-surplus rifles (such as the Carcano carbine involved in the assassination of President John F. Kennedy) and handguns that failed the test of being "particularly suitable for or readily adaptable to sporting purposes" (typically, small, inexpensive handguns).

The motivation for the exemption of privileged "sporting" arms in even draconian prohibitionist schemes has historically been political and economic expediency: it allows governments to outlaw certain firearms while appeasing large political constituencies and economic sectors, namely hunters and "sport" shooters and the economic enterprises dependent on them. In the present day, while the European Economic Community has debated total bans on cross-border transport and civilian-owned firearms, certain "sporting" arms have so far been spared in the interest of commerce.

The concept of "sporting purpose" has also been established as a standard for domestic bans in the U.S. This test was invoked in 1989 to ban, by Executive Order, the importation of certain "assault weapons," consonant with the movement to ban them domestically. In 1994, lack of "sporting purpose" was used for the first time to ban firearms of domestic manufacture under the authority of the Secretary of the Treasury (in this case, the BATF).

iii. Transfer, Sale, and Purchase   The transfer of firearms typically involves either a sale-purchase transaction or the commercial sale of a firearm by a licensed dealer; private transfers between individuals qualified to possess the firearm in question (by sale, barter, gift, or bequest) are generally lawful (with the exception of machine guns, which may be transferred only through a licensed dealer). This is a bone of contention for those who believe that all firearms transfers should be subject to the same regulations. For example, the Gun Control Act of 1968 prohibited only licensed dealers from knowingly transferring a firearm to an underage person or a member of a disqualified category; however, the Firearms Owners Protection Act of 1986 made it unlawful for anyone to do so, thereby including private transfers.

Washington, DC, Chicago, and some other cities ban the sale of handguns, and some states and localities ban the sale of certain small, inexpensive handguns. Where the sale and purchase of firearms is allowed, some regulations affect licensed dealers, while others target purchasers. Firearms dealers are required to have a federal firearms license and some states and localities require state and local licenses as well. The Gun Control Act of 1968 prohibited the sale or delivery of any firearm to anyone from or in another state, except for long guns which could be sold to residents of bordering states. The Firearms Owners Protection Act of 1986 allows long guns to be sold and delivered by licensed dealers directly to qualified individuals in other states in which sale and possession of the firearms are lawful. However, interstate sale and delivery of handguns must be mediated by a licensed dealer in the purchaser's state.

Some states and localities have adopted "gun rationing" laws that prohibit multiple sales and limit how many firearms may be purchased in a given period of time, such as one handgun a month. Advocates argue that this measure obviates multiple purchases by proxy buyers for illegal resale on the black market; opponents argue that notification of multiple purchases is a better

law enforcement mechanism, because it allows investigation and apprehension of strawman buyers.

Federal restrictions on firearms purchasers include a minimum age requirement (18 for long guns, 21 for handguns), a waiting period (where an instant check system is not available), and background clearance on a number of criteria of legal disability for acquiring or possessing a firearm. To the federal criteria for legal disability, some states add criteria such as alcohol addiction.

While the Brady Law established a national application-to-purchase system, state and local law may impose further restrictions on purchasers. There are two such mechanisms: purchase permits and licenses to possess a firearm. Permits to purchase require a background check and may be valid for some period of years and for multiple purchases, after which they can be renewed and at which time a background check may again be required. Alternatively, a separate purchase permit (and background check) may be required for each purchase. Purchase permits are usually required for acquisitions from private individuals as well as for transfers from licensed dealers, and they may apply only to handguns or to all firearms.

Licenses are required for the possession of firearms as well as for making new acquisitions. They also require a background check and commonly take the form of a Firearms Owner Identification Card. Some propose that a national card should be required to possess or purchase any firearm.

iv. Transport   Transport of a firearm simply for purposes of getting it from one location to another can be distinguished from carrying a firearm on or about one's person for purposes of protection. Transport regulations are a form of "place and manner" restriction insofar as they dictate where and in what condition a firearm may be kept for purposes of transporting it off one's own private premises. Transport regulations are of two types: those regulating how a person may privately transport a firearm and those regulating how commercial carriers must transport firearms.

v. Possession ("Keeping and Bearing")   Possession includes legal ownership as well as having a firearm (which one might not own) on one's premises or on or about one's person. Laws or policies regarding possession, in effect, regulate the keeping and bearing of firearms: who may or may not keep or bear them, the places and manners in which they may or may not be kept or carried, and the form of permission required to keep or carry them.

Possession, in the sense of ownership, beyond purchase or acquisition, might be regulated in four ways: (1) a license might be required to own any firearm (or a handgun) in some states or locales; (2) some state or local jurisdictions might require registration of any firearms (or handguns) one owns; and (3) many states require that all firearms be kept secured from unauthorized hands, in particular from children, in certain specified ways (a "manner" restriction) and/or impose criminal liability for firearms that are not properly secured and consequently misused.

Most states have special exemptions, or special carry permits, allowing hunting firearms to be carried openly in vehicles or about one's person in designated areas during hunting season. In general, possession in the sense of carrying a firearm on or about one's person, openly or concealed, is lawful on one's home or business premises, but carrying an uncased firearm, loaded or unloaded, on or about one's person beyond one's private premises is prohibited unless one has a license to do so. Vermont is the one state that allows concealed carry in public without a license, provided that the firearm is lawfully possessed and the bearer has none but lawful intent. Open carry in public is in theory or by default legal in many states, but, in the modern cultural climate and urban or suburban settings, this may cause alarm and be construed as disturbing the peace. On the other hand, in certain rural areas, carrying a long gun or handgun openly may be both lawful and unremarkable.

Besides restricting the manner in which a firearm is carried under a license, federal, state, and local law may restrict the places in which firearms can be carried even by licensed carriers. Possession of a firearm is prohibited in all federal buildings and in airport terminals. Commercial railroad or bus lines can prohibit carry by passengers, and carry by operators is generally prohibited by company policy. Many states prohibit even licensed carriers from carrying in bars (or eating establishments that serve liquor), and in sports stadiums or at sporting events.

Private establishments such as stores, restaurants, shopping malls, and amusement parks may prohibit firearms possession by legal carriers on their premises. In Texas, when the new mandatory carry licensing law took effect in January, 1996, many establishments and commercial chains posted signs prohibiting concealed carry. However, many of these rescinded the prohibition because of (a) threatened boycotts, or (b) because the postings might serve as an invitation to armed robbers, or (c) out of concern for liability in the event of an incident like the Killeen massacre (where Luby's Cafeteria patrons had firearms in their vehicles with which they might have defended against the perpetrator had they been allowed to carry them inside).

Most states prohibit possession on school grounds. Congress passed the Gun Free School Zone Act in 1990 to make this prohibition uniform nationally, but the Supreme Court found the law unconstitutional. An amendment to the Omnibus Consolidated Appropriations Act of 1997 reinstituted a national prohibition on the possession of firearms on school grounds and included findings to show the relevance to interstate commerce and thus to federal jurisdiction.

Federal, state, and local regulations may prohibit the possession of firearms in federal, state, or local parks. Such an ordinance in Tucson, Arizona, was ruled in violation of Arizona state law, which preempts local authorities from regulating the possession or carrying of firearms within the state.

The idea of "gun free zones" (especially when they are hallowed places such as schools for children, churches, or recreational areas for families) may seem unassailable until one examines the logic of such restrictions. However, firearm possession by criminals or minors and firearm use for criminal intent is already outlawed and penalized everywhere. Moreover, according to numerous studies in Texas, Florida, and elsewhere, firearm possession by licensed law-abiding citizens, even in hallowed places, is (a) not a significant problem and (b) useful for deterring criminal violence.

Criminals who possess and carry guns illegally in society, the whole of which is in effect a "free zone" for them, are not likely to be any more respectful of special "gun free zone" laws. However, the effect of such policies is likely to disarm the law abiding, depriving them of the means of self-defense and depriving society of the utility of responsible armed citizens.

Thus, the rationale for many special "gun free zones" appears to be merely symbolic. One might as well call for "bullet free zones," because it is not the presence of guns but rather their misuse that is the greater concern. On reflection, the symbolism of special "gun free zones" is also perverse: it implies that human life is more sacred in some places than in others, as well as that the right to defend innocent life varies with place and, worse, that this right shall be restricted in those very places that society considers most hallowed.

This line of objection to many "place" restrictions on possession of firearms by licensed carriers does concede that there may be places where even lawful, defensive response by armed citizens can be too hazardous to risk. Airliners are a likely candidate, where a stray bullet can compromise the air-worthiness of the aircraft, thereby threatening all aboard; training and marksmanship standards for air marshals, who routinely carry aloft, are consequently higher than for law enforcement generally.

Courthouses and airport terminals are exceptional because they are so closely policed that the law-abiding who are disarmed are less likely to encounter armed criminals who successfully ignore the law. However, schools, workplaces, commercial establishments, and parks are places where some of the worst incidents of mass violence have occurred, violence that might have been averted by armed citizens. The Killeen, Texas, massacre at Luby's Cafeteria is a case in point, and it galvanized the movement to reform the Texas carry law. Dr. Suzanna Gratia watched as her parents were fatally shot at close range before her eyes, knowing that she could have shot the perpetrator with the pistol she had duly left in her vehicle, in order to abide by Texas law at the time. At the least, the controversy over "place" restrictions on possession and carry, whether imposed by government or by private enterprise, calls for close scrutiny of both their empirical and their philosophical rationales.

b. Types of Persons

That certain qualifications should be required for acquiring and possessing firearms, as well as for being licensed to carry or deal in them, is, on its face, among the least controversial of all gun control propositions. Presumably, the general criterion for prohibiting certain types or categories of persons from acquiring or possessing firearms, or certain types of firearm (such as handguns), is being at "high risk" for misusing them criminally or for failing to use them responsibly and safely.

However, the specific criteria employed for determining legal disability are not necessarily relevant to such risk. For example, convicted felons are not permitted firearms regardless of whether the conviction was for a violent crime or for a nonviolent "white collar" crime; minors are not permitted handguns, regardless of the fact that some minors are more responsible than many of their seniors; persons dishonorably discharged from the armed services are not permitted firearms, although a dishonorable discharge does not necessarily equate to being at "high risk" for violence or firearm misadventure. On the other hand, some factors, such as alcohol or drug addiction, mental impairment, or a history of chronic violence, are statistically relevant to being at higher risk for criminal misuse of firearms. Thus, depending on the category in question, it may or may not make sense to consider people who are in that category as "high risk." This raises the question

of what the rationale for a category of legal disability actually is.

The federal Gun Control Act of 1968 as amended by the Firearms Owner Protection Act of 1986, provides the following criteria for legal disability from acquiring, possessing, selling, transporting, or importing firearms: (1) being under indictment or having been convicted of a crime punishable by imprisonment for a term exceeding 1 year; (2) being a fugitive from justice; (3) being an unlawful user of, or addicted to, a controlled substance (as defined in the Controlled Substances Act, 21 U.S.C. 802, Section 102); (4) having been adjudicated as a mental defective or committed to a mental institution; (5) being an illegal alien (firearms possession is not proscribed for legal adult aliens); (6) having been dishonorably discharged from the armed services; and (7) having been a citizen of the United States and having renounced that citizenship. In addition, one must be 18 years of age to acquire a rifle or shotgun and 21 years of age to acquire a handgun.

Some states add addiction to alcohol as a disability, which raises the question of which standards should be used to determine whether a person fits a given criterion. Some criteria carry a cut-and-dried standard: one is either a certain age or not. Similarly for the seven criteria listed above; all are objective measures. But, for example, what is the standard for being addicted to, or an abuser of, alcohol? Some states use the standard of having been convicted of driving while intoxicated a certain number of times. Being a DWI offender may be a good reason for legal disability, but not all DWIs are alcoholics and not all alcoholics are convicted as DWIs. Extending the standard to include other evidence runs afoul of privacy and confidentiality issues regarding therapeutic records and relationships, fairness issues regarding discriminating against alcoholics who seek help, or evidentiary issues regarding the reliability of "expert" opinion or other diagnostic indicators (which are especially fallible predictors of violence predicated on mental or emotional difficulties). Similar problems have been encountered by proposals to extend the standard for mental or emotional impairment beyond adjudication or commitment for same, which are verifiable matters of public record. Current controversy revolves around just such efforts to extend the criteria and standards for "high risk" categories.

c. Types of Firearms and Ammunition

A federal license is required to acquire a fully automatic firearm, but in most states no license is required to acquire other firearms, be they handguns or long guns. However, where licenses are required to purchase or own more ordinary firearms, handguns rather than long guns are typically the targets of the requirement. While federal law prohibits possession of all firearms by convicted felons, some states prohibit only their possession of handguns. Presumably, it is the utility and popularity of handguns for criminal purposes or their alleged susceptibility to misuse in general that motivates their differential treatment. Other gun types selected for special treatment include machine guns (associated in the public mind with indiscriminate or mass violence and with use by gangsters in the 1920s and 1930s) and short-barreled rifles and shotguns (singled out for their concealability and popularity for criminal purposes). In 1986, the Gun Control Act of 1968 was amended by the Firearms Owner Protection Act to double the prescribed penalty for any federal crime, in particular drug offenses, if a machine gun or a firearm equipped with a sound suppressor was used in the commission of the crime. Similar sentence enhancements are prescribed by some state and local laws for the use of an assault weapon in the commission of a crime.

When it comes to the most restrictive form of gun control, outright gun bans, selected targets include handguns generally and specifically the "Saturday Night Special" subcategory of handgun, machine guns (in several states), and "assault weapons."

Certain firearm accessories are also targets of control. For example, detachable magazines holding more than 10 rounds and manufactured after September, 1994, were banned for civilian use by the federal "assault weapon" ban, part of the Violent Crime Control Act of 1994. This act also banned firearms that had any two of the following "military style" accoutrements: a pistol-grip shoulder stock, flash suppressor, or bayonet lug. Specific types of ammunition are also targeted for special regulation or prohibition from civilian use; for example, expanding, hollow-point handgun ammunition and so-called armor-piercing or "cop-killer" bullets.

II. EVALUATING GUN CONTROL POLICY

A. Perspectives on Gun Control

The following are three particularly salient perspectives on gun control that emphasize different sorts of consideration or different priorities vying for public attention and allegiance. Although these perspectives are not mutually exclusive, partisan strategies often assume the authoritative mantle of one or another of them, so it is useful to examine critically how they are employed.

1. Criminology and Criminal Justice

Criminology studies, among other things, the behavior of criminals and influences thereon, including the feasibility and efficacy of policies aimed at reducing criminal violence. Criminal justice, among other things, is concerned with the law and other norms governing agencies and policies tasked with reducing criminal violence. Criminal violence is a natural focus from this perspective, as is gun control policy whose strategic priority is reducing criminal violence, which by some lights was the exclusive focus of gun control research and policy into the 1980s.

The other side of the criminology/criminal justice coin is concern with noncriminals as victims and resistors and noncriminal activities (such as legal firearms commerce and ownership) as enabling or deterrent influences on criminal violence. While criminology and criminal justice heed the distinction between justifiable and criminal homicide, their perspectives may be essentially agnostic regarding how noncriminal violence, such as gun accidents and suicides, should be addressed. However, researchers who are ostensibly criminologists are, fundamentally, sociologists who are not limited by artificial disciplinary boundaries; in fact, they assume a broader social-scientific purview on gun violence and policy that embraces noncriminal violence such as suicide and accidents, and they are duly concerned with the reduction of all forms of gun crime and violence.

2. Public Health

Insofar as an exclusive preoccupation with reducing criminal gun violence is a limited strategic perspective for gun control (fully half of all gun deaths are suicides), the public health perspective that evolved in the 1980s is an important complement. Public health policy today is concerned with addressing many contributing factors to human death and injury, not just disease; hence, the establishment of a division within the National Institutes of Health (NIH) and its Centers for Disease Control (CDC), the National Center for Injury Prevention and Control (NCIPC).

The general perspective of public health as such is properly agnostic on matters of essential concern to the criminology/criminal justice perspective: the distinction between justifiable death or injury and criminal violence and such a positive role as legally held firearms can play in reducing or defending against criminal violence. From a public health perspective, injury is injury and something to be prevented, not just treated: the ramifications of preventative medicine can quite naturally include efforts to reduce access to and use of lethal instruments such as firearms. Hence, several health maintenance organizations encourage doctors to advise their patients against keeping household firearms as a health risk, the American Medical Association has officially supported all manner of gun control proposals at the federal level, and the CDC/NCIPC has supported an intensive research program expressly devised to demonstrate that firearms pose a public health risk far greater than any social benefit attributable to their legal ownership or use.

However, what has come to be known, by advocates and critics alike, as "the public health approach" (PHA) to gun control policy has evolved from a research perspective on noncriminal and unintentional gun injury into a strategic political agenda that has proven to be controversial. It is useful, then, to distinguish between the general public health perspective, which is complementary to the study of human injury (including gun suicide and accidental death), and the PHA as a strategic policy perspective with a specific political agenda.

A general public health strategy aims to reduce all death and injury by gun, specifically avoidable death by suicide and accidental injury. Under the same mantle of medical-scientific authority, the PHA political strategy is to advance this laudable goal by reducing private gun ownership and use. The problem, then, with PHA as a research strategy is its predisposition to find against noncriminal firearm possession and use.

The PHA focus on death and injury and the view that firearms themselves are the "vectors" of death and injury are effectively, if not intentionally, biased in important regards. The analogy of firearms to what epidemiologists call "vectors" of disease, such as bacteria and viruses, is problematic as a premise for research design in two ways: guns are not animate, as are viruses and bacteria; and gun-related injury is also a function of the behavior of animate agents (people) possessing intentionality, unlike viruses and bacteria. The PHA research program, modeled on an epidemiological disease metaphor, quite naturally focuses on firearms-related pathology, death, or injury, but can be regarded as myopic in framing its results.

A telling example of this focus is a highly publicized statistic in the current gun control debate, the finding of a 1986 *New England Journal of Medicine* article that a gun in the home is 43 times more likely to be used to kill a family member or acquaintance than to kill an intruder. This suggests frightfully bad odds for people who keep a gun in the home (86% of the gun fatalities were suicides and 12% accidents, making the ratio of justifiable to criminal homicides 1 to 5,

which still looks like a bad bargain). The imputation is that the presence of guns in homes, like deadly viruses, are much more apt to bring death to a user or her loved ones than anything good. The statistic itself is unassailable, the straightforward result of simple arithmetic on the gun fatalities that occurred over 5 years in homes in King County, Washington. It is the focus on fatalities as the measure of the risks/benefits of household firearms that is misleading: less than 1% of defensive uses of firearms are fatal, so intruders killed, as compared to householders or acquaintances killed, is an incomplete measure, just as the number of felons killed by police officers is not the whole, or the most significant, measure of the protective value of the police force in a society.

In addition, the focus on the gun as the "vector" of the pathology (death), to the exclusion of the characteristics of the killers and their victims, ignores critical dispositional, demographic, or environmental factors: the vast majority of householders and their acquaintances who perpetrate or suffer homicide or fatal accident by gun have certifiable histories of violence, recklessness, substance abuse, or drug dealing and are no more representative of risks endemic to the general population of gun owners than the deaths of people who drink and drive are representative of all drivers' risks. Cruder numbers provide some global perspective: in a given year, the ratio of all gun fatalities (at 40,000) to gun owners (at 60 million) is 0.066%. The horrific-looking *NEJM* odds for people who keep a gun in their home is an artifact of the PHA study's perspective: an exclusive focus on pathology (fatalities), the use of the single criterion of intruders killed rather than a complete view of defensive gun use, and the emphasis on one "disease vector," the gun, to the neglect of well-known criminological factors.

3. Constitutional Law

Constitutional issues regarding gun control can be raised both on the state and federal level. On the federal level, issues regarding the constitutional feasibility and justifiability of gun control policies, or the status of the right of citizens to keep and bear arms, have been raised especially on Second Amendment grounds.

a. State Constitutional Provisions on the Right to Arms

State constitutions tend to be very explicit about the right to arms being both a right of individuals and being for the purpose of self-defense as well as the common defense. For example, this excerpt from the state constitution of Delaware: "A person has the right to keep and bear arms for the defense of self, family, home and State, and for hunting and recreational use." (Article I, Section 20)

In fact, a majority of state constitutional provisions are explicit about issues that are contested by different schools of thought about the Second Amendment to the U.S. Constitution, namely: (1) that the right to arms is an individual right, not merely a collective right of the state to equip and muster a militia; (2) that one function of this right to arms is to ensure effective means for self-defense (some states specify it more broadly to include defense of others and property as well); but (3) that the exercise of this right is properly subject to certain forms of regulation, in particular that the state may regulate the manner in which arms may be carried.

Selective gun bans represent one issue that remains ambiguous or arguable even on state constitutional provisions that are more explicit than the Second Amendment. For example, "assault weapon" bans in California, New Jersey, and Connecticut have survived constitutional challenges. This leads to an interesting line of constitutional argument in favor of selective gun bans, which was used by the Connecticut Supreme Court. The issue is whether the government's power to impose certain regulations even as against an individual right to arms includes the power to prohibit the lawabiding from possessing some types of firearm. The argument on behalf of the Connecticut ban was that it left a sufficient remainder of legal firearms unmolested so as to comport with the state constitution's provision that "every citizen has a right to bear arms in defense of himself and the state."

The generally used term "arms" is ambiguous regarding just what kinds of firearms merit protection. For self-defense purposes, could the state not prescribe a narrow assortment of handguns or long guns as sufficient? Would the right to bear arms in self-defense be violated by being limited to a few kinds of state-approved guns? Of course, there are important intervening empirical issues about what the criminal potential and defensive utility of assault weapons actually are, but the issue of principle concerns the power of the state to define what constitutes a sufficient selection of arms for defensive purposes. What reasons does the state need to constrain the otherwise unfettered choice of arms by citizens? This leads to another related issue: whether another function of the right to arms is to help secure the citizenry against tyranny, an issue central to debate about the Second Amendment.

b. The Second Amendment

A well regulated militia being necessary to the security of a free state, the right of the people to keep and bear arms, shall not be infringed.

The complex of issues about the meaning and scope of the Second Amendment, and the vast scholarship to which they have given rise, are beyond the capacity of this article. An outline of the general lay of the land must therefore suffice.

There are basically two schools of thought: what may be termed the individual right view (IRV), that the Second Amendment refers to a right of individuals; and the states' right view (SRV), that it refers to a collective or state right (as in a right of the several states) to maintain a militia as one check against the federal government, whereby the states retain the discretion to determine how citizens shall be armed and regulated for this purpose. The "militia clause" is taken by the SRV proponents as evidence of this intent, whereas the IRV position observes that the term "the people" is distributively, not collectively, used in other amendments in the Bill of Rights and that "rights" therefore pertain to individual citizens while "powers" pertain to government entities.

Supervening this controversy is the presumption that the "original intent" of the Framers is crucial to the current meaning of the Second Amendment. Some opponents of the idea of an individual right to arms break with this presumption in one of two ways. Some aver that the Framers did indeed hold the IRV but argue that in deciding constitutionality, original intent needs to be balanced against modern exigencies and may be discounted; others accept both the IRV and original intent, but conclude that the amendment should be repealed rather than finessed. The former believe the Framers had no idea what havoc modern firearms technology would produce, so that if they were alive today they would allow that the IRV may be constrained in whatever ways necessary. The second view holds that regardless of what reaction we might presume the Framers would have to the current world, that is not good enough reason to override the protections of the First, Fourth, or Fifth Amendments. The only proper way to correct the constitution, in this view, is by formal repeal or by a counteramendment.

IRV opponents point out that the U.S. Supreme Court has never proscribed gun control on Second Amendment grounds. Since the Supreme Court has addressed Second Amendment issues only once in this century, in a very circumspect decision (U.S. v. Miller,

1939), the only thing that can be fairly said about Supreme Court Second Amendment jurisprudence is that there is a dearth of it to argue about. As to the IRV/SRV controversy, it is argued that *Miller* supports the IRV, but this is true only in dicta, incidental to the decision, which skirts this fundamental issue. The basic fact of the matter about Supreme Court jurisprudence on the Second Amendment is judiciously put by Nowak, Rotunda, and Young in the Third Edition of *Constitutional Law* (1986): "The Supreme Court has not determined, at least not with any clarity, whether the amendment protects only a right of state governments against federal interference with state militia and police forces . . . or a right of individuals against the federal and states government(s)." That this observation is relegated in the text to a footnote is symbolic of the marginal status of the Second Amendment in the purview of the Supreme Court.

SRV advocates gain more ground in their appeal to the authority of lower court decisions, many of which construct an SRV from their interpretations of *Miller*. While SRV advocates arm themselves with the authority of court rulings, IRV supporters appeal to constitutional scholarship, where the weight of authority breaks down as follows. Of the approximately 60 law review/journal articles that have been published on the Second Amendment, they run over 6 to 1 in favor of the IRV position. Among the minority SRV authorities, it is pointed out, most are not law professors but are employees of gun control advocacy organizations; and their articles appear in inferior reviews or invitational symposia that are not peer-reviewed. Among the majority IRV authorities, whose articles appear in the most prestigious peer-reviewed journals, are many of the most distinguished constitutional law professors who happen not to be gun owners and who are personally hostile to firearms and the private use of force. Of course, none of this says anything about the merits of the scholarship or its arguments. But it indicates a remarkable growth in Second Amendment research in general, as well as among scholars who are not by disposition or personal philosphy gun-rights advocates.

III. TRYING THE FACTS

The great enemy of the truth is very often not the lie—deliberate, contrived, and dishonest—but the myth—persistent, persuasive, and unrealistic.

(JOHN F. KENNEDY)

It isn't what folks don't know that's the problem. It's what they know that ain't so.

(WILL ROGERS)

Former President Kennedy's and Will Roger's caveats apply to much of what is taken as conventional wisdom about firearms and violence. Pace Will Rogers, in addition, what people don't know or care to know is also a problem for public policy dispute. Of course, the controversy over guns engages many of the strongest and least attractive of human passions: the fears evoked by the apparent ubiquity or randomness of human violence (fears exacerbated for some, assuaged for others, by the availability of guns); contempt for others with alien, seemingly threatening values (be they "gun nuts" who are seen as "Wild West" vigilantes or do-gooder "gun grabbers" who would throw the citizenry, disarmed, to the wolves); and cultural beliefs akin to apocalyptic religious faith (visions of bloody anarchy or cold-blooded totalitarianism, either of which might bring an end to the world as we wish to know it). Phobia, paranoia, and bigotry reign at both extremes. Extreme control advocates see the gun culture as paranoid and bloodthirsty, but are viewed in turn as paranoid enemies of liberty by their opposite numbers.

Perhaps more than the abortion controversy, which tends to turn on metaphysical and moral issues more than upon empirical matters, the gun control controversy is rife with factual disputes. On the factual front, there is bad news and good news. The good news is that there are many well-researched findings of fact available, as well as informed and reasoned analysis on irreducibly speculative matters. The bad news is that a lot of the comforting faith and conventional wisdom about guns and gun control does not hold up under factual scrutiny. But this bad news should not make a virtue of ignorance: we still need to know what there is to know and to identify what of what we think we know that "ain't so." The following description of factual issues provides only a summary of a sample of the pertinent research.

A. Effects Attributable to Firearms

Presumably, we are interested in factual matters of the following kind for purposes of informing some cost/benefit assessment of private firearm ownership and use (as well as controls thereon), whatever role cost/benefit analyses may play within our respective ethical orientations. For purposes of illustrating the empirical contours of the task of policy evaluation, the following discussion will focus on well-defined indicators of social cost and benefit: the chief categories of firearm fatality, violent crime, and the defensive and deterrent effects of firearms.

1. Criminal Gun Violence

From the indisputable facts that America has a high level of violent crime, a high level of gun ownership, and a high level of crime committed with guns, and the fact that America's levels of both gun ownership and violent crime are higher than other nations, the inference is often drawn that the level of gun ownership "causes" or occasions the higher violent crime rate in America. There are two, decidedly less popular, alternative hypotheses: the substitution hypothesis, that the violent crime rate is accountable to other factors and would occur by other means without the guns, and the reverse causation hypothesis, that the crime rate motivates gun ownership.

There are two possible connections between gun possession and violent crime that need to be distinguished: (a) the effect of illegal gun posession by criminal aggressors on the patterns and lethality of violent crime and (b) the effects of legal gun ownership in the general population on violent crime rates.

a. Effects of Illegal Gun Possession on Criminal Aggression

On the level of individual incidents of violent crime, one question of interest is how the type of weapon possessed by a criminal aggressor influences the disposition to commit aggression via threat, whether threats escalate to attacks, whether in the event of attack injury results, and whether in the event of injurious attack death results. These are questions about what are called instrumentality effects. What are the instrumentality effects of firearms when used by criminal aggressors? Does the use of guns in violent crime tend to increase the likelihood of attack or serious injury and death from attack?

i. Effect on Criminal Threat It has been found that guns are used in homocides more often in the following types of cases (as compared with the reverse situations): where the victim is male, where the attacker is female, where the attacker is under 16 or older than 39, where the victim is 16 to 39 and the attacker is outside this "prime" age span, where there is a single attacker, and where a single aggressor attacks multiple victims. Such homicide data suggest that guns, compared with other weapons, can facilitate criminal aggression where attack is contemplated or where victim resistance is a contem-

plated risk. But these data do not prove that guns induce aggression or attack where they would not otherwise have been attempted for lack of a gun. It is possible that criminal aggressors would be sufficiently motivated to threaten or even attack victims, absent a gun. However, the advantage of a gun as a threat and remote-control weapon might well embolden criminals to be aggressive where they would not do so without a gun. This might be true particularly where the aggressors perceive themselves to be at risk or at a disadvantage as compared with anticipated victims; for example, by virtue of some disparity of bodily force in stature or strength or because of age or gender. A gun can certainly facilitate aggression by equalizing disparities in force, real or perceived.

ii. Effect on Criminal Threat Escalating to Attack Similarly, it seems reasonable to hypothesize that a gun would facilitate weaker or smaller criminals' escalating their aggression from mere threat to attack, even where attack was not originally contemplated, but particularly where victim resistance is seen as a risk. Guns may also enable physically strong and able criminals to commit attacks where they would be loathe to do so with weapons requiring physical contact. This facilitation hypothesis holds that guns enable some criminals to attack in situations where they would not do so with bare hands or contact weapons because guns equalize disparities of force for aggressors (just as they do for victims) or because guns allow attack without requiring contact with the victim.

In addition, a triggering hypothesis holds that guns can increase the likelihood of criminal aggression or attack because their very presence or possession can incite aggression. This has also been called "the weapons effect," because it could apply to other weapons. Experimental studies on this effect are about evenly divided between those that support a triggering effect and those that do not. No study provides evidence that mere possession of a gun by itself stimulates aggression or, as the triggering hypothesis is aptly summarized to hold, that "the trigger pulls the finger." Indeed, some "weapons effect" experiments showed that the mere sight of a weapon could inhibit "aggression," but various expressions of aggression are one thing, while lethal attack is quite another (and certainly not an option for experimental subjects).

A further inhibition hypothesis holds that, probably because a gun creates such a disparity of force and is effective at a distance (the very features delineated by the facilitation hypothesis), when a gun is presented by the aggressor, both the aggressor and the victim tend to refrain from attack or resistance, respectively. The victim is, predictably, more apt to comply with the aggressor's mere threat and, because this is likely, the aggressor is inhibited from gratuitously raising the ante by escalating from threat to attack. Evidence for the inhibition hypothesis comes from victim survey data. Complementary evidence for the inhibition hypothesis is found in the fact that victims who resist aggressors with a gun fare better, for all categories of criminal threat, than victims who do not resist or those who resist by other means.

iii. Effect on the Injuriousness of Completed Attacks

Once an attack ensues, for whatever reason, what effect does the use of a gun by an aggressor have on the likelihood of the attack being completed and resulting in injury? Conversely, how likely is it that an attack involving the firing of a gun (as opposed to using the gun as an impact weapon) will miss and not injure the intended victim, as compared with an edged or impact weapon attack? According to National Crime Survey data for 1990–1987, only 19% of gun attacks resulted in hits on victims. By contrast, NCS data on knife attacks show that they connect 55% of the time. However counter-intuitive it might be for those unfamiliar with the impact of stress in lethal encounters and the difficulty of shooting accurately even at close range, the net effect of the use of firearms in criminal attacks is to reduce the frequency of completed attacks and resultant injury. More generally, it is found that the more lethal the weapon involved in an attack, the less likely it will be used to inflict injury.

iv. Effect on the Fatality of Injurious Attack

It is natural to expect that the surprising infrequency with which gun attacks are completed and prove injurious would be counter-balanced by the greater lethality of the gun-shot wounds that do occur. This intuition turns out to be correct: given an injury, the injury is more likely to prove fatal if it is a gunshot wound than some other kind. Actuarially, there is a hierarchy of fatality running from, at the top, gunshot wounds to knife wounds to blunt-instrument injuries to damage produced by the use of the hands and feet.

How does the greater frequency of fatality from injury interact with the lower frequency of injury from firearms as compared with other modes of attack? The matter is too complex for summary analysis here, but the use of a gun by an aggressor, all things considered, increases the probability of a victim's death by 1.4%. Thus, the countervailing "good news/bad news" effects

of firearm use at different stages of aggression almost cancel one another out.

b. Effects of Legal Gun Ownership on Criminal Violence

The vast majority of violent crime is not committed by law-abiding gun owners who turn rogue, but by small, high-risk or recidivist subsets of the population disposed to criminal violence. Nevertheless, the institution of private gun ownership is suspected of increasing violent crime by increasing general gun availability (for example, for theft), thereby enabling illegal possession and use, and by enabling, or even inducing, legal gun owners to commit violent acts.

The question about gun "availability" as affected by legal gun ownership is whether, or to what extent, the level of lawful ownership of firearms is positively correlated with either criminal gun violence or criminal violence in general. For example, do areas with higher rates of legal gun ownership have more crime? Do crime rates increase over time when gun ownership rates increase? These questions are ambiguous, insofar as a positive correlation between levels of gun ownership and levels of crime could have at least four explanations:

1. Gun ownership enables illegal possession and crime; thus higher levels of gun ownership promote higher levels of crime.
2. Reverse causation: higher levels of crime motivate higher gun ownership.
3. Reciprocal causation: each has a positive effect on the other.
4. Confounding factors: many other variables, demographic and cultural, are determinants of crime rates.

Although space cannot be afforded here to summarize the amount and variety of the research on this matter, the bottom line is instructive: the net impact on violent crime of the various combined effects of gun possession by criminals and by prospective victims (the general public) is a virtual nullity. "Consequently, the assumption that general gun availability positively affects the frequency or average seriousness of violent crimes is not supported. The policy implication is that there appears to be nothing to be gained from reducing the general gun ownership level. Nevertheless, one still cannot reject the possibility that gun ownership among high-risk subsets of the population may increase violent crime rates" (Kleck, 1991). Thus, as a policy matter, while trying to reduce levels of legal gun ownership is not helpful and might even be counter-indicated for reducing the rate and severity of violent crime; it might nonetheless be effective to target illegal gun possession and to screen against high-risk persons' acquiring firearms.

c. International Comparisons

A popular tactic in the U.S. gun control debate, employed by both sides, is to make comparisons between the United States and other countries. Japan and Great Britain, it is observed, have far lower rates of homicide but far stricter gun controls; therefore, America's being awash in uncontrolled guns must be the reason that it is awash in violence. Switzerland, comes the rejoinder, is not only awash in guns but also requires its citizens to keep fully automatic assault rifles in their homes, yet Switzerland has one of the lowest violent crime rates in the world, lower even than Great Britain's. Hence, the availability of guns throughout a given population is not uniformly associated with violent crime.

The obvious difficulty with international comparisons regarding gun ownership/control and violence derives from important cultural differences, such as the relative presence (or absence) of such factors as: social solidarity, ethnic homogeneity, racial conflict, hierarchical rigidity, obedience to authority, and a subjective sense of unjust deprivation. (For example, Switzerland not only keeps and bears its private firearms with noteworthy civil discipline, but is also noteworthy for citizens who pay public transit fees on the honor system.) In many cases, reliable and uniform data are not available either on these and other cultural variables or on gun ownership levels. Consequently, systematic study of a large comparison set is impaired.

However, despite the obstacles in the way of accurate comparisons, certain approaches have proven instructive. For example, to partially control for cultural differences between the U.S. and Japan, Kleck examined homicide rates among Japanese-Americans in the U.S., where gun availability is widespread, with homicide rates in virtually firearm-free Japan, finding rates of 1.04 per 100,000 for the former and 2.45 for the latter. Of course, there could be many cultural differences between Japanese-Americans and Japanese citizens that might defeat this comparison, but that is just the point: international comparisons are readily vitiated. The lesson that Kleck draws from his exercise is that even a simple attempt at controlling for cultural variables can obviate an apparently enormous difference in violence rates.

An example of an obviously fallacious but popular comparison is that between the U.S. and Great Britain: not only is the U.S. overall homicide rate higher, but its gun homicide rate is also higher, which is then taken to imply that the greater rate of gun ownership in the U.S. must account for its higher rate of homicide. But Britain also has lower rates of homicide from the use of the hands and feet, yet no one would suppose that this fact is accountable to Britons' having fewer hands and feet.

Another illustrative study surveyed gun ownership levels in 14 countries and noted, for pair-wise comparisons, that higher gun ownership levels generally correlated with higher total homicide rates and with higher gun homicide rates. What the study did not notice or mention was that greater gun availability correlated equally strongly with higher nongun homicides, which suggests an alternative to the hypothesis that more guns cause more homicide; namely, the reverse causation hypothesis that higher homicide rates motivate higher levels of gun ownership. *A priori,* there seems more reason to expect nongun homicide to motivate gun ownership than to expect gun ownership to motivate nongun homicide. Another alternative explanation is that both the higher levels of gun ownership and the higher homicide levels are correlated with other cultural variables, such as attitudes on the use of lethal weapons against others. In any case, international studies are not yet conclusive on the nature of the relationship between gun ownership levels and violence rates, and they therefore provide no definitive comparisons for the U.S.

d. Demographics

The tendency to isolate firearms as a major factor accounting for American violence is understandable: America has distinctively high levels of gun ownership and also of violent crime and gun crime. However, solutions to the problem of American violence are not apt to become apparent if the problem itself is oversimplified and other factors in the patterns of American violence are ignored.

For example, it is axiomatic that violence correlates to demographics. Perhaps the most distressing recent manifestation of the effect of demographic factors in the U.S. is the sharp rise in violent crime, and gun crime in particular, among juveniles and young adults. It is not surprising, from the criminological perspective, that as the youth cohort of the general population increases the overall crime rate can increase, because the highest rate of crime in any population in every age and country occurs in the subset of those aged roughly 15 to 24. In turn, the highest crime rate in the youth cohort is in the subset of males and the highest crime rate in the male youth cohort is in the subset of the socioeconomically deprived. Despite the steep increase in gun crime among the youth cohort and the increase in the relative size of that cohort in the 1980s in the United States, the overall violent crime rate did not so markedly increase, indicating that in other age groups violent crime actually decreased. Aside from the increase of drug trafficking and associated incentives for American youths to resort to firearms in the 1980s, the general factors of youth, gender, and socioeconomics play an influential role in the national crime rate.

For example, data from the 1992 FBI Uniform Crime Reports and the *Economist,* reported by Jarod Taylor in the May, 1994, *National Review,* show that European murder rates in 1990 per 100,000 people were: Great Britain, 7.4; France, 4.6; Germany, 4.2; and Italy, 6.0; with an average of 5.5, compared to the 1992 U.S. rate of 9.3. If the socioeconomically deprived cohort is removed from the U.S. tally, the U.S. murder rate falls below Great Britain's and compares to the European average. Removing the youth cohort aged 15–24 has a similar, dramatically deflationary effect. This in no way diminishes the more severe violent crime problem in the United States, because the same manipulation would also deflate the murder rates in the European countries. It simply illustrates the magnitude of the association of violence with general demographic factors. The point is not that the problem of violent crime is not significant, but that the problem is not uniform across U.S. society.

Beyond the role of general demographic, socioeconomic, or geographic factors, more specific influences on the patterns of violence in American society can be discerned. Analogous to the question "Why is America more violent than its neighbor to the north, Canada?" is the question "Why was the American western frontier more violent than Canada's?" (Significantly, the American West was no more uniformly violent than American society is today.)

David T. Courtwright explores this question in his article "Violence in America" in the September, 1996, *American Heritage.* He identifies many regional peculiarities and differences in American violence through history that cannot be explained simply by the demographics of age and gender, whereby young men, as in all societies and times, are at highest risk for violent crime and misadventure. More specifically, it is young men who lack parental supervision or marital partners, family, or other communitarian identities, who are at greatest risk. For a variety of reasons and for most of its history, "America has had a higher proportion of itinerant, single men in its population than the nations from which its immigrants, voluntarily or otherwise, came." American immigration patterns were such that there was a surplus of men every year until 1946, producing what Courtwright calls "the abnormal structure of the population" that accounts in significant part for America's abnormal history of violence "played out with a bad hand of cards dealt from a stacked demographic deck." The surplus of men, many of whom would necessarily remain single, combined with "the ubiquity of bachelor vices" (such as liquor, gambling, and prostitution purveyed in places of commercialized vice) created ample opportunity for violent conflict, which in turn created ample reason for this volatile population to resort to arms. Unlike the Canadian frontier, which attracted families and women in greater numbers and was characterized by a more balanced and rooted population, single men disproportionately populated the notoriously violent zones of the American frontier.

Courtwright's case in point is California during the Gold Rush. The population was 95% men in 1849, 20% of whom were dead within 6 months of their arrival from disease, suicide, or violence brought on by competition for scarce prostitutes or gambling quarrels, all of which were exacerbated by alcohol abuse. For a complex of reasons, the excesses and ravages of life in communities dominated by single men abated with the influx of women and, in established communities with more balanced populations, violent conflict was localized to the establishments and mining camps where men exclusively caroused.

Mining communities were several times more violent than urban crime centers today. For example, where the latter post homicide rates of 20 to 30 per 100,000, the former produced rates of 60 to over 110. However, an exception was the Gold Hill area of North Carolina, which was settled by immigrant Cornish miners who brought and created families and suffered nothing like the premature death and homicide rates of the female-scarce and, hence, family-scarce California environs.

By Courtwright's analysis, the key factor differentiating the more violent from the more pacific communities across "frontier" regions as well as across time (as havens of violence became increasingly domesticated and peaceful or vice versa) was the difference in gender balance: the more balanced the population, the greater the social order. The complexion of this relationship, of course, reflects far more than the mere head count of male and female co-inhabitants, but the dynamics of the relationship and the salient role played historically by undomesticated men in America's violent "hot spots" illustrate a level of demographic detail worthy of attention today.

2. Suicide by Gun

There are two different kinds of issues regarding guns and suicide. The empirical questions concern the effect of firearm possession on the frequency of attempted suicide and the effect of the use of a firearm on the success of suicide attempts. While there may be little philosophical question about the propriety of the law being used to try to reduce criminal violence, there is a philosophical question, albeit a delicate one, about the law being used to prevent suicide. If objection can be raised against medical paternalism, it can also be raised against paternalism (limitation on, or interference with, a person's liberty for the presumed good of that person but regardless of, or against, that person's express or apparent wishes) exercised by coercive state authority.

Suicide prevention, at least gun-suicide prevention, is part of the rationale for imposing special criminal liability for negligence in securing firearms from unauthorized hands. And suicide reduction is one rationale for gun bans or gun-scarcity programs, on the assumption that eliminating or reducing gun suicides will reduce total suicides. Prohibiting minors and the mentally/emotionally impaired from possessing guns, imposing liability for the insecure keeping of guns, and banning guns are three different types of gun control aimed at suicide reduction.

A brief summary of the facts and findings about guns and suicide is helpful for determining how suicide-targeted gun controls might be argued. Gun suicides regularly outnumber gun homicides and account for roughly half of all gun deaths. If in a given year gun fatalities were 40,000, 20,000 would typically be suicides, 1,500 accidents, and 18,500 homicides (10 to 15% of which could be in justifiable self-defense).

Guns were used in 57% of U.S. suicides in 1985, compared with hanging, the second most popular method, at 14%. The frequency of both gun suicides and the preference for firearms for suicide in general suggest to some that the immediate availability of a gun can induce suicide (analogous to the "triggering" hypothesis regarding guns and criminal aggression, that "the trigger pulls the finger") or that the general availability of guns is conducive to suicide. Alternative notions are that the suicide who chooses a gun is a determined, not an ambivalent or impulsive, suicide attempter; that the gun is preferred because the suicide attempter wants to ensure success (fatality); that ambivalent or call-for-help suicide attempters, for this reason, do not prefer guns. Proponents of this line of hypothesizing have generated a mass of research, as have its opponents, but it culminates in the substitution hypoth-

esis, which holds that virtually all gun suicides would have been committed by some other means had a gun not been available. The substitution hypothesis is one empirical challenge to proposals to reduce firearm ownership in order to reduce suicide overall.

Overall, by Kleck's analysis (1991) and as is the case in other areas, the research fails to make a case for the effectiveness of gun controls for reducing the overall suicide rate (as opposed to the gun suicide rate). As is the case in other contested areas of research on the efficacy of gun controls, the research is about evenly divided regarding whether any given gun control measure appeared to reduce overall suicide rates or failed to do so.

There are two studies paradigmatic of what can be said for the partisans and opponents of the substitution hypothesis, respectively. A 1990 study of average suicide rates in Toronto 5 years before and after Canada imposed stricter gun controls found a decrease in the gun suicide rate but no significant drop in the overall suicide rate, consonant with the substitution hypothesis. However, a study of the effects of the Washington, DC Firearms Control Act of 1975 (which went into effect in February, 1977) from 1976 to 1977 found that the gun suicide rate decreased by 38% while the total suicide rate decreased by 22%, even as the national suicide rate was increasing. The DC law prohibited handgun sales as well as handgun possession by previous handgun owners who failed to register their handguns prior to passage of the law; it is the latter provision that could have had an impact in the study's short time frame. Factors that detract from the impressive drop in overall suicides include the facts that (a) the study did not control for any other variables besides the handgun ban and (b) that the results represent only a 1-year period. Factors that enhance the impressiveness of the D.C. study's results include the facts that (c) the substitution of more lethal long guns for handguns, if it occurred, left a marked decrease nonetheless, contrary to one version of the substitution hypothesis, and (d) any "leakage" effect from other jurisdictions that helped make Washington the "murder capitol of the world" despite its gun ban evidently did not erase the effect of the handgun ban on the suicide rate in the first year; "leakage" might have more of an effect over time, but suicide attempters are more law-abiding and less apt to seek illegal guns than criminals.

By contrast with the dramatic suicide rate drop and contrary to the study's authors' claim, the DC handgun ban, according to Kleck's analysis, did not result in decreases in overall violent crime. This is consistent with two general facts: few crimes, but most suicides, are committed by people without certifiable criminal identities; broadly targeted gun controls, such as gun bans, reduce gun possession only among the law-abiding if they reduce gun possession at all. While the reliability or generalizability of the DC study's result, limited to 1 year of the past two decades, might be questioned, the study poses an instructive question. The Canadian toughening of gun controls that effected no reduction in total suicides, according to the aforementioned 10-year Toronto study, was not tantamount to a handgun ban. The discrepancy might be taken to suggest that only sufficiently draconian controls, such as outright bans, are rewarded with the intended effect, a net reduction in some category of violence. The challenge, then, is to decide how to weigh the benefits against countervailing costs. Washington, DC is a case in point: on the assumption that overall suicide reduction has remained a result of the 1975 handgun ban, the question is whether the suicides saved counterbalance innocent lives lost to criminal violence for lack of a defensive firearm. Two questions remain: whether the prospect of suicide reduction can itself justify gun bans and, if not, what other forms of gun control might hope to reduce suicide.

There are two important firearm-specific instrumentality effects to consider, whatever one's position on suicide-preventative gun control. (1) Firearms are among the most lethal suicide instruments. Also, delayed-success methods like drug overdoses provide more opportunity to interdict suicide, should that be justifiable. The lethality of guns as suicide instruments suggest that even if gun suicide attempters would have seriously attempted suicide absent the availability of a gun, more attempters might survive (and survive with less damage) absent a gun. (2) A secondary effect of a handgun ban, were it to be effective in reducing handgun possession, could be to induce firearms users to substitute long guns (rifles and shotguns) for handguns; in the case of gun suicide attempters, this substitution would prove yet more lethal. While the Washington, DC handgun ban, at least in the first year, resulted in a significant net decrease in suicides whether or not long guns were substituted as an instrumentality, handgun bans or handgun ammunition bans can still have the peverse effect of inducing some suicide attempters to resort to more lethal firearms.

3. Accidental Death by Gun

As in the case of suicide, there is more philosophical argument about how the law should be used to prevent accidents (which can involve harm to self as well as harm to others) than about how the law should be used to prevent crime (harm to others). As with suicide, accident-prevention measures that target minors or children are less contestable than those that constrain adults for their own safety. With respect to coercive accident-prevention measures aimed at adults for their own safety, some might be welcomed by their supposed beneficiaries, while others can objectionably interfere with the liberty or other interests of their would-be beneficiaries.

Unlike the case of gun suicides, which typically outnumber gun homicides, fatal gun accidents are relatively small in proportion to all gun deaths (typically, less than 5%) and in number (1400 to 1500 per year in the 1990s), and their rate has been steadily decreasing since early in the century. For example, accidental firearm fatalities among children and juveniles age 14 and younger dropped 63% between 1979 and 1993; and the National Center for Health Statistics puts accidental firearm death at the bottom of their list, below drownings, falls, and choking. While 1500 deaths are hardly a negligible issue, the magnitude of the problem they represent is hardly on the order of the "thousands of deaths a year, most of them children" advertised by some gun control proponents. For example, the January 10, 1997, issue of the *Weekly Reader,* self-described as the "largest newspaper for kids in the world," reported that almost 2000 "kids" died in gun accidents in 1992, whereas the total number of fatal gun accidents for all age groups in 1992 was actually 1400.

Despite the low number of fatal gun accidents (FGAs) at, say, 1500 a year, some control advocates argue that FGAs outnumber justifiable gun homicides in the home and that, therefore, the risks of a gun kept in the home for defense outweigh its defensive value. Allowing that not all but most FGAs occur in the home, the problem with this extremely popular argument is that justifiable homicides represent less than 1% of defensive firearms use and are in no way an adequate measure of their defensive value. As advice that people should disarm themselves, it is a bad argument; as a paternalistic argument for disarming defensive gun owners, it is worse.

One reason to expect that the rate of fatal gun accidents would be below drownings, falls, and choking, among other modalities, is that people's exposure rates are also lower: even most gun owners have cause to handle loaded guns far less frequently than they encounter heights and food. We could expect, then, that an increase in the exposure rate would increase the fatal accident rate. Lott and Mustard did a recent study of all counties in the United States on the effects of right-to-carry laws. Where more people are newly licensed to carry concealed handguns, we might expect that more will carry and that fatal gun accidents would increase with this increased exposure (handling a loaded firearm on a daily basis). Lott and Mustard estimated that the increase in right-to-carry laws might increase fatal gun accidents by 9, which would be an increase of 0.6%, if accidental gun deaths were 1500 per year. This increment as a cost would, then, need to be balanced against the benefits of concealed carry found by Lott and Mustard.

Fatal gun accidents fall into two categories: FGAs that involve a person accidentally shooting himself with a gun he is holding and FGA's that involve another person getting shot by the person holding the gun. About half of FGAs are self-inflicted. It is estimated that 5.5–14% of self-inflicted deaths classified as FGAs are actually suicides. This substantially reduces the already relatively small magnitude of the problem of self-inflicted FGAs. For example, if there are 1500 apparent FGAs in a given year, 750 of which are self-inflicted, and if 100 (13%) of these are actually suicides, then there are actually 650 self-inflicted FGAs. What type and magnitude of legal apparatus is appropriate for reducing this number? What proportion of the self-inflicted FGAs involve children shooting themselves with someone else's gun as opposed to qualified adult gun owners shooting themselves with their own gun? It might be that cases of purely paternalistic controls are too difficult to distinguish from harm-to-others controls to raise concern, but it is an issue to watch for as new consumer-product safety measures are proposed.

Of course, the relatively small number of fatalities does not capture the whole problem of concern, accidental gun injury (fatal or not). The Consumer Product Safety Commission (CPSC) estimated from a national sample of emergency room data (which included intentional injuries among youths 15 and younger) that guns accounted for 60,000 injuries. Guns thus ranked 36th among 183 products or groups of products. The CPSC had previously weighted injuries by seriousness. On the CPSC injury index that took into account both frequency and seriousness, guns ranked 46th among 159 products, just behind prescription drugs and three ranks ahead of pens and pencils. Bicycles ranked first, with a rating 15 times as high as firearms. For the prudent, these figures counsel due care. For some policymakers, the implication is that there is always room for more concerted governmental controls. The potential for reducing accidental gun death or injury by government action will be a function of how gun accidents come about.

Using the common "reasonable and prudent person" standard of negligence, the vast majority of gun "accidents" are morally if not actionably negligent. The implication is that gun accidents are occasioned by some manner and discernible degree of carelessness. Even purely mechanical discharges that result from dropping a gun can be foreseeable and avoidable. The keeping of an unsecured and loaded firearm in one's bedroom, where a child or other unauthorized person may find it while one is away, is needless and careless, irresponsible or foreseeably risky. This general characterization of the problem of gun "accidents" comports with specific findings about those who cause or occasion them. In 1987, children under age 10 accounted for 122 of the 1400 victims of FGAs, or 13%. It is estimated that 64% of child FGAs might be caused by other children under 10. Even if all these FGAs were either self-inflicted or involved other children as shooters, children, of course, cannot be accounted "negligent" or responsible. The responsibility, or negligence, lies with the adults who allowed them access to the firearms.

Adults who allow children access to guns match the high-risk/reckless profile of adults and juveniles who are typically the shooters (and also victims) in gun accidents, who in turn match the profile of high-risk/aggressive offenders who perpetrate violent crime. The most accident-prone as well as the most violence-prone categories are these: male, single, 15 to 24 years of age, minorities, socioeconomically deprived, abusive of drugs or alcohol with histories of accidents or violence (such as vehicular accidents and offenses, prior arrests for assault).

By contrast, middle-class professionals are at virtually no risk for gun accidents; indeed, the vast majority of the general population, as well as the population of lawful gun owners, are likewise at negligible risk for gun misadventure of any description. This fact raises a general philosophical question regarding not just gun accidents but also criminal gun violence and gun suicides: How should the vast majority of any population, or their liberty, be restricted in the hopes of restricting the untoward or heinous behavior of a fractional and marginal element (notwithstanding that the effects of this element's behavior are significantly harmful, but granting that would-be controls to date have been largely ineffective)? At bottom, and in the main, the problem of gun accidents is a behavioral problem, not a mechanical safety problem, and this perspective needs to govern the deliberation of gun controls contemplated or crafted to reduce gun accidents.

4. The Defensive Utility of Firearms

The defensive utility of firearms against personal criminal threat (of murder, assault or rape, robbery, or the burglary of inhabited premises) is a quantifiable or actuarial component of their personal protective value as well as their social value and a function of two factors: the frequency and the efficacy of defensive use. The efficacy of defensive use, in turn, has two dimensions: the effect of defense with a firearm on the completion of an attempted crime and on the injuriousness of an attempted crime (including attempted homicide).

Doubt about the defensive utility of firearms is often based on one or more of the following common beliefs: people who own guns hardly ever use them defensively, because the guns are not likely to be available when needed; even whey they are, people who try to defend against crime with guns will not prevail and usually have their guns taken away and used against them; gun-armed defenders just escalate conflict and the likelihood of attack and injury from attack, whereas the best advice is to comply with criminals' terms or run away; civilians lack the ability to use guns effectively and probably shoot more innocent people than criminals; people can and should rely on the police for protection rather than "taking the law into their own hands."

a. The Frequency of Defensive Firearm Use

Kleck and Gertz have conducted a comprehensive critical analysis of all past research on the frequency of the defensive use of firearms as well as the most recent and systematic survey research. The major finding is that guns are used by civilians in defense against criminal threat from 2 million to 2.5 million times a year. Assuming approximate round numbers for gun deaths at 40,000 a year, with 18,500 homicides, 1,500 accidents, and 20,000 suicides (variations in actual numbers in any year will make a negligible difference to the comparisons below), we can derive the following comparative frequency figures based on the Kleck and Gertz finding.

• Guns are probably used defensively to save lives nearly 20 times more often than they are used criminally to take life. Reportedly, 314,000 lives are "almost certainly" saved by the defensive use of firearms; this divided by 16,250 criminal homicides yields 19.28.

• Guns are used 50 times more often to defend against criminal threat than to kill anybody—defensively, criminally, suicidally or by accident. Kleck and Gertz estimate justifiable gun homicides at fewer than 3,000 (or less than 1% of the lives reportedly saved by defensive gun use).

• Guns are used 100 times more often to defend against criminal threat than to kill another person intentionally or to commit suicide. Two million gun defenses divided by 20,000 gun suicides is 100.

• Guns are used 480 times more often by law-abiding citizens to defend against criminal threat than to commit criminal homicide. Assume the finding of Chicago Police Department studies of 20,264 homicides from the period 1965–91 that approximately 75% of criminal homicides are committed by criminals with prior records. Assume 18,500 annual gun homicides and a low rate of justifiable gun homicide at 10% or 1,850, leaving 16,650 criminal homicides. 25% of 16,650 criminal homicides yields 4,163 criminal firearm homicides by people with no prior criminal record.

The last comparative frequency estimate addresses the question of how often previously law-abiding gun owners turn rogue and commit criminal homicide as compared to how often they use guns defensively. It provides perspective for those who presume the worst of gun owners (as one gun ban advocate put it, "the homicide fantasy is the engine that drives America's fascination with guns") and it gainsays widely believed and authoritatively propagated allegations such as "The overwhelming majority of people who shoot to kill are not convicted felons; in fact, most would be considered law-abiding citizens prior to their pulling the trigger."

b. The Efficacy of Defensive Firearm Use

By the forgoing findings, the defensive use of firearms is far more frequent than misuse resulting in criminal homicide, suicide, or accidental death. But just how effective is it? There are at least five significant indicators of the efficacy of gun defense or lack thereof: (i) How effective is defensive gun use in foiling crime? (ii) How many lives are saved? (iii) How well do the gun defenders fare compared to those who do not resist or who use nongun resistance? (iv) Are guns taken away from these defenders and used against them? (v) How often do would-be defenders mistakenly shoot innocent people?

i. Efficacy in Preventing the Completion of Crimes Victims who resisted robbery with a gun or other weapon were less likely to lose property than those who resisted in any other way or those who did not resist. Kleck's analysis of National Crime Survey (NCS) data for 1979 to 1985 found the following completion rates for attempted robberies: guns, 30.9%; knives, 35.2%, other weapon, 28.9%; physical force, 50.1%; threatening or reasoning with robber, 53.7%; no self-protection, 88.5%.

NCS data on rape attempts provided too small a sample to analyze, since fewer than 1% of rape victims report resisting with a gun. Kleck and Sayles grouped resistance with guns, knives, and other weapons together and found that armed resistors to rape were less likely to have the rape completed against them than victims using other methods of resistance (such as reasoning with their assailant) and armed resistors did not suffer greater injury beyond the rape itself. From the finer breakdown of data on completion and injury rates for robbery and assaults, it seems reasonable to infer that the same results would hold for rape: in general, the more lethal the weapon used to resist, the less likely is the chance of completion of the crime.

ii. Estimation of Lives Saved
Defensive gun use is not limited to self-defense but often involves or includes the defense of some person(s) other than or in addition to the gun wielder. The Kleck and Gertz study asked the following question: "If you had not used a gun for protection in this incident, how likely do you think it is that you or someone else would have been killed?" Reportedly, 15.7% of respondents "almost certainly would have been killed," 14.2% "probably would have," and 16.2% "might have," which, given the lower estimate of 2 million defensive gun uses, would translate to 314,000; 598,000; and 922,000 lives saved. At the lower end, the lives reportedly saved by defensive gun use are a good seven times the total gun deaths in any year. If only 15% of the most confident respondent reports were correct, lives saved with guns would still outweigh all gun deaths.

iii. Efficacy in Preventing Attack and Injury
People who defend against criminal insult or threat with a gun are the best off of all the categories of victim-responder regarding the likelihood of suffering injury: better off than those who do not resist, who try to reason with the criminal, who try to flee, or who resist with bare physical force or with any other type of weapon.

Thus, as a matter of actuarial fact, gun defenders are significantly better off than those who employ any of the alternative methods of responding to robbery or assault. This fact contradicts the myths created and propagated by many (not all) police chiefs and other authoritative paternalists to the effect that people are better off not resisting or carrying and using a police whistle or Mace or pepper spray or a "stun gun." Regarding speculation that attempted gun defense is apt to precipitate or escalate a criminal attack, Kleck found

to the contrary that the defensive use of firearms appeared to inhibit attack on defenders in threatening confrontations with criminals as well as, in the event of an attack, to reduce the probability of injury.

iv. Defenders Shot With Their Own Gun
One form of ineptitude attributed to gun defenders by skeptics of the defensive efficacy of private firearms is their liability to having their guns taken away by an assailant and used against them. Because of the prevalence of this allegation, it merits special attention. In fact, this sort of misadventure is extremely rare. By Kleck's analysis, 1% of defensive gun use is the outside estimate for such untoward reversals. These incidents even include situations such as where a burglar did not actually take the gun from the defender's hands but rather confronted an armed defender with another of the defender's guns obtained in the course of the buglary.

v. Defenders' Rate of Mistaken Shootings
Another prevalent myth is that gun defenders are trigger happy, because they are naturally bloodthirsty, skittish, eager to shoot their way into the "Armed Citizen" column of the American Rifleman, and so on. Again by Kleck's analysis, fewer than 2% of fatal gun accidents involve a would-be defender shooting an innocent person who is mistaken for an intruder or assailant. Assuming 1500 unintentional gun fatalities a year, this means 30 fatal mistaken shootings annually. Fatally mistaken shootings then represent 0.0015% of gun defenses.

c. Defensive Firearm Use versus Vigilantism
Vigilantism is historically associated with times and places where no official law enforcement or judicial authority was available to apprehend and punish offenders. Whatever its arguable quasilegal rationale in such times and circumstances, vigilantism in the modern American setting is defined here as the use of force by anyone (whether a civilian, police officer, or government official) to impose punishment without due process of law. As such, it is decidedly a criminal offense. By contrast, the use of deadly force is perfectly lawful in defense of innocent human life against the imminent threat of death or grave bodily harm (and, in some jurisdictions, in defense of property or against trespass, where the law grants the householder the presumption that an unannounced intruder poses actionable risk). The threat of the use of deadly force, especially upon one's own premises, is arguably lawful when the defender has reasonable suspicion of the hostile intent of the offender (akin to the standard for investigative detention by a police officer). Such an action, whose

intent is defensive and not punitive, is, by definition, not vigilantism.

The defensive use of force is often dubiously described as "taking the law into one's own hands." It is, indeed, precisely that, notwithstanding the ambiguity of the metaphor: when the law is "broken" by an offender who poses a threat allowing defensive force (or the threat of defensive force), the defender is allowed to take the broken law into his own hands, as it were, and forcibly make it right. This is not vigilantism, the unlawful taking of the law into one's own hands for purposes of meting out punishment in the absence of due process of law, but a lawful mending of broken law.

5. The Deterrent Value of Firearms

Crime prevention by interdicting or interrupting an attempted crime is different from deterring a person from even attempting a crime in the first place. Crime deterrence means the prevention of the very attempt to commit a crime by people who are or might be otherwise disposed to break the law, presumably by engendering fear of negative consequences. A deterrent effect attributable to private firearms possession would be another component of their protective value and their social value in addition to their defensive utility. While, unlike the defensive utility of firearms, their deterrent value is difficult to determine, let alone quantify, there exist reasonable grounds as well as direct evidence for posting a deterrent effect. There are at least two questions of interest: whether there is reason to assume a deterrent effect and, if so, how to assess its magnitude or significance.

a. A Plausibility Argument for a Deterrent Effect

Apart from direct empirical evidence, there is a plausibility argument to the effect that there probably is a deterrent effect and, whatever its exact magnitude might be, that it is probably greater than, or at least similar to, any deterrent effect attributable to the criminal justice system, whose presumed deterrent effect is itself notoriously hard to prove. Thus, the plausibility argument is conditional: if the justice system has a deterrent effect, the deterrent effect of private firearms and the private use of force is probably greater.

Deterrence theory holds that deterrence, in part, is a function of three factors: (1) the certainty of penalty, (2) the severity of penalty, and (3) the promptness of penalty. Kleck observes that the risk a criminal faces from armed civilians is at least more prompt (the armed victim is, by definition, at the crime scene) and potentially more severe (death or grave injury) than the risk

of penalty from the criminal justice system (where the likely legal penalty for robbery, burglary, rape, assault, or even murder is a few to several years in prison). While less than 1% of defensive gun uses by civilians are fatal, civilians fatally shoot thousands of criminals a year, more than do the police and more than are executed for capital crimes. The frequency of defensive gun uses that involve actual confrontations (at 2,000,000 per year) is twice the 1980 arrest rate for violent crime and burglary (at 988,000), so the risk of confronting an armed citizen is at least as likely as arrest but far more likely than conviction.

Of the estimated 600,000 police officers in the U.S., less than 25%, or 150,000, are on duty at any given time; whereas there are tens of millions of civilians with access to firearms and high motivation to use them for protection of themselves or their families. For example, if 1% of the adult population carries a concealed firearm (in states that have licensed concealed carry, 3–5% of the population are license holders, which need not mean that all of them carry all or most of the time), then there could be more armed civilians abroad than armed police on most shifts. In sum, if there is reason to attribute any deterrent effect to the criminal justice system, there seems to be reason to attribute a deterrent effect of at least similar magnitude to armed civilians.

b. Evidence of a Deterrent Effect

Until recently, the direct evidence for a deterrent effect has been of two kinds: self-reports obtained from surveys of incarcerated criminals, which are extremely persuasive but not conclusive, and quasiexperimental or observational studies of the before-and-after effects of well-publicized firearms training programs. In addition, there is recent evidence, for example, one study by Lott and Mustard of all counties in the United States, on the effects of right-to-carry laws. Insofar as concealed carry by civilians has a deterrent effect, it could affect violent crime abroad or in general, not just violent crime or burglary in the home or business establishments in which guns are apt to be kept.

Kleck reports as follows on the classic Wright and Rossi study (1986) that interviewed 1874 imprisoned felons in 10 states about their encounters with, and their perception of the risks of confrontations with, civilians armed with guns. Interviews of those who admitted having committed a violent crime or burglary in their criminal histories indicated the following: 42% encountered armed victims; 38% were scared off, shot at, wounded, captured, or a combination; 43% on some occasion refrained from a crime because they believed the victim was carrying a gun; 56% agreed with the statement that "most criminals are more worried about meeting an armed victim than they are about running into the police"; 58% agreed that "a store owner who is known to keep a gun on the premises is not going to get robbed very often"; 52% agreed that "a criminal is not going to mess around with a victim he knows is armed with a gun"; 45% of those who had encountered an armed victim thought frequently about the risk of getting shot by a victim, while only 28% of those who had not had such an encounter said the same; and only 27% saw committing a crime against an armed victim as an exciting challenge.

Kleck allows that prisoners are a biased sample because their very imprisonment shows that at least in one instance they were not deterred. It has also been argued that felons who elude arrest might be different in attitude and disposition from those who are captured. However, the latter point suggests only that not all criminals are risk-averse in either attitude or behavior regarding encountering armed victims, which the survey already allows. Moreover, Kleck argues that the bias of the sample renders the survey results more impressive. The prisoners' admissions recounted above are not complimentary; if anything, prisoners' incentive is not to admit such vulnerabilities and concerns, such that the results are likely to underreport the extent of aversion to the risks of encountering armed victims. Because the prisoner sample excludes the criminally disposed who are in fact deterred, the survey results underrepresent the deterrent impact of armed civilians.

B. The Feasibility and Efficacy of Gun Control

Nothing is so firmly believed as that which we least know.

(MONTAIGNE)

Montaigne's remark can be applied to general faith that gun controls actually work as intended or hoped. But what actually is known about the workability and intended impacts of gun controls? And, absent a showing of impact, what remains to be said for them? The following are some examples of gun control policies that have a serious claim to feasibility, efficacy, and justifiability, along with some caveats about their potential controversy.

1. Background screening at points-of-sale by means of a national "instant" records check. The need for uniform screening and centralized, reliable data argues for a

federally mandated, and subsidized, policy. Background screening to obviate the possibility of purchase by disqualified applicants, a corollary of the need to disqualify certain categories of people, is presumably as agreeable as gun controls come. Another law enforcement advantage of an instant check system is the capability it provides to apprehend disqualified applicants who may be dangerous or wanted. However, a computerized and nationally networked instant check system arouses opposition from those who fear, and have reason to fear, the creation of a national (or state or city) registry of legal gun owners: its expediency for the confiscation of firearms. Government's lack of response to this fear is causing gratuitous controversy over a gun control measure that should not be problematic.

2. Required background screening for private transfers. The lack of uniformity enables "leakage" of legally disqualified buyers to private sellers, who lack the means to perform a proper background check. The proposal is for a national policy (some states already have such laws) that require private transfers to be processed through a licensed dealer. This policy may be arguable in its impact on the illicit firearms market, but it is also arguably obligatory to do what we can to prevent illegal firearm acquisitions, regardless of net impact, when the burden to law-abiding gun owners of "doing the right thing" is modest. Private automobile transfers are handled by a similar process, requiring a modest notary fee.

3. Legal disability policy. Laws that prohibit certain categories of people from possessing or using firearms may be the least problematic form of gun control. However, two controversial issues are (a) exactly what categories of people (beyond the "usual suspects" such as minors and those with felony records or certifiable mental disabilities) ought to be disqualified from firearm acquisition, possession, or licensing for concealed carry and (b) the standards for granting relief from legal disability, such as for recovered mental patients or convicted felons after some period of time has passed since they served their sentence. There is no question that certain categories of "high risk" people should be prohibited from possessing firearms, but the expansion of the traditional criteria of disability has proven controversial.

4. Improved, concerted, proactive enforcement of carry and possession laws. Illegal carry of firearms occurs in public and is an easily established offense in that setting; laws prohibiting unlicensed carry are more susceptible of enforcement than laws against general possession, whose enforcement requires access to the criminal's residence. Law enforcement programs that

have intensified, for whatever purposes, street searches have been found effective for interdicting casual weapon carrying. Sentence enhancement for certain firearms-related offenses can prove an effective tool of enhanced enforcement, although discretionary policies are found more effective than the popular mandatory enhancement laws. This is an interesting case where many gun control opponents, on the one hand, argue against gun control nostrums on grounds of their lack of proven efficacy and, on the other hand, persist in pushing "tough on criminal" laws such as mandatory enhanced sentencing for gun crimes only to be hoist upon their own petard: evidence that discretionary systems work better than mandatory ones.

One strategy for reducing overall violence is indirect, trying to do so by reducing overall gun ownership; another is to target and try to reduce gun violence directly and thereby reduce the overall violence rate. In general, gun controls do not reduce general gun ownership, either legal ownership among the general public or illegal keeping of guns among "high-risk" groups. While this suggests that the indirect strategy or its proximate goal of reducing gun ownership is not a promising approach to reducing the overall violence rate, it also suggests that in general gun controls (gun bans excepted) do not impair legal ownership.

However, certain forms of the direct strategy, which targets gun violence specifically rather than gun ownership generally, have demonstrable benefits. Kleck reports on the results of 121 tests of the effects of various types of gun control on crime and violence; in 92% of the cases there was no effect on violence rates. However, 6 tests provided ambiguous evidence of efficacy, while 4 provided unequivocal support. For example, mandatory penalties for illegally carrying a firearm and discretionary (rather than mandatory) additional penalties for felonies committed with a gun evidently reduce robbery rates. One possible explanation is that such laws, by whatever mechanism, reduce casual carrying and thereby reduce casual or opportunistic robbery.

Of course, the fact that the preponderance of gun controls have no demonstrable efficacy in reducing violence does not show that gun control in general can have no such effect, because it might be the case, as advocates insist, that different controls, more controls, or stricter controls would prove effective. The point, rather, is to illustrate that common assumptions about the efficacy of gun control are, more often than not, too facile.

IV. WEIGHING THE VALUES

Regarding the balance of harms against benefits associated with private firearms, a question often asked is: At what point does the good of the many outweigh the freedom of the individual? The way such qeustions are framed often presumes that there exists a net balance of harm or risk to the detriment of the many, putting individuals' entitlement to firearms on trial under a presumption of guilt. Such questions also imply a utilitarian presumption about what is required for proof of innocence, that a showing of net benefit would vindicate the putative right to private arms.

A. The Value of Firearms to Individuals

The potential value of firearms to individuals is twofold: their recreational value and their protective value. Individuals may also take an abiding interest in the residual social and political values of private firearms.

1. Recreational Value and "Sporting Purpose"

An unusual facet of the gun control controversy is what might be called the "sporting purpose hypothesis." The concept of "sporting purpose" is one of the tools for discriminating between "good" and "bad" guns. The mantle of "sporting purpose" protects "good" guns from bans, while its denial helps stigmatize "bad" guns. This argument holds that if a firearm (such as firearms particularly suitable for combat purposes) serves no legitimate sporting purpose, then it may justifiably be banned.

The obvious question is why sporting purpose should come into the question of which guns to ban or not ban. If private firearms are to be banned either because they are fundamentally morally objectionable or because they produce greater social harm than benefit, then their recreational value and "sporting purpose" is certainly not going to be sufficient to prevent such a ban.

The category of "sporting purpose" firearms is a puzzlement because many hunting firearms are far more deadly than the firearms targeted as "assault weapons." For example, the Colt Sporter targeted by the federal assault weapon ban fires a relatively small .223 caliber cartridge, while the Remington 7400 rifle fires the vaunted .30-06 round, a U.S. military cartridge from before WWI to Korea, a favorite of big-game hunters and a far more devastating round than the .223. Why is the lightweight .223 an "assault weapon" and the heavy-duty .30-06 a "sporting" firearm? The answer, gun control opponents argue, is that the "sporting purpose" standard is a temporary expedient for allaying opposition to gun bans and that it provides only temporary immunity for the guns of sport shooters and hunters on the perverse pretext that the recreational value of deadly weapons carries special weight in the balancing of the overall harms and benefits of firearms.

Whatever weight it carries in the social balance scales, the value of the recreational use of firearms is twofold: the residual value of the enjoyment of firearms by recreational shooters, hunters, or collectors regardless of their expectable utility, a value to individuals, and the social utility of their use in lawful hunting, insofar as this recreation serves and raises significant moneys for wildlife conservationist policy and local economies. (For example, the Vermont Fish and Wildlife Department estimated that the 1996 fall hunting season brought $68 million into the state's economy.) In addition, social utility is imputed to reactional training and competitions with combat firearms.

2. Protective Value

The protective value of firearms to individuals also has two dimensions: (a) defensive utility, one measure of which is the actuarial rate at which armed civilians successfully defend against criminal threats (as discussed earlier) and (b) the residual value of the right to firearms as an option in self-defense, irrespective of their defensive utility.

a. Defensive Utility

As has been documented earlier, a firearm happens to be one's best option in the gravest extreme when, by the universal standard of justifiable deadly force, an innocent person is in imminent and otherwise unavoidable danger of death or grave bodily harm. The conventional wisdom notwithstanding, gun owners and carriers know this and wish to preserve this option.

b. Residual Value

The second dimension of the protective value of firearms is the fact of having this option in self-defense regardless of the actuarial utility of using a gun defensively or the likelihood or ever having to use it (which, while nonnegligible, may be very low for many people). A person may value this option in self-defense, and many do, regardless of what the statistics say about the defensive efficacy of firearms or the probability of ever having to ward off predatory criminals.

3. The Question of Police Protection

The protective value of firearms to individuals may take on a different complexion and priority depending on one's view of the efficacy or likelihood of police protection, whose functions are essentially general deterrence and reactive apprehension after the fact. As a matter of law, the police are not responsible for protecting individuals, nor liable for failing to do so, in all but a few special cases where they assume this obligation. The legal fact that police have no general duty to protect is well established by statutory law and case law going back into the 19th century.

In light of the fact that police have neither the duty nor the ability to afford individuals protection and given the nonnegligible actuarial risks of victimization (the National Crime Survey estimates indicate that 83% of Americans, sometime in their lifetime, will be a victim of violent crime), the residual value of private firearms possession for protection is predicated on citizens' ultimate responsibility for their own protection in the gravest extreme. People who value the option of armed defense argue that, if they must bear responsibility for their own protection, the options afforded them should be commensurate.

B. The Social Value of Firearms

1. Security, Tranquility, Civility

On the one hand, the prevalence of private firearms may seem to threaten the social values of security, domestic tranquility, and civility. For example, people who advocate domestic disarmament, a state monopoly on force, and oppose self-help against crime for the sake of domestic tranquility and civility, also uphold the value of the security of life and limb for the sake of enjoying the rest. However, they do not hold with private firearms as a means of securing any of these values.

On the other hand, proponents of self-help in the provision of individual and collective security, and of the right to arms for this purpose, who oppose a state monopoly on all means of force, also uphold the social values of domestic tranquility and civility; but they cleave to very different ideas about the means for securing these values and the apportionment of responsibility. As Jeffrey Snyder argues in *The Public Interest* (Fall, 1993), "How can you rightfully ask another human being to risk his life to protect yours, when you will assume no responsibility yourself?"

2. The Social Utility and Residual Value of Private Firearms

By the Snyder ethic, the social value of private firearms is not limited to their utility in defensive deployment or to their role in the reduction of criminal violence or social disorder by either deterrence or defensive interdiction. Rather, their social value, like their protective value to individuals, is twofold: one part social utility and one part residual value (their value regardless of their expectable utility) held by those who take an abiding interest in lawful citizen participation in the maintenance of civil order. There are the empirical, actuarial questions of utility: Does an armed citizenry collectively deter or reduce crime against the person and thereby provide, on balance, an effective measure of aggregate security from harm? Or, rather, does the keeping or bearing of arms by law-abiding citizens undermine private and public safety?

Besides these empirical questions of social utility, there are also residual moral questions: Are citizens morally obligated to contribute to the public safety, as well as to their own defense, not by vigilantism, but by vigilance and, in the gravest extreme, by responsible armed response? Can citizens be fairly expected to fulfill this civic right and duty without being afforded effective means? Or, rather, should the state be afforded a monopoly of armed force and sole responsibility for maintaining public safety and civil order?

C. The Political Value of Firearms

An important controversy beyond that of the social value of private firearms concerns the value of an armed citizenry. This is a fundamental issue for moral-political philosophy, the question of the monopoly of force as a political matter: whether the distribution of checks and balances of power in the society should not properly allot to the people, the ultimate sovereigns, a fair share in the distribution of force. There is a collateral issue: Who should enjoy the greater presumption of trust, the people or their government, irrespective of actual trustworthiness? This question is analogous to the question of which presumption should rule the institution of criminal law: the presumption of innocence, or the presumption of guilt. Should the government presumptively mistrust the people in the apportionment of liberty? Or should the people presumptively mistrust their government in the apportionment of power?

1. Political Utility and Residual Value

The political value of an armed citizenry is perhaps the most controversial, insofar as its empirical dimension is so largely speculative. This putative value presumably consists in the role of an armed citizenry as a defense or deterrent against government violation of the social contract as well as their utility for the common defense. But this political value is one part expected utility (the

deterrent or defensive efficacy of an armed citizenry against government transgressions and the likelihood of the need therefore, or success) and one part the residual value of citizens' being entrusted with a share of armed force (as against a paternalistic or arrogated monopoly of force by the state).

Again, there are two kinds of question of value. There are the obvious empirical, albeit speculative, utility questions: Whether an armed citizenry is any longer necessary or likely useful for the protection of the state against disorder from within or invasion from without; or, whether an armed citizenry is either a necessary or even viable impediment to governmental abuse of power. Be that as it may, there remain fundamental philosophical questions: the propriety in principle of entrusting the state with a paternalistic monopoly of armed force as versus the value of methodical mistrust of government, the value of sharing all manner of power (including the right to arms) with the people as part and parcel of the system of checks and balances, the value of investing a measure of coercive (not just procedural) power in the people themselves, individually as well as collectively. The residual moral value of so entrusting and empowering the people is not a function of expected utility (whether it is likely that it would ever be necessary or feasible in fact for the people to pose a threat of armed resistance against their government); it is rather a matter of the principles upon which the governance of a free people should arguably be founded, a question of residual moral value rather than expected utility alone.

2. Speculative Issues

The question of the need for an armed citizenry as a check on the abuse of governmental power is simply dismissed by many as both anachronistic and anathema in our modern and high-mindedly optimistic times. But the question is relative, as the need or capacity or efficacy of armed resistance pertains to any level of government: federal, state, or local. In fact, armed American citizens have mustered in order to resist corrupt governmental authority on the local level. That an armed citizenry is a factor to be reckoned with even by a government superior in arms is, by some lights, shown by many insurgency actions around the world, not the least by our own forebears' historic war of independence.

But today the very idea of a people having to take up arms against their own government invites images of anarchy as well as futility and is, in any case, a discomfiting thought. While granting this, Sanford Levinson, in his judicious treatment of the Second Amendment controversy ("The embarrassing Second Amendment," in Cottrol, 1994), provides a temporizing perspective on this sensitive and irreducibly speculative issue: "One would, of course, like to believe that the state, whether at the local or national level, presents no threat to important political values, including liberty. . . . But it seems foolhardy to assume that the armed state will necessarily be benevolent. The American political tradition is, for good or ill, based in large measure on a healthy mistrust of the state . . . . In any event, it is hard for me to see how one can argue that circumstances have so changed as to make mass disarmament constitutionally unproblematic."

In the end, the empirical fact of the matter, the likelihood of whether the people could, or would need to, resist their government in the gravest breach of power, is not dispositive on the moral and political-philosophic question, whether a free people should nonetheless be so empowered. In addition, political-philosophic commitment to such empowerment is part of the residual value of firearms for many individuals, who value it regardless of its speculative utility. The individual, social, and political value of privately owned firearms are all arguable, on both empirical and philosophic grounds. But that is to say that they must be fairly accounted and weighed in the balance scales on their merits, not suumarily ignored as counter-conventional wisdom.

V. PARADIGMS OF RESTRICTIVE AND PERMISSIVE POLICY

Gun bans and permits to carry firearms concealed in public are probably the two most controversial types of gun control measure among political proponents and opponents of gun control, by virtue of the fact that they are viewed, respectively, as extremely (too) restrictive and extremely (too) permissive policies. Both restrictive control advocates and a large part of the public (as reflected in polls) have favored selective bans on certain types of firearm. In the case of "assault weapons," 70% of Americans apparently favored a ban (whatever they may have construed such firearms to be). Prohibitionist control advocates tend to oppose concealed carry permits, at least the more premissive "shall issue" variety. While a 1996 poll found 60% of Americans in favor of permissive licensing for concealed carry, the outcry against such measures has been as intense as the opposition to equally popular "assault weapon" bans. These cases of gun control are useful to examine not only because of their high profile but because corrigible speculation plays a large role in the associated controversy.

A. Gun Bans

While the ultimate social goal of many ban proponents is complete civilian disarmament, selective bans are taken to be politically necessary incremental steps. The ultimate goal of other ban proponents is reduction of criminal violence, and thus they may be more selective in the guns they see fit to ban. In either case, the gun ban proposals on the public agenda at any time are apt to be selective bans, where total and selective prohibitionists can make common cause. Selective gun bans typically target firearms that can be easily stigmatized in some fashion or seem particularly conducive to criminal violence, such as "Saturday Night Specials" and "assault weapons" or even handguns in general. Arguments against banning such highly stigmatized guns will presumably tell against more comprehensive bans, the defense theory being that if the most evil-seeming of "bad" guns may not justifiably be banned, no firearms may justifiably be banned. So, we will focus on the forms of argument about selective bans, in particular bans on so-called assault weapons, but we will first examine the salient tactical role that selective bans play in more comprehensive ban strategies.

1. Comprehensive Bans and Civilian Disarmament

The political feasibility of a total ban or even a general handgun ban is arguably nil, because of the size of the political constituency that value guns of some sort, like sporting arms and handguns. On the occasions when popular referendums on categorical handgun bans have been held, in states where public support had appeared significant before the ban campaign, the proposed bans were defeated by large margins. In view of the fact that 60% of Americans now support permissive right-to-carry laws and handguns are the very guns suitable for concealed carry, even a general handgun ban is not feasible politically.

In addition, the moral right of self-defense, while denied by some on moral grounds, is upheld by the law as well as an overwhelming majority of Americans, as is the moral right to firearms as the most effective means of self-defense (a moral position quite separable from any debate over the meaning of the Second Amendment). The number of people cleaving to both of these putative rights as essentially connected probably pose insuperable political opposition to very comprehensive gun bans. The right of self-defense (tantamount to the right to use deadly force) and the right to possess guns for that purpose are, by some lights, segregatable (for example, English and Australian law uphold the quite universal right of self-defense but deny self-defense as a legitimate reason for possessing firearms). However, convincing most Americans of this, that the former right (self-defense) does not entail the latter (a right to arms), is not likely.

Comprehensive ban proponents know this and consequently adopt an incremental strategy against the general store of private firearms, attacking select types of firearms with smaller constituencies. The long list of protected "sporting purpose" firearms in the federal "assault weapon" ban in the Violent Crime Control Act of 1994 was intended to assure hunters and sport shooters that their favorite firearms were not at risk and thereby allay potential opposition from that large population. The "assult weapon" ban portion of the larger 1994 crime bill was called the Public Safety & Recreational Firearms Use Protection Act to signal its intention to protect "recreational firearms." An important collateral tactic is to assure the large population interested in self-defense guns that "assault weapons" are not legitimate instruments of self-defense.

Similarly, "Saturday Night Special" ban proposals attempt to allay the opposition of both sports shooters and gun-defense advocates alike by arguing that such cheap guns are no good for either purpose, by virtue of being both unsafe and unreliable. "Saturday Night Special" and other stigmatic terms, such as "junk gun," "assault weapon," or "cop-killer gun," are designed to allay public opposition: Who, after all, would want to stand up for "cop-killer guns" or depend for defense on "junk guns"? Ban opponents, in turn, refer to such targeted weapons as "affordable handguns" that are "particularly suitable for defensive purposes."

2. Selective Gun Bans

As a prohibitionist policy, gun banning harks to at least two different strategies, which for convenience of reference may be called the utilitarian ban strategy (UBS) and the fundamental moral objection strategy (FMOS). While there are, in fact, significant numbers of influential gun ban proponents who adhere to or vacillate between each sort of strategy, the UBS and FMOS here serve simply to illustrate radically different approaches to gun bans.

a. The Fundamental Moral Objection Strategy (FMOS)

For the UBS, as will be seen, the ultimate goal is reducing criminal violence; the efficacy of a ban for this purpose is essential to its justifiability. For the FMOS, by contrast, the reduction of the store of private firearms is the ultimate goal as a matter of fundamental moral

objection to private force and firearms, so the efficacy of a ban may be expedient to claim and argue, but it is not taken as critical to the justifiability of the ban. The FMOS affords preeminence to certain moral values, such that trying the facts or weighing the balance of social harms and benefits of private firearms is not dispositive. The individual, social, and political values of private firearms are the very sort found objectionable; so, in principle, they are either dismissed or demoted to inconsequential status (even if in practice they are entertained). Any putative rights to firearms for defense against criminal threat, let alone against the state, will carry no weight with the FMOS.

The FMOS has a counterpart among gun-rights positions that resort to empirical and utilitarian argument about the utility of firearms as a tactic but hold that, in principle, the numbers cannot gainsay what they take to be a fundamental right to arms derived from the paramount right of self-defense. Second Amendment fundamentalists, who believe that the constitutional right in question is not only an individual right but an absolute one, would be one counterpart to FMOS partisans. Such partisanship, based on fundamental and nonnegotiable moral entrenchments inhospitable to empirical considerations, is one reason the gun control controversy is aptly called a "culture war."

b. The Utilitarian Ban Strategy (UBS)

A more prevalent, and more tractable, sort of gun ban strategy is the utilitarian crime-control agenda whose goal is to reduce criminal violence (or, at least, its more indiscriminate, wanton forms, such as mass mayhem and massacres) by reducing criminal access to certain types of firearm with features that are "particularly suitable" to indiscriminate violence or that otherwise make them "criminals' weapons of choice."

Noncriminal misuse of firearms (such as in suicide or gun accidents) is not typically used to promote selective bans, because it is hard to make the case that certain types of firearm are more conducive to gun suicide or accident than any other type. Thus, the UBS seeks to ban certain firearms that are claimed to figure significantly in crime in order to reduce criminal access to these weapons and, thereby, reduce criminal violence. If banning certain weapons did not reduce criminal violence overall, there would be no reason to reduce access to these rather than to other guns according to a utilitarian strategy. Regarding any selective gun ban, then, it is sensible to ask: Why ban these and not other guns, or all guns? From the UBS view, the answer must be that banning certain weapons promises a reduction in criminal violence overall, because there is something special about them that is especially conducive to promoting greater fatality or a greater prevalence of violence.

For example, one feature of handguns that makes them specially suitable to criminal violence and attractive to criminals is the fact that they are convenient to carry and conceal. Handguns are most criminals' weapons of choice and thus are frequently targeted for selective gun bans. But with regard to so-called assault weapons, which include a confusing melange of rifles, shotguns, and pistols, convenience and concealability for carry and stealth cannot be the common features of concern. Thus, the UBS approach can select different guns for banning on the basis of different features, and the specific features are material to the rationale for the ban in question. In fact, it is the specific features that the variety of assault weapons all supposedly have in common that make sense of that very variety. The UBS argument for the efficacy and consequent justifiability of assault weapons bans rests on the following empirical hypotheses and principle of justifiability:

Criminals' Weapons of Choice: Assault weapons are very attractive to violent criminals, making them the criminals' "weapons of choice," which increases the frequency with which they are used in violent crime.

Greater Destructive Potential: Assault weapons are designed to kill or maim many people quickly, even while being fired unaimed from the hip, as in military assaults. They possess certain features that render them capable of perpetrating massive and indiscriminate violence, of shooting more victims, including innocent bystanders, in shorter periods of time than other firearms, because they can fire more rounds more rapidly before being reloaded.

Greater Overall Violence: Given the above factors, criminal use of assault weapons results in higher rates and greater severity of injury overall than would result if no criminals used them.

Reduced Criminal Access: Banning assault weapons will eliminate criminal access or at least reduce criminal access to a negligible level.

Overall Violence Reduction: Banning assault weapons will reduce criminal violence overall, if not its frequency, then the rate and severity of injury resulting from criminal violence.

No Legitimate Sporting Purpose: Assault weapons have no "legitimate sporting purpose," so banning them harms no legitimate recreational or avocational interests.

No Defensive Value: Assault weapons are designed or useful only for military or criminal assault, in neither of which law-abiding citizens have any legitimate interest; at least, assault weapons are unnecessary for self-defense; so, in any case, banning them does no harm to anyone's interest in self-protection.

Since the use or possession of any firearm by criminals or for criminal purpose is already prohibited, extant criminal laws and penalties covering such use and possession have presumably exercised whatever deterrent effect of which they are capable. The UBS proposes to supplement general criminal law with an assault weapon ban in hopes of reducing criminal violence. This is a laudable ambition, but there are problems with each facet of the UBS argument, as follows:

i. Criminals' Weapons of Choice Although it is menacing-looking long guns (such as the AK-47 with its 30-round magazine or the "Streetsweeper" shotgun with its rotund cylinder) that, for rhetorical purposes, are made emblematic of assault weapons, as in ads for assault weapon bans, in fact "normal-looking" semiautomatic pistols are more popular as criminals' weapons of choice. It stands to reason that long guns would not be most criminals' choice because they are less wieldy and less concealable than handguns, the very reason handgun ban advocates give for handguns being criminals' weapons of choice. So-called "assault rifles" figure in perhaps 1% of gun crimes overall (their use varies from 0 to 3% by jurisdiction). For example, in New York City from 1987 through 1992, the highest annual rates of homicide committed with rifles and shotguns were 0.7% and 2%, respectively, according to New York's Division of Criminal Justice Services.

Estimates of assault weapon use in violent crime are inflated by using arbitrary definitions of the term "assault weapon." An example is the Pennsylvania State Police count of the use of such weapons in violent crime in 1994. They used crime data but included in the category of assault weapons not only "military-style rifles and shotguns" (1.33% of the guns used in violent crime) and "high-capacity pistols" (defined as semiautomatic pistols with magazine capacities in excess of 20 cartridges, 1.33%), but also "low-capacity pistols" (9.33%). The federal assault weapon ban defines "high capacity" as over 10 rounds, so the Pennsylvania State Police undercounted, by this standard, while including a category, "low-capacity pistols" (small, concealable semiautomatic pistols), that had not before been regarded as assault weapons.

ii. Greater Destructive Potential Though this hypothesis holds that the use of assault weapons results in more death and injury than the use of other firearms, the "power" and caliber of assault weapon cartridges are actually not greater on average than those of other weapons: cartridges for revolvers and low-capacity semi-automatic pistols cover a comparable range of "power" and caliber, from .22 to .45 caliber, regardless of whether they are categorized as assault weapons; cartridges for what are nominated as "assault rifles" are semiautomatic versions of military rifles, such as the AK-47 in 7.62 × 33 mm or the M16 in .223 (5.56 × 45 mm) and, thus are, on average, less powerful than the wide array of hunting rifle rounds in similar calibers; 12- or 20-gauge shotgun cartridges are as devastating whether fired from a 5-round "sporting" shotgun or an 8-round (or the rare 12-round) combat shotgun. The greater destructive power attributed to assault weapons is rather a function of what is called, ambiguously, their "firepower," which takes into account such factors as ammunition capacity, rate of fire, volume of continuous fire per load, reloading time, and volume of sustained fire per reload.

The hypothesis that assault weapons are potentially more destructive than nonassault weapons will be true in any specific case insofar as the assault weapon in question is capable of higher volumes of fire. However, this factor (and, hence, the validity of the greater destructive potential hypothesis) is arguably inconsequential to the aggregate of death and injury resulting from criminal violence, as will be seen in the discussion of the Greater Overall Violence hypothesis.

iii. Greater Overall Violence

This hypothesis postulates that, given the greater destructive potential of assault weapons, the rate and severity of injury (including death) resulting from their criminal use is greater than would result if no criminals used such weapons. However, criminals are, in the main, notoriously inaccurate with whatever firearms they use, even at close range, at least when they are facing armed defenders. This fact is substantiated by New York Police Department (NYPD) reports of all shooting incidents involving police officers, which shows criminals' hit probability to be on average less than 10%.

Moreover, the same reports show that the number of shots fired by criminals in battles with the police to be fewer than five on average, a number that is attainable by shooting an ordinary revolver. While a high-capacity assault weapon affords the shooter more potentially stray rounds, extrapolation from actual shooting incidents both with police and civilian defenders (where the preprator is being shot at) does not support the hypothesis that criminals would fire more errant shots when shooting at unarmed victims (where they have the time and incentive to place their shots more carefully).

Criminological facts, as gleaned from the NYPD reports and similar incident samples for civilians, indicate that gunfights rarely involve more than a few shots on either side, well within the capability of revolvers or low-capacity long guns. In the rare instance of an extended firefight, armed defenders or police can indeed suffer a disadvantage in "firepower," such as being subjected to the high volume of suppressive fire of which assault weapons are capable. But the relevant question is whether these rare incidents result in injury or fatality as compared to other such extended firefights in which assault weapons are not used.

iv. Overall Violence Reduction

At best, then, assault weapons might account for some marginal increment in the overall rate and severity of injury (including death). The marginality of the risk or potential increment is a function of the extreme rarity of the situations in which assault weapons could actually cause more human carnage than nonassault weapons. The other side of the greater overall violence postulated to result from the use of assault weapons by criminals is the overall violence reduction hypothesized as a benefit of assault weapon bans. But if the former increment is marginal, so is the latter.

v. Reduced Criminal Access

This hypothesis, that banning guns will translate to getting them "off the street" or out of "the wrong hands," is so firmly and widely believed as to be taken as common knowledge. The "uncommon knowledge" view holds that reduction of access to criminals who seek assault weapons is impossible to achieve, because for criminal demand there will always be a supply, even of contraband. In fact, the most seriously violence prone among the criminally disposed are precisely the ones who would be attracted to instruments supposedly capable of wanton and indiscriminate destruction. Such criminals as are willing to commit capital offenses are the least likely to fear the relatively minor penalties imposed by assault weapon bans.

If there is a way to reduce criminal use of assault weapons, it is not by a supply-side prohibition that targets criminal access while also burdening the law-abiding population, many of whom would comply but many others of whom, unjustly disenfranchised by their government in their view, would prepare, as some have already prepared, to resist. The question to assault weapon ban advocates is whether marginal and likely inconsequential criminal compliance is worth the cost of significant, and possibly violent, civil disobedience; whether deterring some people with prior criminal identities is worth generating a large new class of criminals from the stock of disaffected citizens. This question shifts our focus from the presumed but dubious efficacy or social benefits of an assault weapon ban to its social costs and objections against it.

vi. No Sporting Purpose Firearms that are generally recognized as particularly suitable for sporting purposes are presumptively excluded on that basis from proposed gun bans. By contrast, firearms that are particularly suitable for combat (such as assault weapons), but which are assumed to serve no legitimate sporting purpose, are prime targets of proposed gun bans. The objections brought against this hypothesis are three:

1. The "sporting purpose" hypothesis presupposes that government has the authority or competence to judge what counts as "legitimate" leisure, sport, or avocation and the right to curtail socially harmless and even socially useful leisure activities that some majority deems illegitimate.
2. The discriminatory notion of "sporting purpose" is also problematic because it presupposes without argument that "sporting purpose" should carry special privileged weight in the balancing of harms and benefits. On the contrary, the weightiest interest in the balance scales of benefits is not the recreational value of firearms, but rather their protective value to individuals, along with their associated social value and political value.
3. Finally, there is a sport and avocation with ample claim to legitimacy through recreational competition and training with firearms particularly suitable for combat, such as those stigmatized as "assault weapons." The practitioners of combat weaponcraft as a sport or avocation hold that law-abiding civilians have a legitimate interest in combat for their own self-defense. This legitimate interest in combat firearms training for defensive purposes naturally gives rise to both legitimate and socially useful "sporting purposes" for which combat weapons (or assault weapons) are particularly suitable in the sport and avocation known as combat weaponcraft.

vii. No Defensive Value This hypothesis denies that assault weapon gun bans harm the interests of people for whom assault weapons have protective value. This denial is based on one or both of two different arguments.

One argument is that assault weapons are designed solely for military assault (in which civilians as such have no legitimate interest) and are otherwise useful only for criminal assault (in which people obviously have no legitimate interest). That so-called "assault weapons" are inherently "bad" because they are designed only for killing or, worse, only for killing many people quickly, is on the same order of moral obtuseness as the view that assault weapons are "bad" because they are "particularly suitable" for combat rather than for hunting or target shooting. Combat is inherently defensive as well as offensive; its moral or legal justifiability, in either case, must be assessed on the merits of the combat itself and has nothing to do with the instrument used. By the same commonsense reckoning, the martial arts are neither regarded nor outlawed as "assault arts." The good or evil done with a weapon is not a function of the instrument but rather of the intent and consequences of its use. Law-abiding citizens, as well as the police, have use for, and therefore a legitimate interest in, assault weapons for threat management and defensive combat. The fact that assault weapons are not useful solely for indiscriminate murder and mayhem is evident in the interest the police have in these as well as other firearms and the fact that no ban proposes to prohibit their use by the police.

The second argument does not try to obscure the distinction between criminal assault and defense with disingenuous semantic games and does not deny that assault weapons can be used defensively. Rather, it denies that assault weapon bans do any harm to anyone's interest in firearms for protection by alleging that assault weapons are not necessary for defense, that other firearms can serve the defense interest just as well. There is often the added imputation that people who think they "need" an assault weapon lack both good sense and good character. However, recent cases in which semiautomatic shotguns and high-capacity semiautomatic rifles have been dramatically advantageous in deterring packs of rampaging offenders include the Los Angeles riots after the first Rodney King case verdict, the St. Petersburg riots in the fall of 1996, and civil disorders following natural disasters such as Hurricane Andrew.

While extended firefights with multiple assailants are rare, they do indeed occur and represent a nonnegligible risk in the world of random violence. The fact that criminals resort to assault weapons only enhances the argument that assault weapons are reasonably "necessary" defensive options for lawful defense by civilians as well as the police. To ask "What does a decent citizen need with an assault weapon? Why won't more 'refined' firearms do?" is like asking why people "need," or choose to carry, flood insurance in areas where floods rarely occur. The simple answer is: just in case.

B. Right-to-Carry Laws

Basic issues regarding the carrying of firearms in public by law-abiding civilians are: (1) Should this be allowed at all? (2) If so, should it be licensed? (3) If so, by what sort of licensing system?

1. "Shall Issue" versus Discretionary Licensing

Discrimination arises under discretionary licensing systems for concealed carry for two related reasons: that discretion in vetting applications for a license is allowed; and that the typical standards of "special need" or "good reason" exacerbate the inconsistency endemic to discretionary licensing.

Given the judgmental latitude allowed by the subjective nature of such criteria, a licensing official may, at one extreme, effectively institute a ban on concealed carry or, at the other extreme, effectively waive the requirement to show need by approving otherwise qualified applicants who simply cite the general reason of self-defense. In states imposing such subjective criteria, the policies of local officials are notoriously variable between both extremes. Unfairness arises if equally qualified, or equally disqualified, applicants are differentially issued or denied a license on the morally irrelevant basis of where they happen to reside. This is not merely a theoretical possibility but a prevalent reality in states with discretionary licensing (such as New York, Massachusetts, and California). It poses not only problems of fairness, but also criminological problems: (1) where politics or favoritism allows, otherwise unqualified applicants may obtain licenses and (2) where very restrictive discretionary practices are known to be the rule, violent crime may increase as a function of criminals' expectations that victims will be unarmed and there will be a consequent displacement of crime from jurisdictions where more citizens are apt to be armed.

Endemic unfairness notwithstanding, if concealed carry is to be permitted, its opponents may prefer a discretionary system precisely because it is apt to be more restrictive overall in practice. However, the criminological factors, the effects of legal concealed carry on crime and violence in the balance of social harms and benefits have to be reckoned.

2. The Effects of Permissive Carry Laws

Negative reaction against allowing concealed carry where it has been proposed is easy to conjure, along with the dramatic visions of mayhem that sustain it: blood in the streets, shootouts over minor insults and fender benders. More sober speculation holds, not that an armed society would fail to be a polite society, but that any defensive or deterrent utility of allowing concealed carry would be outweighed by criminals becoming preemptively more violent. Contrary to the hypothesis that criminals' uncertainty about whether prospective victims were armed would result in fewer victimizations, opponents of concealed carry hypothesize that criminals would go armed more often themselves and shoot first, to obviate the risk of injury from encountering an armed victim. However, this "preemptive strike" hypothesis does not stand up to the years of victimization survey data analyzed by Kleck: although, by definition, in gun rapes and robberies, criminal assailants pull guns first, they do not tend to shoot first and then rape and rob later. The idea that it would make sense for criminals disposed to commit rape, robbery, or assault to raise the ante to murder or attempted murder as a preemptive strike may seem plausible to some, but it is a phenomenon that has not appeared in the many states where concealed carry has already been permitted for years, nor was there a sudden rise in gun assaults, robbery, or rape in the highly scrutinized states where concealed carry was recently legalized. So, there is no reason to expect that criminals will suddenly become so imprudent in states that pass new concealed carry laws.

Unlike the deliberate violence escalation described above, speculation that the number of gun accidents are likely to increase along with concealed carry stands to reason on reflection. It is reasonable to suppose that the chances for a gun accident will increase as the occasions for people to handle loaded guns increase, which they do when more people start carrying concealed firearms that have to be holstered and unholstered daily. But, instead of speculating about defender and offender misadventure, we need to look at the available evidence.

While, of course, not all law violators are caught, if licensed concealed gun carriers are really gun-flashing or trigger-happy misadventurers, we would expect to find some significant record of revoked licenses, in particular licenses revoked for violent gun crimes. So, the phenomenon is easy to check, especially when new state carry laws mandate close scrutiny of the behavior of license holders. Texas, whose "shall issue" law is among the newest, and Florida, whose law initiated what became a wave of such measures, are two cases in point.

The Texas "shall issue" concealed carry law took effect on January 1, 1996. In the following year 1202 applicants were denied, 111,408 licenses were issued, and there were 57 incidents in which licensees committed offenses on the order of carrying a gun while intoxicated or failing to keep the weapon concealed. The overall offense rate by licensees at that point was 0.05% and the violent offense rate was 0.0009%.

Florida passed a "shall issue" concealed carry law in 1987. The Florida Department of State compiles data on carry licenses denied and revoked and the reasons therefore. According to Secretary of State Sandra Mortham, in a January 11, 1996, letter responding to published criticism of the Florida law, her Department had so far denied 723 applications and had issued 207,978 licenses, of which 324 were revoked for some manner of offense, of which 54 involved a firearm and 5 were violent crimes (none of which resulted in fatalities): thus 0.16% were revoked for some offense, 0.026% for an offense involving a gun and 0.0024% for a violent crime.

One hypothesis to explain the extremely low incidence of (apprehended) misadventure by licensed gun carriers is the training that is required to obtain a carry permit. For example, the Texas law requires a training course that includes not only basic marksmanship, firearm safety, and the law on the use of defensive deadly force, but also techniques of conflict resolution. But while training requirements are typical of the new wave of carry laws, they are by no means universal among the older laws. For example, concealed carry has been permitted without training in Pennsylvania for decades and the record of licensed gun carriers is basically as clean as elsewhere. The violent crime rate in Pennsylvania outside the city of Philadelphia is as low as Europe's. New Hampshire, the "Live Free or Die!" state, likewise has no training requirement and enjoys one of the lowest crime rates in the country. Vermont, which enjoys the lowest of violent crime rates, has neither a training requirement nor even a license requirement: concealed carry with lawful intent is a right of every adult citizen without a criminal record.

3. The Overall Impact of Concealed Carry Laws

The following three studies of the effects of concealed carry laws differ in illustrative ways: one is an intrastate study comparing violent crime across counties whose policies varied widely in permissiveness and restrictiveness under a discretionary licensing system; the second is a before-and-after study of the homicide levels associated with the introduction of "share issue" laws in a collection of five urban areas; and the third is a national study of crime rates across all U.S. countries with all manner of carry laws.

a. The California Study

Cramer and Kopel did a study accounting for demographic factors, comparing violent crime rates by county in California, which has a discretionary carry law resulting in extreme variation in policy from prohibitory to very permissive. They claimed to find that counties with high numbers of licensed concealed gun carriers and permissive policies had lower violent crime rates than counties with restrictive policies, which in turn had lower rates than counties with prohibitive policies.

b. The Violence Research Group Study

McDowall, Loftin, and Wiersema of the Violence Research Group at the University of Maryland did a study that compared gun homicide versus other homicides in five select urban areas in three states before and after new "shall issue" laws went into effect: Tampa, Jacksonville, and Miami, Florida; Jackson, Mississippi; and Portland, Oregon. The study found that after the new laws the number of people killed by guns in four of the cities increased (74% in Jacksonville, 43% in Jackson, 22% in Tampa, 3% in Miami) while the average number of homicides by other means stayed the same. The suggestion is that the relaxation of restrictions in the carry laws is the cause of the homicide increases. (In Portland the homicide rate fell about 12% after the new law, which the researchers suggest could be explained by the fact that Oregon instituted background checks for firearm purchases coincident with the new carry law).

Regarding the relevant homicides committed outside the home, where one would properly look for effects of concealed carry, the authors suggest that while licensed gun carriers may not be committing homicide, the new laws might increase incentive for unlawful carrying by the criminally inclined (which is tantamount to the "preemptive strike" hypothesis discussed above). The study does not distinguish criminal from justifiable homicides, leaving open the alternative to the preemptive strike hypothesis that justifiable homicides might account for the overall increase in homicides, especially in the violent environs studied where licensed gun carriers are apt to be assaulted.

The study's analysis also does not control for confounding factors such as demographic shifts or trends in drug trafficking. Worse, the study results are attributable to the artifact of selecting different stating points for establishing the before-reform homicide baselines, thereby ignoring higher-homicide years that would have shown a post-law decline. Finally, the researchers do not provide a rationale for their particular selection of so few urban areas as opposed to looking at the data for the whole states themselves. Florida's statewide homicide rate fell 21% from 1987 through 1992, after enactment of "shall issue," and has held consistently below the national rate after having been 36% higher before "shall issue." The authors do not explain why their "preemptive strike" hypothesis does not apply to the state as a whole or how the homicide rate in the rest of the state could decrease so far as to greatly offset the increases in Tampa, Jacksonville, and Miami.

Advocates of concealed carry are certainly not willing to grant, as an ethical matter, that an increase in criminal homicide would undermine the defensive efficacy of the practice; quite the contrary, the defensive rationale for concealed carrying and for the right to do so would only increase. To defeat the heavy interest so many have in the arguable right to effective means of self-defense, even on purely utilitarian grounds that grant no presumptive weight to this right, the evidence showing concealed carry laws to be the culprit in any observed increase in criminal violence must be very strong. The Violence Research Group study has been widely touted as proof in the media and by carry critics who see it as the thumb in the dike against the rising tide of "shall issue" laws. But it is not a compelling case for the proposition that laws permitting law-abiding citizens to carry guns for protection are the probable cause of increased criminal homicide.

c. The Lott and Mustard Study

Lott and Mustard (1997) set out to address what they take to be "the crucial question underlying all gun-control laws: What is their net effect? Are more lives lost or saved? Do they deter crime or encourage it?" These questions of efficacy are not the only or last issues for the justifiability of gun controls; there are strong rights-based objections to restrictive gun control on the one hand and, on the other hand, fundamental nonutilitarian moral objections to firearms and their use and, supervening both, the metaissue of how to weigh such residual moral values in the balancing of social goods and ills. But a rigorous address to the efficacy of firearms and their regulation is certainly the foremost if not the final word on justifiability.

Like the Kleck and Gertz study of defensive gun use, the Lott and Mustard study is meticulously designed to anticipate criticism. It analyzed the FBI's crime statistics for all 3054 counties in the United States from 1977 to 1992. Lott and Mustard's (most conservative) estimates and major observations follow:

- "Shall issue" laws reduced murders by 8.5%, rapes by 5%, aggravated assaults by 7%, and robbery by 3%.
- If states that did not permit concealed carry in 1992 had allowed it at that time, the citizenry would have been spared 1570 murders, 4177 rapes, 60,000 aggravated assaults and 12,000 robberies.
- Enjoyment of the deterrent effects quantified above are generally distributed, not limited to those who carry guns and use them defensively. This phenomenon is a major advantage of concealed carry: the uncertainty of who is carrying and the possibility that any potential victim, or potential defender nearby, may be armed renders everyone an unattractive target for many criminals. Unarmed people are thus in effect "free riders" on their armed fellow citizens.
- There is some displacement of criminal activity from violent crimes to property offenses like larceny (such as automobile theft). This is likely an acceptable trade-off in aggregate cost saved, let alone lives.
- In large cities, where typically both crime rates and gun control advocacy are highest, right-to-carry laws produced the largest drops in violent crimes. For areas with concentrated populations of over 200,000, the decrease in murder rate averaged 13%.
- Carry laws seem to benefit women more than men. Murder rates decline regardless of the gender of the gun carrier, but the impact is more pronounced when women are considered separately. An additional female licensed gun carrier reduces the murder rate for women three to four times more than an added male carrier reduces the rate for men. (Victims of violence are typically weaker than their assailants; thus armed women defending themselves enjoy a greater relative increase in their advantage than do armed men.)
- Contrary to the alleged beneficial impact of the Brady Law on crime rates (predicated by defenders simply on the number of applications for purchase denied, without acknowledging the high rate of false positives later corrected or the extremely low yield, 7, of felon-applicants brought to trial), the

law's introduction is associated with higher rates of assaults and rapes.

- While the number of fatal handgun accidents is only 200 a year, if states without "shall issue" laws adopted them, there would be at most nine additional accidental handgun deaths, an increase of 4.5%.

The nearly 50,000 observations in the data set allowed for more rigorous controls for more variables than in any previous gun control study, including regression controls for arrest and conviction rates, prison sentences, changes in handgun laws such as waiting periods and background checks, enhanced-sentencing policies for using a gun in a crime, income, poverty, unemployment, and demographic changes.

Lott has modestly commented that the rigor and results of the study should "give pause" to opponents of permissive "shall issue" concealed carry laws: "The opportunity to reduce the murder rate by simply relaxing a regulation ought to be difficult to ignore."

The initial reaction to the study by many of those opponents was illustrative of how passion can rule the gun control controversy. A public press conference was called by prominent political gun control advocates at which Lott's scholarly integrity was attacked; in particular, it was alleged that he was in the service of the firearms industry. This inference was based on the fact that Lott is the John M. Olin Fellow at the University of Chicago Law School, together with the presumption that the Olin Fellow would be dedicated to the interests of Olin/Winchester, the noted ammunition and firearms manufacturer and a subsidiary of the Olin Corporation.

In fact, the Olin chair is funded by the Olin Foundation, which was created by money from John Olin's personal fortune upon his death, not by the Olin Corporation, which neither chose Lott as a Fellow nor approved his topic. Researchers have since embarked upon the appropriate response to the challenge of the Lott and Mustard study, critical analysis, the first wave of which Lott has rebutted but the most promising of which is yet forthcoming from a new center for violence research at Carnegie Mellon University.

Also See the Following Articles

CONSEQUENTIALISM AND DEONTOLOGY • CRIME AND SOCIETY • HOMICIDE, CRIMINAL VERSUS JUSTIFIABLE • PATERNALISM • UTILITARIANISM

Bibliography

Cottrol, Robert J. (Ed.). (1994). Gun Control and the Constitution: Sources and Explorations of the Second Amendment. Garland Publishing, New York.

Covey, Preston K. (1995). Legitimacy, recreation, sport and leisure: 'Sporting purpose' in the gun-control controversy. Gerald S. Fain (Ed.), Leisure and Ethics, Vol. II. American Association for Leisure and Recreation, Reston VA.

Covey, Preston K., and Stell, Lance. (forthcoming 1998). Gun Control: For and Against. Rowman and Littlefield, Boston.

Kates, Don B., Jr., and Kleck, Gary (Eds.). (1997). The Great American Gun Debate. Pacific Institute for Public Policy Research, San Francisco.

Kleck, Gary. (1991). Point Blank: Guns and Violence in America. Aldine de Gruyter, New York.

Kopel, David B. (1992). The Samurai, the Mountie, and the Cowboy: Should America Adopt the Gun Controls of Other Democracies? Prometheus Books, Buffalo.

Walker, Samuel (1994). Sense and Nonsense about Crime and Drugs, Third Ed. Wadsworth Publishing Co., Belmont, CA.

Wright, James D., and Rossi, Peter H. (1986). Armed and Considered Dangerous: A Survey of Felons and Their Firearms. Aldine de Gruyter, New York.

HAZARDOUS AND TOXIC SUBSTANCES

Kristin Shrader-Frechette
University of South Florida

I. Introduction
II. NIMBY and Equity Issues
III. Consent Issues
IV. Liability Issues
V. Ethical Rules for Behavior under Uncertainty
VI. Conclusion

GLOSSARY

compensating wage differential The increases in individuals' wages that are paid to them in order to compensate them for higher workplace risks that they bear as a consequence of their particular jobs.

discount rate The annual percentage by which economists reduce the sum of money representing the value (the costs or benefits) associated with some event, act, or process that occurs in the future. It is the opposite of an interest rate, the annual percentage by which a sum of money increases.

economies of scale Financial savings that are possible, for example, to a company, because of the great size or volume of the operations.

externality Social costs (such as pollution) or benefits (such as clean air) that are not traded on a market and that are not part of benefit–cost calculations.

genetic damage Damage to the genes and chromosomes that is passed on through heredity to one's descendants.

liability The state of being legally or financially responsible for something or someone.

maximin A rule for decision making, often societal decision making, according to which one acts so as to avoid the worst outcome.

pesticide Chemical used to kill insects or weeds.

risk assessment A set of mathematical and scientific techniques for identifying, estimating, and evaluating the probability and the consequences associated with various public health and environmental threats, such as those from hazardous waste facilities.

statistical casualties Premature deaths calculated to occur on the basis of a particular exposure to a hazard or to a toxic chemical, even though the people killed by a particular threat sometimes are not easily identifiable because their deaths (for example, through cancer) often are not immediate and because the people usually are not under medical examination.

statutory Pertaining to a law, rule, or statute, usually of a government.

toxic tort A civil wrong for which a party injured by toxic chemicals is entitled legally to compensation.

tragedy of the commons The damage that occurs to everyone as a result of some individuals trying to benefit themselves personally by using common resources. For example, everyone is harmed by air pollution because each person attempts to save money by being a polluter.

HAZARDOUS AND TOXIC SUBSTANCES are products or by-products of manufacturing, scientific, medical, and agricultural processes, and they have at least one of four characteristics: ignitability, corrosivity, reactivity, or toxicity (T. P. Wagner, 1990. *Hazardous Waste Identification and Classification Manual*. Van Nostrand–Reinhold, New York). Hazardous and toxic substances become wastes only when they have outlived their economic life. They include solvents, electroplating substances, pesticides such as dioxin, and radioactive wastes. Toxic substances, a subset of hazardous substances, have the characteristic of toxicity: the ability to cause serious injury, illness, or death.

Many people first became aware of the threat of hazardous and toxic substances from Pullitzer Prize nominee Michael Brown's *Laying Waste: The Poisoning of America by Toxic Chemicals* (1979), a frightening account of the cancers, deformities, and deaths caused by hazardous waste in the Love Canal neighborhood in New York. Rachel Carson also helped to educate people to the dangers from hazardous and toxic substances when she wrote *Silent Spring*, her 1962 classic analysis of the dangers of pesticides. U.S. Congressman James Florio said in 1981 that management of hazardous wastes is the single most serious environmental problem (M. Greenberg and R. Anderson, 1984. *Hazardous Waste Sites: The Credibility Gap*. Rutgers, New Brunswick, NJ). In the United States alone, approximately 80% of hazardous and toxic wastes has been dumped into hundreds of landfills, ponds, and pits. It has polluted air, wells, surface water, and groundwater. It has destroyed species, habitats, and ecosystems. It also has caused fires, explosions, direct contact poisoning, cancer, genetic defects, and birth defects.

I. INTRODUCTION

Hazardous and toxic substances are at the center of conflicts between the chemical industry and the public. When the U.S. Environmental Protection Agency in 1995 released its landmark study of the dangers of dioxin, a by-product of manufacturing chlorine, the Chlorine Chemistry Council immediately tried to downplay the dangers. Dioxin causes immune system damage, infertility, cancer, and death. Dioxin is produced whenever industry generates, uses, or burns chlorine or chlorine-derived products. Although PVC (polyvinyl chlorine) plastic is the largest use of chlorine, the pulp and paper industry uses much chlorine in bleaching. As a consequence, incinerating paper, plastic, and other chlorine-containing materials creates dioxin, a dangerous product of many incinerators. In most nations of the world, including the United States,

there are few restrictions on the use of chlorine, and it is widely used in paper and pulp bleaching.

Although regulation of hazardous and toxic substances always lags behind the social, ethical, and political need for such regulation, there are a number of laws aimed at reducing the threat from hazardous and toxic substances. For example, to protect workers and the public from the dangers associated with hazardous substances, the United States has passed laws such as the Hazardous Materials Transportation Act, the Atomic Energy Act, the Clean Water Act, the Clean Air Act, the Resource Conservation and Recovery Act (RCRA), the Toxic Substances Control Act (TSCA), and the Comprehensive Environmental Response, Compensation, and Liability Act (CERCLA or Superfund). Laws such as these have many provisions, including those requiring behavior such as monitoring pollutants, reporting spills, preparation of manifests describing particular wastes, and special packaging for transporting specific types of hazardous materials. Smelter emissions, for instance, are regulated under the Clean Air Act, and mining-caused water pollution is regulated under the Clean Water Act (J. Young, 1992. *Mining the Earth*: Worldwatch Institute, Washington, DC). RCRA was passed to fill a statutory void left by the Clean Air Act and the Clean Water Act; they require removal of hazardous materials from air and water but leave the question of the ultimate deposition of hazardous waste unanswered. RCRA addresses the question of the handling of hazardous waste at current and future facilities, but it does not deal with closed or abandoned sites. CERCLA focuses on hazardous waste contamination when sites or spills have been abandoned; through penalties and taxes on hazardous substances, CERCLA provides for cleaning up abandoned sites.

Despite the various provisions of U.S. laws governing hazardous substances, use of toxins and management of hazardous wastes raise a number of ethical issues that have not been adequately addressed by existing laws and regulations. Most of these ethical questions are related either to the equity of risk distribution or to the assessment and regulation of societal risks associated with hazardous substances. The equity issues include siting facilities that produce or use hazardous materials; rights of future generations to protection against hazardous and toxic substances; worker rights to such protection; public and worker rights to free and informed consent to exposure to hazardous and toxic substances; rights to compensation for risk or damage caused by hazardous or toxic substances; and rights to due process in the event that one is harmed by toxic or hazardous substances through the fault of other people. Questions about risk assessment and regulation include appropriate ethical behavior under conditions of uncertainty about the hazards or toxins; where to place the burden of proof in alleged harms involving hazardous substances; and the right to know of workers and the public who may be exposed to hazardous and toxic substances.

II. NIMBY AND EQUITY ISSUES

In 1996 a scientific team directed by famous lead researcher Herbert Needleman showed that inner-city children with the highest concentrations of lead in their bones were those most likely to exhibit abusive, violent, and delinquent behavior. The lead poisoning—arising from auto exhausts, gasoline fumes, paint, chemicals, and pipes—lowered their intelligence and contributed to impulsive behavior, hyperactivity, and attention-deficit disorder, all of which help cause delinquency. Even after the researchers controlled for factors such as single-parent homes, parents' IQ, and child-rearing practices, they found that lead levels in the bones of young children are accurate predictors of later delinquency and crime as adults. The lead example illustrates clearly that those who can afford to avoid hazardous and toxic substances typically do so. Virtually no people want toxic substances or hazardous wastes used or stored near them. Hence they cry, "not in my backyard"—NIMBY. The NIMBY syndrome also arises because of the fact that any hazardous technology is unavoidably dependent upon fragile and short-lived human institutions and human capabilities. It was not faulty technology, after all, that caused Three Mile Island, Bhopal, Love Canal, or Chernobyl. It was human error. Likewise it could well be human error that is the insoluble problem with using toxics and managing hazardous wastes.

Because of the biological, chemical, or radiological dangers associated with hazardous and toxic substances, and because of the potential human errors associated with their use and disposal, most people try to avoid them. Those who cannot easily do so are usually poor or otherwise disadvantaged, like the inner-city victims of lead poisoning from auto exhausts and gasoline fumes.

Questions about the equity of risk distribution are central to the issue of managing hazardous substances and toxins, because poor, uneducated, or politically powerless people typically bear the gravest threats from such substances. Many people in developing nations—

such as thousands of people in Bhopal, India, for example—have already died as a consequence of exposure to hazardous substances. Such deaths occur because economic comparisons of alternative technologies and different sites for hazardous facilities typically ignore ethical considerations. Instead technological and siting decisions occur because of attempts to minimize market costs. Economists ignore the externalities (or social costs), such as the inequitable distribution of health hazards, associated with toxic chemicals. They also ignore the risk–benefit asymmetries associated with using toxic substances or managing hazardous wastes. Because geographical and intergenerational inequities are typically "external" to the benefit–cost evaluation scheme used as the basis for public policy, such externalities are almost always ignored (K. Shrader-Frechette, 1985. *Science Policy, Ethics, and Economic Methodology.* Kluwer, Boston).

Because rich and poor people are not equally able to avoid threats from hazardous and toxic substances, public and workplace exposure to such hazards raises a number of questions of equity. Many of these questions concern geographical equity, intergenerational equity, or occupational equity. Intergenerational equity problems deal with imposing the risks and costs of hazardous wastes and toxic substances on future generations. The geographical equity issues have to do with where and how to site waste dumps or facilities using toxic substances. The occupational equity problems focus on whether to maximize the safety of the public or that of persons who work with toxic substances or hazardous wastes, since both cannot be accomplished at once (see R. Kasperson, Ed., 1983. *Equity Issues in Radioactive Waste Management.* Oelgelschlager, Gunn, and Hain, Cambridge, MA; K. Shrader-Frechette, 1993. *Burying Uncertainty: Risk and the Case against Geological Disposal of Nuclear Waste.* Univ. of California, Berkeley).

The key ethical issue raised by concerns about intergenerational equity is whether society ought to mortgage the future by imposing its debts of buried hazardous wastes on subsequent generations. In virtually every nuclear nation of the world, current plans for future storage of high-level radioactive waste, for example, require the steel canisters to resist corrosion for as little as 300 years. Nevertheless, the U.S. Department of Energy and the U.S. National Academy of Sciences admit that the waste will remain dangerous for longer than 10,000 years. Government experts agree that, at best, they can merely limit the radioactivity that reaches the environment, and that there is no doubt that the repository will leak over the course of the next 10,000 years (Shrader-Frechette, 1993). If society saddles its descendants with the medical and financial debts of such waste, much of which is extremely long lived, such actions are questionable: this generation has received most of the benefits from the use of industrial and agricultural processes that create hazardous wastes, whereas future persons will bear most of the risks and costs. This risk/cost–benefit asymmetry suggests that, without good reasons or compensating benefits, future generations ought not be saddled with their ancestors' debts (Shrader-Frechette, 1993).

Moreover, any alleged economies associated with long-term storage of hazardous and toxic wastes are in large part questionable because of their dependence on economists' discounting future costs at some rate of x percent per year. For example, at a discount rate of 10%, effects on people's welfare 20 years from now count only for one-tenth of what effects on people's welfare count for now. Or, more graphically, with a discount rate of 5%, a billion deaths in 400 years— caused by leaking toxic wastes—counts the same as 1 death next year. A number of moral philosophers, such as Parfit, have argued that use of a discount rate is unethical, because the moral importance of future events, like the death of a person, does not decline at some x percent per year.

Another issue related to intergenerational equity is what sort of criteria might justify environmentally irreversible damage to the environment, like that caused by deep-well storage of high-level radwaste. Nuclear waste management schemes which are irreversible theoretically impose fewer management burdens on later generations, but they also preempt future choices about how to deal with the waste. On the other hand, schemes which are reversible allow for greater choices for future generations, but they also impose greater management burdens. If society cannot do both, is it ethically desirable to maximize future freedom or to minimize future burdens?

In the absence of knowledge that society can successfully store hazardous waste for centuries, the technical problems associated with it are forcing people to take a great gamble with the freedom and the security of future persons. This is a gamble that today's descendants will not breach the repositories through war, terrorism, or drilling for minerals; that groundwater will not leach out toxins; and that subsequent ice sheets and geological folding will not uncover the wastes.

In addition to temporal inequities associated with different generations, using and storing hazardous and toxic substances also raises questions of spatial or geographical inequity. One such issue is whether it is fair to impose a higher risk (of being harmed by leachate from a hazardous waste dump, for example) on a person just because she lives in a certain part of the community. Likewise, is it ethical for one geographical subset of persons to receive the benefits of products created by using toxic substances, while a much smaller set of persons bears the health risks associated with living near a hazardous waste dump or near an industry employing toxic materials? How does one site (or transport) hazards equitably?

The most serious problems of geographical equity in the distribution of the risks associated with hazardous wastes and toxic substances arise because of developed nations' shipping their toxic substances and hazardous wastes to developing countries. One-third of U.S. pesticide exports, for example, are products that are banned for use in the United States, and many of these exports are responsible for the 40,000 annual deaths caused by pesticides, mainly in developing nations (K. Shrader-Frechette, 1991. *Risk and Rationality*. Univ. of California, Berkeley). The UN estimates that as much as 20% of hazardous wastes is sent to other countries, particularly other nations where health and safety standards are virtually nonexistent. The Organization of African Unity has pleaded with member states to stop such traffic, but corruption and crime have prevented the waste transport from stopping (B. Moyers, 1990. *Global Dumping Ground*. Seven Locks, Washington, DC).

Exporting toxic substances and hazardous wastes may be the current version of infant formula. During the last three decades, U.S. and multinational corporations have profited by exporting infant formula to developing nations. They were able to do so only by coercive sales tactics and by misleading other nations about the relative merits and dangers of the exports. As a consequence, many children in developing nations have died because multinational corporations encouraged their mothers to buy infant formula (even when they had no clean water or sterilization equipment) and to abandon breast feeding.

Some of the greatest risks associated with toxic substances and hazardous wastes, whether in developed or in developing nations, are borne by workers. One of the main questions of occupational equity is whether it is just to impose higher health burdens on workers in exchange for wages. Is it fair to allow persons to trade their health and safety for money? This question is particularly troublesome in the United States, which has a double standard for occupational and public exposures to hazardous and toxic substances. In other nations, such as the Scandinavian countries, Germany, and the former USSR, standards for exposure to public and occupational risks from toxins is approximately the same. Because the United States follows the alleged "compensating wage differential" (CWD) of Adam Smith, U.S. regulators argue that, in exchange for facing higher occupational (than public) risks from toxic substances, workers receive higher wages that compensate them for their burden. Other countries do not accept the theory underlying the CWD and argue for equal health standards (Shrader-Frechette, 1991).

III. CONSENT ISSUES

One reason that the theory underlying the CWD is questionable is that it presupposes that workers exposed to hazards have given free, informed consent to the risks. Siting hazardous facilities and employing persons to work with toxins typically require the consent of those put at risk. Yet, from an ethical point of view, those most able to give free, informed consent—those who are well educated with many job opportunities—are usually unwilling to do so. Those least able to validly consent to a risky workplace or neighborhood—because of their lack of education or information and their financial constraints—are often willing to give alleged consent.

It is true that the 1986 U.S. Right-to-Know Act requires owners or operators of hazardous facilities to notify the Emergency Response Commission in their state that toxins are present at the facility. To some extent, this act contributes to information about hazards, but at least two factors suggest that the requirement is insufficient to provide full conditions for the free, informed consent of persons likely to be harmed by some hazardous substance. One problem is that owners/operators (rather than some more neutral source) provide the information about the hazard. Often those responsible for toxic substances and hazardous wastes do not inform workers and the public of the risks that they face, even after company physicians have documented serious health problems. Moreover, if employers in the chemical industry, for example, expend funds to assess worker health, typically they engage in genetic screening so as to exclude susceptible persons from the workplace, rather than in monitoring their health on the job so as to protect them (Draper, 1991). Another difficulty with ensuring free, informed consent, even under existing right-to-know laws, is that the existence, location, and operational procedures of the dangerous facility itself are likely things to which citizens and workers did not give free, informed consent in the first place, although they may be informed after the fact.

Sociological data reveal that, as education and income rise, persons are less willing to take risky jobs, and those who do so are primarily those who are poorly educated or financially strapped. The data also show that the alleged compensating wage differential does not operate for poor, unskilled, minority, or nonunionized workers. Yet these are precisely the persons most likely to work at risky jobs like storing nuclear waste. This means that the very set of persons *least* able to give free, informed consent to workplace risks from hazardous and toxic substances are precisely those who most *often* work in risky jobs (Shrader-Frechette, 1993).

Likewise, at the international level, the persons and nations least able to give free, informed consent to the location of facilities using toxins are typically those who bear the risks associated with such sites. Hazardous wastes shipped abroad, for example, are usually sent to countries that will take them at the cheapest rate, and these tend to be developing nations that are often ill informed about the risks involved. Recently the United Nations passed a resolution requiring any country receiving hazardous waste to give consent before it is sent. Because socioeconomic conditions and corruption often militate against the exercise of genuine free, informed consent, however, just as they do in the workplace, it is questionable whether the UN resolution will have much effect (Shrader-Frechette, 1991).

If it is difficult to ensure that the risks posed by toxic substances and hazardous wastes are ones to which persons actually give free, informed consent, then medical experimentation may have something to teach society about the ethical constraints on dealing with hazardous waste and toxic substances. Scholars know that the promise of early release for a prisoner who consents to risky medical experimentation provides a highly coercive context which could jeopardize his legitimate consent. So also do high wages for a desperate worker who consents to take a risky job provide a highly coercive context which could jeopardize his legitimate consent. Likewise, providing financial benefits for an economically depressed community provides a coercive context in which the requirements for free, informed consent are unlikely to be met. This means that society must either admit that its classical ethical theory of free, informed consent is wrong or question whether current laws and regulations provide an ethical framework in which those closely affected by hazardous substances genuinely give informed consent to the risk.

One consent-related area of needed improvement in laws regulating hazardous substances, for example, would be to include mining among industries required to report their toxic emissions to state and federal regulators. Utah's Bingham Canyon Copper Mine, owned by Kennecott Copper, ranks fourth in the United States in total toxic releases, yet it and other mining companies are not yet required to report their releases (Young, 1992).

Another aspect of consent problems with hazardous substances is political. Liberty and grassroots self-determination require local control of whether a hazardous facility is sited in a particular area. Yet, equality of consideration for people in all locales, and minimizing overall risk, requires federal control. Should the local community be able to veto a given site, even though that site may be the best in the country and may provide for the most equal protection of all people? Or does one say that the national government can impose a hazardous facility on a local community even though the imposition is at odds with free and self-determined choice?

On the one hand, national supremacy is likely to protect the environment, to avoid the tragedy of the commons, to gain national economies of scale, and to avoid regional disparities in representing all sides of a controversy. National supremacy also is likely to provide for compensation of the victims of one region for spillovers from another locale and to facilitate the politics of sacrifice by imposing equal burdens on all. On the other hand, local autonomy is likely to promote diversity, to offer a more flexible vehicle for experimenting with waste regulations, and to enhance citizens' autonomy and liberty. It also is likely to encourage community coherence through participation in decision making; to avoid inequitable federal policies; and to avoid violations of rights.

IV. LIABILITY ISSUES

One of the greatest ethical problems with regulating hazardous and toxic substances is that current laws do not typically provide for full exercise of due process rights by those who may have been harmed by toxins or by hazardous wastes. One reason is that many of the companies that handle toxic substances do not have either full insurance for their pollution risk or adequate funds themselves to cover damages. In the United States, RCRA and CERCLA, however, require such companies both to show that they are capable of paying at least some of the damages resulting from their activities and to clean up their sites.

Part of the problem is that enforcement of liability and coverage provisions of laws such as RCRA and CERCLA is difficult, and many components of the hazardous waste industries operate outside the law. Another difficulty is that most insurers have withdrawn from the pollution market, claiming that providing such insurance would leave them exposed to enormous payments for claims that would bankrupt them.

But if insurers fear the large liability claims in cases involving hazardous substances, so do members of the public. In Yucca Mountain, Nevada, for example, chosen as the likely site for the world's first, permanent, high-level nuclear waste disposal facility, local residents and the state have asked for unlimited strict liability for any nuclear waste accident or incident. The U.S. Department of Energy position, solidified by the Price–Anderson Act, is on the side of limited liability. The U.S. nuclear program, including radioactive waste management, has a liability limit that is less than 3% of the government-calculated costs of the Chernobyl accident, and Chernobyl was not a worst-case accident (see Shrader-Frechette, 1993).

The ethical judgment that government ought to limit liability for hazardous waste and toxic substances incidents is questionable because liability is a well-known incentive for appropriate, safe behavior. Also, if hazardous and radioactive waste sites are as safe as the government proclaims, then there is nothing to lose from full and strict liability. Third, it is questionable whether government officials should have the right to limit due-process rights under law. Such a limitation may mean that, in the case of an accident at a hazardous waste facility, the main financial burdens will be borne by accident victims rather than by the perpetrators of the hazard. But such a risk–benefit asymmetry appears to be inequitable. Moreover, since much less is known about the dangers from hazardous wastes and toxic substances than about more ordinary risks, it seems reasonable to guarantee full liability. Finally, the safety record of hazardous facilities, in the past, has not been good. Every state and every nation in the world has extensive, long-term pollution from toxins. Even in the United States, the government has been one of the worst offenders. A recent Congressional report argued that cleaning up the hazardous and radioactive wastes at government weapons' facilities is now an impossible task because it would cost more than $300 billion (Shrader-Frechette, 1993). Such revelations suggest that full compensation for potential victims of hazardous substances is ethically desirable (Shrader-Frechette, 1993).

V. ETHICAL RULES FOR BEHAVIOR UNDER UNCERTAINTY

Ethical difficulties such as inadequate compensation for victims of hazardous and toxic substances, and inequitable distribution of the risks associated with hazardous wastes—as well as the uncertainties and potential harm associated with such substances—provide a powerful argument for reducing or eliminating exposure to them. Society needs to move "beyond dumping" and, to some degree, provide market incentives for reducing the volume of toxic substances and hazardous wastes (B. Piasecki, Ed., 1984. *Beyond Dumping: New Strategies for Controlling Toxic Contamination.* Quorum, London.

In 1996, the U.S. National Academy of Sciences began a long-term study of xenoestrogens—hazardous chemicals that look nothing like the female sex hormone estrogen but have similar effects; these chemicals include PCBs, DDT, and other pesticides and industrial chemicals. The organochlorine chemicals that are xenoestrogens essentially behave like female hormones. Even at the lowest levels, parts per trillion, they have caused massive feminization and eventual extinction of amphibian and bird populations and massive decreases in sperm counts. Because of the groundbreaking work of scientists like Dr. Theodora Colborn, people now know that male sperm counts have been steadily decreasing, across all species, in developed nations at least since 1940. Human sperm counts have decreased by 42% since 1940, and female breast cancer has been increasing by at least 1% per year since 1950. The culprit in both cases appears to be extremely low levels of organochlorine chemicals.

Because it is difficult to perform adequate tests for health effects of very low-level chemical exposures—thousands of persons must be tested in order to detect a low-level effect—and because so many toxic substances produce health effects synergistically, there are many uncertainties about actual exposure to hazardous substances and about the effects of such exposures (N. Ashford and C. Miller, 1991. *Chemical Exposures: Low Levels and High Stakes.* Van Nostrand–Reinhold, New York). An additional equity and uncertainty problem is that children are much more susceptible to the effects of hazardous and toxic substances. In 1993, a landmark U.S. National Academy of Sciences Committee (Na-

tional Research Council, 1993. *Pesticides in the Diets of Infants and Children.* NRC, Washington, DC) argued that existing standards for pesticides in the diets of infants and children were not adequate to protect their health. Differences in phenotypical characteristics among individuals often vary by a factor of 200, also causing extreme differences in responses to toxins and contributing to the uncertainty problem. All of these factors cause great uncertainties regarding exposure to, and effects of, hazardous substances.

Moreover, the industries that produce toxic substances and hazardous wastes—and that profit from them—perform almost all of the required tests to determine toxicity and health effects. Pesticide registration decisions in the West, for example, are tied to a risk–benefit standard according to which scientific and economic evidence are considered together. With industry doing most or all of the testing, and with environmental and health groups being forced to argue that the dangers outweigh the economic benefits of a particular pesticide, there is much uncertainty about the real hazards actually faced by workers and consumers.

Human error and crime are also large contributors to uncertainty about the possibility and the effects of exposure to toxins. This uncertainty raises additional questions about appropriate ethical behavior under conditions of uncertainty. Whenever one is dealing with a potentially catastrophic risk, uncertainty about the likelihood of harm arises in part because of human factors. According to risk assessors, for example, 60 to 80% of industrial accidents are due to human error or corruption (Shrader-Frechette, 1993). At the nation's largest incinerator for hazardous wastes, run by Chemical Waste Management, Inc. (CMW), in Chicago, a 1990 grand jury found evidence of criminal conduct, including deliberate mislabeling of many barrels of hazardous waste and deliberate disconnection of pollution-monitoring devices. Moreover, in the United States, corruption in the waste disposal industry has been rampant since the 1940s, when the Mafia won control of the carting business through Local 813 of the International Brotherhood of Teamsters. Today, three Mafia families still dominate hazardous waste disposal and illegal dumping: the Gambino, the Lucchese, and Genovese/Tiere crime groups (see A. Szasz, 1986. *Criminology* **24**, 1–27). Given the potential for human error and corruption, there is great uncertainty regarding whether hazardous wastes and toxic substances will be handled safely, with little threat to workers or to the public.

Because of these unknowns, several moral philosophers have argued that, in potentially catastrophic situations involving hazardous wastes and toxic substances, scientific and probabilistic uncertainty requires ethically conservative behavior (C. Cranor, 1993. *Regulating Toxic Substances*. Oxford Univ. Press, New York; Shrader-Frechette, 1991; Ashford and Miller, 1991). It often requires one to choose a maximin decision rule—to avoid situations with the greatest potential for harm—as John Rawls argued. Such conservatism and maximin decision making in the face of the threat of toxins might require tougher health and safety standards. It might also require greater assurances of free, informed consent and full compensation for victims of toxics. Likewise, it might be important, from an ethical point of view, to ensure that the burden of proof be placed on the users of hazardous substances, rather than on their potential victims. This, in turn, means that society may need many reforms in its law governing so-called "toxic torts" (Cranor, 1993). More generally, it is arguable that in situations of uncertainty, ethical conservatism dictates that one probably ought to minimize type II statistical errors (minimize false negatives, false assertions of no harm from some substance) rather than type I errors (minimize false positives, false assertions of harm from some substance). Most risk assessors, however, in evaluating potentially catastrophic risks from hazardous substances, argue that one ought to minimize type I errors, even though this policy does not contribute to the greatest protection of public health and safety (Shrader-Frechette, 1991).

VI. CONCLUSION

If ethics requires reforms so as to protect future generations, workers, and disenfranchised members of the public, then indeed most law, policy, and regulation regarding hazardous wastes and toxic substances may need revision. Formerly "safe," low-level doses of chemicals such as xenoestrogens or organochlorines are feminizing and then killing off many species, and similar effects on humans have been clear for 50 years. Society requires greater ethical attention to the issues of equity, consent, compensation, and uncertainty that surround its use and disposal of hazardous and toxic substances.

Also See the Following Articles

BIODIVERSITY • ENVIRONMENTAL IMPACT ASSESSMENT • NUCLEAR POWER

Bibliography

Carson, R. (1962). "Silent Spring." Houghton Mifflin, Boston.

Colborn, T., and Clement, C. (Eds.) (1992). "Chemically Induced Alterations in Sexual and Functional Development." Princeton Scientific, Princeton, NJ.

La Dou, J. (1992). First world exports to the third world. *Western J. Med.* 156, 553–554.

National Research Council (NRC) (1993). "Pesticides in the Diets of Infants and Children." NRC, Washington, DC.

Nordquist, J. (1988). "Toxic Waste," Bibliography. Reference and Research Services, Santa Cruz, CA.

Piasecki, B., and Davis, G. (1987). "America's Future in Toxic Waste Management: Lessons from Europe." Quorum, New York.

Postel, S. (1987). "Defusing the Toxics Threat." Worldwatch Institute, Washington, DC.

Samuels, S. (1986). "The Environment of the Workplace and Human Values." Liss, New York.

Wynne, B. (Ed.) (1987). "Risk Management and Hazardous Waste." Springer-Verlag, New York.

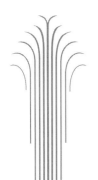

HEALTH AND DISEASE, CONCEPTS OF

Robert Wachbroit
University of Maryland

I. Concepts of Health and Their Impact
II. Articulating a Family of Concepts: Constraints and Proposals
III. The Issue of Normativism

GLOSSARY

biological function The characterization of a biological phenomenon in terms of its achieving a particular goal or effect, rather than in terms of its etiology or cause.
medicalization The process by which a phenomenon or issue not usually seen as a medical problem comes to be regarded as susceptible to medical analysis and response.
physiology The study of how biological systems and processes normally function.

THE CONCEPT OF HEALTH is crucial to medicine because it informs medicine's goals, scope, and criteria of success. To state it roughly and simply, ignoring many subtleties and qualifications, the goal of medicine is to maintain or promote health; the scope of medicine's concern is with problems of health; and when medical practice brings someone back to a state of health, (medical) success is rightly declared. And yet, there is considerable controversy not only over particu-

lar definitions of health but also over the general conditions that any proposed definition should satisfy. The presence of this controversy should not be surprising. Many ethical and public policy issues concerning medicine are, in part, disputes over the definition or analysis of the concept of health and, with that, the concept of disease.

Analyses of the concept have variously described health as complete physical, mental, and social well-being; as what people in a culture value or desire; as whatever the medical profession decides to call "health"; or as nothing more than a theoretical concept in physiological theory. The purpose of this article is not to assess the merits of specific proposals but rather to clarify the general themes and concerns that have shaped the philosophical and ethical literature on the concept of health.

I. CONCEPTS OF HEALTH AND THEIR IMPACT

The significance of the concepts of health and disease can be illustrated in several ways. One of the clearest and most dramatic ways is by looking at the phenomenon of "medicalization."

It is common to come across cases where a problem previously understood in terms of socialization, individual personalities, and the like is now framed in the language of medicine, invoking the terms "health" and "disease." Alcoholics and persistent gamblers, rather than being seen as individuals with various psychological weaknesses or moral failings, may now be regarded as victims of a disease. The restless, rebellious child or the poor learner, rather than merely exhibiting youthful energy, poor upbringing, or mediocre intelligence, may be diagnosed as someone with a disease—for example, attention deficit disorder. Even street violence, a problem many might regard as paradigmatically a social problem, has sometimes been called a "public health problem" or a problem arising from various disorders concerning impulsivity control and aggressive behavior.

In many cases, the warrant for using the language of disease is not some empirical discovery about human physiology but instead a general argument arising from a particular conception of health or disease. For example, if a disease is understood to be an undesirable condition over which the individual has no direct control but that seems to be treatable with certain medications, then alcoholism, on this understanding, is a disease. Once a condition is classified as a disease, several conclusions are often immediately drawn: The condition needs to be *cured;* finding and administering the cure is the responsibility of health professionals (e.g., physicians); the cure may require surgery, medication, or, if the condition is particularly serious and contagious, isolation and quarantine. Plainly, classifying something as a disease is a serious matter.

The enormous impact of the concept of health also appears in disputes over the sort of things to which the concept applies. Everyone agrees that the concept applies to people—it surely makes sense to say that an individual is healthy or has a disease. Common practice would also suggest that the concept applies to animals and plants as well as to parts of individuals—for example, organs and tissues. Controversies arise, however, when we ask whether the concept applies to units larger than an individual or to parts smaller than tissues. Does it make sense to ask whether a particular population or national group is healthy? Does it make sense to talk about the health of a species or a race? Does it make sense to talk about healthy or diseased genes or to invoke the idea of "genetic health?"

The legitimacy of extending the concept in these ways is closely tied up with the issue of eugenics. The aim of eugenics, as it has often been understood in this century, is to improve the health of the species. In this extended sense, health is indicated not simply by the health of current individuals but also by the health of their potential offspring. That is to say, even if individuals show no signs or symptoms of disease, the likelihood of their giving birth to children born with some disease indicates that those individuals have a condition that

constitutes a health problem. Some eugenicists argued that such individuals were not "genetically healthy" and could transmit their disease to the population through reproduction. The cure: ensure that these individuals do not in fact reproduce. The result—the American sterilization laws and the Nazi eugenic practices—was surely one of the darkest events in the history of medicine.

For another, perhaps more contemporary illustration of the significance different concepts of health can have, consider the controversy over human genetic engineering. Many critics believe that there is an important moral difference between manipulating people's genes in order to cure them of some disease—so-called "gene therapy"—and manipulating their genes in order to enhance their physical or intellectual capacities. The former is seen to be on a par with any other therapeutic intervention; the latter, however, is seen to be morally suspect, perhaps a return to discredited eugenics. For example, manipulating a child's genes in order to cure him of dwarfism would not be more morally suspect than any other medical intervention, but manipulating a normal child's genes so that he grows to an above-average height would be seen as morally problematic. The line between therapy and enhancement is nothing other than the line between health and disease.

Finally, the importance of the concepts of health and disease in informing the character of medicine shows itself in this: when we have difficulty identifying a condition as healthy or diseased, it becomes quite unclear what, if anything, medicine should do about it. Consider the case of genetic susceptibilities. These are genetic abnormalities that lead to diseases only when certain environmental (including, in some cases, certain cellular) conditions are present. For example, mutations of the BRCA1 gene can lead to a form of breast cancer, but, it appears, only when certain other conditions, such as a family history of that disease, are present. Is the mere presence of a genetic susceptibility itself a disease? If we were to regard genetic susceptibilities as diseases, then the goal of medicine would become the cure, control, or elimination not only of diseases but also of genetic susceptibilities to disease. This view, however, comes uncomfortably close to some of the older, discredited forms of eugenics, where the goal was not simply health but also a kind of genetic purity. On the other hand, it is difficult to regard genetic susceptibilities as healthy conditions, because a person with a genetic susceptibility is at greater risk of contracting the disease. Presumably, the goal of maintaining health includes reducing the risks to health. The difficulty in construing genetic susceptibilities as either healthy or diseased conditions complicates our efforts to spell out the goals of medicine with respect to these (quite common) susceptibilities.

II. ARTICULATING A FAMILY OF CONCEPTS: CONSTRAINTS AND PROPOSALS

Health and disease are just two members of a family of concepts that includes illness, disorder, normality, abnormality, malady, function, malfunction, dysfunction, trauma, injury, and so forth. Some writers have argued that the relationship between different pairings is often more complicated than either synonymy or antonymy.

For example, is health nothing more than the absence of disease? At first it might seem so, but two considerations have led some to deny this. First, there are many conditions that are not usually called "diseases"—for example, broken bones, motion sickness, wounds, and so on—but whose absence is usually thought to be part of being healthy. Some have therefore tried to identify a generic term to cover all these cases—for example, malady—while others have responded by explicitly stating that the term "disease" is being used in their discussion in an especially broad way somewhat at odds with ordinary usage. A different consideration suggesting that health and disease are not opposites arises from noting certain comparative judgments regarding health. Even if two individuals are both free of disease (even in the broad sense of disease), one might be judged to be healthier than the other because, for example, the first is a star athlete while the other is sedentary. One response to such considerations is to examine first basic or minimal health in the hope that more positive conceptions can be seen as extensions of the basic conception. Furthermore, because incorporating positive conceptions of health into the goals of medicine introduces new controversial issues, establishing the basic conception also has the advantage of beginning the discussion with the simpler case.

Here is another conceptual problem: Are disease and illness the same thing? At first it might seem so. But while a disease can have asymptomatic phases, illness cannot: it would be (linguistically) odd to say of someone that he was physically ill but nevertheless felt fine. Some have claimed that illness is a certain class of disease—a disease that the individual experiences as an undesirable condition. Others have suggested that

illnesses are not a subclass of diseases, because one can in fact be ill without having a disease—as, for instance, when one has a hangover.

The substantive issue underlying these apparently linguistic matters is whether the investigation of health or disease should be directed at the family of ordinary or scientific concepts. That is to say, should the aim be to analyze the concepts of health, disease, and so on, as reflected in everyday usage, or should the aim be to analyze these concepts as they are reflected in biological theories? This question must be addressed prior to any proposed analysis because the answer determines how the resulting analysis should be assessed. The concept of health is one of many concepts—others are those of space, time, heat, force, work, solidity, being a fish, and so on—that have an ordinary and a scientific understanding. The relationship between the ordinary and the scientific concept is a matter of some controversy, and so we cannot assume that the same analysis would apply to both. For example, we would expect an analysis of the ordinary concept of space as reflected in everyday use to be quite different from an analysis of the scientific concept of space as reflected in physicists' theories of the structure of spacetime.

Some commentators have denied that there are scientific concepts of health and disease, insisting that these concepts have no role in biological theories and explanations. But this claim probably reflects the influence of early logical positivism and its suspicion of the use of the concept of function in biology. Few would now deny that at least some members of the family of concepts play a significant role in biological theories. The impact of this acknowledgment on the assessment of proposed analyses should be clear. If the aim is an analysis of the ordinary concepts, then the goal is to construct a definition that captures how these concepts are typically used and understood; a failure to capture *any* ordinary use of the concepts would constitute a prima facie objection to the analysis. On the other hand, if the aim is to analyze the scientific concept, then the goal is to analyze the role these concepts play in the appropriate biological theories and explanations, notably those in physiology; any effort to capture usage outside of these scientific contexts would be beside the point.

Not surprisingly, deciding which investigation is the correct one to pursue is controversial because that decision is tied to the question of the relationship between medicine and biology. Putting the issue in its most extreme form: Are medical concepts simply biological concepts suitably framed and applied? Or is medicine an independent discipline whose use of biology is purely opportunistic? We will return to this dispute over which set of concepts is the appropriate one to analyze.

III. THE ISSUE OF NORMATIVISM

Most of the literature on the concepts of health, disease, and so on has been concerned not with the assessment of particular definitions but with the question of whether the concepts are value-laden. This has been called the issue of "normativism." In order to explain what is at issue, we should begin with the observation that ordinary judgments of health and disease have what we might call a normative "force" or "effect." That is to say, most people regard being healthy as a prima facie good thing and having a disease as a prima facie bad thing. The dispute is over how to explain these conclusions.

According to the normativists, value claims are part of the *meaning* of health and disease. For example, one version of normativism holds that having a disease is having a biological condition that society values negatively. Epilepsy is judged in our society to be a disease because, in part, it is judged to be a bad or undesirable condition. But in another society, where the epileptic's seizure is taken to indicate a valued encounter with the sacred, epilepsy is not judged to be a disease at all. Thus, the normative conclusion is a straightforward inference based solely on the meanings of the terms.

The nonnormativists, on the other hand, hold that the meanings of health and disease can be specified in a value-neutral way. According to one version of nonnormativism, disease is a deviation from normal biological functioning, where what the biological functions are and what counts as normal functioning is specified by biological theory, specifically physiology. (It is usually assumed by both sides that scientific *theory* is value-free. The tenability of scientific *practice* being value-free is a different and more controversial matter.) Epilepsy is a disease because it is a deviation from normal functioning; if another society does not regard it as a disease, then its members are simply wrong about human biology. The normative conclusion does not therefore follow directly from the meanings of "health" and "disease" but requires further premises of an explicitly moral nature. For example, some people have argued that assumptions about a theory of justice are required to explain the normative effect of (some) judgments of health.

It would seem therefore that the difference between the normativists and the nonnormativists turns on who can provide a better semantic theory of medical language. After all, it hardly seems plausible that simple (or sophisticated) introspective observation can determine whether the normative conclusion is based solely on the meanings of the terms or requires additional moral premises. But for the most part, the disputants have not engaged in a discussion of the merits of various semantic theories. Instead, the literature has attended more to constructing and responding to various counterexamples to the specific claims about whether the concepts of health are or are not value-free.

For example, a typical argument nonnormativists use against normativism is to identify cases where having a disease might be thought to be a good thing—for example, an individual might be happy to have flat feet (he wants to avoid the military draft), and people who contract the cowpox disease may count themselves fortunate (because contracting cowpox confers an immunity to the more serious smallpox disease). The thought behind these objections is that if being a bad or undesirable condition were part of the meaning of "disease," then examples such as these would be self-contradictions, which they are not. But this type of argument does not work in the absence of an explicit semantics. Consider a concept that everyone would regard as value-laden—for example, the concept of beauty. We would not conclude that the concept is not value-laden after all because we can imagine cases where someone doesn't want to be beautiful or thinks being plain-looking is a good thing.

On the other hand, the common type of objection against nonnormativism is to point out counterexamples to Boorse's account, which is usually taken to be the paradigm nonnormativist position. Briefly put, Boorse characterizes disease as a departure from normal functioning, where "normal functioning" is understood in terms of what is statistically typical for the species. Thus, if an individual's thyroid—whose function is to secrete hormones important for metabolism—secretes an excessive amount of hormones, compared to what is statistically typical, then the individual has an abnormal—that is, a diseased—thyroid. While normativists may point to various exceptions to Boorse's account, perhaps the clearest counterexample is the one that Boorse himself raises. If malfunctioning is understood as deviation from species typicality, then the account cannot recognize widespread or universal diseases—for example, dental cavities or functional declines associated with old age. Boorse's response is to propose ad hoc additions to his account of disease or to regard such examples as in fact not counterexamples at all but rather themselves "anomalies deserving continued analysis." That is to say, the nonnormativist account is not being proposed as simply descriptive of medical usage; if certain examples cannot fit the account, so much the worse for these examples—we should reconsider calling them diseases. Such a response suggests that the semantics of the concepts of health and disease is not really the issue.

One suggestion for what might be at issue—in contrast to the fairly technical one of semantics—is the objectivity of judgments of health and disease. When a society claims that masturbation is a disease, does that claim rest on a biological fact, which either supports or refutes it, or is the claim nothing more than a society's values dressed up in medical language? If one society claims that homosexuality is a disease while another does not, are the different societies disagreeing about some objective, biological fact or is there no real disagreement, only a difference of culture?

Recasting the dispute in this way clearly assumes that values, and so normative conceptions of health and disease, are not objective. But there are several problems with interpreting the normativism dispute in this way. The move from a debate over whether the semantics of health and disease contain value terms to a metaphysical debate over whether the condition of being healthy or diseased is a fact or a value is a move that many philosophers are hesitant to make: the semantic "is–ought" distinction is far less obscure than the metaphysical fact–value distinction. Consequently, there is considerable controversy among philosophers over what "objectivity" means, so that few would say that the concept of objectivity is clearer or less controversial than the concepts of health and disease. Moreover, and in part because of this controversy, some philosophers would hold that values *are* objective, including some who argue for the normativist position.

Nevertheless, thinking of the dispute as one over the objectivity of judgments of health and disease does seem to point in the right direction. Perhaps a clearer way of identifying the problem would be in terms of the issues we mentioned earlier regarding the contrast between ordinary and scientific concepts of health and disease: Are the concepts of health and disease that characterize the aim, scope, and criteria of success of medicine scientific or ordinary concepts?

By and large, normativists focus on the ordinary concepts and judgments, because their aim seems to be to capture ordinary usage. For the most part they do not seem to be arguing that standard biological theories are (or must be) value-laden. Indeed, they do not seem to be drawing any conclusion regarding biological theories. On the other hand, nonnormativists appear to give pride of place to the scientific concepts and

judgments of health and disease. They appear willing to revise or correct ordinary usage in order to smooth the transition to the scientific concepts. In their view, the apparently normative judgments about disease that the normativist identifies should really be understood as judgments about illness, a quite different concept. Of course, this suggestion is not intended to entail that a normativist could not challenge the value-free claims of biological theories, although the task of arguing the broader claim would dwarf the normativist's thesis regarding health. Similarly, it is conceivable that a nonnormativist would argue that ordinary judgments of health and disease are value-free as they stand, although, given the number and variety of apparent counterexamples that have been proposed, such a position would face considerable difficulties without an appropriate semantic theory of these ordinary concepts.

Once the dispute is cast in terms of a contrast between the ordinary and the scientific, the normativist and nonnormativist positions no longer seem diametrically opposed: The nonnormativist is right in that the concepts of health and disease, considered as scientific concepts in biology, are value-free. The normativist is right in that the concepts of health and disease, considered as ordinary concepts that are shaped by our experiences of illness and disability, are value-laden. The question becomes, however, which set of concepts is appropriate for medicine, for these two kinds of concepts suggest two very different conceptions of medicine. According to one, medicine is the application of biological knowledge to diagnose and correct biological abnormalities. According to the other, medicine is a discipline that uses biological discoveries to advance and maintain certain values.

The second (normative) conception might be objectionable in that it seems open to abuse: the image of health care practitioners advancing a particular agenda of values calls forth all the problems raised by medical paternalism. This might make the apparently more modest first (nonnormative) conception more appealing until we realize that it depicts practitioners as, in effect, morally neutral technicians, which can itself lead to a different kind of abuse. The second conception does make clear that medicine and those who work within it have a distinctive moral responsibility. Presented in this way, the dispute is hardly an academic one.

Also See the Following Articles

EUGENICS • GENE THERAPY • LIFE, CONCEPT OF • MEDICAL CODES AND OATHS • MEDICAL ETHICS, HISTORY OF • MENTAL HEALTH

Bibliography

Boorse, C. (1975). On the distinction between health and disease. *Philosophy & Public Affairs, 5,* 49–68.

Boorse, C. (1977). Health as a theoretical concept. *Philosophy of Science, 44,* 542–573.

Caplan, A. L. (1996). The Concepts of health and disease. In R. M. Veatch (Ed.), *Medical ethics,* pp. 49–62. Boston: Jones and Bartlett.

Caplan, A. L., Engelhardt, H. T., & McCartney, J. J., (Eds.). (1981). *Concepts of health and disease: Interdisciplinary perspectives,* Reading, MA: Addison-Wesley Publishing Co.

Culver, G. M., & Gert, B. (1982). *Philosophy of medicine: Conceptual and ethical issues in medicine and psychiatry,* New York: Oxford University Press.

Daniels, N. (1985). *Just health care.* Cambridge: Cambridge University Press.

Engelhardt, H. T. (1975). The Concepts of Health and Disease. In H. T. Engelhardt & S. Spicker (Eds.), *Evaluation and explanation in the biomedical sciences,* pp. 125–141. Boston: Reidel.

Fulford, K. W. M. (1989). *Moral theory and medical practice.* Cambridge: Cambridge University Press.

King, L. (1954). What is a disease? *Philosophy of Science, 12,* 193–203.

Margolis, J. (1976). The concept of disease. *Journal of Medicine and Philosophy, 1,* 238–255.

Reznek, L. (1987). *The nature of disease.* London: Routledge & Kegan Paul.

Wachbroit, R. (1994a). Distinguishing genetic disease and genetic susceptibility. *American Journal of Medical Genetics, 53,* 236–240.

Wachbroit, R. (1994b). Normality as a biological concept. *Philosophy of Science, 61,* 579–591.

HEALTH CARE FINANCING

Gerald M. Oppenheimer* and Robert A. Padgug†
*Brooklyn College, City University of New York, †Albert Einstein College of Medicine

GLOSSARY

capitation An insurance mechanism in which a fixed amount is paid per person to cover all services provided to patients; capitation may be paid by financers to managed care plans or by health plans to providers.

community rating The fact of charging the same premium to all individuals or groups in a specific "community" or pool.

experience rating The fact of basing the premium rate for a group on its own past or projected health care costs.

health maintenance organization (HMO) A facility or organization that accepts financial risk for providing a range of health care services to a specified population in return for fixed, periodic payment. A type of "managed care" (below) offering services either at fixed sites or through networks of physician and other provider offices (IPAs).

individual practice association (IPA) A type of health maintenance organization that contracts with pri-

vate, office-based physicians, or group practices to treat enrolled members.

managed care In general, the implementation of control over health care provider or patient behavior to reduce health care utilization and costs. More specifically, health plans that use such controls, including health maintenance organizations, preferred provider organizations, point-of-service plans, and "traditional" fee-for-service plans that impose utilization management.

point-of-service (POS) plan A managed care plan that offers coverage for care outside its network of providers, while offering financial incentives (in particular, higher levels of reimbursement) for utilization of in-network care.

preferred provider organization (PPO) A type of managed care in which insurers contract with a network of providers who agree to provide care to covered persons at lower-than-normal rates in exchange for a larger volume of patients.

self-funding (or self-insurance) The fact of using the resources of an employer group to fund health care expenses directly rather than transferring the risk to an insurer.

social insurance Insurance mandated by law for a specified population, often financed by taxes.

third-party payer A payer of health care services other than the patient ("first party") or health care provider ("second party").

HEALTH CARE FINANCING comprises those financial mechanisms that societies use to create, pay for, and provide access to their health care delivery systems. It involves the collection of funds for these purposes, their "pooling" to ensure that those in need receive care, and their use in reimbursement systems to pay for health care. In this article we focus on the origins, nature, and problems of the health care financing system in the United States.

I. INTRODUCTION

A. Common Assumptions and Purposes of Health Care Coverage

All modern industrialized societies assume that health care is different from other services or commodities required by their populations. As a result they have developed public policies to spread access to health care as widely as possible among the populace. They have done so in the belief that medicine is necessary (if not sufficient) to produce health itself, something without which life would be substantially impaired or impossible. These assumptions have led industrialized societies to support or organize "social" financing systems that offer increased access to health care than would otherwise be the case under ordinary "market" conditions.

Although based on shared assumptions, existing health care coverage and reimbursement systems are quite varied in organization and carry out their goals using different means: national health services, national health insurance, private (not-for-profit or commercial) insurance, or combinations of these. Nonetheless, what all these approaches have in common is that they are systems of *pooled* savings that protect individuals and populations against the costs of illness and injury. Pools may be composed of whole societies, the inhabitants of particular geographical subregions, the members of employment-based groups, or the purchasers of private insurance policies. Such systems are viable because all participants contribute to them or have contributions made on their behalf, but only a small fraction of the participants draw upon the pooled savings in any given year; for example, in the United States one percent of the utilizers of health care in any given year account for fully 30% of the costs. Individuals and groups are generally willing to contribute to those pools, even if they are healthy, for two major reasons: their risks of illness and injury are unpredictable at any given moment, and the care they may require is likely to be more expensive than they can ordinarily afford. Pooled savings allow large groups of people to share the risks of costly, unpredictable, but nevertheless likely future events.

All countries with pooled health care reimbursement systems must develop answers to the same set of questions. First, who will be covered by the system? Next, what benefits will be offered, and to whom, within the population covered? Lastly, what will be the sources of funding for those benefits? How a nation chooses to answer these questions affects the form and function of its health care system; it also raises multiple ethical issues. For example, are specific social classes, demographic groups or legal categories excluded from, or under-represented in, the reimbursement system, and do they, as a consequence, have poorer access to health care services? Are benefits uniform and universal or do they vary directly with the need, wealth or power of particular individuals, groups, or institutions? Finally, who pays for the benefits and who is "subsidized" in any given year; that is, how is financial risk shared, what means are used to do so, and are they fair to all participants?

The financing of health care systems can take many forms. Monies can come through general taxation or through payroll taxes, or they can be raised through premiums paid to either nonprofit sickness funds or private firms. The United States, in fact, uses all four approaches, but primarily relies on the last option in the form of private insurers and a private system of provision of care.

B. The United States: Private Insurance and Provision of Care

For most of this century, health care in the United States has been dominated by private, but not-for-profit providers, in particular hospitals, supplemented by public institutions and a small, largely doctor-owned, proprietary sector. In large measure, this was due to the fact that capital and operating funds were difficult to raise except through philanthropy, public funds, and community investment. Even the insurance sector, with its hundreds of commercial (mutual and stock) companies, had a large not-for-profit, community-oriented sector made up of Blue Cross and Blue Shield companies and community-oriented "prepaid group plans" ("health maintenance organizations" since the 1970s). Over the years, however, the balance between not-for-profit and for-profit insurers has changed dramatically, with the latter becoming clearly dominant at the present time. Ironically, this is, in large part, the result of the

TABLE 1
Distribution of Population by Primary Source of Coverage

	1988 Number (millions)	Percent	1995 Number (millions)	Percent
Private coverage	160.2	66.4%	162.7	62.1%
Employer-sponsored	148.2	61.5%	148.3	55.6%
Employees	67.5	28.0%	72.9	27.8%
Dependents	77.6	32.2%	72.9	27.8%
Retirees	3.1	1.3%	2.5	1.0%
Nongroup	12.0	5.0%	14.4	5.5%
Public coverage	50.3	20.9%	59.8	22.8%
Medicare	30.4	12.6%	33.8	12.9%
Medicaid	14.6	6.1%	21.5	8.2%
Other public	5.3	2.2%	4.5	1.7%
Uninsured	30.6	12.7%	39.6	15.1%
Total	241.1	100.0%	262.1	100.0%

Source: Lewin Group estimates from March 1995 Current Population Survey.

enormous growth of pooled savings systems, both private and public, that have added many billions of dollars to the health care system. The effect of this gigantic flow of money has been to render segment after segment of the health care world potential profit centers for for-profit enterprises. These have taken advantage of their new opportunities. We will return to aspects of this theme, insofar as they affect health care financing, in the next section.

The importance of private institutions in the American health financing world can also be seen in its strong emphasis on employer-sponsored health insurance groups. Such groups cover the majority of Americans with third-party coverage (although by no means the majority of costs, because, in general, employees represent the youngest and healthiest parts of the population). Such groups have always been considered the centerpiece of the American coverage system. Other types of third-party insurance (government programs—most notably Medicare and Medicaid—and private insurance purchased by individuals) have been thought of as secondary, created as they largely were to fill "gaps" in employer-sponsored coverage. (See Tables 1 and 2.)

Reliance on employer-sponsored groups to finance the bulk of coverage is not in itself unique to the United States. Many of the developed systems of Europe, for example, rely on similar general methodologies. What provides the American system with its unique character, however, is the amount of power that remains in the

hands of employers: power to decide whether or not to offer coverage at all and broad power to determine the nature and cost of the coverage they do provide. In most other countries these issues are decided by elected legislators and other public officials, who have created by law what are known as "social insurance" systems, in which coverage is virtually universal and uniform. The American system, by contrast, is a "private insurance" system, lacking universality or uniformity.

The American health care financing system can, in sum, be characterized as one based on private, in particular for-profit, insurers and employer-sponsored groups, supplemented by a variety of public programs. Americans have tended to believe that the private sector, utilizing the market and competition among firms, could be relied upon to provide wide access to health care without significant public intervention or control. At the same time, government has, since the 1940s, provided both employers and employees with tax advantages and other privileges that have made employee groups financially feasible.

The use of private organizations—and, in particular, for-profit ones—to meet a social welfare need raises a number of political and ethical concerns. These cluster around a set of closely interrelated issues: Can the American system provide adequate coverage, benefits, and care to all who require it, regardless of individual ability to pay? Can this system spread risk and costs efficiently and equitably within the population? and, Can a system of this sort provide the necessary controls to ensure that it carries out its social purposes both effectively and at the lowest possible costs? In brief, a social system requires equity, while private enterprise operates under competitive market demands of profitability and efficiency. The tension between these differ-

TABLE 2
National Health Expenditures by Source of Funds

	Dollars (Billions)	Percent of total
Total	949.4	100.0
Private	528.6	55.7
Private insurance	313.3	33.0
Consumer (out-of-pocket)	174.9	18.4
Other	80.9	8.5
Public	420.8	44.3
Federal	303.6	32.0
State and local	117.2	12.3

Source: Health Care Financing Administration, Office of the Actuary.

ent principles has been strongly felt since the 1930s in the American health care system. It is worth turning to a brief analysis of key elements of the American system to comprehend this better.

II. THE AMERICAN SYSTEM: FROM INCLUSION TO EXCLUSION

A. Community Rated and Experience-Rated Insurance

In the 1930s, Blue Cross and Blue Shield plans created the insurance policies that served as prototypes for our current reimbursement system. These private, not-for-profit plans determined insurance premiums based upon what is known as community rating. That is, the costs of health care were spread across the entire population—or community—that was covered by a particular type of policy, with premiums set at the same level for everyone (with some adjustment for region and family makeup). This system represented a broad spreading of the risks, and thus of the costs, of health care utilization over a relatively large population. Even under these relatively optimum conditions, the totality of those who could afford insurance was always less than the general population, all of whom were at risk of illness.

In the decades following the Second World War, the original principle of community rating was substantially replaced by what came to be known as experience rating. This was due largely to two related factors. First, employer groups became the main source of financing for health insurance. Such groups had existed as early as the 1930s, but employers in large numbers began to pay premiums on behalf of all of their employees (and often their dependents) only in the 1940s and 1950s. Employer action followed demands by unions, administrative rulings during World War II that fringe benefits were not subject to then-existing wage freezes, and federal legislation (1954) making group health insurance premiums exempt from income tax for employers and employees. The number of participants in employment-related health insurance groups grew rapidly in the postwar period, reaching 123 million by 1958.

Secondly, impressed with the success of Blue Cross and seeing large employer groups as potentially profitable customers, commercial insurers entered the health insurance market during the late 1940s and early 1950s. They successfully offered employers health policies whose rates were based only upon the actual reimbursement experience of their specific employee groups, nor-

mally composed of persons younger and healthier than the general population. Consequently, premiums for large groups would normally be lower than those for the total community, making "experience-rated premiums" attractive to employers.

In order to survive, most Blue Cross and Blue Shield Plans were forced to drop community rating, at least for the majority of their business. This meant that insurance risks were spread less widely than previously and were defined by a relatively narrow, employment-related base. As a result, many small groups and individuals who purchased their own insurance paid higher premiums than they might otherwise have, because they no longer were in the same pools as larger and healthier employer-sponsored groups.

B. Insurance Underwriting

Moreover, many small groups and all individuals became subject to medical underwriting. Through medical underwriting insurers determine "whether and on what basis insurance can be issued at 'standard rates,' offered at higher premium rates or with other limitations (such as the exclusion of a specified medical condition from coverage), or whether insurance should be refused (declined) altogether" (U.S. Congress, Office of Technology Assessment 1988: 5). For small groups and individuals, underwriters determined premium rates and extent of coverage by weighing such variables as age, current and future health status, and type of occupation and geographical location, all of them factors believed to be correlated closely with health care utilization.

After the application of actuarial screens, persons offered insurance were grouped into pools of relatively homogeneous risk and premium levels. As a consequence of underwriting, as of experience rating, the universe of the privately insured was atomized into a multitude of self-contained, self-supporting units, each paying premiums that reflect its past or projected health care costs (rather than a broad, mutually supportive "community-at-risk"). In brief, experience rating led to fragmentation.

C. The Uninsured

Moreover, basing the private insurance system on employee groups and on underwriting tended to lead to the exclusion of risk groups most in need of health care. The elderly, the disabled, those with serious chronic diseases, and the poor were often excluded from private coverage because they were unemployed or high utilizers subject to unaffordably high premiums. In addition, those who were employed by companies that did not provide insurance and many of the self-employed found it difficult to purchase insurance on their own, in particular because the tax laws provided them with small or no subsidies to do so. All of these groups paid, and continue to pay, taxes that are used to subsidize the purchase of insurance for others, without benefitting themselves to any substantial degree. In effect, risk-sharing mechanisms are again narrowed; those who had the greatest financial means and the lowest risk status on average were generally the beneficiaries of the widest risk-sharing. The social aims of insurance pooling were thus unintentionally undermined by the manner in which the system was allowed to operate.

D. Policy Responses to the Problem of the Uninsured

The employment-based system thus left a large portion of the population uncovered. This problem has been dealt with in two ways.

First, access to the health care system has been improved through a succession of large-scale governmental interventions that have created new programs for persons with the least resources and greatest needs for care and whom the private employer-based system, fragmented as it was, was unable or unwilling to include. The most notable of these programs are Medicare (1965), insuring the elderly (and, since 1972, the disabled), and Medicaid (also 1965), insuring the poor, the disabled, and those with large, uncovered health care expenses (such as many of the residents of nursing homes). Medicare is a true social insurance program, covering an entire population, paid for by universal taxes, and uniform in eligibility requirements and benefits provided. Medicaid is also social insurance, paid for by federal, state, and (more rarely, as in New York State) local tax revenues, but is a means-tested program that lacks uniformity and covers only a portion of the needy; each state has its own eligibility requirements and benefits, although federal law mandates minimum levels in each case.

Second, because, in spite of both public and private efforts, a large number of persons remains uncovered by either type (an estimated 40 million in 1995; see Table 1), a variety of more informal methods were developed to pay for their care. Most notable of these is what is often called "cost shifting," through which hospitals (and to a much lesser extent other types of provider) charge higher rates to patients with private or public insurance in order to cross-subsidize the costs of uninsured patients; this is, in effect, an indirect

method of spreading the costs of health care more widely. In some states (such as Maryland and New York), systems of this sort have actually been implemented by legislation aiming to spread the costs of care for the uninsured ("charity care") more widely and more fairly among payers. In most localities, however, the cost-shifting system has remained informal and has had uncertain and incomplete effects.

The American health care financing system has left millions of people uncovered and at risk for receiving insufficient or inadequate health care. For several decades, however, it was assumed by many observers that the system would gradually expand, with more employers offering coverage and public programs covering more of those left out of the private system, until virtually universal coverage would be achieved. This has not occurred; indeed, coverage levels are at present receding in all sectors from the high levels they had attained in the 1980s (see Table 1).

E. Insurance and the Cost Crisis

What analysts failed to take into account was that public and private policy can easily change. Universality was never mandated. Employers were free to decrease or eliminate coverage. Government could reduce funding for politically vulnerable programs. Of equal or greater importance, a system without a concentrated policy-making center or more or less uniform rules and regulations was ill-prepared to meet major crises, in particular the rising costs of health that have challenged the health care coverage systems of all industrialized countries in the 1980s and 1990s.

In our health care reimbursement system, numerous independent parties, none of them powerful enough to achieve control but all with independent power, pursue their own interests. Each party attempts to reduce its own exposure, especially in a period of rapidly rising health care costs. Normally this means shifting costs to other payers or to providers and patients. In the most extreme case, employers and individuals who do not or cannot purchase health insurance depend for medical services on providers funded by others who do; as a consequence, the latter must financially support higher taxes or premiums, and are subsidizing the former. In addition, uninsured individuals often delay or become eligible for medical intervention only when their health conditions become critical, so that the costs of treatment increase. As a consequence, lack of access to health care coverage may raise the aggregate costs of that care—contributing to an inflationary trend that hurts all without being controlled by any.

In brief, lack of internal controls, systemic fragmentation, narrow risk sharing, and a patchwork system have contributed significantly to inefficiencies within the health care sector. These, in turn, have caused participants to react in ways that, ironically, have further increased fragmentation and the inability of the financing system to carry out its purposes.

Even the public sector operates in this manner to some degree. On one level, government represents society as a whole and is supposed to ensure that the social purposes of health care systems are not lost. But on another, more immediate level, government is the administrator of specific programs—that is, particular insurance pools—such as Medicare and Medicaid, which operate in a manner quite similar to those of large employers. These programs use their substantial power to limit, if possible, their own financial exposure, even at the expense of other groups. Indeed, in the early 1990s, Medicare paid hospitals on average only 88% of actual costs for the care of persons covered by it, Medicaid only 82%, while private insurers paid 130%. This type of cost-shifting has little to do with social fairness per se, but rather represents the kind of power large groups may exercise in our system.

Such organizational behavior points up the relatively weak role government plays as a unifying or centralizing force in the U.S. system of health care reimbursement. Currently, state governments may regulate premiums, mandate benefits, and assure the financial viability of health insurance carriers; governments at all levels offer courts for the adjudication of claims and may legislate statutes aimed at reducing discrimination by private insurers against certain classes of the populace, like persons with disabilities. Such regulatory or legislative functions, however, hardly affect the health coverage system as a whole.

In other industrialized countries, governments or quasi-government bodies generally act to control vital aspects of the health care financing system. Those aspects usually include, at a minimum, specifying who is to be covered, defining a minimum package of benefits, and mandating financing sources and levels. Because such actions tend to expand the health care system considerably, governmental or quasi-governmental bodies must develop and apply broad mechanisms to limit rising utilization and costs. Such mechanisms might include negotiated fee schedules between payers and doctors or global budgets for hospitals.

These governmental or quasi-governmental bodies have therefore achieved in large measure what has so far eluded the private, fragmented, decentralized U.S. system: considerable control over utilization and expenditures without a tendency to exclude those whose costs to the reimbursement system might be greater than their payments into it.

F. Self-Funding

By the 1970s, employers, seeking greater control over their plans again strengthened the trend toward fragmentation of the community-at-risk into narrow, self-inclusionary units. In order to reduce costs further and to escape from state legislation and regulation, large employers instituted what is called self-funding or self-insurance, paying the health care costs of their employees directly from their own funds. As a result of this trend, which by the mid-1990s involved a majority of large firms and roughly 40% of all workers with employment-sponsored health insurance in the United States, the costs of health care, which under experience rating were at least shared between employer and insurer, now rest squarely on the employer, unless the latter has purchased relatively expensive "stop-loss" insurance. An employer lacking reinsurance and with any significant number of sick employees could be in danger of serious fiscal hemorrhaging and perhaps insolvency. As a consequence, employers might safeguard themselves by truncating benefits or by reducing the number of those previously covered, thereby further excluding individuals from health insurance.

G. Cost Containment

Starting in the late seventies, insurers and self-funded employers were confronted with more substantial, spiraling increases in the costs of health care. Faced with a massive rise in costs, insurers and employers added to their plans a variety of "cost containment" measures aimed at reducing expenditures for employee health care. Thus, in addition to underwriting techniques, insurers introduced mechanisms to constrain both provider behavior (the introduction of "second opinion" for elective surgery or preauthorization of inpatient hospitalization, for example) and patient demand. Of the procedures to reduce demand, one of the most important was greater "cost-sharing"—for example, charging larger deductibles or higher levels of coinsurance—to those who use health care services.

Unacceptably large increases in the cost of health coverage have led some firms, mainly smaller employers, to drop health insurance entirely, or, more commonly among larger employers, to pass a portion of their costs to the members of the group. Fewer firms, for example, now pay the entire premium for individual or family coverage, especially the latter (with the result that coverage of dependents has dropped dramatically in recent years). At the same time, the majority of employer plans have ceased to reimburse the full costs of even inpatient care, as they did earlier. In addition, employers who are self-funded, and therefore not under the jurisdiction of state insurance laws, can alter their insurance packages to suit their needs, by, for example, increasing employees' deductibles and co-insurance or decreasing the benefits offered.

The private, largely unregulated approach, with its logic of financial "efficiency," had thus by the 1980s resulted in a reimbursement system that was highly fragmented, excluded a large and apparently growing minority of the populace and focused the financial risk of health care costs in increasingly smaller units of population, instead of spreading it as widely as possible. Community rating assumed that insurance benefits should be distributed according to need. Experience rating and underwriting allocate the costs of insurance to those who generate them; at least theoretically, no group or individual pays for anyone else. In the last analysis, each pays for him- or herself. Ultimately, health insurance becomes only a savings plan against future need on the part of those clients accepted by insurance carriers or fortunate enough to have employers willing to finance their care.

III. THE AMERICAN SYSTEM: MANAGED CARE, THE MARKET, AND PROFIT

The American system had reached an impasse by the 1980s. Hundreds of billions of dollars ($949 billion in 1994, for example; see Table 2) flowed into the system, but millions of Americans remained uninsured and an increasingly fragmented system was unable to control costs. The available methods of reducing costs ironically seemed only to add to systemic fragmentation, further reducing the ability of all payers to control costs and adding to the number of the uncovered. Even methods of increasing the number of the covered in an uncontrolled system seemed only to add to systemic costs.

A. Potential Solutions

In such a situation, several potential solutions seemed to offer themselves: reform based on govenment intervention (either some form of national health insurance or, at a minimum, a more uniform degree of regulation and public intervention); a reconstructed and reformed market-based system based on competition and "market forces"; or some combination of these. The aim of any workable solution would, it was widely recognized, have to be to provide the American third-party payment system with what it most lacked: a means of controlling the provision, effectiveness, and costs of health care while providing greater access to care for those currently without insurance. Indeed, many observers of differing political persuasions recognized that effective "cost containment" would be difficult to achieve without universal coverage and vice versa.

By the early 1990s a variety of solutions—both partial and "incremental" and full-scale—were being attempted. Some approaches addressed cost as well as access issues, but most stressed one or the other.

Among the partial solutions, federally mandated increases in eligibility for Medicaid, in particular for women and children, and state legislation regulating small portions of the insurance markets or implementing special state pools for high-risk persons, were most notable. Larger-scale changes were implemented in particular programs, including Medicare and Medicaid, where reimbursement systems incorporating a variety of incentives for cost reduction were implemented (for example, the Medicare prospective hospital payment system and a new fee schedule for physicians).

Public attempts to restructure the health financing system far more radically appeared in the form of a variety of bills introduced into Congress. These took very different approaches: the creation of a true tax-based national health insurance system similar to that in Canada (a "single-payer" approach); the expansion and rationalization of the current system of employer-based insurance through mandated employer- and employee-paid payroll taxes and mainly private coverage; and the elimination of employer groups and public insurance programs, with mandated or voluntary coverage of individuals and families provided by private insurers at the individual level.

The most important of these federal initiatives was that put forward by the Clinton Administration in mid-1994. This attempted to combine public and private approaches by retaining a system of private, employment-based groups and insurers, while adding a good deal of public regulation, including defined minimum benefits, mechanisms for constraining increases in premium levels, and provisions for increased risk-sharing among different covered populations. The Medicaid program would have been folded into the general program—thus eliminating some of the separate tiers of the financing system. Actual coverage would have been provided either by large employee groups (over 5000 members) or through health insurance purchasing agencies set up on a state level to "credential" participating insurers and managed care plans. Such an approach would have restored very large risk-sharing pools for the majority of the population and resolved at least some of the problems associated with continual narrowing of risk pools. The Clinton approach was to a large degree based on what was called "managed competition," developed by Alain Enthoven, Paul Ellwood, and others in the 1970s and 1980s specifically to address the problem of control within a largely private system.

The Clinton proposal failed disastrously by the fall of 1995, largely discrediting, at least for the near future, the idea of large-scale government intervention and regulation. The few state-based more-or-less comprehensive reform efforts that had been attempted in the late 1980s and early 1990s (for example, in Orgeon, Washington, Minnesota, and Massachusetts), had also generally failed by 1995 or had to be scaled back significantly. States found it difficult, if not impossible, to find a satisfactory way of financing major new systems. Finally, they found that federal legislation (in particular the Employee Retirement and Income Security Act of 1974 [ERISA]), which exempted self-funded employer-sponsored groups from state regulation, stood squarely in the way of any reform that chose to rely on financing by employers.

With these failures, governmental reform efforts, except for purely incremental initiatives affecting a relatively small number of persons, essentially came to an end. At both the federal and state level reform efforts receded, while attention to the problem of the uninsured declined.

By the early 1990s a growing movement simply to reduce public expenditures or pass costs directly to providers (in the form of lower reimbursement rates) or enrollees (in the form of larger copayments or more restrictive eligibility rules) had gathered steam. Expansion of Medicaid, a notable feature of the late 1980s, came to a virtual end, the welfare system was altered considerably (with effects on Medicaid and other public health-related programs still unclear), and public financing was reduced (either absolutely or in terms of rate of program growth) wherever possible. The percentage of the population that was poor, at high risk, or uninsured continued to increase, however.

B. The Private Sector and the Market

American health care financing system *was*, nevertheless, undergoing major changes—changes implemented within the private sector itself by employers, insurers and other third-party payers. In the absence of public measures—and often in opposition to them—private payers, in particular employers, began to move the system in new directions in an attempt to control the costs they themselves incurred. Their efforts were far less concerned with the problem of the uninsured than with costs per se, and, in particular with the type and amount of medical care utilized by the members of their own pools.

In keeping with a more general shift in American attitudes away from public programs and initiative and to greater reliance on the market, the assumption that underlay private sector efforts was that a market reformed and controlled by employers and relatively free of public regulation, could most efficiently reduce rates of increases in costs, provide higher standards of care, and produce systemic controls analogous to those of Adam Smith's "invisible hand."

C. Managed Care

The centerpiece of the system developing under the impetus of employers is "managed care," a set of coverage methodologies that to varying degrees eliminate the distinction between the financing and the provision of health care in the interest of cost containment. In the traditional American system, employers, individuals, and government financed health coverage; insurers and other third-party payers created risk-sharing pools; and hospitals, physicians, and other health care institutions and professionals provided care. The normally rigid separation among these parties meant that few controls could be exercised over health care utilization and provider practice.

Managed care is the market approach to providing a "center of control" for the health care system, one strongly supported by larger employers, who have shifted their role from simple financing agents to direct or indirect purchasers of health care for members of their groups. Managed care, especially the HMO, is an attempt, in an otherwise anarchic health care world, to bring all of the elements of health care financing and provision for a specific population (the pool of insured in an employee group or a managed care company) within the control of a single entity. Ironically, a major spur to its success was the Clinton plan itself. By stressing HMOs and other managed care plans as central to a reformed health care system, a significant impetus was provided to their further development; although the Clinton plan was a failure, the managed care plans created to take advantage of it were a success and were, in addition, able to operate virtually free of public regulation.

By combining financing and provision of care, managed care plans redistribute risks among the participants in the health care system. Employers pass much of the risk they formerly bore to managed care organizations. These, in turn, pass as much as they can to providers. Providers, usually physicians or hospitals, either work directly for a plan (with a fixed, agreed-upon salary for all services) or contract with it to provide services to members enrolled in the managed care plan in return for predetermined, often discounted, fees or for some form of capitation. The plan offers its members financial incentives to use the providers with whom it has contracted. Because providers receive, for all or for a large percentage of services, the same reimbursement levels no matter how many services they actually provide, they have an incentive to offer less rather than more to patients. In addition, plans offer providers other inducements to reduce utilization or implement utilization management controls, treatment protocols, and case management programs.

For enrolled beneficiaries, managed care might incorporate underwriting within the group (based on lifestyle or wellness) and flexible benefits that allow the healthier to save by purchasing less coverage. Managed care, therefore, attempts to lower the cost of health care by reducing demand, doing so by shifting at least some of the risk of health care costs to patients and providers. In the process, patients and their providers are supposed to become more sensitive to cost and price, much like ideal purchasers in a typical commodity market. And as in more ordinary markets, competition among managed care organizations—health maintenance organizations (HMOs), independent practice associations (IPAs) and point of service plans (POS)—is intended to promote efficiency and further drive costs down.

Some forms of managed care plan, in particular HMOs, do seem to reduce costs and have the potential to improve quality and continuity of care. Some studies suggest cost reductions on the order of 8 to 12%, but the data on HMOs and its analysis remain incomplete and difficult to interpret. In addition, it is still unclear to what extent managed care organizations have, at least to date, enjoyed positive selection (that is, cover lower-than-average risk populations), although existing evidence suggests that at least some of their savings are due to it.

D. Managed Care as a System: The Market and Profits

The main questions about the developing private sector, in any case, have less to do with cost reductions per se than with the *system* that managed care is part of and is helping to create. Other countries have also become interested in managed care—for example, the Netherlands, the United Kingdom, and some Scandinavian nations—as a means of reducing their (far lower) health care costs. They are implementing elements of managed care, however, within a very different financial and provider system, and the effects will be quite different as well. It is important, therefore, to specify the conditions under which managed care will operate if we are to understand it better.

The emerging managed care system operates in a world with little true public regulation regarding its nature and aims, in particular its social aims. Employers continue to exercise significant power over the system. Hundreds of billions of dollars continue to flow through it, in spite of cost containment efforts, which, at most, have only slowed down the rate of growth. All parties are now in competition with each other. Finally, risk-sharing pools continue to be narrowed.

In these circumstances, the movement toward managed care has had major effects on the organization of health care financing and delivery of care. Among these effects has been a pronounced movement toward mergers, acquisitions, and alliances among financing organizations, and, in particular, provider organizations. For most participants in the health care system, "bigger is better" in that larger size provides negotiating power to organizations that once did not have to compete to any great extent and the ability to retain "market share." It also provides greater access to capital markets, in a world in which public and community-based philanthropic bodies no longer provide capital funds directly or guarantee their repayment to investors.

Of especial importance has been the growing trend for each risk pool to insist on paying for the health care costs of its own members and for no one else. This has been particularly pronounced among employers and the insurers and managed care companies who compete for their premium dollars. To the degree they could, they have used their power to lower the prices *they* pay for health care services.

Other factors associated with the American managed care "revolution" strengthen these tendencies. Competition, by pitting all players against all others, forces participants to seek patients or group members who are lower in risk and are covered by insurance of some sort if they are to survive. The need to generate surplus from direct operations and a rapidly declining capacity to shift costs among payers also renders it difficult or impossible for providers or insurers to continue to subsidize losing "lines of business" such as the uninsured or underinsured.

Providers are increasingly unable, therefore, to muster the funds to treat the uninsured and underinsured. Under community rating, as we have seen, and even under the original version of experience rating, payers cross-subsidized—provided a cushion of funding—to help undewrite the care of the latter two groups. The effect of the present system, however, is to curtail the sharing of financial risk still further and to offer providers disincentives for undertaking charity care.

Consequently, even not-for-profit institutions (especially hospitals) must increasingly act as if they are for-profit, because failure to do so only ensures loss of competitive edge and possible bankruptcy. This has led many such institutions to shift from not-for-profit status to for-profit status. For some, this has been the only way to survive.

E. Managed Care: The Major Questions

The major questions raised by the new system of managed care are: Can a system that is increasingly fragmented, profit-oriented, and competitive succeed in controlling costs, in providing high-quality care to the *entire* population, and in spreading the costs of care fairly among the population? Will the high-risk, sicker parts of the population now become undesirable to *both* insurers and providers? Who will take care of the uninsured and how? What forms of public intervention—both regulatory and financial—will be necessary to ensure that the emerging system carries out both its private and its social aims? What roles will "consumers" of health care, citizens in general, and community-oriented institutions have in the new system?

IV. ETHICAL IMPLICATIONS

In general, the U.S. system demonstrates a tension inherent in meeting a broad social need through a largely private system whose nature and internal development is determined by profitability and cost issues. The most striking aspects of this tension include the desire of each payer to avoid sharing costs with others, as well as the related need of the parts of the system to exclude or reduce benefits to those most in need of health care. It remains problematic whether such a system, so divided, can serve as an efficient, cost-effective *and* fair mechanism for providing access to medical care for the entire community of Americans.

From the forgoing discussion we can raise a number

of ethical issues with which the United States, like other industrialized countries, must contend. These issues assume that the United States, like its peers, remains committed to universal access to medical care.

A. Universality

A fair health care system must develop financial mechanisms to make health care services available to all who need it. Universal access implies universal inclusion in those financial mechanisms. Moreover, any system of health financing must be universal if the costs and benefits of the system are to be spread as widely as possible—broad risk sharing—and if proper controls over cost are to be put into place.

B. Access

A fair health care system must reduce or eliminate barriers that hinder access to medical care, including those that remain once universal financial mechanisms have been put into place. Nonfinancial barriers include regional or institutional shortfalls in equipment, personnel, training facilities, and transportation; but also may include cultural, linguistic, racial, or class differences that make it difficult for individuals or groups to negotiate the health care system. Whatever financing approach the United States develops to achieve universal coverage, the nonfinancial barriers will remain and require long-term resolution.

C. Equitable Financing

Any reformed system must be financed in a fair and equitable manner that puts no undue burden on those with greater need for medical services. Ideally, an equitable financing system would be based on the principle of community rating (equal premiums or other types of payments for equivalent or similar benefit packages), adjusted by income to ensure that wealthier people pay more and less wealthy pay less. This avoids one of the perceived problems of pure community rating, that often in such a system, the low-risk but poor will be unfairly subsidizing the high-risk but well off.

D. Open Enrollment and Risk Adjustment

Assuming the United States will continue to have a system of multiple pools of insured individuals, certain mechanisms must exist in order to achieve fair, equitable financing. First, all pools must be open to enrollment by all persons in the geographical areas covered by them without medical underwriting or other attempts to discriminate among risk statuses. Only in this manner can we begin to ensure that pools attract a more-or-less random selection of health risks.

If there are multiple pools, then there must be some method of risk adjustment to ensure that the pools are relatively equal in risk status and fiscal soundness. Due to differences in the risk status of populations by geographical area, social class, gender, race, ethnicity, employment status, and other demographic characteristics, multiple pools will tend to attract a different mix of high- and low-risk persons. Risk adjustment systems can either be "front-end" systems that provide revenues to pools adjusted for the risk status of their members or "back-end" systems that shift funds from one pool to another after a benefit period, once actual medical utilization is known. In either case, they prevent premiums or benefits from varying excessively among pools. Risk adjustment is especially necessary for reform proposals that are based on competition among health plans, in which plans might reduce costs and charge lower prices by avoiding high-risk enrollees.

E. Uniform Benefits

A fair health care system should assure a uniform, standard benefits package. This provision is not only a question of equity, however. It would also prevent health plans in a multipool environment from decreasing benefits in order to attract only better risks or to lower their costs directly by reducing utilization.

The comprehensiveness of the benefits package should be a matter of debate and public consensus. Although most societies favor as wide a package as possible, financing medical care reduces funding for other services, some of which—like housing—may also affect health. Given finite resources, a fair health care system will also evaluate the effectiveness of medical procedures and technology in order to prevent wasting money.

F. Social Control and Accountability

Under the current system, responses to the crucial questions adumbrated above are made by employers, insurers, providers, and other insular interests, including a burgeoning health care bureaucracy. Lacking are prescribed, meaningful public loci of control or accountability. Many countries, for example, legislate overall health policy, including who is covered, what constitutes the benefit package, and sources of revenue; direct representatives of the public then negotiate with professional groups over specific issues (like physicians' fees) that deeply affect the health care system. All such actions are visible and political, with elected officials ultimately held responsible. Such mechanisms may take many forms. In the United States they may provide greater or lesser roles for competition and the market. Ultimately, they should, however, constitute (1) an effective set of rules, provided or sanctioned by the government and the public, by which the entire system operates and (2) institutions that allow those operations to be held up to public scrutiny and accountability.

Also See the Following Articles

ETHICS AND SOCIAL SERVICES, OVERVIEW • MEDICAL ETHICS, HISTORY OF • RESOURCE ALLOCATION

Bibliography

Aaron, H. J. (1991). *Serious and unstable condition: Financing America's health care.* Washington, DC: Brookings Institution.
Beauchamp, D. E. (1988). *The health of the Republic: Epidemics, medicine, and moralism as challenges to democracy.* Philadelphia, PA: Temple University Press.
Daniels, N., Light D. W., & Caplan, R. L. (1996). *Benchmarks of fairness for health care reform.* New York and Oxford: Oxford University Press.
Enthoven, A. C. (1993). The history and principles of managed competition. *Health Affairs,* 12, Supplement, pp. 24–48.
Glaser, W. A. (1991). *Health insurance in practice: International variations in financing, benefits, and problems.* San Francisco, CA: Jossey-Bass.
Moon, M. (1993). *Medicare now and in the future.* Washington, DC: Urban Institute Press.
Starr, P. (1982). *The social transformation of American medicine: The rise of a sovereign profession and the making of a vast industry.* New York: Basic Books.
United States Congress, Office of Technology Assessment. (1988). *Medical testing and health insurance* (OTA-H-384). Washington, DC: U.S. Government Printing Office.
Weissman, J. S., & Epstein, A. M., (1994). *Falling through the safety net: Insurance status and access to health care.* Baltimore, MD: Johns Hopkins University Press.
White, J. (1995). *Competing solutions: American health care proposals and international experience.* Washington, DC: The Brookings Institution.

HEDONISM

John J. Tilley
Indiana University/Purdue University at Indianapolis

GLOSSARY

ancient hedonism A general term for the normative views of the Cyrenaic and Epicurean philosophers. The Cyrenaics flourished in the fourth century B.C.; the Epicureans in the two centuries following that one. Both groups prescribed pleasure as the goal of life, but they held different views about the essence of pleasure and about the best way to obtain it.

axiological hedonism A theory of intrinsic value, with two core components: first, all pleasure is intrinsically good; and second, nothing but pleasure is intrinsically good.

crude hedonism The view that the best life is a life devoted to pleasure, especially sensual pleasure. Crude hedonism is not an implication of axiological, psychological, or ethical hedonism.

ethical hedonism The view that the moral rightness or wrongness of an act is a function of the pleasure the act produces. This view is logically distinct from axiological hedonism.

extrinsic value The value possessed by a thing owing to its relations to other things of value. For instance, a thing has extrinsic value if it results in, or is a means to, something else of value. Unlike intrinsic value, extrinsic value vanishes if the thing in which it resides is viewed in total abstraction from everything else. (Here and elsewhere, "thing" is used in its broadest sense. It extends not only to tables and chairs, but to pleasure, pain, knowledge, justice, and so forth.)

genetic hedonism The view that all of our present desires arose originally from our desire for pleasure.

instrumental value A type of extrinsic value. A thing has instrumental value insofar as serves as a means to something else of value.

intrinsic value The value a thing possesses insofar as it is valuable *in itself,* taken in abstraction from everything else, including its effects and its accompaniments. Intrinsic value contrasts with extrinsic value, but the two do not exclude each other. A single thing can have both kinds of value.

nonhedonist A person who rejects hedonism. The term is usually used for those who reject axiological hedonism. Some of the latter are *monists* in that they think there is a single intrinsic good, a good that is not pleasure. Others are *pluralists* in that they think there are two or more intrinsic goods, at least one of which is not pleasure. Possible intrinsic goods include (in addition to pleasure) life, love, virtue, justice, beauty, friendship, and knowledge. Some prominent nonhedonists are Plato (428–348 B.C.), Aristotle (384–322 B.C.), Kant (1724–1804), T. H. Green (1836–1882), F. H. Bradley (1846–1924), G. E. Moore (1873–1958), and W. D. Ross (1877–1971).

paradox of hedonism The fact that the single-minded pursuit of pleasure is self-defeating. Often the best way to obtain pleasure is to seek things *other* than pleasure, for example, love, success, and friendship.

prospect hedonism The view that human beings are so constituted that whenever they act, they opt for the alternative the *thought* of which gives them the most pleasure. If the thought of doing D is more pleasing to me than the thought of doing D', and my sole options are D and D', I am sure to do D.

psychological egoism The view that everyone is actuated, ultimately, by nothing but self-interest. Whenever a person acts, her ultimate aim is only to promote her *own* survival, her *own* pleasure, her *own* self-esteem, and so on.

psychological hedonism A version of psychological egoism. It asserts that every purposive human act is motivated, ultimately, by the agent's desire for pleasure—his *own* pleasure.

qualitative hedonism A brand of axiological hedonism according to which the intrinsic value of a pleasure increases with the quantity and *quality* of the pleasure, not with its quantity alone.

quantitative hedonism A brand of axiological hedonism according to which the intrinsic value of a pleasure varies directly, and solely, with the *quantity* of pleasure.

HEDONISM derives its name from the Greek word "hedone," meaning pleasure. It comes in three versions: *axiological hedonism*, according to which pleasure is the sole thing of intrinsic value; *psychological hedonism*, according to which every purposive act is prompted ultimately by the desire for pleasure; and *ethical hedonism*, according to which the moral rightness of an act is a function of the pleasure the act produces. Each version has been held by distinguished philosophers. For example, all three versions were held by Aristippus (435–356 B.C.), Epicurus (342–270 B.C.), Claude-Adrien Helvétius (1715–1771), Jeremy Bentham (1748–1832), James Mill (1773–1836), and John Stuart Mill (1806–1873). For reasons stated in Section II, this article touches only briefly on ethical hedonism, and concentrates on axiological hedonism and psychological hedonism. It begins, however, with a few words about hedonism in ancient times.

I. ANCIENT HEDONISM

"Ancient hedonism" refers to the normative views of the Cyrenaic and Epicurean schools of philosophy. The Cyrenaics flourished in the fourth century B.C.; the Epicureans in the two centuries following that one. The members of these schools not only accepted axiological, psychological, and ethical hedonism, but held detailed views about the best way to achieve a pleasurable life. The Cyrenaics were followers of Aristippus, a student of Socrates who broke with his teacher's philosophy to found his own school in Cyrene, on the coast of North Africa. The Cyrenaics not only prescribed pleasure as the goal of life, but recommended intense, physical, immediate pleasures as those especially to be pursued. (There were exceptions, however. One of them was Hegesias, who stressed the avoidance of pain rather than the active pursuit of pleasure.) This approach to life is famously criticized in Plato's *Philebus*.

The Epicurean school, founded by Epicurus in Athens, identified pleasure with "freedom from pain in the body and from trouble in the mind" (Epicurus, *Letter to Menoeceus*), and taught that the Cyrenaic mode of life was not the best way to obtain pleasure. The Epicureans recommended moderation, rational self-control, and the avoidance of all vain (as opposed to natural) pleasures, especially those most likely bring pain or the loss of mental tranquillity. They recommended these things not as an alternative to seeking pleasure, but as the best way to achieve a genuinely pleasant life. Clearly, the Epicureans were not "epicureans" in the modern sense. Their lives tended toward the ascetic, not toward "pleasure seeking" as it is usually understood.

II. ETHICAL HEDONISM

According to this thesis, whether an act is morally right is a function of the pleasure the act produces (where the function is such that morally right actions are pleasure-*promoting* actions, not pleasure-*diminishing* ones). There are many possible brands of this thesis, depending on how the function in question is specified, and on whose pleasure is relevant. The most common brands are *hedonistic ethical egoism*, according to which an act is right just in case it produces at least as much pleasure for the agent who performs it as any other act available to the agent; and *hedonistic act utilitarianism*, according to which an act is right just in case it produces at least as much pleasure—never mind *whose* pleasure, just pleasure, period—as anything else the agent could do instead.

The first of these views is generally thought to be far less plausible than the second. Indeed, it seems clear that morality and self-gratification can diverge, that what's morally right is not always the same as what maximizes personal pleasure. The second of the two views, hedonistic act utilitarianism, not only is more plausible than the first, but is a serious contender among moral theories. In this article, however, its strengths and weaknesses will not be discussed. This is because utilitarianism is covered elsewhere in this encyclopedia, and because in recent decades the word "hedonism" has been used primarily for psychological hedonism and axiological hedonism. Nowadays, we seldom find it used for a theory of right and wrong.

III. AXIOLOGICAL HEDONISM

A. The Components of Axiological Hedonism

Axiological hedonism is not a theory about the rightness or wrongness of actions, although it figures centrally in many such theories (e.g., Bentham's and J. S. Mill's). It is a theory about intrinsic value, with two core components:

1. Every pleasure has intrinsic value.
2. Nothing but pleasure has intrinsic value.

The word "pleasure" is here understood to include the absence of pain.

Many axiological hedonists (e.g., Bentham), those called *quantitative hedonists,* add the following to (1) and (2):

3. The greater the *quantity* of pleasure, the greater the intrinsic value of the pleasure. More precisely, the intrinsic value of a pleasure varies directly, and solely, with the quantity of pleasure.

But other axiological hedonists (e.g., J. S. Mill) reject (3), maintaining that intrinsic value increases according to the quantity and *quality* of the pleasure, not according to its quantity alone. These hedonists are called *qualitative hedonists.*

A thing has intrinsic value just in case it is valuable in itself, taken in abstraction from everything else, including its results and the ends it promotes. Money has value, but its value is extrinsic rather than intrinsic. It has no value in itself, taken in abstraction from the things we can buy with it and from the satisfaction many receive from acquiring it. In fact, most things of value have only extrinsic value—this is an uncontentious claim that few would deny. Axiological hedonists go a step further and contend that *nothing but pleasure* has intrinsic value. Many other things—for example, life, truth, and beauty—have value, but unlike pleasure, they have no intrinsic value. Axiological hedonists add

to this that *all* pleasures have intrinsic value, including, say, sadistic ones. No doubt sadistic pleasures are normally bad or undesirable, for they contribute to behavior that is pleasure-diminishing for one or more people. This simply means that they are extrinsically bad; it does not refute the claim that they are good *in themselves,* taken in abstraction from everything else. A pleasure can be extrinsically bad (or good) while also being, as all pleasures are, intrinsically good.

B. Common Mistakes about Axiological Hedonism

We must avoid five common errors about axiological hedonism. The first is that of assuming, rather than arguing, that axiological hedonism is about *happiness*—that is, that it's the view that happiness alone has intrinsic value. The latter view is the same as axiological hedonism only if happiness can be identified with pleasure. Many philosophers have argued, plausibly, that the two cannot be identified. Pigeons no doubt feel pleasure, but it's unlikely that pigeons experience happiness. Happiness would seem to require cognitive capacities of a sophisticated sort, capacities that pigeons are unlikely to have. Pleasure, on the other hand, can be experienced by any creature capable of having pleasant physical sensations. This is not to say that "pleasure" refers merely to such sensations. Many philosophers, including many axiological hedonists, would argue that it extends to pleasant experiences or to the hedonic tone—the pleasantness—of such experiences, where neither the experiences nor their pleasantness can be reduced entirely to physical sensations. Also, axiological hedonists treat the *absence of pain* as a form or component of pleasure. They do so by stretching the word "pleasure" just enough to include the absence of pain. In their view this is only a slight stretch, because pain is the opposite of pleasure, just as *east* is the opposite of *west.*

The second error consists of assuming that axiological hedonism is our sole option if we have a scientific outlook—that is, that any view of intrinsic value other than axiological hedonism is somehow unscientific or unempirical. The view that *desire-satisfaction* has intrinsic value fits well with a scientific outlook (partly because desires have a place in the explanatory apparatus of many social sciences), but it conflicts with axiological hedonism. To satisfy a desire is simply to bring about the state of affairs the desire has as its object. For instance, to satisfy my desire to have only one foot I need only cut off a foot, thereby bringing it about *that I have only one foot.* Often, but not always, the satisfaction of the desire produces pleasure, but even when it does, it is not the *same* as pleasure. So the view that desire-satisfaction is intrinsically good is not the view that pleasure is intrinsically good. The general point here is that a person can be a staunch empiricist while holding a nonhedonistic view of intrinsic value.

The third error is that of charging axiological hedonists with the view that our chief aim should be to produce pleasure, either for ourselves or for others. (An even grosser error consists of charging axiological hedonists with the view that our chief interest should be our *own* pleasure. Axiological hedonism is about pleasure *per se,* without regard to *who* experiences it.) The claim that pleasure alone has intrinsic value entails no view about what our chief aims should be. Even if we assume that our aims should be tailored to bring pleasure into the world, axiological hedonism does not imply that we should make the production of pleasure our chief aim. Perhaps the best way to bring pleasure into the world, either for ourselves or for others, is to put pleasure out of our minds and strive directly for such things as peace, knowledge, and friendship—that is, for things *other* than pleasure. This view is compatible with axiological hedonism.

The fourth and fifth errors were touched on in Section A. The fourth is that of thinking that axiological hedonism is about the *sources* of pleasure. According to axiological hedonists, it's not the sources of pleasure—the cognac, the hot bath, the weekend at the beach—that have intrinsic value. Rather, it's the resulting *pleasure* that has such value. More precisely, it is pleasure alone, whatever its source, that has intrinsic value.

The fifth error consists of thinking that according to axiological hedonism, nothing but pleasure has value. Axiological hedonists grant that many things besides pleasure, including many painful things (e.g., tonsillectomies), have value. But they insist that such things have only *extrinsic* value, that pleasure alone has *intrinsic* value. A tonsillectomy has value because it prevents future pain. In other words, it contributes to the *absence of pain,* which is a species or component of pleasure.

C. Arguments for Axiological Hedonism

Arguments 1–4, below, are representative of those used by axiological hedonists. They are arranged in order of increasing credibility. Argument 1 is very weak; argument 2 is only slightly better. Argument 3 is an improvement over 1 and 2; and argument 4 is plausible even if not decisive.

Argument 1 (adapted from Bentham):

(1) "Good" and "pleasurable" are synonymous; so the statement, "Pleasure, and pleasure alone, is intrinsically good" means the same as "Pleasure, and pleasure alone, is intrinsically pleasurable."
(2) Obviously, the sole thing that's intrinsically pleasurable is pleasure itself. In other words, pleasure, and pleasure alone, is intrinsically pleasurable.
(3) Thus (from (1) and (2)), pleasure, and pleasure alone, is intrinsically good.

The first problem with this argument is that premise (2) requires clarification. The term "intrinsically pleasurable" has no familiar meaning; it is not an item of ordinary language. A more serious problem is that premise (1) is false. The word "good" does not mean "pleasurable." Nor does it mean "productive of pleasure." Those who say, "Fairness is good, even when it produces no pleasure," are guilty neither of a contradiction nor of a misuse of language. Perhaps they are guilty of a mistake, but that's another point.

Argument 2 (adapted from chapter 4 of J. S. Mill's *Utilitarianism*):

(1) Happiness is the sole thing people desire for its own sake.
(2) If happiness is the sole thing people desire for its own sake, we have sufficient proof that happiness is the sole thing capable of being desired for its own sake.
(3) "Capable of being desired" means the same as "desirable." So rather than saying that happiness is the sole thing capable of being desired for its own sake, we can say that happiness is the sole thing that's *desirable* for its own sake, which in turn means that it's the sole thing that's intrinsically desirable.
(4) "Desirable" and "good" are interchangeable. So rather than saying that happiness is the sole thing that's intrinsically desirable, we can say that it's the sole thing that's intrinsically good.
(5) Therefore (from (1) through (4)), happiness is the sole thing that's intrinsically good.
(6) Happiness is nothing other than pleasure.
(7) Therefore (from (5) and (6)), pleasure is the sole thing that's intrinsically good.

This argument contains at least two doubtful premises: (1) and (6). Even if we ignore those premises, the argument contains falsehoods unless "desirable" has a different meaning in (4) than it has in (3). In premise (3) it means "capable of being desired." In premise (4) it means "worthy of being desired"; otherwise it is not a stand-in for "good." But if "desirable" has a different meaning in (4) than it has in (3), argument 2 is invalid.

Argument 3 (based on a second, more charitable, look at chapter 4 of Mill's *Utilitarianism*):

(1) Happiness is the sole thing people desire for its own sake.
(2) Although principles concerning what is or is not intrinsically good cannot be proven in a strict sense, they can be shown to be *reasonably acceptable,* meaning acceptable to reasonable and honest people. It is reasonable to accept the principle, "*X* is intrinsically good" if and only if we sincerely desire *X* for its own sake.
(3) Thus, given (1) and (2), it is reasonable to accept the principle that happiness is intrinsically good; it is not reasonable to accept the claim that things other than happiness are intrinsically good. In short, it is reasonable to accept this: "Happiness is the sole thing that's intrinsically good."
(4) Happiness is nothing other than pleasure.
(5) Thus, given (3) and (4), it is reasonable to accept the principle, "Pleasure is the sole thing that's intrinsically good."

Argument 3 does not equivocate on any key terms; in that sense it improves on argument 2. Unfortunately, it contains at least two doubtful premises, namely, (1) and (4). In that respect it is no better than argument 2.

Argument 4 (attributable to R. M. Blake [1889–1950]):

(1) Surely *some* pleasures are intrinsically good. Or if "surely" is too strong a word here, at least this is true: Some pleasures *seem,* upon reflection, to be intrinsically good, and we have no reason to think we are deceived by appearances here.
(2) It is plausible to think this: (a) We can account for the apparent lack of goodness in some pleasures without denying that they have *intrinsic* goodness. Point (a) is plausible because (b) we find upon reflection that whenever a pleasure appears to lack value, this appearance changes if we carefully abstract the pleasure from its effects and accompaniments. For instance, sadistic pleasure seems to lack value, but when we isolate

such pleasure from everything that usually goes with it, including the sadistic deeds to which it contributes, it then seems to have value. The evil that seemed to reside in the pleasure is left behind in the process of abstraction, because it actually resides in things that accompany or result from the pleasure, not in the pleasure itself.
(3) It is also plausible to think this: (c) We can account for the value of things other than pleasure—for example, truth and beauty—without assuming that things other than pleasure have intrinsic value. Point (c) is plausible because (d) we find upon reflection that whenever a thing other than pleasure appears to be valuable, this appearance fades away when the thing is carefully abstracted from the pleasures that accompany or result from it. For instance, beauty appears to have value, but this appearance entirely fades when we consider beauty itself, in abstraction from every pleasure—past, present, and future—that might accompany or result from beauty. The value that seemed to reside in beauty actually resides elsewhere: in the pleasures to which beauty contributes.
(4) Given (1)–(3), it is reasonable to conclude that every pleasure, and nothing but pleasure, is intrinsically valuable.

Although Argument 4 is stronger than 1–3, it contains at least two premises that many philosophers question. These are (2b) and (3d), which essentially say that reflection supports axiological hedonism, where "reflection" refers to thought experiments concerning pleasure and value. Whether thought experiments make hedonism plausible depends on *who* is doing the experiments; thus, argument 4 falls short of *establishing* axiological hedonism. By the same token, antihedonistic arguments that rest on thought experiments do not disprove axiological hedonism. This is one of the key points made by proponents of argument 4.

This is the place to mention a thought experiment made famous by Robert Nozick (1939–). It is widely thought to undermine axiological hedonism. Suppose we can float in a tank the rest of our lives, our brains wired to an *experience machine.* This machine is designed to substitute pseudo-experiences for actual experiences. If we submit to this treatment, we will have no memory of being wired to the machine, and our pseudo-experiences will seem entirely real to us. Suppose also that a "life" on the machine consists entirely of pleasurable pseudo-experiences, the result being a period devoid of pain and filled with far more pleasure than any actual life could be. Would we consent to being wired to the machine? If the answer is no, perhaps this shows that we are not hedonists, that we find intrinsic value in things other than pleasure. We value *doing* certain things and *being* certain kinds of people, and we do so not merely as a means to pleasure. That is why a life floating in a tank, whether pleasurable or not, strikes us as valueless.

D. Problems and Questions for Axiological Hedonists

The first problem, obviously, is that of producing a compelling argument for axiological hedonism, an argument capable of persuading nonhedonists. No one has produced such an argument, but axiological hedonism has a surface plausibility that invites further attempts. The second problem is that of establishing the reality of intrinsic, as opposed to merely extrinsic, value. Some philosophers, notably John Dewey (1859–1952), Sidney Hook (1902–1989), Abraham Kaplan (1918–1993), and Monroe Beardsley (1915–1985), have argued that all value is extrinsic, that nothing has value in complete abstraction from everything else. The third problem is that of quantifying pleasures. The question, Can pleasure be quantified, and if so, how? has produced plenty of thought but little consensus, even among quantitative hedonists.

The third problem should not be overestimated. Perhaps we cannot determine whether two glasses of beer is *twice* as pleasurable as one glass, but we surely can determine whether it is *more* pleasurable. (The example is from E. F. Carritt, *Ethical and Political Thinking*, 1947.) In this case and many others, we can usefully compare two pleasures without the need of any calculus. This is not true in many other cases, especially those in which the two pleasures differ greatly in kind.

Nor should we underestimate the problem by assuming that it can be solved merely by embracing *qualitative* hedonism. Qualitative hedonists do not deny that the intrinsic value of a pleasure varies with its quantity; their point is simply that quality enters the picture as well. Also, qualitative hedonism has problems of its own. For example, E. F. Carritt (1876–1964) compares the qualitative hedonist to the person who says, "I value nothing but money, but I would not come by it dishonestly." Such a person clearly values *honesty* as well as money. Likewise, if a person says that given two pleasures of the same quantity, the one with the higher quality is the more intrinsically valuable of the two, he implies that pleasure is not the sole thing of intrinsic value. This to abandon axiological hedonism.

Or so argues Carritt. His criticism is a standard one, echoing earlier ones by F. H. Bradley and G. E. Moore, and appearing routinely in ethics texts. Whether it ultimately succeeds—that is, whether it's impossible to reconcile the view that (a) nothing but pleasure is intrinsically good with the view that (b) quality must be included in the measurement of a pleasure's intrinsic goodness—is still debated. (See, e.g., the book by Donner in the bibliography.) One thing for sure is that Carritt's criticism must be overcome, or else qualitative hedonism is in trouble.

A fourth problem, closely related to the third, is that of answering the question, What exactly is pleasure? There is no agreement on this issue among axiological hedonists. The problem is complicated by the hedonist's use of "pleasure" so that it extends not only to pleasure as it is usually conceived, but to something quite different, namely, the absence of pain. That these two things differ, that pleasure and pain are not on par like *east* and *west,* is reflected in ordinary language. It makes sense to say, "I'm in pain," which invites from others the question, "Where does it hurt?" But it makes no sense to say, "I'm in pleasure"; the appropriate statement is "I'm experiencing pleasure" or "I find this to be pleasant." And neither of those statements invites the question, "Where does it feel good?" A person who takes pleasure in skydiving cannot *locate* the pleasure in question, indicating that pleasure either is not simply a feeling, or is not a feeling on par with pain.

A natural reply here is that we can revise axiological hedonism along the following lines:

Exactly two things are intrinsically good, neither of which can be reduced to the other. The first is pleasure, whatever its kind or source; the second is the absence of pain.

This thesis is not open to the charge that it puts pleasure and pain on par. The problem, however, is that it makes axiological hedonism a pluralistic, rather than a monistic, theory of intrinsic value. This is a problem because most axiological hedonists see monism not only as an essential element of their theory, but as one of its greatest advantages. If all value can be accounted for in terms of one thing of intrinsic value, then the values of widely different experiences can be compared without much trouble—or so it is commonly thought. But comparisons become difficult if two or more incommensurable things are acknowledged to have intrinsic value.

IV. PSYCHOLOGICAL HEDONISM

A. The Thesis of Psychological Hedonism

The term "psychological hedonism" traditionally refers to the view that every act is prompted, ultimately, by the agent's desire for pleasure (where "pleasure" is understood to include the absence of pain). I say "traditionally" rather than "always," because the term sometimes extends not only to the view just stated, but to various others, including *genetic hedonism,* the view that each of our present desires arose originally from our desire for pleasure; and *prospect hedonism,* the view that whenever we act, we opt for the alternative the *thought* of which gives us the most pleasure. These views differ from the initial one. For example, genetic hedonists can admit that many of our desires are neither egoistic nor concerned with pleasure. Genetic hedonism is about the *origin* of desires, not about their objects or content.

Likewise, prospect hedonists can grant that when Brenda chooses to help Tom rather than to help herself, her ultimate aim is *to help Tom.* She is not helping Tom simply as a means of obtaining pleasure. But if the thought of helping Tom had not been more pleasing than the thought of helping herself, her desire to help Tom would not have won out over her desire to help herself. It would not have become her operative desire, the desire from which she acted. The desire to do *D* becomes operative only if the *thought* of doing *D* is more pleasing than the thought of doing *D'*, more pleasing than the thought of doing *D''*, and so on. This does not mean, however, that the desire to do *D* is a desire for pleasure.

From here on, "psychological hedonism" has its traditional meaning. It refers to this thesis:

> The sole ultimate motive of every purposive human act is the agent's desire for pleasure—her *own* pleasure.

Psychological hedonism is a version of the following view, known as *psychological egoism:*

> Every purposive human act is motivated, ultimately, by the agent's desire for his *own* pleasure, his *own* survival, his *own* advantage, and so on. In short, everyone is actuated, ultimately, by nothing but self-interest.

It is worth noting that although psychological hedonism is held by many philosophers who accept ethical or axiological hedonism, it is logically distinct from those views. Indeed, many of its most insistent critics are axiological or ethical hedonists. An example is Frank Chapman Sharp (1866–1943), whose book *Ethics* (1928) contains a well-known defense of axiological hedonism, and an equally well-known *criticism* of psychological hedonism.

Also worth noting is that psychological hedonism implies none of the following: (1) people do nothing that benefits others; (2) people receive no pleasure from benefiting others; (3) people desire nothing but pleasure; and (4) people are well aware that their deeds spring ultimately from a desire for pleasure. Psychological hedonism does not imply (1) or (2) because although it says that our ultimate goal is pleasure, it says nothing about how we try to attain that goal or about what does or does not produce pleasure. No doubt some people receive pleasure from helping others; so we can expect their desire for pleasure to prompt other-directed actions. Psychological hedonism does not imply (3) because it accommodates the view that people have *subordinate* desires for things other than pleasure. Brenda indeed wants to help Tom, but it's also true that if Brenda were perfectly insightful and honest about her motives, she would agree that she wants to help Tom *as a means of obtaining pleasure.* Her desire to help Tom is subordinate to her desire for pleasure, the latter being her only nonsubordinate (i.e., ultimate) desire. Finally, psychological hedonism does not imply (4) because it accommodates the view that people are skilled at deceiving themselves about their ultimate motives.

B. Arguments for Psychological Hedonism

Psychological hedonism has long been attractive to those who think that cynicism is a badge of social or scientific sophistication. Attractive or not, it is hard to establish. There are two common arguments for it, neither of which is effective.

> *First argument for P.H.:* When we examine our behavior, we often find that our sole motive is to obtain pleasure. Also, when we successfully complete an action, we invariably obtain some pleasure. Taking these facts separately or together, it is reasonable to conclude that every time we act, we do so solely to obtain pleasure.

> *Second argument for P.H.:* Psychological egoism is true, and psychological hedonism is the most

plausible brand of psychological egoism. So we should accept psychological hedonism.

To see the flaws in the first argument, let us number the premises and discuss them in turn:

(1) We often act solely to obtain pleasure.
(2) Whenever we successfully complete an action, we obtain some pleasure.

Premise (1) is true, but it does not warrant the conclusion that we *always* act to obtain pleasure. Such reasoning is similar to thinking, "I often act to obtain chocolate; thus, whenever I act, I do so to obtain some chocolate."

Premise (2) is false. I do not *always* receive pleasure from a successfully performed action. Instead, I receive some *desire-satisfaction*. Because of this, it is easy to think that *I* receive some satisfaction, meaning that I get some pleasure. But there is a confusion here between *satisfying a desire* and *satisfying the person who has the desire*. To satisfy a desire—to "receive some desire-satisfaction"—I need only bring about the state of affairs my desire has as its object. For instance, if I want to die by electrocution, or more precisely, if I want it to be the case *that I die by electrocution*, my desire will be satisfied if that state of affairs is brought about—that is, if I am electrocuted. But I will experience no pleasure when that happens.

Even if premise (2) were true it would not support psychological hedonism. Premise (2) says that whenever I complete an action, I receive some pleasure. This does not imply that whenever I perform an action, I do so to receive pleasure. Think of it this way: Whenever Jim goes home for a visit, he receives a lecture from his mother (on why it's important to attend church on Sunday, and to change his socks regularly). This does not imply that whenever Jim goes home for a visit, he does so to receive a lecture from his mother.

Does psychological hedonism follow from (1) and (2) *combined?* It does not. The view that it does is analogous to the following line of thought, which is plainly fallacious: Because all ships burn coal when they go to sea, and because some ships go to sea to burn their coal (i.e., to *test* their coal), it follows that anytime a ship puts out to sea it does so to consume coal. (The example is from William James, *The Principles of Psychology,* 1890.)

The problem with the second argument for psychological hedonism is that its first premise—that psychological egoism is true—has never been established. Not one of the usual arguments for it is effective. There are at least three such arguments (four actually—one of which we have just discussed):

First argument for P.E.: If we reject egoism we are forced to accept *altruism,* which is an unrealistic, "goody two-shoes" view of human nature. If we are not self-deceptive, if we accept reality, we must grant that people are not angels—and that means accepting egoism.

Second argument for P.E.: Every student of economics knows that people (rational ones, anyway) are *expected utility-maximizers:* they behave in ways that maximize expected utility—their *own* expected utility. That means that people are egoistic. In other words, to deny psychological egoism is to deny that people are utility maximizers, which is to deny a central assumption of economics. But that's grossly unscientific. Thus, if we are scientifically minded we will accept egoism.

Third argument for P.E.: Whenever a person acts, her act is prompted by a desire. But whose desire? A desire of her *own,* of course. For example, if she gives to charity, she does so because *she* wants to. So people are always doing what *they* want to do; they are always acting in their *own* interest. In sum, people are always acting selfishly, even when they seem to be doing otherwise.

The main problem with the first argument is that the antithesis of egoism is not altruism, but simply *nonegoism*—the view that some of our deeds originate from nonselfish desires, meaning desires that are not for our *own* pleasure, our *own* survival, and so on. One way to establish nonegoism would be to show that people sometimes act *maliciously*. That is, they act from a desire to *hurt* others, and not simply as a means of satisfying a more basic, egoistic desire. The ultimate aim of a genuinely malicious deed is the *injury* of another person. Such deeds are as nonselfish as any altruistic one. Thus, if such deeds occur, psychological egoism is false.

The second argument stems from a misunderstanding of the notion of utilty. When economists say that rational people are "utility-maximizers" they do not mean that there is an obtainable *thing* or *feeling* called "utility," and that a rational person strives for as much of it as possible. They mean, roughly, that people act according to their preferences, and that preferences can be numerically measured. This is where the word "utility" enters the picture. Utility is a measure of preference: one thing has a higher utility than another if the relevant person prefers it to the other. So when economists say that people are "utility-maximizers" we should take them to mean, roughly, that people do what they most prefer to do. This is consistent with the assertion that many preferences are unselfish.

The problem with the third argument is that its conclusion—that our behavior is always selfish—could mean either of two things: (a) that we always act from a *selfish* desire, or (b) that we always act from a desire of our *own*. If we read the conclusion as (a), the argument is invalid. The fact that each of my deeds springs from one of *my* desires does not imply that every such deed springs from a *selfish* desire—a desire for *my* pleasure, *my* survival, *my* self-esteem, and so on. Perhaps I have desires for the misery or happiness of others, and such desires cause much of my behavior. This dovetails with the claim that I always do what *I* want to do. The general point is that from the fact that my deeds spring from my own desires, nothing follows about the objects of those desires, and hence about the aims of my actions.

Perhaps we should read the conclusion of the argument as (b). This makes the argument valid, for its conclusion is now a restatement of its central premise. But the conclusion no longer warrants the name "egoism." For it is now compatible with the view that people sometimes act from nonselfish desires, and the latter view is the thesis of *nonegoism*. In other words, to read the conclusion as (b) is to allow the possibility that although people always act from their own desires, some of those desires have as their ultimate object something other than the agent's *own* pleasure, survival, and so on. So the argument no longer supports psychological egoism.

Perhaps the egoist will retort, "But who are *you* to say what 'psychological egoism' means! For me it means the view that people are moved by their *own* desires—for example, that Alf's deeds always spring from *Alf's* motives, not from anyone else's. So my thesis is clearly true."

Indeed it is, but only because it swallows up the opposing thesis. The egoist has defined his view so that most any brand of nonegoism will count as a form of "egoism." When the nonegoist says that people are sometimes moved by other-directed motives, the egoist

will reply: "Fine, but as long as those motives are *their* motives, then you're not opposing my thesis. To oppose it, you must claim that some acts spring from motives that are not the *agent's* motives. Surely you wouldn't claim anything so silly; so you're a psychological egoist, just like me."

This seems clever, but it isn't. It amounts to defining "psychological egoism" so that it extends to virtually every view of motivation, including the view generally known as nonegoism. It amounts to *ignoring* the contrast between egoism and nonegoism, which is a far cry from *refuting* nonegoism. Indeed, the style of reasoning it exhibits is classified as an informal fallacy. It's called the fallacy of *lost contrast,* or of the *suppressed correlative.*

We have been considering the second argument for psychological hedonism, the first premise of which is that psychological egoism is true. We have considered three common arguments for that premise, not one of which is effective. Unless better arguments are forthcoming, psychological egoism is unestablished, and hence the second argument for psychological hedonism is questionable. Thus, we have seen no compelling argument for psychological hedonism.

Also See the Following Articles

EGOISM AND ALTRUISM • EPICUREANISM • GREEK ETHICS, OVERVIEW • PLATONISM • UTILITARIANISM

Bibliography

Barrett, C. L. (1933). *Ethics: An introduction to the philosophy of moral values.* New York: Harper & Brothers.
Donner, W. (1991). *The liberal self: John Stuart Mill's moral and political philosophy.* Ithaca, NY: Cornell University Press.
Garner, R., & Rosen, B. (1967). *Moral philosophy.* New York: Macmillan.
Pojman, L. (Ed.). (1993). *Moral philosophy: A reader.* Indianapolis: Hackett.
Pojman, L. (1995). *Ethics: Discovering right and wrong* (2d ed.). Belmont, CA: Wadsworth.
Snare, F. (1992). *The nature of moral thinking.* London: Routledge.
Sumner, L. W. (1992). Welfare, happiness, and pleasure. *Utilitas* 4(2), 199–223.
Taylor, P. W. (1975). *Principles of ethics.* Belmont, CA: Wadsworth.
Taylor, P. W. (Ed.). (1978). *Problems of moral philosophy* (3d ed). Belmont, CA: Wadsworth.

HIGHER EDUCATION, ETHICS OF

John R. Wilcox
Manhattan College

GLOSSARY

academic freedom The right accorded tenured faculty to present the truth as that faculty member sees it without fear of dismissal.

American higher education Postsecondary schools consisting of two- and four-year colleges (public or state supported and private, secular and religious) granting associate of arts and baccalaureate degrees, and in some cases master's degrees, as well as universities, which may grant the above degrees and doctoral degrees and which, on several levels, engage in research. (Proprietary or for-profit institutions are not considered in this entry.)

ethics The systematic analysis of the moral life of individuals and groups. The analysis generally utilizes theories developed in the Western philosophical tradition and in Jewish and Christian theological traditions, but may also employ theories developed in other cultures and religious traditions such as Buddhism, Hinduism, or Islam. Among the theories employed are consequentialism, duty, natural law, rights, and virtue ethics.

moral agent Individuals or groups in as much as their actions affect other individuals, groups, species, or the environment.

moral life The actions of individuals and groups (moral agents), insofar as the actions affect the dignity, freedom, and rights of other individuals, groups, species, or the environment. The moral life is the data for ethical analysis.

values Those aspects of life, such as calling or family, to which a person or group gives precedence and that play a major role in decision-making and in the formulation of ethical standards.

THE OVERVIEW OF ETHICS IN HIGHER EDUCA-TION describes the responsibilities colleges and universities, as social institutions, have in American society. The article assumes that there is an implicit social contract or charter whereby higher education is given the right to educate the citizens according to the vision and goals of the larger society. Although the vision and goals are fairly general, colleges and universities are moral agents having the responsibility of achieving these goals. In view of moral agency, ethical analysis is brought to bear on the manner in which higher education fulfills the implicit social contract. Colleges and universities are significant actors in American society with weighty social responsibilities. Thus, ethical reflection on moral agency is not an afterthought. Such analysis goes to the heart of the matter: giving attention to the vision and goals of American society and the manner in which higher education realizes them. At the same time, great weight is given to community in higher education and the call to faculty to create purposeful educational communities and to redefine scholarship in an inclusive fashion.

The ethics of higher education goes far beyond administrative, faculty, or student codes of conduct. Of primary importance is the role of higher education in American society. The fundamental ethical issue centers on the responsibility of higher education for the domestic common good or civic life of a constitutional democracy in an increasingly global community and during a period of rapid change in values and culture.

As a way of indicating the intrinsic connection between society and education, a parable is presented. The story indicates how easily the higher education establishment can negate the implicit social contract, but also how easily society itself can lose sight of its vision and goals. One of the best means of addressing ethical issues is through stories. They are a powerful means of making vivid to the reader the problems a society faces. The reader is engaged by the concreteness of the images, by the invitation to identify the characters and to relate personally to the plot. The following story is a parable for our times. Hopefully, it will provide a shock of recognition for the reader who will identify with several of the actors and with the plot. It will serve as a way of introducing the overview of ethics in higher education.

I. HOW THE LITTLE RED SCHOOL HOUSE BECAME A UNIVERSITY

Over the years, it became clear to the growing population of Cascade Corners that attendance at school led to those children being better workers and being more involved in developing the community and the quality of civic life. Gradually, everyone realized that the settlement would be better off if the children attended school. The school grew in size. More and better-qualified teachers were hired. The school day and year lengthened, and Cascade Corners became a city. More schools were founded and eventually the children spent 16 to 20 years attending them because everyone saw how much the prosperity of the city depended on the educational investment now being made by the community. Schooling was becoming more expensive and taxes were raised, but few objected because it was clearly in everyone's interest.

Gradually, the schools with the oldest students, colleges and universities, came to dominate the other schools. There were good reasons for this. All the teachers in the high schools and elementary schools were educated by the colleges and the universities. Furthermore, the graduates attributed their success to the latter schools and gave them more resources than the lower schools. The fame of the higher-education schools spread far and wide, leading more students to seek admission. The colleges and universities grew very wealthy and decided to move out of Cascade Corners in order to expand on nearby large tracts of land. Some citizens objected but the majority agreed because Cascade Corners attributed its own wealth to the education received at the colleges and universities. The latter were still dependent on the citizens for resources, but some of these institutions had become very powerful and set the standard for the others. In any case, all of them were now autonomous and free to set their own goals.

The administration, faculty, and students at the colleges and universities came to care very little for what went on in the mighty metropolis of Cascade Corners. The chief concern was competing with the other colleges and universities to see who had the best students, the most celebrated faculty, the largest endowment. They also tried to compete by means of their sporting teams. The citizenry of Cascade Corners, bored by their prosperity, found these teams a source of great excitement and diversion. Athletics actually prompted more enthusiasm for higher education.

Enticed by the prosperity of Cascade Corners and its excellent educational system, many new settlers sought entrance into the community and its schools. The prospect of foreigners so different from the citizenry provoked an understandable response: "Keep them separate and let them learn the hard way, as we did." The schools followed the same social policy. After all, the educational institutions did have responsibilities to the citizenry. Nevertheless, some professors and administrators, given to critical thinking about their own institutions, sided with the new arrivals and set up alternative schools for them. Within a generation or two, the newcomers found themselves prospering beyond their wildest imaginings. They were extremely grateful to the professors and administrators because, in large part, they attributed their newfound wealth to the higher education establishment. New state-of-the-art colleges and universities were built. The administrators became very powerful, and the faculty did research and published, becoming the envy of the region. Finally, the descendants of the Cascade Corners' original settlers and schools welcomed the new achievers with open arms.

But then clouds appeared on the horizon. A new wave of immigrants inundated Cascade Corners and the metropolitan region. The part of the world from which they migrated was different from the homelands of either the original settlers or the previous newcomers. There were many of them, and their skin color, language, religion, culture, work ethic, and worldview were in sharp contrast to that of the earlier arrivals. At the same time, a severe economic recession hit the region as well as a growing national debt and repeated budget deficits. Consequently, the financial resources of Cascade Corners and its social safety net were severely tried. Resentment toward the new arrivals reached a feverish pitch. Access to work and education by the new wave of immigrants was drastically curtailed because they did not share the same way of thinking and acting as the earlier groups and, in the eyes of the citizens, would probably not contribute to the development of Cascade Corners. Simultaneously, support for higher education by the citizenry was greatly reduced because of the growing economic problems and the perceived wealth, growing isolation, and seeming irrelevance of colleges and universities. These schools now competed among themselves with growing stridency for the decreasing public monies and students. Large amounts of money were poured into recruiting students and developing sports teams, the latter being a tried-and-true method of obtaining lucrative television contracts and maintaining some good will in Cascade Corners. The citizens also competed for scarce resources and they grew increasingly alienated from public life and the growing bureaucracy of government, which, everyone believed, should pay for education, instead of themselves.

II. CONTEXT

A significant characteristic of late twentieth-century American society is concern for and examination of the ethical foundations of its culture and the several institutions (e.g., business, education, entertainment, the family, finance, government, the media, medicine, religion, science) that shape that culture. This article will identify the central ethical concerns of one of these institutions: higher education. It is the educational vision and goals American society has when chartering the institution of higher education that gives rise to the ethical foundations of that institution. As the parable illustrates, the vision and goals can disappear over the years.

As with the other institutions, there is an explicit and an implicit social contract between American society and higher education. The explicit contract is the formal charter that each college or university must obtain from the state that is home to the institution. The implicit contract is ultimately more significant and important. That contract may be described as a collective expectation on the part of the American people that, as a result of the teaching, learning, and research that takes place in academe:

- the society's traditions and its knowledge base will be passed on to future generations;
- critical reflection will be brought to bear on those traditions and that knowledge;
- and a newly formed knowledge base will be created.

More specifically, the collective expectation of the American citizenry is that, as a result of postsecondary education, the students at commencement will not only know, but they will be committed to act in certain ways. Among these actions, which would be the outcomes of higher education, are the following:

- the preservation and enhancement of civic life and constitutional democracy;
- the development of personal and social skills necessary for civic life and democratic governance;
- the personal appropriation of a philosophical knowledge base for self-understanding and life in community with others;
- the identification of and response to one's personal calling and work calling, thereby giving rise to a new generation and to the economic security to maintain social life.

At commencement, it is the transcript that is tangible: the course of study, grades, the grade-point average, all of which indicate a level of cognition. The commitment to action can only be elicited and nurtured. However, without at some point committing to action, the diploma has little value. That is the great challenge and dilemma facing the higher education establishment: to pass on the tradition and yet to be critical of that tradition, to create a new knowledge base and to use it for society's well-being. It is not enough to know, one must also act. Making higher education even more challenging is the fact that the students are exposed to a marketplace of ideas protected by the tradition of academic freedom, a tradition that assumes that exposure to argumentation and the scrutiny of one's peers will lead to a better understanding of truth.

Thus, because higher education has been chartered and given the right by society to educate its citizens, colleges and universities have a corresponding responsibility to meet the expectations of society relative to that education. These institutions, therefore, are moral agents, which means that they are organizations that have the obligation to sustain and enhance individual and social life. The ethics of higher education may, therefore, be defined as the systematic analysis of the moral agency of higher education, or the ways in which colleges and universities respond to the expectations of American society with regard to education.

At the same time, the institution of higher education, as with other social institutions, may challenge the expectations of American society, thus leading to a new understanding of education's role in society and even of the nature of the society itself. Such a challenge is another dimension of responsibility and a part of moral agency as well. Thus, colleges and universities are, at one and the same time, agents of conservation and agents of change.

Unless ethical analysis of a social institution, such as higher education, focuses on the vision and goals of the institution in relation to the expectations of the larger society, the ethical analysis will be artificial, imposed from without, and irrelevant. As already indicated, a social institution such as higher education develops its own ethical analysis of the vision and goals of the larger society, thereby providing a feedback mechanism for critical reflection on the society itself. What makes the analysis even more complex, however, is the fact that American society is undergoing rapid economic, social, and technological change that has a significant impact on the expectations that the society has of higher education. In fact, one could say that the rise of interest in ethics is largely a function of this change. The taken-for-granted norms and the implicit social contract do not function as they did in the past because the society itself is in the process of rapid change. Intense ethical analysis to determine norms and expectations is a function of that change.

Once the implicit social contract between American society and its colleges and universities is examined in this era of rapid change, it becomes quite clear that such analysis is complicated. For instance, what does it mean to "preserve and enhance civic life and constitutional democracy?" To be committed to its preservation and enhancement is important, but what is the nature of civic life and constitutional democracy? How are the citizens to understand the intent of the founding fathers in a society that is racially diverse, and culturally heterogeneous—quite different from that of the founders themselves? According to the norm of academic freedom, higher education has the obligation of raising these questions and then fully presenting the diverse answers and points of view in the belief that such critical thinking will lead to preserving the best of the past while creating a response that meets the challenges of the present day. The college or university thereby becomes a forum for ideas and a crucible for critical reflection on competing visions of the nature of American society and, ultimately, that society's relation to the rest of the world.

Because of its relationship to the larger society by way of its social charter, higher education must address other critical ethical questions arising from its moral agency. Who is to have access to colleges and universities? Rich and poor, only the brightest? Should any preference be given to those who have suffered discrimination? What exactly is to be taught? How is the teaching to be done? What are the responsibilities of the constituent groups in higher education: the administration and the board of trustees, the professoriate, the students, and the state chartering agencies?

In sum, the implicit expectations of the larger society give rise to the vision and goals of colleges and universities and, therefore, to the norms or standards for ethical analysis in higher education. These norms are embedded in the ethical theories that are the rich heritage of Western philosophical and theological traditions, and the traditions of other cultures. As moral agents, each constituent group in academe has a responsibility to engage in this analysis. Moral agency and ethical analysis are thus fundamental to an understanding of higher education and its relation to the larger society. As already stated, ethics is not an extra value added to or simply another dimension of institutional life. It is fundamental to the viability of an institution.

III. FOUR THEMES IN AMERICAN HIGHER EDUCATION

Throughout their history American institutions of higher education have passed judgment on society and have been judged by it. Four related themes emerge in this history to structure the overview of higher education ethics. Colleges and universities:

• have played a significant role in the development of American society,

- prepare people for work and life,
- can both transmit and criticize values, those highly prized aspects of American culture,
- have been, from colonial days, shaped by a moral vision (a vision reflected in public and private college and university curricula if not in research agendas).

The themes require further elaboration.

A. Colleges and Universities Have Played a Significant Role in the Development of American Society

From the earliest days of American higher education, colleges and universities have been viewed as part of the nation-building process. Kimball notes this theme in his discussion of the liberal arts tradition (Kimball, B. A. (1986). Orators and philosophers: A history of the idea of liberal education. New York: Teachers College Press). Historically, colleges functioned as moral enterprises in contrast to the way some think of higher education today: self-serving institutions that motivate students to seek personal interests and careers.

Responsiveness to society's demands is not an unqualified value. American colleges and universities are not simply in the service of the nation. Institutions of higher education bring critical distance to their relationship with society, a distance that yields certain crucial questions. Is higher education the blind servant of professional and corporate elites? What ethical constraints affect the decisions of its scientists, given the rapid pace of scientific discovery and technological application, especially in the military field? For that matter, what is the mission of higher education in view of the lack of consensus on values in society generally? What values should enter into academic decision-making at this point in time?

Another important consideration is the diversity of perspectives from which the approximately 3600 colleges and universities view society. Colleges and universities transmit particular values to their more than 14 million students. Complex state systems run the gamut from research universities to a host of community colleges. A network of private, secular universities and colleges exists alongside loosely affiliated religious institutions in the Jewish, Protestant, and Catholic communities. The present-day heterogeneity of student body and faculty and the pluralism of world views in higher education accurately reflect an American society that, by the year 2000, will be a nation where one of every three persons will be non-White. As an ever-changing society searches for a sense of unifying purpose and community, so also does higher education. Both the larger society and the educational community must assess their goals and the consequences of choice, both of which are ethical issues that call for analysis.

B. Colleges and Universities Prepare People for Work and Life

The evolution of the American university greatly influenced the development of modern research methods, it gave shape to undergraduate education, and it created the disciplines that grant degrees to the professoriate. Implicit in the rise of the university is a tension—that between undergraduate and graduate education and research. This institutional polarity reflects two disparate demands placed on institutions of higher education. On the one hand, the nation's research agenda presses to expand the knowledge base both to advance the economy and for the general social well-being. The satisfaction of these needs has tended to devolve onto graduate education and scholarship. On the other hand, individuals, especially undergraduates, also attend college seeking self-understanding and growth through the humanities and through a liberal education. A cogent moral view of this dilemma must integrate these competing needs.

Two factors seem to have strongly influenced institutions to value graduate-level activities at the expense of an awareness of public mindedness and the vision of the academy as a moral enterprise. First is the rise of the disciplines of knowledge. Intellectual specialization engendered the academic meritocracy and provided entry for the students into high paying careers. The second is the distancing in relationships between academic institutions and two other institutions: church and state. With regard to relationships with these two institutions, there is a consensus in American higher education that the pursuit of truth is integrally related to freedom from both ecclesiastical control and governmental meddling in higher education. While federal and state financial support for higher education is a given in the late twentieth century, freedom from intrusion in the curriculum or in campus life is held as a defining characteristic of colleges and universities. However, these distinguishing features of contemporary American higher education—strong disciplinary fields and freedom from church and state—contribute to the erosion of commitment to civic responsibility and the common good (Laney, J. T. (1990, May). Through thick and thin: Two ways of talking about the academy and moral responsibility.

Ethics and Higher Education. (W. W. Ed.) New York: ACE/Macmillan).

Colleges and universities constitute complex bureaucracies that in turn support meritocracy. The dominant faculty-centered pedagogy emphasizes a lecture method of teaching. Material characteristics such as wealth, fame, and the size of institutions are often thought to be the qualities of a good education. Autonomy, critical thinking, and risk taking on the part of the student are not the valued outcomes (Astin, A. W. (1985). *Achieving educational excellence.* San Francisco: Jossey-Bass).

C. Colleges and Universities Transmit and Criticize Values

Broadly speaking, a tension exists within institutions of higher education between the transmission of civilization and the criticism of it. Some key areas in which such a dilemma exists are: (1) between commitment to the community and the assertion of individualism in American society; (2) between economic and social isolation of professional groups relative to the less well educated; (3) between the demand for personal economic security and the enhancement of the national economy.

Responsiveness to society's demands is not an unqualified value. American colleges and universities are not simply in the service of the nation. Institutions of higher education bring critical distance to their relationship to the wider society, a distance that yields certain crucial ethical questions. Is higher education the servant of groups such as the classic professions of law and medicine or of corporate elites? What moral constraints affect the decisions of scientists (given the rapid pace of scientific discovery and technological application in fields as diverse as computer science and biotechnology)? For that matter, what is the mission of higher education in view of the lack of consensus on values in society generally?

The liberal arts are considered the foundation of higher education in Western civilization. This tradition has its own stresses. There are those, on the one hand, who treasure Western civilization as the font of wisdom and guardian of eternal verities, first principles and authority. Bruce Kimball (Kimball, B. A. (1986). *Orators and philosophers: A history of the idea of liberal education.* New York: Teachers College Press) calls this position the liberal arts or oratorical tradition. Many philosophers, on the other hand, while perhaps treasuring the legacies of Western culture, are skeptical of its traditions and emphasize the tentativeness of a Western philosophy based on its never-ending search for truth and

critical distance. In contrast to the oratorical tradition Kimball calls this the liberal-free or philosophical tradition. This latter humanism sees the West within a larger global matrix and is more comfortable with the discontinuities and compromises of pluralism and relativism.

In the twentieth century, practitioners of the liberal arts in American colleges became investigators and transmitters of knowledge. Now considered by society to be "experts," their elevation to professional status went hand-in-hand with the professionalization of work and careers in American society. The liberal arts themselves increasingly were seen as instrumental, an aspect of professional education. Rapid growth of higher education after World War II fostered universal mass education and the professionalization of the faculty, developments that were increasingly detrimental to the liberal arts tradition. Continued rapid change, however, has precipitated new interest in the liberal arts. The impact of technological revolutions, the growing interdependence of nations, the globalization of economics, the degradation of the world's climate, the championing of social ideals of justice and equality—all of which characterize the fragmentation of and change in American culture—have led to a resurgence of interest in applied ethics as well as the need for a common curriculum.

D. Colleges and Universities Have Been Shaped by a Moral Vision

From its origins at Harvard through the late nineteenth century, the tradition of American higher education sustained a distinctive concern for the development of both personal values and social responsibility. The senior moral philosophy course was the nineteenth-century equivalent of the contemporary capstone course. Ethical sensitivity to the responsibilities of citizenship in a rapidly developing nation was the goal.

Contemporary applied and professional ethics courses have similar goals in a social milieu characterized by change far exceeding the pace of developments in the nineteenth century. Present-day ethics courses tend to focus on specific careers or professions, such as business, engineering, medicine, and law. They are not capstone courses offering an integrated understanding and inculcating responsibility for the commonweal through the practice of civic virtue.

The segmentation of the moral philosophy course mirrors the segmentation of knowledge in higher education that began with the rise of the university in the latter part of the nineteenth century. As the role of the university evolved, it grew in its dedication to the education of the experts as the group to lead society and to meet the challenges facing the United States. The university no longer viewed humanism as an adequate foundation for the project of nation building. The new religion of science, the fragmentation of learning in higher education, and the rise of logical positivism led to the collapse of ethical idealism in institutions of higher education in the 1930s (Sloan, D. (1980). The teaching of ethics in the American undergraduate curriculum, 1876–1976. In D. Callahan & S. Bok (Eds.), *Ethics Teaching in Higher Education,* pp. 1–57. New York: Plenum Press). A corresponding decline in ethics courses took place.

However, it was the pressures arising from the quickened pace of change sparked by the economic, technological, and social revolutions of the last half of the twentieth century that appear to have resulted in a resurgence of interest in the moral life, applied and professional ethics, as well as in values and the valuing process. While moral vision has been a distinctive characteristic of American colleges and universities, any discussion of vision must be tempered by the realization that a renewed emphasis on values and the moral life in higher education is constrained by the fast-paced nature of change in society generally and by the collapse of tradition as a focal point for ethics in American culture. Colleges and universities are part of the larger social matrix. Renewal in the former is in tandem with renewal in the latter.

This article began with a story that described the evolution of higher education in the United States. The parable portrayed the development of an educational system that was not highly reflective and was not ultimately guided by a clear vision and a set of goals. This section then ended on a note of conflict between academe and the community. That conflict was typified by the alienation from government and public life that led individuals to exclaim: "Why should I pay, let the government pay!"

IV. SUGGESTIONS FOR FUTURE DIRECTION

Readers generally prefer a happy ending to a story and there is not much to be gained from painting a picture of the drift in higher education. The intent of this overview is to underscore the fundamental ethical imperative facing higher education: to prepare future generations to preserve and enhance the public life of a constitutional democracy through a broad-based, hu-

manistic, undergraduate education that is coupled with the acquisition of specialized skills for economic security and the betterment of society. The last part of the article examines the challenges presented by this imperative.

A. Creating Community in Higher Education

The reader of the parable was left in the lurch: higher education and society were deeply divided and at odds with each another. In many ways, this is the present situation in the United States. Although they are expert in the scholarship of discovery and invention, faculty are quite reluctant to change the structure, curriculum, or pedagogy of their own institutions. Even in the fast-developing field of applied and professional ethics, the academy only turned its attention to the ethics of higher education very late in the game. This is not at all surprising given the vested interest that is at stake in any restructuring or critical reflection on the academy.

As the Institute for Research in Higher Education (IRHE) has noted (Institute for Research on Higher Education (1996). Shared purposes. *Policy Perspectives,* 6, 4, 1–12.), administrators are the lightning rods most sensitive to the storm of criticism and winds of change that are buffeting the walls of academe. At the same time, they are charged with betrayal and incompetence by the faculty, who view themselves as underpaid and undervalued. Beyond these conflicts, however, is the growing realization that the success of colleges and universities in a period of rapid change is a profound challenge. All sectors must face the task as a cooperative and unified project, what some might call the challenge of building community in higher education.

The difficulty with the appeal to community is that the academic pulse is determined by the heartbeat of the faculty. As professionals, they are the custodians of the knowledge base that drives postmodern society. They qualify the practitioners of business, education, engineering, law, medicine, science, and technology. The preservation, enhancement, and transmission of knowledge is their calling; and the prerogative of life-long tenure protects their mission. Institutional identification and the educational community easily become afterthoughts because the primary allegiance is to the disciplinary guild of scholars itself. Appreciation for social context and institutional accountability are all too often missing. An effective academic community will, therefore, require a paradigm shift by the faculty, a task that is not easily taken up. At the same time, administrators must address the needs that the faculty perceive to be at the heart of their work.

While this discussion of ethics in higher education has focused primarily on administration and faculty, there is a third party that must receive some consideration if the overview is to be complete. Boards of trustees play a largely invisible but important role in American colleges and universities. Such boards are responsible for budget approvals, presidential and other senior administrative hiring, and major policy decisions affecting the institution. Trustees thus play a significant role and have a great deal of power. They chart the direction and they determine major policies of the institution. Board members, therefore, must understand not only the legal obligations they assume, but also the underlying ethical responsibility they have for the institution's immediate well-being and its long-term development.

With regard to long-term issues, the board has a major responsibility for defining institutional identity, understood as a fiduciary responsibility to relate the historical mission of the college or university to the demands of society and the norms of justice in the present. (On this point, see Smith, D. H. (1995). *Entrusted: The moral responsibilities of trusteeship.* Bloomington, IN: Indiana University Press). The college or university is not simply a client for whom the trustee is doing *pro bono* work. The institution is literally entrusted to the board. There is established, as a result, a fiduciary obligation.

A critical issue in relation to the trustees' role is the nature of the appointment itself. Does the president pick his or her own board? Who guards these guardians to assure that they bring a critical perspective to their role? If the president has had a long tenure in office and has had the power to choose the board members, that group may be totally in his or her image and likeness. Given the great power and responsibility of the board, it must not simply be a rubber stamp on presidential decisions. Time and expertise are demanded if budgets are to be analyzed or strategic plans are to be developed. Board members must not be chosen solely because of their potential for monetary contributions or their political influence with legislators. To have such minimal involvement in charting the direction of the college or university would be an abnegation of their ethical responsibility, if not a dereliction of their legal obligations. The fundamental question is whether a president, in choosing his or her board, will invite individuals who will be "a loyal opposition" on the board.

A related problem is the power and influence board members may bring to bear on the senior administration

and other board members. A wealthy board member who has made significant contributions to the institution can make life very difficult for a president if that board member is adamant about retaining a particular coach or athletic director. Boards must also be cautious about potential conflicts of interest if contracts are steered toward past or present trustees on the board. In sum, it is true that, to a large extent, the educational community is made up of students, faculty, administrators, and the several support staffs of the institution. But the powerful, although invisible, presence of the trustees has a significant impact on that community, especially if the college or university is fighting to survive.

The IRHE suggests three steps that may help in making explicit how an effective educational community can function to address the present challenge. These concrete managerial activities would greatly enhance the institution's ability to fulfill the implicit social contract with American society.

1. Establish a framework for debate and decision-making leading to closure, a task in which the administration needs to take the lead, but which must be a joint responsibility of all concerned.
2. Define the issues and assure that all parties have access to information. Excellence in communication is a priority.
3. Resolve the employment function of the faculty. What are the roles, responsibilities, and the obligations of faculty beyond those of the guild itself?

B. The Challenge for the Administration and Faculty

While administrators are portrayed in a leadership role and faculty are asked to redefine their identity, the IRHE underscores the call to common responsibility for meeting the challenge of a rapidly changing society. In a seminal monograph, the Carnegie Foundation for the Advancement of Teaching described this challenge somewhat differently and more comprehensively (The Carnegie Foundation for the Advancement of Teaching (1990). *Campus life: In search of community.* Princeton: The Carnegie Foundation for the Advancement of Teaching). *Campus Life: In Search of Community* provides the foundation on which higher education should be built and it offers six characteristics of campus community: purposefulness, openness, justice, discipline, caring, celebrative.

The first characteristic is of greatest concern to this

overview of ethics in higher education because purposefulness addresses the vision, mission, and goals of the institutions, and it provides the context for the other characteristics. While colleges and universities would appear, by definition, to be educational institutions, Carnegie found that this characteristic was often undermined by the ways in which too many students spent their time outside the classroom: at jobs and in social life, not in study or in the library. At the same time, it is not part of the faculty reward system to mentor students or to develop pedagogies that inspire a love of learning. Learning is a communal process and thus the creation of a college or university community must be identified by the quality of community in the classroom, in curriculum design, and in the culture of learning that should pervade the campus.

There is little doubt that the Carnegie Foundation views the call for a purposeful community primarily as a faculty responsibility. In a companion monograph, *Scholarship Reconsidered: Priorities of the Professoriate,* Ernest Boyer reiterates the leadership role of the administration, especially the president, in restructuring the definition of scholarship (Boyer, E. L. (1990). *Scholarship reconsidered: Priorities of the professoriate.* Princeton: The Carnegie Foundation for the Advancement of Teaching.). However, Boyer also concludes that the primary responsibility for the redefinition is in the hands of the faculty itself. Boyer urges that the scholarship of integration, application, and teaching be given a place of honor beside that of discovery.

Thus, even though the administration is charged explicitly with providing leadership for the colleges and universities, it is the faculty who have the weightiest responsibility in this regard, although that responsibility is implied. From another perspective, it is the faculty who have the greatest rights within the institution: academic freedom through tenuring, teaching the students, and setting the curriculum. Upon this group, which is truly the keystone of the academic arch, is placed the greatest responsibility for maintaining and enhancing the values and ethics that must permeate the culture of higher education.

Also See the Following Article

ETHICS EDUCATION IN SCHOOLS

Bibliography

Cahn, S. M. (Ed.). (1990). *Morality, responsibility, and the university: Studies in academic ethics.* Philadelphia: Temple University Press.

Getman, J. (1992). *In the company of scholars: The struggle for the soul of higher education.* Austin: University of Texas Press.

Kadish, M. R. (1991). *Toward an ethic of higher education.* Stanford, CA: Stanford University Press.

Lappe, F. M., & Du Bois, P. M. (1994). *The quickening of America: Rebuilding our nation, remaking our lives.* San Francisco: Jossey-Bass.

Long, Jr., E. L. (1992). *Higher education as a moral enterprise.* Washington, DC: Georgetown University Press.

Marsden, G. M. (1994). *The soul of the American university: From Protestant establishment to established nonbelief.* New York: Oxford University Press.

May, W. W. (Ed.). (1990). *Ethics and higher education.* New York: ACE/Macmillan Publishing Company.

Mitias, M. H. (Ed.). (1992). *Moral education and the liberal arts.* New York: Greenwood Press.

Rudolph, F. (1990). *The American college and university: A history.* (2nd Ed.). Athens, GA: University of Georgia Press.

Sellers, M. N. S. (Ed.). (1994). *An ethical education: Community and morality in the multicultural university.* Providence, RI: Berg Publishers.

Smith, D. H. (1995). *Entrusted: The moral responsibilities of trusteeship.* Bloomington, IN: Indiana University Press.

Wilcox, J. R. & Ebbs, S. L. (1992). The leadership compass: Values and ethics in higher education. *ASHE-ERIC Higher Education Report No. 1.* Washington, DC: The George Washington University, School of Education and Human Development.

HINDUISM

Robert D. Baird
The University of Iowa

GLOSSARY

ahimsa The Hindu concept of noninjury or nonviolence.

ashrama A term that refers to one's stage in life.

Aurobindo Ghose A highly influential modern religious thinker who was active in the Indian Independence movement and later retreated to a monastery in Pondicherry in south India.

dharma The laws inherent in the universe and also one's duty.

enlightenment (*moksha*) The Hindu goal of liberation from the rounds of rebirth and suffering.

Jains The religious community of India that places strong emphasis on *ahimsa* and traces itself back to Mahavira.

jivanmukti One who is liberated while living.

karma The spiritual law of cause and effect.

maya Usually translated as "illusion," it refers to the idea that the world is not what it appears to be.

Patanjali The thinker responsible for the classical system of yoga.

pativrata A faithful and virtuous wife who is devoted to her husband.

prakriti The active world of matter in Patanjali's yoga system.

purusha The spiritual self in Patanjali's yoga system.

rebirth The Hindu concept of reincarnation whereby the self is reborn after the death of the body.

sannyasin One who has renounced the world.

sati The self-immolation of a widow on the funeral pyre of her husband.

Svadharma One's individual duty as determined by one's class and stage of life.

tapas The heat or pain that comes from practicing asceticism.

HINDUISM has tended to deal with ethics as part of the path toward enlightenment. Since enlightenment is a state of nonattachment, much of Hindu ethics deals with personal qualities and the cultivation of the self. The other side of Hindu ethics deals with *dharma*, one's duty in the socioeconomic world. Hindu ethics can be seen from two levels. On the level of enlightenment, the *jivanmukti* (one who is liberated while living) is beyond ethics. Whatever one does one does spontaneously and without egoism. Hence, while the liberated person is not the embodiment of activism, he is also nonaggressive. On the level of social duty, ethics are preliminary to liberation.

I. WIDE-RANGING DIVERSITY

A discussion of Hindu ethics is susceptible to either a lack of specificity or overgeneralization. First, the term "Hindu" was for a long period of time merely a geographical designation. Not until Muslims invaded India at the beginning of the second millennium (C.E.) did the term take on a religious identification. Muslims used the term to refer to those inhabitants of India who were not Muslim. This meant that the term covered a large number of people who held to a wide range of religious beliefs and practices. Western missionaries later reinforced the religious significance of the term "Hinduism" and, as the Muslims, felt compelled in time to offer a critique of religious and ethical practices of which they did not approve. As the second millennium moved on, and increasingly in the 19th and 20th centuries, Indians accepted the designation and a "Hindu consciousness" developed. Some of the other traditions of thought and practice such as Parsis, Buddhists, and Jains were given their own identifying labels, although there are still some who see Jains as one among many Hindu castes. The term "Hindu," then, was applied to a wide geographical area and to a vast array of cultures long before the diversity it encompassed was adequately appreciated. In the last decade of the 20th century there are continuing discussions concerning how to define "Hinduism." Even the Indian Supreme Court has entered this discussion in clarifying whom is included within the boundaries of "Hindu" law. Since this is the case, it is difficult to know exactly where to draw the line between "Hindus" and non-Hindus. Moreover, wherever one draws the line there is sufficient diversity among "Hindus" that whatever one says about their religious and ethical practices is undoubtedly true for someone and equally untrue for someone else.

In addition to the indefiniteness of the extent of "Hinduism," many modern Hindus see the *Vedas* as basic to their religion. Since some of the *Vedas* were in written form by 1500 B.C.E., and since the Hindu textual corpus has grown from that time to the present, there is a long history involved. Given the wide array of texts from different periods of time, virtually any religious belief or practice can be found. One should approach this topic, then, with the expectation of diversity rather than anticipating a coherent unity. It is begging the question to hold that the many strands that are found are woven together into a single fabric except in the way that history tends to blend extraneous things throughout time.

II. PRESUMPTIVE HOSTILITY TOWARD ETHICS

In his influential *Indian Thought and Its Development* (1936), Albert Schweitzer argued that there were two fundamental problems in all thought. First was the polarity between world and life affirmation and world and life negation. Second was the relationship between ethics and these two approaches to life. In world and life affirmation, which Schweitzer saw as the dominant approach of European thought, human beings see the world as having a value per se and something that human beings are expected to preserve and advance. In world and life negation, which he saw as the dominant approach in Indian thought, the world is meaningless and sorrowful. Rather than seeking to perfect the imperfectable, human beings should renounce attachment to the world and seek to perfect their inner beings. The greatest problem for world and life negation is that it makes no room for an active ethic without compromising its position. It reverts more to inner virtues than outer activity. It asks of human beings more a spirit of kindliness free from hatred than a life of active love.

This Indian approach also involves monism and mysticism rather than the more dualistic and doctrinaire European approach. It seeks to experience the ultimate unity of Reality in a mystical experience. While this mysticism ends in perfection, it is not the perfection of society or the world and therefore, lacking active love, is seen to have no genuine ethical content. The influential ninth century Hindu philosopher Shankara held that ultimate Reality was one and he therefore relegated ethics (which includes distinctions) to a lower level, the level of appearance. The ultimate goal was liberation (*moksha*), which entailed the end of the cycles of rebirth and the realization of ultimate unity without distinction. Ethics were relevant only as a preliminary step on the path to realization, but did not effect liberation. The liberated person was beyond distinctions and hence also beyond ethics. The view that Indian thought, including Hindu thought, lacked a firm foundation for ethics became a standard criticism from the West.

Supporting this judgment was the view that belief in karma (that actions or attitudes are the result of previous actions) negated the human freedom which was basic to ethics. If all of one's acts were simply the result of past karma (past deeds), one could hardly be held accountable for them. Even though Schweitzer was merely asserting that this was a dominant theme in Indian thought, 19th century Western interpreters of

Hinduism picked up on this and saw Hinduism as ethically bankrupt. What can be said of this interpretation?

It must be acknowledged that all historical traditions are subject to change. Whatever the merits of specific interpretations of the past, modern Hindu interpreters often use these sources to move in directions other than those which might have been predicted. S. Radhakrishnan, an Oxford University professor and former president of India, for example, attacked this position by observing that when Shankara held that the world was *maya,* a term usually translated as "illusion," he did not mean that the world did not exist or was meaningless. *Maya* simply meant that the world was not independently real. With this premise, Radhakrishnan went a step further and argued that activity in the world was meaningful so long as the world appeared. When it ceased to appear, all discussion was over anyway. He also dipped into Indian religious history to construct a version of "Hinduism" which included four stages in an individual's life and four classes in society which he argued made ample provision for responsible activity in the world. In the second of life's stages, that of the householder, one's duty was to work in the world for one's family. Moreover, the Kshatriya, Vaishya, and Shudra classes have their own respective duties to perform in the world (see Table I).

Aurobindo Ghose (1872–1950) understood vedanta (Final teaching of Vedas) in such a way that the world was real. Ignorance based on *maya* was the result of seeing only partial reality. When human beings evolve to the level of supramental consciousness they will have an immediate awareness of the One and immediately know how all parts participate in the whole. Using an evolutionary model, Ghose saw the movement from matter to supramental consciousness as an inevitable process, even though human beings have the power to retard it or contribute to it. Ethical action is action that promotes the evolutionary process. That makes it meaningful activity.

Whatever interpretations might be placed on the thought of Shankara, there were other thinkers in classical times who were not monistic. The yoga system of Patanjali (ca. 200 B.C.E.) is dualistic. Both *purusha* (the spiritual self) and *prakriti* (the active material world) are real. The goal of meditation in yoga is to calm the mind (part of *prakriti*) so that it perfectly reflects the spiritual self (*purusha*). The first two steps of yoga are ethical in content. It is true that they center on personal cultivation, but they have implications for life in the world. The first step includes five restraints: noninjury, truthfulness in thought and deed, not taking what is not given, sexual control, and not grasping after things.

The second step of yoga contains five observances: purity of the body, contentment with what one has, austerities or purifying actions, study of sacred texts, and devotion to god. The goal of the ethical life in this system may differ from what Schweitzer desired. While it does center on the cultivation of the self, that does not make it nonethical.

III. UNDERLYING CULTURAL AXIOMS

In order to understand how Hindus view right action, it is necessary to acknowledge the existence of several principles which I will call cultural axioms. In spite of the great geographical and temporal expanse that has resulted in significant diversity, these cultural axioms are not only consciously articulated but often unconsciously assumed by many Hindus. Sometimes they appear in a formal philosophical sense when they have risen to consciousness and have been philosophically articulated and defended. But for many Hindus they are cultural axioms in the sense that they are implicit values and beliefs that are held but seldom articulated. If they are not universally held, they sufficiently permeate the way Hindus conduct themselves that not to call them to mind would place the practical ethics of Hindus beyond understanding.

A. Purity and Impurity

The first such axiom is that certain activities or associations render one pure or impure. Hindu ethical practices take into account who it is that is doing the act, and one of the relevant distinctions is that of gender. Purity (*suddha*) refers to the most desired state of being, and with reference to the human body it is the ideal condition. Its opposite state of being is impurity (*asuddha*), which should be avoided. The quality of purity or impurity can be attributed to animate beings or inanimate objects and places with which one comes into contact in everyday existence. To be in a condition of impurity is to place oneself in a position in which negative results can occur. Purity is a desired state because in that state good fortune is more likely to follow one. This axiomatically accepted principle affects how one lives and what actions are considered good or bad. As stated by T. N. Madan,

> For example, a prepubescent unmarried girl (*kanya*), water from a holy river, unboiled milk, ghee and a temple are *suddha.* On the other hand, contact with certain kinds of human beings (low caste Hindus or non-Hindus), animals (dogs), ob-

jects (goods made of leather), food (beef or food cooked in impure utensils), substances (discharges from the human body), places (cremation ground), etc. causes Brahmans and other upper caste Hindus to become polluted. (1985. In *Purity and Auspiciousness in Indian Society*. J. B. CARMAN AND F. A. MARGLIN (EDS.). BRILL, LEIDEN).

Since discharges from the body are impure, women are particularly susceptible to the state of impurity. Menstruating women should keep out of the kitchen, and birthing, while a joyous occasion, renders both the mother and the newborn impure. People whose occupations place them in contact with death (attendants at cremation grounds, butchers, and leather workers), as well as sweepers, are impure, and contact with them should be avoided by higher class persons lest such contact result in their impurity as well. Until the last century it was assumed that foreign travel would render one impure both through contact with impure persons and through the necessity of eating food that was not pure. Such travel was discouraged and those who traveled abroad anyway were expected to undergo elaborate purification rites upon their return. An astrologer might prescribe that one place powdered gold on one's tongue if a horoscope revealed the potential for calamity. This would be an act of purification and protection against such negative possibilities. Frequent baths in the Ganges river, a temple tank, or even a village pond is a method of purification, even though the water may be muddy. It is clear that this axiom affects not only the things people do and the places they go, but interpersonal associations as well.

Closely related to purity–impurity is auspiciousness and inauspiciousness. Once again, a person may be auspicious but so may a place, an object, or a time. This is frequently determined through astrological calculations. A widow is inauspicious because her husband preceded her in death, and should be kept clear of weddings, which are auspicious events. Certain times are considered auspicious for beginning new ventures. Wedding dates and matrimonial matches are usually determined in consultation with an astrologer, for the marriage of two persons whose horoscopes collide is inauspicious. To do an otherwise "good" thing at the wrong time is inauspicious. Many unhappy occurrences can be avoided by careful attention to a wide range of principles relating to purity–impurity and auspiciousness–inauspiciousness. And, these principles are usually not learned so much through books as through the passage of a living tradition from one generation to the next.

A number of ethical issues converged to encourage child marriage in India. The first is the value of chastity. If one's daughter is to be chaste when married, to arrange that marriage at an early stage of life will help ensure that to be the case. In addition, it was traditionally important that marriage be effected prior to the girl's first menstruation. Since menstruation renders the woman impure, failure to have her married by this time would pass the girl's menstrual impurity onto her father's family. For wives to perform *vrats* (vows) and fast for the well-being of their husbands is considered virtuous action, even though sometimes the husband still dies prematurely. At this point a second cultural axiom comes to bear upon one's understanding of virtuous activity.

B. Karma and Rebirth

A second axiom is the dual concept of karma and rebirth. Hindus have traditionally accepted as self-evident a world in which the spiritual self, at the death of the body, moves on to be reborn in another human or animal form. That is the concept of rebirth. This is linked to the notion of karma, namely, that every act (word, thought, or deed) has its effect upon the actor's spiritual and physical existence. Moreover, every situation in which one finds oneself is the result of acts done in this or previous lives. Nothing is accidental or happenstance. Not until the 19th and 20th centuries do we find Hindus offering philosophical defenses for the doctrine of reincarnation or rebirth. The reason for this is not difficult to find. People do not enter a defense of ideas that are commonly accepted, that is, are taken as axiomatic. Even today, rebirth is part of the vision of the universe for most Hindus, and they would consider it obvious enough not to need defense. Moreover, anthropological studies as well as studies of ancient texts have shown that Hindus believe that some karmic substance can be passed from one person to another. This is often done through sharing food, through passing of bodily fluid from one person to another, or even only through close proximity. Sheryl B. Daniel reports the parting of two college roommates when one became ill and the cause was thought to be the transfer of bad karma from his roommate (1983. *Karma: An Anthropological Inquiry*. C. F. Keyes and E. V. Daniel (Eds.). Univ. of California Press, Berkeley). Not only does this axiom influence what kinds of behavior are considered good, but it is also used to explain why something happened when all other explanations seem to fail.

C. Renunciation and Societal Life

A third axiom is the presumed value of asceticism and renunciation. From as early as the *Upanishads* (600 B.C.E.) a valued strand in the Hindu tradition has been the life of renunciation and asceticism. It is impossible to know how many Hindus actually renounced family life and set out on a full quest for enlightenment (*moksha*). The search for enlightenment and release from the rounds of birth and death was seen as a strenuous undertaking, often accompanied by ascetic practices, and always over a long period of multiple lifetimes. Hindu ascetics were called *sadhus* ("good" or "pious"); they renounced the householder's life and practiced *tapas*. Even some of the gods, most notably Shiva, practiced *tapas*. *Tapas* means "heat," then the pain that comes from heat, and then suffering in general, particularly when it was self-inflicted on the path to enlightenment. Such a vision of the good might not only involve practices in which the body was mortified, but also certain clear ethical principles as well.

No community carried the value of renunciation further than the Jains (dating from Mahavira, 5th century B.C.E.). They emphasized the principle of *ahimsa* (noninjury) to such an extent that it influenced when and where they traveled (so as not to tread on living organisms), made them strict vegetarians, and resulted in particular care in putting away unused food. They also took a vow of truthfulness which necessitated that they never speak without careful deliberation, a vow against taking what is not one's own, and a vow upholding chastity and renouncing of all attachments to pleasant colors, sounds, and smells. Such a renunciant was a homeless wanderer, dependent upon alms giving for food and carrying a bare minimum of possessions.

Alongside this value placed on renunciation, ordinary society continued to exist, without which there would be no one to give alms to renunciants. How was one to reconcile the obvious needs of society with this value placed on renunciation? The most common way was through the fourfold class system and the four stages in life. These are important for they make it clear that some principles are universal only on the sense that they cover all persons at a certain stage in life. What was expected of an individual in terms of ethical action came to be called *dharma*. *Dharma* means law, custom, or appropriate action. It suggests that one's dharma is always appropriate to the way the universe is. There is a certain *dharma* for each stage in life and for each class. At any one point in time, then, one's *svadhamra* (own *dharma*) is determined by these two grids of four.

TABLE I

Hindu Caste System

Brahmin	Highest of the four classes in Hinduism. The spiritual leaders.
Kshatriya	Second of the four classes in Hinduism. Kings and warriors.
Vaishya	Third of the four classes in Hinduism. Concerned with business and commerce.
Shudras	Fourth of the four classes in Hinduism. Servants and those who do manual tasks.
Outcastes	Those who are seen as impure and outside the fourfold class system.

As for the classes, Brahmins are intended to be the spiritual leaders and to meet the religious needs of the people. Even though it was probably never the case that all Brahmins were priests or teachers, that was considered good or appropriate action for them. The second class were Kshatriyas. These were kings and warriors. The *Bhagavadgita,* a highly influential religious text, begins with the moral dilemma of the warrior who does not want to kill because he sees members of his extended family in the opposing army. Krishna, the teacher who is understood to be god as the text unfolds, offers a variety of reasons why the warrior should fight. One of those is that as a Kshatriya it is his *dharma* to do so. While, then, it might be inappropriate for a Brahmin to march into battle and inflict death on the enemy, the Kshatriya is duty bound to do so. The Hindu tradition, then, although it values *ahimsa* or nonviolence, did not promote pacifism.

The Vaishya was the business and economic leader and therefore, however strong the urge to renunciation might be, it would not be appropriate for the Vaishya. The Shudra was a servant who did menial tasks. All such activities were considered good, however, since they were appropriate to the given class into which one was born. In time certain groups of persons were considered outside this system, partially because of occupations that rendered them impure. They came to be called untouchables. (See Table I for a summary of the caste system.)

In addition to the four classes, there developed a scheme which divided life into four stages. An individual lived as a student until marriage when one entered the life of a householder. Then, when one's first grandchild was born one had the option of becoming a "forest-dweller" and seeking to strive toward enlightenment with more intensity. This state and the final one intersects with the goal of renunciation. The final stage was one who was beyond the stages or *ashramas,* and such a person wandered homelessly. Such persons were later called *sannyasins.*

In this way, the Hindu tradition continued to place value on renunciation while making place for ordinary social and economic existence. While it might not be appropriate behavior for a Brahmin renunciate to accumulate material goods, it was certainly quite appropriate for the householder and particularly the Vaishya. If activity connected with death, leather, or human excrement would defile the Brahmin and would therefore be unacceptable behavior, there were always the Shudras or untouchables to carry on such activities. In spite of the inevitable pollution, it was their *dharma* to do such work. And, as the *Bhagavadgita* taught, it is better to act out one's own *dharma,* even if imperfectly, than to seek to imitate the dharma of another. By attending to one's *svadharma* or own duty one was likely to elevate oneself in the next life to a more advantageous class. That different expectations attach to different persons and different stages in life is not merely a theoretical scheme, but again a cultural value that bubbles up and is invoked for purposes of explanation and legitimization from time to time.

IV. THE PLACE OF *AHIMSA*

Because of the place given to the principle of *ahimsa* by the Jain community and by Gandhi in his quest for Indian self-rule, it has often been seen as a basic ingredient of Indian thought, and hence also of Hinduism. However influential *ahimsa* might be, it does not permeate Indian culture to such an extent as to be considered a cultural axiom. The great epics of India, the *Ramayana* and *Mahabharata* (see Table II), center

TABLE II
Influential Hindu Texts

Mahabharata	One of the two great Hindu epics. It is three and a half times the length of the Christian Bible.
Bhagavadgita	An influential Hindu text that is part of the *Mahabharata.*
Ramayana	One of the two great Hindu epics.
Vedas	The earliest religious texts in Hinduism, dating from 1500 B.C.E. Their author(s) is (are) unknown.
Upanishads	An ancient body of philosophical texts which Hindus believe contain the highest teaching of the Vedas.

not so much on the Brahmin as on kings and warriors, that is, the Kshatriya. The *Bhagavadgita,* which is a small part of the *Mahabharata,* makes it clear that it is the duty of a warrior to fight. Gandhi pushed nonviolence so far that he interpreted the setting of the *Bhagavadgita* not as Kurukshetra, a battlefield north of Delhi, but as a struggle that goes on within the heart of any individual. But, whatever one might say of that understanding of the *Bhagavadgita,* it will hardly do to erase the glorification of mighty warriors and battle in the two large epics. *Ahimsa,* then, is an important attitude for understanding a number of Hindu ethical stances. But it does not sufficiently permeate the conscious or unconscious lives of Indians to be called a cultural axiom. This can be seen with reference to the argument for vegetarianism. Many Hindus are vegetarians, but some are meat eaters, and Bengalis commonly exclude fish from the vegetarian principle. Yet, given the importance of *ahimsa* in the life and thought of Gandhi, and given the prominence of Gandhi himself, the term has worked its way into the English language.

Ahimsa is commonly translated as "nonviolence" or "noninjury." For Gandhi it was the foundation of human progress. Nonviolent resistance requires strength of resolve. It means that one is prepared to suffer violence at the hands of another without retaliation or violent defense. *Ahimsa* is not submission to the will of the evildoer, but is resistance to that will, and involves the hope of changing that will in conformity with truth. It is based on the premise that *ahimsa* is equivalent to truth (*satya*) and that even if one perishes while implementing *ahimsa,* truth will prevail and ultimately be realized.

There are three dimensions to *ahimsa.* It begins with nonviolence in thought, which eliminates thinking ill of others or wishing them evil. *Ahimsa* continues with nonviolence in words. Someone practicing *ahimsa* will not speak words that cause pain to others. Truth will be spoken in gentle language. Finally, there is nonviolence in deed where one does not inflict physical injury on others or kill others. *Ahimsa* reinforces the practice of vegetarianism. It is permissible to eat flesh from an animal killed by another carnivorous animal or to use the hides of fallen cattle. But to kill cows or other cattle to fulfill the desire for meat or because they are "worthless" and no longer fill some other human need is unacceptable. It was the argument of *ahimsa* as applied to cattle that led to the formation of *gosadams* or "reservations" where cattle who no longer breed, give milk, or carry cargo can live out their lives and die a natural death. Gandhi held that human beings were superior to the lower animal world and that flesh food was unsuitable to them. He freely associated with meat-eaters, however, for the same principle of *ahimsa* had to be applied to such human relationships.

Gandhi acknowledged that it was never possible to be completely noninjurious. Whatever one eats is bound to cause some death, even though some pressed the principle so far as to subsist on seeds and fruit that had fallen from the tree rather than green leafy vegetables. Even inhaling the air we breathe causes injury to some life-forms. One ought to live, therefore, so as to inflict the barest minimum of injury. Hence the choice of vegetables over meat. By the same token, *ahimsa* does not involve the elimination of jails, but the transformation of jails into institutions of reformation and education. And, how should a woman react to attempted assault? The purity of a fearless woman is her best protection. However perverse the man, he will wilt in shame at her dazzling purity. Even poisonous snakes seldom bite and will not bite unless attacked or cornered. Yet to be willing to give one's life to protect the virtue of a woman is also a manifestation of *ahimsa*. Police are to be armed, but will seldom use those arms. They are to be servants of the people rather than masters. Moreover, if the wealthy act as trustees in a nonviolent state and seek to equalize the economic conditions of the poor, the violence that comes from poverty will be mitigated. Nonviolence, then, begins with the mind, and only after that does it issue in appropriate action. *Ahimsa,* according to this view, is not only negative, that is, to refrain from thinking, speaking, or implementing injury, but also positive. It is the cultivation of goodwill and love toward all.

One should not think that Indian society is governed by such principles any more than any society is an embodiment of its proclaimed ethical principles. It is one way that some Hindus order their lives. One may witness on Indian streets heated arguments, maltreatment of animals, or even physical violence. Nevertheless, the doctrine of *ahimsa* has influenced the way a goodly number of Hindus live their lives.

V. CONTEMPORARY ISSUES

A. Human Rights and Women

It is interesting that the widely circulated monthly newspaper *Hinduism Today,* which is a vehicle for news about international Hinduism and a means of promoting the cause of Hinduism, deals with a wide range of issues effecting modern Hindus, but has thus far given only a low percentage of its space to ethical issues. One

reason for this is that such issues are not as important to modern Hindus as other issues are. A considerable number of ethical issues that are hotly debated among modern Hindus are the result of the confrontation of traditional values with modern human rights ideologies.

It is often argued that the place of women in the Vedic period was high and they were often afforded a position equal to men. Women participated in religious rites, often as equals with men. Some women were scholars and poets, and girls were given the same basic education as boys. There were upper class women who participated in the upanayana (initiation rite) and received the sacred thread as did men of the top three classes. By the time of the epics, however, women were seen as intrinsically evil and impure. In the *Bhagavadgita,* women were classified with sinners, slaves, and Outcastes. Women were unfit for the performance of religious rituals since, regardless of the class of their parents, they were considered as Shudras. For this reason, a man should not eat with his wife and it was meritorious for her if she ate the leavings from her husband's plate. A wife should not walk side by side with her husband, but a few steps behind him. Women were major obstacles to the salvation of men. Benjamin Walker summarizes their status as follows:

> They were considered incapable of controlling themselves, ritually impure at all times, avid for illicit affairs, hard of mind, small in judgment, eager to exhibit their persons. The Creator had implanted in women a love for trinkets, dishonesty, untruth, malice, wickedness, cruelty and impure desires. (1968. *Hindu World,* Vol. II, p. 604. Praeger, London)

Man is often polluted by woman. He emerges from women surrounded by blood and excrement. Women are unclean during menses, pregnancy, and childbirth. Beneath the calm exterior is a raging lust which makes it desirable that a woman always be controlled by a man: first by her father, then her husband or older brother, and finally by her son. When she marries, her sole purpose is to please and protect her husband. The birth of a girl was often unannounced and her status changed only if she bore a son.

Although there are those who paint a more favorable picture of the woman's status and indicate that although she is not equal to her husband, inequality need not imply inferiority, it would seem that many of the more negative attitudes resulted in Hindu reformers of the 19th century championing the cause of women, particularly in the field of education. Legislation on the part of the government has also sought to protect women from subjugation and injustice. The human rights concept of justice is based on the principle of equality rather than inequality. *The Constitution of India,* which has been the norm for Independent India for almost five decades, erases gender as a consideration in determining rights. All persons are to be equal before the law without reference to gender.

The so-called "Hindu Code Bill" that passed the Indian Parliament in 1955–1956 was a systematization as well as a modernization of Hindu law. It passed under four separate bills: the Hindu Marriage Bill, Hindu Succession Bill, Hindu Minority and Guardianship Bill, and Hindu Adoptions and Maintenance Bill. The committee responsible for determining the content of the proposed bills discovered that opposition from Hindus to the changes they intended to make was almost universal. Nevertheless they moved ahead. These bills provided for intercaste marriage, divorce (on an equal basis for men and women), and monogamous marriage (making bigamy punishable by law), and gave a married daughter a share in her father's property.

Those who opposed divorce argued that marriage was a sacrament and created a bond between husband and wife not only in life, but even after death. Although widowers were free to remarry according to tradition, widows should treat their husbands as gods even after death. The traditionalists argued that destitute widows should simply exemplify patient suffering. The committee responded that they were not prepared to extend that principle to men. It was debated whether a man's keeping a concubine was sufficient grounds for divorce. Some argued that it was not unless the man brought the concubine into the house to live. The committee noted that if a woman were discovered to be having an illicit affair it would be grounds for divorce. If that is true for the woman, they concluded, it should also be true for the man.

In addition to the provisions of the Hindu Code Bill, the Dowry Prohibition Act of 1961 outlawed the practice of dowry. The Maternity Benefits Act of 1961 intended to protect women in the workplace, while the Equal Remuneration Act (1976) provided for equal remuneration for men and women for the same work. The Suppression of Immoral Traffic in Women and Girls Act of 1956 intended to suppress prostitution and the keeping of brothels.

All of these acts are based on the ethical principle that women ought to be treated as men are treated and that justice is blind to gender. There are laws against most of the major crimes and injustices against women. That does not mean that they are equally enforced or that the attitudes that result in detrimental treatment of women have been erased.

Indian society is 80% Hindu, and that society remains patriarchal. The dowry system is alive and well. Brides still have "kitchen accidents" in which they are burnt with the use of kerosene when they do not meet the dowry demands of the groom's family. It has gotten to the point that when such a "kitchen accident" takes place, the groom's family is presumed guilty until proven innocent. The desirability of male children and the liability of female children not only feeds sex-determination tests and the abortion of the female fetus, but also has an evaluative effect upon what happens to a girl child after birth. Statistics show that boys are taken for medical treatment three times more frequently than girls. This is not because girls are more healthy and less in need of health care, but because they are given less attention by reason of their lesser value. They are also given less in terms of nutrition. Statistics also show that more girl babies die than boy babies. In some areas infanticide is not uncommon. The Indian Census Report of 1981 records a ratio of 935 females to every 1000 males. Compare this with 946 per thousand males in 1951 and 972 per thousand males in 1901. This is happening at a time when the population of India, which was 684 million in 1981, is projected to reach 1 billion by the turn of the century. The 1981 census placed the literacy level for males at 46.74%, while the level for females was at 24.88%. If one breaks this down in terms of rural and urban, in urban areas 56% of women are illiterate, while in rural areas 88% are illiterate. If the delivery of health care to women is examined, it is also the case that rural women suffer from less availability as well.

B. Suicide

The ancient law books consider suicide a major violation of moral law. Some of the unacceptable reasons for terminating one's life are pride, incurable love, excessive fright, or anger. The methods used to commit suicide were ropes, arms, or poison. The corpse resulting from such a death should not be cremated, have obsequies performed, or tears shed on its behalf. If a relative does that on behalf of a suicide victim, he should have no funeral rites of his own and should be abandoned by his kin (*Arthashastra of Kautilya* 4.7).

Although suicide is generally condemned, there is a long tradition of religious suicide that has been viewed more positively. It was considered auspicious to die under the wheels of the large cart carrying an image of Lord Jagganath in Puri (Orissa) until it was outlawed in the 19th century. The *Laws of Manu* (an ancient law book of considerable authority) recommends one way to end one's life as the Great Journey (*mahaprasthana*). For a disciplined brahman, he might "walk, fully determined and going straight on, in a north-easterly direction, subsisting on water and air, until his body sinks to rest" (6.32).

One form of religious suicide which is supported by a substantial segment of Hindus is *sati*. This is the self-immolation of the widow on the funeral pyre of her husband. The word *sati* comes from the word *sat* and means "goodness" or "virtue." Hence it refers to a virtuous woman who joins her husband in death. In 1812 the British concluded, after consulting with a Hindu Pandit, that *sati* did have religious sanction, but placed certain conditions to its practice. Those conditions were that the woman could not be pregnant, under the age of puberty, the mother of an infant, in a state of impurity (menstruating), or under the influence of drugs. Above all the act of *sati* had to be voluntary. These restrictions did not reduce the number of Hindu widows embarking on *sati*. Rather, the number increased from 378 occurrences in 1815 to 839 occurrences in 1818 in the Bengal Presidency alone. In 1829 the British government backed away from its initial decision to abolish *sati* on the grounds that an alternative existence of ascetic widowhood existed for Hindu widows. Regulation XVII, the Sati Regulation Act, declared that *sati*, whether voluntary or not, was illegal and punishable by the criminal courts.

Although *sati* is a less common occurrence today, the celebrated case of Roop Kanwar in 1987 has served as a rallying point for further legislation and a formulation and hardening of two points of view. The case of Roop Kanwar was the 38th documented case of *sati* since India's Independence in 1947. Married 8 months before, at the age of 18 (her husband was 24), Roop Kanwar's husband died on September 4, 1987, after complaining of stomach pains. She became a *sati* on that same day.

One side saw her as a deeply religious woman and a courageous and devoted wife. The Women and Media Committee describes this view of the event as follows:

> … Roop, after the first shock had worn off, became very calm and reportedly told her father-in-law that she wished to commit sati. Press reports say that she decked herself in bridal finery and, in keeping with the tradition, led the funeral procession to the cremation ground in the center of the village. She then ascended the pyre and placed her husband's head in her lap. Blessing the crowd assembled there and chanting the gayatri mantra, she slowly burnt to death on the pyre. (Bombay Union of Journalists, 1987. *Trial by Fire: A Report on Roop Kanwar's Death*. Bombay)

The values which underlie the affirmation of this act are embodied in the term *pativrata*, a faithful and virtuous wife who is, above all, devoted to her husband. Literally, a *pativrata* has made a vow (*vrat*) to her husband (*pati*). The substance of this vow is to protect him, and this is done through votive observances (*vrata*). Through the performance of these observances, the wife intends to guarantee the health and well-being of her husband and also her children. We have already discussed renunciation as a cultural axiom. From this point of view the *sati* is a heroine because of the self-sacrificial nature of her act. In Rajasthan parallels are drawn between a soldier's death on the battlefield and *satis* who die on their husbands' funeral pyres. Since renunciation produces power, the act of *sati* results in powers that are beneficial to others because of the self-sacrificing nature of the act. One text states that the *sati* ascends to heaven and dwells there many millions of years. She also continues to protect her husband. One ancient text states,

> Even in the case of a husband who has entered into hell itself and who, seized by the servants of Death and bound with terrible bonds, has arrived at the very place of torment; even if he is already standing there, helpless and wretched, quivering with fear because of his evil deeds; even if he is a brahmin-killer or the murderer of a friend, or if he is ungrateful for some service done for him— even then a woman who refuses to become a widow can purify him: in dying, she takes him with her. (*Stridharmapaddhati*)

The benefits which purify the husband also have a good effect on the family by saving it from sickness and financial disaster. Even the larger community is saved from the heartache that future bad behavior might cause.

Those who support *sati* argue that it is a rare occurrence when a woman has such virtue and the power to become a *sati*. A genuine *sati* is necessarily voluntary and the benefits are the result of self-sacrifice. If a woman were compelled or forced to undertake this act, it would not be a genuine *sati*. The practice has the support of the highly regarded Shankaracharya of Puri who sees it as religiously sanctioned and founded on scriptures. "The Vedas, all the *Smritis*, the *Dharam*

Sindhu, Likhit Sindhu, etc., all detail the factors that justify sati—who would become a sati, how one should become a sati, who should not" (*Illustrated Weekly of India.* May 1, 1988).

This position is seen not only in statements by such religious figures and the Shankaracharya of Puri, but also among many of the people themselves. It has been pointed out that not only the local language newspapers, but also the national *Times of India* reported the news with devotion and admiration. And there was widespread popular support for the establishment of a suitable memorial even though it was against the law to do so.

Those on the other side of this issue are firmly convinced that the *sati* is not a heroine, but a victim. She is a victim of a patriarchal society in which women are so oppressed that *sati* begins to appear as the best of a series of bad possibilities. Not only does the widow become as low as an outcast, but she is often blamed for her husband's death. Again, one of our cultural axioms comes into play in that she must have done something in a previous life to merit such punishment. The husband, in effect, is punished for *her* bad karma. Moreover, the sincerity of her devotion, when doing her *vrats,* is thrown into question. The Hindu widow is an inauspicious person, to be kept out of sight during otherwise auspicious events. She should live an austere life so as to atone for previous evil deeds (whether in this life or a previous one) with the hope that she will not become a widow in the next cycle of rebirth. Such a life also has a purifying effect and enables the widow to counter previous bad karma. Officially the woman is not a widow until after the cremation of her husband's body, so the *sati* avoids the stigma attached to widowhood by never having become a widow. The argument continues that since women do not have decision-making power in life, why should it be presumed that they have it in this situation. Often those who oppose *sati* will claim that no widow has ever voluntarily mounted the pyre to be burned.

This debate over *sati* embodies the encounter of tradition and modernity. On the one side there are those who hold to the traditional values and place of women and the family. On the other side are those who champion the cause of women and seek to elevate them to equal standing with men. Traditional texts are based on the principle of inequality. Modern human rights perspectives are based on the presumption of equality. The Shankaracharya of Puri holds passionately that the anti-*sati* act "is against religion, civilisation, culture, ethics, morality. Every Hindu should die opposing it" (*Illustrated Weekly of India.* May 1, 1988). Those who support the anti-*sati* act do so with equal passion. Neither side seems able to compromise nor to enter into genuine discussion with the other. Emotions on this issue are too strong to permit that. It is not that Hindus do not know the truth about suicide and *sati.* They do. But there are two broad interpretations and understandings that are considered true by those who hold them.

C. Abortion

The earliest Hindu texts, the *Vedas,* speak of the god Vishnu as the protector of the "child-to-be" (*Rg-Samhita* VII.36.9). The uniform view is that abortion is a serious crime and the one who extracts the embryo from the womb is an evildoer. Later texts continue this view by stating that a woman who commits abortion loses caste. The *Laws of Manu* forbid ancestral liberations to women who harm the embryo or its mother (V.90). Although the embryo of a Brahmin merits more protection than that of a slave, even harming the embryo of the slave is punishable. Frequently other transgressions such as killing a Brahmin or violating a guru's bed are shown to be heinous by placing them side by side with those who abort an embryo. We have already noted that when the British permitted *sati* with certain conditions, one of the conditions was that the woman not be pregnant. In ancient medical texts abortion is a last resort and is contemplated only when the life of the mother is at stake or if the fetus is thought to be malformed.

The Hindu view behind this is that the human being is a combination of spirit (*atman, purusa*) and matter (*prakrti*). In the *Caraka Samhita* (III.3)

> conception occurs when intercourse takes place in due season between a man of unimpaired semen and a woman whose generative organ, (menstrual) blood and womb are unvitiated—when, in fact, in the event of intercourse thus described, the individual soul (*jiva*) descends into the union of semen and (menstrual) blood in the womb in keeping with the (*karmically* produced) psychic disposition (of the embryonic matter).

This seems to be the dominant view, even though in the *Garbha Upanishad* it is the 7th month in which the fetus is joined to the soul. The fetus in the womb is held to possess consciousness and even a memory of past lives. It is the trauma of birth that wipes such memories from consciousness.

The axioms of karma and rebirth also bear upon the negative valuation given to abortion. Such an action terminates the possibility of the unborn's opportunity to develop through postnatal experiences. The argument that perhaps even abortion is the result of karma is countered by pointing out that the laws of karma do not cancel the necessity of dharmic living in accordance with freedom and responsibility. Hindus speak of "timely" and "untimely" death, the former being death in the fullness of time while the latter is a premature death, a death that takes place before the maturation process is complete.

The importance of sons was another strong reason to protect the pregnant woman and her fetus in traditional India. Sons were necessary to continue the family line and to perform religious ceremonies at the death of the father. Without such rites the father's existence in the afterlife would be hopeless. A careful study of the ancient texts led Julius Lipner to conclude, "In other words, *de facto,* Hindu tradition has always accorded personal moral status to the embryo/fetus throughout pregnancy" (H. G. Coward, J. J. Lipner, and K. K. Young, 1989. *Hindu Ethics,* p. 60. State Univ. of New York Press, Albany). Or, in the words of S. Cromwell Crawford, "The general picture that emerges from this vast literature is that life begins at conception, feticide is a major sin, progeny is a great good, women are worthy of respect and care, and pregnant women are especially to be protected and granted concessions" (S. W. Crawford, 1995. *Dilemmas of Life and Death: Hindu Ethics in a North American Context,* pg. 25. State Univ. of New York Press, Albany).

Against this background it must be noted that in modern India, abortion is legal. In 1992 there were 600,000 recorded abortions in India, not to speak of the many that were unrecorded. The Medical Termination of Pregnancy Act passed by the Government of India in 1971 legalized abortion where the pregnancy would involve a risk to the mother or grave injury to her psychological well-being. The psychological risk comes to play in cases of rape or even if a child is conceived by the failure of a birth control device and the unwanted pregnancy would be presumed to cause the pregnant woman serious mental difficulties. It is clear, then, that the ancient texts notwithstanding, many modern Hindus use abortion as a means of terminating unwanted pregnancies as the result of failed birth control. The existence of widespread abortion as such has not caused a heated discussion, partially because of India's admitted need to control population growth.

What has triggered a heated discussion among modern Hindus is the selective abortion made possible through prenatal sex determination tests. As in the case of *sati,* the two sides are quite inflexible. On the one side are those who support prenatal sex determination tests such as amneocentesis ultrasound as a means of family planning, birth control, and eleviating maternal stress. We have already observed the religious reason for having a son. Although this is still a factor, there are economic reasons as well. These are connected with the practice of dowry. Although dowry was ruled out by the Dowry Prohibition Act of 1961, it is still practiced throughout India. The amount of payment to the family of the groom is determined by the income and means of the bride's family. Incurring huge debts is not uncommon. Marriage and its attendant dowry is also a means of social climbing. Families are often willing to scramble and survive for one daughter, but more than one can impose a life-long debt of considerable magnitude. The argument is that through ultrasound, one can plan the composition of one's family. If one already has a daughter and wants a son to complete the family, female fetuses can be aborted until a male fetus is produced. This is also used to support population control. If one has a daughter and desires a son, and has to have repeated births until the son is conceived, the already oppressive population will be dramatically increased. To continue having children would also weaken the family's economic situation and add stress to the family unit. Since, medical evidence to the contrary, most Hindus blame the woman for the gender of the fetus, repeated attempts for a son places added stress on the mother. These arguments center around the welfare of the family and the benefits to the nation, but the economic issue permeates the arguments.

On the other side stand feminists and those who side with them. For them it is simply one more indignity heaped upon women, this time even before birth. Ultrasound has become a thriving business in modern India. One pitch is printed on billboards throughout the country and may even be blared from loudspeakers: "Pay five hundred rupees now rather than 500,000 rupees later." This clearly targets the female fetus, for the latter figure is an estimated cost of a dowry and wedding. It has been observed that while the abortion issue is an ethical discussion in the West, in Asian countries it is more commonly propelled by practical realities that overshadow issues like rights and when life begins.

One might generalize that laws that place very heavy burdens upon the mass of the population are likely to be unenforceable because they are violated by almost everyone. This was the case with the prohibition of dowry. Those who hold this view support education as the only way to change the existing scenario. Even though the Dowry Prohibition Act was largely ineffectual for that reason, on January 1, 1996, the Government of India put into effect The Pre-Natal Diagnostic

Techniques (Regulation and Prevention of Misuse) Act of 1994. This act makes prenatal tests illegal when their intent is sex determination. Even when necessary for some other reason, the sex of the fetus is not to be revealed to the woman or to her relatives. There are strict penalties (monetary and imprisonment) for a woman who undertakes such tests, for relatives who encourage it, for clinics who advertise the service, and for health workers who might encourage the test. This bill was passed in 1994, but its implementation was delayed until the ban was ratified by the states. Such ratification shows that the bill has widespread public support. Nevertheless, it is too early to see how effective it will be. At the time of this writing no one has yet been prosecuted for offending this bill. One Hindu man laments the consumer society in which he lives, but concedes it is a reality. In his community he reports a saying that sons are referred to as "blank checks."

Hinduism Today (April, 1996) reports that there is already evidence that the tests are being pushed underground. Doctors have become more cautious and all is done through word of mouth. In some places the fee has gone from 700 rupees to 7000 rupees. It may never be possible to know the full extent of this practice since in some localities deaths are not registered.

How have feminists reacted to the enactment of this ban? Some applaud it because it is seen as a protection of the female fetus. Others point out that it takes away from a woman certain options that she had before the ban. If, say pro-abortion advocates, a woman has the right to an abortion, she must also be seen to have the right to selective abortion. And for that she needs the information that an ultrasound test can provide.

Ethics has a long history in Hinduism. While it has tended to concentrate on attitudes and personal cultivation leading to enlightenment, there are resources that can be used to address modern issues as well. Recent books have attempted to use these resources to discuss euthanasia and the environment. Although such topics are relatively undeveloped at present, one might expect more attention to such issues in the future. Hinduism can no longer be treated as simply an Indian religion. Hindu intellectuals have migrated to many countries around the world and are making an increasingly strong impact in those countries. It seems inevitable that as cultures encounter one another, Hindus will look into their tradition for insights into a still wider range of pressing modern issues.

Also See the Following Article

RELIGION AND ETHICS

Bibliography

Baird, R. D. (1991). "Essays in the History of Religions." Lang, New York.

Carman, J. R., and Marglin, F. (Eds.) (1985). "Purity and Auspiciousness in Indian Society." Brill, Leiden.

Coward, H. G., Lipner, J. J., and Young, K. K. (1989). "Hindu Ethics: Purity, Abortion and Euthanasia." State Univ. of New York Press, Albany.

Crawford, S. C. (1974). "The Evolution of Hindu Ethical Ideals." The Univ. Press of Hawaii, Honolulu.

Crawford, S. C. (1995). "Dilemmas of Life and Death: Hindu Ethics in a North American Context." State Univ. of New York Press, Albany.

Jhingran, S. (1989). "Aspects of Hindu Morality." Motilal Banarsidass, Delhi.

Kapur. P. (1993). "Girl Child and Family Violence." Har-Anand, New Delhi.

Mathur, I., and Sharma, S. (Eds.) (1995). "Health Hazards, Gender and Society." Rawat, New Delhi.

Raj, S. L. (Ed.) (1991). "Quest for Gender Justice." Satya Nilayam, Madras.

Schweitzer, A. (1936). "Indian Thought and Its Development." Beacon, Boston.

Sehgal, B. P. S. (1991). "Women, Birth Control and the Law." Deep & Deep, New Delhi.

Singh, I. P. (1989). "Women, Law and Social Change in India." Radiant, New Delhi.

HOMELESSNESS

G. John M. Abbarno
D'Youville College

I. Profile of the Homeless
II. The Causes of Homelessness in the United States
III. The Moral Status of Homelessness

GLOSSARY

deinstitutionalization A trend or policy to decrease the number of hospitalized mental patients.

existentialism A philosophical perspective that studies the meaning of having free choices in a finite existence.

feminization of poverty A condition in which women, especially older women, are at increased economic risk due to lower wages, early pregnancy, divorce, and abandonment.

gentrification An urban transition that typically includes the purchase of low-income housing and its renovation into upper income residences such as condominiums.

homeless People who have no residence address of their own.

marginalization A condition in which policies erode the social standing of a person or group of persons.

negative rights A concept that imposes obligations to refrain from acting in proscribed ways.

positive rights A concept that imposes obligations to act in a required manner or have required goods.

HOMELESSNESS is a complex social problem that reflects swift changes in contemporary culture. It involves diverse groups, all of which are extremely poor. The definition of homelessness approaches circularity; the homeless are people who do not have an address of their own. The Stewart McKinney Act of 1987 provides a more qualified definition of a homeless person: "One who lacks a fixed, permanent nighttime residence or whose nighttime residence is a temporary shelter, welfare hotel, or any public or private place not designed as sleeping accommodations for human beings" (J. Blau, 1992. *The Visible Poor* p. 8 Oxford Univ. Press, New York). This includes those people who reside with family or friends and, after a short stay, either from a sense of pride or personal conflict, join the many who seek refuge on the streets for a place of privacy and safety. The homeless are "basic needs seekers"; they are people without a key to a place of solitude. Homelessness is endemic to the human condition that grips those most vulnerable to economic and political shifts. It is only since the early 1990s that we find philosophers examining this condition.

There are several philosophical perspectives on homelessness. First is the existential viewpoint; having lost more than a personal space, they speak of estrangement from oneself and alienation from their ideals that gave life meaning. Second is the social and political dimensions of homelessness. These are among the most prevalent concerns of those addressing this subject, e.g., matters of public policy formulations that omit consideration of this group, as in the rezoning introduced in some urban areas that would exclude low-income housing, or restrictions imposed on activities that can be conducted in parks that, by circumlocution, discriminate against the homeless dwelling in public places. This domain asks for fair treatment of those groups whose lives have become impoverished while the same principle elevates and enriches the lot of others in society. Third, is the moral perspective where the issue becomes one of access and rights to be treated as persons and not as disposable objects of economic policy. One central question ethicists address is, what moral obligation does a society have to render a group the basic needs to pursue a life of happiness?

I. PROFILE OF THE HOMELESS

A. Misconceptions about Their Composite

The common perception about the homeless is that they are vagabonds, lazy and aimless people who either choose to not have the responsibility of employment and property or, once down on their luck, have no desire to continue in the social system. They are viewed as predominantly unmarried males who are often thought to be mentally ill or addicted to drugs and alcohol. It is also assumed that there is always a suitable place for these people to go, such as shelters or churches, but that they exercise their independence by remaining on the street. Part of the misconception is due to the lack of public policy that attended to the needs of the homeless, so there was not sufficient information of their plight until the late 1960s. Sociologist Peter Rossi (1989. *Down and Out in America.* Univ. of Chicago Press, IL) conducted one of the most concentrated studies of the homeless in Chicago, Illinois, in which he accounts for the changing perspective on this population, which he distinguished as the "old" and "new" homeless. The figure of the old homeless comes out of a study in New York City's Bowery (1969–1972). It found that the old homeless consisted mostly of older white males whose alcohol abuse and the paucity of jobs offered few alternatives to the street life.

The new homeless are younger and have less money than the older group. For example, the reported annual income of Chicago homeless in 1958 was $1058. In 1986, Rossi reports it at $1198 (J. D. Wright, 1989. *Address Unknown.* Aldine de Gruyter, New York). Economic depravation and political marginalization are sustained traits of the new homeless. Surprisingly they are younger and better educated, not as many are alco-

holics, and some have jobs but cannot earn enough to pay for rising rent costs and medical insurance. This transformation of the homeless reflects the changed social and economic conditions for which the attainment of a shelter would not be sufficient as a solution. Proposing shelters as the solution would be equivalent to doing nothing.

B. The New Face of the Homeless

The "new" homeless are a mixed population. Although advocates and social scientists disagree on the number of homeless there are (advocates put the figure at 3 million, whereas analysts believe it is 250,000 to 600,000), this is largely due to counting shelter homeless and street homeless. The ratio between the two gives a sum of how many are in any given area. The advocates always contend that there are a greater number of homeless who are hidden and will not allow themselves to be exposed to publicity. Whatever the actual count is, there is an alarming percentage of mentally ill as part of this group. Researchers indicate that 50% suffer from a form of mental illness, while those who are substance abusers (alcohol and drugs) represent 35–40%. The remaining 10% comprise families and children (M. A. Kraljic, 1992. *The Homeless Problem.* Wilson, New York). The majority of this group is headed by women who cannot afford to pay rent, feed their children, or care for them by purchasing medication when needed. They are quickly growing in number, suggesting that even if they are employed, without affordable housing they move their family to a shelter or the streets. This growing trend is referred to as the "feminization of poverty."

The most devastating effect of homelessness is noticed in the children. Not only is their health in jeopardy due to lack of proper nutrition, but education is interrupted by either the constant mobility of their parent or their own lack of motivation out of embarrassment and resentment. It becomes more difficult for a mother with even the best intentions to hold the unit together as she balances whatever work she can find and a day care for her child to attend, usually at the shelter where they have taken residence. But it is reported that some shelters introduce a new set of challenges: mean-spirited older children and unclean premises.

II. THE CAUSES OF HOMELESSNESS IN THE UNITED STATES

There are five common sources of homelessness: (1) rising unemployment through industrialization; (2) an increase in the number of wage labor opportunities; (3) gentrification of the city and an increased cost of housing; (4) deinstitutionalization of the mentally ill patients from supervised care; and (5) feminization of poverty.

The first two sources can be attributed to diminished corporate loyalty. Pushed by global markets to remain competitive, technological advances are made without consideration of the human factor, employees, and the community. As corporations in the United States increase their production of goods outside the country for lower wages, more unskilled laborers are unemployed and communities reconfigured. Some typical examples include plant relocation, corporate mergers and takeovers of established companies, downsizing, and the restructuring of corporate production.

Since the economy shifted from industrial producers to service (its most rapid phase was from 1979 to 1984), 11.5 million people lost their jobs to deindustrialization (Blau, 1992). By October 1994, the poverty level in the United States recorded its greatest increase in 30 years, at 39 million people (*Washington Post*, Oct. 7, 1994).

The third source of homelessness, the gentrification of the city, stems from the diminishing availability of affordable housing in central urban areas. Gentrification involves the purchase and restoration of older residences by middle-income earners, landlords, and developers. These developers purchase apartments and rooming houses and convert them into single-family upscale apartments or condominiums. Although the old neighborhoods are revitalized by higher income residents, they displace the poor.

The fourth contribution began 30 years ago under President Kennedy: the deinstitutionalization program of mental patients. Mainstreaming patients into community life in conjunction with a network of community mental health centers (CMHCs) was believed to be an asset of this program. The CMHCs were designed to serve the chronically severe patients once released so that there would be continued care. But these centers ended up focusing on preventative care since they were not sufficiently funded to staff appropriate professionals. They spent their time on the "worried well," and those in need wandered the streets since most shelters do not admit people with psychiatric problems.

Feminization of poverty is the final and most recently cited source of homelessness in the United States. This was discussed already as a growing concern that emerges out of the traditional masculine socioeconomic structure. Many women, particularly single parents, are on the threshold of poverty. High costs of child care, health care, and housing often put them on the street.

III. THE MORAL STATUS OF HOMELESSNESS

A. Marginalized Citizenship

As the numbers of homeless increase, they seek dwelling in any available warm cavern: doorways, subways, sidewalk grids over subways, park benches, and public buildings. Tolerance and frustration over the complexity of the condition develop compassion fatigue among many city officials. At the U.S. Mayor's Conference in 1991, it was estimated that homelessness grows at a rate of 25% each year. An example of the exasperation is the callous treatment of the homeless in major American cities. In Seattle, Washington, an attempt was made to "move them away," while in Atlanta, Georgia, Andrew Young offered them a ticket "home"?! In Phoenix, Arizona, garbage was declared public property so that picking through trash was considered theft. Laws have been written to insulate society from this group and have thus invited charges of human rights violations. The late U.S. Supreme Court Justice Thurgood Marshall observed, "The homeless were politically powerless inasmuch as they lack the financial resources necessary to obtain access to the most effective means of persuasion" (N. V. McKittrick, 1988. *Fordham Urban Law Rev.* **16**(3) p. 304).

Moralists and legal scholars have crafted arguments supporting the rights of the homeless to exercise choices worthy of being human. They have addressed the fundamental issues of disenfrachisement, denial of dwelling space, safety, food, and health care (G. J. M. Abbarno, 1997. *The Ethics of Homelessness*. Rodopi, Amsterdam).

B. Moral Rights and Duties

The rights claims made on behalf of the homeless to ensure that basic needs are met are grounded in their value of personhood. These claims honor both positive and negative rights. The argument is made that the duty of a bountiful society to provide liberty, shelter, and food to its citizens is derived from principles of fairness. Each person has a right to satisfy their basic needs and pursue happiness. When the distribution of wealth is concentrated so that it serves to benefit the least needy while the most needy receive woefully less so that their choices cannot be qualitatively changed, an underclass is reinforced. Social position along with a person's self-esteem is profoundly compromised.

Moralists suggest that respecting negative rights of individuals, namely, not to interfere in their lives, is central to autonomy and self-respect. Since certain communities grew tired of the homeless sleeping in parks and doorways, they intervened, sweeping streets and buildings and placing them in shelters. The rationale given is "it is for their own safety." That such occurrences came before conventions questions the sincerity of the intervention. After judicial intervention and social activists championed the homeless cause, the moral imperative of prevention was begun.

In the United States, services have begun to assist low-income renters and homeowners avoid eviction or foreclosure. Mediation between landlords and tenants is sometimes offered, and financial assistance is made available along with household management advice. Such efforts are aimed to keep the family intact. Beyond prevention, some programs are designed to assist homeless to make it back into a stable home life. The Stewart B. McKinney Homelessness Act (1987) has undergone refinements to allocate funding to communities who need shelter, food, and counseling. The Housing and Urban Development (HUD) program responded in 1996 with Shelter Plus Care which provides rent subsidy and case management connected to counseling for the homeless.

Clearly, these are not immediate solutions, but they are recognized social responses to meet the rights claims of the homeless. As homelessness is more carefully followed, its randomness may become more appreciated, and the realization that it could happen to any one of us or our neighbors may have a sobering affect on moral attitudes toward the homeless.

Also See the Following Articles

EXISTENTIALISM • MENTAL ILLNESS, CONCEPT OF • PRIVACY • RIGHTS THEORY • THEORIES OF JUSTICE: HUMAN NEEDS

Bibliography

Abbarno, G. J. M. (1997). Homeless exposure. In "Ethics for Today and Tomorrow" (J. G. Haber, Ed.). Jones and Bartlett, Sudbury, MA.

Anderson, E. (1993). "Value in Ethics and Economics." Harvard Univ. Press, Cambridge, MA.

Giame, B., and Grunberg, J. (1992). "Beyond Homelessness." Univ. of Iowa Press, Iowa City.

Grob, G. (1991). "From Asylum to Community." Princeton Univ. Press, Englewood Cliffs, NJ.

Jencks, C. (1994). "The Homeless." Harvard Univ. Press, Boston, MA.

Ludwig, E. V. (1991). The mentally ill homeless, evolving involuntary commitment issues. *Villanova Law Review,* **36,** pp. 1085–1111.

Orr, L. (Ed.) (1991). "The Homeless. Opposing Viewpoints." Greenhaven, San Diego, CA.

White, R., Jr. (1992). "Rude Awakenings." Center for Self Governance, San Francisco, CA.

HOMICIDE, CRIMINAL VERSUS JUSTIFIABLE

Philip E. Devine
Providence College

GLOSSARY

abortion The killing of an immature human organism in its mother's womb (also called termination or interruption of pregnancy).

conventionalist principle The principle that persons are whoever is defined as such by a given society.

double effect A principle that permits an act resulting in a bad effect, such as the death of a person, so long as that death is foreseen as a consequence rather than the intended result.

euthanasia Killing held to be in the interest of the person or other creature killed.

homicide In the broader sense, the killing of a human being by a human being, including the person who is killed; in the narrower sense, the killing of a human being by *another* human being.

human being Any member of the species *Homo sapiens.*

involuntary Against the will of the person affected.

manslaughter The act or fact of killing a human being in circumstances in which a reasonable person might be overwhelmingly tempted to do so.

murder Homicide that is neither justified nor excused, i.e., no mitigating, or only slightly mitigating, circumstances obtain.

nonvoluntary Without the will of the person affected.

person A subject of rights and duties.

potentiality principle The principle that persons are all those who will, in due course, exercise certain distinctively human capacities.

present possession principle The principle that persons are those who now in possession or enjoyment of distinctively human capacities.

sentience principle The principle that persons are all conscious beings.

species principle The principle that all human beings are persons.

suicide The intentional killing of oneself.

voluntary With the consent of the person affected.

HOMICIDE is regarded as a serious matter by virtually any system of law or ethics. At the same time, virtually every system of law or ethics justifies, or at least excuses, some forms of killing. Moreover, the killing of human beings or persons needs to be distinguished from the killing of nonhuman animals or even of plants. Answers to the resulting questions have always been tightly linked to regligious teachings—and not surprisingly in view of the mysterious character of the death inflicted on the decedent. Nonetheless, it is possible, up to a point, to discuss the ethics of homicide without directly referring to religious issues. That is what I attempt to do here.

Encyclopedia of Applied Ethics, Volume 2

I. PRELIMINARIES

Homicide is regarded as a serious matter by virtually any system of law or ethics. Nonetheless, homicide poses serious conceptual and normative issues, for nearly all systems of ethics hold that homicide is sometimes warranted, and there are situations in which someone will die, whatever we do. Further, issues such as abortion, assisted suicide, capital punishment, euthanasia, and war continue to divide our society. In this entry I shall not attempt a comprehensive discussion of the various grounds—from hunger striking to killing in war—on which homicide or suicide might be justified or excused, but rather I will only elaborate on some principles that apply to all forms of killing.

Homicide is special in that the harm inflicted on the victim, death, is radically incommensurable with other possible forms of harm and with the evils that might flow from continued life. Death is opaque: it resists assimilation into the normal patterns of moral and prudential deliberation. Here I assume, merely for the sake of argument, that death is what it in fact it appears to be, the unequivocal cessation of our existence. An afterlife of whatever sort will complicate the argument, and dealing with the resulting questions is a matter for theology rather than philosophy.

II. CONCEPTUAL ISSUES

A. Homicide

According to a wide definition, homicide is any killing of a human being by a human being, including the person who kills himself; according to a narrower definition, it is the killing of a human being by *another* human being. I will deal with homicide using the second definition first, and then will consider the question of suicide.

B. Murder

Murder is primarily a legal category, but it has a closely associated moral sense as well. In both cases it means the killing of a human being, where that killing is neither justified nor excused, and thus must bear the full onus of criminal liability or moral censure. Usage is often vaguer than this; the cruel or wanton killing of a nonhuman animal, e.g., the poisoning of a pet dog by a neighbor, is sometimes called murder even by people who are not animal rights advocates.

Both law and customary morality recognize a variety of situations in which it is unfair or uncharitable to regard an intentional killer as a murderer, even if his action cannot on the whole be defended. The stock legal example is that of a man who surprises his wife with her lover and proceeds to kill one or both of them. Presumably the same argument would extend to a wife who surprises her husband with his mistress. Kant excuses, though he does not justify, infanticide by a woman whose circumstances do not permit her to care for her infant and dueling among those under severe social pressure to take part. Other plausible examples include forms of self-defense that fall short of full justification (for example, when it is possible to flee, but only with serious loss of reputation) and killing by a conscript soldier on the wrong side of the war, or by a volunteer in unquestioned good faith. Many, though not all, cases of abortion and euthanasia also fall short of murder in the full sense. Both private people and the law make these judgments intuitively rather than on any theory, and the same is true of the defenses of insanity and infancy, which excuse the agent from all culpability, without justifying his action.

C. Human Beings and Persons

1. Preliminaries

Many discussions of life and death issues attempt to distinguish between human beings, or members of the species *homo sapiens,* and persons, or bearers of primary rights and duties. Only the killing of a person, on this view, can be homicide in the moral sense (let alone murder), though it does not necessarily follow that killing a human being who is not a person is morally innocuous. We cannot, however, identify right-holders with subjects of duty, for all of us undergo periods of unconsciousness or incapacity in which we cannot be addressed in terms of duty, though we continue to have rights.

Five principles require consideration here.

1. Conventionalist principle: All and only those creatures defined as such by a given society are persons, i.e., have a right to life
2. Present possession principle: All and only those creatures are persons who have certain distinctively human traits, for example, self-consciousness
3. Sentience principle: All and only those creatures are persons who are conscious, perhaps at a very simple level

4. Potentiality principle: All and only those creatures are persons who now possess, or will in due course possess, certain distinctively human traits

5. Species principle: All and only human beings are persons

2. The Conventionalist Principle

The conventionalist principle assimilates personhood to citizenship, which is often defined by contingent criteria such as birth in the United States rather than Mexico. This criterion provides the strongest ground for drawing the line at birth.

But no clear convention is presently in place about many questions of life and death. Moreover, the conventionalist principle implies that those who have the power to define the rules of society define who is to count as a person—in other words, might makes right. This implication is offensive to conventional opinion itself, which recognizes entrenched systems of injustice such as slavery and massive breakdowns of justice such as the Holocaust—and rightly so, since power relations can change very quickly, as when a member of the elite finds himself alone in a dangerous place.

3. The Present Possession Principle

The present possession principle implies that infants (and in some versions, small children) are not persons. Moreover, only with some strain can it accommodate the personhood of the sleeping, the temporarily comatose, and the curably insane.

4. The Sentience Principle

The sentience principle is a vegetarian principle, since many nonhuman animals are conscious, at least in a rudimentary way. Moreover, it implies that abortion is homicide from (roughly) halfway through pregnancy. Though some writers find these conclusions acceptable, the sentience principle nonetheless suffers from a serious intellectual deficiency. There is no intelligible reasons why the painless killing of a merely sentient being, which will never achieve any further capacity, should bear the heavy burden placed upon killing a human being.

5. The Potentiality Principle

The potentiality principle is like the present possession principle in fixing on distinctively human capacities such as the ability to make moral choices. But it includes in the class of persons not only those creatures who presently have those capacities, but also those who will in due course have them if allowed to live. Hence it protects normal embryos, fetuses, and infants—as well as those suffering from physical handicaps. But it excludes the irreversibly comatose, the seriously retarded, and possibly the severely brain damaged and the incurably insane. These might be protected, however, by prudential considerations, such as the need to protect the boundaries of humanity by defending its most vulnerable members.

6. The Species Principle

The species principle holds that all human beings are persons. It protects all human beings from conception to natural death. There are, however, some important problems for its application.

(a) The definition of death is a highly technical question. A human being can persist even though he has lost all capacity for consciousness, let alone the capacities that are characteristic of human beings. But the mere persistence of cellular life is not enough to make a living human being. Some form of brain-death criterion is therefore required even by the species principle, for the brain is the core organ of a human being, as well as the organ most involved in our distinctively human capacities.

(b) The preembryo, from fertilization to about 14 days thereafter, is capable of twinning or merging with another preembryo in a way that does not conform to our ideas about personal identity. The issue is, in part, whether even the species principle requires exclusive reliance on biological criteria to resolve questions of whether an entity is, in the relevant sense, human. (For a recent discussion of this issue, see M. Johnson and J. Porter, 1995. *Theological Stud.* **56**, 743–770.) Even if we decide this question in the negative, however, some moral restraints are appropriate: it is, in my view, wrong to deliberately bring a preembryo into being while intending or expecting to destroy it afterward.

(c) Virtually everyone finds late abortion more troubling than early abortion, and infanticide more troubling than either. But by the species principle (and the potentiality principle as well) these acts are equally homicidal. Hence "moderates" argue that the fetus is neither a person nor a mere animal, but something intermediate, and "gradualists" argue that it moves by stages into the class of persons. But no one, to my knowledge, has ever worked out a coherent, or even a stable, correlation between stages of fetal development and grounds on which abortion might be justified. Some weight, however, must be given natural human feeling, particularly when dealing with questions of the gravity of the wrong committed.

D. Intention and Foresight

The principle of double effect permits actions that have as their foreseen consequence the death of an innocent person so long as (1) his death is intended neither as an end nor as a means, and (2) there is due proportion between the good sought and the evil accepted. A useful criterion for applying it is to ask the question, "Would we act as we do even if the situation were different only in those respects which yield lethal consequences?" Applying the principle of double effect to the whole range of life and death issues requires some complicated reasoning and close judgments, but the outer limits of the principle should be clear.

It is permissible to give a person dying in pain as much morphine as may be necessary to ease his suffering, even though doing so shortens his life. (If morphine did not inhibit breathing, but only relieved pain, we would still use it.) It is not, however, permissible to use strychnine, or another drug which ends pain only by killing the patient—at least in the absence of some general justification for mercy killing.

It is permissible to bomb an extermination camp in order to stop the killing going on there, even though the innocent inmates die as a result. (If the camp were empty, we would still bomb it.) Shooting enemy soldiers, on the other hand, requires another sort of justification.

Ceasing or omitting medical treatment on the grounds that they are, on the whole, not worth the trouble is not homicide. Examples include not beginning intravenous feeding of a man in a terminal coma resulting from cancer, deciding not to attempt open-heart surgery on a senile patient, and ceasing to pump the lungs of a severely depressed 94-year-old man suffering from pneumonia. (We might omit these treatments even if we expected the patient to survive anyhow.) But to refuse to feed a defective infant is homicide and, unless somehow justified or excused, murder—for even a healthy individual needs food to live.

As this last example shows, the distinction between acting and refraining, though important in law, is of secondary interest in morals. What it does is provide a visible guide to intention for the benefit of those, the agent included, who may be muddled about what is intended.

III. JUSTIFICATIONS FOR HOMICIDE

Let us grant that what is proposed is killing a human being or person. Pacificists in the strict sense hold that the act is for that reason always wrong, but the rest of us admit justifications for some forms of homicide.

A. Other-Regarding Justifications

1. Utility

The simplest argument for killing is that doing so is best on the whole. This warrants atrocious conclusions, such as that it is legitimate to kill a man in order to beget happy children on his wife, or that it is legitimate to kill children on the ground that they are possible rivals for the throne, as was accepted practice among the Ottoman Turks. Few people want to live in a world in which figures in authority—physicians as well as policemen—hold that they have an unlimited license to kill on whatever grounds seem best to them. Furthermore, utilitarianism implies that we may kill one person to secure a slight increase in the happiness of large numbers of others; Rawls' complaint that "classical utilitarianism … fails to take seriously the distinction between persons" (J. Rawls, 1971. *A Theory of Justice,* p. 187). Harvard Univ. Press, Cambridge, MA) is thus in point.

2. Self-Defense, Individual and Collective

The most common alternative to a utilitarian approach to homicide holds that it is wrong to kill the innocent. Moralists thus justify killing in self-defense, both individually and collectively. But the word *innocent* is open to more than one interpretation, as the case of capital punishment makes clear.

John Finnis defends capital punishment on the grounds that "the defining and essential … point of punishing is to restore an order of fairness which was disrupted by the criminal's criminal act" (J. Finnis, 1983. *The Fundamentals of Ethics,* p. 118. Georgetown Univ. Press, Washington, DC). Pope John Paul II, however, argues that punishment

> ought not to go to the extreme of executing the criminal except in cases of absolute necessity: in other words, when it would not be possible otherwise to defend society. Today however, as the result of steady improvements in the organization of the penal system, such cases are very rare, if not non-existent. (John Paul II, n.d. *Encyclical Letter, The Gospel of Life (Evangelium Vitae),* sect. 56, p. 91. Pauline, Boston)

A plausible example of legitimate infliction of the death penalty under this formulation would be the execution of a terrorist whose comrades are prepared to kill in order to secure his release.

To fully resolve this issue would require a deep excursion into the theory of punishment. For present purposes, it is sufficient to note that the notion of *juridical* innocence is here being replaced in the consciousness of morally sensitive persons by that of *causal* innocence (not harming), at least for the purpose of the moral rule against killing. *Moral* innocence has never been the issue, since a soldier on the wrong side of a war, though "guilty" in the causal sense, may be in entire good faith. (A soldier in an international war is moreover juridically innocent, since he has not been, nor justly could be, convicted of any crime.) Nonetheless, controversy persists concerning the legitimacy of killing an unborn child that poses, in all moral and juridical innocence, a clear and present threat to his mother's life.

3. Thomson on Abortion

Judith Jarvis Thomson argues that I am entitled to remove a violinist attached to my kidneys, even though detaching him will cost him his life (1971. *Philos. Public Affairs,* 1). And she builds a wide-ranging defense of abortion on these premises, one that does not require her to deny that the fetus or unborn child has a right to live.

As a general defense of abortion, Thomson's argument is doubly bad. First, when someone performs an abortion, seldom if ever is a fetus merely detached from a pregnant woman; cutting up or poisoning the fetus is the more usual method. Second, in all but rape cases, a pregnant woman has voluntarily risked pregnancy by consenting to intercourse; feminists have endeavored to widen the concept of rape, but it cannot be extended to the majority of heterosexual encounters without undermining the claim that women are, as much as men, free and responsible agents.

Nonetheless, Thomson's argument calls our attention to the fact that, in pregnancy, one person is entirely enclosed in the body of another—a situation unique in human life. While this special circumstance does not resolve all abortion questions, it does affect the judgment of morally sensitive persons in close cases.

4. Extreme Necessity and the Question of Absolutes

Utilitarianism returns to the argument in the guise of certain extreme circumstances which may require us to modify, or make exceptions to, our general rules about killing. For example, is it legitimate to kill an infant to stop him from crying when his cries will attract Nazis on a search-and-destroy mission? May a physician perform an (otherwise unjustified) abortion when the Nazis threaten to kill every pregnant Jewish woman under their control? Assuming that euthanasia is in general wrong, what of cases where pain relievers and other forms of palliative care are not available, for example, that of a man inextricably caught in the burning wreckage of a train?

One way of understanding such cases is that the agent is caught in a "conscience-box" in which every possible action is wrong. (See P. Devine, April 1978. *Ethics.*) The belief that conscience-boxes are impossible seems to me a matter of (possibly rational) faith, rather than of strict logic, which depends for its vindication on the successful completion of the casuistical enterprise. As Fr. Richard McCormick has formulated the point, the casuist "is asked to be both theoretically consistent and practically sensitive to all the complexity and intransigence of reality—in other words to plug all the loopholes in a prudent and persuasive way" (1978. *Doing Evil to Achieve Good* (R. McCormick and P. Ramsey, Eds.), p. 35. Loyola Univ. Press, Chicago). In other words, the casuist attempts to formulate exceptionless moral rules (however complex) in such a way that we are never faced with a forced option of violating at least one of them—a prospect that many people find hopeless. Nonetheless, the complexity of human situations does not establish the impossibility of formulating absolute prohibitions on some sorts of conduct and gives us some reasons for looking for such prohibitions, for without them we might easily find ourselves lost in a trackless moral wildnerness.

B. Decedent-Regarding Justifications

Decedent-regarding justifications for killing are of two sorts: either the person killed has consented to being killed, or being killed is thought to be in that person's interest. These may be combined, as in the argument for voluntary euthanasia.

1. Consensual Homicide

Consensual homicide and assisted suicide raise essentially the same problem, since if both parties to a transaction intend a person's death, it does not matter who pulls the trigger. In both cases there are powerful objections to accepting consent as a justification for homicide. Here I discuss these objections in terms of consensual homicide rather than assisted suicide.

We do not recognize consent to just anything. We do not let people sell themselves into slavery. Most people would not recognize consent to forms of indoctrination, as are believed to be practiced in some "cults," that are designed to extinguish the member's consciences in favor of that of the leader's. Nor do we recognize consent even to an attempt on one's life, as in a duel or in gladitorial combat. Nor do we let people sell their hearts for the benefit of their heirs. Hence there seems no compelling reason to recognize consent to being killed.

Moreover, for consent to be valid, the person consenting must know what he is consenting to: a marriage is invalid if either party does not know what sexual intercourse is. But death is the great unknown, or, more precisely, it is a void opaque to the human intellect and imagination. Even death is not what it appears to be, that is to say, if there is some sort of afterlife, to consent to death is to consent to a venture of the most risky sort imaginable. I consider further on the issue of whether this venture might be acceptable if taken by a person solely on his own responsibility.

Important strands of contemporary secular morality go beyond rejecting consensual homicide to authorizing active interference with the attempt to kill onself, or at least a serious attempt at dissuasion. Michael Walzer makes this argument, not in terms of the "thick" morality of some particular tradition, but of the "thin" morality that leads us to support opposition to tyranny in Beijing or Prague. In his own words,

> We will use force ... to prevent a person from committing suicide, without knowing who he is and where he comes from. Perhaps he has reasons for suicide confirmed by his maximal morality and endorsed by his moral community. Even so, "life" is a reiterated value and defending it is an act of solidarity. And if we give up the forcible defense out of respect for his reasons, we might still criticize the moral culture that provides those reasons; it is insufficiently attentive, we might say, to the value of life. (M. Walzer, 1994. *Thick and Thin,* p. 16. Univ. of Notre Dame Press, Notre Dame, IN)

Nearly everyone would take this view of one common form of would-be suicide: the adolescent facing a world in which he doubts someone with his temperament can find a place.

2. Euthanasia

By euthanasia I mean the killing of a person, whether with his consent or against his will, on the ground that he is better off dead. People have made such judgments about those facing disgrace or despair, but I here discuss euthanasia in a medical context. (Depression represents a borderline region between painful illness and simple unhappiness.) I assume that alternative ways of relieving pain and suffering are available, even if the physician finds them less adequate than killing. But I do not consider the complexities involved in ceasing or omitting life-prolonging treatments—for example, feeding tubes for stroke victims with a bad prognosis. These issues are important, both in theory and in practice, but too technical to discuss here. I shall, however, include physician-assisted suicide, insofar as its primary rationale is the patient's wretched condition rather than his desire to die.

a. Involuntary Euthanasia

Involuntary euthanasia, sometimes called paternalistic killing, is euthanasia carried out against the express will of the person killed. Euthanasia of this sort is conceptually possible, since one can regard a patient's wish to live as based on illusion (say about the next world or about the prospects of recovery). But it is hard to distinguish such euthanasia from murder: consider, for example, a proposal to kill members of some minority to free them from the degradation of living a society that scorns them.

b. Nonvoluntary Euthanasia

Nonvoluntary euthanasia, sometimes called noninvoluntary euthanasia, is euthanasia without the consent of the person affected, but without his express objection either—for example, when he is unconscious, insane, an infant, or otherwise incompetent to understand what is proposed. (Or we might neglect to inform him of the effects of a proposed injection.) Here defenders of euthanasia usually invoke the proxy consent of the patient's family or of the representatives of civil society. (I shall discuss living wills further on.) This form of euthanasia corresponds to the euthanasia of animals—including the killing of unwanted kittens in shelters and the "sacrifice" of experimental subjects. In practice, nonvoluntary euthanasia is little different from involuntary euthanasia, since all people, especially those who are sick enough to be candidates for euthanasia, go through periods of incompetence. And no one really understands what is at stake in a decision to die.

c. Voluntary Euthanasia

Voluntary euthanasia is killing of a person in his own interests, and with his consent. A living will drawn up in anticipation of the occasion is not sufficient to establish consent in such cases: just as even convinced pessimists still jump out of the path of buses, so even lifelong advocates of euthanasia might still tremble at the brink of nothingness. But when killer and decedent concur in their judgment that death is called for, the case for killing is at its apogee.

Nonetheless, the judgment of killer and decedent are vitiated by the opacity of death, which deprives them both of the needed understanding of what is proposed. Moreover, prudential considerations, of the sort usually called "slippery slope," caution us against admitting euthanasia, especially in a society where the costs of medical care have become a serious issue.

An examination of the euthanasia literature quickly discloses that its advocates do not confine themselves to those dying of cancer or AIDS. One writer advocates euthanasia for a woman who is "mildly insane and for no useful reason . . . almost ruining the lives of others" (W. Alvarez, 1972. *Humanistic Perspectives in Medical Ethics* (M. Visscher, Ed.), p. 68. Prometheus, Buffalo, NY). Another speaks of "the wider problem of all those who are burdened with the ills associated with age" (Williams, 1966. "Euthanasia and Abortion." *University of Colorado Law Review* 38, p. 184). Nor have advocates of euthanasia squarely confronted the fact that the Nazis began their extermination campaign not with Jews, Slavs, Gypsies, or homosexuals, but with sick people deemed unworthy of continued life. On the contrary they dismiss the slippery slope argument as "pernicious nonsense" and "obscurantist flim-flam."

IV. SUICIDE

Issues of other-homicide are highly controversial, and the judgments made here are no exception. But all such issues, even abortion, can be discussed, up to a point at least, without engaging our deepest beliefs about the nature of the universe and our place in it. Suicide differs from other-homicide in this respect, with the result that any short discussion will inevitably produce an appearance of relativism. The appearance of relativism would be increased had I space to discuss the views of Schopenhauer, the differences between the Jewish and the Christian traditions, and non-Western traditions such as the Japanese. A discussion of the problems posed by suicides of political protest, aristocratic suicides of honor, and the suicide of a spy to prevent his giving away secrets under torture would engage a still wider range of views. A further set of issues has to do with the relationship between suicide and the ethics of virtue, and in particular the differing understandings of courage in various military traditions.

I accept neither relativism nor the right of the secular-permissive view to rule the public square in a society divided about ultimate issues. But I will not be able to discuss the problems generated by worldviews in conflict with any adequacy here.

A. The Secular-Permissive View

David Hume provides the classic expression of the secular-permissive view of suicide. Rejecting all the traditional arguments against suicide, he treats the act as morally indifferent. In his own words, "no man ever threw away his life when it is worth living" (1964. In *Philosophical Works* (T. H. Green and T. H. Grose, Eds.), p. 414. Aalen, Germany). But Hume also held that practical reason is, and inevitably must be, the slave of the passions—in which he also included the calmer emotions that sustain the ordinary life of society. Hence those in whom suicide prompts either horror or deep sadness are therefore entitled to neglect Hume's argument.

Another source of the secular-permissive view is a denial that there are duties to oneself, or, less misleadingly, that self-regarding acts are within the province of morality. If I am morally free to injure myself in other ways, I am surely free to kill myself as well. This ignores, however, the extreme difficulty of injuring oneself without injuring other people. Moreover, morality is concerned not only with questions of social order, but also with the requirements of a life (or death) worthy of a human being.

Advocates of the secular-permissive view also defend "balance sheet" suicides based on our estimate of the possibilities of life available to us. (The same argument easily extends to the killing of others, at least when these others cannot speak for themselves, as is the case with infants and the insane.) Here they ignore the fact that the choice is not between this or that life course, but between life and death—and death, considered as annihilation, is opaque to understanding, and there is no reason to suppose that suicides will fare well in an afterlife should there be one.

B. The Stoical View

A rationalistic analogue to the secular-permissive view is that of the ancient Stoics. They held that one should accept one's destined place and act appropriately within it, enduring with dignity whatever misfortune such a way of life might entail. But there was one limit to the policy of patient endurance they counselled: one might kill oneself if it was impossible to live with dignity. But in fact this limitation is arbitrary both in theory and in practice, and places no effective limit upon the option of suicide. Seneca argues that suicide is not only the recourse of victims of illness or tyranny, but of those who are disgusted with the world in which they are forced to live.

C. The Kantian View

The central working principle of Kant's moral philosophy is that one ought always treat humanity, whether in oneself or another, as an end-in-itself and never as a means merely. Among the duties to oneself this approach to ethics entails, the chief is a duty not to commit suicide. To kill oneself because one's life lacked the appropriate "quality," as the Stoical and secular approaches both permit us to do, would be to treat one's existence as having not a dignity but a price.

The most plausible exceptions under Kant's principle involve suicide to escape, not pain or disability, but situations in which one's human dignity is systematically denied. No pain need be involved in such situations: imagine killing oneself to avoid the use of one's comatose body as an organ farm, or for purposes of nontherapeutic experimentation. A strict Kantian would respond, however, that even in such cases, there is no essential degradation of the victim, so long as he does not consent to his being abused in this way. (Those who victimize him are of course degraded.) We admire those slaves who did not kill themselves, or even bring about their own deaths by hopeless rebellion, but managed either to escape or to live with some dignity.

D. The Platonic View

At the borderline between philosophy and religion lies the view of Plato. Socrates argues in the *Phaedo* that, though a philosopher naturally desires to escape this earthly prison, nonetheless he must not kill himself, since the gods have placed each of us on earth with a task to perform which we may not abandon under fire. Demythologized, this argument says that each of us has a unique individual destiny to fulfill, and that it is our obligation to persist in this task so long as we can. It involves, however, a lenient casuistry in cases where it is not the individual, but his circumstances, which may be said to have decreed his death. Having made the argument just given, Socrates shows no qualms about cooperating in his own execution.

E. The Christian View

From a Christian point of view, suicide is the worst of sins, so far as overt behavior is concerned—though even in such cases we are not entitled to judge the heart of the sinner. That it may be punished after death and that the suicide lacks the opportunity to repent are secondary issues. In part this judgment is based on "natural law" considerations—that we are naturally disposed to continue ourselves in being. But its deepest source is theological. Christ, we are told, "overcame death by death," and it is the task of each Christian to participate in the saving work of Christ by accepting the death God has ordained for him, rather than taking it upon himself to decree the conditions under which he is prepared to live. We are only stewards of our lives, not full owners.

When it comes to casuistry, the crucial criterion for Christians is that of intention. In decisions whether to cease attempting to prolong life, what matters is not the technical aspects of feeding tubes, but the distinction between decreeing one's own death and the pious acceptance of God's will.

The Christian view is both too fierce and too partisan to claim directly to determine public policy in pluralistic societies (and, in a philosophical context, revelation is not available as a source of premises). But the consciences of Christians, which may require them to keep clear of behavior they abhor, are entitled to at least as much respect as those of anyone else. Moreover, Christians are as much entitled as anyone else to make their voices heard in the public square. Finally, in understanding our present problems we need to understand why our ancestors regarded suicide not just as crime, but in some ways more serious than ordinary murder. We thus reach the limits of what can be argued without putting into question the meaning of our earthly existence. And, when we do so, the claims of Christian faith surprisingly converge with the "animal" impulse to survive, even against the odds.

Acknowledgment

I am grateful to Michael Wreen for his comments on an earlier draft of this article.

Also See the Following Articles

Bibliography

Burke, M. (1996). Sortal essentialism and the potentiality principle. *Rev. Metaphys.* **49**, 491–514.

Devine, P. (1989). "Relativism, Nihilism, and God." Notre Dame Univ. Press, Notre Dame.

Devine, P. (1990). "The Ethics of Homicide." Paperback ed. Notre Dame Univ. Press, Notre Dame.

Devine, P. (1995). A fallacious argument against moral absolutes. *Argumentation* **9**, 611–616.

Devine, P. (1996). "Human Diversity and the Culture Wars." Praeger, Westport, CT.

Finnis, J. (1983). "The Fundamentals of Ethics." Georgetown Univ. Press, Washington, DC.

John Paul II (1994). "Crossing the Threshold of Hope" (V. Messori, Ed.). Transl. J. McPhee and M. McPhee. Knopf, New York.

John Paul II (n.d.). "Encyclical Letter, The Gospel of Life (*Evangelium Vitae*)." Pauline, Boston.

Johnson, M., and Porter, J. (1995). Questio disputata: Delayed hominization. *Theological Stud.* **56**, 743–770.

Schauer, F. (1985). Slippery slopes. *Harvard Law Rev.* **99**, 361ff.

Walzer, M. (1994). "Thick and Thin." Univ. of Notre Dame Press, Notre Dame, IN.

Wolf-Devine, C. (1989). Abortion and the feminine voice. *Public Affairs Quart.* July.

Wreen, M. (1984). In defense of speciesism. *Ethics Animals* **4**(3), 47–66.

Wreen, M. (1996). "Importune Death a While." *Public Affairs Quart.* **10**(2), 153–162.

HOMOSEXUALITY, SOCIETAL ATTITUDES TOWARD

Udo Schüklenk* and Tony Riley†

*University of Central Lancashire Centre for Professional Ethics
†Yale University School of Medicine

GLOSSARY

DSM A system for classifying psychological problems or disorders developed by the American Psychiatric Association and most often used in the United States.

heterosexual A person who directs sexual desires toward another of the opposite sex.

homosexual A person who directs sexual desires toward another of the same sex.

mental illness Psychologically abnormal patterns of functioning that in a given context are deviant, distressful, dysfunctional, and possibly dangerous.

SOCIAL ATTITUDES TOWARD HOMOSEXUALITY have significant influence on individuals' attitudes toward homosexuality in general, and toward gay men and lesbians in particular. People have various beliefs about and attitudes toward homosexuality and homosexuals. Consider, for example, several of the statements contained in a recently created measure of attitudes toward homosexuals: for lesbians, "Female homosexuality is a threat to our basic social institutions," and, "Female homosexuality is an inferior form of sexuality." For gay men, "Male homosexuality is a perversion," and, "Homosexual behavior between two men is just plain wrong" (G. M. Herek, 1994. In *Lesbian and Gay Psychology* (B. Greene and G. M. Herek, Eds.), p. 210. American Psychological Association, Washington, DC). Negative attitudes toward homosexuality are determining factors in irrational fears of homosexuality, a condition labeled by G. Weinberg as "homophobia." These fears have lead to a number of hostile reactions toward homosexual people. For instance, the number of hate crimes committed against gays and lesbians in the USA is on the increase (G. M. Herek and K. T. Berrill, Eds., 1992. *Hate Crimes: Confronting Violence against Lesbians and Gay Men*. Sage, London).

I. A HISTORY OF HOMOPHOBIA AND ITS CONSEQUENCES FOR GAY PEOPLE

Religiously motivated homophobia can be traced back, for instance, in England, to the mid-17th century. Mostly single women were "convicted" of witchcraft and sentenced to death. Official court records indicate that "sexual deviance" was often used as evidence against those women. People in the British Empire were executed because of "sodomy" until 1860. However, religious motivations are only one side of the coin. In nonreligious Nazi Germany tens of thousands of homosexual men were killed in concentration camps.

Interpretations of the German people as a distinct biological race considered homosexuals a threat to the military strength of the Third Reich and the health of the allegedly superior German "race." Homosexuals were also one of the targets of the anticommunist witchhunt organized by McCarthy in the 1950s in the USA. Currently homosexual acts are illegal in the majority of countries on earth (D. Plummer, 1995). *Health Care Analysis* 3, 150–156). For instance, the Republic of Singapore's penal code prescribes prison terms ranging from 2 years up to life imprisonment for consensual homosexual acts among adults. The criminalization of same-sex acts among adults clearly violates the moral limits of the criminal law because no harm to others is done (J. Feinberg, 1984. *The Moral Limits of the Criminal Law: Harm to Others.* Oxford Univ. Press, New York). Even if one were to allege self-harm, Aristotle's *volenti non fit iniuria* would apply and render state interference unjustifiable (*Nicomachean Ethics,* V, 1138a). As he said, "For he suffers voluntarily, but no one is voluntarily treated unjustly. . . . It is not possible to treat oneself unjustly." Even conservative philosophers such as Arthur Schopenhauer seem to agree: "What I do to myself is always only what I will, and consequently it is never a wrong or injustice" (A. Schopenhauer, 1979. *Preisschrift über das Fundament der Moral,* p. 24. Hamburg, Felix Meiner Verlag).

II. THE PREVALENCE OF ANTI-HOMOSEXUAL ATTITUDES

One generalization that emerges from the research on the attitudes of heterosexuals toward gay men and lesbians is that heterosexual men are typically more hostile toward homosexuals than heterosexual women are (e.g., Herek, 1994; M. E. Kite, 1994. In *Lesbian and Gay Psychology* (B. Greene and G. M. Herek, Eds.), pp. 25–53. American Psychological Association, Washington, DC; B. E. Whitley and M. E. Kite, 1995. *Psychological Bulletin, 117,* 146–154). The statements quoted earlier, that is, "Female homosexuality is a threat to our basic social institutions," etc., were taken from Herek's 20-item Attitudes Towards Lesbians and Gay Men (ATLG) scale. Half the items or statements on this scale refer to gay men, and the other half to lesbians; higher scores indicate more negative attitudes toward homosexuals. Herek has found in a series of studies with the ATLG scale involving college students and respondents from the general population that heterosexual men typically score higher than heterosexual women do, indicat-

ing that heterosexual men hold more negative attitudes toward homosexuals. Male college students who hold negative attitudes toward homosexuals were also likely to endorse traditional sex roles, a traditional family ideology, and a dogmatic view of the world; perceive that their friends share their views on homosexuality; and report no positive interaction with gay men or lesbians. The evidence indicates a similar constellation of factors for female college students with negative attitudes toward gay men and lesbians; moreover, they frequently attend religious services and are often members of a conservative religious denomination. Male respondents from the general population have more negative attitudes toward homosexuals than do heterosexual women. These heterosexual men were also more likely to hold traditional attitudes regarding sex roles, adhere to a traditional family ideology, attend religious services often, and hold fundamental religious beliefs.

That heterosexual men hold more negative attitudes toward homosexuals than heterosexual women do is a standard finding. Whitley and Kite wondered whether this finding might change with the level of education of the participants in a review of a series of studies (Kite, 1994). It is generally believed that highly educated persons have more favorable attitudes toward homosexuals (Herek, 1994). Whitley and Kite examined the influence of gender on attitudes toward homosexuals across four levels of education: high school students, college students, graduate students and other professionals, and other adults. They found that the effect of gender on attitudes toward homosexuals was large among high school students, moderate among college students, and slightly less moderate among graduate students and professionals. These findings indicate that male high school students, typically adolescents, hold markedly negative attitudes toward gay men and lesbians. There was no effect of gender on attitudes toward homosexuals among studies involving other adults.

Other reviews of the research (e.g., M. B. Oliver and J. S. Hyde, 1993. *Psychological Bulletin, 114,* 29–51) have noted a relationship between the age of respondents and the effect of gender on attitudes toward homosexuals, indicating that younger male respondents have more negative attitudes. The results of the Whitley and Kite integrative review, however, suggest that this relationship is probably not linear, as the effect of gender on attitudes toward homosexuals remained stable across studies involving college students, graduate students, and other professionals. What this means is that the attitudes of heterosexual men toward homosexuals in the studies involving college students, graduate students, and other professionals were consistently more negative, despite a difference across the samples in average age of about 12 years. The finding that adolescent male high school students are particularly hostile toward gay men and lesbians is important to keep in mind for the subsequent discussion of the incidence of antihomosexual violence. The evidence indicates that the perpetrators of this type of violence are often young male adolescents (A. R. D'Augelli and L. J. Dark, 1994. In *Reason to Hope: A Psychosocial Perspective on Violence & Youth* (L. D. Eron, J. H. Gentry, and P. Schlegel, Eds.). American Psychological Association, Washington, DC).

Another factor that has been of interest to researchers in this area is the effect of contact with gay men and lesbians on heterosexuals' attitudes toward homosexuals. The emerging consensus appears to be that contact positively affects heterosexuals' views of gay men and lesbians. Herek (1994), for example, has reported that those who have had contact with gay men generally have more favorable attitudes toward them. It should be noted that only some heterosexuals were likely to have had more extensive contact with gay men, namely, those who were highly educated, politically liberal, young, and female.

Violence against gay men and lesbians, or persons perceived as such, is at epidemic proportions. D'Augelli and Dark reported that persons believed to be gay or lesbian are the most frequent targets of victimization. A recent longitudinal study found that over a third of a large sample of gay men reported violence during 1 of the 6 years of the study (D'Augelli and Dark, 1994). Fifty-eight percent of a sample of Alaskans and 87% of a sample of Pennsylvanians reported being victims of such violence. Violence against homosexuals increased 127% in a recent six-year period (National Gay and Lesbian Task Force Policy Institute, 1994. *Anti-Gay/Lesbian Violence Fact Sheet: April 1994 Update.* NGLTF, Washington, DC). An earlier report by the same group documented 1822 antigay episodes of violence in 1991, including physical assaults, abuse, and murder. It is not clear whether the increase in reported incidence is a result of an increase in actual hate crimes committed against gay people, or whether it is a result of better reporting.

Plummer reviewed empirical evidence from studies undertaken in the USA and Australia and concluded that antigay violence is often marked by extreme brutality and that it seems to be intent on destroying a person because of his or her sexual orientation. Between 70 and 87% of homosexual people interviewed in these countries report having been subjected to one form or another of antigay/lesbian victimization. Because of the

endemic nature of homophobic prejudices, homosexuals all too often find no support in state agencies such as police stations. Fearing further reprisals, two-thirds of victims in one Australian study did not report the crime committed against them to the police (Plummer, 1995). Large European cities such as Manchester in the United Kingdom and Cologne in Germany have begun to organize joint campaigns of homosexual people and the police force in an effort to curb antigay violence.

III. PROFESSIONAL ATTITUDES TOWARD HOMOSEXUALITY

The influence of societal attitudes toward homosexuality can probably best be described by using the example of the pathologization and depathologization of homosexuality by psychiatry at the end of the 19th and 20th centuries, respectively. The German psychiatrist Richard von Krafft-Ebing was the major force behind the pathologization of homosexuality by mainstream psychiatry at the end of the 19th and beginning of the 20th century. His *Psychopathia Sexualis* was the standard reference work of sex research. Krafft-Ebing's decision to declare homosexuality a mental illness was based on his normative conviction that the *only* purpose of human sexuality was to reproduce. In Darwinian spirit Krafft-Ebing considered any deviation from this purpose as a symptom of a functional degeneration. It did not matter to him whether homosexuals actually suffered inherently from being homosexuals. In fact, it did not matter to him whether homosexuals suffered at all. Krafft-Ebing's thought was based on a number of normative assumptions and decisions about healthy sexual behavior. Any violation of the conclusions based on these views was to be punished by the force of the law. Homosexuals would be put either in jail or in psychiatric hospitals in order to be experimented upon to "heal" them. Some authors have suggested that legal requirements of German prosecutors intent on persecuting homosexual people were the driving force behind Krafft-Ebing's work. Societal attitudes influenced dramatically the construction of homosexuality as a mental illness with all its known harmful consequences for homosexual people.

The pathologization of homosexuality was based on prescriptive, normative, rather than descriptive, views of sexual behavior. The purpose given to sexual behavior was not to enjoy sex but rather (and exclusively so) to reproduce. Obviously, there is no inherent scientific necessity to accept Krafft-Ebing's interpretation of sexual behavior. Still, his views were influential enough to predetermine much of the 20th century's professional psychiatric evaluation of homosexuality.

Changing public perceptions of homosexuality, more self-confidently acting homosexuals, and doubts about the scope of modern psychiatry led to the depathologization of homosexuality by the American Psychiatric Association (APA). Apparently, the profession had to concede that it was incapable of providing even a sound definition of "disorder." As recently as the early 1970s the position in the mental health profession was that homosexuality was a mental illness. It was only in 1973, in response to the sustained lobbying efforts of concerned mental health professionals, that there began a gradual shift in the official definition of homosexuality in the *Diagnostic and Statistical Manual* (DSM). That the redefinition of homosexuality was gradual is important to highlight, since the impression one gets from perusing many contemporary introductory clinical psychology texts suggest otherwise.

The DSM is the manual the American Psychiatric Association has created for labeling various types of mental illness. The third edition of the manual, published in 1980 and referred to as DSM-III, considers a variety of homosexuality as indicating mental illness, what it calls *ego-dystonic homosexuality*. Individuals with this "psychosexual disorder" are described as having a "desire to acquire or increase heterosexual arousal, so that heterosexual relationships can be initiated or maintained," and the manual explicitly states that "a sustained pattern of overt homosexual arousal" is unwanted and hence distressing (p. 281). It was only with the publication of the revised third edition, in 1987, referred to as DSM-III-R, that reference to homosexuality as mental illness was discontinued altogether. It is hard not to suspect that ego-dystonic homosexuality is featured, albeit implicitly, in conversion therapy, the goal of which is to help "distressed" homosexuals become contented heterosexuals. Suffice it to note that the official redefinition of homosexuality, considered a victory among many concerned mental health professionals, was more gradual than is often portrayed, taking almost 15 years to become the official position of the American Psychiatric Association.

Societal attitudes toward homosexuality led to the decision to construct it as a mental illness and changing attitudes have led to its depathologization (U. Schüklenk and M. Ristow, 1996. *J. Homosexuality* 31(3), 5–30). The consequences of this stigmatization of homosexuality for societal attitudes toward homosexuality could be seen everywhere in society. Incredible as it may sound today, the New York Taxi Commission required

homosexual taxi drivers to undergo a psychiatric evaluation twice a year to ensure their fitness to drive, and homosexual Americans were refused a licence to practice law because of the pathologization of homosexuality. Silverstein argued rightly that the pathologization of homosexuality "had served to buttress society's discriminatory practices against gay women and men" (R. Bayer, 1987. *Homosexuality and American Psychiatry: The Politics of Diagnosis.* Princeton Univ. Press, Princeton, NJ). This is still the case in many countries. A National University of Singapore psychiatrist, for instance, reflects his society's attitudes toward homosexuality when he asks whether a (to be found) gay gene should be used in order to undertake "pre-symptomatic testing, for homosexuality in the absence of treatment" (L. C. C. Lim, 1995. *Ann. Acad. Med. Singapore* 24, 759–762). This psychiatrist seems to be unaware of the deletion of the entry homosexuality in the *International Classification of Diseases* (ICD) manual published by the World Health Organisation in 1992.

In a survey of more than 700 gay, lesbian, and bisexual physicians undertaken by the USA Gay and Lesbian Medical Association, 67% reported knowing of patients who received substandard treatment because of their sexual orientation, while 88% mentioned hearing homophobic remarks about gay and lesbian patients made by their heterosexual colleagues and superiors. Undoubtedly, health care professionals' attitudes toward homosexual patients are to a large degree influenced by a professional psychiatric tradition which for most of the 20th century declared homosexuality a mental illness.

Professional attitudes toward homosexuality were clearly influenced over much of the past 100 years by societal attitudes toward it. At the same time, the pathologization of homosexuality, in the absence of any scientific evidence for this judgment, led to the well-known societal perception of homosexuals as "child-molesting perverts." The DSM-III-R points out that most incidents of pedophilia involve men molesting girls below the age of 13, and that pedophilia and homosexuality are unrelated.

The harmful consequences of homophobia also affect the level of homosexual people's self-esteem. It is not hard to imagine that the fairly widespread societal antipathy toward homosexuals negatively impacts their psychological and somatic health. Meyer, for example, described three stressors that gay men typically experience because of their status as gay men: internalized homophobia, stigma, and discrimination and violence (I. H. Meyer, 1995. *J. Health Social Behav.* 36, 38–56). *Internalized homophobia* refers to the extent to which these gay men have accepted society's largely negative views of them, and *stigma* to their expectation and experience of rejection. Each of the three chronic stressors was independently related to psychological distress in the gay men in Meyer's study. Those gay men who experienced these stressors to a greater extent reported higher levels of distress. In some recent research suggesting a possible connection between widespread societal antipathy toward homosexuals and their somatic health, Cole and associates reported higher incidence rates of various physical diseases among HIV-negative gay men who concealed their sexual identity (S. W. Cole, M. E. Kemeney, S. E. Taylor, and B. R. Visscher, 1996. *Health Psychol.* 15, 243–251). Being the targets of widespread societal antipathy and discrimination, then, appears to be both mentally and physically damaging for gay men and lesbians.

IV. RELIGIOUS ATTITUDES TOWARD HOMOSEXUALITY

Religions and religious institutions are influential parts of our traditions. Their influence on societal perceptions and interpretations of homosexuality cannot be underestimated. We will first shed light on religious interpretations of homosexuality and the consequences this has had for homosexual people. An ethical analysis of the religious reasoning as well as its consequences then follow.

Homosexuality has traditionally been seen as ethically wrong by influential religious organizations such as the Roman Catholic Church. The term this organization uses to criticize people engaging in same-sex acts is "sin." Members of the Roman Catholic Church believe that something does exist which has created the earth and the universe, and this entity they call God. A Catholic tradition influenced by the thinking of 13th century theologian Thomas Aquinas claims to know what God likes and dislikes, and asserts that God thinks same-sex acts are "sins against nature." The concept of nature that is used to condemn homosexuality is not a scientific concept of nature, based on a descriptive account of human behavior. Rather, it is a prescriptive account of human nature which defines what human nature should be like (Schüklenk and Ristow, 1996). Every violation of this normative account of human nature is considered immoral, sinful, and so on. Many Christians who share these beliefs have been shown to be highly prejudiced against homosexual people. For instance, studies have demonstrated that many Christian staff members

of a general hospital in New York City would prefer not to be in contact with gay men who have developed AIDS. AIDS is often seen as God's punishment for a "life against nature" (J. J. Wallack, 1989. *Hospital Community Med.* 26, 44–50). American leaders of the Roman Catholic Church have argued vigorously against the extension of equal opportunity legislation to include sexual orientation.

A common assumption is perhaps that holding various religious beliefs predisposes one to negative attitudes toward homosexuals. Herek examined the extent to which hostility toward homosexuals varies by type of religious orientation. He identified two categories of religious persons, those with an extrinsic and those with an intrinsic religious orientation. People with a primarily extrinsic orientation (e.g., attending religious services regularly) view religion as instrumental in their adhering to social conventions, whereas those with an intrinsic orientation view religion as providing "them with a meaning endowing framework in terms of which all life is understood (Herek, 1994, 218). The following quotation from Allport and Ross captures the point of this distinction: "The extrinsically motivated person uses his religion, whereas the intrinsically motivated person lives his religion" (cited in Herek, 1994, 218). The distinction between religious types had no impact on negative attitudes toward homosexuals; rather, the extent to which people subscribed to fundamentalist religious beliefs was significantly associated with their negative attitudes toward gay men and lesbians.

Islamic scholars have argued that all people with AIDS who have contracted the illness by having sex with a partner of the same sex should be killed by stoning them to death. This is in coherence with Islamic teachings which require homosexually active people to be punished. The Koran suggests punishment without going into the particulars of the intended punishment, while the Hadith requires the execution of those involved in homosexual acts. The execution of tens of thousands of Iranians accused or convicted of homosexual acts indicates that Islamic societies are anything but tolerant toward homosexuality. It can safely be assumed that homosexual people who do not hide their sexual orientation in public suffer a variety of discriminations in Islamic countries.

A. Ethical Problems in Regard to Religious Attitudes toward Homosexuality

Two problems occur in regard to the described religiously motivated attitudes toward homosexuality: (i)

Do religious attitudes toward homosexuality have any moral significance? (ii) What relevance should religious attitudes have in regard to homosexuality related legislation in secular and religious societies?

1. Moral Significance of Religious Attitudes toward Homosexuality

The adequate answer to the question of whether religious attitudes have any moral significance is both yes and no. We live today in a multicultural world with people having a large number of different normative views about how we ought to live our lives. There is not one single ethical theory that is universally accepted by everyone. Indeed, there is no way to prove in a manner similar to mathematical or empirical proof that one theory is "right" while another is "wrong." Utilitarians cannot prove deontologists wrong, and proponents of neither of these two ethical theories can prove a Christian ethicist wrong by relying on their own ethical theories. At the same time, however, there are a multitude of ethical theories which provide more or less coherent fundaments for people wishing to base their individual behaviors on them. Some of these theories rely on the existence of a nonhuman entity frequently termed "God." There is no evidence for the existence of God, but that has not prevented people for many centuries to develop ethical theories on the assumption of the existence of an almighty, good God.

People not believing in God have created their own secular theories of correct ethical behavior. Many ethical theories that are based on the idea of the existence of a God condemn homosexuality for a variety of reasons, most of which rely on the claim that these religious people know that God condemns homosexuality. Clearly, for religious people the teachings of their respective religious organizations do have great moral significance. Indeed, religious homosexual people generally accept this situation and attempt to reinterpret the religious scripture on which the condemnation of homosexuality is based in order to be able to live a decent religious *and* homosexual life. It is beyond the scope of this article to consider whether such attempts are prudent.

There is a second point in regard to this question to be made: religious attitudes toward homosexuality carry no normative weight for all those people who subscribe to ethical theories that do not condemn homosexuality. Such people need to provide additional justification should they decide to condemn homosexuality because they cannot reasonably resort to religious judgments about homosexuality.

2. Relevance of Religious Attitudes toward Homosexuality in Secular and Religious Societies

Most Western societies have inscribed in their constitution a separation of state and church, simply because they recognized that religious belief is essentially an activity falling into the private sphere. In general, in liberal secular societies John Stuart Mill's dictum that the autonomous individual is free to do whatever she wants to do in areas that only affect herself has been accepted. Homosexual activities clearly affect only freely consenting adults who are entitled in a liberal society to engage in such activities because they are the only ones affected. Christian philosophers such as H. Tristam Engelhardt, Jr., have proposed that in pluralistic societies we should try to reach a consensus of the kind that people should be legally permitted to do whatever they wish to do in matters that only affect they themselves, while at the same time those who find such behavior wrong should be entitled to damn those who act in such ways. Engelhardt suggests that everyone should have the "freedom to go to hell as one wants," without any interference by the state or fellow citizens (H. T. Engelhardt, Jr., 1994. *The Concept of Moral Consensus* (K. Bayertz, Ed.). Kluwer, Dordrecht).

Another matter pertains to the issue of the adoption of children by homosexual people, the use of *in vitro* fertilization (IVF) technologies by homosexuals, and the issue of homosexuals working as teachers in schools. In most countries homosexuals are barred from adopting children and are barred from access to IVF technologies. In Thailand the Rajabhat Institutes Council, the governing body of all of Thailand's teacher colleges, decided "to bar homosexuals from enrolling in 6 colleges nationwide for fear they will set a bad example for students who go on to teach" (*Bangkok Post,* Dec. 26, 1996). A 1995 survey in the United Kingdom concluded that 75% of heterosexuals were opposed to letting a gay male couple adopt children. The same survey found that 46% thought that gay men should not teach in primary schools. In a liberal society legislation in this regard cannot be determined on the basis of unsubstantiated prejudices about homosexuals being child molesters and the like. It is necessary to analyze the question of whether there is any evidence for the claim that children of homosexual parents are in any way worse off in their childhood or later lives due to their parents' homosexuality. The available evidence indicates that children of gay and lesbian parents are not different in any aspects of their psychological, social, and sexual development from children in heterosexual families

(M. A. Gold, E. C. Perrin, D. Futterman, and S. B. Friedman, 1994. *Pediatric Review* **15**, 354–358). Hence, to prevent homosexual people from adopting children or from raising their own children is incompatible with any liberal society whose goal it is to increase the well-being of its citizens.

How should the problem in religious societies be dealt with? Should homosexuals be punished in Islamic societies where the state's function is primarily seen to uphold religious values? The only appropriate answer seems to be that religious people in religious societies should be judged on the basis of the religion whose teaching they have accepted for themselves. This pertains, of course, only to acts of real or alleged self-harm or violations of religious rules but not acts which affect others. Nonreligious people should not be forced to live their private lives on the basis of religious beliefs they do not subscribe to. It is important, of course, that no citizen is coerced into accepting the state religion. However, it seems reasonable to accept that, for instance, Muslims who voluntarily accept the consequences of Islamic Law should be judged on the basis of legislation they consider ethical.

V. CONCLUSION

A number of ethical theories, most prominently certain utilitarian ones, would hold the position that societal convictions that are based on prejudices are unethical simply because they have been shown to be harmful to healthy and productive members of our societies. Liberal and libertarian, as well as a number of feminist, philosophies would support the utilitarian conclusion even though they would apply different reasoning to support this conclusion.

However, if the history of homophobia is anything to go by, it seems likely that certain segments of our societies will have negative attitudes toward homosexuality and homosexuals. The relevant professions, and here in particular, medical professionals, should try to improve the levels of knowledge in these segments in order to reduce the opportunities for homophobes to repeat their prejudices unchallenged. As far as societal policies toward homosexuality are concerned, it seems clear that individual prejudices should not be allowed to determine public policy. The primary function of any modern society is to increase the overall amount of its citizens' happiness. Discrimination against homosexual people violates this goal and is therefore to be judged unethical. This does not mean that in secular and even in religious societies individuals are not entitled to have negative views toward homosexuality, but they are not ethically entitled to interfere with the lifestyles of homosexual people. It is also important to note that should negative views of homosexuality, which individuals might hold because of their religious or other beliefs or dispositions, have a negative impact on the well-being of homosexuals, they must be regarded as unethical because of their harmful nature (Feinberg, 1984).

Also See the Following Articles

ADOPTION • ARISTOTELIAN ETHICS • DARWINISM • DISCRIMINATION, CONCEPT OF • MENTAL ILLNESS, CONCEPT OF • PSYCHIATRIC ETHICS • SEXUAL ORIENTATION • VICTIMLESS CRIMES

Bibliography

Bayer, R. (1987). "Homosexuality and American Psychiatry: The Politics of Diagnosis." Princeton Univ. Press, Princeton, NJ.
Boswell, J. (1980). "Christianity, Social Tolerance and Homosexuality." Univ. of Chicago Press, Chicago.
Herek, G. M., and Berrill, K. T. (Eds.) (1992). "Hate Crimes: Confronting Violence against Lesbians and Gay Men." Sage, London.
Herek, G. M. (1994). Assessing heterosexuals' attitudes towards lesbians and gay men: A review of empirical research with the ATLG scale. In "Lesbian and Gay Psychology" (B. Greene and G. M. Herek, Eds.), pp. 206–228. American Psychological Association, Washington, DC.
Schmitt, A., and Sofer, J. (Eds.) (1992). "Sexuality and Eroticism among Males in Moslem Societies." Haworth, Binghamton.
Sullivan, G., and Wai-Teng Leong, L. (Eds.) (1995). "Gays and Lesbians in Asia and the Pacific." Haworth, Binghamton.
Weinberg, G. (1972). "Society and the Healthy Homosexual." St. Martin's, New York.

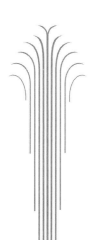

HONOR CODES

Dean A. Steele
United States Air Force Academy

GLOSSARY

academic integrity Adherence to a set of values essential to an academic community, such as honesty, respect, fairness, and advocacy.

cheating Fraudulently presenting the work of others as your own.

confrontation The process of facing an individual suspected of violating the honor code and challenging that individual to explain his or her conduct.

honor Personal integrity maintained without external influence.

honor committee A judicial board consisting of student and/or faculty members who conduct honor hearings.

honor hearing A judicial hearing involving a review of evidence and a determination of guilt or innocence.

honor legislators Students and/or faculty members who decide Honor system policy.

investigation The process of gathering information when an individual is suspected of violating the honor code.

lying Deceiving others in word or conduct for personal gain.

plagiarism Misusing the work of others or failing to acknowledge its use.

stealing Depriving others of their property or ideas without prior permission.

tolerating Observing or acknowledging violations of the honor system without challenge.

violation An infraction of the principles or values of the honor system.

HONOR CODES are promises people make to conduct themselves according to values and principles which are more idealistic than the prescriptions followed by others of that institution or similar organizations. The code might be a written promise, such as a signed declaration, or perhaps a verbal promise in the form of an oath. An honor code might, for example, challenge people to live more ethical lives or to abide by high ethical standards in academia. In addition to a promise to abide by a particular ethical standard, there is also a system which not only chooses the code, but also provides a judicial and an administrative body to maintain it.

The honor code systems with which most are familiar exist at institutions of higher learning. These codes cover student activities in many schools today, ranging from civilian to military schools, and from high schools and preparatory schools to colleges and universities. Honor systems may vary from one establishment to another. Some honor codes may include in their domain of relevant activities only academic endeavors, such as proper exam taking procedures, while other more encompassing systems include all aspects of student life. In addition to the domain of an honor system, there is also a range or extent of influence for the system. The range of a system might be limited to the immediate campus area. However, it might be broad enough to include the local area, or it might even consider location irrelevant to whether the honor code has jurisdiction or not. The domains and ranges of each honor system vary from one system to another. For example, some institutions want to curb cheating at their schools, so the domain of prohibited activities might include class quizzes and exams, homework, papers, and labs or projects. The range of that system might limit itself to the campus proper and activities which directly reflect upon the school. On the other hand, if a school determines that it wants to build student character, then the domain and range of such a system would be much greater. The domain and range of an honor code system depends upon the purpose for which the system was originally established, and the purpose, in turn, depends upon the historical origin of a code and its related ethical point of view.

Throughout history there have existed many ethical points of view, ranging from teachings in religion, to military codes of behavior, and to social ethical values. These moral points of view provided the impetus for creating an honor code based on a need as already described, such as reducing the amount of cheating in the classroom. The historical origin of the code, the moral point of view from which it originated, defined the basic values and principles of the system as well as provided the ethical perspective from which the code compared individuals and their behavior. However, once a system was established, it generally developed around four basic elements. First, there are purposes for which the codes were established. Second, there are methods which will fulfill those purposes. Third, there are common values used by these methods. Finally, each honor system has a similar administrative structure which adjudicates cases and maintains the system.

In addition to the common elements of honor code systems, there are also common problems. The problems range in severity and number, depending on many variables, such as the school environment and ethical norms with which the students are most familiar. The following discussion deals with historical origins of honor codes, honor code systems, and the common problems faced by each system.

I. HISTORICAL ORIGINS

A. General

Every honor code has a history, and some of the honor systems in use today attribute the founding of their system to a particular source. Many codes refer to various religious beliefs, military codes of behavior, and social ethical values as sources for their honor systems. For example, two of the oldest honor codes in civilian universities in the United States are located at the University of Virginia and the College of William and Mary. Both of these schools refer to the fact that they began with a student body primarily from the rich planter class of that era and that social honor was an extremely important quality to foster in their students. Other institutions, such as the United States Military Academy at West Point and the United States Air Force Academy, have systems which reflect the concept of chivalry, religion, and social virtues. There are many different kinds of value systems which have existed throughout history and which have had a great impact on societies and institutions of higher learning. The three previously mentioned are listed most frequently as contributing to the establishment of any particular honor code and system. The following origins of honor codes and honor code systems are not meant to represent a complete set, but rather exemplify some of the more common origins of systems in existence today.

B. Religious Beliefs

Human beings are historically considered religious creatures who honor their dead, believe in a force greater than themselves, and struggle with concepts such as infinity and immortality. Religion played an important role in the formation of societies throughout the world and continues to serve as the basic foundation for social ethical value systems in many cultures. Religious values are incorporated into the very fabric of social norms regardless of any conscious connection to their religious origin. Of the multitude of religions practiced presently, a cursory examination of the major eastern and western religions is sufficient to point out that these value systems focus on character development, a main purpose of many honor code systems. For this reason, many honor code systems reflect, or cite specifically, basic religious values.

Whether one looks toward the East or the West, he or she will encounter at least one of many religions which are followed throughout the world. What are some of the important contributions these religions make toward character development? Hindu values, for example, include truth, self-control, and purity, and each Hindu is part of a vast fellowship of people who accept what is right and earnestly seek the truth. These Hindu values and principles are often reflected in descriptions of honor codes and their foundational principles such as refraining from lying or stealing. Other eastern religions contain sound principles for good character development as well. Buddhism says that one must find the Middle Way between asceticism and self-indulgence in order to achieve a better life—to strive toward concepts like right conduct and right intention. Likewise, Confucianism places a great deal of importance on fostering proper conduct toward others through following basic principles such as treating others as you would like them to treat you.

Many of the basic values and principles espoused in eastern religions exist in western religions as well. The major western religions include Christianity (Catholic and Protestant), Judaism, and Islam. These three share common roots such as serving the same God and following similar laws. One of the important contributions of these three major religions is the Ten Commandments from the Old Testament which forbids, generally, such actions as stealing or lying. Another contribution comes from the Christian Messiah's Sermon on the Mount in which Jesus spoke of good qualities one ought to have, such as a pure or blameless heart and to seek righteousness, that is, to have integrity. Finally, in Islam, like many religions, one encounters an intense desire to know the truth and to do what is right. A desire to seek the truth and do what is right is a purpose many institutions try to nurture in their students and which also serves as a guiding principle of toleration clauses.

Although many honor code systems never cite religion as a contributor to their system, many universities are themselves the direct results of the influence religion played in establishing and preserving educational institutions throughout the world. Therefore, religious principles are ingrained in general school administrations, pedagogy, and values, and continue to provide an indirect, yet important, contribution to honor code systems.

C. Military Codes of Behavior

1. General

Military codes of behavior have numerous origins. Some codes originated from a combination of religious beliefs and social norms, while others were developed because of military necessity. The following discussions of chivalry and the Lieber Rules are provided as examples of military codes of behavior which influenced honor codes.

2. Chivalry

a. Definition

In general, chivalry refers to the medieval institution of knighthood and the principles and values it idealized, such as bravery, honor, courtesy, loyalty, and justice. Although western civilization refers to chivalry of the European knight, other parts of the world share a similar historical period, such as the knight-errant in early Chinese history and the samurai of Japan. The concept of chivalry and the social feudal system in which it thrived developed in the East about 2000 years prior to the rise of feudalism in Europe. However, the ideals and principles are basically the same as those found in medieval Europe. The ensuing discussion covers the European knight as an example of chivalrous behavior and moral codes.

b. European Knight

The knights of medieval Europe arose from the feudal period which existed in Europe at that time. Originally, knights were lesser land owners who worked for the greater lords as soldiers. These earlier knights were much more ruthless and immoral than the knights portrayed in literature and the arts. It was not until the Christian church influenced the process of becoming a knight that the knights began to resemble those gallant and moral beings which story tellers portrayed in their tales. According to Edgar Prestage, in his book, *Chivalry: A Series of Studies to Illustrate Its Historical Significance and Civilizing Influence,* the Council of Clermont made two major contributions to history in 1095 A.D., when the Turks conquered Asia Minor. The first decision the Council made was to declare the beginning of the first Crusade. Its other major impact on history was combining the military servitude of a knight with a purpose other than that of serving the whims of the greater lords. The Council ordered that every male of noble birth, at the age of 12, in essence, would take an oath in the presence of a bishop to defend the oppressed, the widow, and the orphan. This might be considered the birth of the type of knight most often recounted in history.

The Crusades not only marked the beginning of the knight, but also combined the soldier and the church, and fostered the beginning of several Orders of knights such as the Knights Templar, Teutonic knights, the Order of St. John, and the Hospitallers. Each order followed a formal set of ideal values or principles from which more formal codes developed over the next few centuries. Prestage wrote that chivalry was composed of three elements, and that these three components, the military, religious, and social, each provided a set of virtues. The virtues arising from the military character included courage, loyalty, and generosity. The religious contribution was fidelity, obedience, and chastity. Finally, the social addition was courtesy, humility, and beneficence.

c. Importance of Chivalry to Military Codes of Behavior

The ideals preserved from the chivalrous period of ancient China and medieval Europe provided an example for later societies to understand the proper character of a soldier in service to the state. Chivalry provided an ideal soldier. Additionally, the knights of these two early periods provided a concept of honor which not only influenced the military, but the upper social classes as well. The concept of gentlemanly honor is the result of the influence chivalry had on society. Perhaps the most influential and lasting effect of chivalry was in education. The chivalrous concepts of integrity, loyalty, and beneficence, to name a few, were adopted in education as proper character traits for a student to put into practice.

3. Lieber Rules

Unlike chivalry, the Lieber Rules were a legal set of rules rather than a social concept of behavior. The Lieber Rules are a set of 157 rules guiding the behavior of U.S. soldiers in the field. The rules were written during the American Civil War by Francis Lieber, a professor at Colombia University. In 1863, President Abraham Lincoln directed his military staff to develop a set of guiding principles or rules which might alleviate the amount of atrocities experienced in the war, for example, the atrocities committed at Andersonville Prison, the treatment of civilians, the murder of black Union soldiers captured by the Confederates, and the looting by both sides, to name a few. Lincoln's presidential order became General Orders 100, Instructions for the Government of Armies of the United States in the Field, 24 April 1863. These rules were to preserve some humanity in war and greatly influenced later guidelines for conduct of military personnel in the United States and abroad, such as the Hague and Geneva Conventions. According to the Lieber Rules, Article 15, "Men who take up arms against one another in public war do not cease on this account to be moral beings, responsible to one another and to God." These rules tried to remind soldiers of their moral duties and continue to influence the U.S. military today, including its regula-

tions, laws of war, and academy honor codes. Like the codes of chivalry, the legal code established by the Lieber rules offers further guidance to the soldier, as well as the cadet or student, as to the proper conduct of military personnel.

4. Relevance of Military Codes of Behavior to Honor Codes

Military codes of behavior have influenced many military schools throughout the United States, and even the world. The military academies and preparatory schools cite different purposes for establishing honor codes and respective systems, but the influence of their systems on other schools is tremendous. A growing number of schools are becoming more and more concerned with honor and establishing honorable communities at their schools. Many schools share information with each other about their respective systems, and therefore military academies, heavily influenced by military codes of behavior, contribute to the honor codes of many other schools. Additionally, the honor codes at military schools tend to be more holistic, governing all aspects of a student's life rather than just the academic. These schools are historically concerned more with character than civilian schools and consistently demonstrate that concern in their honor systems.

D. Social Ethical Values

Discussions of values and the systems which helped to develop them reach back in ancient history as far as written records exist. There are excellent dialogues written in the 6th century B.C., during the time of Confucius, Buddha, and Taoism's Lao Tsu, as well as in the 4th century B.C. in the early Greek philosophical schools of Plato and Aristotle. These philosophies discuss why virtues are essential to good living as well as methods of achieving them. The importance of these various schools of thought is that they provide a series of methods which may be followed in order to achieve a set of values. Since students arrive at universities with much of their character and value systems already developed, an honor system must find a method which will build upon student value systems and guide students toward recognizing, accepting, and living according to the honor values and principles. Some of the methods still used today include the dialectical method of Socrates and Plato, and the habitualization of virtuous behavior of Aristotle. Another method which is used in many honor code systems today is similar to the social contract discussed by the British philosopher John Locke in the 18th century. Although Locke wrote about social origins and political bodies, the basic principle applies here as well. Institutions establish a basic set of values or principles and a system to enforce conformance to those standards. The system is developed and agreed to by everyone under its scope, either explicitly, such as an oath, or implicitly by accepting matriculation to a school which has an honor system. The value of a social contract is that it is agreed upon by all who fall under its scope and that it is public in the sense that the basic values and principles are known or immediately available in literature or some other public forum. The underlying principle of a social contract is that people make a promise of one form or another to live according to the rules outlined in the contract itself. A challenge of this type of system is trying to teach those who fall under its scope that it is within their best interest to abide by it.

E. Impact of History on Honor Codes

The most important impact of religion, military codes of behavior, and social ethical value systems is their contribution to education. Firstly, theologians and scribes were responsible for preserving scholarly works as well as teaching. Many universities were built by religious organizations as well. Religious values and principles permeate many facets of university life. Secondly, military codes of behavior influenced the establishment of military academies primarily, but also contributed to many social codes such as the concept of "southern honor." The methods used to teach young men the principles of chivalry are still used today in military preparatory schools, such as the New Mexico Military Institute. Finally, social ethical values ranging from those written of in ancient Greece to those of modern times are drawn upon as values essential to fostering an academic community.

All of these historical value systems focused on teaching a way of life—a proper way of living which accomplished a particular purpose by achieving certain goals. Likewise, honor code systems have particular purposes which they are trying to achieve, and the values and principles from these varied sources help institutions define a methodology to reach those goals.

II. HONOR CODE SYSTEMS

A. General

Honor code systems have four basic elements: purpose, method, values, and administrative structure. Once a system determines the purpose for establishing a code, then it must choose a method to fulfill that purpose, including what values are important and an administration which will oversee and sustain the system. Each of these elements is next discussed in more detail.

B. Purpose of an Honor Code

1. General

The purpose for which an honor code was established varies from one institution to another. An institution may want to foster an academic community which is conducive to learning and excelling in academic fields free from the worries and pressures associated with lying, stealing, or cheating. Another system might focus on a minimal set of values and principles which govern student life not only on campus, but off campus as well. Yet other administrations might choose a program to build upon the student's character, preparing them not only to excel in an academic community, but also to be successful in society at large and serve as role models within that society. No matter what the purpose is, it plays an important role in determining several important aspects of that system, such as the methods to fulfill them, the core values and principles, and what administrative structure will succeed in maintaining the system. There are three common purposes found among honor code systems as previously mentioned. Each of these is now discussed in more detail.

2. Establishing an Honorable Academic Community

Many institutions, such as the University of Virginia, wish to develop a "community of trust in which students can enjoy the freedom to develop their intellectual and personal potential" (University of Virginia, 1993. *On My Honor ... Philosophy and Guidelines of the Honor System*). Similarly, Cornell University claims that it is trying to foster a community founded on trust and honesty. What constitutes an honorable academic community? In order to answer this question, one must decide what conditions are necessary for a student to learn freely, unhindered by interference from others. The University of Maryland at College Park suggests that such an environment is attainable if cheating, fabricating, facilitating, and plagiarizing are eliminated, or at least severely limited, within the university. These four areas are rather common among honor code systems and reflect the four basic principles of not cheating, lying, tolerating, or stealing, respectively. These four basic principles are reflected in one form or another in many systems, such as the University of Virginia. Virginia decided upon a concept they refer to as "academic fraud." Academic fraud includes plagiarism, multiple submissions, false citations, and false data. Incidents of academic fraud are merely specific examples of the four basic principles already mentioned. More specifically, plagiarism is stealing the ideas of another, while multiple submissions is a form of cheating. Likewise, both false citations and false data are cases of lying, or even cheating. Virginia suggests that if an institution could eradicate these activities, then the campus environment would be more conducive to academic achievement. Each time a school deters action in these areas, then it is that much closer to achieving an honorable academic community.

3. Maintaining a Minimum Standard

Many of the military preparatory schools and academies state that they are trying to develop a minimum standard of behavior for their respective students which will still provide them with good leaders. They view academic honesty and integrity as character traits essential to their overall objective of producing military leaders. These schools stress the fact that their system is a minimal standard and is not to be taken as a goal in and of itself, but as a baseline dividing acceptable and unacceptable behavior. The challenge of focusing on the minimum standard of acceptable behavior is that students might tend to meet the minimum and go no further. For this reason, these particular schools encourage students to move beyond the minimal standard they are taught under the honor system and to continue their social ethical maturation. The minimum standard view is a difficult goal to achieve and therefore serves more as a bridge between establishing an honorable academic community and building student character than it does as an adequate goal in and of itself. The problems associated with the minimum standard approach are discussed in more detail in Section III.

4. Building Character

The most difficult purpose to achieve in any honor code system is building character in the students of that institution. The College of William and Mary and Duke University are examples of schools trying to develop student character. They wish to build an environment favorable to developing good character by encouraging the use of honorable traits and behaviors in their students. The military academies are also good systems to study when looking at systems trying to build upon or even change a student's character. The domain and range associated with this task are the greatest. For example, military academies are trying to "foster an internal commitment to ethical standards that are beyond reproach," as stated in the *Honor Handbook* at West Point. The range of a system like West Point's cannot be limited by school boundaries, nor can the domain be limited to merely school activities. The standards of good character in such a system must apply at all times, regardless of location or activity. For example, an institution trying to build and improve upon student character as already described might expand the scope of the honor system to cover activities like underage drinking, using false identification cards, or even writing bad checks, such as the University of Virginia includes within its domain of honor violations.

C. Method

Honor code systems utilize codes and oaths as methods of attaining, for example, an honorable academic community or in order to improve upon student character. The codes themselves are methods used to fulfill a purpose of an honor code system. An institution recognizes a need within its community, and to meet that need it establishes an honor code system. Many honor codes have an oath which the students recite or a document which they sign at some point after matriculation. The most common oath is similar to that taken by the cadets at the New Mexico Military Institute (NMMI): "A cadet will not lie, cheat, steal, or tolerate those who do. Every cadet is obligated to support and enforce the honor system." The honor oath is more common among the military academies and preparatory schools, while a written honor statement is more common among civilian universities. Some of the universities demand that all students must sign and be held accountable to a document which declares their willingness to accept and uphold an honor code system. The University of Connecticut, for example, provides a document with the following statement on it for new students to sign upon matriculation to the university: "I hereby certify that the undersigned have completed matriculation at Connecticut College and have been admitted to membership in the college community. In accepting this membership, the student agrees to uphold the Student Government Honor Code and to demonstrate responsibility in the academic and social affairs of the college." This honor statement is similar to those used in other institutions who choose to have written notification from the student that he or she will abide by the honor system. Other universities may not choose to have an oath or statement from their students. These particular schools merely provide students with a briefing given by the Dean, or a similar representative, about the honor system during administrative inprocessing. Although there is little evidence on honor codes that indicate an oath or statement is necessary to the success of the system, histories of other ethical systems demonstrate that some form of public acknowledgment and acceptance of the system will have better results.

Although the honor code itself is an overall method to fulfill the purpose of the system, there are different ways to utilize a code. The code might be a strict legal definition enforced by severe punishments, such as immediate dismissal from the institution. On the other hand, the oath or code may be integrated into a more complex system of methods which are trying to fulfill the institutional purpose of building good character. These two examples represent two methods commonly used in honor code systems. The first is similar to the contract method, while the second is representative of the character method.

1. Contract Method

The contract method is more often used in conjunction with a system which limits its honor code to specific activities, such as plagiarizing or cheating. The contract method is simple in that it outlines unacceptable behavior very specifically by listing the prohibited actions or through basic principles which provide guidance on avoiding those activities. In the contract method, individuals eigher sign a contract, such as the document used by the University of Connecticut, upon matriculation, or swear to an oath in front of witnesses. Students will know just what types of behavior are permitted or which are not. A positive aspect of this method is that it allows students a great deal of flexibility with regard to individual character issues. However, in order for the system to work well, there must be a strong individual or body of individuals to enforce compliance to the system by using whatever action is necessary to deter violations. However, such power is rarely allowed in schools today. Much like the character method, the contract method has merit as well as problems, which will be discussed in Section III. More information on contract theory may be obtained through reading works by Thomas Hobbes and John Locke.

2. Character Method

The character method reflects sound moral principles such as those found in the philosophical teachings of Lao Tsu, Confucius, Socrates, Plato, or Aristotle. Some common elements among these great philosophical teachings are that human beings may be taught good character, that knowledge plays an important role in making sound moral choices, and that becoming good people is a goal in and of itself. Although many of these character views suggest that character development must begin at an early age, the values and principles espoused by these philosophies may be incorporated in an honor code system. For example, the Socratic method of defining a concept, testing the definition against logical analysis, and refining the definition as necessary proves very useful in choosing proper values or even to fully discuss a controversial topic in a focus session. The Aristotelian concept of habitual behavior is also a valuable asset to those honor systems trying to build character. Virtuous actions must be practiced and so ingrained in a person's character that they are habitual. Another contribution of these philosophies is the importance of gaining knowledge and most importantly, wisdom. Good honor education is a necessary aspect of any successful honor code system.

D. Values

In the Introduction an honor code was defined as a kind of promise, an obligation to adhere to a particular standard. The standard is defined through a set of values or principles. The values and principles associated with honor code systems depend upon the purposes or objectives the system wishes to achieve. The most common purpose in many honor code systems is to establish an academic community where students may attain their potential in an honorable manner. In order to establish such an environment, each and every student within that community must understand, accept, and protect a set of values which are conducive to perpetuating that atmosphere. Most honor codes which state that their purpose is to establish an environment such as this, a community of honorable students, cite the following values as those values most important to inculcate in their students: honesty, respect, fairness, and advocacy. These four values are the positive counterparts to the four basic principles mentioned earlier: do not lie, steal, cheat, or tolerate. These standards are important attributes which students must accept and follow in order for the academic community to thrive.

It is clear that in order to have an honorable society, no one should lie, steal, or cheat, and even more importantly, not tolerate those actions in others. However, it is not as obvious when the values the system must choose deal with the overall character a student ought to have. This is the dilemma facing institutions which are trying to build character. Surely the values and principles just covered are good character traits. The question is, are they enough? When an institution wishes to go beyond merely fostering an academic community, when it tries to establish a minimal set of values essential to the school and the community, then the values shift from those needed to foster an honorable academic community toward those essential to a just and honorable society. The schools which state this objective as the purpose for establishing their honor system emphasize those values of good character, such as integrity, moral courage, mutual respect, trust, truthfulness, selflessness, and nontoleration. These institutions want to not only curb the actions in the academic community which detract from good education, but also to discourage activities which are harmful to the community and society at large. The task of choosing the correct values to integrate into the honor system is a difficult one and must take into consideration the short amount of time students are at the institution, the overall influence the school has on individual students, etc.

E. Administration

1. General

The administration of the honor system is extremely important. Without properly educating the students on the system, training the honor representatives and executives of the honor system policies, and promptly dealing with honor code violations, the system will not be able to sustain itself and accomplish its goals. There are several common elements of an honor system administrative body: honor educators, honor representatives, an honor board or committee, and both student and faculty legislators.

2. Honor Educators

Without a doubt the most important aspect of an honor system is the education of the individuals who fall under its purview. The function of the honor educators of the honor system is many fold. They must make available to everyone the various values of the system, their meanings and applications, and the procedures to follow in order to live according to the honor system. In order to have a successful system, each and every student, faculty included, must become familiar with the purpose behind the system, the goals it is trying to achieve, the values it wishes them to follow and incorporate into their way of life, and all aspects of the administration of the code. The purpose and goals of the honor code system are usually provided to the student in a student handbook. These are generally easy to understand. The values upon which the system is based are usually also included in the student hand-

book. However, some institutions do not include more than a general definition for each standard. The most thorough booklets include a variety of examples and explanations of each concept so that a student will have every opportunity to understand just what the value is and how to apply it to everyday life. In addition to the honor handbook, further instruction in the form of classes or seminars, for example, helps the student attain a functional understanding of the honor code values and principles. Some institutions utilize focus sessions where a group of students reads a scenario involving one or even several of the honor values. Once everyone reads it, a facilitator then asks some questions concerning the scenario and directs open discussion. This provides for a good atmosphere at a time and place where students might be more open to discuss honor issues. Other methods might include following a case progression from beginning to end, having students participate in various aspects of the honor case, or requiring students to view an honor hearing early in their student careers.

3. Honor Representatives

The first line of defense in any honor system is the students themselves. However, to facilitate the honor process, honor representatives are tasked to investigate any honor allegation and then forward their findings to the honor committee for review. Honor representatives may be students from all levels of the student body, but usually are students in good standing, academically or otherwise, and are elected to their positions by their peers. In addition to running investigations, honor representatives serve as "lawyers" or "counselors" to the accused student and may help those students with a defense. Additionally, these representatives might eventually become the legislators of the system as they move up in class rank.

4. Honor Committee or Board

Most honor systems are run by honor representatives, and from these representatives and the student body at large are selected a group of individuals who oversee individual cases of honor violations. These honor committees, or boards, vary from one school to another. Some select students from the student body and the only selection criterion is that the student is in good standing, i.e., not on academic probation. Some institutions select a review board for each separate case, while others have an honor board which hears cases for a term of one semester or academic year, and is then replaced by another group of students. Faculty members may even sit on the committee. For example, the

United States Air Force Academy allows for one Commissioned Officer to sit on the board, but she or he does not have any decision-making authority.

The honor board is the central decision-making body concerning individual cases. The specific process involved with any honor code violation depends upon the system the school chooses; however, a general set of steps includes a reported violation, followed by an investigation and then a review and possible hearing by the honor committee. The honor committee or board receives information from the investigative body, which usually consists of selected honor representatives as previously stated above. The board reviews the evidence and decides if the evidence warrants charging the student with violating the honor code and taking the process to the next level, an honor hearing. The board makes many other decisions during the process of reviewing each case as well. They also make decisions regarding students' rights, such as ensuring that the accused student's basic rights were not violated.

Once the decision is made to continue to an honor hearing, the board is the decision-making body which reviews the evidence, hears testimony, and makes a decision of guilt or innocence. Finally, the honor board or committee makes a punitive recommendation if the student is found guilty. A further discussion of punishments follows. The findings of an honor committee, however, are only a recommendation. Most institutional administrative procedures do not allow any other school body to disenroll a student, the most common punishment in cases where a student is found guilty, except the school board or president.

5. Student and Faculty Administrators

The final element of a general honor system includes the student and faculty administrators. The students in nearly all of the honor systems reviewed are the primary legislators of that system. The students choose educators of the system, the representatives, the investigators, and the board members. The students also write policy, design education programs, and maintain many other aspects of the code. The faculty is involved at all levels of the honor system, from administration of the system to following the same basic tenets. Without a faculty which supports the honor code system, any system is doomed to failure. The most successful honor code systems have a good working relationship between the student body and the faculty. Regardless, however, of the extent of faculty involvement, a hard fact of the education system is that violations of school policies, including honor systems, which result in dismissal from that institution must be resolved by the highest levels of the administration of

that school. However, not all punishments include dismissal. Some other forms of punishment might include probation or even restitution to the honor system, victims, and the student body. If a student is dismissed from the school, the transgression may or may not follow that individual, although some institutions list the dismissal due to honor issues on the transcripts. Some institutions, such as the University of Virginia, even help students find enrollment in other schools.

III. COMMON PROBLEMS

At the 1995 United States Air Force Academy Honor Conference, Retired Brigadier General Malham M. Wakin stated that during his more than 35 years of teaching ethics, two problems continued to plague the honor system: a lack of desire to be honorable at all times, and an unwillingness to be responsible for the actions of others. The problem of being honorable all of the time is a very ancient one, found in the dialogues of Plato's *Republic* as well as in student conversations on university campuses around the world today. Why should a student be honorable when he or she can cheat, without getting caught, and excel because of it? A difficult question to answer. General Wakin, as well as many other experts on teaching ethics, consider education an important part of the solution. For this reason, honor education within an honor system is critically important.

Perhaps the most common problem associated with honor code systems is toleration. Toleration is the second of the two most devastating problems encountered in honor code systems today. It is an unwillingness to take responsibility for the actions of others which are counterproductive to the honor concept. Toleration is the backbone of the honor system. No system will endure an internal decay of its principles, which is what occurs when toleration becomes a norm within that system. History serves as a witness to countless ethical systems which failed because people within those systems did not protect the values they swore to uphold. Each year more institutions are adding or expanding current policies on toleration to include making the act of tolerating honor violations a dismissal offense.

There are many reasons why students lack either the desire to be honorable all of the time or to take responsibility for the actions of other students when those students violate the honor code. First, there are strong cultural pressures to violate the honor code principles and values. Cultural pressures range from peer pressure, to family pressures, and to the pressures the system places on students to succeed. Second, it is too easy. There are too few proctors during exams, or teaching methods make it too easy. Third, students lack good role models. Cheating, for example, is a cultural norm. People cheat on everything from their spouses to their taxes. More than 75% of high school students cheat on school work and about 20% of their parents help them do it. Fourth, there are poor student–teacher relationships in educational institutions. Although not a new problem, the relationship between the faculty and the student body is extremely important. Most honor code systems are run by the student body. If students do not trust teachers, then why would they accept a professor's word that a student cheated? They will not if the relationship between students and teachers at that institution is a poor one. A fifth reason is ignorance. Students and faculty may not understand the values and principles of a given honor code system and therefore may make mistakes concerning interpreting how and when they apply in a situation. Finally, and perhaps a major reason for dishonorable behavior among students, is the fear of failure. There are too many pressures on any given student to not fail. This fear is cited in many studies as the number one reason students cheat in school.

How does an institution overcome these problems? Solutions range from, "there are no solutions," to, "educating students and faculty on honor." For instance, schools might try to reduce the number of honor violations by educating the members of its system through conducting courses or seminars in honor concepts. The earlier a student or faculty member becomes involved in the system, the better. Other solutions might try to reduce the temptations to cheat by employing various programs such as tutoring poor students or providing learning assistance courses. Another technique to remove the possibility of cheating is to use more proctors during exams or to use random exams. More complicated problems require more sophisticated solutions, like creating character development centers, using focus sessions, or changing classroom procedures to reflect improved pedagogy consistent with the honor system.

IV. CONCLUSION

Methods used in honor codes have about the same success as those used in education in general. Lectures and similar methods are not as successful as other methods, like combining a lecture with a film clip and a focus session or other group interactive activity. Emotion plays nearly as much of a role in character development and honor education as logic and intellect. If the individuals within an honor system are not emotionally involved in the process, the system will not have much of a chance of succeeding. The success of any system depends upon much more than the system itself. Ultimately, an honor system depends upon the people running the system, including the faculty, the students, society, and the ethical system or principles the system is founded upon. Both the faculty and the student body must share ownership of the honor code system, otherwise, neither group will take responsibility for the system. Additionally, in order to succeed, an honor system must ground itself in a solid ethical foundation, educate those within the system, and hold everyone accountable.

Finally, institutions establishing honor code systems must take advantage of the work which precedes their own. There are many schools which use honor code systems with varying degrees of success. Not only are these schools interacting with each other on a regular basis, they are also, due to the increase in exchange of information, making great improvements in their systems. For example, in more and more institutions today, such as the United States Air Force Academy, there is an emphasis in the honor system on refraining from using negative terms such as not lying, stealing, cheating, or tolerating. The new terminology emphasizes positive values rather than negative ones, and the focus is not on minimal ethics but on ideal standards such as honesty, respect, fairness, and support. The negative values stated in many honor oaths are described in several honor code systems as minimum standards, while the more positive counterparts are considered as ideals to strive for. It may happen that schools choose to change their honor oaths at some future time to reflect this more positive method of instilling values in students.

Changing an environment or even an individual's behavior is no easy task. Change of this nature occurs within a complex web of social interactions, and influenced by habit patterns, signals received from both the institution and individuals, various values and principles and rules of conduct, personal satisfaction, and a supportive environment, as well as by time.

> Never suppose that in any possible situation or under any circumstances that it is best for you to do a dishonorable thing however slightly so it may appear to you. ... Encourage all your virtuous dispositions, and exercise them whenever an opportunity arises, being assured that they will gain strength by exercise ... and that exercise will make them habitual. ... Though you cannot see, when you take one step, what will be the next,

yet follow truth, justice, and plain dealing, and never fear their leading you out of [any difficult situation] in the easiest manner possible. ... (Thomas Jefferson, University of Virginia)

Also See the Following Articles

CODES OF ETHICS • ETHICS EDUCATION IN SCHOOLS • MILITARY CODES OF BEHAVIOR • RELIGION AND ETHICS

Bibliography

College of William and Mary (1993–1994). "William and Mary Student Handbook."

Leming, J. S. (1993). In search of effective character education. *Educational Leadership* Nov., 63–71.

Prestage, E. (1928). "Chivalry: A Series of Studies to Illustrate Its Historical Significance and Civilizing Influence." Kegan Paul, Trench, Trubner, & Co., London.

Schab, F. (1991). Schooling without learning: Thirty years of cheating in high school. *Adolescence* **26**(104), 839–847.

U.S. Air Force Academy (1995). "Honor Code Reference Handbook of the Cadet Wing," vol. 1.

U.S. Air Force Academy (1996). "Honor Code Reference Handbook of the Cadet Wing," vol. 2.

U.S. Air Force Academy. (1994). "Character Development Manual."

University of Virginia. (1993). "On My Honor. ... Philosophy and Guidelines of the Honor System."

Wilcox, J. R., and Ebbs, S. L. (1992). "The Leadership Compass: Values and Ethics in Higher Education." The George Washington Univ., Washington, DC.

HUMAN NATURE, VIEWS OF

Strachan Donnelley
The Hastings Center

I. The Philosophic and Practical Problem
II. Contemporary Applied Ethics and Views of Human Nature
III. Views of Human Nature: Future Tasks

GLOSSARY

determinism The philosophic doctrine that all phenomena and events, natural or human, are determined by antecedent, efficient causes, physical (material) or other.

dualism Philosophic conceptions that posit fundamentally different and independent realms of reality, for example, mind and body (matter) or God and the world.

essentialism The philosophic doctrine that different forms of existence, say a human being or a horse, have a fundamental and unchanging essence (form) or character.

idealism The philosophic doctrine that all phenomena are essentially mental in character, that reality consists of minds and their experiences.

materialism The scientific or philosophic doctrine that all phenomena or reality are essentially material (physical) in character, that reality involves the interactions and causal relations among physical, material forces.

philosophic naturalism Philosophic arguments that find no radical disjunctions between nature and human life (individuals and communities).

worldview An overarching conception or imaginative picture of the origin, nature, and significance of the world and human life.

VIEWS OF HUMAN NATURE, as the histories of religions, philosophy, and ideas tells us, are probably as old as human communities themselves. The views are characteristically a part of a larger imaginative picture that humans fashion about themselves and their world: how the world and they came into being; what the world and they centrally are like; what is the final significance, meaning, or importance of the world and themselves. Views of human nature and accompanying worldviews are central to human cultures at all times and places. There is no escaping them. These views may be thoughtlessly inherited from the past or critically faced in the present. Nevertheless, they importantly rule our human lives. They are how we gain our moral, religious, and cultural orientations. We have the Old Testament Book of Genesis and the latest efforts to come to grips with Darwinian evolutionary biology. Whatever the differences, the human impulse and need are the same: to understand and to orient ourselves in the world. The formal disciplines related to this inquiry are philosophic cosmogony, cosmology, anthropology, and psychology, but in some sense or other we all do it. It is endemic to human and humanly moral life. Thus, views of human nature are and must be central to applied ethics.

I. THE PHILOSOPHIC AND PRACTICAL PROBLEM

Our histories also tell us that worldviews and conceptions of human nature have been innumerably many and remain a fundamental controversial issue. We cannot seem finally to agree upon who we are as human beings. Perhaps this indecision is inescapable, despite the importance of the issue. Views of human nature are strange conceptual beasts, neither fish nor fowl. On one hand, they are meant to describe who we are, to give us the fundamental facts about our nature or mode of being. They are meant to be descriptive and realistic. On the other hand, they tell us humans how we ought or ought not to be, what our particular significance is in the scheme of things, and what we ought to do or become. They are normative and prescriptive.

If views of human nature are inevitably both descriptive and normative, and if in addition humans must start their explorations of themselves from the prevailing ideas and knowledge of their time and place—ideas and knowledge that may not be fully adequate to the task of capturing who we are—then we may better appreciate why these views remain incomplete and controversial. If, moreover, humans in part define or determine who they are—if they are not fully determined by some given and fixed nature—then this also reinforces why each age and human community must decide its "descriptive-normative" view of itself. We are no exception.

No human community starts *de nuovo* with its views of human nature, but exists within historical and cultural traditions that it inherits and that importantly set the stage for contemporary intellectual explorations and speculations. Our Western and increasingly global heritage is exceedingly complex and fateful in determining how we view ourselves and our significance at the end of the twentieth century. Here I can only sketch out a few major issues, bones of contention, and crucial ideas inherited from the past with which we must come to grips in "re-viewing" our human nature. I will then briefly consider the relevance of these ideas for particular issues in contemporary applied ethics.

Traditionally views of human nature have conceived human beings as a species, or as a human community or a "people," or as individual selves. In the spirit of our times, I will focus on our individual selves. What are the major issues and historically the central bones of contention? The fundamental question, of course, is the nature of the human self: its fundamental and abiding character. What determines this character? Is it biology (physical nature), divinity, culture, or society, or the self itself (its reason or will)? Is the self singly and essentially determined by one of these "causes" or is it multiply determined by these several factors together, if not more? Correspondingly, with respect to the human self's status in the scheme of things, what is its relation to nature (its body and physical matter), God, human others, society and community, history, and eternity? Is the relation essential and constitutive of the self or merely accidental, something that does not touch its inner core or nature?

A. The Historical Drama of Ideas

These are philosophic issues that have been fought over for 2000 years or longer in the West. The drama of ideas has both Greek and Judeo-Christian, if not older origins, and I want to fasten on only a few particularly fateful quarrels, for they have crucially influenced rival views of human nature. The first quarrel concerns the human self's relation to the world and the beyond. The Pythagoreans and Plato speculated that the true or higher self had its origins elsewhere, outside the world that we experience in everyday life. Similarly, early Christians and Jews held that we have been created in the image of a God that transcends the natural universe.

The Presocratic Heraclitus retorted that the Pythagoreans spoke nonsense. We, along with everything else, are woven out of the fabric of the natural universe (the "Everliving Fire"). Aristotle analogously played down transcendent origins and emphasized our life within the world: our coming to know the natural universe (the Cosmos) and our active life within the polis or political community.

This fundamental split in worldviews has had a long consequent history. For our purposes, we note certain rival tendencies. First, the Pythagorean/Platonic/Judeo-Christian tradition has fostered various forms of philosophic or theological *dualism* that have tended to set human beings and their cultural communities over and against the natural world. In these dualistic perspectives, the meaning and significance of human life, our particular role in the scheme of things, has little or nothing to do with nature, which tends rather to drag us down and away from our best, most human selves (reason, free will, the capacity for caring love, preparation for an afterlife, etc.).

Closely coupled with the history of dualism is another tendency, again present at the beginnings: *essentialism*. Human nature, if not also the fundamental character of the natural world, is eternally fixed. We all are fundamentally the same. There is a universal human essence. Any differences between us are merely accidental and not finally important. The reason for this abiding human essence is that we are created according to a fixed human form (a "Platonic idea") or in the image of an unchanging God, even if this means that our unchanging nature is the exercise of a free moral will.

The rival tradition of Heraclitus and Aristotle (which later includes David Hume and his moral sentiments) has tended towards a *philosophic naturalism*. The natural world is not seen as an alien or essentially unfriendly place. Rather, it is conceived as a locus for significant and meaningful human activity, and there need not be any radical separation of nature and human culture (human communities). Human life and selfhood, as with Heraclitus, are seen to fit within the natural, worldly scheme of things. It is this tendency toward philosophic naturalism, which includes humans within the wider natural world, that has been more willing to abandon essentialism and look rather for complex and multiple worldly origins of the human self.

The philosophic struggles be can usefully seen in our ongoing disquiet over the issue of *freedom* and *determinism*, which pierces to the quick of our modern notions of ourselves and our human nature. Are we free human agents or are our lives determined by natural (physical, material) causes, cultural or societal forces, or some cosmic or historical fate? Are we swamped by external or internal forces and only have the illusion of individual freedom? The question seems crucial, for if we have no freedom—if we have no real capacity for choosing between viable alternatives of action and for affecting things for better or worse—then we cannot be held morally responsible for what we do. If we consider moral responsibility for ourselves and our world to be importantly constitutive of who we are and to be integral to our human nature, then we are in real trouble. We have lost our traditional philosophic, moral, and cultural moorings. How did we get into this conceptual and existential pickle, which so radically challenges our everyday self-understanding and conceptions of ourselves?

B. The Modern Period and the Legacy of Descartes

Arguably, we can credit this present human or spiritual crisis to a historical and unholy alliance and interweaving of dualism, essentialism, and naturalism. The fateful modern turn came in the seventeenth century with Descartes' particular brand of dualism, his bifurcation of ourselves and our world into mind and body, human beings and nature. Mind is the realm of language,

thought, and freedom (free will), and only humans have minds (originated from a transcendent God). Nature is purely a realm of mechanical, material, blind, and valueless forces, ruled strictly by causal necessity (efficient causes). Perhaps this conception of nature well served the newly emerging Galilean-Cartesian-Newtonian physical sciences, but it has philosophically thrown us off-balance ever since. First and foremost it reinforced a radical distinction between human life (human individuals and their communities) and nature. Philosophically, it left no intelligible relation or connection between ourselves and nature, including our own organic bodies. (Why do we have them?) It thus thwarted any sensible or nuanced naturalism. We and nature were dealt a further blow by Cartesian dualism aligning itself with essentialism. The human self is essentially and eternally the same: reason and will. Nature is essentially and eternally the same: matter or energy ruled by fixed causal laws and principles.

This may be a feast for the mathematically rational mind, as it was for Spinoza, but it has arguably been a disaster for philosophic interpretations of ourselves and our world, both human and natural. It has tended to undermine, skew, or obliterate an understanding of community or togetherness: our understanding of our relations to others, again both human and natural. In the original Cartesian vision there is a radical disjunction of *freedom* (the reason and will of individual humans) and *determinism* (causal necessity). We have "atom-individuals," self-sufficient mental substances essentially unrelated to one another, over and against the universal causal nexus of nature—humans essentially isolated from one another, if not their God, and alien to the "totally other" natural universe. (Note here the origin of later existentialist worldviews and moods of alienation both from nature and other human beings.)

For everyday life, this conceptual picture is untenable, but philosophy and the sciences have been more or less plagued by it ever since. It is hard to live with such a dualism, but if one wishes to escape the split and to side exclusively with the mind, the ploy of philosophic *idealism*, we are left with essentially unrelated mental subjects curiously in touch with mental others while enjoying an experience of a material world that is just that, mere experience or phenomena. (Today we would ask, "Where's the beef?") If this is too much for us to take, we can side with the material body and become philosophic materialists. But this allegiance characteristically has led to a naturalism plagued by essentialism and causal determinism. The human self becomes engulfed and obliterated in the causal mechanisms of nature. Certain forms of *behaviorism* notwithstanding, which espouse this position, this is an equally untenable interpretation of the human self and view of human nature.

In modern forms of *dualism*, *idealism*, and *materialism*, we are more often than not left with individuals understood as autonomous rational agents, laws unto themselves, or "epiphenomenal" selves, lawfully determined and unfree, caught in the universal causal web of nature—that is, no real human selves or agents at all. Often these inconsistent ideas are melded together. We can find the uneasy tension between these rival conceptions of the self expressed within major modern interpretations of human nature, including Darwin, Marx, and Freud. Biological species(understood as populations of constituent individuals), humans included, actively exploit an environment that "mechanistically" or causally determines their genetic and ultimately phenotypical transformations (natural selection). (The relation of organic freedom evidenced at least in the more complex animals and causal necessity implied by evolutionary biology remains a genuine puzzle for most of us.) Political revolutionaries individually and energetically promote a cause that is historically inevitable (the triumph of the proletariat and the communist state under the spur of economic determinism). Patients and therapists freely combine their wits to uncover the underlying causal determinants of behavior or phobias conceived under a theory of psychological determinism. We still witness the ongoing disease in contemporary *sociobiology*, *biomedical genetic research*, and *Skinnerian behaviorism* on the one hand and culturalists, including *deconstructionists* on the other—the modern heirs of materialism and idealism respectively. The one side easily tends to or endorses genetic and environmental (material) determinism; the other often recognize no natural or causal bounds whatsoever (the triumph of the protean mind). Yet we also witness recurrent attempts to overcome the philosophic hangovers of dualism and the ensuing alternatives of materialism and idealism by thinkers in search of a judicious middle way more adequate to our everyday experiences of ourselves and the world (Isaiah Berlin, Mary Midgley, and Hans Jonas, among others).

There are promising attempts to recover the tradition of the philosophic naturalism of a Heraclitus or Aristotle, minus essentialist and deterministic undercurrents or ideologies. There are genuine endeavors to take the worldly life of both humans and nature seriously and to give both human and natural history their due in the ongoing constitution of our human communities and our individual selves. We are still and will long remain on this search to understand ourselves and our nature, but applied ethics cannot await the outcome. On practical matters, we must decide and act now.

II. CONTEMPORARY APPLIED ETHICS AND VIEWS OF HUMAN NATURE

Views of human nature and their accompanying worldviews provide a moral framework or landscape within which to situate ourselves and reflect upon everyday moral quandaries. Presently applied ethics—biomedical, animal, and environmental ethics, among others—are characterized by a variety of moral frameworks and accompanying views of human nature, sometimes complementing one another, other times at loggerheads.

Given our prior historical discussions, I want briefly to sketch out three moral frameworks at work in contemporary ethical debates that (arguably) have their historical roots in idealism, materialism, and philosophic naturalism. We will then consider how well these frameworks elucidate pressing issues in practical ethics. There are, of course, other relevant moral frameworks deriving from various alternate philosophic, religious, or cultural traditions.

The first moral framework derives ultimately from Kant and his particular brand of idealism. According to Kant, the human self is characterized by a practical reason and a free will at least in principle untouched by nature or history. This reason and will and their self-legislating activities are the ground of the individual's moral worth and constitute humans as "ends-in-themselves," worthy of ultimate moral respect and concern. Here is an ethics and moral framework that dominantly emphasizes respect for individual persons, especially their capacities to make autonomous rational and moral decisions. It is also an ethics emphasizing justice: the extension of moral respect and concern to all "ends-in-themselves," human and perhaps other. This "*deontological*" *ethics* is known for rights and duties owed primarily to individuals.

The second moral framework is "*consequentialist*" and is chiefly concerned with the consequences of our actions as they affect the well-being or welfare of individuals or "moral subjects." This welfare is defined in terms of experiential pleasure, pain, and happiness; the capacity to pursue one's own life plans or subjective preferences; or whatever is deemed the moral good to be pursued and the harm to be avoided. Characteristically, this ethics is not rationalistic in the Kantian sense and seems comfortably compatible with, if not derived from materialism and determinism. The welfare of individuals—the pleasures, pains, happinesses, and subjective preferences—may all be caused and beyond the individual's ultimate control. However, if the welfare of individuals—the greatest good for the greatest number—is promoted, that is what morally counts. This too is an ethics of justice and equality—each moral subject is to count as one and only one—but with its emphasis on the summation of overall welfare, it can be less protective of the rights of individuals than deontological ethics. The consequentialist ethics that we know best is *utilitarianism*, derived from Bentham and J.S. Mill in the nineteenth century.

Deontological and utilitarian (consequentialist) ethics are undergirded and dominated by rival conceptions of human nature and the human self—the one more akin to the philosophic and dualistic traditions of Plato and Descartes (the rational self with divine origins); the other more earthbound, if not overtly materialist. Yet both share an emphasis on the individual moral subject, with perhaps an inadequate attention to worldly time, history, and relations to others. It is here that the tradition of philosophic naturalism reenters the picture, under the guise of what we might term contingent or historical naturalism to avoid any deterministic connotations.

Let me briefly characterize this contemporary philosophic naturalism and its conception of human nature. Whatever relations we might have to a divinity or eternity (the beyond), we are to the core worldly selves, fundamentally related to the body and wider nature, to other individuals and human communities, and to historical and cultural contexts. We are genuine human agents or actors, with a circumscribed and context-dependent freedom to choose among alternatives, to act in the world, to become our individual selves. (Nature and freedom are not radically opposed.) We have a genuine, if limited capacity to affect others and the world and thus to influence the future for better or worse. This everyday, commonsense view, which has long been held among moral and political philosophers (for example, Berlin, Midgley, and Jonas), is also supported by recent philosophic interpretations of *evolutionary biology*, which offer a radical critique of both causal determinism and essentialism as applied to organic life and recognize the role of chance and historical contingencies at work in particular natural and cultural contexts (Ernst Mayr).

In sum, this philosophic naturalism proposes that we are "embedded" human selves, with substantive moral responsibilities to ourselves, human others, and the natural world. What we do matters to how we, others,

and the world become. This active implication in the everyday world in part constitutes and engenders our human meaning, significance, and particular, if modest role in the scheme of things.

A. Biomedical Ethics

1. Rehabilitation Medicine

How do such moral frameworks or landscapes contribute to the consideration of particular cases typically confronted in applied ethics? Consider *rehabilitation medicine*, which aims to serve patients suffering from severe and traumatic accidents or chronic and incurable afflictions. Imagine a young athlete, say a soccer player, who has permanently lost the use of his or her leg; or an accomplished cellist who ravaged by MS (Multiple Sclerosis) can no longer play the cello and perform before audiences; or a mother who through mental afflictions can no longer care for her children; or a philosopher who has suffered a major debilitating stroke. What are the typical biomedical ethical issues?

Standard bioethics and the combined moral frameworks of consequentialism and deontology tell us that a first duty is to do no harm, to attend to the individual's welfare and suffering, and above all to respect persons and get a truly *informed consent* for medical procedures or interventions. However, this counsel may be too simplistic, especially if we are imaginatively ruled by a simplified edition of human nature, for example, the idea that from a moral perspective we are essentially minds and rational decision-makers and not full-fledged *human organisms* ("mind-bodies"). From the perspective of philosophic naturalism, how could the patient readily give his or her informed consent? How would he or she know how to decide, given that the particular worldly, historical, and bodily self has been severely challenged or undermined, a core sense of self perhaps temporarily, if not permanently lost? What is the young athlete, the cellist, the mother, or the philosopher to do now? How do they replace the old meaning and significance of their lives? How should they reorient themselves? Should not a primary obligation of health care providers be to help the patient engender a "newly" active self, with new worldly life goals commensurate with new levels of capacity?

Moreover, we not only deal with individual patients, but with their families and friends, all those involved in intricate webs of intimately interconnected lives, each in his or her own way challenged or devastated by the patient's affliction. The whole web, with the patient at the center, needs care and moral attention. This attention may include consideration of particular cultural traditions and even where the rehabilitation ought to take place, especially if the patient and family are deeply rooted in their community and regional home and become disoriented in unfamiliar places. Such is the embeddedness of our individual selves in the everyday world. How well does either deontology or consequentialism, with their essentially "individual" selves, deal with these moral dimensions that arise from essential "worldly" relatedness?

This is not to speak of other patients in rehabilitation settings, the cultural and moral traditions of the health care professionals (which may themselves be diverse and conflicting), and the complex moral and societal context of the health care system in which the rehabilitation medicine is situated. Each of these elements of the moral landscape may or may not have a moral pull in particular decisions concerning the patient's care and rehabilitation. The recognition of this moral complexity is the price we must pay for understanding that we are fundamentally worldly selves, inextricably caught up with one another and the rest of the world.

Recognition of the complexity of our human nature and moral lives may help us understand better other issues in medicine and health care that presently vex us, for example, physician-assisted suicide and organ transplantation.

2. Physician-Assisted Suicide

The central moral imperatives of a bioethics dominantly centered on individuals—consequentialist and deontological injunctions to relieve suffering and to respect persons and their autonomy in decision-making—can powerfully combine to argue the case for *physician-assisted suicide*, which moreover carries its own intuitive appeal. Who would not want to end intractable and unrelievable suffering? Who would want morally to infantilize an individual by taking away moral agency over such an ultimately significant issue as one's own life and death? Yet things are not ethically so simple. We human individuals live with one another in communities that have their own complex habits historically fashioned, upheld, and dynamically transformed over extensive periods of time, stretching from the distant past into the indefinite future. One of our primary human responsibilities is to uphold the cultural and moral fabrics of our communities. Will physician-assisted suicide, primarily meant for individuals in extreme distress, undermine important community habits? Will it lessen our respect for human life and our sense of responsibility for the weak, vulnerable, and infirm, if not lead outright to the taking of lives unwanted by us, but not by the individuals themselves? Will we ordinary

citizens come to ape, in the name of compassion, suicide-assisting physicians? These are real questions that haunt the moral landscape of physician-assisted suicide.

Moreover, how will physician-assisted suicide affect the moral fabric and habits of the health care professions, especially if individual professionals remain divided within themselves or among one another over the issue? Could the professions tolerate a universal right to physician-assisted suicide and still effectively perform their community functions and obligations? Should legitimate moral concerns for individuals trump legitimate moral concerns for the ongoing well-being of professions and communities? (This is a question deontological ethics must seriously ask itself). Does the moral decision moreover depend significantly on the different communities, cultures, and individuals involved? For example, what might prove to be morally tolerable or permissible in the Netherlands might be morally intolerable or dangerous in other countries or societies, given different moral and cultural climates and habits. If we are truly worldly selves, all relevant things must be carefully considered. Ethical concerns for individuals must be matched and balanced by ethical responsibilities to communities and societies.

3. Organ Transplantation

We find a parallel situation with *organ transplantation*, which on the surface seems such a straightforward issue. There is a significant and unmet need of human organs for transplantation into critically ill individuals, irrespective of the quality of their posttransplant lives (a question often overlooked). Human individuals do not need their organs after death and therefore should surrender them upon dying for the sake of the welfare and well-being of others. Within a consequentialist framework, what could be simpler? It seems morally incomprehensible that there remains a chronic shortage of organs for transplantation—unless one considers relevant and differing views of human nature.

Ethical arguments for organ donation work particularly well within dualistic, materialist, and utilitarian views of human nature. If the organic body is a mere mechanism or machine that has nothing essentially to do with our human selves, then it and its parts are of no direct moral concern. The parts of particular bodies, given certain biological limitations, are "fungible" or substitutable for one another. For the welfare of others, we should share these parts when no longer needed and get on with it.

However, if we are essentially worldly, bodily, and historical selves, things are not so straightforward. The human body typically has enormous meaning and significance for us. Think of the role of the human body in art, music, athletics, sexual relations, and family life. Think how important our individual bodies are in our own personal lives. These examples only touch the tip of the iceberg. For us, human bodies are anything but meaningless, insignificant, and valueless. It is not us that are odd, but a science or philosophy that assigns our bodies to a valueless moral limbo.

For morally weighty and altruistic reasons, I might want to give my organs to benefit others in extreme need. But I should not expect my wife and children upon my death easily to surrender my body for the organ harvest. They have long lived with the bodily me, and my body has not been morally and humanly insignificant to them. This goes beyond any erotic intimacy to palpable human realities of warmth and security, the exuberance of physical play, and a religious or philosophic awe before the very fact of intimate, bodily existence, us humanly organic ones mattering so much to one another. Nor should we be surprised at the moral burnout of the medical teams that harvest human organs, especially the nurses. The recently dead individual, just parted from its intricate web of personal lives, is soon a bag of bones and useless parts. This rapid and dramatic transformation seems morally difficult to digest, despite the very real benefits to others, precisely because our bodily nature lies within and not outside of traditional moral and religious landscapes that have a long human past and an abiding hold over us. We are morally and spiritually troubled by doing a good deed and perhaps rightly so.

4. Animal Donors and *Xenografts*

The moral complexity of organ transplantation does not vanish if we turn our attention away from humans to animals as the source of organs. For example, chimpanzees have been considered as a source for "bridge" hearts until a human donor becomes available. (Interestingly, both deontology and consequentialism have wavered on the morality of this proposal, depending on whether or not their respective moral concerns are extended beyond humans to other ("higher") animals.) But chimpanzees are our close evolutionary cousins, remarkably capacitated in their own right, and, unlike ourselves, are threatened with extinction. Baboons have experimentally contributed hearts and livers to human patients, but though not threatened with extinction, we worry about baboons transmitting unknown and lethal viruses into the human population, not to mention the moral obligations we might owe the baboons themselves.

The latest animal organ donor candidate is a transgenic pig so biotechnologically fashioned with human genetic material as to suppress immunological rejection of the foreign organ, for example, a heart. Beyond questions of scientific and biological feasibility, this again may seem morally unproblematic. If we raise pigs for food and other useful products, why not use them for spare organ parts, certainly a more compelling moral justification on consequentialist, if not also deontological grounds? But again this line of argument may put the issue in an overly simplified or reduced ethical landscape incommensurate with our human nature.

As worldly, historical, and bodily beings, we have a long entwined, if checkered history with nature and animals. Nature and animals have multiple values and significance for us, from the biological and economic to the scientific, aesthetic, moral, and religious. In ways that we are only beginning better to understand, nature and animals are complexly and intimately woven into our cultural capacities, habits, and achievements and thus into our very selves. Nature and animals, both positively and negatively, importantly matter to us. Moreover, the future fate of humans, animals, and nature are intimately conjoined.

What will be the moral fallout if transgenic pig hearts become a viable resource for human transplantation? Will we accept the porcine hearts into ourselves without a thought or with a new gratitude for pigs and animal life? Or will we become profoundly disturbed and morally disoriented? Given the central symbolic and iconic significance that our hearts have for us—think of literature (*Heart of Darkness*), ordinary metaphors ("my heart goes out to you;" "our heartland"), and popular songs ("My heart dies for you")—can we readily incorporate the various long-standing cultural and moral meanings of pigs or other animals into the very core of our human bodily being? What will it humanly feel like to be so utterly dependent on another animal's organ? What will it do to our sense of self and moral, religious, and cultural orientations? Perhaps we cannot effectively answer these questions before the event, but this might not be such an easy and minor affair as boosters of organ transplantations (especially, the consequentialists) would like to think. Our human nature, as we find with human organ donation, is not so easily pliable.

B. Environmental Ethics

1. Wild Animals and Nature

Pigs have long been domesticated animals and thus assimilated into our human communities and ordinary cultural routines. For the moral better or worse, we do not give them much thought, and perhaps after all their hearts would slip into our bodies without fanfare. But most of animal life and nature is not domesticated. It has different meanings and significance for us. We have innumerable other relations to animals and nature that have become deeply rooted in our human lives and that require their own moral considerations. In North America we have had a long love–hate relationship with wild nature and animals. This relationship has become part of our collective soul and culture and still strongly animates us. Wild trout, salmon (Pacific and Atlantic), and rivers are a case in point. In various regions of the United States and Canada, there are energetic conservation efforts to save native trout, salmon, rivers, and surrounding watersheds, often met by equally energetic efforts to exploit these and other natural resources.

The conservation and exploitation of nature in North America raise deep moral and human passions, leading on occasion to acts of terrorism for the sakes of forests, wild and domesticated animals, or human communities. These deep-running passions make no sense on human-centered worldviews, deontological, consequentialist, or other. If we are essentially minds unrelated to the body and wider nature—or if we are essentially pleasure seekers and pain avoiders who can get our satisfactions chiefly, if not solely within the confines of human communities—why should we care so much about nature and animal life? How do we explain ongoing and raging controversies over human–nature relations and interactions, which are not considered to be merely pragmatic issues, but characteristically to have a central moral, if not religious significance?

If we adopt a philosophic naturalism and moral framework that presupposes that we are worldly, historical, and bodily beings, then these contemporary moral and political struggles over humans and nature become more readily intelligible and hopefully tractable. We better see what multiple moral needs and interests that we need to take into account. Considering human beings as outside of and radically over against nature blinds us to both what in fact is happening in the world and our moral duties to the future. We need somehow better to think humans and nature together and understand them in the final analysis as involved in a single and dynamic biospheric or worldly whole.

With mention of conserving trout, salmon, and rivers, we of course have entered upon applied environmental and conservation ethics, perhaps the outstanding challenge of our time and of the foreseeable future. The challenge is both practical (moral and political) and theoretical. It underscores that ideas, including ideas of human nature, no matter how speculative, really matter. How we conceive ourselves importantly

determines who we are, how we feel, how we act, what we become. The human–nature crisis, impending and already here, presses us systematically to reconsider ourselves and thoughtfully to begin again, which is the original and ongoing task of philosophy.

III. VIEWS OF HUMAN NATURE: FUTURE TASKS

In this "descriptive-normative" task, we should, I think, embark along certain directions, decidedly beyond inherited frameworks of deontological and consequentialist thought. Again, from a moral, religious, and cultural point of view, we must consider nature and humans' ongoing interactions with nature seriously. This means taking the philosophic measure of contemporary Darwinian evolutionary biology and ecology, as coupled with other dominant cultural orientations towards nature. This enterprise inherently must be both speculative and critical. Certain major themes already seem evident. As against certain atemporal, essentialistic, and deterministic conceptions of humans and nature, the natural world conceived by most evolutionary biologists and ecologists is deeply historical, dynamic, multicaused, contingent (no grand cosmic plan), opportunistic, and context-dependent. Lives are lived and species evolve only in particular bioregional contexts, notwithstanding the complex interactions of bioregions within an overall biosphere.

Similarly, humans have evolved naturally and culturally in historical, dynamic, and bioregional contexts in response to natural, as well as human challenges and opportunities. There is an underlying and deep affinity between the processes of human communities and nature. Indeed this affinity may help to explain why there is so much nature in our human cultures and selves and so much evidence of ourselves in nature, interventions intended or unintended. Human life, immersed and embedded in natural reality, involves the creative modification of nature, in fact and in symbol. This mutual implication or immanence of human individuals, communities, and nature is the backbone of philosophic naturalism and its view of human nature.

This is not a politically innocent or uncontroversial view. No view of human nature, no matter how substantive or minimal (abstract), is uncontentious or above the fray. Philosophic naturalism has definite moral implications. For example, it suggests that our ethics of human–nature interactions should focus on long-term responsibilities to historical and dynamic processes (community and individual) and be regional. Human communities should attend to their regional ecosystems, landscapes, flora, and fauna. We need to understand our regional human and natural past (natural history and human–nature interactions) and opportunities for a vital human and natural future. We need to understand how our regional homes dynamically fit into wider bioregional and global systems (human and natural), influenced and influencing, and to recognize both local and global moral responsibilities. We need to fashion some form of cosmopolitan regionalism if we are practically and morally to save ourselves and nature from the looming pressures of human populations and exploitation of natural resources.

We will not meet this fundamental moral challenge if we do not get our heads straight about our own human nature and our place in the natural scheme of things. Such philosophic exploration is not our only task, but it is indispensable. The human world is ruled by ideas, views of human nature (clashing or convergent) in particular. In our everyday lives, nature and ideas are indissolvable.

Given the history of human life and thought, we should expect and hope that this philosophic naturalism will be fleshed out and corrected, if not superseded by more philosophically and ethically adequate views. Whatever, we must squarely and earnestly face the original and fateful Cartesian disjoining of mind and body, thought and feeling, freedom and determinism, and our human selves and the rest of nature. The subsequent history of moral and political theory and practice has had an ironic, if intelligible course. We have seen an ardent championing of individual freedom that has condoned an irresponsibility for human communities and wider nature. We have had an equally ardent championing of connections to human communities or nature that has meant the denial of individual freedom, selfhood, and thus moral responsibility altogether. Both of these theory-driven tendencies to disjoin individuals, communities, and nature are philosophically and morally bankrupt. We need more judicious and adequate middle way between human individuals, human communities, and the wider nature world. Our ongoing challenge is to conceive together humans and nature, freedom and causal influence. We need ethically to rediscover genuine human moral actors embedded in wider human and natural communities. There is no other sensible way to go. We are still very much amidst this unfinished philosophic and ethical business. In short, we have yet adequately to conceive and appreciate our human nature.

Bibliography

Arnhart, L. (1995). The new Darwinian naturalism in political theory. *American Political Science Review*, **89**:2, 389–400.

Berlin, I. (1979). *Four essays on liberty*. Oxford: Oxford University Press.

Donnelley, S. (1988). Human selves, chronic illness, and the ethics of medicine. *Hastings Center Report*, **18**:1, 5–8.

Donnelley, S. (1989). Hans Jonas, the philosophy of nature, and the ethics of responsibility. *Social Research*, **56**:3, 635–657.

Donnelley, S. (1995). The art of moral ecology. *Ecosystem Health*, **1**:3, 170–176.

Donnelley, S. (1995). Bioethical troubles: Animal individuals and human organisms. *Hastings Center Report*, **25**:7, 21–29.

Jonas, H. (1985). *The imperative of responsibility*. Chicago: The University of Chicago Press.

Mayr, E. (1991) *One long argument*. Cambridge, MA: Harvard University Press.

Midgley, M. (1995). *Beast and man*. London: Routledge.

HUMAN RESEARCH SUBJECTS, SELECTION OF

Richard Ashcroft
University of Bristol

I. Scientific Issues
II. Ethical and Social Issues

GLOSSARY

bias A quantifiable mismeasure of some determinate quantity due to an unrepresentative method of selecting subjects.
harm An actual physical or psychological injury to self or body.
risk A determinable or indeterminable chance of a harm.
subject A participant in research, whose body and/or psychology are the site of scientific investigations into their workings, possibly under the influence of innovative chemical or biological agents, or of some other innovative social or material practice.

THE SELECTION OF HUMAN RESEARCH SUBJECTS in medical and other scientific studies was until recently an issue in scientific methodology alone. Could we validly derive generally true beliefs about human physiology or the efficacy of some treatment from experiments using this subject or sample of subjects? Since the Nuremberg war crimes trials, revelations about scientific "misuse" of human subjects have forced a re-

casting of the selection issue. The contemporary form of the selection issue concentrates on the ethics and justice of enrolling or excluding particular individuals or populations. The watchwords are autonomy, informed consent, and the interests of each subject. More recently the clarity of this model has been clouded by the recognition that the ethical consideration of any selection method and any experiment must consider the wider purpose of the experiment. This consideration must take into account the interests of members of society not selected into the experiment, possibly including future members. This is particularly relevant in cases where the investigation could proceed through a series of linked but limited experiments, or instead through a single (or smaller number of) large-scale inclusive trials which might involve more subjects here and now, but determine answers to more questions and sooner. Recently there has been a shift of emphasis back to issues of research methodology and reliability, as a consequence of the recognition that these issues have an ethical dimension.

I. SCIENTIFIC ISSUES

Scientific soundness is a necessary condition for ethical selection of subjects. In this section I will discuss why this is so, and indicate areas where the distinction between the scientific and the ethical may be confusing.

Encyclopedia of Applied Ethics, Volume 2

A. Researcher Obligations Related to Scientific Validity

The fundamental principle of research ethics is that bad science is bad ethics. The soundness of the scientific research proposal and the research design is a necessary, but not a sufficient, condition for a scientific experiment involving human subjects to be considered ethical. The principle holds good for a number of reasons, and is valid in all sciences where human subjects are used. In the first place, any scientific experiment involving human subjects will involve subjects giving up some of their time on the understanding that they are assisting scientific research. If that research is incompetently framed or carried out so that no reasonable scientific assessor would expect anything useful and novel could be learned in an epistemologically reliable way, then the subject's participation has been gained under false pretenses. This is perhaps no more than a breach of etiquette; but it may be more than that. A special case is the case of experiments carried out for the educational benefit of the student researcher. Here the subject has no right to expect competence from the student, and the subject's enrollment is conditional instead upon the educational utility of the experiment.

I have assumed so far that the experiment offers no significant possibilities of benefit or harm to the subject. I have also assumed that the subject is enrolling for no reason other than altruism, curiosity, or an interest in playing a part in scientific progress. In much research involving human subjects, researchers recognize that the inconvenience of taking part may be in excess of the interest of sufficiently many subjects for the validity of the experiment. Some financial or other inducement may be offered, in order to stimulate enough participants to come forward. This financial or other benefit to participants raises justice issues, which I will discuss in more detail later. But it should remind us here that scientific experiments cost money, and in the competitive environments of private and state scientific funding, it is almost always the case that where one project is funded, several others could not be. The incompetently designed and managed experiment therefore deprives society of the possible benefits of research which was not funded. This represents a waste of scarce resources, which might be regarded as unethical in many cases.

In scientific experiments which involve the use of possibly harmful agents or procedures, the unethical character of the badly designed experiment is more clear-cut. In the first place, the experiment may increase the already existent measure of risk involved in use of this agent or procedure. The researcher is under an obligation to minimize the risks which the subject must undergo, consistent with the aims of the experiment and the informed and reflective agreement of the subject to undergo those risks. Failure to obey this obligation represents negligence, and may do so even where the subject has given her explicit consent. Secondly, the incompetent and dangerous experiment may yield inconclusive results which are due to the performance of the experiment and which may necessitate repetition of the experiment (after redesign) and hence involve exposure of further subjects to the experimental risks, delaying still further the licensing of a beneficial treatment (in medicine) or the proscription of some dangerous substance.

B. Subject Obligations Related to Scientific Validity

It should be noted that while all of these obligations and expectations rest upon the researcher's shoulders, they may also be incurred by the subjects themselves. There is little literature on the obligations incurred by subjects in experiments, largely because, as we shall see, most experimentation ethics is orientated toward a protection standard. Most work in this area is concerned with the safety and dignity of subjects actually enrolled in the study. However, it is clear that a subject who enters a study with a prior intention of breaking the protocol for malicious or self-serving reasons, or who develops such an intention while participating in the study, is acting unethically. This is because the subject's actions may cause the experiment to become invalid, and he is taking the place of some other would-be participant who would have acted according to the spirit of the agreement. It may, in exceptional circumstances, become arguable that an experimental protocol is unethical in its design, and some other principle may override the obligation to honor the agreement made with the researcher on joining the experiment. This is analogous to the arguments which may be made concerning civil disobedience or revolt.

C. Compliance

A second reason may be adduced why the issue of subjects' obligations has not received much attention in the literature. In medical research, the concept of noncompliance is used, which covers all forms of patient nonadherence to treatment instructions. Simply because patients may not comply for many reasons, which may include the side effects of the treatment, the practicalities of taking the treatment, or the inconvenience involved in the treatment, the concept of noncompliance is not a moral one. It is arguable that the medical concept is often applied in a moralistic way, as a mechanism of social control. But we may isolate the intention as the key here, and distinguish deliberate, premeditated noncompliance from other forms. In the same way, we have used the concept of competent design and performance of an experiment to distinguish experiments which are vague, ill thought out, or dangerous from experiments which are sound in conception, but which yield no conclusive or negative findings.

The importance of distinguishing moral from nonmoral uses of the compliance concept is as follows. In any experiment which is designed to test the efficacy and utility of a medical treatment or social policy, it is important to know not only whether it is efficacious in ideal cases, but whether it is "workable." Patients or other subjects must be enrolled in the experiment in a way which will enable the workability of the drug or procedure to be tested. Compliance is a relational property: it is only in extreme cases that a patient may be a "noncomplier" by preference and habit. In most cases, most patients will find some treatments hard to comply with, and vice versa. In some circumstances the researcher may decide that some subject is so unlikely to comply with the experimental protocol that they are unsuitable for enrollment. But, particularly in medical cases, where the researcher is a doctor under an obligation to do the patient some good where possible, this judgment will never be made lightly.

D. Competence, Importance, and Reliability

To define what will count as a competently designed research protocol we need the following. An experiment must be designed such that it can give a reliable answer to a well-posed scientific question which is of importance to the theory or applications of the science in question. The "science" can be construed quite broadly here: any predictive or policy science involving human beings and their behavior, psychology, physiology, biology, or medicine falls within the domain of interest.

Defining "importance" here is difficult to do analytically. As already noted, many experiments involving human subjects are pedagogical exercises rather than being intended to add something new to human knowledge. I will concentrate on experiments which are intended to play a part in research proper rather than in training. The same principles apply in each case. In the training experiment, more is known about the sub-

stance or procedure under investigation, so the principles can be applied more easily (for instance, more is known about the risks, harms, and benefits involved, so they can be explained more exactly and, usually, controlled more precisely). Supervision by a senior researcher is required to ensure that the procedures of the experiment are carried out to the normal standards of safety and competence. Thirdly, and finally, the subject is being asked to participate in a training exercise rather than innovation, and this will have a bearing on how likely each particular person will be to consent and on what his or her expectations are.

The importance of an experiment is contextual: simple experiments are often more important than complex ones; some measurement experiments are of great relevance, while some hypothesis testing may have few practical consequences or theoretical ramifications; and some attempts to replicate earlier data are more significant than the original "discovery." It is possible for a test of some drug's effectiveness as a treatment for most instances of a condition to show that while it is efficacious as an antibiotic, it may be less useful than another treatment for some reason. So giving a definition of "importance" is probably futile. It is a task that is performed sociologically by the grant-application process (albeit in a somewhat unsatisfactory way, if most disappointed researchers are to be believed!).

Reliability in method is easier to determine in most sciences, particularly those of a statistical nature, such as empirical psychology or clinical and social medicine. Mathematical methods exist for determining how many subjects to enroll in a statistical study in order to get a reliable result, conditional on controlling sources of bias. This takes us to our main subject.

Thus far we have seen that even before selecting subjects for research can begin, we must satisfy ourselves that the experiment is capable of giving a satisfactory answer to a well-posed question, which will be of some utility or importance.

E. The Population of Possible Research Subjects

The principles for selection of subjects from research can be approached from this direction. It is crucial for the validity and generalizability of the experimental findings that the group of subjects enrolled into the experiment should be composed so as to permit an adequate answer to the experimental question. This will require a statement in the experimental protocol which determines which biological or social characteristics may be relevant to the substance or procedure under test, and why. These are the characteristics which define the population of possible experimental subjects. Other characteristics may be relevant for ethical or social reasons, which permit secondary selection within that experimental population. But people who do not possess the relevant primary characteristics do not belong in the experiment.

It is essential that the primary characteristics are explicit and open to critical scrutiny. For instance, historically, women were (are?) often excluded from many drug trials, and indeed often from trials which would be of benefit almost exclusively to women, on the grounds that they are "pregnant, pregnable, or once pregnable." This was in fact enshrined in many regulatory codes. But it was not clear whether this was for scientific, ethical, or cultural reasons. Women were not approached to be recruited to such trials, although there was nothing in the scientific hypotheses which warranted this. The decision to risk side effects relevant to childbearing was a secondary tier of selection, properly speaking. To define one's eligible population on social or ethical grounds *before* examining the scientific criteria for determining the study population is to risk greater injustice than one thought to forestall.

It is possible that one might regard gender, or ethnicity or occupation, as a scientific criterion, however. Side effects are a significant part of what one wishes to determine about a treatment or procedure. A series of small trials, each one with relatively exclusive selection criteria related to a specific population, might be regarded as safer, and hence more ethical, because each trial can answer a more precise question, and the influence of more factors can be controlled for.

This is an important argument, but not really relevant here. In the trials where women were excluded for "scientific" reasons, and without consultation, women were often the primary treatment group, not one group among several (two?). And not only were they excluded from a smaller, initial trial on men only, no second trial (on women) occurred. Hence, either the treatment was not licensed for use in women (so that they could not benefit from something which could usually benefit only them), or they were obliged, as a population, to use a treatment untested on them for efficacy or safety. And the only rationale for the test in the first place was to protect women (in fact, anybody) from treatments of unknown safety or efficacy.

The scientific criterion for defining the population of possible research subjects should be interpreted maximally, and in itself will usually involve no explicit selection principle beyond technical criteria such as feasibility of experimentation. It is of course sometimes

the case that some "technical" criteria involve suppressed ethical assumptions. In this case the experimental protocol involves an implicit ethical judgment about the appropriateness of experimentation on a certain subpopulation, or a quasi-ethical judgment about the inconvenience (or disutility) of enrolling a certain class of subjects. In such cases, the ethical status of the protocol is subject to scrutiny using the same principles as any proposal involving an explicit selection principle. Ethical good faith requires transparency here, and passing off ethical judgments as scientific may be regarded as suspicious and bad practice.

F. Sample Size and Control Groups

Once the population of subjects for the experimental hypothesis test or inquiry has been determined in principle, the task of determining how many and which subjects to enroll begins. In some experiments, it may be that only a very few subjects are needed to establish the hypothesis, because all humans are sufficiently similar in the relevant respect that variations between subjects may be ignored. Almost all experimentation on human subjects will involve recognizing that human variation is relevant to the measurement or hypothesis, and so the experiment is statistical in nature. As already remarked, in a statistical experiment a certain mathematical calculation (the "power" calculation or its "Bayesian" analogues) can be used to determine the minimum number of required subjects. An experiment which fails to recruit sufficiently many subjects will produce results which are inconclusive or of uncertain quality. In consequence, an experiment which is unlikely to be able to recruit enough subjects to achieve this minimum size, but which is carried out anyway, is arguably unethical for the same reasons that an inadequately designed experiment is unethical. This objection may be overcome if some reliable method exists of aggregating data from other similar experiments so that a fictional meta-experiment which is of an appropriate size results, but this remains controversial.

The usual method of reducing "sample size" difficulties is to dispense with a control group. Most experimentation using human subjects involves a comparison with a group of subjects who do not receive the substance under test, or who do not undergo the experimental procedure, in order to ensure that any observed effect in the "treatment" group really is due to the new treatment. Usually this means enrolling subjects into the experiment, and assigning some to the treatment group and some to the control (comparison) group by some method (usually random assignment). The alternative is to enroll all subjects into the treatment arm, and to compare each subject with a subject outside the trial (by examination of their medical records, for instance) who is either in a relevantly similar situation now or was in the recent past. This may be done on an individual basis, or it may be done at the level of the group, so that while patient-by-patient similarity may not hold, the two groups share the relevant properties en bloc.

Scientifically, the relevant point is that most statisticians agree that experimentation without a purposely enrolled control group is significantly less reliable than experimentation with such a group. And most agree that unless this group is constructed by assigning subjects at random to the treatment or control groups, the experiment is vulnerable to the effects of unknown, unevenly distributed "confounding" or "nuisance" variables. There are many complex ethical issues related to the ethical merits of these various methods of experimentation which are beyond the scope of this article. Here we should only note that it is important to know how many subjects are required as a minimum, relative to the experimental design (and method of inference) in use.

In some cases no experiment will be possible, simply because the experimental population is smaller than the minimum sample size needed. In this case it may be necessary in *medical* cases to give the treatment to whoever the doctor (in consultation with the patients) deems to require the treatment. Here the patient–subject will be receiving an experimental treatment outside the context of an experiment. This is the situation which obtains in treatments for rare diseases. It will also obtain in the early phase of treatment development, where not enough is known about a treatment for it to be tested experimentally in a rigorous way, but some patients in dire straits may be given the treatment as a last resort, and the consequences observed. Ethically, it is the rarity or extremity of the situation which is relevant, but the issues of risk and benefit and consent are essentially the same as in other circumstances. The distinction should be drawn between these situations and human experimentation proper, because in these situations no true experiment is carried out, although an experimental treatment is used, and data about its effects will be gathered.

Another type of situation where an experiment may prove impossible is the case where a sufficient number of subjects are available, but the rate of recruitment is too low for the experiment to be completed on time. This can be because subjects are unwilling to enroll for ethical or other reasons of their own, or because (in the medical case) physicians are unwilling to put their patients forward as possible subjects. If there is no obvious ethical reason for this, this may represent a case where some inducement might be required. Most experts on research ethics regard inducement as unethical, because it may be considered as either duress or as seducing individuals to act against their own interest or perhaps as destructive of the social virtue of acting altruistically. A distinction may be drawn between overcoming the inconveniences attendant upon participating in an experiment and causing subjects to overlook the additional harms they may undergo as a result of taking part in the experiment. Inducement issues, as with the differential benefits which may accrue to the experimental participant which are unavailable to the nonparticipant, are issues of justice and rights, and I will return to those in the sections on nonscientific issues of selecting subjects.

G. Representativeness

If the necessary minimum sample size is smaller than the size of the experimental subject population, selection on some principle will almost certainly be necessary. In some cases, where the two sizes are of the same order of magnitude, there may be an argument for including the whole population in the experiment, or rather, offering participation to all members of the population. This would be for reasons of equity. This would be a rare event, however. In most cases, a sample of the same approximate size as the minimum is more appropriate. This will be for reasons of convenience and for other ethical reasons.

A smaller experiment will usually be easier to manage and quicker to complete, and so the results will be easier to determine and turn into policy, from which the whole population will benefit. If one of the treatments is harmful, quick completion (or discontinuation) will mean that the group receiving the harmful treatment will be minimized. It is sometimes possible to terminate an experiment "prematurely," that is, before the minimum size experiment has run its course, in cases where the experimental treatment's harm or benefit becomes statistically "obvious." Usually this is not the case, however. The experiment needs to run its course for the results to have any meaning. In each case, running a controlled experiment where some benefit or harm befalls the subjects because of the experiment due to the novel treatment means using a number of subjects who will, after the fact, be seen to have derived less benefit by reason of their allocation to one or the other group alone. It is not predictable in advance which group this will turn out to be—that is the motivation behind the experiment. In order to minimize this after-the-fact (relative) misfortune, it is usual to run experiments close to the minimum size.

Some subjects will be selected for the offer of participation in the experiment while others will not. In general, more subjects will be offered participation than are statistically necessary, simply because some of those subjects will decline participation. In almost all cases, as we shall see, the subject's consent to participate must be sought, and refusal of this consent makes exclusion of the patient from the study compulsory for the researcher. If a patient, who is judged suitable to be offered participation, accepts the offer, in all but a few exceptional circumstances he or she will be admitted to the study (for instance, in the case of medical treatment, his or her condition might change). This may involve more subjects accepting than predicted, so that the sample size is larger than the minimum. Patients are asked for their consent to receive a treatment under the experimental protocol, and have some right to expect that their consent will admit them to the protocol, unless there is some good reason not to include them. Offering participation and withdrawing the offer at a later stage may be regarded, in many circumstances, as at least rude, and at worst cruel, unless something has changed which alters subjects' suitability for participation or the conditions underlying their own grant of consent. Simply being supernumerary does not satisfy this clause.

Which individuals are to be selected for a given experiment? Scientifically, the criterion is suitability as regards a genuine test of the hypothesis under consideration, or an unbiased measurement of the parameter of interest. In the medical case, patients may be ineligible because their condition is so severe (or so mild) that they would not normally receive either treatment; because there is clear reason to suppose that they would benefit from some specific treatment (and so participation in the experiment would not be in that patient's medical best interests); because they are susceptible to some known side effect of the treatment; or because they are "comorbid" (simultaneously ill with another disease or condition), where this comorbidity either will affect the effectiveness of the treatment under study or will require treatment which will affect the effectiveness of the treatment under study.

The main issue which determines patient suitability is the need to construct a sample which will allow generalization of the results of the experiment upon this sample to the population under study. There is a red herring here: representativeness. It is not necessary to construct a sample where the distribution in the sample of the scientifically important characteristics which define the population reflects their distribution in the population itself. In fact, it is very unlikely that such a construction would be possible, if the intention were to construct this model directly. In most nontherapeutic research it is possible to imitate that distribution by random sampling. This may be necessary, scientifically, if one is attempting to describe the features of the population. In cases where the experiment is intended to be beneficial to some or all subjects, in particular in medicine, selection at random means benefit at random. This is an ethically complex issue, as we shall see later. However, and more crucially, in the medical case, the existence of a stable population of subjects with a certain disease is almost always meaningless, and the experiment takes place under the obligation to treat a patient as and when he or she presents (among other medical obligations and patients' rights). Largely the sample constructs itself, and while the researcher can exclude some patients, it will be difficult to actively include patients who do not present themselves for treatment. In some cases this is possible; in others it is also necessary—for instance, in community-based substance abuse research. The sample which constructs itself in this way has no necessary connection in distribution with the population at large.

If the sample is not connected with the population in distribution, it will almost certainly produce results which are biased, that is, results which are significantly different from those which would be obtained if the experiment involved the whole population (past, present, and future). It is sometimes possible to predict that the bias will be in a certain direction, but inference on correction for bias on this prediction may be unreliable. The bias I have described here is patient self-selection bias; in parallel there is researcher selection bias (where consciously or unconsciously a researcher selects more subjects of one kind than another).

From a simplistic "scientific" point of view, the only factors of interest to enrolling the sample are those which define the population under study, and provided that all subjects are members of the population, use of further criteria of selection are "purely" matters of ethics or social policy. However, the truth is more complicated. It is possible that other factors are relevant to the experiment, whose influence we may or may not know about, and which may affect the results of the experiment. Our method of selection may emphasize the influence of these factors (confounding or nuisance variables), causing our inferences to be in error. In order to control the influence of these variables, it is usual to randomize *within* the sample. That is, subjects are assigned at random to one or the other experimental (or control) group. In this way, it is argued, distribution of the nuisance variables will be the same in each group, and their net influence will be balanced out. There are particular ethical issues to do with randomization in medical trials, which are beyond the scope of this article.

The relevance of these matters to selection issues is that representativeness is not a scientific issue. It may become a scientific issue if the attempt to construct a "representative" selection method causes biased results. A socially representative sample may be constructed, but—as with any active selection principle—it may be a source of bias *unless* steps are taken to construct a control group which is parallel in composition to the treatment group. And given the practicalities of research recruitment, the most effective and fairest way to construct this parallel is randomization.

It is important to underline the distinction between scientific and social criteria of inclusion or exclusion. It may be that it is thought ethically or socially important that some definite group be offered (or refused) the opportunity to participate in some experiment. Does this relate to some feature relevant to the hypothesis under test? In some cases it may: for example, many chemotherapeutic treatments are relevant to the treatment of children's cancers. Ignoring the legal issues, note that in many cases such treatments are not tested upon children, and so may, in general, not be used on children. Yet it is probable that they would benefit from such treatments. Should children be included in the trials of these treatments? The rash answer would be yes. But, scientifically, the dosage and side effects of the treatments in children would be significantly different. If the tests were to be done on children, they would have to be done in separate pediatric trials. The ethical issues do not relate to the exclusion of children from adult trials, but to the lack of pediatric trials. On the other hand, exclusion of some ethnic minority patients from a trial is unlikely to have any scientific validity, and so may reflect some social injustice (or indeed some other cultural factor).

II. ETHICAL AND SOCIAL ISSUES

In part I, I discussed the ethical necessity for any scientific experiment using human subjects to be scientifically sound in conception. Merely scientifically sound experiments will not generally be ethically legitimate, however. In this part I will discuss ethical issues of design and recruitment to scientific experiments which are relevant to the method of selecting subjects.

A. Protecting Subjects

Historically, the most significant ethical issue in selection of subjects for research has been the protection of subjects. The main ethical standards in human subjects research have been framed and disseminated in the wake of the Nuremberg war crimes trials, and subsequently these have been reinforced by evidence of other "medical" atrocities. The purpose of these standards has been to protect subjects from actual physical and mental cruelty, and from being treated as "mere means" to ends set in the name of Society or Science (or both). The main focus of the Nuremberg inquiry was upon coerced participation by subjects. Later, attention was turned to enrollment of subjects into experiments without their knowledge, in particular, instances of experiments which were performed without any conceivable benefit to the subject, where actual harm would result, and where subjects were offered financial or other inducements to take part in the experiments.

These concerns focus our attention on the issue of enrolling vulnerable individuals into experiments, and onto the issue of risks, harms, benefits, and interests. It has been established that in all but the most extreme or exceptional cases, no one should be enrolled in an experiment without their explicit and voluntary consent. Particular attention has been devoted to those cases where subjects are incompetent to give or incapable of giving explicit and voluntary consent. These include minors (including, on some interpretations, fetuses), the mentally ill and disabled, and the unconscious. In addition to these cases (which for the most part involve special legal considerations as well as ethical ones), attention has been focused on subjects who may be vulnerable to duress or other kinds of pressure to participate. Such duress might on occasion be held to invalidate any consent such subjects may give, because it vitiates the voluntary character of that consent. The original cases where such concerns were raised were prisoners, members of the armed forces, and students and junior staff in research institutions. More recently, concern has been voiced about subjects at a social disadvantage vis-à-vis the researcher or access to health or social services. Throughout the history of these debates attention has returned again and again to the situation of severely ill subjects who may be able to make reflective judgments, but only at the cost of great suffering, or who may not be able to make judgments "in character" because of their suffering.

B. Limits to the Protective Model

It is clear from this focus on the protection of subjects, and on identification of types of vulnerable subjects who particularly need protection, that the emphasis in research ethics lies on the risks of research, rather than on the benefit. This may be a somewhat misleading or distorting emphasis. Arguably, most research exposes subjects to no risk of physical or psychological suffering or injury, even in the short term. Most social research and most psychological research is of this type. A large portion of medical research on minor conditions and on the delivery of healthcare is of this type, too. Levine has distinguished between harm and inconvenience to subject. We may also note that some research is no more or less harmful or inconvenient than "standard" practice, and that if a protective test is to be applied, it should apply not only to the research intervention but also to the standard intervention. This point may be considered irrelevant to experimental sciences where subjects are actively recruited and enrolled, but it is important in research in medicine or management science (say) where research activity is part of or added on to "ordinary" activity, and the subjects are clients or staff of the service. Related to this, in applied sciences where practices are subject to continuous innovation or adaptation to changing circumstances (surgery is a good example) it is hard to determine where research begins and standard practice ends. The distinction may lie in the deliberate intention to alter a practice in a way which, if successful, will lead to a permanent alteration or extension of the practice, so that the purview of the intention is not simply the case in hand, but all future similar cases.

In medical research, many treatments or practices may be both harmful and beneficial. Chemotherapies are usually physically very unpleasant and their effectiveness lies in their being toxic—but more toxic to the cancerous than to the "normal" cells. The aim of a selection principle in this case will be to select patients as subjects for whom the benefits of the innovation will be in proportion to the harms actually to be undergone, or at risk. In addition the principle holds that the researcher (and a respectable body of professional opinion) must believe that the new treatment will turn out to be at least no less effective (that is, beneficial) than any alternative treatment we could offer. In these cases, focus on risk alone is inappropriate.

What is the nature of the protective standard we seek to apply in such cases? In the first case, where the research presents some inconvenience to the subjects, the consent test merely seeks to ensure that subjects are aware of and agree to undergo the inconvenience. Insofar as this is an ethical issue, it is normally the issue of good manners: putting subjects to inconvenience without their consent will make them (and others) less likely to participate in the future, and this is particularly so when they are at first unaware of the experiment or the inconvenience. Where a subject may feel they have been deceived, misled, or spied upon they become at risk of psychological harm (a sense of violation), and misconduct in the practice of the experiment turns the inconvenience into an actual harm. Finally, covert or deceptive research may be regarded as having serious consequences for the nature of the society permitting such research, indicating as it does a disregard for privacy and individual liberty. Most ethics committees are therefore very unwilling to permit such research, however well motivated. In many cases such research is actually illegal.

In the case where the experimental procedure exposes subjects to risks and benefits of the same degree as standard practice (the benefits of the research being to the organization rather than to the subjects directly), we may argue that first, good manners require informing the subjects, and cooperative subjects may be a source of extra information for the study, and second, the consent of subjects may be required for both experimental and nonexperimental procedures where risk is involved.

The role of consent as a protective test is twofold. First, it alerts the subject to the fact of their possible participation in an experiment, which is a situation where some significant risks or benefits or both will be incompletely known. Secondly, it promotes and legitimizes the subjects knowing acceptance of the chances of harm and benefit and any reasonable consequences of the innovation for the subject. The consent test is antipaternalistic in a number of ways. It makes the choice the subject's choice, rather than that of the researcher. In many situations experiments which a subject might not find objectionable may be ruled out by a too anxious researcher or committee: it may be paternalistic not to offer the subject the choice, in fact. A test based on risk alone may be slightly absurd for the reasons already noted, but it is also seriously expert-centered and paternalistic too. Finally, the consent test, at best, may involve the subject as a partner in the research, rather than as a "subject" in the political sense of the term. Some authors have suggested abandoning the term subject for this very reason, although this may be a case of linguistic usage running ahead of practice.

The consent test does have its pitfalls, however. In Section II.A I mentioned the ways in which consent may not serve the interests of several classes of vulnerable subjects, either by automatically excluding some de facto (the unconscious and the mentally ill or disabled) or de jure (children or prisoners), or by permitting the inclusion of others (the seriously ill or members of vulnerable social groups) against their "best interests" (however they be determined). A further twist is the perception that some professional groups may use the informed consent test as a sort of "buyer beware"—in an exculpatory way. Many patients in medical experiments may regard informed consent cynically (as part of "defensive medicine"), or as the doctor off-loading his responsibility to know, judge, and decide what is best for the patient.

C. Selection and Protection

It is clear that the consent mechanism is a kind of selection mechanism as well as a protection mechanism. Many medical trials have ultimately failed because, while many patients were offered participation, very few accepted the offer. In most cases, the situation is the opposite: the experimental population is large, and enrollment continues until enough suitable subjects have presented and given their consent. The subjects who enroll effectively select themselves from the experimental population. At this point the issue of justice is at least as important as protection. Are certain psychological or cultural types of people more (or less) likely to consent (perhaps because of "intelligence" or "educational level")? Or to present in the first place? Are people of this type unfairly advantaged by their superior access to the benefits of such research? Or unfairly disadvantaged by their exposure to the risks of research? Furthermore, the consent mechanism is one selection mechanism among others.

Subjects in medical trials are "selected" for participation in medical trials of treatment by their misfortune in falling ill with a particular disease, at the given time and in the given place. This is mostly by chance, and may be a blessing or a disadvantage; but in some cases an additional selection factor may combine with this selection by fortune. This is the socioeconomic factor. Being treated at a hospital with a large research load may increase one's chance of participation in a trial, and this may be a good or a bad thing, but one may have a higher prior probability of being treated in such a hospital because of one's inability to pay for care, or alternatively because one lives in the (often) poor neighborhood in which a teaching hospital is found; or perhaps because one has the money and status which make one able to demand "state of the art" treatment.

In any of these cases a "market failure" may be occurring which distorts the just selection of subjects for the risks and benefits of research.

The difficulty in negotiating the issue of justice here is heightened by the time asymmetry. After the fact, when the risks and benefits of the experimental procedure are more clear, it is easier to say that some group was harmed by participation or exclusion, because we can identify whether participation entailed access to net harm or net benefit. Doing this before the fact is much harder—in fact, if it were not we would not need to do the experiment in the first place. But it is not always impossible. Any treatment or procedure will involve some knowable consequences, and some unknown consequences. In a trial of radical mastectomy versus lumpectomy, most of the surgical and psychosocial consequences are predictable; what is not predictable is the relative effectiveness of the two procedures. The doctor and the patient must together determine whether the consequences and risks of each treatment are such that the patient and doctor are able to tolerate the predictable outcomes of either treatment to the extent that they are indifferent between them.

In most cases the researcher will screen some subjects out even before informed consent as unsuitable. Recall that we have assumed that the person under consideration as a subject is a member of the experimental population—if they are not then they are automatically ineligible. Of the possible subjects who present themselves, some will be unsuitable for some reason. In a medical trial, their condition may be too severe or to mild, for example. Informally, some subjects may be ruled out as unlikely to comply, as previously discussed. There is a fine line here between pragmatism and paternalism. The suitability of a subject is another, often informal and private, selection criterion.

In many cases, what counts as unsuitability will turn on unsuitability to give consent rather than medical, social, or psychological unsuitability for participation in the study. A patient, otherwise suitable, may be so distressed by his condition that seeking his participation would be cruel. But in this case it might be that giving them the chance to participate is giving them a measure of control over their situation, which they might not otherwise feel they had, and may be therapeutic of itself. In the wider philosophical context, informed consent is usually not taken to stand on its own as a test (as it does in the Nuremberg Code), but as part of "respect for autonomy" (or self-determination). Here we see a case where overzealous respect for the letter of consent, combined with a somewhat paternalistic desire to protect a patient from the stress of choice (understood as harmful), may actually interfere with the patient's autonomy. In most discussions autonomy is taken to be a reflexive character trait which adds to the moral quality of a person's life and develops through use, but is fundamental to human being. I have not used the concept previously in this entry because it is not philosophically neutral, and perhaps not widely accepted, even though it is widely presumed accepted.

1. Women: Protecting a Possible Fetus?

While many subjects are excluded from a study because they are judged unsuitable on scientific or pragmatic grounds, others are excluded for philosophical or legal reasons, and others are included against their interests, through compulsion or coercion. Women are often excluded, not on any grounds of their own personal safety, but on the grounds of possible harm to actual or future children they may bear. Many drugs are indeed very harmful for fetal development; radiotherapy can certainly promote mutation, and so on. The philosophical question here is, whose risk is this? Is it the (potential) mother's, to take as she sees fit? Or is it the (potential) child's, from whom no consent can be derived either actually or by substituted judgment (no such inference would permit a child to undergo a harm without benefit to the child)? In some cases the treatment will be medically necessary for the mother's survival, and in cases where her survival is necessary for the survival of the child, a law of double effect may apply. These are still open questions, and much discussed. Furthermore, the methods of (temporary) resolution in this area are methods of the law and the court.

2. Protecting the Powerless

Other important exclusions include the exclusion of prisoners and military personnel, and of students and junior staff working for the researcher, or in the researcher's sphere of influence. The argument here is not that such subject cannot genuinely volunteer, nor that they cannot benefit from experimentation, but that their consent is either the result of coercion by the authorities or is distorted by their membership of an institution which has a powerful influence over their future, and may be regarded as having interests other than those of the individual subject at heart. These situations are different from that of the patient in the hospital, precisely because the hospital is supposed to care for the (medical) interests of the patients. In some cases prisoners have been prevented from taking part

in research which would, on their own judgment, have been to their benefit, by overliteral interpretation of regulations forbidding the enrollment of prisoners for their own protection. Yet it is hard to press the charge of paternalism here, simply because the regulations for prisoners and students were framed to curb actual abuses of power.

The way out of this dilemma may be to develop the notion of group or communal consent, not as sufficient for inferring individual consent, but as sufficient for allowing individuals to be approached. This is a subject's rights analogue of the Institutional Review Board or Local Research Ethics Committee. Institutions of this kind have already been established to protect the rights of the Inuit in Canada, Maori communities in New Zealand, and native Americans in the reservations of the United States.

3. Subjects Incompetent to Consent

The most difficult cases in practical research is research on children, unconscious subjects, and the mentally ill or disabled. In such cases the capacity for exercising autonomy or for giving genuinely informed consent is curtailed or absent, yet in other respects the interests are the subjects' own, and are very real. It is arguable that research on these subjects is unethical, if it is not for the benefit of each individual subject him- or herself, and cannot stand the test of what in other circumstances the subject might want and what society in its best intentions might deem decent and dignified. This is an extreme statement. It would rule out child psychological development research as unethical because it has no benefit for the child. So most authorities allow nontherapeutic research which is noninvasive and nonintrusive, and poses "minimal risk" to the child (or other subject).

D. Rights and Duties

The main protective issue in all of these cases is to protect the individual's rights and interests being overridden in the interests of present and future others or "society." This is held to be both respectful of the subject's own rights and person, and also beneficial for the health of society. The main counterargument to this is a mixed authoritarian and utilitarian one, which according to Daniel Rothman was to be found in societies like the USA in the "total wars" of this century. According to this argument, in some circumstances (plagues, wars, or natural disasters) the rights of the individual were subservient to those of society, simply because without the continued existence of that society those rights would be destroyed. And in exceptional circumstances, that society has the right to hold certain individual rights in abeyance. This is a very dangerous argument, but one still familiar among so-called "realists." Many of the most serious medically inflicted harms have been imposed on members of the armed forces by their own side for this reason, and for the reason that in battle, troops may be injured, mutilated, and killed, often voluntarily, to save comrades or for military necessity, and participation in medical experiments was simply another form of this duty.

The duty to participate in experimentation has not found many defenders, although some authors have advanced powerful arguments. We have seen that all subjects have the right not to participate in research, and hence that all researchers have the obligation to honor this right, as well as the obligations we derived in the first part of this article concerning adequate study design. We have just discussed an argument which holds both that these rights are sometimes properly overturned in the "national interest," and like all national interest arguments they are as hard to resist in the real world as they are hard to defend on paper. The other implication of this argument is that subjects have an obligation to participate when necessary. It is a mistake to conflate these two versions of the argument. It is an important error to assume that to every right corresponds a duty, simply because of grammar. A duty is owed by me to someone, while a right may be considered to bind everyone. This is one reason why there are fewer rights than one might hope. My duty—if I have one—to participate in research is owed to no state, but to humanity. And the state has no right to confuse itself with humanity.

In other words, if there is a duty to participate in research, then it is a social duty, not a civic one. So it is of the same kind as the duty to become a blood donor or to give to charity. Caplan and Jonas have both observed that this must be the nature of such a duty, and have both argued that it exists. It is a matter of moral honor to observe the duty, because it is unenforceable.

Jonas concentrates on the case of nontherapeutic research, and Caplan on therapeutic research. The controversial part of Jonas's argument is that he claims that the severely, perhaps terminally, ill are particularly suited to being research volunteers, and especially in research related to their illness. They would make, on Jonas's theory, excellent Phase I and Phase II trial participants, where Phase I determines toxicity, and Phase II tries to determine the range of effective and tolerable

dosage for a drug. Some studies do indicate that certain altruistic terminally ill subjects agree with Jonas in their own case—it feels like paying back something, or leaving something worthwhile behind. It would be stretching a point to call this recognition of a duty. It would be unusual to recognize altruism as a duty. Jonas's argument rests on the harmfulness of the research. Toxicity research is potentially very harmful indeed; would it not be wrong to attempt it on healthy volunteers or curable cases, even with their consent? It may well be that a "good death" might be available in this way, but many people would regard this sort of stoicism in the face of a death made even more painful, rather than less, as inhuman.

Caplan's argument rests on the principle of reciprocity: we all depend on medical research to some degree, and so refusal to participate where one can is a form of "free riding." It is not clear, however, that this rule applies in every case: can one be choosy about which research one participates in? Of course—one should be. And it is certainly clear that the duty is not transferable: just because I would do something gives me no cause to expect my child, my senile relative, or you to do so.

A final issue in this context is the issue of a right to participate in research. This is in effect a justice issue. If I am aware of research on my condition being done, and I believe that it would benefit me, or indeed that nothing else would do so but this research, have I the right to participate? This is part of a larger issue, the issue of whether one has any rights or entitlements to health care in general or of a specific sort. Most human rights theorists argue that everyone has a right to a minimum standard of care, as to food, but not to anything specific (I have no right to caviar). Similarly, I have no right to any particular form of care that I may demand, although I have a right to expect that my doctor will do what is in his power to preserve my life and health. So the right to participation, if it exists, will be of a limited kind, and will rest on equity issues, limited by scientific and pragmatic matters. To these questions I now turn.

E. Justice and Selection

As I have mentioned throughout this paper, the issue of access to experimentation and fair distribution of risks is a crucial topic in research ethics. It is of little importance in minimal risk, minimal benefit research, save perhaps in the sense that enrolling a wide variety of subjects may have a social solidarity effect: encouraging access to, and participation in, science as a part of culture, and reducing the sense that science is a "white man's" game. Even in this sense, however, there is some worry that subjects are subjects rather than participants, and this is an area where development is needed. But in any research where benefits and harms may accrue to subjects, the issue of fair access to the chances of benefit and fair distribution of risks are of obvious importance.

If we recall the discussion in Section I.A of compensation for the inconvenience of participation, it is possible that such compensation may be regarded as an inducement to participate. As such it may be regarded as a benefit in itself, rather than as a reparation of costs, and as a benefit it may be offset against risk or actual harm. It is possible to regard the supply of participants in a trial as a market, where compensation of subjects is a sort of "price" which is to be set to offset the opportunity cost (the economic value of their inconvenience) of the marginal participant (that is, the last to be recruited for the minimum sample size, taken to be the least willing or most inconvenienced). Understood economically, the earlier subjects (ordered by inconvenience) are indeed receiving a direct benefit—a profit of payment over inconvenience. Are they therefore being induced? In this sense they are. Is this harmful? Not if we can distinguish inconvenience and harm. And can we? Only in some cases. In most cases, neither we nor most participants are that sophisticated. Some economists would regard harm as an economic "good" anyway, and as such tradable. These issues are so complex that most research guidelines ignore them, or specify that financial payments in therapeutic research before the fact (and not as compensation for *unexpected* harms) are unethical, and payments to "healthy volunteers" must be small—a gratuity rather than a payment for a service.

Supposing one can distinguish, as Levine does, between risks and harms on the one hand and inconveniences on the other, it is important that, given the definition of the experimental population, and given the protective standards agreed to in our society, any subject should have fair access to the benefits of the experimental process. The issue of priority setting in research is not unrelated, although it is logically distinct. Arguably, as I stated at the end of the last section, no one has a right to participate in a particular experiment. But it seems clear that if experimentation is going on, no one should be systematically excluded from experimentation which they might benefit from participating in. The arguments of women concerning this are well surveyed by Merton. Such exclusion has two forms: first, through formal or informal exclusion of research directly relevant to them, and second, systematic nonperformance of research relevant to some social group. If some group suspects that work relevant to their health or social well-being is regularly assigned low priority, while some other group's sectional interests are regularly given high priority, then that group may have a right to some remedy. This is a matter of justice about the distribution of social power, and may apply to women, children, homosexuals, and members of ethnic or cultural minorities. A controversial instance would be access of the elderly to experimental health care.

The converse of this is where a group is overrepresented in risky research. This can be through deliberate inclusion of the socially marginal or weak (considered expendable) or as an unplanned consequence of some other social injustice. The very poor, who cannot afford health insurance, may be disproportionately exposed to some kinds of research because of their poverty and because of their poverty-related ill health; in many countries, poverty and ethnic group may be linked, so that the injustice acquires (or is caused by) racial discrimination.

In both questions of justice (considered as fairness), there are two elements. The first is the possibility of social, systematic advantage or disadvantage. Whatever one's views about the ethics of access to standard (or even luxury) health care or social services, it is hard to defend inequality in access to experimental risk or harm, in much the same way as it is hard to defend unequal involuntary exposure to infectious disease as a *policy* rather than as a fact of life. As we noted in the scientific aspects of selection there is no necessity for deliberate social representativeness in sampling. But we also saw that there was no harm to validity in seeking just representation, consistent with selecting from the experimental population, provided suitable randomization measures were taken.

The second element is the element of fairness to individuals considered as such. If we rely—as we must, where we can—on consent as a tool to help the individual protect him- or herself, the more important issue is the issue of ensuring fair access to benefits. For the most part this cannot be detached from group justice, as has been noticed, in another context, in the case of affirmative action. Perhaps these two modes of justice conflict, as they seem to in affirmative action. One solution, as has been noted, is the use of group consent as a prior level of protection. This would need to be proactive, in putting forward group members as a class of participants, and defending the members' right to be approached on equal terms. The function of the group consent would be to protect equality rather than to enforce members' individual rights, which, as we have seen, are probably nonexistent. If we suppose that this protection of equality of access is effective, then the fairness to individuals issue can be approached.

Perhaps the fairest way to distribute chances is by lottery. Other methods include ranking subjects by need (of treatment or of benefit), or inversely by vulnerability (the least vulnerable first). In fact, however, this is an open question in research ethics simply because no one has addressed it since Levine's early paper. The question is perhaps analogous to issues about equality of opportunity (as opposed to equality of access to goods). In practice, two methods are used. The first method is the informal allocation of chances, determined largely by technical considerations of suitability and judgments of compliance, to subjects identified as they present themselves to the researcher. There is no guarantee here of fairness, although there is a link in the medical case to the random element in the epidemiology of the condition. The second method is a modification of the former, in which certain groups are actively recruited, where their low participation has been noted and determined to be linked to a social disadvantage or some specific inconvenience. The latter is the outreach approach.

Also See the Following Articles

ANIMAL RESEARCH • INFORMED CONSENT • MEDICAL CODES AND OATHS • RESEARCH ETHICS • RESEARCH METHODS AND POLICIES

Bibliography

Caplan, A. L. (1991). Is there a duty to serve as a subject in biomedical research? In *If I were a rich man could I buy a pancreas? And other essays on the ethics of healthcare* (Chap. 6). Bloomington: Indiana Univ. Press.

Dula, A. (1994). African American suspicion of the healthcare system is justified: What do we do about it? *Cambridge Quarterly of Healthcare Ethics, 3,* 347–357.

Jonas, H. (1969). Philosophical reflections on experimenting with human subjects. *Daedalus, 98,* 219–247.

Levine, R. J. (1978). Appropriate guidelines for the selection of human subjects for participation in biomedical research. In National Commission for the Protection of Human Subjects of Biomedical and Behavioral Research, *The Belmont Report: Ethical guidelines and principles for the protection of human subjects of research* (Appendix 1, part 4). DHEW Publication (OS) 78-0012. Washington, DC: US Government Printing Office.

Levine, R. J. (1986). *Ethics and regulation of clinical research.* Baltimore/Munich: Urban & Schwarzenberg.

Merton, V. (1993). The exclusion of pregnant, pregnable and once-pregnable people (a.k.a. women) from biomedical research. *American Journal of Law and Medicine, XIX,* 369–451.

Senn, S. J. (1995). A personal view of some controversies in allocating treatment to patients in clinical trials. *Statistics in Medicine, 14,* 2661–2674.

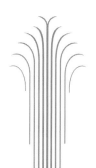

HUMANISM

Eliza Steelwater
University of Illinois at Urbana-Champaign

GLOSSARY

communitarianism The principle that the moral behavior of individuals is best developed within a social community to which they owe certain responsibilities, rather than by the freedom to pursue separate interests.

pragmatism A modern philosophical movement emphasizing the reality of practical experience as the means of evaluating the validity of general principles.

scholasticism A medieval philosophy of Thomas Aquinas, Roger Bacon, and others, based on Aristotelian thought and emphasizing the use of a highly formalized reasoning procedure to analyze moral questions.

secular humanism A term used by critics, for example, fundamentalist Christians, to characterize those aspects of modern humanism that are in conflict with traditional religious teachings such as Biblical infallibility.

Stoicism A classical philosophy of Zeno, Epictetus, Marcus Aurelius, and others, based on the concept of a higher natural law by which the actions of humans may be judged and emphasizing rational behavior free from passion or emotion.

HUMANISM is any philosophical perspective that assigns preeminent value to human beings, their experiences, their interests, and their rights. Humanistic philosophies in this sense can include perspectives as varied as those of Existentialism and of Confucianism—philosophies that are Western or non-Western, modern or ancient. Humanism is also a historical movement in education and scholarship, with influences on political thinking and the arts, that began in Italy in the second half of the fourteenth century. Humanism was short-lived as a coherent movement. It was only one of several competing philosophies within the broader, longer lasting creative outpouring that was the Renaissance. Humanism lasted until about 1500 in Italy, but both began and ended later in other European countries to which it spread. Selected humanist values of the Renaissance, however, contributed to most if not all of the human-centered philosophies that have since developed within the European tradition. These philosophies represent varying combinations of Renaissance humanism, skeptical anti-authoritarianism from the Enlightenment, and a strong emphasis on the inner life or subjectivity of the individual. A historically hybrid "humanist position" can be identified in central ethical debates of the present day.

The word "humanism," coined early in the nineteenth century, came much later than the idea of "humanists" and humanistic scholarship. The meanings of classical Latin *humanitas* are rooted in two distinct Greek concepts: education (*paideia*) and humanitarianism (*philanthropia*). *Philanthropia* relates to the broad definition of humanism: active love and helping concern for human beings. *Paideia,* by contrast, is education in the arts of verbal expression and knowledgeable argumentation that were emphasized as making us human. *Paideia* is the sense of the word humanism that was used by Roman scholars such as Cicero (106–43 B.C.) and Varro (116–27 B.C.) and taken up from them by Renaissance humanists.

"Humanists" during the Renaissance were those who followed the *studia humanitatis* recently revived and modified from ancient Greek and Roman educational practice: grammar, rhetoric, history, poetry, and moral philosophy. More generally, the humanist was a scholar of classical literature. Renaissance humanism was thus a return to antiquity, but the broadest thinkers did not conceive the revival of classical learning as an end in itself. Rather, the five liberal arts and related scholarship were seen as a means of realizing human potential for a freedom based in reason. Although classical scholarship has been progressively deemphasized since the fifteenth century, the development of human potential with "man as the measure of all things" (Protagoras, flourished fifth century B.C.) continues at the center of humanistic philosophies.

I. RENAISSANCE HUMANISM

A. Social Background

As with any tradition of thought, Western humanistic philosophies have developed through the ideas of individual thinkers, through accumulated philosophical discussion, and through the influence of a series of social contexts over time. Historical humanism originated in Italy in the context of urbanization, the local political autonomy of city-states, and prosperous specialties in trade capitalism that marked the Italian city-states of the fourteenth century. In the same period, the weakening of papal authority left the way open for a vigorous secular culture. The society of Italian city-states was inegalitarian and deeply divided. Not being based on inherited land, however, it was relatively fluid. Individuals from essentially middle-class backgrounds could rise to become celebrated scholars and counselors to the *grandi* or patriciate. In turn, this small patrician class of the Italian city-states enthusiastically sponsored humanist learning, with its celebration of the freedom of human will and the potential of human beings for a glorious fulfillment.

Scholars of the Middle Ages had typically been priests, whose function was to train future priests and explicate the Christian faith from a teaching base in universities. Renaissance humanists, often laypersons, took a wider variety of roles. They were particularly influential as civil servants and teachers of secondary-school-aged children of the rich and powerful, whose patronage and company many noted humanists enjoyed. The humanists made up a cadre of perhaps 100 over a century and a half in Italy if one counts only the scholars who made their living from their skill at writing Latin. Such training was coincident with highly developed commerce and the locally based government of city-states, where a great volume of documents led to a large population of notaries. A number of Italian humanists were either notaries or members of notary families. These document handlers and deposition-takers learned excellent Latin (the language of scholars until as late as the 1700s) and were trained in the detailed study of texts. Their skills were particularly valued because the printed word was not current until well after the first printed books appeared in Italy in the 1460s. Texts were still precious possessions to be kept in libraries or copied and carefully circulated.

Petrarch (1304–1374), who can be said to be the first great figure of humanism, exemplifies the humanist of notary origins. Transformed by his first visit to the ruins of ancient Rome, Petrarch initiated the concept of a "dark age" after the glories of classical culture. During this career he discovered texts that had gone unrecognized in Italian libraries, wrote a stream of original works (including poems and biographies) in Latin, attempted to reconcile Christian thought to humanism, attacked scholasticism, and wrote unending letters. Like those of Petrarch, many humanist writings were translations from the Greek, including Plato's complete works, and commentaries on and responses to texts of both ancient Greece and Rome or the early Church fathers. Humanist translations and original writings took the form of letters, ethical essays, histories, scholarly discussions, poetry, plays, and speeches. Scholars from other European countries, notably England, France, the Netherlands, Scotland, and Spain, either came to Italy to study or acquired knowledge of humanism through correspondence or the reading of Italian-authored works.

B. Philosophical Elements of Renaissance Humanism

In terms of knowledge, humanism and Renaissance learning generally continued in the vein of the Middle Ages rather than broke with them. Medieval intellectual forms were based in antiquity, from the use of Latin to

Roman literature, law, and science. The medieval poet Dante Alighieri (1265–1321) paid tribute in *The Divine Comedy* to the Roman poet Virgil (or Vergil, 70–19 B.C.). Medieval mathematics derived from Euclid (flourished 300 B.C.), astronomy from Ptolemy (flourished 130). Arguably, the most important influence on medieval intellectual development was Aristotle (384–322 B.C.). Aristotelian philosophy and methods of observation, as interpreted by Thomas Aquinas (1225–1274) and others, became the basis of the characteristic and lasting medieval philosophy of *scholasticism.*

Scholasticism was a technical philosophical approach emphasizing argument from analogy, and it was typically medieval in taking classical learning as a precursor to Christianity's greater unfolding of wisdom. "Schoolmen" or scholastic thinkers developed and used it to graft a pervasive and militant Christian world view onto the base of information, social organization, and custom inherited from antiquity. By the 1200s, even citizenship was placed within a Christian framework. European governments used legal restrictions and violence to marginalize Jews and Muslims, whose scholarship had earlier been instrumental in bringing classical works to the West. Scholasticism as an ideology was instrumental in rationalizing such developments. But when scholasticism is viewed as a *method,* its ability to transcend Christian concerns and remain relevant in an age of scientific discovery is not surprising. Scholastic commentaries on Aristotle's *Physics* built a base for the work of Renaissance physicists including Galileo (1564–1642).

Both scholastics and early humanists retained a Christian focus for classical study. Initially, skepticism played a small part in humanistic inquiry, and religion remained relevant within the centering of human concerns. Humanists reinstated the texts of early fathers of the Christian church, such as Augustine and Jerome, along with texts of pagan writers such as Cicero, Livy, and Plato. Even a late Italian humanist treatise, Pico della Mirandola's (1463–1494) *Oration on the Dignity of Man,* seeks to place human beings within a God-centered chain of being. But for Pico, both the poignancy and the glory of the human condition lay in the fact of our having no fixed place in the chain, which medieval thinkers had considered rigidly hierarchical. Human beings, through their intellectual capacities and freedom of choice, could imitate beasts or angels.

Such thinking, which began as early as the 1300s, tended to separate philosophy from theology. Even within purely religious debate, an emphasis arose on the imperfectibility of human institutions and the inapplicability of Aristotelian "natural reason" to matters of faith. These attitudes reduced the church's authority and made the religious perspective only one of several ways of understanding human fate. A "probabalistic" level of knowledge gained credibility at the expense of earlier heartfelt certainty in spiritual matters.

A lessening role for theology was accompanied by increasing philosophical acceptance of the world. Success and happiness, and the beauties of literature, art, architecture, and the human body, were enjoyed fully by the patrons of humanism. Both aesthetic pleasure and a growing activism in government and politics developed in direct contradiction to medieval ideals, which (heavily influenced by the classical philosophy of Stoicism) had privileged asceticism and the contemplative life. Some Italian humanists recognized, although with misgivings, that the prosperity and autonomy of the city-states allowed great scope for the kind of rounded human development that Renaissance thinkers prized. Moreover, the lack of a centralized government in Italy left room for questions leading to the birth of modern European political thought. Political thinking interacted with the developing science of history, with its systematic study of human achievements, which some argue did even more than changes within religious thought to lead away from religious teachings as the exclusive source of knowledge about humanity.

The exact content of "civic humanism" can be debated. But a reshaping of Italian political culture, and a redefinition of education and scholarship in relation to society, arguably did take place in Florence and Rome following the end of Florence's war against Milan in 1402. Overlapping Petrarch in time was Colucci Salutati (1331–1406), who became a chancellor, or high government secretary, and sponsored the teaching of Greek. A generation later Leonardo Bruni (1369–1444), through his history of the Florentines, became a leading influence on the civic humanism that Salutati and others had begun to formulate. The significance of Bruni's work is its depiction of Florence's history as owing more to the Etruscan, rather than the later Roman Imperial, influence. According to Bruni, Florence's Etruscan origins provided a political tradition of numerous independent city states and a cultural tradition of liveliness and diversity. Moreover, the history of imperial Rome—traditionally so central to the concept of Italian states—was depicted as expectably finite. Such a depiction represents a significant departure from centering the source of cultural and civic authority on a past golden age.

Tension within civic humanism came from the issue of whether wealth and virtue were compatible. The Roman Stoic tradition held that the source of civic virtue, as well as the basis of empire, was the individually poor members of the smallholder-agriculturalist class. This account, however, did not conform to the Renaissance experience of city-states whose ability to maintain culture, prestige, and political autonomy was based on controlling wealth. Fifteenth-century humanists such as Leon Battista Alberti (1404–1472; in his late work *De Ichiarchia*) argued that whatever serves family and city, such as wealth, health, and personal gifts, must be a good. Numerous humanist authors stressed the centrality of republican thought within Florentine humanism during the first two-thirds of the fifteenth century. But the possibility of combining wealth with civic virtue was increasingly rejected after 1450. The political theorist Niccolò Machiavelli (1469–1527) and others of his generation viewed the civic humanist culture of Florence, at least, as an ideological tool in the hands of the city-state's ruling elite.

Humanists in other European countries shared the varied occupations, the influence on worldly affairs, and the intense focus on classical texts of Italian humanists. Non-Italian humanists thought, however, operated largely within the framework of religious issues that were only one strain of Italian humanism. Northern European humanists' attention to scriptural and church writings facilitated the formation of Protestantism. Desiderius Erasmus (1466–1536), a Dutch monk who never accepted the cloistered life, carried out important translations and corrections of early Christian writings. Reading Erasmus's Greek New Testament of 1516 led Martin Luther (1483–1546) to attack the Church practice of indulgences as having no foundation in Scripture. Erasmus's critical (but not skeptical) spirit, as expressed in his writings, undermined the influence of the scholastics and placed him in opposition to the more dogmatic views of Luther. Erasmus spent portions of his life in England, where he formed close ties with John Colet (1466–1519) and Thomas More (1478–1535). Like Erasmus, Colet was an influential educational reformer and scholar of Scripture who preached in English and modeled himself on Saint Augustine. Colet corresponded with Italian humanists and made use of the work of his contemporary Pico della Mirandola (above). Pico was also a model for Colet's student Thomas More, a lawyer, statesman, and later martyr-saint of the Roman Catholic Church. More's *Utopia* eloquently presents a "Christian Epicureanism" in which pleasure and an ethical life can exist together, very much in the Renaissance humanist spirit.

In Spain, Portugal, and southern France, humanist thought was set against a backdrop of politicized religion that had long supported persecution of the Jews.

Both Michel de Montaigne (1533–1592) and Francisco Sánchez (or Sanches, 1550–1623, a distant cousin born in Portugal) came of Jewish families and were heir to the rich intellectual tradition of Spanish (Sephardic) Judaism. Sánchez's family was of many converted to Christianity to save their lives or avoid expulsion from their country. Montaigne as legislator and mayor of Bordeaux and a former student of the University of Toulouse, and Sánchez, as a physician and professor at Toulouse, maintained ties to other scholars within the university world of southern France and read intensively in classical texts. Montaigne and Sánchez can be classed as skeptics whose outlook was rooted in opposition to the religious fanaticism of their time, but they did not share the extreme empiricism of a Francis Bacon (1561–1626) or the anti-authoritarianism of eighteenth-century thinkers such as François Voltaire (1694–1778). Montaigne's thought matured in the form of highly personal, introspective essays, while Sánchez developed his position of skepticism through systematic critiques of Aristotelian science and Plato's advocacy of mathematics as a basis for knowledge. Montaigne and his student Pierre Charron (1541–1603) were read all over Europe, but Sánchez's work seems never to have become influential.

C. Contributions of Renaissance Humanism

The "liberalizing" trends of humanism gained force in conjunction with intense processes of state formation, both of local states and future nations. These processes occurred during the 1300s and 1400s in England, France, Germany, Italy, and elsewhere. A spirit of protonationalism led new governments to make use of classical and post-classical myths of freedom that were reinforced by the increasing scope of secular life. The reality of individual accomplishment, in an age that allowed some to become prominent based on merit, led to the notion that happiness, worldly achievement, and spiritual excellence could coexist in the same soul. Excellence began to be measured in terms that were human rather than divine. This change paved the way for the secular outlook of humanism and also created a sense of unresolvable relativism in the setting of standards. Relativism was perhaps a basis of the religious toleration for which humanism has always been known. Skepticism also became an influence as increasing religious polarization on the one hand, and a focused program of scientific inquiry on the other, engulfed the earlier open spirit of humanism. This spirit can still be discerned, however. Tolerating diversity, asserting human worth, valuing civic and political life, seeking ethical validity, and believing in the humanizing influence of the historical sense and the liberal arts: these are the legacy of Renaissance humanism.

II. HUMANISTIC PHILOSOPHIES SINCE THE RENAISSANCE

A. Communitarianism

Communitarianism is an ongoing thread of political thought from Aristotle (384–322 B.C.), through such figures as Montesquieu (1689–1754), Jean-Jacques Rousseau (1712–1788), James Harrington (1611–1677), the American republicans of the Federalist period, and Hannah Arendt (1906–1975). Communitarianism can also be seen as a continuation of the civic humanism of Renaissance Florence, Venice, and Rome. Historians and political thinkers such as Salutati, Bruni, and Machiavelli, in spite of differing conclusions, operated from the premise that human development (as a central concern of Renaissance humanism) was best served within the framework of a political community ("the state") rather than by atomistic individuals free to follow their separate interests. During the seventeenth and eighteenth centuries, European and American preoccupation with theories of the nation-state led to intense discussion of alternatives between state supremacy and maximum freedom of the individual. Although the American "Bill of Rights" was essentially an afterthought, the current within American legislation and jurisprudence since 1776 has generally run in favor of individual freedom rather than state authority. This trend is exemplified in the increase of rights over time for persons accused of and convicted of a crime. Today, the debate has been renewed as "liberalism versus communitarianism." The central issue has become whether individual rights, such as freedom of speech, should be absolute or should be tempered by consideration of the harmful effects of exercising the right.

B. Socialist Humanism

In his early work Karl Marx (1818–1883) espoused an explicitly labeled humanism and distinguished among types of humanist thinking. Some followers of Marx, notably Louis Althusser (1918–1990), feel that Marx changed his position after 1845 to decenter human beings within the process of history, replacing their role with that of the relations of economic production as a driving force in history. Nonetheless, socialist human-

ism owes some of its theoretical position to Marx's definition of human nature. Marx conceptualized human beings as *laborers* who (in contrast to other animals) were able to transform the conditions of their own existence through their efforts. He deplored class differences induced by control of production partly because these differences led to self-deception about our own nature. Those who did not labor were able to see themselves as intrinsically different from workers; workers themselves lost sight of their own interests in their desire to emulate privileged nonworkers.

Socialist humanism generally replaces concern for the human individual with concern for equality of power among all persons. Socialist humanists are critical of capitalist society for its consumerism and glorification of individual desires. Some regard the phenomena of high culture, including the plastic and graphic arts, music, drama, and dance, as self-indulgences of the few at the expense of efforts that could be directed toward transformation of the conditions of life for the many. "Social realist" art and many architectural products of International Modernism, such as Brasilia, were influenced by the desire to create an art that would document, celebrate, and transform human existence without resort to elitist criteria.

C. Pragmatic Humanism

Two philosophers at the origins of American pragmatism, F. C. S. Schiller (1864–1937) and William James (1842–1910), referred to the humanist tradition. American pragmatists generally turned away from formalistic philosophical concerns. They emphasized human meaning as rooted in sensory experiences, but denied that positivistic science gave an adequate account of that experience. In 1933, a group of educators including leading pragmatist and philosopher John Dewey (1859–1952), issued the first of two "humanist manifestos." The 1933 document affirmed "religious humanism," noting that "man's [sic] larger understanding of the universe, his scientific achievements, and his deeper appreciation of brotherhood have created a situation which requires a new statement of the means and purposes of religion" (*New Humanist* 6, 3 [May/June 1933]). The manifesto, setting out 15 points, called for basing ethical guidelines on human experience and needs rather than on theistic religious pronouncements. It affirmed evolutionary theory in the formation of the earth and the influence of history and culture on human beings. It called for channeling religious feeling into self-fulfillment and social activism, and it deplored economic inequality and the profit motive.

The *Humanist Manifesto II,* which appeared 40 years later in *The Humanist* (33, 5 [September/October 1973]) signed by B. F. Skinner, Isaac Asimov, and many others, presented itself as an affirmation of human potential in the face of the continued existence of totalitarianism, racism, sexism, and poverty. The second manifesto questioned any religion based on supermaturalism and explicitly identified technology as an agent of human deliverance from social evils. The scientific method, in spite of the role it was said to have played in ecological damage, the creation of dehumanizing institutions, and other human problems, needed to be developed rather than abandoned in order to work positive effects. The manifesto stressed the central importance of the individual, its full and free development (including the right to birth control, abortion, and divorce), and tolerance for individual differences that did not harm others. Other sections of the manifesto called for a world community and affirmed civil liberties, participatory democracy, the separation church and state, "democratization of the economy," universal education, and the elimination of discrimination, racism, sexism, and ageism. The collection of beliefs and positions expressed in *Manifesto II* correspond closely to "secular humanism" as it is usually understood (and not infrequently attacked) today.

D. Existentialist Humanism

Existentialism as a philosophical movement had its heyday in continental Europe in the period of intense philosophical questioning between the two World Wars. It was felt especially keenly in the 1920s and 1930s that the capacity of rational explanation to embrace events had broken down, that science had become dogmatic, and that the individual and her or his inner life were threatened by impersonality, mediocrity, and the rise of totalitarian social structures. A commentator described existentialism as the "reform" of humanism, and certainly existentialism is humanistic in emphasizing free will as a defining human characteristic. Existentialism has had a large number of both Christian and nonbelieving proponents among philosophers, theologians, and theorists of psychotherapy. Among the best known existentialists are Jean-Paul Sartre, Albert Camus, Gabriel Marcel, and Karl Jaspers.

Existentialists turned away from the determinism and positivism of thinkers such as Marx and Sigmund Freud (1856–1939), to emphasize the *meaning* rather than *explanation* of experience. Both Christian and nonbelieving existenialists have drawn on the work of Sören Kierkegaard (1813–1855), Friedrich Nietzsche (1844–

1900), and Martin Heidegger (1889–1976). All three of these philosophers held in one way or another that there is neither a predetermined human destiny nor an ultimate explanation for the fact that we exist. In the old philosophical debate between essence and existence, between reasoning and experiencing as ways to understand human life, existentialism emphasizes the primacy of experience. This does not equate to the Romantic idea that emotion can serve as the basis for making decisions. Still, especially in Sartre's existentialism, only the experience of the "I" is reliable. On this experience meaning (and religious faith, for believers) must be built. In making life's decisions, no valid criteria of choice can be formulated, yet the act of choosing both defines our humanness and gives moral or ethical commitment its only reality. Sartre was heavily influenced by the dictum of René Descartes (1596–1650), "I think, therefore I am." Contrary to Descartes, however, Sartre held that the individual's choice is what links her or him to the rest of humankind. This is the case both because most choices inevitably affect others and because the ongoing sum of individual choices constitutes the very definition of human nature.

III. HUMANISM IN CURRENT ETHICAL DEBATES

A. The Environment

Humanism enters into environmental ethics through the question of whether nonhuman natural entities have rights, and/or a "voice," that should be represented or heard equally with those of human beings. It cannot be claimed that humanistic thought of the Renaissance originated the idea of human beings as "superior" to other natural entities. Only in animistic religion, or animism, are all natural entities endowed with a language that enables them to interact with human beings on an equal or even superior footing. Such natural entities include not only nonhuman animals but also rocks, trees, rivers, and so on. Human beings as the apex of the natural hierarchy are an idea going back, within Judeo-Christian thought, at least as far as the book of Genesis. Medieval European thought, centering on God, tended to see the created world as existing only to reveal God's purposes to human beings, and "reading God's book" of nature was a common metaphor. But Renaissance thought, in moving the emphasis to human rather than divine purposes, did not change the subordinate place of other natural entities.

Accretions to humanism after the Renaissance were particularly effective in confirming nonhuman natural entities in the status of "thing." Descartes identified reason as the very source of existence and (himself an experimenter upon animals) denied that the cries of "nonreasoning" animals could even signify pain. Following Descartes came a tradition of scientific experiment up until the present in which the human being is the controlling "subject" and other natural entities the acted-upon "object." The explicit goal of much experimentation and observation has been technological: the manipulation and control of the nonhuman world and its entities for the well being and profit of humankind. Even though Karl Marx stressed human beings as a part of nature, *Capital* clearly established nonhuman "nature" as destined to become "one of the organs of human activity," annexed to our own bodily organs. Marx's follower George Lukás expressed a similar thought by saying, in *History and Class Consciousness,* that "nature is a societal category."

Most recently, some environmentalists ("social ecologists") have defended the unique position of human beings within nature, based on the claimed ability of human beings to determine their own evolutionary direction. This position stresses the importance of human reasoning power both to defend the rights of all natural entities and to devise balanced environmental outcomes. A concern is that human beings, especially the poor and persons of color, suffer from adverse health and economic effects when too much stress is laid on the preservation of nonhuman nature. Both scientists within the burgeois capitalist world and utopian marxians, then, have found compelling reasons to view the nonhuman world as limited in its rights and purposes independent of human ones.

B. Scientific Inquiry

Present-day disagreements between "scientists" and "humanists" reach back to, and beyond, the late sixteenth and early seventeenth century. "New scientists" such as Bacon, Descartes, and Galileo had commented unfavorably on methods of learning emphasized by Renaissance humanism. Humanist learning was charged with inadequacy for confining itself to the study of ancient texts, and moreover focusing on their style and context rather than their content. In part this critique represents the reluctance of innovators to acknowledge a debt to their predecessors. There is ample evidence, for example, that humanist commentaries on Greek texts were used by, and underlay the achievements of, such scientists as Nicolaus Copernicus (1473–1543) and Johannes Kepler (1571–1630) in astronomy or the sixteenth-century developers of "the new medicine."

But humanism as the study of texts that had already been written inevitably exhausted its scientific contribution. Indeed, the idea of "science" itself, as the systematic exploration of material phenomena exclusively, became current only late in the Renaissance, and humanist learning could not furnish a complete paradigm once the goals of learning themselves had changed. Humanism's historical mode of understanding did not lend itself to systematization and generalization, and text-based learning was no guide to the methodology of experiment and naturalistic observation. The combination of these with argument from first principles (derived from scholasticism) carried the day.

Last, the age of the new science in Europe was an age of seeking secular grounds for knowledge in the midst of religious controversy, and the emergent scientific method was soon carried over from physical to social phenomena. Using mathematically based science as a yardstick, religious and moral convictions could be removed from the sphere of political decision making because their truth or falsehood could not be conclusively demonstrated. Secularism left the field open for rationalistic doctrines, modeled on scientific discovery, to form the basis of public policy. By the nineteenth century, the implications of science for military and commercial technology had become overwhelming. The prestige of science became institutionalized as a program of university instruction and funded, university-based research competitive with "the humanities."

Competition between the two camps is inevitably sharpened by the decline of government and university support. Ironically, however, scientists today are more likely than those they label "humanists" to defend the importance of human beings. Some scientists, especially among theoretical physicists, have come to a more historical and less law-driven account of phenomena; they have also modified their belief in human ability and even right to predict and control. Typically, however, they have not made issues of the human subject or the nature of knowledge. By contrast, many who find themselves on the humanistic side of the controversy are best described not as humanists but (depending on their degree of radicalism) as "antipositivists," "deconstructionists," or "posthumanists." This group of loosely defined positions, best known through the work of Michel Foucault, may question both the existence of a human subject, or knower, and the possibility of obtaining any knowledge of the world by which decisions can be justified.

C. Religion: "Secular Humanism" versus Revealed Religion

The humanist perspective stands in necessary contrast to that of most "revealed" religions in their fundamentalist version. Both humanistic inquiry and revealed religion seek an understanding of the nature and meaning of human existence. Revealed religion places a Supreme Being (God) at the center of this meaning, however, while humanism, as we have seen, places human beings at the center. Various versions of humanism have been deistic or atheistic, and humanistic inquiry can be bound by a starting assumption that there is a Supreme Being. However, humanistic inquiry proceeds by critical discussion in the belief that knowledge is historical and humanly generated, can be modified, and can never be absolutely certain. Toleration of diverse lifeways and the coexistence of differing beliefs, which follow from the humanist perspective, cannot be accepted within the perspective of revealed religion as strictly interpreted. Revealed religion is usually based on a text, document, and body of sayings believed to have been communicated (revealed) by the Supreme Being. Coming directly from the Supreme Being, this authoritative knowledge base cannot logically be dissented from and is not subject to modification. Generally, interpretation of doctrine is handled within an authority structure. Revealed religions as institutional bodies are often set up so that certain members are designated interpreters of doctrine. (Where this is not done, fragmentation into smaller and smaller sects is apt to occur because dissent cannot be tolerated.)

The term fundamentalism derives from a statement of five Protestant "fundamental doctrines" promulgated from 1910 to 1912. The doctrine of Scriptural infallibility has been particularly important in the disagreement between fundamentalist Christians and "secular humanists." The doctrine of Scriptural infallibility prevailed in Roman Catholicism for a relatively short time, mid-seventeenth to mid-nineteenth century, and is now important mainly to certain Protestant denominations. If the Bible is taken as a historically factual and morally complete world view, some or all humanists positions such as those expressed in *Humanists Manifestos I and II* (above) must be seen as unacceptably counter to Biblical doctrine. Examples are nontraditional roles for women and the acceptance of abortion, birth control, suicide and euthanasia, and homosexual relationships.

The authority of scientific inquiry is a particular target of Christian antihumanists, although most technological innovations such as those relating to medical care, transportation, communication, and housing are accepted. For some, objections to science center on its supposed unitary position that human behavior is determined biologically and perhaps by social forces as well. In this characterization, no role is left for "free will." Thus human beings cannot be seen to choose between good and evil; indeed, these concepts, central to the world view of parts of the Bible, are rendered irrelevant.

Perhaps the most sharply drawn issue currently is the literal truth of the Old Testament book of Genesis. This account of the creation of the earth stands in contradiction to evolutionary theories of the earth's formation as developed from the work of Charles Darwin (1809–1882). Those who accept Genesis as factual history object specifically to a scientific and governmental authority structure that leads to the teaching of evolutionary theory in schools.

IV. CONCLUSIONS

Humanism, then, has lately been characterized as positivistic and deterministic, as absurdly unscientific and opposed to reason, as unwarrantedly privileging human beings over either God or the rest of creation, and as abandoning the idea of a "human subject" altogether. Such self-contradictory characterizations remind us that the history of humanism as a cohesive outlook was brief, and its original goals the narrow ones of classical scholarship combined with education in the distinctive disciplines of grammar, rhetoric, history, poetry, and moral philosophy. Humanism's great influences on the West, however, have been its spirit of toleration, its dedication to open inquiry, its emphasis on the individual, and its quest for an ethical public life. These qualities readily attached themselves for good and ill to each successive intellectual trend during and after the Renaissance: secularization, Enlightenment antiauthoritarianism, the synthesis of reason and empiricism, the cult of individualism, the encouragement of science and civic activism as these promoted human self-fulfillment.

It is difficult to imagine either education or democratic government without the influence of humanism, which affirmed each individual as worthy of development. In scientific inquiry, humanistic concerns have maintained breadth of both methodology and subject matter. Arguably, humanist thought led to broadening the very definition of who is human until persons of color and women were at least formally incorporated: allowed to make their own life decisions, vote, receive an education, and compete for jobs. "Public spiritedness" as exemplified in volunteerism, in governmental social programs, and in universal education can be seen as a creation of humanist ideals.

Some would argue that humanism has run its course. Most "humanisms" have emphasized the commonality of human beings. Of late, however, the issue is differences, and particularly inequalities, among individuals and groups based on gender, race, ethnicity, social class, and physical characteristics. Both theorists and activists of "antihumanism" (other than the religious antihumanists) feel that the lumping of all these as "mankind" has masked and propagated a world of unequally distributed resources; further, that the emphasis on human beings comes at the expense of other parts of nature. Reason itself, especially as embodied in the scientific method, is seen as having rendered issues of equity undiscussable; tolerance, in the form of defending individual rights, is seen as having given more power to those with privileged social identities. If rights, reason, and toleration are to be abandoned, however, other criteria of human inquiry must be sought that are equally capable of allowing human societies to continue their quest for models of ethical and equitable human existence.

Also See the Following Articles

ARISTOTELIAN ETHICS • COMMUNITARIANISM • ENVIRONMENTAL ETHICS, OVERVIEW • EXISTENTIALISM • LIBERALISM • STOICISM

Bibliography

Baron, H. (1988). *In search of Florentine civic humanism: Essays on the transition from medieval to modern thought.* Princeton: Princeton University Press.

Bullock, A. (1985). *The humanist tradition in the West.* New York: W. W. Norton.

Ehrenfeld, D. (1978). *The arrogance of humanism.* Oxford: Oxford University Press.

Fromm, E. (Ed.). (1965). *Socialist humanism.* Garden City, NJ: Doubleday.

Grafton, A. (1991). *Defenders of the text: The traditions of scholarship in an age of science, 1450–1800.* Cambridge: Harvard University Press.

Horkheimer, M., & Adorno, T. (1972). *Dialectic of enlightenment* (J. Cumming, Trans.). New York: Herder and Herder.

Kristeller, P. (1979). *Renaissance thought and its sources.* New York: Columbia University Press.

Pico della Mirandola, G. (1965). *On the dignity of man* (P. J. W. Miller, Trans.). Indianapolis: Bobbs-Merrill.

Sartre, J. (1948). *Existentialism and Humanism* (P. Mairet, Trans. and introduction). London: Methuen.

IMPERIALISM

Darrel Moellendorf
University of the Witwatersrand

GLOSSARY

imperialism In its economic usage the most basic sense of this term is the export of capital from one country to another. In its political usage it refers to the military conquest or subordination of one country by another. Difficulties with defining imperialism are discussed immediately below.

labor theory of value The theory of classical economics that the exchange value of a commodity is measured in terms of the value of the labor or labor power consumed in producing it, including labor (power) consumed either directly as the labor (power) of the worker or indirectly as the labor (power) that makes up the value of the technological means of production. The theory has been largely rejected in the twentieth century except by many Marxists.

overaccumulation The condition of an economy in which capital cannot be profitably invested (or not as profitably as in a foreign economy) because there is too much of it for the economy to put to use. Underconsumption is generally thought to amount to the same thing, merely looked at differently.

prima facie evil An act that is wrong or a state of affairs that is bad, the wrongness or badness of which may

under certain circumstances be outweighed by a resulting greater good. Prima facie evil is usually contrasted with all-things-considered evil.

rate of profit Based upon the labor theory of value, it is the ratio (fraction) of surplus value to total value invested (including labor and technology). Many Marxists argue that there is a tendency for the rate of profit to decline as an economy becomes more industrialized; as investment in technology increases, the denominator of the fraction increases and the rate of profit declines. Capitalists are thought to pursue high rates of profits.

surplus value According to classical Marxist theory this is the difference between the value of the labor power of the worker and the value of what she creates in a day's work. It corresponds to the measure of profits of the capitalist and the exploitation of the worker.

underconsumption The condition of an economy in which demand is insufficiently high to attract for reinvestment all of the profits it generates.

ECONOMIC IMPERIALISM, is minimally defined as the export of capital from one country to another. Difficulties in arriving at a more substantive general definition than this are considerable because the very meaning of the term is in great measure dependent upon the particular theoretical framework in which it is employed. All of the frameworks at least look at the causes and consequences of the export of capital, although they differ in what they view these to be. Because of these differences in purported causes and consequences, a more substantive general definition seems impossible. Furthermore, while theorists of imperialism usually wish to show that political imperialism serves economic imperialism, accounts of the former also vary. This has implications for a moral account of imperialism. A general account of the morality of imperialism of necessity will be insensitive to some of the particularities (causes and consequences) of the chief empirical theories.

I. REVIEWING THE EMPIRICAL THEORIES

A general distinction can be drawn in the explanatory goals of pre- and post-World War Two (WW2) empirical theories of imperialism. Pre-WW2 theories sought to explain the increasing competition for control of foreign lands by the major capitalist powers. Post-WW2 theories often sought rather to explain the failures in development of the economies of underdeveloped countries.

Both pre- and post-WW2 theories generally attempt to establish a causal connection between the economics and politics of imperialism. Pre-WW2 theories hold that capitalist competition causes war. Post-WW2 theories are often used to support the claim that the major capitalist powers, in particular the United States, have an interest in preventing, or turning back by military means, democratic change and socialist revolutions in the underdeveloped countries.

A. Pre-World War 2 Theories

The principal theorists of imperialism of this time period are Luxemburg, Hobson, Hilferding, Bukharin, Lenin, and Kautsky. All of them hold that the export of capital is the main cause of the increasing competition of the major capitalist states. Furthermore, with the exception of Hobson they are all Marxists and hold that imperialism, as the export of capital, is a necessary feature of capitalism. And of these Marxists, with the exception of Kautsky, they all see competition erupting into warfare as the necessary consequence of imperialism. For most of the theorists of imperialism of this period then the exposition of imperialism constitutes an important element in the critique of capitalism; capitalism is to be condemned, in part, because of the evil of warfare to which it gives rise.

Generally, these theorists believe that the immediate cause of economic imperialism is overaccumulation. This is subject to empirical verification. If the overaccumulation thesis is true one would expect to see either a decrease in domestic capital investment at roughly the same time as an increase in foreign investment or an overall increase in investment with the increase going abroad.

With the exception of Luxemburg, all of these theorists see the development of monopoly enterprises in previously more competitive economies as causing overaccumulation. This suggests that Luxemburg's theory is consistent with a different set of facts than the others. If the export of capital preceded the development of monopolies, then Luxemburg's account may be correct but the others would appear to be threatened.

Luxemburg (1963) draws attention to what she sees as a chronic problem of underconsumption in capitalist economies that sends business in search of noncapitalist markets for sales. The problem is explained in terms of what Marx referred to as the realization of surplus value. Surplus value is only realized upon sale of the commodity. This is the basis of the capitalist's profits.

On Luxemburg's account it is structurally impossible for all of the surplus value of a capitalist economy to be realized within that economy. The explanation for this seems to be grounded in the following two claims regarding capitalist competition: Competition requires that the capacity for production constantly expand; but the capacity for consumption cannot keep up with production as workers are not sufficiently remunerated and capitalists are interested in plowing profits back into production, not consumption, in order to keep up with the competition.

Hobson (1902) is the first pre-WW2 theorist to assert the causal connection between imperialism and the rise of monopoly influence in capitalist economies. Fierce competition followed by monopoly consolidation gives rise to tremendous profits for a few that cannot be profitably invested in the domestic market. Overaccumulation of capital or underconsumption of goods then motivates the capitalist to look for foreign sources of investment. The main sectional interest involved in the search for foreign investments are the large capital investors and speculators.

Hobson is also the first of this group to contend that economic protectionism serves imperialism. The best way to defend the gains of imperial conquest against economic competitors is through protectionism. Sufficient protection however requires the use of military force. Military force also ensures that foreign debtors are forthcoming with payments. So, economic imperialism is the cause of the politics of imperialism. Unlike the Marxists who succeeded him, Hobson thinks that the economics and politics of imperialism can be excised from the capitalist economy by reforming its functioning, largely through redistributive policies that boost internal demand thereby giving incentive to capital to invest domestically.

Hilferding (1981) lays the basis for the subsequent anticapitalist theories of Lenin and Bukharin, all three of which link the development of imperialism to the rise of finance capital. This is the name that Hilferding gives to capital loaned by banks to be set to use for industrial purposes. Such loans produce an intimate connection between two previously more distinct businesses, banking and industry. Hilferding, unlike Hobson, sees the banks playing an active role in causing monopoly. The demand for bank loans, a demand initially caused by competition, results in the concentration of capital into large monopolies or trusts because the banks' interest in minimizing losses motivates them to discourage competition among industrial firms.

Protective tariffs and monopoly prices allow for increased prices and higher returns on domestic investments. But the increased prices also reduce demand. This underconsumption provides an incentive to search for foreign markets. Import tariffs in other countries motivate the transfer of production to those countries as a means of payment avoidance. This capital exportation leads to three policy objectives: (1) to establish the largest possible economic territory; (2) to close this territory to foreign competition by a wall of protective tariffs; and (3) to reserve the territory for the national monopolies. The militaries of various states play important roles both in opening up new areas and in protecting them. Hilferding thinks that the only way to halt imperialism and to provide for peace is by the expropriation and nationalization of the largest firms of finance capital.

Bukharin (1976) advances at least two explanations of the overaccumulation, and thus the export, of capital. One is based upon the view that the rate of profit declines in the more industrially advanced countries. The declining rate of profit produces an overaccumulation of capital. The second explanation invokes the growth of finance capital in advanced capitalist economies. Competition results in large concentrations of capital in the hands of the winners. The investment of ever-larger sums of capital tends to reduce competition and leads to the development of industrial monopolies dependent on financial capital. Monopoly profits create an overaccumulation of capital. Thus, monopoly cover-age of the domestic market produces international competition among country-based monopolies.

Bukharin argues that tariffs play a new role under conditions of interstate monopoly competition. They allow domestic firms to raise prices giving them the ability to sell below costs (or dump) in international markets. In other words tariffs at home give capital abroad penetrating powers. Although a globally unified monopoly, existing peacefully, is a theoretical possibility, it is a practical impossibility because the fierce competition between country-based monopolies will periodically erupt into war. Bukharin holds that because imperialist wars serve only the interests of the capitalist class, the most effective means of opposing them is through international working class solidarity.

Lenin's (1964) account of imperialism is much less an explanation of the causes and effects of the export of capital than a description of them. The essentials of the description are encapsulated in his list: (1) the concentration of capital has produced monopolies that play an important role in the life of economies; (2) the merging of bank capital with industrial capital has formed oligarchic finance capital; (3) the export of capital has replaced the export of commodities; (4) the formation of international monopolies has resulted in an economic division of the world; and (5) this economic division has resulted in the territorial division of the world amongst the largest capitalist powers.

Lenin, like Bukharin, is keen to establish that a peaceful imperialism through a globally unified monopoly alliance is impossible. Finance capital must seek territorial areas to control in order to maximize profits. This leads to competition among states for areas of control and resistance among those who fall under foreign domination. The result is periodic warfare.

Kautsky (1970) is the only Marxist of this period to contend that the export of capital peacefully coordinated by the major imperialist powers is not only a theoretical possibility but a practical one as well. The political threat of opposition to war from the working classes of these countries and the need to suppress colonial opposition would motivate peaceful cooperation. Kautsky calls this new stage of imperialism "ultra-imperialism." Although Kautsky's theory came under sharp attack from Lenin and Bukharin, it was no endorsement of ultra-imperialism but rather a warning of the kinds of dangers that might be posed by a new, more stable, form of imperialism. Currently the world seems to be better characterized by Kautsky's ultra-imperialism than the intra-imperialist warfare of the other Marxists of this pre-WW2 period.

B. Post-World War 2 Theories

The main post-WW2 theorists of imperialism are Baran, Frank, Wallerstein, Amin, and Emmanuel. Their principal concern is to explain the unequal levels of development around the world, resulting in what they call "underdevelopment." With the exception of Emmanuel the cause of underdevelopment is the capital invested in the less-developed countries and repatriated to the developed countries. Emmanuel locates the cause in unequal trade relations with the developed countries. These, of course, are not incompatible theses. The theories of imperialism of this period are generally intended to be part of a Marxist critique of the capitalist system. Brenner and Warren are in-house critics of these accounts.

The underdevelopment theorists attempt to explain causally the relationship between the development of the advanced developed countries and the underdevelopment of others. Obviously this method relies on the claim that there are underdeveloped countries, a claim that Warren disputes. The causal explanation cannot start with an empirical observation of correlation between development and underdevelopment and move to a causal explanation. For unless "underdevelopment" means complete absence of development, which would render it useless, it cannot be considered merely an observable brute fact. Empirical evidence that some countries are less developed than others does not reveal that they are underdeveloped. This requires showing either that their lack of development is a structural feature of relations between more- and less-developed countries or that it is the result of unfair relations between these countries. Identifying underdevelopment requires significant empirical or moral theory.

There seem to be two possible ways of identifying underdevelopment. Perhaps "underdeveloped" means not as developed as would be absent the causal relations of underdevelopment. In this case, the theories would have to give a speculative account of why certain countries would have been more developed in the absence of certain relations with others. Failing such an account there is the possibility that the less-developed countries would be even less developed without the relations in question. But such speculation may be open to doubt. Alternatively, "underdevelopment" may mean development constrained by terms of relations that are unfair. On this interpretation, it must be explained why the inequalities among countries are unfair because the mere existence of inequality is not evidence of unfairness. In this case the truth of underdevelopment theory is not merely an empirical matter.

Baran's (1978) explanation of the mechanics of imperialism is not particularly new. As with the pre-WW2 monopoly theorists, monopoly coverage yields an overaccumulation of capital or an underconsumption of goods that gives an incentive to invest capital abroad. But his account of the effects of this export is new. For the consequence of capital export to less-developed countries is the transfer of surplus capital (profits) from the less-developed countries back to the more-developed, resulting in the distortion and retardation of the development of the less-developed countries. Baran's thesis sets the stage for the underdevelopment theorists who would follow him.

Frank (1969) argues that the development of underdevelopment is to be traced to three contradictions or tensions in global capitalism. The first is the expropriation/appropriation of the surplus. External monopolies appropriate the surplus of a country and expropriate it to their home countries. The second is polarization of global capitalism between the metropolitan center and the periphery satellites. It is the metropolitan center that benefits from the appropriation of the surplus of the periphery satellites. The third is the continuity and ubiquity of the structural essentials of the development of underdevelopment throughout the course of the expansion of capitalism in all places.

The chain of appropriation and expropriation of surplus capital extends through many intermediary links from the peasant in the underdeveloped periphery to the financial house in the metropolis. The latter's expropriation is the ultimate cause of the former's poverty. These expropriative relations have been going on since capitalism first began to develop and extend, via exploration, beyond its national borders. According to Frank the way out of underdevelopment for the satellite countries must involve breaking the economic relations with the metropolitan center, but doing this requires a socialist revolution.

Following upon Frank's image of the chain of expropriation that extends from within the borders of a country to beyond, Wallerstein (1979) argues that capitalism must be analyzed as a world-system because globally there is a single division of labor within the relations of market transfer. He contends that there are three main components of the capitalist world-system, the core, the semiperiphery, and the periphery. The first and third correspond to Frank's metropolis and satellites.

These three components play different roles in the capitalist world-market. The periphery is characterized as primarily an exporter of low-wage products, the semiperiphery as having a higher-wage sector that produces part of what is consumed on its internal market, but that is dependent for the other part, and the core as a substantial exporter of high-wage products and the major customer for these products. Wallerstein explains the underdevelopment of the periphery in much the same way as does Frank. The development of capitalism in the core has required since its inception that it receive the redistribution of the surplus from the periphery and semi-periphery. Wallerstein maintains that only a socialist world-system can overcome the relations of subordination of the capitalist world-system.

According to Amin (1974) the cause of capital moving to foreign markets is the tendency of the rate of profit to decline in the center (core) countries. This export of capital produces distorted economies in the periphery. Amin seeks to explain these distortions as the result of the primitive accumulation of capital. This is the name that Marxists give to the brutal origins of capitalism in which noncapitalist communal arrangements were destroyed leaving people without options other than becoming wage-laborers. According to Amin, these kinds of events characterize the ongoing relationship between the center and periphery.

The result of these relations is that the economies of the periphery develop only to serve those of the center. Amin calls this the disarticulation of periphery economies. Disarticulation is not quite the equivalent of underdevelopment; rather, it means that the national economies of peripheral states lack internal coherence. Most of the exchanges are not between economic agents internal to the economy but between internal and external agents, with the effect that the surplus flows to the center. But it is hard to see what the problem with this is unless it results in evils like underdevelopment. Amin (1994) contends that the way to overcome these subordinate relations is for periphery countries to delink from relations with the center. The aim of delinking is to establish what Amin refers to as "autocentric" economies in the periphery oriented around developing institutions that service local needs, rather than external profit.

Both Wallerstein and Amin augment their accounts of imperialism by asserting that trade relations between the center (or core) and periphery are exploitative. Emmanuel (1972) first developed this theory of unequal exchange. He argues that free trade can be unequal if the price of wages in the two trading countries is unequal.

Emmanuel assumed that if capital were mobile and labor were not, then the rate of profit around the world would converge while the costs of labor would not. Emmanuel must assume the mobility of capital is sufficient to achieve a unitary rate of profit, but not so great as to have all capital flow to low-wage, low-cost, sites of production. If the rates of profit are to remain the same, then the price of commodities in high-wage countries must be higher than in low-wage countries because of higher production costs. Thus, low-wage countries must pay more for their imports than do high-wage countries, and exchange is unequal.

Emmanuel sees two ways in which unequal exchange might be ameliorated. Either those countries suffering from it must diversify their economy, sending up the prices of their former main exports and sending down the prices of their former imports, or institutions of international redistribution must be implemented in order to compensate the low-wage countries for their loss of income to the high-wage countries.

Although it has been widely held in this time period that imperialism just is the relationship between the developed and the less-developed world such that the development of the former necessarily is financed by the underdevelopment of the latter, views critical of this have been offered by those also working within a Marxist framework.

Brenner's (1977) criticism of underdevelopment theory takes up matters of the theory of capitalist development. He takes issue with the general claim that the capitalist development of the core can be financed only by surplus transfers from the periphery. Brenner's argument involves a distinction between absolute and relative surplus. Feudal economies attempt to increase productivity by requiring the serfs to work longer for the lords. This is an increase in absolute surplus. An increase in relative surplus occurs when workers produce more in the same amount of time.

Brenner argues that capitalist development historically is a function of an increase in relative surplus. Capitalists get more to invest through innovation, which increases labor productivity. Because workers in a capitalist economy are free to sell their labor power, they must be motivated by market incentives and disincentives (pay increases/the threat of sacking) to use innovations to increase productivity. The key to capitalist development historically has been to dispossess some group of people in order to create a class willing to sell its labor power. Thus, the dynamism of capitalist development has less to do with transferring surplus from the periphery to the core and more to do with creating a class of workers who respond to market incentives and disincentives.

Warren's (1978) argument contains a certain irony insofar as it can be characterized as a Marxist defense of imperialism. Warren would likely contend that whatever irony one sees in this has far more to do with the mistakes of Marxism in the twentieth century than with any inconsistencies in his work. For he, quite like Marx, argues that capitalism is historically progressive. He contends further that imperialism is generally progressive because it just is the spread of capitalism.

According to Warren, capitalism is progressive on cultural, economic, and political grounds. It encourages individual development; it increases productivity; and it encourages parliamentary democracy. These are empirical claims, and Warren contends that the record of development verifies them. If the claims are true, whether they amount to evidence for the progressive nature of capitalism is a moral matter. Warren seems to think quite reasonably that these are valuable items in and of themselves, but what is more that Marxists ought to find them especially attractive because they both comprise the ethical foundation of socialism and are necessary preconditions for it.

II. A MODEL OF IMPERIALISM

In order to assess the morality of imperialism in a way that is not dependent on one or another controversial empirical theory, a more general model of imperialism must be employed. Such a model, by definition, will be insensitive to many purported features of imperialism captured by the various empirical theories. But the loss of sensitivity is offset by the gain of generality.

Roemer (1988) has a model that is useful because its empirical commitments are less extensive than any of the theories I have summarized. He analyzes imperialism as a particular kind of exploitation, the exploitation of one state by another. This is based on his model of exploitation among individuals. A worker is exploited when her wages embody less labor than she expends, while a capitalist is an exploiter when his profits embody more labor than he expends. In other words, what the worker receives requires less socially necessary labor to produce (given current levels of technology) than she expends, and what the capitalist receives requires more.

Roemer argues that this unequal outcome may result even under consensual market relations. If the capitalist has more resources at the beginning of the transactions he may either employ the worker or lend to her on terms that are more advantageous to him than working and more advantageous to her than working without those resources (money or productive technology). Because unequal outcomes are not necessarily unfair ones, this is a technical, nonmoral, definition of exploitation. Whether or not a particular exploitative relationship is

fair depends upon the justice of the preexisting distribution between the two parties.

Roemer sees the morality of exploitation, then, as dependent on the morality of the prior distribution of resources. The reason why exploitation under capitalism is immoral is because the property relations that permit private differential ownership cannot be justified. He makes this argument by considering how a justification might be attempted, for example, on the necessity to reward people for risk-taking or entrepreneurial behavior. This fails to justify private differential ownership of capital because it is not obvious that such activity merits reward, and even if it does, it is doubtful that private differential ownership of capital is necessary to provide the reward. Roemer does not consider, but might have, a more egalitarian defense of capitalist property relations, namely, that they are justified if and only if they are to the maximum benefit of the least advantaged. But if he is right about the failure of the previous possible justification, it is also doubtful that this one would pass the test.

Similar reasoning can be applied to the relations between states. Imperialist states are those that export capital and import labor. States that are exploited by imperialism are those that import capital and export labor. The former end up with income that is greater than the labor expended by their citizens, the latter with less; the former are analogous to the employer, the latter to the worker. Whether or not a particular imperialist relationship is unjust depends not on the features of the economic relationship itself (assuming it to be consental) but upon the justice of the international distribution of resources that precedes it.

This model takes states as the agents and victims of imperialism. Strictly speaking "states" must just be shorthand for individuals grouped geopolitically who thereby partially share, although differentially along class lines, the benefits and burdens of certain economic transactions and policies. For although actual states may in certain ways be agents of imperialism through policies encouraging the export of capital and protecting it after export, theorists of imperialism are usually not concerned about the impact of inequality on the life and health of the state, but on individuals.

III. IMPERIALISM AND INTERNATIONAL DISTRIBUTIVE JUSTICE

Beitz (1979) argues that the international distribution of wealth should conform to what Rawls (1971) refers to as the difference principle. The difference principle states that inequalities among individuals must be such that they are to the maximum benefit of the least advantaged. Only inequalities that conform to such a principle can be considered fair or just.

The justification of the difference principle involves utilizing a thought experiment that Rawls calls the original position. We are asked to imagine parties to a convention who are to decide from among competing principles on the ones that they wish to govern their social interaction. The parties, as representatives of others, are assumed to be motivated only by the pursuit of the advantage of those whom they represent.

However, in deciding on the principles they are subject to a number of constraints. The most important one for our purposes is that they are behind the veil of ignorance; they do not know the social position or natural endowments of those whom they represent. They know only that everyone is presumed to want certain basic goods, among which are liberty and wealth. Assuming the above motivation and constraint, Rawls contends that the parties would choose the difference principle as one of the principles to regulate social interaction because the difference principle gives assurance that everyone will benefit from any distribution of wealth.

The original position is intended to model our convictions about impartiality and fairness. For given its setup any principle that calls on us to treat people differently on the basis of race, gender, sexual orientation, creed, and physical and mental abilities would not be chosen. The difference principle appears to be simply the economic expression of equal treatment. All people can agree that they are treated equally by institutions governed by the difference principle because, measured against a benchmark of strict equality in wealth, they have all benefited, and remaining inequalities exist only because the system is designed to make everyone better off than under strict equality.

Rawls (1971, 1993) does not think that the application of the original position to matters of international justice yields a commitment to international egalitarianism. His position has come under criticism by many political philosophers, including Beitz and Pogge (1994). Beitz argues that the original position is useful for thinking about international as well as domestic fairness and impartiality. And contrary to Rawls (1971, 1994), Beitz argues that if the original position is thought to consist of parties representing all the peoples of the world, then they would choose an international difference principle. If this right, it seems most unlikely that presently existing inequalities between the rich and the poor of the world could be thought to be just.

Part of what is required in order to yield the conclusion that Beitz advocates is an empirical claim about the nature of international society. It must be the case that there exists significant international economic interaction in the form of trade and trade treaties. Without significant interaction among people the question of the justice of their relations does not arise. Agreement on this empirical claim is something all theorists of imperialism appear to share. Indeed, nearly all of them offer substantial evidence to support the claim.

If this procedure is used to think about the economic relations among states, some of which are thought to be agents of imperialism and others victims, then it is of no great moral significance what the particular causal mechanisms of the inequalities are. Rather, the imperialism is unjust, if the inequalities that result from it are due to preexisting economic relations that do not conform to the difference principle. On the reasonable assumption that present-day international inequalities are unjust, so then is present-day imperialism.

Although this account is neutral to the causal accounts of international inequality, it seems to correspond roughly with the intuitions of dependency theory, that unequal outcomes from the relations between more- and less-developed countries are unfair. Nonetheless, the account does not necessarily gainsay Warren's contention that capitalism still has a progressive role to play in developing the less-developed economies. The international redistribution required to achieve justice may not address property relations within states.

This model does not capture all current concerns about imperialism. For example, critics of globalization often point to several constraints placed on the economies of states, particularly those with developing economies. One constraint is the need for capital investment that is required, if the economy is to grow. Another is the general, and apparently democracy-constraining, trend of attaching neoliberal macroeconomic conditions to international loans. A third constraint is the progressive reduction of trade barriers that allows capital greater mobility. The second and third serve to punish by disinvestment states pursuing courses of egalitarian development, which punishment retards development. International institutions of redistribution in conformity with the difference principle would, however, provide some relief from the first constraint and, therefore, the second and third.

IV. IMPERIALISM AND WAR

I have argued elsewhere (Moellendorf 1994) that a necessary condition for the justice of war is that it may reasonably be believed to effect the liberation of an oppressed people, or that it may be against a force that if victorious would oppress a people. The terms "liberation" and "oppression" may have the connotation of all or nothing, not subject to degrees of improvement. Because of this, the above criterion should be modified as follows: A necessary condition for the justice of war is that it is reasonable to believe that its outcome will result in morally relevant improvements in the social circumstances of the affected parties, the citizens and residents of the countries fighting. Accounts of what constitutes morally relevant improvements may differ, but I would suggest that standards of human and civil rights, democratic governance, and socioeconomic equality be employed.

This modified criterion focuses on what is often called just cause. Of course there are also other important constraints on the moral permissibility of waging a war, but they need not occupy us here. This criterion of just cause seems reasonable because it is consistent with our ideas that because warfare is a prima facie evil some significant social good should be expected to result from it. But wars that are fought to safeguard the export of capital would seem quite often to fail to meet this condition because they would be fought, at least under unjust background conditions, to preserve unjust relations of inequality and exploitation. The justice of the U.S. Gulf War against Iraq might be challenged in this way.

The connection between unjust economic imperialism and an unjust war is, however, an empirical and not a conceptual one. It is possible to imagine wars that do nothing to challenge unjust imperialism but nonetheless improve the social circumstances of those affected by them, for example, wars that result in arrangements that are no worse from the perspective of distributive justice and improve on the possibilities for respect for human rights and the establishment of democracy. The U.S. intervention in Haiti might be an example of such a war.

The long history of unjust wars conforming to the interests of unjust imperialism raises the question of whether the intervention in Haiti, if it was just, is an exception to the historical rule or the beginning of a new trend. This question cannot be adequately answered in advance, but there are reasons to believe that private ownership over vast productive resources, such as exists under capitalism, increases the likelihood of unjust wars. Roemer (1994) suggests that we look at imperialist wars as public bads to which capitalism is especially susceptible. Wars are evils that the citizenry suffers but under capitalism are often fought to gain or to preserve access to resources from which mainly private parties profit.

Also See the Following Articles

BUSINESS ETHICS, OVERVIEW • MARX AND ETHICS

Bibliography

Amin, S. (1974). *Accumulation on a world scale.* New York: Monthly Review Press.

Amin, S. (1994). *Rereading the postwar period.* New York: Monthly Review Press.

Baran, P. A. (1978). *The political economy of growth.* Harmondsworth: Penguin Books, Ltd.

Beitz, C. R. (1979). *Political theory and international relations.* Princeton: Princeton University Press.

Brenner, R. (1977). The origins of capitalist development: A critique of neo-Smithian Marxism, *New Left Review,* **104**:3, July–Aug.

Bukharin, N. (1976). *Imperialism and world economy.* London: The Merlin Press.

Brewer, A. (1990). *Marxist theories of imperialism: A critical survey.* London: Routledge.

Brewer, A. (1986). Theories of imperialism. In W. J. Mommeson & J. Osterhammel (Eds.), *Imperialism and after continuities and discontinuities.* London: Allen and Unwin.

Emmanuel, A. (1972). *Unequal exchange.* London: Monthly Review Press.

Frank, A. G. (1969). *Capitalism and underdevelopment in Latin America.* New York: Monthly Review Press.

Hilferding, R. (1981). *Finance capital.* London: Routledge and Kegan Paul.

Hobson, J. A. (1902). *Imperialism: A Study.* London: James Nisbet and Co.

Kautsky, K. (1970). Ultra-imperialism, *New Left Review,* **59**:1, Jan.–Feb.

Lenin, V. I. (1964). *Imperialism, the highest stage of capitalism.* In *Collected Works* (Vol. 19.). Moscow: Progress Publishers.

Luxemburg, R. (1963). *The accumulation of capital.* London: Routledge and Kegan Paul Ltd.

Moellendorf, D. (1994). Marxism, internationalism, and the justice of war, *Science and Society,* **58**:2, Fall.

Pogge, T. (1994). An egalitarian law of the peoples, *Philosophy and Public Affairs,* **23**:3, Fall.

Rawls, J. (1971). *A theory of justice.* Cambridge: Harvard University Press.

Rawls, J. (1993). The law of peoples, *Critical Inquiry,* **20**:1, Autumn.

Roemer, J. E. (1988). *Free to lose.* Cambridge: Harvard University Press.

Roemer, J. E. (1994). *A future for socialism.* Cambridge: Harvard University Press.

Wallerstein, I. (1979). *The Capitalist World-Economy.* Cambridge: Cambridge University Press.

Warren, B. (1980). *Imperialism pioneer of capitalism.* London: Verso.

IMPROPER PAYMENTS AND GIFTS

Robert Larmer
University of New Brunswick

I. Swaying Judgments
II. Bribery, Undue Influence, and Extortion:
    Definitional Issues
III. Bribery, Undue Influence, and
     Extortion: Moral Issues

GLOSSARY

bribe A gift or consideration offered with the explicit intention of causing an employee or official to violate her role duties to her employer.

duty That which a particular person is bound morally or legally to do.

extortion To cause someone by illegal force or threat to act in a way he would otherwise not wish to act.

prima facie duty A presumptive duty one has in the absence of a more basic duty that would override it.

tip A gift or consideration offered by a third party to obtain services from an employee in his or her official capacity but without the intention of causing that employee to violate her role duties to her employer.

undue influence A gift or consideration that, without any explicit intention on the part of the giver or receiver to violate the role duties of the employee, may nevertheless lead to the employee failing in his role duties by improperly favoring the giftgiver.

IMPROPER GIFTS AND PAYMENTS are by definition to be avoided. Three categories of improper payments

and gifts must be distinguished. These are undue influence, bribery, and extortion. How each is defined and why each is prima facie immoral is explored. Also explored is the question of how judgments concerning improper gifts and payments can be made cross-culturally.

I. SWAYING JUDGMENTS

A. Undue Influence

In thinking of improper payments and gifts, the initial tendency is to think of bribery. Instances of bribery may provide us with paradigm examples but the category of improper payments and gifts is considerably broader than the category of bribery. Thus, for example, an expensive Christmas gift from a supplier to an ordering clerk in a large business might be considered improper, yet not constitute an attempt on the part of the supplier to bribe the clerk or an implicit acceptance of a bribe by the clerk.

The impropriety of such a gift, even though it can scarcely be described as a bribe, lies in the fact that it might unduly influence the clerk's decisions. Rather than evaluating products from competing suppliers on their own merits, the clerk may come to let her personal liking for the supplier who has given her an expensive gift sway her decision regarding who gets the order. The clerk, possibly without realizing it, may come to act in her own interests, rather than in the interests of her employer. Innocent of any intention to act improperly, she nevertheless acts improperly inasmuch as she has let her duty to act in the best interests of her employer be compromised.

B. The Appearance of Undue Influence

I have suggested that a sufficient condition of a gift being improper is that it might unduly influence an employee's decisions. Might the clerk in our example argue that she is able to accept the expensive gift without it affecting her ability to fulfill her duties to her employer, and hence that there is nothing wrong in accepting the gift? Leaving aside the very real danger of self-deception, it might still be improper for the clerk to accept the gift. It is important not only that she be able to assure herself that she has not been unduly influenced, but that she be able to assure others of this. She must refrain, therefore, from accepting gifts that, by their nature or the context in which they are given, make it reasonable for others to believe she has been unduly influenced—even if this is not in fact the case. Thus, for example, even if the clerk could know beyond a shadow of a doubt that accepting an expensive trip around the world as a gift from the supplier would not influence her ordering decisions, it would still be improper for her to accept such a gift. Her employer, as well as rival suppliers, have legitimate concerns about whether the acceptance of the gift might illegitimately influence her decisions and, unless she is in the unlikely situation of being able to demonstrate that this will not happen, she is not in a position to do justice to these concerns and hence should not accept the gift. In such matters it is important not only that justice be done, but that it be seen to be done.

C. Appropriate Gifts

In our example, we have focused on the impropriety of the clerk accepting an expensive gift from the supplier. What can be said as regards the impropriety of the supplier offering such a gift? It is tempting to suggest that the supplier should in no circumstances offer the clerk a gift. This seems too strong, however, inasmuch as it ignores that business transactions take place in a social context and that it is appropriate for the supplier to seek to be on good terms with the clerk. We would not, for example, accuse the supplier of any immorality if he adopts a friendly manner in their business dealings and is careful to remember the clerk's birthday by sending a card. Neither are we likely to consider it inappropriate for the supplier to send a gift of a calendar or a box of chocolates to the clerk as a Christmas gift, be-

cause such a gift, unlike an expensive trip around the world, is scarcely liable to compromise, or to be perceived as compromising, the clerk's duty and ability to act in the best interests of her employer. The impropriety of the supplier in proffering an expensive gift lies not in the giving of a gift, but in the giving of a type of gift that has the potential, or is liable to be understood as having the potential, to undermine the proper functioning of the clerk as her employer's agent.

The issue, then, is whether, in a particular relationship involving the performance of professional or official duties, the giving and receiving of a gift is appropriate, and, if so, what type of gift is appropriate. This is hardly a question that can be handled in a purely mechanical manner and there can be no substitute for conscientious judgment and good will. Certainly, it is wise for the individuals involved to err on the side of caution and for the organizations they represent to provide general guidelines for employees concerning what is acceptable in this regard.

II. BRIBERY, UNDUE INFLUENCE, AND EXTORTION: DEFINITIONAL ISSUES

A. Bribery Defined

Instances of bribery provide paradigm examples of improper gifts and payment. Unfortunately, this does not mean that defining bribery is a simple task. Uncomplicated though it is to say what constitutes bribery in some instances, it is far from easy to provide a universal definition. We have already suggested that care must be taken to distinguish bribery from gifts and payments that, although inappropriate, could not properly be termed bribes. In addition, we must distinguish bribes from instances of extortion. Also to be considered is the fact that many practices that would be considered bribery in one culture would not only be accepted, but would be expected in other cultures.

Returning to our example of the purchasing clerk, let us suppose that the supplier offers her a large sum of money if she will order supplies from him rather than a rival supplier, and the clerk willingly agrees. This, we will probably agree, constitutes a clear case of bribery. But what makes it such? What are the key elements that enable us to recognize it as an instance of bribery?

Several factors seem relevant. First, it is clearly the intention of the supplier to cause the clerk to violate her duties to act in the best interests of her employer. Second, the clerk is a willing participant; she is in no way forced to violate her duties, yet she agrees to do so in exchange for the reward offered. Third, the duties she is being asked to violate are acquired duties, that is, they are duties she has acquired by virtue of a previous agreement to act in a role of faithful agent for her employer.

Generally, an act of bribery will involve an employee or official, under the influence of a third party offering a reward, illegitimately subverting a prior agreement to act as agent for an employer, thus failing to fulfill the role duties acquired under that agreement. Typically, then, an instance of bribery involves three parties: the person offering the bribe, the employee or official to whom the bribe is offered, and the employer for whom the employee previously agreed to act as an agent. This suggests that bribery essentially involves an intentional and willing alienation of agency by the employee and a third party, without ever informing the original employer that the employee is no longer working as her agent.

Having said this, we do well to recognize that not all bribes are successful. They nevertheless remain bribes, because a bribe, like a gift, is defined not by whether it is accepted, but by the intention of the giver. A bribe remains a bribe whether it is accepted or not but the act of bribery can only occur when the employee consents to take the bribe. Until then we would speak not of bribery, but rather an attempt at bribery.

B. Bribery Distinguished from Undue Influence

This understanding of bribery provides conceptual clarity in several ways. First, it helps explain what we have already noted, namely, that not all improper gifts or payments should be considered bribes. We have suggested that for bribery actually to occur there must be an agreement both on the part of the person offering the reward and the person accepting it, to subvert an existing contract. For an employee to accept a gift even though it might unduly influence him, is quite different than to accept the gift with the explicit intention of violating his duties.

C. Bribery Distinguished from Extortion

Second, this understanding of bribery allows us to distinguish instances of bribery from instances of extortion. Several key differences are clear. One is that whereas bribery involves the willing participation of the person bribed, extortion involves unwilling partici-

pation under duress. We do not speak of the person receiving a bribe as a victim, but we would describe someone as a victim of extortion. Adopting a metaphor, we can say that bribery resembles adultery, extortion rape.

Another difference is that bribery essentially involves the alienation of agency, but extortion does not. One cannot accept a bribe and remain a loyal employee, but it is possible to act under duress, yet remain a loyal employee. For example, an employee told by a corrupt inspector that a shipment of goods up to standards will not be passed unless the inspector receives an expensive "gift" might justifiably regard himself as a loyal agent of his employer in acceding to the inspector's demands, even though he in his role as agent of his employer is a victim of extortion. On the other hand, extortion may involve an alienation of agency, as in the case of an employee, say a night watchman, who under threat does not perform his proper role duties and allows the building he is guarding to be burgled.

Yet another difference is that, whereas bribery always involves the subversion of role duties, extortion does not. One can only be bribed if one is acting as an agent for another, but this is not a necessary condition for being a victim of extortion. One may be a victim of extortion both in instances where one is free to act on one's own behalf or one has acquired duties to act on the behalf of one's employer.

D. Bribery and Culturally Relative Practices

Third, this understanding of bribery provides guidance in assessing practices that would be considered bribery in one culture but are accepted and expected behavior in other cultures. It avoids the conclusion that our definition of bribery must be culturally relative, yet recognizes that what properly counts as bribery may vary from culture to culture. Bribery, we have said, essentially involves an intentional and willing alienation of agency by the employee and a third party, such that the employee illegitimately subverts a prior agreement to act as agent for an employer, thus failing to fulfill the role duties acquired under that prior agreement. This understanding, although not culturally relative, is capable of recognizing that the official duties of employees may vary from culture to culture, so that behavior that in one society would constitute taking a bribe should not be so regarded in another. The key question is not the variability of employee behavior, but whether the employee acts as loyal agent for her employer. This is not to say that if a practice is culturally accepted it does not constitute bribery, but rather that what counts as the official duties of an employee may be culturally relative.

III. BRIBERY, UNDUE INFLUENCE, AND EXTORTION: MORAL ISSUES

Our discussion of bribery has allowed us to distinguish between instances of undue influence, bribes, and extortion. It has also led us to conclude that, although there is no need to define bribery in a culturally relative manner, employee duties may be understood differently in different cultures, so that what counts as taking a bribe may differ from culture to culture. What we must now examine is whether there are circumstances in which one could legitimately exert what we would normally call undue influence, offer a bribe, or extort. Additionally, we must examine whether there are circumstances in which one could legitimately accede to what we would normally call undue influence, accept a bribe, or pay extortion.

A. Undue Influence and Morality

We have said that undue influence occurs when an employee is swayed, or in danger of being swayed, from his duty to act in the best interests of his employer. How then could it ever be morally correct either to exert undue influence or to allow oneself to be unduly influenced? The answer that must be given is that, although there exists a prima facie obligation not to exert undue influence or to allow oneself to be unduly influenced, it seems possible to conceive of situations where this obligation would fail to hold. What if the result of the undue influence is that a great harm would be prevented from occurring or that a great good would be brought about?

It deserves emphasis in this regard that contractual obligations are acquired and cannot legitimately conflict with the more general obligations one has simply by virtue of being a human person. For example, one could never have an acquired duty on the basis of a contract to perform murder, because this would violate one's general duty not to kill. Given that there are general obligations that, in unusual circumstances, would necessitate the suspension of what we would otherwise regard as the legitimate role duties of an employee, it seems permissible in such circumstances to exert, or to allow oneself to be influenced by, what in other circumstances would constitute undue influence.

Suppose, for example, the manager of a shoe store has been instructed by its owner not to extend credit. She is approached by a customer, well known for his honesty and for keeping his word, who in the past has frequently bought shoes for his children and has always paid her cash. The customer informs her that, although he knows she has been instructed not to extend credit, could she nevertheless make an exception in this instance. He tells her that his family recently had a house fire in which they lost all their possessions. The insurance check will cover their losses, but will not be issued for a couple of days, and meanwhile his children require winter footwear. He promises that if she will extend the credit he will not let the fact that she has done so become public knowledge and also that he will provide her with free car washes at his service station. Concerned for the welfare of the children, she agrees to extend the credit and, not wanting to offend or embarrass the customer, promises that she will come in for the free car washes he insists on offering her. In such an instance, although we might say that the manager has a prima facie duty to follow the instructions of her employer and that the customer has a prima facie duty not to seek to cause her to violate her duty to her employer, neither has acted immorally, inasmuch as these primar facie duties are trumped by the more general duty of avoiding a considerable but easily preventable harm to the customer's children. To be noted, of course, is the fact that the manager's motive for extending the credit was based on concern for the customer's children and not on the special treatment she would receive as a result of her decision.

B. Bribery and Morality

Similarly, in the case of bribery, these exists a prima facie obligation for someone in an official position to fulfill her official duties. There exists, therefore, a prima facie obligation not to subvert the fulfillment of positional duties by offering or receiving a bribe. How seriously this prima facie obligation ought to be taken will depend in large part on the institutional and social context in which one finds oneself. Again, the controlling principle is that role or positional duties generated by contractual obligations cannot legitimately conflict with the more general obligations one has simply by virtue of being a human person. It would seem strange, for example, to suggest that in a politically and judicially corrupt regime, someone who bribed a guard to let an innocent prisoner condemned to a lengthy jail sentence escape, was acting immorally. The prima facie duty of the guard not to let the prisoner escape, and the prima facie duty of citizens not to endeavor by means of bribery to cause the guard to fail in his duty are to be respected to the degree that the institutional and social context generating these positional duties is fair and just.

It might be objected that an example such as I have just given demonstrates only that it is morally permissible under some circumstances to offer a bribe, not that it is morally permissible to take a bribe. Would we not want to say that the prison guard should not require a bribe if his action is genuinely morally motivated? To suggest this is to ignore the possibility that, unless the guard receives enough of a bribe to flee the country, his action of letting the prisoner escape will result in his being executed. We could scarcely suggest the guard is morally required to forfeit his own life to prevent an innocent prisoner from serving a lengthy prison sentence, but it does seem clear that in such a situation the guard could morally accept a bribe that enables him, without having to forfeit his own life, to let the prisoner escape.

C. Extortion and Morality

In the normal course of events, extorting someone will be even harder to justify than bribing someone, inasmuch as the person suffering the extortion is a victim rather than an accomplice. Again, any justification of the practice in specific instances will depend on challenging the moral legitimacy of the institutional or social context in which the extortion takes place.

Conversely, paying extortion seems much easier to justify than receiving a bribe. In many instances of extortion one is not acting as an employee or official and thus there are no positional duties to an employer to complicate the question of whether to meet the extortion demands. This is not to suggest that one should automatically give in to the demands of a blackmailer or extortionist in such instances, because one has a prima facie duty to resist the immoral actions of others. There may well, however, be considerations that are capable of overriding this prima facie obligation.

In instances where meeting extortion demands would necessitate failing in positional duties, the question arises as to how greatly the victim or others will suffer if one carries out these duties. For example, we can scarcely fault a clerk for failing in his positional duty by handing over the contents of a cash register to an extortionist if he is faced with the genuine and immediate threat of his home being blown up by a bomb planted by the extortionist. This is not to say that one could never illegitimately subvert one's role duties as an employee by paying extortion. For example,

the clerk would not be justified in handing over the contents of the cash register if the threat was only that his windows would be soaped. But supererogatory acts of moral heroism are not implicit in the contractual agreement by which one acquires role duties.

D. Cultural Differences and Morality

I have suggested that, although the definition of bribery is not culturally relative, what constitutes the official duties of an employee frequently is. This implies that behavior that in one society would count as offering or taking a bribe, that is, behavior that would involve subverting one's official duties, might not so count in another society. In other words, the same behavior might be perfectly consistent with one's official duties. Thus, behavior that in some countries might be construed as offering or demanding a bribe, might in other countries be construed as offering or demanding a tip. The term tip, originally an acronym for the phrase "to insure prompt service," implies no alienation of agency, but rather recognizes that an employee can remain faithful to her employer, even though she is independently receiving payment for service to her employer's customers. In such instances, payment to the employee takes place with the implicit or explicit approval of her employer and tends to become simply a cost of doing business, much as tipping a waitress should be included in estimating the cost of a meal at a restaurant.

Equally, however, it implies that the question of whether certain practices constitute bribery is not to be settled by whether the culture in which they occur considers them bribery, but rather whether in fact these practices are consistent with fulfilling one's official duties. This will also hold true in the case of undue influence and extortion. If we think that undue influence, bribery, and extortion are prima facie immoral we must, in the absence of special circumstances justifying these practices, be prepared to criticize the social environments in which they are condoned.

Even more importantly, we must also be prepared to raise the issue of whether the way a particular culture or society conceives official duties is in accord with the general duties we have simply by virtue of our humanity. As I have argued earlier, role or positional obligations cannot legitimately conflict with these more general obligations. The implication of this is that if a particular society conceives professional duties in such a way that these duties conflict with our more basic human duties, then we must be prepared to raise larger moral issues regarding that society's structuring of its institutions and contractual agreements.

Also See the Following Articles

BUSINESS ETHICS, OVERVIEW • CORPORATIONS, ETHICS IN

Bibliography

Anechiarico, F., & Kuo, L. (1995, Spring). The justified scoundrel: The structural genesis of corruption. *Journal of Social Philosophy,* 25, 1, 147–161.

Berleant, A. (1982, August). Multinationals, local practice, and the problem of ethical consistency. *Journal of Business Ethics,* 1, 3, 185–193.

Carson, T. (1985, Winter). Bribery, extortion, and the foreign corrupt practices act. *Philosophy and Public Affairs,* 14, 1, 66–90.

D'Andrade, K. (1985). Bribery. *Journal of Business Ethics,* 4, 239–248.

Danley, J. Toward a theory of bribery. *Business and Professional Ethics Journal,* 2, 3, 19–39.

Fadiman, J. (1984, July/August). A traveler's guide to gifts and bribes. *Harvard Business Review,* 4, 122–136.

Philips, M. (1984). Bribery. *Ethics,* 94, 621–636.

INDIGENOUS RIGHTS

Jorge M. Valadez
Marquette University

GLOSSARY

cultural integrity The quality that a cultural tradition exhibits when its principal values, customs, and sociopolitical and economic institutions remain relatively cohesive and whole over time.

ethnic group Group of individuals who share a common cultural tradition. In contrast to indigenous groups, when they form part of a multicultural society it is more likely that they are, or wish to be, integrated into the larger society.

globalization The economic, cultural, political, and technological processes through which countries and peoples throughout the world become increasingly interconnected.

indigenous group Group of individuals with a culturally distinctive character who are the living descendents of preinvasion inhabitants. They are part of larger settler societies and they generally have profound connections to their land and a continuity of identity with their ancestral past. Often, the terms

"native" and "aboriginal" are used synonymously with the term "indigenous" to describe this category.

neoliberalism An economic doctrine that emphasizes international free trade, production for export, privatization of national services, minimal government intervention in economic activity, and domestic markets open to foreign investment and ownership.

self-determination The right of a group to control its own destiny by choosing and sustaining its economic and sociopolitical institutions and preserving its cultural heritage.

territorial autonomy The right of a group to control the access and use of a particular territory and its natural resources without interference from the larger society or external societies.

INDIGENOUS RIGHTS are rights designed to protect the vital interests of certain culturally distinctive groups with ancestral connections to precolonial peoples who inhabited areas now occupied by settler societies. What makes indigenous rights different from universally applicable human rights is that they answer to the particular social, political, and economic needs of nondominant indigenous groups who live in societies formed as the result of colonization. Historically, many indigenous groups have been socially and politically marginalized through racial discrimination and have been deprived of ownership and control of their ancestral homelands. According to political philosophers, indigenous leaders, and human rights activists, the special circumstances faced by indigenous groups make it necessary that they be protected by rights that take into account their special group needs and interests. Prominent examples of indigenous rights are the rights of territorial autonomy, self-governance, preservation of cultural integrity, and nondiscrimination.

I. HISTORICAL BACKGROUND

A. Early Treatment of Indigenous Rights

Up until the middle of the 20th century, indigenous rights were generally unrecognized because indigenous groups, occupying an intermediate position between individuals and states, were not regarded as legitimate bearers of rights. According to the 17th and 18th century philosophical model of rights adopted, among others, by Emmerich de Vatell and Thomas Hobbes, rights could be exhaustively divided into the rights of individuals and the rights of states. Since indigenous groups were obviously not individuals, they could be granted collective rights only if they could satisfy the criteria for statehood provided by this state-centered model. But while indigenous groups were collectivities like states, often they did not exhibit the hierarchical, centralized structures of governance and authority characteristic of states. To be sure, some indigenous groups, such as the Aztecs in Mexico and the Incas in Peru, had highly centralized and hierarchical governance structures at the time of the arrival of the European colonizers, while other indigenous groups had complex nonhierarchical sociopolitical systems whose sophistication was denied or ignored by the colonizers. But typically, indigenous groups had horizontal, decentralized political structures, and, unlike states which had clearly delineated territorial boundaries, they often inhabited territories that overlapped with those of other indigenous groups.

Thus indigenous groups did not satisfy the criteria for statehood provided by the state-centered model. Since some of the most important rights of indigenous groups, such as the right to self-determination, are collective in nature, the failure to grant indigenous groups due recognition as rights bearers was an important loss for them. The state-centered model served, whether accidentally or by design, to further colonial interests and empire building. Further, since indigenous people were often regarded as "uncivilized" and "primitive," they were seen as less than fully human and were thus denied even their most basic individual rights. Many indigenous groups suffered brutal injustices at the hands of the colonizers, such as enslavement, mass killings, and forcible displacement from their homelands.

B. Recent Developments Concerning Indigenous Rights

In recent years there has been increased interest in issues related to indigenous rights and a resulting movement toward their legitimation. This has been due to several interconnected factors, the most prominent of which are the greater demand for natural resources found in native homelands, increased awareness and political activity of indigenous groups, and changes in the global political climate.

As nations throughout the world become more integrated into the global economy, and as their populations increase, they are being compelled to make maximal use of their natural resources. Economic integration often means acceptance of the neoliberal paradigm of economic development which emphasizes open access of a country's economy to foreign ownership and investment. Thus indigenous groups find themselves besieged by the territorial intrusions of transnational and domestic companies in the logging, mining, fishing, oil, and agricultural industries as these companies try to identify and exploit new resources.

For example, the Tarahumaras of northern Mexico are battling logging companies and encroachment from settlers; the indigenous peoples of Irian Jaya (West Papua) are engaged in an intense, bloody struggle for control of their lands with the Indonesian government; and the Yupik of Alaska are competing with commercial fishing interests and fighting attempts by the U.S. government to control their hunting and fishing practices. The struggles of indigenous peoples to protect their lands and resources from outside interests and to retain their traditional forms of economic subsistence are a major cause of conflict in the world.

While the "resource wars" many indigenous peoples are engaged in sometimes take the form of violent struggle, oftentimes they proceed through legal battles in domestic and international courts and political participation in national and international forums. Aided by indigenous and nonindigenous human rights activists and organizers, indigenous groups in South America, Asia, North America, Africa, and Australia are taking a more active role in determining their destinies by demanding government compliance of early treaties and legitimation of their collective rights. The realization that their way of life and even their survival as a cultural group are at stake has contributed to a resurgence of political awareness and activity among indigenous groups throughout the world.

Of pivotal importance in the development of this process of heightened indigenous political participation was the International Nongovernmental Organization Conference on Discrimination against Indigenous Populations in the Americas that was held in Geneva in 1977. Representatives from indigenous groups in North and South America initiated a process of political dialogue and engagement that eventually came to include not only peoples in the western hemisphere, but indigenous groups throughout the world. The struggle of indigenous peoples for their collective rights has extended beyond control of land and natural resources to include cultural rights such as the right to an education in their native language and government support of programs that promote the retention of their cultural heritage. The decline of military dictatorships and the process of democratization, particularly in Latin America, has also encouraged the political participation of indigenous groups fighting for their self-determination.

Another factor in the latter part of the 20th century that has facilitated the legitimation of indigenous rights is the changed global political climate. During this period there has been a shift from a state-centered normative framework in which issues such as the ethical treatment of indigenous groups were seen as matters of domestic law to a universalistic framework which focuses on essentialist normative conceptions. According to this universalistic framework the rights of indigenous peoples transcend the particular sociopolitical norms of the settler societies where they reside. The UN now officially disavows both external (overseas) and internal forms of colonialism.

Furthermore, the end of the cold war and the corresponding decrease of ideological polarization has created a more propitious environment in international supragovernmental institutions like the UN for discussing questions of human rights from a universalistic perspective. While the state-centered model still remains the dominant model, the voices and perspectives of nonwestern cultural groups have attained greater prominence in the international community. Having noted the advances made by indigenous groups, it must also be pointed out that formal recognition of the rights of indigenous groups is quite different from the implementation of these rights by the countries where these groups reside. Widescale abuses of indigenous people still take place in many countries.

Three central issues have arisen in discussions of

indigenous rights: (i) the nature and scope of these rights, (ii) their philosophical justification, and (iii) the criteria for determining which groups are entitled to these rights. Each of these issues will be discussed in turn.

II. THE NATURE OF INDIGENOUS RIGHTS

A. Some Philosophical Questions Concerning Indigenous Rights

What kinds of rights are indigenous rights? What areas of life do they affect, i.e., what is their scope? Concerning the first question, a great deal has been written about whether indigenous rights (and more generally, rights granted on the basis of cultural membership) are collective rights that are irreducible to individual rights. For some philosophers a central issue is whether indigenous groups *qua* collectivities are the bearers of rights, that is, whether it is the group that properly speaking is entitled to indigenous rights and not its individual members. Individualists deny the rights-bearing priority of collectivities and maintain that despite the fact that the language of group rights gives the impression that the group is the bearer of rights, ultimately it is the individual members of the group who exercise and are entitled to the rights.

Collectivists, on the other hand, argue that the interests of groups or communities are not identical with, and not exhausted by, the interests of individuals, and that since rights are designed to protect interests, we cannot equate group and individual rights. Thus, concerning a particular indigenous right such as the right to self-governance, the collectivist would emphasize that it is a right that a indigenous community requires to preserve its own existence and that by definition it is a right that only a collectivity can exercise. Individualists, however, would contend that even though self-governance is a right that individuals must exercise within a group context, ultimately it is out of respect for the right of individuals to govern themselves as they see fit that we grant the right in the first place.

It is possible to mediate between the individualist and the collectivist positions by noting that there are different aspects of indigenous rights on which we can focus, and that these rights can be understood as collective or individual rights depending on which of these aspects we emphasize. There are at least four aspects of indigenous rights that we can distinguish: (i) the basis on which indigenous rights are granted, i.e., whether one is entitled to them because of group membership or merely because one is a human being; (ii) the fact that since there are certain characteristics that only groups can exemplify—such as ownership of communal property—only groups can be entitled to rights ensuring the preservation of such characteristics; (iii) the claim that indigenous rights inhere not in collectivities themselves but in the individuals composing those collectivities; and (iv) whether the legal declaration and exercise of indigenous rights is best understood in terms of groups or individuals. It seems reasonable to maintain that indigenous rights are collective rights in senses (i) and (ii), that they are individual rights in sense (iii), and that in sense (iv) they can be seen, depending on the particularities of the case at hand, as either collective or individual rights.

Before proceeding, an additional observation must be made concerning the individualist–collectivist debate. This debate is considered philosophically significant because it has a crucial bearing on the question of whether the community or the individual has moral priority. Adopting a collectivist position would mean that when there are conflicts between the interests of the community and the interests of some of its members we would grant moral priority to the community, while adopting an individualist position would mean favoring the interests of the individual vis-a-vis the community. Despite its prominence in the literature, however, it is not clear whether the individualist–collectivist debate clarifies more than it obfuscates the important issues surrounding indigenous rights. As Will Kymlicka points out, the individualist–collectivist debate, by conceptualizing the issue of indigenous rights in terms of the relative moral primacy of the individual or the community, diverts attention from central questions concerning their function and legitimacy (W. Kymlicka, 1995. *Multicultural Citizenship: A Liberal Theory of Minority Rights.* Clarendon Press, Oxford).

When we take the debate about indigenous rights as essentially a controversy about whether individuals or communities have moral priority, we construe indigenous rights only in terms of the internal restrictions that indigenous communities can place on their members. In other words, we conceive of indigenous rights as rights that an indigenous group can appeal to in order to prohibit or require certain actions of their members. But it is equally important, if not more so, to understand indigenous rights as external protections that indigenous groups can rely on to defend themselves from the detrimental decisions of the larger society. Understanding indigenous rights as external protections is particularly crucial in societies where the rights of minority groups have been systematically violated by majority groups.

To be sure, there are important questions concerning the restrictions that liberal democracies should place on the authority that indigenous groups can exercise over their own members, but clearly the issues concerning indigenous rights are not exhausted by such questions. In addition, taking the individualist–collectivist debate as pivotal to understanding indigenous rights is bound to bias the case against them in societies which prize individual autonomy over collective needs and interests. If we construe support for indigenous rights as support for the primacy of collective over individual interests, it is unlikely that indigenous rights will receive the reasoned and fair consideration that they deserve.

B. The Content and Function of Indigenous Rights

In order to understand more fully the character and function of indigenous rights, it would be instructive to examine some generally recognized indigenous rights and their interconnections. Among the most prominent are the rights of self-determination, territorial autonomy, and preservation of cultural integrity.

Self-determination can be considered as an overarching indigenous right because it incorporates a number of other indigenous rights. At the core of self-determination is the conviction that people should be free to determine their own destinies by choosing and sustaining their own economic and sociopolitical institutions, patterns of governance, and ways of life. Self-governance for indigenous communities means not only political governance that accords with the will of indigenous peoples, but also governance that is consistent with their historical modes of sociopolitical organization. Thus it would not be appropriate to merely incorporate indigenous communities into the existing western political-legal systems, because such systems may be at odds with indigenous patterns of self-governance.

Most indigenous groups have traditionally functioned with consensual systems of decision making and procedures of conflict resolution that differ markedly from those of liberal democratic societies. In contrast to legal systems based on an adversarial orientation, for example, Navajo courts of conflict resolution focus on identifying the reasons why the conflict occurred and strive to restore broken community solidarity. Similarly, consensual decision making is preferred by indigenous communities because systems of democratic majority rule are seen as potentially divisive and unfair since the interests and preferences of those who are outvoted are diminished or neglected. In short, we cannot assume that political inclusion and assimilation to the mainstream society can ensure adequate self-governance for indigenous groups.

In the case of indigenous peoples, self-determination is closely connected with such rights as territorial autonomy and the preservation of cultural integrity. Control of land and natural resources by indigenous people is important for their self-determination because of their profound spiritual and material connections to the land. For many groups their means of subsistence—which typically consist of fishing, hunting, and farming practices—have intrinsic cultural significance. For Maya communities in Guatemala, for example, some of the practices related to the cultivation of corn are replete with religious meaning. The ancestral homelands of indigenous peoples also contain sacred sites and ancient burial grounds that connect the community to earlier generations. Most indigenous groups see themselves as connected to their ancestral past through continued stewardship of the land, and they consider caring for the land that future generations will inhabit as a great moral and cultural responsibility. The land and its creatures are seen as parts of a great biotic web of which the members of the indigenous group are also an integral component. Breaking this connection to the land would mean severing a pervasive bond that they have with the natural world.

The preservation of cultural integrity—which includes maintaining one's language, religion, and economic and sociopolitical institutions—is also important for the exercise of self-determination. Since the preservation of a cultural tradition cannot be carried out by isolated individuals, the right to preserve cultural integrity must take place within a communal context. It is also the case that maintaining cultural integrity is meaningless without the existence of a vibrant indigenous community. In practical terms, this means that positive efforts must be made, and material resources provided, for the development and maintenance of indigenous communities. This is particularly important given the fact that indigenous groups have suffered pervasive racial discrimination, religious bigotry, and attempts at cultural destruction at the hands of the majority society.

In the United States, for example, the General Allotment Act of 1887 negated traditional communal land patterns in Indian reservations and replaced them with a system of individual private property ownership. The destruction of traditional communal ownership was made with the expressed purpose of disrupting the cultural cohesion and communal solidarity of Native American peoples. Other attempts by the U.S. government to undermine the cultural integrity of Native Americans include the subverting of indigenous tribal governments by the assassinations of their leaders, the withholding of official recognition of certain tribes through the Extermination Act of 1953, and the forced schooling of Native American children in English in an effort to eradicate their cultural identity. Indigenous groups in other parts of the world have also faced forced assimilation or attempts at cultural and physical annihilation. This legacy of oppression has typically left indigenous groups socially and politically marginalized, impoverished, and communally fractured. The oppression suffered by indigenous groups strongly supports a remedial component in the right to preserve cultural integrity.

Our observations on self-determination, territorial autonomy, and cultural integrity reveal the special interrelatedness of indigenous rights. In many cases, an indigenous community cannot maintain cultural practices that are central to its cultural integrity without a secure land base. Likewise, granting indigenous groups the right to self-determination involves respecting their reliance on traditional forms of self-governance and dispute resolution, which are essential components of their cultural traditions. We can also readily discern that other generally recognized indigenous rights, like nondiscrimination and the promotion of social welfare, complement and reinforce self-determination. In short, indigenous rights form a cohesive and interconnected set of principles that lay the groundwork for the survival and flourishing of indigenous communities.

III. THE PHILOSOPHICAL JUSTIFICATION OF INDIGENOUS RIGHTS

The justification of certain indigenous rights raises some interesting philosophical issues. Defending certain rights, like the right to nondiscrimination, poses no particular problems because everyone (at least in a liberal democratic society) is recognized as having the right to be protected against invidious and arbitrary discrimination on the basis of race, color, creed, and similar characteristics. Other indigenous rights, however, like the right to territorial autonomy, appear to be problematic. What justifies granting special rights, like the right to fish and hunt in areas that are off limits to others, to the members of certain groups only? In societies that are based on principles of equality and justice, how can we justify rights based on group membership?

Some indigenous rights based on group membership can be justified by reference to the idea of the "inequality of equals." This idea gives due recognition to the fact that in certain situations special protections will be necessary to ensure equal treatment of all members of society. Consider the fundamental right in a democratic multicultural society to pursue one's conception of the good life. For many people this endeavor may involve maintaining their cultural identity, including keeping their language and cultural traditions. Preserving cultural identity may be taken for granted by the members of the majority cultural group because their own language is used in official government transactions and in the schools, the society provides public funds for museums and art organizations that preserve their culture's artistic heritage, the justice system conforms to the conceptions of justice of their cultural tradition, etc.

However, the situation is very different for indigenous groups who are in a position of social and political inequality vis-a-vis the larger society. For them it will be extremely difficult to exercise the right to pursue their vision of the good life because of the lack of support given to their cultural traditions by the majority society. Without rights specifically designed to preserve their cultural heritage, such as rights guaranteeing education in their own language, these indigenous groups will be unable to pursue and realistically achieve their vision of a good and satisfying life. Thus, indigenous rights protecting language and cultural heritage are not designed to provide indigenous groups with special privileges that other members of the society do not have; on the contrary, they are meant to ensure that indigenous groups have the same freedoms and opportunities that everyone else in the society enjoys.

Sometimes the argument is made that group rights protecting cultural integrity would not be necessary if indigenous groups assimilated into the majority society. This view is supported by the claim that it is reasonable for a society to expect that its members assimilate into the national culture. After all, many other ethnic groups who were once discriminated and marginalized have integrated successfully and now enjoy the social benefits that full acceptance and participation in the society bring. By demanding special group rights, indigenous groups willfully separate themselves from the rest of society and thwart the process of assimilation that ethnic minority groups in a pluralistic society must undergo in order to function successfully.

This view fails to make the crucial distinction between ethnic minorities and indigenous groups. Ethnic minorities are groups with a common cultural background who have voluntarily immigrated and who typically favor integration into their adopted country. They have not strenuously resisted assimilation into the mainstream society; in fact, many immigrant parents teach their children only the mainstream language and willingly adopt the prevaling cultural norms of the new country. Even though sometimes the self-identity of first generation immigrants is closely connected with the cultural traditions of their native countries, that is generally not the case with succeeding generations.

Indigenous groups, on the other hand, did not immigrate from a foreign country but were forcefully annexed or conquered by the dominant society. Before the arrival of the settler society, they were self-governing autonomous communities or nations with their own distinctive economic, social, political, and cultural institutions. Most indigenous groups have for many generations vigorously resisted assimilation, and have fought not so much for civil rights that would guarantee them full membership in the society, as for rights of political liberty and self-determination. Keeping in mind the distinction between ethnic minorities and indigenous groups is important for understanding why it may be reasonable to expect the former to integrate into the society but not the latter. Distinguishing clearly the two groups is also helpful for alleviating fears of the larger society that ethnic minorities will use the same reasoning as native groups to demand the same collective rights.

Other indigenous rights have a different justificatory basis. The important right of territorial autonomy, for example, can be defended by reference to the historical injustices committed when disputed indigenous territories were expropriated through conquest or unilaterally annexed by the larger society. The justification here is a kind of compensatory justice where a significant wrong inflicted on a particular group needs to be redressed. Additional support for the moral obligation for rectification comes from the fact that the denial of territorial autonomy for indigenous groups is the cause of continuing social and political oppression. If an indigenous group has maintained a strong continuity of identity with its ancestral past and with its homeland, then the rationale for granting them at least some form of territorial autonomy is compelling.

In justifying the indigenous right of self-determination, several considerations have to be taken into account. Self-determination is a right that is recognized by the international community as belonging to all people, but in the case of indigenous groups it acquires a special meaning. We have already seen how for indigenous people self-determination is closely connected to the rights of territorial autonomy and the preservation of cultural integrity. But the right of self-determination as it applies to indigenous groups must be further qualified by the recognition of the diversity of historical circumstances, present sociopolitical conditions, and collective decisions of particular indigenous groups. For some indigenous groups self-determination may mean having control of their natural resources and of the immigration policies for residency in their homeland, for others it may entail retaining traditional forms of self-governance and dispute resolution, and for yet others it may mean secession from the larger nation-state in order to achieve complete sovereignty.

The right of self-determination has often been equated with the right to secession and independent statehood. Indeed, resistance to claims of self-determination has often been based on this erroneous assumption. Many indigenous groups, however, are not seeking complete sovereignty but some form of political and territorial autonomy within the boundaries of the nation-state where their lands are located. Various types of federalism, where significant control of political, economic, and cultural affairs is devolved to local and regional subunits, could accommodate the demands of some indigenous groups for self-determination.

Thus, different indigenous groups may seek various forms of self-determination. A number of considerations must be kept in mind when attempting to justify particular forms of self-determination. Among the factors to be considered are the needs and interests of the indigenous group in question, the historical facts surrounding the group's colonization or incorporation by the larger society, the cultural cohesiveness of the indigenous group and its continuity of identity with its ancestral communities, the likelihood that the proposed form of self-determination will bring about the survival and flourishing of the indigenous group, and the consequences of the proposed form of self-determination for the larger society. The philosophical justification of the principle of self-determination is a complex matter involving a number of empirical and conceptual considerations.

IV. CRITERIA FOR THE GROUPS ENTITLED TO INDIGENOUS RIGHTS

Different criteria for defining indigenous groups have been proposed in various contexts, and it is difficult to arrive at a universally accepted definition. Governments have sometimes employed excessively narrow criteria of who is indigenous in order to avoid or lessen financial and legal responsibilities. Different indigenous groups have used different criteria for group membership, for tribal voting rights, and for holding office in tribal government. American Indians, for example, have used group membership criteria that range from requiring one-half tribal blood to one-sixteenth. Specifying criteria for indigenous group membership sometimes takes political overtones within the groups themselves, as opinions differ about how to best employ them to maintain community solidarity or achieve political goals. It is important to note that many indigenous groups traditionally took a liberal approach to the question of who is a group member. Nonindigenous persons could be adopted as members of the group if they accepted its perspectives and way of life.

A key issue in defining indigenous groups is whether they are to be characterized primarily in ethnological (racial) or cultural terms. Ethnological criteria are based on percentages of native blood while cultural criteria involve adoption of cultural beliefs and practices and affinity with other group members. There are advantages and disadvantages in using ethnological or cultural criteria for group membership. Ethnological classification can contravene charges of arbitrariness concerning indigenous group membership and can make more compelling the demands for restitution from the colonizing society for past injustices. It would be highly implausible, for example, for a group to demand the return of lands illegitimately expropriated from their ancestors if the group's hereditary connections to those ancestors were nonexistent or indeterminate.

On the other hand, culturally based criteria do not exclude individuals who are deeply committed and knowledgeable of the needs and concerns of the indigenous group but who do not have the required degree of ancestry. In addition, cultural criteria conform more closely with the traits and practices which indigenous groups are concerned with preserving. If the core demand of indigenous groups is to attain self-determination and live according to their chosen way of life, it makes sense to adopt criteria for group membership based on how committed an individual is to defending and embodying that way of life. Cultural criteria based on a set of sociopolitical convictions and commitments are also more likely to enhance the credibility of indigenous group demands in liberal democratic societies that are deeply suspicious of race-based rights and privileges.

Reasonable standards for indigenous group membership should take into account the strengths and liabilities of ethnological and cultural criteria. While ethnological criteria do not appear to be necessary for every case for group membership, a "critical mass" of group members with ancestral connections seems to be an essential component of group identity. Otherwise, as we have seen, the moral legitimacy of certain indigenous rights would be undermined. Indeed, relations of descendance are part of the very meaning of the terms "native" and "indigenous." It is perhaps impossible to determine in precise terms what this critical mass should be, but it is reasonable to suppose that past a certain point of hereditary attenuation, there will be a decline in the moral exigency of some, although not all, indigenous group claims. Besides ethnological considerations there are other criteria that are straightforwardly relevant. The most important of these are that the members be cognizant of the cultural traditions of the group and that they exhibit a discernible commitment to those traditions, that they have a continuity of identity with the group's ancestral past, and that they value the continued existence and intergenerational transmission of the group's cultural heritage.

Ultimately, however, it should be up to indigenous groups themselves to determine the criteria for group membership. There are advantages gained and responsibilities incurred in adopting particular criteria for group membership, and awareness of these should restrain excessively broad or overly restrictive standards for group membership.

V. CONCLUSION: PROSPECTS FOR INDIGENOUS RIGHTS

There are some encouraging developments that support the understanding, development, and recognition of indigenous rights. After centuries of neglect, this subject is currently being researched by philosophers, legal scholars, and political scientists. Interest in indigenous rights has been bolstered by the increasing interest in the cultural pluralism that now characterizes societies throughout the world. Scholars in different disciplines are recognizing that a proper understanding of democracy and human rights must take into account the diversity of perspectives, needs, and interests of the different cultural groups that make up the global human community. Developments in information technologies and telecommunications have also facilitated research and

scholarly exchanges between researchers interested in indigenous groups.

There has also been an increased interest in the legal status of the rights of indigenous peoples by the international community. Of special importance in this connection are the drafts that United Nations committees have written on the rights of indigenous groups, particularly the "Draft United Nations Declaration on the Rights of Indigenous Peoples." This document represents a milestone in the international recognition of indigenous rights.

However, prospects for the implementation of indigenous rights and the preservation of the cultural integrity of indigenous groups are uncertain. Governments routinely give rhetorical recognition to such rights but do little to carry out social welfare projects or enforce formally granted rights. Sometimes this is due to lack of resources and sometimes to neglect or persisting racist attitudes toward indigenous groups. But perhaps the greatest danger to the cultural survival of indigenous groups is the current global western cultural homogenization driven by commercial interests and put into effect by ubiquitous media technologies. Should this process succeed, the world will have lost the cultural richness of indigenous groups which is our common human heritage.

Also See the Following Articles

ETHNOCULTURAL MINORITY GROUPS, STATUS AND TREATMENT OF • ENVIRONMENTAL ETHICS, OVERVIEW • IMPERIALISM • POLITICAL ECOLOGY • RACISM

Bibliography

Anaya, S. J. (1996). "Indigenous Peoples in International Law." Oxford Univ. Press, Oxford.

Buchanan, A. (1993). The role of collective rights in the theory of indigenous peoples' rights. *Transnational Law Contemporary Problem* 3(1), 89–108.

Clinton, R. (1990). The rights of indigenous peoples as collective group rights. *Arizona Law Rev.* 32(4), 739–747.

Jaimes, M. A. (Ed.) (1992). "The State of Native America: Genocide, Colonization, and Resistance." Sound End, Boston.

Kymlicka, W. (1995). "Multicultural Citizenship: A Liberal Theory of Minority Rights." Clarendon Press, Oxford.

Kymlicka, W. (Ed.) (1995). "The Rights of Minority Cultures." Oxford Univ. Press, Oxford.

Pacari, N. (1996). Taking on the neoliberal agenda. *North American Congress on Latin America: Report on the Americas* 29(5), 23–32.

Pevar, S. L. (1992). "The Rights of Indians and Tribes," 2nd ed. Southern Illinois Univ. Press, Carbondale/Edwardsville.

INFERTILITY

Mary Ann McClure
John Jay College of Criminal Justice

GLOSSARY

artificial insemination (AI) A technique in which the male sperm is collected and mechanically introduced into the woman's vagina.

artificial insemination with donor sperm (AID) A type of artificial insemination in which the sperm does not come from the woman's partner but rather from a donor.

coerced infertility The forcing of persons to use contraceptives or to be sterilized against their will.

contractual parenthood A transaction that involves in its most typical form the AI of a woman who agrees to give up the child after birth to be raised by the genetic father and a woman, usually his wife.

cryopreservation A process by which embryos or sperm can be preserved by freezing.

embryo Normally, a fertilized egg that has implanted itself in the wall of the uterus; however, with the advent of reproductive technologies, this term is also applied to fertilized eggs that have been generated by IVF or embryos removed by surgery from the uterine wall.

gamete A mature sperm or egg capable of fusing with a gamete of the opposite sex to produce a fertilized egg.

gamete intrafallopian transfer (GIFT) A technique similar to IVF in which the eggs are placed together with the sperm in the fallopian tubes instead of fertilizing them in the laboratory.

infertility Inability to reproduce, typically defined as the failure to produce offspring after 1 year of regular sexual relations.

***in vitro* fertilization (IVF)** A technology that involves collecting eggs and sperm, combining them in a glass dish, growing any resulting fertilized eggs to the two- to eight-cell stage, and introducing them into a woman's uterus.

reproductive technology A medical intervention that facilitates conception.

transvaginal oocyte retrieval A technique in which eggs are obtained by inserting a needle through the vaginal wall rather than through the abdominal wall by surgery.

INFERTILITY is typically defined as the inability to produce offspring after 1 year of regular sexual relations. In the United States, about 15% of couples of childbearing age are affected by this condition. The ethical issues relating to the problem of human infertility have been reshaped by the emergence, during the last two decades, of new reproductive technologies that facilitate conception. These technologies represent a commitment by society to foster the reproduction of certain privileged groups. Similarly, the issue of coerced infertility focuses on the attempt by society to control the reproduction of those considered to be less desirable or a burden.

For many the new technologies represent powerful tools that promise great benefits to those facing the personal anguish of infertility. But others seriously question the morality and wisdom of having developed these techniques. Some theologians object to the use of any reproductive technology, believing any conception outside of sexuality is unnatural and not in accord with God's plan. Various feminists voice concern about the exploitation of women and children. Still others worry about commercialization, commodification, and the social implications of the expansion of biotechnological control. A sense of uneasiness exists that we may be selling body parts or even selling babies, an anxiety captured by the euphemistic word "donor" when referring to the eggs or sperm involved in the procedures. In most cases these are not gifts, but services exchanged for a fee. Despite these serious objections, these reproductive technologies have been developed and are increasingly being employed, and their use has led to a panoply of moral and legal issues.

I. THE TYPES OF REPRODUCTIVE TECHNOLOGIES

A. Artificial Insemination

The new reproductive technologies include artificial insemination, egg retrieval, *in vitro* fertilization and embryo transfer, and cryopreservation. The simplest and most frequently used of these reproductive interventions is artificial insemination (AI), in which the male sperm is collected and mechanically introduced into the woman's vagina. The sperm may come from the woman's partner, but more often the couple must employ AID, artificial insemination with the sperm of a donor.

B. *In Vitro* Fertilization

The most publicized of these new techologies is *in vitro* fertilization (IVF). In 1978, the birth of Louise Brown, the first human baby resulting from this procedure, seized the public's attention. Although the procedure is understood in the popular imagination as producing "test tube babies," IVF remains connected to natural processes. It represents a complex technology that involves collecting eggs and sperm, combining them in a glass dish, growing any resulting fertilized eggs to the two- to eight-cell stage, and introducing them (the optimum number is four) into a woman's uterus. It requires the transfer of ova and embryos and is sometimes combined with AID and programs of contractual parenthood. Variations on IVF, such as gamete intrafallopian transfer (GIFT) and transvaginal oocyte retrieval, have been developed to reduce the trauma to the woman and to increase the success rate. GIFT involves obtaining eggs as they would be for IVF. But instead of fertilizing them in the laboratory, the eggs are placed together with the sperm in the fallopian tubes. Transvaginal oocyte retrieval offers the advantage of not requiring surgery because eggs are obtained by inserting a needle through the vaginal wall rather than through the abdominal wall.

C. Egg Donation, Embryo Transfer, and Embryo Freezing

The technologies developed for IVF allow for alternative reproductive options, including egg donation, embryo transfer, and embryo freezing. Egg donation allows the woman to be both the gestational and the social mother, if not the genetic one. Eggs are retrieved from one woman and implanted in another. This procedure requires hyperstimulation of the donor's ovaries by hormone treatment and the aspiration of the resultant eggs through the donor's vagina. It not only causes discomfort, but also entails some degree of risk to the donor woman. Even more complex is the ability to transfer a developing fertilized egg from one woman to another, allowing for the possibility of embryo transfer. Embryos can also be preserved by freezing in a process called embryo cryopreservation (CE).

D. Contractual Parenthood

Parenting through contract, also called "surrogate motherhood," in its most typical form involves the AI of a woman who agrees to give up the child after birth to be raised by the genetic father and a woman, usually his wife. However IVF can also be used. Thus the contractual mother can be either the genetic and/or gestational biological parent.

II. MORAL AND LEGAL ISSUES CONCERNING THE USE OF REPRODUCTIVE TECHNOLOGIES

A. Physical Harm and Financial Cost

Most reproductive technologies are painful, invasive, and expensive. AI represents the exception: a relatively simple procedure that costs between $400 and $600 a cycle with a 60% success rate within three to six ovulation cycles. In contrast, IVF is an invasive medical procedure. It involves hormone therapy, frequent monitoring of the woman's blood and urine, surgery, and a period of immobility as well as some degree of risk to the woman's health. Success rates are enhanced if more than one egg or embryo is implanted, but this also poses the risk of multiple pregnancies. It is a costly procedure (one cycle of treatment costs $10,000) with a predicted 10–15% success rate. CE offers the possibility of reducing the physical ordeal of IVF. Since all of the embryos generated from IVF do not have to be immediately implanted, cryopreservation reduces the risk of multiple pregnancy and the trauma of repeated egg removals. However, a low success rate and the possibility of embryonic damage that can result in birth defects have called the practice into question. Nevertheless, IVF (with or without CE) represents a last hope for many couples in their onerous struggle for biological parenthood.

B. The Withholding of Services

Many providers of reproductive technologies routinely withhold services to unmarried individuals. This denial of services can be argued to be morally and legally justified. The assumption is that infertility is not a disease and thus the procedure is not a medical necessity. The autonomy of the physician must be respected as well. She may believe that it is morally wrong to produce a child with only a single parent. Yet the physician does not have a moral right to discriminate, and it is frequently difficult to tease out the bases of such strongly held beliefs about appropriate parenthood from prejudices against single parenthood and prejudices against lesbians in particular.

Nevertheless, it can be argued that physicians who are assisting in bringing children into the world by means of reproductive technologies have some moral responsibility for the outcome in a way that differs from physicians assisting in the birth of a child not conceived through the aid of reproductive technology, since the conception was only possible because of their participa-tion. However, questions then arise about the competence of physicians and institutions that provide reproductive technological services to make decisions about the appropriateness of parenthood.

C. Concerns about Interference with Nature and Tradition

Reproductive technologies splinter elements of procreation which had previously been unified as continuous bodily processes and allow them to be carried out in different ways and by different individuals. Gametes and embryos, as well as sperm, are manipulated both within and outside of women's bodies. At stake is a possible redefinition of what it means to be human and specifically the meaning of human procreation. Traditional notions of parenthood and lineage become problematic.

Expressing concern about the separation of sexuality and procreation, the Vatican Statement of 1987 condemned virtually all of the reproductive technologies, including AID, IVF, and parenting by contract. It argued that children, marriage, and procreation are denigrated when procreation is removed from the realm of bodily love. It also expressed concerns that reproduction would be reduced to a scientific enterprise and warned that a child "cannot be desired or conceived as the product of an intervention of medical or biological techniques; that would be equivalent to reducing him (sic) to an object of scientific technology" (J. C. Ratzinger and A. Bovone, 1987. *Instruction on respect for human life in its origin and on the dignity of procreation* (p. 28). Vatican City: Vatican Polyglot Press). Other theologians have labelled AID adultery because it introduces a third party, the sperm donor, into the marriage relationship.

D. Concerns about Ontological Status

Questions emerge also about the ontological status of the entities produced by the reproductive technologies. Both IVF, which produces surplus fertilized eggs, and CE, which freezes them, raise the familiar issues associated with abortion. At the heart of the abortion debate is the moral status of fetuses. The pro-life perspective defines personhood as starting with fertilization and would thus extend personhood to these embryos. It would find either flushing the embryos or freezing them, which may cause damage, to be equivalent to abortion. This position would advocate that these extra embryos be implanted in some woman's uterus to allow for the possibility that they be brought to term. However, for those opposed to the pro-life position, the ontological status of these embryos, while perhaps ambiguous, is clearly not that of a person. They would argue that a necessary, but not sufficient, condition of personhood is sentience and embryos are not sentient. Furthermore, they would posit that letting the embryo die, or freezing it, is not equivalent to abortion because an abortion is a termination of a pregnancy, and pregnancy depends upon a physiological tie between a woman and an embryo.

E. Moral and Legal Concerns Unique to Individual Technologies

1. Artificial Insemination

With the use of reproductive technologies, the separation of biological and social fatherhood becomes more of a possibility, while motherhood becomes fractured into the multiple components of genetic, gestational, and social, generating multiple parents with sets of conflicting rights. Decisions also have to be made about the disposition of genetic materials when they exist separate from the bodies of either of the originators. The most technologically simple of the reproductive interventions, AI, also presents the least moral and legal entanglements.

Nevertheless, the use of AI is shrouded in secrecy. Many times the couple conceals it, wishing to protect the male partner from the stigma of infertility. Many, however, would argue that responsible parenting demands that the parents be honest with the child about how she was conceived. Similarly, the identity of the donor almost always remains anonymous although enough information about the donor is collected to allow for matching traits, such as race and general physical resemblance. The sperm donor's right to anonymity is upheld to prevent future children from making legal, financial, or emotional claims. However his right to anonymity conflicts with the right of his biological children to know, especially in an era when genetic history is increasingly relevant medical information.

2. Cryopreservation of Embryos

The disposition of existing cryopreserved embryos can present legal problems. Difficulties often emerge when infertile couples, who have been attempting to produce a child aided by CE, break up and divorce. Conflicts occur over who has the right to become, or not become, a parent. In *Davis v. Davis* (1989), a former husband successfully argued that the gestation of cryopreserved embryos, produced while they were married, in his ex-

wife would be a violation of his reproductive rights. Nevertheless, some feminists argue that future-oriented considerations should take precedence. Christine Overall would confer the authority of disposition of these cryopreserved embryos to the woman involved since use of the existing cryopreserved embryos would spare these women from having to undergo expensive and risky future egg retrievals.

3. Contractual Parenthood

Contractual parenthood can be relatively simple, technologically, but socially and morally complex when the contractual mother reconsiders her initial agreement. The Baby M case brought these complexities to the attention of the public when Mary Beth Whitehead, the genetic/gestational mother, sought to maintain custody of the child she had conceived through a contract with William and Elizabeth Stern. This arrangement can be legal and ethical if understood within the context of the model of a contract in which Ms. Whitehead entered into voluntarily. Applying this model, she is understood to have abrogated her maternal rights. Also from an deontological perspective, she has ethically erred by reneging on her agreement, and her rights cannot be honored. It should be noted that the rubric, "surrogate," also insinuates that she is a mere substitute and not the real mother. This was the initial decision of the New Jersey trial court that awarded custody to the Sterns.

But some would question whether the traditional concept of a contract is appropriate for contractual motherhood. Others have found prostitution or baby selling a more appropriate analogy and have worried that contractual parenthood encourages women to engage in commercial transactions over the "products" of their reproductive labor. Indeed the New Jersey Supreme Court, in overruling the lower court in the Baby M case, found contractual parenthood to be a form of baby selling and therefore not a legally binding contract.

Ultimately, the U.S. Supreme Court resolved the dispute using the traditional custody model that ensures that the child receive adequate care and protection from possible harm. They restored custody to the Sterns while acknowledging Ms. Whitehead's maternal rights by allowing her visitation privileges. Some worry that rulings based on the child's best interest make possible interpretations that would always favor the richer parent. Mahowald argues that the child's right to care should not be read as a right to the best possible care but merely care that is good enough.

IVF now allows women to become biological mothers in two distinct ways—genetically and gestational. When the contractual mother is not the genetic mother, some would deny her maternal rights. In 1991, the California Supreme Court ruled against the claims of a gestational mother on the grounds that since she was not the genetic mother, she had no legal rights. Nevertheless, California has a Uniform Parentage Act that upholds the claim of "natural" motherhood to the woman who gives birth. Nelson has presented ethical arguments that grant biological priority to the gestation mother over the genetic mother on the bases of her duration of commitment, risk, necessity, and effectiveness of parental role.

Robertson defends contractual parenthood as differing little from existing practices, specifically non-agency-directed adoption. But those concerned about the underlying commercial nature of contractual parenthood would distinguish it from adoption. They argue that contractual parenthood remains unique because the child is conceived explicitly for the purpose of being given away, or more frankly, of being sold at birth. This turns the child into a commodity. Furthermore, Krimmel argues that the child who discovers the conditions of her birth may grow up with the knowledge that she was created to be "given away" and feel devalued and experience a loss of self-worth.

III. THE SOCIAL AND POLITICAL CONTEXT OF INFERTILITY

Reproductive technologies also have to be evaluated within a social and political context. Many question the wisdom of "creating" new babies in a world where population pressures are increasingly putting strains on the environment. Others worry that the development of reproductive technologies leads to and perpetuates the misuse of scarce medical resources. In economic terms, the cost of something is what one must otherwise forego—in this case, the use of reproductive technologies means medical services are not available for saving lives or improving the quality of existing lives.

On the other hand, it is important to recognize that infertility can be personally devastating. Many of the infertile feel a strong desire to bring into being and rear children who represent an extension of their own bodies and genetic lineage. The urge to reproduce one's self offers a hedge against mortality, and it connects us to past and future generations. It represents a quest for transcendence, and a desire for creativity.

Liberal feminists would argue that women and men should be allowed to use whatever reproductive technologies they want provided that they do no harm in the process. They assert an analogy between a woman's right for reproductive control of her body defended in the pro-choice stance on abortion and her right for reproductive control of her body when faced with infertility. They claim that the ability to choose if and when to have a child is as important for the woman faced with infertility as it is for the woman faced with an unwanted pregnancy.

Others would argue, however, that an individual's desires and preferences are not simply autonomously determined but must be understood within the context of socially constructed meaning. For them, infertility is not merely a biological condition: it's a social category that structures and influences an individual's response to the biological fact of infertility and to the options available. The discovery that one is infertile elicits a diverse repertoire of feelings and behaviors—acceptance, denial, a change in one's partners, or adoption. Sherwin would claim that the emphasis on reproductive technologies as a solution to infertility has weakened the case for nonmedical options. She would have us view infertility within the context of a society that increasingly offers a technological fix for problems that are interpersonal and social.

Many fear that the use of reproductive technologies will lead to many children not being adopted who need to be. Adoption also offers the advantage of not increasing the population. Some believe that we live in a society that overvalues genetic connection and undervalues social linkage. This reinforces the notion that biological children are more one's own than children one has adopted. To help remedy this, Mahoney advocates a concept of parenthood based on nurturing rather than one based on genetics.

Adoption, however, has its own pitfalls. Nurturing can only occur after birth, and in the case of foreign adoptions delays can be lengthy. Adoption can also be costly and time consuming. One has to deal with bureaucracies and protracted waiting. And while adoption is not physically invasive, like the reproductive technologies, many prospective parents find the experience to be degrading and personally intrusive. Nor is this option available to most same-sex couples either because agencies discriminate against them or because most states outlaw same-sex adoptions. Furthermore, IVF and contractual parenthood represent options that are beyond the reach of most infertile women or couples. Some maintain that these expensive reproductive technologies reinforce the message that it is more important for the affluent to reproduce children of their own genetic kind than to adopt children of different backgrounds.

IV. COERCED INFERTILITY

But if an implicit eugenics lurks in society's commitment of vast resources to new reproductive technologies, the issue comes to the foreground in programs of coerced infertility (either temporary or permanent)—that is, actions that attempt to control the reproduction of those considered by society to be undesirable or a burden.

There has been a long history in the United States of nonconsensual sterilization by both private physicians and state and federal authorities for the purpose of limiting the reproduction of poor women and women of color. In addition, women on welfare have been frequently pressured to use the contraceptive Norplant, which must be medically inserted and removed. Once in place, Norplant prevents pregnancy up to 5 years. Judges have also required the implant as a condition of probation for women convicted of drug-related charges or child abuse. The apartheid regime of South Africa injected adolescent black girls with the long-lasting contraceptive Depo-Provera without their consent and black women were required to document their use of birth control before applying for employment. Poor women in Thailand have also been required to accept Depo-Provera before being granted permission to marry.

Sterilization has also frequently been implemented among the disabled and mentally impaired. In all these incidents, a set of issues relating to eugenics becomes explicit. In *Buck v. Bell* (1927) the U.S. Supreme Court ruled that the sterilization of "mental defectives" was constitutional. It held that society has a right to protect itself from the possibility of the dissemination of defective genes and that if sterilized, the person might be more self-supportive. But in *Skinner v. Oklahoma* (1942) the Court overruled an Oklahoma law that mandated sterilization for anyone convicted of three crimes involving "moral turpitude." It found marriage and procreation to be basic civil rights that the state can abridge only on demonstration of compelling state interest. Implicit in the court's decision was a concern about the possibilities for oppression in the implementation of state policies of sterilization.

In conclusion, science is revolutionizing the problem of human infertility. As new techniques continue to be developed, both the popular imagination and the attention of public policy makers will be captured by the unresolved debate about whether such reproductive technologies are moral and about what the consequences of their use will be.

Also See the Following Articles

ADOPTION • EMBRYOLOGY, ETHICS OF • FETUS • POPULATION ETHICS • REPRODUCTIVE TECHNOLOGIES • WOMEN'S RIGHTS

Bibliography

Hartmann, B. (1987). *Reproductive rights and wrongs: The global politics of population-control and contraceptive choice.* New York: Harper and Row.

Krimmel, H. T. (1998). Surrogate mother arrangements from the perspective of the child. *Logos: Philosophic Issues in Christian Perspectives, 9,* 97–112.

Mahoney, J. (1995). Adoption as a feminist alternative to reproductive technologies. In J. C. Callahan (Ed.), *Reproduction, ethics, and the law: Feminist perspectives* (pp. 35–54). Bloomington: Indiana Univ. Press.

Mahowald, M. B. (1993). *Women and children in health care: An unequal majority.* New York: Oxford Univ. Press.

Nelson, H. L., & Nelson, J. L. (1989). Cutting motherhood in two: Some suspicions concerning surrogacy. *Hypatia, 4,* 257–265.

Overall, C. (1995). Frozen embryos and "father's rights": Parenthood and decision-making in the cryopreservation of embryos. In J. C. Callahan (Ed.), *Reproduction, ethics, and the law* (pp. 178–198). Bloomington: Indiana Univ. Press.

Ratzinger, J. C., & Bovone, A. (1987). *Instruction on respect for human life in its origin and on the dignity of procreation: Replies to certain questions of the day.* Vatican City: Vatican Polyglot Press.

Robertson, J. A. (1993). Surrogate motherhood: Not so novel after all. *Hastings Center Report, 13,* 28–34.

Sherwin, S. (1992). *No longer patient: Feminist ethics and health care.* Philadelphia: Temple Univ. Press.

INFORMATION MANAGEMENT

Richard O. Mason
Southern Methodist University

GLOSSARY

exposure by minute description The process of listing every available detail about something or someone in one place in such a way that the whole reveals more than the sum of the parts taken separately.

information The symbolic means by which one mind influences another mind.

information agent The party or parties who are capable of deliberate action and engage in information activities.

information handling The acquiring, processing, storing, disseminating, using, and when received living with of information.

information technology Machines, methods, and skills used to manipulate, store, and move information.

intellectual property Information—a set of symbols—or the know-how for producing it created by the addition of human labor and serving as the externalization of a person's ideas and purposes; usually considered a right.

THE ETHICS OF INFORMATION MANAGEMENT deals with the decisions people make and the norms a society institutes concerning how information will be handled. Information, in its most general form, is the symbolic means by which one mind influences another mind. It takes many familiar forms: reports, books, articles, speeches, radio or TV broadcasts, films, computer databases, statistical displays, Internet home pages, and the like. In modern society, however, it is sometimes difficult to distinguish the information itself from the technologies that process and carry it. Although they are closely related, it is important that the distinction be drawn. Information consists of abstract symbols. Technology consists of machines, methods, and skills for manipulating, storing, and moving these symbols. Examples include paper and quill, the printing press, radio, motion pictures, television, telecommunications, computers, and the Internet. Both information and its enabling technologies confront people with concrete, practical ethical issues. The parties who must resolve these issues are called "information agents" in this article.

In our information society increasingly large numbers of people are spending most of their time handling information. Sometime around 1950, the United States reached a position in which a larger portion of people were employed in information-based occupations than were employed in services, industry, and agriculture. As a result, the handling of information now supersedes the physical manipulation of goods and materials, in-person service, and interpersonal exchange as the prime driver of the economy. This increased centrality of information in our society has been enabled by a vast array of innovations in information technology. Each innovation adds to the amount, speed, and character of the information moving in society, expanding the field of ethical impact and thereby increasing the potential for both good and bad outcomes. The affects are felt at all levels: systemic or societal, organizational, professional, and individual.

Embedding a new technology in a social system can have far-reaching effects due to the ways it disrupts an ongoing society. Jobs and social relationships are changed; problems of security arise. Some of these direct effects of introducing technology into society are discussed in other entries. The more profound effects of introducing a new technology, however, result from the greatly expanded set of information handling activities it affords and the decisions it requires the information agents in society to make.

I. INFORMATION HANDLING ACTIVITIES

A. Acquiring Information

Information handling can be described in terms of six fundamental, though closely related and sometimes overlapping, information activities. All information handling begins with the activity of observing, collecting, or otherwise acquiring information. Information agents face two essential moral questions at this stage: Should this information be collected? If so, by what means? For example, collecting information that invades the privacy of an individual without informed consent is generally considered to be unethical, as is the use of secret, remote electronic surveillance techniques. These questions run deep in an information society because so many people are motivated to take advantage of the abundance of information that is potentially available to them for pursuing their self-interests, and they also desire to use the many economical and effective technologies that are accessible to them.

B. Processing Information

Once acquired, information can be manipulated and compared and inferences drawn from it. The ethical vulnerability created by this processing of information is often undervalued. Pieces of information which taken separately may be inoffensive can, when brought together,

uncover patterns which can compromise people or reveal things about them they do not want others to know. Governments, detectives, and intelligence agencies understand well the power of data manipulation and of exposure by minute description—literally, listing every available detail about something or someone in one place. As Aleksander Solzhenitsyn observes, in a government's dossiers the "answer of just one person to one question in one form" creates a thread which can be linked to hundreds or even millions of other threads and used to create a web that serves to constrain and control that person and others with whom he is associated (1968. *The Cancer Ward* (p. 32), New York: Dial Press.). The moral question here is, should this analysis, comparison, or interpretation be applied to this information?

C. Storing Information

Acquired and processed information can be consumed immediately or it may be stored. One of the most telling attributes of an information society is that it preserves many files and records in either paper or electronic form. Because the cost of storing and retrieving information drops with each technological innovation, there is a strong tendency to continue to add to the existing body of stored information (sometimes misleadingly called "memory" in computer jargon). Historical progress, of course, depends on a society's capacity and willingness to store information from its past and to use it to learn; but, information that is collected in one context or for one purpose and retrieved in another may serve to defeat the moral worthiness of that progress. This means that actions taken to retain information or to destroy it—note the ubiquitous paper shredder in offices—may have pervasive ethical implications. The moral questions are, should this information be preserved or destroyed, and for how long or when?

D. Disseminating Information

The activities of disseminating and using information may coincide but are sufficiently distinct to be considered separately. Inert information, for the most part, possesses only potential ethical value. When it begins to flow, however, it releases that value for either benefit or harm. Rights such as free speech, free press, and academic freedom are predicated on the ethical belief that information generates more positive social value when it flows. Contrary practices such as censorship, secrecy, and confidentiality are based on the belief that some information causes more harm than it does good when it flows. Among the moral questions to be considered concerning the dissemination of information are, should the flow of this information be confined, dammed up? Or, should this information be allowed to flow? If so, to whom, when, and under what conditions?

E. Using Information

The subtle distinction to be made between the dissemination and the use of information is contained in the familiar aphorism, "sticks and stones can break my bones but words will never hurt me." The ethics of information dissemination are based on the belief that words, in and of themselves, if expressed publicly, can either cause harm or, indeed, serve some good. Concerns around the activity of using information takes this belief a step further. It is assumed that by whatever means information is disseminated the very fact that a piece of information serves as a relevant factor in a decision process, one that leads to some form of behavior on the part of an agent, bestows it with moral value. As Marx maintained in a slightly different context, the ethical value of information is revealed by its use. Just as general ethics evaluates an agent's behavior in terms of goodness, rightness, and justice, so information ethics focuses on the role that information plays as a contributing factor to that behavior. Thus, when an agent is in possession of information the questions to be asked are, should I use this information or ignore it? If so, how should I use it? What should I do with it? How can I live with it?

F. Living with Information

Some of the most profound ethical issues are created not by the active use of information but in *not* using it and having to live with that knowledge. For example, say a physician has just completed the many detailed information handling activities needed to complete a genetic test on a newborn child. The tests reveal that the child suffers from Tay-Sachs disease, a condition for which there is no known treatment at this time and which is usually fatal within 3 or 4 years. The great psychological burden brought about by having learned this information cannot be released, unfortunately, through using it directly such as by engaging in surgery or some other treatment (although the information can, of course, figure in the preparations made for the remaining years of the child's life). The physician, the parents, and, perhaps, the child must simply live with this fact and learn to accommodate to it within their ongoing reality. Achieving serenity rather than economic gain is the necessary goal of living with informa-

tion. "Sorrow is knowledge," Byron said, "they who know the most must mourn the deepest o'er the fatal truth."

In an information society the fundamental processes of acquiring, processing, storing, disseminating, and using or living with information assume more importance in the lives of people. Issues in applied ethics stem from the fact that any of these processes, taken either individually or collectively, can serve both to help or to harm people. Undertaking these activities will confront information agents with temptations, confound them with quandaries, require them to conduct some form of self-policing or regulation, and challenge them to criticize the prevailing social system. These are the four general types of challenges agents face when they engage in information handling.

II. FOUR GENERAL TYPES OF ETHICAL CHALLENGES

A. Information Temptations

At a very practical level, an ethical challenge occurs when an agent has access to valuable information or to the processes for handling it and, pursuing his own self-interests, the agent wants to take advantage of the situation; but, he has a moral obligation not to do it (or, indeed, to do something else). This is an information temptation. This ethical challenge abounds in an information society because there is so much information available and so many people are engaged in handling it—and because in our society information garners so much value. It has become, as it were, the new "coin of the realm."

B. Information Quandaries

Equally problematic are situations in which the norms and duties for handling information come into conflict, or for which the available evidence indicates that a given information activity is both morally right and at the same time morally wrong. These are information quandaries. As increasing amounts of information are handled in new and previously unexplored ways, situations occur in which agents must deliberate and struggle to determine their most fundamental ethical beliefs in order to choose a course of action. In some cases there may be no clear moral guidelines.

TABLE I

Ethical Challenges for Information Activities

Information activity	Ethical challenge			
	Temptation	Quandary	Self-regulation	Criticism
Acquiring	Collecting information or using a means of collection an agent knows he should not, but for which the personal gain is so high he does anyway (e.g., invasion of privacy, illegal surveillance)	Deciding whether or not to collect information or to employ a means of surveillance that has both good and bad dimensions to it (e.g., collecting genetic information which could be used for medical diagnosis but also carries a stigma with employers or insurers)	Admonishing, reprimanding, or blowing the whistle on parties who succumb to the temptation to collect prohibited information (e.g., reporting a party who had collected forbidden information to the authorities)	Pointing out flaws, inconsistencies, or inequities in a community's norms and regulations about information collection and suggesting improvements (e.g., writing an article criticizing existing privacy law and working with the U.S. legislature on national privacy protection legislation)
Processing	Knowingly conducting prohibited analysis or comparisons on information for purposes of personal gain (e.g., comparing employees' income from one file with their racial heritage from another legally separate file to conduct a smear campaign)	Deciding whether or not to perform an analysis or comparison, the results of which may have good or bad implications (e.g., comparing peoples' ethnicity with IQ and income knowing that the results can be used for either improving the allocation of social resources or to inflame prejudices)	Stopping a party from conducting an information analysis or comparison activity that violates social norms, or admonishing, reprimanding, or blowing the whistle on parties that do (e.g., inactivating a computer program that does forbidden analysis or complaining to the public that the program exists.	Pointing out flaws and inconsistencies or inequities in a community's norms and regulations about analyzing or comparing information and suggesting improvements (e.g., proposing a new information handling policy for an organization or nation)
Storing	Knowingly keeping information that should be destroyed for purposes of personal gain, or knowingly destroying information because it may implicate the agent in some wrong doing (e.g., keeping a clandestine file on people without their consent in order to control their behavior, or destroying incriminating files prior to an audit)	Decision whether or not to retain information that may have either good or bad implications in the future (e.g., an executive keeping detail files on all of the decisions she made during her tenure, or keeping the results of a genetic screening)	Destroying information that should not have been retained, or admonishing, reprimanding, or blowing the whistle on parties that do (e.g., announcing to the world that an organization has been keeping files and records that are a threat to the social order, or that vital records have been destroyed)	Pointing out flaws and inconsistencies or inequities in a community's norms and regulations for retention and storing information and suggesting improvements (e.g., proposing a new information storage, retention, and retrieval policy for an organization or nation)

C. Information Agents' Responsibility for Self-Policing

Information temptations and quandaries relate specifically to an individual's actions *qua* individual. But, these individuals are also members of a larger social system—a community, an organization, or an entire society—to which they are also responsible. To the extent that information is a principle resource in that social system this responsibility extends beyond their own behavior to include ensuring that all members of the social system engage in ethical information activities; that is, they should work toward creating and maintaining a "good" information society. The ideals from which these social obligations are derived come from two primary sources: the ancient Greeks' notion of "polis" and Hegel's belief that an individual's highest and most complete moral existence is only to be attained as a fully participating member of a social system (i.e., *Sittlichkeit* or ethical substance.) In practical terms, the

TABLE I—*Continued*

Information activity	Ethical challenge			
	Temptation	Quandary	Self-regulation	Criticism
Disseminating	Revealing forbidden information knowingly to others or breaking pledges of confidentiality or secrecy for self-gain (e.g., publicizing confidential information about a political opponent)	Deciding whether or not to release or publish information that could be used for either good or bad purposes (e.g., publishing the results of a controversial study on the relationship between IQ and racial heritage)	Inhibiting a party from revealing forbidden information, or admonishing, reprimanding, or blowing the whistle on parties who do (e.g., censoring publicly offensive information)	Pointing out flaws and inconsistencies or inequities in a community's norms and regulations for retention and storing information and suggesting improvements (e.g., drawing attention to failings in current practices and proposing a new national policy for the freedom of speech)
Using	To knowingly predicate one's decisions or behavior on information gained by an illegal or unethical means for self-gain (e.g., a manufacturer illegally acquires trade secret information about a competitor and uses it to produce a cheaper version of a product)	Possessing information that can be used for either good or evil and having to decide whether or not to use it (e.g., mulling over whether or not to incorporate medical data acquired from slaves and prisoners as corroborating evidence in a larger research study)	Inhibiting a party from using forbidden information, or admonishing, reprimanding, or blowing the whistle on parties who do (e.g., turning in a colleague who falsified research results and used the flawed results to consult with others)	Pointing out flaws and inconsistencies or inequities in a community's norms and regulations for retention and storing information and suggesting improvements (e.g., helping to devise a national information use policy to work in conjunction with land use and other policies)

ideal of a good information society places two additional responsibilities on an individual member. The first is that anytime a member becomes aware that the behavior of another member violates any of the information handling norms the society has instituted, that member has a responsibility to try to stop the deviant behavior and/or to elicit the aid of others in putting a stop to the behavior and punishing the violator. This is the challenge of self-policing or self-regulation.

D. Information Agents' Responsibility for Social Criticism

A second responsibility occurs anytime a member becomes aware of a policy, norm, or other governance mechanism that keeps the social system from achieving its ideal of being a good information society. In this case the member has a responsibility to call public attention to the fault, explain its failings, and suggest improvements. This is the challenge of social criticism. Either of these two responsibilities is justified to the extent that it fixes and puts right deviations from the social ideal.

Table I summarizes the ways that these four ethical challenges manifest themselves during each information handling activity.

III. THE FUNDAMENTAL ETHICAL ISSUES OF AN INFORMATION SOCIETY

A. Information as a Threat to Privacy

Modern information technology makes the acquisition and integration of intimate information about people and their behavior and its storage, processing, dissemination, and use feasible and economical. On the one hand, this information is wanted and needed by decision makers in business, government, and other organizations; on the other hand, some of this information is gathered at the ethical cost of invading individual privacy—the right to control information about one's self and to use it to engage in personal relationships. Sensitive, sometimes quite intimate, information about people is revealed to those who do not have a legitimate need to know it or who are not authorized by the subject party to know it. Members of the society must balance their temptation to acquire this data against their obligation to respect the privacy and autonomy of others.

This ethical issue has led to the adoption of principles of fair information practices based on the concept of informed consent: no personal information should be acquired on a secret basis, an individual should be able to discover what personal information is being kept about him or her, the individual should be able to correct the record, the individual who gives consent for the collection of information for one purpose should be able to prohibit its collection or use for any other purposes, and any party collecting and handling personal information must ensure its accuracy and reliability (see also below), and take reasonable precautions to prevent its misuse. Relevant U.S. legislation includes the Freedom of Information Act of 1966, the Fair Credit Reporting Act of 1970, the Privacy Act of 1974, and the Privacy Protection Act of 1980.

B. Information as Property

Property is something that can be possessed, controlled, or owned while excluding others from these privileges. As John Locke argued in the 17th century, people earn the right to make something their property by virtue of their physical and intellectual labor. It is difficult, however, to exercise this right effectively with intellectual property because of the unique characteristics of information: it consists of symbols; it is intangible and mental; and it is readily reproducible, facilely transmittable, easily sharable, and highly "leakable"—that is, information tends to flow even if one tries to keep it from flowing. One's intellectual property is a source of wealth and value; consequently, other people are motivated, tempted, and, frequently, able to take it without compensating its owner. Members of a society must steward and safeguard their organizations' intellectual property and ensure that their organizations and employees respect the property of others.

This leads to issues such as software piracy, fraud and theft in electronic funds transfers and accounts, and copyright infringements of all types. A related class of issues is program damage such as caused by software viruses, worms, logic bombs, and Trojan horses. Computer security is one response to these threats. Relevant U.S. legislation includes the Copyright Act of 1976, the Electronic Funds Transfer Act of 1980, the Semiconductor Chip Protection Act of 1984, the Computer Fraud and Abuse Act of 1986, and proposed computer virus legislation.

A person's intellectual capability and know-how are also property in the sense used here. Initiatives under the name of artificial intelligence and expert systems— activities undertaken in order to delve into a worker's mind, to capture the principles of his or her reasoning, and to program them into computer systems—may also violate or compromise the property rights of that individual.

C. Accuracy and Reliability of Information

In an information society most people rely on information to make decisions that materially affect their lives and the lives of others. They also depend on computers, communication devices, and other technologies to provide this information. Errors in information can result in bad decisions, personal trauma, and significant harm to other, often innocent, parties. Bias and deception may be even more harmful. Users are entitled to receive information that is accurate, reliable, valid, neutral (unless its bias is carefully specified), and of high quality (at least, adequate for the purposes to which they intend to put it). Meeting this requirement, however, entails a significant opportunity cost. Error-free, high-quality information can be approximated only if substantial resources are allocated to the handling activities by which it is produced. Consequently, information agents must make ethical trade-offs pitting the degree of accuracy they are obligated to provide to meet the legitimate needs of their users against securing other social benefits from alternative allocations of the resources required. In any case, whichever trade-offs are made, a certain minimal, socially acceptable level of accuracy is required of all information and information systems.

D. Burden of Producing Information

The economic and social costs of providing information at any level of accuracy or in any degree of quality is borne, usually, by a limited class of people. Those who benefit from the information are often not the same as those who produced it. For agents, this raises a question of fairness: are the information providers unduly burdened or inadequately compensated for their contributions? At the U.S. governmental level, the Federal Paperwork Reduction Act of 1980, which was passed to relieve citizens of some of the burdens involved in filling out bureaucratic forms, is one response to this problem.

E. Access to Information

As already stated, information is the primary currency of an information society and of information-intensive organizations. Information agents are responsible for its just and equitable allocation. In order to participate effectively in a democratic society people must have access to information concerning things that affect their work and their lives, and, therefore, they must have access to a minimal level of technology for handling information and they must receive an adequate level of general and technological education.

F. Power of Information

Power is the ability to influence or control other individuals or organizations. Its acquisition and use engender responsibility. Information, including the capability to produce and handle it, is a fundamental source of power and, therefore, a generator of responsibility. For example, the principle intent of the strategic and marketing use of information is to enhance the organization's power base. Propaganda, public relations, and advertising share the same intent. Wielding this power, however, may result in considerable help or harm to others. In industry, for instance, capturing vital information sources can result in monopolistic power, which, in a free market economy, raises serious questions for managers and for government as to how this power is to be channeled, allocated, and used responsibly.

G. Technologically Induced Social Change

Technology is generally implemented in order to secure economic and social gains. In the process, however, the flow and the balance of benefits and burdens to the stakeholders in the social system are changed. Some people win; others lose—physically, psychologically, economically, or socially. Resulting from this redistribution of social status is a set of ethical issues that information agents must resolve, such as worker displacement, underemployment or "dumbing down" of jobs, depersonalization, new health hazards, overreliance on technology, spatial reallocation (e.g., telecomputing), technological illiteracy, and the need for education and training.

IV. SUMMARY

The availability of information creates its own demand. Two forces—the continued innovation in information technology which augments society's capacity to handle information and the presence of increasingly strong economic and social incentives for people to use information—collectively serve to exacerbate the ethical issues confronting information agents as outlined in the preceding. In the future, as the increased use of information technology results in more information being made more generally available to more people, the ethics of information management will assume more prominence in our daily lives.

Also See the Following Articles

BROADCAST JOURNALISM • CENSORSHIP • COMPUTER AND INFORMATION ETHICS • CONFIDENTIALITY, GENERAL ISSUES OF • FREEDOM OF THE PRESS IN THE USA • FREEDOM OF SPEECH • MEDIA OWNERSHIP • PRIVACY, GENERAL ISSUES OF • REPUTATION MANAGEMENT BY CORPORATIONS

Bibliography

Johnson, D. G. (1985). *Computer ethics.* Englewood Cliffs, NJ: Prentice-Hall.
Johnson, D. G., & Snapper, J. W. (1985). *Ethical issues in the use of computers.* Belmont, CA: Wadsworth.
Oz, E. (1994). *Ethics for the information age.* Dubuque, IA: Brown.
Mason, R. O., Mason, F. M., & Culnan, M. J. (1995). *Ethics of information management.* Thousand Oaks, CA: Sage.

INFORMED CONSENT

Jonathan D. Moreno,* Arthur L. Caplan,† Paul Root Wolpe†
*SUNY Health Science Center at Brooklyn, †University of Pennsylvania

GLOSSARY

advance directives Instructions given by a patient in anticipation of his or her incapacity concerning wishes for providing or withholding health care during the period of incapacity, including statements about specific interventions or identification of a preferred decision-maker, or both.

authorization The act of signing a form that records consent to an intervention by a health-care professional.

capacity The task-specific ability of an individual to consent to a particular treatment or test, in contrast with the more global concept of competence.

implied consent Inferences about interventions to which it can be assumed a patient consents by the act of presenting to a health-care professional or in a health-care institution for treatment, including routine procedures like taking blood samples, which do not require specific consent.

informed consent The knowledgeable and voluntary agreement by a patient to undergo an intervention by a health-care professional, one that is in accord with the patient's values and preferences.

presumed consent Inferences about likely wishes for intervention by a health-care professional under emergency conditions when consent cannot practically be obtained without endangering the patient's life or limb, consistent with the patient's medical interests, but subsequently revocable by the patient.

therapeutic exception or privilege A traditional and now largely discredited exception to patient consent that allowed physicians wide discretion in withholding medical information from a patient if, in the physician's judgment, that information would be harmful to the patient.

INFORMED CONSENT has become the legal and philosophical cornerstone of physician–patient relationships. Although now deeply embedded in the framework of rights and duties commonly understood to characterize these relationships, especially in the United States, informed consent is relatively recent in its predominance. It is, as well, a conceptual scheme that continues to undergo elaboration and modification due to changes in the nature and economics of health-care delivery and enhanced understanding of obstacles to communicating often complex medical information, as well as other factors. The values underlying informed consent, especially patient self-determination, have also become reference points for identifying acceptable alternatives when a patient lacks capacity to agree to a treatment or test.

In spite of the continuing assessment of the precise implications of informed consent, it has clearly succeeded in replacing historical tendencies to accept physicians' recommendations with little overt resistance, a tradition often pejoratively characterized as "paternalism." The revolution against physician paternalism can partly be ascribed to a number of highly publicized incidents involving the perceived abuse of human subjects of clinical research, and partly to a series of court cases that applied legal rights concerning unconsented touching to physician–patient relationships. Also influencing the rise of informed consent has been the recent explosion of medical knowledge and technology, and the ability of applied biomedical science to affect the human organism within a fair range of predictive accuracy. As the power of medicine has increased, so has the desire for control over its consequences by those directly affected by it. Ironically, the once unquestioned authority of physicians in clinical decision making has declined as their scientifically grounded expertise has grown, to be replaced by patients' and research subjects' insistence on their right to give an informed consent.

Yet, in the context of biomedical ethical analysis, although informed consent gives modern medical ethics its special character, it is by no means the only value that applies to health care decision-making. The patient's interests and societal considerations are among the other values that should often brought to bear in medical decisions.

I. THE LEGAL DOCTRINE OF INFORMED CONSENT

A. Two Legal Standards

The relationship between the legal and philosophical elements of informed consent is a complex one. In the law, a doctrine is a body of legal theory as it applies to a particular subject. Informed consent is a legal doctrine, albeit one with philosophical implications, and one subject to philosophical justification. The philosophical justification for informed consent includes some ideas that are well articulated in the legal doctrine, though of course one cannot be reduced to the other. In general, two legal theories have been applied to the duties of physicians toward their patients. The failure to fulfill a legal duty, whatever the theory upon which that duty is based, constitutes either liability to punishment or an obligation to provide compensation.

According to the theory of battery, the defendent is held liable for any intentional act that results in physical contact for which the plaintiff has not given express or implied permission. Although evil intent and injury are not required for battery, in practice at least one of these conditions must obtain in order for a suit to be worthwhile. The philosophy behind battery or "unconsented touching" is well expressed in a famous statement in a 1914 legal decision (*Schloendorff v. Society of New York Hospitals*) that appears to uphold a right of self-determination:

> Every human being of adult years and sound mind has a right to determine what shall be done with his own body; and a surgeon who performs an operation without his patient's consent commits an assault.

By contrast, under negligence theory the defendent is held liable for a careless action or omission where that defendent had a duty toward the plaintiff and an injury was caused by the carelessness. Negligence, a failure to use due or reasonable care, is the tort of unintentional doing of harm. The standard of reasonable care is that level of care that an ordinary person would regard as appropriate behavior. In professional negligence or malpractice the profession is the group that provides the standards according to which due care is measured. Medical negligence is said to occur when the standard of due care has been violated by a physician, including a failure to appropriately disclose information about a treatment. An action for negligence in informed consent would have to show that a physician breached a duty of due care to inform a patient, that this breach resulted in a financially measurable injury, and that a reasonable person would not have consented.

Negligence is the legal theory of choice in contemporary informed consent liability. Battery is widely viewed as inherently antisocial and not a credible perspective from which to view physician conduct. A minority of commentators, however, contends that battery theory captures the philosophy of self-determination behind informed consent better than does negligence theory. An important issue, for example, is whether the "mere" failure to obtain consent without resulting harm should be recognized as a dignitary injury to bodily integrity and compensated. A battery theory would seem to imply that unconsented touching, even for medical reasons, would be due compensation, while a negligence theory would seem not to require compensation.

B. Standards of Information Disclosure

Several standards have been put forward concerning the content and amount of information that must be disclosed to patients under the law. The professional practice standard requires disclosure according to the customary practices of the professional community under the relevant circumstances. Defenders of this standard argue that only physicians have the expertise to determine what information should and should not be disclosed. Once dominant in the law, the professional practice standard has been criticized for assuming that there is in fact a consensus about disclosure among physicians, for theoretically enabling the withholding of important information from patients if that is what the physician community endorses, and for failing to ensure that the best interests of patients are likely to be advanced by a physician-determined standards of disclosure.

The reasonable-person standard has been urged as more likely to ensure that patient self-determination is respected, and has been adopted by nearly every jurisdiction. According to this standard, information disclosure would be based upon what the "reasonable person" would need to know about the potential harms and benefits of the recommended treatment as well as alternatives. What is material to the disclosure could thus be determined by laypeople rather than physicians. Although adopted in several court cases, critics of this standard argue that it is not in the best interests of patients, that it is too vague to serve as a guide for physicians, and that the idea of a reasonable person is ambiguous.

Some commentators prefer a subjective standard that would require physicians to disclose whatever information is desired by particular patients. Because the goal of informed consent is patient self-determination, it is argued, only a standard that hews closely to what particular patients actually need to know under their specific circumstances can hope to attain this goal. Neither of the other disclosure standards can make such a claim. Opponents contend that physicians would then be legally required to guess what their patients want to know, and that patients could always state later on that at the time they wanted more information than they were given.

These standards and the debate about them are specific to American jurisprudence. Other societies, including those with legal cultures very similar to that in the United States such as the United Kingdom and Canada, would not entertain a subjective standard and do not accept a reasonable person standard, but operate according to the professional practice standard.

C. Legal Exceptions to the Informed Consent Requirement

Courts recognize five exceptions to informed consent: public health emergency, medical emergency, patient incompetence, patient waiver, and therapeutic privilege. However, the last of these, therapeutic privilege, has been drastically narrowed in its applicability in recent years. While at one time physicians were granted substantial authority to determine whether information about the patient's condition should be withheld for the patient's good, it is now generally thought that patient self-determination can be undermined in this manner only if having material information would do serious harm to the patient.

The law recognizes that public health emergencies can justify the suspension of civil liberties, including informed consent and freedom of movement, under specified circumstances for identified populations. The medical emergency exception is quite different: here it is the patient's well-being rather than that of the public that "trumps" informed consent, when a delay in an intervention could mean substantial harm to the patient. If the patient is incapacitated and if it is not believed that he or she would reject the intervention, then the physician's duty to treat rules.

Patient incompetence to give informed consent can be due to many factors. Minors as a class are not viewed as legally competent but individuals may be viewed as such under some state laws if they are emancipated (married or otherwise self-supporting) or if they are seeking reproductive health care. Otherwise, parents or legal guardians must give informed consent to treatment or permission for participation in research. Conversely, all persons who have reached the age of majority are considered competent unless determined to be incompetent due to some impairment. Unless the individual has executed a valid advance directive, such as a living will or durable power-of-attorney for health care, a third party must consent to treatment (except, of course, in emergencies), or permit research participation.

Finally, a patient may waive his or her right to give an informed consent. The waiver itself must be done with understanding of the implications of such an action. The waiver could authorize the treating physician to make the decision but inform the patient, or it could waive information disclosure as well as decision-making. Whether a waiver of informed consent can be legally sound, especially one that involves also a waiver of information disclosure, is uncertain. The ethical argument that a person should not be compelled to learn unwanted information about the details of his or her disease has merit, but is hard to square with the view (implied by the value of self-determination) that one should know what risks might be entailed by that lack of information.

II. THE ELEMENTS OF INFORMED CONSENT IN PHILOSOPHICAL PERSPECTIVE

A. Self-Determination

The legal basis of the doctrine of informed consent is also a philosophical one, that persons have a right to privacy and bodily integrity, and that in general only the person can decide whether to be touched and in what manner. Although there can be disagreement about whether this right is primary or is derived from other, more basic rights, there is no doubt that it is a bulwark of Western liberal political philosophy. When privacy is combined with goal-oriented practices like medical care, it becomes a right of self-determination. In bioethics self-determination is often construed as based on the ethical principle of autonomy, or that moral agents have the capacity for self-government, and that that capacity must be respected.

An analysis in terms of autonomy and self-determination yields a far richer concept of informed consent than one based on privacy, as in the law. The legal doctrine of informed consent based on privacy and bodily integrity can be reduced to two elements: (1) information about the patient's condition and the risks and benefits of a proposed treatment, and (2) the patient's consent to the treatment. These elements cannot be satisfied if the individual is not legally competent to given an informed consent, whether because of membership in a certain group (e.g., minors) or because of a particular disqualifying condition (e.g., severe cognitive disability).

But a philosophical perspective on informed consent goes far beyond these minimal legal requirements because it emphasizes the spirit of the ideal represented in informed consent, that the patient's values are solicited, respected, and advanced in the process of medical decision-making, so that patient-oriented values drive the process. While a document proffered to the patient might satisfy legal requirements in some instances, the informed consent ideal implies at least one personal encounter between the physician and the patient in which each strives to integrate what the other has to offer: the doctor his or her scientific information, technical knowledge, and clinical experience, and the patient his or her fears, concerns, values, and goals.

Some commentators would prefer a more general element that includes self-determination but goes beyond it, to embrace the patient's dignity as well. The National Commission for the Protection of Human Subjects of Biomedical and Behavioral Research (1974–1978) identified "respect for persons" as a basic ethical principle. Respect for persons implies not only that the rights inherent to persons must be honored, such as the capacity for self-determination, but also that persons are entitled to being treated in a dignified manner, whether self-determining or not. Thus, patients who are incompetent should still have their private information closely held, for example. Especially in a society such as ours, which places a high value on self-determination, it is well to be reminded of the respect owed those who are not so situated.

B. Competence and Capacity

Thus the notion of competence, as the initial qualifying condition to give an informed consent, should be subjected to a much closer analysis than is typically the case in the law. Because the ability to perform a certain action, such as making a decision about medical care, is task-specific, the notion of capacity is preferable to the more global notion of competence. In this sense even an individual who is "incompetent" with respect to, say, his or her financial affairs, is not necessarily so incapacitated that he or she cannot make a decision about how much medication can comfortably be tolerated, for example. Even when it has been determined that an individual is incapable of making a particular decision, protestations against continuing even indicated, standard treatment (let alone innovative or investigational therapy), should be taken seriously and weighed carefully against the expected benefits and the amount of time required to manifest them. Alternative approaches should be considered under these circumstances, considering relatively likely benefits to the patient and the inherent cost of forced treatment to the patient's well-being.

C. The Elements of Informed Consent

According to a standard pattern of analysis, the elements of informed consent include information, understanding, consent, and authorization. Patients who are capable of giving informed consent are entitled to information about their condition and about the treatment alternatives, including nontreatment. Included in this disclosure should be an assessment of the potential harms and benefits associated with the alternatives. Risks vary with their likelihood and seriousness. More-serious risks should be disclosed if they occur at least one percent of the time—and some would argue for an even lower threshhold—and less-serious risks if they occur at least 5% of the time. Clearly, no informed consent can be valid if the patient is lacking critical information. Just as clearly, disclosure of the gravity of a patient's condition can be inhumane if conducted in an abrupt and insensitive manner. Also, because respect for the patient's autonomy includes holding information confidential, any effort to enlist the patient's family members or friends for support in the disclosure process can only proceed with the patient's permission to share the information with those the patient has identified as eligible to receive it.

Another element of a valid consent is that the patient understand the information being disclosed. Patient understanding can be facilitated by expressing information in functional rather than in technical medical terms, guided by the practical effects of treatment and rehabilitation on the future of the patient. For example, rather than the technical aspects of cancer chemotherapy, discussion may center on its impact on the patient's quality of life during the therapeutic period. Understanding can also be hampered by any number of factors, from medication to emotional distress. To optimize the patient's comprehension as part of a valid informed consent process it is best that the personal physician initiate a discussion before hospitalization, in his or her own office under relaxed circumstances.

The element of patient consent involves the patient's voluntary and uncoerced choice. Choices may be coerced by obvious pressures exerted by family members or others, however well intended. Voluntariness may also be undermined in less obvious ways, through manipulation or deception. Ideally, a patient's choice is an expression of his or her authentic values, the result of careful deliberation. While coercion and manipulation are unacceptable, patient voluntariness is consistent with a physician's earnest efforts at persuasion that a certain course is in the patient's best interests.

Authorization is required to complete the valid informed-consent process, and can only be administered by the patient (or an appropriately designated surrogate if the patient is incapable). Too often the mere act of signing a form is taken as the informed-consent process itself, and while it is true that in the law a signed form establishes a presumption of informed consent, ethically more must be known about the process that the form is said to record before its significance can be determined.

Many questions can be raised about the idealized, philosophically elaborated conception of informed consent. We will consider some of these questions later in this article. For now it is enough to note that there is precious little empirical information on how well the recommended informed-consent process is carried through in practice.

III. PHYSICIAN–PATIENT RELATIONS BEFORE THE DOCTRINE OF INFORMED CONSENT

Because the assumptions underlying the doctrine of informed consent, and the requirement of informed consent itself, are so familiar, one may fail to appreciate the full significance of the doctrine as a recent innovation in physician–patient relations. Often it is said that the informed-consent requirement represents a "revolution" in that relationship. But talk of revolution may be hyperbolic. After all, consent has been gathering strength for some time, and even now there are significant obstacles to realizing the ideal of informed consent, as we will describe in subsequent sections. Nor is the acceptance of informed-consent doctrine universal, indeed it remains to be embraced even in theory in much of the world.

Still, the modern Western emphasis on informed consent is an important break with medical tradition and its Hippocratic roots. Of the many values articulated in the Hippocratic Oath and other writings attributed to the Hippocratics, none of those critical to informed consent is in evidence. While confidentiality is stressed in the Oath, truth-telling goes unmentioned, as it does in the rest of the Hippocratic corpus, which emphasizes efforts to benefit the patient according to accepted medical standards. The tradition also places great importance upon professional solidarity, all of which gives the impression that expert decision-making for the sake of the patient is the physician's near-sacred province. The doctor–patient relationship was mainly a monologue delivered by the physician for the benefit of the patient.

What is now often derided as a paternalistic medical philosophy in the West was dominant in subsequent eras as well. Patients were to report their condition accurately, along with a thorough history, and were to accept with gratitude the physician's advice. By the nineteenth century advances in the prevention of infectious disease began to force a somewhat different approach, because testing new vaccines involved exposing uninfected individuals to viruses, and the consent of those to be exposed was increasingly thought to be essential. The perceived need for consent in experimental contexts came gradually to influence the conventional treatment setting as well, so that by the 1920s consent to surgical intervention in the United States was often recorded in a written permission form. Like medical experiments, surgery was perceived to be especially risky, and it was undoubtedly the factor of risk that mostly drove early consent practices in both surgery and research. When consent to treatment was recorded in the nineteenth century, it was apparently justified by reference to the benefits that could accrue to the patient by feeling in control of the situation, and not because of an ethic of autonomy.

It is reasonable to assert that the modern legal emphasis on informed consent in the clinical setting is to a large extent a carryover from the scandals and exposés that occurred in the research context, beginning with Nazi experiments on concentration camp inmates during the Holocaust. To be sure, that experiments on otherwise healthy people could not take place without their permission has a self-evident quality that consent to routine beneficial medical care of the sick does not. However, when sufficient weight is placed upon the value of self-determination, as came to be the case in the 1960s and 1970s, then the rationale for informed consent for even therapeutic interventions becomes far more compelling.

IV. THE NUREMBERG CODE AND THE DECLARATION OF HELSINKI

Even though it does not actually use the term informed consent, the Nuremberg Code is perhaps a uniquely important landmark in the legal history of the doctrine. The Code was written by the judges who presided over the Nuremberg Medical Trial, which began in late 1946. Twenty physicians and three Third Reich administrative officials were tried for the unethical exploitation of concentration camp inmates in medical experiments, many of them quite bizarre but some clearly associated with the German war effort, such as studies of hypothermia and exposure to high atmospheric pressures.

In the Trial, the defense argued that there were in fact no well-established international standards for the use of human beings in medical research, and that similar experiments had been conducted by the Allies during World War II. The prosecution countered with the expert testimony of Dr. Andrew Ivy, the American Medical Association's representative at the Trial. With Ivy's guidance, the AMA had adopted several principles on human experimentation late in 1946, just before Ivy left for Germany. At Nuremberg Ivy testified that the defendants were not "motivated by the spirit of the true scientist, namely to seek the truth for the good of humanity." His draft of a memorandum for the judges included language that formed the basis for several principles of the Nuremberg Code.

There is still debate about whether Ivy was factually correct in his assertion that there were internationally recognized rules governing human research. The very recent adoption of the AMA principles itself cast some doubt on this claim, as the defense pointed out. The judges were apparently sufficiently concerned about this question that they saw fit to draft their Code, the first principle of which is that the "voluntary consent" of the subject is "absolutely esential." It is both interesting and ironic that the German Interior Ministry had itself drafted regulations in 1931 that established strict controls over human experimentation, including consent requirements, but these guidelines ("Richtlinien") did not play an important role in the Medical Trial.

Nearly as soon as the Nuremberg Code was promulgated authorities in the world of medical research seem to have recognized its shortcomings as a practical guide. No less a figure than Henry Beecher, a Harvard professor of anesthesiology and a pioneer in research ethics, later commented that the requirement for subject consent "would effectively cripple if not eliminate most research in the field of mental disease." Indeed, any subject population that was incapable of giving voluntary consent, including young children as well as the mentally ill, would therefore be excluded from study.

To address this and other shortcomings of the Nuremberg approach, the World Medical Association (WMA) formally adopted its own code in 1964. Called the Declaration of Helsinki, the WMA code retained a consent requirement but distinguished between therapeutic and nontherapeutic research. The former is defined as offering some potential for therapeutic or diagnostic benefit, while the latter is understood as purely investigational. Unlike nontherapeutic research, within which "informed consent" can never be waived, the Declaration of Helsinki permits considerations of "patient psychology" in deciding whether to offer a consent process to those who stand to benefit from the research, thus condoning the therapeutic privilege as a basis for waiving informed consent. Although such decisions were to be validated by an "independent committee" of review, this position has subjected the WMA's code to severe criticism by those who regard the privilege, even combined with the protection of a review panel, as undermining respect for individual rights.

Whatever the merits of its revision of Nuremberg, the Declaration of Helsinki was surely far more influential in the world of organized medicine than was its predecessor. The AMA, the American Society for Clinical Investigation, and the American Federation for Clinical Research were among the important organizations that either endorsed the Declaration or used it as the basis for their own statements. The same was true of the Food and Drug Administration when it developed its consent requirements.

However, while earlier scholarship has tended to conclude that the Nuremberg Code was virtually without standing in subsequent official developments, in spite of its sentimental and symbolic importance, more recent work has suggested that the picture is somewhat more complicated. For example, in 1953 the United States Department of Defense adopted the Code verbatim as the basis of its policy on the use of human "volunteers" in research on defense against atomic, biological, and chemical weapons. Some of this research included psychological studies of possible panic reactions among soliders deployed during exercises held in close proximity to atomic bomb detonations during the 1950s and early 1960s. A subset of these soldiers who ventured still closer to the blast site signed written consent forms, as was required by the Pentagon policy. Written consent, was, in fact, an addition to the Nuremberg requirements that appeared in the Pentagon policy. This policy continued as part of Defense Department regulations through the mid-1960s, and in at least some cases was entered as a clause in contracts with Pentagon-funded investigators.

V. ORIGINS OF THE TERM "INFORMED CONSENT"

Before the 1950s various terms were used to describe specific permission to be subjected to a medical inter-

vention, whether therapeutic or experimental, including "waiver," "permission," and "consent," or "voluntary consent." It is not clear when "informed consent" entered the lexicon, though the essential legal elements of information disclosure and consent were available since at least the turn of the century.

The first documented use of the term itself occurs in a letter dated November 5, 1947, from the General Manager of the United States Atomic Energy Commission to an AEC contract scientist using radioisotopes supplied by the Commission. The letter set out three general conditions when substances that are known or suspected of being harmful are given to human beings: the potential for patient benefit, written informed consent, and written informed consent of the next of kin. The AEC had legal and public relations concerns that partly motivated these conditions, but their implementation in subsequent years was apparently sporadic. In fact, most of the human research involving AEC-supplied radioisotopes were "tracer" studies, intended to track the course of naturally occurring substances throughout the human body. These were miniscule amounts of radiation that could do no discernible damage but would also be too small to have any therapeutic potential. Hence, even the AEC's requirement for patient benefit could not be met, let alone the informed-consent provisions. Nevertheless, and even though the term does not appear again for another decade, the AEC letter is evidence that the outlines of the later fully fleshed out concept were beginning to emerge around the time of the Nuremberg medical trial.

The AEC letter was apparently the result of careful drafting that involved the agency's legal counsel. That the term was of legal origin is important as one considers the next documented use of informed consent, in the landmark legal case of *Salgo v. Leland Stanford Jr. University Board of Trustees* (1957). Martin Salgo was permanently paralyzed following a translumbar aortography, a diagnostic procedure. Salgo argued that the physicians failed in their duty to disclose risks needed to give consent. In its decision for the plaintiff, the court found that the already recognized duty to obtain consent to treatment, following a disclosure of its nature and consequences, implied also that all factors relevant to a decision must be disclosed. The Salgo decision thus concluded that a true consent must be fully informed by disclosing the risks and benefits of the recommended treatment and of alternative treatments, as well. The decision appeared to draw from both negligence and battery theories in extending the reach of the requirements of patient self-determination.

But just as the AEC did not seem to exercise strenuous efforts to enforce the requirements set out in the 1947 letter among its researchers, the Salgo court left it up to physician discretion to determine how to implement fully the new informed consent. This unresolved question has continued to characterize tensions about the practical significance of the legal doctrine of informed consent.

A related question is when and how informed consent came to be seen as a decision that should be committed to writing, preferably by the patient or subject. As noted, there were various permission and release forms for surgery and some research prior to the 1960s that were to be signed by the patient or next of kin, and the Pentagon's 1953 policy specified written consent. When the National Institutes of Health Clinical Center opened its doors in 1953, the research hospital in Betheda, Maryland, required written consent of its own personnel who were recruited as "normal subjects" of research, and shortly thereafter of all such subjects. By the mid-1960s consent forms for invasive or risky therapy and virtually all research that entailed some risk seemed to be well-established bureaucratic requirements, intended mainly as legal records but also as reminders to physicians and other health care professionals about the need to obtain an informed consent.

VI. ADVANCE DIRECTIVES AND VARIATIONS ON INFORMED CONSENT FOR INCAPACITATED PATIENTS

The legal and ethical embrace of informed consent and the philosophy of patient self-determination has gone well beyond the paradigmatic decisionally capable patient. It has extended to individuals who are able to express their treatment preferences but are not asked about every single intervention (hospital patients), temporarily unable to express their treatment preferences (many emergency room patients), those who are chronically unable to express their treatment preferences (the incapacitated), and even to those who have never been in a position to develop preferences (the very young and the severely cognitively impaired). In other words, the doctrine has become the basis for understanding physician–patient relations in general, but not always in ways that are clear or persuasive.

Not all medical interventions for hospitalized patients are thought to require specific consent. Less invasive and routine procedures, such as venipuncture (drawing blood) are considered covered under the vari-

ation on informed consent known as "implied consent," the rationale being that one who is hospitalized has given implicit permission to be subject to certain routine and nonrisky procedures.

Patients who are temporarily incapacitated but require immediate medical care are, of course, common in the emergency room. In that setting their consent to indicated treatment is "presumed" until they regain their decisional capacity, at which time they may elect to have treatment cease. But incapacitated emergency room patients are not considered to have lost their right of self-determination. Thus, if it is known that they have previously indicated a wish not to undergo cardiopulmonary resuscitation following a myocardial infarction (a "heart attack"), for example, then in theory that directive should be respected.

The 1976 case of Karen Ann Quinlan in New Jersey has become a cultural milestone as well as an important incident in the history of the informed consent doctrine. For although Quinlan was herself in a "persistent vegetative state" and unable to decide about her life-sustaining treatment (specifically the artificial respiratory support that was ultimately withdrawn), the court relied on the idea of the competent patient's right to make medical decisions in finding that one does not lose this right when one is no longer competent. Specifically, it is the individual's constitutionally guaranteed right to privacy that, although not absolute, should prevail absent a compelling state interest to the contrary, according to the Quinlan court. Because the court could find no compelling state interest in this case, Quinlan's right to privacy, as represented in tests of what she would have wanted done under the circumstances, prevailed.

The Quinlan case helped establish the legal priority of "advance directives," statements made by persons in advance of their lack of decisional capacity that are to guide decisions about their treatment. These directives enable a "substituted judgment" concerning the patient's wishes. Advance directives may be either oral or written, but different legal jurisdictions may establish standards of evidence of prior wishes that effectively require them to be written, and of a certain degree of specificity. Thus, the underlying philosophy of informed consent, involving elements such as self-determination and privacy, is arguably preserved.

Many will find that the above circumstances permit a plausible interpretation of the doctrine of informed consent in spite of the absence of an informed and/or consenting patient. Of more difficulty for the doctrine are circumstances in which there is either no reliable information about the incapacitiated patient's prior wishes, or in which the patient is someone who has never even had the opportunity to formulate such personal values. Examples of the latter are the very young and those who have been profoundly cognitively impaired since they were very young. Both courts and bioethical commentators have been divided about how precisely to treat such cases in a fashion that preserves the philosophy behind informed consent. Standards such as the "reasonable person" or the "best interests of the person" have been suggested. These implications of these standards are not always easy to distinguish, do not always generate agreement, and in any case are not conceptually related to self-determination and privacy.

It is doubtful how far beyond some paradigmatic physician–patient relationship the doctrine of informed consent can reach, a relationship in which the capable patient enjoys full disclosure and has the opportunity to act on that information. Even within this relatively limited category there are reasons to be concerned about how informed consent is to be implemented.

VII. OBSTACLES, REFORMS, AND NEW CHALLENGES

A. Cultural and Social Obstacles to Informed Consent

Among the difficulties in achieving the ideal of informed consent are the fundamental problems of communicating technical and value-laden information, particularly to people who are in distress. Physicians are trained in science and are comfortable thinking in terms of probability; many laypeople, especially the poorly educated, do not think in statistical terms and therefore have trouble evaluating what a phrase such as "a 10% chance of complications" might mean. Physicians also tend to present options in purely medical terms, and neglect how different courses of action might effect a patient's life-style or interpersonal relationships. Confronted with a difficult medical decision, lacking a frame of reference for technical differences, uninformed of the nonmedical implications of various courses of action, and intimidated by the prestige and technological sophistication of modern medicine, the majority of patients defer to the physician and accept whatever course of action the physician recommends.

In a pluralistic society such as the United States, the process of informing patients and obtaining consent may be further undermined when different languages, racial and ethnic assumptions, class perspectives, or strategies of decision-making mediate the interaction. Racial and ethnic subcultures often do not share the assumptions, disease definitions, or values of the majority of physicians in the United States. In addition, many minorities view the health-care system with suspicion, if not hostility, and may see malevolent intent behind physician recommendations. Others may baffle physicians by their decision-making processes; many Hmong Vietnamese, for example, defer to a community elder when making important medical decisions, or at least seek the elder's approval. Medical training has not traditionally accommodated cultural and class differences very well, and so provides the physician with few tools to avoid misunderstandings and false impressions.

B. Practical Obstacles to Informed Consent

In spite of the difficulties of applying the philosophy underlying informed consent to the kinds of circumstances above, there is no serious disagreement with the very general view that consent to medical treatment must be obtained from capable patients. Surveys consistently demonstrate a wish among the overwhelming number of patients to be given information and control concerning their medical care. What is at issue (apart from the nature of decisional capacity itself), is exactly what the content and extent of the informed consent interaction should be. For example, it is a commonplace that patient understanding of the details of medical treatment is severely limited. Although limited patient understanding can be attributed to poor communication skills on behalf of physicians, a still more serious obstacle is the fact that neither health insurance arrangements nor the always busy and sometimes chaotic hospital routine lend themselves to the labor-intensive interactions required for these sensitive and sometimes complex communications to achieve their goals.

The combination of legal and administrative requirements for informed consent along with obstacles that can actualize valid informed consent interactions provide ample opportunity for cynicism among those with responsibility for patients. At the very least, there is little doubt that, as a matter of routine, the act of signing a form has come to substitute for the comprehensive process of information disclosure and deliberative choice envisioned in the philosophy underlying informed consent.

Suggestions for reform of the informed-consent process have concentrated on varying the standards of information disclosure depending on the seriousness of the risks associated with the medical intervention. More routine and less potentially harmful procedures would be preceded by a less detailed information disclosure than those that present greater risks. The information would focus on more common and serious problems associated with the proposed treatment. In every case, however, the patient would have the opportunity—or might even be prompted—to ask for more details than had been volunteered. While this proposal probably squares with the reality of many physician–patient encounters, there is no consensus among ethicists about its acceptability. Some would also place a greater responsibility upon the patient than is now the case to be clear about what his or her desires are concerning treatment outcomes, in order to come to a truly collaborative conclusion about the best option.

C. Informed Consent in a Managed Care System: A New Challenge

"Managed" health-care financing systems are an increasingly important part of the health-care insurance marketplace and of efforts to contain the costs of health care. Unlike traditional "fee-for-service" arrangements, which usually pay a portion of whatever a physician or hospital charged (within limits often defined as usual, customary, and reasonable), managed care takes an active role in modifying the way treatment is delivered. Based on consistent evidence that fee-for-service encourages, or fails to discourage, unneccessary testing and treatment, managed-care organizations attempt to modify the behavior of health-care providers through a mix of incentives and disincentives. One of these is per capita prepayment, through which the insurer pays the physician a fixed amount of money per patient each year, out of which fees for testing and referrals to specialists must be paid.

From the standpoint of informed consent, one potential hazard of managed health care would be any disincentive to disclose medical interventions that are not among the plan's "covered services." Fee-for-service arrangements did not present this problem, as any alternative believed to be medically suitable could be covered, even if not the one recommended by the physician. But at least some managed-care organizations have attempted to impose explicit prohibitions on physicians' communicating noncovered alternatives to patients. Of course, even without such "gag rules," providing information about medical options does not imply that an insurer must or will pay for anything that cannot be considered medically necessary.

VIII. INFORMED CONSENT IN CLINICAL RESEARCH

A. A History of Tragedy and Scandal

While legal cases have proven to be landmarks in establishing the legal doctrine of informed consent in the clinical setting, several highly publicized incidents in human research have had much the same function in calling attention to informed consent in medical studies. One result is that informed-consent requirements are far more highly specified and more rigorously enforced in research, reflecting an underlying philosophical view that, when human beings are to be used as means to advance science, special precautions must be taken. These precautions include not only ensuring that their informed consent has been obtained, but also that the research methodology is sound, that all preliminary resarch has been done, that the information cannot be obtained in any other way, and that there is a suitable balance between the importance of the information and the risks involved in obtaining it.

During the early 1960s several tragedies and scandals called public attention to issue in human subjects research. Thalidomide was widely prescribed for nausea in pregnant women in western Europe until it was associated with birth defects. Approval for clinical use in the United States was blocked by the Food and Drug Administration for lack of animal data, thus impressing upon Americans the importance of suitable testing of medications. Shortly thereafter it was revealed that severely ill patients at the Brooklyn Jewish Chronic Disease Hospital had been injected with live cancer cells without their knowledge. Also in New York, a distinguished infectious disease researcher was reported as having exposed profoundly disabled youngsters at the Willowbrook State Hospital to hepatitis virus, a disease that was acquired by most of the young patients during their stays.

The most influential of these episodes was the so-called Tuskegee Syphillis Study, actually a United States Public Health Service project conducted from 1932 until its discovery in the early 1970s. More than 400 Black men, many illiterate, were recruited for an ambitious long-term study of the effects of untreated syphillis. They were not told their diagnosis and were not offered the relatively ineffective treatment then available, nor were they offered penicillin when it became available after World War II. Following the study's revelation, a federal commission was appointed to investigate it and report to the nation, quickly followed by another federal panel that proposed regulations governing the use of human subjects. When in 1991 all federal agencies conducting research with human subjects were required to be bound by them, these regulations came to be known as the "Common Rule."

B. Continuing Issues in Informed Consent and Clinical Research

As in informed consent to a recognized clinical intervention, the ability of the subject to understand the proposed treatment is a matter of ongoing concern. Arguably the provision of information and the subject's ability to assess it is even more problematic in research, where the uncertainties about outcomes are precisely at issue and which may therefore involve subtle calculations of potential risks and benefits. At the same time, concerns have been expressed about the adequacy of consent forms in disclosing questions about the research that investigators and IRB members might themselves have had, and about subjects' exaggerated hopes for personal benefit from the research.

Another continuing problem in clinical research is the fact that the clinical investigator often functions in a dual role, as physician and researcher. In this potentially conflicted capacity as a "double agent," the clinician must be concerned both with the medical best interests of the patient and with the integrity and completion of the research project. Considering the researcher's desire to enroll subjects, some have proposed assigning the informed-consent process to a disinterested third party. So long as the same individual who is responsible for the study recruitment and consent process is also responsible for patient care, there will be an inherent conflict of interest that can raise questions about informed consent in clinical research.

Although no recent case stands as an exemplar of unethical research as did Tuskegee, a number of practices revealed in the intervening years have raised alarms about the adequacy of extant protections. Cases have involved populations often regarded as vulnerable to coercion, including the terminally ill, the mentally ill, and military personnel. Yet there has also been a countervailing tendency among some groups who insist that they ought to be permitted to shoulder more risk than the protectionist system for regulating human subjects research has generally allowed, including especially those who are HIV-positive.

A more recent controversy has erupted over the conduct of research in the emergency room, where patients' capacity to consent is often doubtful at best. Some conditions typically found in the E.R., such as the current or recent myocardial infarction, are important objects of study, but patients are commonly in a distressed state and unable to give valid consent to research. Further, often the prevailing therapies are not very effective and the alternative treatments that are being investigated may hold great promise for future patients and even for the research subjects themselves. In this case the challenge is to protect patients from undue risk. In the United States, federal regulations now permit experimental emergency medical treatments without informed consent for life-threatening situations where available treatment is either unproven or unsatisfactory. But the treatment being studied must present a reasonable risk–benefit ratio and must offer information that cannot be obtained in any other way. An independent physician and an institutional review board must also agree that the study meets these conditions. The community must also be made aware of the fact that the study is taking place through the local emergency room.

Also See the Following Articles

ADVANCE DIRECTIVES • DO-NOT-RESUSCITATE DECISIONS • PATERNALISM

Bibliography

Beauchamp, T., & Childress, J. (1995). *Principles of biomedical ethics* (4th ed.) New York: Oxford University Press.

Buchanan, A., & Brock, D. (1989). *Deciding for others.* New York: Cambridge University Press

Caplan, A. (1990). *When medicine went mad.* Totowa, NJ: Humana Press.

Caplan, A. (1998). *Am I my brother's keeper?* Indiana University Press.

Faden, R., & Beauchamp, T. (1986). *A history and theory of informed consent.* New York: Oxford University Press.

Grodin, M., & Glantz (Eds.). (1995). *Children as research subjects.* New York: Oxford University Press.

Jones, J. H. (1981). *Bad blood.* New York: Free Press.

Katz, J. (1986). *The silent world of doctor and patient.* New York: Free Press.

Levine, R. (1986). *Ethics and the regulation of clinical research.* (2nd Ed.). Baltimore: Urban and Schwarzenberg.

Morreim, H. (1991). *Balancing act: The new medical ethics of medicine's new economics.* Dordrecht: Kluwer.

Wear, S. (1993). *Informed consent: Patient autonomy and physician beneficence within clinical medicine.* Dordrecht: Kluwer.

INSANITY, LEGAL CONCEPT OF

Stephen J. Morse
University of Pennsylvania

GLOSSARY

affirmative defense A defense to criminal liability which, if proved, results in the complete acquittal of a defendant even though the prosecution may have proved beyond a reasonable doubt every element contained in the definition of the crime.

element of a crime A definitional criterion of a crime, such as the prohibited conduct and the mental state that must accompany the prohibited conduct, that the prosecution must prove beyond a reasonable doubt to convict a defendant of the offense.

excuse An affirmative defense, such as duress, infancy, or legal insanity, that relieves the defendant of criminal liability because the defendant is not legally responsible for the criminal behavior.

justification An affirmative defense, such as self-defense or defense of property, that relieves the defendant of criminal liability because, in the specific circumstances, conduct that would otherwise be criminal is legally desirable or at least permissible.

mens rea The mental state element, such as purpose or knowledge, that is part of the definition of a criminal offense.

LEGAL INSANITY is a criminal law excuse that entirely relieves a defendant of criminal responsibility for the crime charged. Although all claims of legal insanity must be based in part on a finding that the defendant suffered from a mental abnormality at the time of the crime, whether the abnormality affected the defendant sufficiently to warrant an excuse is a moral, political, and, ultimately, legal question. The criteria for legal insanity vary slightly across jurisdictions and there is some conflict concerning the precise justification for the insanity defense, but virtually all moral and legal theorists agree that the defense is morally necessary because some mentally disordered defendants do not deserve blame and punishment and should be excused. The insanity defense is not raised frequently in the United States or other common law countries. The best estimate, for example, is that it is raised in only about 1% of American felony prosecutions. The defense is thus not of grave practical importance, but its justification exposes the concepts of personhood and morality that guide the criminal law.

I. THE LAW'S CONCEPT
OF THE PERSON

Intentional human conduct, that is, *action,* unlike other phenomena, can be explained by physical causes *and* by reasons for action. Although physical causes explain the movements of galaxies and planets, molecules, infrahuman species, and all the other moving parts of the physical universe, only human action can also be explained by reasons. It makes no sense to ask a bull that gores a matador, "Why did you do that?", but this question makes sense and is vitally important when it is addressed to a person who sticks a knife into the chest of another human being. It makes a great difference to us if the knife-wielder is a surgeon who is cutting with the patient's consent or a person who is enraged at the victim and intends to kill him.

When one asks about human action, "Why did she do that?", two distinct types of answers may therefore be given. The first, the reason-giving explanation, accounts for human behavior as a product of intentions that arise from the desires and beliefs of the agent. The second type of explanation treats human behavior as simply one more bit of the mechanistic phenomena of the universe, subject to the same natural, physical laws that explain all phenomena. According to this mode of explanation, human action is indistinguishable from any other phenomena in the universe, including the movements of bacteria and the winds.

Most of the sciences adopt the second mode of explanation. The social sciences, including the clinical and experimental sciences of behavior, psychiatry and psychology, are uncomfortably wedged between the reason-giving and mechanistic accounts of human conduct. Sometimes they treat actions as purely physical phenomena, sometimes as texts to be interpreted, and sometimes as a combination of the two.

Law, unlike mechanistic explanation or the conflicted stance of the social sciences, views human action as almost entirely reason-governed. The law's concept of a person is a practical reasoning, rule-following being, most of whose legally relevant movements must be understood in terms of beliefs, desires, and intentions. As a system of rules to guide and govern *human* interaction—the legislatures and courts do not decide what rules infrahuman species must follow—the law presupposes that people use legal rules as premises in the practical syllogisms that guide much human action. No "instinct" governs how fast a person drives on the open highway. But among the various explanatory variables, the posted speed limit and the belief in the proba-

bility of paying the consequences for exceeding it surely play a large role in the driver's choice of speed. For the law, then, a person is a practical reasoner. The legal view of the person is not that all people always reason and behave consistently rationally according to some preordained, normative notion of rationality. It is simply that people are creatures who act for and consistently with their reasons for action and are generally capable of minimal rationality according to mostly conventional, socially constructed standards.

II. REASONS, RESPONSIBILITY,
AND EXCUSES

The law's conception of responsibility follows logically from its conception of the person and the nature of law itself. Once again, law is a system of rules that guides and governs human interaction. It tells citizens what they may and may not do, what they must or must not do, and what they are entitled to. Unless human beings were creatures who could understand and follow the rules of their society, the law would be powerless to affect human action. Rule followers must be creatures who are capable of properly using the rules as premises in practical reasoning. It follows that a legally responsible agent is a person who is so capable according to some contingent, normative notion of both rationality itself and how much capability is required. For example, legal responsibility might require the capability of understanding the reason for an applicable rule, as well as the rule's narrow behavior command. These are matters of moral, political, and, ultimately, legal judgment, about which reasonable people can and do differ. There is no uncontroversial definition of rationality or of what kind and how much is required for responsibility. But the debate is about human action—intentional behavior guided by reasons.

Specific legal responsibility criteria exemplify the foregoing analysis. Consider the criminal law and criminal responsibility. Most substantive criminal laws prohibit harmful conduct. Effective criminal law requires that citizens must understand what conduct is prohibited, the nature of their conduct, and the consequences for doing what the law prohibits. Homicide laws, for example, require that citizens understand that unjustifiably killing other human beings is prohibited, what counts as killing conduct, and that the state will inflict pain if the rule is violated. A person incapable of understanding the rule or the nature of her own conduct, including the context in which it is embedded, could not properly use the rule to guide her conduct. For example, a person who delusionally believed that she was about to be killed by another person and kills the other in the mistaken belief that she must do so to save her own life does not rationally understand what she is doing. She of course knows that she is killing a human being and does so intentionally, but the rule against *unjustifiable* homicide will be ineffective because she delusionally believes that her action is justifiable.

The inability properly to follow the rule is what distinguishes the delusional agent from people who are simply mistaken, but who could have followed the rule by exerting more effort, attention, or the like. We believe that the delusional person's failure to understand is not her fault because she lacked the ability to understand in this context. In contrast, the person capable of rational conduct is at fault if she fails to exercise her rationality. In sum, rationality is required for responsibility, and nonculpable irrationality is an excusing condition. Blaming and punishing an irrational agent for violating a rule she was incapable of following is unfair and an ineffective mechanism of social control.

Responsibility also requires that the agent without compulsion or coercion, even if the agent is fully rational, because it is also unfair to hold people accountable for behavior that is wrongly compelled. For example, suppose a gunslinger threatens to kill you unless you kill another innocent person. The balance of evils is not positive: it is one innocent life or another, so the killing would not be justified. But it might be excused because it is compelled. Compulsion involves a wrongful hard choice that a rational, otherwise responsible agent faces. If she yields to the threat, it will not be because she does not understand the legal rule or what she is doing. She knows it is wrong and acts intentionally precisely to avoid the threatened harm. Still, society, acting through its legal rules governing such cases, might decide that some choices are too hard fairly to expect the agent to behave properly and that people will be excused for making the wrong choice. If the hard choice renders the person irrational and incapable of rationality, then there is no need to resort to notions of compulsion to excuse.

Sometimes a person may cause harm although the agent has not acted. For example, suppose that a driver has a totally unforeseeable seizure while driving on a city street, blacks out, and crashes into and kills an innocent pedestrian. In this case, the agent has surely caused the death of the pedestrian, but she has not acted at all. The crash was not intentional conduct rationalized by her desires and beliefs. The driver is temporarily not a human agent when she crashes and the crash is not the product of human agency.

Cases involving no action often cause confusion in the law, because they are sometimes treated as instances of excused action rather than no action at all, and the characterization makes a legal difference. The definitions of all crimes require that the defendant act intentionally, and the prosecution has the burden of proving beyond a reasonable doubt all definitional elements of the crime charged. If an element is lacking, the defendant is simply not guilty of the crime in the first place, rather than guilty but excused. Thus, if the defendant did not act, she is simply not guilty. As we shall see, mental disorder, even severe mental disorder, rarely interferes with a defendant's ability to act.

In sum, an agent is responsible for a particular *action* if she was capable of rationality and acted without compulsion in this context. If she was incapable of rationality or compelled to perform the particular action, she will be excused.

III. MENTAL DISORDER, PRACTICAL REASON, AND THE EXCUSING CONDITIONS

Mental disorders do not turn people into mechanisms. Even the most wildly delusional or hallucinating person retains the ability to act intentionally, to act for reasons. Actions that irrational perceptions and reasons motivate are nonetheless actions and are therefore distinguishable from involuntary bodily movements that neurological disorders or the like produce. Moreover, irrationally motivated actions in themselves are no more compelled than rationally motivated actions. Consider again the delusional self-defender who kills in response to the mistaken belief that she is about to be killed. Human action to save one's life is not a mechanistic, literally irresistible cause of behavior, and irrational beliefs are no more compelling than rational beliefs. The killing is perfectly intentional—the delusional belief provides the precise reason to form the intention to kill. Moreover, the killing is also not compelled simply because the belief is pathologically produced. A nondelusional but unreasonably mistaken self-defender, who feels the same desire to save her own life, would have no excuse for killing. A desire to save one's own life furnishes an excusing condition only in very limited circumstances. There is also nothing wrong with our defender's "will," properly understood as an intentional executory state that translates desires and beliefs into action. The defender's will operated quite effectively to effectuate her desire to live when she believed that she needed to kill to survive. The real reason our delusional self-defender ought to be excused, of course, is that she is nonculpably irrational. This is the excusing condition that distinguishes her from the nondelusional but unreasonably mistaken self-defender.

Some mental abnormalities, so-called "compulsions," may seem naturally to raise the analogy of mechanism and to suggest that action is lacking or that a compulsion excuse should obtain. In these cases, the analogy to a mechanism is flawed, however, and the compulsion theory of excuse is problematic. Consider, for example, a person who suffers from "substance dependence disorder," or, to use the more common term, "addiction." Possessing and using the substance in question is intentional action. The addict desires either the pleasure of intoxication, the avoidance of the pain of withdrawal, or both. The addict believes that using the substance will satisfy the desire and consequently forms the intention to possess and to use the substance. Or consider a person suffering from "pedophilia," recurrent, strong desires for sexual contact with children that produce distress or dysfunction. If the person yields and has sexual contact with a child, this, too, is surely intentional action. Many people think of the intense cravings or desires of "compulsive" states as an "internal" gun to the head. Whether the analogy is sound is controversial, however. Some try to avoid the problem by claiming that "compulsive" desires are irrational, but this move is also controversial, because no convincing theory of the rationality of desires exists. In any case, the "compelled" behavior is surely action.

It is important to recognize, finally, that terms such as "free will" or "choice," which are often used as the apparent criteria for the moral and legal responsibility of people with mental disorders, are really conclusory labels that are placeholders for the genuine criteria. As we have seen, the actions of people with mental disorders are intentional, not mechanisms, and there is nothing "wrong" with their wills, properly understood. There is no philosophical agreement about what free will is in any case, and irrational people do choose their actions, albeit for irrational reasons or because their symptoms place them in a "hard choice" situation. To see clearly why "free will" and choice are not the issue, consider why we do not hold small children fully morally responsible for their deeds. They choose their conduct and their conduct is no more or less caused than the conduct of adults or infrahuman species. We often say that children do not have free will or free choice, but what we really mean is that they are not fully rational.

However one characterizes the psychological and behavioral problems mental disorder produces, all agree that for the most part agents are not responsible for their signs and symptoms of mental disorder and that mental abnormalities can affect the agent's ability properly to follow the law if signs and symptoms affect the agent's practical reasoning.

IV. THE MORAL BASIS OF THE INSANITY DEFENSE

Whether the law should adopt some form of insanity defense is a normative question that is dependent on one's theory of the justification of criminalization and punishment. If one is a pure consequentialist, for example, excusing people who are legally insane would be justified if and only if retaining the excuse maximized the good the criminal justice system seeks to maximize. Suppose it were uncontroversially agreed that the sole goal of criminal justice was to maximize the social goods of safety and security. It would then be an open empirical question whether convicting and punishing people who commit harms for extremely irrational reasons would produce a net increase or decrease in social welfare. On the other hand, if one believes that it is fair to blame and punish only people who are morally culpable, that is, if desert is a necessary justification, then the defense should be retained if some people with mental disorder are not culpable for their criminal conduct.

Our notion of crime and punishment is not concerned solely with harm and its prevention, with the prediction and control of dangerous agents. Crime and punishment imply a nonconsequential concern with blameworthiness or culpability. Criminal punishment is not pain inflicted for therapeutic purposes. In our system, it is at least in part a deserved response to blameworthy wrongdoing by moral agents to whom blame may properly be ascribed. Moral responsibility and blameworthiness in our criminal justice system are necessary preconditions for justifiable blame and punishment. Indeed, for pure retributivists, blame and punishment are justified solely by the offender's moral desert.

The predominant view of the justification of criminal punishment is a mixed model that blends just deserts and consequential concerns. People may be punished only if they deserve it *and* if the net consequences of doing so are positive. Desert is thus a necessary but not a sufficient justification of punishment. But whether one is a mixed theorist or a pure retributivist, desert is necessary. People who are morally blameless should not be convicted and punished. Some theorists consider this requirement of desert an outmoded relic of a prerational, prescientific age, but this is a minority view. Our system clearly requires moral desert, and the dominant view is that this is desirable because people are moral agents and treating ourselves as such enriches our lives and encourages human flourishing.

Consequential arguments can also justify the insanity defense. For example, some believe that irrational agents who do not understand what they are doing or who do not understand the legal rules cannot be deterred by criminal punishment. Therefore, punishment is not justifiable. But this is an empirical question and it cannot be asked independently of other empirical consequences of maintaining the defense. Perhaps deterrence works for even the most irrational agents. Moreover, even if it does not, perhaps the availability of an excuse that can be faked will encourage people without disorders to engage in criminal conduct. Furthermore, insanity defense trials can be very expensive. Even if deterrence does not work with the most irrational agents, social welfare might be increased if the defense were abandoned. In sum, the consequential justification of the insanity defense depends on facts about the world that are at present unknown.

Some people are undeniably and apparently uncontrollably irrational, and on occasion such people may commit harm for extremely irrational reasons. The central question in a system committed to moral blameworthiness as a precondition to just blame and punishment is whether people who commit harms for irrational reasons are always blameworthy. If they are not, then it is the moral and legal duty of a system committed to justice to devise a mechanism to relieve such people from blame and punishment. The account given in Sections I–III of the law's concept of the person, responsibility, and the excusing conditions should suggest that at least some people who act for sufficiently irrational reasons are so irrational or, perhaps, acting under sufficient compulsion that they are not blameworthy and ought to be excused, unless devising a reasonable excuse is impossible. The law is in accord. Despite consistent criticisms of the operation of the insanity defense, almost all American jurisdictions retain some form of the insanity defense because some people with mental disorders that affect their practical reasoning are not morally responsible agents and do not deserve to be blamed and punished.

A popular counterargument to the moral necessity of the insanity defense *accepts* the moral necessity of

blameworthiness as a precondition to punishment, but rests on a philosophical confusion. The argument correctly observes that poverty is a more criminogenic variable than severe mental disorder. Because strongly criminogenic poverty does not undermine responsibility and is therefore not a morally compelled excuse for crime, the argument continues, weakly criminogenic mental disorder *a fortiori* does not undermine responsibility and warrant an excuse. The implicit premise of the argument is that causation is itself a relevant excusing condition, but this premise erroneously confuses causation with excuse. In a world of universal causation or determinism, all events have causes and therefore all behavior would be excused.

The moral argument against the insanity defense tries to evade this reductio ad absurdum by arguing that responsibility is inversely proportional to the strength of causation: as the strength of the causes of behavior increases, responsibility allegedly decreases proportionately. But this evasion fails, because causation is not a matter of degree. All events are fully caused by their jointly sufficient causes, and causation is not an excuse in any case. No coherent moral theory suggests that causation per se excuses. If a delusional person acts in response to a delusional belief, the delusion is surely a strong cause of the action. The action will not be excused because it is caused, but because it is irrational. If blameworthiness is a precondition of blame and punishment, as it is, the counterargument resting on the confusion of causation with excuse does not permit abandonment of the insanity defense.

V. LEGAL INSANITY TESTS

All tests for legal insanity try to identify those agents whose mental disorder has so affected their practical reasoning that an excuse is appropriate. The specific criteria of a test will instantiate the moral and legal theory of excuse the test implicitly adopts. Section II suggests that irrationality and compulsion are the law's generic excusing conditions, but these terms are hardly self-defining. What is meant by irrationality and how irrational must a defendant be to warrant an excuse? Is compulsion necessarily an excusing condition and, if so, how should compulsion be defined and how much compulsion must be present to excuse? For example, a minimalist definition of rationality would require that a defendant must be capable of knowing a moral or legal rule if the agent will be held responsible for violating it. After all, a defendant incapable of knowing a rule cannot fairly be expected to use the rule as a premise in practical reasoning; the defendant is incapable of rationality in this context. Must the defendant also understand the reason behind the rule or be able to empathize with the pain to his victim a breach of the rule might entail? Does rationality require such understanding or empathy? Moral and legal theorists disagree about such matters, and deciding which definition to adopt is a normative choice. Narrower definitions of irrationality will excuse fewer defendants; wider definitions will excuse more. Either result will be just or unjust depending on one's moral theory about the definition and scope of the excusing condition.

All legal insanity tests require that the defendant must suffer from a mental disorder. Simply being irrational when one commits a crime is insufficient. The requirement of mental disorder satisfies important functions. Because we believe that the irrationality symptomatic or mental disorder is neither the sufferer's fault nor mostly under the sufferer's control, the presence of a disorder suggests that the sufferer is genuinely incapable of rationality. Mental abnormality is also an allegedly gross and verifiable, objective indicator that the sufferer is incapable of rationality.

The presence of mental disorder alone at the time of the crime, even severe disorder, is insufficient to warrant a finding of legal insanity. The mental disorder must also produce an excusing condition. Since the middle of the 19th century, when the modern law of legal insanity was first developed, tests have changed in response to social, political, moral, and legal changes. With rare exception, however, all modern tests of legal insanity address rationality or compulsion criteria.

Modern legal insanity tests begin in England in 1843 with the rule in *M'Naghten's Case*. Daniel M'Naghten delusionally believed that the ruling Tory party in Britain was persecuting and intended to murder him. In response, he killed Edward Drummond, secretary to the Tory Prime Minister, Sir Robert Peel, apparently in the mistaken belief that Drummond was Peel. M'Naghten was found "not guilty by reason of insanity," the standard way of expressing a finding of legal insanity. The acquittal so alarmed Queen Victoria and the public that the "Supreme Court" of Great Britain, the Law Lords in the House of Lords, was asked to formulate the rules governing legal insanity. The most important rule adopted was this:

> ... to establish a defense on the ground of insanity, it must be clearly proved that, at the time of the committing of the act, the party accused was labouring under such a defect of reason, from disease of the mind, as not to know the nature

and quality of the act he was doing; or, if he did know it, that he did not know he was doing what was wrong. (M'Naghten's Case, 1843)

Suffering from a disease that affected one's reason was not sufficient. The disease in addition specifically had to prevent the defendant from knowing what he was doing or that what he was doing was wrong.

The test is a limited irrationality test. For example, if mental disease prevented a defendant from knowing that his victim was a person or that shooting a person can kill, then the defendant would not know the nature and quality of his act. Such a defendant would properly be acquitted because he irrationally misconstrued what he was doing. Or, if a defendant did not know that killing was wrong, then he would be acquitted because he did not rationally understand the applicable conduct-guiding rules. People without mental disorders can of course make such mistakes. We believe, however, that they are capable of rationality and are thus responsible for their mistakes. People with severe mental disorders are not believed capable of rationality when mental disorders affect their practical reasoning and thus they deserve to be excused.

M'Naghten makes clear that cognitive problems are the basis for the excuse, but the meaning of the test is neither transparent nor precise. How narrowly should knowledge of the nature and quality of the act be defined? M'Naghten knew, for example, that he was killing a human being. At that narrow level of knowledge, there was no problem. He was delusionally mistaken, however, about his relationship with the intended victim. Neither Peel nor his party was persecuting or intending to kill M'Naghten, but he believed that they were and killed in response. Should the delusional background belief that motivated his criminal conduct be included in his knowledge of "the nature and quality of his act?" Should someone's reason for action be considered a morally and legally relevant feature of their action, or should simple knowledge of what one is doing suffice? Does knowledge that one's act is "wrong" mean moral or legal wrong? For example, suppose a parent kills his or her child because the parent delusionally believes that God wants the parent to sacrifice the child to produce peace on earth. The parent may know that this is legally impermissible, but may also irrationally believe that it is morally justified, because God's will morally trumps positive law. What the examples demonstrate is that even a seemingly defined cognitive test will be subject to interpretation based on one's best moral theory of excusing.

In response to criticism that narrow "knowledge" of

morality or the law was too constraining, some jurisdictions instead adopted the terms "understand" or "appreciate." Although the test remained primarily cognitive, proponents alleged that this change broadened the type of knowledge that responsibility required, but it is not clear what these terms mean in this context. Some claim that responsibility requires the ability to fuse knowledge with feeling, to "really" understand what the law or morality requires. Even if this concept were clear, however, it is problematic because the law does not excuse psychopaths, who apparently lack precisely this heightened sense of knowledge. Despite these problems, many jurisdictions continue to replace knowledge with these broader terms in their insanity tests.

A persistent criticism of *M'Naghten* was that its apparently exclusive focus on cognitive functioning was too narrow. Critics claimed that human psychology cannot be successfully divided as *M'Naghten's* implicit and outmoded "faculty psychology" would suggest. Cognitive functions allegedly cannot be carved out from the entire psychology of the person, which is composed of inextricably interdependent functions. Consequently, the test failed to excuse people who were cognitively intact, but who allegedly could not control themselves. Critics also feared that *M'Naghten's* narrowness prevented mental health experts from testifying about the complete state of the defendant's psyche, thus preventing judges and juries from hearing all the relevant evidence that would permit a reasonable conclusion about legal sanity.

In response to such criticisms, many jurisdictions supplemented *M'Naghten* with a so-called "irresistible impulse," "control," or "volitional" test that was adopted to excuse cognitively intact defendants who were nonetheless unable to control their criminal conduct as a result of mental disorder. The usual interpretation of control tests required the defendant to lose all ability to control criminal conduct before an excuse was warranted.

The control tests, although purportedly an advance on cognitive tests like *M'Naghten*, also received substantial criticism. They, too, tended to be stated in all-or-none terms, thus ignoring that psychopathology and responsibility were both matters of degree. Moreover, impulses could build slowly and inexorably, rather than striking overwhelmingly and without warning. And even the control tests seemed overly mechanical and narrow. The "whole" person could easily be lost.

Two reformist responses tried to address the various criticisms of cognitive and control tests. The first, the "product rule" announced by the U.S. Court of Appeals for the District of Columbia in *Durham v. United States*

(1954), received wide scholarly attention but had little impact on state legislatures or other U.S. Courts of Appeals. Although one state had adopted a similar test since the late 19th century, the test received little discussion until it was adopted by the *Durham* decision.

The product test held that a defendant was not guilty by reason of insanity if "his unlawful conduct was the product of mental disease or defect." Although the test gave experts wide scope to provide judges and juries with a clear picture of a defendant's psyche, it provided no real guidance about responsibility because causation is not itself an excuse and the test provided no criteria for an excusing condition, like irrationality, that mental disorder might produce. After all, we might conclude that a defendant is legally responsible even though mental disorder might be a "but-for" cause of criminal behavior. The central moral and legal issue about responsibility was submerged by disputes about which conditions were mental disorders and whether they were sufficient causes. The product test was unworkable and by 1972 the U.S. Court of Appeals for the District of Columbia abandoned it in favor of the second reformist test, the American Law Institute's *Model Penal Code* (MPC) test, which had already been adopted in many states and in other U.S. Courts of Appeals.

The MPC test for legal insanity is an amalgam of cognitive and control tests that is not stated in all-or-none terms. Under this test, a defendant is not responsible for criminal conduct if at the time of the crime, ". . . as a result of mental disease or defect he lacks substantial capacity either to appreciate the criminality [wrongfulness] of his conduct or to conform his conduct to the requirements of law." (Model Penal Code, Sec. 4.01(1)) The MPC test appeared to satisfy most of the criticisms of existing tests and it was widely influential. On the other hand, empirical research and anecdotal evidence suggested that the test used made little difference in the outcome of insanity trials, and theoretical and practical criticism of the control prong of the test persisted. Nonetheless, many proponents of a control test argued that it was morally required because some cognitively intact defendants simply did not seem able to control themselves. Moreover, some empirical evidence suggests that the general public believes a control test is warranted. Abandoning it might thus cast some doubt on the criminal law's moral legitimacy.

The criticism of the control prong of the MPC test and control tests in general peaked in 1982 when John Hinckley, Jr., was acquitted by reason of insanity for the attempted assassination of President Reagan. Although the jury's precise reason for finding Hinckley legally insane was unclear, widespread dissatisfaction with the verdict led to intense efforts to narrow the defense. In particular, critics claimed that neither theory nor science supported a control test, and both Congress and many state legislatures rushed to reform their insanity laws.

Most jurisdictions that reformed their insanity tests in the wake of the Hinckley verdict adopted some version of the cognitive test. The Federal insanity defense test, adopted by Congress in 1984 and applicable in all federal courts, is representative. It reads as follows:

> It is an affirmative defense to a prosecution under any Federal statute that, at the time of the commission of the acts constituting the offense, the defendant, as the result of severe mental diseaase or defect, was unable to appreciate the nature and quality of the wrongfulness of his acts. (18 United States Code, Sec. 17(a))

Although very much like *M'Naghten,* the test also requires that the necessary disease be severe to avoid the acquittal of people with mental disorders whose rationality was not grossly impaired. Moreover, it adopts the term, "appreciate," one of the allegedly broader criteria within a cognitive test.

Because the insanity defense is an affirmative defense, a state may place the burden of proving legal insanity, of proving that the defendant's conduct met the applicable insanity test, on the defendant. Many jurisdictions nevertheless placed the burden on the prosecution to prove that the defendant was legally sane. After Hinckley, however, large numbers of states and the Federal criminal code shifted the burden of persuasion to the defendant, rendering it more difficult to succeed with the defense. Some empirical evidence suggests that shifting the burden of persuasion in this way had more effect on the outcome of insanity cases than alterations in the test itself.

VI. OBJECTIONS TO THE INSANITY DEFENSE

There are a number of objections to the insanity defense that are frequently raised but appear insubstantial. That is, either they are based on false empirical assumptions and incorrect logic or they prove too much and thus fail to provide objections specific to the insanity defense.

A. The Insanity Defense Produces "Wrong" Verdicts

Unlike many other criteria for criminal liability, the insanity defense tests do not raise strictly factual questions. Rather, the judgment made about the defendant's mental state at the time of the crime is primarily a legal, moral, and social judgment. Drawing the line between guilt and innocence is the task of the fact finder as the moral representative of the community. Except at the extremes, there are rarely determinate answers to such moral questions.

If there is no substantial error in the presentation of the evidence or the instructions to the jury, most insanity verdicts are presumptively reasonable. The question is one of applying community standards in light of legal precedents and there are few determinate, objectively correct, clear cases that reach the jury. The fact finder may be swayed by prejudice, or may willfully refuse to apply the test properly in the rare clear cases, but this is possible with all indeterminate, morally based criteria, and there is no reason to believe it happens disproportionately often in insanity defense cases. Furthermore, even if insanity defense verdicts can be objectively wrong, again there is no reason to believe this occurs disproportionately often with this particular defense.

B. Insanity Defendants "Beat the Rap"

Few defendants "beat the rap" with the insanity defense. There is variation across jurisdictions in the rate of cases that raise the insanity defense, but the best estimate is that the insanity defense is raised in about 1% of federal and state trials, and in most jurisdictions it is rarely successful. In a few jurisdictions the defense does succeed in a substantial number of cases. The reason for the success rate in those jurisdictions is unclear, but even in those jurisdictions most insanity claims fail and the total number of cases is small. The complaint that this defense allows large numbers of criminals to avoid conviction and punishment is simply unfounded. Prosecutors and defense attorneys generally recognize that insanity is a defense of last resort that betokens an otherwise weak defense and that rarely succeeds. Insanity acquittals are far too infrequent to communicate the message that the criminal justice system is "soft" or fails to protect society. It is impossible to measure precisely the symbolic value of these acquittals, but it is also hard to believe that they have much impact on social or individual perceptions. So few insanity pleas succeed that neither aspiring criminals nor society assume that conviction and punishment will be averted by raising the defense.

Most important, defendants properly found not guilty by reason of insanity—and most verdicts of legal insanity or pleas of not guilty by reason of insanity that the prosecutor accepts are presumptively proper—are not beating a rap in any case. They are genuinely not guilty and do not deserve blame and punishment. Indeed, in jurisdictions in which insanity cases are routinely handled by plea agreement rather than by trial, prosecutors readily accept that in some cases in which mental disorder motivates criminal conduct, there is no justification for blame and punishment.

C. The Insanity Defense Deflects Attention from the Needs of Disordered Jail and Prison Inmates

It is improbable that the existence of the insanity defense deflects attention from the condition and the needs of the many disordered persons in jail and prison who do not raise or fail with the defense. Mental health (and other medical) services in jails and prisons are admittedly insufficient to meet the needs of disordered inmates. Nevertheless, it is unimaginable that the neglect of this population stems in whole or in substantial part from the existence of the insanity defense and the attention it receives. Substandard jail and prison conditions exist because society believes that criminals deserve fewer resources than other claimants.

D. The Insanity Defense Is an Historical Accident

Some critics try to demonstrate that the insanity defense is an historical accident and thus does not deserve the veneration it receives. Although historical evidence supports the contrary position, too, the history is irrelevant in determining if the defense is morally necessary and practically workable: only moral and practical counterarguments can defeat moral and practical arguments for the existence of the defense. Past practice is only as strong as the arguments that support it. The place of insanity and its manner of adjudication in the past are not dispositive of what its place *should be* and whether it can be workable today.

E. Insanity Is a Rich Person's Defense

It is often claimed that insanity is a rich person's defense—the Hinckley verdict is a particularly popular example—but this claim proves too much. Wealthier defendants can almost always retain the best attorneys and experts in all types of cases, both civil and criminal. Although this economic reality may be especially disquieting in the criminal justice system, where liberty and stigma are at stake, it is no more problematic in insanity defense trials than in other criminal cases. Abolishing the insanity defense would not abolish the inequities of the criminal justice system admittedly caused by financial inequality. In any case, probably only a few rich defendants raise the insanity defense, and, as noted above, few defendants of any economic status succeed with it. Overall, the better solution is systemic: reasonable attempts must be made to ensure that all defendants receive decent representation. All defendants with a credible claim for the defense must be given a reasonable opportunity to pursue the defense properly by providing them with qualified experts and other necessary resources. If the defense is morally required, however, society must be willing to bear the reasonable costs of its fair adjudication.

F. The Insanity Defense Is Raised Too Infrequently to Be Worth the Trouble

Some argue that the insanity defense is raised too infrequently to be worth the trouble it causes. But other defenses such as duress and necessity are also raised infrequently and are also difficult to "adjudicate." If a defense is morally required then it should be retained, even if only a few defendants quality for it. Because it is unfair to punish those who are legally insane, society should bear the cost of avoiding such injustice.

G. Past Mental States Cannot Be Determined

Critics claim that the insanity defense is unworkable because neither experts nor laypersons can reconstruct the defendant's mental state at the time of the crime; it is too hard to enter the mind of another, especially when considering past events. Consequently, the usual prescription is to consider the defendant's mental disorder only at the time of sentencing. This argument proves too much. If these critics concede, as almost all do, the necessity of proving *mens rea* before punishment may justly be imposed, then their argument against the insanity defense must fail unless assessing past intent, knowledge, and other types of *mens rea* is easier than assessing past irrationality. After all, both *mens rea* and legal insanity refer to past mental states that must be inferred from the defendant's actions, including utterances. Indeed, the substantial irrationality that warrants a finding of not guilty by reason of insanity is probably easier to establish than ordinary *mens rea* because it is, by definition, obvious. Moreover, if sentencing is based in part on desert, then the defendant's responsibility, based on mental state at the time of the crime, must be assessed. Although it is admittedly difficult to determine the mental state of another, it is nevertheless utterly necessary to make moral judgments about the actor. Both the law and lay judgments individuate an actor's culpability according to the mental states that accompany actions. Unless one wishes the law to stop treating persons as persons—as beings deserving of praise and blame—and wishes the law, instead, to treat them as machines that need only be adjusted, criticism of the law's assessment of mental states is misguided.

VII. RELATED DOCTRINES

The three major doctrines that must be distinguished from the insanity defense are "incompetence to stand trial," "diminished capacity," and "guilty but mentally ill" (GBMI).

Incompetence to stand trial refers to whether mental abnormality prevents a defendant from receiving a fair trial. Unlike the insanity defense, which asks a retrospective question about a defendant's mental state at the time of the crime, incompetence to stand trial addresses a defendant's present mental state at the time of trial. Although the tests vary across jurisdictions, virtually all inquire whether a defendant has a rational understanding of the nature of the charges and the proceedings and is able to assist counsel. In a series of decisions, the U.S. Supreme Court has held that trying an incompetent defendant violates due process because doing so undermines the dignity of the proceedings and the accuracy of the outcome.

Because legal insanity and incompetence to stand trial concern a defendant's mental state at different times and address different questions, it is perfectly possible that a defendant might meet just one or both standards. For example, a defendant who was legally insane at the time of the crime may later be competent to stand trial, either because the defendant recovered or because the defendant's particular mental disorder does not affect his trial competence, even if it bars responsibility for the alleged criminal conduct. Similarly, a responsible criminal may be incompetent to stand trial either because the defendant became disordered between the time of the crime and that of the trial or because the particular disorder affects trial competence but not criminal responsibility. The third alternative is also possible: A defendant's persistent mental disorder may render the defendant both legally insane at the time of the crime and incompetent to stand trial. Of course, unless a defendant is ultimately found competent to stand trial, no formal adjudication of legal insanity will occur.

"Diminished capacity" is an imprecise and imprecisely used phrase to cover a congeries of legal doctrines, which have a variety of names. Whatever they are called, however, there are only two types of claims covered by these doctrines. The first may be termed the *"mens rea"* claim. Most crimes require a mental state element as part of their definition. For example, a standard definition of first degree murder is the *premeditated, intentional* killing of another human being. If a defendant kills without premeditation, the defendant cannot be guilty of first degree murder. The *mens rea* claim is simply that evidence of mental abnormality casts doubt on whether a defendant possessed a requisite *mens rea*. To continue the example, a defendant who kills spontaneously in response to a command hallucination does not premeditate and cannot be guilty of first degree murder.

Many, but not all, American jurisdictions permit such claims, but it should be recognized that the *mens rea* claim is not really an excuse. It is a pure "not guilty" claim, based on the absence of a defining element of the crime charged. The defendant in the example might still be guilty of intentional killing, however, but then could try to avoid culpability by raising the genuine excuse of legal insanity.

The second variant of diminished capacity may be termed the "partial responsibility" claim. This is a genuine partial excuse, a defense of "partial legal insanity." The defendant is claiming that although his or her behavior may have satisfied all the definitional elements of the crime charged and he or she is legally sane, as a result of mental abnormality, the defendant is not fully rational and responsible. Neither American nor English criminal law contains a generic partial excuse of this type, but such claims are addressed by various doctrines and at sentencing.

The most common doctrinal expression of "partial responsibility" is found in the law of homicide. A defendant who kills intentionally and would otherwise be guilty of murder may be found guilty instead of the lesser crime of manslaughter if the killing occured while the defendant was not fully rational. The Model Penal Code test for this mitigation, which has been adopted in many American jurisdictions, asks whether the defendant suffered from an "extreme mental or emotional disturbance for which there is reasonable explantion or excuse." (Model Penal Code, Sec. 210.3(1)(b).) The English expression of this doctrine, known as "diminished responsibility," reduces a murder to manslaughter if the defendant suffered from "such abnormality of mind . . . as substantially impaired the mental responsibility." (5 & 6 Eliz. II, ch. II, Sec. 2(1).) Notice that, in principle, these are generic partial responsibility formulas that could be applied to the commission of any crime. Nonetheless, American and English law have limited their application to the law of homicide. In England, the possibility of raising diminished responsibility in response to a murder charge has effectively ended the use of the insanity defense in murder prosecutions, because murder defendants are in general better off being convicted of manslaughter than found not guilty by reason of insanity.

The most frequent application of partial responsibility occurs at sentencing. Mental abnormality is a standard mitigating condition that presentence reports will address and sentencing judges will consider. Defendants who suffer from a mental abnormality routinely claims that they are therefore less responsible and should receive a reduced sentence. In many capital sentencing statutes, mental abnormality is listed specifically as a mitigating factor that must be considered.

"Guilty but mentally ill" is an additional verdict alternative that has been adopted by a substantial minority of American jurisdictions. It does not replace the insanity defense; it is an alternative that a jury may find instead. A defendant is GBMI if the defendant was guilty, mentally disordered, and *not* legally insane. The purpose of this verdict is ostensibly to ensure that responsible but disordered defendants receive better treatment, but the verdict does not guarantee this. Judges can send GBMI defendants to prison and GBMI defendants may even be sentenced to death. If they are sent to hospital for treatment rather than to prison, they must be treated, but when the treatment is complete, GBMI defendants can be returned to prison to complete their sentences. Moreover, defendants simply found "guilty" who suffer from mental disorders are routinely treated in prison or, if the prison is unable to treat them, are transferred to hospitals for treatment. Even without a special verdict, simple humanity and the federal Constitution requires that all prisoners who are ill—whether physically or mentally—must receive minimally adequate treatment. A jury verdict is not the appropriate means to reach diagnoses or to ensure treatment.

If the purpose of GBMI is to ensure punishment of nonresponsible persons, then it is morally objectionable. Societal concerns about releasing dangerous, disordered defendants should not be assuaged by convicting those who do not deserve conviction. Rather, persons who were fundamentally irrational at the time of their crimes should found legally insane and societal safety should be ensured by rational post-acquittal procedures. It makes no sense to sentence an irrational defendant to a term based on culpability when the defendant is not culpable. If the defendant is culpable, a simple guilty verdict is appropriate.

Furthermore, GBMI may encourage jurors who believe a defendant is legally insane but who dislike or distrust the insanity defense to compromise on an improper GBMI verdict. GBMI thus creates the potential of unfair verdicts without yielding dependable benefits, benefits that a rational and humane system could provide without it. Finally, if, as some critics claim, the insanity defense confuses juries, then, *a fortiori,* a combination of the insanity defense and GBMI will prove even more confusing.

VIII. ALTERNATIVES TO THE INSANITY DEFENSE

Some critics concede the moral point that legal recognition of the impact of mental abnormality on rationality and responsibility is important, but believe that this can be accomplished without maintaining a separate defense of legal insanity.

The major alternative to the insanity defense—the "elements" approach—holds that mental disorder is fairly considered if it is used only to disprove the act or mental state elements required by the definition of the offense. It would in effect substitute the *mens rea* claim of diminished capacity, which is not an excuse, for the excuse of legal insanity. A small number of states have adopted this approach. Arguably, however, the elements approach ignores morally relevant effects of mental disorder on behavior and operates unfairly. As a factual matter, mental disorder, even of the extreme variety, rarely negates the requirements of an act and appropriate mental state. People with mental disorders are not automatons. Unlike sleepwalkers or persons acting reflexively who do not act and thus do not meet the act requirement for the crime, disordered persons' acts are intentional even if they are the result of irrational reasons or compulsion. Moreover, virtually all people with mental disorders know, in the strictest sense, what they are doing and intend to do it. A person who kills another because of a delusional belief is aware of killing a human being and does so intentionally. If such a person is to be acquitted, it must be because the person deserves an excuse, not because the state has failed to prove the definitional elements of the crime.

Other doctrines of excuse or justification such as duress, mistake, or self-defense will not help either. These excuses will typically be irrelevant, or, if relevant, will succeed only if acted on reasonably. For instance, the traditional excuse of duress will not be available to a defendant who killed another acting upon a delusional belief because there is no threat by another person. Mistake, too, will typically be irrelevant because the type of mistake produced by mental disorder usually involves the defendant's motive instead of negating *mens rea*. Finally, where the crazy person's belief is relevant, it is, by definition, unreasonable. Moreover, it is not the product of negligence, but rather of apparently uncontrollable, albeit largely unidentified, factors.

In most cases, doctrines other than legal insanity will fail to excuse even the most irrational defendant. Unless the criminal justice system is willing to convict people who lack moral agency, legal insanity must be retained. For example, a person who kills in response to the delusional belief that it is necessary to do so to save one's own life kills intentionally and will not succeed with the defense of self-defense. That person may be guilty only of negligent or reckless homicide, but such a verdict is not responsive to the moral character of the killing. Such a person is not properly viewed as a negligent or reckless killer who should be convicted of a risk-creation type of homicide. Rather, the act is fundamentally irrational and committed by an agent incapable of rationality in the circumstances. Such an agent should be excused. The immorality of convicting such persons of some degree of homicide can be avoided only by an insanity defense and not, as proponents of the elements approach claim, by lesser conviction or punishment.

IX. POST-INSANITY ACQUITTAL PROCEDURES

In all American jurisdictions and in England, a defendant found not guilty by reason of insanity will be committed to a mental hospital for evaluation to determine if he or she still suffers from a mental disorder and is still dangerous to society. Although the standards and procedures for postevaluation commitment to the hospital vary, in general if mental disorder and dangerousness persist, the defendant will be judicially committed to the hospital to ensure the safety of the community and to provide the patient treatment.

The length of post-insanity acquittal commitment terms varies across jurisdictions, but theoretically they may be indefinite. The patient has been acquitted, so there is no principle of proportionality to dictate the length of incarceration as there is when a culpable defendant is convicted. Some jurisdictions recognize the potential unfairness of hospitalizing a patient for longer than the prison term the patient would have served if convicted and have set limits on the ultimate term of commitment, but most have not. In general, post-insanity commitments tend to be of about the same length as the prison term provided for the crime charged.

Post-acquittal commitments must be periodically reviewed, but if at any time the patient recovers so that he or she is no longer suffering from mental disorder or is no longer dangerous, then the patient must be released. After all, if the mental disorder that rendered the patient dangerous justified the commitment, the absence of these criteria deprives the commitment of that justification. Many fear that normality is easy to fake and that mental health professionals are poor predictors of future violence. These fears have merit, but are overwrought. Mistakes can be made and harm can ensue. Legally insane defendants are not culpable, however, and should not remain involuntarily hospitalized when, in our best judgment, hospitalization is no longer necessary. In a free society, we must be willing to take some risks to provide liberty, and the data suggest that the risk in these cases is not high.

Also See the Following Articles

AUTONOMY • HOMICIDE, CRIMINAL VERSUS JUSTIFIABLE • JURY CONDUCT • LEGAL ETHICS, OVERVIEW • MENTAL ILLNESS, CONCEPT OF • PSYCHIATRIC ETHICS

Bibliography

American Law Institute (1985). *Model penal code and commentaries: Part I, secs. 3.01–5.07.* Philadelphia: The American Law Institute.
Fingarette, H., & Hasse, A. (1979). *Mental disabilities and criminal responsibility.* Berkeley: Univ. of California Press.
Goldstein, A. (1967). *The insanity defense.* New Haven, CT: Yale Univ. Press.
M'Naghten's Case, 10 Cl. & F. 200 (H.L. 1843).
Moore, M. (1980). Legal conceptions of mental illness. In B. Brody and H. T. Engelhardt (Eds.), *Mental illness: Law and public policy* (pp. 24–69). Dordrecht: Reidel.
Morris, N. (1982). *Madness and the criminal law.* Chicago: Univ. of Chicago Press.
Morse, S. (1985). Excusing the crazy: The insanity defense reconsidered. *Southern California Law Review,* **58,** 777–836.
Steadman, H., *et al.* (1993). *Before and after Hinckley: Evaluating insanity defense reform.* New York: Guilford.

INTELLIGENCE TESTING

Edward Johnson
University of New Orleans

GLOSSARY

disinformation Information, usually false, that is designed to mislead.

environmentalism The view that ability is primarily determined by conditions of upbringing or other environmental factors.

g The factor of general intelligence, hypothesized by Charles Spearman and other psychometricians.

hereditarianism The view that ability is primarily determined by genetic heritage.

psychometrics The science (or, in some views, pseudoscience) of mental measurement.

scientific racism The deployment of the trappings of science to support racist attitudes.

INTELLIGENCE TESTING refers to the practice and theory of measuring people's performance on various diagnostic instruments (intelligence tests) as a tool for predicting future behavior and life prospects, or as a tool for identifying interventions (such as educational programs). Such determinations are one kind of "psy-

chological assessment," which is a broader notion that includes characteristics (such as personality) distinct from intelligence. Such assessment can be referred to as "mental measurement" (psychometry) or "mental testing," but these phrases are most commonly associated with intelligence (or IQ) testing. In popular parlance, "intelligence" and "IQ" are often interchangeable. This creates an ambiguity, with IQ referring sometimes to a *score* on a test and sometimes to a (single?) *characteristic*, intelligence, which is the (inherent?) cause of the score. British psychometrician Cyril Burt went so far as to claim, albeit implausibly, that the modern sense of "intelligence" is derivative from the technical work of psychologists, though there is little doubt that that work influenced twentieth-century usage.

The history of IQ tests and their interpretation is too complex and controversial to be recounted here except in its broadest outline, which can be conveniently divided into four periods: (1) a prehistory from about 1865 until 1904; (2) a period of emergence and development, from 1905 until after the Second World War; (3) a period of intense social scrutiny from the late 1960s into the early 1980s; and (4) a resurgence of social controversy in the mid-1990s.

I. THE ERA OF EUGENICS

The idea of sorting individuals according to intellectual ability and the idea of eugenics are as old as Plato, who two dozen centuries ago made a case for both in his

Republic, where he supported ability testing and social sorting as a scheme for (utopian) social improvement. Whether the "elitism" of knowledge can be reconciled with the clamor of democracy has been debated ever since.

A. Galton and Social Darwinism

Darwin's cousin, Francis Galton (1822–1911), helped bring numbers to social science, developing statistical methods (correlation and regression) essential to the development of IQ theory. Douglas Lee Eckberg, in *Intelligence and Race: The Origins and Dimensions of the IQ Controversy* (1979), follows others in suggesting that "Galton's development of statistical procedures was done in order to demonstrate the primacy of heredity in human ability." It is clear, in any event, that by 1865 Galton was convinced that outstanding human ability was transmitted through heredity. With Galton's *Hereditary Genius:* (1869), the idea of eugenics was born, although it was not baptized until 1883.

Eugenics can be seen as one aspect of the Social Darwinism which tried to adapt Darwin's ideas about natural selection—announced in *The Origin of Species* (1859)—to apply to society. Although it may be, as some have claimed, that "Darwin himself was not an unequivocal social Darwinist," in discussing the social implications of an evolutionary view of human beings at the end of *The Descent of Man* (1871), Darwin seemed to speak plainly: ". . . as Mr. Galton has remarked, if the prudent avoid marriage, whilst the reckless marry, the inferior members tend to supplant the better members of society. Man, like every other animal, has no doubt advanced to his present high condition through a struggle for existence consequent on his rapid multiplication; and if he is to advance still higher, it is to be feared that he must remain subject to a severe struggle. Otherwise he would sink into indolence, and the more gifted men would not be more successful than the less gifted. Hence our natural rate of increase, though leading to many and obvious evils, must not be greatly diminished by any means. There should be open competition for all men; and the most able should not be prevented by laws or customs from succeeding best and rearing the largest number of offspring."

B. Dysgenics

The goal of eugenics is, at a minimum, to discourage dysgenics, which William Schockley has concisely defined as "retrogressive evolution through disproportionate reproduction of the genetically disadvantage."

The idea is that for society to be well off, those with highly undesirable (and heritable) characteristics should have fewer children (ideally, none) than those more favored. The fear that the lower classes and the "feeble-minded" (often conflated) will outbreed their betters stretches from the nineteenth century, through Supreme Court Justice Oliver Wendell Holmes's worry about "our being swamped with incompetence" (in his notorious majority opinion in the 1927 case, *Buck v. Bell,* legitimizing sterilization of imbeciles), all the way up to the lament in *The Bell Curve* (1994) that "the most efficient way to raise the IQ of a society is for smarter women to have higher birth rates than duller women. Instead, America is going in the opposite direction."

In a 1970 critique of Jensen in the *Bulletin of the Atomic Scientists*—soon reprinted in Ashley Montagu's *Race and IQ* (1975) and in Ned Block's and Gerald Dworkin's indispensable *The IQ Controversy* (1976)— geneticist Richard Lewontin argued that it had been shown "the old story that lower IQ classes out-breed higher IQ classes was the erroneous result of an egregious statistical blunder: They forgot to count women who had no children! In fact, women with low IQs have much bigger families when they have a family, but many fewer of them have families. The result is that the reproductive rate of the highest IQ classes is actually the highest." This argument was reiterated by others, such as Paul Ehrlich and Shirley Feldman in *The Race Bomb: Skin Color, Prejudice, and Intelligence* (1977). Herrnstein and Murray reject the argument, suggesting among other things that comparisons between generations may have been contaminated by the Flynn effect: "James Flynn has by now convinced everyone that IQ scores rise over time, more or less everywhere they are studied, but there remains little agreement about what that means. For those who believe that the increase in scores represents authentic gains in cognitive ability, the dysgenic effects may be largely swamped by overall gains in the general environment. For those who believe that the increases in scores are primarily due to increased test sophistication . . . the Flynn effect is merely a statistical complication." However, Claude Fischer and his colleagues insist that "the historical data are clear and imply that intelligence has been sharply elevated by changing social environments."

C. Sterilization and Immigration

Concern about the comparative reproductive success of different groups seemed to eugenists to imply that the "fit" should have more children and that the "unfit" should have none. And so concern about dysgenics led to the idea of sterilization, voluntary or involuntary. In the United States, in the early decades of the twentieth century, eugenic concerns led, it has been argued, both to *restrictive immigration* policies and to legislatively approved programs of involuntary *sterilization*. (As late as the 1970s, Nobel laureate William Shockley was advocating a program which would pay individuals with below-average IQs to accept voluntary sterilization.)

D. Statistics and Genetics

The work of Galton and his followers, such as Karl Pearson (1857–1936), by the end of the nineteeth century helped set the stage for the emergence of IQ practice and theory, both by encouraging the statistical approach to human life—an important general phenomenon discussed in Gerd Gigerenzer *et al., The Empire of Chance: How Probability Changes Science and Everyday Life* (1989), and Ian Hacking, *The Taming of Chance* (1990)—and by emphasizing the tension of "nature versus nurture," a theme that would long define the debate between *hereditarians* (friends of "nature") and *environmentalists* (advocates of "nurture").

This same period was also the prehistory of genetics. The discoveries of the Austrian monk Gregor Mendel were published, in an obscure local journal, in 1865, but remained unrecognized during the remainder of the century. Only with their "rediscovery" in 1900 does modern genetics begin its period of astonishing development. It is worth remembering that during the eugenic prehistory of the IQ movement, nothing was yet known about the actual mechanism of heredity.

II. THE EPOCH OF PSYCHOMETRICS

A. Binet and the Practice of Testing

Although the term "mental tests" was introduced in 1890, it is generally agreed that the modern intelligence test was born in 1905. In 1904, Alfred Binet (1857–1911) undertook a commission from the French government to discover a means of identifying students unlikely to benefit from ordinary school instruction. He identified questions and actions that most children of a given age could get right, and others which they could not (but older children could). This allowed him to define children's "mental age" as younger, older, or the same as their biological age. Students whose mental age lagged significantly behind their biological age re-

quired special treatment. Binet, with his colleague T. Simon, published the first practical test in 1905.

It is often suggested that it was never part of Binet's idea that the intellectual problems identified by his tests be seen as irremediable limitations on intelligence dictated by a child's heredity. According to this view, Binet himself did not consider intelligence to be immutable, but many of those who followed him did. Other critics, however, view Binet's ideas as less benign. Henry Goddard (1866–1957) translated the Binet-Simon scales into English in 1909. In 1912, the German Wilhelm Stern (1871–1938) suggested dividing mental age by chronological age to produce an "intelligence quotient." In 1916, Lewis Terman (1877–1956) abbreviated this to IQ, and suggested multiplying it by 100, to get rid of decimal points; he also published the Stanford-Binet Intelligence Scale, one of the most influential of all IQ tests. Binet's tests were adapted for British life by Cyril Burt.

With Goddard and Terman and Burt, if not with Binet himself, the goals of testing come into contact with the hereditarian attitudes of the eugenics movement. The two decades between Binet's commission in 1904 and the U.S. Congress's Immigration Restriction Act of 1924 saw the active depolyment of intelligence testing, particularly in the notorious Army Alpha and Beta tests, which proceeded from the distorted examination of soldiers to the astonishing conclusion that the average mental age of the country was 13! Carl Brigham's book, *A Study of American Intelligence* (1923), helped popularize these ideas, although he subsequently recanted. He defended the use of questions about such matters as the name of the Brooklyn National League baseball team: "If the tests used included some mysterious type of situation that was 'typically American', we are indeed fortunate, for this is America, and the purpose of our inquiry is that of obtaining a measure of the character of our immigration. Inability to respond to a 'typically American' situation is obviously an undesirable trait." (He went on to develop the Scholastic Aptitude Test.) According to critics such as Leon Kamin and Stephen Jay Gould, such ideas exerted an influence on the restrictive immigration policy; others (including Richard Herrnstein) have questioned this. It is obviously insufficient to respond to this history by saying, as John C. Loehlin and his colleagues do, in their influential hereditarian study *Race Differences in Intelligence* (1975), that "it is not too difficult to find both good things and bad in the history of the intelligence-testing movement. Kamin, for whatever reasons, has elected to report only the bad."

B. Spearman and the Theory of Intelligence

If 1904 was a significant year for IQ practice, with Binet's commission, it was also a banner year for theory, for it was in that year that Charles Spearman (1863–1945) published his account of *factor analysis,* which was to play a central role in the development of psychometrics. As Hearnshaw says in his biography of Burt: "The time was a momentous one in the history of psychometrics. Binet's original scale had just appeared in Paris; Spearman's factor theory, published in America in 1904, seemed to provide a justification for the concept of intelligence." J. P. Guilford, who later proposed between 120 and 150 factors, said: "No single event in the history of mental testing has proved to be of such momentous importance as Spearman's proposal of his famous two-factor theory." In this theory, Spearman distinguished between a *general factor* of intelligence (known as "g"), necessary for success on all sorts of mental tests, and *specific factors* relevant only to specific kinds of tests. Spearman put emphasis on g, as an actual thing (a kind of "mental energy"), which served to explain the positive correlations among tests.

In the 1930s, Louis L. Thurstone (1887–1955) developed mathematical methods (involving the rotation of factor axes) that permitted him to argue that the general factor was not paramount, but only a second-order phenomenon, growing out of a number of "primary mental abilities," such as verbal comprehension, word fluency, and so on. By thus putting the emphasis on the specific factors, Thurstone in effect argued that intelligence is not a single thing, but many (actually, seven) things.

In Stephen Jay Gould's view, "Thurstone dethroned g not by being right with his alternate system, but by being equally wrong—and thus exposing the methodological errors of the entire enterprise." We can believe with Spearman in a powerful g and weak secondary factors, or we can believe with Thurstone in a number of primary mental abilities and a weak, second-order g. The data are compatible with either interpretation, which suggests to Gould that g should not be thought of as a real thing: "In this perspective, g cannot have any inherent reality, for g emerges in one form of mathematical representation for correlations among tests, and disappears (or at least greatly attenuates) in other forms that are entirely equivalent in amounts of information explained."

Some psychologists have found Gould's analysis persuasive—for example, Howard Gardner, whose theory of "multiple intelligences" (discussed below) can be viewed as an extension, more or less radical, of Thurstone's approach. But the psychometric friends of g have mostly been unmoved by Gould's arguments, content with the second-order g which derives from the positive correlation of axes in Thurstone's scheme. Thus, Nathan Brody, in a 1985 article, observes: "Although it is certainly the case that one can factor analyze a matrix of ability using oblique factor-analytic methods and find a factor solution that does not include a general factor, it should be noted that the obliquely defined factors will themselves be correlated and that tests that load highly on the primary factors will also have substantial loading on the g factor." Jensen makes similar observations. But Gould objects: "Jensen has missed or ignored Thurstone's repeated claim about this indirect form of g: it is generally a weak, secondary effect accounting for a small percentage of total variance among all tests. Jensen's argument requires not merely that g exist, but that it be, quantitatively, the major source of variance."

C. Two Kinds of Environmentalism

Radical critics of IQ testing think Gould has not gone far enough. Thus, Elaine Mensh and Harry Mensh see environmentalists such as Gould as still guilty of taking IQ too seriously: "Instead of taking note of such mundane matters at the dropping of test items that do not produce the desired correlations, Gould offered a mystifying presentation of the debate between . . . Spearman and . . . Thurstone, over the cause of the correlations. . . . So far as understanding mental measurement is concerned, all one actually need know about factor analysis is the role it plays in mystifying this pseudoscience." More generally, they claim that "as a thesis that accepts the claimed racial and class intelligence differentials and advances its own interpretation of the disparities it assumes, environmentalism necessarily sustains the rival hereditarian interpretation of the presupposed differentials." Thus, in their view, "environmentalism also serves as a rationale for the social order."

In the nature-versus-nurture debate, both hereditarians and environmentalists assume that there is such a thing (or things) as intelligence, which can be measured (by IQ tests, or whatever). It is precisely this that the radical critic of IQ testing disputes. In popular usage, "IQ" is ambiguous, referring sometimes to a *score* on a test and sometimes to a *characteristic* (intelligence) of which the score is supposed to be the consequence and sign. Obviously, intelligence (whatever it might be) is quite a different kind of thing from a score.

For the hereditarian, intelligence is largely fixed by genetic heritage, and therefore in a certain sense so is one's score. In the view of the environmentalist, intelligence is significantly open to environmental influence, and therefore one's score can improve, given the right environmental changes (which may or may not be possible in practice).

A low score, for hereditarians, must count straightforwardly as an indication of low intelligence, about which (they assume) little can be done. For the environmentalist, a low score need not indicate low intelligence: some environmental fact may be interfering. And even if not, still there is (they assume) the possibility of improvement through appropriate environmental enrichment. Thus, both environmentalist and hereditarian assume that the score indicates something about the person tested (intelligence), and both may assume that whether the person's intelligence is immutable depends on whether it is, or is not, largely inherited. The latter assumption, however, is both false and unnecessary. Neither hereditarian nor environmentalist need believe (and it is a mistake to believe) that what is inherited cannot be changed by environment, or that what is not inherited must be changeable. Geneticists have repeatedly emphasized this. As Ehrlich and Feldman put the point, "whether the heritability of IQ within a given group in a given environment is .00 or .81, changing the environment can both change the IQ directly and affect the degree of heritability itself."

In sum, both hereditarian and environmentalist take "IQ" to mean intelligence. The environmentalist is trying to account for environmental effects on intelligence. The radical critic, however, does not concede that the IQ score is a valid sign of intelligence. The radical appeals to environmental factors (including such things as politics) as a way of explaining how the score comes into being. The radical denies the correlations—more exactly, refuses to explain the correlations in terms of any facts about the individual. Accordingly, the radical either dismisses the correlations as chance rather than causation (i.e., as really just inexplicable correlations) or accounts for the correlations in terms of external factors (cultural bias, etc.). Thus, a radical position on the correlations of IQ scores is that they are an artifact of the procedures (politics) of test construction. As Evans and Waites point out, in *IQ and Mental Testing: An Unnatural Science and Its Social History* (1981), "the cultural bias [i.e., the radical] and cultural deprivation [i.e., the environmentalist] interpretations cannot easily be disentangled. . . . Although they have profoundly different implications for psychometrics, they can both be classed as environmental interpretations."

III. THE AGE OF ENVIRONMENTALISM

The Second World War opened a period of reconsideration of attitudes about the social status of both "blacks" and women. The enormities of Nazi racial ideology and the genocide of "inferior races" could not help but prompt reflection. More concretely, the war effort had required the utilization of all available manpower and womanpower, in ways that revealed new possibilities of accomplishment and equality. Rosie the Riveter and the desegregation of the army had promised a new world. But after the war, women were expected to return to the kitchen and "blacks" were expected to move to the back of the bus. Out of the tensions created by this state of affairs, the civil rights movement took shape in the 1950s, culminating in the Civil Rights Act of 1964, which, among other things, mandated equal educational opportunity. Half a decade later, when Arthur Jensen's critique of compensatory education appeared, a new round of debate about hereditarian claims was sparked. Now, however, the hereditarian claim was no longer the dominant voice in the debate.

A. Jensen and His Critics

A century after the modern debate about genetic influence on intelligence began, it was reignited by Arthur Jensen's article, "How Much Can We Boost IQ and Scholastic Achievement?" published in the *Harvard Educational Review* in 1969. "Compensatory education has been tried and it apparently has failed," declared Jensen. (Of course, it has not been tried for very long.) On Jensen's account, the undisputed gap between average IQ scores in "white" and "black" populations (100 and 85, respectively) should be understood in terms of heritable average group limitations on intelligence. This article ignited a storm of controversy, and not only among scholars: Jensen became an object of popular vilification.

In the succeeding decades, however, Jensen stood his ground concerning both the significance of racial differences and the propriety of their investigation. In 1972, he noted: "I find myself in agreement with Professor Dwight Ingle, who has said, 'If there are important average differences in genetic potential for intelligence between Negroes and non-Negroes, it may be that one necessary means for Negroes to achieve true equality is biological'. The possible consequences of our failure to seriously study these questions may well be viewed by future generations as our society's greatest injustice to Negro Americans." He expressed resentment at having been cast in the role of villain, "as if ethical behavior were the sole possession of the environmental dogmatists."

Jensen's critics often viewed such remarks, along with his professed commitment to objectivity and individualism, as so much camouflage for racism. What legitimate purpose could be served by an argument that racial discrepancies in IQ are genetically based? Jensen and his supporters answer by appealing to the intrinsic value of truth, as well as to the fact/value gap. Jensen insists that "to fear research on genetic racial differences, or the possible existence of a biological basis for differences in abilities, is, in a sense, to grant the racist's assumption: that if it should be established beyond reasonable doubt that there are biological or genetically conditioned differences in mental abilities among individuals or groups, then we are justified in oppressing or exploiting those who are most limited in genetic endowment." This, he suggests, would be a mistake: "Equality of human rights does not depend upon the proposition that there are no genetically conditioned individual differences or group differences. Equality of rights is a moral axiom: it does not follow from any set of scientific data."

Even among psychometricians, the issue remains controversial. Paul Kline, for example, in his primer *Intelligence: The Psychometric View* (1991), views it as "disingenuous for Jensen to claim that he is interested only in the scientific truth and to ignore the political and social consequences of his work. ... especially since the evidence is not unequivocal." Kline argues that "the only advantage in setting out the different scores on IQ tests of different racial groups is to give ammunition to those who wish to decry them," and he declines to do so.

Other critics dispute the basic assumptions of Jensen's psychometric approach. Stephen Jay Gould applies his arguments against Spearman's *g* to Jensen's position as well. He also argues that Jensen conflates a harmless technical sense of "bias"(a test is biased in the "statistical sense" if the same score has a different meaning for different populations) with the everyday sense of "bias" (a test is biased in the "vernacular sense" if it is unfair or culture-loaded).

Beginning with Richard Lewontin in 1970, some critics have faulted Jensen for confused genetics: "The fundamental error of Jensen's argument is to confuse heritability of a character within a population with heritability of the difference between two populations." But geneticist Theodosius Dobzhansky dissents, in *Genetic Diversity and Human Equality* (1973): "Jensen ... is fully aware of the fact that a heritability estimate for *intra*pop-

ulational variability does not necessarily tell us anything about the magnitude of the genetic component in an *inter*populational difference of means. ... Even if the intrapopulation heritability were 100 percent, the interracial differences could be wholly environmental. Nevertheless Jensen argues, and rightly in my opinion, that it is not valid to attribute the interracial differences in IQ averages to undefinable differences between environments. ... One can only conclude that the degree to which differences in the IQ arrays between races are genetically conditioned is at present an unsolved problem."

By the early 1970s, however, the debate over "Jensenism" was partly supplanted by the debate over the posthumously revealed foibles of Cyril Burt (1883–1971), whom Lewontin has called "perhaps the most influential psychologist of the twentieth century."

B. The Question of Cyril Burt's Data

In 1972, a year after Burt's death, Princeton psychologist Leon Kamin began to reexamine Burt's data, pointing out that many of the precise numbers Burt had reported curiously failed to change over time, even though the sample size increased. This seemed statistically improbable and, combined with the vagueness of Burt's reports, served to cast grave doubt over some of Burt's work. Kamin concluded *The Science and Politics of I.Q.* (1974) cautiously: "The numbers left behind by Professor Burt are simply not worthy of our current scientific attention."

Suspicion became scandal in 1976, when a writer for the London *Sunday Times,* Oliver Gillie, reported that crucial data had been faked by Burt. This conclusion was based partly on his inability to locate some of Burt's alleged co-workers. Finally in 1979, L. S. Hearnshaw's *Cyril Burt, Psychologist*—an authorized biography by a sometime admirer—confirmed the claims of falsification, from an examination of Burt's diaries.

A decade later, an attempt to resuscitate Burt's reputation began in Robert B. Joynson's *The Burt Affair* (1989) and Ronald Fletcher's *Science, Ideology and the Media: The Cyril Burt Scandal* (1991). Even Daniel Seligman's generous 1992 judgment conceded: "While Burt was almost certainly not fabricating data, he seems to have grown more careless in his handling of it. In addition, he was encouraging readers—perhaps deliberately—to think that he was contributing more to the debate on heritability than in fact he was." The thrust of this attempt at rehabilitation has been to make it possible to view Burt as guilty of an old man's carelessness and vanity, rather than of deception and fraud.

Kamin finds Hearnshaw's condemnation insufficiently severe, and laments that "Hearnshaw's biography essentially saves the face of psychometry by probing the individual psychology of Burt." The complexities of the situation forestall simple judgment, however, because Burt's distortions in later life extended to insisting on obviously false claims about the independence of his work in factor analysis from Spearman's influence.

C. The Environmentalist Critique

In 1974, Kamin argued: "There exist no data which should lead a prudent man to accept the hypothesis that I.Q. test scores are in any degree heritable." Even radical critics of IQ testing, such as Brian Evans and Bernard Waites, found the claim extreme, suggesting that "a reasonable man would consider that there is enough evidence to reject Kamin's zero heritability hypothesis, and to conclude that inherited differences have *some* effect on IQ." They suggest that Kamin's "defence of the pure environmentalist hypothesis is essentially a heuristic device, adopted in order to demonstrate the methodological shortcomings of kinship investigations."

Kamin's opinion had not much changed a decade after his original statement. In *Not in Our Genes: Biology, Ideology, and Human Nature* (1984), written by Kamin with Richard Lewontin and Steven Rose, the authors conclude: "The data simply do not allow us to calculate a reasonable estimate of genetic variation for IQ in any population. For all we know, the heritability may be zero. ...." But the degree of heritability does not matter, they argue, since heritability does not entail immutability. Their work is directed primarily against "biological determinism," but they criticize "cultural determinism" as well: "The post-1968 New Left in Britain and the United States has shown a tendency to see human nature as almost infinitely plastic, to deny biology and acknowledge only social construction. The helplessness of childhood, the existential pain of madness, the frailties of old age were all transmuted to mere labels reflecting disparities in power. But this denial of biology is so contrary to actual lived experience that it has rendered people the more ideologically vulnerable to the 'commonsense' appeal of reemerging biological determinism. Indeed ... cultural determinism can be as oppressive in obfuscating real knowledge about the complexity of the world we live in as is biological determinism."

The intercorrelations that have inspired psychometricians since Spearman are seen as artifacts of test construction. The authors emphasize the fact that test items

that result in unwanted discriminations are removed during the process of test construction: "Test items that differentiated boys from girls, for example, were removed, since the tests were not meant to make that distinction; differences between social classes, or between ethnic groups or races, however, have not been massaged away, precisely because it is these differences that the tests are meant to measure." In addition, the decision to treat IQ scores as satisfying a so-called "normal" distribution (the bell curve) is seen as an arbitrary, if not indeed a political, decision. "Biology is not committed to bell-shaped curves."

IV. THE LAST DECADE

A. The Multiplicity of Intelligence

By the mid-1980s, many psychologists were seeking alternatives to "classical" psychometrics. Two of the most prolific and influential were Howard Gardner and Robert Sternberg, who agreed in seeing intelligence as neither single nor immutable. (Herrnstein and Murray call Sternberg a "revisionist" and Gardner a "radical.")

Gardner articulates his "theory of multiple intelligences" in *Frames of Mind* (1985) and subsequent books, such as *Multiple Intelligences: The Theory in Practice* (1993). He believes that it is necessary to go beyond mere criticism of unitary views of intelligence: "we should get away altogether from tests and correlations among tests, and look instead at more naturalistic sources of information about how peoples around the world develop skills important to their way of life." Gardner ends up recognizing seven more or less distinct intelligences: linguistic, logical-mathematical, spatial, musical, bodily-kinesthetic, interpersonal, and intrapersonal.

Gardner's views have been widely influential, especially in the educational community. Critics question, however, whether all his "intelligences" are really intelligence. They also question the claim of relative independence. Sternberg, for example, insists: "Gardner is correct in noting that there are multiple aspects of intelligent mental self-management. The notion that these different aspects are independent, however, is simply wrong. There is overwhelming statistical evidence against this view, and not citing it does not eliminate it. This evidence takes the form of positive correlations among most ability tests: people who do better on one tend to do better on others too."

Sternberg began articulating his own model in *Intelligence, Information Processing and Analogical Reasoning:*

The Componential Analysis of Human Abilities (1977) and has continued the analysis in many subsequent books, such as *Beyond IQ* (1985), *The Triarchic Mind* (1988), and *Successful Intelligence* (1996). The point of an information-processing model is to shed some light on the component processes that make up intelligent activity. Gardner has expressed skepticism about whether it is possible to "envision a decisive test between one information-processing approach and another," in order to choose among competing simulations. Still, he sees "many intriguing points of contact" between his theory and Sternberg's. Sternberg thinks "it is not clear that there has been even a single piece of research that could be interpreted as supporting, or even as testing" Gardner's theory. Their criticisms of each other have a friendly flavor. Sternberg concludes: "Whether we agree with the theory of multiple intelligences or not, it is, I believe, fundamentally important in recognizing the multiple nature of intelligence and that theories of a single ability just do not take into account the complexity of the human mind. In my view, as a theory of single intelligence, IQ fails to do just that."

Although Sternberg does not reject testing or correlations, his views are regarded with ambivalence within the psychometric community. For Paul Kline, "Sternberg has embraced under intelligence almost all human behaviour and has gone well beyond what most people would mean by the term. ... It also appears to be concerned with aspects of motivation and includes, further, social competence." More significantly, Kline argues that component processes amount to "pseudo-empirical psychology" because "the concepts in the main are not empirically supportable but are non-contingent, inevitable notions given the language in which we talk of problem solving and thinking."

It thus remains to be seen whether multiple "intelligences", seen as either independent or only semi-independent, can provide deeper insight into the problem of intelligence than either the conventional psychometric view or the radical environmental view.

B. *The Bell Curve* and Equality

A quarter century after Jensen's article, the publication in 1994 of *The Bell Curve* met with much publicity and considerable hostility. Its basic idea had been articulated by Richard Herrnstein long before. In 1971, he published in the *Atlantic Monthly* an article, "IQ," sympathetic to Jensen. This was expanded into *IQ in the Meritocracy* (1973). In this book, Herrnstein declared: "By removing artificial barriers between classes, society has encouraged the creation of biological barriers. When people can take their natural level in society, the upper classes will, by definition, have greater capacity than the lower."

The Bell Curve develops this idea in ways which managed to anger or annoy most of its readers. *New York Times* columnist Bob Herbert said that "the book is just a genteel way of calling somebody a nigger." Jacqueline Jones called it "hate literature with footnotes." Charles Lane, in the *New York Review of Books*, criticized the use of "tainted sources." Leon Kamin, reviewing for *Scientific American*, judged that "the caliber of the data cited by Herrnstein and Murray is, at many critical points, pathetic—and their citations of those weak data are often inaccurate." John B. Judis, writing for *The New Republic*, complained: "Their arguments are sophisticated only in the sense that they repeatedly acknowledge the obvious objections to them. But then they blithely ignore these objections." Stephen Jay Gould, in the *New Yorker*, complained about their failure to deal seriously with methodological issues: "Nothing in *The Bell Curve* angered me more than the authors' failure to supply any justification for their central claim ... the reality of IQ as a number that measures a real property in the head, the celebrated 'general factor' of intelligence (known as *g*). ... The fact that Herrnstein and Murray barely mention the factor analytic argument ... provides a central indictment and illustration of the [book's] vacuousness."

In fact, the way Herrnstein and Murray handle this matter is characteristic. At the beginning, they mention factor analysis and concede: "The evidence for a general factor in intelligence was pervasive but circumstantial, based on statistical analysis rather than direct observation. Its reality therefore was, and remains, arguable." Later, however, they assert that the conclusion that there is such a thing as a general factor of cognitive ability is "now beyond significant technical dispute." They grant that the "received wisdom in the media is roughly 180 degrees opposite" to this—an opinion they see Gould's *The Mismeasure of Man* as having "cemented". They decline, however, to devote any of their 870 pages to actually answering Gould's critique of *g*. "To prove our case, taking each point and amassing a full account of the evidence for and against, would lead us to write a book just about them. Such books have already been written. There is no point in our trying to duplicate them."

They rest their case on appeal to two books. One is Daniel Seligman's popular survey, *A Question of Intelligence: The IQ Debate in America* (1992), which they call an "accurate and highly readable summary of the major points." Seligman does not pretend to be more than "a journalist." He responds to Gould's book by pointing out that the book with its "wild proposition was reviewed enthusiastically." The only other references to Gould dismiss his account of abuses in brain-size research, and take issue with his claims about the Immigration Restriction Act. None of this constitutes a defense of *g*. All Seligman has to offer on this subject is an appeal to the work of Jensen, and an appeal to the claim that "a substantial majority of psychologists agree with him". To support this latter claim, Seligman cites (as do Herrnstein and Murray) Mark Snyderman and Stanley Rothman's *The IQ Controversy: The Media and Public Policy* (1988), a work emphasizing the contrast between expert opinion and media treatment, based on a questionnaire sent to a large number of scholars.

The other book Herrnstein and Murray point to, as having obviated a need for them to defend their central assumptions about IQ, is Jensen's *Bias in Mental Testing* (1980), which they say "remains an authoritative statement on most of the basic issues despite the passage of time since it was published." This was, of course, the very book against whose defense of *g* Gould's critique was originally directed. It is easy to understand why Gould reacted with anger to this dismissal of his arguments.

The many additional criticisms of *The Bell Curve* have been collected in a number of anthologies. In a book-length treatment, Claude S. Fischer, *et al.*, *Inequality by Design: Cracking the Bell Curve Myth* (1996), a half-dozen members of the Sociology Department of the University of California, Berkeley argue that "intelligence is not single, unitary, and fixed"; that even if it were, intelligence was not well measured by the primary data Herrnstein and Murray utilized; and that, even if those data "were a good measure of intelligence, the socioeconomic status of people's parents and their broader social environment more strongly determine ... who becomes poor."

Even in the view of a conservative critic like Thomas Sowell, *The Bell Curve* fails. In *Knowledge and Decisions* (1980, rev. 1996), Sowell lamented that the "dogmatic conclusions about racial inferiority which reigned supreme among 'experts' in the 1910s and 1920s were replaced with equally dogmatic conclusions about scientific proof of racial equality in the same field by the 1940s and 1950s." In Sowell's view, Jensen appeared as a kind of hero, a challenger of the current dogmatism. But though Sowell praises Herrnstein and Murray for their "candor" and "clarity," he objects that they seem not to grasp how the Flynn effect "undermines the case for a genetic explanation of interracial IQ differences." Other critics have made the same point.

Herrnstein and Murray themselves acknowledge that in the last half-century "national averages have in fact changed by amounts that are comparable to the fifteen or so IQ points separating whites and blacks in America." There is no reason why blacks could not gain, they argue, "but also no reason to believe that white and Asian means can be made to stand still while the Flynn effect works its magic." They thus presuppose that the gap would continue indefinitely, a result that seems unlikely in view of the fact that various immigrant populations at the beginning of the century suffered from a similar IQ gap, but have since achieved parity.

IQ tests have often been praised by their defenders as instruments of egalitarianism. H. J. Butcher, in *Human Intelligence: Its Nature and Assessment* (1968), notes: "Many of the pioneers of psychological testing, such as Godfrey Thomson and Cyril Burt, saw it as a potent means of furthering social equality and of ensuring that able children, whose ability would otherwise have been submerged by poverty and environmental handicaps, should have the opportunity of an education commensurate with their talent." Even severe critics of IQ testing, such as Brian Evans and Bernard Waites, sometimes concede this point: "We should not forget that the mental testing movement had a progressive phase in Britain when, for a time, IQ tests may very well have increased the chances for working-class children to be upwardly socially mobile; but IQ arguments are nowadays employed solely to draw pessimistic conclusions about social mobility, and to oppose egalitarian doctrines."

The same point was urged in *Larry P. v. Wilson Riles*, the 1970s California case, in which the judge declared: "The use of IQ tests which had a disproportionate effect on Black children violated ... the 14th Amendment when used to place children in EMR [educable mentally retarded] classes." In this case, the plaintiffs' claims were supported by testimony from Leon Kamin on the discriminatory history of IQ testing, and also by testimony from Jane Mercer, who had discussed the discriminatory effects of labeling in *Labeling the Mentally Retarded* (1973). In his review of the case, Robert Kaplan notes: "Banning the use of IQ tests opens the door to completely subjective judgments, which may be even more racist than the test results. Opponents of the Larry P. decision cite many instances in which gifted black children were assumed to be average by their teachers but were recognized as highly intelligent because of IQ test scores."

Those who believe that IQ tests genuinely establish significant group differences typically emphasize that these differences do not, need not, and should not determine how *individuals* are treated. Thus, Arthur Jensen ends his treatise, *Bias in Mental Testing* (1980): "Whatever may be the causes of group differences that remain after test bias is eliminated, the practical applications of sound psychometrics can help to reinforce the democratic ideal of treating every person according to the person's *individual* characteristics, rather than according to his or her sex, race, social class, religion, or national origin." A dozen years later, journalist Daniel Seligman ends his account (and defense) of IQ testing, *A Question of Intelligence* (1992), on a similar note: "One major message of the IQ data is that groups are different. A major policy implication of the data, I would argue, is that people should not be treated as members of groups but as individuals." Richard Herrnstein and Charles Murray—who, as we have seen, offer reference to these two books in lieu of an argument for six key assumptions about IQ which they claim are "now beyond significant technical dispute"—reiterate the sentiment: "... group differences in cognitive ability, so desperately denied for so long, can best be handled—can *only* be handled—by a return to individualism. A person should not be judged as a member of a group but as an individual."

Critics regard such assertions as vacuous, if not disingenuous. It may be true that, as Jensen puts it, test scores "never compel", but only "indicate *probabilities* of success." Yet it remains the case that often, as Jensen says further down the same page, "the best predictors ... must be relied upon for the selection of the aspirants who are statistically the most likely to succeed." It is one thing to insist on separating the idea of moral esteem from the idea of intellectual assessment, as Herrnstein and Murray (and others) suggest: "Measures of intelligence have reliable statistical relationships with important social phenomena, but they are a limited tool for deciding what to make of any given individual. . . . This thing we know as IQ is important but not a synonym for human excellence." It is, however, another thing to keep the way individuals are treated from being affected by how they are grouped. In personal relations, it may be possible, it may even make sense, to treat people in ways not determined by ideas about their group memberships. But there is a difficulty when we come to public policy. For the way public policies treat individuals is determined at least to some extent by the groups to which they belong. The obvious way to mitigate the difficulty would be to have flexible policies that allow for appropriate exceptions. But of course that flexibility would also provide room for "special treatment."

Flexibility is a keynote in the concept of "intelligent testing" defended by Alan Kaufman. He argues that bias is not intrinsic to testing, but "may easily be the product of educational decisions made by test users who pay homage to global IQs, perceive these IQs to be immutable reflections of the magical *g* factor, and pay nothing more than lip service to the need for supplementary tests." For Kaufman, IQ tests are valuable when they are viewed as *clinical* tools; and they are necessary. "Children who are referred for evaluation have problems, and we can help solve those problems by interpreting IQ tests intelligently. I've seen so much stupid testing—then and now—and I remain a strong advocate of intelligent testing." We should neither abandon IQ tests, he thinks, nor put up with the many varieties of test misuse: "... test abuse, in the form of deification of the test itself, overvaluation of global IQs, equation of test scores with genetic potential, and interpretation of low IQs as a call to passive placement rather than active intervention, must be squelched. The flaws of intelligence tests need to be understood by all test uses—not to impel examiners to reject the tests or to ignore fluctuations among subscores, but to facilitate a more incisive interpretation of what the scores mean." In Kaufman's view, the failure of most anti-IQ critics is their focus on group tests rather than individual tests, such as the Wechsler Intelligence Scale for Children (WISC-III). Other assessment approaches he sees as supplements, rather than alternatives.

Kaufman's comprehensive, practical, humane approach is very attractive. It assumes, of course, that a variety of difficulties can be overcome—for example, that bureaucrats can be brought to see the error of mandating precise cutoff points; that examiners who lack "research knowledge, theoretical sophistication, and clinical acumen" will understand that they "are not supposed to *give* the WISC-III, much less interpret it"; that society will see that, to be intelligent, intelligence testing must be individualized. Such commitments have absorbed the point of many of the criticisms leveled against IQ testing. But how much of this can realistically be achieved remains in doubt.

There is little question that intelligent flexibility would be a better clinical practice than stupid bureaucratic rigidity. Yet bureaucratic inefficiencies and inequities are likely to persist. In addition, it is worth remembering that not only does flexibility require talent and money, it also has its own temptations. Hearnshaw describes Burt's early work as England's first educational psychologist: "As a practical psychologist Burt felt justified in making commonsense allowances and 'adjustments.' 'I did not take my test results just as they stood,' he writes. 'They were carefully discussed with teachers, and freely corrected whenever it seemed likely that the teacher's view of the relative merits of his own pupils gave a better estimate than the crude test marks.' For the practical psychologist who had to work with teachers this was a sensible procedure; for the future researcher it could only be regarded as scientifically dubious."

A public policy, of course, can seem justified as long as it achieves its overall goals, even if it gets many particular cases wrong. One may not be surprised, therefore, to find Jensen declaring: "Such questions of fairness and unfairness ultimately lead to metaphysical debate and practically defy objective agreement. In the face of metaphysical disagreements we are thrown back on utilitarian considerations that at least are more amenable to objective analysis with the techniques of psychometrics and statistics." In Jensen's view, "concepts of 'fairness' or 'unfairness' belong more to moral philosophy than to psychometrics." And so they do. But that does not mean that the moral questions can be dismissed.

Pediatricians Michael Lewis and Margaret Wolan Sullivan, in their 1985 review of the assessment of IQ scores of infants (!), argue for the radical position: "When science fails to recognize the values associated with the particular scientific effort, scientists fall prey to bias. ... If it is true that all the features inherent in the concept of IQ have sociopolitical aspects, it may not be too strong to suggest that the IQ score up until now has been more of a sociopolitical than a scientific construct." Of course, *too much* focus on the values at stake can also lead to bias. But at least the latter explicitly invites moral argument of a kind that positivism and would-be "value neutrality" mistakenly, and sometimes disingenuously, evade.

In the end, the debate between hereditarians and environmentalists too often boils down to each side accusing the other of having failed to establish its case. Both sides are no doubt right on this point, but little progress can be expected from a struggle over who has the burden of proof.

Evans and Waites, among others, point out that the only falsifiable hypotheses produced by the debate are (1) that *all* variance in IQ is due to heredity, and (2) that *all* variance in IQ is due to environment. But participants on both sides of the issue agree that nobody on *their* side holds the extreme position. Thus, environmentalist Gould contrasts "pure hereditarianism (which Spearman and Burt came close to promulgating) and pure environmentalism (which no major thinker has ever been foolish enough to propose)"—a claim that either ignores Kamin and Lewontin or relies on a nu-

anced reading of "propose." Evans and Waites criticize Jensen for "setting up and then refuting specific environmentalist explanations for black-white differences" that "turn out to be very much men of straw." Hereditarian enthusiast Daniel Seligman asserts: "Scholars arguing for the possibility of a zero heritability (most of them seem to be Marxists) have ... dodged the issue, using up most of their firepower in detailed critiques of studies arguing a case for substantial heritability (and seldom explicitly making an affirmative case of their own for zero).... You cannot find a psychometrician or behavioral geneticist arguing that differences in IQ are explained entirely by genes."

Each side represents its opponent as (almost) defending an extreme and implausible view, and attempts to claim the middle ground for itself. Each side in fact recognizes that both nature and nurture are involved, but insinuates that the other side denies this. For environmentalists, recognition of this mixed reality means a rejection of (extreme) hereditarianism and a triumph for (moderate) environmentalism. For hereditarians, the same facts imply a rejection of (extreme) environmentalism and a triumph for (moderate) hereditarianism.

Thus, Herrnstein and Murray claim that "the genetic component of IQ is unlikely to be smaller than 40 percent or higher than 80 percent" and indifferently "adopt a middling estimate of 60 percent heritability." This casualness is methodologically suspect ("let's split the difference" is hardly a reliable scientific principle), the range discussed is open to debate, and the idea that we know (in a scientific sense) anything about the heritability of intelligence, let alone IQ, has been challenged. But none of this really matters to the authors of *The Bell Curve,* because they see themselves as rejecting the extremes and claiming the middle ground.

The problem persists whether we think that we do not know *exactly* how heritable intelligence is, or think that we do not know it *at all* (as when Lewontin, Rose, and Kamin say that heritability might be 0 or 50%). The problem persists because, though we may not know, we still have to make judgments, settle policies, and so on—in short, *act* on the basis of currently plausible belief. Biologists often point out that the heritability question does not matter, unless we confuse heritability with immutability, and environmental determinability with plasticity. That is true, but does not alter the need to act on the basis of currently plausible belief. It may be that, as geneticists argue, knowing that a trait is 100% heritable will not tell us about what would be the case in some other environment. But that does not mean that no practical, common-sense judgments can or should be made, pending future research.

Hereditarians call for more research to settle the question of group differences and limits on plasticity. Environmentalists call for more research too, albeit of a different kind. Environmentalists argue that we cannot know what is environmentally modifiable until we try. As Evans and Waites put it: "Any new method of teaching introduces a novel element into the environment, and its effect cannot be known until it has been tried."

Although each side welcomes research which supports its view, it sees the other side's appeal to future research as a masked political agenda. Thus Fischer and his Berkeley colleagues note that Thomas Jefferson "dealt with the dissonance [between his egalitarian principles and his slave practice] by suggesting that the question of innate inferiority be left to future scientific observation, a solution remarkably similar to that disingenuously advanced by Herrnstein and Murray." The comparison is perhaps a little unfair to Jefferson. To be sure, his confidence that a black "could scarcely be found capable of tracing and comprehending the investigations of Euclid" was refuted in his own time by the example of the distinguished scientist Benjamin Banneker. But Jefferson later recognized this and sought to publicize it, rather than manipulating the evidence. (It is an interesting question how much, if at all, his being "a man of his times" should count in mitigation of his moral failings.)

In criticizing the funding source for much of the race-differences "research," John Sedgwick argues: "By positing that the races are inherently unequal because of their respective IQ scores, the Pioneer Fund dismisses one of our nation's central tenets, the unifying idea that opens the Declaration of Independence ... 'All men are created equal.'" But, of course, this criticism conflates factual equality with moral or political equality in the way criticized by Jensen as well as by many moral philosophers. Peter Singer, for example, argues: "Perhaps all of the important differences will eventually prove to be environmental rather than genetic. Anyone opposed to racism and sexism will certainly hope that this will be so, for it will make the task of ending discrimination a lot easier; nevertheless it would be dangerous to rest the case against racism and sexism on the belief that all significant differences are environmental in origin. ... Equality is a moral idea, not a simple assertion of fact."

One of the many beneficiaries of Pioneer Fund support has been J. Philippe Rushton, whose peculiar and controversial work (on racial differences in intelligence, brain size, genital size, etc.) led in 1991 to a call for his expulsion from the University of Western Ontario. The call appealed in part to an established government antihate policy, which states: "All doctrines and practices of racial superiority are scientifically false, morally reprehensible, and socially destructive, and are contrary to the policies of this government, and are unacceptable in Ontario." One may think Rushton's work silly (or repulsive, or dangerous) and still find disturbing the idea of a government body legislating scientific truth. Surely what is scientifically false cannot be determined by what is "unacceptable in Ontario." Irving Louis Horowitz, who quotes the policy, reminds us that "those truths held to be self-evident are those which are most in need of reexamination."

In a similar spirit, Charles Locurto, in *Sense and Nonsense about IQ* (1991), argues: "New ways of thinking about IQ are more likely at times to come from the extremes than from the moderate middle. Then, too, each extreme serves to police the worst offenses of the other. We are in this way as much indebted to Leon Kamin for forcing hereditarians to better scrutinize their work as we are to Arthur Jensen for forcing environmentalists to take seriously propositions about human differences that they seem disinclined to explore." It is tempting to end on this note of intellectual tolerance. But a difficult question remains: Do all views deserve serious consideration?

William Tucker, at the end of *The Science and Politics of Racial Research* (1994), notes: "Every neo-Nazi organization is obsessed with the 'scientific evaluation' of races, and their literature regularly refers to the work of such scientists as Jensen, Eysenck, Shockley, Cattell, and now Rushton as the justification for oppressive political positions. At times the scientists have willingly contributed to these publications. Though such an act is, naturally, their right as citizens, no one should be misled into thinking their involvement is anything but political. ... If the century and a half of research into racial differences had at least unearthed some shard of scientific fact, political misuse might be the necessary price for scientific progress. Sadly, however, the legitimation of racist ideology has been its major accomplishment."

In *Denying the Holocaust: The Growing Assault on Truth and Memory* (1994), Deborah Lipstadt chronicles the development of the ideologically motivated revisionist historiography that simply denies that the Nazis killed millions of Jews, dismissing or explaining away the overwhelming evidence. She argues that a "willingness to ascribe to the deniers and their myths the legitimacy of a point of view is of as great, if not greater, concern than are the activities of the deniers themselves." Lipstadt does not dispute that the deniers have an "absolute right" to promulgate their doctrine. But, she argues, to insist that such views receive a fair hearing is to fail to recognize their racist basis, and their function as disinformation. "There is a qualitative difference between barring someone's right to speech and providing him or her with a platform from which to deliver a message."

It is also, she thinks, to fail to recognize the way in which treating the advocate of such ideas as an equal partner in a serious intellectual debate can exert a corrupting effect on public awareness. "Before long he has become 'the controversial Prof. X' and his theory is discussed seriously by nonprofessionals, that is, journalists. He soon becomes a familiar figure on television and radio, where he 'explains' his ideas to interviewers who cannot challenge him or demonstrate the fallaciousness of his argument."

The dangers are real. Ingo Hasselbach, in *Führer-Ex: Memoirs of a Former Neo-Nazi* (1996), describes the powerful impact on him and his fellows of Fred Leuchter's (pseudoscientific) "proof" that there were no gas chambers. Gary Esolen has provided a particularly instructive study of the ways in which the media's built-in vulnerabilities have been exploited by "controversial" political figures such as David Duke. As the power of media representations increases, the gap between scientific fact and public perception grows more troublesome. On one side, the dangers of "political correctness"; on the other, the threat of disinformation: finding safe passage will take all our intelligence, and more.

Also See the Following Articles

AFFIRMATIVE ACTION • DARWINISM • EUGENICS • GENETICS AND BEHAVIOR • MEDIA OWNERSHIP • NATURE VERSUS NURTURE • PLURALISM IN EDUCATION • POLITICAL CORRECTNESS • RACISM

Bibliography

Ceci, S. J. (1996). *On intelligence*. Cambridge, MA: Harvard University Press.

Dubow, S. (1995). *Scientific racism in modern South Africa*. Cambridge: Cambridge University Press.

Esolen, G. (1992). More than a pretty face: David Duke's use of television as a political tool. In D. D. Rose (Ed.), *The emergence of David Duke and the politics of race*, pp. 136–155. Chapel Hill: University of North Carolina Press.

Fischer, C. S., et al. (1996). *Inequality by design: Cracking the bell curve myth*. Princeton: Princeton University Press.

Fraser, S. (Ed.). (1995). *The bell curve wars: Race, intelligence, and the future of America*. New York: Basic Books.

Gould, S. J. (1996). *The mismeasure of man*. New York: W. W. Norton.

Hoberman, J. (1997). *Darwin's athletes*. Boston: Houghton Mifflin.

Jacoby, R. & Glauberman, N. (Eds.). (1995). *The bell curve debate: History, documents, opinions*. New York: Times Books.

Kaufman, A. S. (1994). *Intelligent testing with the WISC-III*. New York: John Wiley.

Kline, P. (1991). *Intelligence: The psychometric view*. London: Routledge.

Mensh, E., & Mensh, H. (1991). *The IQ mythology: Class, race, gender, and inequality*. Carbondale: Southern Illinois University Press.

Tucker, W. H. (1994). *The science and politics of racial research*. Urbana: University of Illinois Press.

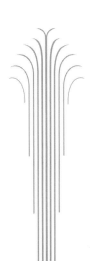

INTERNET PROTOCOL

Duncan Langford
University of Kent at Canterbury

GLOSSARY

electronic address A unique address detailing the name, organization, type of organization and usually also the country of a company or individual.

electronically published Describing or relating to information that has been created, distributed, or made available over networked computers.

electronic communication Interaction between two or more individuals carried out by means of networked computers.

E-mail Short for electronic mail; messages sent between individuals over networked computers.

Internet A high-speed worldwide network of computers.

mailing list A means of distributing e-mail to a group of individuals.

modem A device to connect a computer to a telephone line.

network A group of computers connected in such a way that their users may share information.

newsgroup The name given to the equivalent of a global electronic notice board, classified under a subject heading. Electronic messages posted to it by individuals may be accessed and replied to by any interested person.

newsreader A computer application used to access newsgroups.

on-line/Internet community Those individuals who have access to the wider Internet.

(on-line) service provider An organization that exists to provide a connection to the wider Internet.

site The name given to a specific location on the Internet.

World Wide Web (WWW) or the Web An approach to Internet use, potentially incorporating text, graphics, video, and sound. An individual establishes contact with a specific site containing desired information and accesses it directly. WWW documents, or pages, may be readily connected together.

INTERNET PROTOCOL describes the expectations on the part of existing users of the Internet of the manner in which users should behave. For many years after establishment in the 1960s of the original precursor to the Internet (ARPAnet), the users of globally networked computers tended to be predominantly academic, and to have a strong belief in the virtues of free speech and individual responsibility, together with stress on shared information, rather than proprietary or secret knowledge. This collective view led to the establishment of written and unwritten rules which, through the impossibility of local or national enforcement, were adhered to by members of the Internet itself. This shared acceptance of a protocol allowed the Internet to function efficiently and productively.

However, in recent years newcomers to the Internet, increasingly unaware of this underlying philosophy, have wittingly and unwittingly acted to undermine the protocols. What was originally viewed as a cognate national environment has become a diverse, global one. For the Internet to continue functioning, there is an urgent need to re-establish acceptance by its users of the existing Internet protocol, or establishment of a workable replacement.

I. NETWORKS AND THE INTERNET

A. What Is the Internet?

1. Background

The creation of globally interconnected networks of computers has given individuals the ability to directly communicate with each other, linking across national and international boundaries as easily as across the street. Global publication is trivially easy; this means, for example, that views which may be abhorrent to large numbers of individuals can be propagated and automatically distributed. Material such as pornography, instructions on breaking into computer systems, or even details on building bombs is potentially freely available. However, despite the wishes of politicians and others, it is technically quite impossible to realistically censor or otherwise limit electronically published material. Although national policing may be attempted, operation of the global computer networks known generically as the Internet is, quite literally, out of political control.

2. Networking in Practice

Wide-scale networking means, in effect, that any person or organization possessing a suitable computer, together with a telephone line and modem, has the ability to establish links with other computers. Such links are normally made through a paid-for commercial link to a service provider, the Internet equivalent of a telephone company, offering a connection to the wider Internet community. (For many office workers, connection to a service provider is frequently provided automatically by an employer.) Once joined to any Internet-connected network, a user has the ability to post messages to any connected electronic address, situated anywhere in the world.

Begun as a vehicle for experimental network re-

search, the Internet was originally designed to survive nuclear war. In consequence, there is no central control whatever—any part of it may be removed without damage to the whole.

In attempting to understand how such a devolved system can work, it is essential to appreciate the very strong ethos of the Internet. Its users are very much in favor of internal control and against outside influence. In effect, the Internet is a fully functioning anarchy. Until comparatively recently, most actual users of the Internet were technically aware individuals who understood the technical background to this form of networking and who (because of their experience and background) were perhaps biased in favor of academic freedom and individual autonomy.

What is ethically appropriate must reflect what is technically possible. In order to appropriately consider protocols in electronic communication, there is consequently a need for some understanding of the technical setting. A brief description of the background to computer networking and the Internet therefore precedes consideration of some potential ethical problems involved in networked communications.

Use of the Internet is typically through three main channels—electronic mail, newsgroups, and the World Wide Web.

3. Personal Mail—"E-mail"

Once a service provider has allowed connection, electronic messages may be generated from any computer connected to the Internet. Messages can be "mailed" or "posted" to any user with a similarly connected computer. Given the electronic address of a target, electronic mail can be dispatched in seconds to someone working at the next desk, or on the next continent.

4. Newsgroups

Connection to the Internet also allows access to an enormous number of newsgroups, which cover the whole range of human activity. Although those newsgroups concerned with sexual matters may have gained a high profile, there are, literally, tens of thousands of others. Reading the contents of an Internet newsgroup is very straightforward; simple newsreaders are available for virtually every Internet-linked computer.

"Posting" an article simply involves sending mail to the electronic address of a newsgroup, rather than directing mail to an individual. Although some newsgroups are moderated, which means a human acts as a filter for postings to them, the huge majority have no such control. Whatever is posted to the newsgroup is then automatically distributed to every Internet site subscribing to it. Posting to an Internet newsgroup is consequently the nearest thing on earth to absolute free speech—unmediated, uncensored, and far reaching.

B. How Newsgroups Work

As will be further discussed, there have been demands that the Internet and its newsgroups be censored. Once the workings of the Internet are understood, though, it will be seen that, even if justified, such censorship is technically impossible.

Electronic messages are constantly being sent along links between service providers, or "sites." When a site receives a message, it checks that the newsgroup to which the message belongs is accepted by that site. The message is then made available to a site's individual members by storing a copy "on site." The site will also send a cloned copy of each message to the next site in the wider network. Millions of messages are continually passing around the Internet in this way.

In the typical example illustrated in Figure 1, a message originates at site A and is passed to site B, which distributes it not only to its own subscribers, but also onward, to site C. Copies of the message will then move on to subsequent sites in the network.

What would happen if, instead of passing on the message, site B decided it was subversive of morals or authority, and refused to circulate either the message or the newsgroup to which it belonged? Clearly, those users who depended directly upon the site (site B users) would be unable to access the newsgroup. However, site C and its users, downstream in Figure 1, would be only temporarily inconvenienced. The Internet is not called "net" casually. The pattern of its links forms a spider's web; so, if one connection is damaged, information can be obtained from any other. The Internet interprets censorship as damage, and, of course, it was designed from the first to survive massive damage. Site C can consequently obtain a "censored" newsgroup from any other of

its connections—or it may readily establish a new connection to an unrestricted news "feed."

This pattern holds at whatever scale the Internet is viewed. A single user banned from accessing or contributing to a newsgroup can just telephone a different service provider, while, even if a whole country decided to ban a particular newsgroup, at worst this would only effect the country itself. The global Internet community would continue.

It is very important to keep this state of affairs in mind, not only when considering requests for punitive action against publications on the Internet, but when debating appropriate user conduct.

C. How the World Wide Web Works

The World Wide Web (WWW), graphically based and consequently very visual in nature, is inherently easy to use. In structure, it can be considered as a static approach to service provision. Here, instead of the contents of a newsgroup being constantly transmitted around the world, an individual uses freely available software to establish direct contact with a site containing desired information and specifically accesses it. A great advantage of this approach is that Web sites are easily connected to each other. A user may, by clicking buttons on their personal computer's screen, move between the display of Web pages in different states—or different continents—without realizing they are doing more than accessing the next page of data. Communication may be two-way: companies and individuals may establish their own Web sites; any connected computer may then read presented information. Access to Web sites is very easy indeed—they form the simplest way of accessing electronic information, and have played a large part in the recent enormous growth of the Internet (see Fig. 2).

Although their purposes—access to desired information—may seem similar, Internet Web sites and Internet newsgroups are very different. A newsgroup has no "real" location and cannot therefore be said to exist

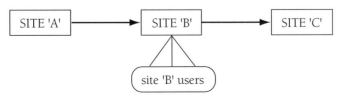

FIGURE 1   Transmission of typical newsgroup message.

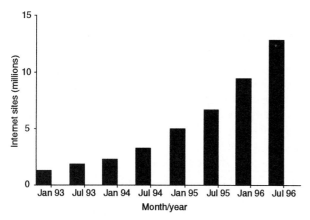

FIGURE 2 *Source:* Network Wizards Internet Domain Survey.

in any one place, while a Web site must, by definition, have a unique home address.

D. Summary

Anyone with a full Internet connection may post electronic messages to any Internet address anywhere in the world. In addition, anyone may read from and contribute to Internet newsgroups, which cover the whole range of human activity. Such groups cannot effectively be banned. Graphically based, World Wide Web sites also contain information, but such sites, unlike newsgroups, have specific locations. Both rely on the Internet, a paradoxically unorganized and ad hoc arrangement of connected computers which has evolved to its present position of global dominance from an origin as a nuclear attack-proof research network.

The underlying ethos shared by long-standing users of the Internet has always been very strongly in favor of freedom from external controls and internal self-regulation.

II. PROBLEMS IN ELECTRONIC COMMUNICATION

In considering appropriate protocols, two areas of computer networking and communications may be viewed as particularly relevant. The first relates to *individual* communications, and the second is concerned with *publication*—that is, reading or publishing information through access to newsgroups and World Wide Web sites.

A. Ethical Issues in Individual Communications

When moving into new circumstances, it is natural to assume previous experience may be relevant. Consider an apparently simple task, such as writing a letter. It may seem logical to bring to composing and sending an electronic letter an established cognitive model which has worked well in generating similar paper mail. However, unthinking transference to the Internet of experience gained in other settings may lead to serious problems.

One such problem lies in classifying an electronic message. Is it, for instance, best treated as a traditional paper memo? There can be similarities, but there are also important differences. A typed memo involves several stages, at each of which an author may modify the text, or even decide to scrap the whole idea. This extended process does not fit the generation of an electronic message, which, in contrast, is very quick and easy to produce. Many people create and send e-mail spontaneously, often without pausing to consider use of tone and language, or even if the message is really appropriate or necessary. Of course, an electronic message can easily be printed as well, so a casual electronic jotting may instantly and unexpectedly achieve the formal authority of a typed memo.

Unlike paper communications, electronic mail appears transitory. A message can flash across a screen before seeming to vanish into electronic limbo. However, it is a serious mistake to think of e-mail as temporary. Although messages can certainly be impermanent, the opposite is also true. Once sent, a copy of an unguarded personal message may easily be stored by a recipient, perhaps for years, before, in the memorable phrase of one businessman, "It comes back to haunt you."

This is an instance of an individual problem which is likely to follow misunderstanding of the electronic medium, possibly leading to the inappropriate establishment of protocols—protocols which may have been quite appropriate in a different setting. For example, sending a paper letter is predicated upon the assumption that its contents will remain personal to the addressee. It is therefore both logical and appropriate to use a paper letter to convey confidential information, and to consider that a third party who then reads it is, normally, acting unethically.

However, in addition to the potential problems already described, there are also manifold possibilities for inadvertent distribution of electronic mail. Accidentally posting to a mailing list (which copies mail to everyone on the list) or unthinkingly sending multiple copies is deceptively easy. Given such a very different distribution model, transference of paper mail protocols to electronic mail is not appropriate.

This e-mail example illustrates the importance of applying an appropriate cognitive model to the consideration of electronic communication. In this case, the protocol which has evolved with the Internet itself suggests it is unethical to distribute electronic mail inappropriately, or to publish personal messages.

B. Ethical Issues in Networked Communications

In addition to the issues concerning personal communication, networked computers allow spreading of information in a way which is directly analogous to traditional broadcasting, or publishing on paper. Once distributed electronically, such "published" information is potentially seen by very large numbers of individuals indeed. Discussed next are two illustrative examples of inappropriate Internet broadcasting.

1. Personal—"Spamming"

Sending multiple copies of messages to many different newsgroups, although very easy, is always considered inappropriate. Doing so is called, in Netspeak, "spamming," after an old Monty Python sketch.

Distributing many hundreds of thousands of copies of your message and presenting it to the readers of every newsgroup might, perhaps, be useful to you, but the disadvantages to everyone else are very clear. Who does this, and why?

The most infamous example to date was probably the 1994 Green Card Lottery Spam, perpetrated by the U.S. law firm of Canter & Siegel. The firm considered the Internet to be an ideal, low-cost, and perfectly legitimate way to target their advertising at people likely to be potential clients. Although spreading their "spam" message cost others thousands of dollars, and much inconvenience, they had done nothing illegal or, in their consideration, improper. Among Internet users this was certainly a minority view—the reaction of the Internet population was overwhelmingly hostile.

Users felt that, firstly, Internet newsgroups were the wrong place to conduct commercial business. Its origins, and long-standing academic bias, had created a long tradition of non-commercialism. Secondly, although it may not be obvious to users, global use of the Internet is not free—the costs of infrastructure, transmission, and storage must be borne by someone. Canter & Siegel were alleged to have posted to over 6000 groups, which must surely have involved expenditure of quite a lot of other people's money.

Finally, in order to be established, newsgroups have individual "charters," setting out their aims. Many of the charters of the Internet newsgroups and connected sites specifically prohibit offers to do business. (A few do accept them, but restrict buyers and sellers to individuals, not companies.) Of course, being the Internet, such charters have only moral force. Understandably, though, people reading a particular newsgroup can become very annoyed by irrelevant postings concerning subjects outside the group's charter. This is analogous to, say, a neighborhood group meeting together to discuss the needs of their local school and being constantly interrupted in their debate by someone trying to sell telephone chat lines.

Noncommercial spamming may be used by antisocial individuals as a deliberate irritation; to this a typical response would be "flaming," which is the sending of personally abusive e-mail or the posting of similarly abusive news items.

Respecting the rights of groups and individuals is part of the Internet ethic. Someone who, for their own purposes, casually overrides the interests of other users by generating spams is consequently acting unethically.

2. Technical—Broadcasting of "Inappropriate" Material

Once a computer is connected to the Internet, running appropriate software allows easy creation of a World Wide Web site. Tens of thousands of such sites exist, and numbers are increasing exponentially. Most such sites are well designed and well conducted—but there are some WWW sites, for example, which exist to distribute pornography, both hard and soft, as well as those devoted to propagating extremist political views. All that is needed to view them is the correct electronic address.

As was mentioned earlier, Internet newsgroups are only controllable by refusing to allow news packages to enter a service provider's site. Newsgroup access may also be made more difficult by a "censoring" site refusing to pass information along the networked chain of computers.

In contrast, a Web site cannot be controlled at all, beyond refusing it permission to exist at a particular location. Sites created by individuals but felt to be unsuitable by their service providers have been closed down, but there is no way whatever of forbidding them to exist. A closed site may just spring up somewhere else—potentially, even in a different country, perhaps in the Third World. Such use is directly analogous to telephone sex lines in the United Kingdom. Although protests resulted in them being banned by United Kingdom operators, the lines continued—using numbers located outside the United Kingdom.

The ethical issues involved here are inherently enormously complex, and this complexity is exacerbated in the electronic world. It would be foolish to pretend there are easy or obvious solutions. The mix of Internet users is increasingly being diluted from its specialist origins by a vast influx of additional users from a range of different backgrounds. The well-established Internet philosophy of open access and free communication is consequently in direct conflict with the social and moral mores of many of its new users. If the trend continues, the philosophy itself must, at best, be in a state of flux. What is certain, however, is the inescapable fact that censorship is not possible. Whatever decisions are eventually reached must inevitably reflect this reality.

III. THE ISSUES

So far we have discussed a selection of examples intended to illustrate some problems in using the Internet. These range from minor difficulties—unexpected responses to personal mail—to the more serious, and potentially involve abuse or limitation of free speech.

Difficulties faced by new users in attempts to communicate effectively by electronic mail are probably typical of the teething problems to be anticipated in the use of most new facilities. Advice to tread warily, together with effective education, should go a long way to answering their problems.

In contrast, the impossibility of exerting effective censorship is hard for many individuals to understand. Politicians, especially, are understandably reluctant to consider anything other than legislation as the ultimate sanction on behavior. Within the Internet, though, local or even national legislation simply will not work.

There are two main reasons why this is so. Policing the Internet is technically impossible, and, in any event, much of the Internet lies beyond the reach of any national police force. This means that any Internet site may make available whatever it likes, provided only that the country *within which it is located* does not object. Although access to such sites from the United States may be officially forbidden, it would be as difficult to prevent as a ruling forbidding faxes. Anyone with a computer and telephone could access any site. In reality, enforcement is quite impractical.

Given the impossibility of exercising political or technical control over the Internet, the need for appropriate education is growing increasingly urgent. In the past, the Internet worked well; it has done so since it was first established. The principal reason we are experiencing problems now lies in a dramatic shift which has taken place in the Internet population. No longer are the majority of users experienced in the use of computers, familiar with an academic approach to free speech, and aware of established expectations of user behavior. Letting loose new users on the Internet without training or education is perhaps analogous to letting loose new drivers without instruction—except that even the worst new driver does not have the ability to inconvenience several million people, a task well within the powers of even a neophyte Internet user.

Quite apart from a massive increase in personal use, we are also seeing an explosion in commercial use of the Internet, principally through the World Wide Web. What was formerly a largely academic network is now a promotional goldrush. Hundreds, if not thousands, of companies from the very large to the very small are racing to seize the enormous potential market represented by those with Internet connections. This commercial rush shows no signs of decreasing—indeed, all the indications are that it will continue to accelerate. What decisions should be taken on defining what is appropriate commercial use of the Internet, and who should be responsible for framing such definitions? How long can the established ethic, which is essentially a shared understanding on the part of users, be sustained under a stunningly rapid dilution of user experience? There appears a real need for establishment of an updated 'Internet ethic', if only an acceptable defining body can be found or established.

IV. CONCLUSIONS

This entry has outlined some of the practical and ethical problems concerned with appropriate behavior in electronic communication. It has emphasized the impossibility of effective network policing, and the associated need for a greatly increased level of education.

Before the advent of the Internet, few individuals could expect to have their views and opinions considered by more than a handful of friends and acquaintances. In contrast, a simple posting to a popular Internet newsgroup may potentially be read by hundreds of thousands of people.

It seems clear that automatic carrying over of "small-scale" behavior into a large-scale forum will lead to inevitable difficulties. Such difficulties are likely to be compounded by the greatly increased opportunities the Internet offers for antisocial behavior. Users with even limited knowledge may, for example, employ electronic mail to "spam" newsgroups, while the more technically advanced may use the World Wide Web to distribute extreme political propaganda.

Until now, the Internet has worked through acceptance on the part of its users of a belief, which might perhaps be viewed as an evolved general ethic of behavior. While reflecting what may be a purely pragmatic approach to Internet use, this evolved approach has proved both effective and functional. Six protocols have been particularly emphasized:

- The Internet is very strongly against external control and in favor of internal self-regulation
- Rights of groups and individuals should always be respected
- Individual actions should always reflect awareness of the wider Internet community
- Person-to-person communications should be private
- No message should be broadcast without proper cause
- The ability to post globally is so powerful it must always be voluntarily limited

Underlying these points is the well-established Internet philosophy of open access and free communication.

As the number and variety of new Internet users are constantly increasing, the situation is dynamic, and prediction risky. However, there is a strong case for some form of coordinated encouragement of appropriate ethical standards, ideally founded upon those established during development of the Internet. If such standards are agreed upon, they might then be included in appropriate education of new users of the Internet. New users surely need to demonstrate awareness of the responsibilities, as well as the advantages, of Internet use. Further research into the ethos of the Internet is clearly essential.

The Internet undoubtedly provides a tremendous global opportunity, analogous to the invention of the printing press in its power to educate and inform. Should it develop without an ethical foundation known to all users, we should all surely be the poorer.

Also See the Following Articles

ADVERTISING • CENSORSHIP • COMPUTER AND INFORMATION ETHICS • COMPUTER SECURITY • MEDIA OWNERSHIP • PORNOGRAPHY • PRIVACY

Bibliography

Bynum, T. W. (1997). *Information ethics: An introduction.* Oxford: Blackwell.

Gotternbarn, D. (1996). Establishing standards of professional practice. In Myers, Hall, Pitt (Eds.), *The responsible software engineer.* London: Springer.

Johnson, D. G. (1994). *Computer ethics,* 2nd ed. Englewood Cliffs, NJ: Prentice-Hall.

Langford, D. (1995). *Practical computer ethics.* London: McGraw-Hill.

Langford, D. (1997). Ethical issues in network system design. *Australian Journal of Information Systems* May, 4(2).

Rogerson, S., and Bynum, T. W. (Eds.) (1997). *A reader in information ethics.* Oxford: Blackwell.

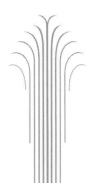

ISLAM

John J. Shepherd
University College of St. Martin

I. Sources and Resources
II. Normative Issues
III. Theoretical Issues
IV. Conclusion

GLOSSARY

hadith A report or tradition containing sayings and actions attributed to Muhammad, and hence conveying his exemplary conduct as a normative ideal and authoritative precedent (cf. Sunna).
Shi'ites An overall minority in the Muslim world constituted by a number of "sects," the largest of which is the Twelver Shi'ism predominant in Iran. They differ from Sunnis in a number of ways, including doctrines of religious leadership, forms of religious authority, and methods of legal interpretation.
Sunnis (Sunna) Adherents of the mainstream development in Islam are called Sunnis, in contrast to the Shi'ite minority. They claim fidelity to the sunna, or normative practice, of Muhammad, although the point is contested by Shi'ites.

ISLAM developed largely as a religion of law in which a synthesis of religion, morality, and religious law (*shari'a*) prevailed. In this respect three prime sources and resources for Islamic ethics may be identified: the

Qur'an, the Sunna, and the shari'a. In addition, "dialectical theology" (*kalam*) and the rival intellectual tradition of philosophy (*falsafa*) both contributed significantly to the theological ethics that eventually emerged. Finally, two other sources of ethical inspiration were writings in a particular literary genre, *adab,* and a variety of impulses originating in Sufism.

With regard to normative issues, the division of the Muslim world into Sunnis and Shi'ites is of relatively little practical relevance. With regard to theoretical issues, while a traditionalist theology (Ash'arism) largely antipathetic to independent rational argument came to exercise effective hegemony in the Sunni world, an outlook similar to that of the rival Mu'tazilite theologians became absorbed into Shi'ism.

I. SOURCES AND RESOURCES

1. *Qur'an.* Muslims regard their sacred text as the infallible repository of God's final, perfect revelation to humanity mediated through Muhammad (570–632 C.E.). The message of the Qur'an centers on (i) religious doctrines (concerning the oneness of God, the role of Muhammad as God's messenger, etc.), (ii) religious duties (e.g., prayer, fasting, alms, and pilgrimage, and (iii) moral teachings.

2. *Sunna.* Muhammad is generally believed to have led an exemplary life: indeed, Muslim theology developed a doctrine of his sinlessness. The record of this normative example is to be found in authoritative col-

lections of hadiths (Shi'ites have their own), which function in practice as virtually equivalent in status to the Qur'an, despite not themselves constituting actual revelation.

3. *Shari'a.* The early, fluid period of Islamic thought led to the development of a complex pattern of religious law, shari'a. According to the classical jurisprudence (*fiqh*) developed by the jurist al-Shafi'i (d. 820), there are four main roots to the law: the basic two are the Qur'an and Sunna, to which are added the method of analogical reasoning (*qiyas*) and the consensus (*ijma*) of all Muslims (later, less idealistically, the consensus of expert jurists). Four Sunni schools of shari'a prevailed (the Hanafi, Maliki, Shafi'i, and Hanbali schools), while Twelver Shi'ites have their own legal tradition. The contents of the shari'a are conventionally divided into two categories, duties to God and duties to fellow humans. All are construed as centering on divine commands and prohibitions, although in due course a famous fivefold classification of actions emerged: obligatory, recommended, permissible, reprehensible, and forbidden. Actions in the fifth category, e.g., murder or theft, have legally prescribed punishments attached.

Shari'a literature is the largest single genre in Islam; hence the possible designation of Islam as a religion of law. "Law" here has, however, significantly different connotations from its use in Western culture. On the one hand it is not promulgated by the state, and it is not codified, relying instead on legal precedent established by recourse to compendia of previous juridical interpretations and rulings. On the other hand it incorporates obligations which in largely secular cultures have been separated out as belonging to other spheres, notably religion and morality, but also etiquette and personal hygiene.

4. *Kalam.* Although the development of religious law predominated, vigorous theological debates also occurred in classical Islam. Two schools of thought to note are the Mu'tazilites and the Ash'arites, their opposing convictions being prominently aired in the ninth century, but concerning issues with a distinctly modern ring.

5. *Falsafah, Akhlaq.* Serious attempts were made to integrate the Greek philosophical inheritance into Islam, and a number of prominent philosophers emerged, including Avicenna (or Ibn Sina, d. 1037) and Averroes (or Ibn Rushd, d. 1198). To the religious scholars, however, philosophers seemed to be subordinating revelation to reason in an impious way, and their work was eclipsed by traditionalist theology, especially Ash'arite. Nevertheless, an important corpus of work has been handed down.

Some of this material is clearly focused on ethics, drawing inspiration in particular from Plato's *Republic* and Aristotle's *Nichomachean Ethics.* This tradition of philosophical ethics is known as *akhlaq.* It contains analyses of the soul, classifications of the virtues, and expositions of the contribution of the virtues to the perfection of the soul. Two principal exponents (both Shi'ites) were Miskawayh (d. 1030), with his book, *Refinement of Character,* and Nasir al-Din Tusi (d. 1274), with his *Nasirean Ethics.*

6. *Adab.* This genre of literature, popular in courtly circles in particular, expounded ideals of noble conduct in advice to secretaries, physicians, etc., and to rulers in the "Mirrors for Princes" literature.

7. *Sufism.* Sufism is a complex strand of Islam which includes mysticism, asceticism, devotion to saints, and welfare, education, and missionary activities. It is associated with an emphasis on God's love more than his justice, and an attendant antilegalist outlook, though typically it aims to complement the shari'a and influence its interpretation, not to supplant it.

The ideals, theories, and arguments to be found in these sources and resources for ethics may receive a largely historical exposition (cf. M. Fakhry, 1991. *Ethical theories in Islam.* Leiden/New York: Brill). Here a thematic approach is adopted, beginning with the normative base before considering the key theoretical issues that arise.

II. NORMATIVE ISSUES

In Islam, as in the related religions of Judaism and Christianity, there is scope both for an ethic of puritan rigor and for an ethic of humane compassion. Exclusive focus on the former by external critics represents unwarranted prejudice. On the other hand, the existence, for example, of harsh penalties for certain offenses cannot be overlooked, and is a focus of internal Muslim controversy as well as evoking criticism from outsiders.

There is merit, though, in placing Muslims in three broad camps: (i) conservatives or traditionalists, who continue to uphold the whole shari'a inheritance; (ii) fundamentalists or Islamists, who are impatient of much traditional juristic methodology and learning, but keen to reintroduce some of the controversial shari'a penalties in the framework of an Islam that has been both policitized and, by their standards, purified; and (iii) liberals (reformers, modernists) who advocate rethinking Islam in modern terms in a way that is sensitive to what is best in non-Islamic thought and culture. While there is appreciable ethical overlap between all three, the differences may generate mutual suspicions and antagonisms.

Muslim normative teachings range from the general to the particular. General injunctions include the pivotal requirement of faith, and the equally pivotal requirement to let faith issue in good works—recurrent Qur'anic themes. The necessity of obedience to God's commands has its counterpoint in the importance of seeking to imitate his justice and compassion, and to persevere in patience, humility, and fortitude. There is apparent equivocation in the Qur'anic teaching both to repay evil with evil (Qur'an 4:123, 28:84) and to repay evil with good (23:96, 41:34), with unequivocal emphasis on kindness to the orphan, giving alms to the poor, and succoring the needy. Honesty is imperative.

Among the specific teachings are a prohibition of pork, alcohol, gambling (extended by jurists to include life insurance), and usury. Harsh mandatory punishments (known as *hadd,* pl. *hudud,* punishments), based on the Qur'an and Sunna, are prescribed in classical shari'a for certain crimes, notably adultery, fornication, theft, apostasy, and drunkenness, and there is renewed focus on these as fundamentalists campaign for their strict implementation, contrary to the generally prevailing Muslim ethos. The death penalty may be incurred for murder, based on the principle of retribution, but settlement by payment of blood money to the family of the deceased is a "recommended" action in the classical fivefold scheme, which may be opted for (cf. Qur'an 5:45, 42:40). Thus murder remains in an important respect a private crime despite the public involvement of the state.

Two important fields of normative teaching concern marriage and sexual morality. Traditional cautious approval of polygamy, up to a maximum of four wives (provided they can be treated equally, Qur'an 4:3), has been replaced with endorsement of monogamy by liberal Muslims. Divorce is permitted, but it remains controversially very much easier for a man to divorce his wife than vice versa, and custody of children passes to him from the mother in due course. Legal adoption, with rights of inheritance, is not permitted.

The position and status of women are in general hotly disputed topics, with conservatives emphasizing the benefits brought by Islam (e.g., the granting of legal status; rights to ownership of the dower, to inheritance, and to divorce; and the prohibition of female infanticide), while liberals advocate moving beyond the stated ideal of equal dignity to equal rights, with full legal and social equality. Modest dress is enjoined (for both sexes), but face veiling of women and seclusion (*pur-*

dah) are cultural accretions not directly sanctioned by revelation. Traditional emphases on wives being obedient to husbands, and always sexually available to them, evoke the ire of critics, as does the permission for men to enjoy sexual relations with concubines (Qur'an 70:30), although slavery has now been discontinued. Adultery carries the death penalty in principle (as does homosexual activity), but proof of guilt requires the evidence of four eyewitnesses, an illustration of how *hadd* penalties may be tempered by the strictness of the conditions of their application, enabling a less punitive and more widely acceptable ethos to flourish, to the anger of fundamentalists.

The traditional principle of holy war, *jihad,* is generally construed as a principle of purely defensive just war, although it has also inspired anticolonialist movements, and is currently construed by some fundamentalist groups as a license for acts of terrorism which contravene traditional teachings on general noncombatant immunity and traditional prohibitions on hostage taking, as well as the traditional Sunni teaching that an unjust ruler should be endured rather than overthrown (rather different developments in Shi'ite teaching helped motivate the 1979 Iranian revolution). Martyrdom in battle is rewarded with Paradise, but should not be courted unnecessarily in order to avoid being classed as suicide.

The principle of democratic government is generally accepted, drawing on the Qur'anic principle of *shura,* consultation. For many fundamentalists (and conservatives), though, the prime condition of just rule is government in accordance with the shari'a, and Western-style liberal democracy is decried as un-Islamic (a view which generally entails prescribing protected status for non-Muslims in an Islamic state, but not full equal rights of citizenship). Traditional endorsement of social hierarchy has been reasserted against the social egalitarianism of Islamic socialism, though vigorous efforts are directed toward developing an Islamic economics as an alternative to socialism and capitalism (but so far leaning more towards the latter). Experiments in interest-free Islamic banking are based on—though not, charge critics, a necessary inference from—the traditional rejection of usury.

In medical ethics, Muslims oppose abortion (unless the mother's life is at stake), along with suicide and euthanasia, since the taking of life remains God's prerogative. Contraception is permitted, although some Muslims disapprove of it as encouraging promiscuity. *In vitro* fertilization receives cautious approval, but both surrogacy and sterilization are rejected. Blood transfusions and organ transplants are permissible.

With its emphasis on the worldwide *umma*, or community of the faithful, Islam has a strong communitarian character which can be in tension with the pronounced individualism of Western liberalism. Thus while the human rights agenda of the latter receives strong support (though the claim that duties have priority over rights is frequently voiced), reservations are entered by conservative and fundamentalist Muslims, e.g., in respect of women's rights. The 1990 Cairo Declaration on Human Rights in Islam specified, as did previous documents, that human rights be subject to the provisions of the shari'a.

Discussion of environmental issues and animal rights is relatively limited, but the ritual slaughter of animals for halal meat is claimed to be humane because it is swift and painless.

III. THEORETICAL ISSUES

A. Ethics and Religion

The way in which Western culture and philosophy have increasingly effected a disjunction between morality and religion contrasts markedly with the ethicoreligious or theologicojuridical framework of most Muslim thinkers. Nevertheless, key questions have been debated which imply a logical separation of spheres.

1. Epistemology: The Sources of Moral Knowledge

The key question here concerns the relationship between revelation and reason. Most traditionalist Sunni theologians, from al-Ashari (d. 935) onward, have broadly insisted that it is impossible to ascertain what is right by independent reason. We have to rely for such knowledge on revelation, with reason being granted the purely dependent role of interpreting the Qur'an (or, for most thinkers, the Qur'an and Sunna). The strictly opposing view, that we can always ascertain what is right by independent reason, appears to be the tacit presupposition of the Islamic philosophers.

This latter view faces the charge of contradicting Islam by rendering revelation superfluous. The traditionalist view, however, is exposed to the charge, leveled by the Mu'tazilites and others (including non-Muslims), that it disregards, or fails to account for, the existence of true moral judgments outside Islam (and outside other religions of revelation revered by Muslims, such as Christianity and Judaism). Moreover, the Qur'an itself arguably presupposes, or implies, that pagans and idolaters are to be condemned, not because they are wholly ignorant of what is right (although ignorance is indeed a major theme), but because they have failed to live in accordance with what is right (e.g., Qur'an 74:42–4; 90:8–16).

The intermediate position, according to which revelation and reason are mutually complementary sources of moral knowledge, was proposed by the Mu'tazilites, with different blends of the two being advocated by different theorists. According to one view, while reason can ascertain moral truth, revelation is necessary in order to present it in the vivid and inspiring form crucial to its effectiveness. Another view maintains that while reason can uncover some, or much, moral truth, revelation is a necessary supplement in certain key respects (e.g., the moral importance of prayer in the formation of character).

Partly for political reasons, the Mu'tazilite view was eclipsed by the Ash'arite view, except among Shi'ites, only to be revived by the modernists.

2. Ontology: Theories of Moral Value

At issue here is what is known in Western philosophy as the Euthyphro dilemma, or the divine command theory of ethics: is an action right because God commands it, or does God command it because it is right? In the classical Islamic debate on the topic, the Ash'arites espoused the first horn of the dilemma, and the Mu'tazilites the second. Attention focused in particular on the elucidation of conceptions of divine justice and power.

For the Mu'tazilites, the Qur'anic emphasis on the God of justice was to be construed in terms of divine conformity with objective standards of justice (discoverable, at least to a great extent, by independent human reason). A correlative claim was advanced in respect of moral values in general.

The Ash'arites retorted that such a view entailed limits to God's power, thus contradicting the doctrine of divine omnipotence. In an attempt to safeguard the latter, they insisted that justice, and moral values in general, had to be understood simply as what God commands. Thus morality was rooted in God's will, a form of theistic subjectivism or ethical voluntarism.

The classic objection to this, within Islam as elsewhere, is that rooting God's actions in his unrestricted will and power renders morality ultimately arbitrary. It implies that God could in principle, even if in practice he chooses not to, command anything to be right, including actions universally condemned as immoral. This inference, unacceptable to the Mu'tazilites, was unavoidable for the Ash'arites, who in logical consistency accepted it, and it has remained the predominant Sunni view ever since. Its acceptance has been facilitated by related emphases on the divine mystery on the one hand, and the importance of faith on the other. Theological propositions unfathomable by human reason may need to be accepted *bila kayfa,* "without questioning how."

3. Theories of Moral Responsibility: Free Will and Determinism

Here we have a third strand of the classical kalam controversies, and this too revolved around conceptions of divine justice. A prominent theme in the Qur'an is the promise of paradise and the threat of hell as reward and punishment for human conduct. The Mu'tazilites insisted that God's justice could only be upheld if the allocation of reward and punishment were to proceed on a fair basis, and that this entailed free will; for to punish miscreants whose evil had been unavoidable because determined would be a flagrant injustice and incompatible with God's nature.

However, while the Qur'an (and the Sunna) could be quoted in support of free will and human responsibility, it could also be quoted in support of divine predestination and determinism (e.g. Qur'an 74:31: "God misleads whom he will and guides whom he pleases"). The Ash'arites were naturally sensitive to the link between divine predestination and divine omnipotence, and endorsed the former as being entailed by the latter. At the same time, the logic of the Mu'tazilite position was not without its effect, and the strict determinism canvassed by some was eschewed in favor of an attempted compromise involving a "doctrine of acquisition." It was proposed that while, in accordance with God's omnipotence, human acts are all divine creations, in accordance with human responsibility we have the power to "acquire" them. Yet for al-Ash'ari, the power to "acquire" is also created by God, leaving critics unpersuaded of the doctrine's plausibility as a safeguard of human responsibility. Indeed, subsequent traditionalist theologians essayed a number of variations on this theme in an attempt to infuse greater clarity and coherence— with what degree of success remaining a matter of dispute.

Despite its pronounced theoretical character, this debate is of practical relevance in that acceptance of the doctrine of predestination may be thought to condone an attitude of fatalism inimical to ethical endeavor, a consideration not overlooked by the theologians, and a charge leveled at times by external critics of Islam. Ironically, a precisely opposite implication was drawn by Max Weber in his famous "Protestant Ethic" essay, in respect of another predestinarian tradition, Calvinism.

4. Theories of Moral Motivation

According to a well-known hadith, "actions will be judged according to intentions," and the importance of right intentions became firmly fixed in Muslim thought from early on. Indeed, according to the Qur'an itself, conduct that is outwardly ethical but rooted in wrong intentions is unacceptable to God. A range of motives may be identified.

According to one influential study, the essential motive of virtuous conduct in the Qur'an is fear of God, or awe. In general, too, Muslims emphasize the importance of fear of the Day of Judgment and of the anticipated torments of hell as a sadly necessary deterrent against evil actions. The theme of rewards and punishments is very pronounced, evoking the criticism that Islam enshrines a form of religioethical egoism. The value of right action undertaken without thought for recompense does appear in the Qur'an, but tends to be linked, if not with fear of God, then with action undertaken for his sake only, rather than with action undertaken for the sake of the right action alone, out of unalloyed altruism (Qur'an 92:18–21, 76:4–9). Nevertheless altruism is apparent, for example, in an Islamic formulation of the Golden Rule found in the Sunna: "None of you truly has faith if he does not desire for his brother what he desires for himself."

In addition, we find the notion of right conduct undertaken for the love of God (cf. Qur'an 2:177), a view developed and emphasized above all by the Sufis. Sufism is generally understood to have been in part a reaction to the growing legalism in Islam consequent upon the elaboration of the shari'a. An overemphasis on religious law may lead to an undue focus on observable compliance with, or indeed mechanical observance of, its precepts. Conversely, though, an overreaction to such legalism may lead to outright antinomianism, as happened with some of the Sufis. A powerful warning against this was issued by *al-Ghazali* (d. 1111), whose treatise, *The Revival of the Religious Sciences,* is widely regarded as an authoritative synthesis of classical Islamic theology. Making love of God supreme in his system, he linked the shari'a's prescription that every act should be preceded by a properly formulated intention to the Sufi emphasis on the intention of the heart, thus emphasizing the ethical dimension of obedience to the law.

In Islam as a whole, then, Qur'anic emphasis on the fear of God is balanced by an emphasis on the love of God, and while "Islam" itself means "submission" (to God's command), the obedience that is enjoined is not a routinized heteronomy. The Qur'an constantly links together "faith and good works": the latter spring from the former, which in turn is linked not only to fear and love, but to a range of other attitudes, including gratitude to God for his revelations and his mercies, as well as humility before God in his majesty and power.

5. Analyses of Moral Character and the Virtues

In philosophical ethics, typically, we find an analysis of the soul and its faculties, followed by an ethics of virtue. In the case of Miskawayh the four cardinal virtues of wisdom, temperance, courage, and justice are first identified and then subdivided into numerous categories (e.g., wisdom is analyzed into intelligence, retention, rationality, etc.). Further elucidation utilizes Aristotle's doctrine of the mean. Methods toward the refinement of character are recommended, so that the soul may move toward its perfection. A discussion of eudaimonia links happiness with life after death, but there is little here that is distinctively Muslim (piety, for example, is listed as a subdivision of justice, but also, confusingly, of temperance), hence, indeed, the widespread disapprobation of the philosophers by the theologians.

The theologian al-Ghazali, though, incorporates much of Miskawayh's ethics. Character is defined as an established state of the soul from which actions proceed easily, without any need for reflection and deliberation, and good actions are those which are praised by reason and the shari'a. The soul has four faculties, knowledge, anger, desire, and justice, and when functioning soundly these reflect the four cardinal virtues of wisdom, courage, temperance, and justice. Justice thus appears, exceptionally, as both a faculty and a virtue. It is further exceptional as a virtue in not representing a mean (contrary to Miskawayh, and also Aristotle). The mean is relative to person and circumstance, and is to be ascertained by reason and the shari'a. Emphasis on the latter distinguishes Ghazali from the philosophers, and he further emphasizes theological virtues, e.g., gratitude and trust, alongside the philosophical ones. Again, understanding of the shari'a can be at different levels: most believers can attain only proximate happiness, while the highest level of moral insight, leading to ultimate happiness, is gained by a minority infused with the mystical virtues, culminating in union with God in love. Thus Ghazali seeks a synthesis of shari'a, kalam, philosophy, and Sufism in one overarching theological vision.

6. Types of Moral Theory

A morality of divine commandments construed as categorical prescriptions invites interpretation as a deonto-

logical ethic of duty, and certainly this is a major factor. On the other hand, Muslim ethics can also be regarded as teleogical in character. In thinkers like Miskawayh and Ghazali the teleology in question takes the form of eudaimonism, or virtue ethics. Here morality is not merely externally related to an ultimate goal, but internally related to an overarching conception of well-being, with morality itself as a form of human flourishing (ideally exemplified in Muhammad). In the hands of the traditionalist theologians, on the other hand, certainly at times, the teleology is more akin to what we might call theological or eschatological utilitarianism. Here right conduct appears to function as a prelude to postmortem bliss, to which it is merely externally related, just as in classical utilitarianism morality is instrumental to the achievement of a nonmoral good. There are also, it seems, elements of ethical egoism, as noted in Section III.A.4.

B. Ethics and Law

Islam is often claimed to embody an admirable synthesis of morality and law. A key difference between the two in Western thought is that for infringements of the law, but not for purely moral infringements, there are statutory punishments (cf. the absence of punishments for actions classed as recommended, permissible, and reprehensible in the classical fivefold schema). Nevertheless, Islam has tended to blur this distinction, partly by emphasizing the affinity between legal punishments in this world and divine punishments in the next, and partly by maintaining strong elements of legal moralism, e.g., in matters of sexual morality. Yet reformers argue that failure to maintain a sufficiently sharp distinction between the two, or failure to draw it in the right place, has led to serious distortions of true Islamic values. The point may be argued in different ways.

One is to begin by pointing to an equivocation in the use of the term shari'a. It may designate an ideal, the full set of God's prescriptions for humanity, or it may be equivalent to *fiqh,* and designate the cumulative deliverances of the jurists, developed within the classically established framework of criteria and procedures (see Section I.3). Used equivocally, epithets appropriate to the former (e.g., comprehensive and eternally valid) become applied, somewhat unrealistically, to the latter, and a mindset that permits elision of the two tacitly encourages an incautious elevation of legal rules to the status of *expressions* of God's commands, rather than preserving their more modest status as *interpretations* of God's commands. The practical effect, it is claimed, is the cherishing of legal anachronisms and undue rigidity in the face of rapid social change and a globalizing culture. Admittedly, jurists have gained a degree of flexibility and liberalisation by "patching" (*talfiq*), combining elements from the different schools of law in a spirit of humane pragmatism. Yet liberals seek more wholesale reform.

Here the distinction between morality and law may be adduced as an essential solvent of the difficulties, albeit with proposals ranging from the relatively cautious to the more radical. The common key moves, however, are to argue that legal rules reflect moral precepts (or that norms reflect values); to seek support for this in the Qur'an itself (and, indeed, in the shari'a); to maintain that ultimately God's will is to be primarily discerned in morality rather than law; and finally to argue that therefore either the shari'a should be discarded as obsolete or, less drastically, the harsh penalties attached to "forbidden" actions must in principle be subject to ethical revision, and its inherited rigors softened.

The strategy by liberals provides appreciable leeway for constructive debate within Islam, while at the same time evoking considerable opposition from conservatives. It is perhaps most effective when the proposed revision of the law has the clear support of a moral principle enunciated in the Qur'an. Thus the world has become aware, through the Salman Rushdie affair, that Islam has traditionally contained the death penalty for apostasy, yet this contradicts Qur'an 2:256, that "there is no compulsion in religion."

The strategy has also been widely used in connection with the status of women. The Qur'an contains certain notoriously controversial utterances, e.g., "women are your fields, enter them at will," or "men have authority over women because God has made the one superior to the other" (2:223, 4:34). Yet elsewhere it implies equal status (cf. 33:35, 4:1). Again, the jurists inferred from the reference in Qur'an 2:282 to summoning two female witnesses alongside one male, that one male witness is equal to two female witnesses—a further case of alleged masculine superiority. Yet elsewhere this gender differentiation of witnesses is not observed (cf. Qur'an 5:106, 24:6–9). Where skeptics would allege contradiction (as happens too with the Bible), reformers advocate contextualization and a harmonization of verses based on their liberal Muslim scale of moral priorities in order to undermine perceived sexual discrimination.

Greater difficulties occur when Qur'anic teachings are themselves morally controversial yet apparently unambiguous and uncontradicted. One example of this is the *hadd* penalty (Section II) of the cutting off of the hand for theft (Qur'an 5:38). Although still advocated (and practiced) by a minority of strict Muslims, e.g., in Saudi Arabia, invoking the principle of just deserts and a deterrent theory of punishment, it is generally circumvented by insisting that what was sadly necessary in Muhammad's Arabia is no longer necessary in a modern state, and not being required practically is not binding morally. Thus in effect the letter of the Qur'an is subordinated to its spirit, construed in terms of mercy, forgiveness, and a humanitarian Islam.

Another example of this difficulty is the *hadd* penalty of stoning to death for adultery. Here, in fact, Islam has allowed the Sunna to trump the Qur'an, which makes no provision for stoning. This invites the argument, common among reformers, that the superior authority of the Qur'an should be reaffirmed. However, the Qur'an specifies either that offending women should be imprisoned in their houses until they die or repent (4:15), or that both offenders should be flogged with a hundred lashes (24:2). Neither penalty appeals to the liberal conscience, yet in respect of the flogging the Qur'an continues: "And do not let compassion prevent you from executing the decree of God." As with theft, however, it may be argued that radically changed circumstances render such draconian punishments otiose. Conversely, though, conservatives and fundamentalists (e.g., in Pakistan) may insist on their continued application despite the virtual impossibility of satisfying the shari'a requirement of the evidence of four impeccable eyewitnesses.

There are also other ways in which the importance of the distinction between law and ethics may be approached. For example, the jurists have been accused of category confusion by imposing legal penalties for purely moral infractions (i.e., actions deemed to be immoral within Islam), thus espousing legal moralism. Apostasy is a case in point. In the Qur'an (4:137) this is a matter between God and the individual, and while the offense is grave, punishment is reserved for the hereafter, and does not require earthly punishment.

What all these moves imply is a reduction in the scope of religious law as such, especially in respect of freedom of religion, the status of women, and the *hadd* punishments, in favor of an enlarged sphere of more clearly differentiated morality. In effect this means safeguarding a sphere of private morals in the spirit of J. S. Mill, and as with Mill, one important goal would be to provide a firm basis for tolerance. Correlatively, liberals argue, there would be an enlarged sphere for the exercise of individual conscience. Traditionalists respond, however, by charging Western liberalism with having licensed moral laxity and the permissive society.

At issue, ultimately, are contending conceptions of social justice, and of the relationship between the individual and society.

The opposition between these two standpoints emerges in sharp relief with regard to increasingly confident claims to respect advanced by Muslim communities in Western societies. Liberalism may seek to accommodate religious communitarianism by a fresh acknowledgment of minority group rights in addition to the classic individual rights, but is unlikely to sacrifice the latter to the former in cases of conflict involving basic human rights.

Another line of specifically Muslim argument is to claim that Islam has neglected part of its own shari'a heritage, namely, the criterion of *maslahah,* the public good. Traditionally subordinated to other criteria, especially the "four roots" of the law (Section I.3), the suggestion now is that it should be accorded greater prominence and receive a more detailed modern elucidation. Moreover, a case can be made for the view that what counts as the public good is partly dependent upon time and circumstance, and that therefore rulings from distant times and different circumstances may need to be considered afresh. Here the argument becomes part of a wider debate about the need to exercise *ijtihad,* or independent reasoning and judgment, there being a widespread (though questionable) view that "the gates of ijtihad" were closed by the jurists centuries ago. The call for them to be reopened has been a longstanding rallying cry for reformers, as has been the claim that ijtihad may legitimately be exercised by nonjurists.

IV. CONCLUSION

Typically, the stance taken on matters of morality and law is influenced by the stance taken on issues in theology and metaethics. For example, the application of the criterion of the public good is likely to be more radical among those who allow at least a partial autonomy of ethics as opposed to a strict ethical voluntarism. The same is true of thinkers who allow a partly independent role for reason in relation to revelation. Moreover, both are more likely to be liberal on normative issues. The resultant patterns give meaning and value to categories like "conservative," "fundamentalist," and "liberal," despite their relative imprecision.

Conservatives and fundamentalists are desperate not to squander a precious heritage, while liberals seek a principled and truly Islamic basis of reform that will differentiate them from secular Westernizers and thus avert the charge of having betrayed their faith. One is left with a vivid sense of controversy and plurality: for "Islam" read "Islams."

Also See the Following Article

RELIGION AND ETHICS

Bibliography

An-Naim, A. A. (1990). *Toward an Islamic reformation: Civil liberties, human rights, and international law.* Syracuse, NY: Syracuse Univ. Press.

Esposito, J. L. (1995). *The Oxford encyclopedia of the modern Islamic world.* Oxford/New York: Oxford Univ. Press.

Goodman, L. E. (1997). Morals and society in Islamic philosophy. In B. Carr and I. Mahalingam (Eds.), *Companion encyclopedia of Asian philosophy.* London/New York: Routledge.

Hourani, G. F. (1985). *Reason and tradition in Islamic ethics.* Cambridge: Cambridge Univ. Press.

Hovannisian, R. (Ed.) (1985). *Ethics in Islam.* Malibu, CA: Undena.

Mayer, A. E. (1991). *Islam and human rights: Tradition and politics.* Boulder, CO/San Francisco: Westview; London: Pinter.

Weeramantry, C. G. (1988). *Islamic jurisprudence: An international perspective.* London: Macmillan.

ISBN 0-12-227067-3

9 780122 270673   90038